MILLER'S

Antiques Shops, Fairs & Auctions 2002

MILLER'S

Antiques Shops, Fairs & Auctions 2002

MILLER'S ANTIQUES SHOPS, FAIRS AND AUCTIONS 2002

Compiled, edited and designed by Miller's Publications Ltd
The Cellars, High Street, Tenterden, Kent TN30 6BN
Tel: 01580 766411 Fax: 01580 766100

Project Director Valerie Lewis
Executive Art Editor Victoria Bevan
Project Co-ordinator David Penfold
Assistant Project Co-ordinator Elizabeth Ellender
Researched by Caroline Bugeja, Rosemary Cooke, Carol Woodcock
Art Editor Colin Goody
Jacket Design Rhonda Fisher
Designers Simon Cook, Philip Hannath, Kari Reeves
Production Controller Angela Couchman
Advertising Executive Joanna Hill

First published in Great Britain in 2002 by Miller's,
a division of Mitchell Beazley, imprints of Octopus Publishing Group Ltd,
2–4 Heron Quays, London E14 4JP

ISBN 1 84000 569 6

Printed and bound by Aubin Imprimeur Press

Scotland
Northern Ireland
North East
North West
Yorks & Lincs
Republic of Ireland
Midlands
East
Wales
Heart of England
South
South East
West Country
LONDON
Channel Islands

CONTENTS

8 **HOW TO USE THIS BOOK**

9 **INTRODUCTION**

11 **ANTIQUE SHOPS, CENTRES & AUCTION HOUSES**

12 **SOUTH EAST**
Kent, East Sussex

44 **LONDON**
East, North, South, West, Middlesex

107 **SOUTH**
Berkshire, Hampshire, Isle of Wight, Surrey, West Sussex

146 **WEST COUNTRY**
Cornwall, Devon, Dorset, Somerset, Wiltshire

199 **EAST**
Cambridge, Essex, Suffolk, Norfolk

232 **HEART OF ENGLAND**
Bedfordshire, Buckinghamshire, Gloucestershire, Herefordshire, Hertfordshire, Oxfordshire

268 **MIDLANDS**
Derbyshire, Leicestershire, Northamptonshire, Nottinghamshire, Rutland, Shropshire, Staffordshire, Warwickshire, West Midlands, Worcestershire

315 **YORKS & LINCS**
East Riding of Yorkshire, North Yorkshire, South Yorkshire, West Yorkshire, Lincolnshire

349 **NORTH EAST**
Co Durham, Northumberland, Tyne & Wear

356 **NORTH WEST**
Cheshire, Cumbria, Greater Manchester, Lancashire, Merseyside

387 **WALES**
Carmarthenshire, Ceredigion, Conwy, Denbighshire, Gwynedd, Flintshire, Isle of Angelsey, Mid Glamorgan, Monmouthshire, Pembrokeshire, Powys, South Glamorgan, West Glamorgan

404 **SCOTLAND**
Edinburgh, Glasgow, Aberdeenshire, Angus, Argyle & Bute, Dumfries & Galloway, East Ayrshire, East Lothian, Fife, Highland, Midlothian, Moray, North Ayrshire, Perth & Kinross, Renfrewshire, Scottish Borders, South Ayrshire, South Lanarkshire, Stirling, West Lothian

428 **CHANNEL ISLANDS**
Guernsey, Jersey

431 **NORTHERN IRELAND**
Co Antrim, Co Armagh, Co Down, Co Fermanagh, Co Londonderry, Co Tyrone

441 **REPUBLIC OF IRELAND**
Co Carlow, Co Cavan, Co Clare, Co Cork, Co Donegal, Co Dublin, Co Galway, Co Kerry, Co Kildare, Co Kilkenny, Co Laois, Co Leitrim, Co Limerick, Co Louth, Co Mayo, Co Meath, Co Offaly, Co Sligo, Co Tipperary, Co Waterford, Co Wexford, Co Wicklow

457 **ASSOCIATED SERVICES**

505 **FAIRS**

556 **KEY TO MEMBER ORGANISATIONS**

557 **INDEX OF ADVERTISERS**

558 **INDEX OF SPECIALISTS**

570 **INDEX OF PLACE NAMES**

578 **GENERAL INDEX**

608 **FORM FOR NEW ENTRIES**

HOW TO USE THIS BOOK

It is our aim to make Miller's Antiques Shops, Fairs & Auctions simple to use. In order to make it easier to find entries, the book has been divided into three main sections: Dealers, Antiques Centres and Auction Houses; Associated Services; and Fairs.

Key to Symbols

- ⊞ Dealer
- Auction House
- Antiques Centre
- ⊠ Address
- P Parking
- ☎ Telephone No.
- M Mobile No.
- F Fax No.
- E E-mail address
- W Web Address

SOUTH

HAMPSHIRE • ANDOVER

☎ 01962 732188 F 01962 732998
M 07769 715510
E anthony.l.d.oxley@ukgateway.net
Est. 1950
Stock Victorian watercolours, old maps, antiquarian books
Open Mon–Sat 9am–5pm
Fairs Chelsea Book Fair
Services Restorations, picture framing

⊞ Tudor Antiques and Fine Arts Ltd (AAFAA)
Contact Eric or Penelope Tudor
⊠ **The Old Exchange, Station Road, Alresford, Hampshire, SO24 9JG** P
☎ 01962 735345 F 01962 736345
M 07774 908888
E e&ptudor@tudor-antiques.co.uk
W www.tudor-antiques.co.uk
Est. 1980 *Stock size* Large
Stock 17th–19thC English, French, Oriental furniture, objets d'art
Open Mon–Sat 10am–4pm Sun by appointment
Services Valuations, shipping arranged

⊞ Underwood Oak
Contact Ms Ann Egerton
⊠ **49 West Street, Alresford, Hampshire, SO24 9AB** P
☎ 01962 735677 F 01730 267797
E antiques@underwoodoak.co.uk
Est. 1999 *Stock size* Medium
Stock 17th–19thC oak, country furniture
Open Mon–Sat 10am–5pm closed Wed
Fairs Avington
Services Valuations, restorations

☎ 01420 560055 F 01420 560050
E jardinique@aol.com
W www.jardinique.co.uk
Est. 1994 *Stock size* Large
Stock Statuary, sundials, urns, gardenalia, seats, fountains, stone troughs, staddle stones
Open Tues–Sat 10am–5pm or by appointment
Services Valuations

ANDOVER

Andover Saleroom
Contact Mrs J Henry
⊠ **41a London Street, Andover, Hampshire, SP10 2NU** P
☎ 01264 364820 F 01264 323402
Est. 1979
Open Mon–Fri 8.30am–6pm
Sales Pictures and jewellery Sat, antique and general Mon, viewing Fri 9am–9pm Sat 9am–6pm. Advisable to telephone for details
Frequency Fortnightly
Catalogues Yes

Ludgershall Antiques Centre
Contact Mrs I Haylen
⊠ **4–6 Andover Road, Ludgershall, Andover, Hampshire, SP11 9LZ** P
☎ 01264 791372 F 01264 710704
E lac@hayland.demon.co.uk
Est. 1996 *Stock size* Medium
Stock Furniture, jewellery, silver, bronzes, paintings, porcelain, objets d'art
Open Tues–Sat 10am–5pm Sun 11am–4pm

SOUTH

Dealers, Auction Houses and Antiques Centres

The United Kingdom has been divided into geographical regions, which are listed in the Contents on page 7. There is also a section for the Republic of Ireland. Each region is divided into counties and within each county, cities, towns and villages are listed alphabetically. Indexes to company name and place name can be found at the end of this Directory.

Each entry shows information such as address, phone number, opening hours, e-mail address and website, member organizations (eg LAPADA) and year established. Each **Dealer** entry contains details of stock and any services they provide. **Auction House** entries include information about their sales, frequency of sales and if catalogues are available. Entries for **Antiques Centres** include the number of dealers within the centre. **Associated Services** such as restorers, packers and valuers etc are listed alphabetically according to the service offered.

The **Fairs** section lists in date order, antiques fairs that will take place in the UK and Ireland throughout 2002. It is always advisable to contact the organisers in advance to check that information has not changed since going to press.

There are Indexes of **Specialists, Place Names** and a **General Index**, which are to be found beginning on page 555.

INTRODUCTION

Shopping for antiques and collectables is perhaps one of the greatest pleasures that Britain has to offer. How many people spend their weekends visiting antiques fairs and centres to indulge in collecting one of our most popular national hobbies? How many tourists come to the UK, not just to see our great cities and rural beauty spots, but to take home a little bit of 3D history from one of our antique shops?

As this guide shows, what an astonishing range there is to choose from. Leaf through its pages and you will find specialists in everything from antiquities to telephones, from fine furniture to children's toys, to breweriana. Having edited *Miller's Collectables Price Guide* for several years, I know from experience that there is not only a collector for every subject under the sun, but also a supplier. This invaluable book lists shops, auction houses and antiques fairs throughout Britain and Ireland, its 7000 entries reflecting the huge explosion of interest in antiques and collectables in every field.

As the market has expanded, it has also changed, and not always for the better. Rising business rates have forced many antiques dealers (along with other small traders) out of our town centres, leaving them blander and less attractive places. Variety is the spice of life and the essence of shopping. One of the reasons people collect is the sheer pleasure of owning unusual, rare and sometimes unique items. Tracking them down is half the fun and always an adventure. You can never be sure what you will find at the end of an antiques hunt but thanks to this book, at least you will know where to begin looking.

Britain is lucky enough to have some of the finest dealers and auction houses in the world. It was in order to recognize this fact that Miller's in Association with *BBC Homes and Antiques Magazine* launched the BACAs, the annual British Antiques and Collectables Awards. Categories cover all areas of the market and nominations are received from the general public. If in the course of buying antiques and collectables in Britain and Ireland you come across a dealer, auction house or antiques fair that you feel deserves particular recognition for knowledge, service and quality of material, please let us know.

All the BACA judges (of which I am one) were given a copy of this guide, and very useful we found it. Antique dealers' opening times can be as strange and idiosyncratic as their stock and it is always worth ringing up before visiting. It is also useful (and enjoyable) to see what other shops can be found in the same area as your intended quarry, though I have to admit this knowledge has cost me dear in terms of time and money. To an enthusiast, an antiques shop or collectors' fair is irresistible, and the downside of working in a field that you love is that it can cost you a fortune!

I hope you find this guide as helpful as I do and that you will have a good time visiting the places listed. It was Napoleon who famously described England as "a nation of shop keepers". Were he alive today, he could well have called Britain a nation of antique shop keepers.
Happy Hunting!

Madeleine Marsh

Antiques Shops, Centres & Auction Houses

If you wish your company to be entered in the next edition of the Directory, please complete the form at the end of the book or go to our website: http://www.mitchell-beazley.co.uk/mbeazley/miller/antiques_shops.htm

SOUTH EAST

EAST SUSSEX

ALFRISTON

⊞ Alfriston Antiques
Contact John Tourell
✉ **The Square, Alfriston, East Sussex, BN26 5UD** Ⓟ
☎ 01323 870498 Ⓕ 01323 870498
Est. 1967 *Stock size* Large
Stock Small collectables, porcelain, silver, jewellery, clocks
Open Wed–Sat 11am–5pm Sun 2.30–4.30pm
Services Valuations

⊞ The Old Apiary
Contact Tony Phillimore
✉ **High Street, Alfriston, East Sussex, BN26 5TB** Ⓟ
☎ 01323 870730
Est. 1995 *Stock size* Small
Stock Small furniture, decorative china
Open Mon–Sun 10am–5.30pm

BATTLE

⊞ Barnaby's of Battle
Contact Mr Barney Hance
✉ **50 High Street, Battle, East Sussex, TN33 0AN** Ⓟ
☎ 01424 772221
Est. 1997 *Stock size* Medium
Stock Old pine, oak and hardwood furniture
Open Mon–Sat 10am–6pm
Services Restorations

Burstow & Hewett
Contact Mr R Ellin
✉ **Abbey Auction Galleries & Granary Salerooms, Lower Lake, Battle, East Sussex, TN33 0AT** Ⓟ
☎ 01424 772374 Ⓕ 01424 772302
Est. 1790
Open Mon–Fri 9am–5.30pm
Sales Sales of general antiques
Frequency Monthly
Catalogues Yes

⊞ Lavande
Contact Aryo Bakker or Sophie Hartley
✉ **53 High Street, Battle, East Sussex, TN33 0EN** Ⓟ
☎ 01424 774474 Ⓕ 01424 774474
Ⓜ 07710 098642
Ⓔ info@lavande.co.uk
Ⓦ www.lavande.co.uk
Est. 1998 *Stock size* Medium
Stock French18th–19thC furniture and accessories
Open Mon–Sat 9.30am–5.30pm Sun by appointment
Fairs Decorative Antiques and Textiles Fair, Battersea
Services Upholstery, interior design

⊞ Spectrum Fine Jewellery Ltd (NAG, IPG)
Contact Mr Keith Ingram
✉ **46 High Street, Battle, East Sussex, TN33 0EE** Ⓟ
☎ 01424 774404
Est. 1975 *Stock size* Medium
Stock Jewellery, silver
Open Tues–Sat 9.30am–5.30pm
Fairs NEC
Services Repairs, enamelling, commissions

BEXHILL-ON-SEA

⊞ Acme Inc.
Contact Mrs Ruth Hardie
✉ **5 Wickham Avenue, Bexhill-on-Sea, East Sussex, TN39 3EP** Ⓟ
☎ 01424 211848
Ⓜ 07773 402404
Ⓔ ruth@acme-inc.com
Ⓦ www.acme-inc.com
Est. 1993 *Stock size* Large
Stock 19th–20thC decorative arts, furniture
Open Mon Thurs Fri 11am–noon 2.30–4pm Sat 3–5pm Sun 3–4pm or by appointment
Fairs Ardingly, Swinderby

⊞ Annie's
Contact Priscilla Ann Rose
✉ **4 Bixlea Parade, Little Common Road, Little Common, Bexhill-on-Sea, East Sussex, TN39 4SD** Ⓟ
☎ 01424 846966
Est. 1992 *Stock size* Large
Stock Small pieces of furniture, collectables
Open Mon–Fri 10am–4pm Sat 10am–1pm closed Wed

⊞ Bexhill Antique Exporters
Contact Kim Abbott
✉ **56 Turkey Road, Bexhill-on-Sea, East Sussex, TN39 5HE** Ⓟ
☎ 01424 225103 Ⓕ 01424 731430
Ⓜ 07702 006982
Est. 1986 *Stock size* Large
Stock Furniture for the Spanish, Italian and French markets
Open Mon–Fri 10am–5pm Sat Sun by appointment
Services Exporters

Gorringes Auction Galleries (SOFA, ISVA)
Contact Mr Mark Hudson

✉ Terminus Road, Bexhill-on-Sea, East Sussex, TN39 3LR P
☎ 01424 212994 F 01424 224035
E auctions@gorringes.co.uk
W www.gorringes.co.uk
Est. 1926
Open Mon–Fri 8.30am–5.30pm Sat 9am–noon
Sales Fine art, antiques, collectables, Tues and Wed at 10am, viewing Fri 10am–5pm Sat 9.30am–4pm
Frequency 6 weeks
Catalogues Yes

⊞ Sivyer's
Contact Mrs V Sivyer
✉ **7 Sackville Road, Bexhill-on-Sea, East Sussex, TN39 3JB** P
☎ 01424 733821
Est. 1990 *Stock size* Medium
Stock General antiques, kitchenalia
Open Mon–Sat 10am–5pm

⊞ Springfield Antiques
Contact Mr C Georgiou
✉ **127 Ninfield Road, Bexhill-on-Sea, East Sussex, TN39 5BD** P
☎ 01424 211225
M 07973 969244
Est. 1972 *Stock size* Large
Stock Original old English pine furniture, kitchenware
Open Mon–Sun 10am–5.30pm

BISHOPSTONE

⊞ The Titus Gallery (LAPADA)
Contact Mrs C A Grice
✉ **The Studio, Norton, Bishopstone, East Sussex, BN25 2UW** P
☎ 01323 873912 F 01323 873912
M 07710 036080
E tiartgal@aol.com or tiartgal@ic24.nett
Est. 1975 *Stock size* Large
Stock Paintings, objets d'art
Open By appointment only
Fairs LAPADA, Bailey
Services Valuations, cleaning and restoration of oil paintings

BRIGHTON

⊞ Alexandria Antiques
Contact Mr A H Ahmed
✉ **3 Hanover Place, Brighton, East Sussex, BN2 2SD** P
☎ 01273 688793 F 01273 688793
M 07880 625558
Est. 1978 *Stock size* Medium
Stock 18th–19thC furniture, porcelain, bronzes, paintings, decorative objects
Open Mon–Fri 9.30am–5.30pm Sat Sun by appointment
Fairs Newark, Ardingly
Services Valuations, restorations

⊞ Alexandria Antiques
Contact Mr A H Ahmed
✉ **33 Upper North Street, Brighton, East Sussex, BN1 3FG** P
☎ 01273 328072 F 01273 688793
M 07880 625558
Est. 1978 *Stock size* Medium
Stock 18th–19thC furniture, porcelain, bronzes, paintings, decorative objects
Open Mon–Fri 9.30am–5.30pm Sat Sun by appointment
Fairs Newark, Ardingly
Services Valuations, restorations

⊞ Art Deco Etc
Contact Mr J Clark
✉ **73 Upper Gloucester Road, Brighton, East Sussex, BN1 3LQ** P
☎ 01273 329268 F 01273 329268
M 07971 268302
Est. 1979 *Stock size* Medium
Stock Pottery, glass, 1860–1980s, lighting, small furniture, metalwork
Open By appointment only
Fairs Newark, Alexandra Palace, Ardingly, Battersea
Services Valuations and insurance claims

⊞ The Bookmark
Contact Sally May
✉ **91–93 Dyke Road, Brighton, East Sussex, BN1 3JE** P
☎ 01273 735577
Est. 1994 *Stock size* Medium
Stock General stock of antiquarian and modern books
Open Mon 1.30–6pm Tues–Fri 11.30am–6.30pm Sat 10.30am–6pm

⊞ Bright Helm Antiques & Interiors
Contact Mr Matthew Winter
✉ **40 Sydney Street, North Lanes, Brighton, East Sussex, BN1 4EP** P
☎ 01273 572059
E brighthelm.antiques@fastnet.co.uk
W www.sexualpine.co.uk
Est. 1997 *Stock size* Large
Stock Pine and painted furniture, architectural salvage
Open Mon–Sun 10am–6pm or by appointment
Services Restorations, repairs

⊞ Brighton Architectural Salvage
Contact Mr R L Legendre
✉ **33–34 Gloucester Road, Brighton, East Sussex, BN1 4AQ**
☎ 01273 681656 F 01273 681656
M 07979 966245
Est. 1979 *Stock size* Large
Stock Restored architectural antiques, fireplaces, reclaimed flooring
Open Mon–Sat 10am–5pm
Services Fireplace installation

⊞ Brighton Flea Market
Contact Mr A R Wilkinson
✉ **31a Upper St James's Street, Brighton, East Sussex, BN2 1JN**
☎ 01273 624006 F 01273 328665
E arwilkinson@aol.com
Est. 1988 *Stock size* Large
Stock Antiques, bric-a-brac, collectables
Open Mon–Sun 9.30am–5.30pm

⊞ Brighton Postcard Shop (PTA)
Contact Mr K Davies
✉ **38 Beaconsfield Road, Brighton, East Sussex, BN1 4QH** P
☎ 01273 600035 F 01273 628660
E keith.davies@pobox.com
W www.visitweb.com/adultglam. Backnumbers www.postcard.co.uk/flair
Est. 1987 *Stock size* Large
Stock Postcards, ephemera, vintage glamour magazines
Open Tues–Sat 10am–4pm
Fairs Bloomsbury Fairs, Alexandra Palace
Services Mail order

⊞ Brighton Retro
Contact Greg Wish
✉ **102a North Road, Brighton, East Sussex, BN1 1YE** P
☎ 01273 628444
M 07801 546709
Est. 1996 *Stock size* Medium
Stock Arts and Crafts, early 20thC furniture, retro furniture clothes and fabrics
Open Mon–Sat 11am–6pm Sun noon–4pm
Services Valuations, restorations

SOUTH EAST

EAST SUSSEX • BRIGHTON

⊞ Tony Broadfoot Antiques
Contact Mr Tony Broadfoot
✉ **39 Upper Gardner Street, Brighton, East Sussex, BN1 4AN** 🅿
☎ 01273 695457 Ⓕ 01273 620365
Est. 1982 *Stock size* Large
Stock Antique furniture
Open Mon–Fri 9am–5pm

⊞ C A R S (Classic Automobilia and Regalia Specialists)
Contact Mr G G Weiner
✉ **4–4a Chapel Terrace Mews, Kemp Town, Brighton, East Sussex, BN2 1HU** 🅿
☎ 01273 622722/601960
Ⓕ 01273 601960
Ⓜ 07890 836734
Ⓔ cars@kemptown-brighton.freeserve.co.uk
Ⓦ www.carsofbrighton.co.uk
www.brmmbrmm.com/pedalcars
Est. 1981 *Stock size* Medium
Stock Automobilia, collectors' car badges and mascots, hand-built collectors' and children's pedal cars
Open Mon–Sat 10am–6pm or by appointment
Fairs Classic car shows at NEC, Alexandra Palace
Services Valuations

⊞ Clock Tower Antiques
Contact Mr D Goss
✉ **128d Queens Road, Brighton, East Sussex, BN1 3WB** 🅿
☎ 01273 747666 Ⓕ 01273 747666
Est. 1985 *Stock size* Large
Stock Antique pine furniture
Open Mon–Sun 9.30am–5.30pm
Services Kitchen specialists

⊞ Decorative Arts
Contact Anthony White
✉ **27 Gloucester Road, Brighton, East Sussex, BN1 4AQ** 🅿
☎ 01273 676486
Ⓜ 07788 107101
Ⓦ www.decarts.net
Est. 1996 *Stock size* Medium
Stock Oak furniture 1880–1970, decorative arts, 1970s leather furniture
Open Mon–Sat 10am–5.30pm
Sun by appointment

⊞ Enhancements
Contact Lucille Robinson
✉ **11a Cavendish Street, Brighton, East Sussex, BN2 1RN** 🅿
☎ 01273 677303
Ⓜ 07788 727878
Ⓔ lue80@hotmail.com
Est. 1992 *Stock size* Medium
Stock Kitchenware, tools, beds, pine furniture, shabby chic furniture
Open Mon–Sat 10am–5.30pm
Services Free delivery

⊞ Alan Fitchett Antiques
Contact Mr A Fitchett
✉ **5–5a Upper Gardner Street, Brighton, East Sussex, BN1 4AN**
☎ 01273 600894 Ⓕ 01273 600894
Est. 1969 *Stock size* Large
Stock Furniture
Open Mon–Fri 9am–5.30pm

⊞ Georgina's Antiques
Contact Mrs Heldman
✉ **45 High Street, Rottingdean, Brighton, East Sussex, BN2 7HE** 🅿
☎ 01273 308699
Est. 1995 *Stock size* Medium
Stock Antiques, collectables
Open Mon–Sat 9.30am–5pm
Sun noon–5pm

⊞ Julie Griffin Antiques
Contact Julie Griffin
✉ **13a Prince Albert Street, Brighton, East Sussex, BN1 1HE** 🅿
☎ 01273 773895
Est. 1996 *Stock size* Large
Stock Antique, reproduction and reclaimed pine furniture, mahogany, decorative pieces
Open Mon–Sat 10am–5pm

⊞ Hallmark Jewellers
Contact Mr J Hersheson
✉ **4 Union Street, The Lanes, Brighton, East Sussex, BN1 1HA** 🅿
☎ 01273 725477 Ⓕ 01273 725477
Ⓜ 07885 298494
Est. 1959 *Stock size* Large
Stock Antique and modern silver, silver collectables, jewellery
Open Mon–Sat 9am–5pm
Sun 11am–4pm
Services Valuations

⊞ The House of Antiques (LAPADA)
Contact Mr A Margiotta
✉ **39 Upper North Street, Brighton, East Sussex, BN1 3FH** 🅿
☎ 01273 327680 Ⓕ 01273 324961
Est. 1959 *Stock size* Medium
Stock General antiques, furniture, bronzes, porcelain, clocks
Open Mon–Fri 10am–5pm closed 1–2.15pm
Services Pawnbrokers

⊞ Dudley Hume
Contact Mr D Hume
✉ **46 Upper North Street, Brighton, East Sussex, BN1 3FH**
☎ 01273 323461 Ⓕ 01273 240422
Ⓜ 07977 598627
Ⓔ dudley@dudleyhume.freeserve.co.uk
Est. 1973 *Stock size* Medium
Stock 18th–19thC furniture, decorative items
Open Mon–Fri 10.30am–4.30pm
Sat 10am–noon
Fairs Olympia

Raymond P Inman
Contact Robert Inman
✉ **35 & 40 Temple Street, Brighton, East Sussex, BN1 3BH** 🅿
☎ 01273 774777 Ⓕ 01273 735660
Ⓔ r.p.inman@talk21.com
Est. 1929
Open Mon–Fri 9am–5pm
Sales General antique sales
Frequency 10 a year
Catalogues Yes

⊞ Jezebel
Contact Mrs A Davis
✉ **14 Prince Albert Street, Brighton, East Sussex, BN1 1HE** 🅿
☎ 01273 206091 Ⓕ 01273 206091
Est. 1989 *Stock size* Medium
Stock Art Deco, Art Nouveau, costumes, vintage clothing, costume jewellery
Open Mon–Sat 11am–5.30pm
Fairs Newark

⊞ The Lanes Armoury
Contact Mark or David Hawkins
✉ **26 Meeting House Lane, Brighton, East Sussex, BN1 1HB** 🅿
☎ 01273 321357 Ⓕ 01273 326453
Ⓔ hawkinsarms@hotmail.com
Ⓦ www.thelanesarmoury.co.uk
Est. 1992 *Stock size* Large
Stock Arms, armour, militaria and books from 1stC AD–WWII
Open Mon–Sat 10am–5.15pm

Patrick Moorhead Antiques
Contact Mr P Moorhead
Spring Gardens, 76 Church Street, Brighton, East Sussex, BN1 1RL
01273 779696 01273 220196
07785 725202
patrick.moorhead@virgin.net
Est. 1984 *Stock size* Large
Stock 18th–19thC furniture, European and Oriental ceramics, paintings, clocks
Open Mon–Fri 9.30am–5.30pm
Services Valuations, restorations

Oasis
Contact Mr I Stevenson
39 Kensington Gardens, Brighton, East Sussex, BN1 4AL
01273 683885
Est. 1979 *Stock size* Medium
Stock Period lighting, telephones, gramophones, furniture, Art Deco, Art Nouveau, watches, lighters, glass, textiles, clothes from 1920s and 1930s
Open Mon–Sat 10am–5.30pm

Odin Antiques
Contact Mr A Sjovold
43 Preston Street, Brighton, East Sussex, BN1 2HP
01273 732738
www.odinantiques.co.uk
Est. 1979 *Stock size* Medium
Stock Antique furniture, maritime items, telescopes
Open Mon–Sat 10.30am–5.30pm

The Old Picture Shop
Contact Mr S Clark
2 Nile Street, Brighton, East Sussex, BN1 1HW
01273 725609
Est. 1959 *Stock size* Medium
Stock Old paintings, watercolours, period furniture
Open Mon–Sat 10am–5pm
Services Valuations

Colin Page Antiquarian Books (ABA)
Contact Mr J Loska
36 Duke Street, Brighton, East Sussex, BN1 1AG
01273 325954 01273 746246
cpage@pavilion.co.uk
Est. 1969 *Stock size* Large
Stock Antiquarian and second-hand books, literature, natural history, plate books, bindings
Open Mon–Sat 9.30am–5.30pm
Fairs ABA, Olympia, Chelsea
Services Valuations

Dermot & Jill Palmer Antiques
Contact Jill Palmer
7–8 Union Street, Brighton, East Sussex, BN1 1HA
01273 328669 01273 777641
07771 614331
Est. 1969 *Stock size* Large
Stock Mainly 19thC French and English furniture
Open Mon–Sat 9am–6pm or by appointment
Fairs Olympia

Sue Pearson Antique Dolls & Teddy Bears
Contact Sue Pearson
13½ Prince Albert Street, Brighton, East Sussex, BN1 1HE
01273 329247 01273 494600
enquire@sue-pearson.co.uk
www.sue-pearson.co.uk
Est. 1981 *Stock size* Large
Stock Antique and modern bears, soft toys, dolls
Open Mon–Sat 10am–5pm
Fairs Kensington Town Hall
Services Repair of dolls/bears

Ben Ponting Antiques
Contact Michelle Ponting
53 Upper North Street, Brighton, East Sussex, BN1 3FH
01273 329409 01273 558749
pontingco@aol.com
Est. 1976 *Stock size* Large
Stock English Georgian–Edwardian antique furniture
Open Mon–Fri 9am–5pm
Services Valuations, restorations

Rin-Tin-Tin (ESoc)
Contact Mr Rick Irvine
34 North Road, Brighton, East Sussex, BN1 1YB
01273 672424 01273 672424
Est. 1982 *Stock size* Medium
Stock Old advertising, promotional matter, magazines, early glamour, games, toys, plastics, 20thC fixtures and fittings
Open Mon–Sat 11am–5.30pm
Fairs Alexandra Palace, Juke Box Fairs
Services Framing

Savery Antiques
Contact Ann Savery
257 Ditchling Road, Fireways, Brighton, East Sussex, BN1 6JH
01273 564899
hjamsavery@aol.com
Est. 1968 *Stock size* Medium
Stock Small furniture, porcelain, glass, metalwork
Open Mon 10.30am–5pm Thurs–Sat 9.30am–5pm
Fairs Ardingly, Sandown Park

Savery Books
Contact Mr James Savery
300 Ditchling Road, Brighton, East Sussex, BN1 6JG
01273 503030
Est. 1990 *Stock size* Large
Stock Second-hand books
Open Wed–Sat 10am–4.30pm

Snooper's Paradise
Contact Mr N Drinkwater
7–8 Kensington Gardens, Brighton, East Sussex, BN1 4AL
01273 602558 01273 686611
snoopersparadisebrighton@btinternet.com
www.snoopersparadise.co.uk
Est. 1994 *Stock size* Large
No. of dealers 70–80
Stock China, pictures, 1970s items, clothes and fabric, kitchenware, ephemera, jewellery, watches, records and CDs, phones and electrical, Art Deco, glass, treen, furniture, photographic, pens and lighters, militaria etc
Open Mon–Sat 9.30am–5.30pm Sun 11am–4pm

Studio Bookshop
Contact Mr P Brown
68 St James's Street, Brighton, East Sussex, BN2 1PJ
01273 691253
paul@studiobookshop.demon.co.uk
Est. 1995 *Stock size* Medium
Stock Reference books on glass, art and antiques
Open Mon–Sat 10am–6pm
Fairs Glass fairs
Services Catalogue, telephone orders

Valelink Ltd
Contact Mr J Trory
26 Queen's Road, Brighton, East Sussex, BN1 3XA

SOUTH EAST

EAST SUSSEX • BURWASH

☎ 01273 202906
Est. 1970 *Stock size* Medium
Stock Collectables
Open Mon–Sat 10am–6pm
Fairs Brighton Centre

⊞ Wardrobe
Contact Mr Clive Parks or Mr Philip Parfitt
✉ **51 Upper North Street, Brighton, East Sussex, BN1 3FH** 🅿
☎ 01273 202201 Ⓕ 01273 202201
Ⓜ 07802 483056
Est. 1986 *Stock size* Medium
Stock Vintage clothing and accessories, textiles, jewellery, Art Deco, bakelite, collectable plastics
Open Wed–Sat 10am–5pm or by appointment
Fairs Alexandra Palace, Sandown Park, Horticultural Hall

⊞ Graham Webb Musical Boxes
Contact Mr Graham Webb
✉ **59a Ship Street, Brighton, East Sussex, BN1 1AE** 🅿
☎ 01273 321803 Ⓕ 01273 321803
Ⓔ gwebb@musicalbox.demon.co.uk
Est. 1961 *Stock size* Large
Stock Musical boxes
Open Mon–Fri 10am–5pm
Services Valuations, restorations, shipping

⊞ E & B White
Contact Elizabeth or Ben White
✉ **43 & 47 Upper North Street, Brighton, East Sussex, BN1 3FH**
☎ 01273 328706 Ⓕ 01273 207035
Est. 1965 *Stock size* Medium
Stock Antique and decorative furniture
Open Mon–Fri 9.30am–5pm Sat 9.30am–1pm

⊞ Wilkinsons
Contact Mrs Wilkinson
✉ **11 Church Street, Brighton, East Sussex, BN1 1US** 🅿
☎ 01273 328665 Ⓕ 01273 328665
Ⓜ 07801 418495
Ⓔ arwilkinsn@aol.com
Est. 1991 *Stock size* Large
Stock Furniture, decorative objects, lighting
Open Mon–Sat 10am–5.30pm Sun noon–5pm
Services Free delivery, gift wrap, wedding lists

⊞ The Witch Ball
Contact Gina Daniels
✉ **48 Meeting House Lane, Brighton, East Sussex, BN1 1HB** 🅿
☎ 01273 326618
Ⓦ www.antiques-index.com
Est. 1967 *Stock size* Large
Stock 1550–1850 prints and maps
Open Mon–Sat 10.30am–6pm
Services Lists on request

⊞ Pamela Wright
Contact Mrs P Wright
✉ **45 Upper North Street, Brighton, East Sussex, BN1 3FH**
☎ 01273 738838 Ⓕ 01273 724047
Est. 1987 *Stock size* Large
Stock Period furniture and metal, light fittings, paintings
Open Mon–Fri 10am–5pm

BURWASH

⊞ Chateaubriand Antiques Centre
Contact John Barker or Nick Morgan
✉ **High Street, Burwash, East Sussex, TN19 7ES** 🅿
☎ 01435 882535
Ⓔ chateauframe@hotmail.com
Est. 1984 *Stock size* Large
Stock 4 showrooms. Furniture, pictures, prints, brass, copper, china, maps
Open Mon–Sat 10am–5pm Sun noon–5pm
Services Valuations, tea room, picture framing

CROWBOROUGH

⊞ Ashdown Antiques
Contact Mrs J Lowther
✉ **The Wool Shop, Croft Road, Crowborough, East Sussex, TN6 1DL** 🅿
☎ 01892 664180
Est. 1994 *Stock size* Large
Stock Furniture, jewellery, ceramics, silver, Art Deco, glass, Victoriana
Open Mon–Sat 10am–4pm
Fairs Ardingly
Services Valuations, jewellery repairs

EASTBOURNE

⌂ Antique Grove
Contact Mimi Boogaert or George Gauntlett
✉ **43 Grove Road, Eastbourne, East Sussex, BN21 4TX** 🅿
☎ 01323 645587 Ⓜ 07803 900202
Ⓔ mimi_antiques@hotmail.com
Est. 1999 *Stock size* Large
No. of dealers 17
Stock Glass, silver, ceramics, jewellery, Hornby and Dinky toys, furniture, perfume bottles, embroidery, paintings
Open Mon–Sat 10am–5.30pm

⊞ Camillas Bookshop
Contact Ms C Francombe or Mr S Broad
✉ **57 Grove Road, Eastbourne, East Sussex, BN21 4TX** 🅿
☎ 01323 736001
Est. 1975 *Stock size* Large
Stock Antiquarian and second-hand books, postcards, ephemera, children's books, needlework, military/nautical topics a speciality
Open Mon–Sat 10am–5.30pm
Services Valuations, book search

⊞ Francois Celada
Contact Francois Celada
✉ **26 South Street, Eastbourne, East Sussex, BN21 4XB** 🅿
☎ 01323 644464 Ⓕ 01323 644464
Est. 1996 *Stock size* Large
Stock Postcards, stamps, cigarette cards, medals, coins, collectables
Open Mon–Sat 9.30am–5pm Wed 2–5pm
Services Valuations

⊞ Cornfield Antiques & Collectables
Contact Mrs D Wolff or Mr F Wolff
✉ **18 Cornfield Terrace, Eastbourne, East Sussex, BN21 4NS** 🅿
☎ 01323 733345 Ⓕ 01323 638315
Ⓔ cornfieldantiqueseastbourne@barclays.net
Est. 1996 *Stock size* Large
Stock Paintings, furniture, silver, crystal, glass, jewellery, porcelain, pottery, perfume bottles, collectables
Open Mon–Sat 10am–5pm
Services Multilingual service

⊞ John Cowderoy Antiques (LAPADA)
Contact Mr Richard Cowderoy
✉ **42 South Street, Eastbourne, East Sussex, BN21 4XB** 🅿

☎ 01323 720058 Ⓕ 01323 410163
Ⓔ john@cowderoyantiques.co.uk
Ⓦ cowderoyantiques.co.uk
Est. 1973 *Stock size* Large
Stock General antiques, collectables, clocks, musical boxes
Open Mon–Sat 8.30am–5pm closed Wed pm
Services Restorations

Crest Collectables
Contact Mr C Powell
✉ **54 Grove Road, Eastbourne, East Sussex, BN21 4UD** Ⓟ
☎ 01323 721185
Est. 1986 *Stock size* Medium
Stock Teddy bears, dolls, soft toys, collectables
Open Mon–Sat 10.30am–4pm closed Wed

Eastbourne Antiques Market
Contact Mr P C Barltrop
✉ **80 Seaside, Eastbourne, East Sussex, BN22 7QP** Ⓟ
☎ 01323 642233
Est. 1969 *Stock size* Large
No. of dealers 25
Stock Antiques, collectables
Open Mon–Fri 10am–5.30pm Sat 10am–5pm

The Enterprise Collectors Market
Contact Mr Lovegrove
✉ **Enterprise Centre, Station Parade, Eastbourne, East Sussex, BN21 1BD** Ⓟ
☎ 01323 732690
Est. 1988 *Stock size* Large
No. of dealers 15
Stock Antiques, collectables
Open Mon–Sat 9.30am–5pm

Charles French
Contact Mr C McCleave
✉ **2 Kings Drive, Eastbourne, East Sussex, BN21 2NU** Ⓟ
☎ 01323 720128
Est. 1969 *Stock size* Medium
Stock General antiques
Open Mon–Fri 10am–5.30pm
Services House clearance

A & T Gibbard (PBFA)
Contact Mrs M T Gibbard
✉ **30 South Street, Eastbourne, East Sussex, BN21 4XB** Ⓟ
☎ 01323 734128 Ⓕ 01323 734128
Est. 1910 *Stock size* Large
Stock Antiquarian and second-hand books, specializing in natural history, travel, topography, leather-bound books
Open Mon–Sat 9.30am–5.30pm
Fairs Russell Hotel

Edgar Horn's Fine Art Auctioneers
Contact Sue Thomas
✉ **46–50 South Street, Eastbourne, East Sussex, BN21 4XB** Ⓟ
☎ 01323 410419 Ⓕ 01323 416540
Ⓦ www.edgarhorns.com
Est. 1924
Open Mon–Fri 9am–5pm
Sales General sales, Victorian and later effects, Tues 10am, viewing Sat 9am–12.30pm Mon 9am–7pm. 6 Antique sales per annum, Wed 10am, viewing prior Sat 9am–12.30pm, Mon 9am–7pm, Tues 9am–5pm
Frequency Fortnightly
Catalogues Yes

The Old Town Antiques Centre
Contact Mrs V Franklin
✉ **52 Ocklynge Road, Eastbourne, East Sussex, BN21 1PR** Ⓟ
☎ 01323 416016
Est. 1989 *Stock size* Large
No. of dealers 16
Stock Mixed antiques, furniture, fine porcelain, glass, silver, Beswick, Copenhagen figures etc
Open Mon–Sat 10am–5pm
Services Valuations, restorations

Timothy Partridge Antiques
✉ **46 Ocklynge Road, Eastbourne, East Sussex, BN21 1PP**
☎ 01323 638731
Ⓜ 07860 864709
Stock size Medium
Stock General pre-war goods, furniture, smalls
Open Mon–Fri 10am–1pm 2–5pm

Pharoahs Antiques
Contact Mr W Pharoah
✉ **28 South Street, Eastbourne, East Sussex, BN21 4XB** Ⓟ
☎ 01323 738655
Ⓜ 0771 4398870
Est. 1988 *Stock size* Medium
Stock Lighting, linen, china, furniture, medical instruments, the bizarre, architectural ironmongery
Open Mon–Sat 10am–5pm
Fairs Ardingly

Seaquel Antiques & Collectors Market
Contact Mrs P Mornington-West
✉ **37 Seaside Road, Eastbourne, East Sussex, BN21 3PP** Ⓟ
☎ 01323 645032
Ⓔ c.mornington@hotmail.com
Est. 1998 *Stock size* Large
No. of dealers 18
Stock Furniture, collectables, bric-a-brac
Open Mon–Sat 10am–5pm Sun 11am–5pm

Shine's Antiques and Collectables
Contact Brian Shine
✉ **8 Crown Street, Eastbourne, East Sussex, BN21 1NX** Ⓟ
☎ 01323 726261
Est. 1999 *Stock size* Large
Stock Antiques, collectables
Open Mon–Sat 10am–5pm

South Coast Collectables
Contact Sylvia Redford
✉ **85 Seaside Road, Eastbourne, East Sussex, BN21 3PL** Ⓟ
☎ 01323 648811
Est. 1997 *Stock size* Large
No. of dealers 18
Stock Antiques, collectables, Georgian–Edwardian furniture
Open Mon–Sat 10am–5pm

FOREST ROW

Cadari Ltd
Contact Marie Camp
✉ **6 Newlands Place, Hartfield Road, Forest Row, East Sussex, RH18 5DQ** Ⓟ
☎ 01342 826644 Ⓕ 01342 826655
Est. 1995 *Stock size* Medium
Stock English antiques, Georgian–Victorian furniture, French antiques, smalls
Open Tues–Sat 10am–5pm
Fairs Ardingly

The Dandelion Clock
Contact Mrs L Chapman
✉ **Lewes Road, Forest Row, East Sussex, RH18 5ES** Ⓟ
☎ 01342 822335

SOUTH EAST

EAST SUSSEX • GOLDEN CROSS

Ⓦ www.dandelion-clock.co.uk.
Est. 1994 *Stock size* Large
No. of dealers 12
Stock Pine and country furniture, antiques, collectables
Open Mon–Sat 10am–5.30pm
Services Local delivery available

Falcon Antiques
Contact Mr Fallon
The Square, Lewes Road, Forrest Row, East Sussex, RH18 5ES
☎ 01342 826224 Ⓕ 01342 811127
Ⓜ 07939 365703
Est. 2000 *Stock size* Medium
Stock Furniture, 18th–early 20thC paintings, porcelain, silver
Open Mon Tues 10am–5pm
Wed 10am–12.30pm
Thurs–Sat 10am–5.30pm
Fairs Olympia, Goodwood

Jeroen Markies Antiques Ltd
Contact Mr J Markies
14–16 Hartfield Road, Forest Row, East Sussex, RH18 5HE
☎ 01342 824980 Ⓕ 01342 823677
Ⓔ sales@markies.co.uk
Ⓦ www.markies.co.uk
Est. 1981 *Stock size* Large
Stock 18th–19thC fine antique furniture, decorative objects, silver
Open Mon–Sat 9.30am–5.30pm
Services Restorations

Trojan Antiques
Contact Mr Warren Hall
The Square, Forest Row, East Sussex, RH18 5HD
☎ 01342 826766 Ⓕ 01342 826766
Ⓜ 0788 788 1301
Est. 1998 *Stock size* Large
Stock Country furniture and associated items for home and garden
Open Mon–Sat 10am–5.30pm
Services Free delivery

GOLDEN CROSS

Golden Cross Antiques
Contact Mrs R R Buchan
A22, Golden Cross, Hailsham, East Sussex, BN27 4AN
☎ 01825 872144 Ⓕ 01825 872144
Ⓜ 07957 224165
Ⓔ info@goldencrossantiques.co.uk
Ⓦ www.goldencrossantiques.co.uk
Est. 1974 *Stock size* Medium
Stock Furniture, collectables, silver
Open Mon–Sat 9am–6pm
Sun 10am–6pm
Fairs Crowborough, Felbridge

GUESTLING

Hearth & Home
Contact Mr D Hance
Rye Road, Guestling Green, Hastings, East Sussex, TN35 4LS
☎ 01424 813220 Ⓕ 01424 813220
Est. 1984 *Stock size* Medium
Stock Original Victorian and cast-iron fireplaces
Open Mon–Sat 9am–1pm
2–5.30pm
Services Advice, installation

HADLOW DOWN

Hadlow Down Antiques
Contact Mr Adrian Butler
Hastingford Farm, School Lane, Hadlow Down, Uckfield, East Sussex, TN22 4DY
☎ 01825 830707 Ⓕ 01825 830172
Ⓜ 07730 332331
Ⓔ hdantiques@talk21.com
Est. 1989 *Stock size* Large
Stock Antiques, decorative furniture, accessories
Open Mon–Sun 10am–5pm closed Wed or by appointment
Services Valuations, restorations, custom-made oak furniture

HAILSHAM

Hawkswood Antiques
Contact Mr Barry Richardson
9–10 Carew Court, Hawkswood Road, Hailsham, East Sussex, BN27 1UL
☎ 01323 844454
Est. 1989 *Stock size* Medium
Stock General antiques, collectables
Open Mon–Fri 9.30am–5.30pm
Sat 9.30am–1pm closed Wed pm
Services Free local delivery

Horsebridge Antique Centre
Contact Roger Lane
1 North Street, Lower Horsebridge, Hailsham, East Sussex, BN27 4DJ
☎ 01323 844414 Ⓕ 01323 844000
Ⓔ lane_roger@hotmail.com
Est. 1978 *Stock size* Medium
Stock General antiques
Open By appointment

Stable Doors
Contact Mr K Skinner or Mr B Skinner
Market Street, Hailsham, East Sussex, BN27 2AE
☎ 01323 844033
Est. 1996 *Stock size* Large
Stock Antiques, collectables
Open Mon–Sat 9am–5pm
Sun 10am-4pm
Fairs Ardingly

Sunburst Antiques & Art Furniture
Contact Mr John Clements
1 Carriers Path, High Street, Hailsham, East Sussex, BN27 1AP
☎ 01323 441191
Est. 1998 *Stock size* Large
Stock Late 19thC furniture
Open Mon–Sat 10am–5.30pm
Services Restorations

Wealth of Weights (Cambridge Paperweight Circle)
Contact Mrs J Skinner or Mr K Skinner
Stable Doors, Market Street, Hailsham, East Sussex, BN27 2AE
☎ 01323 441150
Ⓔ jaqui@weights.co.uk
Ⓦ www.weights.co.uk
Est. 1997 *Stock size* Large
Stock Largest selection of paperweights in the South of England
Open Mon–Sun 9am–5pm
Fairs Effingham Park, Copthorne, Woking Glass Fair
Services Valuations, collections bought

HASTINGS

Book Centre
Contact Mr R Naylor
18 West Street, Hastings, East Sussex, TN34 3AN
☎ 01424 729866
Est. 1996 *Stock size* Large
Stock Antiquarian and second-hand books
Open Mon–Sun 9am–5pm
Services Book search

Coach House Antiques
Contact Mr R J Luck
42 George Street, Hastings, East Sussex, TN34 3EA
☎ 01424 461849 Ⓕ 01424 461849

Ⓜ 07710 234803
Est. 1979 *Stock size* Large
Stock Longcase clocks, Victorian furniture, Dinky toys
Open Mon–Sun 10am–5pm
Services Valuations, restorations

John & Noel Connell
Contact Mr or Mrs J Connell
✉ **52–54 George Street, Hastings, East Sussex, TN34 3EE**
☎ 01424 434373
Est. 1999 *Stock size* Medium
Stock Furniture, silver, glass
Open Thurs–Sun 11am–4pm or by appointment

K M & J Garwood
Contact Mrs J Garwood
✉ **The Garwood Gallery, 26 George Street, Hastings, East Sussex, TN34 3EA** Ⓟ
☎ 01424 429973
Est. 1971 *Stock size* Medium
Stock Art, antiques, Oriental and tribal antiquities
Open Mon–Sun 9am–5pm

George Street Antiques Centre
Contact Mrs F Stanley
✉ **47 George Street, Hastings, East Sussex, TN34 3EA** Ⓟ
☎ 01424 429339
Est. 1984 *Stock size* Large
No. of dealers 8
Stock Collectables
Open Mon–Fri 9am–5pm Sat 10am–5pm Sun 11am–5pm

Howes Bookshop Ltd (ABA, PBFA)
Contact Mr M Bartley
✉ **Trinity Hall, Braybroke Terrace, Hastings, East Sussex, TN34 1HQ** Ⓟ
☎ 01424 423437 Ⓕ 01424 460620
Ⓔ rarebooks@howes.co.uk
Ⓦ www.howes.co.uk
Est. 1946 *Stock size* Large
Stock Antiquarian and second-hand books, arts and humanities a speciality
Open Tues–Sat 9.30am–5pm
Fairs Olympia, Chelsea
Services Valuations

Nakota Curios
Contact Mr R Kelly
✉ **12 Courthouse Street, Hastings, East Sussex, TN34 3AU** Ⓟ
☎ 01424 438900
Est. 1969 *Stock size* Large
Stock Chandeliers, decorative china, silverware, rugs, pictures, mirrors
Open Mon–Sat 10.30am–1pm 2pm–4.30pm

Old Hastings Bookshop
Contact Mr Brian Richers
✉ **15 George Street, Hastings, East Sussex, TN34 3EG** Ⓟ
☎ 01424 425989
Est. 1983 *Stock size* Small
Stock Antiquarian, rare and second-hand books
Open Mon–Sat 10am–4pm closed Wed

Reeves & Son
Contact Mr C Hawkins
✉ **4–6 Courthouse Street, Hastings, East Sussex, TN34 3AU** Ⓟ
☎ 01424 437672
Ⓜ 07778 311803
Est. 1818 *Stock size* Large
Stock Military collectables, china, smalls, books
Open Mon–Sat 9am–5pm
Services House clearance

John & Shahin Wilbraham
Contact Mr J Wilbraham
✉ **16 George Street, Hastings, East Sussex, TN34 3EG**
☎ 01424 446413
Ⓔ john@wilbraham.demon.co.uk
Ⓦ www.wilbraham.demon.co.uk
Est. 1980 *Stock size* Medium
Stock Antiquarian and second-hand books, literature and children's books a speciality
Open Mon–Sat 10am–5pm closed 1–2pm closed Wed
Services 4 catalogues issued per annum

HEATHFIELD

Colonial Times
Contact Tony Skinner
✉ **Lewes Road, Cross In Hand, Heathfield, East Sussex, TN21 0TA** Ⓟ
☎ 01435 866442/862962
Ⓜ 07860 441922
Ⓔ colonial.times@easynet.co.uk
Ⓦ www.easyweb.easynet.co.uk/~colonial.times
Est. 1978 *Stock size* Large
Stock Furniture imported from India, China and the Far East
Open Mon–Sat 10am–5pm
Fairs Newark
Services Restorations

The Pig Sty
Contact Mrs Worton
✉ **49 High Street, Heathfield, East Sussex, TN21 8HU** Ⓟ
☎ 01435 866671
Est. 1997 *Stock size* Medium
No. of dealers 10
Stock General antiques and collectables
Open Mon–Sat 9am–5pm
Services Coffee shop

Toad Hall Antique Centre
Contact Patsy Quick
✉ **57 High Street, Heathfield, East Sussex, TN21 8HU** Ⓟ
☎ 01435 863535 Ⓕ 01435 863535
Est. 1996 *Stock size* Large
No. of dealers 16
Stock Furniture, general antiques, collectables
Open Mon–Sat 9am–5.30pm Sun 11am–4pm

HORAM

John Botting
Contact Mr J Botting
✉ **Winston House, High Street, Horam, East Sussex, TN21 0ER**
☎ 01435 813553
Est. 1981 *Stock size* Medium
Stock Georgian–Edwardian furniture and effects
Open By appointment only
Fairs Ardingly, Newark

HOVE

Antiques et Cetera
Contact Mr Ken Bomzer
✉ **190 Portland Road, Hove, East Sussex, BN3 5QN** Ⓟ
☎ 01273 746159 Ⓕ 01273 746159
Est. 1994 *Stock size* Large
Stock 18thC–modern porcelain, gold, silver, glassware, pictures, furniture, chandeliers, lighting, costume jewellery
Open Mon–Fri 10am–4pm Sat 10am–1pm
Services Valuations of jewellery

Bonhams & Brooks
Contact Tim Squire-Sanders
✉ **19 Palmeira Square, Hove, East Sussex, BN3 2JN** Ⓟ

☎ 01273 220000 🄕 01273 220335
🄔 sussex@bonhams.com
🅦 www.bonhams.com
Est. 1793
Open Mon–Fri 9am–5.30pm
Sales Regional representative for Sussex, Surrey and Hampshire See Head Office (London) for details

⊞ J S Carter
Contact Mr J Carter
✉ **9 Boundary Road, Hove, East Sussex, BN3 4EH** 🅿
☎ 01273 439678 🄕 01273 416053
Est. 1974 *Stock size* Large
Stock Georgian–Edwardian furniture
Open Mon–Fri 9.30am–6pm
Services Restorations

⊞ Simon Hunter Antique Maps
Contact Mr Simon Hunter
✉ **21 St Johns Road, Hove, East Sussex, BN3 2FB** 🅿
☎ 01273 746983 🄕 01273 746983
🄔 simonhunter@fastnet.co.uk
🅦 www.antiquemaps.org.uk
Est. 1989 *Stock size* Large
Stock Antique maps
Open By appointment
Fairs AMPS Bonnington Hotel

⊞ Michael Norman Antiques Ltd (BADA)
Contact Michael Keehan
✉ **Palmeira House, 82 Western Road, Hove, East Sussex, BN3 1JB** 🅿
☎ 01273 329253/326712 🄕 01273 206556
🄔 antiques@michaelnorman.com
🅦 www.michaelnorman.com
Est. 1964 *Stock size* Large
Stock 18th–19thC English furniture
Open Mon–Sat 9am–5.30pm closed 1–2pm

⚒ Scarborough Perry Fine Arts
Contact Mr S Perry
✉ **Hove Auction Rooms, Hove Street, Hove, East Sussex, BN3 2GL** 🅿
☎ 01273 735266 🄕 01273 723813
🄔 gspfa@pavilion.co.uk
🅦 www.scarboroughperry.co.uk
Est. 1897
Open Mon–Fri 9am–5.30pm Sat 9am–noon
Sales General antique sales Thurs–Fri 10.30am, viewing Tues–Wed 10am–4.30pm Tues 6–8pm. Occasional special sales
Frequency 5–6 weeks
Catalogues Yes

⊞ Shirley-Ann's Antiques & Decorative Furniture
Contact Mrs S A Downes
✉ **69 Church Road, Hove, East Sussex, BN3 2BB** 🅿
☎ 01273 770045
Est. 1985 *Stock size* Large
Stock Georgian–Edwardian furniture and antiques
Open Mon–Sat 10am–5.30pm
Services Free delivery

⊞ Yellow Lantern Antiques (LAPADA)
Contact B. Higgins
✉ **34 Holland Road, Hove, East Sussex, BN3 1JL** 🅿
☎ 01273 771572 🄕 01273 455476
Ⓜ 07860 342976
Est. 1950 *Stock size* Medium
Stock Period English town furniture pre 1840, ormolu and bronzes
Open Mon–Fri 10am–5.30pm Sat 10am–4pm
Fairs Olympia, Buxton
Services Valuations, restorations

HURST GREEN

⊞ Delmar Antiques
Contact Mr Harry Nicol
✉ **77 London Road, Hurst Green, East Sussex, TN19 7PN** 🅿
☎ 01580 860345 🄕 01435 882039
Ⓜ 07712 543749
Est. 1951 *Stock size* Medium
Stock Period/Regency furniture, oils, watercolours, silver, clocks
Open Sat 9am–6pm or by appointment
Fairs NEC
Services Valuations, repairs

⊞ Hurst Green Antiques
Contact Mr S Atkinson
✉ **79 London Road, Hurst Green, East Sussex, TN19 7PN** 🅿
☎ 01580 860317
🅦 www.hurstgreenantiques.com
Est. 1988 *Stock size* Large
Stock English and French period furnishings for house and garden
Open Tues–Sat 9.30am–5.30pm

⊞ Libra Antiques
Contact Mrs Janice Hebert
✉ **81 London Road, Hurst Green, East Sussex, TN19 7PN** 🅿
☎ 01580 860569
Est. 1985 *Stock size* Medium
Stock Antique lamps, pine, collectables
Open Tues–Sat 9.30am–6pm Sun Mon by appointment

LEWES

⊞ Antique Interiors for Home & Garden
Contact Mr Kevin Hillman
✉ **7 Malling Street, Lewes, East Sussex, BN7 2RA** 🅿
☎ 01273 486822
Ⓜ 01273 486481
Est. 1990 *Stock size* Medium
Stock General antiques, decorative items, garden furniture, country pine
Open Mon–Sat 9.30am–5.30pm or by appointment
Fairs Ardingly, Newark

⊞ Ashcombe Coach House Antiques (BADA, CINOA)
Contact Mr Roy Green
✉ **Ashcombe Coach House, Brighton Road, Lewes, East Sussex, BN7 3JR** 🅿
☎ 01273 474794 🄕 01273 705959
Ⓜ 07803 180098/0589 127273
🄔 anglocont@applied-tech.com
Est. 1953 *Stock size* Large
Stock 18th–early 19thC furniture, decorative objects
Open By appointment only
Fairs Olympia, BADA

⊞ Bow Windows Bookshop (ABA, PBFA)
Contact Jennifer Shelley
✉ **175 High Street, Lewes, East Sussex, BN7 1YE**
☎ 01273 480780 🄕 01273 486686
🄔 rarebooks@bowwindows.com
🅦 www.bowwindows.com
Est. 1964 *Stock size* Medium
Stock General antiquarian books, all subjects
Open Mon–Sat 9.30am–5pm
Fairs Russell Hotel, International Book Fairs London
Services Valuations, 3/4 catalogues per year

⊞ David Cardoza Antiques
Contact David or Christina Cardoza

✉ **Milwards Farm, Lewes Road, Laughton, Lewes, East Sussex, BN8 6BN** P
☎ 01323 811155
Ⓜ 07855 835991
Ⓔ dcardozaantiques@aol.com
Est. 1996 *Stock size* Large
Stock French furniture, armchairs, bedside tables, beds and bedroom suites
Open Every day by appointment only
Fairs Galloway
Services Restorations upholstery

Castle Antiques
Contact Mr Christopher Harris
✉ **163a High Street, Lewes, East Sussex, BN7 1XU** P
☎ 01273 475176
Est. 1984 *Stock size* Medium
Stock Pine furniture
Open Mon–Sat 10am–5pm
Sun 11am–5pm

Church Hill Antique Centre
Contact Susan Miller or Simon Ramm
✉ **6 Station Street, Lewes, East Sussex, BN7 2DA** P
☎ 01273 474842 Ⓕ 01273 846799
Ⓦ www.church-hill-antiques.co.uk
Est. 1995 *Stock size* Large
No. of dealers 60
Stock Art, collectables
Open Mon–Sat 9.30am–5pm or by appointment
Services Valuations

Cliffe Antiques Centre
Contact The Manager
✉ **47 Cliffe High Street, Lewes, East Sussex, BN7 2AN** P
☎ 01273 473266 Ⓕ 01273 473266
Est. 1981 *Stock size* Medium
No. of dealers 15
Stock Wide range of antiques, collectables
Open Mon–Sat 9.30am–5pm

A & Y Cumming Ltd (ABA)
Contact Andrew Cumming
✉ **84 High Street, Lewes, East Sussex, BN7 1XN** P
☎ 01273 472319 Ⓕ 01273 486364
Ⓔ a.y.cumming@ukgateway.net
Est. 1976 *Stock size* Large
Stock Antiquarian and second-hand books on travel, natural history, colour plate books, 1st editions, leather bound
Open Mon–Fri 10am–5pm
Sat 10am–5.30pm
Fairs Olympia (June), Chelsea Book Fair
Services Valuations

The Elephants Trunk
Contact Mr J Milbank
✉ **The Needlemakers, West Street, Lewes, East Sussex, BN7 2NZ** P
☎ 01273 480230
Est. 1997 *Stock size* Large
Stock Antiques, collectables, furniture, lighting, mirrors
Open Mon–Sat 10am–5pm
Sun 11am–4pm
Fairs Magnum Fairs, Midhurst
Services China restoration

The Emporium Antiques Centre
Contact Michelle Doyle or Steven Madigan
✉ **42 Cliffe High Street, Lewes, East Sussex, BN7 2AN** P
☎ 01273 486866
Est. 1993 *Stock size* Large
No. of dealers 60
Stock General antiques, collectables, studio ceramics, toys, textiles, silver, jewellery, books, clocks
Open Mon–Sat 9.30am–5.30pm
Sun noon–4pm

The Emporium Antiques Centre Too
Contact Sean Lewis
✉ **24 High Street, Lewes, East Sussex, BN7 2LU** P
☎ 01273 477979
Est. 1989 *Stock size* Large
No. of dealers 100
Stock Antiques, collectables, furniture
Open Mon–Sat 9.30am–5pm
Sun noon–5pm

The Fifteenth Century Bookshop (PBFA)
Contact Mrs Miraband
✉ **99–100 High Street, Lewes, East Sussex, BN7 1XH** P
☎ 01273 474160
Est. 1930 *Stock size* Medium
Stock General stock, collectable children's books
Open Mon–Sat 10am–5.30pm
Sun 10.30am–4.30pm
Services Book search for children's books

Gorringes Incorporating Julian Dawson(SOFA)
Contact Mr Julian Dawson
✉ **56 High Street, Lewes, East Sussex, BN7 1XE** P
☎ 01273 478221 Ⓕ 01273 487369
Ⓔ auctions@gorringes.co.uk
Ⓦ www.gorringes.co.uk
Est. 1920
Open Mon–Fri 9am–5.30pm
Sat 9am–12.30pm
Sales Sales of general antiques and collectables on Mon (not Bank Hols) 10am. Viewing Fri 10am–5pm Sat 9am–12.30pm
Frequency Weekly
Catalogues No

Gorringes Incorporating Julian Dawson (SOFA, ISVA)
Contact Mr P Taylor
✉ **15 North Street, Lewes, East Sussex, BN7 2PD** P
☎ 01273 472503 Ⓕ 01273 479559
Ⓔ auctions@gorringes.co.uk
Ⓦ www.gorringes.co.uk
Est. 1926
Open Mon–Fri 8.30am–5.15pm
Sat 9am–11.45am
Sales Fine art and antiques 3-day sale Tues–Thurs at 10am, viewing Fri 10am–5pm, Sat 9.30am–4pm prior. Occasional house sales
Frequency 6 weeks
Catalogues Yes

Bob Hoare Antiques
Contact Bob Hoare
✉ **Unit Q, Phoenix Place, North Street, Lewes, East Sussex, BN7 2DQ** P
☎ 01273 480557 Ⓕ 01273 471298
Ⓔ bob@antiquebob.demon.co.uk
Ⓦ www.antiquebob.demon.co.uk
Est. 1980 *Stock size* Large
Stock Pine furniture, linen presses and pine dressers, decorative objects, etc
Open Mon–Fri 8am–6pm
Sat 9am–1pm
Services Restorations

Lewes Antique Centre
✉ **20 Cliffe High Street, Lewes, East Sussex, BN7 2AH** P
☎ 01273 476148/472173
Ⓕ 01273 476148
Est. 1968 *Stock size* Large
No. of dealers 60+
Stock Furniture, architectural salvage, bric-a-brac, china, clocks, metalware, glass

SOUTH EAST

EAST SUSSEX • NEWHAVEN

Open Mon–Sat 9.30am–5pm
Sun Bank Hols 12.30am–4.30pm
Services Storage, delivery, pine stripping, restorations,valuations

Lewes Book Centre
Contact Mr David Summerfield
38 Cliffe High Street, Lewes, East Sussex, BN7 2AN P
01273 487053
Est. 1993 *Stock size* Medium
Stock Antiquarian and second-hand books to suit all tastes, military topics a speciality
Open Mon–Sat 10am–5pm

The Lewes Clock Shop
Contact R I McColl
4 North Street, Lewes, East Sussex, BN7 2PA P
01273 473123 F 01273 473123
E rmccoll@lineone.net
Est. 1991 *Stock size* Medium
Stock Restored antique clocks
Open Mon–Sat 9am–4pm closed Wed
Services Valuations, restorations, shipping

Lewes Flea Market
Contact Mr A R Wilkinson
14a Market Street, Lewes, East Sussex, BN7 2NB P
01273 480328 F 01273 328665
M 07801 4118496
E arwilkinson@aol.com
Est. 1993 *Stock size* Large
Stock Antiques, collectables, bric-a-brac
Open Mon–Fri 9.30am–5pm
Sat Sun 10.30am–5pm

Pastorale Antiques
Contact Mr Soucek
15 Malling Street, Lewes, East Sussex, BN7 2RA P
01273 473259 F 01273 473259
Est. 1980 *Stock size* Large
Stock English, French, East European and pine furniture, garden furniture and ornaments
Open Mon–Sat 10am–5pm
Services Restorations

School Hill Antiques
Contact Mrs Tina Allen
207 High Street, Lewes, East Sussex, BN7 2NS P
01273 477782 F 01273 477782
Est. 1998 *Stock size* Medium
Stock Victorian–Edwardian furniture, decorative items
Open Mon–Sat 10am–5pm
Services Valuations, advice on decorations

The Treasury
Contact Pamela Marshall
89 High Street, Lewes, East Sussex, BN7 1XN P
01273 480446 F 01273 838785
Est. 1986 *Stock size* Medium
Stock Collectables, small antiques, out-of-production figurines
Open Thurs–Sat 10am–5pm
Services Mail order

Wallis & Wallis
Contact Mr Roy Butler
West Street Auction Galleries, Lewes, East Sussex, BN7 2NJ P
01273 480208 F 01273 476562
E auctions@wallisandwallis.co.uk
W www.wallisandwallis.co.uk
Est. 1928
Open Mon–Fri 9am–5.30pm closed 1–2pm
Sales 9 militaria, medals, coins, arms and armour per annum, 2 connoisseur arms and armour per annum, Tues Wed 11am, 8 die-cast and tinplate toys per annum, Mon 10.30am, viewing prior Fri 9am–5pm Sat 9am–1pm, morning of sale 9am–10.30pm
Frequency 6 Weeks
Catalogues Yes

NEWHAVEN

Newhaven Flea Market
Contact Mr R Mayne
28 Southway, Newhaven, East Sussex, BN9 9LA P
01273 516065
M 0771 4660522
Est. 1979 *Stock size* Large
No. of dealers 40
Stock Furniture, collectables, bric-a-brac
Open Mon–Sun 10am–5.30pm

NUTLEY

Nutley Antiques
Contact Anne Marie Dickinson
Libra House, High Street, Nutley, East Sussex, TN22 3NF P
01825 713220
Est. 1986 *Stock size* Large
Stock Rustic, country and decorative items
Open Mon–Sat 10am–5pm
Sun 1.30–5pm
Fairs Ardingly
Services Caning, rushing

PEVENSEY

The Old Mint House
Contact Mr Andrew Nicholson
High Street, Pevensey, East Sussex, BN24 5LF P
01323 762337 F 01323 762337
E antiques@minthouse.co.uk
W www.minthouse.co.uk
Est. 1966 *Stock size* Large
Stock General antiques
Open Mon–Fri 9am–5pm
Sat 10.30am–4pm
Services Shipping

POLEGATE

Graham Price Antiques Ltd
Contact Mr G Price
Applestore, Chaucer Industrial Estate, Dittons Road, Polegate, East Sussex, BN26 6JF P
01323 487167 F 01323 483904
E mail@grahampriceantiques.co.uk
W www.grahampriceantiques.co.uk
Est. 1984 *Stock size* Large
Stock Decorative and antique country furniture, rural artefacts
Open Mon–Fri 8am–5pm
Fairs Newark
Services Packing, shipping

PORTSLADE

K Edwards Antiques
Contact Mr K Edwards
Unit 2, Bestwood Works, Drove Road, Portslade, Brighton, East Sussex, BN41 2PA P
01273 420866
E kedwa31024@aol.com
W www.kedwardsantiques.co.uk
Est. 1988 *Stock size* Large
Stock Furniture, mainly chests-of-drawers
Open Mon–Fri 7.30am–6pm
Services Restorations

J Powell (Hove) Ltd (LAPADA)
Contact Mr Paul Van Brockhoven
20 Wellington Road, Portslade, Brighton, East Sussex, BN41 1DN P
01273 411599 F 01273 421591
E j-powell-hove-ltd@cwcom.net
W www.antiquesweb.co.uk/jpowell
Est. 1965 *Stock size* Large
Stock Georgian–Edwardian furniture
Open Mon–Fri 7.30am–5.30pm
Services Restorations

ROTHERFIELD

6a Antiques
Contact Mr B Samworth
6 High Street, Rotherfield, Crowborough, East Sussex, TN6 3LL
01892 852008
Est. 1979 *Stock size* Medium
Stock Georgian–Victorian furniture, antique pine
Open Mon–Sun 10am–5pm closed Wed

Forge Interiors
Contact Mr D Masham
South Street, Rotherfield, Crowborough, East Sussex, TN6 3LN
01892 853000 F 01892 853122
asiandecor@forgeinteriors.com
www.forgeinteriors.com
Est. 1999 *Stock size* Medium
Stock Asian and English furniture, decorative items
Open Tues–Sat 10am–1pm 2pm–5pm Sun 2pm–5pm
Services Chair caning

Olinda House Antiques
Contact David Hinton
Olinda House, South Street, Rotherfield, Crowborough, East Sussex, TN6 3LL
01892 852609/852412
Est. 1996 *Stock size* Large
No. of dealers 15
Stock Furniture, china, silver, glass
Open Mon–Sat 10am–5pm Sun 11am–4pm

RYE

Bears Galore
Contact Richard Tatham
c/o The Corner House, 27 High Street, Rye, East Sussex, TN31 7JF
01797 223187
bearsinrye@aol.com
www.bearsgalore.co.uk
Est. 1994 *Stock size* Medium
Stock Hand-made collectable teddy bears
Open Mon–Sat 10am–4.30pm Sun noon–4.30pm
Services Mail order

Bragge & Sons
Contact Mr John Bragge
Landgate House, Landgate, Rye, East Sussex, TN31 7LH
01797 223358 F 01797 223358
Est. 1849
Stock 18thC English furniture and works of art
Open By appointment
Services Valuations, restorations

Chapter & Verse Book Sellers
Contact Mr Spencer Rogers
105 High Street, Rye, East Sussex, TN31 7JE
01797 222692 M 07970 386905
chapterandverse@btconnect.com
Est. 1976 *Stock size* Medium
Stock Antiquarian and out-of-print books
Open Mon–Sat 9.30am–5pm closed Tues
Services Free book search

Cheyne House
Contact Keith Marshall
108 High Street, Rye, East Sussex, TN31 7JE
01797 222612
cheynehouse@ryeantiques.fsnet.co.uk
Est. 1999 *Stock size* Small
Stock Furniture, boxes
Open Mon–Sun 10am–5.30pm closed Tues

Herbert G Gasson
Contact Mr T J Booth
Lion Galleries, Lion Street, Rye, East Sussex, TN31 7LB
01797 222208 F 01797 222208
M 07703 349431
hgassonantiques@hotmail.com
Est. 1909 *Stock size* Large
Stock Early oak, country, walnut, mahogany furniture
Open Mon–Sat 10am–5.30pm

Landgate Books
Contact Mr Bill Menniss
Tower Forge, Hilders Cliff, Rye, East Sussex, TN31 7LD
01797 222280
M 07946 486445
billmenniss@hotmail.com
Est. 1987 *Stock size* Medium
Stock General second-hand and antiquarian books
Open Mon–Sat 10.30am–5pm Thurs Sun 11.15am–5pm closed Tues
Services Book search

Ann Lingard Ropewalk Antiques (LAPADA, BACA Award Winner 2001)
Contact Ann Lingard
18–22 Ropewalk, Rye, East Sussex, TN31 7NA
01797 223486 F 01797 224700
ann-lingard@ropewalkantiques.freeserve.co.uk
Est. 1976 *Stock size* Large
Stock English antique pine furniture, glass, copper, wooden items, garden items, kitchen shop
Open Mon–Fri 9am–5pm Sat 10am–4.30pm

Masons Yard
Contact Mr A Frame
17 Wish Street, Rye, East Sussex, TN31 7DA
01797 224437
Est. 1996 *Stock size* Large
Stock Antique furniture, 1920s artefacts, lighting
Open Mon–Sun 10am–5pm

Mint Antiques
Contact Mr Charles Booth
54 The Mint, Rye, East Sussex, TN31 7EN
01797 224055
Est. 1984 *Stock size* Medium
Stock Antique furniture, decorative items
Open Phone call recommended

Mint Arcade
Contact John Bartholomew
71 The Mint, Rye, East Sussex, TN31 7EW
01797 225952 F 01797 224834
johnbartholomew@freenet.co.uk
Est. 1982 *Stock size* Large
No. of dealers 5
Stock Jewellery, dolls house furniture, hand-made military figures, chess sets, picture frames and mounts, cigarette and trade cards, framed sets of cards
Open Mon–Sun 10am–4.30pm

Needles Antique Centre
Contact Jenny King
15 Cinque Ports Street, Rye, East Sussex, TN31 7AD
01797 225064
needles.antiques@btinternet.com
www.btinternet.com/~needles_antiques_online/
Est. 1996 *Stock size* Large
No. of dealers 5
Stock Small antiques, collectables
Open Mon–Sun 10am–5pm

Quayside Antiques
Contact G T D Niall

SOUTH EAST

EAST SUSSEX • SEAFORD

✉ **The Corn Exchange, The Strand, Rye, East Sussex, TN31 7DB** 🅿
☎ 01797 227088
Est. 1997 *Stock size* Large
Stock French antique furniture
Open Mon–Sun 11am–5pm

Rye Auction Galleries
Contact Mr A Paine
✉ **Rock Channel, Rye, East Sussex, TN31 7HL** 🅿
☎ 01797 222124 Ⓕ 01797 222126
Ⓜ 07769 674328
Est. 1989
Open Mon–Fri 8.30am–5pm
Sales Antique and general sales 1st and 3rd Fri of each month 9.30am, viewing Thurs 9am–5pm
Frequency Bi-monthly
Catalogues Yes

Rye Old Books
Contact Miss A Coleman
✉ **7 Lion Street, Rye, East Sussex, TN31 7LB** 🅿
☎ 01797 225410 Ⓕ 01797 225410
Est. 1993 *Stock size* Medium
Stock Antiquarian and second-hand books, illustrated, fine bindings
Open Mon–Sat 10.30am–5.30pm Sun 2–5pm by appointment on Sundays during winter
Services Valuations

Strand Quay Antiques
Contact Ann Marie Sutherland
✉ **1–2 The Strand, Rye, East Sussex, TN31 7DB** 🅿
☎ 01797 226790 Ⓜ 07788 806552
Est. 1994 *Stock size* Large
No. of dealers 12
Stock Victorian–Edwardian furniture, porcelain, glass, pictures, collectables
Open Mon–Sun 10am–5pm

Wish Barn Antiques
Contact Mr Robert Wheeler or Mr Joe Dearden
✉ **Wish Street, Rye, East Sussex, TN31 7DA** 🅿
☎ 01797 226797 Ⓕ 01797 226797
Est. 1993 *Stock size* Large
Stock 19thC pine, country and mahogany furniture
Open Mon–Sun 10am–5pm

SEAFORD

The Barn Collectors Market & Bookshop
Contact Mr B J Wicks
✉ **Church Lane, Seaford, East Sussex, BN25 1HL** 🅿
☎ 01323 890010
Est. 1969 *Stock size* Medium
No. of dealers 20
Stock Collectables, books, militaria, jewellery
Open Mon–Sat 9.30am–5pm

Colonial Times II
Contact Tony Skinner
✉ **25–27 High Street, Seaford, East Sussex, BN25 1PA** 🅿
☎ 01323 492200 Ⓕ 01323 492200
Ⓜ 07860 441922
Ⓔ colonial.times@easynet.co.uk
Ⓦ www.easyweb.easynet.co.uk/~colonial.times
Est. 1978 *Stock size* Large
Stock Furniture imported from India, China, the Far East
Open Mon–Sat 9.30am–5.30pm
Fairs Newark
Services Restoration, polishing

The Little Shop
Contact Mr C Keane
✉ **6 High Street, Seaford, East Sussex, BN25 1PG** 🅿
☎ 01323 490742
Est. 1987 *Stock size* Large
Stock General curios, collectables, dolls' house furniture
Open Mon–Sat 9.30am–6pm

ST LEONARDS-ON-SEA

The Antique Shop
Contact A. Dwight
✉ **121 Bohemia Road, St Leonards-on-Sea, East Sussex, TN37 6RL** 🅿
☎ 01424 423049
Est. 2001 *Stock size* Small
Stock Chinese and European ceramics, English and Continental glass
Open By appointment

The Book Jungle
Contact Mr M Gowen
✉ **24 North Street, St Leonards-on-Sea, East Sussex, TN38 0EX** 🅿
☎ 01424 421187
Est. 1990 *Stock size* Medium
Stock Antiquarian and second-hand books
Open Mon–Sat 10am–5pm closed Wed

Bookman's Halt
Contact Mr C Linklater
✉ **127 Bohemia Road, St Leonards-on-Sea, East Sussex, TN37 6RL** 🅿
☎ 01424 421413
Est. 1980 *Stock size* Medium
Stock Low-key general stock of antiquarian and second-hand books
Open Mon–Sat 10am–1pm 2.30pm–5pm closed Wed

Makins & Bailey
Contact Barbara Makins
✉ **42 Norman Road, St Leonards-on-Sea, East Sussex, TN38 0EG** 🅿
☎ 01424 440777
Est. 2001 *Stock size* Small
Stock Antique and decorative furniture
Open Mon–Fri 10am–5pm Sat 10am–1pm closed Wed
Services Valuations

Monarch Antiques
Contact Mr Marcus King
✉ **6 & 19 Grand Parade, St Leonards-on-Sea, East Sussex, TN38 0DD** 🅿
☎ 01424 445841 Ⓕ 01424 445841
Ⓜ 07802 217842/07809 027930
Ⓔ monarch.antiques@virgin.net
Ⓦ www.monarch-antiques.co.uk
Est. 1981 *Stock size* Large
Stock Victorian–Edwardian furniture, pine, bamboo, decorative items
Open Mon–Sat 8.30am–5.30pm or by appointment
Fairs Newark
Services Valuations, restorations

Woodstock Antiques
Contact Mr P Bebb
✉ **68 Norman Road, St Leonards-on-Sea, East Sussex, TN38 0EJ** 🅿
Ⓜ 07720 086889
Est. 1994 *Stock size* Medium
Stock Architectural and garden antiques, contemporary garden ornaments
Open Mon–Sat 10am–5pm
Services Valuations, design, search

TICEHURST

Piccadilly Rare Books (ABA, PBFA)
Contact Mr P Minet
✉ **Church Street, Ticehurst, East Sussex, TN5 7AA** 🅿
☎ 01580 201221 Ⓕ 01580 200957

ⓔ minet.royalty@btinternet.com
ⓦ www.abebooks.com/home/piccadilly
Est. 1968 *Stock size* Large
Stock Antiquarian and second-hand books
Open Mon–Sat 10am–5pm
Services Valuations

WADHURST

Browsers Barn
Contact Brian Langridge
New Pond Farm, High Street, Wallcrouch, Wadhurst, East Sussex, TN5 7JN Ⓟ
☎ 01580 200938 ⓕ 01580 200885
ⓜ 07809 836662
ⓔ brian.langridge@talk21.com
ⓦ www.browsers-barn.co.uk
Est. 1973 *Stock size* Large
Stock General antiques and collectables
Open Mon–Sat 9am–5pm Sun 10.30am–4pm
Services Shipping

Park View Antiques
Contact Bunty Ross
High Street, Durgates, Wadhurst, East Sussex, TN5 6DE Ⓟ
☎ 01892 783630 ⓕ 01892 740264
ⓜ 07974 655120
ⓦ www.parkviewantiques.co.uk
Est. 1988 *Stock size* Medium
Stock Country furniture, stripped pine, artefacts, rural items, vintage tools, period oak
Open Wed–Sun 10am–4pm and by appointment
Services Restorations

KENT

APPLEDORE

Appledore Antiques Centre
Contact Ken Thompsett
The Old Forge, High Street, Appledore, Kent, TN26 2BX Ⓟ
☎ 01233 758272
Est. 1985
No. of dealers 25
Stock General antiques
Open Mon–Sat 10am–5pm Sun 11am–5pm

ASH

Henry's of Ash
Contact Mr P Robinson
51 The Street, Ash, Canterbury, Kent, CT3 2EN Ⓟ
☎ 01304 812600
Est. 1988 *Stock size* Medium
Stock Victorian, Art Deco, pre-1950s items, general antiques, linens
Open Mon Thurs–Sat 10am–noon 2–5pm Tues 10am–noon
Fairs Copthorne, Great Danes, Ashford International

ASHFORD

Hobbs Parker
Contact Marie Sessford
Monument Way, Orbital Park, Ashford, Kent, TN24 0HB Ⓟ
☎ 01233 502222 ⓕ 01233 502211
ⓔ antiques@hobbsparker.co.uk
ⓦ www.hobbsparker.co.uk
Est. 1850
Open Mon–Fri 9am–5.30pm
Sales Regular sales of antiques and collectables in the Amos Hall
Frequency Regular
Catalogues Yes

Parkinson Auctioneers
Contact Mrs L Parkinson
46 Beaver Road, Ashford, Kent, TN23 7RP Ⓟ
☎ 01233 624426 ⓕ 01233 624426
ⓔ auctions@parkinson-uk.com
ⓦ www.parkinson-uk.com
Est. 1979
Open Mon–Fri 9am–5pm
Sales General sale Mon 10am, viewing Sat 9am–1pm
Frequency Monthly
Catalogues Yes

BECKENHAM

Stabledoors and Co
Contact Mr R Pike
94–98 High Street, Beckenham, Kent, BR3 1ED
☎ 020 8650 9270 ⓕ 020 8650 9563
ⓜ 07899 892071
Est. 1967
Open Mon–Fri 9.30am–5.30pm
Sales General antiques sale Thurs 10am, viewing Wed 10am–4pm
Frequency Fortnightly
Catalogues Yes

BENENDEN

Mervyn Carey
Contact Mr M Carey
Twysden Cottage, Benenden, Cranbrook, Kent, TN17 4LD Ⓟ
☎ 01580 240283 ⓕ 01580 240283
Est. 1991
Sales Antiques sales at Church Hall, Church Road, Tenterden, Kent. Further details by post
Frequency Quarterly
Catalogues Yes

BETHERSDEN

Stevenson Brothers (British Toymakers Guild)
Contact Mark Stevenson or Sue Russell
The Workshop, Ashford Road, Bethersden, Ashford, Kent, TN26 3AP Ⓟ
☎ 01233 820363 ⓕ 01233 820580
ⓔ sale@stevensonbros.com
ⓦ www.stevensonbros.com
Est. 1982 *Stock size* Large
Stock Antique and new rocking horses
Open Mon–Fri 9am–6pm Sat 10am–1pm
Services Restorations of children's classic cars

BEXLEY

Classical Deco
Contact Mr Terry Clarke
40 Bexley High Street, Bexley, Kent, DA5 1AH Ⓟ
☎ 01322 558527 ⓕ 01322 558527
ⓜ 07979 805892
ⓔ deco@ndirect.co.uk
ⓦ www.artdeco.ndirect.co.uk
Est. 1999 *Stock size* Medium
Stock Art Deco furniture, mirrors, lighting, figures, clocks, Clarice Cliff
Open Wed–Sat 10.30am–5pm
Services Wanted list

Ellenor Hospice Care Shop
Contact Mrs June Lynch
18–20 High Street, Bexley, Kent, DA5 1AD Ⓟ
☎ 01322 553996
Est. 1996 *Stock size* Large
Stock General antiques. All profits raised support hospice care in North West Kent and London Borough of Bexley
Open Mon–Sat 9.30am–4.30pm

BIDDENDEN

Period Piano Company
Contact David Winston
Park Farm Oast, Hareplain Road, Biddenden, Nr Ashford, Kent, TN27 8LJ Ⓟ
☎ 01580 291393

Ⓕ 01580 291393
Ⓔ periodpiano@talk21.com
Ⓦ www.periodpiano.com
Est. 1980 *Stock size* Medium
Stock 1760–1930 pianos, piano stools, music stands, music cabinets
Open By appointment
Services Valuations, restorations, shipping

BILSINGTON

The Barn at Bilsington
Contact Gabrielle de Giles
Swanton Lane, Bilsington, Ashford, Kent, TN25 7JR Ⓟ
☎ 01233 720917 Ⓕ 01233 720156
Ⓜ 07721 015263
Est. 1984 *Stock size* Large
Stock Antique and country furniture, architectural items
Open By appointment
Fairs Battersea Decorative Antique & Textile Fair
Services Valuations, restorations

BIRCHINGTON

Birchington Antiques
Contact Mr G Booker
63 Station Road, Birchington, Kent, CT7 9RE Ⓟ
☎ 01843 842811
Est. 1997 *Stock size* Medium
Stock Reupholstered antique furniture, mostly Georgian–Edwardian mahogany and walnut, china, glass
Open Mon–Sat 10am–5pm
Services Reupholstery

Galleria Pinocchio
Contact Frank or Olga Tramontin
28 Station Approach, Birchington, Kent, CT7 9RD Ⓟ
☎ 01843 847592
Ⓔ olga@galpin.fsnet.co.uk
Est. 1997 *Stock size* Small
Stock General antiques and bric-a-brac, fishing tackle, militaria
Open Mon–Sat 10am–5pm
Services Valuations

Silvesters (LAPADA)
Contact Mr S N Hartley
Albion Chambers, 1 Albion Road, Birchington, Kent, CT7 9DN Ⓟ
☎ 01843 841524 Ⓕ 01843 845131
Est. 1954
Stock Decorative items, furniture, Georgian, Victorian, silver, porcelain, glass
Open By appointment only
Services Valuations

BLUEWATER

Famously Yours Ltd
Contact Lee Croxon
Upper Thames Walk, Unit U090B, Bluewater, Greenhithe, Kent, DA9 9SR Ⓟ
☎ 01322 427072 Ⓕ 01322 427072
Ⓔ enquiries@famouslyyours.com
Ⓦ www.famouslyyours.com
Est. 1996 *Stock size* Large
Stock Autographed memorabilia
Open Mon–Fri 10am–9pm Sat 9am–8pm Sun 11am–5pm

BRASTED

David Barrington
Contact Mr D Barrington
High Street, Brasted, Kent, TN16 1JL Ⓟ
☎ 01959 562537
Est. 1947 *Stock size* Medium
Stock General antiques
Open Mon–Sun 9am–5pm or by appointment

Bigwood Antiques
Contact Steven Bigwood
Roshleigh, High Street, Brasted, Kent, TN16 1JA Ⓟ
☎ 01474 823866 Ⓕ 01474 823866
Ⓔ steve@sbigwood.force9.co.uk
Est. 1996 *Stock size* Medium
Stock Furniture
Open Mon–Sat 10.30am–5pm Sun 1.30–5pm
Services Restorations, upholstery

Cooper Fine Arts
Contact Mr Jonathan Hill-Reid
Swan House, High Street, Brasted, Kent, TN16 1JJ Ⓟ
☎ 01959 565818
Est. 1980 *Stock size* Medium
Stock Paintings and furniture
Open Mon–Sat 10am–6pm
Services Framing, restoration of oils/watercolours

Courtyard Antiques
Contact Gill Whyman
High Street, Brasted, Kent, TN16 1JE Ⓟ
☎ 01959 564483 Ⓕ 01732 454726
Est. 1982 *Stock size* Large
Stock Silver, jewellery, ceramics, 19thC furniture including extending dining tables, chairs, Tunbridge ware, glass, copper, brass, watercolours, oils, prints, objets d'art
Open Mon–Sat 10am–5pm Sun and Bank Hols 12.30–4.30pm
Services Furniture restoration, French polishing, re-leathering

Celia Jennings
Contact Celia Jennings
High Street, Brasted, Kent, TN16 1JE Ⓟ
☎ 01959 563616 Ⓕ 01689 853250
Ⓜ 07860 483292
Est. 1965 *Stock size* Medium
Stock Early European wood carvings, sculpture
Open Mon–Sat 9.30am–5.30pm
Fairs Summer Olympia

Keymer Son & Co Ltd
Contact P T Keymer
Swaylands Place, The Green, High Street, Brasted, Kent, TN16 1JY Ⓟ
☎ 01959 564203 Ⓕ 01959 561138
Est. 1977 *Stock size* Small
Stock Small 19thC furniture
Open Mon–Fri 9.30am–5.30pm

Roy Massingham Antiques (LAPADA)
Contact Mr R Massingham
The Coach House, High Street, Brasted, Kent, TN16 1JJ Ⓟ
☎ 01959 562408 Ⓕ 01959 562408
Est. 1967 *Stock size* Large
Stock 18th/19thC furniture, pictures and objects
Open By appointment any time
Services Buying 'pre-valued' antiques

Southdown House Antique Galleries
Contact Mr Graham Stead
High Street, Brasted, Kent, TN16 1JE Ⓟ
☎ 01959 563522
Est. 1978 *Stock size* Medium
Stock 18th/19thC furniture, textiles, porcelain, glass, metalware
Open Mon–Sat 10am–5pm
Services Valuations, restorations, shipping

Dinah Stoodley
Contact Mrs D Stoodley
High Street, Brasted, Kent, TN16 1JE Ⓟ

☎ 01959 563616
Est. 1965 *Stock size* Medium
Stock Early oak, country furniture
Open Mon–Sat 9.30am–5.30pm

Village Antique Centre
Contact Karen Phillips
4 High Street, Brasted, Westerham, Kent, TN16 1RF
☎ 01959 564545
Est. 1993 *Stock size* Large
No. of dealers 25
Stock Antiques up to 1930s, jewellery, pictures, country oak, teddy bears, mirrors, porcelain
Open Mon–Fri 10am–5pm Sat 10am–5.30pm Sun 11am–5pm
Services Valuations

W W Warner Antiques (BADA)
Contact Mr Chris Jowitt
The Old Forge, The Green, Brasted, Kent, TN16 1JL
☎ 01959 563698 Ⓕ 01959 563698
Est. 1957 *Stock size* Medium
Stock 18th–19thC porcelain, glass, pottery.
Open Mon–Sat 10am–5pm

BROADSTAIRS

Gillycraft
Contact Mrs Gill Faulkner
15 Albion Street, Broadstairs, Kent, CT10 1LU
☎ 01843 867983
Est. 1992 *Stock size* Large
Stock Dressed collector bears, accessories
Open Mon–Sat 9.30am–4.30pm or by appointment
Services Promotional bears, fund raising bears, personalized bears

Market Fayre
Contact Margaret Sage
69 High Street, Broadstairs, Kent, CT10 1NQ
☎ 01843 862563
Est. 1989 *Stock size* Medium
Stock Antique bric-a-brac, china, glass, dolls' houses, dolls' house furniture, limited-edition bears
Open Mon–Sat 9.30am–4.30pm

Secondhand Department
Contact Mr Alan Kemp
44 Albion Street, Broadstairs, Kent, CT10 1NE
☎ 01843 862876 Ⓕ 01843 860084
Est. 1956 *Stock size* Large
Stock Antiquarian and second-hand books
Open Mon–Sat 9am–5.30pm Sun 10.30am–4.30pm

BROMLEY

Bears 'n' Bunnies
Contact Mrs C Sales
18 The Mall, High Street, Bromley, Kent, BR1 1TS
☎ 020 8466 9520 Ⓕ 020 8466 9570
Ⓔ bearsnbunnies@btinternet.com
Ⓦ www.bearsnbunnies.btinternet.com
Est. 1995 *Stock size* Large
Stock Collectable bears from leading manufacturers
Open Mon–Sat 10am–5pm

Peter Morris (BNTA)
Contact Mr P Morris
1 Station Concourse, Bromley North Station, Bromley, Kent, BR1 4EQ
☎ 020 8313 3410 Ⓕ 020 8466 8502
Ⓔ coins@petermorris.co.uk
Ⓦ www.petermorris.co.uk
Est. 1983 *Stock size* Large
Stock Coins, medals, bank notes, antiquities
Open Mon–Fri 10am–6pm Sat 9am–2pm closed Wed
Fairs BNTA Coinex
Services Mail order, 4 illustrated lists, valuations

Past & Present
Contact Mrs Jan Sibley
22 Plaistow Lane, Bromley, Kent, BR1 3PA
☎ 020 8466 7056
Ⓜ 07961 995303
Est. 1992 *Stock size* Large
Stock Varied range of antiques, furniture, china, tools, records, books, garden items
Open Mon–Sat 9am–5.30pm
Services House clearance

The Studio
Contact Mr Ian Burt
2 Sundridge Parade, Plaistow Lane, Bromley, Kent, BR1 4DT
☎ 020 8466 9010
Est. 1998 *Stock size* Large
Stock Georgian–Edwardian furniture, Art Deco, ceramics
Open Tues–Sat 11am–4.30pm or by appointment closed Thurs

CANTERBURY

Antique & Design
Contact Mr S Couchman
The Old Oast, Hollow Lane, Canterbury, Kent, CT1 3SA
☎ 01227 762871 Ⓕ 01227 780970
Est. 1987 *Stock size* Large
Stock English and Continental pine furniture
Open Mon–Sat 9am–6pm Sun 11am–5pm

Bygones Reclamation (Canterbury) Ltd
Contact Bob Thorpe
Nackington Road, Canterbury, Kent, CT4 7BA
☎ 01227 767453 Ⓕ 01227 762153
Ⓜ 07802 278424
Ⓔ bob@bygones.net
Ⓦ www.bygones.net
Est. 1991 *Stock size* Large
Stock Victorian fireplaces, cast-iron radiators, building materials, architectural salvage, 1000s of reclaimed items
Open Mon–Sun 9am–5.30pm
Services Paint stripping, spraying, sand blasting, welding repairs

The Canterbury Auction Galleries (SOFAA)
Contact Christine Wacker
40 Station Road West, Canterbury, Kent, CT2 8AN
☎ 01227 763337 Ⓕ 01227 456770
Est. 1911
Open Mon–Fri 9am–1pm 2–5pm
Sales 6 specialist sales a year. Monthly sales of Victorian and later furniture
Frequency Bi-monthly
Catalogues Yes

The Canterbury Book Shop (PBFA, ABA)
Contact David Miles
37 Northgate, Canterbury, Kent, CT1 1BL
☎ 01227 464773 Ⓕ 01227 780073
Est. 1980 *Stock size* Medium
Stock Antiquarian and second-hand books
Open Mon–Sat 10am–5pm
Fairs PBFA fairs, ABA London
Services Valuations

Chaucer Bookshop (ABA)
Contact Robert Sherston-Baker
6–7 Beer Cart Lane, Canterbury, Kent, CT1 2NY

☎ 01227 453912 Ⓕ 01227 451893
Ⓔ chaucerbooks@canterbury.dialnet.com
Ⓦ www.chaucer-bookshop.co.uk/main.html
Est. 1957 *Stock size* Large
Stock Antiquarian and out-of-print books
Open Mon–Sat 10am–5pm or by appointment
Services Valuations, Shipping

W J Christophers
Contact Mr W Christophers
9 The Borough, Canterbury, Kent, CT1 2DR Ⓟ
☎ 01227 451968
Est. 1970 *Stock size* Large
Stock General antiques, 1720s–1950s, pottery, porcelain, clocks, furniture, prints, books
Open Mon–Sat 9am–5pm

The Coach House Antique Centre
Contact Manager
2a Duck Lane, Northgate, Canterbury, Kent, CT1 2AE Ⓟ
☎ 01227 463117
Est. 1975 *Stock size* Large
No. of dealers 10
Stock General antiques, collectables, pressed glass
Open Mon–Sat 10am–4pm

Conquest House Antiques
Contact Mrs C Hill
17 Palace Street, Canterbury, Kent, CT1 2DZ Ⓟ
☎ 01227 464587 Ⓕ 01227 451375
Ⓔ empire@empire-antiques.co.uk
Ⓦ www.empire-antiques.co.uk
Est. 1994 *Stock size* Large
Stock Georgian–Victorian furniture, small items, paintings, chandeliers, rugs
Open Mon–Sat 10am–5pm
Services Valuations, restorations

G W Finn and Son Auctioneers (RICS)
Contact Mr James Linington
Canterbury Auction Market, Market Way, Canterbury, Kent, CT2 7JG Ⓟ
☎ 01227 767751 Ⓕ 01227 478566
Ⓦ www.thesaurus.co.uk/gwfinn
Est. 1880
Open Mon–Fri 9am–1pm
Sales Antiques and fine art sales, general household sales
Frequency Monthly
Catalogues Yes

Stuart Heggie (Photographic Collectors Club)
Contact Mr Stuart Heggie
14 The Borough, Northgate, Canterbury, Kent, CT1 2DR Ⓟ
☎ 01227 470422 Ⓕ 01227 470422
Ⓔ heggie.cameras@virgin.net
Est. 1980 *Stock size* Medium
Stock Vintage cameras, optical toys, photographic images
Open Fri–Sat 10am–5pm
Fairs South London Photographic Fair, Photographica
Services Valuations, restorations

Housepoints
Contact Mr Robin Ross Hunt
13 The Borough, Canterbury, Kent, CT1 2DR Ⓟ
☎ 01227 451350
Ⓜ 07808 784638
Est. 1984 *Stock size* Large
Stock French country pine furniture, Victorian–Edwardian pieces
Open Mon–Fri 10am–5pm Sat 9.30am–6pm
Services Restorations

The Neville Pundole Gallery
Contact Neville Pundole
8a and 9 The Friars, Canterbury, Kent, CT1 2AS Ⓟ
☎ 01227 453471 Ⓕ 01227 453471
Ⓔ neville@pundole.co.uk
Ⓦ www.pundole.co.uk
Est. 1986 *Stock size* Large
Stock Moorcroft and contemporary pottery, glass
Open Mon–Sat 10am–5pm or by appointment
Services Valuations

Phillips International Auctioneers and Valuers
27 Watling Street, Canterbury, Kent, CT1 2UD
☎ 01227 819000 Ⓕ 01227 819003
Ⓦ www.phillips-auction.com
Sales Regional Office. Telephone for details

Pinetum
Contact Mr Alan Pattinson
25 Oaten Hill, Canterbury, Kent, CT1 3HZ Ⓟ
☎ 01227 780365 Ⓕ 01227 780365
Est. 1972 *Stock size* Medium
Stock Pine and country furniture
Open Mon–Sat 9.30am–5pm Sun 10am–3pm
Services Valuations, polishing

Whatever Comics
Contact Mr M Armario
2 Burgate Lane, Canterbury, Kent, CT1 2HH Ⓟ
☎ 01227 453226
Est. 1988 *Stock size* Large
Stock Die-cast cars, *Star Trek*, *Star Wars* toys, movie-related items, sci-fi collectables, Beanie Babies, action figures
Open Mon–Sat 10am–5.30pm

World Coins
Contact David Mason
35–36 Broad Street, Canterbury, Kent, CT1 2LR Ⓟ
☎ 01227 768887
Ⓔ worldcoins@bigfoot.com
Ⓦ www.worldcoins.freeservers.com
Est. 1970 *Stock size* Large
Stock Coins, medals, militaria, bank notes, stamps, medallions, tokens
Open Mon–Sat 9.30am–5pm closed Thurs pm
Services Valuations, identification, quarterly catalogue

CHATHAM

The American Comic Shop
Contact Mr K Earl
1 Church Street, Chatham, Kent, ME4 4BS Ⓟ
☎ 01634 817410
Est. 1993 *Stock size* Large
Stock American imported comics, graphic novels, collectable toys, posters
Open Mon Wed–Fri 10am–5.30pm Tues 10am–5pm Sat 9am–5.30pm
Fairs Science Fiction Fair
Services Valuations, mail order, standing order

CHISLEHURST

Chislehurst Antiques (LAPADA)
Contact Margaret Crawley
7 Royal Parade, Chislehurst, Kent, BR7 6NR Ⓟ
☎ 020 8467 1530 Ⓕ 020 8249 7705
Ⓜ 07768 081577
Est. 1978 *Stock size* Large
Stock 1860–1910 lighting, mirrors, 1760–1900 furniture
Open Fri Sat Mon 10am–5pm Sun 11am–4pm or by appointment

Michael Sim (LAPADA)
Contact Mr M Sim
1 Royal Parade, Chislehurst, Kent, BR7 6NR
020 8467 7040 020 8467 4352
Est. 1983 *Stock size* Large
Stock Clocks, barometers, Georgian furniture
Open Mon–Sat 9am–6pm
Services Restorations

Wrattan Antique & Craft Mews
Contact Mrs M Brown
51–53 High Street, Chislehurst, Kent, BR7 5AF
020 8295 5933
Est. 1996 *Stock size* Large
No. of dealers 45
Stock Antiques, collectables, crafts
Open Mon–Sat 9.30am–5pm
Services Café

CLIFTONVILLE

Cliftonville Antiques
Contact Mr F Al-Aldan
161 Northdown Road, Cliftonville, Margate, Kent, CT9 2PA
01843 223470 01843 223470
Est. 1994 *Stock size* Large
Stock Antique furniture, silver, china, clocks
Open Mon–Sat 10am–5pm

Cottage Antiques
Contact Mr P J Emsley
172 Northdown Road, Cliftonville, Margate, Kent, CT9 2RB
01843 298214/299166
07771 542872
Est. 1990 *Stock size* Large
Stock Georgian–1930s antiques, oak, china, silver, smalls
Open Mon–Sat 10am–5pm
Services Valuations

CRANBROOK

Bentleys Fine Art Auctioneers (RADS)
Contact Mr Raj Bisram
The Old Granary, Waterloo Road, Cranbrook, Kent, TN17 3JQ
01580 715857 01580 715857
cranauct@aol.com
Est. 1995
Open Mon–Fri 10am–5pm
Sat 10am–1pm
Sales 1st Sat monthly antiques and fine art sale 11am, viewing 3 days prior 10am–6.30pm. Specialist sales throughout the year
Frequency Monthly
Catalogues Yes

Douglas Bryan Antiques (BADA, LAPADA)
Contact Douglas Bryan
The Old Bakery, St Davids Bridge, Cranbrook, Kent, TN17 3HN
01580 713103 01580 712407
Est. 1980 *Stock size* Medium
Stock 17th–18thC oak furniture, associated items
Open Thurs–Sat 10am–5pm or by appointment
Fairs Olympia, BADA

Cranbrook Antiques
Contact Sue Bisram
15 High Street, Cranbrook, Kent, TN17 3EB
01580 712173
07714 391230
RBisramthe@aol.com
Est. 1989 *Stock size* Large
No. of dealers 10
Stock 19thC country antiques, silver, small items of furniture, ceramics, prints
Open Mon–Sat 10am–5pm

The Old Tackle Box
Contact Richard Dowson
PO Box 55, Cranbrook, Kent, TN17 3ZY
01580 713979 01580 713979
Est. 1994 *Stock size* Large
Stock Antique fishing tackle
Open By appointment
Services Valuations and mail order

Swan & Foxhole Antiques
Contact Mr Robert White
Albert House, Stone Street, Cranbrook, Kent, TN17 3HG
01580 712720
www.cranbrookpc.freeserve.co.uk
Est. 1979 *Stock size* Medium
Stock Folk art, country decorated furniture
Open Tues Thurs–Sat 10am–1pm 2pm–5pm closed Mon Wed
Fairs Olympia, Decorative Fair, Battersea
Services Restorations, chair caning, valuations

Tudor House Antiques
Contact Phil or Eileen Prosser
Stone Street, Cranbrook, Kent, TN17 3HE
01580 715845
Est. 1993 *Stock size* Large
Stock Decorative items, textiles, 18thC oak, general furniture
Open Mon–Sat 10am–5pm Wed 11am–3.30pm

Vestry Antiques
Contact Mrs L Dawkins
3a Stone Street, Cranbrook, Kent, TN17 3HF
01580 713563
Est. 1994 *Stock size* Large
Stock 18th–early 19thC pine, oak, mahogany furniture, decorative items
Open Mon–Sat 9.30am–5pm
Services Local delivery, full or part house clearance, single items purchased

DARTFORD

Wot-a-Racket (GCS [GB, USA], TCS)
Contact Mr B Casey
250 Shepherds Lane, Dartford, Kent, DA1 2PN
01322 220619 01322 220619
07808 593467
wot-a-racket@talk21.com
Est. 1981 *Stock size* Large
Stock Sporting memorabilia
Open By appointment
Fairs Newark, Ardingly, Sandown Park, Alexandra Palace

DEAL

Decors
Contact Nicole Loftus-Potter
67a Beach Street, Deal, Kent, CT14 6HY
01304 368030 01304 368030
Est. 1990 *Stock size* Medium
Stock 17th–19thC antiques, modern St Louis, Baccarat, non-renewable pieces, textiles
Open Mon–Sun 10am–7pm or by appointment

Delpierre Antiques
Contact Margery Borley
132 High Street, Deal, Kent, CT14 6BE
01304 371300
07771 864231
Est. 1998 *Stock size* Medium

SOUTH EAST

KENT • EAST PECKHAM

Stock Individual and specialist pieces, lighting, Art Deco, Art Nouveau, Oriental, French furniture
Open Tues–Sat 9.30am–5pm or by appointment
Services Valuations

⊞ Fordham's
Contact Mr A Fordham
✉ **3a Victoria Road, Deal, Kent, CT14 7AS** Ⓟ
☎ 01304 373599 Ⓕ 01304 389333
Est. 1974 *Stock size* Medium
Stock Silver, furniture, general antiques, antiquities, second-hand and antiquarian books
Open Mon–Sat 9.30am–4.30pm or by appointment
Services Valuations for probate/insurance

⊞ Mulbery Antiques
Contact Mrs Nina Spencer
✉ **7 St Georges Passage, Deal, Kent, CT14 6TA**
☎ 01304 381800 Ⓕ 01304 381800
Est. 1988 *Stock size* Medium
Stock General antiques, furniture, glass, china, textiles, lamps, lighting, jewellery
Open Tues Thurs–Sat 10am–4pm
Services Commissions undertaken

⊞ Pretty Bizarre
Contact Phillip Hartley
✉ **170 High Street, Deal, Kent, CT14 6BQ** Ⓟ
Ⓜ 07973 794537
Est. 1991 *Stock size* Medium
Stock General antiques including Art Deco
Open Fri–Sat 10am–4pm

⊞ Quill Antiques
Contact Mr A J Young
✉ **12 Alfred Square, Deal, Kent, CT14 6LR** Ⓟ
☎ 01304 375958
Est. 1969 *Stock size* Small
Stock General small antiques
Open Mon–Sat 9am–5pm

⊞ Ron's Emporium
Contact Mr Ron Blown
✉ **98 Church Lane, Sholden, Deal, Kent, CT14 9QL** Ⓟ
☎ 01304 374784 Ⓕ 01304 380294
Est. 1979 *Stock size* Large
Stock Unusual items, clocks, phone boxes, antique furniture, snooker tables, collectables
Open Mon–Sat 9.30am–5.30pm closed Thurs
Services House clearance

⊞ Serendipity
Contact Marion Short or Jayne Eschalier
✉ **125 High Street, Deal, Kent, CT14 6BB** Ⓟ
☎ 01304 369165
Ⓔ dipityantiques@aol.com
Est. 1979 *Stock size* Large
Stock Small furniture, ceramics, pictures
Open Mon–Wed Fri 10am–4.30pm closed 12.30–2pm Sat 9.30am–4.30pm or by appointment
Fairs Sandown Park
Services Restoration of pictures

⊞ Toby Jug Collectables
Contact Mrs S Pettit
✉ **South Toll House, Deal Pier Beach Street, Deal, Kent, CT14 6HZ** Ⓟ
☎ 01304 369917
Est. 1996 *Stock size* Large
Stock Royal Doulton, discontinued Toby and character jugs, other china collectables
Open Tues–Sun 11am–5.30pm closed 1.30–2.30pm

EAST PECKHAM

⊞ Desmond and Amanda North
Contact Desmond North
✉ **The Orchard, 186 Hale Street, East Peckham, Kent, TN12 5JB** Ⓟ
☎ 01622 871353 Ⓕ 01622 872998
Est. 1971 *Stock size* Medium
Stock Persian and other Oriental rugs, carpets, runners, and cushions 1800–1939
Open Mon–Sun appointment advisable
Services Valuations, restorations

EDENBRIDGE

⊞ Lennox Cato Antiques (BADA, LAPADA, WKADA, CINOA)
Contact Lennox or Susan Cato
✉ **1 The Square, Church Street, Edenbridge, Kent, TN8 5BD** Ⓟ
☎ 01732 865988 Ⓕ 01732 865988
Ⓜ 07836 233473
Ⓔ cato@lennoxcato.com
Ⓦ www.lennoxcato.com
Est. 1979 *Stock size* Medium
Stock 18th–19thC furniture, works of art, accessories
Open Mon–Sat 9.30am–5.30pm
Fairs Olympia, BADA, Harrogate
Services Valuations, consultancy, restorations

⊞ Chevertons of Edenbridge Ltd (LAPADA)
Contact Angus or David Adam
✉ **67–73 High Street, Edenbridge, Kent, TN8 5AL** Ⓟ
☎ 01732 863196 Ⓕ 01732 864298
Ⓜ 07711 234010
Ⓔ chevertons@msn.com
Ⓦ www.chevertons.com
Est. 1959 *Stock size* Large
Stock English and Continental antique and decorative furniture, accessories
Open Mon–Sat 9am–5.30pm
Fairs NEC, Olympia

⊞ Way Back When
Contact Mrs L Hayward
✉ **25 High Street, Edenbridge, Kent, TN8 5AB** Ⓟ
☎ 01732 868280 Ⓕ 01732 868280
Est. 1995 *Stock size* Large
Stock Worcester, Derby, Crown Derby, jewellery, clocks, furniture, general antiques, 18thC glass and silver
Open Tues–Sat 10am–5.30pm

⊞ Yew Tree Antiques
Contact Mr Bob Carter
✉ **Crossways, Four Elms Road, Edenbridge, Kent, TN8 6AF** Ⓟ
☎ 01732 700215
Est. 1984 *Stock size* Large
Stock Small furniture, bric-a-brac, books, linen, pictures
Open Mon 1.30–5pm Tues–Sat 10am–5pm Sun 1.30–5pm
Services House clearance

ELHAM

⊞ Elham Antiques
Contact Mr Julian Chambers
✉ **High Street, Elham, Kent, CT17 9AH** Ⓟ
☎ 01303 840085
Est. 1989 *Stock size* Large
Stock Architectural antiques, old metal toys
Open Tues–Sat 10.30am–5.30pm
Fairs Sandown Park, Newark
Services Valuations

Elham Valley Book Shop (PBFA)
Contact Mr Tim Parsons
St Mary's Road, Elham, Canterbury, Kent, CT4 6TH
01303 840359 01303 840359
books@elham-valley.demon.co.uk or etchinghill@hotmail.com
www.elham-valley.demon.co.uk
Est. 1992 *Stock size* Large
Stock Rare and second-hand books including those on art, travel, topography, modern 1st editions, illustrated, natural history, private press a speciality
Open Tues Thurs 2–4.30pm Fri 11.30am–4.30pm Sat 11am–5pm Sun noon–4pm closed Mon and Wed
Services Valuations

ERITH

Belmont Jewellers
Contact Mr S J Girt
5 Belmont Road, Northumberland Heath, Erith, Kent, DA8 1JY
01322 339646
Est. 1986 *Stock size* Small
Stock Jewellery, furniture, pictures, silver, silver plate
Open Mon–Sat 9am–5pm
Fairs Ardingly
Services Valuations, jewellery repairs

FARNBOROUGH

Farnborough Antiques
Contact Mr D Phillips
119 High Street, Farnborough, Orpington, Kent, BR6 7AZ
01689 855461
07932 628836
Est. 1984 *Stock size* Medium
Stock Antique lighting, furniture
Open Mon–Wed Fri Sat 9.30am–6pm Thurs 9.30am–noon
Services Lighting restorations, repairs

FARNINGHAM

Adams Arts & Antiques Ltd
Contact Mr M Adams
The Old Forge, 1 High Street, Farningham, Dartford, Kent, DA4 0DG
01322 866877 01322 866877
Est. 1998 *Stock size* Medium
Stock Mainly metalware, stoneware, garden statuary
Open Mon–Sun 9am–5pm

P T Beasley
Contact Mrs R Beasley
Forge Yard, High Street, Farningham, Dartford, Kent, DA4 0DB
01322 862453
Est. 1964 *Stock size* Large
Stock 17th–19thC furniture, small items, brass, pewter
Open Mon–Sun 9am–5pm or by appointment

Farningham Pine
Contact Mr P Dzierzek
The Old Bull Stores, Farningham, Kent, DA4 0DG
01322 863230 01322 863168
Est. 1987 *Stock size* Large
Stock Pine furniture
Open Mon–Sat 10am–5pm Sun 11am–3pm closed Wed

FAVERSHAM

Collectors' Corner
Contact Mrs Mavis Mileham
East Street, Crescent Road, Faversham, Kent, ME13 8AD
01795 539721
Est. 1988 *Stock size* Medium
Stock Second-hand tools, brassware, door knobs, furniture, coins, pictures, cigarette cards
Open Mon–Sat 10am–5pm closed Wed Thurs

Faversham Antiques and Collectables
Contact Mr Ralph Lane
7 Court Street, Faversham, Kent, ME13 7AN
01795 591471
Est. 1997 *Stock size* Large
Stock General furniture, collectables, blue and white china, Osborne plaques, jewellery
Open Mon–Sat 10am–5pm
Fairs Ardingly

Squires Antiques
Contact Ann Squires
3 Jacob Yard, Preston Street, Faversham, Kent, ME13 8NY
01795 531503 01795 591600
Est. 1984 *Stock size* Large
Stock General antiques
Open Mon Tues Fri Sat 10am–5pm

FOLKESTONE

Bespoke Furniture
Contact Mr M McEwan
55 Sandgate High Street, Folkestone, Kent, CT20 3AA
01303 249515 01303 249515
Est. 1994
Stock Chairs, tables, cabinets
Open Mon–Fri 8.30am–5pm Sat 9am–2pm Sun by appointment
Services Restorations

Bookstop
Contact Jenny Hurst
21 Tontine Street, Folkestone, Kent, CT20 1JT
01303 227333 01303 863583
hx69@dial.pipex.com
Est. 1995 *Stock size* Medium
Stock Antiquarian, second-hand, out-of-print books
Open Mon–Sat 10am–5am closed Wed winter openings call first
Services Book search

Hogben Auctioneers & Valuers Ltd
Contact Mr M Hogben
Unit C, Highfields Industrial Estate, Warren Road, Folkestone, Kent, CT19 6DD
01303 246810 01303 246256
hogbenauctions@btconnect.com
www.hogbenauctioneers.com
Est. 1986
Open Mon–Fri 9am–5pm
Sales 3 weekly. Sat fine art and collectables, Sun Victorian and later, viewing Thurs 10am–6pm Fri 10am–8pm. Specialist jewellery, ephemera, books and Art Deco sales throughout the year
Catalogues Yes

Lawton's Antiques
Contact Ian Lawton
26 Canterbury Road, Folkestone, Kent, CT19 5NG
01303 246418
Est. 1987 *Stock size* Medium
Stock General antiques
Open Mon–Sat 9am–6pm
Services Valuations

Alan Lord Antiques
Contact Mr R Lord
71 Tontine Street, Folkestone, Kent, CT20 1JR

☎ 01303 253674 Ⓕ 01303 240284
Est. 1953 *Stock size* Large
Stock General antiques, unrestored furniture
Open Mon–Fri 9am–5pm Sat 10am–1pm
Services House clearance of antiques to 1930

G & DI Marrin & Son (ABA & PBFA)
Contact John or Patrick Marrin
✉ **149 Sandgate Road, Folkestone, Kent, CT20 2DA** Ⓟ
☎ 01303 253016 Ⓕ 01303 850956
Ⓜ 07768 961495/6
Ⓔ marrinbook@clara.co.uk
Ⓦ www.marrinbook.clara.net
Est. 1947 *Stock size* Medium
Stock Books on topography of Kent, history and literature of the Great War, prints, maps
Open Tues–Sat 9.30am–5.30pm
Fairs PBFA London Book Fair, Russell Hotel – Monthly, major events in the UK and overseas
Services Valuations

GOUDHURST

Mill House Antiques
Contact Brad Russell
✉ **Unit 3, Fountain House, High Street, Goudhurst, Kent, TN17 1AL** Ⓟ
☎ 01580 212476
Est. 1991 *Stock size* Medium
Stock Pine and country antiques, complementary items
Open Tues–Sat 10am–5pm
Services Valuations

GRAVESEND

Courtyard Antiques
Contact Mrs J Giles
✉ **7a Manor Road, Gravesend, Kent, DA12 1AA**
☎ 01474 369399
Est. 1987 *Stock size* Medium
Stock Victorian–1930s furniture, collectables
Open Mon–Sat 10am–4.30pm
Services Restorations

GREEN STREET GREEN

Antica Antiques
Contact Mrs Muccio
✉ **48 High Street, Green Street Green, Orpington, Kent, BR6 6BJ** Ⓟ
☎ 01689 851181
Est. 1980 *Stock size* Medium
Stock General antiques, bric-a-brac
Open Mon–Sat 10am–5pm closed Thurs

GREENHITHE

Bears 'n' Bunnies
Contact Mrs C Sales
✉ **Bluewater Shopping Centre, Upper Thames Walk, Greenhithe, Kent, DA9 9SR** Ⓟ
☎ 01322 624997
Ⓦ www.bearsnbunnies.com
Est. 1999 *Stock size* Large
Stock Collectable bears from leading manufacturers and artists
Open Mon–Fri 10am–9pm Sat 9am–8pm Sun 11am–5pm

HADLOW

Lime Tree House Antiques
Contact Wendy Thomas
✉ **Lime Tree House, 2 High Street, Hadlow, Kent, TN11 0EE** Ⓟ
☎ 01732 852002 Ⓕ 01732 852002
Est. 1987 *Stock size* Large
Stock Oak, mahogany and decorative furniture
Open Tues–Sun 10am–4pm
Fairs Newark, Ardingly
Services Valuations, restorations

HAMSTREET

Woodville Antiques
Contact Andrew MacBean
✉ **The Street, Hamstreet, Ashford, Kent, TN26 2HG** Ⓟ
☎ 01233 732981 Ⓕ 01233 732981
Ⓜ 07762783354
Ⓔ woodvilleantique@netscapeonline.co.uk
Est. 1988 *Stock size* Medium
Stock Antique and collectable tools, glass, furniture
Open Tues–Sun 10am–5.30pm
Services Valuations

HARRIETSHAM

B J Norris
Contact Mrs Norris
✉ **The Quest, West Street, Harrietsham, Maidstone, Kent, ME17 1JD** Ⓟ
☎ 01622 859515/692515
Ⓕ 01622 859515
Ⓔ norris02@globalnet.co.uk
Ⓦ www.antiquesbulletin.com/bjnorris
Est. 1972
Open Mon–Fri 9am–5pm
Sales General antiques sale Thurs 10am, viewing Thurs 8am–1pm prior to sale
Frequency Fortnightly

HAYES

Allbrooks
Contact Nina Allbutt
✉ **16 Station Approach, Hayes, Bromley, Kent, BR2 7EH** Ⓟ
☎ 020 8462 3772
Ⓜ 07930 166290
Ⓔ carole@allbrooks.fsbusiness.co.uk
Est. 1999 *Stock size* Large
No. of dealers 20
Stock Antiques, curiosities
Open Mon–Sat 10am–5pm

HEADCORN

Headcorn Antiques
Contact Mr or Mrs Smith
✉ **61 High Street, Headcorn, Ashford, Kent, TN27 9QA** Ⓟ
☎ 01622 890050 Ⓕ 01622 890050
Est. 1994 *Stock size* Medium
Stock General antiques, Continental pine, mahogany, oak
Open Mon–Sat 10am–5pm Sun 11am–4pm

Penny Lampard
Contact Mrs Lampard
✉ **31–33 High Street, Headcorn, Ashford, Kent, TN27 9NE** Ⓟ
☎ 01622 890682
Est. 1985 *Stock size* Large
Stock Decorative pieces for the interior design trade
Open Mon–Sat 9.30am–5.30pm Sun 11am–5pm
Fairs Detling
Services Tea shop

HERNE BAY

Archaic Artifacts
Contact Miss E J Hooper
✉ **Wealden Forest Park, Herne Common, Herne Bay, Kent, CT6 7LQ** Ⓟ
☎ 01227 711840 Ⓕ 01227 711840
Est. 1996 *Stock size* Large
Stock Oak beams, bricks, slates, Kent peg tiles, floor tiles,

architectural salvage, fireplaces, doors, floor boarding
Open Mon–Sat 9am–5pm Sun 10am–4pm
Services Demolition

HIGH HALDEN

High Halden Antiques
Contact Mr Jennings
Ashford Road, High Halden, Ashford, Kent, TN26 3BY
☎ 01233 850195
Est. 40 years *Stock size* Medium
Stock Victorian–Edwardian furniture, mahogany
Open Tues–Sat 10am–5pm
Services Valuations, restorations

Rother Reclamation (SALVO)
Contact Mrs Symonds
The Old Tile Centre, Ashford Road, High Halden, Tenterden, Kent, TN26 3BP
☎ 01233 850075 F 01233 850955
M 07889 387136
Est. 1960 *Stock size* Medium
Stock Renovation materials, bricks, tiles, oak beams, flooring, doors, slate, stone, railway sleepers, garden statuary, pine furniture, sanitary ware etc
Open Mon–Sat 8am–5pm
Services Delivery (south east) & special requests

HYTHE

Malthouse Arcade
Contact Mr or Mrs Maxtone Graham
High Street, Hythe, Kent, CT21 5BW
☎ 01303 260103 F 01304 615436
E rmg@postmaster.co.uk
Est. 1974 *Stock size* Large
No. of dealers 37
Stock General antiques
Open Fri Sat 9.30am–5.30pm
Services Café

Owlets
Contact Mrs A Maurice
99 High Street, Hythe, Kent, CT21 5JH
☎ 01303 230333
W www.owlets.co.uk
www.millenniumjewellers.co.uk
www.kentjewellers.co.uk
Est. 1955 *Stock size* Large
Stock Antique and estate jewellery, silver
Open Mon–Sat 9.30am–5pm closed Wed
Services Valuations, restorations, jewellery repairs

Second Treasures
Contact Mr Alan Fairbairn
18 High Street, Hythe, Kent, CT14 5AT
☎ 01303 267801 F 0870 0554727
E ha@applesys.demon.co.uk
Est. 1995 *Stock size* Large
Stock General antiques, clocks, collectables
Open Mon–Sat 10am–4.30pm
Services Clock repair and restoration

LAMBERHURST

Ascension Interiors
Contact Sonya Murton
Forstal Farm, Goudhurst Road, Lamberhurst, Kent, TN3 8AG
☎ 01892 890102
E sonya.murton@lineone.net
W www.asint.co.uk
Est. 2001 *Stock size* Small
Stock Decorative French and English furnishings, exterior stonework design
Open By appointment
Fairs Ardingly
Services Interior design service

Forstal Farm Antique Workshops
Contact Mr D Johnstone
Forstal Farm, Goudhurst Road, Lamberhurst, Kent, TN3 8AG
☎ 01892 891189 F 01892 891189
W www.forstalantiques.com
Est. 1997 *Stock size* Large
Stock Hand-painted beds and armoires, general bedroom furniture
Open Mon–Sun 10am–5pm or by appointment

Junk & Disorderly
Contact Rupert Chipchase
Forstal Farm, Goudhurst Road, Lamberhurst, Kent, TN3 8AG
☎ 01892 890102
E chipchase@compuserve.com
Est. 1998 *Stock size* Large
Stock Antiques, decorative items, French country furniture
Open Daily by appointment
Fairs Ardingly
Services House clearance

LITTLEBOURNE

Jimmy Warren
Contact Mr J Warren
Cedar Lodge, 28 The Hill, Littlebourne, Canterbury, Kent, CT3 1TA
☎ 01227 721510 F 01227 722431
E enquiries@jimmywarren.co.uk
W www.jimmywarren.co.uk
Est. 1973 *Stock size* Large
Stock Unusual antiques, garden ornaments
Open Mon–Sun 10am–5pm
Services Valuations

LOOSE

Loose Valley Antiques
Contact Mrs V Gibbons
Scriba House, Loose Road, Loose, Maidstone, Kent, ME15 0AA
☎ 01622 743950
Est. 1998 *Stock size* Large
Stock Oak furniture, collectables, pine
Open Tues–Sat 10am–5pm Sun 10am–4pm
Services Free local delivery

LYMINGE

Valley Auctions
Contact Mr E T Hall
Claygate, Brady Road, Lyminge, Folkestone, Kent, CT18 8EU
☎ 01303 862134 F 01303 862134
Est. 1978
Open Mon–Fri 9am–5pm
Sales General antiques sale Sun 9.30am, viewing Sat 1–6pm
Frequency Monthly
Catalogues Yes

MAIDSTONE

Cobnar Books (PBFA)
Contact Larry Icott
567 Red Hill, Wateringbury, Maidstone, Kent, ME18 5BE
☎ 01622 813230
E books@cobnar.demon.co.uk
Est. 1994
Stock Antiquarian and English topography books
Open Mail order only
Fairs Royal National Hotel Book Fair
Services Valuations, books on the Internet

SOUTH EAST

KENT • NEW ROMNEY

Crackpots
Contact Annie Smith
1b Hamilton House, Heath Road, Coxheath, Maidstone, Kent, ME17 4DF
01622 741200
Est. 1984 *Stock size* Medium
Stock Furniture, bric-a-brac
Open Mon–Sat 10am–5pm closed Wed

Gem Antiques
Contact Mark Rackham
10 Gabriels Hill, Maidstone, Kent, ME15 6JG
01622 763344
markrackham@ukonline.co.uk
Est. 1994 *Stock size* Medium
Stock Jewellery, pocket watches, objets d'art
Open Mon–Sat 10am–5pm
Services Valuations, repairs

Newnham Court Antiques
Contact Mrs S Draper
Newnham Court Shopping Village, Bearsted Road, Weavering, Maidstone, Kent, ME14 5LH
01622 631526
newnhamcourt@antikes.co.uk
www.antikes.co.uk
Est. 1993 *Stock size* Large
No. of dealers 3+
Stock Collectables, ceramics, dining furniture
Open Mon–Sat 9.30am–5.30pm Sun 10am–5pm

Sutton Valence Antiques (LAPADA, CINOA)
Contact Nigel Mullarkey
Unit 4, Haslemere Estate, Sutton Road, Maidstone, Kent, ME15 9NL
01622 675332 01622 692593
svantiques@aol.com
www.svantiques.co.uk
Est. 1977 *Stock size* Large
Stock Furniture
Open Mon–Sat 9am–5.30pm Sun 11am–4pm
Services Valuations, restorations, shipping

Whatever Comics
Contact Mr M Armario
5 Middle Row, High Street, Maidstone, Kent, ME14 1TF
01622 681041
Est. 1988 *Stock size* Medium
Stock Second-hand comics, *Star Trek* and *Star Wars* toys, movie related items, sci-fi collectables, Beanie Babies, action figures
Open Mon–Sat 10am–5.30pm

NEW ROMNEY

The House Clearance Shop
Contact Mrs C S Bray
48 High Street, New Romney, Kent, TN28 8AT
01797 363000
Est. 1994 *Stock size* Medium
Stock Brass, copper, pictures, glass, mirrors, furniture
Open Mon–Sat Sun in Summer 9am–5pm
Services House clearance

NORTHFLEET

Northfleet Hill Antiques
Contact Martine Kilby
36 The Hill, Northfleet, Gravesend, Kent, DA11 9EX
01474 321521 01474 350921
07770 993906
Est. 1986 *Stock size* Medium
Stock Furniture, collectables, glass, china
Open Mon Tues Fri 10am–5pm
Fairs Mainwarings Chelsea Antiques Fair
Services Upholstery

ORPINGTON

Crescent Antiques
Contact Mrs B Harris
19 Crescent Way, Orpington, Kent, BR6 9LS
01689 857711
ca@curioquest.com
www.curioquest.com
Est. 1998 *Stock size* Large
Stock Victorian–modern collectables, china, glass, small items of furniture
Open Mon–Sat 10am–5.30pm closed Thurs
Services Valuations, auction sale agents

OTFORD

Ellenor Hospice Care Shop
Contact Mrs Gill Saunderson
11a High Street, Otford, Kent, TN14 5PG
01959 524322
Est. 1995 *Stock size* Medium
Stock General antiques
Open Mon–Sat 10am–5pm April–October, 10am–4pm November–March
Services Tea rooms

Mandarin Gallery
Contact Mr Joseph Liu
The Mill Pond, 16 High Street, Otford, Sevenoaks, Kent, TN14 5PQ
01959 522778 01732 457399
mandarin.gallery@which.net
Est. 1984 *Stock size* Medium
Stock Mainly Chinese Oriental furniture, ivory, wood carvings, silk, paintings
Open Mon–Sat 10am–5pm closed Wed
Services Restorations

Otford Antique and Collectors Centre
Contact Mr David Lowrie
26–28 High Street, Otford, Sevenoaks, Kent, TN14 5PQ
01959 522025 01959 525858
info@otfordantiques.co.uk
www.otfordantiques.co.uk
Est. 1997 *Stock size* Large
No. of dealers 34
Stock General antiques, collectables
Open Mon–Sat 10am–5pm Sun 11am–4pm
Services Restorations, valuations, upholstery

John M Peyto & Co Ltd
Contact Mr J Peyto
The Coach House, Rowdow Lane, Otford Hill, Sevenoaks, Kent, TN15 6XN
01959 524022 01959 522100
07860 516040
Est. 1985
Open Mon–Fri 7am–7pm Sat 8am–2pm
Sales Large house sales on site
Frequency Every 2 weeks
Catalogues Yes

PETTS WOOD

Memory Lane
Contact Mr R K Ludlam
105 Queensway, Petts Wood, Orpington, Kent, BR5 1DG
01689 826832

Est. 1972 *Stock size* Large
Stock General antiques
Open Mon–Sat 9.30am–5.30pm
Fairs Ardingly
Services House Clearance

PLUCKLEY

⊞ Catchpole and Rye (SALVO)
Contact Diana Rabjohns or Tony O'Donnel
✉ **Saracen's Dairy, Pluckley Road, Pluckley, Kent, TN27 0SA** 🅿
☎ 01233 840457
ⓔ info@crye.co.uk
ⓦ www.crye.co.uk
Est. 1991 *Stock size* Large
Stock Baths, basins, cisterns, taps, sanitary ware
Open Mon–Fri 9am–5pm Sat by appointment
Services Design Service

RAINHAM

⊞ The Bookmark
Contact Mr G Harrison
✉ **Unit 15c, Rainham Shopping Centre, Rainham, Gillingham, Kent, ME8 7HW** 🅿
☎ 01634 365987/401893
Est. 1992 *Stock size* Large
Stock Antiquarian, second-hand, general books, fiction, non-fiction
Open Mon–Sat 9.30am–5.30pm

RAMSGATE

⊞ B & D Collectors' Toys
Contact Mr R Smith
✉ **332 Margate Road, Ramsgate, Kent, CT12 6SQ** 🅿
☎ 01843 589606 ⓕ 01843 589606
Est. 1991 *Stock size* Large
Stock Old and obsolete toys, Dinky, Corgi etc, new collectable toys, *Star Wars*
Open Mon–Thur 9.30am–5.30pm Wed 9.30am–1pm Fri Sat 9.30am–6pm
Services Valuations, mail order

⊞ Granny's Attic
Contact Miss Penny Warn
✉ **2 Addington Street, Ramsgate, Kent, CT11 9JL** 🅿
☎ 01843 588955/596288
ⓜ 07773 155339
Est. 1986 *Stock size* Large
Stock Victorian, Edwardian, pre-1930s furniture, china, silver, glass, mirrors, pictures etc
Open Mon–Sat 10am–5pm closed 1–2pm Thurs 10am–1pm
Services Free local delivery, delivery in UK and abroad can be arranged

⊞ Thanet Antiques Trading Centre
Contact Mr Roy Fomison
✉ **45 Albert Street, Ramsgate, Kent, CT11 9EX** 🅿
☎ 01843 597336
Est. 1983 *Stock size* Large
Stock General antiques, furniture, collectables
Open Mon–Sat 9am–5pm
Fairs Ardingly

⊞ Yesteryear Railwayana
Contact Patrick or Mary Mullen
✉ **Stablings Cottage, Goodwin Road, Ramsgate, Kent, CT11 0JJ**
☎ 01843 587283 ⓕ 01843 587283
ⓔ mullen@yesrail.com
ⓦ www.yesrail.com
Est. 1980 *Stock size* Medium
Stock Out-of-print and scarce books, illustrations, documentation, printed ephemera, both important and trivial
Open Mail order only
Services Catalogue monthly

ROCHESTER

Amhuerst Auctions
Contact Ms S Duke
✉ **375 High Street, Rochester, Kent, ME1 1DA** 🅿
☎ 01634 844759 ⓕ 01634 815713
ⓦ www.Angelfire.com/NT/AmhuerstAuctions
Est. 1999
Open Mon–Sat 9am–5.30pm
Sales Antiques, collectables and general household sale Sat noon, viewing Fri 2–5pm Sat 9am–noon prior to sale
Frequency Weekly
Catalogues Yes

⊞ Baggins Book Bazaar
Contact Mr Godfrey George
✉ **19 High Street, Rochester, Kent, ME1 1PY** 🅿
☎ 01634 811651 ⓕ 01634 840591
ⓔ bagginsbookbazaarltd@btinternet.com
ⓦ www.bagginsbooks.co.uk
Est. 1986 *Stock size* Large
Stock Antiquarian, rare, second-hand books
Open Mon–Sun 10am–6pm
Services Book search, ordering service

⊞ Baggins too
Contact Gillian Emerson
✉ **63 High Street, Rochester, Kent, ME1 1LX** 🅿
☎ 01634 409868
ⓔ bagginsbookbazaarltd@btinternet.com
ⓦ www.bagginsbooks.co.uk
Est. 2000 *Stock size* Medium
Stock Antiquarian, rare, second-hand books
Open Mon–Sun 10am–6pm
Services Book search, new book ordering service

⊞ Castlebridge Antiques
Contact Hazel Duckworth or Gemma Glover
✉ **30 High Street, Rochester, Kent, ME1 1LD** 🅿
☎ 01634 880037
Est. 1996 *Stock size* Large
Stock Antiques, collectables
Open Mon–Fri 10am-4pm Sat 9.30am-5pm
Fairs Sandown Park, Ardingly
Services House clearance

⊞ Cathedral Antiques
Contact Jeanette Dickson
✉ **83 High Street, Rochester, Kent, ME1 1LX** 🅿
☎ 01634 842735 ⓕ 01634 826480
ⓜ 07802 177800
Est. 1974 *Stock size* Large
Stock 17thC–1910 furniture
Open Mon–Sat 9.30am–5pm
Services Valuations for probate/insurance

⊞ City Antiques Ltd
Contact Mrs Pam Ware
✉ **78 High Street, Rochester, Kent, ME1 1JY** 🅿
☎ 01634 841278
ⓜ 07979 494614
Est. 1997 *Stock size* Large
Stock Clocks, barometers, Georgian, Victorian, Edwardian furniture
Open Mon–Sat 10am–5pm closed some Wed
Services Clock and barometer repair, furniture restorations

SOUTH EAST

KENT • ROLVENDEN

Collectables
Contact Mrs Pat Lucas
23 High Street, Rochester, Kent, ME1 1LN
01634 880555
07976 565092
medauc@dircon.co.uk
Est. 1990 *Stock size* Large
Stock Collectables, curios including badges, glass, ceramics
Open Mon–Sat 10am–4.30pm

Cottage Style Antiques
Contact Mr W Miskimmin
24 Bill Street Road, Frindsbury, Rochester, Kent, ME2 4RB
01634 717623
Est. 1982 *Stock size* Large
Stock Collectables, architectural salvage, fireplaces, interesting pieces
Open Mon–Sat 9.30am–5.30pm
Services Restorations, repairs

Dragonlee Collectables
Contact Janet Davies
Memories, 128 High Street, Rochester, Kent, ME1 1JT
01622 729502
07761 400128
Est. 1995 *Stock size* Medium
Stock Noritake, ceramic collectables, furniture
Open Tues Wed 9am–5pm
Fairs Detling

Field, Staff & Woods
Contact Jim Field
93 High Street, Rochester, Kent, ME1 1LX
01634 846144/840108
john@woods-of-rochester.co.uk
Est. 1996 *Stock size* Large
Stock Furniture, small items, clocks, collectables, silver
Open Mon–Sat 10am–5pm call for seasonal Sun opening
Services Valuations, clock repairs and restorations

Kaizen International Ltd
Contact Jason Hunt or Jo Olivares
88 The High Street, Rochester, Kent, ME1 1JT
01634 814132
Est. 1997 *Stock size* Large
Stock Jewellery, silver, furniture, wine-related items
Open Mon–Sat 10am–5.30pm
Services Valuations

Medway Auctions
Contact Mr Bill Lucas
23 High Street, Rochester, Kent, ME1 1LN
01634 847444 F 01634 880555
medauc@dircon.co.uk
Est. 1997
Open Mon–Sat 10am–4.30pm
Sales General sales 1st or 2nd Wed, antiques and collectables sale quarterly, specialist sale each month except December of toys, postcards, ephemera, books, military, scientific and communications. Contact auction office for details and viewing times
Catalogues Yes by subscription

Memories
Contact Mrs V Lhermette
128 High Street, Rochester, Kent, ME1 1JT
01634 811044
Est. 1985 *Stock size* Large
No. of dealers 15
Stock Small furniture, china, general antiques
Open Mon–Sat 9am–5pm Sun 11am–5pm

ROLVENDEN

Falstaff Antiques
Contact C M Booth
63–67 High Street, Rolvenden, Kent, TN17 4LP
01580 241234
Est. 1964 *Stock size* Medium
Stock General antiques and reproductions
Open Mon–Sat 10am–6pm

J D and R M Walters
Contact Mr John Walters
10 Regent Street, Rolvenden, Cranbrook, Kent, TN17 4PE
01580 241563
Est. 1979 *Stock size* Medium
Stock 18th–19thC mahogany
Open Mon–Fri 8am–6pm Sat 11am–4.30pm or by appointment
Services Restorations

SANDGATE

Christopher Buck Antiques (BADA)
Contact Christopher Buck
56–60 Sandgate High Street, Sandgate, Folkestone, Kent, CT20 3AP
01303 221229 F 01303 221229
07836 551515
chrisbuck@throwley.freeserve.co.uk
Est. 1983
Stock 18thC and early 19thC English furniture and associated items
Open Mon–Sat 9.30am–5pm
Fairs Olympia, BADA
Services Valuations, restorations

Emporium Antiques
Contact Mr West
31–33 Sandgate High Street, Sandgate, Folkestone, Kent, CT20 3AH
01303 244430
07860 149387
Est. 1984 *Stock size* Medium
Stock Antique and decorative furniture
Open By appointment

Michael W Fitch Antiques (LAPADA)
Contact Mr Michael Fitch
99, 97, 95 Sandgate High Street, Sandgate, Kent, CT20 3BY
01303 249600 F 01303 249600
Est. 1977 *Stock size* Large
Stock 18th–19thC furniture, furnishings, clocks
Open Mon–Sat 10am–5.30pm
Services Valuations

Freeman and Lloyd Antiques (BADA, LAPADA)
Contact Mr K Freeman or Mr R Lloyd
44 High Street, Sandgate, Folkestone, Kent, CT20 3AP
01303 248986 F 01303 241353
07860 100073
freemanandlloyd@ukgateway.net
Est. 1968 *Stock size* Large
Stock 18th–early 19thC furniture, accessories, pictures, clocks, bronzes
Open Tues Thurs–Sat 10am–5pm
Fairs Olympia (February, June, November), BADA (March)
Services Valuations

David Gilbert Antiques
Contact Mr D Gilbert
30 Sandgate High Street, Sandgate, Folkestone, Kent, CT20 3AP
01303 850491
Est. 1984 *Stock size* Large

Stock Edwardian–Victorian Arts and Crafts
Open Mon–Sat 9.30am–4.30pm or by appointment
Services Delivery

Jonathan Greenwall Antiques (LAPADA)
Contact Mr J Greenwall
61–63 Sandgate High Street, Sandgate, Folkestone, Kent, CT20 3AH P
01303 248987 F 01303 248987
M 07799 133700
Est. 1969 *Stock size* Large
Stock Jewellery, clocks, watches, furniture, pictures, prints, glass
Open Mon–Sat 9.30am–5pm Sun Bank Hols by appointment
Services Valuations, watch/clock jewellery repair

David M Lancefield Antiques (LAPADA)
Contact Mr D Lancefield
53 Sandgate High Street, Sandgate, Folkestone, Kent, CT20 3AH P
01303 850149 F 01303 850149
Est. 1976 *Stock size* Large
Stock 17th–20thC antiques, decorative arts
Open Mon–Sat 10am–6pm Sun Bank Holidays 11am–5pm
Services Restorations

John McMaster
Contact Mr J McMaster
56a Sandgate High Street, Sandgate, Folkestone, Kent, CT20 3AP P
01303 252725
M 07774 451179
Est. 1847 *Stock size* Large
Stock 18th–early 19thC English furniture, engravings
Open Mon–Sat 9.30am–5pm or by appointment
Fairs Goodwood, Guildford
Services Print and watercolour restorations

Sandgate Passage
Contact Mr John Rendle
82 Sandgate High Street, Sandgate, Folkestone, Kent, CT20 3BX P
01303 850973
Est. 1987 *Stock size* Medium
Stock Old postcards, prints
Open Mon–Sat 10.30am–4.30pm
Fairs DMG Detling, York, Twickenham, Guildford, Woking
Services Valuations

SANDWICH

All Our Yesterdays
Contact Sandy Baker
3 Cattle Market, Sandwich, Kent, CT13 9AE P
01304 614756
E chrisbaker@u.k.packardbell.org
Est. 1994 *Stock size* Medium
Stock General antiques, collectables, unusual items
Open Mon–Sat 10.30am–2.30pm or by appointment closed Wed
Services Gramophone repairs

Chris Baker Gramophones (CLPGS)
Contact Mr Chris Baker
3 Cattle Market, Sandwich, Kent, CT13 9AE P
01304 614756/375767
F 01304 614696
M 07808 831462
E chrisbaker@u.k.packardbell.org
Est. 1996 *Stock size* Large
Stock Mechanical music
Open Mon–Sat 10.30am–2.30pm closed Wed
Services Repairs, stock list available on request

Delf Stream Gallery
Contact Nick Rocke
14 New Street, Sandwich, Kent, CT13 9AB P
01304 617684 F 01304 615479
E oastman@aol.com
W www.delfstreamgallery.com
Est. 1984 *Stock size* Large
Stock 19th–20thC European and American art pottery
Open Mon Thurs–Sat 10am–5pm or by appointment
Fairs NEC
Services Valuations

Roses Antiques
Contact Mrs D Clark
60 King Street, Sandwich, Kent, CT13 6BT P
01304 615303 F 01304 615303
M 07831 214067
E DClark6689@aol.com
Est. 1989 *Stock size* Large
Stock Furniture, collectables, silver, jewellery, paintings
Open Mon–Sat 9am–5.30pm closed Wed

Sandwich Fine Books (ABA PBFA)
Contact Mr Nick McConnell
Cambridge House, 41 New Street, Sandwich, Kent, CT13 9BB P
01304 620300 F 01304 620300
M 07977 573766
E nick.mcconnell@exl.co.uk
Est. 1976 *Stock size* Small
Stock Antiquarian and second-hand books
Open By appointment
Fairs Russell Square
Services Valuations

SEAL

Campbell and Archard (BADA)
Contact Paul Archard
Lychgate House, Church Street, Seal, Kent, TN15 0AR P
01732 761153
E pnarchard@aol.com
Est. 1970 *Stock size* Large
Stock Austro-Hungarian 1790–1850 clocks and regulators, English regulators and bracket clocks
Open By appointment
Fairs Olympia
Services Restorations

SEVENOAKS

Emma Antiques
Contact Mrs I Crow
28a Holly Bush Lane, Sevenoaks, Kent, TN13 3TH P
01732 459794
Est. 1979 *Stock size* Medium
Stock General antiques, furniture, china, silver, pictures, tapestry cushions
Open Mon Fri 2–5.15pm Tues Thurs 10am–5pm Sat 10am–1pm

Furniture and Effects
Contact Mr A Hardman
3 St Botolphs Road, Sevenoaks, Kent, TN13 3AJ P
01732 460400
Est. 1994 *Stock size* Large
Stock General antiques, furniture
Open Mon–Sat 10am–6pm
Services Valuations, restorations

Gem Antiques
Contact Mr M Rackham
28 London Road, Sevenoaks, Kent, TN13 1AP P
01732 743540
Est. 1994 *Stock size* Medium

SOUTH EAST

KENT • SIDCUP

Stock Clocks, jewellery
Open Mon–Sat 10am–5pm
Services Clock repairs

Ibbett Mosely
Contact Mr Hodge
125 High Street, Sevenoaks, Kent, TN13 1UT
☎ 01732 456731 Ⓕ 01732 740910
Est. 1935
Open Office hours Mon–Fri 9am–5.30pm
Sales General antiques, 9 sales a year, call for viewing times
Frequency 9 a year
Catalogues Yes

Phillips International Auctioneers and Valuers
49 London Road, Sevenoaks, Kent, TN13 1AR
☎ 01732 740310 Ⓕ 01732 741842
Ⓦ www.phillips-auction.com
Sales Regional Saleroom. Telephone for details

SIDCUP

Memory Lane Antiques and Collectables
Contact Lynn Brackley
143 Station Road, Sidcup, Kent, DA15 7AA
☎ 020 8300 0552
Ⓜ 0794 6649843
Est. 1998 *Stock size* Medium
Stock General antiques, collectables
Open Mon–Sat 10am–5.30pm closed Wed

SITTINGBOURNE

Newington Antiques
Contact Georgina McKinnon
58–60 High Street, Newington, Sittingbourne, Kent, ME9 7JL
☎ 01795 844448 Ⓕ 01795 841448
Ⓜ 07802 844448
Ⓔ newington.antiques@lineone.net
Ⓦ www.newingtonantiques.freeserve.co.uk
Est. 1994 *Stock size* Medium
Stock Decorative, antique furniture, small items, lighting, general antiques
Open Tues Thurs–Sat 10am–5pm Sun 10am–2pm or by appointment
Fairs Ardingly, Kempton
Services Valuations, restorations, shipping

Past Sentence
Contact Mrs J Colbran
70 High Street, Sittingbourne, Kent, ME10 4PB
☎ 01795 428787
Est. 1997 *Stock size* Small
Stock Second-hand and antiquarian books
Open Mon–Sat 9.30am–5.30pm

SPELDHURST

Bonhams & Brooks
Contact Ray Calcutt
Northleigh Cottage, Speldhurst, Kent, TN3 0QD
☎ 01892 863082 Ⓕ 01892 863082
Ⓦ www.bonhams.com
Open Mon–Fri 9am–5pm
Sales Regional Representative for Kent

STOCKBURY

Steppes Hill Farm Antiques (BADA)
Contact Mr William Buck
Steppes Hill Farm, Stockbury, Sittingbourne, Kent, ME9 7RB
☎ 01795 842205
Stock General antiques, porcelain
Open Mon–Fri 9am–5pm
Fairs Olympia, Chelsea
Services Valuations, restorations

SUTTON VALENCE

Sutton Valence Antiques (LAPADA, CINOA)
Contact Judith Mullarkey
North Street, Sutton Valence, Maidstone, Kent, ME17 3AP
☎ 01622 843333 Ⓕ 01622 843499
Ⓔ svantiques@aol.com
Ⓦ www.svantiques.co.uk
Est. 1978 *Stock size* Large
Stock 18th–19thC furniture, clocks, china, glass
Open Mon–Fri 9.30am–5pm Sat 10am–5pm Sun 11am–4pm
Services Valuations, restorations, shipping, container packing

TENTERDEN

Flower House Antiques
Contact Mr Q Johnson
90 High Street, Tenterden, Kent, TN30 6JB
☎ 01580 763764
Ⓕ 01580 291251/01797 270386
Est. 1995 *Stock size* Large
Stock 17th–early 19thC furniture, objets d'art, chandeliers, worldwide general antiques
Open Mon–Sat 9.30am–5.30pm Sun by appointment
Services Valuations, restorations

Gaby's Clocks and Things
Contact Gaby Gunst
140 High Street, Tenterden, Kent, TN30 6HT
☎ 01580 765818 Ⓕ 01580 765818
Est. 1969 *Stock size* Medium
Stock Clocks, barometers
Open Mon–Sat 10.30am–5pm
Services Clock and barometer restoration

Heirloom Antiques
Contact Jan Byhurst
68 High Street, Tenterden, Kent, TN30 6AU
☎ 01580 765535
Est. 1994 *Stock size* Medium
No. of dealers 6
Stock Dolls, teddies, porcelain, prints, pictures, books, Winstanley cats and dogs, jewellery, furniture, militaria
Open Mon–Sat 10am–5pm Sun 11am–5pm

J & M Collectables (PTA)
Contact Maurice Coombs
66a High Street, Tenterden, Kent, TN30 6AU
☎ 01580 891657
Ⓔ jandmcollectables@tinyonline.co.uk
Est. 1993 *Stock size* Variable
Stock Postcards, crested china, Osborne plaques, other small collectables including Wade, Doulton etc
Open Mon–Sat 10am–5pm Sun 11am–5pm
Services Major credit/debit cards accepted, mail order considered

Lambert and Foster
Contact Mrs G Brazier
102 High Street, Tenterden, Kent, TN30 6HT
☎ 01580 762083 Ⓕ 01580 764317
Ⓔ saleroom@lambertandfoster.co.uk
Ⓦ www.lambertandfoster.co.uk
Est. 1830
Open Mon–Fri 9am–5.30pm
Sales General antiques sale Thurs 9.30am, viewing Sun 10.30am–4pm Tues 9.30am–4.30pm

Frequency Monthly
Catalogues Yes

Memories
Contact Mr Mark Lloyds
74 High Street, Tenterden, Kent, TN30 6AU
01580 763416
Est. 1995 *Stock size* Large
Stock Antiques, collectables, small furniture
Open Mon–Sat 10am–5pm Sun 11am–4pm

Tenterden Antique & Silver Vaults (BSSA)
Contact T Smith
66 High Street, Tenterden, Kent, TN30 6AU
01580 765885
Est. 1991 *Stock size* Large
Stock Clocks, silver, china, furniture, glass, collectables, jewellery
Open Mon–Sat 10am–5pm Sun 11am–5pm
Services House clearance

Tenterden Antiques Centre
Contact Mick Ellin
66a High Street, Tenterden, Kent, TN30 6AU
01580 765655
07776 203755
Est. 1990 *Stock size* Large
No. of dealers 20
Stock Furniture, Deco, china, clocks, silver, jewellery, militaria, postcards, porcelain, bric-a-brac
Open Mon–Sat 10am–5pm Sun 11am–5pm

TEYNHAM

Company of Bears
Contact Mrs K Davis
16 Station Row, Barrow Green, Teynham, Kent, ME9 9EA
01795 520920 01795 520920
hugs@companyofbears.com
www.companyofbears.com
Est. 1998 *Stock size* Medium
Stock Collectable bears, Steiff, Dean's and Hermann bears
Open Mail order only

Jackson-Grant Antiques
Contact Mr David Jackson-Grant
133 London Road, Teynham, Sittingbourne, Kent, ME9 9QJ
01795 522027 01795 522027
07831 591881
david.jackson-grant@talk21.com
www.jackson-grantantiques.co.uk
Est. 1966 *Stock size* Large
Stock Antique furniture, small items
Open Mon–Sat 10am–5pm Sun 1–5pm
Services Valuations

TONBRIDGE

Barden House Antiques
Contact Mrs Brenda Parsons
1 & 3 Priory Street, Tonbridge, Kent, TN2 2AP
01732 350142
Est. 1959 *Stock size* Large
No. of dealers 4
Stock General antiques, prints, watercolours, jewellery, china, small pieces of furniture
Open Tues–Sat 10am–5pm

Greta May Antiques
Contact Mrs G May
The New Curiosity Shop, Tollgate Buildings, Hadlow Road, Tonbridge, Kent, TN9 1NX
01732 366730
Est. 1988 *Stock size* Medium
Stock Furniture, silver, silver plate, china, glass
Open Tues Thurs–Sat 10am–4.30pm
Fairs Great Danes
Services Teddy bear repairs

Derek Roberts Antiques (BADA)
Contact Mr Derek Roberts
25 Shipbourne Road, Tonbridge, Kent, TN10 3DN
01732 358986 01732 771842
drclocks@clara.net
www.qualityantiqueclocks.com
Est. 1968 *Stock size* Large
Stock 17th–19thC clocks, books about clocks and barometers
Open Mon–Sat 9.30am–5.30pm
Services Valuations, restorations, annual lists

TUNBRIDGE WELLS

Aaron Antiques (RADS)
Contact Ron Goodman
77 St Johns Road, Tunbridge Wells, Kent, TN4 9TT
01892 517644
Est. 1967 *Stock size* Large
Stock Coins, medals, clocks, china, silver, paintings, prints, scientific and musical instruments, furniture, Chinese porcelain
Open Mon–Sat 10am–5pm or by appointment

The Antiques Shop
Contact Joanne Chipchase
77a St John's Road, Tunbridge Wells, Kent, TN4 9TT
01892 676637
theantiquesshop@amserve.net
Est. 1998 *Stock size* Medium
Stock Decorative antiques and country furniture
Open Mon–Sat 10am–5pm
Fairs Ardingly

Architectural Emporium (SALVO)
Contact Nick Bates
55 St Johns Road, Tunbridge Wells, Kent, TN4 9TP
01892 540368
www.architecturalemporium.com
Est. 1985 *Stock size* Large
Stock Decorative architectural salvage, 18th–19thC fireplaces, garden statuary, door furniture
Open Tues–Sat 9am–5.30pm
Fairs Decorative Fair (Battersea)

Henry Baines (LAPADA)
Contact Mr H Baines
14 Church Road, Southborough, Tunbridge Wells, Kent, TN4 0RX
01892 532099 01892 545992
07973 214406
Est. 1968 *Stock size* Large
Stock Oak, country furniture
Open Prior phone call advised
Fairs Olympia

Beau Nash Antiques
Contact Mr David Wrenn or Mrs Gina Rowlett
29 Lower Walk, The Pantiles, Tunbridge Wells, Kent, TN2 5TD
01892 537810
Est. 1990 *Stock size* Large
Stock Georgian–Edwardian period furniture, associated decorative items
Open Tues–Sat 11am–5pm

Bracketts Fine Arts
Contact Mr James Braxton ARICS
Auction Hall, Pantiles, Tunbridge Wells, Kent, TN1 1UU

SOUTH EAST

KENT • TUNBRIDGE WELLS

☎ 01892 544500 Ⓕ 01892 515191
Ⓦ www.bfaa.co.uk
Est. 1828
Open Mon–Fri 9am–5pm
Sales 2 monthly antiques sales Fri 10am, viewing Thurs 9am–7pm. Antiques and general sale Fri 10am, viewing Thurs 9am–7pm
Catalogues Yes

Calverley Antiques
Contact Mr P Nimmo
✉ **30 Crescent Road, Tunbridge Wells, Kent, TN1 2LZ** Ⓟ
☎ 01892 538254
Est. 1984 *Stock size* Large
Stock Pine, decorative and painted furniture
Open Mon–Sun 9.30am–5.30pm
Fairs Ardingly
Services House clearance

Chapel Place Antiques
Contact Mrs J A Clare
✉ **9 Chapel Place, Tunbridge Wells, Kent, TN1 1YQ**
☎ 01892 546561 Ⓕ 01892 546561
Est. 1984 *Stock size* Large
Stock Antique and modern silver, hand-painted Limoges boxes, amber jewellery, silver photo frames, old silver plate, claret jugs
Open Mon–Sat 9am–6pm
Services Valuations

Claremont Antiques
Contact Mr A Broad
✉ **48 St Johns Road, Tunbridge Wells, Kent, TN4 9NY** Ⓟ
☎ 01892 511651 Ⓕ 01892 517360
Ⓜ 07788 452382
Ⓔ ant@claremontantiques.com
Ⓦ www.claremontantiques.com
Est. 1995 *Stock size* Large
Stock Pine, hardwood, painted country furniture
Open Mon–Sat 10am–5.30pm

Corn Exchange Antiques Centre
Contact Mrs D Long
✉ **64 The Pantiles, Tunbridge Wells, Kent, TN2 5TN** Ⓟ
☎ 01892 539652 Ⓕ 01892 538454
Ⓔ chris@alvesden.freeserve.co.uk
Est. 1999 *Stock size* Large
No. of dealers 11
Stock Pictures, tapestry, glass, silver, furniture, musical boxes, china
Open Mon–Sat 10am–5pm

Culverden Antiques
Contact Mr D Mason
✉ **49 St Johns Road, Tunbridge Wells, Kent, TN4 9TP** Ⓟ
☎ 01892 515264
Est. 1985 *Stock size* Medium
Stock 19thC furniture, decorative pieces
Open Tues–Sat 10am–5.30pm

Downlane Hall Antiques
Contact Mrs Hayes
✉ **Culverden Down, St Johns, Tunbridge Wells, Kent, TN4 9SA** Ⓟ
☎ 01892 522440
Est. 1980 *Stock size* Large
Stock Georgian–Victorian furniture
Open Mon–Sat 10am–4pm
Services Restorations

Glassdrumman
Contact Mr or Mrs G Dyson Rooke
✉ **7 Union Square, The Pantiles, Tunbridge Wells, Kent, TN4 8HE** Ⓟ
☎ 01892 538615
Est. 1989 *Stock size* Large
Stock Georgian, Victorian, second-hand jewellery, silver, pocket watches, decorative items, furniture
Open Tues–Sat 10am–5.30pm closed Mon
Services Repairs

Pamela Goodwin
Contact Pamela Goodwin
✉ **11 The Pantiles, Tunbridge Wells, Kent, TN2 5TD** Ⓟ
☎ 01892 618200 Ⓕ 01892 618200
Ⓜ 07885 259577
Est. 1998 *Stock size* Large
Stock 18th–20thC furniture, clocks, silver, English porcelain, Moorcroft, Doulton, glass, sewing collectables
Open Mon–Fri 9.30am–5pm Sat 9.30am–5.30pm

Gorringes (SOFA)
Contact Mr Leslie Gillham
✉ **15 The Pantiles, Tunbridge Wells, Kent, TN2 5TD** Ⓟ
☎ 01892 619670 Ⓕ 01892 619671
Ⓔ tunbridge.wells@gorringes.co.uk
Ⓦ www.gorringes.co.uk
Est. 1926
Open Mon–Fri 8.30am–5.30pm Sat 9am–noon
Sales Fine art and antiques sales at The Spa Hotel, Tunbridge Wells, Tues 11.30am, viewing noon–8pm Mon prior and day of sale 8.30–11am
Frequency Quarterly
Catalogues Yes

Peter Hoare Antiques
Contact Peter Hoare
✉ **35 London Road, Southborough, Tunbridge Wells, Kent, TN4 0PB** Ⓟ
☎ 01892 524623
Est. 1983 *Stock size* Medium
Stock Arts and Crafts furniture
Open Tues–Sat 10am–6pm
Services Valuations

Old Colonial
Contact Suzy Rees or Dee Martyn
✉ **56 St Johns Road, Tunbridge Wells, Kent, TN4 9NY** Ⓟ
☎ 01892 533993 Ⓕ 01892 513281
Est. 1994 *Stock size* Large
Stock Country antiques, decorative items, painted furniture
Open Mon–Sat 10am–5.30pm or by appointment

Pantiles Antiques
Contact Mrs E M Blackburn
✉ **31 The Pantiles, Tunbridge Wells, Kent, TN2 5TD** Ⓟ
☎ 01892 531291
Est. 1981 *Stock size* Medium
Stock Georgian and Edwardian furniture, porcelain, decorative pieces
Open Mon–Sat 9.30am–5pm
Fairs Copthorne
Services Restorations, upholstery

Pantiles Spa Antiques
Contact Mrs J A Cowpland
✉ **4–6 Union House, The Pantiles, Tunbridge Wells, Kent, TN4 8HE** Ⓟ
☎ 01892 541377 Ⓕ 01435 865660
Ⓜ 07711 283655
Ⓔ psa.wells@btinternet.com

Ⓦ www.antiques-tun-wells-kent.co.uk
Est. 1987 *Stock size* Large
Stock Specialist dining room tables and chairs, furniture, dolls, porcelain, glass, prints, watercolours, maps, clocks, silver
Open Mon–Fri 9.30am–5pm Sat 9.30am–5.30pm
Services Free delivery within 30 mile radius

⊞ Phoenix Antiques (WKADA)
Contact Robert Pilbeam, Jane Stott or Peter Janes
✉ 51–53 St Johns Road, Tunbridge Wells, Kent, TN4 9TP **P**
☎ 01892 549099 Ⓕ 01424 844365
Ⓔ Pilbeamrj@aol.com
Est. 1989 *Stock size* Large
Stock 18th–19thC English and French country furniture, overmantel mirrors, associated decorative items
Open Mon–Sat 10am–5.30pm or by appointment

⊞ Sporting Antiques
Contact Mr L Franklin
✉ 10 Union Square, The Pantiles, Tunbridge Wells, Kent, TN4 8HE **P**
☎ 01892 522661 Ⓕ 01892 522661
Est. 1993 *Stock size* Large
Stock Sporting antiques, arms, armour, technical instruments, tools
Open Mon–Fri 9.30am–5pm Sat 9.30am–5.30pm closed Wed

⊞ John Thompson
Contact Mr J Thompson
✉ 27 The Pantiles, Tunbridge Wells, Kent, TN2 5TD **P**
☎ 01892 547215
Est. 1982 *Stock size* Medium
Stock 18th–early 19thC furniture, late 17th–20thC paintings, glass, porcelain
Open Mon–Sat 9.30am–1pm 2–5pm

⊞ Tunbridge Wells Antiques
Contact Mr Nick Harding
✉ Union Square, The Pantiles, Tunbridge Wells, Kent, TN4 8HE **P**
☎ 01892 533708
Ⓔ nick@staffordshirefigures.com
Ⓦ www.staffordshirefigures.com
Est. 1986 *Stock size* Large
Stock Tunbridge Ware, Staffordshire figures, watches, clocks, silver, porcelain, pottery, furniture
Open Mon–Sat 9.30am–5pm
Services Valuations, restorations

⊞ Up Country Ltd
Contact Mr C Springett
✉ The Old Corn Stores, 68 St Johns Road, Tunbridge Wells, Kent, TN4 9PE **P**
☎ 01892 523341 Ⓕ 01892 530382
Ⓦ www.upcountryantiques.co.uk
Est. 1988 *Stock size* Large
Stock Antique and decorative country furniture, rural artefacts
Open Mon–Sat 9am–5.30pm

⊞ World War Books (OMRS)
Contact Mr Tim Harper
✉ Oaklands, Camden Park, Tunbridge Wells, Kent, TN2 5AE
☎ 01892 538465 Ⓕ 01892 538465
Ⓔ wwarbooks@btinternet.com
Est. 1988 *Stock size* Large
Stock Military books including manuals, weapon books, regimental histories, maps, photographs, diaries
Open Mail order only
Fairs Arms and Armour Fair (Birmingham), World War Book Fair
Services Valuations, probate, book search, catalogue

WALMER

⊞ Grandma's Attic
Contact S J Marsh
✉ 60 The Strand, Walmer, Kent, CT14 7DP **P**
☎ 01304 380121
Est. 1986 *Stock size* Medium
Stock Second-hand and antiques, mirrors
Open Mon–Sat 9.30am–5.30pm Sun by appointment
Services Restorations, gilding

WELLING

⌂ The Emporium Antiques, Collectables & Crafts Centre
Contact Miss J Marshall
✉ 138–140 Upper Wickham Lane, Welling, Kent, DA16 3DP **P**
☎ 020 8855 8308 Ⓕ 020 8855 8308
Ⓔ tony@gearya.freeserve.co.uk
Est. 1999 *Stock size* Large
No. of dealers 30
Stock Antiques, collectables, craft ware
Open Mon–Sat 10am–5pm

WEST KINGSDOWN

⊞ East Meets West Antiques
Contact Philippa Dudley
✉ Unit 7, West Kingsdown Industrial Estate, London Road, West Kingsdown, Kent, TN15 6EL **P**
☎ 01474 854807 Ⓕ 01474 852839
Ⓜ 07973 756302
Ⓔ info@eastmeetswestantiques.co.uk
Ⓦ eastmeetswestantiques.co.uk
Est. 2001 *Stock size* Medium
Stock Furniture
Open Mon–Fri 10am–4pm Sat Sun 11am–3pm
Services Valuations, restorations

WEST MALLING

⊞ The Old Clock Shop
✉ 63 High Street, West Malling, Kent, ME19 6NA **P**
☎ 01732 843246 Ⓕ 01732 843246
Ⓦ www.theoldclockshop.co.uk
Est. 1975 *Stock size* Medium
Stock Clocks, barometers
Open Mon–Sat 9am–5pm
Services Restorations

⊞ Rose and Crown Antiques
Contact Mrs Candy Lovegrove
✉ 40 High Street, West Malling, Kent, ME19 6QR **P**
☎ 01732 872707 Ⓕ 01732 872810
Ⓔ c_lovegrove@hotmail.com
Ⓦ www.antiqueswestmalling.co.uk
Est. 1995 *Stock size* Medium
Stock 18th–early 20thC furniture, small items
Open Tues–Sat 9.30am–5.30pm
Fairs Alexandra Palace
Services Restorations, upholstery

WEST WICKHAM

⊞ Nightingale Antiques and Craft Centre
Contact Maureen Haggerty
✉ 89–91 High Street, West Wickham, Kent, BR4 0LS **P**
☎ 020 8777 0335 Ⓕ 020 8776 2777

SOUTH EAST

KENT • WESTERHAM

Est. 1998 *Stock size* Large
Stock Victorian–Edwardian furniture, 1930s oak, china
Open Mon–Sat 10am–5pm

West Wickham Bookshop (PBFA)
Contact Mr Ronald Davies
5 Bell Parade, Wickham Court Road, West Wickham, Kent, BR4 0RH
☎ 020 8777 3982 Ⓕ 020 8777 3982
Ⓔ ron.davies@btinternet.com
Est. 1995 *Stock size* Medium
Stock General stock including antiquarian, military topics a speciality
Open Mon–Sat 10am–5pm
Fairs Bloomsbury (H D Book Fairs), all Title Page Book Fairs
Services Book binding

WESTERHAM

20th Century Marks
Contact Mr M Marks
12 Market Square, Westerham, Kent, TN16 1AW
☎ 01959 562221 Ⓕ 01959 569385
Ⓜ 07831 778992
Ⓔ TCM@marks.plus.com
Ⓦ www.20thcenturymarks.co.uk
Est. 1960 *Stock size* Large
Stock Classic 20thC designs
Open Tues–Sat 10am–6pm Sun noon–6pm
Services Valuations, restorations

Apollo Galleries (LAPADA)
Contact Mr S M Barr
19–21 Market Square, Westerham, Kent, TN16 1AN
☎ 01959 562200 Ⓕ 01959 562986
Ⓔ apollogalleries@city2000.com
Est. 1974 *Stock size* Large
Stock Mainly Georgian–Edwardian furniture, bronzes, oil paintings, watercolours, mirrors, objets d'art
Open Mon–Sat 9.30am–5.30pm
Fairs Olympia

Castle Antique Centre Ltd
Contact Stewart Ward Properties
1 London Road, Westerham, Kent, TN16 1BB
☎ 01959 562492
Est. 1986 *Stock size* Large
No. of dealers 8
Stock 4 showrooms. Linen, tools, silver, jewellery, china, glass, books, 19thC clothing, kitsch, retro clothing, small furniture
Open Mon–Sat 10am–5pm Sun 1–6pm
Services Valuations, advice, house clearance

Peter Dyke
Contact Mr Peter Dyke
3 The Green, Westerham, Kent, TN16 1AS
☎ 01959 565020
Est. 1993 *Stock size* Medium
Stock 18th–19thC furniture and works of art
Open Mon–Sat 10am–5pm

Anthony Hook Antiques
Contact Mr Anthony Hook
The Green, Westerham, Kent, TN16 1AS
☎ 01959 562161 Ⓕ 01959 562191
Ⓜ 07860 277099
Est. 1948 *Stock size* Medium
Stock Period furniture, shipping goods, reproduction garden statuary
Open Mon–Fri 9am–5.30pm Sat 10.30am–4.30pm
Services Valuations

London House Antiques
Contact Vivienne Graham
4 Market Square, Westerham, Kent, TN16 1AW
☎ 01959 564479 Ⓕ 01959 565424
Est. 1995 *Stock size* Large
No. of dealers 4
Stock Furniture, clocks, bears, dolls, porcelain, glass
Open Mon–Sat 10am–5pm or by appointment

Marks Antiques
Contact Mr M Marks
5 The Green, Westerham, Kent, TN16 1AS
☎ 01959 562017 Ⓕ 01959 562017
Ⓔ lambarda@btconnect.com
Est. 1960 *Stock size* Medium
Stock Fine 18th–19thC furniture, objets d'art
Open Mon–Sat 9.30am–5pm
Services Valuations, restorations

More Than Music Collectables
Contact Mike Vandenbosch
PO Box 68, Westerham, Kent, TN16 1ZF
☎ 01959 565514 Ⓕ 01959 565510
Ⓔ morethnmus@aol.com
Ⓦ www.mtmglobal.com
Est. 1995 *Stock size* Medium
Stock Vinyl, books, magazines, posters etc
Open Mon–Fri 10am–5.30pm Sat 10am–1pm
Services Worldwide mail order service

Barbara Ann Newman
Contact Barbara Ann Newman
London House Antiques, 4 Market Square, Westerham, Kent, TN16 1AW
☎ 01959 564479
Ⓜ 07850 016729
Est. 1991 *Stock size* Medium
Stock Antique dolls, teddy bears, children's antique furniture, rocking horses
Open Mon–Sat 10am–5pm
Fairs Kensington, Birmingham Doll Fair, Chelsea
Services Shipping

Regal Antiques (WKADA)
Contact Mrs T Lawrence
2 Market Square, Westerham, Kent, TN16 1AW
☎ 01959 561778 Ⓕ 01959 561778
Est. 1991 *Stock size* Medium
Stock Antique jewellery, portrait miniatures, porcelain, watches, fine paintings
Open Wed–Sat 11am–5pm
Services Watch repairs

D H Sargeant
Contact Mr D H Sargeant
21 The Green, Westerham, Kent, TN16 1AX
☎ 01959 562130 Ⓕ 01959 561989
Est. 1949 *Stock size* Large
Stock Chandeliers, table glass, glass wall lights
Open Mon–Sat 9am–5.30pm

Taylor-Smith Antiques (LAPADA)
Contact Ashton Taylor-Smith
4 The Grange, High Street, Westerham, Kent, TN16 1AH
☎ 01959 563100 Ⓕ 01959 565300
Ⓔ mountjoy@dircon.co.uk
Est. 1974 *Stock size* Medium
Stock Fine 18th and early 19thC furniture, objets d'art
Open Mon–Sat 10am–5pm closed Wed

Westerham House Antiques (LAPADA)
Contact Mr Raymond Barr

✉ The Old Sorting Office, Fullers Hill, Westerham, Kent, TN16 1AA P
☎ 01959 561622 F 01959 562986
M 07885 883441
E westhouse.antiques@virgin.net
Est. 1995 *Stock size* Large
Stock Georgian–Edwardian furniture, decorative items
Open Mon–Sat 10am–6pm
Fairs Olympia, NEC
Services Valuations

WESTGATE ON SEA

Westgate Auctions
Contact Mr Colin Langston
✉ **Rear of 70 St Mildred's Road, Westgate on Sea, Kent, CT8 8RF** P
☎ 01843 834891
Est. 1982
Open Mon–Sat 9am–5pm
Sales Antique and modern furniture and effects Sat 9am, viewing Fri 9.30am–5pm
Frequency Monthly
Catalogues Yes

WHITSTABLE

Bonhams & Brooks
Contact Christopher Hodgson
✉ **95–97 Tankerton Road, Whitstable, Kent, CT5 2AJ** P
☎ 01227 275007 F 01227 266443
E kent@bonhams.com
W www.bonhams.com
Open Mon–Fri 9am–5.30pm Sun 9am–3pm
Sales Regional Representative for Kent. Contact Head Office (London) for details

Book & Pieces
Contact Mrs J Harvey
✉ **48 Oxford Street, Whitstable, Kent, CT5 1DG** P
☎ 01227 771333
Est. 1990 *Stock size* Large
Stock Some antiquarian books, general second-hand books
Open Mon–Sat 9.45am–4pm closed Wed

Boulevard Antiques
Contact Mrs J Baker
✉ **139 Tankerton Road, Whitstable, Kent, CT5 2AW** P
☎ 01227 273335
Est. 1997 *Stock size* Large
No. of dealers 5
Stock China, Art Deco, glass, furniture, postcards, books, records, Osborne plaques, dolls, toys, silver, silver plate
Open Mon–Sat 9.30am–5pm
Services Valuations

Laurens Antiques
Contact Mr G Laurens
✉ **2 Harbour Street, Whitstable, Kent, CT5 1AG** P
☎ 01227 261940
Est. 1965 *Stock size* Large
Stock General antiques
Open Mon–Sat 10am–5pm closed Wed
Services Valuations

Tankerton Antiques (BHI)
Contact Mr Paul Wrighton
✉ **136 Tankerton Road, Whitstable, Kent, CT5 2AN** P
☎ 01227 266490
M 07702 244064
Est. 1985 *Stock size* Medium
Stock Antiques, 18th–19thC clocks, watches, china, furniture, fabrics, ceramics
Open Tues Wed 10am–1pm Thurs–Sat 10am–5pm
Fairs Brunel Clock and Watch Fair, Ardingly

WITTERSHAM

Old Corner House Antiques
Contact Gillian Shepherd
✉ **4 Poplar Road, Wittersham, Kent, TN30 7PG** P
☎ 01797 270326
Est. 1986 *Stock size* Medium
Stock Early English ceramics, needleworks, carvings, country furniture
Open Mon–Thurs Sat 10am–5pm
Fairs Bishop's Stortford, Rhodes Centre, Ardingly

WROTHAM

Barnaby's Antiques
Contact Cordelia McCartney
✉ **High Street, Wrotham, Kent, TN15 7AD** P
☎ 01732 886887 F 01732 886887
E cordelia@cordeliamc.free-online.co.uk
Est. 1996 *Stock size* Small
Stock Smalls, collectables, country furniture
Open Mon–Sat 9am–5pm or by appointment

LONDON

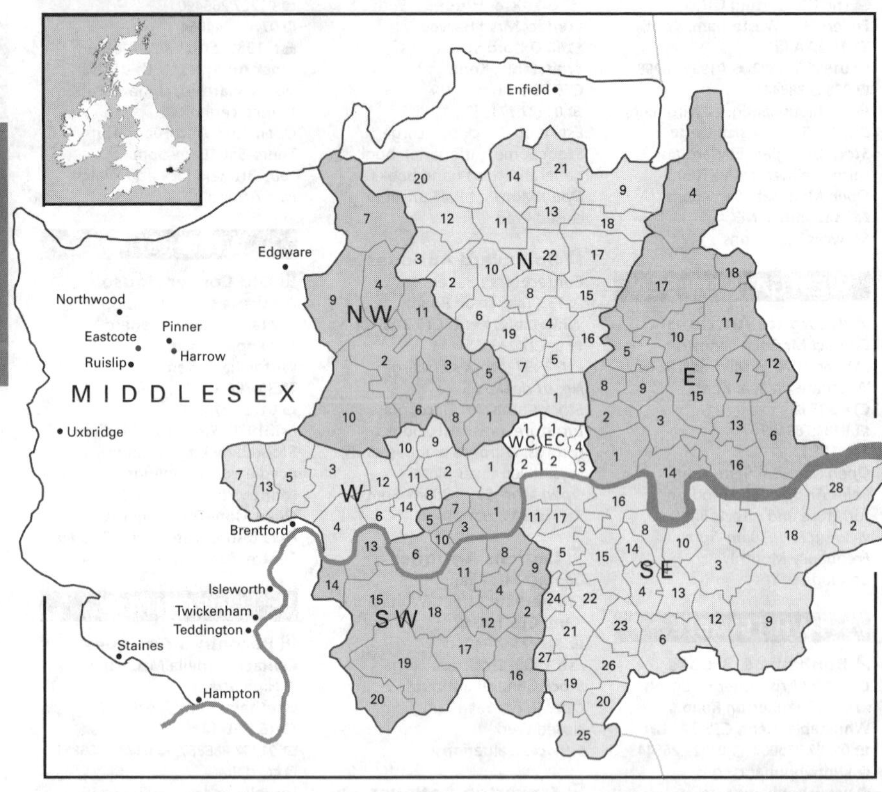

EAST

E1

Acme Planet
Contact Mr D Everington
Unit B1L/15, Metropolitan Wharf, Wapping Wall, London, E1 9SS
☎ 020 7480 5880 Ⓕ 020 7480 5881
Ⓔ acme@planet.co.uk
Ⓦ www.acmeplanet.co.uk
Est. 1996 *Stock size* Large
Stock Sci-fi, monster toys, bygones, kitsch
Open By appointment

Eat My Handbag Bitch
Contact George Enoch or Georgina Stead
6 Dray Walk, Off 91–95 Brick Lane, London, E1 6QL
☎ 020 7375 3100 Ⓕ 020 7375 0959
Ⓜ 0780 350 2249
Ⓔ georges@eatmyhandbagbitch.co.uk
Ⓦ www.eatmyhandbagbitch.co.uk
Est. 1999 *Stock size* Large
Stock Post-war design, furniture, glass, small decorative items, clocks, ceramics, stereos, televisions, lighting
Open Mon noon–7pm Wed Thurs 11am–7pm Fri 11am–5pm Sat Sun 11am–7pm closed Tues
Services Valuations

La Maison
Contact Mr Guillaume Bacou
107–108 Shoreditch High Street, London, E1 6JN
☎ 020 7729 9646 Ⓕ 020 7729 6399
Ⓔ gui@lamaison.com
Ⓦ www.lamaison.co.uk
Est. 1991 *Stock size* Medium
Stock French and Italian beds
Open Mon–Sat 10am–6pm
Services Restorations, upholstery

E2

John Jackson (LAPADA)
Contact Fiona Atkins
116 Columbia Road, London, E2 7RG
☎ 020 7613 2866 Ⓕ 020 7354 9591
Ⓜ 07711 319237
Est. 1984 *Stock size* Medium
Stock French and English decorative antiques and furniture
Open Sun 9am–2pm or by appointment

John Jackson (LAPADA)
Contact Fiona Atkins
5 Fournier Street, London, E1 6QE
☎ 020 7247 4745 Ⓕ 020 7354 9591
Ⓜ 07711 319237
Est. 1984 *Stock size* Large
Stock Early and Georgian furniture, decorative items
Open Thurs–Sat 10am–5pm or by appointment

George Rankin Coin Co Ltd
Contact Mr G Rankin
325 Bethnal Green Road, London, E2 6AH
020 7729 1280 020 7729 5023
Est. 1969 *Stock size* Large
Stock Period, modern coins, medals, banknotes, jewellery
Open Mon–Sat 10am–6pm
Fairs Coinex, Cumberland and Europa
Services Valuations

E4

Record Detector
Contact Mr J Salter
3–4 Station Approach, Chingford, London, E4 6AL
020 8529 6361
nick@salter.co.uk
www.salter.co.uk
Est. 1991 *Stock size* Large
Stock Second-hand records, CDs, 1950–1990s, videos, magazines
Open Mon–Sat 9.30am–6pm

Nicholas Salter Antiques
Contact Mrs S Salter
8 Station Approach, Chingford, London, E4 6AL
020 8529 2938
nick@salter.co.uk
www.salter.co.uk
Est. 1969 *Stock size* Large
Stock General antiques
Open Mon–Wed 10am–5pm Fri Sat 10am–6pm

E11

I D Edrich
Contact Mr I Edrich
17 Selsdon Road, London, E11 2QF
020 8989 9541 020 8989 9541
edrich@lineone.net
www.website.lineone.net/edrichid
Est. 1965 *Stock size* Large
Stock First editions, antiquarian books, literary periodicals, literature a speciality
Open By appointment

Forrest & Co Ltd
Contact Mr J Wiggett
Lancaster House, Lancaster Road, Leytonstone, London, E11 3EJ
020 8556 7009 020 8532 8292
Est. 1965
Open Mon–Fri 9am–5pm
Sales Sale 11am Thurs, viewing Wed 10am–5pm
Frequency Fortnightly
Catalogues Yes

Wanstead Antiques Centre
Contact Mr Gill
21 High Street, Wanstead, London, E11 2AA
020 8532 9844
Est. 1992 *Stock size* Medium
Stock Georgian–Victorian furniture, ceramics, vintage radios, vintage pens, collectables
Open Mon–Sat 10am–5.30pm Sun 11am–4pm

E15

Robert Bush Antiques
Contact Mr Robert Bush
Bermondsey Antique Arches, 84 St James Road, Bermondsey, London, E15 1RN
07836 236911
bush.antiques@virgin.net
Stock Antique and decorative furniture
Open Mon–Thurs 9.30am–5pm Fri 7.30am–4pm

E17

Peter Davis Antiques
Contact Mr P Davis
1 Georgian Village, 100 Wood Street, London, E17 3HX
020 8520 6638 020 8520 6638
Est. 1972 *Stock size* Small
Stock Walking sticks, postcards, small silver, collectables
Open Mon–Wed 10.30am–4.30pm

E18

Thornwood Auction
Contact Mrs D Green
Thornwood Village Hall, Weald Hall Lane, Thornwood, Epping, London, E18
020 8553 1242
07860 905667
Est. 1985
Open Mon–Fri 9am–5pm
Sales Antiques and general Mon 6.30pm
Frequency Fortnightly
Catalogues Yes

Victoria Antiques
Contact Mr M Holman
166a George Lane, London, E18 1AY
020 8989 1002
Est. 1998 *Stock size* Medium
Stock Silver, silver-plate, brass, china, carved items, small furniture, coins, clocks
Open Mon–Sat 11am–5pm closed Tues Thurs
Services Valuations

Woodford Auctions
Contact Mrs D Green
209 High Road, South Woodford, London, E18 2PA
020 8553 1242
07860 905667
Est. 1994
Open Mon–Fri 9am–5pm
Sales Antiques and general sale Mon 6.30pm, viewing Mon 4pm prior to sale
Frequency Fortnightly
Catalogues Yes

EC1

Boutle and King (PBFA)
Contact Mr C Boutle
23 Arlington Way, London, EC1R 1UY
020 7278 4497 020 7278 4497
Est. 1987 *Stock size* Medium
Stock Antiquarian and second-hand books, genealogy, architecture, publishing a speciality
Open Mon–Fri 10.30am–7pm Sat 10.30am–6pm
Fairs City Book Market

Eldridge London
Contact Mr B Eldridge
99–101 Farringdon Road, London, EC1R 3BN
020 7837 0379 020 7278 6167
Est. 1955 *Stock size* Large
Stock 18th–19thC English furniture, treen, items of social and historic interest
Open Mon–Fri noon–5pm 1st Sat of month 11am–5pm closed Wed

Andrew Lowe Antiques
Contact Gloria Wenhan
18 Exmouth Market, London, EC1R 4QE
020 7837 6699 020 7837 3735
Est. 1998 *Stock size* Medium

Stock 19thC French mirrors, period furniture
Open Mon–Sat 10am–6.30pm or Sun by appointment

⊞ Paragon Art
Contact Mr Hassbani
✉ **Office 7, 34–35 Hatton Garden, London, EC1 N8PJ** Ⓟ
☎ 020 7404 3207 Ⓕ 020 8551 4487
Ⓔ hassbanis@aol.com
Est. 1993 *Stock size* Large
Stock Ancient and Islamic art 2000BC–18thC
Open By appointment only

⊞ Andrew R Ullmann Ltd
Contact Mr J Ullmann
✉ **10 Hatton Garden, London, EC1N 8AH** Ⓟ
☎ 020 7405 1877 Ⓕ 020 7404 7071
Est. 1950 *Stock size* Large
Stock Antique gold and gem jewellery, clocks, silver, objets d'art, watches
Open Mon–Fri 9am–5pm Sat 9.30am–5pm
Services Restorations

EC2

⊞ Atlas Books
Contact Mr B Burdett
✉ **55–57 Tabernacle Street, London, EC2A 4AA** Ⓟ
☎ 020 7490 4540 Ⓕ 020 7490 4514
Ⓔ bn@atlasgallery.com
Ⓦ www.atlasgallery.com
Est. 1993 *Stock size* Medium
Stock Antiquarian, rare, second-hand books, travel a speciality
Open Mon–Fri 9am–5.30pm
Fairs Bloomsbury, Phillips
Services Valuations, book search

⊞ LASSCO St Michael's (LAPADA, SALVO, BACA Award Winner 2001)
Contact Jack Nott-Bower or Anthony Reeve
✉ **St Michael's Church, Mark Street (Off Paul Street), London, EC2A 4ER** Ⓟ
☎ 020 7749 9944 Ⓕ 020 7749 9941
Ⓔ st.michaels@lassco.co.uk
Ⓦ www.lassco.co.uk
Est. 1978 *Stock size* Large
Stock Architectural antiques, chimney pieces, overmantels, carved stonework, panelled rooms, statuary, garden ornaments and furniture, stained glass, metalwork
Open Mon–Fri 9.30am–5.30pm Sat 10am–5pm
Services Shipping

⊞ Westland and Co (SALVO)
Contact Mr R Muirhead
✉ **St Michael's Church, Leonard Street, London, EC2A 4ER** Ⓟ
☎ 020 7739 8094 Ⓕ 020 7729 3620
Ⓔ westland@westland.co.uk
Ⓦ www.westland.co.uk
Est. 1963 *Stock size* Large
Stock Architectural elements, paintings, lighting, statuary, furniture, period, decorative chimneys
Open Mon–Fri 9am–6pm Sat Sun 10am–5pm
Services Valuations, restorations

EC3

⊞ Halcyon Days (BADA)
Contact Georgina Foster or Cheska Moon
✉ **4 Royal Exchange, London, EC3V 3LL** Ⓟ
☎ 020 7626 1120 Ⓕ 020 7283 1876
Ⓔ info@halcyondays.co.uk
Ⓦ www.halcyondays.co.uk
Est. 1950 *Stock size* Small
Stock Enamels, fans, snuff boxes, objects of virtue, *tôle peinte*, papier mâché, porcelain
Open Mon–Fri 10am–5.30pm
Fairs Grosvenor House

NORTH

N1

⊞ After Noah
Contact Simon Tarr
✉ **121 Upper Street, London, N1 1QP** Ⓟ
☎ 020 7359 4281 Ⓕ 020 7359 4281
Ⓔ mailorder@afternoah.com
Ⓦ www.afternoah.com
Est. 1989 *Stock size* Medium
Stock Antique and contemporary furniture & houseware
Open Mon–Sat 10am–6pm Sun noon–5pm
Services Restorations

⊞ Annie's Vintage Costume and Textiles
Contact Mrs Annie Moss
✉ **10 Camden Passage, Islington, London, N1 8ED** Ⓟ
☎ 020 7359 0796 Ⓕ 020 7359 9608
Est. 1975 *Stock size* Small
Stock 1900–1940s costume, linen, textiles
Open Mon Tues Thurs Fri 11am–6pm Wed Sat 9am–6pm

⊞ The Antique Trader at the Millinery Works
Contact Mr B Thompson
✉ **85–87 Southgate Road, London, N1 3JS** Ⓟ
☎ 020 7359 2019 Ⓕ 020 7359 5792
Ⓔ antiquetrader@millinery.demon.co.uk
Ⓦ www.millineryworks.co.uk
Est. 1970 *Stock size* Large
Stock Arts and Crafts movement, furniture, effects
Open Tues–Sat 11am–6pm Sun noon–5pm or by appointment
Services Valuations

⊞ Art Nouveau Originals C1900 (LAPADA)
Contact Mrs C Turner
✉ **4–5 Pierrepont Row Arcade, Camden Passage, London, N1 8EF**
☎ 020 7359 4127 Ⓕ 01733 244717
Ⓜ 07774 718096
Ⓔ anoc1900@compuserve.com
Est. 1997 *Stock size* Medium
Stock Art Nouveau furniture, ceramics, bronzes, pictures, jewellery
Open Sat Wed 9am–4pm
Fairs NEC, LAPADA

⊞ Banana Dance Ltd
Contact Jonathan Daltrey
✉ **16 The Mall, 359 Upper Street, Camden Passage, Islington, London, N1 0PP** Ⓟ
☎ 020 8699 7728/020 7354 3125
Ⓕ 020 8699 7728
Ⓜ 07976 296987
Ⓔ jonathan@bananadance.com
Ⓦ www.bananadance.com
Est. 1989 *Stock size* Large
Stock Clarice Cliff, 20thC ceramics
Open Wed Fri Sat 9am–5pm
Fairs NEC, Alexandra Palace
Services Valuations, shipping, mail order

⊞ David Bowden Chinese and Japanese Art
Contact David Bowden
✉ **12 The Mall, Upper Street, Islington, London, N1 0PD** Ⓟ
☎ 020 7226 3033
Est. 1980 *Stock size* Large
Stock Japanese netsuke, works of art, Chinese works of art

Open Wed–Fri 11am–3pm
Sat 10am–4pm
Fairs NEC

Camden Passage Antiques Market
Contact Mrs S Lemkow
12 Camden Passage, London, N1 8ED
020 7359 0190 F 020 7704 2095
Est. 1960 *Stock size* Large
No. of dealers 300
Stock General antiques and specialist shops
Open Wed Sat 8am–3pm stalls 8am–5pm shops

Camel Art Deco (LPTA)
Contact Mrs E Durack
34 Islington Green, London, N1 8DU
020 7359 5242
Est. 1996 *Stock size* Small
Stock Art Deco ceramics, furniture, lighting
Open Wed 9am–3.30pm Thurs Fri noon–5pm Sat 9am–6pm
Fairs Specialist Art Deco fairs
Services French polishing, reupholstering of Lloyd Loom furniture

Patric Capon (BADA)
Contact Patric Capon
350 Upper Street, Islington, London, N1 0PD
020 7354 0487 F 020 7295 1475
M 07831 444924
E patric.capon@netway.co.uk
Est. 1975 *Stock size* Medium
Stock Antique clocks, marine chronometers, barometers
Open Wed–Sat only
Fairs Olympia (Summer)
Services Valuations, restorations, shipping

Castle Gibson
Contact Joyce Gibson
106a Upper Street, London, N1 1QN
020 7704 0927 F 020 7704 0927
Stock size Large
Stock 19thC–1940s office furniture, polished metal items, 1930s leather chairs, sofas, early 20thC industrial furniture, 1920s–1940s shop fittings, garden furniture
Open Mon–Sat 10am–6pm Sun noon–5pm
Services Deliveries within London

Chancery Antiques Ltd
Contact Mr R Rote
10 The Mall, 357a Upper Street, London, N1 0PD
020 7359 9035 F 020 7359 9035
Est. 1951 *Stock size* Medium
Stock Japanese porcelain, pottery, ivory, 19thC Continental works of art, cloisonné
Open Tues–Sat 10.30am–5pm or by appointment closed Thurs

Peter Chapman Antiques and Restoration (LAPADA, CINOA)
Contact Peter Chapman or Zac Chapman
10 Theberton Street, Islington, London, N1 0QX
020 7226 5565 F 020 8348 4846
M 07831 093662
E pchapmanantiques@easynet.co.uk
W www.antiques-peterchapman.co.uk
Est. 1971 *Stock size* Medium
Stock English and Continental furniture 1700–1900, mirrors, Grand Tour souvenirs, bronzes, spelters and other smalls, paintings, lighting, hall lanterns, stained glass, architectural, garden and decorative items
Open Mon–Sat 9.30am–6pm or by appointment
Services Valuations, restorations, shipping

Charlton House Antiques
Contact Mr S Burrows or Mr R Sims
18–20 Camden Passage, Islington, London, N1 8ED
020 7226 3141 F 020 7226 3141
E charlhse@aol.com
Est. 1979 *Stock size* Large
Stock Antique furniture
Open Mon–Sat 9.30am–5pm
Services Shipping

Charlton House Antiques
Contact Mr S Burrows or Mr R Sims
35 Camden Passage, London, N1 8EA
020 7226 3141 F 020 7226 3141
E charlhse@aol.com
Est. 1979 *Stock size* Large
Stock English and European 19thC furniture, decorative items
Open Mon–Sat 9.30am–5pm

Cloud Cuckoo Land
Contact Mrs C Harper
6 Charlton Place, London, N1 8AJ
020 7354 3141
E info@cloudcuckooland.org.uk
W www.cloudcuckooland.org.uk
Est. 1981 *Stock size* Medium
Stock Vintage clothes, accessories, 1850s–1950s, some later
Open Mon–Sat 9.30am–5.30pm

Peter Collingridge
Contact Mr Peter Collingridge
6 The Hall, 359 Upper Street, London, N1 0PD
020 7354 9189
Est. 1987 *Stock size* Large
Stock 18th–19thC brassware
Open Wed 7.30am–5pm Fri 11am–4pm Sat 9am–5pm
Fairs NEC
Services Valuations, restorations

Rosemary Conquest
Contact Mrs R Conquest
4 Charlton Place, London, N1 8AJ
020 7359 0616
Est. 1996 *Stock size* Large
Stock Continental and Dutch lighting, decorative items
Open Tue Thurs Fri 11am–5.30pm Wed Sat 9am–5.30pm

Criterion Auctioneers
Contact Daniel Webster
53 Essex Road, Islington, London, N1 2SF
020 7359 5707 F 020 7354 9843
E info@criterion-auctioneers.co.uk
W www.criterion-auctioneers.co.uk
Est. 1989
Open Mon–Fri 9.30am–6pm
Sales Mon 5pm sale of antiques and decorative furnishings. Better quality antiques sales held monthly, telephone for details, viewing Fri 4–8pm Sat Sun 10am–6pm and on the day of sale 10am–5pm
Frequency Weekly
Catalogues Yes

Carlton Davidson Antiques
Contact Mr Carlton Davidson
33 Camden Passage, London, N1 8EA
020 7226 7491 F 020 7226 7491
Est. 1982 *Stock size* Medium

Stock Decorative French items, including lighting
Open Wed–Sat 10am–4pm

⊞ Deans Antiques
Contact Mr D Gipson
✉ **25 Camden Passage, London, N1 8EA** 🅿
☎ 020 7354 9940 Ⓕ 020 7704 0020
Ⓜ 07770 231687
Ⓔ dean.antiques@virgin.net
Est. 1988 *Stock size* Large
Stock French decorative antiques
Open Wed–Sat 9am–5pm or by appointment
Fairs Battersea Decorative Antiques and Textiles Fair

⊞ Decodence
Contact Mr Gadd Sassower
✉ **21 The Mall, 359 Upper Street, London, N1 0PD** 🅿
☎ 020 7354 4473 Ⓕ 020 7689 0680
Ⓜ 07831 326326
Ⓔ gad@decodence.demon.co.uk
Est. 1989 *Stock size* Medium
Stock Anything celluloid or Bakelite, radios, lighting, telephones etc
Open Wed–Sat 10am–5pm or by appointment
Services Valuations

⊞ Eclectica
Contact Liz Wilson
✉ **2 Charlton Place, London, N1 8AJ** 🅿
☎ 020 7226 5625 Ⓕ 020 7226 5625
Est. 1988 *Stock size* Large
Stock Vintage costume jewellery, 1920s–1960s
Open Wed–Sat 9am–6pm Mon Tues Thurs Fri 11am–6pm
Services Theatre/film hire

⊞ Fandango
Contact Jonathan Ellis or Henrietta Palmer
✉ **50 Cross Street, Islington, London, N1 2BA** 🅿
☎ 020 7226 1777 Ⓕ 020 7226 1777
Ⓜ 07979 650805
Ⓔ shop@fandango.uk.com
Ⓦ www.fandango.uk.com
Est. 1997 *Stock size* Medium
Stock Post-war design lighting and furniture
Open Wed–Sat 11am–6pm Sun noon–5pm
Services Valuations, interior design

⊞ Feljoy Antiques
Contact Mrs Joy Humphreys
✉ **3 Angel Arcade, Camden Passage, London, N1 8EA** 🅿
☎ 020 7354 5336 Ⓕ 020 7831 3485
Ⓔ joy@feljoy-antiques.demon.co.uk
Ⓦ www.chintz.net/feljoy
Est. 1985 *Stock size* Large
Stock Chintzware, textiles, cushions, shawls, small decorative furniture, decorative items including beadwork cushions
Open Wed 8am–3.30pm Sat 10am–4pm
Services Mail order

⊞ Vincent Freeman
Contact Mr V Freeman
✉ **1 Camden Passage, Islington, London, N1 8EA** 🅿
☎ 020 7226 6178 Ⓕ 020 7226 7231
Ⓜ 0589 966880
Est. 1966 *Stock size* Large
Stock General including furniture, 19thC musical boxes both disc and cylinder
Open Wed–Sat 9am–5pm or by appointment
Fairs Olympia (June)

⊞ Furniture Vault
Contact Mr David Loveday
✉ **50 Camden Passage, London, N1 8AE**
☎ 020 7354 1047 Ⓕ 020 7354 1047
Est. 1984 *Stock size* Large
Stock 18th–19thC furniture
Open Tues–Sat 9.30am–4.30pm

⌂ Gateway Arcade Antiques Market
Contact Mike Spooner
✉ **357 Upper Street, Camden Passage, London, N1 0PD** 🅿
☎ 020 7969 1500 Ⓕ 020 7969 1639
Est. 2000 *Stock size* Large
No. of dealers 50
Stock Jewellery, silver, collectables, watches, militaria
Open Wed 6am–2pm Sat 8am–2pm

⊞ Gazebo (PTA)
Contact Mrs D Brennan
✉ **Top Floor, The Flea Market, Pierrepont Row, Camden Passage, Islington, London, N1 8EE** 🅿
☎ 020 7226 6627
Est. 1961 *Stock size* Large
Stock Disney, Warner Brothers, McDonalds items, egg cups, postcards, song sheets, ephemera, fashion plates
Open Wed Sat 9.30am–3.30pm
Fairs British Picture Postcard Fair
Services Valuations, Postcard Collectors Club

⌂ The Georgian Village Antique Centre
Contact Mr D Turner
✉ **30–31 Islington Green, London, N1 8DU** 🅿
☎ 020 7226 1571
Est. 1978 *Stock size* Large
No. of dealers 45–50
Stock Wide range of antiques, collectables
Open Tues–Fri 9am–1pm Wed 8.30am–4pm Sat 1–4pm

⊞ Goodison & Paraskeva
Contact Mr J Goodison
✉ **16 Camden Passage, London, N1 8ED** 🅿
☎ 020 7226 2423 Ⓕ 01273 501969
Est. 1985 *Stock size* Large
Stock Decorative antiques, papier mâché, lighting, garden furniture, statuary
Open Wed–Sat 9am–4pm
Fairs Decorative Antiques Fair, Great Antiques Fair

⊞ Hallmark Antiques
Contact Mr Ralph
✉ **359 Upper Street, London, N1 0PD** 🅿
☎ 020 7354 1616
Est. 1979 *Stock size* Medium
Stock Victorian–Edwardian jewellery, silver, silver photo frames
Open Tues Thurs Fri 10am–2pm Wed Sat 10am–5pm

⊞ Rosemary Hart
Contact Rosemary Hart
✉ **8 Angel Arcade, 116 Islington High Street, London, N1 8EG** 🅿
☎ 020 7359 6839
Ⓔ rosemaryhart@cwcom.net
Est. 1980 *Stock size* Small
Stock Small plated tableware and silver pieces, decorative pieces and mother-of-pearl
Open Wed 9am–4pm Fri Sat by appointemnt

⊞ Heather Antiques
Contact Heather Cohen
✉ **25 The Mall, 359 Upper Street, London, N1 8EG** 🅿

☎ 020 7226 2412 Ⓕ 020 7226 2412
Est. 1969 *Stock size* Medium
Stock Silver, silver-plate decorative items, flatware
Open Tues–Sat 10am–5pm
Services Valuations, restorations

⊞ Diana Huntley (LAPADA)
Contact Mrs Ross
✉ **8 Camden Passage, London, N1 8ED** Ⓟ
☎ 020 7226 4605 Ⓕ 020 7359 0240
Ⓔ diana@dianahuntleyantiques.co.uk
Ⓦ www.dianahuntleyantiques.co.uk
Est. 1970 *Stock size* Large
Stock Fine quality 19thC porcelain, Meissen, major English factories
Open Tues Fri Sat 10am–4pm Wed 7am–4pm

⊞ Japanese Gallery Ltd (Ukiyo-e Society)
Contact Mr C D Wertheim
✉ **23 Camden Passage, London, N1 8EA** Ⓟ
☎ 020 7226 3347 Ⓕ 020 7229 2934
Ⓜ 07930 411991
Ⓔ princyw@hotmail.com
japanesegallerylondon@hotmail.com
Est. 1980 *Stock size* Large
Stock Japanese woodcut prints, Japanese ceramics, sword armour, Japanese dolls
Open Mon–Fri 9.30am–4.30pm Sat 10am–5pm
Services Restorations, free authentification

⊞ Jonathan James (LAPADA)
Contact Norman or James Petre
✉ **52–53 Camden Passage, London, N1 8EA** Ⓟ
☎ 020 7704 8266
Est. 1994 *Stock size* Medium
Stock 18th–19thC English furniture
Open Tues–Sat 10am-5pm
Services Valuations

⊞ Judith Lassalle (PBFA)
Contact Mrs J Lassalle
✉ **7 Pierrepont Arcade, London, N1 8EF** Ⓟ
☎ 020 7607 7121
Est. 1765 *Stock size* Small
Stock Toys, games, books, optical toys, ephemera, all pre-1914
Open Wed 7.30am–4pm Sat 9.30am–4pm or by appointment
Fairs English and American ephemera fairs, PBFA Bookfair at Russell Hotel

⊞ LASSCO Warehouse (SALVO)
Contact Jesse Carrington
✉ **101–108 Britannia Walk, London, N1 7LU** Ⓟ
☎ 020 7490 1000 Ⓕ 020 7490 0908
Ⓔ warehouse@lassco.co.uk
Ⓦ www.lassco.co.uk
Est. 1978 *Stock size* Large
Stock Architectural reclamation and salvage
Open Mon–Sat 10am–5pm
Services Shipping

⊞ John Laurie (LAPADA)
Contact Mr John Laurie
✉ **352 Upper Street, London, N1 0PD** Ⓟ
☎ 020 7226 0913 Ⓕ 020 7226 4599
Ⓔ jjgewirtz@aol.com
Est. 1963 *Stock size* Large
Stock Antique and modern silver, silver plate
Open Mon–Sat 9.30am–5pm
Services Restorations, re-plating

⊞ Leolinda
Contact Ms Leolinda Costa
✉ **33 Islington Green, London, N1 8DU** Ⓟ
☎ 020 7226 3450 Ⓕ 020 7209 0143
Ⓦ www.islington.co.uk/leolinda
Est. 1989 *Stock size* Small
Stock Old and new silver jewellery, gemstone necklaces, ethnic art, jewellery
Open Wed and Sat 10am–5pm
Services After sales service

⊞ Andrew Lineham Fine Glass (BADA, CINOA)
Contact Mr A Lineham
✉ **19 The Mall, Camden Passage, London, N1 8EA** Ⓟ
☎ 020 7704 0195 Ⓕ 01243 576241
Ⓜ 07767 702722
Ⓔ andrewlineham@onetel.net.uk
Ⓦ www.andrewlineham.co.uk
Est. 1979 *Stock size* Large
Stock 19th–20thC colourful glass, porcelain
Open Wed 8am–3pm Sat 10.30am–4pm or by appointment
Fairs Olympia (Jun Nov)
Services Valuations, hire

⊞ Mah's Antiques
Contact Mr Mah
✉ **49 Camden Passage, London, N1 8EA** Ⓟ
☎ 020 7354 1860
Est. 1984 *Stock size* Medium
Stock Oriental and European porcelain, works of art
Open Tues–Sat 10.30am–4.30pm closed Thurs
Services Valuations, restorations

The Mall Antiques Arcade
Contact Mike Spooner
✉ **359 Upper Street, Camden Passage, London, N1 0PD** Ⓟ
☎ 020 7351 5353 Ⓕ 020 7351 5350
Ⓔ antique@dial.pipex.com
Est. 1979 *Stock size* Large
No. of dealers 35
Stock Furniture, decorative antiques
Open Tues Thurs Fri 10am–5pm Wed 7.30am–5pm Sat 9am–5.45pm

⊞ Mario & Sabre (CPADA)
Contact Ms S Gilmartin
✉ **23 The Mall, 359 Upper Street, Islington, London, N1 0PD** Ⓟ
☎ 020 7226 2426 Ⓕ 020 8873 1315
Ⓜ 07956 963531
Ⓔ sabgilmar@aol.com
Ⓦ www.antiques-net.com
Est. 1998 *Stock size* Medium
Stock English and European porcelain, fine glass
Open Wed–Sat 9am–5pm or by appointment
Fairs NEC, Olympia (June)

⊞ Metro Retro
Contact Mr Saxon Durrant
✉ **1 White Conduit Street, London, N1 9EL**
☎ 020 7278 4884 Ⓕ 01245 442047
Ⓜ 07850 319116
Ⓔ saxon@metroretro.demon.co.uk
Ⓦ www.metroretro.co.uk
Est. 1994 *Stock size* Large
Stock Industrial style and stripped-steel furniture, lighting, home accessories
Open Tues–Sat 11am–6pm Sun 10am–2pm
Fairs Syon Park, Jukebox Madness, Chiswick, Battersea
Services Props hire, consultancy

⊞ Michel André Morin (CPTA)
Contact Brian Trotman
✉ **12b Camden Passage on Charlton Place, Islington, London, N1 8ED** Ⓟ
☎ 020 7226 3803 Ⓕ 020 7704 0708

Ⓜ 07802 832496
Ⓔ michel.morin@virgin.net
Est. 1989 *Stock size* Medium
Stock French decorative furniture, chandeliers, items for interior decorators
Open Wed–Sat 7.30am–4.30pm or by appointment
Fairs Olympia, Battersea Decorative Antiques and Textiles Fair

⊞ Michel André Morin (CPTA)
Contact Brian Trotman
⊠ **27 Charlton Place, Islington, London, N1 8AQ** Ⓟ
☎ 020 7226 3803 Ⓕ 020 7704 0708
Ⓜ 07802 832496
Ⓔ michel.morin@virgin.net
Est. 1989 *Stock size* Medium
Stock French decorative furniture, chandeliers, items for interior decorators
Open Wed–Sat 7.30am–4.30pm or by appointment
Fairs Olympia, Battersea Decorative Antiques and Textiles Fair
Services Valuations, restorations

⊞ Chris Newland Antiques
Contact Chris or George Newland
⊠ **The Lower Level Georgian Village, 30–31 Islington Green, London, N1 8DU** Ⓟ
☎ 020 7359 9805
Est. 1968 *Stock size* Large
Stock 18th–19thC period furniture, objets d'art
Open Tues–Sat 9.30am–4.30pm
Services Restorations

⊞ Number 19
Contact Mr D Griffith
⊠ **19 Camden Passage, London, N1 8EA** Ⓟ
☎ 020 7226 1999 Ⓕ 020 7226 1126
Est. 1982 *Stock size* Large
Stock Decorative antiques, campaign furniture, vintage shop fittings, leather seating, decorative accessories
Open Tues–Sat 10am–5pm closed Thurs

⊞ Out of Time
Contact Mr E Farlow
⊠ **21 Canonbury Lane, London, N1 2AS** Ⓟ
☎ 020 7354 5755 Ⓕ 020 7354 5755
Est. 1969 *Stock size* Large
Stock 1940s–1950s homestyle furniture, glass, fridges, tables, chairs
Open Mon–Sun 10am–6pm
Fairs Jukebox Madness, Ascot
Services Valuations, restorations

⊞ Kevin Page Oriental Art Ltd (LAPADA, CPADA)
Contact Mr K Page
⊠ **2–6 Camden Passage, Islington, London, N1 8ED** Ⓟ
☎ 020 7226 8558 Ⓕ 020 7354 9145
Ⓔ kpageoriental@aol.com
Ⓦ www.kevinpage.co.uk
Est. 1969 *Stock size* Large
Stock Oriental art, bronze, lacquer, porcelain, ivory
Trade only Trade and export only
Open Tues–Sat 10.30am–4.30pm

⊞ John Pearman
Contact John Pearman
⊠ **24 The Mall, Upper Street, London, N1 0PD** Ⓟ
☎ 020 7359 0591 Ⓕ 020 7359 0591
Ⓔ john.pearman@talk21.com
Est. 1983 *Stock size* Medium
Stock 19thC glass, ceramics
Open Wed 9am–5pm Sat 10am–5pm or by appointment

⊞ Phoenix Oriental Art (LAPADA)
Contact Elena Edwards
⊠ **No 6 the Lower Mall, 359 Upper Street, Islington, London, N1 0PD** Ⓟ
☎ 020 7226 4474 Ⓕ 020 8521 8846
Ⓔ okinasan@aol.com
Ⓦ www.trocadero.com/okinasan
Est. 1981 *Stock size* Large
Stock Chinese and Japanese bronze from the last 1000 years
Open Wed Sat 10am–4pm or by appointment

⊞ Sylvia Powell Decorative Arts (LAPADA)
Contact Mr D Powell
⊠ **18 The Mall, Camden Passage, London, N1 0PD** Ⓟ
☎ 020 7354 2977 Ⓕ 020 8458 2769
Ⓜ 07802 714998
Ⓔ dpowell909@aol.com
Ⓦ www.sylvia-powell.com
Est. 1987 *Stock size* Large
Stock Art pottery, 20thC decorative arts
Open Wed 8am–5pm Sat 9am–5pm or by appointment
Fairs Olympia Feb, June LAPADA London, NEC
Services Valuations

⊞ Piers Rankin
Contact Mr P Rankin
⊠ **14 Camden Passage, London, N1 8ED** Ⓟ
☎ 020 7354 3349 Ⓕ 020 7359 8138
Est. 1979 *Stock size* Large
Stock Silver, silver plate
Open Tues–Sat 9.30am–5.30pm
Services Packing for export

⊞ Regent Antiques
Contact Mr Tino Quaradeghini
⊠ **Barpart House, York Way, London, N1 0UZ** Ⓟ
☎ 020 7833 5545 Ⓕ 020 7278 2236
Ⓜ 07836 294074
Ⓔ tilno@aol.com
Est. 1974 *Stock size* Large
Stock 18thC–Edwardian furniture
Open Mon–Fri 9am–5.30pm
Services Restoration of furniture

⊞ Relic Antiques
Contact Mr Gliksten
⊠ **21 Camden Passage, London, N1 8EA** Ⓟ
☎ 020 7359 2597 Ⓕ 020 7388 2691
Ⓜ 07831 785059
Est. 1994 *Stock size* Large
Stock Decorative antiques, folk art, fairground art, country pieces, marine, architectural, trade signs, shop fittings
Open Wed–Sat 10am–4pm or by appointment
Services Valuations

⊞ Rookery Farm Antiques
Contact Mrs S Lemkow
⊠ **12 Camden Passage, London, N1 8ED** Ⓟ
☎ 020 7359 0190 Ⓕ 020 7704 2095
Ⓔ saralemkow@btinternet.com
Ⓦ www.antique-kitchenalia.co.uk
Est. 1989 *Stock size* Large
Stock Kitchenware, French enamel, brass, copper, country furniture
Open Mon–Sun 10.30am–5pm

⊞ Marcus Ross Antiques
Contact Mr M Ross
⊠ **16 Pierrepont Row, Camden Passage, Islington, London, N1 8EE** Ⓟ
☎ 020 7359 8494 Ⓕ 020 7359 0240
Est. 1973 *Stock size* Large
Stock Japanese and Chinese porcelain, 17thC onwards
Open Tues–Sat 10am–4pm closed Thurs

⊞ Rumours (LAPADA)
Contact John Donovan
✉ **4 The Mall, Upper Street, Camden Passage, Islington, London, N1 0PD** 🅿
☎ 020 7704 6549
Ⓜ 07836 277274 or 07831 103748
Ⓔ rumdec@aol.com
Est. 1988 *Stock size* Large
Stock Pottery
Open Wed Sat 8am–4pm
Fairs NEC
Services Valuations

⊞ Sanz & Pottle (CPTA)
Contact Mr B Pottle
✉ **Shops C & D, Angel Arcade, Camden Passage, London, N1 8EA** 🅿
☎ 020 7704 9884 Ⓕ 01386 840099
Est. 1969 *Stock size* Medium
Stock Bamboo furniture, general decorative antiques
Open Wed 7am–4pm Sat 8.30am–4.30pm
Services Valuations, restorations

⊞ At the Sign of the Chest of Drawers
Contact Mr Tony Harms
✉ **281 Upper Street, London, N1 2TZ** 🅿
☎ 020 7359 5909 Ⓕ 020 7359 5909
Est. 1986 *Stock size* Large
Stock Soft and hardwood old furniture, wooden and metal beds, chests-of-drawers, sofas, armchairs, wardrobes
Open Mon–Sun 10am–6pm
Services Valuations, restorations

⊞ Keith Skeel Antiques (LAPADA)
Contact Mr N McKay
✉ **46 Essex Road, London, N1 8LN** 🅿
☎ 020 7359 5633 Ⓕ 020 7226 3780
Ⓔ neil@mail.keithskeel.com
Ⓦ www.keithskeel.com
Est. 1975 *Stock size* Large
Stock 18th–19thC furniture, accessories
Open Mon–Sat 9am–6pm

⊞ Staffordshire Pride
Contact Sharon Racklyeft
✉ **4B Pierrepont Arcade, Camden Passage, London, N1 8EF**
☎ 020 7359 4127
Ⓜ 07958 453295
Est. 1975 *Stock size* Large
Stock 18thC–1900 Staffordshire
Open Sat Wed 9am–4pm

⊞ Sugar Antiques (CPTA)
Contact Mr T Sugarman
✉ **8–9 Pierrepont Arcade, Pierrepont Row, London, N1 8EF** 🅿
☎ 020 7354 9896 Ⓕ 020 7931 5642
Ⓜ 07973 179980
Ⓔ tony@sugar-antiques.demon.co.uk
Ⓦ www.sugar-antiques.demon.co.uk
Est. 1990 *Stock size* Large
Stock Wristwatches, pocket watches, pens, lighters, costume jewellery
Open Wed–Sat 8am–3.30pm
Services Valuations, restorations, shipping, book search, repairs

⊞ Chris Tapsell at Christopher House (CPADA)
Contact Mr C Tapsell
✉ **5 Camden Passage, Islington, London, N1 8EA** 🅿
☎ 020 7354 3603
Est. 1993 *Stock size* Medium
Stock 18th–19thC English and Continental furniture, Oriental ceramics, Georgian–Victorian mirrors
Open Tues Wed10am–5pm Fri Sat 10am–5pm or by appointment
Services Valuations, restorations

⊞ Pam Taylor Antiques (CPADA)
Contact Mrs P Taylor
✉ **Shop 4, 34 Islington Green, Camden Passage, London, N1 8DU** 🅿
☎ 020 7704 2253 Ⓕ 020 8343 0071
Ⓔ pamlet@globalnet.co.uk
Est. 1982 *Stock size* Medium
Stock Late 19th–early 20thC ceramics, glass, oil lamps
Open Wed 9am–4pm Sat 10am–4pm
Fairs Bowman, Stafford, NEC

⊞ Templar Antiques
Contact Mrs P Wilson
✉ **28 The Hall Antiques Centre, 359 Upper Street, London, N1 0PD** 🅿
☎ 020 7704 9448 Ⓕ 01621 819737
Ⓦ www.templar-antiques.co.uk
Est. 1974 *Stock size* Medium
Stock 18th–19thC glass, English, Irish, Bohemian
Open Mon–Sat 9am–5.40pm
Services Valuations, restorations

⊞ R J Tredwen
Contact Mr R Tredwen
✉ **3 Phelps Cottage, 357 Upper Street, London, N1 0PD** 🅿
☎ 020 7359 2224 Ⓕ 020 8467 7027
Ⓜ 07850 031 056
Ⓔ mantique@tredwen7.freeserve.co.uk
Est. 1970 *Stock size* Large
Stock Helmets, uniforms, guns, caps, swords, badges
Open Tues–Sat 11am–4.30pm
Fairs NEC, Nottingham Arms Fair
Services Valuations, hire service

⊞ Mike Weedon (LAPADA, CPADA)
✉ **7 Camden Passage, Islington, London, N1 8EA** 🅿
☎ 020 7226 5319/020 7609 6826
Ⓕ 0207 700 6389
Est. 1979 *Stock size* Large
Stock Art Nouveau, Art Deco, general antiques
Open Wed 9am–5pm Sat 10am–5pm or by appointment
Fairs Olympia

⊞ Agnes Wilton
Contact Mrs A Wilton
✉ **3 Islington High Street, Camden Passage, London, N1 0PG** 🅿
☎ 020 7226 5679
Est. 1972 *Stock size* Large
Stock Silver, furniture, decorative antiques
Open Mon–Sat 9.30am–3pm
Services Valuations

⊞ Woodage Antiques (LAPADA)
Contact Mr C Woodage
✉ **359 Upper Street, London, N1 0PD** 🅿
☎ 020 7226 4173 Ⓕ 01753 529 047
Ⓔ woodage.antiques@btinternet.com
Est. 1995 *Stock size* Large
Stock 18th–20thC furniture
Open Wed 7.30am–5pm Sat 9am–5pm
Fairs TVADA

⊞ York Gallery Ltd
Contact Mr G Beyer
✉ **51 Camden Passage, Islington, London, N1 8EA** 🅿
☎ 020 7354 8012 Ⓕ 020 7354 8012
Est. 1989 *Stock size* Large
Stock 17th–19thC engravings
Open Wed–Sat 10am–5pm
Services Picture framing

Michael Young
Contact M Young
22 The Mall, 359 Upper Street, Camden Passage, London, N1 0PD P
☎ 020 7226 2225
Est. 1985 *Stock size* Medium
Stock Marine models, pond yachts, general antiquities
Open Wed–Sat 9am–4pm
Services Valuations

N2

Martin Henham
Contact Mr M Henham
218 High Road, London, N2 9AY P
☎ 020 8444 5274
Est. 1963 *Stock size* Medium
Stock 18th–20thC Victoriana, bronzes, ceramics, porcelain
Open Tues–Sat 10am–6pm closed Thurs or by appointment
Services Furniture restoration

N3

Church End Antiques
Contact Mr A Martin
54 Hendon Lane, London, N3 1TT P
☎ 020 8346 6500
churchant@saqnet.co.uk
Est. 1997 *Stock size* Small
Stock Continental and English decorative antiques, Victorian, 19thC furniture
Open Tues–Sat 10.30am–5pm or by appointment
Services Valuations, restorations, French polishing

Martin Gladman Second-hand Books
Contact Mr M Gladman
235 Nether Street, London, N3 1NT P
☎ 020 8343 3023
Est. 1991 *Stock size* Large
Stock Large range of rare and antiquarian books through the humanities, history, military history
Open Sat 10am–6pm Tues–Fri 11am–8pm
Services Valuations

Intercol (ITA, Coin, Banknote and Map Collectors Societies)
Contact Mr Yasha Beresiner
43 Templars Crescent, London, N3 3QR P
☎ 020 8349 2207 F 020 8346 9539
yasha@compuserve.com
www.intercol.co.uk
Est. 1981 *Stock size* Medium
Stock Maps, charts, books, playing cards, currency
Open Wed Sat 9.30am–5pm or by appointment
Fairs Playing cards fairs, Map Society fairs (phone for details)
Services Valuations

N5

Gathering Moss
Contact Mrs S Murnane
193 Blackstock Road, London, N5 2LL P
☎ 020 7354 3034
Est. 1999 *Stock size* Medium
Stock Furniture, gifts, reclaimed timber items
Open Thurs 11am–7pm Sun 11am–5pm

Nicholas Goodyer (PBFA, ABA)
Contact Mr N Goodyer
15 Calabria Road, London, N5 1JB P
☎ 020 7226 5682 F 020 7354 4716
email@nicholasgoodyer.com
Est. 1950 *Stock size* Medium
Stock Antiquarian and rare books on architecture, travel, design, illustrated, natural history, colour plate books
Open Mon–Fri 9am–5pm or by appointment, prior call advised
Fairs PBFA Russell, ABA N6
Services Valuations, restorations, shipping, book search

Strike One Antique Clocks, Barometers & Music Boxes (BADA)
Contact Mr J G Mighell
48a Highbury Hill, London, N5 1AP P
☎ 020 7354 2790 F 020 7354 2790
M 07860 335933
milo@strikeone.co.uk
www.strikeone.co.uk
Est. 1968 *Stock size* Medium
Stock Antique clocks, barometers, music boxes, 1700–1900 English tavern clocks a speciality
Open By appointment only
Services Valuations, repairs

N6

Fisher & Sperr (ABA)
46 Highgate High Street, London, N6 5JB P
☎ 0208 3407244 F 0208 3484293
Est. 1945
Stock General second-hand and antiquarian books
Open Mon–Sat 10am–5pm
Services Valuations

Ripping Yarns (PBFA)
Contact Mrs C Mitchell
355 Archway Road, London, N6 4EJ P
☎ 020 8341 6111 F 020 7482 5056
yarns@rippingyarns.co.uk
www.rippingyarns.co.uk
Est. 1982 *Stock size* Large
Stock General stock, antiquarian and second-hand books including children's fiction, illustrated
Open Mon–Fri 10.30am–5.30pm Sat 10am–5pm Sun 11am–4pm
Fairs PBFA
Services Book search, French/Spanish spoken, annual catalogue

At the Sign of the Chest of Drawers
Contact Mr. Vincent Glanvill
164 Archway Road, London, N6 5BB P
☎ 020 8340 7652 F 020 8340 7652
Est. 1999 *Stock size* Large
Stock Soft and hardwood old furniture, wooden and metal beds, chests-of-drawers, wardrobes
Open Tues–Sat 10am–6pm
Services Restorations

N7

Back in Time
Contact Mr Demetriou
93 Holloway Road, London, N7 8LT P
☎ 020 7700 0744
Est. 1996 *Stock size* Large
Stock 1950s–1970s furniture, metal wardrobes, decorative items, metal kitchen furniture
Open Mon–Sat 10am–6pm
Services Valuations, restorations

Dome Antiques (LAPADA)
Contact Mr A Woolf
40 Queensland Road, London, N7 7AJ P
☎ 020 7700 6266 F 020 7609 1692

Ⓜ 07831 805888
Ⓔ dome.antiques@dial.pipex.com
Ⓦ www.domeantiques.co.uk
Est. 1974 ***Stock size*** Large
Stock 19thC decorative furniture
Open Mon–Fri 9am–5pm
Fairs NEC, Olympia
Services Restorations

N8

Hornsey Auctions Ltd
Contact Miss C Connoly
✉ **54–56 High Street, Hornsey, London, N8 7NX** Ⓟ
☎ 020 8340 5334 Ⓕ 020 8340 5334
Ⓔ hornseyauctions@ic24.net
Est. 1983
Open Thurs Fri 9.30am–5.30pm Sat 10am–4pm
Sales Antiques and general sale Wed 6.30pm, viewing Tues 5–8pm Wed 10am–6.30pm prior to sale
Frequency Weekly
Catalogues Yes

Of Special Interest
Contact Mr S Loftus
✉ **42–46 Park Road, London, N8 8TD** Ⓟ
☎ 020 8340 0909 Ⓕ 020 8374 6990
Est. 1988 ***Stock size*** Large
Stock Antique pine furniture, porcelain, fabrics, Indian items, garden furniture
Open Mon–Fri noon–7pm Sat 10am–6pm Sun noon–4pm

N11

A Pine Romance (BSSA)
Contact Mr A Gray
✉ **111 Friern Barnett Road, New Southgate, London, N11 3EU** Ⓟ
☎ 020 8361 5860 Ⓕ 020 83614697
Est. 1989 ***Stock size*** Medium
Stock British and Continental pine furniture, manufacturers of furniture from reclaimed timber
Open Mon–Sat 10am–5.30pm
Services Valuations, restorations

N12

Dean's Antiques Emporium
Contact Mr Dean Georgiou
✉ **7 Halliwick Court Parade, Woodhouse Road, London, N12 0NB** Ⓟ
☎ 020 8368 1858 Ⓕ 020 8368 1858
Ⓜ 07770 445338
Ⓔ dean@dean-antiques.com
Ⓦ www.dean-antiques.com
Est. 1996 ***Stock size*** Large
Stock English, Continental, Edwardian, Victorian furniture
Open Mon–Sat 10am–6pm closed Wed
Fairs Newark, Ardingly
Services Valuations, restorations

Nash & Company
Contact Mr S Nash
✉ **Lodge House, 9–17 Lodge Lane, London, N12 8JH** Ⓟ
☎ 020 8445 9000 Ⓕ 020 8446 6068
Est. 1977
Open Mon–Fri 9am–5.30pm
Sales Antiques and general sale Mon 5pm, viewing Sun 9am–1pm Mon 9am–5pm
Frequency Weekly
Catalogues Yes

The New Curiosity Shop
Contact Mrs T Robins
✉ **211 Woodhouse Road, Friern Barnet, London, N12 9AY** Ⓟ
☎ 020 8368 2117 Ⓕ 020 83682117
Est. 1994 ***Stock size*** Medium
Stock Coins, stamps, banknotes, sci-fi memorabilia, pop memorabilia, *Star Wars* toys, Corgi, Dinky, Matchbox collectables
Open Mon–Sat 10am–5.30pm
Services Valuations

N13

Palmers Green Antiques Centre
Contact Michael Webb
✉ **472 Green Lanes, Palmers Green, London, N13 5PA** Ⓟ
☎ 020 8350 0878
Ⓜ 07855 067544
Est. 1996 ***Stock size*** Large
No. of dealers 40+
Stock Furniture, clocks, pictures, jewellery, porcelain, china, glass, silver, lighting, general antiques
Open Mon Wed–Sat 10am–5.30pm Sun 11am–5pm
Services Valuations, house clearance

N14

Southgate Auction Rooms
Contact Mr J Nolan
✉ **55 High Street, Southgate, London, N14 6LD** Ⓟ
☎ 020 8886 7888 Ⓕ 020 8882 4421
Ⓦ www.southgateauctionrooms.com
Est. 1986
Open Mon–Fri 9am–5.30pm
Sales General and antiques sales Mon 5pm, viewing Sat 9am–1pm Mon 9am–5pm prior to sale
Frequency Weekly
Catalogues Yes

Southgate Bookshop
Contact Mr W Lobo
✉ **62 Chase Side, Southgate, London, N14 5PA** Ⓟ
☎ 020 8886 4805 Ⓕ 020 8363 8625
Est. 1985 ***Stock size*** Small
Stock Antiquarian, new and old books, furniture, silver, sport
Open Mon–Sat 11am–5.30pm
Services Valuations, book search

N15

Krypton Komics
Contact Mr G Ochiltree
✉ **252 High Road, Tottenham, London, N15 4AJ** Ⓟ
☎ 020 8801 5378 Ⓕ 020 8376 3174
Ⓔ krypton.komics@virgin.net
Ⓦ www.kryptonkomics.com
Est. 1980 ***Stock size*** Large
Stock 1950s–present day American comics
Open Mon–Fri 10.30am–6pm Sat 10am–6pm Sun 11am–6pm
Fairs Comic Convention at the Royal National Hotel
Services Valuations, mail order catalogue

M A Stroh Bookseller
Contact Mr M Stroh
✉ **1st Floor, 74–80 Markfield Road, Tottenham, London, N15 4QF** Ⓟ
☎ 020 8885 2112 Ⓕ 020 8885 2112
Ⓜ 07974 413039
Ⓔ patents@stroh.demon.co.uk
Ⓦ www.webspawner.com/users/buttonbook
Est. 1957 ***Stock size*** Medium
Stock Books, patents 1617–1970, journals, scientific papers, ephemera, old bindings, dissertations
Open By appointment

N16

I Ehrnfeld (NAWCC)
Contact Isaac Ehrnfeld
29 Leweston Place,
London, N16 6RJ
020 8802 4584 020 8800 1364
07966 136495
Est. 1989 *Stock size* Medium
Stock Watches, wrist watches, ceramics, porcelain
Open By appointment
Fairs Major antiques fairs, clock and watch fairs
Services Shipping

N19

Old School
Contact Mr F Lascelles
130c Junction Road,
Tufnell Park,
London, N19 5LB
020 7272 5603 020 7272 5603
Est. 1996 *Stock size* Large
Stock Garden furniture, statuary, antique furniture, made-to-measure furniture
Open Mon–Sun 11am–6pm
Fairs Newark, Ardingly

N20

The Totteridge Gallery
Contact Mrs J Clarke
61 Totteridge Lane,
London, N20 0HD
020 8446 7896 020 8446 7541
07836 777773
janet@totteridgegallery.com
www.totteridgegallery.com
Est. 1987 *Stock size* Large
Stock Fine art, 18th–20thC British and Continental oil paintings, watercolours, limited-edition Sir William Russell Flint prints
Open Mon–Sat 11am–6.30pm
Services Valuations, restorations

N21

Dollyland (Steiff Club)
864 Greenlanes, Winchmore Hill, London, N21 2RS
020 8360 1053 020 8364 1370
0780 821773
www.dollyland.com
Est. 1986 *Stock size* Large
Stock Dolls, Steiff bears, Scalextric, trains, die-cast toys
Open Tues Thurs–Sat 9.30am–4.30pm
Fairs Hugglets, Kensington Town Hall

Past Present Toys
Contact Mr Jim Parsons
862 Green Lanes,
London, N21 2RS
020 8364 1370 020 8364 1370
Est. 1986 *Stock size* Large
Stock Dinkys, Hornby railways, tin-plate toys, Corgi, Matchbox
Open Tues Thurs–Sat 9.30am–4.30pm

Winchmore Antiques
Contact Mr D Hicks
Mr S Christian
14 The Green,
London, N21 1AY
020 8882 4800
wa@keristal.freeuk.com
Est. 1980 *Stock size* Medium
Stock General antiques, furniture, porcelain, glass, china, silver, oil lamps and parts, architectural fittings, fireside accessories
Open Tues–Sat 9.30am–5.30pm
Services Valuations, restorations

NW1

Archive Books and Music
Contact Mr T Meaker
83 Bell Street, Marylebone,
London, NW1 6TB
020 7402 8212
Est. 1975 *Stock size* Small
Stock Antiquarian and modern books, printed pop and classical music
Open Mon–Sat 10.30am–6pm

Art Furniture
Contact Liam Scanlon
158 Camden Street,
London, NW1 9PA
020 7267 4324 020 7267 5199
arts-and-crafts@artfurniture.co.uk
www.artfurniture.co.uk
Est. 1989 *Stock size* Large
Stock Arts and crafts furniture and objects including Liberty, Heals, Shapland and Petter
Open Mon–Sun noon–5pm
Services Shipping, restoration

Comic Book Postal Auctions Ltd (Eagle Society)
Contact Malcolm Phillips
40–42 Osnaburgh Street,
London, NW1 3ND
020 7424 0007 020 7424 0008
comicbook@compuserve.com
www.compalcomics.com
Est. 1992
Open By appointment
Sales Quarterly, British and American comics, 1900–1970s, also annuals, artwork, TV-related merchandise. Sales in Mar, Jun, Sept, Dec
Frequency Quarterly
Catalogues Yes

Madeline Crispin Antiques
Contact Mrs M Crispin or David Thomas
95 Lisson Grove,
London, NW1 6UP
020 7402 6845
07956 289906
david@crispinantiques.fsnet.co.uk
Est. 1979 *Stock size* Medium
Stock Furniture, decorative items
Open Mon–Fri 10.30am–5pm Sat 10.30am–3pm
Services Valuations

The Military History Bookshop (ABA)
Contact Mr M Murphy
77–81 Bell Street,
London, NW1 6TA
020 7723 2095 020 7723 4665
sales@tmhbs.force9.co.uk
www.militaryhistorybooks.com
Est. 1972 *Stock size* Large
Stock BC–date military books
Open Mon–Fri 10am–5pm Sat 10am–2pm
Services Book search, mail order

Planet Bazaar
Contact Maureen Silverman
151 Drummond Street,
London, NW1 2PB
020 7387 8326 020 7387 8326
maureen@planetbazaar.demon.co.uk
www.planetbazaar.co.uk
Est. 1997 *Stock size* Medium
Stock 1950–1980 designer furniture, art, glass, lighting, ceramics, books, eccentricities
Open Tues–Sat 11.30am–7pm and by appointment

The Relic Antiques Trade Warehouse
Contact Mr Gilksten
127 Pancras Road,
London, NW1 1JN
020 7387 6039 020 7388 2691
Est. 1972 *Stock size* Large
Stock Decorative antiques, folk art, fairground art, Black Forest carvings, country pieces,

architectural, marine, trade signs, shop fittings
Open Mon–Fri 10am–6pm Sat by appointment
Services Valuations, framing, mirror restoration

Travers Antiques
Contact Mr S Kluth
71 Bell Street, London, NW1 6SX P
020 7723 4376
Est. 1976 *Stock size* Large
Stock 1820–1920 furniture, decorative items
Open Mon–Sat 10.30am–5pm
Services Valuations, restorations

NW2

G and F Gillingham Ltd
Contact Mr Gillingham
62 Menelik Road, London, NW2 3RH
020 7435 5644 F 020 7435 5644
M 07958 484140
Est. 1960
Stock 1750–1950 furniture
Open By appointment
Services Valuations, exports, restorations

Gladstone's Furniture
Contact Mr Anthony Dwyer
1 Gladstone Parade, Off Edgware Road, London, NW2 1UJ P
020 8208 1010 F 020 8450 9296
E info@qfw.co.uk
W www.qfw.co.uk
Est. 1998 *Stock size* Medium
Stock Reproduction Italian and French ormolu furniture, Victorian–Edwardian furniture
Open Mon–Sun 10.30am–6pm
Fairs Newark, Wembley
Services Repair, restoration

Quality Furniture Warehouse
Contact Mr Anthony Dwyer
Ionna House, Humber Road, London, NW2 6EN P
020 8830 5888 F 020 8450 9296
E info@qfw.co.uk
W www.qfw.co.uk
Est. 1981 *Stock size* Large
Stock Victorian–Edwardian furniture and earlier, quality used furniture, English and Continental, reproduction French and Italian ormolu furniture

Open Sat Sun 10.30am–5.30pm or by appointment
Fairs Newark, Wembley
Services Restorations, repairs

NW3

Brian Fielden (BADA)
Contact Brian Fielden
7 Chalcot Gardens, London, NW3 4YB P
020 7722 9192 F 020 7722 9192
Est. 1965 *Stock size* Small
Stock English 18th–early 19thC furniture
Open By appointment

Gillian Gould Antiques
Contact Gill Gould
18a Belsize Park Gardens, Belsize Park, London, NW3 4LH P
020 7419 0500 F 020 7419 0400
M 07831 150060
E gillgould@dealwith.com
Est. 1989 *Stock size* Small
Stock Scientific, marine, general gifts
Open By appointment only
Services Valuations, restorations

Hampstead Antique and Craft Emporium
Contact Mrs N Apple
12 Heath Street, London, NW3 6TE P
020 7794 3297 F 020 7794 4620
Est. 1976 *Stock size* Large
No. of dealers 20
Stock Furniture, jewellery, first-edition teddy bears, trimmings, buttons, paintings, prints, gifts
Open Tues–Fri 10.30am–5.30pm Sat 10am–6pm courtyard open Sun 11.30am–5.30pm
Services Coffee shop

Recollections Antiques Ltd
Contact Mrs June Gilbert
The Courtyard, Hampstead Antiques Emporium, 12 Heath Street, Hampstead, London, NW3 6TE P
020 7431 9907 F 020 7794 9743
M 07930 394 014
Est. 1991 *Stock size* Large
Stock Early 19thC blue-and-white transfer-printed pottery, early pine, miniature furniture, children's highchairs, kitchenware, collectors' teddy bears

Open Mon–Fri 10.30am–5pm Sat 10.30am–6pm

Villa Grisebach Art Auctions
Contact Mrs Sabina Fliri
27 Kemplay Road, London, NW3 1TA
020 7431 9882 F 020 7431 9756
W www.villa-grisebach.de
Est. 1986
Open By appointment
Sales 19th–20thC art and photography, phone for details
Frequency Bi-annual in Berlin
Catalogues Yes

David Wainwright
Contact Mr D Wainwright
28 Rosslyn Hill, London, NW3 1NH
020 7431 5900
Stock Antique and old furniture, decorative items from India, Indonesia, China
Open Mon–Sat 10am–7pm Sun 11am–7pm
Services Delivery

NW4

Murray Cards (International) Ltd
Contact Mr I Murray
51 Watford Way, London, NW4 3JH P
020 8202 5688 F 020 8203 7878
E murraycards@ukbusiness.com
W www.murraycards.com
Est. 1965 *Stock size* Large
Stock Cigarette and trade cards, albums, frames, books
Open Mon–Fri 9am–5pm
Fairs Royal National Hotel
Services Annual catalogue, auction catalogues

The Talking Machine
Contact Mr D Smith
30 Watford Way, London, NW4 3AL P
020 8202 3473
M 07774 103139
E davepaul50@hotmail.com
W www.gramophones.endirect.co.uk
Est. 1975 *Stock size* Large
Stock Mechanical antiques, typewriters, radios, music boxes, photographs, sewing machines, juke boxes, calculators, televisions
Open Variable or by appointment
Services Valuations, restorations

NW6

Brondesbury Architectural Reclamation (SALVO)
Contact Tony Carroll
✉ **The Yard, 136 Willesden Lane, London, NW6 7TE** P
☎ 020 7328 0820 F 020 7328 0280
Est. 1993 *Stock size* Large
Stock Period fireplaces, cast-iron radiators, period doors, garden statuary, door furniture, sanitary ware, stained glass
Open Mon–Sat 10am–6pm

Frosts
Contact Mrs D Frost
✉ **205–207 West End Lane, London, NW6 1XF**
☎ 020 7372 5788 F 020 7372 5788
Est. 1989 *Stock size* Medium
Stock Pine, painted country furniture, textiles, porcelain, blue-and-white china, kitchenware
Open Mon–Sat 11am–5.30pm

Gallery Kaleidoscope incorporating Scope Antiques
Contact Mr K Barrie
✉ **64–66 Willesden Lane, London, NW6 7SX** P
☎ 020 7328 5833 F 020 7624 2913
Est. 1970 *Stock size* Large
Stock Furniture, interior decorators' pieces, paintings, prints, sculptures, glass
Open Tues–Sat 10am–6pm
Services Valuations, framing, silverwork

NW8

Alfie's Antique Market
Contact Rosalind Mena
✉ **13–25 Church Street, London, NW8 8DT** P
☎ 020 7723 6066 F 020 7724 0999
E post@ealfies.com
W www.ealfies.com
No. of dealers 200
Stock General antiques, collectables, 20thC design
Open Tues–Sat 10am–6pm
Services Restoration, bureau de change, rooftop restaurant

Beverley
Contact Beverley
✉ **30 Church Street, Marylebone, London, NW8 8EP** P
☎ 020 7262 1576 F 020 7262 1576
M 07776 136003
Est. 1958 *Stock size* Large
Stock 1850–1950 English ceramics, glass, metal, wood, pottery, collectables, decorative items
Open Mon–Fri 10.30am–6pm Sat 9.30am–6pm or by appointment
Fairs NEC, Peterborough Festival of Antiques
Services Mail order worldwide

D and A Binder
Contact Mr D Binder
✉ **34 Church Street, London, NW8 8EP** P
☎ 020 7723 0542 F 020 7607 7800
Est. 1979 *Stock size* Large
Stock Period shop fittings, counters, cabinets
Open Tues–Sat 10am–5pm
Services Restorations

Bizarre
Contact Mr V Conti or Mr A Taramasco
✉ **24 Church Street, London, NW8 8EP** P
☎ 020 7724 1305 F 020 7724 1316
Est. 1982 *Stock size* Large
Stock Art Deco, Continental furniture, wrought iron, glass, ceramics
Open Mon–Fri 10am–5pm Sat 10am–4pm
Services Interior design

S Brunswick
Contact Ms S Brunswick
✉ **Alfie's, Antique Market 13 Church Street, London, NW8 8DT** P
☎ 020 7724 9097 F 020 8902 5656
Est. 1988 *Stock size* Large
Stock Functional and decorative furnishings for house, garden, conservatory
Open Tues–Sat 10am–6pm
Services Restorations, delivery

Camden Art Gallery
Contact Robert Gordon or Alan Silver
✉ **22 Church Street, London, NW8 8EP**
☎ 020 7262 3613 F 020 7723 1010
Stock size Large
Stock Paintings, 18th–early 20thC furniture
Open Tues–Sat 10am–6pm

Church Street Antiques
Contact Stuart Shuster
✉ **8 Church Street, London, NW8 8ED** P
☎ 020 7723 7415 F 020 7723 7415
Est. 1980 *Stock size* Large
Stock 18th–20thC furniture, decorative items
Open Tues–Sat 10am–6pm

Gallery of Antique Costume & Textiles
Contact L Segal
✉ **2 Church Street, London, NW8 8ED** P
☎ 020 7723 9981 F 020 7723 9981
E info@gact.co.uk
W www.gact.co.uk
Est. 1980 *Stock size* Medium
Stock Antique textiles, curtains, cushions, antique costumes, mainly 1920s and 1930s, textiles by Lalya Moussa
Open Mon–Sat 10am–5.30pm
Fairs HALI Antique Textile Art Fair, Olympia

Gardiner & Gardiner
Contact Mrs H Gardiner
✉ **Stand FO13, Alfie's Antique Market, Church Street, London, NW8 8DT** P
☎ 020 7723 5595
Est. 1969 *Stock size* Medium
Stock Decorative items, interior accessories, Paisley and cashmere shawls
Open Tues–Sat 10am–6pm

Goldsmith & Perris (LAPADA)
Contact Mrs Goldsmith
✉ **13 Church Street, London, NW8 8DT** P
☎ 020 7724 7051 F 020 7724 7051
M 07831 447432
E goldperri@alfies.fsnet.co.uk
Est. 1975 *Stock size* Medium
Stock Antique silver, silver plate, lamps, collectables, cocktail shakers
Open Tues–Sat 10am–6pm
Fairs Portobello, Covent Garden
Services Valuations

Patricia Harvey Antiques (LAPADA)
Contact Mrs P Harvey
✉ **42 Church Street, London, NW8 8EP** P
☎ 020 7262 8989/020 7624 5173
F 020 7625 8326/020 7262 8989

fairs@harveymanagement.fsnet.co.uk
Est. 1960 *Stock size* Large
Stock 18th–19thC English, French furniture, decorative, unusual objects
Open Mon–Sat 10am–5.30pm
Fairs Decorative Antiques & Textiles Fair (Jan, April, Sept)
Services Valuations

Tara Antiques
Contact Mr G Robinson
6 Church Street, London, NW8 8ED
020 7724 2405
Est. 1984 *Stock size* Large
Stock Eclectic mix of decorative furniture and items, ivories, sculptures
Open Tues–Fri 10am–6pm Sat 1.30–6pm
Fairs Fine Art, Olympia, Decorative Textile Fairs, Battersea

Tin Tin Collectables
Contact Mr P Pinnington
Ground Units 38–42, Antique Market, 13–25 Church Street, London, NW8 8DT
020 7258 1305
tin.tin@teleregion.co.uk
www.tintincollectables.com
Est. 1995 *Stock size* Large
Stock Handbags, Victorian–present day, decorative evening bags, luggage
Open Tues–Sat 10am–6pm
Fairs Sandown Park, Bath, Manchester
Services Valuations, film/TV hire

Wellington Gallery (LAPADA)
Contact Mrs M Barclay
1 St John's Wood High Street, London, NW8 7NG
020 7586 2620 020 7483 0716
Est. 1979
Stock Porcelain, silver, general antiques
Open Mon–Fri 10.30am–6pm Sat 10am–6pm

NW10

Retrouvius Architectural Reclamation (SALVO)
Contact Adam Hills
2A Ravensworth Road, London, NW10 5NR
020 7724 3387
07778 210855
mail@retrouvius.com
www.retrouvius.com
Est. 1992 *Stock size* Medium
Stock Architectural antiques, reclamation
Open By appointment
Fairs Newark
Services Design service

Willesden Green Architectural Salvage
Contact Mr D Harkin
189 High Road, Willesden, London, NW10 2SD
020 8459 2947 020 8451 1515
Est. 1994 *Stock size* Large
Stock Radiators, stained glass windows, pine doors, lighting, architectural salvage, fireplaces
Open Mon–Sat 9am–6pm
Services Stripping

SOUTH

SE1

The Antiques Exchange
Contact Ray Gibbs
170–172 Tower Bridge Road, London, SE1 3LS
020 7403 5568 020 7378 8828
info@antiquesexchange.com
www.antiquesexchange.com
Est. 1966 *Stock size* Large
Stock Furniture, glass, china, collectables, reproduction Tiffany lamps
Open Mon–Fri 10am–6pm Sat Sun 10.30am–5pm
Services Exchange deal for trade

Antiques Trade Warehouse
Contact Mrs McCarthy
1 Bermondsey Square, London, SE1 3UN
020 7394 7856
Est. 1979 *Stock size* Medium
Stock Wide range of furniture, collectors' items
Open By appointment, trade welcome
Services Shipping

Sebastiano Barbagallo Antiques
Contact Mr S Barbagallo
Universal House, 294–304 St James's Road, London, SE1 5JX
020 7231 3680 020 7231 3680
Est. 1978 *Stock size* Large
Stock Chinese furniture, Indian and Tibetan antiques, crafts
Open By appointment only

Bermondsey Antiques Market
Contact Mike Spooner
Corner of Long Lane, Bermondsey Street, Bermondsey Square, London, SE1 3TQ
020 7969 1500 020 7969 1639
Est. 1950 *Stock size* Large
No. of dealers 400
Stock Wide range of general antiques and collectables, including specialists in jewellery and silver
Open Fri 5am–2pm and Bank Holidays

Victor Burness Antiques
241 Long Lane, Bermondsey, London, SE1 4PR
01732 454591
Est. 1975
Stock Scientific instruments
Open Fri 6am–12.30pm
Services Valuations, restorations

The Galleries Ltd
Contact Alan Bennett
157 Tower Bridge Road, London, SE1 3LW
020 7407 5371 020 7403 0359
Est. 1993 *Stock size* Large
No. of dealers 28
Stock Victorian, Edwardian, reproduction furniture, Arts and Crafts, Art Nouveau, reproduction leather Chesterfields
Open Mon–Thurs 9.30am–5.30pm Fri 8am–4pm Sat noon–6pm Sun noon–5pm

LASSCO Flooring (SALVO, Timber Trade Federation, TRADA)
Contact Bob Lovell
41 Maltby Street, London, SE1 3PA
020 7237 4488 020 7237 2564
flooring@lassco.co.uk
www.lassco.co.uk
Est. 1978 *Stock size* Large
Stock Reclaimed timber flooring in parquet strip and board
Open Mon–Sat 10am–5pm
Services Shipping

LASSCO RBK (SALVO, Institute of Plumbing)
Contact Bill Murphy or Douglas Kirk
41 Maltby Street, London, SE1 3PA
020 7336 8221 F 020 7336 8224
E rbk@lassco.co.uk
W www.lassco.co.uk
Est. 1978 *Stock size* Large
Stock Reclaimed radiators, bathrooms, kitchens
Open Mon–Sat 10am–5pm
Services Shipping

Radio Days
Contact Mrs C Layzell
87 Lower Marsh, London, SE1 7AB
020 7928 0800 F 020 7928 0800
Est. 1993 *Stock size* Large
Stock 1930s–1970s lighting, telephones, radios, clothing, magazines, cocktail bars
Open Mon–Sat 11am–5pm or by appointment

G Viventi
Contact Giorgio
173 Bermondsey Street, London, SE1 3UW
020 7403 0022 F 020 7403 6808
E viventi@btinternet.com
Est. 1977 *Stock size* Large
Stock Period furniture, silver, silver plate
Open Mon–Fri 9am–6pm

G Viventi
Contact Giorgio
160 Tower Bridge Road, London, SE1 3LS
020 7357 8951
E viventi@btinternet.com
Est. 2000 *Stock size* Large
Stock Wide range of furniture, styles and periods
Open Mon–Sat 9.30am–6pm

Wissinger Antiques (LAPADA)
Contact Mr G S Wissinger
166 Bermondsey Street, London, SE1 3TQ
020 7407 5795 F 020 7407 5795
M 07836 605292
Est. 1969 *Stock size* Large
Stock 17th–late 19thC furniture, paintings, porcelain, books
Open Mon–Fri 9am–5.30pm
Services Valuations, restorations

SE3

The Bookshop Blackheath Ltd (ABA)
Contact Mr L Leff
74 Tranquil Vale, London, SE3 0BN
020 8852 4786
Est. 1947 *Stock size* Large
Stock Second-hand, new, antiquarian books, prints, maps
Open Mon–Sat 9am–4.30pm
Services Valuations, book search

SE4

Original Door Specialist (SALVO)
Contact Mr D Slattery
93 Endwell Road, Brockley Cross, London, SE4 2NF
020 7252 8109
Stock Doors, tables, flooring, handles, general architectural salvage
Open Mon–Sat 9am–6pm

SE5

Architectural Rescue
Contact Mr J Powell
1 Southampton Way, London, SE5 7JH
020 7277 0081 F 020 7277 0081
Est. 1993 *Stock size* Large
Stock Flooring, radiators, sanitary ware, doors, door furniture, fireplaces a speciality, York stone
Open Mon–Sat 10am–5pm Sun 10am–2pm
Fairs Newark, Swinderby

Camberwell Architectural Salvage & Antiques
Contact Mr M Tree
47 Southampton Way, London, SE5 7SW
020 7277 0315 F 020 7701 5735
M 07957 249722
E casa@tinyonline.co.uk
Est. 1993 *Stock size* Medium
Stock Period doors, floor boards, stained glass windows, fireplaces, cast-iron radiators, fixtures, fittings, hospital furniture, sinks, basins, roll-top baths, taps
Open Tues–Sat 10am–5pm or by appointment

SE6

The Old Mill
Contact Mr A Jackson
358 Bromley Road, Catford, London, SE6 2RT
020 8697 8006
Est. 1845 *Stock size* Medium
Stock Garden statuary, fireplaces
Open Mon–Sat 9.30am–5pm

SE8

Antique Warehouse (GOMC)
Contact Mrs Tillet
9–14 Deptford Broadway, London, SE8 4PA
020 8691 3062 F 020 8469 0295
E martin@antiquewarehouse.co.uk
W www.antiquewarehouse.co.uk
Est. 1983 *Stock size* Large
Stock General antiques
Open Mon–Sat 10am–6pm Sun 11am–4pm
Services Valuations via website

SE9

Chapman Antiques
Contact Mrs P Chapman
34 Well Hall Road, Eltham, London, SE9 6SF
020 8850 6464
Est. 1995 *Stock size* Large
Stock Pine furniture, china, collectables, mirrors, glass, garden ornaments
Open Mon–Fri 10am–6pm Sat 4–6pm Sun 2–4pm
Fairs Newark, Ardingly

Cobwebs
Contact Martin Baker
73 Avery Hill Road, New Eltham, London, SE9 2BJ
020 8850 5611
M 0771 243 5842
Est. 1995 *Stock size* Medium
Stock Furniture, general antiques, collectables
Open Mon 2pm–5.30pm Tues Wed Fri Sat 10am–5.30pm Sun 10am–2pm
Fairs Crook Log, Bexley Heath
Services Valuations

SE10

Beaumont Travel Books (ABA, PBFA, ILAB)
Contact Mr G Beaumont

✉ **Unit 6–9, Skillion Business Centre, 49 Greenwich High Road, London, SE10 8JL** 🅿
☎ 020 8691 2023 Ⓕ 020 8691 2023
Ⓔ beaumont@dircon.co.uk
Ⓦ www.abebooks.com/home/beaumont
Est. 1996 ***Stock size*** Large
Stock Antiquarian, rare, second-hand books, anthropology, military, history, travel, exploration a speciality
Open Mon–Fri 9.30am–2pm or by appointment
Services Valuations, book search

🏛 Cassidy's Gallery
Contact Mr M Cassidy
✉ **20 College Approach, Greenwich, London, SE10 9HY** 🅿
☎ 020 8858 7197 Ⓕ 020 8858 7197
Ⓜ 07710 012128
Ⓔ cassidysgallery@aol.com
Est. 1984 ***Stock size*** Small
Stock Antiquarian, plate books, atlases, illustrated books, maps, prints
Open By appointment
Fairs International Trade Antique Print and Plate Book Dealers Fair

🏛 Creek Antiques
Contact Dave
✉ **23 Greenwich South Street, London, SE10 8NW** 🅿
☎ 020 8293 5721
Ⓜ 07778 427521
Est. 1986 ***Stock size*** Medium
Stock Jewellery, silver, enamel signs, amusement machines
Open By appointment
Fairs Sandown, Newark, Bermondsey

🏛 Decomania
Contact Mrs J Crompton
✉ **9 College Approach, London, SE10 9HY** 🅿
☎ 020 8858 8180
Ⓦ www.decormania.co.uk
Est. 1998 ***Stock size*** Large
Stock Rare pieces of 1920s–1930s Art Deco, pictures, mirrors, furniture, decorative items, jewellery
Open Wed–Sun 10.30am–5.30pm or by appointment
Services Delivery, shipping

🏛 Finds
Contact Jeni Ferns
✉ **73 Trafalgar Road, London, SE10 9TS** 🅿
☎ 020 8305 9665
Ⓜ 07778 013096
Est. 1997 ***Stock size*** Medium
Stock Collectables, furniture, books, pictures, mirrors
Open Mon–Sat 10am–5pm Sun 11am–5pm closed Wed
Fairs Detling, Ardingly
Services Book search

🏛 Flying Duck Enterprises
Contact Mr J Lowe or Ms C Shrosbree
✉ **320–322 Creek Road, Greenwich, London, SE10 9SW** 🅿
☎ 020 8858 1964 Ⓕ 020 8852 3215
Ⓜ 07831 273303
Ⓔ jimllkitschit@flying-duck.com
Est. 1985 ***Stock size*** Large
Stock 1950–1970s items, cocktail bars, furniture, lighting, fabrics, dinette sets, glassware, china, 1950s fridges
Open Tues–Fri noon–6pm Sat Sun 10.30am–6pm
Services Mail order

🏛 Greenwich Collectables
Contact Lynn Lennon or Steve Mead
✉ **3–4 Nelson Road, London, SE10 9JB** 🅿
☎ 020 8858 3311 Ⓕ 020 8858 3311
Ⓦ www.greenwichcollectables.com
Est. 1998 ***Stock size*** Large
Stock Ceramics, teddies
Open Mon–Sun 10am–5pm

🏛 The Junk Box
Contact Mrs M Dodd
✉ **47 Old Woolwich Road, Greenwich, London, SE10 9PP** 🅿
☎ 020 8293 5715
Est. 1988 ***Stock size*** Large
Stock Antiques, collectables, Victorian furniture, china, glass, copper, brass, kitchenware
Open Mon–Sun 10am–5pm
Services Bespoke framing, valuations

🏛 Lamont Antiques Ltd (LAPADA)
Contact Mr F Llewellyn
✉ **Unit K, Tunnel Avenue Trading Estate, Greenwich, London, SE10 0QH** 🅿
☎ 020 8305 2230 Ⓕ 020 8305 1805
Est. 1974 ***Stock size*** Large
Stock Architectural items, stained glass, pub and restaurant fixtures, fittings
Open Mon–Fri 9.30am–5pm

🏛 Peter Laurie Maritime Antiques
Contact Mr P Laurie
✉ **28 Greenwich Church Street, Greenwich, London, SE10 9BJ** 🅿
☎ 020 8853 5777 Ⓕ 020 8853 5777
Ⓜ 0771 8033150
Ⓔ plaurie@maritimeantiques-uk.com
Ⓦ www.maritimeantiques-uk.com
Est. 1978 ***Stock size*** Large
Stock Nautical, maritime items, navigational, scientific instruments, clocks, barometers, regalia, antique prints
Open Mon–Thurs Sat Sun 10.30am–5pm Fri 1–5pm

🏛 Marcet Books (PBFA)
Contact Mr M Kemp
✉ **49 Nelson Road, Greenwich, London, SE10 9JB** 🅿
☎ 020 8853 5408 Ⓕ 020 8853 5408
Ⓔ marcet@dircon.co.uk
Ⓦ www.marcet.dircon.co.uk
Est. 1980 ***Stock size*** Medium
Stock Antiquarian, rare, second-hand books, maritime, foreign travel, British topography, art, natural history, poetry topic, specialities
Open Mon–Sun 10am–5.30pm
Fairs PBFA, Russell Hotel
Services Valuations

🏛 The Old Bottle Shop
Contact D Farrell
✉ **Unit 7, 17–18 Stockwell Street, Greenwich, London, SE10 9JN** 🅿
☎ 020 8488 7048
Ⓜ 07930 200584
Est. 1999 ***Stock size*** Large
Stock Antique bottles, breweriana
Open Mon Wed 10.30am–4pm Fri 2–4pm Sat 10.30am–5.30pm Sun 8.30am–5.30pm
Fairs Ardingly
Services Valuations, shipping

🏛 Relcy Antiques
Contact Mr R Challis
✉ **9 Nelson Road, London, SE10 9JB** 🅿
☎ 020 8858 2812 Ⓕ 020 8293 9848
Est. 1956 ***Stock size*** Large
Stock 18th–19thC English and Continental furniture, pictures, prints, marine and scientific instruments, ship models
Open Mon–Sat 10am–6pm Sun 11am–6pm
Services Valuations, restorations

Rogers Turner Books (ABA, PBFA)
Contact Mr P Rogers
23a Nelson Road, Greenwich, London, SE10 9JB P
☎ 020 8853 5271 F 020 8853 5271
E rogersturner@compuserve.com
Est. 1976 *Stock size* Medium
Stock Rare, antiquarian and second-hand books on experimental science, scientific instruments, horology, dialling a speciality
Open Thurs Fri 10am–6pm or by appointment
Fairs ABA Fairs, Olympia, PBFA London (monthly)
Services Valuations, catalogues

The Warwick Leadlay Gallery (FATG)
Contact Mr Anthony Cross
5 Nelson Road, London, SE10 9JB P
☎ 020 8858 0317 F 020 8853 1773
E wlg@ceasynet.co.uk
W www.wlgonline.com
Est. 1974 *Stock size* Large
Stock Antique maps, decorative maritime prints, fine arts, curios
Open Mon–Sat 9.30am–5.30pm Sun 11.30am–5.30pm
Services Valuations, restorations, conservation, framing

Robert Whitfield (LAPADA)
Contact Mr R Whitfield
Unit K, Tunnel Avenue Trading Estate, Greenwich, London, SE10 0QH P
☎ 020 8305 2230 F 020 8305 1805
Est. 1974 *Stock size* Large
Stock Oak, mahogany and walnut furniture
Open Mon–Fri 9am–5pm or by appointment

SE11

Kear of Kennington Antiques
Contact Mr S A Kear
4 Windmill Row, London, SE11 5DW P
☎ 020 7735 1304
Est. 1968 *Stock size* Small
Stock 18thC English drinking glasses, pottery, porcelain
Open By appointment

SE12

Book Aid Charitable Trust
Contact Mrs A Hiley
Christian Fellowship, Mayeswood Road, Grove Park, London, SE12 P
☎ 020 8857 7794 F 020 8653 6577
Est. 1987 *Stock size* Large
Stock Antiquarian, rare, second-hand religious books, bibles, general books
Open Thurs 9am–5pm or by appointment

SE13

The Old Station
Contact Mr R Jacob
72 Loampit Hill, Lewisham, London, SE13 7SX P
☎ 020 8694 6540/020 8692 8395
F 020 8692 6824
M 07710 489895
E rob.jacob@btinternet.com
W www.the-old-station.co.uk
Est. 1995 *Stock size* Large
Stock Large varied stock, architectural salvage, fireplaces, antique furniture, chimney pieces, sanitary ware
Open Mon–Sat 10am–5pm Sun by appointment only
Fairs Newark, Ardingly
Services Door stripping, fireplace restoration

SE17

Pub Paraphernalia UK Ltd
Contact Mr M Ellis
Unit 13, Newington Industrial Estate, Crampton Street, London, SE17 3AZ
☎ 020 7701 8913 F 020 7277 4100
E sales@pub-paraphanalia.com
W www.pub-paraphanalia.com
Est. 1980
Stock Water jugs, bar towels, beer mats, glassware, ashtrays, mirrors
Open Mon–Fri 9am–5pm by appointment
Fairs NEC (Spring)

SE19

The Book Palace
Contact Mr K Harman or Mr G West
Jubilee House, Bedwardine Road, London, SE19 3AP P
☎ 020 8768 0022 F 020 8768 0563
E david@totalise.co.uk
W www.bookpalace.com
Est. 1996 *Stock size* Large
Stock Histories of comics and popular media, art books, science fiction, film and TV biographies, Disney, animation, old US and UK comics, pulps, paperbacks, graphic novels
Open Mon–Fri 10am–6pm or by appointment
Fairs CIAMA, London Memorabilia Fair, NEC
Services Valuations, wanted titles list

SE20

Bearly Trading of London
Contact Cindy Hamilton-Aust
202 High Street, London, SE20 7QB P
☎ 020 8659 0500/8466 6696 F 020 8460 3166
Est. 1998 *Stock size* Large
Stock Old and new artists' teddy bears, rocking horses, antique furniture
Open Sat 10am–6pm or by appointment
Fairs Kensington Bear Fair (Nov)
Services Lay-a-way, mail order

SE21

Francis Jevons
Contact Mr F Jevons
80 Dulwich Village, London, SE21 7AJ P
☎ 020 8693 1991
Est. 1983 *Stock size* Small
Stock Antique furniture, china, glass, interior design items
Open Mon–Fri 9.30am–1pm 2.30–5.30pm Sat close 5pm closed Wed
Services Valuations, restorations

SE22

Melbourne Antiques & Interiors
Contact Ian Peters
67 Lordship Lane, London, SE22 8EP P
☎ 020 8299 6565 F 020 8299 4257
E melbourneantiques@lineone.net
Est. 1998 *Stock size* Large
Stock French furniture, mirrors, chandeliers, armoires, beds, commodes, linens, fire surrounds
Open Mon–Sat 10am–6pm

Melbourne Antiques & Interiors
Contact Ian Peters
8 Melbourne Grove, London, SE22 8QZ
020 8299 6565 Ⓕ 020 8299 4257
Ⓔ melbourneantiques@lineone.net
Est. 1998 *Stock size* Large
Stock French furniture, mirrors, chandeliers, armoires, linens, beds, commodes, fire surrounds
Open Mon–Sat 10am–6pm or by appointment

Still Useful
Contact Mr R H Honour
52 Grove Vale, London, SE22 8DY
020 8299 2515
Est. 1979 *Stock size* Large
Stock Oak and mahogany furniture, decorative items, lighting
Open Mon–Sat 10am–5pm

SE26

Grenadiers
Contact Mr C Chin-See
102 Sydenham Road, London, SE26 5JX
020 8659 1588 Ⓕ 020 8659 1588
Ⓔ grenadiers@btinternet.com
Ⓦ www.grenadiers.co.uk
Est. 1998 *Stock size* Medium
Stock Wide range of militaria
Open Mon–Fri 9.30am–6pm Sat 9.30am–5.30pm

Oola Boola Antiques London
Contact Mrs S Bramley
139–147 Kirkdale, London, SE26 4QJ
020 8291 9999 Ⓕ 020 8291 5759
Ⓜ 07956 261252
Ⓔ oola.boola@telco4u.net
Est. 1970 *Stock size* Large
Stock Victorian, Edwardian, Art Nouveau, Art Deco, Arts and Crafts furniture
Open Mon–Sat 10am–6pm, Sun 11am–5pm
Services Restorations, shipping

Sydenham Antiques Centre
Contact Mr P Cockton
48 Sydenham Road, London, SE26 5QF
020 8778 1706
Est. 1996 *Stock size* Large
No. of dealers 10
Stock Antiques, china, glass, furniture, jewellery, pictures, silver
Open Mon–Sat 10am–5pm

SE27

Rosebery Fine Art Ltd (ISVA)
Contact Miss L Lloyd
74–76 Knights Hill, London, SE27 0JD
020 8761 2522 Ⓕ 020 8761 2524
Ⓔ auctions@roseberys.co.uk
Ⓦ www.auctions@roseberys.co.uk
Est. 1987
Open Mon–Fri 9.30am–5.30pm
Sales Antiques and collectors' sale Tues Wed noon. General sale Tues noon, viewing Sun 2.30–5.30pm Mon 10am–7pm Tues 9.30am–12pm Wed 9.30am–noon prior to sale. Quarterly specialist sale, music, decorative arts, books, toys
Frequency Monthly
Catalogues Yes

SW1

ADC Heritage Ltd (BADA)
Contact Francis Raeymaekers or Elisabeth Bellord
95a Charlwood Street, London, SW1V 4PB
020 7976 5271 Ⓕ 020 7828 7432
Ⓜ 07747 692554
Ⓔ elbellord@btinternet.com
Est. 1980 *Stock size* Small
Stock Antique English silver and old Sheffield plate
Open By appointment only
Services Valuations, restorations

Albert Amor (RWHA)
Contact Mark Law or Nicholas Lyne
37 Bury Street, London, SW1Y 6AU
020 7930 2444 Ⓕ 020 7930 9067
Ⓔ infor@albertamor.co.uk
Ⓦ www.albertamor.co.uk
Est. 1899 *Stock size* Small
Stock 18thC English porcelain
Open Mon–Fri 9.30am–5pm
Fairs Park Lane International Ceramics Fair

Anno Domini Antiques (BADA)
Contact Mr D Cohen
66 Pimlico Road, London, SW1W 8LS
020 7730 5496
Est. 1969 *Stock size* Large
Stock 18th–19thC furniture, mirrors, pictures, glass, porcelain
Open Mon–Fri 10am–1pm 2.15–5.30pm Sat 10am–3pm or by appointment
Services Valuations, restorations

The Armoury of St James (OMRS, GOMC)
Contact Mr Rawlins or Mr Davis
17 Piccadilly Arcade, London, SW1Y 6NH
020 7493 5082 Ⓕ 020 7499 4422
Ⓔ welcome@armoury.co.uk
Ⓦ www.armoury.co.uk/home
Est. 1969 *Stock size* Large
Stock Royal memorablilia, model soldiers
Open Mon–Fri 10am–6pm Sat noon–6pm
Services Valuations, world orders, decorations

Blanchard Ltd (LAPADA)
Contact Mr Piers Ingall
86–88 Pimlico Road, London, SW1W 8PL
020 7823 6310 Ⓕ 020 7823 6303
Est. 1989 *Stock size* Medium
Stock English and Continental furniture, decorative items, works of art
Open Mon–Fri 10am–6pm Sat 10am–3pm
Fairs Olympia (June)
Services Valuations, restorations, shipping

John Bly (BADA, LAPADA, CINOA)
Contact Mr John Bly or Mr James Bly
27 Bury Street, London, SW1Y 6AL
020 7930 1292 Ⓕ 020 7839 4775
Ⓔ james@johnbly.com
Ⓦ www.johnbly.com
Est. 1891 *Stock size* Large
Stock 18th–19thC English furniture, works of art, objets d'art, paintings, silver, glass, porcelain, tapestries
Open Mon–Fri 9.30am–5.30pm Sat by appointment
Fairs Olympia (June), BADA (March), Palm Beach, Florida (Feb)
Services Valuations, restorations

⊞ J H Bourdon-Smith Ltd (BADA, CINOA)
Contact Mr J Bourdon-Smith
✉ **24 Masons Yard, Duke Street, St James's, London, SW1Y 6BU** P
☎ 020 7839 4714 F 020 7839 3951
Est. 1953 *Stock size* Large
Stock Georgian–Victorian silver, modern reproduction silver
Open Mon–Fri 9.30am–6pm
Fairs Grosvenor House, BADA, Olympia (Nov)

⊞ Andre de Cacqueray
Contact Mr A de Cacqueray
✉ **227 Ebury Street, London, SW1W 8UT** P
☎ 020 7730 5000 F 020 7730 0005
Est. 1984 *Stock size* Medium
Stock 18th–19thC Continental antique furniture, objets d'art
Open Mon–Fri 10am–6pm or Sat by appointment
Services Interior design

⊞ John Carlton-Smith (BADA)
Contact Mr J Carlton-Smith
✉ **17 Ryder Street, London, SW1Y 6PY** P
☎ 020 7930 6622 F 020 7930 6622
E jcarltonsm@aol.com
W www.fineartantiqueclocks.com
Est. 1968 *Stock size* Large
Stock Fine antique clocks and barometers
Open Mon–Fri 9am–5.30pm
Fairs March BADA, Grosvenor House, Winter Olympia
Services Valuations

⊞ Chelsea Antique Mirrors
Contact Mr A Koll
✉ **72 Pimlico Road, London, SW1W 8LS** P
☎ 020 7824 8024 F 020 7824 8233
Est. 1980 *Stock size* Medium
Stock 18th–19thC mirrors, furniture
Open Mon–Fri 10am–6pm Sat 10am–2pm
Services Restorations

Christie's
✉ **8 King Street, London, SW1Y 6QT** P
☎ 020 7839 9060 F 020 7839 1611
W www.christies.com
Est. 1766
Open Mon–Fri 9am–5pm
Sales Sales throughout the year, except Aug and Jan, viewing 4 days prior to sales and weekends, evenings. Free verbal auction estimates
Catalogues Yes

⊞ Ciancimino Ltd
Contact Mr J Ciancimino
✉ **99 Pimlico Road, London, SW1W 8PH** P
☎ 020 7730 9950 F 020 7730 5365
E info@ciancimino.com
W www.ciancimino.com
Est. 1965 *Stock size* Medium
Stock Art Deco furniture, Oriental furniture, ethnography
Open Mon–Fri 10am–6pm Sat by appointment
Fairs International Fine Art & Antique Dealers Show, New York

⊞ Classic Bindings
Contact Mr S Poklewski-Koziell
✉ **61 Cambridge Street, London, SW1V 4PS** P
☎ 020 7834 5554 F 020 7630 6632
E info@classicbindings.net
W www.classicbindings.net
Est. 1990 *Stock size* Large
Stock General antiquarian books, classic bindings
Open Mon–Fri 9.30am–5.30pm or by appointment
Services Valuations

⊞ Crowther (SALVO)
Contact Mrs S Powell
✉ **77 Pimlico Road, London, SW1W 8PH** P
☎ 020 7730 8668 F 020 7730 3005
E sales@crowthersyonlodge.com
W www.crowthersyonlodge.com
Est. 1876 *Stock size* Large
Stock Decorative period garden ornaments, sculptures, urns, chimney pieces, paintings, mirrors
Open Mon–Fri 10am–6pm Sat 11am–3pm
Fairs Olympia (June, Feb), Chelsea Flower Show
Services Hand carving, period-style panelled rooms, blacksmith

⊞ Peter Dale Ltd (LAPADA)
Contact Mr Robin Dale
✉ **12 Royal Opera Arcade, London, SW1Y 4UY** P
☎ 020 7930 3695 F 020 7930 2223
M 07785 580396
E robin@peterdaleltd.com
Est. 1960 *Stock size* Medium
Stock European antique arms and armour
Open Mon–Fri 9.15am–5pm
Fairs London Arms Fair
Services Valuations

⊞ Kenneth Davis (Works of Art) Ltd
Contact Danielle Fluer
✉ **15 King Street, London, SW1Y 6QU** P
☎ 020 7930 0313 F 020 7976 1306
Est. 1965 *Stock size* Medium
Stock Antique English and Continental silver, works of art
Open Mon–Fri 9.30am–5pm
Services Valuations, restorations

⊞ Alastair Dickenson Fine Silver Ltd (BADA)
Contact Mr A Dickenson or Mrs M Cuchet
✉ **90 Jermyn Street, London, SW1Y 6JD** P
☎ 020 7839 2808 F 020 7839 2809
M 07976 283530
Est. 1996 *Stock size* Small
Stock 16th–19thC fine, rare English silver
Open Mon–Fri 9.30am–5.30pm
Services Valuations, restorations

⊞ Didier Aaron (London) Ltd (BADA)
Contact Didier Leblanc
✉ **21 Ryder Street, London, SW1Y 6PX** P
☎ 0207 8394716 F 0207 9306699
E contact@didieraaronltd.com
Est. 2985 *Stock size* Medium
Stock 18thC and early 19thC Continental furniture, old master drawings, paintings
Open Mon–Fri by appointment
Fairs Maastricht, Paris Bienniale

⊞ N & I Franklin (BADA)
Contact Mr N Franklin or Mr I Franklin
✉ **11 Bury Street, London, SW1Y 6AB**
☎ 020 7839 3131 F 020 7839 3132
Est. 1980 *Stock size* Large
Stock 17th–18thC English domestic silver
Open Mon–Fri 10am–5pm or by appointment
Fairs BADA Duke of York's
Services Valuations

⊞ J A L Franks and Co
Contact Mr G Franks
✉ **7 Allington Street, London, SW1E 5EB** P
☎ 020 7233 8433 F 020 7233 8655
E jalfranks@btinternet.com

Ⓦ www.jalfranks.btinternet.co.uk
Est. 1947 *Stock size* Medium
Stock 16th–19thC antique maps
Open Mon–Fri 9am–5pm
Fairs Bonnington, IMCOS

Victor Franses Gallery (BADA)
Contact Graham Franses
✉ **57 Jermyn Street, St James's, London, SW1Y 6LX**
☎ 020 7493 6284/7629 1144
Ⓕ 020 7495 3668
Ⓔ bronzes@vfranses.com
Ⓦ www.vfranses.com
Est. 1972 *Stock size* Large
Stock 19thC animalier sculpture, paintings, drawings, watercolours
Open Mon–Fri 10am–5pm or by appointment
Fairs Grosvenor House
Services Valuations, restorations

Nicholas Gifford-Mead (BADA, LAPADA)
Contact Mr N Gifford-Mead
✉ **68 Pimlico Road, London, SW1W 8LS** Ⓟ
☎ 020 7730 6233 Ⓕ 020 7730 6239
Est. 1969 *Stock size* Medium
Stock Pre-1840 English and European chimney pieces, sculpture
Open Mon–Fri 9.30am–5.30pm
Services Valuations

Ross Hamilton (Antiques) Ltd (LAPADA, CINOA)
Contact Mr C M Boyce
✉ **95 Pimlico Road, London, SW1W 8PH** Ⓟ
☎ 020 7730 3015 Ⓕ 020 7730 3015
Ⓦ www.lapada.co.uk/rosshamilton/
Est. 1973 *Stock size* Large
Stock 17th–19thC fine English and Continental furniture, 16th–20thC paintings, Oriental porcelain, objets d'art, bronzes
Open Mon–Fri 9am–6pm, Sat 10.30am–4pm
Services Shipping worldwide

Brian Harkins
Contact Ms Erica Quan or Brian Harkins
✉ **3 Bury Street, St James's, London, SW1Y 6AB** Ⓟ
☎ 020 7839 3338 Ⓕ 020 7839 9339
Ⓔ info@brianharkins@co.uk
Ⓦ www.brianharkins.co.uk
Est. 1978
Stock Chinese and Japanese antiques, scholars' items, furniture, decorative items, ceramics, bronzes, rocks, baskets
Open Mon–Fri 10am–6pm

Harvey & Gore (BADA)
Contact Barry Norman
✉ **41 Duke Street, St James's, London, SW1Y 6DF** Ⓟ
☎ 020 7839 4033 Ⓕ 020 7839 3313
Ⓔ norman@harveyandgore.co.uk
Est. 1723 *Stock size* Large
Stock Jewellery, bijouterie, snuff boxes, old Sheffield plate, minatures
Open Mon–Fri 9.30am–5pm
Fairs BADA
Services Valuations, restorations, VAT margin and standard

Thomas Heneage Art Books (ABA, LAPADA)
Contact Antonia Howard-Sneyd
✉ **42 Duke Street, St James's, London, SW1Y 6DJ** Ⓟ
☎ 020 7930 9223 Ⓕ 020 7839 9223
Ⓔ artbooks@heneage.com
Ⓦ www.heneage.com
Stock size Large
Stock Art reference books
Open Mon–Fri 9.30am–6pm or by appointment
Services Valuations

Hermitage Antiques Plc
Contact Mr Vieux-Pernon
✉ **97 Pimlico Road, London, SW1W 8PH** Ⓟ
☎ 020 7730 1973 Ⓕ 020 7730 6586
Ⓔ info@hermitage-antiques.co.uk
Ⓦ www.hermitage-antiques.co.uk
Est. 1970 *Stock size* Large
Stock Biedermeier and Russian furniture, chandeliers, oil paintings, decorative arts, bronzes
Open Mon–Fri 10am–6pm Sat 10am–5pm
Fairs Olympia (June)
Services Consultancy

John Hobbs Ltd (BADA)
Contact Mr C Mortimer or Mr R Hobbs
✉ **107a Pimlico Road, London, SW1W 8PH** Ⓟ
☎ 020 7730 8369 Ⓕ 020 7730 0437
Ⓔ info@johnhobbs.demon.co.uk
Ⓦ www.johnhobbs.co.uk
Est. 1994 *Stock size* Large
Stock 18th–19thC Continental and English furniture, objets d'art, statuary
Open Mon–Fri 9am–6pm Sat 11am–4pm

Christopher Hodsoll Ltd (BADA)
Contact Mr C Hodsoll
✉ **89–91 Pimlico Road, ondon, SW1W 8PH** Ⓟ
☎ 020 7730 3370 Ⓕ 020 7730 1516
Ⓔ c.hodsoll@btinternet.com
Ⓦ www.hodsoll.com
Est. 1991 *Stock size* Large
Stock 18th–19thC furniture, works of art
Open Mon–Fri 9am–6pm Sat 10am–5pm
Fairs Olympia
Services Finders service, interior design

Hotspur Ltd (BADA)
Contact Mr R Kern
✉ **14 Lowndes Street, London, SW1X 9EX** Ⓟ
☎ 020 7235 1918 Ⓕ 020 7235 4371
Ⓔ hotspurltd@msn.com
Est. 1924 *Stock size* Medium
Stock 18thC quality furniture, works of art
Open Mon–Fri 9am–6pm Sat 9am–1pm
Fairs Grosvenor House

Christopher Howe Antiques
Contact Sara Bratby or Christopher Howe
✉ **93 Pimlico Road, London, SW1W 8PH** Ⓟ
☎ 020 7730 7987 Ⓕ 020 7730 0157
Ⓜ 07711 560348
Ⓔ c.howe@easynet.co.uk
Est. 1987 *Stock size* Large
Stock English Regency–20thC modern design classic furniture
Open Mon–Fri 9am–6pm Sat 10.30am–4.30pm
Fairs Olympia (June)

Humphrey-Carrasco
Contact Mr David Humphrey
✉ **43 Pimlico Road, London, SW1W 8NE** Ⓟ
☎ 020 7730 9911 Ⓕ 020 7730 9944
Ⓔ hc@humphreycarrasco.demon.co.uk
Est. 1990 *Stock size* Medium
Stock English furniture, 18th–19thC objects
Open Mon–Fri 10am–6pm Sat 10am–5pm
Fairs Olympia (Nov)

⊞ Jeremy Ltd (BADA)
Contact Mr M Hill
✉ **29 Lowndes Street, London, SW1X 9HX** 🅿
☎ 020 7823 2923 Ⓕ 020 7245 6197
Ⓔ jeremy@jeremique.co.uk
Ⓦ www.jeremy.ltd.co.uk
Est. 1946 *Stock size* Large
Stock 18th–early 19thC English and Continental furniture, works of art, clocks, antiques
Open Mon–Fri 8.30am–6pm Sat 9am–1pm
Fairs Grosvenor House, New York

⊞ Daniel Katz Ltd (SLAD)
Contact Daniel Katz or Stuart Lochhead
✉ **59 Jermyn Street, London, SW1Y 6LX**
☎ 020 7493 0688 Ⓕ 020 7499 7493
Ⓔ info@katz.co.uk
Ⓦ www.katz.co.uk
Est. 1969 *Stock size* Large
Stock European sculpture, works of art, old master paintings
Open Mon–Fri 9am–6pm

⊞ Keshishian (BADA)
Contact Mr Arto or Eddy Keshishian
✉ **73 Pimlico Road, London, SW1W 8NE** 🅿
☎ 020 7730 8810
Est. 1989 *Stock size* Large
Stock Aubussons, British Arts and Crafts, Art Deco, antique and modernist carpets and tapestries
Open Mon–Fri 9.30am–6pm Sat 10am–5pm

⊞ John King (BADA)
Contact Mr J King
✉ **74 Pimlico Road, London, SW1W 8LS** 🅿
☎ 020 7730 0427 Ⓕ 020 7730 2515
Est. 1967 *Stock size* Large
Stock Period furniture, associated items, 20thC items
Open Mon–Fri 10am–6pm or by appointment
Fairs Olympia (June)

⊞ Knightsbridge Coins (BNTA)
Contact Mr J Brown
✉ **43 Duke Street, London, SW1Y 6DD** 🅿
☎ 020 7930 8215 Ⓕ 020 7930 8214
Est. 1975
Stock English and foreign medieval–present day coins
Open Mon–Fri 10.15am–6pm
Fairs Coinex, Cumberland
Services Valuations

⊞ M & D Lewis
Contact Mr D Vaughan
✉ **84 Pimlico Road, London, SW1W 8PL** 🅿
☎ 020 7730 1015
Est. 1959 *Stock size* Large
Stock English and Continental furniture, Oriental porcelain
Open Mon–Fri 10am–5pm Sat 10am–noon

⊞ Jeremy Mason
Contact Mr J Mason
✉ **145 Ebury Street, London, SW1W 9QN** 🅿
☎ 020 7730 8331 Ⓕ 020 7730 8334
Est. 1974 *Stock size* Small
Stock Oriental works of art from all periods
Open By appointment only

⊞ McClenaghan
Contact Ms Bob Gilhooly
✉ **69 Pimlico Road, London, SW1W 8NE** 🅿
☎ 020 7730 4187 Ⓕ 020 7730 4187
Ⓔ mcclenaghan.mcced@virgin.net
Est. 1990 *Stock size* Medium
Stock Period lighting, English country house furniture
Open Mon–Thurs 10am–6pm Fri 10am–5pm Sat 10.30am–4.30pm

⊞ Peter Nahum at the Leicester Galleries (BADA)
Contact Peter Nahum
✉ **5 Ryder Street, London, SW1Y 6PY** 🅿
☎ 020 7930 6059 Ⓕ 020 7930 4678
Ⓜ 07770 220851
Ⓔ peternahum@leicestergalleries.com
Ⓦ www.leicestergalleries.com
Est. 1984 *Stock size* Large
Stock 19th–20thC paintings, drawings, sculpture
Open Mon–Fri 9.30am–6pm
Fairs Grosvenor House Art and Antiques Fair, London and International Fine Art Fair, New York
Services Valuations, restorations, shipping, book search

⊞ Odyssey Fine Arts Ltd (LAPADA)
Contact Mr M Macrodain
✉ **24 Holbein Place, London, SW1W 8NL** 🅿
☎ 020 7730 9942 Ⓕ 020 7259 9941
Ⓦ www.odysseyart.co.uk
Est. 1993 *Stock size* Medium
Stock 18th–19thC French, English painted furniture, engravings, Chinese watercolours
Open Mon–Fri 10.30am–5.30pm Sat 10.30am–3.30pm
Fairs LAPADA, Royal College of Art, Olympia (Feb, Nov)

⊞ Ossowski (BADA)
Contact Mr M Ossowski
✉ **83 Pimlico Road, London, SW1W 8PH**
☎ 020 7730 3256 Ⓕ 020 7823 4500
Ⓔ markossowski@msn.com
Est. 1960 *Stock size* Large
Stock 18thC English giltwood mirrors, tables, decorative wood carving
Open Mon–Fri 10am–6pm Sat 10am–1pm
Fairs Olympia (June), Palm Beach (Feb)
Services Restorations

⊞ Anthony Outred Antiques Ltd (BADA)
Contact Felicity Wilde, Paul Hardy, Ferrous Auger
✉ **46 Pimlico Road, London, SW1W 8LP** 🅿
☎ 020 7730 4782 Ⓕ 020 7730 5643
Ⓔ antiques@outred.co.uk
Ⓦ www.outred.co.uk
Est. 1977 *Stock size* Medium
Stock 18th–19thC English, Irish and Continental furniture, sculptures, lighting, oil paintings
Open Mon–Fri 9am–6pm Sat 10am–5pm
Fairs Olympia (June, Nov)

⊞ Trevor Philip & Son Ltd (BADA)
Contact Mr T Waterman
✉ **75a Jermyn Street, St. James's, London, SW1Y 6NP** 🅿
☎ 020 7930 2954 Ⓕ 020 7321 0212
Ⓔ globe@trevorphilip.com
Ⓦ www.trevorphilip.com
Est. 1972 *Stock size* Large
Stock Ships' models, marine and navigation instruments
Open Mon–Fri 9am–6pm Sat 10am–4pm or by appointment
Fairs Grosvenor House
Services Valuations, restorations

⊞ Pullman Gallery Ltd
Contact Mr S Khachadourian
✉ **14 King Street, St James's, London, SW1Y 6QU** 🅿
☎ 020 7930 9595 Ⓕ 020 7930 9494
Ⓔ pullman.gallery@dial.pipex.com

Ⓦ www.pullmangallery.com
Est. 1998 *Stock size* Large
Stock Cocktail shakers, bar accessories, smoking accessories, automobilia, vintage Louis Vuitton and Hermès luggage, motor racing posters, René Lalique glass, 1900–1940
Open Mon–Fri 10am–6pm or by appointment
Services Usual gallery services

Mark Ransom Ltd
Contact Mr C Walker or Mr M James
62/64 Pimlico Road, London, SW1W 8LS
☎ 020 7259 0220 Ⓕ 020 7259 0323
Ⓔ contact@markransom.co.uk
Ⓦ www.markransom.co.uk
Stock size Medium
Stock Russian and French Empire, Continental furniture, decorative items, objets d'art, prints, pictures
Open Mon–Sat 10am–6pm

Mark Ransom Ltd
Contact Mr C Walker or Mr M James
105 Pimlico Road, London, SW1W 8LS
☎ 020 7259 0220 Ⓕ 020 7259 0323
Ⓔ contact@markransom.co.uk
Ⓦ www.markransom.co.uk
Stock size Medium
Stock Russian and French Empire, Continental furniture, decorative items, objets d'art, prints, pictures
Open Mon–Sat 10am–6pm

Rogier Antiques
Contact Mr Elene Rogier
20a Pimlico Road, London, SW1W 8LJ
☎ 020 7823 4780 Ⓕ 020 7823 4780
Est. 1988 *Stock size* Medium
Stock French and Continental 18th–19thC decorative furniture, unusual lamps, reproductions, lighting
Open Mon–Fri 10am–6pm Sat 11am–4pm
Services Restorations

Rossi & Rossi Ltd
Contact Mr Fabio Rossi
Barrington Court, 91c Jermyn Street, London, SW1Y 6JB
☎ 020 7321 0208 Ⓕ 020 7321 0546
Ⓔ rossirossi@compuserve.com
Ⓦ www.asianar.com/rossi
Est. 1986 *Stock size* Medium
Stock Asian art, sculpture, paintings from India, the Himalayas, Chinese textiles
Open Mon–Fri 10.30am–5.30pm

The Silver Fund Ltd (LAPADA)
Contact A Crawford
40 Bury Street, London, SW1Y 6AU
☎ 020 7839 7664 Ⓕ 020 7839 8935
Ⓔ dealers@thesilverfund.com
Ⓦ www.thesilverfund.com
Est. 1996 *Stock size* Large
Stock Georg Jensen, Tiffany, Martele and Puiforcat silver
Open Mon–Fri 9am–6pm
Fairs NEC, LAPADA, Claridges
Services Valuations

Sims Reed Ltd (ABA)
Contact Mr J Sims
43a Duke Street, St James's, London, SW1Y 6DD
☎ 020 7493 5660 Ⓕ 020 7493 8468
Ⓔ info@simsreed.com
Ⓦ www.simsreed.com
Est. 1977 *Stock size* Large
Stock Antiquarian, rare, second-hand books, including books illustrated by artists, books on fine and applied arts
Open Mon–Fri 10am–6pm or by appointment
Fairs ABA, Olympia

Peta Smyth Antique Textiles (LAPADA, CINOA)
Contact Mrs P Smyth
42 Moreton Street, London, SW1V 2PB
☎ 020 7630 9898 Ⓕ 020 7630 5398
Est. 1975 *Stock size* Large
Stock Early European textiles, needlework, silks, tapestries, hangings
Open Mon–Fri 9.30am–5.30pm
Fairs Olympia (June, Nov)
Services Valuations

Somlo Antiques Ltd (BADA)
Contact Mr Charles Tearle
7 Piccadilly Arcade, London, SW1Y 6NH
☎ 020 7499 6526 Ⓕ 020 7499 0603
Ⓔ mail@somlo.com
Ⓦ www.somloantiques.com
Est. 1970 *Stock size* Large
Stock Vintage wristwatches, antique pocket watches
Open Mon–Fri 10am–5.30pm Sat 10.30am–5.30pm
Fairs Olympia (Feb, June)
Services Valuations, repairs

Un Français à Londres
Contact Mr P Sumner
202 Ebury Street, London, SW1W 8UN
☎ 020 7730 1771 Ⓕ 020 7730 1661
Ⓔ eburystreet@aol.com
Ⓦ www.unfrancaisalondres.com
Est. 1998 *Stock size* Large
Stock French and Continental furniture, works of art, 17th–19thC
Open Mon–Fri 10am–6pm Sat 10am–4pm or by appointment
Services Valuations, restorations, upholstery

Westenholz Antiques Ltd
Contact Andrew Damonte
76–78 Pimlico Road, London, SW1W 8PL
☎ 020 7824 8090 Ⓕ 020 7823 5913
Ⓔ shop@westenholz.co.uk
Ⓦ www.westenholz.co.uk
Stock 18th–19thC English furniture, decorative items
Open Mon–Fri 8.30am–6pm
Fairs Olympia (June, Nov)
Services Interior design

SW3

Norman Adams Ltd (BADA, BACA Award Winner 2001)
Contact R S G Whittington or C Claxton-Stevens
8–10 Hans Road, London, SW3 1RX
☎ 020 7589 5266 Ⓕ 020 7589 1968
Ⓔ antiques@normanadams.com
Ⓦ www.normanadams.com
Est. 1923 *Stock size* Large
Stock Fine 18thC English furniture, works of art, mirrors, paintings, chandeliers
Open Mon–Fri 9am–5.30pm or Sat Sun by appointment
Fairs BADA (March), Grosvenor House (June)
Services Annual catalogue

After Noah
Contact Simon Tarr
261 King's Road, London, SW3 5EL
☎ 020 7351 2610
Ⓔ mailorder@afternoah.com
Ⓦ www.afternoah.com

Est. 1995 *Stock size* Medium
Stock Antique and contemporary furniture and houseware
Open Mon–Sat 10am–6pm Sun noon–5pm
Services Restorations

Antiquarius Antique Centre
Contact Mike Spooner
131–141 Kings Road, London, SW3 4PW
020 7351 5353 020 7351 5350
antique@dial.pipex.com
Est. 1969 *Stock size* Large
No. of dealers 100+
Stock General and specialist antiques of all periods
Open Mon–Sat 10am–6pm

Apter-Fredericks Ltd (BADA)
Contact Mr H Apter
265–267 Fulham Road, London, SW3 6HY
020 7352 2188 020 7376 5619
antiques@apter-fredericks.demon.co.uk
Est. 1946 *Stock size* Large
Stock 18thC English furniture
Open Mon–Fri 9.30am–5.30pm
Fairs Grosvenor House

Joanna Booth (BADA, CINOA)
Contact Joanna Booth
247 King's Road, London, SW3 5EL
020 7352 8998 020 7376 7350
joannabooth@londonweb.net
www.joannabooth.co.uk
Est. 1966 *Stock size* Large
Stock Old master drawings, early sculptures, tapestries, oak furniture, textiles
Open Mon–Sat 10am–6pm
Fairs Olympia
Services Valuations, restorations

Bourbon Hanby Antique Centre
Contact Mr I Towning
151 Sydney Street, London, SW3 6NT
020 7352 2106 020 7565 0003
www.antiques-uk.co.uk/bourbon-hanby
Est. 1974 *Stock size* Large
No. of dealers 30
Stock China, glass, silver, porcelain, jewellery, textiles, furniture, carpets, rugs, paintings
Open Mon–Sat 10am–6pm
Sun 11am–5pm
Services Restorations, jewellery manufacturing

Jasmin Cameron (Glass Circle)
Contact Jasmin Cameron
Stand M16, Antiquarius, 131–141 Kings Road, London, SW3 4PW
0207 351 4154 0207 351 4154
07774 871257
jasmin.cameron@mail.com
Est. 1989 *Stock size* Large
Stock 18th–19thC drinking glasses, decanters, fountain pens, writing materials
Open Mon–Sat 10am–5.30pm
Fairs Glass and Ceramics Fair, Kensington
Services Valuations, restorations

Chelsea Clocks and Antiques
Contact Mr Donald Lynch
Stands H 3–4, Antiquarius, 131–141 Kings Road, London, SW3 4PW
020 7352 8646 020 7376 4591
info@chelseaclocks.co.uk
www.chelseaclocks.co.uk
Est. 1979 *Stock size* Medium
Stock Clocks, scales, boxes, collectables, ink stands and wells
Open Mon–Sat 10am–5.30pm

Chelsea Military Antiques
Contact Richard Black
Stands N13–N14, Antiquarius, 131–141 Kings Road, London, SW3 4PW
020 7352 0308 020 7352 0308
richard@chelseamilitaria.com
www.chelseamilitaria.com
Est. 1996 *Stock size* Large
Stock British campaign medals, 19th and 20thC Allied and Axis militaria
Open Mon–Sat 10.30am–5.30pm
Fairs Britannia and South England Miitaria Fairs
Services Valuations, medal mounting

Classic Fabrics with Robin Haydock (LAPADA)
Contact Robin Haydock
18 Bourbon Hanby Antiques Centre, 151 Sydney Street, Chelsea, London, SW3 6NT
020 7349 9110 020 7349 9110
Est. 1996 *Stock size* Medium
Stock Antique textiles, mostly 18thC European and earlier, decorative furnishings
Open Tues–Sat 10.30am–6pm
Sun 11am–5pm
Fairs Olympia (June) Decorative Antiques & Textile Fairs
Services Valuations, restorations

Classic Prints
Contact Mr Paul Dowling
265 King's Road, London, SW3 5EL
020 7376 5056 020 7460 5356
07770 431855
art@classicprints.com
www.classicprints.com
Est. 1983 *Stock size* Large
Stock Antique prints of all ages, maps
Open Mon–Sat 10am–6pm Sun noon–5pm
Services Valuations

L and D Collins
Contact Louise Collins or David Collins
020 7584 0712 020 7584 0712
Est. 1994 *Stock size* Medium
Stock Paintings, fans, decorative objects
Open By appointment
Fairs Decorative Antiques and Textiles Fair, Penman Fairs

Richard Courtney Ltd (BADA)
Contact Mr R Courtney
114 Fulham Road, London, SW3 6HU
020 7370 4020 020 7370 4020
Est. 1965 *Stock size* Large
Stock Finest early 18thC English walnut furniture
Open Mon–Fri 9.30am–5.30pm
Fairs Grosvenor House, BADA Duke of York's

Jesse Davis Antiques (LAPADA)
Contact Mr J Davis
Stands A9–11, Antiquarius, 131–141 Kings Road, London, SW3 4PW
020 7352 4314
Est. 1984 *Stock size* Large
Stock 19thC pottery, majolica, Staffordshire and other collectable factories, decorative objects
Open Mon–Sat 10.30am–6pm
Fairs Olympia (June), LAPADA Fair, Decorative Antiques and Textiles Fair

Dernier and Hamlyn Ltd
3 Egerton Terrace, London, SW3 2EJ
020 7225 5030 020 7838 1030
www.dernier-hamlyn.com
Stock size Large
Stock Fine lighting, high-quality period lighting
Open Mon–Sat 10am–7pm
Services Restorations

Robert Dickson and Lesley Rendall Antiques (BADA)
Contact Robert Dickson or Lesley Randall
263 Fulham Road, London, SW3 6HY
020 7351 0330
www.dicksonrendallantiques.co.uk
Est. 1969 *Stock size* Large
Stock Antique furniture, English and French works of art, English Regency
Open Mon–Fri 10am–6pm Sat 10am–4.30pm
Services Valuations, restorations

Eclectic Antiques and Interiors
Contact Graham Tomlinson
Stands T3–4, Antiquarius, 131–141 Kings Road, London, SW3 4PW
020 7286 7608 020 7286 7608
07778 470983 *Stock size* Medium
Stock English and French decorative antiques and furniture
Open Mon–Sat 10am–6pm
Services Shipping, valuations

Michael Foster (BADA)
Contact Margaret Susands
118 Fulham Road, Chelsea, London, SW3 6HU
020 7373 3636 020 7373 4042
Est. 1967 *Stock size* Medium
Stock Fine 18th–early 19thC furniture, works of art
Open Mon–Fri 9.30am–5.30pm
Fairs Grosvenor House, Olympia
Services Valuations

Hayman & Hayman
Contact Georgina Hayman
Antiquarius, 131–141 Kings Road, London, SW3 4PW
020 7351 6568
hayman@wahlgren.demon.co.uk
Est. 1976 *Stock size* Large
Stock Photograph frames, Limoges boxes, scent bottles
Open Mon–Sat 10am–5.30pm
Services Valuations, restorations, shipping

Peter Herington Antiquarian Bookseller (ABA, PBFA)
Contact Kevin Finch
100 Fulham Road, Chelsea, London, SW3 6HS
020 7591 0220 020 7225 7054
mail@peter-herington-books.com
www.peter-herington-books.com
Est. 1969 *Stock size* Large
Stock Antiquarian books, illustrated, fine bindings, English literature, travel, children's etc, modern first editions
Open Mon–Sat 10am–6pm
Fairs Olympia ABA, Chelsea ABA

Hill House Antiques & Decorative Arts
Contact S Benhalim
PO Box 17320, London, SW3 3WE
07973 842777
sbhhouse@aol.com
Est. 1999 *Stock size* Small
Stock Small furniture, metalware, ceramics, decorative arts
Open By appointment
Fairs P & A fairs, Take Five Fairs
Services Sourcing, design consultancy

Paul Howard
Contact Mr P Howard
Within Bourbon Hanby Antique Centre, Shop 2, 151 Sydney Street, Chelsea, London, SW3 6NT
020 7352 4113 020 7351 0003
07881 862375
Est. 1972 *Stock size* Medium
Stock Antique sextants, octants, theodolites, microscopes, telescopes, scientific instruments, other related items
Open Mon–Sat 10am–6pm

Michael Hughes (BADA)
Contact Michael Hughes
88 Fulham Road, London, SW3 6HR
020 7589 0660 020 7823 7618
antiques@michaelhughes.freeserve.com
Est. 1995 *Stock size* Large
Stock 18th–early 19thC English furniture and works of art
Open Mon–Fri 9.30am–5.30pm
Fairs Olympia

Anthony James & Son Ltd (BADA, CINOA)
Contact James Millard
88 Fulham Road, London, SW3 6HR
020 7584 1120 020 7823 7618
anthony.james10@virgin.net
www.anthony-james.com
Est. 1949 *Stock size* Large
Stock Fine 18th–19thC English and Continental furniture, decorative items
Open Mon–Fri 9.30am–5.45pm
Fairs Olympia (June, Nov)
Services Valuations, restorations

John Keil Ltd (BADA)
Contact Diana Yates-Watson
First Floor, 154 Brompton Road, London, SW3 1HX
020 7589 6454 020 7823 8235
antiques@johnkeil.com
www.johnkeil.com
Est. 1959 *Stock size* Medium
Stock 18thC English furniture
Open Mon–Fri 9.30am–5.30pm

M Lexton
Contact Michael Lexton
Antiquarius, 131–141 Kings Road, London, SW3 4PW
0207 351 5980 0207 351 5980
mlextonltd@hotmail.com
Stock size Medium
Stock Silver
Open Mon–Sat 10.30am–6pm
Services Valuations, restorations

Lini Designs
Contact Rupali Varma
121 Sydney Street, London, SW3 6NR
020 7795 0077 020 7376 8593
linidesign@aol.com
Stock size Medium
Stock Antique Indian furniture, cushions, artefacts, Christmas decorations
Open Mon–Sat 11am–6pm Sun noon–6pm
Fairs Top Drawer, NEC

Michael Lipitch (BADA)
Contact Mr M Lipitch
98 Fulham Road, London, SW3 6HS
020 7589 7327 020 7823 9106

LONDON

Est. 1969 *Stock size* Large
Stock 18th–19thC fine furniture, mirrors, objets d'art
Open Mon–Fri 9am–6pm Sat 10am–5pm
Fairs Grosvenor House
Services Specialist advice on forming collections

⊞ Peter Lipitch Ltd (BADA)
Contact Melvyn Lipitch
✉ **120–124 Fulham Road, London, SW3 6HU** Ⓟ
☎ 020 7373 3328 Ⓕ 020 7373 8888
Ⓔ lipitch.al@aol.com
Est. 1950 *Stock size* Medium
Stock 18thC English furniture
Open Mon–Fri 9.30am–5.30pm Sat 10am–2pm

⊞ Little River Oriental Antiques
Contact Mr D Dykes
✉ **Antiquarius, 131–141 Kings Road, London, SW3 4PW** Ⓟ
☎ 020 7349 9080 Ⓕ 01342 300131
Est. 1997 *Stock size* Large
Stock Chinese antiquities, domestic ceramics
Open Mon–Sat 10am–6pm
Services Restorations

⊞ The Map House (BADA, ABA)
Contact Mr P Stuchlik
✉ **54 Beauchamp Place, London, SW3 1NY**
☎ 020 7584 8559 Ⓕ 020 7589 1041
Ⓔ maps@themaphouse.com
Ⓦ www.themaphouse.com
Est. 1973 *Stock size* Large
Stock Antique maps, 15th–19thC, decorative engravings, 16th–19thC, globes, atlases
Open Mon–Fri 9.45am–5.45pm Sat 10.30am–5pm
Services Valuations

⊞ Mariad Antiques
Contact Mrs H McClean
✉ **Antiquarius, 131–141 King's Road, London, SW3 6NT** Ⓟ
☎ 020 7351 9526
Est. 1971 *Stock size* Large
Stock Georgian, Victorian, Edwardian jewellery, cold-painted Vienna bronzes, animal subjects
Open Mon–Sun 10am–6pm
Fairs NEC
Services Valuations, restorations

⊞ Gerald Mathias
Contact Mr G Mathias
✉ **Stands R5–8, Antiquarius, 131–141 Kings Road, London, SW3 4PW** Ⓟ
☎ 020 7351 0484 Ⓕ 020 7351 0484
Ⓔ gm@geraldmathias.com
Ⓦ www.geraldmathias.com
Est. 1979 *Stock size* Large
Stock Antique wooden boxes, Georgian tea caddies
Open Mon–Sat 10am–5.30pm

⊞ Sue Mautner Costume Jewellery
Contact Mrs S Mautner
✉ **Stand P13, Antiquarius, 131–141 Kings Road, London, SW3 4PW** Ⓟ
☎ 020 7376 4419
Est. 1990 *Stock size* Large
Stock 1940s–1950s costume jewellery, Christian Dior, Miriam Haskell, Schiaparelli, Coppolo Toppo, Har, Schreiner
Open Mon–Sat 10.30am–5pm

⊞ Michael's Boxes Ltd
Contact Michael Cassidy
✉ **Unit V4, Antiquarius, 131–141 Kings Road, Chelsea, London, SW3 4PW** Ⓟ
☎ 020 7351 5644 Ⓕ 020 8930 8318
Ⓔ info@michaelsboxes.com
Ⓦ www.michaelsboxes.com
Est. 1997 *Stock size* Large
Stock Limoges, enamel antique boxes
Open Mon–Sat 10am–6pm Sun 11am–5pm
Fairs Portobello
Services Personalized boxes

⊞ No. 12
Contact Mrs Isabel Haines
✉ **12 Cale Street, London, SW3 3QU** Ⓟ
☎ 020 7581 5022 Ⓕ 020 7581 3966
Est. 1990 *Stock size* Large
Stock French country antiques
Open Mon–Sat 10am–6pm
Services Interior design

⊞ Jacqueline Oosthuizen Antiques (LAPADA)
Contact Mrs J Oosthuizen
✉ **23 Cale Street, Chelsea, London, SW3 3QR** Ⓟ
☎ 020 7352 6071 Ⓕ 020 7376 3852
Ⓜ 07785 258806
Est. 1979 *Stock size* Large
Stock Staffordshire animals, cottages, figures, jewellery
Open Mon–Sat 10am–5pm Sun by appointment only

⊞ Rogers de Rin (BADA)
Contact Mrs V De Rin
✉ **76 Royal Hospital Road, London, SW3 4HN** Ⓟ
☎ 020 7352 9007 Ⓕ 020 7351 9407
Ⓔ rogersderin@rogersderin.co.uk
Est. 1965 *Stock size* Medium
Stock Collectors' Items, snuff boxes, enamels, Vienna bronzes, Staffordshire, Scottish Wemyss ware
Open Mon–Fri 10am–5.30pm Sat 10am–1pm
Fairs Olympia (June, Nov), BADA (March)
Services Shipping arranged

⊞ Salamanca
Contact Mrs Martin
✉ **Stands 14–15, Antiquarius, 131–141 Kings Road, London, SW3 4PW** Ⓟ
☎ 020 7351 5829 Ⓕ 020 7351 5829
Est. 1976 *Stock size* Large
Stock Moorcroft pottery, Sabino glass, porcelain, silver
Open Mon–Sat 10.30am–5.30pm
Services Valuations, restorations

⊞ Charles Saunders Antiques
Contact Mr Charles Saunders
✉ **255 Fulham Road, London, SW3 6HY** Ⓟ
☎ 020 7351 5242 Ⓕ 020 7352 8142
Est. 1987 *Stock size* Medium
Stock Antique lighting, English and Continental 18th–19thC furniture, objects, decorations
Open Mon–Fri 9.30am–5.30pm Sat 10am–5pm

⊞ Christine Schell (LAPADA)
Contact Ms Christine King
✉ **15 Cale Street, London, SW3 3QS** Ⓟ
☎ 020 7352 5563 Ⓕ 020 7589 7161
Ⓔ c.schell@eidosnet.co.uk
Est. 1973 *Stock size* Medium
Stock Tortoiseshell, ivory, silver, Arts and Crafts, decorative items, mirrors
Open Mon–Sat 10am–5.30pm
Services Valuations, restorations

⊞ Snap Dragon
Contact Leonie Whittle
✉ **247 Fulham Road, London, SW3 6HY** Ⓟ

☎ 020 7376 8889
Ⓔ leonie@snapdragon.sonnet.co.uk
Stock size Large
Stock 18th–19thC Chinese furniture, chairs
Open Mon–Sat 10am–6pm

Miwa Thorpe
Contact Ms Miwa Thorpe
✉ **Stands M8–M9, Antiquarius, 131–141 Kings Road, London, SW3 4PW** Ⓟ
☎ 020 7351 2911 Ⓕ 020 7351 6690
Ⓜ 07768 455679
Est. 1987 *Stock size* Medium
Stock Jewellery and decorative silver
Open Mon–Sat 10am–6pm

Geoffrey Waters Ltd (LAPADA)
Contact Mr G Waters
✉ **Stands F1–F6, Antiquarius, 131–141 Kings Road, London, SW3 4PW** Ⓟ
☎ 020 7376 5467 Ⓕ 020 7376 5467
Est. 1992 *Stock size* Large
Stock Chinese export porcelain, *famille rose*, *famille verte*, Chinese Imari, 16th–18thC blue and white porcelain
Open Mon–Sat 10am–5.30pm

Gordon Watson Ltd (LAPADA)
Contact Mr S Berg
✉ **50 Fulham Road, London, SW3 6HH** Ⓟ
☎ 020 7589 3108 Ⓕ 020 7584 6328
Stock size Medium
Stock Art Deco furniture, lighting
Open Mon–Sat 11am–6pm
Fairs Olympia

O F Wilson Ltd (BADA, LAPADA)
Contact Mr P Jackson
✉ **Queens Elm Parade, Old Church Street, Chelsea, London, SW3 6EJ** Ⓟ
☎ 020 7352 9554 Ⓕ 020 7351 0765
Ⓔ ofw@email.msn.com
Est. 1949 *Stock size* Medium
Stock Continental furniture, French chimney pieces, English painted decorative furniture, mirrors
Open Mon–Fri 9.30am–5.30pm Sat 10.30am–1pm
Fairs Grosvenor House
Services Valuations

The World of Antiques (UK) Ltd
Contact Yves De Keersmaeker
✉ **151 Sydney Street, Chelsea, London, SW3 6NT** Ⓟ
☎ 00 32 2 4612429
Ⓕ 00 32 2 4610889
Ⓜ 00 32 7580 6443
Ⓔ worldofantiques@pophost.eunet.be
Ⓦ www.theworldofantiques.com
Est. 2000 *Stock size* Medium
Stock Decorative antiques, English and French furniture, hotel silver plate
Open Mon–Sat 10am–7pm
Fairs Decorative Antiques Fair London
Services Shipping

World's End Bookshop
Contact Mr S Dickson
✉ **357 King's Road, London, SW3 5ES** Ⓟ
☎ 020 7352 9376
Ⓜ 07961 316 918
Ⓔ stephen.dickson@virgin.net
Est. 1999 *Stock size* Medium
Stock Antiquarian, rare, second-hand books on non-fiction, art, literature etc.
Open Mon–Sun 10am–6.30pm
Fairs Royal National Hotel, Bloomsbury (H D)
Services Valuations

SW4

Antiques and Things
Contact Mrs V Crowther
☎ 020 7498 1303 Ⓕ 020 7498 1303
Ⓜ 07767 262096
Ⓔ val@antiquesandthings.co.uk
Ⓦ www.antiquesandthings.co.uk
Est. 1985 *Stock size* Medium
Stock Lighting, chandeliers, curtain furniture, accessories, French decorative furniture, textiles
Open Mon–Fri 10am–5pm by appointment
Fairs Decorative Antiques and Textiles Fair

Places and Spaces
Contact Paul Carroll or Nick Hannam
✉ **30 Old Town, Clapham, London, SW4 0LB** Ⓟ
☎ 020 7498 0998 Ⓕ 020 7498 0998
Ⓔ contact@placesandspaces.com
Ⓦ www.placesandspaces.com
Est. 1997 *Stock size* Large
Stock 20thC classic designs, 1950s Scandinavian furniture, Italian lighting, Eames, Panton
Open Tues–Sat 10.30am–6pm Sun noon–4pm
Fairs Knee Deep in Design (Sept), 100% Design
Services Valuations, design consultancy

SW6

275 Antiques
Contact Mr D Fisher
✉ **275 Lillie Road, London, SW6 7LL** Ⓟ
☎ 020 7386 7382 Ⓕ 020 7381 8320
Est. 1991 *Stock size* Large
Stock 1880s–1930s furniture, decorative items, American Lucite furniture, lighting, 1930s–1970s
Open Mon–Sat 10am–5.30pm

The Antique Mirror Gallery
✉ **7 New King's Road, London, SW6 4SB** Ⓟ
☎ 020 7731 7341 Ⓕ 020 7731 7341
Est. 1997 *Stock size* Large
Stock 18th–19thC gilt mirrors, gilt furniture
Open Mon–Sat 11am–5.30pm
Services Valuations, restorations

Sebastiano Barbagallo Antiques
Contact Mr S Barbagallo
✉ **61 Fulham Road, London, SW6 5PZ** Ⓟ
☎ 020 7751 0691 Ⓕ 020 7751 0691
Est. 1978 *Stock size* Large
Stock Chinese furniture, Indian and Tibetan antiques, crafts
Open Mon–Sun 10am–6pm

Sebastiano Barbagallo Antiques
Contact Mr S Barbagallo
✉ **3110 Wandsworth Bridge Road, London, SW6 2UA** Ⓟ
☎ 020 7751 0586 Ⓕ 020 7751 0586
Est. 1978 *Stock size* Medium
Stock Chinese furniture, objects
Open Mon–Sun 10am–6pm

Big Ben Clocks and Antiques
Contact Mr R Lascelles
✉ **5 Broxholme House, New King's Road, London, SW6 4AA** Ⓟ
☎ 020 7736 1770 Ⓕ 020 7384 1957
Ⓔ info@lasc.demon.co.uk
Est. 1974 *Stock size* Large

Stock Longcase, mantel, and traditional reproduction clocks
Open Tues–Sat 10am–5pm

Alasdair Brown
Contact Mr A Brown
3–4 The Cranewell, The Gas Works, 2 Michael Road, London, SW6 2AD
020 7736 6661 F 020 7384 3334
M 07836 672857
E ab@ajcb.demon.co.uk
Est. 1984 *Stock size* Medium
Stock 19th–20thC furniture, lighting, upholstery, unusual items
Open Wed Thurs 10am–6pm
Fairs Winter Olympia
Services Valuations

I and J L Brown Ltd
Contact Mr S Hilton
632–636 King's Road, London, SW6 2DU
020 7736 4141 F 020 7736 9164
E enquiries@brownantiques.com
W www.brownantiques.com
Est. 1978 *Stock size* Large
Stock English country, French provincial antique and reproduction furniture, extensive range of decorative items
Open Mon–Sat 9am–5.30pm or by appointment
Services Restorations, re-rushing

Rupert Cavendish Antiques
Contact Mr Francois Valcke
610 King's Road, London, SW6 2DX
020 7731 7041 F 020 7731 8302
E rcavendish@aol.com
W www.rupertcavendish.co.uk
Est. 1984 *Stock size* Large
Stock European 20thC paintings
Open Mon–Sat 10am–6pm

Fergus Cochrane Leigh Warren
Contact Mr F Cochrane
570 King's Road, London, SW6 2DY
020 7736 9166 F 020 7736 6687
Est. 1979 *Stock size* Large
Stock 19th–20thC lighting
Open Mon–Fri 10am–5pm Sat 10am–4pm

Marc Costantini Antiques
Contact Mr M Costantini
313 Lillie Road, London, SW6 7LL
020 7610 2380 F 020 7610 2380
M 07941 075289
Est. 1999 *Stock size* Large
Stock English and Continental antique furniture
Open Mon–Sat 10.30am–5.30pm

Decorative Antiques (LAPADA)
Contact Mr T Harley
284 Lillie Road, Fulham, London, SW6 7PX
020 7610 2694 F 020 7386 0103
Est. 1992 *Stock size* Large
Stock 18th–19thC French provincial furniture, Irish furniture
Open Mon–Sat 10am–5.30pm

Charles Edwards (BADA, CINOA)
Contact Annabel or Louise
19a Rumbold Road, London, SW6 2HX
020 7736 7172 F 020 7731 7388
E charles@charlesedwards.demon.co.uk
Est. 1969 *Stock size* Medium
Stock Antique lighting, 18th–19thC furniture, bookcases, general antiques
Open Mon–Fri 9.30am–6pm Sat 10am–5pm

Nicole Fabre French Antiques (LAPADA)
Contact Mrs N Fabre
592 King's Road, London, SW6 2DX
020 7384 3112 F 020 7610 6410
Stock size Medium
Stock French Provençale furniture and beds, Provençale quilts, linens, textiles, 18th–19thC toiles, decorative items
Open Mon–Fri 10am–6pm Sat 11am–5pm
Fairs Decorative Antiques and Textiles Fair
Services Represents Christopher Moore and the Lady Huntly Collection

Hector Finch Lighting
Contact Mr H Finch
88–90 Wandsworth Bridge Road, London, SW6 2TF
020 7731 8886 F 020 7731 7408
E hector@hectorfinch.com
W www.hectorfinch.com
Est. 1987 *Stock size* Large
Stock Specialist period lighting shop, large range of antique and contemporary decorative lighting
Open Mon–Sat 10am–5.30pm

Birdie Fortescue Antiques (LAPADA)
Contact Birdie Fortescue
Unit GJ, Cooper House, 2 Michael Road, London, SW6 2AD
01206 337567 F 01206 337557
M 07778 263467
Est. 1991 *Stock size* Large
Stock 18th–early 19thC Continental furniture
Open By appointment
Fairs Olympia (Feb, June), Decorative Antiques Fair, Battersea Park (Jan, April, Sept), LAPADA

Fulham Antiques
Contact Mr A Eves
320 Munster Road, London, SW6 6BH
020 7610 3644
Est. 1993 *Stock size* Large
Stock Antique and decorative furniture, lighting, mirrors
Open Mon–Sat 10am–5.30pm
Services Delivery

Ena Green
Contact Ms Ena Green
566 King's Road, London, SW6 2DY
020 7736 2485 F 020 7610 9028
M 07831 106002
Est. 1979 *Stock size* Medium
Stock 18th–20thC painted furniture, lighting, mirrors, decorative items
Open Mon–Sat 10.30am–5.30pm

Judy Greenwood Antiques
Contact Ms J Greenwood
657 Fulham Road, London, SW6 5PY
020 7736 6037 F 020 7736 1941
M 07768 347669
E judyg@dial.pipex.com
Est. 1978 *Stock size* Large
Stock 19th–20thC French decorative items, beds, textiles, lighting, furniture, mirrors, quilts
Open Mon–Fri 10am–5.30pm Sat 10am–5pm
Services Restorations, painting

H R W Antiques Ltd (LAPADA)
Contact Mr I Henderson-Russell

✉ 26 Sulivan Road,
London, SW6 3DT 🅿
☎ 020 7371 7995 🅕 020 7371 9522
🅔 ian@hrw-antiques.freeserve.co.uk
🅦 www.hrw-antiques.com
Est. 1988 *Stock size* Large
Stock Decorative items
Open Mon–Fri 9am–5pm

Nigel Hindley
Contact Mr N Hindley
✉ **281 Lillie Road,**
London, SW6 7LL 🅿
☎ 020 7385 0706
Est. 1979 *Stock size* Large
Stock English period antiques, French furniture, eccentricities
Open Mon–Sat 10.30am–5pm
Services Valuations

Holt & Company (GTA)
Contact Mr N Holt
✉ **5 Rickett Street, West Brompton, London, SW6 1RU** 🅿
☎ 020 7385 9558 🅕 020 7385 9558
🅔 enquiries@holtandcompany.co.uk.
Est. 1993
Open Mon–Fri 9am–5pm
Sales Modern and antique gun sales at the Duke of York's Barracks, King's Road, London Wed 2pm, viewing Mon 9am–8pm Tues 9am–8pm Wed 9am–12.30pm
Frequency 6 per annum
Catalogues Yes

Indigo
Contact Marion Bender
✉ **275 New King's Road,**
London, SW6 4RD 🅿
☎ 020 7384 3101 🅕 020 7384 3102
🅔 indigo_uk@compuserve.com
Est. 1982 *Stock size* Large
Stock Indian and Chinese furniture, decorative items, handicrafts, Indonesian furniture from recycled teakwood
Open Mon–Sat 10am–6pm
Fairs House and Garden Fair

Jackdawes (LAPADA)
Contact Princess Sevilla Hercolani
✉ **297 Lillie Road,**
London, SW6 7LL 🅿
☎ 020 7386 0880 🅕 020 7602 4800
Est. 1989 *Stock size* Large
Stock Decorative French, Italian, and English painted furniture, lighting, gilded mirrors
Open Mon–Sat 10.30am–5.30pm
Fairs Decorative Fair, Battersea, Kensington Penman Fair
Services Restorations

Christopher Jones Antiques
Contact Rene Sanderson
✉ **618–620 King's Road,**
London, SW6 2DU 🅿
☎ 020 7731 4655 🅕 020 7371 8682
🅔 florehouse@msn.com
🅦 www.christopherjonesantiques.co.uk
Est. 1984 *Stock size* Large
Stock French furniture, mirrors, screens, 1860–1890 Chinese porcelain
Open Mon–Sat 10am–5.30pm

King's Court Galleries
Contact Mrs J Joel
✉ **949–953 Fulham Road,**
London, SW6 5HY 🅿
☎ 020 7610 6939 🅕 020 7731 4737
🅔 sales@kingscourtgalleries.co.uk
🅦 www.kingscourtgalleries.co.uk
Est. 1984 *Stock size* Large
Stock Antique maps, engravings, sporting, decorative prints
Open Mon–Sat 10am–5.30pm
Services Framing

L & E Kreckovic
Contact Joanna Christopher
✉ **559 King's Road,**
London, SW6 2EB 🅿
☎ 020 7736 0753 🅕 020 7731 5904
Est. 1969 *Stock size* Large
Stock Early 18th–19thC furniture
Open Mon–Sat 10am–6pm
Services Valuations, restorations

L'Accademia Antiques
Contact Mrs P Villanueva
✉ **643c Fulham Road,**
London, SW6 5PU 🅿
☎ 020 7736 7088
Est. 1996 *Stock size* Large
Stock Antiques, decorative items, chandeliers, bedroom furniture, mirrors, French and Italian furniture
Open Mon–Sat 10am–6pm

Roger Lascelles Clocks Ltd
Contact Mr R Lascelles
✉ **29 Carnwath Road,**
London,
SW6 3HR 🅿
☎ 020 7731 0072 🅕 020 7384 1957
🅔 info@lasc.demon.co.uk
Est. 1984 *Stock size* Large
Stock Antique & reproduction clocks
Open Mon–Fri 10am–5pm
Fairs Birmingham, Frankfurt, New York Gift Fair
Services Annual catalogue

M Luther Antiques
Contact Mr M Luther
✉ **590 King's Road,**
Chelsea,
London, SW6 2DX 🅿
☎ 020 7371 8492 🅕 020 7371 8492
Est. 1992 *Stock size* Medium
Stock 18th–19thC English and Continental furniture, tables, chairs, mirrors, lighting etc
Open Mon–Sat 9.30am–6pm

Michael Marriott
Contact Mr M Marriott
✉ **588 Fulham Road,**
Fulham,
London, SW6 5NT 🅿
☎ 020 7736 3110 🅕 020 7736 0568
Est. 1979 *Stock size* Medium
Stock English 18th–19thC furniture, antiquarian prints
Open Mon–Fri 8.30am–5pm Sat 9am–1pm
Services Valuations, restorations

David Martin-Taylor Antiques (LAPADA)
Contact Mr Cavet
✉ **558 King's Road,**
London, SW6 2DZ 🅿
☎ 020 7731 4135 🅕 020 7371 0029
🅜 07889 437306
🅔 dmt@davidmartintaylor.com
🅦 www.davidmartintaylor.com
Est. 1965 *Stock size* Large
Stock 18th–19thC Continental and English furniture, objets d'art, decorative art, from the eccentric to the unusual
Open Mon–Fri 10am–6pm Sat 11am–4.30pm or by appointment
Fairs Olympia (June), London Decorative Arts

Ann May
Contact Mrs A May
✉ **80 Wandsworth Bridge Road,**
London, SW6 2TF 🅿
☎ 020 7731 0862
Est. 1969 *Stock size* Medium
Stock Painted French furniture, decorative items
Open Mon–Sat 10am–6pm

Mark Maynard
Contact Mr M Maynard
✉ **651 Fulham Road,**
London, SW6 5PU 🅿
☎ 020 7731 3533
Est. 1985 *Stock size* Medium
Stock Painted French furniture, decorative items
Open Mon–Sat 10am–6pm

Mora & Upham Antiques
Contact Mr M Upham
✉ **584 King's Road, London, SW6 2DX** Ⓟ
☎ 020 7731 4444 Ⓕ 020 7736 0440
Ⓔ mora.upham@talk21.com
Est. 1980 *Stock size* Large
Stock Gilded French chairs, antique chandeliers, 18th–19thC English and Continental furniture, mirrors
Open Mon–Sat 10am–6pm

Sylvia Napier Ltd
Contact Mrs S Napier
✉ **554 King's Road, London, SW6 2DZ** Ⓟ
☎ 020 7371 5881
Ⓜ 07802 309081
Est. 1981 *Stock size* Large
Stock Painted Continental furniture, ironwork, chandeliers, urns
Open Mon–Sat 10am–6pm

Nimmo & Spooner
Contact Myra Spooner or Catherine Nimmo
✉ **277 Lillie Road, London, SW6 7LL** Ⓟ
☎ 020 7385 2724 Ⓕ 020 7385 2724
Est. 1990 *Stock size* Medium
Stock Decorative antiques, unusual objects, 18thC French furniture
Open Mon–Sat 10am–5.30pm
Fairs Decorative Antiques and Textiles Fair

Old World Trading Co
Contact Mr R Campion
✉ **565 King's Road, London, SW6 2EB** Ⓟ
☎ 020 7731 4708 Ⓕ 020 7731 1291
Ⓔ oldworld@btinternet.com
Est. 1970 *Stock size* Large
Stock 18th–19thC English and French chimney places, fire dogs, grates
Open Mon–Fri 9.30am–6pm Sat 10am–3pm
Services Valuations, restorations

Onslow Auctions Ltd
Contact Patrick Bogue
✉ **The Depot, 2 Michael Road, London, SW6 2AD** Ⓟ
☎ 020 7371 0505 Ⓕ 020 7384 2682
Ⓔ onslow.auctions@btinternet.com
Ⓦ www.auctions-on-line.com/onslows
Est. 1984
Open Mon–Fri 9.30am–5pm by appointment
Sales Collectors' sales, vintage travel, aeronautical, posters, railways, motoring, Titanic, ocean liners, advisable to phone for details
Frequency 4 per annum
Catalogues Yes

Orient Expressions Ltd (BABAADA)
Contact Amanda Leader
✉ **Studio 3B2, 3rd Floor, Cooper House, 2 Michael Road, London, SW6 2AD** Ⓟ
☎ 020 7610 9311 Ⓕ 020 7610 6872
Ⓜ 07887 770406
Ⓔ amandaleader@compuserve.com
Ⓦ www.antiquesbulletin.com/orientexpressions
Est. 1996 *Stock size* Medium
Stock Mostly early 19thC provincial Chinese furniture, accessories
Open By appointment

Rainbow Antiques
Contact Mr Fabio Bergomi
✉ **329 Lillie Road, London, SW6 7NR** Ⓟ
☎ 020 7385 1323
Ⓜ 07879 811077
Ⓔ rainbowantiques@aol.com
Est. 1998 *Stock size* Large
Stock Italian, French 1880–1940 period lighting, chandeliers, lamps, lanterns
Open Mon–Sat 10.30am–5.30pm or by appointment
Fairs Battersea Decorative Antiques Fair, House and Garden
Services Restorations, re-wiring

Rainbow Too Interiors
Contact Mr Fabio Bergomi
✉ **303 Munster Road, Fulham, London, SW6 6BJ** Ⓟ
☎ 020 7385 1323
Ⓜ 07879 811077
Ⓔ rainbowantiques@aol.com
Est. 1999 *Stock size* Large
Stock Italian and French period and decorative lighting
Open Mon–Sat 10.30am–5.30pm or by appointment
Fairs Battersea Decorative Antiques Fair, House & Garden
Services Restorations

Daphne Rankin & Ian Conn Oriental Antiques (LAPADA)
Contact Ms Sara Reynolds
✉ **608 King's Road, London, SW6 2DX** Ⓟ
☎ 020 7384 1847 Ⓕ 020 7384 1847
Ⓜ 07774 487713
Est. 1979 *Stock size* Large
Stock 17th–19thC Japanese Imari, Chinese export porcelain, Rose Mandarin, Blue Canton, tortoiseshell tea caddies
Open Mon–Sat 10.30am–6pm or by appointment
Fairs Olympia (June, Nov)

Red Room
Contact Ms Lei Jia
✉ **72 Farm Lane, Fulham, London, SW6 1QA** Ⓟ
☎ 020 7386 8777 Ⓕ 020 7385 3747
Ⓜ 07798 801707
Ⓔ compact@red-room.com
Ⓦ www.red-room.com
Est. 1997 *Stock size* Medium
Stock 18th–19thC Chinese decorative antique furniture
Open Wed–Fri 11am–5pm Sat 11am–3pm
Fairs Battersea

Soosan
Contact Suzanna Murray
✉ **598a King's Road, London, SW6 2DX** Ⓟ
☎ 020 7731 2063 Ⓕ 020 7731 1566
Ⓦ www.soosan.co.uk
Est. 1996 *Stock size* Large
Stock Asian interiors
Open Mon–Sat 10am–6pm
Services Restorations

Stephen Sprake Antiques
Contact Mr S Sprake
✉ **283 Lillie Road, London, SW6 7LL** Ⓟ
☎ 020 7381 3209 Ⓕ 020 7381 9502
Ⓜ 07710 922225
Est. 1998 *Stock size* Medium
Stock 18th–20thC English and French furniture, lighting, unusual architectural pieces
Open Mon–Sat 10.30am–5.30pm

Through The Looking Glass
Contact John Pulton
✉ **563 King's Road, London, SW6 2EB**
☎ 020 7736 7799 Ⓕ 020 7602 3678
Stock size Large
Stock 19thC mirrors
Open Mon–Sat 10am–5.30pm closed Sun

Whiteway & Waldron Ltd
Contact Mr G Kirkland
305 Munster Road, London, SW6 6BJ
020 7381 3195 020 7381 3195
sales@whiteway-waldron.co.uk
www.whiteway-waldron.co.uk
Est. 1978 *Stock size* Large
Stock Religious Victoriana, statues, chalices, sanctuary lamps, crucifixes, candlesticks
Open Mon–Fri 10am–6pm Sat 11am–4pm

York Gallery Ltd
Contact Mr G Beyer
569 King's Road, London, SW6 2EB
020 7736 2260 020 7736 2260
Est. 1989 *Stock size* Large
Stock Antique prints
Open Mon–Sat 10.30am–5.30pm
Services Picture framing

SW7

Atlantic Bay Gallery (BADA)
Contact Mr Wojtek Grodzinski
14 Gloucester Road, London, SW7 4RB
020 7589 8489 020 7589 8189
07831 455492
atlanticbaygallery@btinternet.com
www.atlanticbaycarpet.com
Est. 1945 *Stock size* Large
Stock Oriental and European carpets and textiles, Islamic and Indian art
Open Mon–Fri 9am–5.30pm
Services Valuations, restorations

Bonhams & Brooks
Montpelier Street, London, SW7 1HH
020 7393 3900 020 7393 3905
info@bonhams.com
www.bonhams.com
Est. 1793
Open Mon–Fri 9am–4.30pm Sun 11am–3pm
Sales Regular sales of antique and modern guns and militaria, antiquities, books, maps and manuscripts, clocks and watches, coins, collectables, including toys, scientific instruments and entertainment memorabilia, carpets and rugs, contemporary ceramics, ceramics and glass, decorative arts, design, furniture, Islamic works of art, jewellery, musical instruments, pictures, frames, Oriental works of art, portrait miniatures, silver, textiles, tribal art and vintage pens. In addition to general sales, regional salerooms offer more specialized areas of interest including sporting memorabilia and wines and spirits. Regular house and attic sales across the country; contact London offices for further details (London)
Catalogues Yes

Christie's South Kensington
85 Old Brompton Road, London, SW7 3LD
020 7581 7611 020 7321 3311
www.christies.com
Est. 1766
Open Tues–Fri 9am–5pm Mon 9am–7.30pm
Sales Weekly furniture sale Wed 10.30am. Fortnightly sale of silver Tues 2pm and ceramics Tues 10.30am and 2pm. Fortnightly jewellery sale Tues 2pm and pictures Thurs 10.30am, viewing Sun 1–4pm Mon 9am–7.30pm Tues–Fri 9am–5pm
Catalogues Yes

Julie Collino
Contact Julie Collino
15 Glendower Place, South Kensington, London, SW7 3DR
020 7584 4733
Est. 1968 *Stock size* Medium
Stock Furniture, fabrics, pottery, watercolours, etchings
Open Mon–Fri 11am–6pm Sat 2–6pm or by appointment

Gloucester Road Bookshop
Contact Mrs Meagan Thompson
123 Gloucester Road, London, SW7 4TE
020 7370 3503 020 7373 0610
manager@gloucesterbooks.co.uk
www.gloucesterbooks.co.uk
Est. 1983 *Stock size* Large
Stock Antiquarian, rare, second-hand books, modern literature, academic, art, first editions
Open Mon–Fri 8.30am–10.30pm Sat Sun 10.30am–6.30pm
Services Catalogues, shipping, booksearch

M P Levene Ltd (BADA)
Contact Mr Martin Levene
5 Thurloe Place, London, SW7 2RR
020 7589 3755 020 7589 9908
silver@mplevene.co.uk
mplevene.co.uk
Est. 1989 *Stock size* Medium
Stock Antique and modern English silver, silver cufflinks, cutlery sets, handmade silver scale models
Open Mon–Fri 9am–6pm Sat 9am–1.30pm
Services Valuations

SW8

French House Antiques
Contact Marcus Hazell
125 Queenstown Road, Battersea, London, SW8 3RH
020 7978 2228 020 7978 2340
info@thefrenchhouse.co.uk
www.thefrenchhouse.co.uk
Est. 1998 *Stock size* Medium
Stock French furniture, beds, mirrors
Open Mon–Sat 10am–6pm

Paul Orssich (PBFA)
Contact Paul Orssich
2 St Stephen's Terrace, South Lambeth, London, SW8 1DH
020 7787 0030 020 7735 9612
paulo@orssich.com
www.orssich.com
Est. 1980 *Stock size* Large
Stock Antiquarian, rare and out-of-print books on Hispanic topics
Open By appointment
Fairs Bonnington North Map Fair
Services Valuations, book search

SW10

Adam & Eve Books
Contact Mr S Dickson
18a Basement, Redcliffe Square, London, SW10 9JZ
020 7370 4535
07961 316 918
stephen.dickson@virgin.net
Est. 1999 *Stock size* Small
Stock Antiquarian, Middle East, travel, first editions, modern first editions a speciality
Open Mon–Fri 11am–4pm
Fairs Royal National Hotel Book Fair

Paul Andrews Antiques
Contact Lizzie Bluff
The Furniture Cave, 533 King's Road, London, SW10 0TZ P
☎ 020 7352 4584 F 020 7351 7815
E mail@paulandrews.co.uk
W www.paulandrewsantiques.co.uk
Est. 1969 *Stock size* Large
Stock Eclectic furniture, sculpture, tapestries, paintings, works of art
Open Mon–Sat 10am–6pm Sun noon–5pm

Bonhams & Brooks
65–69 Lots Road, London, SW10 0RN
☎ 020 7393 3900 F 020 7393 3906
E info@bonhams.com
W www.bonhams.com
Est. 1793
Open 9am–4.30pm Mon–Fri 11am–3pm Sun, viewing only
Sales Regular sales of furniture, carpets, ceramics, glass, Oriental works of art, 19thC oils, watercolours, modern pictures, prints, frames, toys, dolls, textiles, rock and pop, tribal art, decorative arts
Catalogues Yes

Brown's
Contact Mr N McAuliffe
First Floor, The Furniture Cave, 533 King's Road, London, SW10 0TZ P
☎ 020 7352 2046
W www.thecave.co.uk
Est. 1972 *Stock size* Medium
Stock 18th–20thC furniture, chandeliers, lighting, tapestries, furniture, accessories
Open Mon–Sat 10am–6pm Sun noon–4pm

Chelsea Gallery and Il Libro (LAPADA)
Contact Mr S Toscani
The Plaza, 535 King's Road, Chelsea, London, SW10 0SZ P
☎ 020 7823 3248 F 020 7352 1579
Est. 1978 *Stock size* Medium
Stock Antique illustrated books, literature, prints, maps, specializing in natural history, travel, architecture, history
Open Mon–Sat 10am–7pm
Services Framing

The Classic Library
Contact Gerry Freeman
1st floor, 533 King's Road, London, SW10 0TZ
☎ 020 7376 7653 F 020 7376 7653
Stock size Large
Stock Antiquarian books, bookcases, library furniture, prints
Open Mon–Sat 10am–6pm Sun noon–5pm

Kenneth Harvey Antiques (LAPADA)
Contact Mr K Harvey
The Furniture Cave, 533 King's Road, London, SW10 0TZ P
☎ 020 7352 3775 F 020 7352 3759
E mail@kennethharvey.com
Est. 1982 *Stock size* Large
Stock English–French furniture, chandeliers, mirrors, late 17thC–20thC, leather armchairs
Open Mon–Sat 10am–6pm Sun 11am–5pm

Simon Hatchwell Antiques
Contact Mr A Hatchwell
533 King's Road, London, SW10 0TZ P
☎ 020 7351 2344 F 020 7351 3520
E hatchwell@callnetuk.com
Est. 1961 *Stock size* Large
Stock English and Continental furniture, early 19th–20thC chandeliers, lighting, bronzes, barometers, clocks including grandfather clocks
Open Mon–Sat 10am–6pm Sun 11.30am–5pm
Fairs Olympia (June)
Services Valuations, restorations

John Nicholas Antiques
Contact Mr Nicholas McAuliffe
First Floor, 533 King's Road, London, SW10 0TZ P
☎ 020 7352 2046
W www.thecave.co.uk
Est. 1999 *Stock size* Medium
Stock 18th–20thC furniture, accessories, chandeliers, lighting, tapestries
Open Mon–Sat 10am–6pm Sun noon–4pm

L'Encoignure
Contact Thomas Kerr
517 King's Road, London, SW10 0TX P
☎ 020 7351 6465 F 020 7351 4744
E kerrant@globalnet.co.uk
Est. 1994 *Stock size* Large
Stock 18th–19thC French furniture, decorative items, Continental furniture
Open Mon–Sat 10am–6pm
Services Interior design

Langfords Marine Antiques (BADA, LAPADA)
Contact Mrs J Langford
The Plaza, 535 King's Road, London, SW10 0SZ P
☎ 020 7351 4881 F 020 7352 0763
E langford@dircon.co.uk
W www.langfords.co.uk
Est. 1950 *Stock size* Large
Stock Nautical artefacts
Open Mon–Sat 10am–5.30pm

Stephen Long
Contact Mr S Long
348 Fulham Road, London, SW10 9UH P
☎ 020 7352 8226
Est. 1966 *Stock size* Medium
Stock Painted furniture, small decorative items, English pottery, 1780–1850
Open Mon–Fri 9.30am–1pm 2.15–5pm Sat 10am–12.30pm

Lots Road Galleries
Contact Patricia Roos or Melina Papadopolous
71–73 Lots Road, Chelsea, London, SW10 0RM P
☎ 020 7351 7771 F 020 7376 6899
E info@lotsroad.com
W www.lotsroad.com
Est. 1979
Open Mon–Wed 9am–6pm Thurs 9am–7pm Fri 9am–4pm Sat 10am–4pm Sun 10am–7pm
Sales 2 sales each Monday, 1pm modern and reproduction furnishings, 6pm antiques sale, viewing Thurs 5–7pm Fri–Sun 10am–4pm Mon 9am–6pm
Frequency 2 per month
Catalogues Yes

Phoenix Trading Co
Contact Mr T Shalloe
The Furniture Cave, 533 King's Road, London, SW10 0TZ P
☎ 020 7351 6543 F 020 7352 9803
W www.phoenixtrading.co.uk.
Est. 1979 *Stock size* Large
Stock Antique and reproduction decorative accessories, furniture, porcelain, bronze, marble
Open Mon–Sat 10am–6pm Sun 11am–5pm

H W Poulter & Son
Contact Mr D Poulter
279 Fulham Road, London, SW10 9PZ P
020 7352 7268 F 020 7351 0984
Est. 1946 *Stock size* Large
Stock 18th–19thC marble, wooden, stone fireplaces, accessories
Open Mon–Fri 9am–5pm Sat 9am–noon
Services Restoration of marble

Francis Smith Ltd
Contact Mr Norman Ashford
107 Lots Road, Chelsea, London, SW10 0RN P
020 7349 0011 F 020 7349 0770
Est. 1835
Open Mon–Fri 9am–6pm
Sales Antiques and general sale Tues 6pm, viewing Sun 11am–4pm Mon 9am–7pm Tues 9am–6pm prior to sale
Frequency Fortnightly
Catalogues Yes

John Thornton
Contact John or Caroline Thornton
455 Fulham Road, London, SW10 9UZ P
020 7352 8810
Est. 1964 *Stock size* Medium
Stock Antiquarian and second-hand books, Catholic and Anglo-Catholic theology
Open Mon–Sat 10am–5.30pm

SW11

Banana Dance Ltd
Contact Mr J Daltrey
Unit 20, The Northcote Road, Antiques Market, 155a Northcote Road, Battersea, London, SW11 2QT P
020 8699 7728/7354 3125
F 020 8699 7728
M 07976 296987
E jonathan@bananadance.com
W www.bananadance.com
Est. 1988 *Stock size* Large
Stock Clarice Cliff, Art Deco, ceramics, silver, silver plate
Open Mon–Sat 10am–6pm Sun noon–5pm
Fairs NEC, Alexandra Palace
Services Valuations, mail order

Battersea Collectables
Contact Mr David Nurse
495 Battersea Park Road, London, SW11 4LW P
020 7228 8820 F 020 7978 6188
M 07939 087757
E revdavidnurse@onetel.net.uk
Est. 1998 *Stock size* Medium
Stock China, clocks, furniture, pictures, mirrors, collectables, Asian Far East furniture
Open Mon–Sat 10am–6pm
Services Valuations, shipping

Braemar Antiques
Contact Mrs Marlis Ramos de Deus
Braemar Villas, 113 Northcote Road, London, SW11 6PW P
020 7924 5628
Est. 1994 *Stock size* Medium
Stock Decorative antiques, furniture, chandeliers, mirrors, fabrics
Open Mon–Sat 10am–5.30pm
Fairs Horticultural Hall, Kensington Brocante

Eccles Road Antiques
Contact Mrs H Rix
60 Eccles Road, London, SW11 1LX P
020 7228 1638 F 020 8767 5313
M 07885 172087
Est. 1985 *Stock size* Large
Stock Victoriana, pine and mahogany furniture, collectables, kitchenware
Open Tues–Sat 10am–5pm Sun noon–5pm
Fairs Ardingly

Garland Antiques
Contact Mrs Garland Beech
74 Chatham Road, London, SW11 6HG P
020 7924 4284 F 020 7924 4284
Est. 1998 *Stock size* Medium
Stock English and Continental furniture, decorative items
Open Tues–Sat 10am–6pm Sun noon–5pm
Services Pine stripping

Northcote Road Antiques Market
Contact Mrs Gill Wilkins
155a Northcote Road, London, SW11 6QB P
020 7228 6850
Est. 1986 *Stock size* Large
No. of dealers 30
Stock Jewellery, prints, pictures, glass, Victoriana, Art Deco, furniture, lighting, silver, plate, textiles, old advertising
Open Mon–Sat 10am–6pm Sun noon–5pm
Services Café

Pairs Antiques
Contact Iain Brunt
Unit 6, Parkfields Industrial Estate, Culvert Road, Battersea, London, SW11 5BA P
020 7622 6446 F 0870 1273570
M 07798 684694
E pairs2@aol.com
W www.pairsantiques.co.uk
Est. 1995 *Stock size* Large
Stock 18th–19thC English and Continental pairs of furniture
Open Wed 10am–4pm Sat 10am–2pm or by appointment
Services Valuations, restorations, shipping, upholstery

Wood Pigeon
Contact Mr J Taylor or Mrs B Cunnell
71 Webb's Road, London, SW11 6SD P
020 7223 8668 F 020 8647 8790
M 07958 787676/07932 780707
Est. 1996 *Stock size* Medium
Stock French, country, painted, upholstered furniture, decorative items
Open Tues–Sat 10.30am–5.30pm Sun noon–4pm
Services Decorative furniture painting, upholstery

Robert Young Antiques (BADA)
Contact Sharon Fraser
68 Battersea Bridge Road, London, SW11 3AG P
020 7228 7847 F 020 7585 0489
E r.yantiques@aol.com
Est. 1975 *Stock size* Medium
Stock Country furniture, folk art, treen
Open Tues–Fri 9.30am–6pm Sat 10am–5pm
Fairs Olympia (June), Chelsea

SW13

Christine Bridge Antiques (BADA, LAPADA, CINOA)
Contact Christine Bridge or Darryl Bowles
78 Castelnau, London, SW13 9EX P
07000 4 GLASS/020 8741 5501
F 07000 FAX GLASS/020 8255 0172
M 07831 126668
E christine@bridge-antiques.com

LONDON

Ⓦ www.bridge-antiques.com or www.antiqueglass.co.uk
Est. 1970 *Stock size* Medium
Stock 18thC collectors' glass, 19thC coloured and decorative glass
Open By appointment
Fairs BADA, Olympia, fairs in USA and Far East

Simon Coleman Antiques
Contact Simon Coleman
40 White Hart Lane, Barnes, London, SW13 0PZ P
☎ 020 8878 5037
Est. 1977 *Stock size* Large
Stock Fully restored farmhouse tables, narrow serving tables
Open Mon–Fri 9.30am–6pm Sat 9.30am–5pm

Joy McDonald Antiques
Contact Ms Angela McDonald
50 Station Road, London, SW13 0LP P
☎ 020 8876 6184 Ⓕ 020 8876 6184
Est. 1966 *Stock size* Large
Stock 18th–20thC mirrors, country furniture, decorative items
Open Tues–Sat 10am–5.30pm

Tobias & The Angel
Contact Angel Hughes
68 White Hart Lane, London, SW13 0PZ P
☎ 020 8878 8902 Ⓕ 020 8296 0058
Est. 1985 *Stock size* Large
Stock Country antiques, furniture, lampshades, pictures, mirrors, linen, pretty and useful objects for the home
Open Mon–Sat 10am–6pm
Services Mail order, bespoke furniture

SW14

The Arts and Crafts Furniture Co Ltd
Contact Mr P Rogers
49 Sheen Lane, East Sheen, London, SW14 8AB P
☎ 020 8876 6544 Ⓕ 020 8876 6544
Ⓔ acfc@49sheen.fsnetco.uk
Ⓦ www.acsc.co.uk
Est. 1989 *Stock size* Large
Stock Arts and Crafts furniture, copperware, ceramics, fabrics, artworks
Open Mon–Fri 10am–6pm Sat 10am–5pm
Services Restorations

Paul Foster Books (ABA PBFA)
Contact P Foster
119 Sheen Lane, East Sheen, London, SW14 8AE P
☎ 020 8876 7424 Ⓕ 020 8876 7424
Ⓔ paulfosterbooks@btinternet.com
Est. 1990 *Stock size* Medium
Stock Antiquarian, rare, second-hand, out-of-print books
Open Mon–Sat 10.30am–6pm
Fairs Olympia, Chelsea

SW15

30th Century Comics (BSSA)
Contact Mr H Stangroom
18 Lower Richmond Road, London, SW15 1JP P
☎ 020 8788 2052
Ⓔ rob@thirtiethcentury.free-online.co.uk
Est. 1994 *Stock size* Large
Stock British and American vintage and new collectors' comics, annuals, 1930s–1970s
Open Mon–Wed Sat 10.30am–6pm Thurs Fri 10.30am–7pm Sun 11am–5pm
Fairs Royal National Comic Marts, Camden Centre Comic Marts
Services Quarterly catalogue

The Clock Clinic Ltd (LAPADA)
Contact Mr R Pedler FBHI
85 Lower Richmond Road, Putney, London, SW15 1EU P
☎ 020 8788 1407 Ⓕ 020 8780 2838
Ⓔ clockclinic@btconnect.com
Ⓦ www.clockclinic.co.uk
Est. 1971 *Stock size* Medium
Stock Antique clocks, barometers, all overhauled and guaranteed
Open Tues–Fri 9am–6pm Sat 9am–1pm
Fairs Olympia (Feb, June, Nov)
Services Valuations, restorations, repairs

Hanshan Tang Books (ABA)
Contact Mr J Cayley
Unit 3, Ashburton Centre, 276 Cortis Road, London, SW15 3AY P
☎ 020 8788 4464 Ⓕ 020 8780 1565
Ⓔ hst@hanshan.com
Ⓦ www.hanshan.com
Est. 1974 *Stock size* Medium
Stock East Asian art, archaeology
Open By appointment
Services Book search, library purchases

Jorgens Antiques
Contact Mr J Dolleris
40 Lower Richmond Road, London, SW15 1JP P
☎ 020 8789 7329 Ⓕ 020 8789 7329
Est. 1969 *Stock size* Large
Stock 18th–early 19thC Scandinavian, English, and Continental antique furniture, china, decorative items, mirrors, objets d'art
Open Tues–Fri 11am–5pm Sat by appointment

Lloyds International Auction Galleries Ltd
Contact Mr Mick Bown
118 Putney Bridge Road, London, SW15 2NQ P
☎ 020 8788 7777 Ⓕ 020 8874 5390
Ⓔ lloyds_international@compuserve.com
Ⓦ www.lloyds-auction.co.uk
Est. 1944
Open Mon–Fri 9.30am–5.30pm
Sales Furniture, paintings and collectables sale Sat 11am, viewing Fri 10.30am–7.30pm Sat 9am prior to sale. Jewellery sale Tues 11am, viewing Mon 9.30am–4pm. General Met Police 'Lost Property' sale Wed 5pm, viewing Wed 10.30am–4.45pm prior to sale
Frequency Fortnightly all sales
Catalogues Yes

SW16

H C Baxter & Sons (BADA, LAPADA)
Contact Mr G Baxter
40 Drewstead Road, London, SW16 1AB P
☎ 020 8769 5969 Ⓕ 020 8769 0898
Ⓔ partners@hcbaxter.co.uk
Ⓦ www.hcbaxter.co.uk
Est. 1928 *Stock size* Medium
Stock 18th–19thC English furniture, decorative items
Trade only Public by appointment only
Open Wed Thurs 9am–5pm
Fairs Olympia (Nov, Feb) BADA, Duke of York, Grosvenor House
Services Valuations

A and J Fowle
Contact Mr A Fowle
542 Streatham High Road, London, SW16 3QF
020 8764 2896
0796 8058790
Est. 1950 *Stock size* Medium
Stock General antiques, furniture, silver, china, paintings
Open Mon–Sun 9am–6pm or by appointment
Fairs Ardingly

Kantuta
Contact Mrs N Wright
1d Gleneagle Road, London, SW16 6AX
020 8677 6701
Est. 1986 *Stock size* Medium
Stock Antique furniture
Open Mon–Sat 10am–6pm
Services Restorations

Rapscallion Ltd
Contact Mrs P Barry
25 Shrubbery Road, London, SW16 2AS
020 8769 8078
Est. 1981 *Stock size* Large
Stock Victoriana, collectables
Open Tues Wed Fri Sat 10am–5pm

SW17

Kerry Ward Antiques
Contact Mrs K Sparkes
30 Bellevue Road, London, SW17 7EF
020 8682 2682
Est. 1993 *Stock size* Large
Stock 19thC painted French furniture, country-look items, French shutters
Open Tues–Sat 10.30am–5.30pm Sun noon–4pm

SW18

Bertie's
Contact Mrs B Ferguson
1st Floor, 284 Merton Road, London, SW18 5JN
020 8874 2520
Est. 1985 *Stock size* Small
Stock Antique and reproduction pine furniture, china, collectables
Open Tues–Sat 9.30am–5.30pm
Services Bespoke pine furniture

The Earlsfield Bookshop
Contact Mr C Dixon
513 Garratt Lane, Wandsworth, London, SW18 4SW
020 8946 3744
Est. 1994 *Stock size* Medium
Stock General books
Open Mon–Thurs 4am–6pm Fri 11am–6pm Sat 10am–5pm
Fairs Kempton Park, Bloomsbury
Services Valuations

Eastern Books of London
Contact Mr P Eastman
81 Replingham Road, London, SW18 5LU
020 8871 0880 020 8877 9757
info@easternbooks.com
www.easternbooks.com
Est. 1989 *Stock size* Large
Stock Antiquarian, rare, and second-hand books, Oriental, Middle Eastern, African, maps, prints
Open Mon–Sun noon–7pm
Services Valuations, book search, library building

The House Hospital
Contact Mr J Brunton
9 Ferrier Street, London, SW18 1SW
020 8870 8202
Est. 1983 *Stock size* Medium
Stock Fireplaces, cast-iron radiators, doors, handles, general architectural salvage
Open Mon–Sat 10am–5pm
Services Sandblasting, paint stripping

Just a Second
Contact Mr J Ferguson
284 Merton Road, London, SW18 5JN
020 8874 2520
Est. 1980 *Stock size* Medium
Stock General antiques, good quality furniture
Open Tues–Sat 9.30am–5.30pm
Services Valuations, restorations

SW19

Adams Rooms Antiques and Interiors (LAPADA)
Contact Mrs Seymour-Cole
18–20 The Ridgeway, Wimbledon Village, London, SW19 4QN
020 8946 7047 020 8946 7476
info@antiques-index.com
www.antiques-index.com
Est. 1973 *Stock size* Large
Stock 18th–19thC English and French furniture, objects
Open Mon–Sat 10am–5pm
Services Valuations, restorations, shipping

Coromandel
Contact Barbara Leigh
PO Box 9772, London, SW19 3ZG
0208 543 9115 0208 543 6225
info@antiqueboxes.com
Est. 1996
Stock Colonial antiques, decorative arts
Open By appointment
Services Ivory and tortoiseshell restorations

Priestley and Ferraro
Contact David Priestley
17 King Street, London, SW19 6QU
020 7930 6228 020 7930 6226
info@priestleyandferraro.com
www.priestleyandferraro.com
Est. 1994 *Stock size* Medium
Stock Early Chinese art
Open Mon–Fri 9.30am–5.30pm
Fairs International Ceramics Fair, Asian Art

Mark J West (BADA)
Contact Mr M West
39b High Street, London, SW19 5BY
020 8946 2811
Est. 1977 *Stock size* Large
Stock 18th–19thC English and Continental glassware
Open Mon–Sat 10am–5.30pm

SW20

W F Turk Fine Antique Clocks (LAPADA, CINOA)
Contact Mr W Turk
355 Kingston Road, London, SW20 8JX
020 8543 3231 020 8543 3231
Est. 1979 *Stock size* Large
Stock Antique clocks, 17th–19thC longcase and bracket clocks, French decorative mantel and carriage clocks
Open Tues–Fri 9am–5.30pm Sat 9am–4pm
Fairs Olympia, LAPADA, NEC
Services Valuations, restorations, repairs, sales

WEST

W1

⊞ David Aaron
Contact Mr David Aaron
✉ **22 Berkeley Square, London, W1J 6EH** Ⓟ
☎ 020 7491 9588 Ⓕ 020 7491 9522
Est. 1910 *Stock size* Large
Stock Worldwide ancient art, rare carpets
Open Mon–Fri 9am–6pm Sat by appointment only
Services Valuations, restorations

⊞ Adrian Alan Ltd (BADA, LAPADA)
Contact Miss H Alan
✉ **63 & 66–67 South Audley Street, London, W1Y 5FB** Ⓟ
☎ 020 7495 2324 Ⓕ 020 7495 0204
Ⓔ enquiries@adrianalan.com
Ⓦ www.adrianalan.com
Est. 1964 *Stock size* Large
Stock Furniture, light fittings, mirrors, objets d'art, paintings, statues, garden furniture, pianos, 19thC Continental furniture a speciality
Open Mon–Fri 9.30am–6pm
Fairs Olympia (June)
Services Restorations, shipping, storage

⊞ Altea Maps and Books (PBFA, ABA)
Contact Mr M Demartini
✉ **3rd Floor, 91 Regent Street, London, W1R 7TB** Ⓟ
☎ 020 7494 9060 Ⓕ 020 7287 7938
Ⓔ altea@antique-maps.co.uk
Ⓦ www.antique-maps.co.uk
Est. 1993 *Stock size* Medium
Stock 15th–19thC maps, atlases, travel books
Open By appointment
Fairs PBFA, Russell Hotel, Chelsea Book Fair
Services Valuations, sale on commission

⊞ Aytac Antiques (NAWCC)
Contact Mr O Aytac
✉ **Grays Antiques Market, Unit 331–332, 5–8 Davies Street, London, W1Y 1LB** Ⓟ
☎ 020 7629 7380 Ⓕ 020 7629 7380
Ⓔ o.aytac@virgin.com
Est. 1982 *Stock size* Large
Stock Vintage wristwatches, clocks, 19thC French bronzes
Open Mon–Fri 10.30am–5pm
Services Wristwatch restoration, repair

⊞ J and A Beare Ltd (BADA)
Contact Simon Morris or Frances Gilham
✉ **30 Queen Anne Street, London, W1G 8HX** Ⓟ
☎ 020 7307 9666 Ⓕ 020 7307 9651
Ⓔ violins@beares.com
Ⓦ www.beares.com
Stock size Large
Stock Musical instruments of the violin family
Open Mon–Fri 10am–12.30pm 1.30pm–5pm
Services Valuations

⊞ Linda Bee
Contact Linda Bee
✉ **1–7 Davies Mews, London, W1Y 1AR** Ⓟ
☎ 020 7629 5921 Ⓕ 020 7629 5921
Ⓜ 07956 276384
Ⓦ www.emews.com
Est. 1992 *Stock size* Large
Stock Vintage fashion accessories, handbags, perfume bottles, powder compacts, costume jewellery
Open Mon–Fri 1–6pm or by appointment
Fairs Alexandra Palace
Services Valuations

⊞ Brian Beet
Contact Mr B Beet
✉ **Bond Street Silver Galleries, 111 New Bond Street, London, W1S 1DP** Ⓟ
☎ 020 7437 4975 Ⓕ 020 7495 8635
Est. 1979 *Stock size* Medium
Stock Provincial and Colonial silver, paktong, silvered brass, small silver collectables
Open By appointment
Fairs Summer Olympia

⊞ Daniel Bexfield Antiques (LAPADA, CINOA)
Contact Mr D Bexfield
✉ **26 Burlington Arcade, Mayfair, London, W1V 9AD** Ⓟ
☎ 020 7491 1720 Ⓕ 020 7491 1730
Ⓔ antiques@bexfield.co.uk
Ⓦ www.bexfield.co.uk
Est. 1981 *Stock size* Large
Stock Fine quality silver, objects of virtue, 17th–20thC
Open Mon–Sat 9am–6pm
Fairs LAPADA, Chelsea
Services Valuations, restorations

⊞ H Blairman & Sons Ltd (BADA)
Contact Martin Levy, Patricia Levy or Sara Sowerby
✉ **119 Mount Street, London, W1K 3NL** Ⓟ
☎ 020 7493 0444 Ⓕ 020 7495 0766
Ⓔ blairman@atlas.co.uk
Est. 1884 *Stock size* Large
Stock 18th–19thC furniture, works of art
Open Mon–Fri 9am–6pm or by appointment
Fairs Grosvenor House Fair, International Fine Art & Antique Dealers Show, New York
Services Catalogues

⊞ N Bloom and Son (1912) Ltd (LAPADA, CINOA, BACA Award Winner 2001)
Contact Ian Harris
✉ **Bond Street Antiques Centre, 124 New Bond Street, London, W1S 1DX**
☎ 020 7629 5060 Ⓕ 020 7493 2528
Ⓔ nbloom@nbloom.com
Ⓦ www.nbloom.com
Est. 1912 *Stock size* Large
Stock 1860–1960 jewellery, silver
Open Mon–Fri 10.30am–5.30pm Sat 11am–5.30pm
Fairs Olympia (June), LAPADA, Claridges (April), Miami (Jan)
Services Valuations, restorations, catalogue

⊞ Blunderbuss Antiques
Contact Mr C Greenaway
✉ **29 Thayer Street, London, W1U 2QW** Ⓟ
☎ 020 7486 2444 Ⓕ 020 7935 1645
Ⓔ mail@blunderbuss-antiques.co.uk
Ⓦ www.blunderbuss-antiques.co.uk
Est. 1968 *Stock size* Large
Stock 16thC–WWII weapons, militaria
Open Tues–Fri 9.30am–4.30pm

⌂ The Bond Street Antiques Centre
Contact Neil Jackson
✉ **124 New Bond Street, London, W1Y 9AE** Ⓟ
☎ 020 7493 1854 Ⓕ 020 7351 5350
Ⓔ antique@dial.pipex.com
Est. 1968 *Stock size* Large
No. of dealers 35

Stock Jewellery, silver, fine vintage watches
Open Mon–Fri 10am–6.45pm Sat 11am–5.30pm

Tony Booth (PADA)
Contact Mr Tony Booth
Grays Antique Market, Stall 322, 58 Davies Street, London, W1
☎ 020 7491 1718 Ⓕ 020 8810 6339
Ⓜ 07770 390749
Ⓔ tonybooth44@hotmail.com
Est. 1990 *Stock size* Medium
Stock Silver
Open Mon–Fri 10am–6pm
Fairs Ardingly, NEC

Patrick Boyd-Carpenter
Contact Mr P Boyd-Carpenter
Grays Antique Market, 58 Davies Street, London, W1Y 2LP
☎ 020 7491 7623 Ⓕ 020 7491 7623
Ⓔ patrickboyd_carpenter@hotmail.com
Est. 1986 *Stock size* Large
Stock Wide range of antiques, 16th–18thC sculpture, paintings, prints
Open Mon–Fri 10.30am–5.30pm or by appointment
Services Valuations, restorations

Brandt Oriental Antiques (BADA)
Contact Robert Brandt
1st Floor, 29 New Bond Street, London, W1S 2RL
☎ 020 7499 8835 Ⓕ 020 7409 1882
Ⓜ 07774 989661
Ⓔ brandt@nildram.co.uk
Est. 1980 *Stock size* Medium
Stock Japanese metalwork and screens, the China trade
Open By appointment
Fairs June Olympia, New York

Paul Champkins Oriental Art (BADA)
Contact Mr P Champkins
41 Dover Street, London, W1X 3RB
☎ 020 7495 4600 Ⓕ 01235 751658
Ⓔ pc@paulchampkins.demon.co.uk
Est. 1995 *Stock size* Medium
Stock Chinese, Korean, Japanese porcelain, works of art
Open By appointment
Fairs Grosvenor House, International Asian Art Fair New York, Olympia (Winter)
Services Valuations, restorations, auction purchasing advice

Antoine Chenevière Fine Arts Ltd (BADA)
Contact Mr Chenevière
27 Bruton Street, London, W1X 7DB
☎ 020 7491 1007 Ⓕ 020 7495 6173
Ⓔ finearts@antoinecheneviere.com
Stock size Medium
Stock 18th–19thC Russian, Austrian, German and Italian furniture, objets d'art
Open Mon–Sat 9.30am–6pm
Fairs Grosvenor House, The Armoury Fair

Classical Numismatic Group Inc. (BNTA)
Contact Mrs C Wingate
14 Old Bond Street, London, W1X 3DB
☎ 020 7495 1888 Ⓕ 020 7499 5916
Ⓔ cng@historicalcoins.com
Ⓦ www.historicalcoins.com
Est. 1990
Stock Coins, Greek, Roman, Medieval, European to end of 18thC
Open Mon–Fri 9.30am–5.30pm
Fairs Coinex, Marriott
Services Valuations, auctions, phone for details

Sandra Cronan Ltd (BADA)
Contact Sandra Cronan or Blane Thompson
18 Burlington Arcade, London, W1J 0PN
☎ 020 7491 4851 Ⓕ 020 7493 2758
Ⓔ sandracronanltd@btinternet.com
Est. 1978 *Stock size* Medium
Stock 18th–early 20thC jewellery
Open Mon–Fri 10am–5pm
Fairs Grosvenor House, March BADA, The Armoury
Services Valuations, restorations, repairs, design commission

Cyjer Jewellery Ltd
Contact Mrs E M Plampton
143/144 , Grays Antique Market, 58 Davies Street, London, W1Y 2LP
☎ 020 7629 3206
Est. 1989 *Stock size* Large
Stock Georgian–Edwardian, Art Deco, modern jewellery
Open Mon–Fri 10.30am–5.30pm closed Tues
Fairs Copthorne Hotel, Runnymede Hotel
Services Restorations

Barry Davies Oriental Art (BADA)
Contact Barry Davies
1 Davies Street, London, W1K 3DB
☎ 020 7408 0207 Ⓕ 020 7493 3422
Ⓔ bdoa@btinternet.com
Ⓦ www.barrydavies.com
Est. 1976 *Stock size* Large
Stock Japanese works of art
Open Mon–Fri 9am–6pm

Adèle De Havilland
Contact Adèle De Havilland
The Bond Street Antique Centre, 124 New Bond Street, London, W1S 1DX
☎ 020 7499 7127
Est. 1971 *Stock size* Medium
Stock Oriental porcelain, netsuke, jade, ivory carvings, bronze figures, objects of virtue
Open Mon–Sat 10am–4pm

Deacon Antiques (GAGB)
Contact Mrs Deacon
L17 Grays Mews Antique Market, Davies Mews, London, W1K 5AB
☎ 020 7499 0911
Est. 1985 *Stock size* Small
Stock Decorative items of silver
Open Mon–Fri 10am–6pm

Dix Noonan Webb (BNTA, OMRS, OMSA)
Contact Mr C Webb
1 Old Bond Street, London, W1S 4PB
☎ 020 7499 5022 Ⓕ 020 7499 5023
Ⓔ auction@dnw.co.uk
Ⓦ www.dnw.co.uk
Est. 1991
Open Mon–Fri 8.30am–5.30pm
Sales Coins and military medals sale Wed, viewing Tues noon–1pm prior to sale
Frequency 10 per annum
Catalogues Yes

Charles Ede Ltd (BADA, ADA, IADA)
Contact Mr J Ede
20 Brook Street, London, W1K 5DE
☎ 020 7493 4944 Ⓕ 020 7491 2548
Ⓔ charlesede@attglobal.net
Ⓦ www.charlesede.com
Est. 1976 *Stock size* Medium
Stock Egyptian, Greek, Roman classical and pre-classical antiquities

Open Tues–Fri 12.30–4.30pm or by appointment
Fairs Grosvenor House
Services Valuations, bidding at auction, mail order

Peter Edwards
Contact Mr P Edwards
58 Davies Street, London, W1Y 2LP
020 7493 6044 F 020 7493 1440
Est. 1966 *Stock size* Medium
Stock 20thC jewellery, signed pieces
Open Mon–Fri 10am–6pm
Fairs Olympia, Harrogate
Services Valuations, restorations

Elvisly Yours
Contact Mr Sid Shaw
233 Baker Street, London, NW1 6XE
020 7486 2005
elvisly@globalnet.co.uk
www.elvisly-yours.com
Est. 1978 *Stock size* Large
Stock Elvis memorabilia
Open Mon–Sat 11am–9pm Sun 11am–8pm

Eskenazi Ltd (BADA)
Contact Mr J Eskenazi
10 Clifford Street, London, W1S 2LJ
020 7493 5464 F 020 7499 3136
eskArt@ad.com
Est. 1960 *Stock size* Medium
Stock Early Chinese works of art
Open Mon–Fri 9am–5.30pm

John Eskenazi Ltd (BADA)
Contact Kate Cook
15 Old Bond Street, London, W1S 4AX
020 7409 3001 F 020 7629 2146
john.eskenazi@john-eskenazi.com
www.john-eskenazi.com
Est. 1994 *Stock size* Medium
Stock South East Asian, Himalayan and Indian works of art, Oriental textiles and carpets
Open Mon–Fri 9am–6pm or by appointment
Fairs International Asian Art Fair

Simon Finch Rare Books (ABA, PBFA)
Contact Mr S Finch
53 Maddox Street, London, W1S 2PN
020 7499 0974 F 020 7499 0799
rarebooks@simonfinch.com
www.simonfinch.com
Est. 1982 *Stock size* Medium
Stock 15th–20thC books on art, architecture, literature, science, medicine
Open Mon–Fri 10am–6pm
Fairs Olympia, Chelsea, Grosvenor House
Services Valuations, library advice

J First Antiques
Contact Mr J First
Stand 310, Grays Antique Market, 58 Davies Street, London, W1Y 1LB
020 7409 2722 F 020 7409 2722
www.firstsilver18@hotmail.com
Est. 1967 *Stock size* Large
Stock Antique English silver collectables
Open Mon–Fri 10am–6pm
Fairs NEC

Matthew Foster
Contact Mr M Foster or Mr J Silver
Units 4, 5 & 6, Bond Street Antiques Centre, 124 New Bond Street, London, W1S 1DX
020 7629 4977 F 020 7629 4977
Est. 1987 *Stock size* Large
Stock Large stock of Victorian gold jewellery
Open Mon–Fri 10am–5.30pm Sat 11am–5.30pm
Fairs Olympia (June)

O Frydman
Contact Mr G Barnett
The Bond Street Silver Galleries, 111–112 New Bond Street, London, W1S 1DP
020 7493 4895 F 020 7493 4895
Est. 1929 *Stock size* Medium
Stock Second-hand and antique silver, Victorian silver, old Sheffield plate
Open Mon–Fri 9.30am–5.30pm
Services Valuations, renovations

Peter Gaunt
Contact Mr P Gaunt
Stand 120, Grays Antique Market, 58 Davies Street, London, W1K 5JF
020 7629 1072 F 020 7629 5253
ptg@peter-gaunt.fsnet.co.uk
Est. 1978 *Stock size* Large
Stock Antique silver including Georgian teaspoons, 17thC candlesticks
Open Mon–Fri 10am–5pm
Services Valuations

Gentry Antiques
Contact Marilyn Gentry
Grays Antiques Market Mews, Davies Street, London, W1Y 2LP
01993 832252
info@cornishwarecollector.co.uk
www.cornishwarecollector.co.uk
Est. 1998 *Stock size* Medium
Stock T G Green Cornish ware and other kitchenware
Open Mon–Fri 11am–5pm

The Gilded Lily (LAPADA, CINOA)
Contact Ms Korin Harvey
Stand 145–146, Grays Antique Market, 58 Davies Street, London, W1K 5LP
020 7499 6260 F 020 7499 6260
korinh@freenetname.co.uk
www.graysantiques.com
Est. 1970 *Stock size* Large
Stock Glamorous jewellery, signed pieces
Open Mon–Fri 10am–6pm
Fairs Olympia, LAPADA, Miami Beach, Hong Kong

Glendining's (BNTA, SFAA)
Contact Mr A Litherland
101 New Bond Street, London, W1S 1SR
020 7493 2445
Est. 1900
Open Mon–Fri 8.30am–5pm
Sales 4 coin sales, 3 medal sales, also arms, armour, militaria
Frequency 7 per annum
Catalogues Yes

Gordon's Medals (OMRS)
Contact Mr M Gordon
Stand G14–16, Grays Mews Antiques Market, Davies Mews, London, W1K 5AB
020 7495 0900 F 020 7495 0115
M 07976 266293
malcolm@gordonsmedals.co.uk
www.gordonsmedals.co.uk
Est. 1979 *Stock size* Large
Stock Militaria, uniforms, headgear, badges, medals, documents
Open Mon–Fri 10.30am–6pm
Fairs Brittania Fair, OMRS
Services Valuations

The Graham Gallery (LAPADA)
Contact Mr G Whittall
60 South Audley Street, Mayfair, London, W1K 2QW
☎ 020 7495 3151 Ⓕ 020 7495 3171
Ⓜ 07710 407 885
Est. 1979 *Stock size* Large
Stock 18–19thC furniture, 19thC oil paintings, objets d'art
Open Mon–Fri 10.30am–6pm or by appointment
Fairs Olympia (June), LAPADA

Graus Antiques
Contact Jackie Stern
Bond Street Silver Galleries, 111–112 New Bond Street, London, W1S 1DP
☎ 020 7629 6680 Ⓕ 020 7629 6651
Ⓔ eric@graus-antiques.demon.co.uk
Est. 1945 *Stock size* Large
Stock Antique pocket watches, jewellery
Open Mon–Fri 9am–5pm

Anita Gray (LAPADA)
Contact Mrs A Gray
Grays Antique Market, 58 Davies Street, London, W1Y 2LP
☎ 020 7408 1638 Ⓕ 020 7495 0707
Ⓔ info@chinese-porcelain.com
Ⓦ www.chinese-porcelain.com
Est. 1975 *Stock size* Medium
Stock Asian and European porcelain, works of art, 16th–18thC
Open Mon–Fri 10am–6pm
Fairs International Ceramics Fair

Grays Antique Market
Contact Caroline Churchill
58 Davies Street, London, W1K 5AB
☎ 020 7629 7034 Ⓕ 020 7493 9344
Ⓔ grays@clara.net
Ⓦ www.egrays.com
Est. 1978 *Stock size* Large
No. of dealers 300
Stock Asian art, jewellery, glass, collectables, silver, books
Open Mon–Fri 10am–6pm
Services Café

Anthony Green Antiques
Contact Anthony Green
Unit 39, The Bond Street Antiques Centre, 124 New Bond Street, London, W1S 1DX
☎ 0207 409 2854 Ⓕ 0207 409 7032
Ⓜ 07900 681469
Ⓔ vintagewatches@hotmail.com
Ⓦ www.anthonygreen.com
Est. 1985 *Stock size* Large
Stock Vintage wristwatches and antique pocket watches
Open Mon–Fri 10am–5pm Sat 11am–5pm

Simon Griffin Antiques Ltd
Contact Mr S Griffin
3 Royal Arcade, 28 Old Bond Street, London, W1S 4SB
☎ 020 7491 7367
Est. 1979 *Stock size* Medium
Stock Antique, modern silverware, old Sheffield plate
Open Mon–Sat 10am–5.30pm

Nicholas Grindley (BADA)
Contact Ms Rebecca Sullivan
13 Old Burlington Street, London, W1X 1LA
☎ 020 7437 5449 Ⓕ 020 7494 2446
Ⓔ nick@nicholasgrindley.co.uk
Est. 1993 *Stock size* Small
Stock Chinese works of art, sculptures, wall paintings, furniture etc
Open Mon–Fri 2–5pm or by appointment
Fairs Asian Art, London (Nov)
Services Valuations by mail

Sarah Groombridge (LAPADA)
Contact Sarah Groombridge
Stand 335, 58 Davies Street, London, W1Y 1LB
☎ 020 7629 0225 Ⓕ 01252 616201
Ⓜ 07770 920277
Est. 1974 *Stock size* Medium
Stock Fine antique jewellery, Georgian–1920s including natural pearls, cameos
Open Mon–Fri 10am–6pm
Fairs Olympia (Nov, June) Miami Jan

Guest and Gray
Contact Anthony Gray
1–7 Davies Mews, London, W1Y 2LP
☎ 020 7408 1252 Ⓕ 020 7499 1445
Ⓜ 07968 719496
Ⓔ anthony@guest-gray.demon.co.uk
Ⓦ www.guest-gray.demon.co.uk
Est. 1970 *Stock size* Large
Stock Asian and European ceramics, works of art and art reference books
Open 10am–6pm Mon–Fri
Fairs International Ceramics Fair, Olympia
Services Valuations

Claire Guest at Thomas Goode & Co. Ltd
Contact Claire Guest
19 South Audley Street, London, W1Y 6BH
☎ 020 7499 2823/7243 1423
Ⓕ 020 7629 4230/7792 5450
Est. 1969 *Stock size* Medium
Stock Antique furniture, silver, silver plate, glass, china
Open Mon–Sat 10am–6pm

Hadji Baba Ancient Art Ltd (IADA)
Contact R Soleimani
34a Davies Street, London, W1K 4NE
☎ 020 7499 9363 Ⓕ 020 7493 5504
Ⓔ info@hadjibaba.co.uk
Ⓦ www.hadjibaba.co.uk
Est. 1979 *Stock size* Medium
Stock Near and Middle East antiquities
Open Mon–Fri 10am–6pm
Services Valuations

Halcyon Days (BADA)
Contact Cheska Moon or Susan Benjamin
14 Brook Street, London, W1S 1BD
☎ 020 7629 8811 Ⓕ 020 7409 7223
Ⓔ info@halycondays.co.uk
Ⓦ www.halcyondays.co.uk
Est. 1950 *Stock size* Small
Stock 18thC English enamels, fans, objects of virtue, tortoiseshell, pique, scent bottles
Open Mon–Fri 9.30am–6pm Sat 10am–6pm
Fairs Grosvenor House

Robert Hall (BADA)
Contact Mr R Hall
15c Clifford Street, London, W1X 1RF
☎ 020 7734 4008 Ⓕ 020 7734 4408
Ⓔ roberthall@snuffbottle.com
Ⓦ www.snuffbottle.com.
Est. 1976 *Stock size* Large
Stock 18th–19thC Chinese snuff bottles
Open Mon–Fri 10am–5.30pm or by appointment
Fairs Grosvenor House
Services Valuations, bi-annual catalogues

LONDON

⊞ Hancocks and Co (Jewellers) Ltd (BADA)
Contact Mr Steven Burton
✉ **52–53 Burlington Arcade, London, W1J 0HH**
☎ 020 7493 8904 Ⓕ 020 7493 8905
Ⓔ info@hancockslondon.com
Ⓦ www.hancockslondon.com
Est. 1849 *Stock size* Large
Stock Jewellery, silver
Open Mon–Fri 9.30am–5pm Sat 10am–4pm
Fairs Grosvenor House, Maastricht, The Armoury, Palm Beach
Services Valuations, restorations, purchase of second-hand items

⊞ Brian Haughton Antiques
Contact Brian Haughton
✉ **3b Burlington Gardens, London, W1X 1LE** Ⓟ
☎ 020 7734 5491 Ⓕ 020 7494 4604
Ⓔ info@haughton.com
Ⓦ www.haughton.com
Est. 1965 *Stock size* Large
Stock 18th–19thC English and European porcelain, pottery
Open Mon–Fri 10am–5pm
Fairs International Ceramics Fair and Seminar (June), The International Fine Art & Antique Dealers Show, New York (Oct)

⊞ Gerard Hawthorn Ltd (BADA)
Contact Mr G Hawthorn
✉ **104 Mount Street, London, W1K 2TL** Ⓟ
☎ 020 7409 2888 Ⓕ 020 7409 2777
Ⓜ 07775 917487
Ⓔ mail@gerardhawthorn.com
Est. 1996 *Stock size* Medium
Stock Chinese, Japanese, Korean ceramics, works of art
Open Mon–Fri 10am–late
Fairs 2 exhibitions at gallery (June, Nov), International Asian Art Fair, New York (March)
Services Valuations, restorations, photography

⊞ Brian and Lynn Holmes (LAPADA)
Contact Brian or Lynn Holmes
✉ **Stand 304–306, Grays Antique Market, 58 Davies Street, London, W1Y 2LP** Ⓟ
☎ 020 7629 7327 Ⓕ 020 7629 7327
Ⓦ www.graysantiques.com
Est. 1971 *Stock size* Large
Stock Georgian–Victorian silver, gold, jewellery, Scottish antique jewellery
Open Mon–Fri 10am–6pm
Services Valuations, restorations

⊞ C John Ltd (BADA)
Contact Mr L Sassoon
✉ **70 South Audley Street, London, W1K 2RA** Ⓟ
☎ 020 7493 5288 Ⓕ 020 7409 7030
Ⓔ cjohn@dircom.co.uk
Est. 1948 *Stock size* Large
Stock Persian, French, Russian, Caucasian tapestries, Indian, Turkish, Chinese carpets, rugs, textiles
Open Mon–Fri 9.30am–5pm
Fairs Grosvenor House
Services Valuations, restorations

⊞ Johnson Walker Ltd (BADA)
Contact Miss R Gill
✉ **64 Burlington Arcade, London, W1J 0QT** Ⓟ
☎ 020 7629 2615/6
Ⓕ 020 7409 0709
Est. 1849 *Stock size* Medium
Stock Jewellery, bijouterie
Open Mon–Sat 9.30am–5.30pm
Services Valuations, repairs

⊞ John Joseph (LAPADA, LJAJDA)
Contact Mr J Joseph
✉ **Stand 34b, Grays Antique Market, 58 Davies Street, London, W1Y 2LP** Ⓟ
☎ 020 7629 1140 Ⓕ 020 7629 1140
Ⓔ jewellery@john-joseph.co.uk
Ⓦ www.john-joseph.co.uk
Est. 1995 *Stock size* Large
Stock Victorian, Edwardian, Art Deco jewellery, gem set, gold, platinum
Open Mon–Fri 10am–6pm
Fairs Olympia (June)

⊞ Roger Keverne Ltd (BADA)
Contact Mr R Keverne
✉ **2nd Floor, 16 Clifford Street, London, W12 3RG** Ⓟ
☎ 020 7434 9100 Ⓕ 020 7434 9101
Ⓔ rogerkeverne@keverne.co.uk
Ⓦ www.keverne.co.uk
Est. 1996 *Stock size* Large
Stock Chinese ceramics, jade, lacquer, bronzes, enamels, hard stones, ivory, bamboo
Open Mon–Fri 9.30am–5.30pm Sat for exhibitions
Fairs Exhibition at 16 Clifford Street (Jun, Nov), International Asian Art Fair, New York (March)
Services Valuations, restorations

⊞ D S Lavender Antiques Ltd (BADA)
Contact Mr D Lavender
✉ **26 Conduit Street, London, W1S 2XX** Ⓟ
☎ 020 7409 2305 Ⓕ 020 7629 3106
Ⓔ dslavender@clara.net
Est. 1946 *Stock size* Large
Stock Gold, silver, enamel fine snuff boxes, fine jewels, 16th–early 19thC portrait miniatures
Open Mon–Fri 9.30am–5pm
Fairs Grosvenor House
Services Valuations, restorations

⊞ Leuchers & Jefferson
Contact Mr H Leuchers
✉ **94 Mount Street, London, W1Y 5HG** Ⓟ
☎ 020 7491 4931 Ⓕ 020 7491 5027
Est. 1829 *Stock size* Medium
Stock 18thC English furniture, decorative items
Open Mon–Sat 9.30am–5.30pm
Services Valuations, restorations

⊞ Sanda Lipton (BADA, CINOA)
Contact Sanda Lipton
✉ **3rd Floor, Elliot House, 28A Devonshire Street, London, W1G 6PS** Ⓟ
☎ 020 7431 2688 Ⓕ 020 7431 3224
Ⓜ 07836 660008
Ⓔ sanda@antique-silver.com
Ⓦ www.antique-silver.com
Est. 1979 *Stock size* Medium
Stock 16th–mid 19thC silver, collectors' items, early English spoons, historical medals
Open By appointment
Fairs Olympia, March BADA
Services Valuations, restorations, consultancy, bidding at auction

⊞ Monty Lo Antiques
Contact Mr M Lo
✉ **Grays Antique Market, 58 Davies Street, London, W1Y 1LB** Ⓟ
☎ 020 7493 9457
Est. 1980 *Stock size* Medium
Stock European and English ceramics, glass
Open Mon–Fri 10am–6pm
Services Valuations, repair

Michael Longmore and Trianon Antiques Ltd (LAPADA, LJAJDA)
Contact Mr Bruce Rowley
Stand 378, Grays Antiques Market, 58 Davies Street, London, W1K 5LP
020 7491 2764 020 7409 1587
michaellongmore@aol.com
Est. 1974 *Stock size* Large
Stock Fine jewellery, objets d'art
Open Mon–Fri 10am–5.30pm
Fairs Olympia (June)

Maggs Bros Ltd (ABA, BADA)
Contact Mr Edward F Maggs
50 Berkeley Square, London, W1J 5BA
020 7493 7160 020 7499 2007
ed@maggs.com
www.maggs.com
Est. 1853 *Stock size* Large
Stock Military history, travel, natural history, science, modern literature, early English and Continental books, illustrated manuscripts, autographed letters
Open Mon–Fri 9.30am–5pm
Fairs Olympia
Services Catalogues issued by all departments

Mallett (BADA)
Bourden House, 2 Davies Street, London, W1K 3DJ
020 7629 2444 020 7499 2670
antiques@mallett.co.uk
www.mallett.co.uk
Est. 1865 *Stock size* Large
Stock Fine antique furniture, works of art, glass, paintings, watercolours, needlework
Open Mon–Fri 9am–6pm Sat 10am–4pm
Fairs Grosvenor House, International Ceramics Fair

Mallett (BADA)
141 New Bond Street, London, W1S 2BS
020 7499 7411 020 7495 3179
antiques@mallett.co.uk
www.mallett.co.uk
Est. 1865 *Stock size* Large
Stock Fine antique furniture, works of art, glass, paintings, watercolours, needlework
Open Mon–Fri 9am–6pm Sat 10am–4pm
Fairs Grosvenor House, International Ceramics Fair

Carol Manheim at Biblion (ABA, PBFA)
Contact Carol Manheim
Grays, 1–7 Davies Mews, London, W1Y 2LP
020 89949740
art.photo@lineone.net
wwwcarolmanheimartbooks.co.uk
Est. 1984
Stock 20thC fine art monographs and illustrated books, exhibition catalogues
Open Mon–Sat 10am–6pm
Fairs ABA

Map World (IMCOS)
Contact Cathy Chivers
25 Burlington Arcade, Piccadilly, London, W1V 9AD
020 7495 5377 020 7495 5377
info@map-world.com
www.map-world.com
Est. 1982 *Stock size* Large
Stock 15th–19thC antique maps
Open Mon–Sat 10am–5.30pm
Services Valuations

Marks Antiques (BADA, LAPADA)
Contact Anthony Marks
49 Curzon Street, London, W1J 7UN
020 7499 1788 020 7409 3183
marks@marksantiques.com
www.marksantiques.com
Est. 1921 *Stock size* Large
Stock Antique silver
Open Mon–Fri 9.30am–6pm Sat 9.30am–5pm
Fairs Olympia, BADA Duke of York's
Services Valuations, Shipping

Marlborough Rare Books Ltd (ABA)
Contact Jonathan Gestetner
4th Floor, 144–146 New Bond Street, London, W1S 2TR
020 7493 6993 020 7499 2479
sales@mrb-books.co.uk
Est. 1948 *Stock size* Medium
Stock Antiquarian books on rare art, architecture and topography also illustrated, colour plate, fine bindings and English literature
Open Mon–Fri 9.30am–5.30pm
Fairs Olympia, Chelsea
Services Valuations

Massada Antiques (LAPADA, LJAJDA)
Contact Mr B Yacobi
Bond Street Antiques Centre, 124 New Bond Street, London, W1S 1DX
020 7493 5610 020 7491 9852
Est. 1970 *Stock size* Large
Stock Georgian–Edwardian wearable, decorative jewellery
Open Mon–Fri 10am–5.30pm
Fairs Olympia (June, Nov)
Services Valuations, repairs

Mayfair Gallery Ltd
Contact Mrs C Giese
39 South Audley Street, London, W1K 2PP
020 7491 3435/3436
020 7491 3437
mayfair.gallery@dial.pipex.com
www.artnet.com/mayfairgallery.html
Est. 1974 *Stock size* Large
Stock 19thC antiques, decorative arts, bronzes, marbles, Continental porcelain, furniture
Open Mon–Fri 9.30am–6pm Sat by appointment
Services Valuations, restorations

Pete McAskie Toys
Contact Mr P McAskie
Stand A12–13, Basement, 1–7 Davies Mews, London, W1Y 2LP
020 7629 2813 020 7493 9344
Est. 1976 *Stock size* Large
Stock Tin toys, 1895–1980, die-cast toys, robots, battery-operated toys, lead figures
Open Mon–Fri 10am–6pm
Fairs Sandown Park Toy Show, Reading Vintage Toy Show.

The Mews Antique Market
Contact Caroline Churchill
1–7 Davies Mews, London, W1K 5AB
020 7629 7034 020 7493 9344
grays@clara.net
http://ethemews.com
Est. 1976 *Stock size* Large
No. of dealers 100
Stock Collectables, glass, medals, coins, Oriental, Islamic antiques, antiquities, toys, dolls, antiquarian books
Open Mon–Fri 10am–6pm
Services Restorations

Sydney L Moss Ltd (BADA)
Contact Paul G Moss or Mr D Wright
51 Brook Street, London, W1Y 1AU

☎ 020 7629 4670 ⓕ 020 7491 9278
ⓜ 07850 778746
ⓔ slmoss@freeserve.uk
Est. 1904 *Stock size* Large
Stock Chinese and Japanese antiques, works of art, paintings
Open Mon–Fri 10am–5.30pm
Fairs International Asian Art Fair New York
Services Valuations

⊞ Morris Namdar

Contact Mr Morris Namdar
✉ **Grays Mews Antiques Market, 1–7 Davies Mews, Stand B18, London, W1K 5AB** Ⓟ
☎ 020 7629 1183 ⓕ 020 7493 9344
Est. 1979 *Stock size* Medium
Stock Chinese, Japanese, European ceramics, glass, textiles
Open Mon–Fri 10am–6pm

⊞ The O'Shea Gallery (BADA)

Contact Mr D Isaac
✉ **120a Mount Street, London, W1Y 5HB** Ⓟ
☎ 020 7629 1122 ⓕ 020 7629 1116
ⓔ osheagallery@paston.co.uk
Est. 1969 *Stock size* Large
Stock 15th–19thC maps, decorative, natural history, sporting, marine prints, publisher of Annie Tempest, Tottering-by-Gently cartoons
Open Mon–Fri 9.30am–6pm
Fairs Grosvenor House, BADA, New York International
Services Restorations, framing

⊞ Pendulum of Mayfair

Contact Mr J Clements
✉ **King House, 51 Maddox Street, London, W1R 9LA** Ⓟ
☎ 020 7629 6606
ⓦ www.pendulumofmayfair.com
Est. 1995 *Stock size* Large
Stock Clocks, including longcase, bracket, wall, Georgian period furniture
Open Mon–Fri 10am–6pm Sat 10am–5pm or by appointment

🔨 Phillips International Auctioneers and Valuers (BADA, BACA Award Winner 2001)

✉ **101 New Bond Street, London, W1Y 9LG** Ⓟ
☎ 020 7629 6602 ⓕ 020 7629 8876
ⓦ www.phillips-auction.com
Est. 1796
Sales Head Office and International Saleroom. Sales of arms and armour, automobilia, bonds and banknotes, books, atlases, manuscripts and photographs, clocks, watches, scientific and nautical instruments, coins, collectors' items, contemporary ceramics, European ceramics and glass, furniture, golfing equipment, jewellery, late 19th–20thC decorative arts, 20thC design and modernism, medals, Ministry of Defence sales, musical instruments, Oriental carpets and rugs, Oriental ceramics and works of art, pianos and keyboards, pictures, postage stamps and covers, silver, sporting memorabilia, rivercraft and maritime memorabilia, textiles, costumes, lace and fans, tribal art and antiquities, wine, works of art and metalware, writing equipment
Catalogues Yes

⊞ Ronald Phillips Ltd (BADA)

Contact Mr S Phillips
✉ **26 Bruton Street, London, W1J 6QL** Ⓟ
☎ 020 7493 2341 ⓕ 020 7495 0843
ⓔ ronphill@aol.com.
ⓦ www.rp-antique-furniture.com
Est. 1952 *Stock size* Large
Stock 18thC English furniture, glass, clocks, barometers, mirrors
Open Mon–Fri 9am–5.30pm Sat by appointment
Fairs Grosvenor House

⊞ S J Phillips Ltd (BADA)

Contact Mr F Norton
✉ **139 New Bond Street, London, W1A 3DL**
☎ 020 7629 6261 ⓕ 020 7495 6180
ⓔ enquiries@sjphillips.com
ⓦ www.sjphillips.com
Est. 1869 *Stock size* Large
Stock Silver jewellery, snuff boxes
Open Mon–Fri 10am–5pm
Fairs Grosvenor House, TEFAF, Maastricht
Services Restorations

⊞ Pickering and Chatto (ABA, PBFA)

Contact Mr J Hudson
✉ **36 St George Street, London, W1R 9FA** Ⓟ
☎ 020 7491 2656 ⓕ 020 7491 9161
ⓔ rarebook@pickering-chatto.com
ⓦ www.pickering-chatto.com
Est. 1820 *Stock size* Medium
Stock Antiquarian, rare, second-hand books on economics, philosophy, medicine, general literature
Open Mon–Fri 9.30am–5.30pm or by appointment
Fairs Olympia
Services Book search valuations

⊞ Pieces of Time (BADA)

Contact Mr J Wachsmann
✉ **1–7 Davies Mews, London, W1Y 2LP** Ⓟ
☎ 020 7629 2422 ⓕ 020 7409 1625
ⓔ info@antique-watch.com
ⓦ www.antique-watch.com
Est. 1973 *Stock size* Large
Stock Antique pocket watches, Judaica
Open Mon–Fri 10.30am–5pm
Services Valuations

⊞ Nicholas S Pitcher Oriental Art

Contact Mr N S Pitcher
✉ **1st Floor, 29 New Bond Street, London, W1S 2RL** Ⓟ
☎ 020 7499 6621 ⓕ 020 7499 6621
ⓜ 07831 391574
ⓔ nickpitcher@cs.com
Est. 1990 *Stock size* Medium
Stock Early Chinese ceramics, works of art
Open By appointment
Fairs Arts of Pacific Asia Show, New York
Services Valuations

⊞ Jonathan Potter Ltd (ABA, BADA, LAPADA, PBFA)

Contact Mr J Potter
✉ **125 New Bond Street, London, W1Y 9AF** Ⓟ
☎ 020 7491 3520 ⓕ 020 7491 9754
ⓔ jpmaps@attglobal.net
ⓦ www.jpmaps.co.uk
Est. 1974 *Stock size* Large
Stock History of cartography books, atlases, maps, reproduction globes
Open Mon–Fri 10am–6pm
Fairs ABA, Olympia, IMCoS, International Map Fair
Services Valuations, restorations, framing

⊞ Bernard Quaritch Ltd (PBFA, ABA, BADA)

Contact Mr I Smith
✉ **5–8 Lower John Street, London, W1R 4AU**
☎ 020 7734 2983 ⓕ 020 7734 0967

rarebooks@quaritch.com
www.quaritch.com
Est. 1847 *Stock size* Large
Stock Antiquarian books
Open Mon–Fri 9am–5.30pm
Fairs Olympia
Services Valuations

Retrouvius Architectural Reclamation (SALVO)
Contact Adam Hills or Maria Speake
32 York House, Upper Montague Street, London, W1H 1FR
warehouse: 020 8960 6060 office: 020 7724 3387
07778 210855
mail@retrouvius.com
Est. 1992 *Stock size* Medium
Stock Architectural antiques, reclamation
Open By appointment
Fairs Newark
Services Design service

David Richards & Sons (LAPADA)
Contact Mr Richards
10 New Cavendish Street, London, W1G 8UL
020 7935 3206/0322
020 7224 4423
Est. 1970 *Stock size* Large
Stock Modern and antique silver-plate, decorative items, flatware
Open Mon–Fri 9.30am–5.30pm
Services Valuations, restorations

Samiramis (LAPADA)
Contact Mr H Ismael
M14–16 Grays Mews, Davies Mews, London, W1Y 1FH
020 7629 1161 020 7493 5106
Est. 1978 *Stock size* Medium
Stock Islamic pottery, silver, Eastern items, calligraphy
Open Mon–Fri 10am–6pm

Alistair Sampson Antiques Ltd (BADA)
Contact Mr A Sampson
120 Mount Street, London, W1K 3NN
020 7409 1799 020 7409 7717
info@alistairsampson.com
www.alistairsampson.com
Est. 1969 *Stock size* Large
Stock English pottery, oak, country furniture, metalwork, needlework, pictures, 17th–18thC decorative items
Open Mon–Fri 9.30am–5.30pm or Sat by appointment
Fairs Olympia, Grosvenor House

Bernard J Shapero Rare Books (ABA, PBFA, BADA)
Contact Lucinda Boyle
32 St George Street, London, W1S 2EA
020 7493 0876 020 7229 7860
rarebooks@shapero.com
www.shapero.com
Est. 1979 *Stock size* Large
Stock 16th–20thC guide books, antiquarian and rare books, English and Continental literature, specializing in travel, natural history, colour plate
Open Mon–Fri 9.30am–6.30pm Sat 11am–5pm August Mon–Fri 10am–5pm
Fairs Olympia
Services Valuations, restorations

Shapiro & Co. (LAPADA)
Contact Sheldon Shapiro
Stand 380, Gray's Antique Market, 58 Davies Street, London, W1K 5JF
020 74912710 020 74912710
07768 840930
Est. 1982
Stock Jewellery, silver, objets d'art, Imperial Russian works of art
Open Mon–Fri 10am–6pm
Fairs Olympia, NEC

Shiraz Antiques (BADA)
Contact Mr Reza Kiadeh
1 Davies Mews, London, W1K 5AB
020 7495 0635 020 7495 0635
Est. 1990 *Stock size* Medium
Stock Asian art, antiquities, glass, marble, pottery
Open Mon–Fri 10am–6pm
Fairs BADA

R Solaimany
Contact Mr R Solaimany
Unit H, Davies Mews, London, W1K 5AB
020 7491 2562 020 7493 9344
Est. 1981 *Stock size* Medium
Stock Oriental ceramics, bronzes, Roman glass
Open Mon–Fri 10am–6pm

Sotheby's
34–35 New Bond Street, London, W1A 2AA
020 72935000
www.sothebys.com
Est. 1744
Open Mon–Fri 9am–5.30pm
Sales International auctioneer of fine art, furniture, jewellery, decorative arts, collectables and more. Services included restoration, valuation, financial service, picture library, on-line auctions, Sotheby's International Realty and Sotheby's bookshop
Frequency Varies by month
Catalogues Yes

Henry Sotheran Ltd (ABA, PBFA, ILAB)
Contact Mr A McGeachin
2 Sackville Street, Piccadilly, London, W1S 3DP
020 7439 6151 020 7434 709
sotherans@sotherans.co.uk
www.sotherans.co.uk
Est. 1761 *Stock size* Large
Stock Antiquarian books on English literature, natural history, travel, children's illustrated, modern first editions, prints, art, architecture
Open Mon–Fri 9.30am–6pm Sat 10am–4pm

Spectrum
Contact Mrs S Spectrum
Stand 372, Grays Antique Market, 58 Davies Street, London, W1K 5LP0
020 7629 3501 020 8883 5030
07770 753302
Est. 1979 *Stock size* Large
Stock Georgian seedpearl necklaces, brooches, Georgian–Victorian jewellery, Georg Jensen jewellery
Open Mon–Fri 10am–6pm
Services Valuations, repairs, stringing, designing

A and J Speelman Ltd (BADA)
Contact Mr J Speelman or J Mann
129 Mount Street, London, W1K 3NX
020 7499 5126 020 7355 3391
speelman@enterprise.net
Est. 1976 *Stock size* Large
Stock Oriental furniture, porcelain, works of art
Open Mon–Fri 10am–6pm
Fairs New York, Asian Art Fair
Services Valuations, restorations

⊞ St. Petersburg Collection Ltd
Contact Mr B Lynch
✉ **42 Burlington Arcade, London, W1J 0QG** Ⓟ
☎ 020 7495 2883 Ⓕ 01895 810566
Ⓔ creations@stpetersburgcollection.com
Ⓦ www.stpetersburgcollection.com
Est. 1989 *Stock size* Medium
Stock English and French objets d'art, boxes, 19th–20thC silver, glass, ormolu
Open Mon–Sat 10am–5pm

⊞ Stair & Company Ltd (BADA, CINOA)
Contact Mr M Pick
✉ **14 Mount Street, London, W1Y 5RA** Ⓟ
☎ 020 7499 1784 Ⓕ 020 7269 1050
Ⓔ stairandcompany@talk21.com
Ⓦ www.stairandcompany.com
Est. 1911 *Stock size* Large
Stock 18thC fine English furniture, works of art
Open Mon–Fri 9.30am–5.30pm or by appointment
Fairs Grosvenor House
Services Valuations, restorations

⊞ Jacob Stodel (BADA)
Contact Jacob Stodel
✉ **Flat 53, Macready House, 75 Crawford Street, London, W1H 5LP** Ⓟ
☎ 020 7723 3732
Ⓔ jacobstodel@aol.com
Stock 18thC English and Continental furniture, 17th–early 19thC Oriental and European ceramics and works of art
Open By appointment
Fairs Maastricht
Services Valuations

⊞ E Swonnell Ltd
Contact Miss S Swonnell
✉ **111–112 New Bond Street, London, W1Y 0BQ** Ⓟ
☎ 020 7629 9649 Ⓕ 020 7629 9649
Est. 1957 *Stock size* Large
Stock 17th–19thC silver and plate, large decorative items
Open Mon–Fri 10am–5pm
Services Valuations, restorations

⊞ Tagore Ltd
Contact Mr R Falloon
✉ **Stand 302, Grays Antique Market, 58 Davies Street, London, W1Y 2LP** Ⓟ
☎ 020 7499 0158 Ⓕ 020 7499 0158
Ⓔ grays@clara.net
Est. 1977 *Stock size* Large
Stock 20thC drinking, smoking, and gambling collectors' items, silver, glass
Open Mon–Fri 10am–6pm
Services Valuations

⊞ Textile-Art: The Textile Gallery (BADA)
Contact Michael Franses or Nicholas Waterhouse
✉ **12 Queen Street, Mayfair, London, W1J 5PG** Ⓟ
☎ 020 7499 7979 Ⓕ 020 7409 2596
Ⓜ 07836 321461
Ⓔ post@textile-art.com
Ⓦ www.textile-art.com
Est. 1972
Stock 300BC–17thC textile art from China, Central Asia, India and Ottoman Empire, 1400–1700 classical carpets
Open Mon–Fri by appointment 10.30am–6pm
Fairs The European Fine Art Fair, Maastricht, Asian Art in London
Services Conservation of important textiles to museum standards

⊞ Tosi Gold Ltd
Contact Sergio Tencati
✉ **Unit 16, Bond Street Antiques Centre, 124 New Bond Street, London, W1Y 9AE** Ⓟ
☎ 020 7493 6272 Ⓕ 020 7493 6272
Ⓜ 07929 875822
Est. 1897 *Stock size* Medium
Stock Antique and contemporary 18ct gold jewellery
Open Mon–Sat 10.30am–5.30pm
Services Valuations, repair, shipping

⊞ Toynbee-Clarke Interiors Ltd
Contact Mrs Daphne Toynbee-Clarke
✉ **95 Mount Street, London, W1Y 5HG** Ⓟ
☎ 020 7499 4472 Ⓕ 020 7495 1204
Est. 1959 *Stock size* Medium
Stock Continental furniture, works of art, 18th–19thC Chinese hand-painted export wallpapers, early 19thC French panoramic papers
Open Mon–Fri 11am–5.30pm or by appointment
Services Restorations

⊞ Trianon Antiques Ltd and Michael Longmore (LAPADA, LJAJDA)
Contact Miss L Horton
✉ **Bond Street Antiques Centre, 124 New Bond Street, London, W1Y 9AE** Ⓟ
☎ 020 7629 6678 Ⓕ 020 7355 2055
Est. 1974 *Stock size* Large
Stock Fine jewellery, objets d'art
Open Mon–Fri 10am–5.30pm
Fairs Olympia (June)

⊞ Jan Van Beers Oriental Art (BADA)
Contact Mr J Van Beers
✉ **34 Davies Street, London, W1Y 1LG** Ⓟ
☎ 020 7408 0434 Ⓕ 020 7355 1397
Ⓔ jan@vanbeers.demon.co.uk
Est. 1978 *Stock size* Large
Stock Chinese and Japanese antiques, ceramics, works of art
Open Mon–Fri 10am–6pm
Services Valuations

⊞ Vinci Antiques
Contact Mr A Vinci
✉ **27 Avery Row, London, W1X 9HD** Ⓟ
☎ 020 7499 1041
Est. 1974 *Stock size* Large
Stock Objets d'art, objects of virtue, silver, porcelain, glass, paintings, Russian icons, jewellery
Open Mon–Sat 9am–7pm
Services Valuations, restorations

⊞ Rupert Wace Ancient Art Ltd (ADA, IADAA, BADA)
Contact Mr R Wace
✉ **14 Old Bond Street, London, W1X 3DB** Ⓟ
☎ 020 7495 1623 Ⓕ 020 7495 8495
Ⓔ rupert.wace@btinternet.com
Est. 1987 *Stock size* Large
Stock Antiquities, Greek, Roman, ancient Egyptian, Near Eastern, Celtic, Dark Ages
Open Mon–Fri 10am–5pm or by appointment
Fairs Olympia (June, Feb)
Services Valuations

⊞ Westminster Group Antique Jewellery (LAPADA)
Contact Mr R Harrison
✉ **Stand 150, Grays Antique Market, 58 Davies Street, London, W1K 2LP** Ⓟ
☎ 020 7493 8672 Ⓕ 020 7493 8672

Est. 1976 *Stock size* Large
Stock Victorian–Edwardian second-hand jewellery, watches
Open Mon–Fri 10am–6pm

Wimpole Antiques (LAPADA)
Contact Lyn Lindsay
Stand 349, Grays Antiques Market, Davies Street, London, W1Y 1LB
020 7499 2889 Ⓕ 020 7372 2405
Ⓔ 100046.1430@compuserve.com
Est. 1977 *Stock size* Large
Stock Affordable, wearable jewellery, 1780–1960, Victorian jewellery
Open Mon–Fri 10am–6pm
Fairs Olympia, NEC, LAPADA
Services Valuations, repairs

Yamamoto Antiques
Contact Mrs M Yamamoto
Units 14 & 15, Bond Street Antique Centre, 124 New Bond Street, London, W1Y 9AE
0207 491 0983 Ⓕ 0207 491 0983
Ⓔ m@bondst.plus.com
Est. 1995 *Stock size* Medium
Stock Jewellery, porcelain
Open Mon–Sat 11am–5.30pm
Services Shipping

W2

Mark Gallery (BADA, CINOA)
Contact Helen Mark
9 Porchester Place, Marble Arch, London, W2 2BS
020 7262 4906 Ⓕ 020 7224 9416
Est. 1970
Stock 16th–19thC Russian and Greek icons, contemporary and modern French lithographs and etchings
Open Mon–Fri 10am–1pm 2pm–6pm Sat by appointment 11am–1pm
Fairs Olympia, Cologne
Services Valuations, restorations

Phillips International Auctioneers and Valuers
10 Salem Road, Bayswater, London, W2 4DL
020 7229 9090 Ⓕ 020 7313 2701
Ⓦ www.phillips-auction.com
Est. 1796
Sales Saleroom
Catalogues Yes

Quest
Contact Fay Lambert
1 Garway Road, Bayswater, London, W2 4PH
020 7221 1863 Ⓕ 020 7221 1863
Ⓜ 07850 878994
Ⓔ fay.lambert@btinternet.com
Est. 1995
Stock Fine art, decorative antiques
Open By appointment
Services Acquisition/disposal of fine art/antiques

Reel Poster Gallery
Contact Mr Tony Nourmand
72 Westbourne Grove, London, W2 5SH
020 7727 4488 Ⓕ 020 7727 4499
Ⓔ info@reelposter.com
Ⓦ www.reelposter.com
Est. 1989
Stock Original vintage film posters
Open Mon–Fri 11am–7pm Sat noon–6pm
Services Valuations, annual catalogue

W3

Chiswick Auctions
Contact Mr D Wells
1 Colville Road, London, W3 8BL
020 8992 4442 Ⓕ 020 8896 0541
Est. 1992
Open Mon–Fri 10am–6pm
Sales Antiques and general effects Mon 5pm, viewing Sat 10am–6pm Sun noon–6pm Mon 10am–5pm
Frequency Weekly
Catalogues Yes

W4

Chiswick Park Antiques
Contact Mr Azzariti
2 Chiswick Park Station, London, W4 5EB
020 8995 8930
Est. 1965 *Stock size* Medium
Stock Mirrors, furniture, clocks
Open Mon–Sat 11am–6pm
Services Valuations, restorations

David Edmonds Indian Furniture
1–4 Prince of Wales Terrace, London, W4 2EY
020 8742 1920 Ⓕ 020 8742 3030
Ⓜ 07831 666436
Ⓔ dareindia@aol.com
Est. 1987 *Stock size* Large
Stock Fine quality Indian furniture, antiques, architectural items
Open Mon–Sat 11am–6pm Sun noon–4pm
Services Valuations, repairs

W A Foster (PBFA)
Contact Mr Foster
183 Chiswick High Road, London, W4 2DR
020 8995 2768
Est. 1968 *Stock size* Medium
Stock Antiquarian, rare, second-hand books, fine bindings, illustrated children's books
Open Thurs–Sat 10.30am–5.30pm
Fairs PBFA Hotel Russell

Harmers of London Stamp Auctioneer Ltd (Philatelic Traders Society)
Contact Mr G Childs
111 Power Road, Chiswick, London, W4 5PY
020 8747 6100 Ⓕ 020 8996 0649
Ⓔ auctions@harmers.demon.co.uk
Ⓦ www.harmers.com
Est. 1918
Open Mon–Fri 9am–5pm
Sales Philatelic auctions every 6 weeks, ring for details
Frequency Every 6 weeks
Catalogues Yes

The Old Cinema (LAPADA)
Contact Mr K Norris
160 Chiswick High Road, London, W4 1PR
020 8995 4166 Ⓕ 020 8995 4167
Ⓔ theoldcinema@antiques-uk.co.uk
Ⓦ www.antiques-uk.co.uk/theoldcinema
Est. 1980 *Stock size* Large
Stock Georgian–Art Deco furniture, large items of furniture, clocks, silver
Open Mon–Sat 9.30am–6pm Sun noon–5pm

Strand Antiques
Contact Mrs A Brown
46 Devonshire Road, London, W4 2HD
020 8994 1912
Est. 1977 *Stock size* Large
Stock English and French furniture, glass, lighting,

jewellery, silver, garden items, kitchenware, books, prints, textiles, collectables
Open Mon–Sat 10.30am–5.30pm
Services Furniture restoration

W5

⊞ Aberdeen House Antiques (LAPADA, CINOA)
Contact Mr N Schwartz
✉ **75 St Mary's Road, London, W5 5RH** P
☎ 020 8567 1223
Est. 1972 *Stock size* Medium
Stock 18th–19thC antiques, decorative items, lighting, furniture, mirrors
Open Mon–Sat 10am–5.30pm or by appointment
Fairs Olympia (June)
Services Valuations

⊞ Harold's Place
Contact Mr H Bowman
✉ **148 South Ealing Road, Ealing, London, W5 4QJ** P
☎ 020 8579 4825
Est. 1976 *Stock size* Medium
Stock Antique china, glass, decorative items
Open Mon–Sat 9.30am–5.30pm closed Wed

⊞ Kitchenalia
Contact Miss P Clewer
✉ **122 Pitshanger Lane, Ealing, London, W5 1QP** P
☎ 020 8991 1786
Ⓔ polly@kitchenalia.fsnet.co.uk
Est. 1996 *Stock size* Medium
Stock Antique tables, chairs, porcelain, glass, silver plate, mirrors, second-hand furniture
Open Mon–Sat 10.15am–6pm Sun noon–4pm
Fairs Swan Antiques Centre, Tetsworth

⊞ Terrace Antiques
Contact Mr N Schwartz
✉ **10–12 South Ealing Road, London, W5 4QA** P
☎ 020 8567 5194
Est. 1972 *Stock size* Medium
Stock Furniture, collectables, china, silver plate, glass
Open Mon–Sat 10am–5.30pm or by appointment
Services Valuations

W6

⊞ Zoom
Contact Eddie Sandham
✉ **Arch 65, Cambridge Grove, Hammersmith, London, W6 0LD** P
☎ 07000 9666 2002
Ⓕ 020 8287 4962/020 8404 6099
Ⓜ 07958 372975
Ⓔ eddiesandham@hotmail.com
Ⓦ www.retrozoom.com
Est. 1981 *Stock size* Large
Stock 1950s–1970s furniture, lighting
Open Mon–Fri 10am–8pm
Fairs Newark, Olympia
Services Prop hire, sales

W8

⊞ Abstract/Noonstar (LAPADA)
Contact Galya Aytac or Juliette Boagers
✉ **58–60 Kensington Church Street, London, W8 4DB**
☎ 020 7376 2652 Ⓕ 020 7376 2652
Ⓜ 07770 281301
Ⓔ galya53@aol.com
Ⓦ www.abstract-antiques.com
Est. 1980 *Stock size* Medium
Stock 20thC Decorative Arts, Art Nouveau, Art Deco
Open Mon–Sat 11am–5pm
Services Valuations, shipping

⊞ Antiquewest Ltd at Patrick Sandberg Antiques (CINOA)
Contact Mr J Robinson
✉ **150 Kensington Church Street, London, W8 4BH** P
☎ 020 7229 4115 Ⓕ 020 7792 3467
Ⓔ china@antikwest.com
Ⓦ www.antikwest.com
Est. 1980 *Stock size* Large
Stock Oriental porcelain, pottery, Chinese carpets, furniture
Open Mon–Fri 10am–6pm Sat 10am–4pm
Fairs Olympia (June), Gothenburg, Sweden (Oct)
Services Valuations, restorations

⊞ Artemis Decorative Arts Ltd (LAPADA)
Contact Mr M Jones
✉ **36 Kensington Church Street, London, W8 4BX** P
☎ 020 7376 0377 Ⓕ 020 7376 0377
Ⓔ artemis.w8@btinternet.com
Est. 1994 *Stock size* Medium
Stock Art Nouveau, Art Deco, glass, bronze, ivory, furniture
Open Mon–Sat 10am–6pm

⊞ Garry Atkins
Contact Mr G Atkins
✉ **107 Kensington Church Street, London, W8 7LN** P
☎ 020 7727 8737 Ⓕ 020 7792 9010
Ⓔ garry.atkins@englishpottery.com
Ⓦ www.englishpottery.com
Est. 1983 *Stock size* Large
Stock English and Continental pottery, 18thC and earlier
Open Mon–Fri 10am–5.30pm
Fairs New York Ceramics Fair

⊞ Gregg Baker Asian Art (BADA, LAPADA, CINOA)
Contact Mr G Baker
✉ **132 Kensington Church Street, London, W8 4BH** P
☎ 020 7221 3533 Ⓕ 020 7221 4410
Ⓔ gbakerart@aol.com
Ⓦ www.greggbaker.com
Est. 1984 *Stock size* Medium
Stock Japanese and Chinese works of art
Open Mon–Fri 10am–6pm or by appointment
Fairs Olympia

⊞ Eddy Bardawil (BADA)
Contact Mr E Bardawil
✉ **106 Kensington Church Street, London, W8 4BH** P
☎ 020 7221 3967 Ⓕ 020 7221 5124
Est. 1982 *Stock size* Medium
Stock 18th–19thC English furniture, works of art
Open Mon–Fri 10am–6pm Sat 10am–1pm
Services Restorations

⊞ Nigel Benson 20th Century Glass (KCSADA)
Contact Mr N Benson
✉ **Unit 7, The Antique Centre, 58–60 Kensington Church Street, London, W8 4DB** P
☎ 020 7938 1137 Ⓕ 020 7729 9875
Ⓜ 07971 859848
Est. 1986 *Stock size* Large
Stock 1870–1980 British glass, post-war Scandinavian, Continental glass
Open Thurs–Sat noon–6pm or by appointment
Fairs NEC (April, August, November), Glass Fair, Birmingham

Berwald Oriental Art (BADA, CINOA)
Contact Isabella Corble
101 Kensington Church Street, London, W8 7LN
020 7229 0800 020 7229 1101
berwald@aapi.co.uk
www.berwald-oriental.com
Est. 1986 *Stock size* Medium
Stock Fine Chinese pottery and porcelain, Han to Qing and Chinese works of art
Open Mon–Fri 10am–6pm or by appointment

Nicolaus Boston Antiques
Contact Mr N Boston
58–60 Kensington Church Street, London, W8 4DB
020 7937 2237 020 8944 1280
sales@majolica.co.uk
www.majolica.co.uk
Est. 1983 *Stock size* Large
Stock Majolica, Christopher Dresser, aesthetic pottery
Open Fri Sat 10am–6pm
Fairs Olympia, Ceramic Fair, New York

David Brower (KCSADA)
Contact Mr D Brower
113 Kensington Church Street, London, W8 7LN
020 7221 4155 020 7221 6211
07831 234343
David@davidbrower-antiques.com
www.davidbrower-antiques.com
Est. 1969 *Stock size* Large
Stock Meissen, KPM, European and Asian porcelain, French bronzes, Japanese works of art
Open Mon–Fri 10am–6pm Sat by appointment
Fairs Olympia (June)

Cohen & Cohen (BADA, KCSADA)
Contact Mr M Cohen
101b Kensington Church Street, London, W8 7LN
020 7727 7677 020 7229 9653
cohenandcohen@aol.com
www.artnet.com
Est. 1973 *Stock size* Large
Stock Chinese export porcelain, works of art
Open Mon–Fri 10am–6pm Sat 10am–4pm
Fairs New York Ceramics Fair, Palm Beach

Davies Antiques (LAPADA)
Contact Mr H Davies
40 Kensington Church Street, London, W8 4BX
020 7937 9216 020 7938 2032
hugh.davies@btconnect.com
Est. 1975 *Stock size* Large
Stock 1710–Art Deco Continental porcelain, Meissen porcelain
Open Mon–Fri 10am–5.30pm Sat 10am–3pm

Richard Dennis Gallery
Contact Mr P Babb
144 Kensington Church Street, London, W8 4BH
020 7727 2061 020 7221 1283
paul@dennispublns.freeserve.co.uk
Est. 1967 *Stock size* Medium
Stock Antique and modern studio ceramics, 1850–present day contemporary ceramics
Open Mon–Sat 10am–5.30pm
Services Valuations, collectors' ceramics books published, exhibition catalogues

Denton Antiques
Contact Mr N Denton
156 Kensington Church Street, London, W8 4BN
020 7229 5866 020 7792 1073
Est. 1897 *Stock size* Large
Stock French and English chandeliers, lighting, table lamps, 1750–1920
Open Mon–Fri 9.30am–5.30pm

Didier Antiques (LAPADA)
Contact Didier Haspeslagh
58–60 Kensington Church Street, Kensington, London, W8 4DB
020 7938 2537 020 7938 2537
didier.antiques@virgin.net.
www.didierantiques.com
Est. 1989 *Stock size* Large
Stock Late 19th–early 20thC Arts and Crafts, Art Nouveau, jewellery, silver, 1960s–1970s designer jewellery
Open Tues–Sat noon–6pm
Fairs Olympia (June, Nov)

C. Fredericks and Son (BADA, KCSADA)
Contact Richard Fredericks
142 Kensington Church Street, London, W8 4BN
020 7727 2240 020 7727 2240
antiques@cfredericksandson.freeserve.co.uk
Est. 1947 *Stock size* Medium
Stock 18thC English furniture
Open Mon–Fri 9.30am–5.30pm
Fairs BADA Olympia (Nov)
Services Restorations

Michael German Antiques (BADA, LAPADA)
Contact Mr M German
38b Kensington Church Street, London, W8 4BX
020 7937 2771 020 7937 8566
michael@antiquecanes.com
michael@antiqueweapons.com
www.antiquecanes.com
www.antiqueweapons.com
Est. 1973 *Stock size* Large
Stock Antique walking canes, antique arms, armour
Open Mon–Fri 10am–5pm Sat 10am–1pm

Robert Hales Antiques
Contact Mr R Hales
131 Kensington Church Street, London, W8 7LP
020 7229 3887 020 7229 3887
RHAntique@aol.com
Est. 1967 *Stock size* Medium
Stock Oriental and Islamic arms, armour, medieval–19thC
Open Tues–Fri 9.30am–5.30pm
Fairs Park Lane Arms Fair
Services Valuations

Adrian Harrington Antiquarian Bookseller (ABA, PBFA)
Contact Mr Pierre Lambardini
64a Kensington Church Street, London, W8 4DB
020 7937 1465 020 7368 0912
rare@harringtonbooks.co.uk
www.harringtonbooks.co.uk
Est. 1964 *Stock size* Large
Stock Antiquarian, rare, second-hand books on literature, children's illustrated, travel
Open Mon–Sat 10am–6pm
Fairs Olympia, Chelsea Town Hall
Services Valuations

Jeanette Hayhurst (BADA)
Contact Mrs J Hayhurst
32a Kensington Church Street, London, W8 4HA
020 7938 1539
Est. 1979 *Stock size* Medium
Stock 18thC glass, specializing in English drinking glasses

Open Mon–Fri 10am–5pm Sat noon–5pm or by appointment
Fairs BADA, Harrogate, NEC

D Holmes
Contact Mr D Holmes
47c Earls Court Road, in Abingdon Villas, London, W8 6EE
020 7937 6961 F 020 8880 254
M 07710 249471
Est. 1965 *Stock size* Small
Stock 18th–19thC English mahogany furniture
Open Fri 9am–7pm Sat 9am–3pm
Fairs Olympia (June)
Services Also showrooms at Oudenaarde, Belgium

Hope & Glory
Contact Mr J Pym
131a Kensington Church Street (Entrance in Peel Street), London, W8 7LP
020 7727 8424
Est. 1982 *Stock size* Large
Stock Commemorative ceramics, Royal, political etc
Open Mon–Sat 10am–5pm

Jonathan Horne (BADA, CINOA)
Contact Mr S Westman or Jonathan Horne
66c Kensington Church Street, London, W8 4BY
020 7221 5658 F 020 7792 3090
E jh@jonathanhorne.co.uk
W www.jonathanhorne.co.uk
Est. 1968 *Stock size* Large
Stock Early English pottery, medieval–1820
Open Mon–Fri 9.30am–5.30pm
Fairs BADA, Olympia (June, Nov)
Services Valuations

Valerie Howard (LAPADA)
Contact Mrs Valerie Howard
4 Campden Street, London, W8 7EP
020 7792 9702 F 020 7221 7008
E valeriehoward@quimperpottery.com
W www.masonsironstonechina.com or www.quimperpottery.com
Est. 1988 *Stock size* Medium
Stock Mason's ironstone, other English ironstone, Miles Mason porcelain 1796–1840, Quimper pottery 19thC–1920
Open Mon–Fri 10am–5.30pm Sat 10am–4.30pm
Fairs International Ceramics Fair and Seminar
Services Valuations, Shippings

Isaac Carpets
Contact Mr Javid
347 Kensington High Street, London, W8 6NW
020 7603 6655/020 8838 3399
F 020 8388 3102
Est. 1978 *Stock size* Large
Stock Antique Oriental carpets, European carpets, tapestries
Open Mon–Sat 10am–6pm
Services Valuations, repair, cleaning

J A N Fine Art (KCSADA)
Contact F K Shimizu
134 Kensington Church Street, Kensington, London, W8 4BH
020 7792 0736 F 020 7221 1380
Est. 1979 *Stock size* Medium
Stock Japanese, Chinese, Korean ceramics, bronzes, works of art
Open Mon–Fri 10am–6pm Sat by appointment
Services Restorations

Jag Applied and Decorative Arts (Decorative Arts Society)
Contact C A Warner, G J Morgan or G S Strickland
58–60 Kensington Church Street, London, W8 4DB
020 7938 4404 F 020 7938 4404
M 07974 567507
E jag@jagdecorativearts.com
W www.jagdecorativearts.com
Est. 1990 *Stock size* Medium
Stock Liberty pewter and silver, Art Nouveau metal, glass decorative items
Open Mon–Sat 10.30am–5.30pm

Japanese Gallery Ltd (Ukiyo-e Society)
Contact Mr C D Wertheim
66D Kensington Church Street, London, W8 4BY
020 7229 2934 F 020 7229 2934
M 07930 411991
E princyw@hotmail.com
Est. 1978 *Stock size* Large
Stock Japanese woodcut prints, Japanese ceramics, sword armour, Japanese dolls
Open Mon–Sat 10am–6pm
Services Exhibitions every 3 months of Japanese print, Japanese-speaking staff

Roderick Jellicoe (BADA, KSADA, BACA Award Winner 2001)
3a Campden Street, off Kensington Church Street, London, W8 7EP
020 7727 1571 F 020 7727 1805
Est. 1975
Stock 18thC English porcelain
Open Mon–Fri 10am–5.30pm Sat 10am–1pm
Fairs ICF, NY Ceramics fair

John Jesse
Contact John Jesse
160 Kensington Church Street, London, W8 4BN
020 7229 0312 F 020 7229 4732
M 07767 497880
E jj@johnjesse.com
W www.johnjesse.com
Est. 1963 *Stock size* Medium
Stock 20thC decorative arts, sculpture, glass, ceramics, silver, jewellery
Open Mon–Fri 10am–5.30pm Sat 11am–4pm

Howard Jones Antiques (LAPADA)
Contact Mr Tristan Wright
43 Kensington Church Street, London, W8 4BA
020 7937 4359 F 020 7937 4359
Est. 1979 *Stock size* Small
Stock Antique and modern silver, trinket boxes, picture frames, cufflinks
Open Mon–Sat 9.30am–5.30pm

Peter Kemp
Contact Mr P Kemp
170 Kensington Church Street, London, W8 4BN
020 7229 2988 F 020 7229 2988
E peterkemp@btinternet.com
Est. 1971 *Stock size* Large
Stock 18thC Oriental, European porcelain, works of art
Open Mon–Fri 10.30am–5.30pm or by appointment

Kensington Church Street Antique Centre
Contact Jody Barry
58–60 Kensington Church Street, London, W8 4DB
020 7937 4600 F 020 7937 3400
E themanager@vh-businesscentres.com
W www.vh-businesscentres.com
Est. 1989 *Stock size* Large

No. of dealers 9
Stock 19th–20thC Decorative arts, Oriental and English ceramics
Open Mon–Sat 10am–6pm
Services Valuations, restorations, shipping

The Lacquer Chest
Contact Mrs G Andersen
75 Kensington Church Street, London, W8 4BG
020 7937 1306 020 7376 0223
Est. 1959 *Stock size* Large
Stock Military chests, china, clocks, samplers, lamps
Open Mon–Fri 9.30am–5.30pm Sat 11am–3pm
Services Prop hire of antiques

Lev Antiques Ltd (GOMC)
Contact Alyson Lawrence
97a Kensington Church Street, London, W8 7LN
020 7727 9248 020 7727 9248
alyson@richardlawrence.co.uk
Est. 1882 *Stock size* Medium
Stock Jewellery, silver, paintings, objets d'art, antiquities
Open Tues–Sat 10.30am–5.45pm Mon noon–5.30pm
Services Oil painting restoration

Lewis & Lloyd (BADA)
Contact Mr Paul C Lewis
65 Kensington Church Street, London, W8 4BA
020 7938 3323 020 7361 0086
paulclewis@aol.com
www.lewisandlloyd.co.uk
Est. 1977 *Stock size* Medium
Stock 18th–early 19thC English and Continental furniture
Open Mon–Fri 10.15am–5.15pm
Fairs Olympia (June, Nov)

Libra Antiques
Contact Mrs A Wolsey
131d Kensington Church Street, London, W8 7PT
020 7727 2990
Est. 1979 *Stock size* Large
Stock English blue-and-white pottery 1790–1820, creamware
Open Mon–Fri 10am–5pm Sat 10am–4pm

London Antique Gallery
Contact Mr C D Wertheim
66e Kensington Church Street, London, W8 4BY
020 7229 2934 020 7229 2934
07930 411991
centrallondon@hotmail.com
Est. 1996 *Stock size* Medium
Stock Meissen, Dresden, Worcester, Minton, Shelley, Sèvre, Lalique, bisque dolls
Open Mon–Sat 10am–6pm
Services Restorations, framing

Mah's Antiques
Contact Mr Mah
141 Kensington Church Street, London, W8 7LP
020 7229 9047 020 7354 1860
Est. 1994 *Stock size* Large
Stock Oriental and European porcelain, works of art
Open Mon–Fri 10.30am–5.30pm
Services Valuations, restorations

C H Major
Contact Sally Major
154 Kensington Church Street, London, W8 4BN
020 7229 1162 020 7221 9676
Est. 1919 *Stock size* Large
Stock 18th–19thC English furniture
Open Mon–Fri 10am–5.30pm Sat 10am–2pm
Services Valuations, restorations

E and H Manners (BADA)
Contact Errol Manners
66a Kensington Church Street, London, W8 4BY
020 7229 5516 020 7229 5516
manners@europeanporcelain.com
www.europeanporcelain.com
Est. 1986 *Stock size* Medium
Stock 18thC European porcelain, pottery
Open Mon–Fri 10am–5.30pm
Fairs International Ceramics Fair

S Marchant & Son (BADA, KCSADA)
Contact Mr S Marchant or Mr R Marchant
120 Kensington Church Street, London, W8 4BH
020 7229 5319 020 7792 8979
marchant@dircon.co.uk
www.marchantasianart.com
Est. 1925 *Stock size* Large
Stock Chinese porcelain, works of art, snuff bottles, jade
Open Mon–Fri 9.30am–5.30pm
Fairs Grosvenor House, International Asian Art
Services Valuations

Michael Coins
Contact Mr M Gouby
6 Hillgate Street, London, W8 7SR
020 7727 1518 020 7727 1518
Est. 1966 *Stock size* Medium
Stock English and foreign, medieval–present day coins, banknotes
Open Tues–Fri 10am–5pm

Colin D Monk
Contact Mr C Monk
58–60 Kensington Church Street, London, W8 4DB
020 7229 3727 020 7376 1501
Stock size Medium
Stock Oriental porcelain
Open Mon–Sat 11am–5pm

Nassirzadeh Antiques
Contact Mr Houshang
178 Kensington Church Street, London, W8 4DP
020 7243 8262 020 7243 8262
07958 626777
Est. 1984 *Stock size* Large
Stock Porcelain, glass, textiles
Open Mon–Sat 11am–6pm

New Century
Contact Mr H Lyons
69 Kensington Church Street, London, W8 4BG
020 7937 2410 020 7937 2410
07711 098941
Est. 1989 *Stock size* Medium
Stock Design 1860–1910
Open Mon–Sat 10am–6pm

Mrs Quick Chandeliers
Contact Mr N Denton
166 Kensington Church Street, London, W8 4BN
020 7229 1338 020 7792 1073
Est. 1897 *Stock size* Large
Stock French and English chandeliers, lighting, table lamps, 1750–1920
Open Mon–Fri 9.30am–5.30pm

Paul Reeves
Contact Mr P Reeves or S Barrett
32b Kensington Church Street, London, W8 4HA
020 7937 1594 020 7938 2163
Est. 1976 *Stock size* Large
Stock Victorian–Edwardian furniture, artefacts, textiles, glass, ceramics, metalwork, Arts and Crafts, aesthetic movement, gothic revival
Open Mon–Fri 10am–6pm Sat 11am–4pm

⊞ Reindeer Antiques Ltd (BADA, LAPADA)
Contact Adrian Butterworth
✉ **81 Kensington Church Street, London, W8 4BG** P
☎ 020 7937 3754 Ⓕ 020 7937 7199
Ⓔ adrianbutterworth@btinternet.com
Ⓦ www.reindeerantiques.co.uk
Est. 1969 *Stock size* Large
Stock Fine period English furniture, 17th–19thC mahogany, walnut, oak mirrors, paintings, objets d'art
Open Mon–Fri 9.30am–6pm Sat 10am–5pm
Fairs BADA (March), LAPADA (Oct), NEC
Services Valuations, restorations

⊞ Roderick Antiques (LAPADA, KCSADA)
Contact Mr R Mee
✉ **23 Vicarage Gate, (Junction Kensington Church Street), London, W8 4AA** P
☎ 020 7937 8517 Ⓕ 020 7937 8517
Est. 1975 *Stock size* Large
Stock Antique clocks, 1700–1900, including bracket, Vienna, longcase, carriage, English, French, German
Open Mon–Fri 10am–5.30pm Sat 10am–4pm
Services Valuations, repairs

⊞ Brian Rolleston Antiques Ltd (BADA)
Contact Mr B Rolleston
✉ **104a Kensington Church Street, London, W8 4BU** P
☎ 020 7229 5892 Ⓕ 020 7229 5892
Est. 1955 *Stock size* Medium
Stock 18thC English furniture
Open Mon–Fri 10am–1pm 2–5.30pm
Fairs Grosvenor House

⊞ Dyala Salam Antiques (KCSADA)
Contact Miss Dyala Salam
✉ **174a Kensington Church Street, London, W8 4DP** P
☎ 020 7229 4045 Ⓕ 020 7229 2433
Est. 1991 *Stock size* Large
Stock 18th–19thC Ottoman antiques, textiles, Bohemian glass, Islamic furniture
Open Mon–Fri 11am–6pm Sat 11.30am–3.30pm

⊞ Patrick Sandberg Antiques (BADA, CINOA)
Contact Mr C Radford
✉ **150–152 Kensington Church Street, London, W8 4BH** P
☎ 020 7229 0373 Ⓕ 020 7792 3467
Ⓔ psand@antiquefurniture.net
Ⓦ www.antiquefurniture.net
Est. 1983 *Stock size* Large
Stock 18th–19thC English furniture, mirrors, accessories
Open Mon–Fri 10am–6pm Sat 10am–4pm
Fairs Olympia

⊞ Santos (BADA)
Contact Mr A Santos
✉ **21 Old Court House, London, W8 4PD** P
☎ 020 7937 6000 Ⓕ 020 7937 3351
Ⓦ www.santoslondon.com
Est. 1979 *Stock size* Small
Stock 17th–18thC Chinese Export porcelain
Open By appointment only
Fairs International Ceramics Fair & Seminar London, The International Asian Art Fair, New York, Palm Beach, The New York Ceramics Fair

⊞ M & D Seligman (BADA, CINOA)
Contact Mr D Seligman
✉ **37 Kensington Church Street, London, W8 4LL** P
☎ 020 7937 0400 Ⓕ 020 7722 4315
Ⓜ 07946 634429
Est. 1974 *Stock size* Medium
Stock Vernacular furniture, 16th–early 19thC, mainly oak, treen, works of art
Open Mon–Fri 10.30am–5.30pm or by appointment
Fairs Olympia (June, Nov), BADA

⊞ Simon Spero
Contact Mr S Spero
✉ **109 Kensington Church Street, London, W8 7LN** P
☎ 020 7727 7413 Ⓕ 020 7727 7414
Est. 1964 *Stock size* Large
Stock 18thC English porcelain, enamels
Open Mon–Fri 10am–5pm closed 1–2pm
Fairs International Ceramics Fair
Services Valuations, author of 4 reference books, lecturer

⊞ Stockspring Antiques (BADA, LAPADA, KCSADA)
Contact Mrs F Marno
✉ **114 Kensington Church Street, London, W8 4BH**
☎ 020 7727 7995 Ⓕ 020 7727 7995
Ⓔ stockspring@antique-porcelain.co.uk
Ⓦ www.antique-porcelain.co.uk
Est. 1979 *Stock size* Large
Stock 18thC English porcelain, 1745–1835, figures, tea ware, dinnerware, decorative ware
Open Mon–Fri 10am–5.30pm Sat 10am–1pm
Fairs Olympia (Nov, June), Harrogate (Sept)
Services Packing, shipping

⊞ Through The Looking Glass
Contact Mr J Pulton
✉ **137 Kensington Church Street, London, W8 7LP** P
☎ 020 7221 4026 Ⓕ 020 7602 3678
Est. 1988 *Stock size* Large
Stock 19thC mirrors
Open Mon–Sat 10am–5.30pm

⊞ Jorge Welsh (BADA)
Contact Mr J Welsh
✉ **116 Kensington Church Street, London, W8 4BH** P
☎ 020 7229 2140 Ⓕ 020 7792 3535
Ⓔ uk@jorgewelsh.com
Ⓦ www.jorgewelsh.com
Est. 1997 *Stock size* Large
Stock Chinese porcelain
Open Mon–Fri 10am–5.30pm Sat 10am–2pm
Fairs International Ceramics Fair, Olympia (June)

⊞ Mary Wise & Grosvenor Antiques (BADA)
Contact Mrs M Wise
✉ **27 Holland Street, London, W8 4NA** P
☎ 020 7937 8649 Ⓕ 020 7937 7179
Ⓜ 07850 863 050
Ⓔ info@wiseantiques.com
Ⓦ www.wiseantiques.com
Est. 1970 *Stock size* Small
Stock Porcelain, small bronzes, works of art, Chinese watercolours on pith paper
Open Mon–Fri 10am–5pm
Fairs New York Ceramics Fair, San Francisco Fall Antiques Show
Services Bid at auction

⊞ The Woolahra Trading Co Ltd (Syndicate des Antiquaires)
Contact Robert or Judith Compton-Jones
✉ **5 Bedford Gardens, London, W8 7ED** P

☎ 020 7727 6996 Ⓕ 020 7727 6996
Est. 1970
Stock 16th–18thC European ceramics and oil paintings
Open By appointment only
Fairs International Ceramics Fair, Biennale Paris
Services Valuations

⊞ Zeitgeist Antiques
Contact Mr A Self
✉ **58 Kensington Church Street, London, W8 4DB** Ⓟ
☎ 020 7938 4817 Ⓕ 020 7938 4817
Ⓔ zeitgeistantiques@virgin.net
Ⓦ www.zeitgeistantiques.com
Est. 1988 *Stock size* Small
Stock Art Nouveau, Art Deco, glass, ceramics, metalware
Open Mon–Sat 10am–6pm
Fairs 20thC Olympia, Great Antiques Fair

W9

⊞ Vale Antiques
Contact Mr P Gooley
✉ **245 Elgin Avenue, Maida Vale, London, W9 1NJ** Ⓟ
☎ 020 7328 4796
Est. 1973 *Stock size* Large
Stock Eclectic mix of antiques, Victorian–1950s, pictures, mirrors, silver, silver plate, china etc
Open Mon–Sat 10am–6pm
Services Restorations, pearl stringing, clock/watch repairs, framing

W10

⊞ 88 Antiques
Contact Mr D Lucas
✉ **88 Golborne Road, London, W10 5PS** Ⓟ
☎ 020 8960 0827
Est. 1977 *Stock size* Large
Stock Antique pine, country furniture
Open Tues–Sat 10am–6pm
Services Makers of tables from reclaimed 100-year-old wood

⊞ Bazar
Contact Ms M Davis or Ms C Rogers
✉ **82 Golborne Road, London, W10 5PS** Ⓟ
☎ 020 8969 6262
Est. 1992 *Stock size* Medium
Stock French decorative country furniture, beds, tables, armchairs, kitchenware, garden furniture etc
Open Tues–Thurs 10am–5pm
Fri Sat 9.30am–5.30pm

⊞ David Wainwright
Contact Mr Jeremy Schroder
✉ **16–18 Malton Road, London, W10 5UP**
☎ 020 8960 8181
Stock size Large
Stock Antique and old furniture, decorative items from India, Indonesia, China
Open By appointment
Services Delivery

W11

⊞ 51 Antiques
Contact Mr Justin Raccanello
✉ **51 Ledbury Road, London, W11 2AA** Ⓟ
☎ 020 7229 6153 Ⓕ 020 7229 6153
Est. 1975 *Stock size* Medium
Stock Italian ceramics, 1500–1900, Venetian glass
Open Mon–Fri 9.30am–5.30pm
Sat 9.30am–1pm

⊞ Alice's
Contact Mrs D Carter
✉ **86 Portobello Road, London, W11 2QD** Ⓟ
☎ 020 7229 8187 Ⓕ 020 7792 2456
Est. 1887 *Stock size* Large
Stock Painted furniture, decorative items, general antiques
Open Tues–Fri 9am–5pm
Sat 7am–4pm

⊞ Anthea's Antiques
Contact A Mcilroy
✉ **Burtons Arcade, 296 Westbourne Grove, Portobello Market, London, W11 2PS** Ⓟ
☎ 020 8690 7207
Ⓜ 07961 838780
Est. 1985 *Stock size* Medium
Stock 19thC English and Continental glass and ceramics
Trade only Yes
Open Sat 7am–4pm
Fairs Newark, Ardingly
Services Will arrange shipping if required

⊞ Arbras
Contact Mr Peter Hornby
✉ **Arbras Gallery, 292 Westbourne Grove, London, W11 2PS** Ⓟ
☎ 020 7229 6772 Ⓕ 020 7229 6772
Ⓔ info@arbras.freeserve.co.uk
Ⓦ www.arbras.freeserve.co.uk
Est. 1973 *Stock size* Large
Stock Silver picture frames, giftware
Open Mon–Fri 10am–4.30pm
Sat 7am–4.30pm
Services Mail order

⊞ Arenski Fine Art (BADA, LAPADA)
Contact Katie Kirkland
✉ **The Coach House, Ledbury Mews North, London, W11 2AF** Ⓟ
☎ 020 7727 8599 Ⓕ 020 7727 7584
Ⓔ arenski@netcomuk.co.uk
Ⓦ www.arenski.com
Stock size Large
Stock Exotic, unusual and colonial furniture, sculpture, animals in art
Open By appointment only
Fairs Olympia (summer and winter), Dallas, Palm Beach

⊞ Atlam Sales and Service (PADA)
Contact B Skogland-Kirk
✉ **111 Portobello Road, London, W11 2QB** Ⓟ
☎ 020 7602 7573 Ⓕ 020 7602 2997
Ⓔ info@atlam-watches.co.uk
Ⓦ www.atlam-watches.co.uk/ www.atlamsilver.com
Est. 1979 *Stock size* Large
Stock Silver and antique pocket watches, decorative silver
Open Mon–Fri 9am–5pm
Sat 8am–5pm

⊞ B and T Antiques Ltd (LAPADA, PADA)
Contact Bernadette Lewis or Vigi Sawdon
✉ **79–81 Ledbury Road, London, W11 2AG** Ⓟ
☎ 020 7229 7001 Ⓕ 020 7229 2033
Ⓔ bt.antiques@virgin.net
Est. 1994 *Stock size* Large
Stock Decorative antiques, Art Deco furniture and objects
Open Mon–Sat 10am–6pm
Services Restorations, gilding

⊞ Sebastiano Barbagallo Antiques
Contact Mr S Barbagallo
✉ **15 Pembridge Road, London, W11 3HG** Ⓟ
☎ 020 7792 3320 Ⓕ 020 7792 3320
Est. 1978 *Stock size* Large

Stock Chinese furniture, Indian and Tibetan antiques, crafts
Open Mon–Fri 10.30am–6.30pm Sat 9am–7pm Sun 10.30am–5pm

⊞ Barham Antiques (PADA)
Contact Mr M Barham
✉ **83 Portobello Road, London, W11 2QB** 🅿
☎ 020 7727 3845 Ⓕ 020 7727 3845
Ⓔ mchlbarham@aol.com
Est. 1970 *Stock size* Large
Stock Boxes, caddies, inkwells, clocks, glassware, inkstands, small furniture, silver plate
Open Mon–Fri 10am–4.30pm Sat 7am–5pm
Services Valuations, restorations

⊞ P R Barham (LAPADA)
Contact Mr P Barham
✉ **111 Portobello Road, London, W11 2QB** 🅿
☎ 020 7727 3397 Ⓕ 020 7243 1719
Est. 1967 *Stock size* Large
Stock Victorian and decorative furniture, clocks, paintings, objets d'art
Open Mon–Sat 9am–5pm
Fairs Olympia, NEC
Services Restorations

⊞ Beagle Gallery and Asian Antiques
Contact Mr Beagle
✉ **303 Westbourne Grove, London, W11 2QA** 🅿
☎ 020 7229 9524 Ⓕ 020 7792 0333
Est. 1984 *Stock size* Medium
Stock Oriental furniture, sculpture
Open By appointment

⊞ Book and Comic Exchange
Contact Mrs S Dawson
✉ **14 Pembridge Road, London, W11 3HL** 🅿
☎ 020 7229 8420
Ⓦ www.buy-sell-trade.co.uk
Est. 1967 *Stock size* Medium
Stock Modern first editions, cult books, comics
Open Mon–Sun 10am–8pm

⊞ Tony Booth Antiques (PADA)
Contact Mr Tony Booth
✉ **135 Portobello Road, London, W11 2DY** 🅿
☎ 020 8810 6339 Ⓕ 020 8810 6339
Ⓜ 07770 390749
Ⓔ tonybooth44@hotmail.com
Est. 1990 *Stock size* Medium
Stock Silver
Open Sat 7am–5pm
Fairs Ardingly, NEC

Key to Symbols
⊞ = Dealer
⌂ = Antiques Centre
⚒ = Auction House
✉ = Address
🅿 = Parking
☎ = Telephone No.
Ⓜ = Mobile tel No.
Ⓕ = Fax No.
Ⓔ = E-mail address
Ⓦ = Website address

⊞ Butchoff Antiques (LAPADA)
Contact Mr A Kaye
✉ **220 Westbourne Grove, London, W11 2RH** 🅿
☎ 020 7221 8174 Ⓕ 020 7792 8923
Ⓔ ian@butchoff.com
Ⓦ www.butchoff.com
Est. 1999 *Stock size* Medium
Stock One-off items, textiles, collectables, dining tables, chairs, consoles, accessories
Open Mon–Fri 9.30am–6pm Sat 9.30am–5pm

⊞ Canonbury Antiques Ltd
Contact Miss A Worster
✉ **174 Westbourne Grove, London, W11 2RW** 🅿
☎ 020 7229 2786 Ⓕ 020 7229 5840
Ⓔ martin@canonbury-antiques.co.uk
Est. 1964 *Stock size* Large
Stock 18th–19thC furniture, reproduction furniture, accessories
Open Mon–Sat 10am–5.30pm
Fairs Newark
Services Restorations

⊞ Aurea Carter (LAPADA)
Contact Aurea Carter
✉ **Burton's Antique Arcade, 296 Westbourne Grove, London, W11 2PS** 🅿
☎ 020 7731 3486 Ⓕ 020 7731 3486
Ⓜ 07815 912477
Ⓔ aureacarter@englishceramics.com
Ⓦ www.englishceramics.com
Est. 1980 *Stock size* Large
Stock 18th–early 19thC English pottery and porcelain
Open Sat 7.30am–2.30pm Fri afternoon by appointment
Fairs Olympia, New York Ceramic Fair
Services Valuations, shipping

⊞ Jack Casimir Ltd (BADA, LAPADA)
✉ **23 Pembridge Road, London, W11 3HG** 🅿
☎ 020 7727 8643
Est. 1931 *Stock size* Large
Stock 16th–19thC British and European domestic brass, copper, pewter, paktong
Open Mon–Sat 9.30am–5.30pm
Services Shipping

⊞ Chamade Antiques
Contact George Walters
✉ **65 Portobello Road, London, W11 2QB** 🅿
☎ 020 8446 0130
Stock size Medium
Stock Antique Rolex watches
Open Sat 7am–3pm

⊞ Nicholas Chandor Antiques
Contact Mr N Chandor
✉ **4a Ladbroke Grove, London, W11 3BG** 🅿
☎ 020 7229 4044 Ⓕ 020 7229 4044
Ⓔ nicholaschandor@aol.com
Est. 1990 *Stock size* Medium
Stock Eclectic Continental furniture
Open Tues–Sat 10am–6pm

⊞ Cohen & Cohen Portobello Road (BADA)
Contact Mr M Cohen
✉ **84 Portobello Road, London, W11 2QD** 🅿
☎ 020 7229 9458 Ⓕ 020 7229 9653
Ⓔ cohenandcohen@aol.com
Ⓦ www.artnet.com/cohen&cohen.html
Est. 1973 *Stock size* Large
Stock Chinese Export porcelain, works of art
Open Fri 9am–4pm Sat 8am–4pm

⊞ Sheila Cook Textiles
Contact Mrs S Cook
✉ **283 Westbourne Grove, London, W11 2QA** 🅿
☎ 020 7792 8001 Ⓕ 020 7229 3855
Ⓔ sheilacook@sheilacook.co.uk
Ⓦ www.sheilacook.co.uk
Est. 1970 *Stock size* Small
Stock Mid-18thC–1970s European costume, textiles, accessories
Open Tues–Sat 10am–6pm
Services Valuations

Stuart Craig (PADA)
Contact Stuart Craig
Unit 72, Ground Floor, Admiral Vernon Antiques Market, 141–149 Portobello Road, London, W11 2DY P
☎ 020 7221 8662
Ⓜ 07947 889012
Est. 1991 *Stock size* Medium
Stock Early 19thC–1950s antique ladies' clothing, accessories
Open Sat 8.30am–4pm or by appointment

Cura Antiques
Contact Mr Cura
34 Ledbury Road, London, W11 2AB P
☎ 020 7229 6880 Ⓕ 020 7792 3731
Ⓔ mail@cura-antiques.com
Ⓦ www.artnet.com/cura.html
Est. 1969 *Stock size* Medium
Stock Continental works of art, furniture, old master paintings
Open Mon–Fri 10.30am–5.30pm Sat 10am–1pm
Fairs Olympia (June)
Services Restorations

John Dale Antiques (PADA)
Contact Mrs Jo Cairns
87 Portobello Road, London, W11 2QB P
☎ 020 7727 1304
Est. 1960 *Stock size* Medium
No. of dealers 6
Stock Stained glass, books, prints, antiquities, collectables, cameras, decorative antiques
Open Sat 7am–5pm Mon–Fri 11am–4pm or by appointment

Simon Finch (ABA, PBFA)
Contact Simon Finch
61a Ledbury Road, London, W11 2AL P
☎ 020 7792 3303
Ⓔ rarebooks@simonfinch.com
Ⓦ www.simonfinch.com
Est. 1982 *Stock size* Medium
Stock Modern first editions, art and photography
Open Mon–Sat 10am-6pm
Fairs Olympia, Chelsea, Grosvenor House

J Freeman (LAPADA)
Contact Mr J Freeman
85a Portobello Road, London, W11 2QB P
☎ 020 7221 5076 Ⓕ 020 7221 5329
Est. 1949 *Stock size* Medium
Stock Victorian–Edwardian silver, silver plate
Open Mon–Sat 9am–5pm

Henry Gregory (PADA)
Contact Camy Gregory
82E Portobello Road, London, W11 2QD P
☎ 020 7792 9221
Est. 1970 *Stock size* Medium
Stock Silver plate, silver, sporting goods, decorative antiques
Open Mon–Fri 10am–4.30pm Sat 8am–4.30pm
Services Shipping

Hampton Antiques (PADA)
Contact Mark Goodger
Crown Arcade, 119 Portobello Road, London, W11 2QB P
☎ 01604 764298 Ⓕ 01604 764298
Stock size Medium
Stock Antique boxes (including tortoiseshell and ivory), objets d'art, small furniture
Trade only Yes
Open Sat 6.30am–3pm or by appointment
Fairs Newark, Ardingly
Services Restorations

Hart & Rosenberg
Contact Mrs E Hart
Units L52/L53, Lower Trading Hall, Admiral Vernon Antiques Market, 141–149 Portobello Road, London, W11 2DY P
☎ 020 7359 6839 Ⓕ 020 7359 6839
Est. 1968 *Stock size* Large
Stock Oriental and Continental ceramics, decorative items
Open Wed–Sat 10am–5pm Tues–Fri 10.30am–5pm or by appointment
Services Valuations, restorations

Helios Gallery (ADA, PADA, BABAADA)
Contact Rolf Kiaer
292 Westbourne Grove, London, W11 2PS P
Ⓕ 01225 336097
Ⓜ 07711 955997
Ⓔ heliosgallery@btinternet.com
Ⓦ www.heliosgallery.com
Est. 1995 *Stock size* Medium
Stock Roman, Greek, Egyptian, Chinese, ancient art
Open Sat 8am–4pm or by appointment
Fairs ADA Fair
Services Valuations, restorations, shipping

Hirst Antiques
Contact Mrs S Hirst
59 Pembridge Road, London, W11 3HN P
☎ 020 7727 9364 Ⓕ 020 7460 6480
Est. 1969 *Stock size* Large
Stock General antique furniture, antique beds, bronzes, sculpture, pictures
Open Mon–Sat 10am–6pm

Erna Hiscock (PADA)
Contact Erna Hiscock
Chelsea Galleries, 69 Portobello Road, London, W11 2PS
☎ 01233 661407 Ⓕ 01233 661407
Est. 1975 *Stock size* Large
Stock 17th–19thC samplers, needlework
Open Sat 7am–3pm
Fairs NEC
Services Valuations

Kleanthous Antiques Ltd (LAPADA)
Contact Mr C Kleanthous
144 Portobello Road, London, W11 2DZ P
☎ 020 7727 3649 Ⓕ 020 7243 2488
Ⓜ 07850 375501
Ⓔ antiques@kleanthaus.com
Est. 1969 *Stock size* Medium
Stock Jewellery, wristwatches, furniture, clocks, pocket watches, porcelain, china, silver, works of art, 20thC decorative items
Open Sat 8am–4pm or by appointment
Fairs Olympia

M & D Lewis
Contact Mr M Lewis
83–85 Ledbury Road, London, W11 2AG P
☎ 020 7727 3908 Ⓕ 020 7727 3908
Est. 1959 *Stock size* Large
Stock English and Continental furniture, Oriental porcelain
Open Mon–Fri 10am–5pm Sat 10am–4pm

M & D Lewis (PADA)
Contact Mr M Lewis
1 Lonsdale Road, London, W11 2BY P
☎ 020 7727 3908 Ⓕ 020 7727 3908
Est. 1959 *Stock size* Large

Stock English and Continental furniture, Oriental porcelain
Open Mon–Fri 10am–5pm
Sat 10am–4pm

M & D Lewis
Contact Mr M Lewis
172 Westbourne Grove, London, W11 2RW
020 7727 3908 F 020 7727 3908
Est. 1959 *Stock size* Large
Stock English and Continental furniture, Oriental porcelain
Open Mon–Fri 10am-5pm
Sat 10am–3pm

Caira Mandaglio
Contact Anne or Sharon
31 Pembridge Road, London, W11 3HG
020 7727 5496 F 020 7229 4889
Est. 1998 *Stock size* Large
Stock 14th–20thC furniture, lighting, glassware, objets d'art, chandeliers
Open Tues–Fri 11am–5pm
Sat 10.30am–5.30pm

Robin Martin Antiques
Contact Mr P Martin
44 Ledbury Road, London, W11 2AB
020 7727 1301 F 020 7727 1301
E paul.martinll@virgin.net
Est. 1971 *Stock size* Medium
Stock Mirrors, Regency furniture, Continental furniture, works of art, lighting
Open Mon–Fri 10am–6pm
Sat 10am–1pm
Fairs Olympia (June, Nov)

Mayflower Antiques (PADA)
Contact Mr John Odgers
117 Portobello Road, London, W11 2DY
020 7727 0381
M 07860 843579
E antiques@johnodgers.com
Est. 1970 *Stock size* Medium
Stock Music boxes, clocks, dolls, scientific instruments, pistols, collectable items
Open Sat 7am–4pm
Fairs Newark, Ardingly

MCN Antiques
Contact Makoto Umezawa
183 Westbourne Grove, London, W11 2SB
020 7727 3796 F 020 7229 8839
Est. 1980 *Stock size* Large
Stock Japanese porcelain, works of art
Open Mon–Fri 10am–6pm
Sat 11am–3pm

Mercury Antiques (BADA)
Contact Mrs Liane Richards
1 Ladbroke Road, Kensington, London, W11 3PA
020 7727 5106 F 020 7229 3738
Est. 1963
Stock 18th–early 19thC pottery, porcelain, Delft, glass
Open Mon–Fri 10am–5.30pm
Sat 10am–12.30pm
Fairs International Ceramics Fair
Services Valuations

Mimi Fifi
Contact Rita Delaforge
27 Pembridge Road, Notting Hill Gate, London, W11 3HG
020 7243 3154 F 020 7938 4222
M 07956 222238
E info@mimififi.com
W www.mimififi.com
Est. 1992 *Stock size* Large
Stock Collectors' and vintage toys, Coca-Cola memorabilia, Pokémon, perfume-related items, vintage badges, tobacco memorabilia, Michelin memorabilia, Kewpie dolls, Astro Boy
Open Mon–Fri 11am–7pm
Sat 10am–7pm
Services Overseas postal service

Terence Morse & Son
Contact Mr G Morse
237 Westbourne Grove, London, W11 2SE
020 7229 4059 F 020 7792 3284
Est. 1948 *Stock size* Large
Stock 18th–19thC fine English and Continental furniture, linen presses, library furniture
Open Mon–Fri 10am–6pm
Sat 11am–2pm

Myriad Antiques
Contact Mrs S Nickerson
131 Portland Road, London, W11 4LW
020 7229 1709 F 020 7221 3882
Est. 1975 *Stock size* Large
Stock French painted furniture, garden furniture, bamboo, Victorian–Edwardian upholstered chairs, mirrors, objets d'art
Open Tues–Sat 11am–6pm

Ormonde Gallery (LAPADA)
Contact Mr F Ormonde
156 Portobello Road, London, W11 2EB
020 7229 9800 F 020 7792 2418
Stock size Large
Stock 19thC Chinese and Indonesian furniture, ceramics 2000BC–Ching Dynasty, Oriental art, jade, snuff bottles
Open Mon–Fri 10am–6pm
Sat 9am–6pm

Peter Petrou (BADA, LAPADA)
Contact Katie Kirkland
The Coach House, Ledbury Mews North, London, W11 2AF
020 7229 9575 F 020 7727 7584
E peterpetrou@btinternet.com
W www.peterpetrou.com
Est. 1974 *Stock size* Large
Stock Exotic, unusual and colonial furniture, sculpture, animals in art
Open By appointment only
Fairs Olympia (summer and winter), Dallas, Palm Beach

Portobello Antique Store
Contact Mr J Ewing
79 Portobello Road, London, W11 2QB
020 7221 1994 F 020 7221 1994
Est. 1984 *Stock size* Large
Stock Silver, silver plate, decorative items, flatware
Open Tues–Fri 10am–4pm
Sat 8.15am–4pm

Principia Fine Art
Contact Mr M Forrer
Stand 9–!0, Lipka Arcade, 282 Westbourne Grove, London, W11 2DX
01488 682873 F 01672 511551
M 07899 926020
W www.antiquesportfolio.com
Est. 1970 *Stock size* Large
Stock Scientific instruments, small furniture, Oriental art, books, paintings, works of art
Open Sat 7am–12.30pm
Services Valuations, restorations, shipping, book search

Rogers Antiques Gallery
Contact Mike Spooner
65 Portobello Road, London, W11 2QB

☎ 020 7969 1500 ⓕ 020 7969 1639
Est. 1969 *Stock size* Large
No. of dealers 65
Stock Wide range of antiques and collectables, specialist dealers in most fields
Open Sat 7am–4.30pm
Services Valuations

⊞ Schredds of Portobello (LAPADA, CINOA, PADA)
Contact George R Schrager
✉ **107 Portobello Road, London, W11 2QB** Ⓟ
☎ 020 8348 3314 ⓕ 020 8341 5971
ⓔ silver@schredds.demon.co.uk
ⓦ www.schredds.com
Est. 1972 *Stock size* Large
Stock Small pieces of pre-1880 silver
Open Sat 7am–2.30pm
Fairs Penman fairs
Services Valuations, shipping

⊞ Justin F Skrebowski Prints (PBFA, PADA)
Contact Mr J Skrebowski
✉ **Ground Floor, 177 Portobello Road, London, W11 2DY** Ⓟ
☎ 020 7792 9742 ⓕ 020 7792 9742
Ⓜ 07774 612474
ⓔ justin@skreb.co.uk
ⓦ www.skreb.co.uk
Est. 1979 *Stock size* Large
Stock 18–19thC decorative prints, 18th–20thC frames for prints and watercolours, oils, watercolours
Open Sat 9am–4pm or by appointment
Fairs PBFA, Russell Hotel
Services Folio stands, easels, display equipment

⊞ Solaris Antiques
Contact Hassan Abdullah
✉ **170 Westbourne Grove, London, W11 2RW** Ⓟ
☎ 020 7229 8100 ⓕ 020 7229 8300
Est. 1994 *Stock size* Medium
Stock Decorative antiques from France and Sweden, all periods up to 1970s
Open Mon–Sat 10.30–6pm
Fairs Battersea Antiques Fair
Services Restorations, upholstery

⊞ June and Tony Stone Fine Antique Boxes (PADA LAPADA)
Contact Tony Stone
✉ **75 Portobello Road, London, W11 2QB** Ⓟ
☎ 07092 106600 ⓕ 07092 106611
ⓔ jts@boxes.co.uk
ⓦ www.boxes.co.uk
Est. 1990 *Stock size* Large
Stock 18th–19thC boxes, rare and unusual tea caddies
Open Mon–Fri 10.30am–4.30pm Sat 8am–5pm
Fairs All Olympias, LAPADA
Services Shipping included in prices

⊞ Virginia
Contact Mrs V Bates
✉ **98 Portland Road, London, W11 4LQ** Ⓟ
☎ 020 7727 9908 ⓕ 020 7229 2198
Est. 1971 *Stock size* Medium
Stock Vintage clothes, late 19thC–late 1930s
Open 11am–6pm by appointment only

⊞ Visto
Contact Mrs H Little
✉ **41 Pembridge Road, Notting Hill, London, W11 3HG** Ⓟ
☎ 020 7243 4392 ⓕ 020 7243 1374
Ⓜ 07788 136906
Est. 1997 *Stock size* Medium
Stock 1950s–1960s collectables, lighting, textiles, furniture, ceramics, glass
Open Mon–Fri 11am–6pm Sat 10am–6pm

⊞ David Wainwright
Contact Mr D Wainwright
✉ **63 Portobello Road, London, W11 3DB**
☎ 020 7727 0707 *Stock size* Small
Stock Antique and old furniture, decorative items from India, Indonesia, China
Open Mon–Sat 9am–6pm
Services Delivery

⊞ David Wainwright
Contact Mr D Wainwright
✉ **251 Portobello Road, London, W11 1LT**
☎ 020 7792 1988
Stock size Medium
Stock Antique and old furniture, decorative items from India, Indonesia, China
Open Mon–Sat 9.30am–6.30pm Sun 11am–6pm
Services Delivery

⊞ Trude Weaver (LAPADA)
Contact Mr B Weaver
✉ **71 Portobello Road, London, W11 2QB** Ⓟ
☎ 020 7229 8738 ⓕ 020 7229 8738
Ⓜ 07768 551269
Est. 1968 *Stock size* Large
Stock 18th–19thC English and Continental furniture, complementary accessories
Open Wed–Sat 9.30am–5.30pm
Fairs Olympia (June, Nov)

W12

Neil Freeman Angling Auctions
Contact Mr N Freeman
✉ **PO Box 2095, London, W12 8RU** Ⓟ
☎ 020 8749 4175 ⓕ 020 8743 4855
Ⓜ 07785 281349
ⓔ neil@anglingauctions.demon.co.uk.
ⓦ www.thesaurus.co.uk/angling-auctions/
Est. 1990
Sales Angling auctions twice yearly, first Sat April noon, first Sat October noon, viewing The Grand Hall, Chiswick Town Hall, Heathfield Terrace, London W4 prior Fri 1.30–7pm day of sale 8.30am–noon
Frequency Twice yearly
Catalogues yes

W13

⊞ C and L Burman (BADA)
Contact Charles Truman or Lucy Burniston
✉ **5 Vigo Street, London, W13 3HF** Ⓟ
☎ 020 7439 6604 ⓕ 020 7439 6605
ⓔ charles-truman@lineone.net
Est. 2001 *Stock size* Medium
Stock Antiques and works of art including silver, glass, ceramics, furniture, sculpture
Open By appointment
Fairs March BADA, Grosvenor House, Winter Olympia
Services Valuations, restorations

W14

⊞ Asenbaum Fine Arts Ltd
Contact Mrs C Fells
✉ **10 Carlton Mansions, Holland Park Gardens, London, W14 8DW** Ⓟ
☎ 020 7602 5373 ⓕ 020 7602 5373
Est. 1998 *Stock size* Medium
Stock English and Viennese

silver, Viennese furniture, Victorian jewellery
Trade only Yes
Open By appointment only

Kate Thurlow (LAPADA, CINOA)
Contact Kate Thurlow
The Warehouse, 7A North End Road, London, W14 8ST
☎ 020 7602 8388 Ⓕ 020 7602 8388
Ⓔ kate.thurlow@btinternet.com
Est. 1978 *Stock size* Medium
Stock 16th–17thC European furniture, associated works of art
Open By appointment
Fairs Olympia
Services Restorations

WC1

Amherst Antiques (LAPADA)
Contact Mrs Dianne Brick
Monomark House, 27 Old Gloucester Street, London, WC1 N3XX
☎ 01892 725552 Ⓕ 01892 725552
Ⓜ 07850 350212
Est. 1987 *Stock size* Medium
Stock Tunbridge ware, 19thC English ceramics, coloured glass, silver
Open By appointment
Fairs Olympia, NEC, Chester, Buxton, Petersfield
Services Valuations of Tunbridge ware

The Bloomsbury Bookshop
Contact Mr M Thompson
12 Bury Place, London, WC1A 2JL
☎ 020 7404 7433
Ⓔ dullbooks@aol.com
Est. 1989 *Stock size* Large
Stock Non-fiction, history, humanities, social sciences
Open Mon–Sat 11am–6pm Sun 11am–5pm
Services Valuations, book search

Book Art and Architecture Ltd
Contact Mr D C Sharp
12 Woburn Walk, London, WC1H 0JL
☎ 020 7387 5006 Ⓕ 0170 7875286
Ⓜ 07710 207404
Ⓔ sharpd@globalnet.co.uk
Est. 1998 *Stock size* Large
Stock Antiquarian, rare, out-of-print, second-hand books, also the volume gallery, modern architecture, art, design a speciality
Open Mon–Fri 11am–6pm
Fairs Russell Hotel, Hatfield
Services Book searches, valuations, library lists

Coincraft (ADA, IBNS, PNG, ANA)
Contact Mr B Clayden
44–45 Great Russell Street, London, WC1B 3LU
☎ 020 7636 1188 Ⓕ 020 7323 2860
Ⓔ info@coincraft.com
Ⓦ ww.coincraft.com
Est. 1955
Stock Greek, Roman, English, medieval–present day coins, British and foreign banknotes, ancient artefacts
Open Mon–Fri 9.30am–5pm Sat 10am–2.30pm or by appointment
Fairs Marriott, Cumberland
Services Catalogue of British coins

Collinge & Clark (PBFA)
Contact Mr O Clark
13 Leigh Street, London, WC1H 9EW
☎ 020 7387 7105 Ⓕ 020 7388 1315
Est. 1989 *Stock size* Medium
Stock Antiquarian, rare, second-hand books, private press books, limited editions, 18th–19thC political/social history, typography
Open Mon–Fri 11am–6.30pm Sat 11am–3.30pm

Fine Books Oriental Ltd (PBFA)
Contact Mr J Somers
38 Museum Street, London, WC1A 1LP
☎ 020 7242 5288 Ⓕ 020 7242 5344
Ⓔ oriental@finebooks.demon.co.uk
Ⓦ www.finebooks.demon.co.uk
Est. 1977 *Stock size* Medium
Stock South Asian and Indian, out-of-print, rare books
Open Mon–Fri 9.30am–6pm Sat 11am–6pm
Fairs PBFA, Russell Hotel
Services Valuations

Robert Frew Ltd (PBFA, ABA)
Contact Mr R Frew
106 Great Russell Street, London, WC1B 3NB
☎ 020 7580 2311 Ⓕ 020 7580 2313
Ⓔ shop@robertfrew.com
Ⓦ www.robertfrew.com
Est. 1976 *Stock size* Medium
Stock Antiquarian and rare books, travel, literature, classics, maps, prints
Open Mon–Fri 10am–6pm Sat 10am–2pm
Fairs PBFA Bookfairs, Russell Hotel, ABA Olympia Chelsea

R A Gekoski Booksellers (ABA, ILAD)
Contact Rick Gekoski
Pied Bull Yard, 15a Bloomsbury Square, London, WC1A 2LP
☎ 0207 4046676 Ⓕ 0207 4046595
Ⓔ gekoski@dircon.co.uk
Est. 1984
Stock First editions, letters, paintings, manuscripts
Open Mon–Fri 10am–5.30pm
Fairs ABA
Services Valuations

Griffith & Partners Ltd
Contact David Griffith
31–35 Great Ormond Street, London, WC1N 3HZ
☎ 020 7430 1394
Est. 1992 *Stock size* Medium
Stock Antiquarian, rare, second-hand books, London topography, Middle East, poetry, Anglo and Welsh topics a speciality
Open Mon–Fri noon–6pm or by appointment
Services Valuations, book search, catalogues, mail order

Jarndyce Antiquarian Booksellers (ABA, PBFA)
Contact Mr B Lake or Ms Janet Nassau
46 Great Russell Street, London, WC1B 3PA
☎ 020 7631 4220 Ⓕ 020 7631 1882
Ⓔ books@jarndyce.com
Ⓦ www.jarndyce.com
Est. 1969 *Stock size* Large
Stock Antiquarian, rare, second-hand books on English language, English literature, Dickens, 18th–20thC economic and social history
Open Mon–Fri 10.30am–5.30pm
Fairs Olympia, Chelsea ABA, York PBFA
Services Valuations, catalogues

Robert Johnson Coin Co
Contact Mr R Johnson
15 Bury Place, London, WC1A 2JB
020 7831 0305 Ⓕ 01494 681084
Est. 1971
Stock Greek, Roman, English, hammered and milled coins
Open Mon–Fri 10am–6pm Sat 11am–4pm
Services Valuations

Marchmont Bookshop
Contact Mr D Holder
39 Burton Street, London, WC1H 9AL
020 7387 7989 Ⓕ 020 7387 7989
Est. 1977 *Stock size* Medium
Stock Rare, antiquarian, second-hand books, literature, poetry a speciality
Open Mon–Fri 11am–6.30pm

Rennies (ESoc)
Contact Mr P Rennie
13 Rugby Street, London, WC1N 3QT
020 7405 0220 Ⓕ 020 7405 0220
Ⓔ Rennart@aol.com
Ⓦ www.rennart.co.uk
Est. 1990 *Stock size* Small
Stock 20thC art and design, inter-war period posters, graphics
Open Tues–Sat noon–6.30pm
Services Valuations

Roe and Moore
Contact Mr T Roe
29 Museum Street, London, WC1A 1LH
020 7636 4787 Ⓕ 020 7636 6110
Ⓔ roe&moore@fsbdial.co.uk
Ⓦ www.abebooks.com
Est. 1992 *Stock size* Medium
Stock Prints, posters, 19th–20thC rare books, children's books, photography, European language books
Open Mon–Sat 10.30am–6pm

Simmons Gallery (BNTA)
Contact Mr H Simmons
53 Lambs Conduit Street, London, WC1N 3NB
020 7831 2080 Ⓕ 020 7831 2090
Ⓔ info@simmonsgallery.co.uk
Ⓦ www.simmonsgallery.co.uk
Est. 1982 *Stock size* Large
Stock Worldwide coins, contemporary, prize, commemorative medals, art, sculpture, jewellery
Open Mon–Fri 9.30am–5.30pm or by appointment
Fairs London Coin Fair, Coinex, Affordable Art Fair
Services Valuations, bi-annual metrology mail auction

Skoob Books Ltd
Contact Mr I Ong or Mark Lovell
15 Sicilian Avenue, off Southampton Row, London, WC1A 2QH
020 7404 3063 Ⓕ 020 7404 4398
Ⓔ books@skoob.com
Ⓦ www.skoob.com
Est. 1980 *Stock size* Large
Stock Second-hand, antiquarian books, philosophy a speciality
Open Mon–Sat 10.30am–6.30pm Sun noon–5pm

Unsworths Booksellers Ltd (ABA, PBFA)
12 Bloomsbury Street, London, WC1B 3QA
020 7436 9836 Ⓕ 020 7637 7334
Ⓔ books@unsworths.com
Ⓦ www.unsworths.com
Est. 1986 *Stock size* Large
Stock Antiquarian, second-hand and remainder books on the humanities
Open Mon–Sat 10am–8pm Sun noon–8pm
Fairs See website for details

Woburn Book Shop (PBFA)
Contact Mr B Buitekant
10 Woburn Walk, London, WC1H 0JL
020 7388 7278 Ⓕ 020 7263 5196
Ⓔ bb@ukgateway.net
Est. 1994 *Stock size* Medium
Stock Second-hand and antiquarian books on social history, psychoanalysis, philosophy
Open Mon–Fri 11am–6pm Sat 11am–5pm

WC2

Anchor Antiques Ltd
Contact Mrs Samne
26 Charing Cross Road, London, WC2H 0DG
020 7836 5686
Est. 1964 *Stock size* Medium
Stock European and Oriental ceramics
Trade only Yes
Open By appointment
Services Book search

Any Amount of Books (PBFA, ABA, ILAB)
Contact N Burwood
62 Charing Cross Road, London, WC2H 0BB
020 7240 8140 Ⓕ 020 7240 1769
Ⓔ charingx@anyamountofbooks.com
Ⓦ www.anyamountofbooks.com
Est. 1975 *Stock size* Large
Stock Antiquarian, rare, second-hand books
Open Mon–Sat 10.30am–9.30pm Sun 11.30am–8.30pm
Fairs PBFA Russell Hotel, Olympia
Services Shipping

Argenteus Ltd (LAPADA)
Contact Mr M Feldman
Vault 2, The London Silver Vaults, 53 Chancery Lane, London, WC2A 1QS
020 7831 3637 Ⓕ 020 7430 0126
Est. 1991 *Stock size* Medium
Stock Antique silver, Sheffield plate, flatware
Open Mon–Fri 9am–5.30pm Sat 9am–1pm

A H Baldwin and Son (BADA)
Contact Tim Wilkes
11 Adelphi Terrace, London, WC2N 6BJ
020 7930 6879 Ⓕ 020 7930 9450
Ⓔ coins@baldwin.sh
Ⓦ www.baldwin.sh
Est. 1872
Stock Coins, commemorative medals
Open Mon–Fri 9am–5pm
Services Valuations

Bell, Book and Radnell (ABA)
Contact Mr John Bell or Mr James Tindley
4 Cecil Court, London, WC2N 4HE
020 7240 2161 Ⓕ 020 7379 1062
Ⓔ bellbr@dial.pipex.com
Est. 1972 *Stock size* Medium
Stock 20thC first editions, literature, novels, poetry
Open Mon–Fri 10am–5.30pm Sat 11am–4pm
Services Valuations

Malcolm Bord
Contact Mr M Bord
16 Charing Cross Road, London, WC2H 0HR
020 7836 0631 Ⓕ 020 7240 1920

Est. 1970 *Stock size* Large
Stock Worldwide old silver and bronze coins
Open Mon–Sat 10.30am–5.30pm
Services Valuations

Charing Cross Markets
Contact Rodney Bolwell
1 Embankment Place, London, WC2N 6NN
01483 281771 ⓕ 01483 281771
rodney@chicane.fsbusiness.co.uk
Est. 1974 *Stock size* Large
No. of dealers 35
Stock Stamps, postcards, coins
Open Sat 7.30am–3pm

Coins and Bullion (BNTA, ANA)
Contact Mr P Cohen
20 Cecil Court, London, WC2N 4HE
020 7379 0615
Est. 1977
Stock British coins from 1500, world coins
Open Mon–Fri 10.30am–5.30pm
Sat 1–5pm
Services Valuations

Paul Daniel (LSVA)
Contact Paul Daniel
51 The London Silver Vaults, Chancery Lane, London, WC2A 1QS
020 7430 1327 ⓕ 020 7430 1327
ⓜ 07831 338461
paveldaniel@aol.com
Est. 1979 *Stock size* Medium
Stock Commercial English and Continental silver
Open Mon–Fri 10am–4pm
Services Valuations, restorations

Bryan Douglas (LAPADA)
Contact Mr B Douglas
12 & 14 The London Silver Vaults, Chancery Lane, London, WC2A
020 7242 7073 ⓕ 020 7242 7073
sales@bryandouglas.co.uk
www.bryandouglas.co.uk
Est. 1971 *Stock size* Large
Stock Antique, vintage, modern silver, silver plate, old Sheffield plate
Open Mon–Fri 9.30am–5pm
Sat 9.30am–1pm
Services Valuations

R Feldman Ltd Antique Silver (LAPADA)
Contact Mr R Feldman
4 & 6 The London Silver Vaults, 53 Chancery Lane, London, WC2A 1QB
020 7405 6111 ⓕ 020 7430 0126
rfeldman@rfeldman.co.uk
www.rfeldman.co.uk
Est. 1954 *Stock size* Large
Stock Victorian silver, old Sheffield plate
Open Mon–Fri 9am–5.30pm
Sat 9am–1pm
Services Valuations, repairs

Frasers Autographs (IADA, UACC)
Contact Poppy Collinson
399 The Strand, London, WC2R 0LX
020 7836 9325 ⓕ 020 7836 7342
sales@frasersautographs.co.uk
www.frasersautographs.co.uk
Est. 1978 *Stock size* Large
Stock Signed photos, letters, documents, stage and film costumes and props, signed guitars, sports equipment
Open Mon–Sat 9.30am–5.30pm
Sun 10am–4pm
Fairs Stanley Gibbons Fairs
Services Valuations, want list, bi-monthly postal Internet autograph auction, lifetime authenticity guarantee

Stanley Gibbons Auctions Ltd
Contact Mr Colin Avery
399 Strand, London, WC2R 0LX
020 7836 8444 ⓕ 020 7836 7342
auctions@stanleygibbons.co.uk
www.stanleygibbons.com
Est. 1856
Open Mon–Fri 9am–5pm
Sat 9.30am–5.30pm
Sales 4–5 worldwide stamp auctions, 2–3 rarities and specialized auctions, phone for details. Postal auction, 6 per year, web auction monthly
Frequency Every 6-8 weeks
Catalogues Yes

Gillian Gould Antiques
Contact Gill Gould
Ocean Leisure, 11–14 Northumberland Avenue, London, WC2N 5AQ
020 7419 0500 ⓕ 020 7419 0400
ⓜ 07831 150060
gillgould@dealwith.com
Est. 1989 *Stock size* Small
Stock Scientific, marine, general gifts
Open By appointment only
Services Valuations, restorations

Grosvenor Prints
Contact Ms McDiarmid
28 Shelton Street, London, WC2H 9JE
020 7836 1979 ⓕ 020 7379 6695
grosvenorprints@btinternet.com
www.grosvenorprints.com
Est. 1976 *Stock size* Large
Stock Topographical, sporting, dogs, portraits, decorative prints
Open Mon–Fri 10am–6pm
Sat 11am–4pm

M & J Hamilton
Contact Mr M Hamilton
25 The London Silver Vaults, Chancery Lane, London, WC2A 1QS
020 7831 7030 ⓕ 020 7831 5483
Stock size Large
Stock Antique silver, flatware services a speciality
Open Mon–Fri 9.30am–5.30pm
Sat 9.30am–1pm

Handsworth Books (PBFA)
Contact Mr S Glover
148 Charing Cross Road, London, WC2H 0LB
020 7240 3566
ⓜ 07976 329042
steve@handsworthbooks.demon.co.uk
www.abebooks.com/home/handsworth
Est. 1987 *Stock size* Medium
Stock Rare, second-hand, antiquarian books on history, literature, the arts, academic and scholarly topics a speciality
Open Mon–Sat 11am–7pm
Sun noon–5pm

P J Hilton Books
Contact Mr P Hilton
12 Cecil Court, London, WC2N 4HE
020 7379 9825
paul.hilton@rarebook.globalnet.co.uk
www.rarebookweb.com
Est. 1986 *Stock size* Medium
Stock Antiquarian, second-hand, rare books, pre-1700 a speciality
Open Mon–Fri 10.30am–6pm
Sat 10.30am–5pm
Services Book search

⊞ Raymond D Holdich (OMRS)
Contact Mr R Holdich
⊠ **7 Whitcomb Street, London, WC2H 7HA** 🅿
☎ 020 7930 1979 ⓕ 020 7930 1152
ⓜ 07774 133493
ⓔ rdhmedals@aol.com
ⓦ www.rdhmedals.com
Est. 1969 *Stock size* Large
Stock Cap badges, militaria including medals, orders, decorations
Open Mon–Fri 10am–5pm
Fairs OMRS
Services Valuations

⊞ Lee Jackson (IMCOS, AMPF)
⊠ **2 Southampton Street, London, WC2E 7HA** 🅿
☎ 020 7240 1970 ⓕ 020 7836 9323
ⓔ leejackson@btinternet.com
ⓦ www.leejackson.btinternet.co.uk
Est. 1973 *Stock size* Medium
Stock Antique maps, charts, topographical views
Open Mon–Fri 10am–5.30pm

⊞ S & H Jewell Ltd (Guild of Master Craftsmen)
Contact Mr R Jewell or Mr G Korkis
⊠ **26 Parker Street, London, WC2B 5PH** 🅿
☎ 020 7405 8520 ⓕ 020 7405 8521
ⓜ 07973 406 255
Est. 1830 *Stock size* Large
Stock Quality English antique and period style 19th–20thC furniture
Open Mon–Fri 9am–5.30pm other times by appointment
Fairs Newark
Services Valuations, restorations

⊞ Stephen Kalms Antiques (LAPADA)
Contact Mr S Kalms
⊠ **The London Silver Vaults, Chancery Lane, London, WC2A 1QS** 🅿
☎ 020 7430 1254 ⓕ 020 7405 6206
ⓔ stephen@kalms.freeserve.co.uk
Est. 1990 *Stock size* Large
Stock Victorian–Edwardian silver, silver plate, decorative items
Open Mon–Fri 9am–5.30pm Sat 9am–1pm
Fairs Olympia (June)
Services Valuations, restorations, repairs

⊞ Nat Leslie Ltd
Contact Mr M Hyams
⊠ **21 The London Silver Vaults, 53 Chancery Lane, London, WC2A 1QS** 🅿
☎ 020 7242 4787
Est. 1947 *Stock size* Large
Stock Modern, antique, contemporary silverware, silver-plate, flatware a speciality
Open Mon–Fri 9.30am–5pm

⊞ C and T Mammon (LSVA)
Contact Mr C Mammon
⊠ **55 and 64 The London Silver Vaults, Chancery Lane, London, WC2A 1QT** 🅿
☎ 020 7405 2397 ⓕ 020 7405 4900
ⓜ 07785 325642
Est. 1969 *Stock size* Large
Stock Decorative silver, silver-plate items
Open Mon–Fri 9am–5.30pm or by appointment
Services Valuations

⊞ E W Marchpane Ltd (ABA, PBFA)
Contact K Fuller
⊠ **16 Cecil Court, Charing Cross Road, London, WC2N 4HE** 🅿
☎ 020 7836 8661 ⓕ 020 7497 0567
ⓔ kenneth@marchpane.com
ⓦ www.marchpane.com
Est. 1989 *Stock size* Medium
Stock Antiquarian, rare, second-hand books, children's and illustrated books a speciality
Open Mon–Sat 10.30am–6.30pm

⊞ Arthur Middleton Ltd (SIS)
Contact Mr A Middleton or Miss Morgan
⊠ **12 New Row, London, WC2N 4LF** 🅿
☎ 020 7836 7042 ⓕ 020 7497 2486
ⓔ arthur@antique-globes.com
ⓦ www.antique-globes.com
Est. 1978 *Stock size* Large
Stock Marine and scientific instruments, globes
Open Mon–Fri 10am–6pm
Fairs Scientific Instruments Fair, Portman Hotel (April, Oct)
Services Valuations

⊞ E C Molan
Contact Mr E Molan
⊠ **1 Cecil Court, London, WC2N 4EZ** 🅿
☎ 020 7497 9228 ⓕ 020 7497 2328
Est. 1971 *Stock size* Small
Stock Prints, maps, antiquarian books
Open Mon–Sat 10.30am–6.30pm

⊞ Murray Cards (International) Ltd (GOMC)
Contact Mr I Murray
⊠ **20 Cecil Court, London, WC2N 4HE**
☎ 020 8202 5688 ⓕ 020 8203 7878
ⓔ murraycards@ukbusiness.com
ⓦ www.murraycards.com
Est. 1965 *Stock size* Large
Stock Cigarette and trading cards, albums, frames, books
Open Mon–Sat 10.30am–5.30pm
Services Annual Catalogue, auction catalogue

⊞ Colin Narbeth and Son (IBNS)
Contact Mr Simon Narbeth
⊠ **20 Cecil Court, London, WC2N 4HE**
☎ 020 7379 6975 ⓕ 017 2 811244
ⓔ colin.narbeth@btinternet.com
ⓦ www.colin-narbeth.com
Est. 1982 *Stock size* Large
Stock Banknotes, bonds, shares of all countries and periods
Open Mon Sat 10.30am–4pm Tues–Fri 10am–5pm
Fairs Bonnington Paper Money Fair, IBNS (Oct)

⊞ Percy's Ltd (LAPADA)
Contact Mr D Simmons
⊠ **16 The London Silver Vaults, Chancery Lane, London, WC2A 1QS** 🅿
☎ 020 7242 3618
ⓕ 020 7831 6541
ⓔ sales@percys-silver.com
ⓦ www.percys-silver.com
Est. 1935 *Stock size* Large
Stock 18th–19thC decorative silver and plate
Open Mon–Fri 9.30am–5pm Sat 10am–1pm
Fairs Olympia (June, Nov)
Services Valuations, repairs

⊞ Henry Pordes Books Ltd
Contact Mr G Della-Ragione
⊠ **58–60 Charing Cross Road, London, WC2H 0BB**
☎ 020 7836 9031 ⓕ 020 7240 4232
ⓔ henrypordes@clara.net
ⓦ www.home.clara.net/henrypordes
Est. 1983 *Stock size* Medium

Stock Remainders, second-hand, antiquarian books, art, literature, Judaica a speciality
Open Mon–Sat 10am–7pm

Quinto Bookshop
Contact Mr I Marchant
48a Charing Cross Road, London, WC2H 0BB
020 7379 7669
Est. 1979 *Stock size* Medium
Stock General second-hand, antiquarian books
Open Mon–Sat 9am–9pm
Sun noon–7pm

Rare Art Ltd (BADA)
Contact Mr L Smith
London Silver Vaults, Chancery Lane, London, WC2A 1QS
020 7242 7624 F 020 7831 0221
E rareart@compuserve.com
W www.artnet.com/koopmdn.html
Est. 1984 *Stock size* Large
Stock Antique silver
Open Mon–Fri 9am–5.30pm
Sat 10am–1pm
Fairs Olympia (June), IFAADS, New York

Reg & Philip Remington (ABA)
Contact Mr R Remington
18 Cecil Court, London, WC2N 4HE
020 7836 9771 F 020 7497 2526
E philip@remingtonbooks.com
W remingtonbooks.com
Est. 1979 *Stock size* Medium
Stock Antiquarian, rare, second-hand books, voyages, travel books a speciality
Open Mon–Fri 9am–5pm
Fairs Olympia

Bertram Rota Ltd (ABA)
Contact Mr A Rota
1st Floor, 31 Long Acre, London, WC2E 9LT
020 7836 0723 F 020 7497 9058
E bertramrota@compuserve.com
W www.ourworld.compuserve.com/homepages/bertramrota
Est. 1923 *Stock size* Small
Stock Antiquarian, rare, second-hand books, 1890–present day first editions of English and American literature
Open Mon–Fri 9.30am–5.30pm
Services Valuations, book search, catalogues (4–6 a year)

Silstar Antiques Ltd
Contact Mr J Langer
29 The London Silver Vaults, Chancery Lane, London, WC2A 1QS
020 7242 6740 F 020 7430 1745
Est. 1955 *Stock size* Large
Stock Antique and modern silver of all descriptions
Open Mon–Fri 10am–5pm

B Silverman (BADA)
Contact Robin Silverman or Bill Brackenbury
26 London Silver Vaults, Chancery Lane, London, WC2A 1QS
020 7242 3269 F 020 7430 1949
E silverman@cocoon.co.uk
W www.silverman-london.com
Stock size Large
Stock 17th–19thC fine English silverware, silver flatware
Open Mon–Fri 9am–5pm
Sat 9am–1pm
Fairs Olympia, BADA
Services Valuations

Jack Simons Antiques Ltd (LAPADA)
Contact Mr J Simons
37 The London Silver Vaults, Chancery Lane, London, WC2A 1QS
020 7242 3221 F 020 7831 6541
Est. 1955 *Stock size* Large
Stock Fine antique English and Continental silver, objets d'art
Open Mon–Fri 9.30am–5pm
Services Valuations, restorations

Stage Door Prints (UACC)
Contact Mr A L Reynold
9 Cecil Court, St Martins Lane, London, WC2N 4EZ
020 7240 1683 F 020 7379 5598
Est. 1979 *Stock size* Large
Stock Antique prints, maps, autographs, movie posters, out-of-print books, film memorabilia, Victorian cards, Valentines
Open Mon–Fri 11am–6pm
Sat 11.30am–6pm

S & J Stodel (BADA)
Contact Mr S Stodel
24 The London Silver Vaults, Chancery Lane, London, WC2A 1QS
020 7405 7009 F 020 7242 6366
W www.chinesesilver.co.uk
Est. 1973
Stock Chinese Export silver, Art Deco silver, antique silver flatware
Open Mon–Fri 9.30am–5.30pm
Sat 9am–1pm
Fairs Olympia (June)

Tom Tom
Contact Gary Mitchell
42 New Compton Street, London, WC2H 8DA
020 7240 7909 F 020 7240 7909
E sales@tomtomshop.co.uk
W www.tomtomshop.co.uk
Est. 1993 *Stock size* Large
Stock Post-war designer furniture/technology, classics by Eames, Jacobsen, Saarinen
Open Tues–Fri noon–7pm Sat 11am–6pm or by appointment
Services Valuations

Travis & Emery Books on Music (ABA)
Contact Mr Coleman
17 Cecil Court, London, WC2N 4EZ
020 7240 2129 F 020 7497 0790
E enquiries@travis-and-emery.com
Est. 1960 *Stock size* Medium
Stock Antiquarian sheet music, prints, ephemera, books on music
Open Mon–Sat 11am–6pm Sun noon–4pm or by appointment
Services Valuations

William Walter Antiques Ltd (BADA, LAPADA)
Contact Miss E Simpson
3 The London Silver Vaults, Chancery Lane, London, WC2A 1QS
020 7242 3248 F 020 7404 1280
E enq@wwantiques.plestel.co.uk
W www.williamwalter.co.uk
Est. 1949 *Stock size* Large
Stock Georgian silver, decorative silver, flatware etc.
Open Mon–Fri 9.30am–5.30pm
Sat 9.30am–1pm
Services Valuations, repairs

Peter K Weiss
Contact Mr P Weiss
18 The London Silver Vaults, Chancery Lane, London, WC2A 8QS
020 7242 8100
E peterweiss@mymailstation.com
Est. 1958 *Stock size* Large
Stock Antique clocks, watches, objets d'art

Open Mon–Fri 10am–4pm
Sat 10am–1pm
Services Valuations, restorations

Nigel Williams Rare Books (PBFA, ABA)
Contact Mr Nigel Williams
22 Cecil Court, London, WC2N 4HE
020 7836 7757 020 7379 5918
nwrarebook@tcp.co.uk
www.nigelwilliams.com
Est. 1989 *Stock size* Medium
Stock Antiquarian, rare, second-hand books, collectable children's, illustrated, 19th–20thC first editions
Open Mon–Sat 10am–6pm
Fairs Olympia, Russell Hotel
Services Monthly catalogue

MIDDLESEX

ASHFORD

Magnet Antiques
Contact Mr Ted Pullen
23 Woodthorpe Road, Ashford, Middlesex, TW15 2RP
01784 253107
Est. 1989 *Stock size* Medium
Stock Victorian–Edwardian reproduction furniture, Doulton, Beswick, Kevin Francis ceramics
Open Mon–Sat 10am–5pm

BRENTFORD

West Middlesex Auction Rooms
Contact Mr T Keane
113–114 High Street, Brentford, Middlesex, TW8 8AT
020 8568 9080
Est. 1999
Open Mon–Fri 9.30am–6pm
Sales Antiques and general sale Sat 11am, viewing Fri 10am–8.30pm Sat 9am–11am
Frequency Fortnightly
Catalogues Yes

EASTCOTE

Eastcote Bookshop (PBFA)
Contact Mrs E May
156–160 Field End Road, Eastcote, Middlesex, HA5 1RH
020 8866 9888 020 8985 9383
Est. 1994 *Stock size* Large
Stock Antiquarian, rare, second-hand books
Open Tues–Sat 10am–5pm
Fairs Russell Hotel

ENFIELD

Designer Classics
Contact Mr L Wilkin
70 Goat Lane, Enfield, Middlesex, EN1 4UB
020 8342 1221 020 8366 8786
mail@designclassic.com
www.designclassic.com
Est. 1998 *Stock size* Large
Stock 1950s–present day classics by famous designers, Bellini, Herman Miller, Verna Panton, computers, hi-fi, radios etc
Open Mail order via Internet

Enfield Collectors Centre
Contact Mr R E Kent
St Onge Parade, 6 Genotin Road, Enfield, Middlesex, EN1 1YU
020 8363 9375
Est. 1970 *Stock size* Large
Stock Militaria, old toys, Dinky, Corgi, Meccano, pocket watches, wind-up gramophones, cigarette cards, postcards, coins
Open Mon–Sat 10am–5pm
Fairs Lea Valley Leisure Centre
Services Medal mounting

Gallerie Veronique
Contact Ms V Aslangul
66 Chase Side, Enfield, Middlesex, EN2 6NJ
020 8342 1005 020 8342 1005
07770 410041
antiques@gallerieveronique.co.uk
Est. 1993 *Stock size* Large
Stock Victorian–Edwardian, 1930s furniture, reproduction, teddy bears
Open Mon–Fri 10am–3pm
Sat 10am–5pm
Services Restorations

Griffin Antiques
Contact Mr J Gardner
6 Chase Side, Enfield, Middlesex, EN2 6NF
020 8366 5959
Est. 1970 *Stock size* Medium
Stock Wide range of antiques, porcelain, silver, metalware, scales, weights, measures, candlesticks
Open Mon–Fri 10.30am–6pm
Sat 4.30am–6pm
Fairs Newark
Services Valuations

La Trouvaille
Contact Mrs Cicely M Waring
1a Windmill Hill, Enfield, Middlesex, EN2 6SE
020 8367 1080
Est. 1981 *Stock size* Medium
Stock 1800–1950 small furniture, porcelain, glass, silver, prints, mirrors
Open Tues Thurs Fri 10am–5pm
Sat 9.30am–5.30pm

Period Style Lighting (Lighting Association)
Contact Gillian Day
8–9 The Antiques Village, East Lodge Lane, Botany Bay, Enfield, Middlesex, EN2 8AS
020 8363 9789
Est. 1991 *Stock size* Large
Stock Antique and period lighting, chandeliers
Open Tues–Sun 10am–5pm
Services Valuations, restorations

HAMPTON

Hunters of Hampton
Contact Mr R Hunter
76 Station Road, Hampton, Middlesex, TW12 2AX
020 8979 5624 020 8979 5624
Est. 1991 *Stock size* Large
Stock Victorian–Edwardian furniture, clocks
Open Mon 10am–5.30pm Fri Sat 10am–6pm or by appointment

HAREFIELD

David Ansell (BHI, BAFRA)
Contact David Ansell
48 Dellside, Harefield, Middlesex, UB9 6AX
01895 824648
07976 222610
dansell@globalnet.co.uk
Est. 1990 *Stock size* Medium
Stock Clocks, photographica
Open Mon–Sun 8.30am–5.30pm or by appointment
Fairs NEC, Newark
Services Restorations

Harefield Antiques
Contact Mrs J Davie
42 High Street, Harefield, Uxbridge, Middlesex, UB9 6BX
01895 825224
antiques@nildram.co.uk
www.homepages.nildram.co.uk/~antiques
Est. 1998 *Stock size* Medium

No. of dealers 10
Stock Furniture, china, glass, stamps, radios, militaria, civil war books, sporting memorabilia, jewellery, collectables
Open Mon–Sat 10am–5.30pm Sun 11am–5pm
Services Finding service

HARROW

Alberts of Kensington
Contact Mrs J A Wooster
PO Box 491, Harrow, Middlesex, HA2 8YN
☎ 020 8426 4321 Ⓕ 020 8426 4111
Est. 1964
Open Tues–Fri 10am–6pm Sat 10am–4pm postal only
Sales 10–12 postal auctions of cigarette cards and ephemera per year
Catalogues Yes

The Collectors Shop (PTA, ESoc)
Contact Mr I Crawford
16 Village Way East, Rayners Lane, Harrow, Middlesex, HA2 7LU
☎ 020 8866 1053
Est. 1992 *Stock size* Large
Stock Postcards, cigarette cards, illustrated sheet music, toys, sporting items, records, illustrated song sheets, film memorabilia, militaria, china, collectables
Open Mon–Sat 9.30am–4.30pm closed Wed
Services Valuations

Kathleen Mann Antiques
Contact Mrs K Mann
49 High Street, Harrow on the Hill, Middlesex, HA1 3HT
☎ 020 8422 1892 Ⓕ 020 8864 2796
Ⓔ 106076.2024@compuserve.com
Ⓦ www.iss.u-net.com/kmann/km.htm
Est. 1972 *Stock size* Small
Stock Mainly furniture, decorative items, silver, prints, pictures
Open Thurs–Sat 9.30am–5pm
Services Valuations

HATCH END

Calvers Collectables
Contact Mrs I Calver
266–268 Uxbridge Road, Hatch End, Middlesex, HA5 4HS
☎ 020 8421 1653
Est. 1994 *Stock size* Large
No. of dealers 26
Stock Doulton, Art Deco, ceramics, small furniture, collectables
Open Mon–Sat 10am–5.30pm Sun 11.30am–4pm
Services Ceramic repairs

HAYES

Hussar Military Miniatures
Contact Mr M Hearn
3 Third Avenue, Hayes, Middlesex, UB3 2EF
☎ 020 8573 4597 Ⓕ 020 8573 1414
Est. 1981 *Stock size* Large
Stock Vast range of military figures, mostly medieval hand-painted collectors' items
Open By appointment only
Services Catalogues, mail order

ISLEWORTH

Antique Traders
Contact Mr T Keane
156 London Road, Isleworth, Middlesex, TW7 5BG
☎ 020 8847 1020 Ⓕ 020 8847 1020
Est. 1997 *Stock size* Large
Stock Wide range of antiques, furniture, porcelain, glass, pictures, mirrors
Open Mon–Sun 10.30am–6pm
Services Valuations

Crowther of Syon Lodge Ltd
Contact Ms S Powell
Busch Corner, London Road, Isleworth, Middlesex, TW7 5BH
☎ 020 8560 7978 Ⓕ 020 8568 7572
Ⓔ sales@crowthersyonlodge.com
Ⓦ www.crowthersyonlodge-com
Est. 1876 *Stock size* Large
Stock Period garden ornaments, urns, fountains, statues, temples, chimney pieces, panelled rooms
Open Mon–Fri 9am–5pm Sat Sun 11am–4pm
Fairs Olympia (June, Feb), Chelsea Flower Show
Services Hand-carved ornamental work, period-style panelled rooms, blacksmith

LALEHAM

Laleham Antiques
Contact Mrs H Potter
23 Shepperton Road, Laleham, Middlesex, TW18 1SE
☎ 01784 450353
Est. 1973 *Stock size* Medium
Stock Antique and reproduction furniture, old pine, silver, plated items, pictures, brass, copper, jewellery, collectables
Open Mon–Sat 10.30am–5.30pm closed Wed

NORTHWOOD HILLS

Golden Days
Contact Mrs J Bryne
37 The Broadway, Joel Street, Northwood Hills, Middlesex, HA6 1NZ
☎ 01923 841255
Est. 1996 *Stock size* Large
Stock Antique furniture, ceramics, brass, mirrors, lighting, collectables
Open Mon–Sat 10am–4.30pm closed Wed or by appointment
Services Valuations, glass and china repairs, re-planing, house clearance

PINNER

The Curiosity Shop
Contact Mr P August
7 High Street, Pinner, Middlesex, HA5 5PJ
☎ 020 8868 9953 Ⓕ 020 8429 1585
Ⓦ www.the-curiosity-shop.co.uk
Est. 1987 *Stock size* Medium
Stock Antique maps, engravings, Georgian–Victorian silver, decorative items
Open Mon–Sat 10am–5pm
Services Valuations, restorations

RUISLIP

Hobday Toys (Hornby Railway Collectors Association, Dolls Club)
Contact Wendy Hobday
☎ 01895 636737 Ⓕ 01895 621042
Ⓔ wendyhobday@freenet.co.uk
Est. 1985 *Stock size* Large
Stock O-gauge trains, dolls houses and furniture, tin-plate toys
Open By appointment
Fairs Sandown, Rugby
Services Valuations

The Old Trinket Box
Contact Eilleen Cameron
1B High Street, Ruislip, Middlesex, HA4 7AU
01895 675658
Est. 1995 *Stock size* Medium
No. of dealers 10
Stock Wide range of collectables, antiques
Open Mon–Sat 10am–5pm Sun 11am–4pm

STAINES

K W Dunster Antiques
Contact Mr K W Dunster
23 Church Street, Staines, Middlesex, TW18 4EN
01784 453297 F 01784 483146
M 07831 649626
Est. 1973 *Stock size* Medium
Stock Brass, furniture, jewellery, marine items
Open Mon–Sat 9am–4pm
Services Valuations, house clearance

Staines Antiques
Contact Mr D Smith
145–147 Kingston Road, Staines, Middlesex, TW18 1PD
01784 461306 F 01784 461306
Est. 1978 *Stock size* Large
Stock Furniture, ceramics
Open Mon–Sat 9am–5.30pm
Services Valuations, restorations

TEDDINGTON

Chris Hollingshead
Contact Chris Hollingshead
10 Linden Grove, Teddington, Middlesex, TW11 8LT
020 8255 4774
E c.hollingshead@btinternet.com
Est. 1993 *Stock size* Medium
Stock Scarce, out-of-print, antiquarian books on landscape, architecture, garden design, botany, horticulture, funeral customs, cemeteries
Open 9.30am–6pm
Services Mail order, annual catalogue

Waldegrave Antiques
Contact Mrs J Murray
197 Waldegrave Road, Teddington, Middlesex, TW11 8LX
020 8404 0162
M 07946 506145
Est. 1997 *Stock size* Large
Stock Wide selection of antiques, furniture, silver, porcelain, glass etc
Open Mon–Sat 10.30am–5.30pm
Fairs Kempton Park

TWICKENHAM

Antique Interiors
Contact Mr A Mundy
93 Crown Road, Twickenham, Middlesex, TW1 3EX
020 8607 9853
Est. 1995 *Stock size* Medium
Stock English, French and 19thC mahogany and old pine furniture, other quality English items
Open Tues–Sat 10am–5.30pm
Services Restorations, upholstery

Cheyne Galleries
Contact Mrs C Cox
8 Crown Road, Twickenham, Middlesex, TW1 3EE
020 8892 6932
Est. 1977 *Stock size* Medium
Stock Wide range of antique and second-hand items, collectables
Open Mon–Sat 10am–6pm closed Wed
Services Valuations, house clearance

Anthony C Hall (ABA, PBFA)
Contact Mr A C Hall
30 Staines Road, Twickenham, Middlesex, TW2 5AH
020 8898 2638 F 020 8893 8855
E achallbooks@internet.co.uk
W www.hallbooks.co.uk
Est. 1966 *Stock size* Large
Stock Out-of-print and rare books, Russian and eastern European topics a speciality
Open Mon–Sat 9am–5.30pm closed Wed
Fairs Richmond Book Fair

John Ives (PBFA)
Contact Mr J Ives
5 Normanhurst Drive, Twickenham, Middlesex, TW1 1NA
020 8892 6265 F 020 8744 3944
E jives@btconnect.com
Est. 1979
Stock Reference books on antiques and collecting, 1,000s of titles in stock including scarce items
Open By appointment
Services Mail order only, catalogue

David Morley Antiques
Contact Mr D Morley
371 Richmond Road, Twickenham, Middlesex, TW1 2EF
020 8892 2986
Est. 1968 *Stock size* Large
Stock Wide range of antiques including small furniture, silver, porcelain, silver plate, telephones, old toys
Open Mon Tues Thurs –Sat 10am–5pm closed 1–2pm
Services Valuations

Phelps Ltd (LAPADA)
Contact Robert Phelps
133–135 St Margaret's Road, East Twickenham, Middlesex, TW1 1RG
020 8892 1778/7129
F 020 8892 3661
E antiques@phelps.co.uk
W www.phelps.co.uk
Est. 1870 *Stock size* Large
No. of dealers 16
Stock Antique furniture
Open Mon–Fri 9am–5.30pm Sat 9.30am–5.30pm Sun noon–4pm
Services Restorations

The Twickenham Antiques Warehouse
Contact Mr A Clubb
80 Colne Road, Twickenham, Middlesex, TW2 6QE
020 8894 5555
M 07973 132847
Est. 1984 *Stock size* Large
Stock English and Continental furniture, 1700–1930s, decorative items
Open Mon–Sat 9.30am–5pm
Services Valuations, restorations

UXBRIDGE

Antiques Warehouse & Restoration
Contact Mr M Allenby
34 Rockingham Road, Uxbridge, Middlesex, UB8 2TZ
01895 256963
Est. 1979 *Stock size* Large
Stock 1800–1950 furniture, collectables
Open Mon–Sat 10am–6pm
Services Restorations

⊞ Anthony Smith
Contact Mr Anthony Smith
✉ **45 Windsor Street, Uxbridge, Middlesex, UB8 1AB** 🅿
☎ 01895 814442 Ⓕ 01895 253756
Est. 1997 *Stock size* Large
Stock Georgian–Edwardian furniture
Open Mon–Sat 10am–6pm Sun 11am-4pm
Services Restorations, upholstery

WEST RUISLIP

A Bainbridge & Co
Contact Mr P Bainbridge
✉ **The Auction House, Ickenham Road, West Ruislip, Middlesex, HA4 7DL** 🅿
☎ 01895 621991 Ⓕ 01895 623621
Est. 1979
Open Mon–Fri 9am–5pm
Sales Antiques and general effects Thurs 11am, viewing Wed 1–7pm Thurs from 9.30am
Frequency Every 4 weeks
Catalogues Yes

WRAYSBURY

⊞ Wyrardisbury Antiques
Contact Mr C Tuffs
✉ **23 High Street, Wraysbury, Staines, Middlesex, TW19 5DA** 🅿
☎ 01784 483225 Ⓕ 01784 483225
Est. 1978 *Stock size* Medium
Stock All types, ages of clocks up to Edwardian, small furniture, barometers
Open Tues–Sat 10am–5pm
Services Valuations, repairs

BERKSHIRE

ALDERMASTON

⊞ Village Antiques Aldermaston

Contact Mrs Vivian Green
✉ **The Old Dispensary, The Street, Aldermaston, Reading, Berkshire, RG7 4LW** 🅿
☎ 0118 971 2370
Est. 1997 *Stock size* Large
Stock Clocks, architectural antiques, furniture, china, glass, silver, garden items
Open Tues–Sun 10am–5.30pm

ASCOT

⊞ The Coworth Gallery

Contact Mr S Paddon
✉ **9 Coworth Road, Ascot, Berkshire, SL5 0NX** 🅿
☎ 01344 626532 Ⓕ 01344 626532
Ⓜ 07831 182076
Est. 1990 *Stock size* Small
Stock French provincial, English country furniture, decorative items, statuary, architectural antiques
Open By appointment
Services Garden design

Edwards and Elliott

Contact Mr Francis Ogley
✉ **32 High Street, Ascot, Berkshire, SL5 7HG** 🅿
☎ 01344 872588 Ⓕ 01344 624700
Ⓜ 07885 333627
Ⓔ edwards2@netcomuk.co.uk
Ⓦ www.edwardsandelliott.co.uk
Est. 1994
Open Mon–Fri 9am–5.30pm Sat 10am–4pm Sun 10am–2pm
Sales Wed Thurs every 5–6 weeks antiques and modern, view day of sale 9am–noon. Held at Silver Ring Grandstand, Ascot Racecourse
Frequency Every 5–6 weeks
Catalogues Yes

⊞ Melnick House Antiques (ESOC)

Contact Mrs J Collins
✉ **16 Brockenhurst Road, Ascot, Berkshire, SL5 9DL** 🅿
☎ 01344 297517/628383
Ⓕ 01344 291800
Ⓔ antiquarian@melnick-house.demon.co.uk
Est. 1972 *Stock size* Large
Stock Antique maps, prints, furniture, decorative antiques
Open Tues–Sat 10am–5pm
Services Restorations, free postage worldwide

BRIMPTON

Law Fine Art Ltd

Contact Mr Mark Law
✉ **Firs Cottage, Brimpton, Berkshire, RG7 4TJ** 🅿
☎ 01189 710353 Ⓕ 01189 713741
Ⓔ info@LawFineArt.co.uk
Ⓦ www.LawFineArt.co.uk
Est. 2000
Open Mon–Fri 9am–6pm Sat 9am–1pm
Sales Quarterly sales of general antiques, 8 specialist ceramic sales per annum
Frequency Monthly
Catalogues Yes

CAVERSHAM

⊞ Amber Antiques

Contact Clair Hughes
✉ **12 Bridge Street, Caversham, Berkshire, RG4 8AA**
☎ 01189 541394 Ⓕ 01189 541394
Ⓜ 07977 499234
Ⓔ amberantiques@btinternet.com
Ⓦ www.amberantiques.co.uk
Est. 1995 *Stock size* Medium
Stock French antiques, decorative items
Open Mon–Sat 10.30am–5.30pm
Fairs TVADA
Services Restorations, in house traditional upholstery

⊞ D Card (BHI)

Contact D Card
✉ **1a Chester Street, Caversham, Reading, Berkshire, RG4 8JH** 🅿
☎ 0118 947 0777 Ⓕ 0118 947 0777
Ⓔ d.card@ntlworld.com
Est. 1971 *Stock size* Small
Stock Longcase, carriage and table clocks, music boxes
Open Mon–Fri 9am–5pm appointment preferred
Services Valuations, restorations

⊞ The Clock Workshop (LAPADA, TVADA, FBHI)
Contact Mr J Yealland
✉ **17 Prospect Street, Caversham, Reading, Berkshire, RG4 8JB** P
☎ 0118 947 0741
Ⓦ www.lapada.co.uk
Est. 1981 *Stock size* Medium
Stock English clocks, French carriage clocks
Open Mon–Fri 9.30am–5.30pm Sat 10am–1pm
Fairs Olympia, LAPADA, TVADA
Services Valuations, restorations

COOKHAM

⊞ Cookham Antiques
Contact Mr G Wallis
✉ **35 Station Parade, Cookham, Maidenhead, Berkshire, SL6 9BR** P
☎ 01628 523224
Ⓜ 07778 020536
Est. 1989 *Stock size* Large
Stock Furniture, decorative items, architectural
Open Mon–Sat 10am–5pm Sun 11am–5pm
Services Valuations

DONNINGTON

Dreweatt Neate (SOFA, ARVA)
Contact Clive Stewart-Lockhart
✉ **Donnington Priory, Donnington, Newbury, Berkshire, RG14 2JE** P
☎ 01635 553553 Ⓕ 01635 553599
Ⓔ auctions@dreweatt-neate.co.uk fineart@dreweatt-neate.co.uk
Est. 1759
Open Mon–Fri 9am–5.30pm Sat 9am–12.30pm
Sales General sales fortnightly Tues at 10am, antiques sales every six weeks Wed 10am. Viewing prior Sat 9am–12.30pm Mon 9.30am–7pm and 9.30am–4pm for Wed sales
Frequency Six weeks
Catalogues Yes

ETON

⊞ Art and Antiques (Eton Traders)
Contact Mrs V Rand
✉ **69 High Street, Eton, Windsor, Berkshire, SL4 6AA** P
☎ 01753 855727
Ⓜ 07977 748696
Est. 1982 *Stock size* Large
Stock Furniture, china, brass, silver-plate, jewellery, collectors' items
Open Mon–Fri 10.30am–5.30pm Sat 10.30am–6pm Sun 2.30–6pm

⊞ Roger Barnett
Contact Roger Barnett
✉ **91 High Street, Eton, Windsor, Berkshire, SL4 6AF** P
☎ 01753 867785
Est. 1976 *Stock size* Medium
Stock Brown furniture, brass, longcase clocks
Open Variable

⊞ Eton Antiques
Contact Mr M Procter
✉ **80 High Street, Eton, Windsor, Berkshire, SL4 6AF** P
☎ 01753 860752 Ⓕ 01753 818222
Ⓦ www.etonantiques.com
Est. 1969 *Stock size* Large
Stock 18th–19thC English furniture
Open Mon–Sat 10am–5pm Sun 2.30–5pm
Services Valuations, restorations, shipping

⊞ Marcelline Herald Antiques (LAPADA, TVADA)
Contact Marcelline Herald
✉ **41 High Street, Eton, Windsor, Berkshire, SL4 6BD** P
☎ 01753 833924 Ⓕ 0118 9714683
Ⓦ www.tvada.co.uk
Est. 1998 *Stock size* Medium
Stock 17thC shop in historic Eton High Street selling18th–19thC furniture, mirrors and decorative items
Open Tues–Sat 10am–5pm
Fairs Decorative Fair Battersea, TVADA
Services Valuations

⊞ Peter J Martin (TVADA, LAPADA)
Contact Mr P Martin
✉ **40 High Street, Eton, Windsor, Berkshire, SL4 6BD** P
☎ 01753 864901
Est. 1967 *Stock size* Large
Stock 18th–20thC furniture, copper, brass, mirrors
Open Mon–Fri 9am–5pm closed 1–2pm Sat 10am–1pm or by appointment
Services Restorations

⊞ Mostly Boxes
Contact Mr G Munday
✉ **93 High Street, Eton, Windsor, Berkshire, SL4 6AF** P
☎ 01753 858470 Ⓕ 01753 887212
Est. 1982 *Stock size* Large
Stock Ivory, tortoiseshell, and decorative antique boxes
Open Mon–Sat 10am–6.30pm
Fairs K & M London

⊞ Sebastian of Eton
Contact Hannah West
✉ **4 High Street, Eton, Berkshire, SL4 6AS**

☎ 01753 851897 Ⓕ 01753 851897
Ⓔ sebastians@wingchairs.co.uk
Est. 2000 *Stock size* Small
Stock Antiques and decorative items
Open Mon–Sat 10am–6pm

Studio 101
Contact Anthony Cove
✉ **101 High Street, Eton, Berkshire, SL4 6AF** Ⓟ
☎ 01753 863333
Est. 1959 *Stock size* Small
Stock General antiques
Open By appointment

Times Past Antiques (MBHI)
Contact Mr P Jackson
✉ **59 High Street, Eton, Windsor, Berkshire, SL4 6BL** Ⓟ
☎ 01753 856392 Ⓕ 01753 856392
Ⓜ 07768 454444
Ⓔ phillipstimespast@aol.com
Est. 1974 *Stock size* Medium
Stock Clocks, barometers, small furniture
Open By appointment
Services Valuations, restorations

Turks Head Antiques
Contact Mrs A Baillie or Mr A Reeve
✉ **98 High Street, Eton, Windsor, Berkshire, SL4 6AF** Ⓟ
☎ 01753 863939
Est. 1975 *Stock size* Large
Stock Small furniture, porcelain, silver, glass, pictures
Open Mon–Sat 10am–5pm
Services Restorations of porcelain, silver-plating

Windsor & Eton Antiques Centre
Contact Mrs Thomas
✉ **17 High Street, Eton, Berkshire, SL4 6AX** Ⓟ
☎ 01753 840412 Ⓕ 01628 630041
Est. 2000 *Stock size* Medium
No. of dealers 22
Stock General antiques and collectables
Open Mon–Fri 10.30am–5pm Sun 1–4pm
Services Valuations

GORING ON THAMES

Barbara's Antiques and Bric-a-Brac
Contact Mrs M Bateman
✉ **Wheel Orchard, Station Road, Goring on Thames, Reading, Berkshire, RG8 9HB** Ⓟ
☎ 01491 873032
Est. 1981 *Stock size* Large
Stock Furniture, linen, lace, jewellery, china, brass, silver, plate, railwayana
Open Mon–Sat 10am–1pm 2.15–5pm

HUNGERFORD

Beedham Antiques Ltd (BADA)
Contact Herbert or Paul Beedham
✉ **26 Charnham Street, Hungerford, Berkshire, RG17 0EJ** Ⓟ
☎ 01488 684141 Ⓕ 01488 684050
Est. 1971 *Stock size* Medium
Stock 16th–17thC English and continental oak furniture
Open Mon–Sat 11am–5pm or by appointment
Fairs Olympia June, Nov

Below Stairs of Hungerford
Contact Stewart Hofgartner
✉ **103 High Street, Hungerford, Berkshire, RG17 0NB** Ⓟ
☎ 01488 682317 Ⓕ 01488 684294
Ⓔ stewart@belowstairs.co.uk
Ⓦ www.belowstairs.co.uk
Est. 1972 *Stock size* Large
Stock Collectables, furniture, taxidermy, garden items, kitchenalia, lighting, interior fittings
Open Mon–Sun 10am–6pm
Services Valuations

William Bentley Billiards
Contact Charles Saunders
✉ **Standen Manor Farm, Hungerford, Berkshire, RG17 0RB** Ⓟ
☎ 01488 681711 Ⓕ 01488 685197
Ⓦ www.billiards.co.uk
Stock size Large
Stock Billiard tables, accessories, build contemporary and traditional billiard tables including convertible dining and billiard tables
Open Mon–Sun or by appointment
Fairs Daily Telegraph House and Garden, Ideal homes
Services Valuations, restorations

Bowhouse Antiques
Contact Jo Preston
✉ **3–4 Faulkener Square, Charnham Street, Hungerford, Berkshire, RG17 0EP** Ⓟ
☎ 01488 680826 Ⓕ 01488 608593
Ⓜ 07710 921331
Est. 2000 *Stock size* Large
Stock 19thC decorative interiors
Open Mon–Sat 9.30am–5.30pm Sun 11am–4pm
Services Upholstery

Bridge House Antiques & Interiors
Contact Kate Pols
✉ **7 Bridge Street, Hungerford, Berkshire, RG17 0EH** Ⓟ
☎ 01488 681999 Ⓕ 01488 681999
Ⓔ bridgehouse@kpols.fsnet.co.uk
Est. 1992 *Stock size* Medium
Stock Antiques, decorative items for interiors
Open Tues–Sat 10am–5.30pm
Services Shipping

Countryside Books (PBFA)
Contact Mr Martin Smith
✉ **The Hungerford Antiques Centre, High Street, Hungerford, Berkshire, RG17 0NB**
☎ 01264 773943
Est. 1980 *Stock size* Medium
Stock Antiquarian, rare, second-hand books
Open Mon–Fri 9.15am–5.30pm Sat 9.15am–6pm Sun 11am–5pm
Fairs PBFA fair, Russell Hotel

The Fireplace (Hungerford) Ltd
Contact Mr E B Smith
✉ **The Old Fire Station, 3 Charnham Street, Hungerford, Berkshire, RG17 0EP** Ⓟ
☎ 01488 683420
Est. 1975 *Stock size* Large
Stock Fireplaces, fireplace furnishings, fenders, fire irons, dog baskets, firebacks, paintings
Open Mon–Sat 10am–1pm 2.15–5pm
Services Valuations, restorations of fireplace furnishings

Franklin Antiques
Contact Mrs L Franklin
✉ **25 Charnham Street, Hungerford, Berkshire, RG17 0EJ** Ⓟ
☎ 01488 682404 Ⓕ 01488 686069
Ⓔ antiques@lyndafranklin.com
Est. 1974 *Stock size* Large

Stock 18th–19thC English and French furniture
Open Mon–Sat 10am–5.30pm
Services Interior decoration

⊞ Garden Art
Contact Mr Arnie Knowles
✉ **Barrs Yard, 1 Bath Road, Hungerford, Berkshire, RG17 0HE** 🅿
☎ 01488 681881 Ⓕ 01488 681882
Ⓔ garden.art@dial.pipex.com
Est. 1976 *Stock size* Large
Stock Architectural antiques for the garden including gates, neo-classical statuary, bronze
Open Mon–Sat 10am–6pm Sun 11am–4pm or by appointment
Services Valuations, restorations, garden design

Great Grooms of Hungerford
Contact Mr J Podger
✉ **Riverside House, Charnham Street, Hungerford, Berkshire, RG17 0EP** 🅿
☎ 01488 682314 Ⓕ 01488 686677
Ⓔ antiques@great-grooms.co.uk
Ⓦ www.great-grooms.co.uk
Est. 1998 *Stock size* Large
No. of dealers 65
Stock General antiques, furnishings, country furniture, porcelain, clocks, silver, rugs, glass, bronzes, lighting, pictures
Open Mon–Sat 9.30am–5.30pm Sun 10am–6pm
Services Valuations, restorations

Hungerford Arcade
Contact Trevor Butcher
✉ **26 High Street, Hungerford, Berkshire, RG17 0ER** 🅿
☎ 01488 683701
Est. 1978 *Stock size* Large
No. of dealers 80
Stock General antiques and collectables
Open Mon–Sun 9.15am–5.30pm

⊞ Roger King Antiques
Contact Mrs A King
✉ **111 High Street, Hungerford, Berkshire, RG17 0NB** 🅿
☎ 01488 682256
Est. 1974 *Stock size* Large
Stock Georgian–Edwardian furniture
Open Mon–Sat 9.30am–5pm Sun 11am–5pm

⊞ M J M Antiques
Contact Michael Mancey
✉ **13 Bridge Street, Hungerford, Berkshire, RG17 0EH** 🅿
☎ 01488 684905 Ⓕ 01488 684090
Ⓜ 07774 479997
Ⓔ mike@oldguns.co.uk
Ⓦ www.oldguns.co.uk
Est. 1999 *Stock size* Medium
Stock Fine antique arms
Open Mon–Sat 10am–5pm or by appointment
Fairs Arms & Armour Fairs
Services Valuations

⊞ Medalcrest Ltd
Contact Mrs M Farrow
✉ **Charnham House, 29–30 Charnham Street, Hungerford, Berkshire, RG17 0EJ** 🅿
☎ 01488 684157 Ⓕ 01488 684157
Ⓜ 07901 898585
Est. 1974 *Stock size* Large
Stock 18th–19thC walnut, mahogany, oak, and country furniture, barometers
Open Mon–Sat 10am–5.30pm Sun by appointment

⊞ The Old Malthouse (BADA, CINOA)
Contact Mr or Mrs P Hunwick
✉ **15 Bridge Street, Hungerford, Berkshire, RG17 0EG** 🅿
☎ 01488 682209 Ⓕ 01488 682209
Ⓜ 07771 862257
Ⓔ hunwick@oldmalthouse30.freeserve.co.uk
Est. 1959 *Stock size* Large
Stock 18th–19thC furniture, brass, mirrors, paintings, clocks, barometers, decorative items
Open Mon–Sat 10am–5.30pm
Fairs Chelsea
Services Valuations

⊞ Principia Fine Art
Contact Mr M Forrer
✉ **35a High Street, Hungerford, Berkshire, RG17 0NF** 🅿
☎ 01488 682873 Ⓕ 01672 511551
Ⓜ 07899 926020
Ⓦ www.antiquesportfolio.com
Est. 1970 *Stock size* Large
Stock Scientific instruments, small furniture, Oriental art, books, paintings, works of art
Open Mon–Sat 9.30am–5.30pm Sun by appointment
Services Valuations, restorations, shipping, book search

⊞ Turpins Antiques (BADA, LAPADA, CINOA)
Contact Mrs J Summer
✉ **17 Bridge Street, Hungerford, Berkshire, RG17 0EG** 🅿
☎ 01488 681886
Est. 1959 *Stock size* Medium
Stock 18thC English and Regency walnut furniture
Open Wed Fri Sat 10am–5pm or by appointment
Fairs Olympia

⊞ Youll's Antiques
Contact Mr B Youll
✉ **27–28 Charnham Street, Hungerford, Berkshire, RG17 0EJ** 🅿
☎ 01488 682046 Ⓕ 01488 684335
Ⓔ bruce.youll@talk21.com
Ⓦ www.youll.com
Est. 1935 *Stock size* Large
Stock 17th–20thC English and French furniture, porcelain, silver, decorative items
Open Mon–Sun 10.30am–5.30pm
Fairs Newark
Services Valuations, restorations

HURST

⊞ Christopher Edwards (ABA)
Contact Mr C Edwards
✉ **Hatch Gate Farmhouse, Lines Road, Hurst, Berkshire, RG10 0SP** 🅿
☎ 0118 934 0531 Ⓕ 0118 934 0539
Ⓔ chr.edwards@which.net
Est. 1992 *Stock size* Small
Stock Antiquarian English literature, early Continental books, manuscripts
Open By appointment
Fairs London Antiquarian Book Fair, Chelsea
Services Valuations

KINGSCLERE

⊞ Wyseby House Books (PBFA)
Contact Mrs A Oldham
✉ **Kingsclere Old Bookshop, 2a George Street, Kingsclere, Newbury, Berkshire, RG20 5NQ** 🅿
☎ 01635 297995 Ⓕ 01635 297677
Ⓔ info@wyseby.co.uk
Ⓦ www.wyseby.co.uk
Est. 1978 *Stock size* Large
Stock General antiquarian, rare,

second-hand books, fine art, decorative arts, architectural a speciality
Open Mon–Sat 10am–5pm
Services Catalogue 10 times a year

LECKHAMPSTEAD

Hill Farm Antiques
Contact Mr M Beesley
Hill Farm, Shop Lane, Leckhampstead, Newbury, Berkshire, RG20 8QG
01488 638541/638361
01488 638541
beesley@hillfarmantiques.demon.co.uk
Est. 1987 ***Stock size*** Large
Stock 19thC extending dining tables in mahogany, oak, walnut
Open Mon–Sat 10am–5pm Sun by appointment

MIDGHAM

Berkshire Antiques Centre
Contact Mrs J Bradley
Unit 1, Kennet Holme Farm Buildings, Bath Road, Midgham, Berkshire, RG7 5UX
01189 710477 01189 710477
enquiries@berkshire-antiques.fsnet.co.uk
Est. 2000 ***Stock size*** Large
No. of dealers 10
Stock Furniture, general antiques and collectables
Open Mon–Sun 10.30am–4.30pm closed Wed

Special Auction Services
Contact Andrew Hilton
The Coach House, Midgham Park, Reading, Berkshire, RG7 5UG
0118 971 2949 0118 971 2420
Est. 1991
Open 8.30am–6pm by appointment
Sales Special auctions of commemoratives, pot lids, Prattware, fairings, Goss and Crested, Baxter and Le Blond prints. Please phone for details. Held at The Courtyard Hotel, Padworth, Nr Reading
Frequency March, June, Sept, Nov
Catalogues Yes

MORTIMER

Frank Milward (BNTA, ANA)
Contact Mr F Milward
2 Ravensworth Road, Mortimer, Reading, Berkshire, RG7 3UU
0118 933 2843 0118 933 2843
Est. 1975 ***Stock size*** Medium
Stock English and foreign coins, banknotes
Open By appointment
Fairs International Coin Fair, Coinex, London
Services Valuations

NEWBURY

Invicta Bookshop (PBFA)
Contact Mr S Hall
8 Cromwell Place, Newbury, Berkshire, RG14 1AF
01635 31176
Est. 1969 ***Stock size*** Medium
Stock Antiquarian, rare, second-hand books, cookery, cricket, military topics a speciality
Open Mon–Sat 10.30am–5.30pm closed Wed
Fairs Oxford, Bath PBFA
Services Book search

Newbury Salvage Ltd (FOCC)
Contact Mrs H Bromhead
Kelvin Road, Newbury, Berkshire, RG14 2DB
01635 528120 01635 551007
07785 518869
Est. 1988 ***Stock size*** Large
Stock Bricks, tiles, slates, chimney pots, fireplaces, doors, windows, statuary, sanitary ware, oak beams
Open Mon–Fri 8am–5pm Sat 9am–1pm

Alan Walker (BADA, TVADA)
Contact Mr A Walker
Halfway Manor, Halfway, Newbury, Berkshire, RG20 8NR
01488 657670 01488 657670
www.alanwalker-barometers.com
Est. 1987 ***Stock size*** Large
Stock 18th–19thC barometers, barographs, related instruments
Open By appointment
Fairs Olympia, BADA, Duke of York's
Services Valuations, restorations, barometers purchased

PANGBOURNE

R Butler
Contact Rita Butler
4 Station Road, Pangbourne, Reading, Berkshire, RG8 7AN
0118 984 5522 0118 984 4520
Est. 1999 ***Stock size*** Medium
No. of dealers 5
Stock Small to medium-sized furniture 17th–20thC, Art Deco, decorative interiors, Georgian and other glass
Open Wed–Mon 10am–5pm closed Sun
Services Valuations

READING

Addington Antiques
Contact Paul Schneiderman
41 Addington Road, Reading, Berkshire, RG1 5PZ
0118 935 3435
Est. 1996 ***Stock size*** Small
Stock General antiques 18thC–1960s design
Open Thurs–Sat 10am–6pm
Fairs Newark, Ardingly

P D Leatherland Antiques (TVADA)
Contact Mr P D Leatherland
68 London Street, Reading, Berkshire, RG1 4SQ
0118 958 1960
Est. 1965 ***Stock size*** Large
Stock 18th–19thC furniture, porcelain, clocks, paintings, decorative items
Open Mon–Sat 9am–5.15pm Sun 10am–4pm

Stables Antiques Centre
Contact Ms S A Bunce
1a Merchants Place, Reading, Berkshire, RG1 1DT
0118 959 0290
Est. 1965 ***Stock size*** Large
No. of dealers 40
Stock Furniture, silver, china, jewellery, collectables, models, coins, militaria
Open Mon–Sat 10am–5pm

SLOUGH

Randtiques
Contact Mr Tony Lowe
23 Stoke Road, Slough, Berkshire, SL2 5AH
01753 572512
Est. 1984 ***Stock size*** Medium
Stock Furniture, china, glass, pine, prints, watercolours
Open Mon–Sat 10am–5pm closed Wed
Services Framing, paint stripping

SONNING-ON-THAMES

Cavendish Fine Art (BADA)
Contact Janet Middlemiss
Dower House, Pearson Road, Sonning-on-Thames, Berkshire, RG4 6UL
0118 969 1904
07831 295575
info@cavendishfineart.com
www.cavendishfineart.com
Est. 1973 ***Stock size*** Large
Stock Georgian furniture
Open By appointment
Fairs Olympia, BADA

TWYFORD

Bell Antiques
Contact Mr N Timms
2b High Street, Twyford, Reading, Berkshire, RG10 9AE
0118 934 2501
Est. 1989 ***Stock size*** Large
Stock General antiques, collectables
Open Mon–Sat 9.30am–5.30pm Sun 10am–5.30pm

Brocante Antiques & Interiors
Contact Tony Wilkinson
19–21 Church Street, Twyford, Reading, Berkshire, RG10 9DN
0118 932 0850
brocante.wilkinson@virgin.net
Est. 2000 ***Stock size*** Medium
Stock Late 18thC–early 19thC French and Oriental furniture, decorative items
Open Wed–Sun 10.30am–5.30pm
Fairs East Berkshire Antique Fair, Newark, Ardingly
Services Valuations, restorations

Jem's Collectables
Contact Mr Belli
7 The High Street, Twyford, Reading, Berkshire, RG10 9AB
0118 932 1414
Est. 1993 ***Stock size*** Medium
Stock Bunnykins, Royal Doulton, collectables
Open Mon–Sat 10am–5.30pm Sun 11am–4.30pm
Services Valuations

Loddon Lily Antiques
Contact Mrs S Rose
1 High Street, Twyford, Reading, Berkshire, RG10 9AB
0118 934 2161
Est. 1979 ***Stock size*** Large
No. of dealers 20
Stock Antiques, collectables
Open Mon–Sat 9.30am–5.30pm Sun 10.30am–5pm

WARFIELD

Moss End Antiques Centre (TVADA)
Contact Maureeen Staite or Maura Dorrington
Moss End, Warfield, Berkshire, RG42 6EJ
01344 861942
Est. 1988 ***Stock size*** Large
No. of dealers 20
Stock Furniture, clocks, silver, glass, porcelain, linen, collectables
Open Tues–Sun 10.30am–5pm
Services Restorations, coffee shop

WARGRAVE

Ferry Antiques
Contact Peter or Kate Turner
70 High Street, Wargrave, Berkshire, RG10 8BY
0118 940 4415
07778 615975
Est. 1993 ***Stock size*** Medium
Stock 18th–19thC furniture, general antiques, glass, porcelain, silver, decorative objects
Open Wed–Sun 10am–5.30pm
Fairs The East Berkshire Antiques Fair
Services Valuations, restorations

Wargrave Antiques
Contact Mr J Connell
66 High Street, Wargrave, Berkshire, RG10 8BY
0118 940 2914
Est. 1979 ***Stock size*** Large
Stock Furniture, porcelain, glass, silver, copper, brass, 19thC furniture a speciality
Open Wed–Sun 10am–5pm
Services Valuations, restorations

WINDSOR

Berkshire Antiques Co Ltd
Contact Mr Sutton
42 Thames Street, Windsor, Berkshire, SL4 1YY
01753 830100 01753 832278
jewels@dircon.co.uk
Est. 1981 ***Stock size*** Large
Stock Silver, dolls, jewellery, furniture, pictures, porcelain, Art Deco, Art Nouveau, commemorative memorabilia, royal commemoratives
Open Mon–Sat 10.30am–5.30pm Sun 1–5.30pm
Services Valuations, restorations

Dee's Antique Pine
Contact Mrs Dee Waghorn
89 Grove Road, Windsor, Berkshire, SL4 1HT
01753 865627 01753 850926
deesantiquepine@aol.com
Stock size Large
Stock Decorative items, furniture
Open Tues–Sat 10.30am–6pm or by appointment

Jan Hicks Antiques (TVADA, LAPADA, Decorative Antiques and Textiles Fair)
Contact Jan Hicks
Fifield, Near Windsor, Berkshire
01488 683986 01488 683986
07770 230686
antiques@janhicks.com
Est. 1987 ***Stock size*** Large
Stock French provincial furniture, particularly armoires, beds, farm tables, buffets, mirrors, chandeliers, decorative items
Open By appointment

Old Barn Antiques (BSSA)
Contact Mrs Sue Lakey
Wyedale Garden Centre, Dedworth Road, Windsor, Berkshire, SL4 4LH
01753 833099
Est. 1991 ***Stock size*** Large
Stock Furniture, porcelain,

jewellery, garden antiquities, militaria, silver, dolls, glassware
Open Mon–Sat 10am–5pm Sun 10.30am–4.30pm

Rule's Antiques (TVADA)
Contact Miss Sue Rule
62 St Leonards Road, Windsor, Berkshire, SL4 3BY
01753 833210
Est. 1995 *Stock size* Medium
Stock Decorative pieces, brass, lighting, door furniture and fittings
Open Mon–Sat 10.30am–6pm
Fairs TVADA

WOKINGHAM

Barkham Antiques Centre
Contact Len or Mary Collins
Barkham Street, Wokingham, Berkshire, RG40 4PJ
01189 761355
www.neatsite.com
Est. 1984 *Stock size* Large
Stock Collectables, toy specialists, Doulton, general antiques, architectural salvage
Open Mon–Sun 10.30am–5pm
Services Restorations

Nicholas, Martin & Pole
Contact Mr G J R Lewis
The Auction House, Milton Road, Wokingham, Berkshire, RG40 1DB
0118 979 0460 F 0118 977 6166
a@martinpole.co.uk
www.martinpole.co.uk
Est. 1846
Open Mon–Fri 9am–5pm
Sales Monthly antiques and collectables, also modern and household. No sales in August. Phone for details
Frequency 2 per month
Catalogues Yes

WOOLHAMPTON

The Old Bakery Antiques
Contact Susan Everard
Bath Road, Woolhampton, Reading, Berkshire, RG10 8BY
0118 971 2116
Est. 1974 *Stock size* Medium
Stock Antiques and collectables
Open Thurs–Sat 10am–5pm
Fairs Newark, Ardingly

HAMPSHIRE

ALDERSHOT

Aldershot Antiques
Contact Mr N Powell-Pelly
2a Elms Road, Aldershot, Hampshire, GU11 1LJ
01252 408408 F 01252 408408
M 07768 722152
Est. 1979 *Stock size* Small
Stock Furniture including pine
Open By appointment
Services Valuations

Traders Antiques and Country Pine Centre
Contact Mrs J Burns
Norfolk House, 131 Grosvenor Road, Aldershot, Hampshire, GU11 3ER
01252 322055
Est. 1969 *Stock size* Large
Stock Furniture, fireplaces, doors, pine, mahogany, oak
Open Mon–Sat 10am–5.30pm
Services Restorations, French polishing

ALRESFORD

Artemesia (LAPADA)
Contact Mr Tim Wright
16 West Street, Alresford, Hampshire, SO24 9AT
01962 732277
Est. 1969 *Stock size* Large
Stock English and Continental furniture, ceramics, works of art
Open Mon–Sat 10am–1pm 2–5pm
Services Valuations

Laurence Oxley (ABA)
Contact Anthony Oxley
17 Broad Street, Alresford, Hampshire, S024 9AW
01962 732188 F 01962 732998
M 07769 715510
anthony.l.d.oxley@ukgateway.net
Est. 1950
Stock Victorian watercolours, old maps, antiquarian books
Open Mon–Sat 9am–5pm
Fairs Chelsea Book Fair
Services Restorations, picture framing

Tudor Antiques and Fine Arts Ltd (AAFAA)
Contact Eric or Penelope Tudor
The Old Exchange, Station Road, Alresford, Hampshire, SO24 9JG
01962 735345 F 01962 736345
M 07774 908888
e&ptudor@tudor-antiques.co.uk
www.tudor-antiques.co.uk
Est. 1980 *Stock size* Large
Stock 17th–19thC English, French, Oriental furniture, objets d'art
Open Mon–Sat 10am–4pm Sun by appointment
Services Valuations, shipping arranged

Underwood Oak
Contact Ms Ann Egerton
49 West Street, Alresford, Hampshire, SO24 9AB
01962 735677 F 01730 267797
antiques@underwoodoak.co.uk
Est. 1999 *Stock size* Medium
Stock 17th–19thC oak, country furniture
Open Mon–Sat 10am–5pm closed Wed
Fairs Avington
Services Valuations, restorations

ALTON

Artisan Restoration
Contact Mr W Dalton
86 Victoria Road, Alton, Hampshire, GU34 2DD
01420 549554
artisan@britannia.uk.com
Est. 1984 *Stock size* Medium
Stock Antique writing furniture, display cabinets, rocking horses
Open Mon–Sat 9am–1pm or by appointment
Services Restorations

Jardinique (SALVO)
Contact Mr Edward Neish
Old Park Farm, Abbey Road, Beech, Alton, Hampshire, GU34 4AW
01420 560055 F 01420 560050
jardinique@aol.com
www.jardinique.co.uk
Est. 1994 *Stock size* Large
Stock Statuary, sundials, urns, gardenalia, seats, fountains, stone troughs, staddle stones
Open Tues–Sat 10am–5pm or by appointment
Services Valuations

ANDOVER

Andover Saleroom (Pearsons)
Contact Dominic Foster

SOUTH

✉ **41a London Street, Andover, Hampshire, SP10 2NU** 🅿
☎ 01264 364820 Ⓕ 01264 323402
Ⓦ www.pearsons.com
Est. 1979
Open Mon–Fri 8.30am–6pm
Sales Pictures and jewellery Sat, antique and general Mon, viewing Fri 9am–9pm Sat 9am–6pm. Advisable to telephone for details
Frequency Fortnightly
Catalogues Yes

Ludgershall Antiques Centre
Contact Mrs I Haylen
✉ **4–6 Andover Road, Ludgershall, Andover, Hampshire, SP11 9LZ** 🅿
☎ 01264 791372 Ⓕ 01264 710704
Ⓔ lac@hayland.demon.co.uk
Est. 1996 *Stock size* Medium
Stock Furniture, jewellery, silver, bronzes, paintings, porcelain, objets d'art
Open Tues–Sat 10am–5pm Sun 11am–4pm
Services Valuations, free local delivery

May and Son (NAEA)
Contact Miss N Gibbs
✉ **18 Bridge Street, Andover, Hampshire, SP10 1BH** 🅿
☎ 01264 323417 Ⓕ 01264 338841
Ⓜ 07710 001660
Ⓔ mayandson@enterprise.net
Est. 1925
Open Mon–Fri 9am–5pm Sat 9am–noon
Sales Antique furniture and effects 3rd Wed of the month, viewing Tues 8.30am–6.30pm and morning of sale from 8.30am. Sales take place in Village Hall, Penton Mewsey, Andover. No buyer's premium. Periodic specialist auctions
Frequency Monthly
Catalogues Yes

BASINGSTOKE

Anticks
Contact Jean Stone
✉ **5 Church Street, Basingstoke, Hampshire, RG21 7QH** 🅿
☎ 01256 471000
Est. 1995 *Stock size* Medium
Stock Jewellery, antiques and collectable china
Open Mon–Sat 10am–5pm closed Tues
Fairs Magnum
Services Jewellery repairs

Hickley's Cards
Contact Mr R Hickley
✉ **PO Box 6090, Basingstoke, Hampshire, RG23 8YR**
☎ 01256 411893 Ⓕ 01256 411894
Ⓔ sales@hickleysautographs.com
Ⓦ www.hickleysautographs.com
Est. 1993 *Stock size* Large
Stock Japanese and American music memorabilia
Open By appointment only
Services Valuations, search service

The Squirrel Antique & Collectors Centre
✉ **Joyce's Yard, 9a New Street, Basingstoke, Hampshire, RG21 7DE**
☎ 01256 464885
Est. 1981 *Stock size* Large
Stock Jewellery, silver, dolls, teddy bears, Art Deco ceramics, china, furniture
Open Mon–Sat 10am–5.30pm
Services Valuations

BROCKENHURST

Antiquiteas
Contact Mr R Wolstenholme
✉ **37 Brockley Road, Brockenhurst, Hampshire, SO42 7RB** 🅿
☎ 01590 622120
Ⓔ antiquiteas@aol.com
Ⓦ www.antiquiteas.co.uk
Est. 1999 *Stock size* Medium
Stock Pine furniture, copper, brass, porcelain, watercolour originals, prints
Open Mon–Sat 10am–5pm Sun 10am–4pm

Squirrels
Contact Sue Crocket
✉ **Lyndhurst Road, Brockenhurst, Hampshire, S042 7RL** 🅿
☎ 01590 622433
Est. 1989 *Stock size* Medium
Stock Antiques, collectables, stripped pine, furniture, Victoriana, Art Deco, Art Nouveau, kitchenware, garden items, pictures, mirrors
Open Wed–Sun 10am–5pm 10am–4pm in winter

CHANDLERS FORD

Boris Books (PBFA)
Contact Mrs P Stevenson
✉ **2 Holland Close, Chandlers Ford, Eastleigh, Hampshire, SO53 3NA** 🅿
☎ 023 8027 5496 Ⓕ 023 8027 5496
Ⓜ 0780 1111886
Ⓔ borisbooks@aol.com
Est. 1995 *Stock size* Small
Stock Antiquarian, rare, collectable, second-hand books, specializing in literature, music, children's, illustrated
Open By appointment
Fairs Romsey Antique and Collectors Fair, Forest Fairs
Services Book search

EMSWORTH

Antique Bed Company
Contact Mr I Trewick
✉ **32 North Street, Emsworth, Hampshire, PO10 7DG** 🅿
☎ 01243 376074 Ⓕ 01243 376074
Ⓔ antiquebed@aol.com
Est. 1992 *Stock size* Large
Stock Victorian–Edwardian brass, iron and wooden beds
Open Mon–Sat 9am–5.30pm
Services Valuations, restorations

Bookends
Contact Mrs C Waldron
✉ **7 High Street, Emsworth, Hampshire, PO10 7AQ** 🅿
☎ 01243 372154 Ⓕ 01243 372154
Ⓜ 07968 417395
Ⓔ cawaldron@tinyworld.co.uk
Est. 1982 *Stock size* Medium
Stock Antiquarian, rare, second-hand books, sheet music
Open Mon–Sat 9.30am–5pm Sun 10.30am–3pm
Services Valuations, book search

Dolphin Quay Antique Centre
Contact Mrs N Farmer or Mr G Farmer
✉ **Queen Street, Emsworth, Hampshire, PO10 7BU** 🅿
☎ 01243 379994 Ⓕ 01243 379251
Ⓜ 07803 056513
Ⓔ enquiries@dolphin-quay-antiques
Ⓦ www.dolphin-quay-antiques.co.uk
Est. 1969 *Stock size* Large
No. of dealers 30+
Stock Fine antique furniture, porcelain, clocks, watches, jewellery, silver

Open Mon–Sat 10am–5pm
Sun 10am–4pm
Services Restorations, furniture upholstery

EVERSLEY

Eversley Antiques
Contact Hilary Craven
Church Lane, Eversley, Hampshire, RG27 0PX P
☎ 0118 932 8518
Est. 1998 ***Stock size*** Large
No. of dealers 11
Stock General antiques, collectables
Open Mon Thurs–Sun 10.30am–5.30pm
Services Delivery

FLEET

Bona Art Deco Store (ADDA)
Contact Mr J Motley
The Hart Shopping Centre, Fleet, Hampshire, GU13 8AZ P
☎ 01252 372188 F 01252 615855
E artdeco@bona.co.uk
W www.clariceclift.co.uk
Est. 1973 ***Stock size*** Large
Stock 20thC ceramics, Clarice Cliff, English pressed glass, furniture, lighting
Open Mon–Sat 10am–5pm
Services Valuations, restorations, archive information

Yesterdays
258 Fleet Street, Fleet, Hampshire, GU13 8BX P
☎ 01252 669971 F 01252 669971
E enquiries@yesterdays.co.uk
W www.yesterdays.co.uk
Est. 1998 ***Stock size*** Large
Stock Georgian–1940s furniture, glass, china, collectables
Open Mon–Wed Fri 10.30am–5.30pm Thurs 10.30am–5pm Sun 11am–4.30pm

FORDINGBRIDGE

Bonhams & Brooks
Contact Charles Leith
Frogham Mount, Frogham, Fordingbridge, Hampshire, SP6 2HW
☎ 01425 652216 F 01425 653458
W www.bonhams.com
Open Mon–Fri 9am–5pm
Sales Regional Representative for Hampshire and Dorset

Bristow and Garland
Contact Mr David Bristow
45–47 Salisbury Street, Fordingbridge, Hampshire, SP6 1AB
☎ 01425 657337 F 01425 657337
E davidbristow@bristowandgarland.fonet.co.uk
Est. 1960 ***Stock size*** Small
Stock Antiquarian, rare, second-hand books, manuscripts, ephemera
Open Mon–Sat 9.30am–5pm closed Wed

West Essex Coin Investments (BNTA, IBNS)
Contact Mr R Norbury
Croft Cottage, Station Road, Alderholt, Fordingbridge, Hampshire, SP6 3AZ
☎ 01425 656459 F 01425 656459
Est. 1977 ***Stock size*** Medium
Stock English coinage medieval–present day including English milled, British colonial, coins of the USA
Open By appointment only
Fairs York Racecourse, BNTA Fairs
Services Valuations

GOSPORT

Easter Antiques
Contact Mr R Easter
333 Forton Road, Gosport, Hampshire, PO12 3HF P
☎ 023 9250 3621
Est. 1984 ***Stock size*** Small
Stock Small decorative items
Open Mon–Sat 10am–5pm closed Wed
Services Valuations, restorations

Former Glory
Contact Mr L Brannon
49 Whitworth Road, Gosport, Hampshire, PO12 3NJ P
☎ 023 9250 4869
Est. 1986 ***Stock size*** Medium
Stock Victorian–Edwardian furniture, china
Open Mon–Sat 9am–5pm closed Wed
Services Restorations, traditional upholstery

HARTLEY WINTNEY

Nicholas Abbott (LAPADA)
Contact Mr C N Abbott
High Street, Hartley Wintney, Hook, Hampshire, RG27 8NY P
☎ 01252 842365 F 01252 842365
E nicholasabbott@web-hq.com
W nicholas-abbott.com
Est. 1964 ***Stock size*** Medium
Stock 18thC furniture
Open Mon–Sat 9.30am–5.30pm

Andwells Antiques (LAPADA)
Contact Alastair Mackenzie
The Row, High Street, Hartley Wintney, Hampshire, RG27 8NY P
☎ 01252 842305 F 01252 845149
Est. 1967 ***Stock size*** Large
Stock 18thC English furniture
Open Mon–Fri 9am–5.30pm Sat 9.30am–5.30pm

Antique House
Contact P Weaver
22 High Street, Hartley Wintney, Hook, Hampshire, RG27 8NY P
☎ 01252 844499 F 01252 845270
M 07467 603443
E paul.a.weaver@nationwideisp.net
Est. 1977 ***Stock size*** Large
Stock Georgian–Victorian mahogany and walnut furniture
Open Mon–Sat 9.30am–5.30pm
Services Valuations, restorations

The Antiques Centre
Contact Mrs S Lister
Primrose House, London Road, Hartley Wintney, Hampshire, RG27 8RG P
☎ 01252 843393 F 0118 934 9311
M 07836 734838
Est. 1996 ***Stock size*** Large
No. of dealers 9
Stock Georgian–Victorian, fine and country furniture, clocks, paintings, china (including Art Deco)
Open Mon–Sat 10am–5pm Sun noon–4pm
Services Shipping

Cedar Antiques Centre Ltd
Contact Derek Green
High Street, Hartley Wintney, Hampshire, RG27 8NY P
☎ 01252 843222 F 01252 842111
E cac@cedar-ltd.demon.co.uk
W www.cedar-antiques.com
Est. 1998 ***Stock size*** Large
No. of dealers 50
Stock Early English furniture, silver, glass, watercolours, carpets

Open Mon–Sat 10am–5.30pm
Sun 11am–5pm
Services Café, Museum of T G Green pottery

⊞ Cedar Antiques Ltd
Contact Sally Green
✉ **High Street, Hartley Wintney, Hampshire, RG27 8NT** 🅿
☎ 01252 843252
Est. 1964 *Stock size* Large
Stock 17th–20thC English and continental country furniture with colour
Open Mon–Sat 10am–5pm
Services Valuations, restorations

⊞ Bryan Clisby (LAPADA)
Contact Mr B Clisby
✉ **High Street, Hartley Wintney, Hampshire, RG27 8NY** 🅿
☎ 01252 716436 🅕 01252 716436
🅔 bryanclisby@cwcom.net
Est. 1978 *Stock size* Large
Stock Longcase, bracket, wall clocks, mantel clocks, barometers
Open Mon–Sat 9.30am–5.30pm
Services Restorations

⊞ Deva Antiques
Contact Mr A Gratwick
✉ **High Street, Hartley Wintney, Hook, Hampshire, RG27 8NY** 🅿
☎ 01252 834538 🅕 01252 842946
🅔 devaants@aol.com
🅦 www.deva-antiques.com
Est. 1986 *Stock size* Medium
Stock 18th–19thC mahogany, walnut, country furniture, decorative accessories
Open Mon–Sat 9am–5.30pm
Services Collection from BR station by arrangement

⊞ Sally Green Designs
Contact Sally Green
✉ **63 High Street, Hartley Wintney, Hampshire, RG27 8NT** 🅿
☎ 01252 843252 🅕 01252 842111
🅔 sg@cedar-ltd.deom.co.uk
🅦 www.cedar-antiques.com
Est. 1965 *Stock size* Medium
Stock 18th–19thC English and continental country furniture
Open Mon–Sat 10am–5pm

⊞ David Lazarus Antiques (BADA)
Contact Mr D Lazarus
✉ **High Street, Hartley Wintney, Hook, Hampshire, RG27 8NS** 🅿
☎ 01252 842272 🅕 01252 842272
Est. 1973 *Stock size* Medium
Stock Furniture, sculpture, objets d'art
Open Mon–Sat 9.30am–5.30pm
Services Valuations

⊞ Phoenix Green Antiques (LAPADA)
Contact Mr J Biles or Mr Gregory Woodcock
✉ **London Road, Hartley Wintney, Hook, Hampshire, RG27 8RT** 🅿
☎ 01252 844430/843647
🅕 01252 849992
🅔 johnbiles@phoenixgreenantiques.com
🅦 www.phoenixgreenantiques.com
Est. 1981 *Stock size* Large
Stock 18th–19thC English and Continental furniture
Open Mon–Sat 9am–6pm
Sun 10–5pm
Fairs Guildford, Buxton
Services Valuations, restorations

HEADLEY

⊞ Victorian Dreams
Contact Mrs S Kay
✉ **The Old School, Crabtree Lane, Headley, Bordon, Hampshire, GU35 8QH** 🅿
☎ 01428 717000 🅕 01428 717111
🅔 sales@victorian-dreams.co.uk
🅦 www.victorian-dreams.co.uk
Est. 1985 *Stock size* Large
Stock Brass, iron, wooden, upholstered and caned bedsteads
Open Mon–Sat 9am–5.30pm
Sun 10am–4pm
Fairs Newark, Ardingly
Services Valuations, restorations, world and nationwide delivery

HIGHBRIDGE

⊞ Brambridge Antiques
Contact Mr D May
✉ **Bugle Farm, Highbridge Road, Highbridge, Eastleigh, Hampshire, SO50 6HS** 🅿
☎ 01962 714386
Est. 1973 *Stock size* Medium
Stock Mahogany and walnut furniture
Open Mon–Sat 9am–5pm
Services Restorations

HORNDEAN

⊞ The Goss & Crested China Club
Contact Lynda Pine
✉ **62 Murray Road, Horndean, Hampshire, PO8 9JL** 🅿
☎ 023 9259 7440 🅕 023 9259 1975
🅔 info@gosschinaclub.demon.co.uk
🅦 www.gosschinaclub.demon.co.uk
Est. 1969 *Stock size* Large
Stock Over 5,000 pieces of Goss and Crested china
Open Mon–Sat 9am–5pm
Services Monthly mail order catalogue, museum on site, search service for wants lists

LISS

⊞ Mother Hubbard Antiques
Contact Mr J Worboys
✉ **20 Station Road, Liss, Hampshire, GU33 7DT** 🅿
☎ 01730 894989 🅕 01252 812311
Est. 1975 *Stock size* Medium
Stock Pine furniture
Open Mon–Sat 9am–6pm
Sun 11am–3pm
Services Restorations, paint stripping

⊞ Plestor Barn Antiques
Contact Mr McCarthy
✉ **Farnham Road, Liss, Hampshire, GU33 6JQ** 🅿
☎ 01730 893922
🅜 07850 539998
Est. 1984 *Stock size* Medium
Stock Victorian–Edwardian, stripped pine, 1920s furniture, used and reproduction soft furnishings
Open Mon–Fri 10am–5pm
Sat 10am–2pm
Services Light removals service

LYMINGTON

⊞ Beagle Books (PBFA)
Contact Mr A F Blakeley
✉ **1 Middle Road, Sway, Lymington, Hampshire, SO41 6AT**
☎ 01590 683421
Est. 1974 *Stock size* Medium
Stock Books on natural history, country life, hunting, shooting, fishing, gardening
Open Mail order only
Services Book search

⊞ Carlsen's Antiques and Fine Arts
Contact Mr D Carlsen
✉ **8 St Thomas Street, Lymington, Hampshire, SO41 9NA** 🅿

☎ 01590 676370
Est. 1987 *Stock size* Large
Stock Watercolours, pencils, etchings, mirrors, small Georgian–Victorian furniture
Open Mon–Sat 9.30am–5.30pm
Fairs Winchester, Lymington
Services Valuations

Corfield Ltd
Contact Mr A Roberts
✉ **120 High Street, Lymington, Hampshire, SO41 9AQ** P
☎ 01590 673532 F 01590 678855
Est. 1995 *Stock size* Medium
Stock Porcelain, paintings, Regency, Georgian, Victorian furniture
Open Mon–Sat 9.30am–5.30pm
Services Restorations

George Kidner
Contact Mrs K Chamberlain
✉ **The Old School, The Square, Pennington, Lymington, Hampshire, SO41 8GN** P
☎ 01590 670070 F 01590 675167
E info@georgekidner.freeserve.co.uk
Est. 1991
Open Mon–Fri 9am–5pm
Sales Furniture and decorative items, silver, jewellery, paintings, collectors items. Sales on Wed, viewing Sat 9.30am–1pm Mon 9.30am–4.30pm Tues 9.30am–7pm
Frequency Monthly
Catalogues Yes

Landfall
Contact Mrs E P Moody
✉ **96 High Street, Milford on Sea, Lymington, Hampshire, SO41 0QE** P
☎ 01590 643951
Est. 1973 *Stock size* Small
Stock General, small furniture, pictures, clothes, books, jewellery, linen
Open Mon–Sat 9am–5.30pm Sun 2–5pm

Lymington Antique Centre
Contact Lisa Reeves
✉ **76 High Street, Lymington, Hampshire, SO41 9AL**
☎ 01590 670934
Est. 1990 *Stock size* Large
No. of dealers 30
Stock Furniture, porcelain, books, jewellery, silver, pictures
Open Mon–Fri 10am–5pm Sat 9am–5pm
Services Restorations

Platt's of Lymington
Contact Mrs Kay Boyd-Platt
✉ **15 St Thomas Street, Lymington, Hampshire, SO41 9NB** P
☎ 01590 688769
Est. 1997 *Stock size* Large
Stock Superb selection of good quality porcelain, furniture, especially small pieces, all stock dated, priced, guaranteed
Open Wed–Sat 10am–5pm or by appointment, longer hours during December, please phone to check
Services Valuations

Treasure Trove
Contact Mrs M Wall
✉ **1a Captain's Row, Lymington, Hampshire, SO41 9RP** P
☎ 01590 673974
Est. 1993 *Stock size* Medium
Stock Collectables, glass, clocks
Open Tues–Sat 10am–4pm

Wick Antiques (LAPADA, CINOA)
Contact Mr Charlie Wallrock
✉ **Fairlea House, 110–112 Marsh Lane, Lymington, Hampshire, SO4 19EE** P
☎ 01590 677558 F 01590 677558
E charles@wickantiques.co.uk
W www.wickantiques.co.uk
Est. 1984 *Stock size* Large
Stock 18th–19thC English and French furniture
Open Mon–Sat 9am–5pm
Fairs Olympia Fine Arts Fair
Services Restorations

LYNDHURST

Lita Kaye Antiques
Contact Mr S Ferder
✉ **13 High Street, Lyndhurst, Hampshire, SO43 7BB** P
☎ 023 8028 2337
Est. 1950 *Stock size* Large
Stock English period, 18thC Regency furniture, porcelain, decorative items
Open Mon–Sat 9.30am–5.30pm

Lyndhurst Antique Centre
Contact Mrs G Ashley
✉ **19–21 High Street, Lyndhurst, Hampshire, SO43 7BB** P
☎ 023 8028 4000
Est. 1998 *Stock size* Large
No. of dealers 50
Stock Collectables, furniture, militaria
Open Mon–Sun 10am–5pm

MATTINGLEY

Odiham Auction Sales
Contact Mr S R Thomas
✉ **Unit 4, Priors Farm, West Green Road, Mattingley, Hampshire, RG29 8JU** P
☎ 01189 326824 F 01189 326797
M 07836 201764
Est. 1989
Open Mon–Fri 9.30am–4pm
Sales General antiques sales Wed. Smalls sales at 2pm, furniture sales at 6.30pm, viewing Tues 6–9pm Wed 9am–2pm
Frequency Fortnightly
Catalogues Yes

NEW MILTON

Forest House Antiques
Contact Mr K Plater
✉ **4 Winston Parade, Lymington Road, New Milton, Hampshire, BH25 6PT** P
☎ 01425 614441
Est. 1984 *Stock size* Large
Stock 18th–19thC English furniture, ceramics, collectables
Open Mon–Sat 10am–5pm closed Wed
Fairs Antiques for Everyone, Newark
Services Valuations, restorations

NORTH WARNBOROUGH

Second Chance Antique Centre
Contact Mrs Paula Vaisey
✉ **The Albion Centre, Dunleys Hill, North Warnborough, Near Odiham, Hampshire, RG25 1DX** P
☎ 01256 704273
M 07932 664086
Stock size Large
No. of dealers 18
Stock General antiques
Open Mon–Sat 10am–5.30pm Sun 11am–5.30pm

OLD BEDHAMPTON

J F F Militaria & Fire Brigade Collectables
Contact Mr J Franklin
Ye Olde Coach House, Mill Lane, Old Bedhampton, Hampshire, PO9 3JH P
023 9248 6485
07802 483869
Est. 1995 *Stock size* Medium
Stock Militaria, brass fire helmets, medals, badges, cloth insignia, equipment, buttons
Open By appointment only
Fairs Stoneleigh, Beltring
Services Valuations

PETERSFIELD

Wayne Buckner Antiques
Contact Audrey Buckner
62 Station Road, Petersfield, Hampshire, GU32 3ES P
01730 268822 F 02392 327584
07801 254494
Est. 1996 *Stock size* Medium
Stock Collectables, clocks, small items of furniture, music boxes, barometers, china toys, meccano, steam engines
Open Wed–Sat 9.30am–4pm or by appointment
Fairs Kempton, Goodwood
Services Valuations, restorations, house clearance

Dragon Treasures
Contact Elizabeth or Rose
10–12 College Street, Petersfield, Hampshire, GU31 4AD P
01730 269888
Est. 1998 *Stock size* Medium
Stock Small items of furniture, china, glass, gold and silver jewellery, pictures, prints
Open Mon–Sat 9.30am–5pm

Folly Four Antiques & Collectables
Contact Diane
10–12 College Street, Petersfield, Hampshire, GU31 4AD P
01730 266650
Est. 1999 *Stock size* Small
Stock Antiques and collectables
Open Mon–Sat 9.30am–5pm

Jacobs and Hunt Fine Art Auctioneers
Contact Mr C Jacobs
26 Lavant Street, Petersfield, Hampshire, GU32 3EF P
01730 233933 F 01730 231393
W www.jacobsandhunt.co.uk
Est. 1895
Open Mon–Fri 9am–5pm Sat 9am–noon
Sales General antiques sales, viewing day before sale 10am–6.30pm and morning of sale from 9am. Advisable to telephone for details
Frequency 6–8 weeks
Catalogues Yes

The Petersfield Bookshop (ABA, PBFA)
Contact Frank Westwood
16a Chapel Street, Petersfield, Hampshire, GU32 3DS P
01730 263438 F 01730 269426
E sales@petersfieldbookshop.com
W www.petersfieldbookshop.com
Est. 1918 *Stock size* Large
Stock Antiquarian and modern books
Open Mon–Sat 9am–5.30pm
Fairs ABA, Olympia, Chelsea
Services Valuations, quarterly catalogues

PORTSMOUTH

The Architectural Warehouse
Contact Mr Byng
17 Beck Street, Portsmouth, Hampshire, PO1 3AN P
023 9287 7070 F 023 92294777
E des_res@hotmail.com
Est. 2000 *Stock size* Large
Stock Architectural antiques, doors, baths, sinks, stained glass, pine flooring, fireplaces
Open Mon–Sat 9am–5pm

Good Day Antiques and Decor
Contact Mrs G Day
22 The Green, Rowlands Castle, Portsmouth, Hampshire, PO9 6AB P
023 9241 2924
0795 8619413
E Gillday@aol.com
Est. 1979 *Stock size* Medium
Stock Victorian furniture, small cabinets, jewellery, silver, porcelain, pottery, pictures
Open Thurs–Mon 11am–5pm
Services Silver plating, gilding, engraving

Alexandra Gray
Contact Mrs A Gray
129–131 Havant Road, Drayton, Portsmouth, Hampshire, PO6 2AA P
023 9237 6379
07811 778601
Est. 1969 *Stock size* Large
Stock English Georgian–Edwardian furniture, pictures, porcelain, French beds, oil lamps
Open Mon–Sat 10am–5pm Sun noon–4pm closed Wed

RINGWOOD

E Chalmers Hallam (PBFA)
Contact Mrs L Hiscock
9 Post Office Lane, St Ives, Ringwood, Hampshire, BH24 2PG P
01425 470060 F 01425 470060
E laura@chalmershallam.freeserve.co.uk
Est. 1946 *Stock size* Large
Stock Antiquarian, rare, second-hand books, angling, field sports, travel, Africana
Open By appointment
Services Valuations

Hugh and Favia Lister
Contact Mrs Favia Lister
Ringwood Road, Burley, Ringwood, Hampshire, BH24 4BU P
01425 402404
Est. 1974 *Stock size* Small
Stock Porcelain, small collectables
Open Mon–Sun 10am–5pm
Services Repairs to jewellery including re-threading, plating, silver, small furniture

Millers Antiques Ltd (LAPADA)
Contact Mr A J Miller
Netherbrook House, Christchurch Road, Ringwood, Hampshire, BH24 1DR P
01425 472062 F 01425 472727
07806 711280
E millant@millers-antiques.co.uk
W www.millers-antiques.co.uk
Est. 1897 *Stock size* Large
Stock English and Continental country furniture, 19thC majolica, Quimper, treen, decorative items
Open Mon–Fri 9am–5pm Sat 10am–4pm

Fairs Decorative Antiques and Textiles Fair, Great Antiques Fair
Services Restorations, packing, shipping

Robert Morgan Antiques
Contact Mr C King
90 Christchurch Road, Ringwood, Hampshire, BH24 1DR
01425 479400 01425 479400
07767 416106
Est. 1985 *Stock size* Medium
Stock Small furniture, unusual items, medals, coins
Open Mon–Sat 10am–5pm
Fairs Kempton Park, Newark
Services Valuations

The Old Toyshop
Contact Mr David Wells
PO Box 4389, Ringwood, Hampshire, BH24 1YN
01425 476899
07802 924775
enquiries@theoldtoyshop.com
www.theoldtoyshop.com
Est. 1979 *Stock size* Large
Stock Old collectables, vintage toys
Open By appointment only
Services Mail order world wide

Phillips International Auctioneers and Valuers
54 Southampton Road, Ringwood, Hampshire, BH24 1JD
01425 473333 01425 470989
www.phillips-auction.com
Sales Regional Saleroom. Telephone for details

Sci-Fi World
Contact Mr J Wilson
42a High Street, Ringwood, Hampshire, BH24 1AG
01425 474506
james.wilson5@virgin.net
Est. 1996 *Stock size* Medium
Stock Cards, badges, mugs, videos, books, toys
Open Mon–Sat 10am–5pm
Services Valuations

Lorraine Tarrant Antiques
Contact Mrs L Tarrant
23 Market Place, Ringwood, Hampshire, BH24 1AN
01425 461123
Est. 1991 *Stock size* Medium
Stock Furniture, carved oak, old pine, bears, collectors' items, tapestry cushions
Open Tues–Sat 10am–5pm

ROMSEY

Antique Enterprises
Contact Mr M Presterfield
19 Cavendish Close, Romsey, Hampshire, SO51 7HT
01794 515589
Est. 1976 *Stock size* Medium
Stock Furniture, china, glass, collectables
Open By appointment

Bell Antiques (Gemmological Association)
Contact Mr M Gay
8 Bell Street, Romsey, Hampshire, SO51 8GA
01794 514719
Est. 1979 *Stock size* Large
Stock Jewellery, silver, glass, china, small furniture, maps, topographical prints
Open Mon–Sat 9.30am–5.30pm closed Wed in Winter

Cambridge Antiques (LAPADA)
Contact Mr T Cambridge
PO Box 169, Romsey, Hampshire, SO51 6XU
01794 324499/322125 01794 324411
post@cambridgeantiques.co.uk
www.cambridgeantiques.co.uk
Est. 1973 *Stock size* Medium
Stock General, furniture, porcelain, clocks, paintings
Trade only Yes
Open By appointment only
Services Valuations

Rick Hubbard Art Deco
Contact Rick Hubbard
3 Tee Court, Bell Street, Romsey, Hampshire, SO51 8GY
01794 513133
07767 267607
www.rickhubbard-artdeco.co.uk
Est. 1995 *Stock size* Large
Stock 20thC ceramics
Open Mon–Fri 10am–3pm Sat 9am–4pm
Fairs Alexander Palace, Shelley Collectors Fair

Romsey Auction Rooms
Contact Mrs Vanessa Blair
86 The Hundred, Romsey, Hampshire, SO51 8BX
01794 513331 01794 511770
gavelman@waitrose.com
Est. 1966
Open Mon–Thurs 9am–5.30pm Fri 9am–5pm
Sales General antiques sales monthly, first or second Tues. 5 silver sales and 3 toy sales a year, viewing day before sale noon–7.30pm. Advisable to phone for sale details
Frequency Monthly
Catalogues Yes

Romsey Medals (OMRS, LAPADA)
Contact Mr T Cambridge
PO Box 169, Romsey, Hampshire, SO51 6XU
01794 324488/322125 evenings
01794 324411
post@romseymedals.co.uk
www.romseymedals.co.uk
Est. 1973 *Stock size* Large
Stock British orders, gallantry and campaign groups, British cap badges, medals
Trade only Yes
Open By appointment only
Fairs Orders and Medals Research Society Fair
Services Valuations, restorations

SOUTHAMPTON

Amber Antiques
Contact Mr R Boyle
115 Portswood Road, Portswood, Southampton, Hampshire, SO17 2FX
023 8058 3645 023 8058 3645
Est. 1970 *Stock size* Large
Stock Furniture
Open Mon–Sun 9am–5pm
Services Restorations

The Antique Centre
Contact Mrs S O'Shea
Britannia Road, Southampton, Hampshire, SO14 0QL
023 8022 1022
Est. 1999 *Stock size* Large
No. of dealers 40
Stock Furniture, porcelain, jewellery, pictures, glass, medals, ocean memorabilia, Clarice Cliff
Open Mon–Sat 10am–5.30pm Sun 10.30am–4pm
Services Restorations, upholstery

Athena Antiques
Contact Mr Alan Tonks
31 Newtown Road, Warsash, Southampton, Hampshire, SO31 9FY
01489 578093
athenaantq@aol.com
Est. 1980 *Stock size* Large
Stock China, glass, figurines, chandeliers, railwayana
Open Telephone for opening hours
Fairs Athena Fayres, Antiques and Collectables Fairs at Wickham, Locks Heath, Minstead

The Brompton Gallery
Contact Mr C Browne
21 Old Northam Road, Southampton, Hampshire, SO14 0NZ
023 8021 1591
Est. 1996 *Stock size* Medium
Stock Contemporary paintings, sculpture, ceramics, etchings, prints
Open Mon–Fri 9.30am–4.30pm Sat 11am–5pm

Clocktower Antiques Centre
Contact Mr Chris White
1 Manor Farm Road, Bitterne Park Triangle, Southampton, Hampshire, SO18 1DE
023 8055 4303
Est. 1999 *Stock size* Large
No. of dealers 20
Stock Furniture, porcelain, brass, silver, clocks
Open Mon–Sat 10am–5.30pm
Services Valuations

Cobwebs
Contact Mr P Boyd-Smith
78 Northam Road, Southampton, Hampshire, SO14 0PB
023 8022 7458 023 8022 7458
www.cobwebs.uk.com
Est. 1974 *Stock size* Large
Stock Ocean liner memorabilia, Titanic and White Star Line, Aviation items, Royal and Merchant Navy items
Open Mon–Sat 10am–4pm closed Wed
Fairs Transportation 2000, British Titanic Convention
Services Valuations

H M Gilbert (PBFA)
Contact Richard Gilbert
2½ Portland Street, Southampton, Hampshire, SO14 7EB
023 80 226420 023 80 227382
Est. 1859
Stock British topography, English literature, military and maritime books
Open Mon–Fri 9am–5pm Sat 8.30am–5pm
Fairs Chelsea Book fair, PBFA

Highfield Antiques
Contact Clive Madge
33 Highfield Lane, Southampton, Hampshire, SO17 1QD
023 8032 2025
cmadge@aol.com
Est. 1983 *Stock size* Medium
Stock Georgian–1930s furniture, pictures, prints, garden furniture, ceramics, glass, toys
Open Mon–Sat 9am–5.30pm
Fairs Swinderby, Kempton
Services Free delivery

Memory Lane
Contact Mr A Dittrich
26 Manor Farm Road, Southampton, Hampshire, SO18 1HP
023 8055 1166
Est. 1997 *Stock size* Medium
Stock Furniture, pictures, collectables
Open Mon–Sat 10am–5pm closed Wed
Services House clearance

Nova Foresta Books (PBFA)
Contact Mr Peter Roberts
185 Lyndhurst Road, Ashurst, Southampton, Hampshire, SO40 7AR
023 8029 3389
Est. 1994 *Stock size* Medium
Stock Antiquarian, rare, second-hand books, New Forest, 20thC literature and art a speciality
Open Tues–Sat 10am–5.30pm
Fairs PBFA fairs
Services Valuations, book search

Pennyfarthing Antiques
Contact Roberta Payne
Lymington Antiques Centre, 76 High Street, Lymington, Hampshire, SO41 9AL
023 8086 0846
07970 847690
Est. 1996 *Stock size* Large
Stock Georgian–Edwardian furniture, clocks, Oriental items, watches
Open Mon–Sat 10am–5pm
Services Valuations, restorations

Peter Rhodes Books
Contact Peter Rhodes
21 Portswood Road, Southampton, Hampshire, SO17 2ES
023 8039 9003
peterrhodes21@hotmail.com
Est. 1997 *Stock size* Large
Stock Antiquarian, rare, second-hand books, architecture, art, design, illustrators a speciality
Open Mon–Sat 11am–5pm
Fairs HD Fairs
Services Valuations, book search

Kenneth Standrin
Contact Mr K Standrin
307a Burlesdon Road, Southampton, Hampshire, SO19 8NE
023 8044 4200
Est. 1998 *Stock size* Small
Stock Antique furniture, mirrors, decorative items
Open Mon–Sat 9am–5pm
Services Restorations

SOUTHSEA

Book Academy (ABA)
Contact Mr Robinson
13 Marmion Road, Southsea, Hampshire, PO5 2AT
023 9281 6632 023 9281 6632
bacademy@globalnet.co.uk
Est. 1970 *Stock size* Large
Stock Antiquarian and new, reformed theology books including bibles, prayer, hymn books, Dickens, Hampshire a speciality
Open Mon–Sat 9.30am–4.30pm
Services Valuations, book repair, rebinding

The Clock Shop
Contact Mr G Carrington
155 Highland Road, Southsea, Hampshire, PO4 9EY
023 9285 1649
Est. 1999 *Stock size* Large
Stock Clocks, watches, general antiques
Open Wed–Sat 9am–5pm

Fairs Kempton Park, DMG
Services Valuations, clock restorations

Design Explosion
Contact Susan Mosely
2 Exmouth Road, Southsea, Hampshire, PO5 2QL
023 9229 3040
07850 131414
susan.moseley@btclick.com
www.ianparmiter.co.uk
Est. 1998 *Stock size* Medium
Stock 1950s–1970s china, glass, lighting, furniture
Open Fri Sat 9am–5pm
Fairs Ardingly

A Fleming (Southsea) Ltd (BADA)
Contact Mr Alfred Fleming
The Clock Tower, Castle Road, Southsea, Hampshire, PO5 3DE
023 9282 2934 F 023 9229 3501
07885 334545
mail@flemingsantiques.fsnet.co.uk
www.flemingsantiques.com
Est. 1908 *Stock size* Medium
Stock 18th–19thC English and Continental furniture, silver, boxes, barometers
Open Mon–Fri 9.30am–5.30pm Sat 9.30am–1pm or by appointment
Fairs Kensington, Goodwood
Services Valuations, furniture and silver restorations

Langford Antiques
Contact Mr I Langford
70 Albert Road, Southsea, Hampshire, PO5 2SL
023 9283 0517
Est. 1982 *Stock size* Medium
Stock Victorian–20thC furniture, collectables, silver, costume jewellery
Open Mon–Fri 11am–5pm Sat 10am–6pm closed Wed

D M Nesbit & Co
Contact Mr M Jarrett
7 Clarendon Road, Southsea, Hampshire, PO5 2ED
023 9286 4321 F 023 9229 5522
auctions@nesbits.co.uk
www.invaluable.com/dmnesbit@co
Est. 1921
Open Mon–Fri 9.30am–5pm
Sales General antiques sale monthly. Phone for details
Catalogues Yes

Ian Parmiter
Contact Mr I Parmiter
18a Albert Road, Southsea, Hampshire, PO5 2SH
023 9229 3040
www.ianparmiter.co.uk
Est. 1987 *Stock size* Medium
Stock Architectural antiques, unusual items
Open Mon 11am–2.30pm Fri Sat 11am–5pm or by appointment

STOCKBRIDGE

Evans and Partridge
Contact John Partridge
Agriculture House, Stockbridge, Hampshire, SO20 6HF
01264 810702 F 01264 810944
Est. 1973
Open Mon–Fri 9am–5.30pm Sat 9am–4pm
Sales Sales of early and modern fishing tackle, sporting guns, antique weapons, steam, tractors and farming bygones
Frequency Annual
Catalogues Yes

Lane Antiques
Contact Mrs E Lane
High Street, Stockbridge, Hampshire, SO20 6EU
01264 810435
Est. 1982 *Stock size* Medium
Stock 18th–19thC porcelain, silver, glass, small furniture, objets d'art, fine art
Open By appointment

Elizabeth Viney (BADA)
Contact Miss E A Viney MBE
Jacobs House, High Street, Stockbridge, Hampshire, SO20 6HF
01264 810761
Est. 1967 *Stock size* Small
Stock 18th–19thC furniture, treen, domestic metalware, brass, candlesticks, police truncheons
Open By appointment only

TITCHFIELD

Robin Howard Antiques
Contact Mr R Howard
6 South Street, Titchfield, Fareham, Hampshire, PO14 4DJ
01329 842794
Est. 1985 *Stock size* Small
Stock Antique and modern silver, jewellery, objects of virtue
Open Mon–Sat 9.30am–5pm

WARSASH

Solent Railwayana
Contact Mr Alan Tonks
31 Newtown Road, Warsash, Nr Southampton, Hampshire, SO31 9FY
01489 578093
solentrly@aol.com
Est. 1992 *Stock size* Medium
Stock General railwayana
Open Mon–Sat 10am–5.15pm closed 1–2.15pm closed Mon pm telephone before travelling
Fairs Athena Fayres–Minstead, Wickham

WICKHAM

Solent Railwayana Auctions
Contact Mr Alan Tonks
Community Centre, Mill Lane, Wickham, Hampshire, PO17 5AL
01489 584633
solentry@aol.com
Est. 1992
Open Sale 11am–5pm
Sales Phone for details
Frequency 3 per annum
Catalogues Yes

WINCHESTER

Burns and Graham (BADA)
Contact Mr Graham Rollitt
27 St Thomas Street, Winchester, Hampshire, SO23 9HJ
01962 853852 F 01962 853852
07771 960313
Est. 1971 *Stock size* Medium
Stock 17th–19thC furniture, decorative items
Open Mon–Sat 9.30am–5pm
Fairs BADA fairs
Services Restorations

The Clock-Work-Shop (Winchester) (BHI, AHS)
Contact Mr P Ponsford-Jones
6a Parchment Street, Winchester, Hampshire, SO23 8AT
01962 842331
07973 736155

SOUTH

Est. 1994 *Stock size* Large
Stock Furniture, clocks, barometers
Open Mon–Sat 9am–5pm
Services Restorations of clocks and barometers

G E Marsh (Antique Clocks) Ltd (BADA, CINOA, CC, BHI, NAWCC)
Contact Mr D Dipper
32a The Square, Winchester, Hampshire, SO23 9EX
☎ 01962 844443 Ⓕ 01962 844443
Ⓔ gem@marshclocks.co.uk
Ⓦ www.marshclocks.co.uk
Est. 1947 *Stock size* Medium
Stock Carriage clocks, English longcase clocks, Continental clocks
Open Mon–Fri 9.30am–5pm Sat 9.30am–1pm 2–5pm
Services Valuations, restorations, home visits

Phillips International Auctioneers and Valuers
The Red House, Hyde Street, Winchester, Hampshire, SO23 7DX
☎ 01962 862515 Ⓕ 01962 865166
Ⓦ www.phillips-auction.com
Sales Regional Saleroom. Telephone for details

The Pine Barn
Contact Mr P Chant
Folly Farm, Crawley, Winchester, Hampshire, SO21 2PH
☎ 01962 776687 Ⓕ 01962 776687
Est. 1987 *Stock size* Large
Stock Furniture made from reclaimed pine, antique and reproduction pine furniture
Open Mon–Sat 9am–5pm Sun 10am–4pm
Services Valuations, restorations, shipping

The Pine Cellars
Contact Mr N Brain
39 Jewry Street, Winchester, Hampshire, SO23 8RY
☎ 01962 777546
Est. 1971 *Stock size* Large
Stock Antique pine, country furniture
Open Mon–Sat 9.30am–5.30pm
Services Restorations

The Silver Shop
Contact Christopher Barbour
Unit 3, Antique Market, Kings Walk, Winchester, Hampshire, SO23 8AF
☎ 01962 855575
Ⓔ acbsilwin@aol.com
Est. 1992 *Stock size* Small
Stock Antique silver, jewellery and plate
Open Mon–Sat 10.30am–4.30pm
Services Valuations, restorations

Studio Coins (BNTA)
Contact Mr S Mitchell
16 Kilham Lane, Winchester, Hampshire, SO22 5PT
☎ 01962 853156 Ⓕ 01962 624246
Est. 1987
Stock Old English coins
Open By appointment only
Fairs Coinex, Cumberland, York
Services Free bi-monthly list

Todd & Austin Antiques & Fine Art
Contact Gerald Austin
2 Andover Road, Winchester, Hampshire, SO23 7BS
☎ 01962 869824
Est. 1974 *Stock size* Medium
Stock 18th–early 20thC pottery, porcelain, glass paperweights 1845–60, decorative silver, boxes, silver plate, Oriental arts, 18th–19thC glass, objets d'art
Open Tues–Fri 9.30am–5pm (Nov Dec Sat 9am–noon)
Services Valuations

Irene S Trudgett Collectables
Contact Irene S Trudgett
3 Andover Road, Winchester, Hampshire, SO23 7BS
☎ 01962 854132/862070
Est. 1966 *Stock size* Medium
Stock Pottery, porcelain, cigarette cards, Goss and Crested china, glass, collectables
Open Mon–Fri 9.15am–4pm Thurs Sat 9.15am–noon
Services Valuations, restorations, book search

Winchester Antiques
Contact Mr D Letts
20–20a Jewry Street, Winchester, Hampshire, SO23 8RZ
☎ 01962 850123
Est. 1998 *Stock size* Large
No. of dealers 20
Stock Furniture, silver, jewellery, glass, porcelain, pine
Open Mon–Sat 10am–5pm

The Winchester Bookshop (PBFA)
Contact Mr M Green
10a St George's Street, Winchester, Hampshire, SO23 8BG
☎ 01962 855630
Est. 1991 *Stock size* Medium
Stock Antiquarian, rare, second-hand books, topography, archaeology, travel, literature a speciality
Open Mon–Sat 10am–5.30pm
Fairs PBFA fairs
Services Valuations, book search

ISLE OF WIGHT

BEMBRIDGE

Cobwebs Antiques and Collectables (GADAR)
Contact Mrs Sue Williams
Foreland Road, Bembridge, Isle of Wight, PO35 5XN
☎ 01983 874487
Est. 1997 *Stock size* Medium
Stock Bunnykins, Beatrix Potter, Doulton
Open Tues–Sat 10am–5pm

COWES

Copperwheat Restoration (RICS)
Contact Carole Copperwheat
Rear of Pascall Atkey, 29–30 High Street, Cowes, Isle of Wight, PO31 7RX
☎ 01983 281011
Ⓜ 07720 399670
Est. 1985 *Stock size* Small
Stock 17th–18thC furniture, metalware, ceramics
Open Any time by prior phone call
Services Valuations, restorations

Flagstaff Antiques
Contact Mr T A M Cockram
Tudor House, Bath Road, Cowes, Isle of Wight, PO31 7RH
☎ 01983 200138
Est. 1995 *Stock size* Medium
Stock Jewellery, porcelain, silver
Open Mon–Sat 10.30am–4pm closed Wed
Fairs Miami, Florida
Services Valuations

⊞ Gaby Goldscheider (ABA)
Contact Miss G Goldscheider
✉ **Charles Dickens Bookshop, 65 High Street, Cowes, Isle of Wight, PO31 7RL** Ⓟ
☎ 01983 280586
Est. 1987 *Stock size* Medium
Stock Second-hand, antiquarian, rare books, prints, children's books, literature, fiction, topography, travel, nautical a speciality
Open By appointment
Fairs ABA fairs at Chelsea, Bath
Services Catalogues

⊞ Royal Standard Antiques
Contact Mrs C Bradbury
✉ **70–72 Park Road, Cowes, Isle of Wight, PO31 7LY** Ⓟ
☎ 01983 281672
Ⓜ 07741 041902
Ⓔ caroline@royalstandardantiques.fsbusiness.co.uk
Ⓦ www.royalstandardantiques.fsbusiness.co.uk
Est. 1994 *Stock size* Medium
Stock Georgian–Edwardian English and French furniture, pictures, engravings, commemoratives, architectural antiques
Open Mon–Sat 10.30am–5.30pm Wed 10.30am–1pm or by appointment
Services Furniture restoration, stained glass restoration, upholstery, chair caning

FRESHWATER

⊞ Aladdin's Cave
Contact Mrs Dunn
✉ **147–149 School Green Road, Freshwater, Isle of Wight, PO40 9BB** Ⓟ
☎ 01983 752934/753846
Ⓜ 07867 558424
Est. 1984 *Stock size* Large
Stock Old pine furniture, glass, china, collectables
Open Mon–Sat 9.30am–4.30pm
Services House clearance

⊞ The Old Village Clock Shop
Contact Mr R Taylor
✉ **3 Moa Place, Freshwater, Isle of Wight, PO40 9DS** Ⓟ
☎ 01983 754193
Est. 1970 *Stock size* Medium
Stock 17th–19thC English longcase and dial clocks, Vienna regulators, early German, English bracket, French ormolu, carriage clocks
Open Mon Wed Fri Sat 9.30am–1pm or by appointment
Services Valuations

GODSHILL

⊞ Style
Contact Mrs R Brooks
✉ **High Street, Godshill, Isle of Wight, PO38 3HH** Ⓟ
☎ 01983 840194 Ⓕ 01983 840438
Est. 1992 *Stock size* Large
Stock China, glass, collectables, items of interest, furniture
Open Mon–Sun 10am–5pm

NEWPORT

⊞ Mike Heath Antiques
Contact Mr M Heath
✉ **3–4 Holyrood Street, Newport, Isle of Wight, PO30 5AU** Ⓟ
☎ 01983 525748
Est. 1979 *Stock size* Medium
Stock Furniture, oil lamps, porcelain, glass, collectables
Open Mon–Sat 9.30am–5pm closed Thurs
Services Metal restoration, polishing

⊞ Lugley Street Antiques
Contact Mr D Newman
✉ **13 Lugley Street, Newport, Isle of Wight, PO30 5HD** Ⓟ
☎ 01983 523348
Est. 1986 *Stock size* Large
Stock Furniture, clocks, china, collectables, 19thC furniture a speciality
Open Mon–Sat 9.30am–5pm closed Thurs

⊞ Online
Contact Kim or Steve Snow
✉ **5 Watchbell Lane, Newport, Isle of Wight, PO30 5XU** Ⓟ
☎ 01983 526282
Ⓔ vintage.uk@virgin.net
Ⓦ www.vintage-uk.com
Est. 2001 *Stock size* Small
Stock Anything old and interesting
Open Mon–Sat 10am–4pm

RYDE

⊞ Antiques Etc
Contact Mr B Walker
✉ **27 Cross Street, Ryde, Isle of Wight, PO33 2AA** Ⓟ
Ⓜ 07790 874181
Est. 1969 *Stock size* Large
Stock China, collectables, glass, furniture
Open Mon–Sat 10am–4pm

⊞ Hayter's Antique and Modern Furniture
Contact Mr R W Hayter
✉ **18–20 Cross Street, Ryde, Isle of Wight, PO33 2AD** Ⓟ
☎ 01983 563795 Ⓕ 01983 566196
Est. 1957 *Stock size* Medium
Stock Antique, Victorian and modern furniture
Open Mon–Sat 9am–1pm 2.15–5pm closed Thurs

⊞ Heritage Books
Contact Rev D H Nearn
✉ **7 Cross Street, Ryde, Isle of Wight, PO33 2AD** Ⓟ
☎ 01983 562933 Ⓕ 01983 812634
Ⓔ dhnearn.heritagebooksryde@virgin.net
Est. 1977 *Stock size* Medium
Stock General, Isle of Wight antiquarian prints, books on modern theology, history, culture of Africa a speciality
Open Mon–Sat 10am–5pm closed Thurs
Fairs Guildford Book Fair
Services Book search

⊞ Nooks and Crannies
Contact Mr D Burnett
✉ **60 High Street, Ryde, Isle of Wight, PO33 2RJ** Ⓟ
☎ 01983 568984
Est. 1986 *Stock size* Medium
Stock Collectables, lamps, 78 rpm records, telephones, radios, glass, china, furniture
Open Mon–Sat 9.30am–1.30pm 2.30–5pm closed Thurs pm
Fairs Ardingly

⊞ Ryde Antiques
Contact Mr Roger Rowan
✉ **61 High Street, Ryde, Isle of Wight, PO33 2RJ** Ⓟ
☎ 01983 615703
Ⓔ rydeantiques@iow-home.freeserve.co.uk
Est. 1979 *Stock size* Medium

Stock Jewellery, militaria
Open Mon–Sat 10am–4pm
Services Valuations, restorations

Ways
Contact Mr T L Smith
✉ **The Auction House, Garfield Road, Ryde, Isle of Wight, PO33 2PT** Ⓟ
☎ 01983 562255 Ⓕ 01983 565108
Ⓦ www.waysauctionrooms.fsbusiness.co.uk
Est. 1815
Open Mon–Fri 9am–5pm
Sales Antique and modern furnishings sale on Thurs, viewing day prior 10am–6pm. No buyer's premium
Frequency Every 5 weeks
Catalogues Yes

SANDOWN

Lake Antiques
Contact Mrs J Marchant
✉ **18 Sandown Road, Sandown, Isle of Wight, PO36 9JP** Ⓟ
☎ 01983 406888
Ⓜ 07710 067678
Est. 1982 *Stock size* Medium
Stock Antique furniture, clocks, pictures, decorative items
Open Mon–Sat 10am–4pm closed Wed or by appointment
Services Valuations, mainland deliveries arranged

SEAVIEW

Rex Gully Antiques
Contact Mr R Gully
✉ **Regent House, High Street, Seaview, Isle of Wight, PO34 5EX** Ⓟ
☎ 01983 613362/872725
Ⓜ 07860 499608
Ⓔ rexgully@amserve.net
Est. 1978 *Stock size* Medium
Stock Antique pine, blue and white pottery, brass and copper
Open Mon–Fri 10am–1pm Sat 10am–5pm or by appointment
Services Delivery service

SHANKLIN

Regency Antiques
Contact Mr D Cooper
✉ **64 Regent Street, Shanklin, Isle of Wight, PO37 7AE** Ⓟ
☎ 01983 868444
Est. 1955 *Stock size* Medium
Stock Oriental and English antiques
Open Mon–Sat 11am–2pm or by appointment
Services Valuations

Shanklin Auction Rooms (NAVA)
Contact Mr H Riches
✉ **79 Regent Street, Shanklin, Isle of Wight, PO37 7AP** Ⓟ
☎ 01983 863441 Ⓕ 01983 863890
Ⓔ shanklin.auction@tesco.net
Est. 1850
Open Mon–Fri 9am–5pm
Sales Collective antiques monthly. Antiques quarterly. Phone for details
Frequency Monthly
Catalogues Yes

VENTNOR

Curios
Contact Mr M Gregory
✉ **3 Church Place, Chale, Ventnor, Isle of Wight, PO38 2HA** Ⓟ
☎ 01983 730230
Est. 1995 *Stock size* Large
Stock Taxidermy, architectural antiques, fireplaces, staddle stones, unusual curiosities
Open Mon–Sun noon–5.30pm
Services Valuations

Plumridge Antiques
Contact Mr R Plumridge
✉ **Unit 2, Caxton House, Ventnor Industrial Estate, Ventnor, Isle of Wight, PO38 1DX** Ⓟ
☎ 01983 856666 Ⓕ 01983 855325
Ⓜ 07855 649297
Ⓔ plumridge@lineone.net
Est. 1999 *Stock size* Large
Stock Pianos, furniture
Open Mon–Fri 8.30am–5pm Sat 8.30am–1pm
Services Packers, shippers

Ultramarine
Contact Mrs M Stevens
✉ **40b High Street, Ventnor, Isle of Wight, PO38 1RZ** Ⓟ
☎ 01983 854062
Est. 1999 *Stock size* Large
Stock Collectables, costume jewellery, china, stoneware, glass
Open Mon Tues 10am–1pm Thurs Fri Sat 10am–2pm closed Wed

Ventnor Antiques Centre
Contact Mrs P Huntley
✉ **66 High Street, Ventnor, Isle of Wight, PO38 1LU** Ⓟ
☎ 01983 855302 Ⓕ 01983 855325
Est. 1994 *Stock size* Medium
No. of dealers 4
Stock General antiques, collectables, furniture
Open Mon–Sat 10am–5pm
Services Valuations, delivery

Ventnor Junction
Contact Mr or Mrs P Dolby
✉ **48 High Street, Ventnor, Isle of Wight, PO38 1LT** Ⓟ
☎ 01983 853996
Ⓔ shop@ventjunc.demon.co.uk
Ⓦ www.ventjunc.demon.co.uk
Est. 1987 *Stock size* Large
Stock Old toys, collectables, tin trains
Open Most mornings or by appointment
Fairs Sandown Park Toy Fair, Esher
Services Mail order

YARMOUTH

Yarmouth Antiques and Books
Contact Mrs V Blakeley & Mr M Coyle
✉ **The House, The Square, Yarmouth, Isle of Wight, PO41 0NP** Ⓟ
☎ 01983 760046
Ⓔ yarmouth-antiquesiow@btinternet.com
Est. 1996 *Stock size* Medium
Stock Antiquarian, second-hand books, china, collectables
Open Mon–Sun 10am–5pm
Fairs Kempton Park, February

SURREY

ABINGER HAMMER

Abinger Bazaar
Contact Mike Gammon
✉ **Guildford Road, Abinger Hammer, Dorking, Surrey, RH5 6QA** Ⓟ
☎ 01306 730756
Ⓔ g.tovey@virgin.net
Est. 1979 *Stock size* Medium
Stock French Art Deco stoves, porcelain, books, Victorian fireplaces, dolls' houses
Open Tues–Sun 10am–6pm

Stirling Antiques
Contact Mr U Burrell
✉ **Aberdeen House, Guildford Road, Abinger Hammer, Dorking, Surrey, RH5 6RY** Ⓟ

☎ 01306 730706 Ⓕ 01306 731575
Ⓜ 07748 005619
Est. 1968 *Stock size* Medium
Stock Architectural stained glass, metalware, furniture, jewellery, silver, curios
Open Mon–Sat 9.30am–6pm closed Thurs

ADDLESTONEMOOR

Small Wood Ltd
Contact Julian Faulkner
✉ **The Elephant House, Addlestonemoor, Surrey, KT15 2QF** Ⓟ
☎ 01932 848122 Ⓕ 01932 831690
Ⓔ enquiries@small-wood.com
Est. 1998 *Stock size* Medium
Stock Architectural salvage, contemporary furniture, art and antiques
Open Mon–Sat 10am–5pm

ASHTEAD

Bumbles
Contact Mrs B Kay
✉ **90 The Street, Ashtead, Surrey, KT21 1AW** Ⓟ
☎ 01372 276219 Ⓕ 01798 875545
Est. 1978 *Stock size* Medium
Stock General furniture, clocks, porcelain, silver, coins, cigarette cards, lighting, oil lamp parts
Open Mon–Sat 10am–5.30pm
Services Furniture restorations, re-upholstery

BETCHWORTH

Dorking Desk Shop (LAPADA, DADA)
Contact J G Elias
✉ **Stoney Croft Farm, Reigate Road, Betchworth, Surrey, RH3 7EY** Ⓟ
☎ 01737 845215 Ⓕ 01306 875363
Ⓦ www.thesaurus.co.uk/dorking/desk/shop/
Est. 1973 *Stock size* Large
Stock Library and writing furniture, dining tables, sets of chairs, sideboards, oak and country furniture, wardrobes, four poster beds, bookcases, chests
Open Mon–Fri 8am–5.30pm Sat 10.30am–5.30pm
Services Finding service

BLETCHINGLEY

John Anthony
Contact Mrs N Hart
✉ **71 High Street, Bletchingley, Redhill, Surrey, RH1 4LJ** Ⓟ
☎ 01883 743197 Ⓕ 01883 742108
Ⓜ 07836 221689
Ⓔ johnanthonyantiques@hotmail.com
Est. 1974 *Stock size* Medium
Stock 18th–19thC furniture
Open By appointment only

Lawrences Auctioneers Ltd
Contact Miss S Debnam
✉ **Norfolk House, High Street, Bletchingley, Redhill, Surrey, RH1 4PA** Ⓟ
☎ 01883 743323 Ⓕ 01883 744578
Ⓦ www.lawrencesbletchingley.co.uk
Est. 1960
Open Mon–Fri 9am–5pm
Sales General antiques sales on Tues Wed Thurs, viewing Fri, Sat 10am–5pm
Frequency Every 6 weeks
Catalogues Yes

Post House Antiques
Contact Mr P Bradley
✉ **High Street, Bletchingley, Surrey, RH1 4PA** Ⓟ
☎ 01883 743317 Ⓕ 01883 743317
Est. 1975 *Stock size* Large
Stock Antique lighting
Open Mon–Sat 10am–5pm
Services Restorations

Quill Antiques
Contact Mrs J Davis
✉ **86 High Street, Bletchingley, Surrey, RH1 4PA** Ⓟ
☎ 01883 743755
Est. 1973 *Stock size* Large
Stock Agricultural, rural bygones, copper, brass, glass, porcelain
Open Tues–Sat 10am–5.30pm
Fairs Dorking

BRAMLEY

Memories Antiques
Contact Mrs P S Kelsey
✉ **High Street, Bramley, Guildford, Surrey, GU5 0HB** Ⓟ
☎ 01483 892205
Ⓜ 07774 885014
Est. 1985 *Stock size* Medium
No. of dealers 8
Stock Georgian–Victorian French, pine furniture, silver, jewellery, porcelain, collectables, garden items, kitchenware, French antiques
Open Mon–Sat 10am–5pm
Services 'Wanted' service

The Old Works Antiques
Contact Mr A Sutherland
✉ **24 High Street, Bramley, Guildford, Surrey, GU5 0HB** Ⓟ
☎ 01483 894648
Ⓜ 07968 971444
Est. 1994 *Stock size* Medium
Stock English, Continental, Victorian, pre-Victorian furniture
Open Mon–Fri 9am–5.30pm Sat 9.30am–5pm Sun 10.30am–4pm
Services Restorations

BROCKHAM

Cartels Auctioneers and Valuers
Contact Mr Carter
✉ **2 Tanners Court, Middle Street, Brockham, Dorking, (on A25) Surrey, RH3 7NH** Ⓟ
☎ 01737 844646 Ⓕ 01737 844646
Ⓜ 07768 004293
Est. 1978
Open Mon–Fri 9.30am–5pm
Sales General antiques, fine art, pre-1930s, viewing all day Fri 10am–7pm and morning of sale 8.30–10am
Frequency Monthly excluding August
Catalogues Yes

CARSHALTON

Cherub Antiques
Contact Mr M Wisdom
✉ **312–314 Carshalton Road, Carshalton, Surrey, SM5 3QB** Ⓟ
☎ 020 8643 0028
Ⓜ 07740 178093
Est. 1985 *Stock size* Large
Stock Continental and English antique pine, mahogany
Open Mon–Sat 10am–5.30pm
Services Pine stripping, French polishing

The Clock House (BWCG)
Contact Mark Cocklin
✉ **75 Pound Street, Carshalton, Surrey, SM5 3PG** Ⓟ
☎ 020 8773 4844
Ⓜ 07850 363317
Ⓔ mark@theclockhouse.co.uk
Ⓦ www.theclockhouse.co.uk
Est. 1989 *Stock size* Medium

Stock Antiquarian horology, longcase clocks
Open Tues–Fri 9.30am–4.30pm Sat 9am–6pm or by appointment
Fairs Brunel University
Services Valuations, restorations, spares

Collectors Corner
Contact Mr A Wilton
3 The Square, Carshalton, Surrey, SM5 3BN
020 8669 7377
Est. 1979 *Stock size* Medium
Stock Collectable items, china, glassware, coins, postcards, medals, stamps
Open Mon–Fri 11.30am–3.30pm Sat 10am–5.30pm closed Wed
Services Valuations, restorations

CATERHAM

Chaldon Books and Records
Contact Mr K Chesson
1 High Street, Caterham, Surrey, CR3 5UE
01883 348583
Est. 1994 *Stock size* Medium
Stock Rare and second-hand books
Open Mon–Sat 9.30am–5.30pm
Services Book search

CHEAM

Parkins
Contact Mrs Mary Zenthon
18 Malden Road, Cheam, Surrey, SM3 8QF
020 8644 6633
www.urus.globalnet.co.uk/~parkins
Est. 1945
Open Mon–Fri 9am–1pm 2–5pm
Sales Antique furniture and effects 1st Mon of month 10am, general furniture and effects 2nd and 4th Mon of month 10am, viewing Fri 2–4pm, Sat 10am–4pm. Smaller antiques and collectables monthly evening sale, viewing 2–7pm
Catalogues Yes

Village Antiques
Contact Miss S Jenner
16 Malden Road, Cheam, Sutton, Surrey, SM3 8QF
020 8644 8567
Est. 1986 *Stock size* Large
Stock Furniture, lighting, porcelain, glass, silver, jewellery, collectors' items
Open Mon–Sat 11am–5pm closed Tues Thurs
Services House clearance

CHERTSEY

Chertsey Antiques
Contact Judy Carroway
10 Windsor Street, Chertsey, Surrey, KT16 8AS
0118 976 1355
Est. 1996 *Stock size* Medium
No. of dealers 6
Stock Collectables, furniture, clocks, silver, jewellery, memorabilia
Open Mon–Fri 10am–5pm Sat 10am–5.30pm

D'Eyncourt Antiques
Contact Mr G D H Davies
21 Windsor Street, Chertsey, Surrey, KT16 8AY
01932 563411
Est. 1970 *Stock size* Large
Stock Furniture, jewellery, china, collectables, cigarette lighters a speciality
Open Mon–Fri 10am–5.15pm Sat 7am–5.30pm Sun 11am–4pm
Fairs London Photographic Fair
Services Valuations

Glasheen's Bookshop
Contact Mr P Glasheen
5 Burwood Parade, Guildford Street, Chertsey, Surrey, KT16 9AE
01932 562555
orders@glasheens-books.demon.co.uk
Est. 1996 *Stock size* Small
Stock Second-hand books
Open Mon–Sat 9.30am–5pm
Services Book search, shippping

CHOBHAM

Chobham Antique Clocks (BHI)
Contact Mike Morris
73–75 High Street, Chobham, Woking, Surrey, GU24 8AF
01276 682560
Est. 1989 *Stock size* Medium
Stock Antique clocks, barometers
Open Tues–Sat 10am–5pm
Services Valuations, restorations

Mimbridge Antiques and Collectables
Contact Mrs J Monteath Scott
Mimbridge Garden Centre, Station Road, Chobham, Woking, Surrey, GU24 8AS
01276 855736
0771 862284
Est. 1987 *Stock size* Medium
Stock Small antiques, pictures, prints, maps, garden items, period furniture, decorative items, porcelain, glass, dolls
Open Mon–Sun 10am–5pm
Fairs Kempton
Services Picture framing

COBHAM

Cobham Galleries (LAPADA)
Contact Mrs Jerry Burkard
65 Portsmouth Road, Cobham, Surrey, KT11 1JQ
01932 867909 01932 845360
07850 651743
jerryburkard@aol.com
Est. 1960 *Stock size* Medium
Stock 19th–early 20thC oil paintings, watercolours, 19thC rosewood and mahogany furniture
Open Tues–Sat 10am–5pm Sun 11am–5pm
Fairs LAPADA, NEC
Services Bidding on behalf

Village Antiques
Contact Mr N Tsangari
38 Portsmouth Road, Cobham, Surrey, KT11 1HZ
01932 589841
07973 549221
Est. 1998 *Stock size* Medium
Stock General antiques, small furniture, pictures, porcelain, glass
Open Mon–Fri 10am–6pm or by appointment
Services Picture restoration

COMPTON

Country Rustics
Contact Veronica Dewey
45 The Street, Compton, Guildford, Surrey, GU3 1EG
01483 810505
Est. 2001 *Stock size* Small
Stock Rustic furniture and collectables
Open Tues–Sun 10am–6pm

Old Barn Antiques
Contact Mrs Chris Thurner
Old Barn, The Street, Compton, Guildford, Surrey, GU3 1EB P
☎ 01483 810819
Est. 1993 *Stock size* Small
No. of dealers 6
Stock Country items, blue-and-white, Victoriana, china, glass, collectables
Open Mon–Sat 10am–4pm

CROYDON

Beddington Antiques and Clearance Centre at Lawmans
Contact Mr Peter Lawman
32 Beddington Lane, Beddington, Croydon, Surrey, CR0 4TB P
☎ 020 8401 0877 F 020 8688 3362
Est. 1974 *Stock size* Large
Stock Georgian–Edwardian furniture, collectables, Victoriana
Open Mon–Sat 9.30am–5.30pm Sun 10am–4pm
Services Restorations

Croydon Coin Auctions
Contact Mr G J Monk
PO Box 201, Croydon, Surrey, CR9 7AQ P
☎ 020 8656 4583 F 020 8656 4583
E cca@eigo.co.uk
W www.eigo.co.uk/cca
Est. 1983
Open Mon–Fri 9am–5pm
Sales 6 sales a year of English, foreign and ancient coins, medallions, tokens and bank notes. Held at the United Reformed Church Hall, East Croydon Tues noon
Frequency Bi-monthly

McNally Antiques
Contact I McNally
322 Brighton Road, South Croydon, Surrey, CR2 6AJ P
☎ 020 8686 8387 F 020 8686 8387
Est. 1972 *Stock size* Large
Stock Oak, walnut, mahogany furniture
Open Mon–Fri 9.30am–5.30pm Sat 9.30am–1pm or by appointment
Services Shipping

Miss Ellany
Contact Mr or Mrs J A Cusden
28 Croham Road, South Croydon, Surrey, CR2 7BA P
☎ 020 8688 338
Est. 1984 *Stock size* Small
Stock Antiquarian, rare, second-hand books, transport a speciality
Open Mon–Sat 11am–4pm closed Thurs

DORKING

Antique Clocks by Patrick Thomas
Contact Mr P Thomas
62a West Street, Dorking, Surrey, RH4 1BS P
☎ 01306 743661 F 01306 743661
M 07779 640319
Est. 1992 *Stock size* Large
Stock Clocks, scientific instruments, sporting antiques
Open Mon–Sat 9.30am–5.30pm Sun 11am–4pm
Services Valuations, restorations

G D Blay Antiques (BADA)
Contact Geoffrey Blay
56 West Street, Dorking, Surrey, RH4 1BS P
☎ 01306 743398
M 07785 767718
E gblayantiques@gblay.freeserve.co.uk
W www.gdblayantiques.com
Stock size Medium
Stock Pre-1830s furniture
Open Tues–Sat 10am–5pm or by appointment
Fairs Summer and Winter Olympia, BADA Chelsea

J and M Coombes (DADA)
Contact Mr M Coombes
44 West Street, Dorking, Surrey, RH4 1BU P
☎ 01306 885479 F 01306 885479
Est. 1967 *Stock size* Large
Stock Victorian–Edwardian furniture
Open Mon–Fri 9am–5pm Sat 10am–5pm Sun 1–4pm

Crows Auction Gallery
Contact Mrs H Farquhar
Rear of Dorking Halls, Reigate Road, Dorking, Surrey, RH4 1SG P
☎ 01306 740382 F 01306 881672
Est. 1988
Open Mon–Fri 9am–4pm Sat 9am–noon
Sales Antiques and collectables sale last Wed in month 10am, viewing Sat 9am–1pm Mon–Tues 9am–4pm and morning of sale
Frequency Monthly
Catalogues Yes

Dolphin Square Antiques
Contact Diana Jones
42 West Street, Dorking, Surrey, RH4 1BU P
☎ 01306 887901
Est. 1995 *Stock size* Medium
Stock Georgian–Edwardian furniture, clocks, mirrors, Staffordshire, porcelain, glass, copper, brass ware, bronzes
Open Mon–Sat 10am–5.30pm

Dorking Desk Shop (LAPADA, DADA)
Contact J G Elias
41 West Street, Dorking, Surrey, RH4 1BU
☎ 01306 883327 F 01306 875363
W www.desk.uk.com
Est. 1973 *Stock size* Large
Stock Library and writing furniture, pedestal and partner desks
Open Mon–Fri 8am–5.30pm Sat 10.30am–5.30pm
Services Desk finding service

Dorking House Antiques
Contact Mrs G Emburey
17–18 West Street, Dorking, Surrey, RH4 1BL P
☎ 01306 740915
Est. 1988 *Stock size* Large
No. of dealers 25
Stock Period furniture, silver, porcelain, paintings, 19thC Oriental furniture, clocks
Open Mon–Sat 10am–5pm
Services Restorations

Gallery Eleven (LAPADA)
11 West Street, Dorking, Surrey, RH4 1BL P
☎ 01306 887771 F 01306 887771
Est. 1990 *Stock size* Large
Stock Fine 18th–19thC furniture, quality ceramics, decorative items
Open Mon–Sat 10am–5pm
Services Valuations

Hampshires of Dorking (LAPADA)
Contact Mr Arkell
50–52 West Street, Dorking, Surrey, RH4 1BU
01306 887076 01306 881029
07973 819783
sales@hampshires.co.uk
www.hampshires.co.uk
Est. 1970 *Stock size* Large
Stock Georgian–Edwardian furniture, satinwood
Open Mon–Sat 9.30am–5pm
Fairs Louise Walker Harrogate

Harmans Antiques (LAPADA)
Contact Mr P Harman
19 West Street, Dorking, Surrey, RH4 1QH
01306 743330 01306 742593
enquiries@harmans-antiques.co.uk
www.harmans-antiques.co.uk
Est. 1956 *Stock size* Large
Stock Georgian–Edwardian furniture
Open Mon–Sat 10am–5pm Sun 11am–4pm
Fairs Guildford
Services Restorations

Howard Gallery (LAPADA)
Contact Mrs F Howard
1 West Street, Dorking, Surrey, RH4 1BL
01306 880022 01273 857742
www.thehowardgallery.article7.co.uk
Est. 1989 *Stock size* Medium
Stock 17th–18thC early Georgian, Queen Anne, Regency, oak, country furniture, longcase, bracket clocks
Open Wed–Sat 11am–5pm
Services Restorations, shipping

King's Court Galleries (FATG)
Contact Mrs J Joel
54 West Street, Dorking, Surrey, RH4 1BS
01306 881757 01306 875305
kingscourt.dorking@lineone.net.
www.kingscourtgalleries.co.uk
Est. 1984 *Stock size* Large
Stock Antique maps, engravings, sporting and decorative prints
Open Mon–Sat 9.30am–5.30pm
Services Bespoke framing, mounting

Malthouse Antiques
Contact Mr N Arkell
49 West Street, Dorking, Surrey, RH4 1BU
01306 886169
Est. 1993 *Stock size* Large
No. of dealers 9
Stock 18th–19thC antiques
Open Mon–Sat 10am–5pm

Mayfair Antiques
43 West Street, Dorking, Surrey, RH4 1BU
01306 885007 01306 742636
Est. 1968
Stock General antiques, furniture
Open Mon–Sat 10am–5.30pm
Services Restorations

Norfolk House Galleries Ltd
Contact Mr M Share
48 West Street, Dorking, Surrey, RH4 1BU
01306 881028
Est. 1975 *Stock size* Large
Stock 18th–19thC furniture
Open Mon–Sat 10am–5pm
Services Valuations, shipping

The Olde Bakehouse Antiques
Contact Mr D Kenney
1a West Street, Dorking, Surrey, RH4 1BL
01306 876646
Est. 1987 *Stock size* Large
Stock George III–Edwardian mahogany furniture, decorative items, china, pictures, silver, books
Open Tues–Sat 10.30am–5pm

Pilgrims Antique Centre
Contact Mrs M Pritchard
7 West Street, Dorking, Surrey, RH4 1BL
01306 875028
Est. 1990 *Stock size* Medium
No. of dealers 10
Stock Glass, furniture, paintings, books, Art Deco, barometers, Jobling glass, collectables
Open Mon–Fri 10am–5pm Sat 10am–5.30pm
Services Restaurant

The Refectory
Contact Mr Chris Marks
38 West Street, Dorking, Surrey, RH4 1BU
01306 742111 01306 742111
Est. 1995
Stock 16th–19thC English country furniture, refectory tables, coffers, Windsor chairs, country items
Open Mon–Sat 10.30am–5.30pm Sun by appointment

Eric Tombs
Contact Mr Eric Tombs
62a West Street, Dorking, Surrey, RH4 1BS
01306 743661
07801 183685
ertombs@aol.com
Est. 1992 *Stock size* Medium
Stock Scientific instruments
Open Mon–Sat 9.30am–5.30pm Sun 11am–4pm
Fairs Scientific Instruments Fair
Services Valuations, restorations

Victoria and Edward Antique Centre (WSADA)
Contact Mr Tony Crowe
61 West Street, Dorking, Surrey, RH4 1BS
01306 889645
Est. 1983 *Stock size* Large
No. of dealers 26
Stock General antiques, furniture, metalware, porcelain, jewellery, silver
Open Mon–Sat 9.30am–5.30pm

The Vinery Antiques
Contact Cindy King or Pauline Schwarz
55 West Street, Dorking, Surrey, RH4 1BS
01306 743440 01306 743440
Stock size Medium
Stock 18th–19thC mahogany, walnut furniture, upholstery, early porcelain, decorative items
Open Tues–Sat 10.30am–5pm or by appointment
Services Valuations, restorations, furniture search

West Street Antiques
Contact Mr J G Spooner
63 West Street, Dorking, Surrey, RH4 1BS
01306 883487 01306 883487
weststant@aol.com
antiquearmsandarmour.com
Est. 1986 *Stock size* Medium
Stock English furniture, arms, armour
Open Mon–Sat 9.30am–1pm 2.15–5.30pm or by appointment
Fairs London Arms Fair, Park Lane Arms Fair
Services Valuations

P F Windibank
Contact Mr S Windibank
Dorking Halls, Reigate Road, Dorking, Surrey, RH4 1SG
01306 884556 01306 884669
sjw@windibank.co.uk
www.windibank.co.uk
Est. 1945
Open Mon–Fri 9am–5pm
Sat 10am–1pm
Sales Antique and quality sales on Sat, viewing Thurs 5–9pm
Fri 9am–5pm
Frequency 4–6 weeks
Catalogues Yes

EAST MOLESEY

Antique Centre
Contact Mr Stuart James
77 Bridge Road, East Molesey, Surrey, KT8 9HH
020 8979 7954
Est. 1972 *Stock size* Large
No. of dealers 8
Stock Furniture, silver, glass, ceramics, jewellery, collectors' items
Open Mon–Sat 10am–5pm
Sun noon–5pm

Books Bought and Sold
Contact Mr P Sheridan
68 Walton Road, East Molesey, Surrey, KT8 0DL
020 8224 3232 020 8224 3576
booksbought@yahoo.co.uk
Est. 1973 *Stock size* Medium
Stock Antiquarian, rare, second-hand books, transport, collectable children's books a speciality
Open Tues–Sat 10am–5pm
Fairs H D Book Fairs

Elizabeth R Antiques
Contact E L Mallah
39 Bridge Road, Hampton Court, East Molesey, Surrey, KT8 9ER
020 8979 4004 020 8979 4004
lizaantiques@hotmail.com
Est. 1994 *Stock size* Large
No. of dealers 10
Stock 18th–19thC furniture, porcelain, glass, jewellery, 20thC dolls and toys
Open Tues–Sun 10am–4.30pm
Services Valuations, restorations

Hampton Court Antiques
Contact Mr Leon Abbott
75 Bridge Road, East Molesey, Surrey, KT8 9HH
020 8941 6398
leonabbott@freeuk.com
Est. 1969 *Stock size* Large
Stock Furniture, porcelain, silver, glass, jewellery, clocks
Open Mon–Sat 10am–5pm
Services Valuations

The Hampton Court Emporium
Contact Mr A Smith
52–54 Bridge Road, East Molesey, Surrey, KT8 9HA
020 8941 8876
Est. 1992 *Stock size* Large
No. of dealers 16
Stock Cameras, books, brass, copper, toys, war ephemera, French arts, bronzes, furniture
Open Mon–Sat 10am–5.30pm
Sun 11am–5.30pm

Howard Hope Phonographs & Gramophones
Contact Mr H Hope
21 Bridge Road, East Molesey, Surrey, KT8 9EU
020 8941 2472 020 8398 7630
phonoking@hotmail.com
www.thesaurus.co.uk/hope/
Est. 1975 *Stock size* Large
Stock Phonographs, gramophones, mainly 1895–1930
Open Fri Sat 10am–5pm or by appointment
Services Valuations, props for hire for filming, theatre, etc

Nicholas Antiques
Contact Mr N Wallace
31 Bridge Road, East Molesey, Surrey, KT8 9ER
020 8979 0354 020 8979 0354
Est. 1971 *Stock size* Medium
Stock Mirrors, decorative items, Georgian–Victorian, decorative furniture
Open Mon–Sat 9.30am–5.30pm
Services Valuations

Nostradamus
Contact Heather Ferri
30 & 32 Bridge Road, East Molesey, Surrey, KT8 9HA
020 8979 6766
07979 591022
Est. 1998 *Stock size* Large
No. of dealers 20
Stock General antiques, old cameras, brass, porcelain, Art Deco, jewellery, furniture
Open Tues–Sun 10am–5.30pm

Nostradamus II
Contact Kristina Carson
53 Bridge Road, East Molesey, Surrey, KT8 9HA
020 8783 0595
Est. 1980 *Stock size* Medium
No. of dealers 20
Stock Furniture, crystal, silver, old toys, Art Deco
Open Tues–Sun 10am–5.30pm

Palace Antiques
Contact John Prince
29 Bridge Road, East Molesey, Surrey, KT8 9ER
020 8979 2182
Est. 2000 *Stock size* Large
No. of dealers 10
Stock General antiques
Open Mon–Sun 10am–6pm

Rhombus
Contact Jackie Griffin
28 Bridge Road, East Molesey, Surrey, KT8 9HA
020 8224 5035
07941 292049
Est. 2000 *Stock size* Medium
No. of dealers 4
Stock Art Deco centre
Open Tues–Sun 11am–5.30pm
closed Fri

Alexis F J Turner Antiques
Contact Mr Turner
Antiques at 144a Bridge Road, East Molesey, Surrey, KT8 9HW
020 8542 5926
07770 880960
Est. 1992 *Stock size* Medium
Stock Natural history, taxidermy, gentlemen's effects, curiosities
Open Tues and Sat 10am–5pm

ESHER

Esher Antiques Centre
Contact David Martin or Paula den Besten
128 High Street, Esher, Surrey, KT10 9QJ
01372 468788 01372 471199
07710 741442
www.antiquesportfolio.com
Est. 1997 *Stock size* Large
Stock Furniture, general antiques
Open Mon–Sat 10am–5.30pm

Sun 11am–4pm
Services Public gallery consignment service

EWELL

A E Booth and Son (BAFRA, AMUSF)
Contact Mrs Ann Booth
9 High Street, Ewell, Epsom, Surrey, KT17 1SG
020 8393 5245 Ⓕ 020 8393 5245
Est. 1934 *Stock size* Large
Stock Georgian–Victorian furniture
Open Mon–Sat 9am–4.45pm
Services Restorations

Julian Eade
Ewell, Surrey
020 7304 7413
Ⓜ 07973 542971
Ⓔ julian.eade@insignia-re.com
Est. 1983 *Stock size* Medium
Stock Worcester, Minton, Derby, Doulton stoneware
Open By appointment
Fairs NEC
Services Valuations

J W McKenzie
Contact Mr J W McKenzie
12 Stoneleigh Park Road, Ewell, Epsom, Surrey, KT19 0QT
020 8393 7700 Ⓕ 020 8393 1694
Ⓔ jwmck@netcomuk.co.uk
Ⓦ www.mckenzie-cricket.co.uk
Est. 1972 *Stock size* Medium
Stock Antiquarian, rare, second-hand cricket books
Open Mon–Fri 9.30am–5.30pm Sat 10am–noon or by appointment

FARNHAM

The Antiques Warehouse
Contact Mrs H Burroughs
Badshot Farm, St George's Road, Runfold, Farnham, Surrey, GU9 9HY
01252 317590 Ⓕ 01252 879751
Ⓔ hilary@prjbol.globalnet.co.uk
Est. 1995 *Stock size* Large
No. of dealers 40
Stock Wide variety of antiques including militaria, glass, silver, china, furniture, paintings, prints, garden artefacts
Open Mon–Sun 10am–5.30pm including Bank Holidays
Services Restorations, caning

Bourne Mill Antiques
Contact Mrs Vicky Bowers
39–43 Guildford Road, Farnham, Surrey, GU9 9PY
01252 716663
Est. 1960 *Stock size* Large
No. of dealers 65–85
Stock Antiques, collectables in 38 rooms
Open Mon–Sat 9.30am–5pm Sun 10am–5pm

Casque and Gauntlet Militaria
Contact R L Colt or A Colt
57 Badshot Lea Road, Badshot Lea, Farnham, Surrey, GU9 9LP
01252 320745 Ⓕ 01252 320745
Ⓦ www.armsandarmour.co.uk/dealers/casque/casque.htm
Est. 1972 *Stock size* Large
Stock Militaria, 15thC–modern including swords, bayonets, armour
Open Mon–Sat 11am–5pm
Services Restoration of antique weapons

Childhood Memories
Contact Miss M Stanford
57 Downing Street, Farnham, Surrey, GU9 7PN
01252 724475 Ⓕ 01252 793704
Ⓔ maureen@childhood-memories.co.uk
Ⓦ www.childhood-memories.co.uk
Est. 1976 *Stock size* Large
Stock Antique toys including dolls, cars, aeroplanes, *Star Wars* collectables, bears
Open Mon–Sat 10am–5pm
Services Valuations, restorations

Christopher's Antiques
Contact Mr C Booth
39a West Street, Farnham, Surrey, GU9 7DX
01252 713794 Ⓕ 01252 713266
Ⓔ cbooth7956@aol.com
Est. 1972 *Stock size* Large
Stock French provincial country furniture
Open Mon–Fri 8am–5.30pm Sat 8am–noon
Services Valuations, restorations

Churt Curiosity Shop
Contact Mrs G Gregory
Crossways, Churt, Farnham, Surrey, GU10 2JE
01428 714096
Est. 1995 *Stock size* Medium
Stock Victorian–Edwardian small furniture, Victorian china, glass, collectables
Open Tues–Sat 10.15am–5pm closed Wed

Honey Pot Antiques Centre
Contact Mr B Holroyd
Milford Road, Elstead, Farnham, Surrey, GU8 6HR
01252 703614 Ⓕ 01252 733909
Est. 1996 *Stock size* Large
No. of dealers 20
Stock Furniture, silver, militaria, pictures, kitchenalia, lights, tools
Open Mon–Sat 10am–5.30pm Sun 11am–5.30pm

FERNHURST

John Nicholson Fine Art Auctioneers
Contact Mr G Nugent
The Auction Rooms, Longfield, Midhurst Road, Fernhurst, Surrey, GU27 3HA
01428 653727 Ⓕ 01428 641509
Ⓔ nicholfineart@aol.com
Ⓦ www.antiquestradegazetter.co.uk
Est. 1992
Open Mon–Fri 9am–5.30pm
Sales Fine art auctions 6 weekly Wed Thurs. Paintings, prints, antiquarian books 3–4 times a year
Catalogues Yes

GODALMING

Michael Andrews Antiques
Contact Mr M Andrews
Portsmouth Road, Milford, Godalming, Surrey, GU8 5AU
01483 420765
Est. 1982 *Stock size* Medium
Stock 18th–early 19thC furniture, mainly mahogany
Open Mon–Sat 9.30am–5.30pm closed Thurs or by appointment

E Bailey
Contact E Bailey
Portsmouth Road, Milford, Godalming, Surrey, GU8 5DR
01483 422943
Est. 1978 *Stock size* Medium
Stock General antiques, collectables, curios, golf clubs, woodworking, engineering tools
Open Mon–Sat 8.30am–5pm closed Thurs

Church Street Antiques
Contact Mr L Bambridge
10 Church Street, Godalming, Surrey, GU7 1EH
01483 860894
churchst.antiques@virgin.net
www.freespace.virgin.net/churchstreetantiques
Est. 1984 *Stock size* Large
Stock Early 19th–20thC ceramics
Open Mon–Sat 10am–5pm Wed 10am–1pm
Services Valuations

Godalming Antiques
Contact Gillian Noble-Jones
72a Ockford Road, Godalming, Surrey, GU7 1RF
01483 414428
Est. 1993 *Stock size* Medium
No. of dealers 7
Stock Antiques, furniture, collectables, uniforms, books, trivia, memorabilia
Open Mon–Sat 10am–4.30pm

Hamptons International Auctioneers and Valuers
Contact Liz Bryder
Queen Street Salerooms, Queen Street, Godalming, Surrey, GU7 1BA
01483 423497 01483 415699
queenstreetauctions@hamptons-int.com
www.hamptons.co.uk
Open Mon–Fri 9am–5.30pm Sat 8.30am–12.30pm (sale days only)
Sales Victorian, Edwardian and later furniture and effects sales on Sat at 9.30am, viewing Fri 10am–7pm Sat 8.30–9.30am
Frequency Fortnightly
Catalogues Yes

Hamptons International Auctioneers and Valuers
Contact Liz Bryder
Baverstock House, 93 High Street, Godalming, Surrey, GU7 1AL
01483 423567 01483 426392
fineartauctions@hamptons-int.com
www.hamptons.co.uk
Est. 1996
Open Mon–Fri 9am–5.30pm
Sales Sales of antiques, furniture, carpets, pictures, clocks, china, glass, jewellery, silver, objects of virtue take place on Wed and Thurs at 11am, viewing Sat 9.30am–12.30pm Mon 9.30am–7pm Tues 9.30am–3pm and up to 10.30am on day of sale
Frequency 4 sales every 6–8 weeks
Catalogues Yes

Heath-Bullocks (BADA)
Contact Mrs Mary Heath-Bullock
8 Meadrow, Godalming, Surrey, GU7 3HN
01483 422562 01483 426077
rogrheathbullock@aol.com
www.heath-bullocks.com
Est. 1925 *Stock size* Large
Stock 17th–19thC furniture
Open Fri Sat 10am–5pm and by appointment
Fairs BADA, The Surrey Antiques Fair, The Buxton Antiques Fair
Services Valuations, restorations, upholstery

Honeypot Antiques
Contact Bob Holroyd
Milford Road, Elstead, Godalming, Surrey, GU8 6HR
01252 703614 01252 733909
Est. 1996 *Stock size* Large
No. of dealers 25
Stock General antiques and collectables
Open Mon–Sat 10am–5.30pm Sun 11am–5.30pm

GOMERSHALL

Reeves Restoration at the Coach House Antiques
Contact Mr P W Reeves
The Coach House, 60 Station Road, Gomershall, Guildford, Surrey, GU5 9NP
01483 203838 01483 202999
07774 729325
coach_house.antiques@virgin.net
www.coachhouseantiques.com
Est. 1984 *Stock size* Large
Stock Regency, William IV furniture
Open Mon–Sun 10am–5pm closed Thurs
Fairs Guildford, Olympia
Services Restorations

GOMSHALL

The Studio
Contact Mrs M Ellenger
Station Road, Gomshall, Guildford, Surrey, GU5 9LQ
01483 202449
Est. 1984 *Stock size* Large
Stock Furniture, china, silver, pictures
Open Mon–Sun noon–5pm

GREAT BOOKHAM

Memory Lane Antiques
Contact Mrs J Westwood
30 Church Road, Great Bookham, Leatherhead, Surrey, KT23 3PW
01372 459908
Est. 1984 *Stock size* Medium
Stock Antiques, toys
Open Mon–Fri 10am–5pm Sat 10am–2pm closed Wed

GUILDFORD

Clarke Gammon Auctioneers and Valuers (RICS)
Bedford Road, Guildford, Surrey, GU1 4SJ
01483 880915 01483 880918
Est. 1919
Open Mon–Fri 9am–5.30pm
Sales Fine art, antiques and collectors' sales, viewing Sat 9am–noon Mon 9am–7pm prior to sale
Frequency 6 weeks
Catalogues Yes

Denning Antiques
Contact Mrs C Denning
1 Chapel Street, Guildford, Surrey, GU1 3UH
01483 539595
Est. 1984 *Stock size* Large
Stock Silver, textiles, jewellery
Open Mon–Fri 10am–5pm Sat 9.45am–4.45pm

Horological Workshops (BADA, BHI)
Contact Mr M D Tooke
204 Worplesdon Road, Guildford, Surrey, GU2 9UY
01483 576496 01483 452212
enquiries@horologicalworkshops.com
Est. 1968 *Stock size* Large
Stock Clocks, watches, barometers
Open Tues–Fri 8.30am–5.30pm Sat 9am–12.30pm
Services Valuations, restorations, shipping

Pew Corner Ltd (SALVO)
Contact David Bouldin
Artington Manor Farm, Old Portsmouth Road, Guildford, Surrey, GU3 1LP
01483 533337 F 01483 535554
E pewcorner@pewcorner.co.uk
W www.pewcorner.co.uk
Est. 1988 *Stock size* Large
Stock Period ecclesiastical interiors, furniture, hand-made furniture
Open Mon–Sat 10am–5pm Sun 11am–5pm

Phillips International Auctioneers and Valuers
Millfield, Guildford, Surrey, GU2 5BE
01483 504030 F 01483 450205
W www.phillips-auction.com
Sales Regional Saleroom. Telephone for details

Thomas Thorp
Contact Mr J Thorp
170 High Street, Guildford, Surrey, GU1 3HP
01483 562770 F 01438 562770
W www.thorpsbooks.co.uk
Est. 1883 *Stock size* Medium
Stock Antiquarian, rare, and second-hand books
Open Mon–Sat 9am–5.30pm

Charles W Traylen (ABA)
Contact Mr C W Traylen
Castle House, 49–50 Quarry Street, Guildford, Surrey, GU1 3UA
01483 572424 F 01483 450048
Est. 1945 *Stock size* Large
Stock Antiquarian, rare, and second-hand books
Open Tues–Sat 9am–5pm
Fairs Olympia Book Fair, Chelsea
Services Book search

Wellers Auctioneers (ISVA)
Contact Mr Glen Snelgar or Mr Mark Longson
70 Guildford Street, Chertsey, Surrey, KT16 9BB
01932 568678 F 01932 568626
Est. 1980
Open Mon–Fri 9am–5.30pm
Sales Antique sales 2nd Sat monthly at 9.30am, Bygones auction March and September
Frequency Monthly
Catalogues Yes

HAM COMMON

Glencorse Antiques (LAPADA)
Contact Mr Prydal
321 Richmond Road, Ham Common, Surrey, KT2 5QU
020 8541 0871 M 07740 779917
Est. 1983 *Stock size* Medium
Stock 19thC furniture, Victorian, modern British paintings
Open Mon–Sat 10am–5.30pm
Fairs Olympia (Spring), Claridges (April), Harrogate (May)

HAMPTON WICK

Gill Parkin Furniture
Contact Mr D Beard
7 High Street, Hampton Wick, Kingston upon Thames, Surrey, KT1 4DA
020 8977 5402 F 020 8977 5403
Est. 1980 *Stock size* Medium
Stock Handcrafted 17th and 18thC-style oak and country furniture
Open Mon–Sat 9am–5.30pm or by appointment

HASLEMERE

Serendipity
Contact Mrs E Moore
7 Petworth Road, Haslemere, Surrey, TU27 2BJ
01428 642682
Est. 1997 *Stock size* Medium
No. of dealers 14
Stock Period, pine furniture, china, glass, books, maps, pictures, collectables
Open Mon–Sat 10am–5pm

West Street Antiques
Contact Mr M Holden
8–10 West Street, Haslemere, Surrey, GU27 2AB
01428 644911
W www.weststreetantiques.co.uk
Est. 1998 *Stock size* Medium
Stock 17thC–early 20thC furniture, dinner services, maps, prints, Georgian and Victorian silver
Open Mon–Sat 9.30am–5pm
Services Valuations, restorations

Woods Wharf Antiques Market
Contact Mrs C Lunnon
56 High Street, Haslemere, Surrey, GU27 2LA
01428 642125 F 01428 642125
Est. 1975 *Stock size* Medium
No. of dealers 8
Stock Antiques, collectables
Open Mon–Sat 9.30am–5pm

HINDHEAD

Albany Antiques
Contact Mr T Winstanley
8–10 London Road, Hindhead, Surrey, GU26 6AF
01428 605528 F 01428 605528
M 07931 672345
Est. 1949 *Stock size* Large
Stock Georgian furniture, 18thC brass, Victorian antiques, porcelain, statuary
Open Mon–Sat 9.30am–5pm or by appointment

M J Bowdery (BADA)
Contact Mr Malcolm John Bowdery
12 London Road, Hindhead, Surrey, GU26 6AF
01428 606376
M 07774 821444
Est. 1970 *Stock size* Small
Stock 18th–19thC furniture
Open Mon–Sat 9am–1pm or by appointment
Fairs The Buxton Antiques Fair, Surrey Antiques Fair
Services Valuations

Drummonds Architectural Antiques Ltd (SALVO)
Contact Mr Drummond Shaw
The Kirkpatrick Buildings, 25 London Road, Hindhead, Surrey, GU26 6AB
01428 609444 F 01428 609445
E info@drummonds-arch.co.uk
W www.drummonds-arch.co.uk
Est. 1989 *Stock size* Large
Stock Period bathrooms, oak and pine flooring, fireplaces, statues, garden furniture and lighting, brass door furniture and fittings, radiators, furniture, windows, doors, gates, railings, conservatories
Open Mon–Fri 9am–6pm Sat Sun 10am–5pm

Grayshott Pine
Contact Julia Dickens
5 Victoria Terrace, Crossways Road, Grayshott, Hindhead, Surrey, GU26 6HF
01428 607478
Est. 1960 *Stock size* Large

Stock Pine, painted furniture, kitchenware
Open Mon–Sat 10am–1pm 2–5pm closed Wed
Services Restorations

HORLEY

Surrey Antiques
Contact Mr M Bradnum
3 Central Parade, Massetts Road, Horley, Surrey, RH6 7PP
01293 775522 F 01293 773097
Est. 1989 *Stock size* Large
No. of dealers 3
Stock Antiques, collectables, furniture, silver, china, glass, brass, linen
Open Mon–Fri 10am–5pm Sat 10am–4pm
Services House clearance

KINGSTON-UPON-THAMES

Glydon and Guess (NAG, NPA, GMC)
Contact Mr A Fleckney
14 Applemarket, Kingston-upon-Thames, Surrey, KT1 1JE
020 8546 3758 F 020 8541 5743
Est. 1940 *Stock size* Medium
Stock Jewellery, antique and modern furniture, clocks, barometers
Open Mon–Sat 9.30am–5pm
Services Valuations, restorations, pawnbrokers

The Kingston Antiques Centre
Contact Miss R Bean
29–31 London Road, Kingston-upon-Thames, Surrey, KT2 6ND
020 8549 2004 F 020 8549 3839
E enquiries@antiquesmarket.co.uk
W www.kingstonantiquescentre.co.uk
Est. 1996 *Stock size* Large
No. of dealers 80+
Stock Furniture, jewellery, porcelain, silver, pictures, 20thC design, lighting, Oriental
Open Mon–Sat 9.30am–6pm Sun 10am–6pm

LEATHERHEAD

Alan's Antiques
Contact Mr M Laikin
1–3 Church Street, Leatherhead, Surrey, KT22 8DN
01372 360646
E michael.laikin@virgin.net
Est. 1989 *Stock size* Medium
Stock Furniture, glass, china, silver, lighting
Open Mon–Sat 9am–5.30pm
Fairs Sandown, Grasshopper Westerham
Services Valuations, restorations

MERSTHAM

Elm House Antiques
3 High Street, Merstham, Redhill, Surrey, RH1 3BA
01737 643983
Est. 1995 *Stock size* Medium
Stock General antiques, decorative items, mahogany, oak, pine furniture
Open Mon–Sat 11am–6pm
Services Furniture and textile valuations, restorations

OXTED

Books in the Basement
Contact Mr David Neal
Wagstaffs, 80–84 Station Road East, Oxted, Surrey, RH8 OPG
01883 723131
Est. 1999 *Stock size* Medium
Stock General second-hand books
Open Mon–Sat 9.30am–5.30pm
Fairs H & D, Titlepage

The Second-Hand Bookshop
Contact Mr David Neal
56 Station Road West, Oxted, Surrey, RH8 9EU
01883 715755
Est. 1994 *Stock size* Medium
Stock Rare, second-hand books, mainly non-fiction
Open Mon–Sat 10am–5pm
Fairs H & D, Titlepage
Services Valuations

PURLEY

Aladdin's Antiques
Contact Mrs I Ford
947 Brighton Road, Purley, Surrey, CR8 2BP
020 8668 5600
Est. 1997 *Stock size* Medium
Stock Porcelain, furniture, mirrors, pictures, collectables
Open Mon–Sat 10am–5.30pm closed Wed
Services Valuations

REDHILL

F G Lawrence and Son
Contact Mr C Lawrence
Rear of 89 Brighton Road, Redhill, Surrey, RH1 6PS
01737 764196 F 01737 764196
M 07850 787873
E catherine.lawrence@btinternet.com
Est. 1890 *Stock size* Large
Stock Georgian–Edwardian, 1920s furniture
Open Mon–Fri 9am–5pm Sat 9am–1pm
Fairs Newark
Services Valuations, restorations

REIGATE

Reigate Galleries Ltd (PBFA)
Contact J S Morrish
45a Bell Street, Reigate, Surrey, RH2 7AQ
01737 246055 F 01737 246055
Est. 1958 *Stock size* Large
Stock Antiquarian, rare, second-hand books, antique engravings
Open Mon–Sat 9am–5.30pm Wed 9am–1pm
Fairs PBFA fairs in London

M & M White Antiques and Reproduction Centre
Contact Mr M White
57 High Street, Reigate, Surrey, RH2 9AE
01737 222331
Est. 1994 *Stock size* Medium
Stock Regency, Victorian, reproduction furniture
Open Mon–Sat 10am–5.30pm
Fairs Newark, Ardingly

RICHMOND

Antigone
Contact Mr S Bolster
3 Brewers Lane, Richmond, Surrey, TW9 1HH
020 8940 6894
M 07785 222082
Est. 1982 *Stock size* Large
Stock Antique jewellery, objects of virtue
Open Mon–Sat 10am–5pm
Services Valuations, probate

Antique Mart
Contact Mr G Katz
72–74 Hill Rise, Richmond, Surrey, TW10 6UB
020 8940 6942 F 020 8715 4668
M 07775 626423

Est. 1963 *Stock size* Medium
Stock 18th–19thC furniture
Open Thurs–Sun 2–5.15pm or by appointment

Lawrence Churchill London Ltd
Contact Mr R Taylor
10a Cambrian Road, Richmond, Surrey, TW10 6JQ
020 8940 9517 020 8332 7774
Est. 1996 *Stock size* Medium
Stock General antiques including glass, porcelain, pewter, Art Nouveau reproductions
Open Sat only 7am–5.30pm
Fairs Newark, Ardingly

Andrew Davis Antiques
Contact Mr A Davis
6 Mortlake Terrace, Kew Green, Richmond, Surrey, TW9 3DT
020 8948 4911
07768 904041
Est. 1969 *Stock size* Medium
Stock General antiques, furniture, clocks, pictures, prints, ceramics, glass
Open Open most days and by appointment
Services Valuations, house clearance

The Gooday Gallery
Contact Mrs D Gooday
14 Richmond Hill, Richmond, Surrey, TW10 6QX
020 8940 8652
07710 124540
Est. 1971 *Stock size* Medium
Stock Arts and Crafts, Art Nouveau, Art Deco, postmodernism, tribal art, African and oceanic masks
Open Thurs–Sat 11am–5pm or by appointment
Services Valuations

F and T Lawson Antiques
Contact Mr Lawson
13 Hill Rise, Richmond, Surrey, TW10 6UQ
020 8940 0461
Est. 1965 *Stock size* Medium
Stock Furniture, collectables, brass, copper, costume jewellery, china
Open Mon–Sat 11am–5.30pm closed Wed
Services Valuations

Linden Antique Prints
Contact Mr M Synan
1a Church Court, Richmond, Surrey, TW9 1JL
020 8332 7019
020 8223 26516
martin@lindenprints.com
www.lindenprints.com
Est. 1997 *Stock size* Medium
Stock Antique prints, maps, watercolours
Open Mon–Fri 10.30am–5.30pm or by appointment
Fairs Royal National

Marryat Antiques Ltd (LAPADA)
Contact Mrs M Samuels
88 Sheen Road, Richmond, Surrey, TW9 1UF
020 8332 0262 020 8332 0256
Est. 1990 *Stock size* Large
Stock Furniture, pictures, silver, porcelain, Oriental antiques
Open Mon–Fri 10am–5.30pm Sat 9.30am–6pm Sun by appointment
Services Restorations

Richmond Hill Antiques
Contact Mrs M Hobson
82 Hill Rise, Richmond, Surrey, TW10 6UB
020 8940 5755 020 8940 5755
07909 912382
richmondhillant@hotmail.com
Est. 1970 *Stock size* Medium
Stock Georgian and Victorian furniture
Open Mon Thurs Fri noon–4pm Tues–Wed by appointment
Services Valuations, restorations, shipping

Succession
Contact Michael John
18 Richmond Hill, Richmond, Surrey, TW10 6QX
020 8940 6774
07885 275694
Est. 1969 *Stock size* Medium
Stock Art Nouveau, Art Deco, furniture, bronzes, glass, pictures
Open Fri Sat 11am–6pm Sun 1–6pm or by appointment
Fairs Olympia Spring, 20thC Specialist Fair

Vellantiques
Contact S Vella
127 Kew Road, Richmond, Surrey, TW9 2PN
020 8940 5392
Est. 1983 *Stock size* Large
Stock Furniture, pictures, jewellery
Open Mon–Sat 10am–6pm
Fairs Ardingly, Kempton
Services Valuations

RIPLEY

J Hartley Antiques Ltd (LAPADA)
Contact Mr J Hartley
186 High Street, Ripley, Woking, Surrey, GU23 6BB
01483 224318
Est. 1973 *Stock size* Medium
Stock Antique furniture
Open Mon–Fri 9am–6pm Sat 9.30am–5pm
Services Free local delivery

The Lamp Gallery
Contact Graham Jones
Talbot Walk Antique Centre, Talbot Hotel, High Street, Ripley, Surrey, GU23 6BB
01483 211724 01483 211724
Est. 1999 *Stock size* Medium
Stock Interior lighting, including Art Nouveau and Art Deco lamps
Open Mon–Sat 10am–5pm Sun 11am–4pm or by appointment
Services Valuations, restorations, shipping

Ripley Antiques (LAPADA)
Contact Mrs H Denham
67 High Street, Ripley, Surrey, GU23 6AX
01483 224981 01483 224333
Est. 1959 *Stock size* Large
Stock Large showrooms specializing in English and French 18th–19thC furniture, decorative items for trade and export
Open Mon–Sat 9.30am–5.30pm
Services Shipping

Talbot Walk Antique Centre
Contact Graham Jones
Talbot Hotel, High Street, Ripley, Surrey, GU23 6BB
01483 211724 01483 211724
Est. 1999 *Stock size* Medium
No. of dealers 40
Stock Interior lighting, including Art Nouveau and Art Deco lamps
Open Mon–Sat 10am–5pm Sun 11am–4pm
Services Valuations, restorations, shipping

⊞ Anthony Welling (BADA)
Contact Mr A Welling
✉ **Broadway Barn, High Street, Ripley, Woking, Surrey, GU23 6AQ** Ⓟ
☎ 01483 225384 ⓕ 01483 225384
Est. 1970 *Stock size* Medium
Stock Large 17th–18thC oak, country furniture
Open Mon–Sat 9.30am–5pm
Services Valuations, restorations

RUNFOLD

The Packhouse Antiques Centre
Contact Rachel Pickering
✉ **Hewetts Kilns, Tongham Road, Runfold, Farnham, Surrey, GU10 1PQ** Ⓟ
☎ 01252 781010 ⓕ 01252 783876
ⓔ hewett@cix.co.uk
ⓦ www.packhouse.com
Est. 1990 *Stock size* Large
No. of dealers 80
Stock General antiques including jewellery, antique baths, clocks, paintings
Open Mon–Fri 10.30am–5.30pm Sat–Sun 10am–5.30pm
Services Delivery service, book search

SHERE

⊞ Helena's Collectables
Contact Miss H White
✉ **Middle Street, Shere, Guildford, Surrey, GU5 9HF** Ⓟ
☎ 01483 203039 ⓕ 01483 203039
ⓔ helena@collectables.demon.co.uk
ⓦ www.collectables.demon.co.uk
Est. 1996 *Stock size* Large
Stock Doulton, Beswick, classic Disney, porcelain, collectable ceramics
Open Mon–Sat 9.30am–5.30pm Sun 10.30am–4.30pm
Fairs Detling, Newark, Ardingly
Services Mail order service

⊞ Shere Antiques Centre
Contact Mrs Jean Watson
✉ **Middle Street, Shere, Guildford, Surrey, GU5 9HF** Ⓟ
☎ 01483 202846 ⓕ 01483 830762
ⓔ jeanwatson@glenturret.co.uk
ⓦ www.glenturret.co.uk/shereantiques
Est. 1987 *Stock size* Large
Stock Majolica, flow blue, Continental ceramics, chintz, silver, antique furniture, maps, prints
Open Mon–Fri 10am–5pm Sat 10am–5pm Sun 11am–5pm or by appointment
Services Restorations, shipping, house clearance

SOUTH HOLMWOOD

⊞ Holmwood Antiques
Contact R Dewdney
✉ **Charlwyns, Norfolk Road, South Holmwood, Dorking, Surrey, RH5 4LA** Ⓟ
☎ 01306 888468 ⓕ 01306 742636
Est. 1968
Stock General antiques
Open Mon–Fri 9am–6pm or by appointment
Services Restorations

SURBITON

⊞ Maple Antiques
Contact Lynda or Geof Morris
✉ **4 Maple Road, Surbiton, Surrey, KT6 4AB** Ⓟ
☎ 020 8399 6718
Est. 1981 *Stock size* Medium
Stock Mahogany, pine, oak, walnut furniture, mirrors, rugs, garden art
Open Mon–Sat 10am–5.30pm
Fairs Ardingly, Kempton Park
Services Valuations

SUTTON

⊞ David Aldous-Cook
Contact David Aldous-Cook
✉ **PO Box 413, Sutton, Surrey, SM3 8SZ**
☎ 020 8642 4842 ⓕ 020 8642 4842
Est. 1979 *Stock size* Large
Stock Reference books on antiques and collectables
Open Mon–Fri 9am–5pm
Fairs NEC
Services Mail order, credit cards accepted

TADWORTH

⊞ Ian Caldwell (LAPADA)
Contact Mr I Caldwell
✉ **9a The Green, Dorking Road, Tadworth, Surrey, KT20 5SQ** Ⓟ
☎ 01737 813969
ⓔ caldwell.antiques@virgin.net
ⓦ www.lapada.co.uk/homepages/2486.htm
Est. 1978 *Stock size* Medium
Stock Town furniture, William and Mary–Edwardian
Open Mon–Sat 10am–5pm closed Wed
Services Valuations, restorations

THAMES DITTON

⊞ Clifford and Roger Dade
Contact Mr C Clifford
✉ **Boldre House, Weston Green, Hampton Court Way, Thames Ditton, Surrey, KT7 0JP** Ⓟ
☎ 020 8398 6293 ⓕ 020 8398 6293
Ⓜ 07932 158949
Est. 1937 *Stock size* Medium
Stock Georgian furniture, particularly mahogany
Open Sat 9.30am–5pm or by appointment

WALLINGTON

⊞ An-Toy-Ques
Contact Mrs Britt Grace
✉ **85 Stafford Road, Wallington, Surrey, SM6 9AP** Ⓟ
☎ 020 8288 8124
Ⓜ 077 478 31043
ⓔ antoyques@tinyworld.co.uk
Est. 1994 *Stock size* Large
Stock Old toys including dolls, dolls' houses, bears, trains, lead figures
Open Tues–Sat 10.30am–5pm closed Wed
Fairs Sandown Park, Train fairs, Reading Vintage
Services Valuations, restorations

WALTON-ON-THAMES

⊞ Antique Church Furnishings (SALVO)
Contact Mr L Skilling
✉ **Rivernook Farm, Sunnyside, Walton-on-Thames, Surrey, KT12 2ET** Ⓟ
☎ 01932 252736 ⓕ 01932 252736
ⓔ antchurch@aol.com
ⓦ www.churchantiques.com
Est. 1989 *Stock size* Large
Stock Church furniture, fixtures and fittings
Open Mon–Fri 10am–6pm

⊞ Chancellors Church Furnishings (SALVO)
Contact Mr S Williams
✉ **Rivernook Farm, Sunnyside, Walton-on-Thames, Surrey, KT12 2ET** Ⓟ
☎ 01932 230284 ⓕ 01932 230284
Ⓜ 07973 139308

e antchurch@aol.com
w www.churchantiques.com
Est. 1992 *Stock size* Large
Stock All pre-war church furnishings, fixtures and fittings
Open Mon–Fri 10am–6pm

WARLINGHAM

Trengove Antiques
Contact Mr B Trengove
397 Limpsfield Road, Warlingham, Surrey, CR6 9LA P
☎ 01883 624422
Est. 1900 *Stock size* Large
Stock Small pieces of furniture, china, glass, silver, objets d'art
Open Thurs Fri 9.30am–12.30pm or by appointment

WEST BYFLEET

Academy Billiard Company (GOMC)
Contact Robert Donachie
5 Camp Hill, Camphill Road, West Byfleet, Surrey, KT14 6EW P
☎ 01932 352067 F 01932 353904
Est. 1983 *Stock size* Large
Stock Antique and modern games room equipment
Open By appointment
Services Valuations, restorations, shipping

WEYBRIDGE

Ariel Antiques
Contact Mrs Pat Harvey or Gail Rees
89 Queens Road, Weybridge, Surrey, KT13 9UQ P
☎ 01932 850135
e gailrees@compuserve.com
Est. 1994 *Stock size* Medium
Stock Furniture, porcelain, mirrors, silver, jewellery
Open Mon–Sat 10am–5pm
Services Porcelain, furniture restorations

Church House Antiques (LAPADA)
Contact Mary Foster
42 Church Street, Weybridge, Surrey, KT13 8DP P
☎ 01932 842190
Est. 1886 *Stock size* Medium
Stock Antique jewellery, furniture, silver, decorative accessories
Open Thurs–Sat 10am–5.30pm

The Clockshop
Contact Mr A Forster
64 Church Street, Weybridge, Surrey, KT13 8DL P
☎ 01932 855503 F 01932 840407
Est. 1969 *Stock size* Large
Stock Antique clocks, barometers
Open Mon–Sat 10am–6pm closed Wed
Services Restorations

Village Antiques
Contact Barry Mulvany
39 St Marys Road, Weybridge, Surrey, KT13 9PT P
☎ 01932 846554
M 07803 372399
w www.villantiques.co.uk
Est. 1980 *Stock size* Medium
Stock Mahogany, pine furniture, silver
Open Mon–Sat 10am–3pm

WHYTELEAFE

Modellers Loft
Contact Mr A Hall
4 Wellesley Parade, Godstone Road, Whyteleafe, Surrey, CR3 0BL P
☎ 01883 625417 F 01883 625417
e info@modellersloft.co.uk
w www.modellersloft.co.uk
Est. 1980 *Stock size* Large
Stock Action Man, both old and new, soldiers, Dinky, Corgi, Scalextric, railways, all scale, *Star Wars*, sci-fi collectables
Open Mon–Sat 9am–5.15pm
Fairs Lee Valley Park, Sandown Park

WOKING

Barbers Fine Art Auctioneers (West Sussex Estate Agents, Surveyors and Auctioneers)
Contact Mr K Mansfield
Mayford Centre, Mayford Green, Woking, Surrey, GU22 0PP P
☎ 01483 728939 F 01483 762552
Est. 1971
Open Mon–Sat 9am–1pm
Sales General and fine art sales. Please telephone for further details
Frequency Every 5–6 weeks
Catalogues Yes

Ewbank Fine Art Auctioneers (SOFAA)
Contact Mr C T J Ewbank
Burnt Common Auction Rooms, London Road, Send, Woking, Surrey, GU23 7LN P
☎ 01483 223101 F 01483 222171
e antiques@ewbankauctions.co.uk
w www.ewbankauctions.co.uk
Est. 1994
Open Mon–Fri 9.30am–5pm
Sales 4 antiques sales and 14 sales of Victorian and later furnishings annually, viewing Tues week of sale 2–5pm and Wed 10am–8pm. Phone for sale details
Frequency Monthly
Catalogues Yes

Philip Gilbert
Contact Mr P Gilbert
77 High Street, Horsell, Woking, Surrey, GU21 4UA P
☎ 01483 756807
e philip@pgilbert.fsnet.co.uk
Est. 1975 *Stock size* Small
Stock Georgian–Edwardian furniture
Open Mon–Fri 10.30am–5.30pm Sat 10am–1pm
Services Restorations

Goldsworth Books and Prints (PBFA)
Contact Mr Brian Hartles
47 Goldsworth Road, Woking, Surrey, GU21 1JY P
☎ 01483 767670 F 01483 767670
e goldsworth@cwcom.net
Est. 1986 *Stock size* Medium
Stock Antiquarian, rare, second-hand books, antiquarian maps, books illustrated by Arthur Rackham a speciality
Open Tues–Sat 10am–5pm Sat 9am–4.30pm
Fairs Russell Hotel, London, York National
Services Worldwide book search

WEST SUSSEX

ARDINGLY

Ardingly Antiques
Contact Mary Burke
64 High Street, Ardingly, Haywards Heath, West Sussex, RH17 6TD P
☎ 01444 892680
Est. 1990 *Stock size* Medium
Stock General antiques and collectables
Open Mon–Sun 2–5.30pm closed Tues
Fairs Ardingly, Sandown Park

⌂ Rocking Horse Antique Market
Contact Mrs J Livett or Mr P Livett
✉ **16 High Street, Ardingly, West Sussex, RH17 7TD** Ⓟ
☎ 01444 892205
Est. 1993 *Stock size* Large
No. of dealers 20
Stock Antiques, collectables, books, ephemera
Open Mon–Sat 9.30am–5.30pm Sun 10am–5.30pm winter 5pm

ARUNDEL

⊞ Antiquities
Contact Mr Ian Fenwick or Mrs Christina Fenwick
✉ **5–7 Tarrant Street, Arundel, West Sussex, BN18 9DG** Ⓟ
☎ 01903 884355 Ⓕ 01903 884355
Ⓔ antiquities@montal-internet.co.uk
Est. 1991 *Stock size* Large
Stock 19thC English and French furniture, decorative items, majolica, blue and white, pond boats, French mirrors
Trade only Trade and export, public by appointment
Open Mon–Sat 10am–5pm or by appointment
Services Shipping, major credit cards accepted

⊞ Arundel Antique Galleries
Contact Herbert Smith
✉ **Castle Mews, Tarrant Street, Arundel, West Sussex, BN18 9DG** Ⓟ
☎ 01903 883066
Est. 1980 *Stock size* Medium
Stock Georgian–Edwardian furniture
Open Mon–Sat 10.30am–4.30pm Sun 2.30–4.30pm

⌂ Arundel Antiques Centre
✉ **51 High Street, Arundel, West Sussex, BN18 9AJ** Ⓟ
☎ 01903 882749
Est. 1975
No. of dealers 30
Stock Furniture, china, silver, porcelain, general antiques
Open Mon–Sun 10am–5pm
Services Valuations

⊞ The Arundel Bookshop
Contact G or A Shepherd
✉ **10 High Street, Arundel, West Sussex, BN18 9AB** Ⓟ
☎ 01903 882680
Est. 1977 *Stock size* Medium
Stock Rare, antiquarian, second-hand books
Open Mon–Sat 9.30am–1pm 2.15–5.30pm

⊞ Castle Antiques
Contact Mr J Hughes
✉ **34 High Street, Arundel, West Sussex, BN18 9AB** Ⓟ
☎ 01903 882208
Est. 1990 *Stock size* Medium
Stock Georgian–Edwardian furniture
Open Mon–Sat 10am–5pm

⊞ Decorum
Contact Caroline Baker
✉ **9 Tarrant Street, Arundel, West Sussex, BN18 9DG** Ⓟ
☎ 01903 884436 Ⓕ 01903 889527
Ⓔ caroline@decorum@-arundel.co.uk
Est. 1989 *Stock size* Medium
Stock French furniture and antiques
Open Mon–Sun 10am–5pm

⊞ The Jolly Pedlars
Contact Mr Travers
✉ **43 High Street, Arundel, West Sussex, BN18 9AG** Ⓟ
☎ 01903 884401 Ⓕ 01903 723381
Est. 1982 *Stock size* Medium
Stock General antiques, collectables, toys, dolls
Open Mon–Sun 10.30am–4.30pm

⌂ The Old Cornstore Antiques Centre
Contact Peter Francis
✉ **31 High Street, Arundel, West Sussex, BN18 9AG** Ⓟ
☎ 01903 885456 Ⓕ 01903 892481
Est. 2001 *Stock size* Large
No. of dealers 30
Stock Georgian–Edwardian furniture, jewellery ceramics, silver, paintings, clocks
Open Mon–Sat 10am–5pm Sun 11am–5pm closed Wed
Services Valuations, shipping

⊞ Passageway Antiques
Contact J Saxon
✉ **18 High Street, Arundel, West Sussex, BN18 9AB** Ⓟ
☎ 01903 884602
Est. 1994 *Stock size* Large
Stock Antiques, collectables
Open Mon–Sat 10am–5pm Sun 11am–5pm
Services Valuations

⊞ Spencer Swaffer (LAPADA)
Contact Spencer Swaffer
✉ **30 High Street, Arundel, West Sussex, BN18 9AB** Ⓟ
☎ 01903 882132 Ⓕ 01903 884564
Ⓔ spencerswaffer@btconnect.com
Est. 1974 *Stock size* Large
Stock Eclectic mix of decorative items
Open Mon–Sat 9am–6pm Sun 10am–6pm

⌂ Tarrant Street Antique Centre
Contact Louis de Marigny
✉ **Nineveh House, Tarrant Street, Arundel, West Sussex, BN18 9DJ** Ⓟ
☎ 01903 884307
Est. 1989 *Stock size* Large
No. of dealers 14
Stock Furniture, clocks, jewellery, brass, silver, porcelain, French antique furniture
Open Mon–Fri 10am–5pm Sat 9.30am–5pm Sun 11am–5pm

⊞ Wilson's Antiques (LAPADA)
Contact Mr F Wilson
✉ **13 High Street, Arundel, West Sussex, BN18 9AD** Ⓟ
☎ 01903 882448
Ⓜ 07778 813395
Ⓔ frank@wilsons-antiques.com
Ⓦ www.wilsons-antiques.com
Est. 1936 *Stock size* Medium
Stock Georgian–Edwardian furniture, paintings, china, glass, silver
Open Tues–Sat 10am–5pm
Fairs Olympia, Goodwood House
Services Valuations

BALCOMBE

⊞ Woodall & Emery Ltd
Contact Mrs Chinn
✉ **Haywards Heath Road, Balcombe, Haywards Heath, West Sussex, RH17 6PG** Ⓟ
☎ 01444 811608 Ⓕ 01444 811608
Est. 1860 *Stock size* Large
Stock Antique lighting, chandeliers, table lights, lanterns
Open Mon–Sat 10am–5pm closed Wed

BARNHAM

Howard's Reclamation
Contact Craig Howard
The Yard,
Lake Lane,
Barnham,
West Sussex, PO22 0AE
01243 552095
howardsreclaim@callnetuk.com
Est. 1971 *Stock size* Large
Stock Old and new planked timber floors, oak beams, oak sleepers, telegraph poles, bricks, doors, stone, fireplaces and architectural antiquities
Open Mon–Fri 9am–1pm 2–5pm Sat 8am–1pm closed Wed

BILLINGSHURST

Great Grooms Antique Centre
Contact Mr J Podger
Great Grooms,
Parbrook, Billingshurst,
West Sussex, RH14 9EU
01403 786202 F 01403 786224
antiques@great-grooms.co.uk
www.great-grooms.co.uk
Est. 1993 *Stock size* Large
Stock Furniture, porcelain, jewellery, silver, glass, pictures
Open Mon–Sat 9.30am–5.30pm Sun 10am–6pm
Services Valuations, restorations, interior design

Old House Antiques Centre
Contact Mr D Jull
Adversane, Billingshurst,
West Sussex, RH14 9JJ
01403 782186
Est. 1976 *Stock size* Medium
Stock Antiques, collectables
Open Mon–Sun 10am–5pm

The Old Orchard Antique Market
Contact Jean & Sheila
Old House, Adversane,
Billingshurst,
West Sussex, RH14 9JF
01403 783594
Est. 1985 *Stock size* Medium
Stock China, glass, collectables
Open Mon–Sun 10am–5pm

Nicholas Shaw Antiques (BADA, LAPADA, CINOA, BACA Award Winner 2001)
Contact Nicholas Shaw
Great Grooms Antiques Centre, Parbrook, Billingshurst,
West Sussex, RH14 9EU
01403 786656 F 01403 786656
M 07885 643000
silver@nicholas-shaw.com
www.nicholas-shaw.com
Est. 1992 *Stock size* Large
Stock Scottish and Irish fine silver, small silver collectors' items
Open Mon–Sat 9.30am–5.30pm Sun 10am–6pm
Fairs BADA Fair, Olympia, Antiques for Everyone, LAPADA
Services Valuations, restorations

Sotheby's South
Contact Mrs J Clarke
Summers Place, Billingshurst,
West Sussex, RH14 9AD
01403 833500 F 01403 833699
www.sothebys.com
Est. 1744
Open Mon–Fri 9.30am–4.30pm Sat 9.30am–12.30pm
Sales International sales of furniture, pictures, ceramics, clocks, silver, works of art. Decorative sales including oak and architectural features. Monthly arcade auctions. Special sales of garden statuary, arms and armour, sporting guns. Internet auctions
Frequency Weekly (140 per year)
Catalogues Yes

BOSHAM

Mr Pickett's
Contact Mr M Pickett
Top Barn, Old Park Lane,
Bosham, Nr Chichester,
West Sussex, PO18 8EX
01243 574573 F 01243 572255
M 07779 997012
info@mrpicketts.com
www.mrpicketts.com
Est. 1991 *Stock size* Large
Stock Victorian pine furniture
Open Mon–Fri 8am–5pm Sat 8am–4pm Sun by appointment
Services Stripping, restoration, bespoke pine furniture

BUCKS GREEN

Music Room Antiques (BADA)
Contact Andrew Lancaster
School House, Bucks Green,
Horsham, West Sussex, RH12 3JP
01403 822189 F 01403 823089
M 07744 986926
andrew@musicroomantiques.co.uk
www.musicroomantiques.co.uk
Est. 1986 *Stock size* Medium
Stock Square pianos and associated music-related antiques
Open By appointment
Fairs BADA fair, Harrogate Antique Fair
Services Restorations

BURGESS HILL

British Antique Replicas
22 School Close,
Queen Elizabeth Avenue,
Burgess Hill,
West Sussex, RH15 9RX
01444 245577 F 01444 232014
www.1760.com
Est..1963 *Stock size* Large
Stock English replica antique furniture
Open Mon–Sat 9am–5.30pm
Services Restoration of antique furniture

CHICHESTER

Henry Adams Fine Art Auctioneers (ARVA, SOFA)
Contact Kate Lawson-Paul
Baffins Hall,
Baffins Lane,
Chichester,
West Sussex, PO19 1UA
01243 532223 F 01243 532299
enquiries@henryadamsfineart.co.uk
www.henryadamsfineart.co.uk
Est. 2000
Open Mon–Fri 9am–5.30pm
Sales Antiques and fine art
Frequency Six weekly
Catalogues Yes

Antics
Contact Peter German
19 The Hornet, Chichester,
West Sussex, PO19 4JL
01243 786327
Est. 1981 *Stock size* Small
Stock General antiques
Open Mon–Sat 9am–4pm

Antiques and Bygones
Contact Mrs M Haydon
24 The Buttermarket,
North Street, Chichester,
West Sussex, PO19 1LQ
01243 788071

Est. 1975 *Stock size* Medium
Stock China, glass, collectors' items
Open Tues–Sat 10am–4pm

Barnett Antiques
Contact Mrs U Barnett
Unit 1, Almshouse Arcade, 19 The Harnet, Chichester, West Sussex, PO19 4JL
01243 528089
Est. 1970 *Stock size* Medium
Stock Furniture, china, toys
Open Mon–Sat 10am–4.30pm

Canon Gate Bookshop (PBFA)
Contact W or P Pegler
28 South Street, Chichester, West Sussex, PO19 1EL
01243 778477
Est. 1980 *Stock size* Medium
Stock Rare, antiquarian, second-hand books
Open Mon–Sat 10.30am–5pm

Chichester Antiques Centre
Contact Michael Carter
46–48 The Hornet, Chichester, West Sussex, PO19 4JG
01243 530100
www.antiqueschichester.com
Est. 1994 *Stock size* Large
No. of dealers 40
Stock General antiques, collectables, 18th–20thC furniture
Open Mon–Sat 10am–5pm Sun 11am–5pm
Services Valuations

The Chichester Bookshop
Contact Mr N Howell
39 Southgate, Chichester, West Sussex, PO19 1DP
01243 785473
chibooks@supanet.com
Est. 1965 *Stock size* Large
Stock Rare, second-hand books, specialists in railway books, Sussex books, maps, prints
Open Mon–Sat 9.30am–5pm
Services Book search

Gems
Contact Maureen Hancock
39 West Street, Chichester, West Sussex, PO19 1RP
01243 786173 F 01243 778865
Est. 1985 *Stock size* Large
Stock Edwardian furniture, dolls, Staffordshire, Dresden
Open Tues–Sat 10am–1pm 2.30–5pm or by other appointment
Services Restorations

Peter Hancock
Contact Peter Hancock
40 West Street, Chichester, West Sussex, PO19 1RP
01243 786173 F 01243 778865
Est. 1965 *Stock size* Large
Stock A comprehensive range of antiques and collectables
Open Tues–Sat 10am–1pm 2.15–5.30pm or by appointment
Services Restorations

Heirloom Antiques
Contact Alan Hayes
57 Pound Farm Road, Chichester, West Sussex, PO19 2LU
01243 530489
Est. 1986 *Stock size* Large
Stock Furniture, collectables, curios
Open Mon–Sat 9.30am–5pm Sun 11am–4pm
Fairs Goodwood, Kempton

Heritage Antiques
Contact Mr D Grover
77d, 83 & 84 St Pancras, Chichester, West Sussex, PO19 4LS
01243 783796
Est. 1987 *Stock size* Medium
Stock Georgian–Edwardian, 1920s furniture
Open Mon–Sat 9am–5.30pm

Phillips International Auctioneers and Valuers
Baffins Hall, Baffins Lane, Chichester, West Sussex, PO19 1UA
01243 787548 F 01243 538110
www.phillips-auction.com
Sales Regional Office. Telephone for details

W D Priddy Antiques, Chichester Furniture Warehouse
Contact Mr W D Priddy
Unit 6, Terminus Mill, Terminus Road, Chichester, West Sussex, PO19 2UN
01243 783960 F 01243 783960
M 07712 002371
bill@priddyantiques.fsnet.co.uk
www.priddyantiques.co.uk
Est. 1983 *Stock size* Medium
Stock Georgian–Edwardian furniture
Open Mon–Fri 10am–4pm Sat 10am–5pm variable Sundays 11am–4pm or by appointment

J and M Riley
Contact Mr J Riley
Frensham House, Hunston, Chichester, West Sussex, PO20 6NX
01243 782660
Est. 1966 *Stock size* Medium
Stock 18thC English furniture
Open Mon–Sat 9am–6pm and by appointment

St Pancras Antiques
Contact Mr R Willatt
150 St Pancras, Chichester, West Sussex, PO19 1SH
01243 787645
Est. 1980 *Stock size* Medium
Stock Arms, armour, pre-1800 furniture, ceramics, numismatics, militaria
Open Mon–Sat 9.30am–5pm Thurs 9.30am–1pm
Services Valuations

Stride & Son
Contact Mr M Hewitt or Mr K Warne
Southdown House, St Johns Street, Chichester, West Sussex, PO19 1XQ
01243 780207 F 01243 786713
stride-auctions@cyberquest.co.uk
www.strideandson.co.uk
Est. 1890
Open Mon–Fri 9am–5.30pm closed 1–2pm
Sales Monthly sale of general antiques, periodic book auctions
Frequency Monthly
Catalogues Yes

COLGATE

Sayer Antiques
Contact Jennie Sayer
Unit 5, Blackhouse Farm, Blackhouse Road, Colgate, West Sussex, RH13 6HS
01293 852515 F 01293 852516
M 07885 191652
sayerantiques@lasource.freeserve.co.uk
Est. 1975 *Stock size* Large
Stock French and Italian antique and decorative furniture
Trade only Yes
Open By appointment
Services Valuations, restorations

CRAWLEY

⊞ Hickmet Fine Arts (LAPADA, CINOA)
Contact D Hickmet
✉ PO Box 470, Crawley, West Sussex, RH10 3FA P
☎ 01293 885670 Ⓕ 01293 882908
Ⓔ hickmet@lineone.net
Ⓦ www.internetantiques.co.uk
Est. 1936 *Stock size* Medium
Stock Bronze sculptures, decorative glass
Open Selling mainly via the Internet, fairs or by appointment
Fairs NEC, LAPADA
Services Valuations for probate insurance, interior design

CUCKFIELD

⊞ David Foord-Brown Antiques (LAPADA, BADA)
Contact David Foord-Brown
✉ 3 Bank Buildings, High Street, Cuckfield, West Sussex, RH17 5JU P
☎ 01444 414418
Ⓜ 07850 188250
Est. 1988 *Stock size* Large
Stock 18th–19thC furniture, porcelain, silver, glass
Open Mon–Sat 10am–5.30pm and by appointment
Fairs BADA Fair

DITCHLING

⊞ Dycheling Antiques
Contact Mrs E A Hudson
✉ 34 High Street, Ditchling, West Sussex, BN6 8TA P
☎ 01273 842929 Ⓕ 01273 841929
Ⓜ 07785 456341
Ⓔ hudson@icsgroup.demon.co.uk
Est. 1979 *Stock size* Large
Stock Sets of Georgian–Victorian dining furniture, upholstered furniture, chiffoniers, dining tables
Open Tues Thurs–Sat 10.30am–5.30pm or by appointment
Services Chair search service

HAYWARDS HEATH

⊞ Roundabout Antiques
Contact Angie Craik
✉ 7 Commercial Square, Haywards Heath, West Sussex, RH16 1DW P
☎ 01273 835926 Ⓕ 01273 835659
Ⓔ roundabout@mistral.co.uk
Est. 1993 *Stock size* Medium
Stock Collectables, silver, jewellery, furniture, musical instruments
Open Mon–Sat 9.30am–5.30pm

HENFIELD

⊞ Henfield Antiques and Collectables
Contact Mrs D Evans
✉ 2 Commercial Buildings, High Street, Henfield, West Sussex, BN5 9DE P
☎ 01273 495300
Est. 1999 *Stock size* Large
Stock Kitchenware, pine furniture, Beswick, Wade
Open Mon–Sun 10.30am–5pm
Services Verbal valuations

HORSHAM

Denham's
Contact Kate Tyekiff or Louise Shelley
✉ The Auction Galleries, Warnham, Horsham, West Sussex, RH12 3RZ P
☎ 01403 255699 Ⓕ 01403 253837
Ⓔ denhams@lineone.net
Ⓦ www.catalogs.icollector.com/denhams
Est. 1884
Open Mon–Fri 9am–5.30pm Sat 9am–noon
Sales Sales of antiques and collectors' items every four weeks
Frequency Every 4 weeks
Catalogues Yes

The Horsham Antiques Centre
Contact Mr T Costin
✉ 7–9 Park Place, Horsham, West Sussex, RH12 1DF P
☎ 01403 259181 Ⓕ 01403 259181
Est. 1997 *Stock size* Large
No. of dealers 25
Stock Furniture, pictures, pottery, toys, porcelain, glass, silver, jewellery, other collectables
Open Tues–Sat 10am–5.30pm Sun 10.30am–4pm

⊞ The Horsham Bookshop
Contact Mr T Costin
✉ 4 Park Place, Horsham, West Sussex, RH12 1DG P
☎ 01403 252187
Ⓔ horshambs@btinternet.com
Ⓦ www.horshambookshop.com
Est. 1986 *Stock size* Medium
Stock Rare, antiquarian, second-hand books, cricket, aviation a speciality
Open Tues–Sat 9.30am–5.15pm
Services Book search

⊞ Murray and Kemmett
Contact J Murray
✉ 102 Bishopric, Horsham, West Sussex, RH12 1QN
☎ 01403 254847
Est. 1980 *Stock size* Medium
Stock Rare, second-hand books, crime fiction, religious books a speciality
Open Mon–Sat 9.15am–1pm 2–5pm
Services Book search

Rupert Toovey & Co (RICS)
Contact Alan Toovey
✉ Star Road, Partridge Green, Horsham, West Sussex, RH13 8RA P
☎ 01403 711744 Ⓕ 01403 711919
Ⓔ auctions@rupert-toovey.com
Ⓦ www.rupert-toovey.com
Est. 1995
Open Mon–Fri 9am–5pm
Sales Monthly sales of antiques, fine art, collectables, silver, jewellery, clocks and furniture. Sales of books and postcards 2–3 times a year
Frequency Monthly
Catalogues Yes

HOUGHTON

⊞ Stable Antiques at Houghton
Contact Ian Wadey
✉ Main Road (B2139), Houghton, West Sussex, BN18 9LW P
☎ 01798 839555/01903 740555
Ⓕ 01903 740441
Ⓦ www.stableantiques.co.uk
Est. 2000 *Stock size* Medium
Stock Antiques, furniture and design
Open Tues–Sun 11am–4pm

HURSTPIERPOINT

⊞ Heather Boardman Antiques
Contact Heather Boardman
✉ 40 High Street, Hurstpierpoint, West Sussex, BN16 9RG P
☎ 01273 832101
Est. 1987 *Stock size* Small
Stock Decorative items, collectables

SOUTH

Open Mon–Sat 9.30am–5pm closed Wed
Fairs Ardingly

Graham Foster Antiques
Contact Graham Foster
The Old Telephone Exchange, 41 Cuckfield Road, Hurstpierpoint, West Sussex, BN6 9RW
01273 833099
07850 576434
Stock size Large
Stock Iron gates, furniture
Open Mon–Sat 8.30am–6pm
Fairs Ardingly, Newark
Services Restorations

Julian Antiques (LAPADA)
Contact Mrs C Ingram or Mr J Ingram
124 High Street, Hurstpierpoint, West Sussex, BN6 9PX
01273 832145
Est. 1969 *Stock size* Medium
Stock 19thC French mirrors, clocks, candelabra, fireplaces, bronzes, sculptures, fenders, furniture
Open By appointment
Fairs Olympia
Services Shipping

Samuel Orr (LAPADA)
Contact Mr S Orr
34–36 High Street, Hurstpierpoint, West Sussex, BN6 9RG
01273 832081 01273 832081
07860 230888
clocks@samorr.co.uk
www.samorr.co.uk
Est. 1977 *Stock size* Large
Stock Antique clocks, barometers
Services Clock restoration

LINDFIELD

Lindfield Galleries (BADA)
Contact David Adam
62 High Street, Lindfield, West Sussex, RH16 2HL
01444 483817 01444 484682
david@orientalandantiquerugs.com
www.orientalandantiquerugs.com
Est. 1973 *Stock size* Large
Stock Oriental carpets and tapestries
Open Tues–Fri 9.30am–5pm Sat 10am–4pm
Services Valuations, restorations

Spongs Antique Centre
Contact Ashley or Karen Rchardson
102 High Street, Lindfield, West Sussex, RH16 2HS
01444 487566
Est. 2000 *Stock size* Medium
No. of dealers 34
Stock Furniture, china, silver, ceramics, Carlton ware
Open Mon–Fri 10am–5pm Sun 2–5pm
Services Restorations

Stable Antiques
Contact Adrian Hoyle
98a High Street, Lindfield, West Sussex, RH16 2HP
01444 483662 01444 483662
Est. 1989 *Stock size* Large
Stock George III, Regency, Victorian, Edwardian furniture, antique country pine 1850–1920, some porcelain
Open Mon–Sun 10am–5.30pm
Services Free local delivery

LITTLEHAMPTON

Peter Cheney Auctioneers and Valuers (SSA)
Contact Mr P Cheney
Western Road Auction Rooms, Western Road, Littlehampton, West Sussex, BH17 5NP
01903 722264/713418
01903 713418
Est. 1940
Open Mon–Fri 9am–1pm 2–5pm
Sales Monthly auction sales of antiques, furniture, pictures, silver, porcelain and collectors' items. Valuations for insurance and probate. No buyer's premium
Frequency Monthly
Catalogues Yes

LITTLEHAMPTON

Joan's Antiques
Contact Mrs J Walkden
1 New Road, Littlehampton, West Sussex, BN17 5AX
01903 722422
Est. 1977 *Stock size* Large
Stock China, glass, 1930s items, Victoriana, collectables
Open Thurs–Sat 10.30am–4.30pm
Fairs Goodwood

MIDHURST

Churchill Clocks (BHI)
Contact Mr W P Tyrell
Rumbolds Hill, Midhurst, West Sussex, GU29 9BZ
01730 813891
info@churchillclocks.co.uk
www.churchillclocks.co.uk
Est. 1970 *Stock size* Medium
Stock Clocks, longcase, mantel, French bracket etc
Open Mon–Sat 9am–5pm closed Wed pm
Services Valuations, restorations, shipping

The Old Town Hall Antiques Centre
Contact Mr P Baker
The Old Town Hall, Market Square, Midhurst, West Sussex, GU29 9HJ
01730 817166
Est. 1974 *Stock size* Medium
Stock Furniture, glass, porcelain
Open Mon–Sat 10am–5pm

PETWORTH

Angel Antiques
Contact Nick or Barbara Swanson
Church Street, Petworth, West Sussex, GU28 0AD
01798 343306 01798 342665
swan189@aol.com
www.angelantiques.com
Est. 1991 *Stock size* Medium
Stock Oak and country furniture, decorative items
Open Mon–Sat 10am–5.30pm or by appointment

Antiquated (LAPADA)
Contact Vicki Emery
10 New Street, Petworth, West Sussex, GU28 OAS
01798 344011 01798 344011
Est. 1989 *Stock size* Medium
Stock 18th–19thC painted furniture, 19thC rocking horses
Open Mon–Sat 10am–5.30pm

Bacchus Gallery
Contact Mr R Gillett
Lombard Street, Petworth, West Sussex, GU28 OAG
01798 342844 01798 342634
bacchus@cavovin.com

Est. 1988 *Stock size* Medium
Stock Decanters, glasses, corkscrews, anniversary wines
Open Mon–Sat 10am–5pm

Baskerville Antiques (BADA)
Contact Mr B Baskerville
Saddlers House, Saddlers Row, Petworth, West Sussex, GU28 0AH P
☎ 01798 342067 F 01798 343956
E brianbaskerville@aol.com
Est. 1971 *Stock size* Medium
Stock Antiquarian horologist, clocks, barometers
Open Tues–Sat 10am–6pm

John Bird Antiques
Contact John Bird
High Street, Petworth, West Sussex, GU28 P
☎ 01798 343933 F 01273 483366
M 07973 421070/07970 683949
E bird.puttnam@virgin.net
Est. 1976 *Stock size* Medium
Stock Decorative objects and furniture, upholstery, Arts and Crafts
Open Mon–Sat 10.15am–5.15 pm
Fairs Olympia

Bradley's Past and Present Shop
Contact Mr & Mrs M Bradley
21 High Street, Petworth, West Sussex, GU28 0AU P
☎ 01798 343533
Est. 1979 *Stock size* Medium
Stock Furniture and bygones
Open Tues–Sat 10am–1pm 2–5pm
Services Restoration of gramophones

Lesley Bragge Antiques (LAPADA, PAADA)
Contact Ms L Bragge
Fairfield House, High Street, Petworth, West Sussex, GU28 0AU P
☎ 01798 342324 F 01798 344988
W www.antiquesavenue.com
Est. 1982 *Stock size* Medium
Stock 18th–19thC decorative furniture, lighting, silver, porcelain
Open Mon–Sat 10am–5.30pm
Services Restoration, upholstery, valuations

Callingham Antiques Ltd
Contact Nigel Callingham
Northchapel, Petworth, West Sussex, GU28 9HL P
☎ 01428 707379
Est. 1979 *Stock size* Medium
Stock 17th–18thC English furniture
Open Mon–Sat 9am–5.30pm closed Wed
Services Restorations

Ronald G Chambers – Fine Antiques (LAPADA, CINOA, PAADA)
Contact Mr R G Chambers or Mrs J F Tudor
Market Square, Petworth, West Sussex, GU28 0AH P
☎ 01798 342305 F 01798 342724
M 07932 161968
E jackie@ronaldchambers.com
W www.ronaldchambers.com
Est. 1985 *Stock size* Large
Stock Fine-quality antique furniture & objets d'art Queen Anne–Edwardian period, paintings, longcase clocks, gilded mirrors, bronze statuary and decorative items, jewellery
Open Mon–Sun 10am–5.30pm
Services Valuations, restorations, exchange and finder service, shipping

Du Cros Antiques
Contact Mr J Du Cros
1 Pound Street, Petworth, West Sussex, GU28 0DX P
☎ 01798 342071
Est. 1982 *Stock size* Medium
Stock 17th–19thC English furniture, metalware
Open Mon–Sat 10am–5.30pm
Services Verbal valuations

Elliott's (PAADA)
Contact Mrs P Elliott
19 East Street, Petworth, West Sussex, GU28 0AB P
☎ 01798 343408
Est. 1993 *Stock size* Large
Stock Georgian–Edwardian furniture
Open Wed Fri Sat 10am–5pm

The French Room (PAADA)
Contact Jennie Sayer
5–6 The High Street, Petworth, West Sussex, GU28 0AU P
☎ 01798 344454 F 01293 852516
E SayerAntiques@LaSource.freeserve.co.uk
Est. 1979 *Stock size* Large
Stock French period furniture, decorative wares
Open Mon–Sat 9.30am–5.30pm
Services Valuations, restorations, design service

Richard Gardner Antiques (LAPADA, CINOA, PAADA)
Contact Richard Gardner
Market Square, Petworth, West Sussex, GU28 0AN P
☎ 01798 343411
E rg@richardgardnerantiques.co.uk
W www.richardgardnerantiques.co.uk
Est. 1990 *Stock size* Large
Stock Fine period furniture, works of art including bronzes, Staffordshire figures, paintings, silver, mirrors, 18th–19thC porcelain, etchings
Open Mon–Sat 10am–5.30pm Sun 10am–5pm

Granville Antiques (BADA)
Contact Mr Ian Miller
6 High Street, Petworth, West Sussex, GU28 0AU P
☎ 01798 343250 F 01798 343250
M 07966 279761
Est. 1985 *Stock size* Large
Stock Furniture, fine art, decorative antiques
Open Mon–Sat 9.30am–5.30pm
Services Valuations

John Harris Antiques and Restorations
Contact Mr J Harris
Stables, London Road, Northchapel, Petworth, West Sussex, GU28 9EQ P
☎ 01428 707667
Est. 1976 *Stock size* Medium
Stock 18th–19thC furniture, decorative items
Open Mon–Sat 8am–5pm
Services Restorations

John's Corner Allsorts
Contact Mr J H Mason
Market Square, Petworth, West Sussex, GU28 0AH P
☎ 01798 343270
E johns@corner99.freeserve.co.uk
Est. 1991 *Stock size* Medium
Stock Netsuke, okimonos, ivory, small bronzes, silver
Open Mon–Sat 10am–5pm
Fairs Ardingly

Madison Gallery (PAADA)
Contact Mr G Mott
Swan House, Market Square, Petworth, West Sussex, GU28 0AH
☎ 01798 343638
Ⓜ 0797 1521373
Est. 1987 *Stock size* Large
Stock Oak, walnut, mahogany furniture, country furniture, silver, porcelain, decorative items, paintings
Open Mon–Sun 10am–5pm
Services Valuations, restorations

Octavia Antiques (PAADA)
Contact Aline Bell
East Street, Petworth, West Sussex, GU28 0AB
☎ 01798 342771
Est. 1972 *Stock size* Small
Stock Decorative antiques, small furniture, mirrors, lamps, chairs, china
Open Mon–Sat 10.30am–5.30pm closed Fri

Petworth Antique Market
Contact Mrs D M Rayment
East Street, Petworth, West Sussex, GU28 0AB
☎ 01798 342073 Ⓕ 01798 344566
Est. 1974 *Stock size* Large
Stock English oak furniture, silver, linen, books, soft furnishings, porcelain, glass, fans, general antiques
Open Mon–Sat 10am–5.30pm

Petworth Collectables and Bookshop
Contact Mr Hanson
Middle Street, Petworth, West Sussex, GU28 0BE
☎ 01798 342154
Est. 1987 *Stock size* Large
Stock Rare, second-hand, out-of-print books and collectables
Open Mon–Sat 10am–6pm

Annette Puttnam Antiques
Contact Annette Puttnam
2 Leppards, High Street, Petworth, West Sussex, GU28 0AU
☎ 01798 343933 Ⓕ 01798 343933
Ⓜ 07973 421070/07970 683940
Ⓔ bird.puttnam@virgin.net
Est. 1986 *Stock size* Medium
Stock Decorative objects and furniture, upholstery
Open Mon–Sat 10.15am–5.15 pm
Fairs Olympia

Red Lion Antiques (LAPADA)
Contact Mr R Wilson
New Street, Petworth, West Sussex, GU28 0AS
☎ 01798 344485 Ⓕ 01798 342367
Ⓔ rod@redlion-antiques.com
Ⓦ www.redlion-antiques.com
Est. 1980 *Stock size* Large
Stock 17th–19thC furniture
Open Mon–Sat 10am–5.30pm or by appointment
Fairs LAPADA

Riverbank Gallery Ltd (PAADA)
Contact Linda Burke White
High Street, Petworth, West Sussex, GU28 0AU
☎ 01798 344401 Ⓕ 01798 343135
Ⓔ riverbank@riverbank-antiques.com
Est. 1997 *Stock size* Large
Stock Large English 18th–19thC furniture, decorative items, garden furniture, decorative paintings
Open Mon–Sat 10am–5.30pm

Roughshed
Contact Kirstine St John Best
Pound Street, Petworth, West Sussex, GU28 0DX
☎ 01798 344446
Ⓜ 07970 599464
Ⓔ sk.best.roughshed@cwcom.net
Ⓦ www.roughshed.co.uk
Est. 2000 *Stock size* Medium
Stock French and English decorative antiques
Open Fri Sat 10am–5pm or by appointment
Services Design service

Ruddy Antiques
Contact Robin Ruddy
10a New Street, Petworth, West Sussex, GU28 0AS
☎ 01798 344622
Ⓜ 07710 346222
Ⓔ ruddy.antiques@virgin.net
Est. 1981 *Stock size* Medium
Stock Decorative, painted furniture, garden furniture
Open Mon–Sat 10am–5pm

H G Saunders Fine Antiques (LAPADA)
Contact H G Saunders
Market Square, Petworth, West Sussex, GU28 0AH
☎ 01798 344333 Ⓕ 01798 342724
Ⓔ jackie@ronaldchambers.com
Ⓦ www.ronaldchambers.com
Est. 1986 *Stock size* Medium
Stock 18th–19thC furniture, paintings, objets d'art, jewellery
Open Mon–Sun 10am–5.30pm
Services Valuations, restorations

Stewart Antiques
Contact J Moore
High Street, Petworth, West Sussex, GU28 0AU
☎ 01798 342136
Est. 1980 *Stock size* Large
Stock Victorian, Edwardian stripped pine and fruitwood furniture, kitchenware, Continental decorative items
Open Mon–Sat 10am–5.30pm

T and S Blues Antiques
Contact Susan Boyles and Albert Thomas
The Hut, Lombard Street, Petworth, West Sussex, GU28 0AG
☎ 01798 344155 Ⓕ 01798 344155
Est. 2001 *Stock size* Medium
Stock French furniture, 20thC British pictures
Open Mon–Sat 10am–5.30pm
Services Small restorations

Tudor Rose Antique Centre
Contact Elizabeth Lee
East Street, Petworth, West Sussex, GU28 0AB
☎ 01798 343621 Ⓕ 01798 344951
Ⓜ 07980 927331
Est. 2001 *Stock size* Large
No. of dealers 12
Stock General antiques, brown and decorative furniture, silver, porcelain, blue and white, books, reclamation, William Hockley, early country furniture and interiors
Open Mon–Sat 10am–5.15pm Sun 11am–4.15pm

J C Tutt Antiques
Contact J C Tutt
Angel Street, Petworth, West Sussex, GU28 0BQ
☎ 01798 343221 Ⓕ 01798 343221
Est. 1984 *Stock size* Large
Stock Mahogany, country furniture, accessories
Open Mon–Sat 10am–5pm

T G Wilkinson Antiques Ltd (BADA)
Contact Mr T G Wilkinson
Lombard Street, Petworth, West Sussex, GU28 0AG
01798 344443
07771 515064
Est. 1978 *Stock size* Medium
Stock 18th–19thC English furniture, related items
Open Mon–Sat 10am–5.30pm

PULBOROUGH

Brand Inglis (BADA)
Contact Brand Inglis or Jackie Kyte
Besley Farmhouse, Pulborough, West Sussex, RH20 1NG
01798 839180 F 01798 839180
07950 931911
Est. 1975 *Stock size* Medium
Stock Silver
Open By appointment only
Fairs BADA (Mar), Olympia (Nov)
Services Valuations for insurance, probate or family division

Thakeham Furniture
Contact Mr T Chavasse
Mare Hill Road, Pulborough, West Sussex, RH20 2DY
01798 872006
Est. 1979 *Stock size* Medium
Stock 18th–19thC English furniture, 19thC mahogany a speciality
Open Mon–Fri 9am–5pm
Fairs Malthouse Dorking
Services Restorations

SHOREHAM BY SEA

Bookworms of Shoreham
Contact Mrs P A Liddell
4 High Street, Shoreham by Sea, West Sussex, BN43 5DA
01273 453856
Est. 1992 *Stock size* Medium
Stock Rare, second-hand books, military, modern art, Sussex topography a speciality
Open Tues–Sat 10am–5pm

SMALL DOLE

Alexander Antiques
Contact Judith Goodinge,
Small Dole, Henfield, West Sussex, BN5 9XE
01273 493121
Est. 1972 *Stock size* Medium
Stock Country furniture, treen, boxes, brass, copper
Open Telephone call advisable
Fairs Chester, Petersfield

STORRINGTON

Stable Antiques
Contact Ian Wadey
46 West Street, Storrington, West Sussex, RH20 4EE
01903 740555/01798 839555
F 01903 740441
W www.stableantiques.co.uk
Est. 1993 *Stock size* Large
Stock Antiques, furniture and bric-a-brac
Open Mon–Sun 10am–6pm

STREAT

Fisher Nautical (PBFA)
Contact S D Fisher
Huntswood House, St Helena Lane, Streat, Hassocks, West Sussex, BN16 8SD
01273 890273 F 01273 891439
E fishernautical@seabooks.fsnet.co.uk
Est. 1963 *Stock size* Large
Stock Rare, antiquarian, second-hand nautical books
Open Mail order Mon–Fri 9am–5pm
Services Mail order

TURNERS HILL

Albion House Antiques
Contact Janet Avery
Albion House, North Street, Turners Hill, Worth, West Sussex, RH10 4NS
01342 715670
Est. 1971 *Stock size* Large
Stock 18th–19thC brass, copper, furniture, collectables
Open Mon–Sun 9am–6pm during Summer 9am–7pm

WORTHING

Acorn Antiques
Contact Henry Nicholls
91 Rowlands Road, Worthing, West Sussex, BN11 3JX
01903 216926
E hnick@pavilion.co.uk
Est. 1992 *Stock size* Large
Stock Georgian–Edwardian furniture, china, silver, jewellery
Open Mon–Sat 9am–5.30pm
Services Valuations, restorations

Badgers Books
Contact Ray Potter
8–10 Gratwicke Road, Worthing, West Sussex, BN11 4BH
01903 211816 F 01903 211816
Est. 1982 *Stock size* Large
Stock Rare, antiquarian, second-hand books
Open Mon–Sat 9am–5.30pm

Chloe Antiques
Contact Mrs Dorothy Peters
61 Brighton Road, Worthing, West Sussex, BN11 3EE
01903 202697
Est. 1967 *Stock size* Large
Stock Small collectables, jewellery, china, glass
Open Mon–Sat 10am–4.30pm closed Wed

Corner Antiques
Contact Richard Mihok
9–10 Havercroft Building, North Street, Worthing, West Sussex, BN11 1DY
01903 537669 F 01903 206881
E corner.antiques@lineone.net
W www.website@lineone.net/~Ram
Est. 1997 *Stock size* Small
Stock General antiques, textiles, collectables
Open Mon–Sat 10am–5pm
Fairs Charmandan Centre Worthing

R H Ellis and Son Auctioneers and Valuers
Contact Mr K Ellis
44–46 High Street, Worthing, West Sussex, BN11 1LL
01903 238999 F 01903 215959
W www.rhellisestateagents.co.uk
Est. 1928
Open Mon–Fri 9am–1pm 2–5pm
Sales Monthly sales of Edwardian–Victorian furniture and collectables. Quarterly sales of silver, paintings, Oriental and rugs, Sat, viewing 9am–1pm 2–4pm prior to sale
Frequency Monthly and quarterly
Catalogues Yes

Interiors and Antiques
Contact Pat or Janet Cassie
162 Findon Road, Worthing, West Sussex, BN14 0EL
01903 261134

Est. 1998 ***Stock size*** Medium
Stock Furniture, china, glass, garden statues, bird baths
Open Mon–Sun 10am–6pm closed Tues

⊞ Postcard Cabin
Contact Colin Clissold
⊠ **1 West Buildings, Worthing, West Sussex, BN11 3BS** 🅿
☎ 01903 823126 Ⓕ 01903 236254
Est. 1988 ***Stock size*** Medium
Stock Postcards, coins, medals, bank notes
Open Mon–Fri 10am–5pm Sat 10am–2pm closed Wed

⊞ R Warner and Son
Contact Mr R Warner
⊠ **1–13 South Farm Road, Worthing, West Sussex, BN14 7AB** 🅿
☎ 01903 232710 Ⓕ 01903 217515
Est. 1942 ***Stock size*** Large
Stock Antique furniture
Open Mon–Sat 9am–5pm closed 1–2pm and Wed pm
Services Packers, shippers, courier service

⊞ Wilson's Antiques (LAPADA)
Contact Mr F Wilson
⊠ **45–47 New Broadway, Tarring Road, Worthing, West Sussex, BN11 4HS** 🅿
☎ 01903 202059
Ⓜ 0778 813395
Ⓔ frank@wilsons-antiques.com
Ⓦ www.wilsons-antiques.com
Est. 1936 ***Stock size*** Large
Stock Georgian–Edwardian formal English furniture
Open Mon–Fri 10am–5pm other times by appointment
Fairs Olympia, NEC Antiques for Everyone
Services Valuations for insurance and probate

Worthing Auction Galleries Ltd
Contact Mr R Rood
⊠ **Fleet House, Teville Gate, Worthing, West Sussex, BN11 1UA** 🅿
☎ 01903 205565 Ⓕ 01903 214365
Ⓦ www.worthing-auctions.co.uk
Est. 1964
Open Mon–Fri 8.30am–5pm closed 1–2pm
Sales Monthly sales of general antiques
Frequency Monthly
Catalogues No

WEST COUNTRY

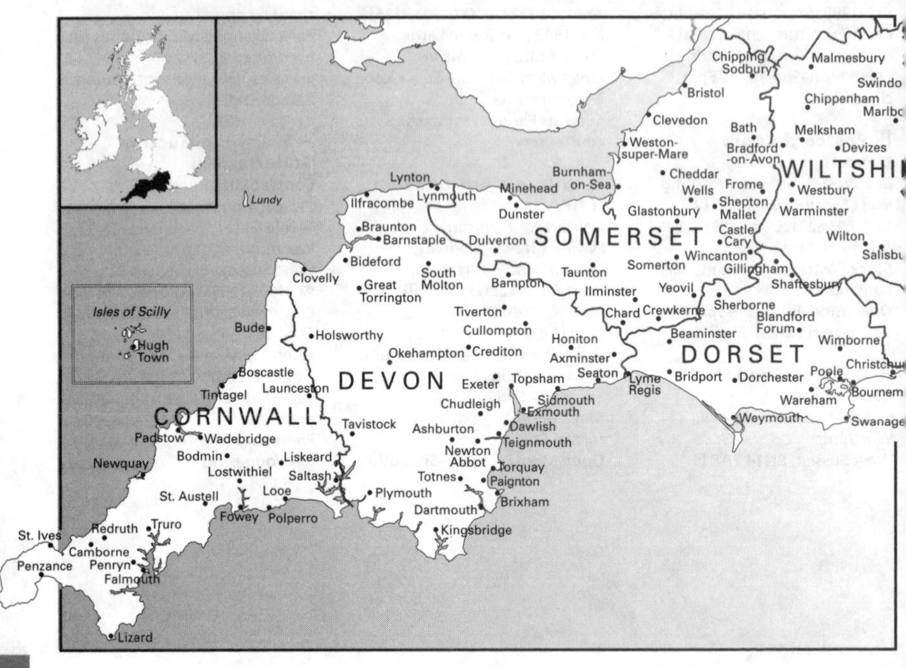

CORNWALL

BODMIN

Bodmin Antiques Centre
Contact Ralph Solomons
Townend, Bodmin, Cornwall, PL31 2LN P
☎ 01208 78661
Ⓜ 07712 431837
Ⓔ bodminantiques@hotmail.com
Est. 1996 *Stock size* Large
Stock General antiques, small items, porcelain, pottery, commemoratives, jewellery, collectables, furniture, glass
Open Mon–Sat 10am–4pm
Services Valuations

BOSCASTLE

Pickwick Antiques
Contact David Lamond
Dunn Street, Boscastle, Cornwall, PL35 0AA P
☎ 01840 250770
Est. 1970 *Stock size* Large
Stock Flatware, silver, small furniture, porcelain, jewellery
Open Mon–Sat 10am–4pm Sun 1–4pm closed Fri
Services Valuations for silver and glass

CAMBORNE

The Victoria Gallery and Bookshop
Contact Jennifer Maker
28 Cross Street, Camborne, Cornwall, TR14 8EX P
☎ 01209 719268
Est. 1983 *Stock size* Medium
Stock Antiquarian and second-hand books, general antiques, silver, jewellery
Open Mon–Fri 10.30am–5.15pm
Services Valuations for insurance, probate, china and furniture restoration, jewellery repairs

CAMELFORD

Corner Shop Antiques
Contact Mr P J Tillett
68 Fore Street, Camelford, Cornwall, PL32 9PG P
☎ 01840 212573
Ⓜ 07884 456247
Est. 1989 *Stock size* Medium
Stock General antiques, collectables
Open Mon–Sat 9.30am–5.30pm

CHACEWATER

Chacewater Antiques
Contact Mrs McCall
5 Fore Street, Chacewater, Truro, Cornwall, TR4 8PS P
☎ 01872 561411
Est. 1992 *Stock size* Medium
Stock Georgian–Edwardian furniture, paintings, 19thC brass ware
Open Mon–Fri 10.30am–4pm closed Wed Sat 10am–1pm

FALMOUTH

Arcade Antiques
Contact G Springfield
16 St George's Arcade, Church Street, Falmouth, Cornwall, TR11 3DH P
☎ 01326 212472
Est. 1995 *Stock size* Medium
Stock General antiques, clocks
Open Mon–Sat 10.30am–5pm

⊞ Browsers Bookshop
Contact Mr Floyd
✉ **13–15 St George's Arcade, Church Street, Falmouth, Cornwall, TR11 3DH** P
☎ 01326 313464
Est. 1981 *Stock size* Medium
Stock Antiquarian and second-hand books, printed music
Open Mon–Sat 9.30am–5pm
Services Valuations

⊞ Marine Instruments
Contact Alistair Heane
✉ **The Wheelhouse, Upton Slip, Falmouth, Cornwall, TR11 3DQ** P
☎ 01326 312414 F 01326 211414
E info@marineinstruments.co.uk
W www.marineinstruments.co.uk
Est. 1960 *Stock size* Large
Stock Marine-related charts, publications, sextants, compasses
Open Mon–Fri 9am–5pm Sat 9am–4pm
Services Worldwide mail order, valuations, repair of sextants and compasses

⊞ Old Town Hall Antiques
Contact Terry Brandreth or Mary Sheppard
✉ **Old Town Hall, 3 High Street, Falmouth, Cornwall, TR11 2AB** P
☎ 01326 319437
Est. 1986 *Stock size* Large
Stock 17th–early 20thC furniture, general antiques and collectables
Open Mon–Sat 10am–5.30pm
Services Deliveries abroad

⊞ P S I Collectables
Contact Phil Hart
✉ **2a Berkeley Court, Falmouth, Cornwall, TR11 3XE** P
☎ 01326 212540 F 01326 212540
M 07929 880230
E psico@madasafish.com
Est. 1998 *Stock size* Medium
Stock Wade, American comics, collectable bears, annuals
Open Mon–Sat 10am–5pm

Waterfront Antiques Market
Contact Mr Rickard
✉ **4 Quay Street, Falmouth, Cornwall, TR11 3HH** P
☎ 01326 311491
Est. 1984 *Stock size* Medium
No. of dealers 20
Stock Furniture, brass, copper, silver, glass, porcelain, pictures, prints, linen, collectables
Open Mon–Sat 10am–4.30pm

FOWEY

⊞ Bookends of Fowey (IPG)
Contact Mrs C Alexander
✉ **4 South Street, Fowey, Cornwall, PL23 1AR** P
☎ 01726 833361 F 01726 833900
E alex@nder.com
W www.nder.com
Est. 1987 *Stock size* Large
Stock Antiquarian and second-hand books, publishers of Cornish literature books
Open Mon–Sat 9.30am–1pm 2.30–6pm
Services Valuations, book search

GRAMPOUND

⊞ Pine & Period Furniture
Contact Simon Payne
✉ **Fore Street, Grampound, Cornwall, TR2 4QT** P
☎ 01726 883117
M 07850 318298
Est. 1971 *Stock size* Medium
Stock Pine and period furniture
Open Mon–Sat 10.30am–5pm
Services Restorations

HELSTON

⊞ Butchers Antiques
Contact Howard Jones
✉ **12 Wendron Street, Helston, Cornwall, TR13 8PS** P
☎ 01326 565117
Est. 1991 *Stock size* Medium
Stock Country and pine furniture, cottageware and very unusual items
Open Mon–Sat 8am–5pm

⊞ The Helston Bookworm (PBFA)
Contact Mr and Mrs Summers
✉ **9 Church Street, Helston, Cornwall, TR13 8TA** P
☎ 01326 565079
Est. 1994 *Stock size* Medium
Stock Antiquarian and second-hand books
Open Mon–Fri 10am–5.30pm Sat 10am–2pm
Fairs Local fairs (phone for details)
Services Restorations, book search

LAUNCESTON

⊞ Antique Chairs and Museum
Contact Alice or Tom Brown
✉ **Colhay Farm, Polson, Launceston, Cornwall, PL15 9QS** P
☎ 01566 777485 F 01566 777485
Est. 1987 *Stock size* Large
Stock Period chairs
Open Mon–Sat 9am–5.30pm
Services Restorations, upholstery

⊞ Todd's Antiques
Contact Mr T Mead
✉ **2 High Street, Launceston, Cornwall, PL15 8ER** P
☎ 01566 775007 F 01566 775007
Est. 1997 *Stock size* Large
Stock Small furniture, collectables, ceramics
Open Mon–Fri 9am–5pm Thurs–Sat 9am–4pm

⊞ Wayfarer Books (PBFA)
Contact Mr R F or Mr B V Brown
✉ **3 Highgrove, Trevadlock Hall, Launceston, Cornwall, PL15 7PW**
☎ 01566 782325 F 01566 782325
E beebeebrownwayfarer@eclipse.co.uk
Est. 1974 *Stock size* Small
Stock Antiquarian, second-hand books by mail order
Open Mail order
Services Free book search

LISKEARD

⊞ Collage
Contact Mrs Dempsey
✉ **Station Road, Liskeard, Cornwall, PL14 4BX**
☎ 01579 348471
Est. 1995 *Stock size* Medium
Stock Antique furniture, new pine, crafts, juggling equipment
Open Mon–Sat 10am–5pm

⊞ Olden Days
Contact Mrs F Nancarrow
✉ **Five Lanes, Dobwalls, Liskeard, Cornwall, PL14 6JD** P
☎ 01579 321577 F 01579 321577
M 07780 687944
Est. 1989 *Stock size* Medium
Stock General antiques, old furniture, new pine
Open Mon–Sun 10am–5pm
Services Bespoke fitted kitchens, bedrooms etc

LOOE

⊞ Tony Martin
Contact Mr Tony Martin
✉ Fore Street, East Looe, Looe, Cornwall, PL13 1AE Ⓟ
☎ 01503 262734
Est. 1965 *Stock size* Medium
Stock General small furniture, china, ceramics, pictures
Open Appointment advisable

LOSTWITHIEL

⊞ John Bragg Antiques
Contact Ann Bragg
✉ **35 Fore Street, Lostwithiel, Cornwall, PL22 0BN** Ⓟ
☎ 01208 872827
Est. 1973 *Stock size* Large
Stock Period furniture
Open Mon–Sat 10am–5pm closed Wed pm
Services Valuations

⊞ Deja-Vu Antiques & Collectables
Contact Adrian or Marianne Barratt
✉ **31 Fore Street, Lostwithiel, Cornwall, PL22 0BN** Ⓟ
☎ 01208 873912
Ⓔ antiquedejavu@hotmail.com
Est. 1998 *Stock size* Medium
Stock Furniture, pictures, collectables, curios, silver, large selection of books
Open Mon–Sat 10am–5pm closed Wed pm
Fairs Charlestown, Trenython Manor
Services Book search

⊞ The Furniture Store
Contact Mike Edwards
✉ **2 Queen Street, Lostwithiel, Cornwall, PL22 0AB**
☎ 01208 873408 Ⓕ 01208 873408
Ⓜ 07790 759540
Est. 1986 *Stock size* Large
Stock Pine furniture, turn-of-the-century oak, Bakelite radios
Open Mon–Sat 10am–5.30pm Wed closed 1pm

⊞ The Higgins Press
Contact Doris Roberts
✉ **South Street, Lostwithiel, Cornwall, TL22 0BZ** Ⓟ
☎ 01208 872755
Est. 1980 *Stock size* Medium
Stock Antiques and collectables
Open Mon–Sat 10am–4pm closed Wed pm

⚒ Jefferys
Contact Ian Morris
✉ **5 Fore Street, Lostwithiel, Cornwall, PL22 0BP** Ⓟ
☎ 01208 872245 Ⓕ 01208 873260
Ⓔ jefferys.lostwithiel@btinternet.com
Ⓦ www.jefferys.uk.com
Est. 1865
Open Mon–Fri 9am–5.30
Sales Antique and fine art sales every two months Wed 10am. Viewing prior Mon 2–7pm Tues 10am–1pm 2pm–5pm. General household sales fortnightly Wed 10am, viewing prior Tues 10am–1pm 2–5pm
Frequency 8 weekly
Catalogues Yes

⊞ The Old Palace Antiques
Contact Mrs D Bryant
✉ **Quay Street, Lostwithiel, Cornwall, PL22 0BS** Ⓟ
☎ 01208 872909
Est. 1979 *Stock size* Medium
Stock Pine furniture, china, brass, prints, postcards
Open Mon–Sat 10am–5pm closed 1–2pm and Wed pm

⊞ Yesterdays
Contact John Fairclough
✉ **9 Fore Street, Lostwithiel, Cornwall, TL22 0BP** Ⓟ
☎ 01208 872344 Ⓕ 01208 872344
Est. 1997 *Stock size* Medium
Stock Antique pine furniture, prints, watercolours, brass, ceramics
Open Tues–Sat 10am–5pm
Services Picture framing

MEVAGISSEY

⊞ Cloud Cuckoo Land (UACC)
Contact Paul Mulvey
✉ **12 Fore Street, Mevagissey, St Austell, Cornwall, PL26 6UQ** Ⓟ
☎ 01726 842364
Ⓜ 07973 135906
Ⓔ oy91@dial.pipex.com
Est. 1993 *Stock size* Medium
Stock Autographs
Open Mon–Sun 10am–5pm

MILLENDREATH

⚒ County Auctions
Contact Mrs Joy Walker
✉ **Millendreath, Looe, Cornwall, PL13 1NY** Ⓟ
☎ 01503 265553 Ⓕ 01503 264467
Est. 1995
Open Tues–Thurs 10am–5pm
Sales Quarterly antiques sale Thurs 10am
Frequency Quarterly

PADSTOW

⊞ Jacob & His Fiery Angel
Contact Mrs Sonya Fancett
✉ **7 Middle Street, Padstow, Cornwall, PL28 8AP** Ⓟ
☎ 01841 532130/01209 831616
Ⓕ 01841 532130
Ⓔ debbiemorriskirby@tesco.net
Ⓦ www.jacobandhisfieryangel.com
Est. 1992 *Stock size* Large
Stock Antiques, eccentricities, eg angels, chandeliers, cats, curiosities. Taxidermy (birds)
Open Mon–Sat 11am–5pm winter: Mon Thurs Sat noon–4pm or by appointment

⊞ Padstow Antiques
Contact K J Webb
✉ **21–23 New Street, Padstow, Cornwall, PL28 8EA** Ⓟ
☎ 01841 532914 Ⓕ 01841 532914
Ⓔ info@gardenbygones.demon.co.uk
Ⓦ www.gardenbygones.demon.co.uk
Est. 1988 *Stock size* Large
Stock Garden antiques including statuary, furniture, animalier
Open Mon–Sat 10am–5pm
Services Delivery and shipping

⊞ Taclow Coth
Contact Patricia or Malcolm McCarthy
✉ **The Drang, South Quay, Padstow, Cornwall, PL28 8BL** Ⓟ
☎ 01841 532326
Est. 1998 *Stock size* Medium
Stock Cutlery, antiques and collectables
Open Mon–Sat 10am–6pm

PAR

⚒ Phillips International Auctioneers and Valuers
✉ **Cornubia Hall, Eastcliffe Road, Par, Cornwall, PL24 2AQ**
☎ 01726 814047 Ⓕ 01726 817979
Ⓦ www.phillips-auction.com
Sales Regional Saleroom. Telephone for details

PENRYN

The Old School Antiques
Contact Mr J Gavin
The Old School, Church Road, Penryn, Cornwall, TR10 8DA
01326 375092
Est. 1985 *Stock size* Large
Stock Antique furniture, glass, china, clocks
Open Mon–Sun 9am–5.30pm
Services Clock repairs and furniture restoration

Leon Robertson Antiques
Contact Mr L Robertson
Unit 2, The Old School, Church Road, Penryn, Cornwall, TR10 8DA
01326 372767
07971 171909
Est. 1973 *Stock size* Medium
Stock Furniture, paintings, general antiques
Open Mon–Sun 9am–5.30pm
Services Valuations

PENZANCE

Antiques and Fine Art
Contact Elinor Davies or Geoffrey Mills
1–3 Queens Buildings, The Promenade, Penzance, Cornwall, TR18 4HH
01736 350509
Est. 1994 *Stock size* Medium
Stock Georgian–Edwardian furniture
Open Mon–Sat 10am–4pm
Services Valuations, restorations and upholstery

Chapel Street Arcades
Contact Mr Bentley
61–62 Chapel Street, Penzance, Cornwall, TR18 4AE
01736 363267
Est. 1984 *Stock size* Medium
No. of dealers 20–25
Stock Furniture, brass, copper, silver, glass, porcelain, pictures, prints, linen, collectors' items
Open Mon–Sat 10am–5pm

R W Jeffery
Contact Mr R W Jeffery
Trebehor, St Levan, Penzance, Cornwall, TR19 6LX
01736 871263
Est. 1968 *Stock size* Large
Stock Coins, banknotes
Open By appointment

Peter Johnson
Contact Mr P Johnson
62 Chapel Street, Penzance, Cornwall, TR18 4AE
01736 363267
Est. 1992 *Stock size* Small
Stock Period lighting, Asian ceramics, furniture, handmade silk lampshades
Open Tue–Sat 9.30am–5pm
Services Valuations

W H Lane & Son, Fine Art Auctioneer and Valuers
Contact Graham J Bazley
Jubilee House, Queen Street, Penzance, Cornwall, TR18 4DF
01736 361447 01736 350097
graham.bazley@excite.com
Est. 1934
Open Mon–Fri 9am–5.30pm
Sales 6 major picture sales per annum, occasional country house sales
Frequency 6+ per annum
Catalogues Yes

David Lay (FRICS, RICS)
Contact Mr D Lay FRICS
The Penzance Auction House, Alverton, Penzance, Cornwall, TR18 4RE
01736 361414 01736 360035
dlay@pzsw.fsnet.co.uk
www.catalogs.icollector.com/Dlay
Est. 1985
Open Mon–Fri 9am–5pm
Sales Auctioneers and valuers General sales every 3 weeks Tues 10am, viewing Sat 9am–1pm, Mon 9am–5pm. Bi-monthly 2 day antiques auctions Thurs Fri 10am, viewing Sat, day prior and day of sale 8.30am–10am. Traditional contemporary art auctions 3 per annum Feb June Oct Thurs 11am, viewing Sat 9am–1pm, day prior 9am–5pm, day of sale 8.30am–11am. Book and Collectors sales 2 per annum Aug and Dec Tues 10am, viewing Sat 9am–1pm, day prior 9am–5pm, morning of sale 8.30–10am
Catalogues Yes

New Street Books
Contact Mr K Hearn
4 New Street, Penzance, Cornwall, TR18 2LZ
01736 362758
eankelvin@yahoo.com
Est. 1991 *Stock size* Medium
Stock Antiquarian and second-hand books, Cornish topics a speciality
Open Mon–Sat 10am–5pm
Services Book search

The Old Custom House
Contact Mr M Bauer
53 Chapel Street, Penzance, Cornwall, TR18 4AF
01736 331030 01736 331030
Est. 1997 *Stock size* Medium
Stock Glass, china
Open Mon–Sat 9am–5.30pm Sun by appointment

Penzance Rare Books
Contact Pat Johnstone
43 Causewayhead, Penzance, Cornwall, TR18 2SS
01736 362140
pat@boscathnoe.free-online.co.uk
Est. 1991 *Stock size* Large
Stock Antiquarian and second-hand books
Open Mon–Sat 10am–5pm
Services Valuations

Tony Sanders Gallery
Contact Mr Tony Sanders
14 Chapel Street, Penzance, Cornwall, TR18 4AW
01736 366620
Est. 1969 *Stock size* Large
Stock Antique furniture, paintings, silver, glass, Newlyn copper
Open Mon–Sat 9am–5.30pm

Shiver Me Timbers
Contact Mr T R E Gray
Station Road, Long Rock, Penzance, Cornwall, TR20 9TT
01736 711338
Est. 1983 *Stock size* Medium
Stock Reclaimed materials, makes reproduction furniture
Open Mon–Sat 9am–6pm
Services Hire of materials to film companies

Ursus
Contact Judith Piper
1 Arcade Steps, Market Jew Street, Penzance, Cornwall, TR18 2HW
01736 364605/871537

Ⓜ 07790 442827
Ⓔ piper@tredavoe.freeserve.co.uk
Ⓦ www.ursus.co.uk
Est. 1999 *Stock size* Medium
Stock Old teddy bears and their toy box companions
Open Ring for opening hours
Services Repairs to bears, identifications, valuations, mail order

POLPERRO

Antiques & Things
Contact I Dickerson
Kirk House, Talland Hill, Polperro, Cornwall, PL13 2RE
☎ 01503 272552
Est. 1997 *Stock size* Medium
Stock Furniture, lamps, etc
Open Mon–Sat 10.30am–5.30pm

Expectations
Contact Irene Dickerson or John Walker
Fore Street, Polperro, Cornwall, PL13 2RS
☎ 01503 272552
Est. 2000 *Stock size* Medium
Stock Mirrors, lamps, pine furniture, brass
Open Mon–Sun 10.30am–6.30pm winter times vary

Gentry Antiques
Contact Pauline Black
Little Green, Polperro, Cornwall, PL13 2RF
☎ 01503 272361
Ⓔ info@gentryantiques.co.uk
Ⓦ www.gentryantiques.co.uk
Est. 1998 *Stock size* Medium
Stock Country pine, oak, pottery, porcelains and decorative items
Open Mon–Sun 10am–5pm
Fairs Battersea Antiques and Decorators Fair

Past & Presents
Contact Joe Askew
1 Lansalos, Polperro, Cornwall, PL13 2QU Ⓟ
☎ 01503 272737
Ⓔ askew/wray@landawiddy.freeserve.co.uk
Est. 2000 *Stock size* Medium
Stock Stripped pine and dark wood furniture, other antiques
Open Mon–Sun 10am–5pm

REDRUTH

The Old Steam Bakery
Contact Mr Stephen Phillips
60a Fore Street, Redruth, Cornwall, TR15 2AF Ⓟ
☎ 01209 315099
Est. 1994 *Stock size* Large
Stock Late Victorian and Edwardian oak and pine furniture
Open Mon–Sat 10.30am–5pm
Services Restorations, furniture designed and made to order

Pool Auctions
Contact Mr or Mrs Duncan
Unit 1, Trevenson Road, Pool, Redruth, Cornwall, TR15 3PH Ⓟ
☎ 01209 717111
Est. 1995
Open Mon–Fri 9am–3pm
Sales Antiques and general household sale Tues 6pm, viewing Tues 9am–6pm prior to sale
Frequency Weekly
Catalogues No

Richards Son & Murdoch
Contact Mr Eddy
Alma Place, Redruth, Cornwall, TR15 2AT Ⓟ
☎ 01209 216367 Ⓕ 01209 314959
Est. 1876
Open Mon–Fri 9am–1pm 2–5pm Sat 9am–noon
Sales Tuesday, general antiques, household furniture, 11am
Frequency 5-6 weekly
Catalogues Yes

Romantiques
Contact Patrick Ludford
Old Rectory, Churchtown, Redruth, Cornwall, TR15 3BT Ⓟ
☎ 07980 500490
Est. 1999 *Stock size* Medium
Stock Period antiques and ornamental garden antiques, staddle stones, troughs
Open Mon–Sat 10am–5pm or by appointment

SALTASH

Eric Distin Auctioneers and Chartered Surveyors
Contact Mr E Distin
46 Fore Street, Saltash, Cornwall, PL12 6JL Ⓟ
☎ 01752 842355 Ⓕ 01752 843768
Est. 1973
Open Mon–Fri 9am–5pm
Sales Antiques and collectables sale Sat 10.30am at New Road, Callington, viewing morning of sale
Frequency Fortnightly
Catalogues Yes

ST AUSTELL

Once Upon a Time
Contact Pippa and Graham Kennedy
The Old Workshop, Charles Town, St Austell, Cornwall, PL25 3NJ Ⓟ
☎ 01726 76018 Ⓕ 01872 262520
Est. 1992 *Stock size* Large
Stock China, furniture, garden statuary, coins, general antiques
Open Mon–Sat 10am–4.30pm
Services Valuations, house clearances

ST COLUMB

M R Dingle
Contact Mr Dingle
Station Yard, Station Approach, St Columb Road, St Columb, Cornwall, TR9 6QR Ⓟ
☎ 01726 861119
Est. 1989 *Stock size* Large
Stock Architectural antiques including reclaimed timber
Open Mon–Fri 8am–5pm Sat 8am–noon

ST IVES

The Book Gallery
Contact David and Tina Wilkinson
2 Bedford Road, St Ives, Cornwall, TR26 1SP
☎ 01736 793545
Est. 1991 *Stock size* Medium
Stock Antiquarian and second-hand books. Art on St Ives a speciality
Open Mon–Fri 10am–5pm Sat 10am–2pm winter closed Mon
Services Book search and catalogue on St Ives books

Collectors Corner (PTA)
Contact Steve Prescott
Market Place, St Ives, Cornwall, TR26 1RZ
☎ 01736 798484 Ⓕ 01736 798417

E cprescott@btclick.com
Est. 1985 *Stock size* Small
Stock Stamps, postcards, cigarette cards, coins
Open Mon–Sat 10am–5pm
Fairs Shepton Mallet

Courtyard Collectables
Contact Janice Mosedale
Cyril Noall Square, Fore Street, St Ives, Cornwall, TR26 1HE
☎ 01736 798809
Est. 1994 *Stock size* Large
Stock General collectables
Open May–October Mon–Sun 10am–10pm Nov–April Mon–Sat 10am–5pm Sun noon–5pm

Dragons Hoard
Contact Chris Prescott
2 Tre-Pol-Pen, Street-an-Pol, St Ives, Cornwall, TR26 2DS
☎ 01736 798484 **F** 01736 798417
E dragonshoard@dragonshoard.ws
W www.dragonshoard.ws
Est. 1985 *Stock size* Small
Stock Collectables, bottles, cigarette cards, sugarlump labels
Open Mon–Fri 1.30pm–5pm
Fairs Newark

Mike Read Antique Sciences (SIS)
Contact Mr M Read
1 Abbey Meadow, Lelant, St Ives, Cornwall, TR26 3LL P
☎ 01736 757237 **F** 01736 757237
E mikeread@appleonline.net
Est. 1978 *Stock size* Medium
Stock Scientific instruments, maritime works of art and nautical artefacts
Open By appointment
Fairs International Antique Scientific and Medical Instruments Fair, Portman Square
Services Valuations

Tremayne Applied Arts
Contact Roger or Anne Tonkinson
Street-an-Pol, St Ives, Cornwall, TR26 2DS
☎ 01736 797779 **F** 01736 793222
Est. 1997 *Stock size* Large
Stock 20thC antiques, 1960s, Arts and Crafts, Art Deco, Art Nouveau
Open Summer Mon–Fri 10.30am–4.30pm closed Wed Sat 9.30am–1.30pm winter by appointment

ST JUST

St Just Bygones
Contact S A Wallis
42 Fore Street, St Just, Penzance, Cornwall, TR19 7LJ P
☎ 01736 787860
Est. 1990 *Stock size* Large
Stock Furniture, general antiques, bric-a-brac
Open Mon–Sat 9.30am–5pm

TREGONY

Clock Tower Antiques
Contact Mrs P M Warne
57 Fore Street, Tregony, Truro, Cornwall, TR2 5RW P
☎ 01872 530225
Est. 1987 *Stock size* Medium
Stock General antiques including Doulton stoneware
Open Mon–Sat 9.30am–5pm or by appointment

TRURO

Alan Bennett
Contact Mr A Bennett
24 New Bridge Street, Truro, Cornwall, TR1 2AA P
☎ 01872 273296
Est. 1945 *Stock size* Large
Stock General antiques, furniture
Open Mon–Sat 9am–5.30pm
Services Valuations

Blackwater Pine Antiques
Contact Linda Cropper
Blackwater, Truro, Cornwall, TR4 8ET P
☎ 01872 560919 **F** 01872 560919
Est. 1989 *Stock size* Large
Stock Antique pine, oak, mahogany furniture
Open Mon–Sat 10am–5.30pm closed Wed
Services Valuations, restorations, furniture made to order, pine stripping

Bonython Bookshop
Contact Mrs R Carpenter
16 Kenwyn Street, Truro, Cornwall, TR1 3BU
☎ 01872 262886
Est. 1996 *Stock size* Small
Stock Antiquarian, second-hand and art books. Cornish interest a speciality
Open Mon–Sat 10.30am–4.30pm
Services Valuations, book search

Bric-a-Brac
Contact Richard Bonehill
16a Walsingham Place, Truro, Cornwall, TR1 2RP P
☎ 01872 225200
E richard@bonehill3.freeserve.co.uk
W www.bonehill3.freeserve.co.uk
Est. 1974 *Stock size* Large
Stock Militaria, small collectables, Royal commemorative china
Open Mon–Sat 9.30am–5pm

Philip Buddell
Contact Linda Buddell
19 St Mary's Street, Truro, Cornwall, TR1 2AF
☎ 01872 260021
M 0797 4022893
Est. 1989
Open Mon–Fri 9.30am–5.30pm Sat 9.30am–1pm non-sale days
Sales Antiques and general household sale Sat 10am viewing Fri 10am–5pm. Specialist wine sale, toy sale and book sale bi-annually. Phone for details
Frequency Fortnightly
Catalogues Yes

Philip Buddell Antiques
Contact Philip or Linda Buddell
The Elms, Tresillian, Truro, Cornwall, TR2 4BA P
☎ 01872 520173
Est. 2000 *Stock size* Medium
Stock Fine furniture, paintings
Open Mon–Fri 10am–5pm Sat 10am–1pm or by appointment
Services Valuations

Coinage Hall Antique Centre
Contact Tony Martin
1 Boscawen Street, Truro, Cornwall, TR1 2QV P
☎ 01872 262520 **F** 01872 261133
Est. 1996 *Stock size* Medium
No. of dealers 6
Stock Fine furniture, collectables, general antiques, fabrics, fine art
Open Mon–Sat 10am–4.30pm
Services Valuations

Collectors Corner
Contact Alan McLoughlin
Unit 45–46, Pannier Market, Back Quay, Truro, Cornwall, TR1 2LL P
☎ 01872 272729
E almacmedal@aol.com
W www.militarycollectables.co.uk
Est. 1997 *Stock size* Medium

Stock Coins, banknotes, medals, militaria, stamps, postcards, cigarette cards
Open Mon–Sat 9.30am–4.30pm
Services Valuations, medal mounting

Count House Antiques
Contact Mrs M Such
Coinage Hall, 1 Princess Street, Truro, Cornwall, TR1 2ES
☎ 01872 264269
Est. 1998 *Stock size* Medium
Stock General antiques
Open Mon–Sat 10am–4.30pm
Fairs Exeter

Just Books
Contact Wendy Barritt
9 Pydar Mews, Truro, Cornwall, TR1 2UX
☎ 01872 242532
Est. 1986 *Stock size* Small
Stock Antiquarian, second-hand and out-of-print books, antiquarian maps and prints, Cornish topography
Open Mon–Sat 10am–5pm closed Thurs
Services Valuations, book search, repairs advice

Lodge and Thomas
Contact Mr Lodge
58 Lemon Street, Truro, Cornwall, TR1 2PY
☎ 01872 272722 Ⓕ 01872 223665
Ⓔ l&t@cwcom.net
Ⓦ www.lodgeandthomas.co.uk
Est. 1892
Open Mon–Fri 9am–5.30pm Sat 9am–noon
Sales General antiques and collectables sale, viewing 9–11am prior to sale. Phone for details. Sales held at Ludgvan Community Hall, Ludgvan, Penzance, Cornwall
Frequency 8 per year
Catalogues Yes

Pydar Antiques
Contact Mrs Judy Poole
People's Palace, Pydar Street, Truro, Cornwall, TR1 2AZ
☎ 01872 223516 Ⓕ 01872 510485
Est. 1968 *Stock size* Medium
Stock 16th–20thC furniture, paintings, artefacts
Open Mon–Sat 10.30am–5pm
Services Valuations

Radnor House Antiques
Contact Geoff or Penny Hodgson
Fore Street, Grampound, Truro, Cornwall, TR2 4QT
☎ 01726 882921
Est. 1975 *Stock size* Medium
Stock Georgian–Edwardian oak, pine and mahogany furniture
Open Mon–Sat 10am–6pm

Taylors Collectables (FBS)
Contact Mr D Taylor
The Antique Centre (Upstairs), 1 Princes Street, Truro, Cornwall, TR1 2ER
☎ 01872 262336
Ⓜ 07775 811686
Est. 1996 *Stock size* Large
Stock Collectables, postcards, coins, medals, stamps, ceramics, books, toys, cigarette cards, militaria
Open Mon–Sat 10am–4pm
Fairs Ardingly, Newark, Westpoint, Brentwood
Services Valuations

The Truro Auction Centre
Contact Martyn Rowe
City Wharf, Malpas Road, Truro, Cornwall, TR1 1QH
☎ 01872 260020 Ⓕ 01872 261794
Est. 1990
Open Mon–Fri 9am–5.30pm Wed 9am–6pm Sat 9am–1pm
Sales Victorian and general sale every Thurs 10am, viewing Wed 2–6pm. Antiques and picture sale, also collectors and sporting sale every 6 to 8 weeks Fri 10.30am, viewing Wed 2–6pm Thurs 2–4pm. 3 vintage and classic automobile sales every year, telephone for details
Frequency Weekly
Catalogues Yes

WADEBRIDGE

Lambrays
Contact Richard J Hamm
Polmorla Walk, The Platt, Wadebridge, Cornwall, PL27 7AE
☎ 01208 813593 Ⓕ 01208 814986
Est. 1981
Open Mon–Fri 9am–5.30pm Sat (prior to sale) 9am–noon
Sales Quarterly specialist antique sales. Victoriana sales every other Mon at 11am
Frequency Fortnightly
Catalogues Yes

Polmorla Bookshop
Contact Joan Buck
1 Polmorla Road, Wadebridge, Cornwall, PL27 7NB
☎ 01208 814399
Est. 1991 *Stock size* Large
Stock Antiquarian, rare, second-hand and out-of-print books
Open Mon–Sat 10.30am–5pm
Services Valuations, house clearance, book search

Relics
Contact Mr K Brenton
4 Polmorla Road, Wadebridge, Cornwall, PL27 7NB
☎ 01208 815383
Est. 1991 *Stock size* Large
Stock Furniture, china, brass, kitchenware, pictures
Open Mon–Sat 10am–5pm

Victoria Antiques
Contact Mr Daly
21 Molesworth Street, Wadebridge, Cornwall, PL27 7DD
☎ 01208 814160 Ⓕ 01208 814160
Est. 1974 *Stock size* Large
Stock General antiques, clocks, barometers, period furniture
Open Mon–Sat 9am–5pm

DEVON

ASHBURTON

Adrian F Ager, Ashburton Marbles
Contact Tony Bayliss
Great Hall, North Street, Ashburton, Newton Abbot, Devon, TQ13 7QD
☎ 01364 653189
Est. 1972 *Stock size* Large
Stock Marble fireplaces, furniture, carpets, lighting, garden statuary
Open Mon–Fri 8am–5pm Sat 10am–4pm

The Dartmoor Bookshop (PBFA)
Contact Mr Paul Heatley
2 Kingsbridge Lane, Ashburton, Newton Abbot, Devon, TQ13 7DK
☎ 01364 653356
Ⓔ Dartmoorbks@aol.com

www.dartmoorbks.dabsol.co.uk
Est. 1974 *Stock size* Large
Stock Antiquarian, second-hand, rare and out-of-print books
Open Mon–Sat 9.30am–5.30pm

Kessler Ford Antiques
Contact Matthew Ford or Elizabeth Kessler
9 North Street, Ashburton, Devon, TQ13 7QJ
01364 654310 F 01364 654141
M 07770 782402
E kessler.ford@netmatters.co.uk
Est. 1998 *Stock size* Medium
Stock 17th–18thC English oak and mahogany furniture
Open Tues–Sat 10am–5pm closed Wed or by appointment

Memories
Contact Julia Walters
Globe Buildings, 15 North Street, Ashburton, Devon, TQ13 7QH
01364 654681
M 07773 795777
Est. 1996 *Stock size* Medium
Stock A varied range of period furniture Georgian–Edwardian, collectables
Open Mon–Sat 10am–4pm closed Wed pm
Fairs Shepton Mallet, Westpoint, Exeter
Services Restorations

Moor Antiques
Contact Mr T Gatland
19a North Street, Ashburton, Newton Abbot, Devon, TQ13 7QH
01364 653767
M 07720 183414
Est. 1984 *Stock size* Medium
Stock 18th–19thC furniture, silver, glass, porcelain, clocks, jewellery
Open Mon Tues Thurs–Sat 10am–4.30pm Wed 10am–1pm
Services Valuations

Rendells
Contact Mr Clive Morgan
Stonepark, Ashburton, Newton Abbot, Devon, TQ13 7RH
01364 653017 F 01364 654251
E stonepark@rendells.co.uk
W www.rendells.co.uk
Est. 1816
Open Mon–Fri 9am–5.30pm
Sales Antiques and selected items monthly Thurs Fri 10am viewing Tues 10am–7pm Wed 10am–5pm
Frequency Monthly
Catalogues Yes

The Shambles
Contact Mrs Pam Paice
22 North Street, Ashburton, Devon, TQ13 7QD
01364 653848
Est. 1986 *Stock size* Large
Stock Furniture, collectables, marine antiques, textiles, pictures, rugs, silver, Staffordshire figures
Open Mon–Sat 10am–5pm

The Snug
Contact Jill Stubbs or Ros Gregg
15 North Street, Ashburton, Devon, TQ13 7QH
01364 653096
Est. 1991 *Stock size* Medium
Stock Antiques, decorative items and textiles
Open Mon–Sat 10am–4.30pm
Fairs Hyson Fairs Textiles

Taylors
Contact Wendy Taylor
5 North Street, Ashburton, Devon, TQ13 7QJ
01364 652631
Est. 1985 *Stock size* Medium
Stock 18thC–Edwardian oak furniture, 18thC blue-and-white Chinese porcelain
Open Mon–Sat 10am–5pm Wed closed pm

AXMINSTER

South Street Antiques
Contact Philip Atkins
South Street, Axminster, Devon, EX13 5AD
01297 33701
Est. 1987 *Stock size* Medium
Stock General antiques
Open Mon–Sat 9.30am–5pm
Fairs Shepton Mallet
Services Valuations

Symonds & Sampson
Contact Piers Pisani
The Market, Axminster, Devon, EX13 5AW
01297 35693 F 01297 35693
E general@symsam-a-i-s.co.uk
W www.symsam.a-i-s.co.uk
Est. 1858
Open Mon–Fri 9am–1pm Wed 9am–5pm
Sales General antiques sale last Wed of the month
Frequency Monthly
Catalogues No

BARNSTAPLE

The Barn Antiques
Contact Mr T Cusack
73 Newport Road, Barnstaple, Devon, EX32 9BG
01271 323131
Est. 1987 *Stock size* Large
Stock General antiques
Open Mon–Sat 9.30am–5pm half day Wed
Services Valuations, restorations

Barnstaple Auctions
Contact Mr Mugleston
Pilton Quay, Barnstaple, Devon, EX31 1PB
01271 327087 F 01271 327087
Est. 1993
Open Mon–Fri 9am–5pm Sat 10am–2pm
Sales General antiques sale last Thurs 6.30pm every month, viewing Wed 4–7pm
Frequency Monthly
Catalogues Yes

North Devon Antiques Centre
Contact Patrick Broome
The Old Church, Cross Street, Barnstaple, Devon, EX31 1BD
01271 375788 F 01271 375788
M 07967 930917
E partick-broome@top-finish-designs.freeserve.co.uk
Est. 1998 *Stock size* Large
No. of dealers 27
Stock Georgian to contemporary furniture, Royal Worcester, Clarice Cliff, Crested china ware, Barum and Brannam, militaria, clocks, architectural salvage, pictures and prints, Art Deco
Open Mon–Sat 10am–4.30pm
Services Restorations, café also open 6 days

Phillips International Auctioneers and Valuers
10 Taw Vale, Barnstaple, Devon, EX32 8NJ
01271 374487 F 01271 324269
W www.phillips-auction.com
Sales Regional Office. Ring for details

⊞ Selected Antiques and Collectables
Contact Helen Chugg
✉ **19 Newport Road, Barnstaple, Devon, EX32 9BG** Ⓟ
☎ 01271 321338
Ⓜ 07866 024831
Est. 1994 *Stock size* Large
Stock General antiques, collectables, linen, glass, toys, books, porcelain, memorabilia, North Devon Pottery
Open Tues–Sat 9.45am–4.30pm
Fairs Local only
Services Valuations free in shop, restorations

⊞ Tarka Books (BA, Henry Williamson Society)
Contact Kevin Allcoat
✉ **5 Bear Street, Barnstaple, Devon, EX32 7BU** Ⓟ
☎ 01271 374997
Ⓔ info@tarkabooks.co.uk
Ⓦ www.tarkabooks.co.uk
Est. 1987 *Stock size* Large
Stock Second-hand books. Henry Williamson titles a speciality
Open Mon–Sat 9.45am–5pm
Services Book search

BEER

⊞ Beer Collectables
Contact Mr Forkes
✉ **Dolphin Hotel, Fore Street, Beer, Seaton, Devon, EX12 3EQ** Ⓟ
☎ 01297 24362
Est. 1993 *Stock size* Medium
Stock Collectables, china, glass, fishing tackle, jewellery
Open Mon–Sun 10am–5pm
Fairs Exeter Livestock, Salisbury, T&T Fairs
Services Valuations, restorations

⊞ Dolphin Antiques
Contact Ms Banfield
✉ **Fore Street, Beer, Seaton, Devon, EX12 3EQ** Ⓟ
☎ 01297 625800
Ⓜ 07971 271539
Est. 1989 *Stock size* Medium
Stock Georgian–Edwardian furniture, interior pieces
Open Mon–Sun 10am–5pm closed Tues

BIDEFORD

⊞ J Collins & Son (BADA, LAPADA, CINOA)
Contact Mr John Biggs
✉ **28 High Street, Bideford, Devon, EX39 2AN** Ⓟ
☎ 01237 473103 Ⓕ 01273 475658
Ⓔ 101726.2263@compuserve.com
Est. 1953 *Stock size* Large
Stock Georgian and Regency furniture, Victorian oil paintings, watercolours
Open By appointment only
Fairs BADA, Olympia (June, Nov), Harrogate (Sept)
Services Restorations of English furniture, watercolours and oil paintings

⊞ Peter Hames (PBFA)
Contact Mr P Hames
✉ **Old Bridge Antiques Centre, Market Place, Bideford, Devon, EX39 2DR**
☎ 01237 421065 Ⓕ 01237 421065
Ⓔ peterhames@hotmail.com
Ⓦ www.members.aol.com/tarkabooks
Est. 1979 *Stock size* Medium
Stock Small selection of general books. Jazz and North Devon books a speciality
Open Mon–Sat 9am–5.30pm
Fairs PBFA

⊞ Stuff
Contact David Marochan
✉ **27 Market Place, Bideford, Devon, EX39 2DR** Ⓟ
☎ 01237 423535
Ⓜ 07788 467727
Est. 1988 *Stock size* Medium
Stock General antiques, collectables, furniture, smalls
Open Mon–Sat 10am–4pm
Fairs Westpoint, Exeter Livestock

BRAUNTON

⊞ Book Cellar
Contact Mr Dennis Stow
✉ **5a The Square, East Street, Braunton, Devon, EX33 2JD** Ⓟ
☎ 01271 815655 Ⓕ 01271 815655
Est. 1988 *Stock size* Large
Stock Antiquarian and second-hand books
Open Summer Mon–Sat 10am–5pm (closed Wed) Winter Tues Thurs Sat 10am–4pm

BRIXHAM

⊞ John Luce Antiques
Contact Mr J Luce
✉ **King Street Rooms, King Street, Brixham, Devon, TQ5 9TF** Ⓟ
☎ 01803 858303
Est. 1971 *Stock size* Medium
Stock Early motoring, clocks, general antiques
Open Mon–Sat 10am–5pm
Services Restoration of woodwork and clocks

⊞ John Prestige Antiques
Contact Mr Prestige
✉ **Greenswood Court, Greenswood Road, Brixham, Devon, TQ5 9HN** Ⓟ
☎ 01803 856141 Ⓕ 01803 851649
Ⓔ sales@john-prestige.co.uk
Ⓦ www.john-prestige.co.uk
Est. 1971 *Stock size* Large
Stock Furniture, small paintings, mirrors, ceramics
Trade only Yes
Open Mon–Fri 8.30am–6pm or by appointment
Services Valuations, restorations

BUDLEIGH SALTERTON

⊞ Alison Gosling Antiques
Contact Mrs Gosling
✉ **46a High Street, Budleigh Salterton, Devon, EX9 6LJ** Ⓟ
☎ 01395 443737/271451
Ⓜ 07798 782444
Est. 1983 *Stock size* Medium
Stock Late Georgian–1930s decorative items, early 18thC–1830s period furniture, mostly Georgian and Regency
Open Mon 11am–5pm Tues Wed 3–5pm Fri 11.30am–5pm or by appointment
Services Valuations

⊞ B & T Thorn and Son
Contact Mr D Thorn
✉ **2 High Street, Budleigh Salterton, Devon, EX9 6LQ** Ⓟ
☎ 01395 442448
Est. 1950 *Stock size* Medium
Stock Ceramics, English pottery and porcelain
Open Tues Fri Sat 10am–1pm
Services Valuations

CATTLEDOWN

Plymouth Auction Rooms
Contact Mr P Keen
✉ **Edwin House, St John's Road, Cattedown, Plymouth, Devon, PL4 0NZ** Ⓟ
☎ 01752 254740 Ⓕ 01752 254740

Ⓔ paulkeen@plymouthauctions.freeserve.co.uk
Ⓦ www.invaluable.com/plymouth-auctions
Est. 1992
Open Mon–Fri 9am–5pm
Sales Antiques and collectables every 3 weeks Wed 10.30am, viewing Tues 10am–7pm Wed 9–10.30am. Monthly general sale of modern, reproduction furniture Sat 10.30am, viewing Fri 2–6pm Sat 9–10.30am
Frequency Every 3 weeks
Catalogues Yes

CHULMLEIGH

Youll's Antiques
Contact Michael Youll
Tremchard Farm, Egglesford, Chulmleigh, Devon, EX18 7QJ Ⓟ
☎ 01363 83167 Ⓕ 01363 83972
Ⓔ mikeyoull@aol.com
Ⓦ www.youll.com
Est. Pre-1900 *Stock size* Large
Stock French armoires and chests, buffets, furniture, upholstery, bamboo
Open Mon–Sun 9am–5pm
Fairs Newark
Services Valuations, restorations

COLYTON

D Barney
Contact Mr D Barney
Greenfield, Colyton Hill, Colyton, Devon, EX24 6HY Ⓟ
☎ 01297 552702 Ⓕ 01297 552702
Ⓔ doug.barney@ondigital.com
Est. 1969 *Stock size* Medium
Stock English and foreign coins
Open By appointment and mail order
Services Valuations

Colyton Antique Centre
Contact R C Hunt
Dolphin Street, Colyton, Devon, EX24 6LU Ⓟ
☎ 01297 552339 Ⓕ 01297 552339
Ⓜ 07973 678989
Ⓔ colytonantiques@modelgarage.co.uk
Ⓦ www.modelgarage.co.uk
Est. 1988 *Stock size* Medium
No. of dealers 20+
Stock Antiques and collectables
Open Summer 10am–5pm winter Bank Holidays 11am–4pm

COMBE MARTIN

Combe Martin Clock Shop
Contact Robin Westcott
1 High Street, Combe Martin, Ilfracombe, Devon, EX34 0EP Ⓟ
☎ 01271 882607
Ⓔ robin@robinw.force9.co.uk
Ⓦ www.robinw.force9.co.uk
Est. 1980 *Stock size* Medium
Stock Clocks from longcase to mantel, barometers
Open Mon–Sat 9am–6pm
Services Restorations of clocks

CREDITON

Mid Devon Antiques
Contact Colin Knowles
The Corn Store, Morchard Road, Copplestone, Crediton, Devon, EX17 5LP Ⓟ
☎ 01363 84066
Ⓜ 07718 583086
Est. 1965 *Stock size* Medium
Stock Country furniture, tables, beds
Open By appointment
Services Restorations, repairs

Musgrave Bickford Antiques (BHI)
Contact Dennis Bickford
15 East Street, Crediton, Devon, EX17 3AT Ⓟ
☎ 01363 775042
Est. 1987 *Stock size* Medium
Stock Clocks, barometers, small furniture
Open By appointment
Fairs Westpoint, Shepton Mallet
Services Valuations, restorations

Woods Emporium
Contact Martin Wood
1 Exeter Road, Crediton, Devon, EX17 3BH
☎ 01363 774702/772503
Ⓕ 01363 776082
Ⓔ woodsgroup@eclipse.co.uk
Est. 1972 *Stock size* Large
Stock Marine antiques
Open Mon–Fri 9am–5.30pm Sat 9am–3.30pm

Woods Emporium
Contact Martin Wood
32 Exeter Road, Crediton, Devon, EX17 3BP Ⓟ
☎ 01363 772503 Ⓕ 01363 776082
Ⓔ woodsgroup@eclipse.co.uk
Est. 1972 *Stock size* Large
Stock Government surplus Navy equipment
Open Mon–Fri 9am–5.30pm Sat 9am–3.30pm

CULLOMPTON

Country Antiques & Interiors
Contact Mr M C Mead
The Old Brewery, High Street, Uffculme, Cullompton, Devon, EX15 3AB Ⓟ
☎ 01803 845480 or 01884 841110
Ⓕ 01803 845480
Ⓜ 07768 328433
Ⓔ country.antiques@cosmic.org.uk
Ⓦ www.eastdevon.net/country.antiques
Est. 1994 *Stock size* Medium
Stock Country furniture, decorative items
Open Mon–Fri 9am–6pm by appointment
Services Shipping arranged

Cullompton Old Tannery Antiques
Contact George Mills
The Old Tannery, Exeter Road, Cullompton, Devon, EX15 1DT Ⓟ
☎ 01884 38476 Ⓕ 01884 38476
Ⓔ mail@cullompton-antiques.ltd.uk
Ⓦ www.cullompton-antiques.ltd.uk
Est. 1987 *Stock size* Large
Stock Antique country furniture, English, French and European clocks, mirrors, decorative items
Open Mon–Sat 10am–5pm
Services Shipping, courier

English Country Antiques
Contact Mr M C Mead
The Old Brewery, High Street, Uffculme, Cullompton, Devon, EX15 3AB Ⓟ
☎ 01803 845480 Ⓕ 01803 845480
Ⓜ 07768 328 433
Ⓔ country.antiques@cosmic.org.uk
Ⓦ www.eastdevon.net/country.antiques/
Est. 1984 *Stock size* Medium
Stock Country antiques, decorative items of all types
Open Mon–Sat 9am–6pm or by appointment
Services Shipping arranged

Oaks and Partners
Contact Katy Rombold
Unit 1, Granary Court, Kingsmill Estate, Cullompton, Devon, EX15 1BS Ⓟ
☎ 01884 35848 Ⓕ 01884 35848

Est. 1979
Open Mon–Fri 9am–4pm
Sales Antiques and general sale Sat 10.30am, viewing Thurs 9am–5pm Fri 9am–8pm
Frequency Monthly
Catalogues Yes

DARTMOUTH

The Dartmouth Antique Company
Contact Mr John Smith
The Old Fire Station, Flavell Place, Dartmouth, Devon, TQ6 9ND
☎ 01803 833309
Est. 1999 *Stock size* Large
Stock Period and Victorian furniture, smalls, carpets
Open Mon–Sun 10am–5pm

Looking Back
Contact Paddy Distin
32 Lower Street, Dartmouth, Devon, TQ6 9AN
☎ 01803 832615
Est. 1990 *Stock size* Medium
Stock General antiques
Open Summer Mon–Sat 9.30am–10.30pm Sun 10am–5pm winter Mon–Sun 10am-5pm
Services House clearance

DAWLISH

Emporium
Contact Michael Peters
40b The Strand, Dawlish, Devon, EX7 9PT
☎ 01626 862222 Ⓕ 01626 774689
Ⓜ 07768 076360
Est. 1983 *Stock size* Medium
Stock General antiques
Open Tues–Sat 10am–5pm
Fairs Westpoint, Shepton Mallet
Services Valuations

EXETER

Bearnes (SOFAA)
Contact Mr R Barlow
St Edmund's Court, Okehampton Street, Exeter, Devon, EX4 1DU
☎ 01392 422800 Ⓕ 01392 207007
Ⓔ enquiries@bearnes.co.uk
Ⓦ www.bearnes.co.uk
Est. 1945
Open Mon–Fri 9.30am–5pm
Sales General sale Tues am, viewing Sat am Mon 9.30am–7.30pm. Specialist sale 3 times a year Tues Wed. Phone for details
Frequency Fortnightly
Catalogues Yes

Lisa Cox Music (ABA)
Contact Lisa Cox
Heath House, Heath Lane, Whitestone, Exeter, Devon, EX4 2HJ
☎ 01647 61140 Ⓕ 01647 61138
Ⓔ music@lisacoxmusic.co.uk
Ⓦ www.lisacoxmusic.co.uk
Est. 1984 *Stock size* Large
Stock Antiquarian music, pictures, ephemera, autographs
Open By appointment
Services Valuations

Eclectique
Contact Sue Bellamy
26–27 Commercial Road, The Quay, Exeter, Devon, EX2 4AE
☎ 01392 250799
Est. 1994 *Stock size* Medium
Stock Antique and painted furniture, ceramics, lamps, objets d'art, collectables
Open Mon–Sun 11am–5.30pm
Services Interior design

Exeter Antique Lighting
Contact Julian Wood
Cellar 15, The Quay, Exeter, Devon, EX2 4AP
☎ 01392 490848
Ⓜ 07702 969438
Est. 1990 *Stock size* Large
Stock Antique lighting, fireplaces, iron beds
Open Mon-Sun 11am-5pm or by appointment
Fairs Newark, Ardingly
Services Valuations, restorations

Exeter Rare Books (ABA, PBFA)
Contact Mr R C Parry
12a Guildhall Shopping Centre, Exeter, Devon, EX4 3HG
☎ 01392 436021
Est. 1974 *Stock size* Medium
Stock Antiquarian, rare, and second-hand-books. West Country interest a speciality
Open Mon–Sat 10am–1pm 2–5pm
Fairs Chelsea ABA, Olympia Hilton
Services Valuations

Exeter's Antiques Centre on the Quay
Contact Patsy Bliss
The Quay, Exeter, Devon, EX2 4AN
☎ 01392 493501
Ⓦ www.exeterquayantiques.co.uk
Est. 1984 *Stock size* Large
No. of dealers 21 dealers
Stock Antiques, collectables, books, postcards, jewellery, tools, cameras etc
Open Mon–Sun summer 10am–6pm winter 10am–5pm
Services Restaurant

Isabelline Books
Contact Mr M Whetman
19 Victoria Park Road, Exeter, Devon, EX2 4NT
☎ 01392 201296 Ⓕ 01392 201663
Ⓔ mikann@beakbook.demon.co.uk
Ⓦ www.beakbook.demon.co.uk
Est. 1997 *Stock size* Small
Stock Antiquarian books on ornithology
Open By appointment
Services Valuations, 3 catalogues a year

McBains Antiques (LAPADA)
Contact Mr Gordon McBain
Exeter Airport Industrial Estate, Exeter, Devon, EX5 2BA
☎ 01392 366261 Ⓕ 01392 365572
Ⓔ mcbains@netcomuk.co.uk.
Est. 1980 *Stock size* Large
Stock Georgian–Edwardian furniture, also selection of French and Continental furniture
Open Mon–Fri 9am–6pm Sat 10.30am–1pm
Fairs Newark
Services Full container and export facility

Mortimers
Contact Ian Watson
87 Queen Street, Exeter, Devon, EX4 3RP
☎ 01392 279994
Ⓜ 07767 492815
Est. 1970 *Stock size* Large
Stock Antique jewellery, watches, clocks and silver
Open Mon–Sat 9.30am–5pm
Services Valuations, restorations

Pennies Antiques
Contact David Clark
Unit 2, Wesses Estate, Station Road, St David's, Exeter, Devon, EX4 4NZ
01392 271928
Est. 1979 *Stock size* Large
Stock General antiques and second-hand furniture
Trade only Yes
Open Mon–Sat 9am–6pm Sun 10am–4pm
Services Deliveries

Phantique
Contact Hazel Price
Unit 5–7, 47 The Quay, Exeter, Devon, EX2 4AN
01392 498995
www.phantique.co.uk
Est. 1996 *Stock size* Large
No. of dealers 9
Stock General antiques, collectables, prints, books
Open Summer 10.30am–5.30pm winter 10.30am–5pm

Phillips International Auctioneers and Valuers
Alphin Brook Road, Alphington, Exeter, Devon, EX2 8TH
01392 439025 F 01392 410361
www.phillips-auction.com
Sales Regional Saleroom. Ring for details

The Quay Gallery Antiques Emporium
Contact James Gould or Stephanie Hornsey
43 The Quay, Exeter, Devon, EX2 4AP
01392 213283
Est. 1984 *Stock size* Large
Stock Fine mahogany and oak furniture, maritime, porcelain, silver, glass, paintings, prints, general antiques, antiquities, clocks
Open Mon–Sun 10am–5pm
Fairs Westpoint, Shepton Mallet
Services Valuations

St David's Auctions
Contact Nick Magnum
1–2 Wessex Estate, Station Road, Exeter, Devon, EX4 4NZ
01392 217412/3 F 01392 217414
M 07788 428931
info@stdavidsauctions.co.uk
www.stdavidsauctions.co.uk
Est. 2001
Open Mon–Sat 9am–5pm
Sales General antiques sale Sat viewing Fri 9am–7pm
Frequency Weekly
Catalogues Yes

Tobys (SALVO)
Contact Mr P Norrish
Station House, Station Road, Exminster, Exeter, Devon, EX6 8DZ
01392 833499 F 01392 833429
paul@tobys-antiques.freeserve.co.uk
www.tobysreclamation.co.uk
Est. 1983 *Stock size* Large
Stock Architectural antiques, sanitary ware, fireplaces, reclaimed building materials
Open Mon–Fri 9am–5pm Sat 9.30am–4.30pm Sun and Bank Holidays 10.30am–4.30pm
Fairs Exeter Ideal Home, Devon County Show
Services House clearance, nationwide delivery

Tredantiques
Contact Jon Tredant
Adjacent to Exeter Airport, Exeter, Devon, EX5 2BA
01392 447082
M 07967 447082
www.tredantiques.com
Est. 1982 *Stock size* Large
Stock Good quality furniture and decorative items
Open Mon–Fri 9am–6pm or Sat by appointment
Fairs Newark, Decorative Antiques and Textiles Fair (Battersea)

Victoriana Antiques and Kents Jewellers
Contact Mr Kent
68 Sidwell Street, Exeter, Devon, EX4 6PH
01392 275204/275291
Est. 1964 *Stock size* Medium
Stock General antiques, porcelain, jewellery, silver
Open Mon Tues Thurs–Sat 9.15am–5pm
Services Jewellery, silver and porcelain restorations and repair

A E Wakeman and Sons Ltd
Contact Mr Wakeman
Newhouse Farm, Tedburn St Mary, Exeter, Devon, EX6 6AL
01647 61254 F 01647 61254
M 07836 284765/636525
aewakeman@hotmail.com
Est. 1971 *Stock size* Medium
Stock 19thC furniture
Trade only Yes
Open Mon–Fri 8.30am–5.30pm
Fairs Newark

EXMOUTH

Antiques and Collectables
Contact Antonio Newton
Unit 3, The Indoor Market, The Strand, Exmouth, Devon, EX8 1AB
M 07831 095951
Est. 1990 *Stock size* Medium
Stock Jewellery, clocks, Art Deco, glass, Beswick, Wade, commemorative ware, Poole, Royal Doulton
Open Mon–Sat 9am–5.30pm
Services Valuations, restorations

Browsers
Contact Mr or Mrs Spiller
1–2 The Strand, Exmouth, Devon, EX8 1HL
01395 265010
Est. 1988 *Stock size* Large
Stock Collectables, toys, advertising, books, china
Open Mon–Sat 10.30am–6pm

Martin Spencer-Thomas (NAVA)
Contact Mr M Spencer-Thomas
Bicton Street Auction Rooms, Bicton Street, Exmouth, Devon, EX8 2RT
01395 267403 F 01395 222598
martin@martinspencerthomas.co.uk
www.martinspencerthomas.co.uk
Est. 1984
Open Mon–Fri 9am–5pm
Sales Antiques sale Mon 1.30pm, modern furniture sale Mon 10.30am, viewing Thurs 9am–6pm Fri 9am–5pm Sat 10am–4pm
Frequency 5 weeks
Catalogues Yes

HATHERLEIGH

Hatherleigh Antiques (BADA)
Contact Michael Dann
15 Bridge Street, Hatherleigh, Devon, EX20 3HU
01837 810159 *Stock size* Large
Stock Gothic and Renaissance furniture

Open Mon–Sat please telephone to confirm opening times
Services Valuations, restorations

HELE

Fagins Antiques
Contact Jean Pearson
Old Whiteways Cider Factory, Hele, Exeter, Devon, EX5 4PW
01392 882062 F 01392 882194
E cstrong@fagins-antiques.co.uk
W www.fagins-antiques.co.uk
Est. 1978 *Stock size* Large
Stock Stripped pine, dark wood, general antiques, china, architectural antiques
Open Mon–Fri 9.15am–5pm Sat 11am–5pm
Services Pine stripping

HOLSWORTHY

The Mill Emporium
Contact Tim Coleman
Bude Road, Holsworthy, Devon, EX22 6HZ
01409 254800
Est. 1996 *Stock size* Large
Stock Pine, mahogany and oak furniture, china and general antiques
Open Tues–Sat 9am–5pm
Fairs Westpoint
Services Restorations, pine stripping, re-upholstery

West Country Auctions
Contact Mr Tony King
The Memorial Hall, Holsworthy, Devon
01409 281238 F 01409 281238
M 07970 989227
Est. 1997
Open Mon–Fri 8am–8pm
Sales 15 sales a year of approximately 1200 lots, lists of dates available
Catalogues No

HONITON

Abingdon House Antique Centre
Contact Nick Thompson
136 High Street, Honiton, Devon, EX14 1JP
01404 42108
Est. 1985 *Stock size* Large
Stock General antiques, 17th–20th century furniture, country, tools, prints, equestrian
Open Mon–Sat 9.30 am–5.30pm April–Dec Sun 11am–5pm

Antique Toys
38 High Street, Honiton, Devon, EX14 1PJ
01404 41194
E honitonantiquetoys38@hotmail.com
Est. 1976 *Stock size* Large
Stock Toys, teddies, dolls
Open Tues–Sat 10.30am–5pm closed Mon Thurs
Services Dolls' hospital

Jane Barnes Antiques and Interiors
Contact Mrs Barnes
59 High Street, Honiton, Devon, EX14 1PW
01404 41712 F 01404 861300
M 07971 328618
Est. 1985 *Stock size* Large
Stock General antiques, Victorian and Edwardian
Open Mon–Sat 10am–4pm closed Wed or by appointment
Services Restorations

Bonhams & Brooks West Country
Contact Duncan Chilcott
Dowell Street, Honiton, Devon, EX14 8LX
01404 41872 F 01404 43137
E west_country@bonhams.com
W www.bonhams.com
Open Mon–Fri 9am–5pm
Sales Regional saleroom for Devon and the West Country
Frequency Ring for details
Catalogues Yes

Roderick Butler (BADA)
Contact Mr R Butler or Mrs V Butler
Marwood House, Honiton, Devon, EX14 1PY
01404 42169
Est. 1948 *Stock size* Large
Stock 17th–18thC Regency furniture, works of art and metalwork
Open Mon–Sat 9.30am–5pm by appointment in August
Services Restorations

Collectables
Contact Mr Chris Guthrie
134B High Street, Honiton, Devon, EX14 1JP
01404 47024
E chris@collectables.uk.net
W www.collectables.uk.net
Est. 1995 *Stock size* Large
Stock Ceramics, Wade, cameras, railwayana, toys, militaria, annuals, phone cards, cigarette cards, breweriana, commemorative, games, postcards, Crested china
Open Mon–Sat 10am–5pm

Colystock Antiques
Contact Dave McCollum
Rising Sun Farm, Stockland, Honiton, Devon, EX14 9NH
01404 861271 F 01404 861271
Est. 1985 *Stock size* Large
Stock 18th–19thC pine and reproduction furniture, reclaimed pine kitchens
Open Mon–Sat 8.30am–6pm Sun 1–4pm

Fountain Antiques
Contact J Palmer or G York
132 High Street, Honiton, Devon, EX14 1JP
01404 42074 F 01404 44993
M 07831 138011
E antiques@gyork.co.uk
Est. 1988 *Stock size* Large
No. of dealers 15
Stock Linen, books, cutlery, telephones, china, furniture, lighting
Open Mon–Sat 9.30am–5.30pm

The Globe Antiques & Art Centre
Contact A J Littler
165 High Street, Honiton, Devon, EX14 1LQ
01404 549372 F 01404 41465
E theglobe@honitonantiques.com
W www.honitonantiques.com
Est. 2000 *Stock size* Large
No. of dealers 25
Stock Period furniture, Art Deco, silver, porcelain, glass, corkscrews, lamps, ephemera, collectables, bespoke furniture, Oriental rugs, clocks, barometers, jewellery, permanent art exhibition, pictures
Open Mon–Sat 10am–5pm
Services Restorations

The Grove Antique Centre
Contact Lesley Phillips
55 High Street, Honiton, Devon, EX14 1PW
01404 43377 F 01404 43390
M 07980 202976
E info@groveantiquescentre.com
W www.groveantiquescentre.com
Est. 1998 *Stock size* Medium
Stock Bears, silver, porcelain, 18th–20thC furniture,

collectables, paintings, clocks, barometers, rugs, decorative items
Open Mon–Sat 10am–5pm Sun 11am–4pm
Services Shipping deliveries

⊞ Hermitage Antiques
Contact Christian Giltsoff
✉ **37 High Street, Honiton, Devon, EX14 8PW** Ⓟ
☎ 01404 44406 Ⓕ 01404 42471
Ⓜ 07768 960144
Ⓔ antiquesmerchant@ndirect.co
Est. 1980 *Stock size* Large
Stock General antiques, furniture
Open Mon–Sat 10am–5pm
Services Valuations, buying and selling

⊞ High Street Books (PBFA)
Contact Geoff Tyson
✉ **150 High Street, Honiton, Devon, EX14 8JX** Ⓟ
☎ 01404 45570 Ⓕ 01404 45570
Ⓜ 07930 171380
Ⓔ shegeoff@ukonline.co.uk
Est. 1982 *Stock size* Medium
Stock Antiquarian, books, maps, prints
Open Mon–Sat 10am–5pm
Fairs PBFA
Services Valuations

⊞ The Honiton Lace Shop
Contact Jonathan Page
✉ **44 High Street, Honiton, Devon, EX14 1PJ** Ⓟ
☎ 01404 42416 Ⓕ 01404 47797
Ⓔ shop@honitonlace.com
Ⓦ www.honitonlace.com
Est. 1984 *Stock size* Large
Stock Antique lace, textiles, bobbins and lace-making equipment
Open Mon–Sat 9.30am–1pm 2–5pm
Services Restoration and cleaning of antique lace

⊞ Honiton Old Book Shop (PBFA, ABA)
Contact Roger Collicott
✉ **Felix House, 51 High Street, Honiton, Devon, EX14 1PW** Ⓟ
☎ 01404 47180
Est. 1978 *Stock size* Medium
Stock Antiquarian, rare and second-hand books, leather bindings, West Country antiquarian maps and prints. British topography, travel and natural history topics a speciality
Open Mon–Sat 10am–5.30pm
Fairs PBFA, Russell, ABA, Chelsea Town Hall, November Hilton, Olympia (June)
Services Valuations, 3 catalogues a year

⊞ Kings Arms Antiques Centre
Contact Mrs Heather Grabham
✉ **56 High Street, Honiton, Devon, EX14 1PQ** Ⓟ
☎ 01404 46269
Est. 1989 *Stock size* Large
Stock General antiques, early oak to reproduction furniture
Open Mon–Sat 10am–4.30pm half day Thurs or by appointment

⊞ Kingsway House Antiques
Contact Mrs M Peache
✉ **3 High Street, Honiton, Devon, EX14 8PR** Ⓟ
☎ 01404 46213
Est. 1981 *Stock size* Medium
Stock Georgian furniture, china, clocks
Open Mon–Sat 10am–5.30pm or by appointment

⊞ Maya Antiques
Contact Pauline Brown
✉ **46 High Street, Honiton, Devon, EX14 1PJ**
☎ 01404 46009
Est. 1997 *Stock size* Large
Stock Large Georgian–Edwardian furniture
Open Mon–Sat 10am–5pm
Services Restorations

⊞ Merchant House Antiques
Contact Christian Giltsoff
✉ **19 High Street, Honiton, Devon, EX14 1PR** Ⓟ
☎ 01404 42694 Ⓕ 01404 42471
Ⓔ antiquesmerchant@ndirect.co
Est. 1980 *Stock size* Large
Stock Fine furniture, general antiques and collectables
Open Mon–Sat 10am–5pm
Services Valuations and interior design

⊞ Otter Antiques
Contact Kate Skailes
✉ **69 High Street, Honiton, Devon, EX14 1PW**
☎ 01404 42627 Ⓕ 01404 43337
Ⓔ otterantiques@jspencer.co.
Ⓦ www.jspencer.co.uk
Est. 1979 *Stock size* Large
Stock Fine and antique silver, silver plate
Open Mon–Sat 9.30am–5pm Thurs 9.30am–1.30pm
Services Valuations, restorations, silver-plating, engraving

⊞ Alexander Paul Restorations
Contact Dave Steele
✉ **Fenny Bridges, Honiton, Devon, EX14 1PJ** Ⓟ
☎ 01404 850881 Ⓕ 01404 850881
Ⓔ alexanderpaulre@aol.com
Est. 2000 *Stock size* Medium
Stock French and English country furniture
Open Mon–Fri 9am–5.30pm Sat 10am–4pm
Services Restorations

⊞ Pilgrim Antiques (LAPADA)
Contact Mrs Mills
✉ **145 High Street, Honiton, Devon, EX14 1LJ** Ⓟ
☎ 01404 41219 Ⓕ 01404 45317
Est. 1971 *Stock size* Large
Stock 17th–18thC English and French oak and country furniture, longcase clocks
Open Mon–Sat 9am–5.30pm
Services Valuations, shipping

⊞ Plympton Antiques
Contact Mr Button-Stephens
✉ **59 High Street, Honiton, Devon, EX14 8PW** Ⓟ
☎ 01404 42640
Est. 1966 *Stock size* Medium
Stock Mostly mahogany furniture, copper, brass, porcelain
Open Mon–Sat 10am–4.30pm

⊞ Pughs Antiques
Contact Mr Guy Garner
✉ **Pughs Farm, Monkton, Honiton, Devon, EX14 9QH** Ⓟ
☎ 01404 42860 Ⓕ 01404 47792
Ⓔ sales@pughs-antiques-export.co.uk
Ⓦ www.pughs-antiques-export.co.uk
Est. 1986 *Stock size* Large
Stock Victorian–Edwardian furniture in mahogany, oak, walnut and pine, French furniture, antique beds
Trade only Mainly trade
Open Mon–Sat 9am–5.30pm
Services Export

Jane Strickland & Daughters (LAPADA)
Contact Jane Strickland
71 High Street, Honiton, Devon, EX14 1PW
01404 44221
JSandDaughtersUK@aol.com
Est. 1980 *Stock size* Medium
Stock 18th–19thC English and Continental furniture, upholstery, mirrors, lights, Aubussons, needlepoints
Open Mon–Sat 10am–5pm

Taylors
Contact Mr M J Taylor
Honiton Galleries, 205 High Street, Honiton, Devon, EX14 1LQ
01404 42404 01404 46510
taylorshoniton@compuserve.com
www.invaluable.co.uk/taylors
Est. 1949
Open Mon–Fri 9am–5pm
Sales Antiques and collectors' items bi-monthly Fri 10.30am, viewing Thurs 9am–7pm Fri 9–10.30am. Oil paintings, watercolours and prints Fri 11am, viewing Thurs 9am–5pm Fri 9–10.30am. Trade viewing by appointment. Digital photo of any lot sent by e-mail
Frequency 6 picture and 6 antiques sales
Catalogues Yes

Wickham Antiques
Contact Edwin Waymouth
191 High Street, Honiton, Devon, EX14 8LQ
01404 44654
Est. 1970
Stock Mainly 18th–19thC mahogany furniture
Open Mon–Sat 9am–6pm closed Thursday

Geoffrey M Woodhead
Contact Mr G Woodhead
Monkton House, 53 High Street, Honiton, Devon, EX14 1PW
01404 42969
Est. 1950 *Stock size* Large
Stock General antiques and books
Open Mon–Sat 9.30am–1pm 2.15–5pm
Fairs Westpoint, Shepton Mallet, Livestock Centre Matford Exeter

ILFRACOMBE

Relics
Contact Nicola Bradshaw
113 High Street, Ilfracombe, Devon, EX34 9ET
01271 865486
07967 892998
Est. 1980 *Stock size* Medium
Stock General antiques and collectables
Open Mon–Sat 10am–5pm

Sherbrook Antiques & Collectables
Contact Mr T Pickard
1 Borough Road, Combe Martin, Ilfracombe, Devon, EX34 0AN
01271 889060
07887 806493
Est. 2000 *Stock size* Medium
Stock General antiques, glass ceramics, small furniture
Open Mon–Sun 10am–5.30pm closed Wed
Fairs Westpoint, Exeter
Services Valuations

KINGSBRIDGE

Avon House Antiques
Contact Mrs Hayward
13 Church Street, Kingsbridge, Devon, TQ7 1BT
01548 853718
07977 451223
Est. 1969 *Stock size* Medium
Stock General antiques and collectables
Open Mon–Sat 10am–5pm half day Thurs Sat
Fairs Devon County Antiques Fairs
Services Valuations, restorations

Curiosity Shop
Contact Miss Williams
9 Church Street, Kingsbridge, Devon, TQ7 1BT
01548 857117/01548 853824
Est. 1997 *Stock size* Small
Stock Antiques, bric-a-brac
Open Mon–Fri 10am–5pm Sat 10am–1pm

Haywards Antiques & Avon House Antiques
Contact Mr D Hayward
13 Church Street, Kingsbridge, Devon, TQ7 1BT
01548 853718
07977 451223
www.haywardsantiques.fsbusiness.co.uk
Est. 1985 *Stock size* Large
Stock General antiques and collectables
Open Mon–Wed 10am–5pm Thurs Fri Sat 10am–1pm
Fairs Westpoint, Exeter
Services Valuations

Kingsbridge Collectors' Accessories in association with Salters Bookshelf
Contact Steve Salter
89 Fore Street, Kingsbridge, Devon, TQ7 1AB
01548 857503 01548 857503
Est. 1997 *Stock size* Medium
Stock Picture postcards, postal history, revenue stamps, postal stationery
Open Mon–Sat 9am–5.30pm Sun 10am–2.30pm in summer

LYNTON

Farthings (BSSA)
Contact Jane or Lucy Farthing
Church Hill House, Church Hill, Lynton, Devon, EX35 6HY
01598 753744 01598 753744
jane@farthings1.freeserve.co.uk
farthings.theshoppe.com
Est. 1984 *Stock size* Large
Stock Furniture, pictures, sporting accessories
Open Mon–Sun 10am–5pm
Services Search service, delivery

Wood's Antiques
Contact Mr or Mrs Wood
29a Lee Road, Lynton, Devon, EX35 6BS
01598 752722
Est. 1995 *Stock size* Medium
Stock Antiques, collectables, furniture, clocks
Open Mon–Sun 9am–6pm closed Thurs

MODBURY

Collectors Choice
Contact Allan Jenkins
27 Church Street, Modbury, Ivybridge, Devon, PL21 0QR
01548 831111
07884 365361
Est. 1994 *Stock size* Medium
Stock Small furniture, ceramics, Bakelite, radios, fountain pens, clocks, general antiques

Open Mon–Sat 10am–5.30pm closed Wed
Services Valuations, restorations of valve radios and clocks

NEWTON ABBOT

The Attic
Contact Mr Gillman
9 Union Street, Newton Abbot, Devon, TQ12 2JX
01626 355124
Est. 1976 *Stock size* Large
Stock General antiques and small furniture
Open Tues–Sat 9am–5.30pm closed Thurs

Bonstow and Crawshay Antiques
Contact Simon Crawshay
12a Torquay Road, Kingskerswell, Newton Abbot, Devon, TQ12 5EZ
01803 874291 F 01803 874291
Est. 1996 *Stock size* Medium
Stock Pre-1830 period English furniture, decorative items
Open Mon–Sat 10am–5pm closed Tues
Fairs Westpoint
Services Valuations, restorations

Michael J Bowman ARICS (ICA)
Contact Mr M Bowman
6 Haccombe House, Netherton, Newton Abbot, Devon, TQ12 4SJ
01626 872890 F 01626 872890
Est. 1986
Open By appointment
Sales 7 antiques and effects sales per annum Sat 2pm, viewing Fri 4.30–8.30pm. Held at Chudleigh Town Hall, also free valuations Mon 2–5pm at same venue
Frequency 7 per annum
Catalogues Yes

The Jolly Roger
Contact Mr Chris Sims
4 Western Units, Pottery Road, Newton Abbot, Devon, TQ13 9JJ
01626 835105 F 01626 835105
M 07860 680181
E jollyrog@eclipse.co.uk
W www.jollyroger.eclipse.co.uk
Est. 1994 *Stock size* Large
Stock General antiques and nautical antiques
Open Mon–Fri 9am–4pm Sat 9am–noon phone first
Fairs Newark
Services Valuations and restorations of nautical antiques

St Leonards Antiques and Craft Centre
Contact Mr Derick Wilson
St Leonards, Wolborough Street, Newton Abbot, Devon, TQ12 1JQ
01626 335666 F 01626 335666
M 07860 178969
Est. 1999 *Stock size* Large
Stock General antiques, furniture, jewellery
Open Mon–Sun 10am–4.30pm

Tobys (SALVO)
Contact Mr P Norrish
Brunel Road, Newton Abbot, Devon, TQ12 4PB
01626 351767 F 01626 336788
E paul@tobys-antiques.freeserve.co.uk
W www.tobysreclamation.co.uk
Est. 1985 *Stock size* Large
Stock General antiques, reclaimed material
Open Mon–Fri 9am–5pm Sat 9.30am–4.30pm
Fairs Exeter Ideal Home, Devon County Show
Services House clearance

NEWTON FERRERS

Bonhams & Brooks
Contact Michael Newman ARICS
Parsonage Road, Newton Ferrers, Plymouth, Devon, PL8 1AT
01752 872 150 F 01752 872 797
W www.bonhams.com
Sales Regional representative for Cornwall, Plymouth, see Bonhams West Country Office, Honiton for details

Toad Hall Medals (OMRS, MCCC)
Contact Mr Hitchings
Toad Hall, Court Road, Newton Ferrers, Plymouth, Devon, PL8 1DH
01752 872672 F 01752 872723
E chrissie@toadhallmedals.com
W www.toadhallmedals.com
Est. 1974 *Stock size* Large
Stock Collectors' replacement and veterans' medals
Open Mail order only
Fairs Britannia (London)
Services Valuations

OKEHAMPTON

Alan Jones Antiques
Contact Mr A Jones
Fatherford Farm, Okehampton, Devon, EX20 1QQ
01837 52970 F 01837 53404
M 07836 530819
Est. 1974 *Stock size* Large
Stock Furniture up to Edwardian period
Open Mon–Sat 8.30am–5.30pm or by appointment
Services Delivery can be arranged to most parts of the world

Tarka Antiques
Contact Henrietta Robertshaw
52 Red Lion Yard, Okehampton, Devon, EX20 1AW
01837 54222
Est. 1998 *Stock size* Large
Stock Traditional upholstery, porcelain, glass, lighting, furniture, Lloyd Loom, decorative items
Open Mon–Sat 10am–5pm closed Wed or by appointment
Fairs Westpoint
Services Upholstery

PAIGNTON

Hyde Road Antiques
Contact David Pentecost
23 Hyde Road, Paignton, Devon, TQ4 5BW
01803 554000
Est. 1992 *Stock size* Large
Stock General antiques and collectables
Open Mon–Sat 10am–5pm
Fairs Westpoint, Exeter Livestock
Services Valuations and ceramic repairs

The Pocket Bookshop
Contact Mr L Corrall
159 Winner Street, Paignton, Devon, TQ3 3BP
01803 529804
Est. 1985 *Stock size* Large
Stock Antiquarian, second-hand and out-of-print books
Open Summer Mon–Sat 10.30am–5.30pm winter Tues–Sat 10.30am–5.30pm

PLYMOUTH

Anita's Antiques
Contact Anita Walker
27 New Street, Plymouth, Devon, PL1 2NB
01752 269622
Est. 1984 *Stock size* Large
Stock Furniture, silver, china, jewellery, lighting, glass, clocks, barometers, general antiques
Open Mon–Sat 9am–5pm May–Sept Sun 11am–4pm

Annterior Antiques
Contact Anne Tregenza
22 Molesworth Road, Stoke, Plymouth, Devon, PL1 5LZ
01752 558277 01752 564471
07815 618659
sales@annterior.co.uk
Est. 1984 *Stock size* Medium
Stock 19th–early 20thC country furniture, stripped pine, small accessories
Open Mon–Fri 9.30am–5.30pm Sat 10am–5pm Closed Tues
Services Restorations and finding service

Antique Fireplace Centre
Contact Brian Taylor
30 Molesworth Road, Stoke, Plymouth, Devon, PL1 5NA
01752 559441 01752 605964
antique.fireplaces@2vu.com
www.2vu.com/antique.fireplaces
Est. 1989 *Stock size* Large
Stock 18th–20thC fireplaces, fire irons, spark guards, overmantels, fenders and coal helmets
Open Mon–Sat 10am–5pm
Services Installation, valuations for insurance

Barbican Antique Centre
Contact Tony Cremer-Price
82–84 Vauxhall Street, Plymouth, Devon, PL4 0EX
01752 201752 020 8546 1618
07836 291791
Est. 1971 *Stock size* Large
No. of dealers 60
Stock Silver, jewellery, porcelain, glass, pictures, furniture, collectables
Open Mon–Sat 9.30am–5pm

Eric Distin Auctioneers & Chartered Surveyors (RICS)
Contact Mr E Distin
72 Mutley Plain, Plymouth, Devon, PL4 6LF
01752 663046 01752 255371
Est. 1973
Sales Antiques and collectables Saturday 10.30am, viewing morning of sale or afternoon prior. Coins & stamps 2nd Monday monthly, viewing from 4pm
Frequency Fortnightly
Catalogues Yes

Grosvenor Chambers Restoration
Contact Robert Miller
180 Rendle Street, Plymouth, Devon, PL1 1UQ
01752 257544
robbie@grosvenor-restoration.co.uk
Est. 1989 *Stock size* Large
Stock General architectural antiques, pine furniture, lighting, etc
Open Mon–Sat 9am–5.30pm
Services Valuations, restorations, wood and metal stripping

Frederick Harrison
Contact Mr Harrison
43 Bridwell Road, Weston Mill, Plymouth, Devon, PL5 1AB
01752 365595
Est. 1974 *Stock size* Large
Stock Antiquarian, rare and second-hand books, particularly on diving, Dartmoor and local topography
Open By appointment
Services Valuations

New Street Antique and Craft Centre
Contact Mrs Cuthill
27 New Street, Barbican, Plymouth, Devon, PL1 2NB
01752 256265 01752 256265
Est. 1980 *Stock size* Large
No. of dealers 11
Stock General collectables, books, stamps, postcards, craft materials, locally made crafts
Open Mon–Sat Sun during holiday season 10am–5pm
Services Café

Parade Antiques
Contact Mr Cabello
17 The Parade, The Barbican, Plymouth, Devon, PL1 2JW
01752 221443
Est. 1992 *Stock size* Large
Stock General antiques, militaria
Open Mon–Sun 10am–5pm
Services Tea room

G S Shobrook and Co incorporating Fieldens (RICS)
Contact Roger Shobrook
20 Western Approach, Plymouth, Devon, PL1 1TG
01752 663341 01752 255157
Est. 1920
Open Mon–Fri 9am–5pm Sat 9am–11am
Sales Antiques and collectables sale Wed 1.30pm, viewing Tues 9am-5pm or by appointment. Weekly general household sale Wed 10am, viewing Tues 9am-5pm
Frequency Monthly
Catalogues Yes

Michael Wood Fine Art
Contact Alvin Tull
The Gallery, 1 Southside Ope, The Barbican, Plymouth, Devon, PL1 2LL
01752 225533 01752 225533
Est. 1967 *Stock size* Medium
Stock 1850–present day paintings watercolours, original prints, sculptures, art pottery, studio glass
Open Mon–Sat 10am–6pm
Fairs NEC, Battersea Contemporary Art Fair

Woodford Antiques & Collectables
Contact Mr Bill Humphries
17–18 New Street, The Barbican, Plymouth, Devon, PL1 2NA
01752 344562 01752 344562
07711 723006
Est. 1996 *Stock size* Medium
Stock Ceramics, kitchenware, general antiques and Torquay pottery
Open Mon–Sat 10am–4.30pm Sun noon–4.30pm
Fairs Westpoint, Devon Ceramic Fairs
Services Shipping

PLYMPTON

Eldreds Auctioneers and Valuers
Contact Anthony Eldred
13–15 Ridge Park Road, Plympton, Plymouth, Devon, PL7 2BS

☎ 01752 340066 Ⓕ 01752 341760
Ⓦ www.invaluable.com/eldreds
Est. 1992
Open Mon–Fri 9am–5pm
Sales Fortnightly 19th–20thC sales, 6–8 weekly antiques and specialist sales, phone for details
Frequency Fortnightly
Catalogues Yes

Plympton Reclamation and Architectural Salvage Ltd (SALVO)
Contact Ian Bryans or Glyn Thompson
✉ **Huxley Close, Newnham Industrial Estate, Plympton, Plymouth, Devon, PL7 4JN** Ⓟ
☎ 01752 336996 Ⓕ 01752 345736
Ⓔ plympton.reclamation@btinternet.com
Ⓦ www.ukreclamation.co.uk
Est. 1998 *Stock size* Large
Stock Architectural antiques including granite and slate flooring
Open Mon–Sat 9am–5pm Sun 10am–1pm
Services Cast-iron fireplace and door stripping, deliveries

SEATON

Carol's Curiosity Shop
Contact Mrs Spurgeon
✉ **4 Marine Crescent, Seaton, Devon, EX12 2QN** Ⓟ
☎ 01297 22039
Est. 1996 *Stock size* Large
No. of dealers 5
Stock General antiques, English ceramics, Oriental, lace, books
Open Mon–Sun 10am–6pm

Etcetera Etc Antiques
Contact Mrs Rymer
✉ **12 Beer Road, Seaton, Devon, EX12 2PA** Ⓟ
☎ 01297 21965
Ⓜ 07780 840507
Est. 1965 *Stock size* Large
Stock Furniture and small items
Open Mon–Sat 10am–1pm 2pm–5pm closed Thurs
Services Restorations, house clearances, shipping

SIDMOUTH

Gainsborough House Antiques
Contact Mr K Scratchley
✉ **Libra Court, Fore Street, Sidmouth, Devon, EX10 8AJ** Ⓟ
☎ 01395 514394
Ⓔ kscratchley@freenet.co.uk
Est. 1936 *Stock size* Medium
Stock Military specialists and general antiques
Open Mon–Sat 9am–5pm half days Thurs Sat
Services Valuations

The Old Curiosity Shop
Contact Mr or Mrs T Koch
✉ **Old Fore Street, Sidmouth, Devon, EX10 8LP** Ⓟ
☎ 01395 515299
Est. 1995 *Stock size* Large
Stock General collectables
Open Mon–Sun 9am–5.30pm
Services China restorations

Sidmouth Antiques Centre
Contact Mr R Hair
✉ **Devonshire House, All Saints Road, Sidmouth, Devon, EX10 8ES** Ⓟ
☎ 01395 512588
Ⓜ 07714 376918
Ⓦ www.sidmouthantiques.com
Est. 1994 *Stock size* Medium
No. of dealers 10
Stock General antiques, antiquarian books
Open Mon–Sat 10am–5pm summer Sun 2–5pm

SOUTH MOLTON

Antique Centre
Contact Bob Golding
✉ **14a Barnstaple Street, South Molton, Devon, EX36 3BQ** Ⓟ
☎ 01769 573401
Est. 1990 *Stock size* Large
No. of dealers 10
Stock General antiques, furniture, clocks, bric-a-brac
Open Tues–Sat 10am–5pm

Bonhams & Brooks
Contact John Sampson
✉ **PO Box 10, South Molton, Devon, EX36 4YY** Ⓟ
☎ 01769 550910 Ⓕ 01769 550910
Open Mon–Fri 9am–5pm
Sales Regional Representative for Devon

C R Boumphrey
Contact Mr Boumphrey
✉ **Finehay, Mariansleigh, South Molton, Devon, EX36 4LL** Ⓟ
☎ 01769 550419
Est. 1969
Stock 17th–18thC furniture
Open By appointment
Services Finds and orders stock

The Dragon
Contact Jenny Aker
✉ **80 South Street, South Molton, Devon, EX36 4AG** Ⓟ
☎ 01769 572374
Ⓜ 07712 079818
Ⓔ snapdragonantiques@hotmail.com
Ⓦ www.snapdragoncollectables-northdevon.co.uk
Est. 1998 *Stock size* Medium
Stock General antiques, furniture, books, collectables
Open Mon–Sat 9.30am–4.30pm

Snapdragon
Contact Jenny Aker
✉ **77 South Street, South Molton, Devon, EX36 3AG** Ⓟ
☎ 01769 572374
Ⓜ 07712 079818
Ⓔ snapdragonantiques@hotmail.com
Ⓦ www.snapdragoncollectables-northdevon.co.uk.
Est. 1998 *Stock size* Medium
Stock General antiques, pine furniture, books, farming bygones, kitchenware
Open Mon–Sat 9.30am–4.30pm

R M Young Bookseller
Contact Mr M Young
✉ **17 Broad Street, South Molton, Devon, EX36 3AQ** Ⓟ
☎ 01769 573350
Est. 1985 *Stock size* Large
Stock Antiquarian, second-hand, rare and out-of-print books. Countryside topics a speciality
Open Mon–Sat 10am–5pm
Services Book search, book binding

TAVISTOCK

Archways
Contact Mrs Diana Hunter
✉ **Court Gate, Bedford Square, Tavistock, Devon, PL19 0AE**
☎ 01822 612773
Est. 1989 *Stock size* Medium
Stock General antiques, small items, clocks
Open Tues–Sat 10am–4pm closed Thurs

⊞ Den of Antiquity
Contact Shelly Barlow
⊠ **7 Pixon Lane, Crelake Industrial Estate, Tavistock, Devon, PL19 8DH** Ⓟ
☎ 01822 610274
Ⓜ 07971 182381
Est. 1999 *Stock size* Large
Stock Georgian–Edwardian and French furniture
Open Mon–Sat 10am–5.30pm Sun 2–5pm

Robin A Fenner and Co
Contact Mr Fenner
⊠ **Stannary Gallery, Drake Road, Tavistock, Devon, PL19 0AX** Ⓟ
☎ 01822 617799 Ⓕ 01822 617595
Ⓜ 0771 287 4689
Ⓔ raf2536500@aol.com
Ⓦ www.invaluable.com/rafenner/
Est. 1968
Open Mon–Fri 9am–5pm
Sales 6 antiques, 2 vintage toys and models, 2 collectors', 1 antiquarian books and ephemera and 1 postcards and cigarette cards sale every year. All sales Mon 11am, viewing Fri–Sun noon–5pm. Phone for dates
Frequency Irregular
Catalogues Yes

⊞ J J Books and Antiques
Contact Mr J J Bassett
⊠ **11a Mount Tavy Road, Tavistock, Devon, PL19 9JB** Ⓟ
☎ 01822 617599
Est. 1990 *Stock size* Medium
Stock Antiquarian books and smalls
Open Mon–Sat 10am–6pm closed Tues half day Wed
Services Valuations, china and book restorations

⊞ Tavistock Books
Contact D or J Byass
⊠ **5 Pepper Street, Tavistock, Devon, PL19 0BD** Ⓟ
☎ 01822 616077
Ⓔ d.byass@clara.net
Est. 1990 *Stock size* Medium
Stock Antiquarian, second-hand and out-of-print books. History of ideas books a speciality
Open Tues–Sat 10am–5pm closed Wed
Services Valuations, book search

⊞ Tavistock Furniture Store
Contact Shelley Barlow
⊠ **7 Pixon Lane, Tavistock, Devon, PL19 9AZ** Ⓟ
☎ 01822 610274
Ⓔ doa@pixonlane.fsnet.co.uk
Est. 1999 *Stock size* Large
Stock English and French country furniture and decorative items
Open Mon–Sat 10am–5pm

Ward and Chowen Auction Rooms
Contact Mrs Pat Smith
⊠ **Market Road, Tavistock, Devon, PL19 0BW** Ⓟ
☎ 01822 612603 Ⓕ 01822 617311
Est. 1978
Open Mon–Fri 8.30am–4.30pm
Sales Antiques sale. Fortnightly general household sale Thurs 10am (no catalogue), viewing Wed 1–6pm
Frequency Quarterly
Catalogues Yes

TEIGNMOUTH

⊞ Leigh Extence Antique Clocks (BHI)
Contact Mr Leigh Extence
⊠ **49 Fore Street, Shaldon, Teignmouth, Devon, TQ14 0EA** Ⓟ
☎ 01626 872636 Ⓕ 01626 872636
Ⓜ 07967 802160
Ⓔ clocks@extence.co.uk
Ⓦ www.extence.co.uk
Est. 1981 *Stock size* Medium
Stock Clocks, barometers
Open Tues–Sat 10am–1pm 2.15–5pm closed Thurs
Services Valuations, restorations, clock research

⊞ Extence Antiques
Contact Mr T E or L E Extence
⊠ **2 Wellington Street, Teignmouth, Devon, TQ14 8HH** Ⓟ
☎ 01626 773353
Est. 1928 *Stock size* Large
Stock Jewellery, silver and objets d'art
Open Mon–Sat 10am–5pm
Services Valuations, repair and restoration of jewellery and silver

⊞ The Old Salty
Contact Kate Worden
⊠ **42 Northumberland Place, Teignmouth, Devon, TQ14 8DE**
☎ 01626 775754
Est. 1978 *Stock size* Medium
Stock Old and new nautical items, bygones, kitchenware, decorative items, collectable teddy bears
Open Tues–Sat 10am–4pm closed Thurs

⊞ Queens House Antiques
Contact Teresa Nicholls
⊠ **3 Waterloo Street, Teignmouth, Devon, TQ14 8AS** Ⓟ
☎ 01626 776675 Ⓕ 01626 774689
Est. 1976 *Stock size* Medium
Stock General antiques
Open Mon–Sat 10am–5pm
Fairs Westpoint, Livestock – Exeter
Services Valuations

⊞ Timepiece Antiques
Contact Clive or Willow Pople
⊠ **125 Bitton Park Road, Teignmouth, Devon, TQ14 9BZ** Ⓟ
☎ 01626 770275
Est. 1988 *Stock size* Medium
Stock Country, pine, mahogany and oak furniture, longcase clocks, brass, copper, metalware, gramophones, general antiques
Open Tues–Sat 9.30am–5.30pm

TIVERTON

⊞ Judith Christie
Contact Judith Christie
⊠ **42 Gold Street, Tiverton, Devon, EX16 6PX** Ⓟ
☎ 01884 258795
Ⓜ 07770 741885
Est. 1974 *Stock size* Medium
Stock General antiques,interiors and decorative arts
Open Tues Fri Sat 10.30am–5pm

TOPSHAM

⊞ Bizarre!
Contact Alexandra Fairweather
⊠ **The Quay Antiques Centre, The Quay, Topsham, Exeter, Devon, EX3 OJA** Ⓟ
☎ 01392 874006
Ⓔ office@antiquesattopshamquay.co.uk
Ⓦ www.antiquesattopshamquay.co.uk
Est. 1991 *Stock size* Large
Stock Vintage clothes, textiles and accessories
Open Mon–Sun 10am–5pm
Fairs Hammersmith Textile and Costume, Hyson Textile Fair

Bounty Antiques
Contact J Harding or J Purves
⊠ **76 Fore Street, Topsham, Devon, EX3 0HQ** Ⓟ

☎ 01395 266007
Ⓜ 07939 526504
Est. 1997 *Stock size* Large
No. of dealers 18
Stock General antiques, collectables, scientific instruments, maritime items
Open Mon–Sat 9.30am–5pm
Services Valuations

Charis
Contact Chris Evans
✉ **The Quay Antiques Centre, The Quay, Topsham, Exeter, Devon, EX3 OJA** 🅿
☎ 01392 874006
Ⓔ office@antiquesattopshamquay.co.uk
Ⓦ www.antiquesattopshamquay.co.uk
Est. 1993 *Stock size* Medium
Stock Old glass, crystal, china, jewellery
Open Mon–Sun 10am–5pm

Curzon Pictures
✉ **The Quay Antiques Centre, The Quay, Topsham, Exeter, Devon, EX3 OJA** 🅿
☎ 01392 874006
Ⓔ office@antiquesattopshamquay.co.uk
Ⓦ www.antiquesattopshamquay.co.uk
Est. 1993 *Stock size* Medium
Stock Prints, Louis Wain, Sir W Russell Flint
Open Mon–Sun 10am–5pm

Gudrun Doel
Contact Gudrun (Goody) Doel
✉ **The Quay Antiques Centre, The Quay, Topsham, Exeter, Devon, EX3 OJA** 🅿
☎ 01392 874006
Ⓔ office@antiquesattopshamquay.co.uk
Ⓦ www.antiquesattopshamquay.co.uk
Est. 1993 *Stock size* Medium
Stock Decorative items, porcelain, glass, pictures, silver, textiles
Open Mon–Sun 10am–5pm
Fairs Livestock Centre, Exeter

Farthings
✉ **The Quay Antiques Centre, The Quay, Topsham, Exeter, Devon, EX3 OJA** 🅿
☎ 01392 874006
Ⓔ office@antiquesattopshamquay.co.uk
Ⓦ www.antiquesattopshamquay.co.uk
Est. 1993 *Stock size* Medium
Stock Ceramics, commemorative china
Open Mon–Sun 10am–5pm

Rob Gee
Contact Rob Gee
✉ **The Quay Antiques Centre, The Quay, Topsham, Exeter, Devon, EX3 OJA** 🅿
☎ 01392 874006
Ⓔ office@antiquesattopshamquay.co.uk
Ⓦ www.antiquesattopshamquay.co.uk
Est. 1993
Stock Pot lids, Pratt ware, chemist items, steam and toy locomotives
Open Mon–Sun 10am–5pm

Nicky Gowing
Contact Nicky Gowing
✉ **The Quay Antiques Centre, The Quay, Topsham, Exeter, Devon, EX3 OJA** 🅿
☎ 01392 874006
Ⓔ office@antiquesattopshamquay.co.uk
Ⓦ www.antiquesattopshamquay.co.uk
Est. 1993 *Stock size* Medium
Stock Decorative china, character jugs, Toby jugs
Open Mon–Sun 10am–5pm

Sheila Hyson
Contact Sheila Hyson
✉ **The Quay Antiques Centre, The Quay, Topsham, Exeter, Devon, EX3 OJA** 🅿
☎ 01392 874006
Ⓜ 07798 808701
Ⓔ shyson@freenetname.co.uk
Ⓦ www.antiquesattopshamquay.co.uk
Est. 1993 *Stock size* Large
Stock Kitchenware
Open Mon–Sun 10am–5pm
Fairs Hyson Fairs, Deco '50s and '60s Fair, Exmouth Fair

Robin Jeffreys
Contact Robin Jeffreys
✉ **The Quay Antiques Centre, The Quay, Topsham, Exeter, Devon, EX3 OJA** 🅿
☎ 01392 874006
Ⓔ office@antiquesattopshamquay.co.uk
Ⓦ www.antiquesattopshamquay.co.uk
Est. 1966 *Stock size* Large
Stock Ceramics and Oriental ware
Open Mon–Sun 10am–4pm
Fairs Hyson Pottery and Glass Fair, Chafford Antiques and Collectors Fair

Bart and Julie Lemmy
Contact Bart and Julie Lemmy
✉ **The Quay Antiques Centre, The Quay, Topsham, Exeter, Devon, EX3 OJA** 🅿
☎ 01392 874006
Ⓜ 07809 172468
Ⓔ rosettibrides@btinternet.com
Ⓦ www.antiquesattopshamquay.co.uk
Est. 1993
Stock Royal Doulton figurines
Open Mon–Sun 10am–5pm
Services Shipping furniture

Betty Lovell
Contact Betty Lovell
✉ **The Quay Antiques Centre, The Quay, Topsham, Exeter, Devon, EX3 OJA** 🅿
☎ 01392 874006
Ⓔ office@antiquesattopshamquay.co.uk
Ⓦ www.antiquesattopshamquay.co.uk
Est. 1993 *Stock size* Medium
Stock Linen and lace
Open Mon–Sun 10am–5pm
Fairs Hysons Textile Fair

D Lovell
Contact D Lovell
✉ **The Quay Antiques Centre, The Quay, Topsham, Exeter, Devon, EX3 OJA** 🅿
☎ 01392 874006
Ⓔ office@antiquesattopshamquay.co.uk
Ⓦ www.antiquesattopshamquay.co.uk
Est. 1986 *Stock size* Medium
Stock Silver and silver plate
Open Mon–Sun 10am–5pm

Mere Antiques (LAPADA)
Contact Mrs M Hawkins or Mrs M Reed
✉ **13 Fore Street, Topsham, Exeter, Devon, EX3 OHF** 🅿
☎ 01392 874224 Ⓕ 01392 874224
Ⓜ 07957 867751
Ⓔ mad@mereantiques.co.uk
Ⓦ www.mereantiques.co.uk
Est. 1986 *Stock size* Medium
Stock 18th–19thC porcelain, Japanese Satsuma ware, small period furniture
Open Mon–Sat 10am–5.30pm
Fairs NEC (LAPADA and Antiques for Everyone)
Services Appraisals, deliveries

Number 38
Contact Stuart Westaway
✉ **The Quay Antiques Centre, The Quay, Topsham, Exeter, Devon, EX3 OJA** 🅿
☎ 01392 874006
Ⓔ office@antiquesattopshamquay.co.uk
Ⓦ www.antiquesattopshamquay.co.uk
Est. 1993 *Stock size* Medium
Stock Restored period lighting
Open Mon–Sun 10am–5pm
Services Restorations

Old Tools Feel Better!
Contact Barry Cook
The Quay Antiques Centre, The Quay, Topsham, Exeter, Devon, EX3 OJA
01392 874006 01392 874006
07799 054565
office@antiquesattopshamquay.co.uk
www.antiquesattopshamquay.co.uk
Est. 1993 *Stock size* Large
Stock Antique and collectable quality used tools
Open Mon–Sun 10am–5pm

Pennies
Contact Mrs Clark
40 Fore Street, Topsham, Exeter, Devon, EX3 0HU
01392 877020
www.penniesantiques.co.uk
Est. 1979 *Stock size* Medium
Stock General antiques
Open Mon–Sat 10am–5pm

The Quay Centre
Contact Beverley Cook
The Quay, Topsham, Exeter, Devon, EX3 OJA
01392 874006
office@antiquesattopshamquay.co.uk
www.antiquesattopshamquay.co.uk
Est. 1993 *Stock size* Large
No. of dealers 80
Stock Furniture, collectables, ephemera, Exeter silver, Torquay ware, studio pottery, jewellery, tools, period lighting, textiles
Open Mon–Sun 10am–5pm
Services Cards accepted, online buying, shipping advice

Joel Segal Books
Contact Mrs Neal
27 Fore Street, Topsham, Exeter, Devon, EX3 0HD
01392 877895
Est. 1993 *Stock size* Large
Stock Antique, rare and second-hand books
Open Mon–Sat 10.30am–5pm

Traditional Telephones
Contact Gary Richardson
The Quay Antiques Centre, The Quay, Topsham, Exeter, Devon, EX3 OJA
01752 845188
www.traditionaltelephones.co.uk
Est. 1993 *Stock size* Medium
Stock Restored and vintage telephones, converted and working
Open Mon–Sun 10am–5pm

The Venerable Bead
Contact Daphne King
The Quay Antiques Centre, The Quay, Topsham, Exeter, Devon, EX3 OJA
01392 874006
07787 561681
office@antiquesattopshamquay.co.uk
www.antiquesattopshamquay.co.uk
Est. 1993 *Stock size* Large
Stock Costume jewellery
Open Mon–Sun 10am–4pm
Fairs Westpoint, Shepton Mallett

S Vye
Contact S Vye
The Quay Antiques Centre, The Quay, Topsham, Exeter, Devon, EX3 OJA
01392 874006
s.vye@virgin.net
www.antiquesattopshamquay.co.uk
Est. 1993 *Stock size* Medium
Stock Furniture, ceramics, paintings, samplers
Open Mon–Sun 10am–5pm

Yesteryears
Contact Paul Gowing
The Quay Antiques Centre, The Quay, Topsham, Exeter, Devon, EX3 OJA
01392 874006
07813 569391
www.antiquesattopshamquay.co.uk
Est. 1993 *Stock size* Medium
Stock Furniture, including compactums, wardrobes, dressing tables
Open Mon–Sun 10am–5pm

TORQUAY

The Old Cop Shop
Contact Mr L Rolfe
Castle Lane, Torquay, Devon, TQ1 3AN
01803 294484 01803 316620
Est. 1974 *Stock size* Large
Stock General antiques
Open Mon–Sat 9am–5pm
Services Valuations

Tobys (SALVO)
Contact Mr P Norrish
Torre Station, Newton Road, Torquay, Devon, TQ2 2DD
01803 212222 01803 200523
paul@tobys-antiques.freeserve.co.uk
www.tobysreclamation.co.uk
Est. 1985 *Stock size* Large
Stock General antiques, furniture, architectural antiques, gifts
Open Mon–Fri 9am–5pm Sat 9.30am–4.30pm Sun and Bank Holidays 10.30am–4.30pm
Fairs Exeter Ideal Home, Devon County Show
Services House clearance, nationwide delivery

Upstairs Downstairs
Contact Ms Linda Nicholls
53 Fore Street, St Marychurch, Torquay, Devon, TQ1 4PR
01803 313010
Est. 1997 *Stock size* Large
Stock Antique and modern jewellery, glass, rocking horses, paintings, china, furniture
Open Mon–Sat 9am–5pm
Services Valuations

West Country Old Books (PBFA)
Contact Mr D Neil
22 Perinville Road, Torquay, Devon, TQ1 3NZ
01803 322712
Est. 1989 *Stock size* Small
Stock Antiquarian and good quality second-hand books. Specializing in topography, and literature
Open By appointment only
Fairs PBFA
Services Valuations and books bought

West of England Auctions
Contact Mr Warren Hunt
3 Warren Road, Torquay, Devon, TQ2 5TQ
01803 211266 01803 212286
Est. 1949
Open Mon–Fri 9am–1pm 2pm–5pm
Sales Sales of antiques, silver, jewellery Mon 11am. Viewing Sat 9am–noon Sun 1–5pm Mon 9–11am prior to sale
Frequency Fortnightly
Catalogues yes

TORRINGTON

C Short
Contact Mr C Short
12 Potacne, Torrington, Devon, EX38 8BH

☎ 01805 624796
Est. 1984 *Stock size* Large
Stock Furniture
Open Mon Tues Thurs Fri 10am–4pm Sat Wed 10am–1pm

TOTNES

Bogan House Antiques
Contact Mr M Mitchell
43 High Street, Totnes, Devon, TQ9 5NP
☎ 01803 862075
Ⓜ 07974 808005
Est. 1989 *Stock size* Large
Stock Silver, wood, brass, glass, Japanese woodblock prints
Open Tues noon–4.30pm Fri 10am–4.30pm Sat 10.30am–4.30pm

The Exchange
Contact John Caley
76 High Street, Totnes, Devon, TQ9 5SN
☎ 01803 866836
Est. 1996 *Stock size* Large
No. of dealers 7
Stock Books, printed ephemera, tools, brass, African things, china, stamps, toys, records, musical instruments and postcards
Open Mon–Sat 10am–5pm summer 10am–5.30pm
Services Valuations, restorations to instruments

Fine Pine
Contact Nick or Linda Gildersleve
Woodland Road, Harbertonford, Totnes, Devon, TQ9 7SU
☎ 01803 732465 Ⓕ 01803 732771
Ⓔ finepine@freeuk.com
Est. 1973 *Stock size* Medium
Stock Pine and country antiques
Open Mon–Sat 9.30am–5pm Sun 11am–4pm
Services Valuations, restorations and stripping

Pandora's Box
Contact Sarah Mimpriss
5b High Street, Totnes, Devon, TQ9 5NN
☎ 01803 867799
Ⓜ 07747 772527
Est. 1999 *Stock size* Small
Stock Georgian–Edwardian furniture, mirrors, china, collectables
Open Tues Thurs Fri Sat 10.30am–4pm

Past and Present James Sturges Antiques
Contact Mr J Sturges
94 High Street, The Narrows, Totnes, Devon, TQ9 5SN
☎ 01803 866086 Ⓕ 01803 866086
Est. 1980 *Stock size* Small
Stock Georgian–early 20thC furniture and small items
Open Mon–Sat 10am–5pm closed Thurs

Pedlar's Pack Books (PBFA)
Contact Peter or Angela Elliott
4 The Plains, Totnes, Devon, TQ9 5DR
☎ 01803 866423
Ⓔ pedlar@aol.com
Est. 1983 *Stock size* Medium
Stock Antiquarian, second-hand, rare and modern books. Art and history books a speciality
Open Mon–Sat 9am–5pm summer Sun 10am–4pm
Fairs Local PBFA, also others (phone for details)
Services Valuations, book binding, book search

Rotherfold Antiqeus
Contact Miss Myra Van Heck
2 Rotherfold, Totnes, Devon, TQ9 5ST
☎ 01803 840303
Ⓔ rotherfoldantiques@yahoo.co.uk
Est. 1999 *Stock size* Large
Stock Interesting antiques, ceramics, pictures, rugs, furniture, lights, objets d'art, fabrics, etc
Open Mon–Sat 10am–5pm half day Thurs

TYTHERLEIGH

The Trading Post Antique Centre
Contact Mr Remfry
Main Road, Tytherleigh, Axminster, Devon, EX13 7BE
☎ 01460 221330 Ⓕ 01460 57005
Ⓜ 07971 863192
Est. 1987 *Stock size* Large
No. of dealers 30
Stock General antiques, furniture, collectables, etc
Open Summer Mon–Sat 10am–5pm Sun 10am–4pm Winter Mon–Sat 10am–4.30pm
Services Valuations, restorations, clock repairs

DORSET

BEAMINSTER

Good Hope Antiques
Contact Mr D R Beney
2 Hogshill Street, Beaminster, Dorset, DT8 3AE
☎ 01308 862119
Est. 1979 *Stock size* Medium
Stock Longcase, bracket and wall clocks, period furniture, barometers
Open Mon–Sat 10am–4.30pm closed Wed
Services Restorations of clocks and barometers

BERE REGIS

Dorset Reclamation (SALVO)
Contact David Kirk or Steven Haycock
Cow Drove, Bere Regis, Wareham, Dorset, BH20 7JZ
☎ 01929 472200 Ⓕ 01929 472292
Ⓔ info@dorsetrec.u-net.com
Ⓦ www.dorset-reclamation.co.uk
Est. 1992 *Stock size* Large
Stock Decorative architectural and garden antiques including flagstones, flooring, bathrooms, fittings, radiators, chimney pieces, traditional building materials
Open Mon–Fri 8am–5pm Sat 9am–4pm
Services Delivery

Legg of Dorchester
Contact Mrs H Legg
The Old Mill, West Street, Bere Regis, Wareham, Dorset, BH20 7HS
☎ 01305 264964
Est. 1930 *Stock size* Large
Stock General, mostly furniture
Open Mon–Sat 9.30am–5.30pm

BLANDFORD FORUM

Antiques for All
Higher Shaftesbury Road, Blandford Forum, Dorset, DT11 7TA
☎ 01258 458011 Ⓕ 01258 458022
Est. 1997 *Stock size* Large
No. of dealers 100+
Stock Antique furniture, lighting, collectables
Open Mon–Sat 9.30am–5pm Sun 10.30am–5pm

⊞ Milton Antiques & Restoration
Contact Nigel Church
✉ **Bere's Yard, Market Place, Blandford Forum, Dorset, DT11 7HV** P
☎ 01258 450100
Est. 1989 *Stock size* Medium
Stock Period furniture
Open Mon–Sat 9am–5pm
Services Restorations

Robert A Warry Auctioneer (FNAVA)
Contact Mr R Warry
✉ **1a Alfred Street, Blandford Forum, Dorset, DT11 7JJ** P
☎ 01258 452454 F 01258 452454
E auctioneers@rwarry.freeserve.co.uk
W www.rwarry.freeserve.co.uk
Est. 1956
Open Mon–Fri 9am–5pm
Sales Antiques and collectable sale every three weeks, sale Fri 10am, viewing Wed 2–5pm, Thurs 9.30am–7.30pm and morning of sale
Frequency Every 3 weeks
Catalogues Yes

BOURNEMOUTH

⊞ Abbey Models
Contact Nick Powner
✉ **42 Littledown Drive, Littledown, Bournemouth, Dorset, BH7 7AQ** P
☎ 01202 395999 F 01202 395999
E npowner@bournemouth.demon.co.uk
W www.the-internet-agency.com/abbeymodels
Est. 1992 *Stock size* Large
Stock Old toys, Dinky, Corgi, Matchbox
Open By appointment
Fairs Sandown Park, NEC–toys
Services Valuations, mail order catalogues available

⊞ The Antiques Exchange
Contact Ray Gibbs
✉ **877 Christchurch Road, Boscombe, Bournemouth, Dorset, BH7 6AT** P
☎ 01202 433456
E info@antiquesexchange.com
W www.antiquesexchange.com
Est. 1966 *Stock size* Large
Stock Furniture, glass, china, collectables, reproduction Tiffany lamps
Open Mon–Fri 10am–6pm
Sat Sun 10.30am–5pm
Services Exchange deal for trade

⊞ Arcade Antiques
Contact Mr R Samuel
✉ **6 Westbourne Arcade, Westbourne, Bournemouth, Dorset, BH4 9AY** P
☎ 01202 764800 F 01202 769537
Est. 1990 *Stock size* Medium
Stock General antiques, Poole pottery
Open Mon–Sat 10am–4.30pm
Wed 10am–2pm

⊞ Books & Maps
Contact Mr R J Browne
✉ **1–3 Jewelbox Buildings, Cardigan Road, Winton, Bournemouth, Dorset, BH9 1BB** P
☎ 01202 521373 F 01202 529403
E sales@booksandmaps.freeserve.co.uk
W www.booksandmaps.freeserve.co.uk
Est. 1984 *Stock size* Large
Stock Antiquarian, rare, second-hand books, maps. Books on Africa and dogs a speciality
Open Mon–Sat 9am–5.30pm
Fairs Russell Hotel
Services Valuations

⊞ Boscombe Militaria
Contact Mr E A Browne
✉ **86 Palmerston Road, Bournemouth, Dorset, BH1 4HU** P
☎ 01202 304250 F 01202 733696
Est. 1982 *Stock size* Medium
Stock 20thC militaria, uniforms, medals, badges
Open Mon–Sat 10am–1pm 2–5pm closed Wed
Fairs Farnham, Aldershot

⊞ Chorley–Burdett Antiques
Contact Ray Burdett
✉ **828 Christchurch Road, Bournemouth, Dorset, BH7 6DF** P
☎ 01202 423363 F 01202 423363
Est. 1992 *Stock size* Medium
Stock Victorian–Edwardian furniture, oak, mahogany, new and reclaimed pine
Open Mon–Sat 9am–5.30pm

Dalkeith Auctions Bournemouth
Contact Mr P Howard
✉ **Dalkeith Hall, Dalkeith Steps, rear of 81 Old Christchurch Road, Bournemouth, Dorset, BH1 1YL** P
☎ 01202 292905 F 01202 292931
E how@dalkeith-auctions.co.uk
W www.dalkeith-auctions.co.uk
Est. 1992
Open Mon–Sat 9am–3pm
Sales Collectors' sales of ephemera and other collectors' items 1st Sat of month 11am, viewing week before 9am–3pm
Frequency Monthly
Catalogues Yes

The Emporium Antiques Centre
Contact Rebecca Hood
✉ **908 Christchurch Road, Boscombe, Bournemouth, Dorset, BH7 6DL** P
☎ 01202 422380 F 01202 433348
Est. 1996 *Stock size* Large
No. of dealers 10
Stock General antiques, decorative arts
Open Mon–Sat 9.30am–5.30pm
Services Tea shop

⊞ Lionel Geneen Ltd (LAPADA)
Contact Mr Robert Geneen
✉ **811 Christchurch Road, Boscombe, Bournemouth, Dorset, BH7 6AP** P
☎ 01202 422961/520417
F 01202 422961
M 07770 596781
Est. 1902 *Stock size* Medium
Stock 19thC English, Continental, Oriental furniture, porcelain, bronzes, glass. Ornamental decorative pieces, dessert services, tea and dinner services
Open Mon–Fri 9am–1pm 2–5pm Sat 9am–noon other times by appointment
Services Valuations

⊞ Hardy's Collectables
Contact Mr J Hardy
✉ **862 Christchurch Road, Boscombe, Bournemouth, Dorset, BH7 6DQ** P
☎ 01202 422407
M 07970 056858/613077
Est. 1987 *Stock size* Large
Stock 20thC collectables, mainly smalls, toys, metalware, ceramics
Open Mon–Sat 10am–5pm
Fairs Alexandra Palace, Kempton

Holloway's Antiques
Contact Mr M C Holloway
731 Christchurch Road, Bournemouth, Dorset, BH7 6AQ P
01202 300330
Est. 1998 *Stock size* Large
Stock Victorian–Edwardian furniture, imports from the Far East
Open Mon–Sat 10am–5pm

Kebo Antiques Market
Contact Mr K Lawrence
823a Christchurch Road, Bournemouth, Dorset, BH7 6AP P
01202 417052
Est. 1989 *Stock size* Small
No. of dealers 5
Stock General antiques
Open Mon–Sat 10am–5pm
Services Valuations

Manor Antiques
Contact D R or T W Vendy
739 Christchurch Road, Bournemouth, Dorset, BH7 6AN P
01202 392779
Est. 1969 *Stock size* Large
Stock General antiques, furniture, silver, porcelain
Open Mon–Sat 10am–1pm 2–5pm

Norman D Landing Militaria
Contact Mr Kenneth Lewis
76 Alma Road, Winton, Bournemouth, Dorset, BH9 1AN P
01202 521944 F 01202 521944
M 07711 790044
E kenneth@44doughboy.fsnet.co.uk
W www.norman-d-landing.com
Est. 1995 *Stock size* Large
Stock US uniforms and equipment (1900–1945)
Open Thurs–Sat 10am–5pm, Mon–Wed by appointment
Fairs Stoneleigh, Warwicks (Jan), Beltring, Kent (July)
Services Valuations, mail order, hires to film and TV

Not Just Antiques
Contact Simon or Bryn Davies
Northbourne House, 1262 Wimborne Road, Bournemouth, Dorset, BH10 7AQ P
01202 572315
M 07970 376817
Est. 2000 *Stock size* Medium
Stock A varied selection of English and French furniture, collectables, garden and decorative items
Open Mon–Sat 9.30am–5.30pm Sun 10.30am–4pm
Services Upholstery

Pokesdown Antique Centre
Contact Mr C Lane
848 Christchurch Road, Boscombe, Bournemouth, Dorset, BH7 6AP P
01202 433263
Est. 1989 *Stock size* Large
No. of dealers 10
Stock Decorative antiques, wristwatches, lighting, pine, Georgian–modern collectables, paintings
Open Mon–Sat 9am–5.30pm
Services Valuations, delivery, wristwatch repairs

Portabellows
Contact Mrs V A McKnight
819 Christchurch Road, Boscombe, Bournemouth, Dorset, BH7 6AP P
01202 432928
Stock General, mainly furniture
Open Mon–Sat 10am–4.30pm closed Wed

Rawlinsons
Contact Mr M Rawlinson
884 Christchurch Road, Bournemouth, Dorset, BH7 6DJ P
01202 433394
Est. 1983 *Stock size* Large
Stock General, smalls, furniture, glass, china, metalware, clocks, Art Deco
Open Mon–Sat 10am–5.30pm

Recollections
Contact Mrs B Francis
5 Royal Arcade, Boscombe, Bournemouth, Dorset, BH1 4BT P
01202 304441
E recollections@cwcom.net
W www.recollections.mcmail.com
Est. 1994 *Stock size* Large
Stock Collectables, china, Poole pottery, commemoratives, Beatrix Potter figures, Art Deco
Open Mon Thurs–Sat last Sunday every month 9.30am–5pm

Riddetts of Bournemouth
Contact Keith Harris
177 Holdenhurst Road, Bournemouth, Dorset, BH8 8DQ P
01202 555686 F 01202 311004
E auctions@riddetts.co.uk
Est. 1879
Open Mon–Fri 9am–5.30pm closed 1–2pm
Sales Sales usually Tues or Wed
Frequency Fortnightly
Catalogues Yes

H Rowan
Contact Mr H Rowan
459 Christchurch Road, Boscombe, Bournemouth, Dorset, BH1 4AD P
01202 398820
Est. 1968 *Stock size* Large
Stock Antiquarian books, second-hand books, maps, prints. Local interest, art and antiques topics a speciality
Open Mon–Sat 9.30am–5.30pm
Services Valuations

The Sage Door
Contact Philip Richards
920 Christchurch Road, Bournemouth, Dorset, BH7 6DL P
01202 434771
Est. 1975 *Stock size* Large
Stock Antique and decorative furniture, lighting, soft furnishings
Open Mon–Sat 10am–5pm
Services Interior design

Sainsburys of Bournemouth Ltd (LAPADA)
Contact Jonathan Sainsbury
23–25 Abbott Road, Bournemouth, Dorset, BH9 1EU P
01202 529271 F 01202 510028
E sales@sainsburys-antiques.com
Est. 1918 *Stock size* Large
Stock Antique furniture and accessories, replica chairs
Open By appointment
Services Furniture made from antique timbers

Sandy's Antiques
Contact Michael Sandy
790–792 Christchurch Road, Boscombe, Bournemouth, Dorset, BH7 6DD P

☎ 01202 301190 Ⓕ 01202 301190
Est. 1970 *Stock size* Large
Stock Edwardian, Victorian, shipping, furniture
Open Mon–Sat 10am–5.30pm

Smith & Sons
Contact Matthew Smith
903 Christchurch Road, Bournemouth, Dorset, BH7 6AX
☎ 01202 429523/01425 476705
Ⓔ enquiries@dsmithandsons.demon.co.uk
Ⓦ www.dsmithandsons.demon.co.uk
Est. 1968 *Stock size* Medium
Stock Country furniture and china
Open Mon–Sat 10am–5pm
Services Restorations

Southbourne Antiques
Contact Mr Guyatt
23 Southbourne Grove, Southbourne, Bournemouth, Dorset, BH6 3QS
☎ 01202 430313
Est. 2000 *Stock size* Medium
Stock Collectables, curios, lighting, records, jewellery
Open Mon–Sat 10am–5.30pm

Southern Stoves & Fireplaces
Contact Ms L Godfrey
797 Christchurch Road, Pokestown, Bournemouth, Dorset, BH7 6AW
☎ 01202 430050 Ⓕ 01202 430050
Ⓦ www.southernoriginalfireplaces.co.uk
Est. 1996 *Stock size* Small
Stock Architectural antiques, stoves, original cast-iron fireplaces
Open Mon–Sat 10am–6pm or by appointment
Services Valuations, restorations

Sterling Coins and Medals (OMRS)
Contact Mr V Henstridge
2 Somerset Road, Boscombe, Bournemouth, Dorset, BH7 6JH
☎ 01202 423881 Ⓕ 01202 423881
Ⓔ agagia@aol.com
Est. 1985 *Stock size* Medium
Stock Coins and medals
Open Mon–Sat 9am–3.30pm Wed 9am–12.15pm
Services Valuations and medal mounting

Victorian Chairman
Contact Mrs M Leo
883 Christchurch Road, Bournemouth, Dorset, BH7 6AU
☎ 01202 420996
Est. 1977 *Stock size* Medium
Stock Victorian tables and chairs, wrought iron, glass tables
Open Mon–Sat 10am–5pm
Services Upholstery restoration, French polishing

Volume One Books and Records (NMTA)
Contact Richard Cargill
1073 Christchurch Road, Boscombe East, Bournemouth, Dorset, BH7 6BE
☎ 01202 417652 Ⓕ 01202 483686
Est. 1989 *Stock size* Large
Stock Books, LP records, cassettes and CDs (classical, easy listening, jazz, stage and screen, country, rock and pop)
Open Mon Tues Fri 10am–5.30pm Wed 10am–1pm Sat 10am–2pm closed 3rd Sat in each month
Fairs Midhurst Monthly Market, Sussex; others – please phone
Services Record search and mail order

Wonderworld
Contact Mr David Hern
623 Christchurch Road, Boscombe, Bournemouth, Dorset, BH1 4BP
☎ 01202 394918 Ⓕ 01202 393613
Ⓔ davejh4000@aol.com
Ⓦ www.members.aol.com/davejh4000/ww.htm
Est. 1977 *Stock size* Large
Stock Modern collectables, *Star Wars*, comics, Beanie Babies
Open Mon–Sat 10am–6pm

Woodies Tools
Contact Mr Peter Woodford
856 Wimbourne Road, Moordown, Bournemouth, Dorset, BH9 2DS
☎ 01202 527596
Est. 1980 *Stock size* Large
Stock Antique and collectable tools, some modern
Open Mon–Sun 10am–4pm

Yesterdays Books (PBFA)
Contact David Weir
6 Cecil Avenue, Bournemouth, Dorset, BH8 9EH
☎ 01202 522442
Ⓔ david@yesterdaysbooks.demon.co.uk
Est. 1974 *Stock size* Medium
Stock Antiquarian books, African topics a speciality
Open By appointment
Fairs PBFA at London, Oxford and elsewhere, the London Travel Bookfair
Services Valuations, book search

BRIDPORT

The Auction House Bridport
Contact Michael Dark
38a St Michael Trading Estate, Bridport, Dorset, DT6 3RR
☎ 01308 459400 Ⓕ 01308 459685
Ⓜ 07768 298003
Ⓔ sales@theauctionhouse.dabsol.co.uk
Ⓦ www.theauctionhouse.dabsol.co.uk
Est. 1998
Open Mon–Fri 8am–5pm
Sales Antiques and modern sale last Fri each month 10am, viewing prior Wed Thurs 10am–6pm
Frequency Monthly
Catalogues Yes

P E L Bedford
Contact Patrick Bedford
81 East Street, Bridport, Dorset, DT6 3LB
☎ 01308 421370
Est. 1956 *Stock size* Large
Stock Oriental and general antiques, porcelain, paintings, jewellery
Open Variable telephone call advisable

Bridport Antique Centre
Contact Mr John Higgins
5 West Allington, Bridport, Dorset, DT6 5BJ
☎ 01308 425885
Est. 1970 *Stock size* Large
No. of dealers 6
Stock Collectables, general antiques, pine furniture
Open Mon–Sat 9.30am–5pm

Bridport Old Books (PBFA)
Contact Ms C MacTaggart
11 South Street, Bridport, Dorset, DT6 3NR
☎ 01308 425689
Est. 1998 *Stock size* Medium
Stock Antiquarian, second-hand,

children's illustrated, WWI, T E Lawrence, modern first edition books
Open Mon–Sat 10am–5pm
Services Valuations

⊞ Jack's
Contact Mrs Jini Emery
✉ **24 South Street, Bridport, Dorset, DT6 3NQ** P
☎ 01308 420700
Est. 1985 ***Stock size*** Medium
Stock Oriental rugs, pine furniture, antiques, collectables
Open Mon–Sat 9am–5pm
Services Restorations (rugs)

William Morey & Son
Contact Mr B J Newman
✉ **The Sale Room, St Michael's Lane, Bridport, Dorset, DT6 3RB** P
☎ 01308 422078 F 01308 422078
Est. 1870
Open Mon–Fri 9am–5pm
Sales Antiques sale Thurs 9.30am, viewing Wed 9am–4pm
Frequency Every 4 weeks
Catalogues Yes

CHRISTCHURCH

⊞ Ancient and Gothic (ADA)
Contact Mr C Belton
✉ **PO Box 356, Christchurch, Dorset, BH23 1XQ**
☎ 01202 431721
Est. 1977
Stock Prehistoric, ancient and medieval antiquities, mail order only
Open Mon–Sat 11am–7pm
Services Bi-monthly sales list

⊞ Antique Pine Stores
Contact Russell Davy
✉ **91 Bargates, Christchurch, Dorset, BH23 1QQ** P
☎ 01202 475515
W www.antiquepinestore.com
Est. 2001 ***Stock size*** Large
Stock Antique pine furniture from Eastern Europe
Open Mon–Sat 10am–4.30pm

⊞ Classic Pictures (Postcard Traders Association)
Contact Betty Underwood
✉ **12a Castle Street, Christchurch, Dorset, BH23 1DT** P
☎ 01202 470276
E classicpictures@talk21.com
Est. 1989 ***Stock size*** Large
Stock Old postcards, Edwardian pictures, prints
Open Tues–Sat 9.30am–5pm
Fairs New Forest Show, Bournemouth International Centre
Services Valuations

⊞ H L B Antiques
Contact Mr H L Blechman
✉ **139 Barrack Road, Christchurch, Dorset, BH23 2AW** P
☎ 01202 482388
Est. 1967 ***Stock size*** Medium
Stock General collectables, gramophones, postcards, walking sticks, Art Deco, ivory
Open Sat 10am–4pm or by appointment on 01202 429252
Fairs New Caledonian Market in Bermondsey
Services Valuations

⊞ Gerald Hampton
Contact Gerald Hampton
✉ **12 Purewell, Christchurch, Dorset, BH23 1EP** P
☎ 01202 484000
Est. 1930 ***Stock size*** Medium
Stock General antiques
Trade only Yes
Open By appointment

⊞ Past 'n' Present
Contact Pete Woodford
✉ **4 St Catherine's Parade, Fairmile Road, Christchurch, Dorset, BH23 2LQ** P
☎ 01202 478900
Est. 1997 ***Stock size*** Large
Stock Collectables
Open Mon–Sat 9.30am–5pm
Services Valuations, restorations

⊞ Tudor House Antiques (LAPADA)
Contact Mrs P Knight or Mrs D Burton
✉ **420 Lymington Road, Highcliffe, Christchurch, Dorset, BH23 5HE** P
☎ 01425 280440
Est. 1940 ***Stock size*** Medium
Stock General
Open Tues–Sat 10am–5pm closed Wed

CRANBORNE

⊞ Tower Antiques
Contact Mr P White
✉ **The Square, Cranbourne, Dorset, BH21 5PR** P
☎ 01725 517552
Est. 1973 ***Stock size*** Small
Stock Georgian, Victorian furniture
Open Mon–Sat 8.30am–5.30pm

DORCHESTER

⊞ Antique Map and Bookshop (PBFA, ABA)
Contact Mrs H M Proctor
✉ **32 High Street, Puddletown, Dorchester, Dorset, DT2 8RU** P
☎ 01305 848633 F 01305 848992
Est. 1976 ***Stock size*** Medium
Stock Antique maps, antiquarian, second-hand books
Open Mon–Sat 9am–5pm
Fairs Russell Hotel (June) – PBFA
Services Valuations, restorations, book catalogues (4–6 a year)

⊞ The Antiques Emporium
Contact Bruce Clarke-Williams
✉ **9 High East Street, Dorchester, Dorset, DT1 1HS** P
☎ 01305 261546
Est. 1997 ***Stock size*** Medium
Open Mon–Sat 9.30am–5.30pm

⊞ Box of Porcelain
Contact Robert Lunn
✉ **51d Icen Way, Dorchester, Dorset, DT1 1EW** P
☎ 01305 250856 F 01305 265517
M 07721 351761
E rlunn@btconnect.com
W www.boxofporcelain.com
Est. 1987 ***Stock size*** Large
Stock Doulton, Beswick, Royal Worcester, Spode
Open Mon–Sat 10.30am–5pm closed Thurs
Services Valuations

⊞ Chattels
✉ **Colliton Antique Centre, 3 Colliton Street, Dorchester, Dorset, DT1 1XH** P
☎ 01305 263620
Est. 1993 ***Stock size*** Large
Stock General, Victorian–Edwardian furniture
Open Mon–Sat 9am–5pm

Colliton Antique Centre
Contact Tony Phillips
3 Colliton Street, Dorchester, Dorset, DT1 1XH
01305 269398/260115
Est. 1983 *Stock size* Large
No. of dealers 6
Stock General antiques, Georgian–Edwardian furniture, jewellery, silver, old pine
Open Mon–Sat 9am–5pm Sun by appointment
Services Restorations of metalwork, silver and jewellery valuations

The Dorchester Bookshop
Contact Michael Edmonds
3 Nappers Court, Charles Street, Dorchester, Dorset, DT1 1EE
01305 269919
Est. 1993 *Stock size* Medium
Stock Second-hand and antiquarian books
Open Tues–Sat 10am–5pm
Fairs Local book fairs
Services Valuations, restorations and book search

Hy Duke & Son (SOFAA)
Contact Mr Guy Schwinge or Mr Gary Batt
The Dorchester Fine Art Salerooms, Weymouth Avenue, Dorchester, Dorset, DT1 1QS
01305 265080 F 01305 260101
M 07778 523962
Est. 1823
Open Mon–Fri some Sats 9am–1pm 2–5.30pm
Sales Specialist sales of paintings, furniture, ceramics, silver, jewellery and furniture, viewing week prior Sat 9.30am–noon Mon 9.30am–5pm Tues 9.30am–7pm Wed 9.30am–5pm morning of sale
Frequency 9 per annum
Catalogues Yes

Fordington Antiques
Contact Brian Dodington
60 Kings Road, Dorchester, Dorset, DT1 1NH
01305 251502
Est. 1999 *Stock size* Large
Stock Country furniture, tools, garden items, kitchenware
Open Mon–Sat 8am–6.30pm

Legg of Dorchester
Contact Mrs H Legg
Regency House, 51 High East Street, Dorchester, Dorset, DT1 1HU
01305 264964
Est. 1930 *Stock size* Large
Stock General, mostly furniture
Open Mon–Sat 9.30am–5.30pm

Santiques
Contact Tony Phillips
Collition Antique Centre, 3 Colliton Street, Dorchester, Dorset, DT1 1XH
01305 260115
Est. 1975 *Stock size* Medium
Stock Jewellery, silver, china, furniture
Open Mon–Sat 9am–5pm Sun by appointment
Services Restorations of metal and woodwork, silver and jewellery valuations

John Walker Antiques (BADA)
Contact Mr J Walker
52 High West Street, Dorchester, Dorset, DT1 1UT
01305 260324
M 07880 528436
Est. 1973 *Stock size* Medium
Stock Early oak, textiles, ceramics, metalwork
Open Tues–Sat 9.30am–5pm

GILLINGHAM

Talisman (LAPADA)
Contact Mr Ken Bolan
The Old Brewery, Wyke Road, Gillingham, Dorset, SP8 4NW
01747 824423 F 01747 823544
E arcadia@talisman-antiques.co.uk
W www.talisman-antiques.co.uk
Est. 1979 *Stock size* Large
Stock Antiques and garden statuary
Open Mon–Fri 9am–5pm Sat 10am–4pm
Fairs Summer Olympia

LYME REGIS

The Commemorative Man
Contact Mr Harris
Lyme Regis Antiques & Craft Centre, Marine Parade, Lyme Regis, Dorset, DT7 3JH
01297 32682
Est. 1994 *Stock size* Large
Stock Political and sporting commemoratives
Open April–Oct Mon–Sun 11am–6.30pm Nov–Mar Fri Sat Sun 11am–4.30pm
Services Mail order and search service

Patsy Lewis
Contact Mrs P Lewis
Lyme Regis Antiques & Craft Centre, Marine Parade, Lyme Regis, Dorset, DT7 3JH
01297 445053
Est. 1990 *Stock size* Medium
Stock Linen, tablecloths, sheets and pillowcases
Open Apr–Oct Mon–Sun 11am–6.30pm Nov–Mar Fri Sat Sun 11am–4.30pm

Lyme Regis Antiques & Craft Centre
Contact Mr C Willis
Marine Parade, Lyme Regis, Dorset, DT7 3JH
01297 445053
Est. 1995 *Stock size* Large
No. of dealers 35
Stock Commemoratives, stamps, coins, toys, linen, brass taps, Art Deco, lamps, lighting
Open Apr–Oct Mon–Sun 11am–6.30pm Nov–Mar Fri Sat Sun 11am–4.30pm

MAIDEN NEWTON

Dynasty Antiques
Contact Gareth Clarke-Williams
Newton Hall, Dorchester Road, Maiden Newton, Dorchester, Dorset, DT2 0BD
01300 321313
M 07966 256648
W www.dynastyantiques.co.uk
Est. 2000 *Stock size* Medium
Stock Chinese, Tibetan antique furniture
Open By appointment

MELBURY OSMOND

Hardy Country
Contact Mr S Groves
Meadow View, Drive End, Melbury Osmond, Dorchester, Dorset, DT2 0NA
01935 83440
M 07778 658581
Est. 1972 *Stock size* Large
Stock Old pine

Open Mon–Sat 9am–6pm
Sun by appointment
Services Valuations, restorations

POOLE

Bonhams & Brooks
Contact James Roberts
3 Parkstone Road, Poole, Dorset, BH15 2NN
01202 666662 F 01202 666663
bournemouth@bonhams.com
www.bonhams.com
Open Mon–Fri 9am–5pm
Sales Regional Representative for West Hampshire, Dorset, Southampton and Isle of Wight. See Head Office (London) for details

Castle Books
Contact Mr Clark
2 North Street, Poole, Dorset, BH15 1NX
01202 660295
Est. 1980 *Stock size* Medium
Stock Antiquarian, modern second-hand, collectable books
Open Mon–Sat 10am–5pm
Fairs London Book Fairs (June), HD promotions
Services Valuations

Davey & Davey (NAVA)
Contact Neil Davey
13 St Peters Road, Parkstone, Poole, Dorset, BH14 0NZ
01202 748567 F 01202 716258
Est. 1946
Open Mon–Fri 9am–1pm 2–5.30pm
Sales General antiques and collectables every 2 months, Tues 10am, viewing Mon 10am–4pm
Frequency Every 2 months
Catalogues Yes

Dorset Coin Company (BNTA, IBNS)
Contact Ernie Parsons
193 Ashley Road, Parkstone, Poole, Dorset, BH14 9DL
01202 739606 F 01202 739230
coinsdcc@freenetname.co.uk
www.dorsetcoincompany.co.uk
Est. 1974 *Stock size* Large
Stock Coins, medals, banknotes
Open Mon–Fri 9am–4pm
Fairs BNTA (London – October, Harrogate – April)
Services Valuations

Down To The Woods Ltd
Contact Vanessa Harris
92 The Dolphin Centre, Poole, Dorset, BH15 1SR
01202 669448
downttw@globalnet.co.uk
Est. 1998 *Stock size* Large
Stock Bears, soft toys, bean-bag collections, dolls' houses. Collectables rather than antiques
Open Mon–Sat 9.30am–5.30pm
Services Layaway, mail order

Fireplaces 'n' Things
Contact Mr D L Shackford
87–89 Alder Road, Parkstone, Poole, Dorset, BH12 2AB
01202 735301 F 01202 735301
Est. 1980 *Stock size* Large
Stock Antique and reproduction fireplaces
Open Mon–Sat 10am–5pm half day Wed
Services Valuations, restorations

Great Expectations
Contact Mr Carter
115 Penn Hill Avenue, Lower Parkstone, Poole, Dorset, BH14 9LY
01202 740645
Est. 2000 *Stock size* Medium
Stock General antiques, paintings, prints, objets d'art
Open Wed–Sat 10.30am–5pm

W A Howe
Contact Mr W A Howe
5 Merrow Avenue, Branksome, Poole, Dorset, BH12 1PY
01202 743350
M 01202 743350
Est. 1999 *Stock size* Small
Stock Antiquarian and second-hand books. Children's illustrated books a speciality. Modern first editions, cookery, golf
Open Mon–Sun 8am–8pm
Fairs Local book fairs
Services Valuations

Laburnum Antiques
Contact Mrs D Mills
Lonbourne House, 250 Bournemouth Road, Poole, Dorset, BH14 9HZ
01202 746222 F 01202 746222
enquiries@laburnumantiques.co.uk
www.laburnumantiques.co.uk
Est. 1997 *Stock size* Medium
Stock Georgian–Edwardian furniture, accessories, ottomans, stools and cushions
Open Tues–Sat 10am–5.30pm
Services Full upholstery service and fully qualified furniture restorations

Stocks and Chairs
Contact Mrs Carole Holding-Parsons
11 Bank Chambers, Penn Hill Avenue, Poole, Dorset, BH14 9NB
01202 718618
www.stocksandchairsantiques.com
Est. 1979 *Stock size* Large
Stock 18th–19thC furniture, some smalls
Open Mon–Sat 11am–5pm closed Wed
Services Restoration of hand-dyed leather

Stocks and Chairs
Contact Mrs Carole Holding-Parsons
The Old Church Hall, Hardy Road, Poole, Dorset, BH14 9HN
01202 718418 F 01202 718918
www.stocksandchairsantiques.com
Est. 1979 *Stock size* Large
Stock Antique leather chairs and settees
Open Mon–Fri 8.30am–5.30pm and by appointment
Services Restoration of hand-dyed leather

Christopher Williams (PBFA)
Contact Mr C Williams
19 Morrison Avenue, Poole, Dorset, BH12 4AD
01202 743157 F 01202 743157
cw4finebooks@lineone.net
www.abebooks.com/home/cw
Est. 1967 *Stock size* Small
Stock Antiquarian books and fine modern books. Lace-making, needlework, cookery, art, antiques, collecting and local history topics a speciality
Open By appointment. Trades mostly through fairs or postal order
Fairs PBFA fairs
Services Valuations

SEMLEY

Semley Auctioneers
Contact Mr Simon Pearce
Station Road, Semley, Shaftesbury, Dorset, SP7 9AN
01747 855122 F 01747 855222

Ⓔ simon.pearce@semleyauctioneers.com
Ⓦ www.semleyauctioneers.com
Est. 1990
Open Mon–Fri 9am–5pm
Sales Sat 10am, viewing Friday prior 9am–9pm and morning of sale. Items of higher quality appear in these sales about every 6 weeks
Frequency Fortnightly
Catalogues Yes

SHAFTESBURY

Chapman, Moore & Mugford
Contact Mr W Moore
✉ **9 High Street, Shaftesbury, Dorset, SP7 8JB** Ⓟ
☎ 01747 852400 Ⓕ 01747 853614
Ⓔ whsmoore@talk21.com
Est. 1970
Open Mon–Fri 9am–5.30pm
Sales Antiques and collectables every 6–8 weeks Fri 6pm. Musical instruments 2 per annum Fri 6pm, viewing Fri 10.30am–6pm for both
Catalogues Yes

Dairy House Antiques
Contact Isabel Moyes
✉ **Station Road, Semley, Shaftesbury, Dorset, SP7 9AN** Ⓟ
☎ 01747 853317
Est. 1998 *Stock size* Large
Stock 17th–19thC paintings, furniture, ceramics, textiles
Open Mon–Sat 9am–5pm

Mr Punch's Antique Market
Contact Mr C Jolliffe
✉ **33 Bell Street, Shaftesbury, Dorset, SP7 8AE** Ⓟ
☎ 01747 855775 Ⓕ 01747 855775
Est. 1994 *Stock size* Large
No. of dealers 20
Stock General, furniture, collectables, a Punch museum, militaria
Open Mon–Sat 10am–6pm
Services Valuations, restorations, pine stripping, house clearance

Shaston Antiques
Contact Mr J D Hine
✉ **16a Bell Street, Shaftesbury, Dorset, SP7 8AE**
☎ 01747 850405 Ⓕ 01747 850405
Est. 1996 *Stock size* Medium
Stock Georgian, Regency, Victorian quality furniture
Open Mon–Sat 9am–5pm
half day Wed
Services Restorations

SHERBORNE

Antiques of Sherborne (SAADA)
Contact Clive or Linda Greenslade
✉ **1 The Green, Sherborne, Dorset, DT9 3HZ** Ⓟ
☎ 01935 816549 Ⓕ 01935 816549
Ⓜ 07971 019173
Ⓔ clive@antiquesofsherborne.fsnet.co.uk
Est. 1988 *Stock size* Medium
Stock Furniture, town and country, Georgian–Edwardian, period soft upholstery, pottery, chess sets, games
Open Mon–Sat 10am–5pm
Fairs Shepton Mallet
Services Valuations, upholstery

Chapter House Books (PBFA, Booksellers Association)
Contact Mr or Mrs Hutchison
✉ **Trendle Street, Sherborne, Dorset, DT9 3NT**
☎ 01935 816262
Est. 1988 *Stock size* Large
Stock Antiquarian books (mostly hardback), out-of-print, paperbacks, pictures
Open Mon–Sat 10am–5pm
Services Valuations, book repair, book search

Arnold Dick Antiques
Contact Mr A Dick
✉ **17 Newland, Sherborne, Dorset, DT9 3JG** Ⓟ
☎ 01935 813464 Ⓕ 01935 813464
Est. 1984 *Stock size* Medium
Stock General, clocks
Open Mon–Sat 9.30am–5pm
Services Valuations

Geometrica (SAADA)
Contact Mr A Warne-Cleave
✉ **3 Westbury, Sherborne, Dorset, DT9 3EH** Ⓟ
☎ 01935 814392
Ⓜ 07974 055783
Ⓔ andrew.wc@virgin.net
Est. 1999 *Stock size* Medium
Stock Decorative Arts, 20thC ceramics, furniture, studio pottery
Open Fri–Sat 10am–4pm or by prior arrangement
Fairs Battersea, Mitcham and Brighton
Services Delivery

Greystoke Antiques
Contact Mr F Butcher
✉ **4 Swan Yard, Cheap Street, Sherborne, Dorset, DT9 3AX** Ⓟ
☎ 01935 812833
Est. 1974 *Stock size* Large
Stock Silver, Georgian and Victorian
Open Mon–Sat 10am–4.30pm closed Wed
Services Valuations, restorations

Keeble Antiques
Contact Mr C Keeble
✉ **2 Tilton Court, Digby Road, Sherborne, Dorset, DT9 3NL** Ⓟ
☎ 01935 816199 Ⓕ 01935 816199
Ⓔ clivekeeble@btconnect.com
Ⓦ www.keebleantbks.co.uk
Est. 1969 *Stock size* Medium
Stock Eclectic pieces, pictures, mirrors, clocks, boxes, antique and fine art books
Open Mon–Sat 8am–6pm
Sun 9.30am–5.30pm
Services Book search

The Nook Antiques (SAADA)
Contact Mrs Jill Morley
✉ **South Street, Sherborne, Dorset, DT9 3LX**
☎ 01935 813987
Est. 1969 *Stock size* Large
Stock Small, useful, refurbished furniture. China, glass, brass, copper and collectables.
Open Tues–Sat 10am–5pm

Phillips International Auctioneers and Valuers
✉ **3 Cheap Street, Sherborne, Dorset, DT9 3PT**
☎ 01935 815271 Ⓕ 01935 816416
Ⓦ www.phillips-auction.com
Sales Regional Saleroom. Ring for details

Phoenix Antiques (SAADA)
Contact Neil or Sally Brent Jones
✉ **21 Cheap Street, Sherborne, Dorset, DT9 3PU** Ⓟ
☎ 01935 812788
Est. 1982 *Stock size* Medium
Stock 18th–20thC English and Continental furniture. Mahogany, rosewood, painted

country furniture, furnishings and lighting
Open Mon–Sat 9.30am–5.30pm or by appointment

Piers Pisani Antiques (SAADA)
Contact Mr Piers Pisani
The Music House, The Green, Sherborne, Dorset, DT9 3HX
01935 815209 01935 815209
antiques@pierspisani.sagehost.co.uk
www.pierspisani.com
Est. 1987 ***Stock size*** Large
Stock English and French furniture, upholstery
Open Mon–Sat 10am–5pm
Services Valuations, restorations, furniture copy

Renaissance
Contact Malcolm Heygate-Browne
South Street, Sherborne, Dorset, DT9 3NG
01935 815487 01935 815487
Est. 1984 ***Stock size*** Large
Stock English 18th–19thC furniture, pottery, porcelain, Middle Eastern carpets
Open Mon–Sat 10am–5pm Sun 11am–3pm
Services Valuations, restorations

Sherborne World of Antiques
Contact Mr T F J Jeans
Long Street, Sherborne, Dorset, DT9 3BS
01935 816451 01935 816240
info@sherborneworldofantiques.co.uk
www.sherborneworldofantiques.co.uk
Est. 2000 ***Stock size*** Large
No. of dealers 40
Stock General antiques, fine art, jewellery, clocks, porcelain
Open Mon–Sat 9.30am–5pm
Services Valuations, restorations, shipping, book search

Timecraft Clocks (BHI)
Contact Mr G Smith
Unit 2, 24 Cheap Street, Sherborne, Dorset, DT9 3PX
01935 817771
Est. 1994 ***Stock size*** Small
Stock Clocks, barometers, musical boxes
Open Tue–Fri 10.30am–5.30pm Sat 10.30am–5pm
Services Restorations, repairs

Victor & Co (SAADA)
Contact Victor Barwick
The Stores, Trendle Street, Sherborne, Dorset, DT9 3NT
01935 817595
Est. 1995 ***Stock size*** Large
Stock Domestic antiques, textiles, glass, china
Open Mon–Sat 9.30am–5pm

Wessex Antiques (SAADA)
Contact Frances Bryant
6 Cheap Street, Sherborne, Dorset, DT9 3PX
01935 816816 01935 816816
drucie.bryant@virgin.co.uk
Est. 1986 ***Stock size*** Small
Stock Furniture, Staffordshire figures, 19thC glass, Oriental rugs
Open Tues–Sat 10am–5pm

SWANAGE

New, Secondhand & Antiquarian Books
Contact Mrs J Blanchard
35 Station Road, Swanage, Dorset, BH19 1AD
01929 424088
Est. 1987 ***Stock size*** Large
Stock New, second-hand and antiquarian books. Also first and pocket editions.
Open Summer Mon–Sun 9.30am–5.00pm Winter closed Sun

WAREHAM

Cottees of Wareham
Contact Mr Bullock
The Market, East Street, Wareham, Dorset, BH20 4NR
01929 552826 01929 554916
auctions@cottees.fsnet.co.uk
www.auctionsatcottees.co.uk
Est. 1902
Open Mon–Fri 9am–5pm closed 1–2pm
Sales General antiques sales fortnightly Tues 10am and 2pm, viewing Mon 10am–1pm 2–5pm 6–8pm. Regular quality antique and fine art sales. Poole Pottery, Clarice Cliff, Moorcroft pottery, Art Deco and collectable toy sales
Frequency Fortnightly
Catalogues Yes

Yesterdays
Contact Mrs Joyce Hardie
32 South Street, Wareham, Dorset, BH20 4LU
01929 550505
Est. 1994 ***Stock size*** Large
Stock 1920–1930s porcelain and china, Poole, Shelley, Carlton ware, Susie Cooper, modern collectables
Open Mon–Sat 10am–4.30pm closed half day Wed in winter
Fairs Shepton Mallet, Exeter Livestock
Services Postal

WEYMOUTH

P Barrett
Contact Mr P Barrett
29 East Street, Weymouth, Dorset, DT4 8BN
01305 772757
Est. 1969 ***Stock size*** Medium
Stock Curios, coins, medals, local prints, brass, copper, china, army badges
Open Mon–Sat 10am–5pm closed 1–2.30pm half day Wed
Services Medal mounting, full size or miniature medals

Books Afloat
Contact John Ritchie
66 Park Street, Weymouth, Dorset, DT4 7DE
01305 779774
Est. 1983 ***Stock size*** Large
Stock Antiquarian, rare and second-hand books. Shipping, naval antiques and memorabilia. Old postcards. Ship models, paintings
Open Mon–Sat 9.30am–5.30pm

The Crows Nest
Contact Julia Marko
3 Hope Square, Weymouth, Dorset, DT4 8TR
01305 786930 01305 786930
Est. 1992 ***Stock size*** Large
Stock China, glass, pictures, farming, ships' lamps, nautical, collectables
Open Mon–Sun 10am–5pm
Fairs Shepton Mallet, Exeter Livestock Market
Services Restorations

The Curiosity Shop on the Quay
Contact David Pinches
13 Trinity Road, Weymouth, Dorset, DT4 8TJ

☎ 01305 769988 ℗ 01305 769988
Est. 1990 *Stock size* Large
Stock General collectors' shop, Victoriana, collectables, Moorcroft, Poole pottery and Pendelfin
Open Mon–Sun 10am–5pm
Fairs Shepton Mallet, Exeter Westpoint

Hy Duke & Son (SOFAA)
Contact Bob Bover
✉ **The Weymouth Auction Rooms, St Nicholas Street, Weymouth, Dorset, DT4 8AA** Ⓟ
☎ 01305 761499
Ⓜ 01305 260101
Est. 1823
Open Mon–Fri 9am–5.30pm closed 1–2pm
Sales Twice monthly sales on Tues at 10.30am of general antiques and household effects. Viewing Mon prior 9.30am–5pm
Catalogues No

Nautical Antique Centre
Contact Mr D C Warwick
✉ **Old Harbour Passage, 3A Hope Square, Weymouth, Dorset, DT4 8TR** Ⓟ
☎ 01305 777838/783180
Ⓜ 07833 707247
Ⓔ nauticalantiques@tinyworld.co.uk
Est. 1988 *Stock size* Large
Stock Original maritime equipment, ships' souvenirs and instruments, etc, nautical collectables and memorabilia
Open Tues–Fri 10am–1pm 2–5pm (please ring in case shop is closed for fairs) open evenings and weekends by appointment

Paddy Cliff's Clarice! (CCCC)
Contact Mrs Joan Ferguson
✉ **77 Coombe Valley Road, Preston, Weymouth, Dorset, DT3 6NL**
☎ 01305 834945 ℗ 01305 837369
Ⓜ 07930 116265
Ⓔ bizarre@uk.packardbell.org
Ⓦ www.paddycliff.com
Est. 1999 *Stock size* Large
Stock Clarice Cliff pieces sold by mail order or via Internet
Open By appointment
Fairs NEC, Leeds Royal Armoury

The Shrubbery
Contact Mrs Sally Dench
✉ **The Colwell Centre, Weymouth, Dorset, DT4 8NJ** Ⓟ
☎ 01305 768240
Ⓔ sarah@dolls-direct.co.uk
Ⓦ www.dolls-direct.co.uk
Est. 1997 *Stock size* Large
Stock Collectable dolls, dolls' houses, toys
Open Mon–Sat 9am–5pm
Fairs Weymouth (Dec)

WIMBORNE

Minster Books
Contact Mr or Mrs Child
✉ **12 Cornmarket, Wimborne, Dorset, BH21 1JL**
☎ 01202 883355
Est. 1991 *Stock size* Large
Stock Antiquarian and second-hand books
Open Mon–Sat 10am–5pm
Services Valuations, restorations

Rectory Rocking Horses
Contact Geoff Boyd
✉ **The Barn, Pamphill Dairy, Pamphill, Wimborne, Dorset, BH21 4ED** Ⓟ
☎ 01202 881100 ℗ 01202 881100
Ⓦ www.antiquerockinghorses.co.uk
Est. 1997 *Stock size* Medium
Stock Antique rocking horses
Open Tues–Fri 10am–5pm Sat Sun 11am–3pm
Services Restorations

SOMERSET

ABBOTS LEIGH

David & Sally March Antiques (LAPADA, CINOA)
Contact David March
✉ **Oak Wood Lodge, Stoke Leigh Woods, Abbots Leigh, Bristol, BS8 3QB** Ⓟ
☎ 01275 372422 ℗ 01275 372422
Ⓜ 07774 838376
Ⓔ david.march@lineone.net
Est. 1973 *Stock size* Medium
Stock 18thC English porcelain figures
Open By appointment only
Fairs LAPADA, NEC
Services Valuations

AXBRIDGE

The Old Post House
Contact Ray or Mollie Seaman
✉ **Turnpike Road, Lower Weare, Axbridge, Somerset, BS26 2JF** Ⓟ
☎ 01934 732372 ℗ 01934 733377
Est. 1981 *Stock size* Medium
Stock General antiques, country pine furniture, paintings
Open Tues–Sat 10am–5pm
Services Free delivery (25 miles radius)

BATH

A J Antiques (BABAADA)
Contact Patrick Anketell-Jones
✉ **13 Broad Street, Bath, Somerset, BA1 5LJ**
☎ 01225 447765 ℗ 01225 447765
Est. 1977 *Stock size* Medium
Stock Georgian–1950s furniture
Open Mon–Sat 10am–5.30pm

Abbey Galleries (NAG, NPA)
Contact Richard Dickson
✉ **9 Abbey Church Yard, Bath, Somerset, BA1 1LY**
☎ 01225 460565 ℗ 01225 484192
Est. 1950 *Stock size* Large
Stock Jewellery, Oriental porcelain, silver
Trade only Yes
Open Mon–Sat 10.30am–5pm
Fairs Antiques for Everyone (April, Aug, Nov)
Services Restorations

Alderson (BADA, CINOA)
Contact Mr C J R Alderson
✉ **2 Princes Buildings, George Street, Bath, Somerset, BA1 2ED** Ⓟ
☎ 01225 421652 ℗ 01225 421652
Est. 1976 *Stock size* Medium
Stock 18th–19thC furniture and works of art
Open Mon–Fri 9.30am–5.30pm closed 1–2pm, Sat 9.30am–1pm or by appointment
Fairs BADA, Olympia

Aldridges of Bath
Contact Mr I Street
✉ **Newark House, 26–45 Cheltenham Street, Bath, Somerset, BA2 3EX** Ⓟ
☎ 01225 462830 ℗ 01225 311319
Ⓦ www.invaluable.com/aldridges
Est. 1740

Open Mon–Fri 9am–5pm
Sat 9am–noon
Sales All sales on Tues 10am, Victorian and general sales fortnightly, specialist antiques sales 6–8 weeks, collectors' sales 6–8 weeks
Catalogues Yes

⊞ Antique Glass (BABAADA)
Contact Margaret Hopkins
✉ **33 Belvedere, Lansdown Road, Bath, Somerset, BA1 5HR** 🅿
☎ 01225 312367 Ⓕ 01225 312367
Ⓔ antique.glass@which.net
Ⓦ www.antique-glass.co.uk
Est. 1988 ***Stock size*** Medium
Stock Georgian glass, collectors' drinking glasses, rummers, ales, friggers, decanters, other curiosities
Open Tues–Sat 10am–6pm
Fairs London Glass Fairs at Commonwealth Institute, BABAADA Fair
Services Search

⊞ Antique Linens & Lace (BABAADA)
Contact Rosalind Mellor
✉ **11 Pulteney Bridge, Bath, Somerset, BA2 4AY** 🅿
☎ 01225 465782 Ⓕ 01225 754067
Ⓔ rosalind.mellor@telinco.co.uk
Est. 1969 ***Stock size*** Large
Stock Tablecloths, bed linen, cushions, baby bonnets, wedding veils, shawls, christening gowns, textiles, quilts, bead bags
Open Mon–Sat 10am–5.30pm or by appointment

⊞ Antique Textiles and Lighting (BABAADA)
Contact Joanna Proops
✉ **34 Belvedere, Lansdown Road, Bath, Somerset, BA1 5HR** 🅿
☎ 01225 310795 Ⓕ 01225 443884
Ⓦ www.antiquetextiles.co.uk
Est. 1970 ***Stock size*** Large
Stock Antique textiles, tapestries, samplers, Paisleys, fans, beadwork, linen, lace, wall and ceiling lighting, chandeliers
Open Tues–Fri 10am–5pm
Sat 9am–1pm
Fairs Bath Decorative Fair
Services Valuations

⊞ Antiques of Bath (BABAADA)
Contact Mr Patrick Beetholme-Smith
✉ **12 Margaret's Buildings, Brock Street, Bath, Somerset, BA1 2LP** 🅿
☎ 01225 448432 Ⓕ 01225 448432
Ⓜ 07860 750559
Ⓔ sales@antiques-of-bath.co.uk
Ⓦ www.antiques-of-bath.co.uk
Est. 1969 ***Stock size*** Medium
Stock Furniture, clocks, paintings, silver, decorative items
Open Wed–Sun 10am–5.30pm or by appointment (call mobile number)
Services Restorations, shipping

⊞ The Antiques Warehouse (BABAADA)
Contact Mr or Mrs R D Waterfall
✉ **57 Walcot Street, Bath, Somerset, BA1 5BN** 🅿
☎ 01225 444201
Ⓜ 07990 690240
Est. 1991 ***Stock size*** Medium
Stock Georgian, Victorian and early 20thC furniture and collectables
Open Mon–Sat 10.30am–5.30pm
Services Deliveries

⌂ Assembly Antiques Centre (BABAADA)
Contact Linda Brine
✉ **5–8 Saville Row, Bath, Somerset, BA1 5PF** 🅿
☎ 01225 426288 Ⓕ 01225 429661
Ⓦ www.assemblyantiques.co.uk
Est. 1969 ***Stock size*** Large
No. of dealers 5
Stock 18th–19thC furniture, lighting, chess sets, tea caddies, jewellery, scent bottles, porcelain
Open Mon–Sat 10am–5pm
Wed 8am–5pm
Services Valuations, restorations and gemologist

⌂ Bartlett Street Antiques Centre (BABAADA)
Contact Anne Linham
✉ **5–10 Bartlett Street, Bath, Somerset, BA1 2QZ** 🅿
☎ 01225 469998 Ⓕ 01225 444146
Ⓔ info@antiques-centre.co.uk
Ⓦ www.antiques-centre.co.uk
Est. 1983 ***Stock size*** Large
No. of dealers 50 + 160 show cases
Stock Antiques and collectables
Open Mon–Sat 9.30am–5pm
Wed 8am–5pm
Services Restaurant

⌂ Bath Antiquities Centre
Contact Antonia Kent
✉ **4 Bladud Buildings, Bath, Somerset, BA1 5LS**
Ⓕ 01225 316889
Est. 1998 ***Stock size*** Medium
No. of dealers 9
Stock Prehistoric, neolithic, medieval, Chinese, Greek, Egyptian antiques
Open Mon–Sat 9.30am–5pm

⊞ Bath Old Books (PBFA)
Contact Steven Ferdinando
✉ **9c Margaret's Buildings, Bath, Somerset, BA1 2LP** 🅿
☎ 01225 422244
Est. 1991 ***Stock size*** Medium
Stock Antiquarian and second-hand books
Open Mon–Sat 10am–5pm
Fairs PBFA
Services Valuations, book binding, book searches

⊞ George Bayntun (ABA)
Contact Mr Bayntun-Coward
✉ **Manvers Street, Bath, Somerset, BA1 1JW** 🅿
☎ 01225 466000 Ⓕ 01225 482122
Ⓔ EBayntun@aol.com
Est. 1894 ***Stock size*** Large
Stock Antiquarian and rare books, English literature first editions, fine bindings
Open Mon–Fri 9am–5.30pm
Sat 9am–1pm
Services Valuations, restorations, binding service

⊞ Bedsteads (BABAADA)
Contact Nicola Ashton
✉ **2 Walcot Buildings, London Road, Bath, Somerset, BA1 6AD** 🅿
☎ 01225 339182
Ⓦ bed-steads.co.uk
Est. 1990 ***Stock size*** Medium
Stock Antique bedsteads in iron, brass and exotic woods
Open Mon–Sat 10am–6pm Sun by appointment
Services Restorations

⊞ Geoffrey Breeze (BABAADA, LAPADA)
Contact Mr Breeze
✉ **6 George Street, Bath, Somerset, BA1 2EH** 🅿
☎ 01225 466499 Ⓕ 01225 466499
Ⓔ gebreeze@aol.com
Est. 1972 ***Stock size*** Medium
Stock 19thC furniture

Open Mon–Sat 10am–5pm
Fairs Bath Decorative and Antiques Fair

Lynda Brine Antiques
Contact Lynda Brine
Assembly Antique Centre, 5–8 Saville Row, Bath, Somerset, BA1 2QP
01225 448488 F 01225 429661
M 07715 673716
Est. 1986 *Stock size* Large
Stock Perfume bottles, vinaigrettes, pomanders, objects of virtue
Open Mon–Sat 10am–5pm
Fairs NEC, USA
Services Valuations

Bryers Antiques
Contact Sheila Haines
Guildhall Market, High Street, Bath, Somerset, BA2 4AW
01225 460535
Est. 1945 *Stock size* Medium
Stock Silver, silver plate, china, antique glass
Open Mon–Sat 10am–5.30pm

Camden Books (PBFA)
Contact Victor or Elizabeth Suchar
146 Walcot Street, Bath, Somerset, BA1 5BL
01225 461606 F 01225 461606
E suchcam@msn.com
W www.camdenbooks.com
Est. 1984 *Stock size* Large
Stock Antiquarian books, architecture, philosophy and science
Open Mon–Sat 10am–5pm
Fairs PBFA

Julia Craig (BABAADA)
Contact Julia Craig
Bartlett Street Antique Centre, 5–10 Bartlett Street, Bath, Somerset, BA1 2QZ
01225 448202/310457
F 01225 444432
M 07771 786846
Est. 1980 *Stock size* Large
Stock Antique lace and linen, costumes, costume accessories
Open Mon–Sat 10am–5pm
Fairs Horticultural Hall Fair
Services Valuations

Brian and Caroline Craik Ltd
Contact Mrs C Craik
8 Margaret's Buildings, Bath, Somerset, BA1 2LP
01225 337161
Est. 1962 *Stock size* Medium
Stock General portable items, china and metalwork
Open Mon–Sat 10am–4pm

Mary Cruz Antiques (LAPADA, CINOA, BABAADA)
Contact Ms M Cruz
5 Broad Street, Bath, Somerset, BA1 5LJ
01225 334174 F 01225 423300
Est. 1974 *Stock size* Large
Stock 18th–19thC English and French furniture, 18th–20thC paintings, bronze and marble statues
Open Mon–Sat 10am–7pm
Services Valuations, restorations

Andrew Dando (BADA, LAPADA)
Contact Andrew Dando
4 Wood Street, Bath, Somerset, BA1 2JQ
01225 422702
E andrew@andrewdando.co.uk
W www.andrewdando.co.uk
Est. 1915 *Stock size* Large
Stock Pottery and porcelain 1750–1870
Open Mon–Fri 10am–5pm Sat 10am–1pm
Fairs BADA

D & B Dickinson (BADA, BABAADA)
Contact Mr Dickinson
22 New Bond Street, Bath, Somerset, BA1 1BA
01225 466502
Est. 1917 *Stock size* Large
Stock Silver, jewellery, silver plate
Open Mon–Sat 9.30am–1pm 2–5pm

Frank Dux Antiques (BABAADA)
Contact Mr F Dux
33 Belvedere, Lansdown Road, Bath, Somerset, BA1 5HR
01225 312367 F 01225 312367
E antique.glass@bath.co.uk
W www.antique-glass.co.uk
Est. 1988 *Stock size* Medium
Stock 18th–19thC glass, country oak furniture
Open Tues–Sat 10am–6pm
Fairs London Glass Fairs (Commonwealth Institute, Kensington)
Services Search

Frogmore House Antiques
Contact Andrew Tinson
Bartlett Street Antique Centre, Bartlett Street, Bath, Somerset, BA1 2QZ
01225 445054 F 01225 445054
M 07976 225988
Est. 1976 *Stock size* Large
Stock Novelties, objects of virtue, silver, good smalls
Open Mon–Sat 9.30am–5pm Wed Trade day 8am–5pm
Fairs NEC, Newark

Christina Grant
Contact Mr P Scott
Bartlett Street Antiques Centre, Bath, Somerset, BA1 2QZ
01225 310457 F 01225 319821
M 07850 639770
Est. 1981 *Stock size* Medium
Stock Antique prints, decorative items
Open Mon–Sat 9.30am–5pm

George Gregory
Contact Mr Bayntun-Coward
Manvers Street, Bath, Somerset, BA1 1JW
01225 466055 F 01225 482122
Est. 1846 *Stock size* Large
Stock Antiquarian books, prints
Open Mon–Fri 9am–5.30pm Sat 9am–1pm

Indigo
Contact Marion Bender
59 Walcot Street, Bath, Somerset, BA1 5BN
01225 311795
E indigo_uk@compuserve.com
Est. 1982 *Stock size* Medium
Stock Indian and Chinese antique furniture, small handicraft and decorative items, furniture from Indonesia made from recycled teak
Open Mon–Sat 10am–6pm
Fairs House and Garden fair, DMG fairs
Services Restorations

Simon and Frauke Jackson
Contact Mr Simon Jackson
24 Mount Road, Southdown, Bath, Somerset, BA2 1LD
01225 422221 F 01225 422221
M 07771 887771
Est. 1987 *Stock size* Medium

WEST COUNTRY

Stock Antique furniture
Open By appointment
Services Restorations

Jadis Antiques Ltd (BABAADA)

Contact Ms M Taylor
14, 15 & 17 Walcot Buildings, London Road, Bath, Somerset, BA1 6AD
☎ 01225 333130 Ⓕ 01225 338797
Ⓜ 07768 232133
Ⓔ jadpalad@aol.com
Ⓦ www.jadis.co.uk
Est. 1970 *Stock size* Large
Stock French furniture and decorative items
Open Mon–Sat 9.30am–6pm or by appointment
Fairs Bath Decorative and Antiques Fair
Services Design service, mural painting

Kembery Antique Clocks (BABAADA)

Contact Mr Paul Kembery
Bartlett Street Antique Centre, 5–10 Bartlett Street, Bath, Somerset, BA1 2QZ
☎ 0117 9565281 Ⓕ 0117 9565281
Ⓜ 07850 623237
Ⓔ kembery@kdclocks.co.uk
Ⓦ www.kdclocks.co.uk
Est. 1993 *Stock size* Medium
Stock Longcase, wall, mantel, bracket, carriage clocks and barometers
Open Mon–Sat 9.30am–5pm
Fairs NEC
Services Valuations, restorations, shipping

Ann King Antique Clothes

Contact Mrs Ann King
38 Belvedere, Lansdown Road, Bath, Somerset, BA1 5HR
☎ 01225 336245
Est. 1980 *Stock size* Medium
Stock Antique clothes, quilts, lace
Open Mon–Sat 10am–5pm
Services Valuations

Lansdown Antiques (BABAADA)

Contact Chris or Ann Kemp
23 Belvedere, Lansdown Road, Bath, Somerset, BA1 5ED
☎ 01225 313417
Ⓜ 07801 013663
Ⓔ lansdownantiques@lineone.net
Est. 1983 *Stock size* Medium
Stock Painted pine and country furniture, metalware, decorative items
Open Mon–Sat 9.30am–5.30pm From 8am on Wed
Fairs Bath Decorative and Antiques Fair

Le Boudoir

Contact Sue Turner
Bartlett Street Antique Centre, 5–10 Bartlett Street, Bath, Somerset, BA1 2QZ
☎ 01225 311061 Ⓕ 0117 9608 309
Ⓔ info@bathantiquesonline.com
Ⓦ www.bathantiquesonline.com
Est. 1988 *Stock size* Large
Stock Perfume bottles, dolls, decorative interior items, jewellery, Art Deco ceramics, Bakelite, petit point and beaded purses
Open Mon–Sat 9am–5pm Wed 8am–5pm
Services Valuations, restorations of ceramics

E P Mallory and Son Ltd (BADA)

Contact N Hall or P Mallory
1–4 Bridge Street, Bath, Somerset, BA2 4AP
☎ 01225 788800 Ⓕ 01225 442210
Ⓔ mail@mallory-jewellers.com
Ⓦ www.mallory-jewellers.com
Est. 1898 *Stock size* Large
Stock Silver, jewellery
Open Mon–Sat 9.30am–5pm
Services Valuations

J & S Millard Antiques (BABADA)

Contact Mr Millard
Assembly Antiques, 5–8 Saville Row, Bath, Somerset, BA1 2QP
☎ 01225 448488 Ⓕ 01225 429661
Ⓜ 07711 425629
Ⓔ tmillard@dircon.co.uk
Est. 1987 *Stock size* Large
Stock 18th–19thC decorative furniture, boxes, tea caddies, chess sets
Open Mon–Sat 10am–5pm Wed 7.30am–5pm
Fairs NEC
Services Valuations, restorations, insurance

Montague Antiques (BABAADA)

Contact Alex Schlesinger or David Moore
16 Walcot Buildings, London Road, Bath, Somerset, BA1 6AD
☎ 01225 469282
Est. 1987 *Stock size* Large
Stock General, furniture from 18thC to 1920s, decorative and collectors' items
Open Mon–Sat 10am–6pm Sun 11am–4pm closed Thurs
Services Valuations

Orient Expressions Ltd (BABAADA)

Contact Patricia Wilkinson
Assembly Antiques Centre, 5–8 Saville Row, Bath, Somerset, BA1 2QP
☎ 01225 313399 Ⓕ 020 7610 6872
Ⓔ amandaleader@compuserve.com
Ⓦ www.antiquesbulletin.com/orientexpressions
Est. 1999 *Stock size* Medium
Stock Mostly early 19thC provincial Chinese furniture, accessories
Open Mon–Sat 10am–5pm

Penny Philip

Contact Mrs P Philip
Abbey House, Abbey Green, Bath, Somerset, BA1 1NR
☎ 01225 469564 Ⓕ 01225 469564
Est. 1979 *Stock size* Small
Stock Dyed antique linen sheets
Open By appointment

Phillips International Auctioneers and Valuers

1 Old King Street, Bath, Somerset, BA1 2JT
☎ 01225 310609 Ⓕ 01225 446675
Ⓦ www.phillips-auction.com
Sales Regional Saleroom. Ring for details

Piccadilly Antiques (BABAADA)

Contact John Davies
280 High Street, Batheaston, Bath, Somerset, BA1 2QZ
☎ 01225 851494 Ⓕ 01225 851120
Ⓔ piccadillyantiques@ukonline.co.uk
Est. 2001 *Stock size* Medium
Stock English and French furniture, decorative accessories aimed at the US market
Open Mon–Sat 9.30am–5.30pm Sun 10.30am–4.30 pm or by appointment

Quiet Street Antiques (BABAADA)
Contact Mr Kerry Hastings-Spital
14–15 John Street, Bath, Somerset, BA1 2JG
01225 483003
07860 818212
kerry@quietstreetantiques.co.uk
www.quietstreetantiques.co.uk
Est. 1985 *Stock size* Large
Stock 18th–19thC furniture, clocks, tea caddies, boxes, mirrors, Royal Worcester, works of art
Open Mon–Sat 10am–6pm
Services Valuations, free delivery within 100 miles, export services

Quiet Street Antiques (BABAADA)
Contact Mr Kerry Hastings-Spital
3 Quiet Street, Bath, Somerset, BA1 2JS
01225 315727 01225 448300
07860 818212
kerry@quietstreetantiques.co.uk
www.quietstreetantiques.co.uk
Est. 1985 *Stock size* Large
Stock 18th–19thC furniture, clocks, tea caddies, boxes, mirrors, Royal Worcester, works of art
Open Mon–Sat 10am–6pm
Services Valuations, free delivery within 100 miles and export services

Roland Gallery (BABAADA)
Contact Mike Pettitt
33 Monmouth Street, Bath, BA1 2AN
01225 312330/319464
01225 312330
07889 723272
therolandgallery@aol.com
Est. 2000 *Stock size* Large
Stock Eclectic mix of 20thC design including silver, ivory, decorative items, paintings
Open Wed Sat 10am–5pm or by appointment

Michael Saffell Antiques (BABAADA)
Contact Mr M Saffell
3 Walcot Buildings, London Road, Bath, Somerset, BA1 6AD
01225 315857 01225 315857
07794 115 8049
michael.saffell@virgin.net
Est. 1975 *Stock size* Medium
Stock Advertising items, British tins (biscuit, tobacco, confectionery, mustard etc), decorative items
Open Mon–Fri 9am–5pm best to phone in advance or by appointment
Fairs Newark
Services Valuations

Peter Scott
Contact Mr P Scott
Bartlett Street Antiques Centre, 5–10 Bartlett Street, Bath, Somerset, BA1 2QZ
01225 310457 01225 319821
07850 639770
Est. 1984 *Stock size* Large
Stock White transfer ware, early English pottery including Mason's
Open Mon–Sat 9.30am–5pm
Fairs Newton, Shepton Mallett

Tim Snell Antiques (BABAADA)
Contact Tim Snell
5–6 Cleveland Terrace, Bath, Somerset, BA1 5DF
01225 423045 01225 423045
Est. 1979 *Stock size* Large
Stock 19th–20thC oak furniture, Arts and Crafts
Open Mon–Sat 9am–5pm
Services Valuations, restorations, house clearances

Source (BABAADA)
Contact Mr R Donaldson
93–95 Walcot Street, Bath, Somerset, BA1 3SD
01225 469200
www.source-antiques.co.uk
Est. 1978 *Stock size* Medium
Stock Architectural antiques and lights including 1950s aluminium kitchens
Open Tues–Fri 10am–5pm Sat 9am–5pm
Fairs Bath Decorative and Antiques Fair
Services Valuations

Susannah (BABAADA, The Textiles Society)
Contact Mrs S Holley
25 Broad Street, Bath, Somerset, BA1 5LW
01225 445069 01225 339004
Est. 1989 *Stock size* Medium
Stock General, decorative items, textiles
Open Mon–Sat 10am–5pm please telephone in advance
Fairs Bath Decorative and Antiques Fair, Kensington Brocante, The Textiles Society Fair in Manchester

James Townshend Antiques (BABAADA)
Contact Mr Townshend
1 Saville Row, Bath, Somerset, BA1 2QP
01225 332290 01225 332290
01225 332290
sales@jtownshendantiques.co.uk
www.jtownshendantiques.co.uk
Stock size Large
Stock 19thC furniture, decorative items, mirrors
Open Mon–Sat 10am–5pm
Fairs Kempton
Services Valuations, restorations

Vintage to Vogue (BABAADA)
Contact Teresa Langton
28 Milsom Street (entry in the passage off Broad Street car park), Bath, BA1 1DG
01225 337323
www.vintagetovoguebath.com
Est. 1994 *Stock size* Large
Stock 1850s–1950s period clothing and accessories, costume lace, white linens, textiles
Open Tues–Sat 10.30am–5pm

Walcot Reclamation Ltd (BABAADA)
Contact Colin Blair
108 Walcot Street, Bath, Somerset, BA1 5BG
01225 444404 01225 448163
rick@walcot.com
www.walcot.com
Est. 1975 *Stock size* Large
Stock Architectural antiques including bathrooms, radiators, fireplaces, garden furniture and reproductions of hard-to-find items
Open Mon–Fri 9am–5.30pm
Fairs The Country Living Fairs, Business Design Centre Islington (spring)
Services Restorations of marble, stone and old radiators

BITTON

Barrow Lodge Antiques
Contact Derek Wookey
Kings Square, Bitton, Bristol, BS30 6HR
0117 9324205

Ⓜ 07836 293993
Est. 1975 *Stock size* Large
Stock Furniture
Open By appointment
Fairs Newark, Ardingly
Services Restorations, stripping

BRIDGWATER

Tamlyn and Son
Contact David Knight
✉ **56 High Street, Bridgwater, Somerset, TA6 3BN** Ⓟ
☎ 01278 458241 Ⓕ 01278 458242
Est. 1893
Open Mon–Fri 9am–5.30pm
Sales Antiques and general sales monthly, 2 catalogue sales per annum May and Nov, viewing day before sale
Frequency Monthly
Catalogues Yes

BRISTOL

A & C Antique Clocks
Contact Mr David Andrews
✉ **The Clock Shop, No 86 Bryants Hill, Hanham, Bristol, BS5 8QT** Ⓟ
☎ 01179 476141
Est. 1992 *Stock size* Large
Stock Clocks, furniture, ceramics, Winstanley cats, antique clocks, restorations
Open Tues–Sat 10am–4pm closed Wed
Services Clock repair service, valuations, restorations, shipping

The Antiques Warehouse Ltd (RADS)
Contact Chris Winsor
✉ **430 Gloucester Road, Horfield, Bristol, BS7 8TX** Ⓟ
☎ 0117 942 4500 Ⓕ 0117 942 4140
Ⓔ chriswinsor@theantiqueswarehouseltd.co.uk
Ⓦ www.theantiqueswarehouseltd.co.uk
Est. 1994 *Stock size* Large
Stock Georgian–Edwardian and post-Edwardian furniture, carpets, mirrors
Open Mon–Sun 10am–6pm
Services Valuations, restorations and reupholstery

Arcadia Antiques
Contact Julia Irish
✉ **4 Boyces Avenue, Clifton, Bristol, BS8 4AA**
☎ 0117 914 4479 Ⓕ 0117 923 9308
Ⓔ r.irish@phoenix-net.co.uk
Est. 1994 *Stock size* Small
Stock Furniture, collectables, upholstery, prints, paintings
Open Tues–Sat 10am–5.30pm

Gloria Barnes of Clifton Antiques Centre
Contact Gloria Barnes
✉ **The Clifton Antiques Centre, 18 The Mall, Clifton, Bristol, BS8 4DR** Ⓟ
☎ 0117 973 7843
Ⓔ jonathanbarnes@hotmail.com
Est. 1979 *Stock size* Medium
Stock Sir William Russell Flint prints, paintings, Indian art, stone jewellery
Open Tues–Sat 10am–6pm
Services Valuations

The Bed Workshop
Contact Dr Scott Jones
✉ **The Old Pickle Factory, Braunton Road, Bristol, BS3 3AA** Ⓟ
☎ 0117 963 6659
Ⓔ thebedworkshop@aol.com
Est. 1981 *Stock size* Large
Stock French antique furniture
Open Mon–Sat 9.30am–6pm

Bedsteads (BABAADA)
Contact Nicola Ashton
✉ **15 Regent Street, Clifton, Bristol, BS8 4HW** Ⓟ
☎ 0117 923 9181 Ⓕ 0117 923 9181
Ⓦ www.bed-steads.co.uk
Est. 1990 *Stock size* Medium
Stock Antique bedsteads in iron, brass and exotic woods
Open Mon 11.30am–5.30pm Tues–Sat 10am–6pm
Services Restorations

Paula Biggs
Contact Paula Biggs
✉ **12 Clifton Arcade, Boyces Avenue, Clifton, Bristol, BS8 4AA** Ⓟ
☎ 0117 974 3630/973 9528
Ⓕ 0117 973 1436
Ⓜ 07974 777257
Ⓔ john@thebiggs.co.uk
Est. 1978 *Stock size* Large
Stock Antiques, collectable silver items, objects of virtue
Open Tues–Sat 10am–5.30pm
Fairs NEC 3 times

Bishopston Books
Contact Bill Singleton
✉ **259 Gloucester Road, Bishopston, Bristol, BS7 8NY** Ⓟ
☎ 0117 944 5303
Ⓔ bishopstonbook@btinternet.com
Est. 1993 *Stock size* Small
Stock Antiquarian and second-hand books
Open Thurs Fri 10am–5.30pm Sat 9.30am–4.30pm
Services Book search

Bristol Auction Rooms
Contact David Rees
✉ **St John's Place, Apsley Road, Clifton, Bristol, BS8 2ST** Ⓟ
☎ 0117 973 7201 Ⓕ 0117 973 5671
Ⓔ info@bristolauctionrooms.co.uk
Ⓦ www.bristolauctionrooms.co.uk
Est. 1858
Open Mon–Fri 8.45am–6pm
Sales Antiques and decorative items. Sale Tues 10.30am, viewing Sat 9.30am–1pm Mon 9.30am–7pm day of sale from 9am
Frequency Monthly
Catalogues Yes

Bristol Auction Rooms
Contact David Rees
✉ **Saleroom 2, Baynton Road, Ashton, Bristol, BS3 2EB** Ⓟ
☎ 0117 953 1603 Ⓕ 0117 953 1598
Ⓔ info@bristolauctionrooms.co.uk
Ⓦ www.bristolauctionrooms.co.uk
Est. 1858
Open Mon–Fri 8.45am–6pm
Sales Victorian and modern furniture and effects sale Thurs 10.30am, viewing Wed 11am–6pm, day of sale from 9am
Frequency Fortnightly
Catalogues Yes

Bristol Brocante
Contact David or Elizabeth Durant
✉ **123 St Georges Road, College Green, Hotwells, Bristol, BS1 5UW** Ⓟ
☎ 0117 909 6688
Est. 1970 *Stock size* Large
Stock French antiques
Open Mon–Sat 11am–6pm
Fairs Newark, Kensington Brocante (September), Sandown Park Fair (October)

Bristol Trade Antiques
Contact Mr L Dyke
✉ **192 Cheltenham Road, Bristol, BS6 5RB** Ⓟ
☎ 0117 942 2790
Est. 1969 *Stock size* Medium
Stock Victorian and Edwardian furniture

Open Mon–Sat 9am–5.30pm
Services Valuations, exports to the USA

Caledonia Antiques
Contact Mrs M T Kerridge
6 The Mall, Clifton, Bristol, BS8 4DR
0117 974 3582 F 0117 946 7997
M 07710 434431
Est. 1981 *Stock size* Medium
Stock Jewellery and silver
Open Mon–Sat 10am–5.30pm

Chandos Books
Contact George Janssen
8 Chandos Road, Bristol, BS6 6PE
0117 974 1166
E chandosbooks@hotmail.com
Stock size Medium
Stock Antiquarian, travel, transport, natural history and local interest illustrated books
Open Mon–Sat 10am–6pm
Fairs PBFA
Services Valuations, book search, restoration

Circle Books
Contact Mr Mike Piddock
65 North Street, Bedminster, Bristol, BS3 1ES
0117 966 2622
Est. 1999 *Stock size* Medium
Stock Antiquarian, second-hand, rare and out-of-print books. History, health and well-being books a speciality
Open Mon–Sat 10am–5.30pm closed Tues
Services Valuations and book binding, café in shop

Clifton Antique Centre
Contact Mrs Barnes or Marlene Risdale
18 The Mall, Clifton, Bristol, BS8 4DR
0117 973 7843
Est. 1965 *Stock size* Large
No. of dealers 6
Stock Silver, silver plate, paintings, clocks, ceramics, Moorcroft
Open Tues–Sat 10am–6pm
Services Valuations

Clifton Hill Textiles
Contact Mrs Hodder
4 Lower Clifton Hill, Clifton, Bristol, BS8 1BT
0117 929 0644
E cliftex@yahoo.com.co.uk
Est. 1984 *Stock size* Large
Stock Textiles, buttons, buckles
Open Mon–Sat 11am–5.30pm
Services Valuations

Cotham Antiques
Contact Susan Miller
39a Cotham Hill, Cotham, Bristol, BS6 6JZ
0117 973 3326
Est. 1983 *Stock size* Medium
Stock General
Open Tues–Sat 10.30am–5.30pm
Services Friendly advice

Cotham Galleries
Contact Mr D Jury
22 Cotham Hill, Bristol, BS6 6LF
0117 973 6026
M 07885 166811
Est. 1969 *Stock size* Medium
Stock General
Open Mon–Fri 9am–5.30pm Sat 10am–noon
Services Valuations, restorations

Cotham Hill Bookshop (PBFA)
Contact Roger Plant
39a Cotham Hill, Bristol, BS6 6JY
0117 973 2344
Est. 1975 *Stock size* Medium
Stock Antiquarian and second-hand books and antiquarian prints
Open Mon–Sat 9.30am–5.30pm
Fairs PBFA
Services Valuations

Focus on the Past
Contact Mrs Alison Roylance
25 Waterloo Street, Clifton, Bristol, BS8 4BT
0117 973 8080
Est. 1978 *Stock size* Large
Stock Furniture, pine, kitchenware, china, glass and books, jewellery, 20thC collectables
Open Mon–Sat 9.30am–5.30pm Sun 11am–5.30pm
Fairs Ardingly, Newark

Grey-Harris & Co
Contact Mr Grey-Harris
12 Princess Victoria Street, Clifton, Bristol, BS8 4BP
0117 973 7365
Est. 1969 *Stock size* Large
Stock Antique jewellery, silver
Open Mon–Sat 9am–6pm
Services Valuations, restorations

Grimes Militaria
Contact Christopher or Hazel Grimes
13–14 Lower Park Row, Bristol, BS1 5BN
0117 929 8205
Est. 1967 *Stock size* Medium
Stock Scientific instruments, nautical memorabilia, militaria
Open Mon–Sat 11am–6pm
Fairs Newark, Shepton Mallet
Services Valuations

Margaret R Jubb
Contact Mrs Jubb
6 The Clifton Arcade, Boyces Avenue, Clifton, Bristol, BS8 4AA
0117 973 3105
M 07974 095554
E maggsy@kenmoor.demon.co.uk
W www.kenmoor.demon.co.uk/antiques
Est. 1974 *Stock size* Medium
Stock General antiques
Open Mon–Fri 10am–6pm Sat 10.30am–6pm
Services Valuations

Marlenes
Contact Marlene Risdale
Clifton Antiques Centre, 18 The Mall, Clifton, Bristol, BS8 4DR
0117 973 7645
Est. 1958 *Stock size* Medium
Stock Silver, jewellery
Open Tues–Sat 10am–6pm
Fairs Sandown, Stafford
Services Valuations

Robert Mills Architectural Antiques (SALVO)
Contact Bob Mills
Narroways Road, Eastville, Bristol, BS2 9XB
0117 955 6542 F 0117 9558146
E sales@rmills.co.uk
W www.rmills.co.uk
Est. 1970 *Stock size* Large
Stock Architectural antiques including Gothic church fittings, stained glass, pub interiors
Open Mon–Fri 9.30am–5.30pm Sat 10am–5pm

Jan Morrison
Contact Jan Morrison
5 Clifton Arcade, Boyces Avenue, Clifton, Bristol, BS8 4AA
0117 970 6822 F 0117 970 6822

Est. 1979 *Stock size* Medium
Stock Silver, 18th–19thC glass, jewellery
Open Tues–Sat 10am–5.30pm
Fairs DMG, Shepton Mallet
Services Valuations

Pastimes (OMRS)
Contact Mr A H Stevens
22 Lower Park Row, Bristol, BS1 5BN
0117 929 9330
Est. 1974 *Stock size* Large
Stock Militaria
Open Mon–Sat 10.30am–1.45pm 2.45–5pm Wed 11am–5pm
Fairs Mark Carter Fairs
Services Medal mounting

Piano Export
Contact Mr T W Smallridge
Bridge Road, Kingswood, Bristol, BS15 4FW
0117 956 8300
Est. 1982 *Stock size* Medium
Stock Steinway and Bechstein grand pianos, decorative pianos
Open Mon–Fri or by appointment

Porchester Antiques
Contact Mrs Devonia Andrews
58 The Mall, Clifton, Bristol, BS8 4JG
0117 373 0256 01275 810629
07970 970449
Est. 1978 *Stock size* Medium
Stock Moorcroft, enamels and pottery, Okra glass, Sally Tuffin pottery, jewellery
Open Tues–Sat 10am–6pm
Services Valuations

Pride & Joy Antiques
Contact Martin Williams
25 North View, Westbury Park, Bristol, Bristol, BS6 7SD
0117 973 5806
Est. 1994 *Stock size* Medium
Stock Victorian–Edwardian furniture
Open Mon–Sat 10.30am–1pm 2–5pm
Services Reupholstery

Raw Deluxe
Contact Mr J Stewart
148 Gloucester Road, Bishopston, Bristol, BS7 8NT
0117 942 6998
Est. 1998 *Stock size* Medium
Stock General antiques, collectables
Open Mon–Sat 10am–5pm closed Wed
Services Restorations

Vincents of Clifton
Contact Vincent Risdale
Clifton Antique Centre, 18 The Mall, Clifton, Bristol, BS8 4DR
0117 973 7645
Est. 1984 *Stock size* Medium
Stock Jewellery, silver and gold
Open Tues–Sat 10am–6pm
Fairs Cheltenham, Sandown and Stafford

Whiteladies Antiques & Collectables
Contact Sylvia Skerritt
49c Whiteladies Road, Clifton, Bristol, BS8 2LS
0117 973 5766
Est. 2001 *Stock size* Large
No. of dealers 25
Stock Antiques, collectables, small furniture
Open Mon–Sat 10.30am–5pm Sun noon–4pm

BROOMFIELD

Pines Antique & Gift Centre
Contact Sue Keohane
The Pines, Buncombe Hill, Broomfield, Taunton, Somerset, TA5 1AX
01823 451704 01278 671864
Est. 1999 *Stock size* Small
Stock Bric-a-brac
Open Wed–Sun 10.30am–5.30pm

BRUTON

The Antiques Shop Bruton
Contact David Gwilliam
5 High Street, Bruton, Somerset, BA10 0AB
01749 813264
Est. 1976 *Stock size* Medium
Stock Furniture, brass, copper, jewellery, silver, china, collectables
Open Thurs Fri Sat 10am–5.30pm
Services Jewellery repairs

European Accent
Contact Steve Green
Station Road, Bruton, Somerset, BA10 0EH
01749 812460 01749 813932
0797 7496762
enquiries@europeanaccent.co.uk
www.europeanaccent.co.uk
Est. 1998 *Stock size* Medium
Stock Country decorative, painted, pine and fruitwood furniture, smalls
Open Mon–Fri 8.30am–5.30pm Sat 9am–1pm for trade
Fairs Newark, Shepton Mallet
Services Valuations

M G R Exports
Contact Mr M Read
Station Road, Bruton, Somerset, BA10 0EH
01749 812460 01749 812882
enquiries@mgrexports.co.uk
www.mgrexports.co.uk
Est. 1979 *Stock size* Large
Stock General
Open Mon–Fri 8.30am–5.30pm Sat 9am–1pm for trade
Services Packing, shipping and containers packed

Mr Gompy's Antiques & Curious
Contact Anne Sidford
6 High Street, Bruton, Somerset, BA10 0AA
01749 813238
Est. 1993 *Stock size* Large
Stock Country furniture, soft furnishings, minatures, dolls and dolls' houses
Open Thurs–Fri 9.30am–1pm 2–5.30pm Sat 9.30am–1pm 2pm–4pm
Services Restorations, upholstery

BURNHAM-ON-SEA

Adam Antiques
Contact Mrs R Combes
30 Adam Street, Burnham-on-Sea, Somerset, TA8 1PQ
01278 783193 01278 793709
Est. 1977 *Stock size* Large
Stock General wide range of antiques and collectables
Open Mon–Sat 9am–5pm

Adams Auctions
Contact Mrs R Combes
28 Adam Street, Burnham-on-Sea, Somerset, TA8 1PQ
01278 793709 01278 793709
Est. 1993
Open Mon–Sat 10am–5pm

Sales Antique and general sales, monthly, Wed 6pm viewing Tues 2–6pm Wed 10am–6pm
Frequency Monthly
Catalogues Yes

The Burnham Model & Collectors Shop
Contact W Loudon
3 College Court, College Street, Burnham-on-Sea, Somerset, TA8 1AR
01278 780066 01278 780066
Est. 1994 *Stock size* Large
Stock Ephemera, postcards, banknotes, coins, medals, die-cast models, cigarette cards
Open Mon–Sat 9.30am–5pm
Services Valuations

Heape's (FATG)
Contact Mrs M Heap
39 Victoria Street, Burnham-on-Sea, Somerset, TA8 1AN
01278 782131 01278 782131
pfheap@aol.com
Est. 1988 *Stock size* Large
Stock Porcelain, silverware, fine art, glass, collectables
Open Tues Thurs–Sat 10am–4.30pm Wed 10am–1pm
Services Bespoke framing, hand-made lampshades, specialist table lamps

CASTLE CARY

Cary Antiques
Contact Mrs J A Oldham
2 High Street, Castle Cary, Somerset, BA7 7AW
01963 350437
Est. 1977 *Stock size* Large
Stock General antiques
Open Tues–Sat 10.30am–5pm closed Wed
Fairs Shepton Mallet
Services Picture framing

Pandora's Box
Contact Sally Comer
Fore Street, Castle Cary, Somerset, BA7 7BG
01963 350926
07798 692633
Est. 1988 *Stock size* Medium
Stock Furniture, quilts, textiles and decorative items
Open Mon–Sat 9.30am–5.30pm
Fairs Newark, Shepton Mallet

CHARD

Chard Antiques Centre
Contact Julie Hills or Alistair Smith
23 High Street, Chard, Somerset, TA20 1QF
01460 63517
julie@chardantiques.fsnet.co.uk
Est. 1997 *Stock size* Medium
No. of dealers 9
Stock General antiques, furniture, ceramics and decorative items
Open Mon–Sat 10am–5pm or by appointment

Chez Chalon
Contact Nick or Jake Chalon
Field Barshouse, Shepards Lane, High Street, Chard, Somerset, TA20 1QX
01460 68679 01460 239005
antiques@chezchalon.freeserve.co.uk
Est. 1972 *Stock size* Large
Stock Period English and French country furniture
Open By appointment
Services Restorations

CHILCOMPTON

Billiard Room Antiques (LAPADA, BABAADA, CINOA)
Contact Mrs J Mckeivor
The Old School, Church Lane, Chilcompton, Bath, Somerset, BA3 4HP
01761 232839 01761 232839
info@billiardroom.co.uk
www.billiardroom.co.uk
Est. 1990 *Stock size* Medium
Stock Billiard room furnishings
Open By appointment only
Fairs Olympia
Services Valuations, restoration and shipping

CHIPPING SODBURY

Sodbury Antiques
Contact Millicent Brown
70 Broad Street, Chipping Sodbury, Bristol, BS37 6AG
01454 273369 01454 273369
Est. 1989 *Stock size* Medium
Stock China, jewellery and bric-a-brac
Open Mon–Sat 9.30am–5.30pm closed Wed

CLEVEDON

Clevedon Books (PBFA)
Contact Mr or Mrs Douthwaite
The Gallery, 29 Copse Road, Clevedon, Somerset, BS21 7QN
01275 790579/872304
01275 342817
clevedonbooks@globalnet.co.uk
Est. 1970 *Stock size* Medium
Stock Antiquarian books, maps and prints, second-hand books. History, science and technology a speciality
Open Thurs–Sat 11am–4.30pm
Fairs PBFA
Services Print and map colouring

The Collector
Contact Malcolm or Tina Simmonds
14 The Beach, Clevedon, Somerset, BS21 7QU
01275 875066
Est. 1992 *Stock size* Small
Stock Smalls and collectables including Beatrix Potter figures
Open Mon–Sat 10am–5pm Sun noon–5pm closed Thurs
Fairs Malvern Three Counties, Brunel Temple Meads, Bristol
Services Valuations

Nostalgia
Contact Wendy Moore
65a Hill Road, Clevedon, Somerset, BS21 7PD
01275 342587
Est. 1984 *Stock size* Medium
Stock General antiques, linen, furniture, china
Open Tues–Sat 10am–4.30pm
Services House calls to buy

COXLEY

Mrs Mitchell
Contact Mrs Mitchell
Clover Close House, Main Road, Coxley, Somerset, BA5 1QZ
01749 679533
Est. 1984 *Stock size* Medium
Stock General antiques
Open Mon–Sat 9am–5pm
Services Valuations, caning and upholstery

CREWKERNE

Antiques and Country Pine
Contact Mrs Wheeler

✉ 14 East Street, Crewkerne, Somerset, TA18 7AG
☎ 01460 75623
Est. 1979 *Stock size* Medium
Stock Antique and country pine furniture
Open Tues–Sat 10am–5pm

Books Galore
Contact Mrs Hall
✉ The Old Warehouse, North Street, Crewkerne, Somerset, TA18 7AJ
☎ 01460 74465 Ⓕ 01460 74465
Ⓜ 07957 986053
Ⓔ hallbook@aol.com
Est. 1969 *Stock size* Large
Stock Second-hand books. Countryside topics a speciality
Open Mon–Sat 10am–1pm 2.30–5pm
Services Book search

The Bookshop
Contact Mr Lemmey
✉ 15 Falkland Square, Crewkerne, Somerset, TA18 7JS
☎ 01460 76579
Est. 1990 *Stock size* Medium
Stock Antiquarian and second-hand books, early Penguins a speciality
Open Mon–Sat 10am–5pm

Crewkerne Antiques
Contact Frank Martin
✉ 16 Market Street, Crewkerne, Somerset, TA18 7LA
☎ 01460 77111 Ⓕ 01460 77111
Est. 1991 *Stock size* Medium
No. of dealers 20+
Stock General antiques
Open Tues–Sat 9.30am–4.30pm
Services Valuations, restorations

East Street Antique Centre
Contact Mr C Hennessy
✉ 42 East Street, Crewkerne, Somerset, TA18 7AG
☎ 01460 78600 Ⓕ 01460 78600
Ⓔ info@veryold.co.uk
Ⓦ www.veryold.co.uk
Est. 1974 *Stock size* Large
No. of dealers 8
Stock French and English country furniture, decorative items, architectural pieces, pine furniture
Open Mon–Sat 10am–5pm or by appointment

Gresham Books (PBFA, ABA)
Contact James Hine
✉ 31 Market Street, Crewkerne, Somerset, TA18 7JU
☎ 01460 77726 Ⓕ 01460 52479
Ⓔ jameshine@gresham-books.demon.co.uk
Est. 1972 *Stock size* Large
Stock Antiquarian and second-hand books including early cookery and architectural
Open Mon–Sat 10am–5pm
Fairs London Bookfair (monthly), most major book fairs (phone for details)
Services Valuations

Hennessy
Contact Carl Hennessy
✉ 42 East Street, Crewkerne, Somerset, TA18 7AG
☎ 01460 78600 Ⓕ 01460 78600
Ⓜ 07768 286455
Ⓔ carl@veryold.co.uk
Ⓦ www.veryold.co.uk
Est. 1974 *Stock size* Large
Stock Antique pine, country furniture, decorative items
Open Mon–Sat 10am–5pm

Lawrence Fine Art Auctioneers Ltd (ARVA, SOFAA)
Contact Erica Horsley
✉ 4 Linen Yard, South Street, Crewkerne, Somerset, TA18 8AB
☎ 01460 73041 Ⓕ 01460 74627
Ⓔ enquiries@lawrences.co.uk
Ⓦ www.lawrences.co.uk
Est. 1900
Open Mon–Fri 9am–5pm
Sales Fine art sale third week every month Thurs 11am, viewing Sat 9.30am–12.30pm Mon 10am–4.30pm Tues 10am–7pm Wed 10am–4.30pm Thurs prior to sale. General household sale every Wed 9.30am, viewing Tues 9.30am–7pm
Frequency Monthly – fine art Weekly – general
Catalogues Yes

CROWCOMBE

Newmans (BAFRA)
Contact Tony Newman
✉ Tithe Barn, Crowbombe, Somerset, TA4 4AQ
Ⓜ 07778 615945
Ⓔ tony@cheddon.fsnet.co.uk
Est. 1991 *Stock size* Small
Stock 18th–19thC furniture
Open Sun–Mon 9am–5pm or by appointment
Services Valuations, restorations

DULVERTON

Acorn Antiques
Contact Peter Hounslow
✉ 39 High Street, Dulverton, Somerset, TA22 9DW
☎ 01398 323286
Ⓔ peter@acornantiques.fsnet.co.uk
Ⓦ www.acornantiquesexmoor.co.uk
Est. 1988 *Stock size* Medium
Stock 18th–19thC furniture, decorative items and general antiques
Trade only Yes
Open Mon–Sat 9.30am–5.30pm or Sun by appointment
Services Interior design

Guy Dennler
Contact Mr G Dennler
✉ The White Hart, 23 High Street, Dulverton, Somerset, TA22 9HB
☎ 01398 324300 Ⓕ 01398 324301
Est. 1979 *Stock size* Medium
Stock 18th–19thC English furniture, decorative items
Open Mon–Sat 10am–5pm
Fairs Battersea Decorative Fair
Services Restorations

Out Of The Blue
Contact Finny or Nigel Muers-Raby
✉ 4 Fore Street, Dulverton, Somerset, PA22 9EX
☎ 01398 324155
Est. 2001 *Stock size* Medium
Stock Decorative items for you and your home
Open Tues–Sat 10.30am–4pm

Anthony Sampson
Contact Mr A Sampson
✉ Holland House, Bridge Street, Dulverton, Somerset, TA22 9HJ
☎ 01398 324247 Ⓕ 01398 324027
Ⓜ 07767 842409
Est. 1968 *Stock size* Medium
Stock Furniture, general antiques
Open Mon–Sat 9.30am–5.30pm Sun by appointment
Services Valuations

DUNSTER

The Crooked Window
Contact Robert Ricketts
7 High Street, Dunster, Somerset, TA24 6SF
01643 821606
077641 75627
Est. 1987 *Stock size* Medium
Stock 17th–18thC English furniture, Chinese and European ceramics and works of art, including jade
Open Mon–Sat 10am–5.30pm
Fairs Wilton House
Services Valuations

The Linen Press
Contact Anne Fisher
22 Church Street, Dunster, Somerset, TA24 6SH
01643 821802
Est. 1986 *Stock size* Large
Stock Antique and new English and French linen and textiles
Open Mon–Sun 10.30am–5pm
Services Mail order

FRESHFORD

Freshfords (LAPADA, CINOA, BABAADA)
Contact Mr Simon Powell
High Street, Freshford, Bath, Somerset, BA2 7WF
01225 722111 01225 722991
07970 517332 or 07720838877
antiques@freshfords.com
www.freshfords.com
Est. 1973 *Stock size* Large
Stock Regency period furniture
Open Mon–Fri 10am–5pm Sat 10am–1pm by appointment
Fairs Olympia, Chelsea
Services Valuations, restorations, shipping, book search

FROME

Antiques and Country Living
Contact Mrs D M Williams
43–44 Vallis Way, Frome, Somerset, BA11 3BA
01373 463015
07780 8933076
Est. 1994 *Stock size* Large
No. of dealers 4
Stock 18th–19thC pottery and porcelain, Georgian–Edwardian furniture, books
Open Mon–Sun 9.30am–5.30pm

Steve Vee Bransgrove Collectables
Contact Steve
6 Catherine Hill, Frome, Somerset, BA11 1BY
01373 453225
07977 694537
Est. 1995 *Stock size* Medium
Stock Collectables, advertising, vintage magazines, ephemera, nostalgia
Open Mon–Sat 10am–5pm Thurs closed in winter 10am–2pm in summer
Services Valuations

Cooper and Tanner Chartered Surveyors
Contact Gillian Holland
The Agricultural Centre, Standerwick, Frome, Somerset, BA11 2QB
01373 831010 01373 831103
Est. 1900
Open Mon–Fri 9am–5pm
Sales Furniture, fine art and antiques sale Wed 10.30am, viewing Wed 7.30am prior to sale
Frequency Weekly
Catalogues No

Frome Reclamation (SALVO)
Contact Steve Horler
Station Approach, Frome, Somerset, BA11 1RE
01373 463919 01373 453122
07836 277507
Est. 1987 *Stock size* Large
Stock Architectural antiques, including roofing, flooring, period fireplaces, doors, bathrooms, etc
Open Mon–Fri 8am–5.30pm Sat 8am–4.30pm

GLASTONBURY

Bookbarn Ltd
17 Market Place, Glastonbury, Somerset, BA6 9HL
01458 835698
bookbarn@netcomuk.co.uk
Est. 1997 *Stock size* Large
Stock Antiquarian and second-hand books
Open Mon–Sat 10am–6pm Sun noon–5pm
Services Valuations, book search

Courtyard Books
Contact Mr Mills
2–4 High Street, Glastonbury, Somerset, BA6 9DU
01458 831800
Est. 1995 *Stock size* Large
Stock Antiquarian, esoteric, New Age and magic books
Open Mon–Sun 9.30am–5.30pm

Metropolis Art Deco (SCC)
Contact Helen Smith
3 Monarch Mews, 15 High Street, Glastonbury, Somerset, BA6 9DP
01458 833240/253120
www.metropolisartdeco.co.uk
Est. 1984 *Stock size* Large
Stock Art Deco including ceramics, light fittings, Moorcroft, Susie Cooper, Clarice Cliff, small furniture, Shelley
Open Thurs–Sat 10am–4.30pm closed Wed or by appointment
Fairs Battersea Art Deco,
Services Valuations, selling on commission

HIGHBRIDGE

Colin Dyte Exports Ltd
Contact Mr C Dyte
The Old Bacon Factory, Huntspill Road, Highbridge, Somerset, TA9 3DE
01278 788590 01278 788604
07836 594610/572323
Est. 1949 *Stock size* Large
Stock General antiques and shipping
Open Mon–Sat 7.30am–6pm or by appointment
Fairs Newark, Ardingly
Services Packing service

ILCHESTER

Gilbert and Dale
Contact Roy Gilbert or Joan Dale
The Old Chapel, Church Street, Ilchester, Yeovil, Somerset, BA22 8LN
01935 840464 01935 841599
Est. 1969 *Stock size* Medium
Stock English and French country furniture and accessories
Trade only Mainly trade
Open Mon–Fri 9am–5.30pm

ILMINSTER

Ilminster Auctions
Contact Mrs J Purchase

✉ Rear of 21 West Street, Ilminster, Somerset, TA19 9AA 🅿
☎ 01460 64151 🅕 01460 54261
Est. 1979
Open Tues Fri 11am–5.30pm or by appointment
Sales Antiques and collectors' sales, normally last Sat in month, or Thurs at 6pm, best to check in advance. Sales start at 10.30am on Sat and previews are Fri 9am–7pm
Frequency Monthly
Catalogues Yes

LANGPORT

⊞ Myrtle Antiques
Contact David or Chris Knight
✉ **Staceys Court, Bow Street, Langport, Somerset, TA10 9PQ** 🅿
☎ 01458 252666 🅕 01458 252666
Ⓜ 07967 355490
Ⓦ www.myrtleantiques.co.uk
Est. 1992 *Stock size* Medium
Stock English and European furniture, also reproduction pine and elm
Open Mon–Fri 9am–5.30pm Sat 9.30am–3pm
Services Restoration and furniture makers

LYDEARD ST LAWRENCE

The Coach House
Contact Clare Roberts
✉ **Handycross Farmhouse, Handycross, Lydeard St Lawrence, Somerset, TA4 3PL** 🅿
☎ 01984 667568
Est. 1996 *Stock size* Large
No. of dealers 11
Stock A wide range of furniture, collectables, silver, ceramics
Open Thurs–Sun Bank Holidays 11am–5pm

MARTOCK

⊞ Bowen & Co
Contact Jason Bowen
✉ **9B The Green, Martock, Somerset, TA12 6NE**
☎ 01935 822100
Est. 2001 *Stock size* Medium
Stock Furniture, jewellery, china, crystals, coins
Open Wed–Sun 9.30am–5.30pm
Fairs Wembley
Services Restorations

⊞ Castle Reclamation (SALVO)
Contact Mr A Wills
✉ **Parrett Works, Martock, Somerset, TA12 6AE** 🅿
☎ 01935 826483 🅕 01935 826791
Ⓔ info@castlereclamation.com
Ⓦ www.castlereclamation.com
Est. 1989 *Stock size* Medium
Stock Architectural antiques, stone masonry, fireplaces
Open Mon–Fri 8.30am–5pm Sat 10am–1pm

MIDSOMER NORTON

⊞ Somervale Antiques (BADA, LAPADA, CINOA, BABAADA)
Contact Wing Commander Ron Thomas
✉ **The Poplars, 6 Radstock Road, Midsomer Norton, Bath, Somerset, BA3 2AJ** 🅿
☎ 01761 412686 🅕 01761 412686
Ⓜ 07885 088022
Ⓔ ronthomas@somervaleantiquesglass.co.uk
Ⓦ www.somervaleantiquesglass.co.uk
Est. 1972 *Stock size* Large
Stock English 18th–19thC drinking glasses, decanters, cut and coloured, Bristol and Nailsea glass, scent bottles
Open By appointment. Trains to Bath met by arrangement
Services Valuations

MINEHEAD

⊞ Memory Lane
Contact Mr M Ryan
✉ **53a The Avenue, Minehead, Somerset, TA24 5BB** 🅿
☎ 01643 708991
Est. 1998 *Stock size* Large
Stock Furniture, collectables
Open Mon–Sat 10am–4pm Sat 10am–1pm closed Wed
Services Valuations

NORTH PETHERTON

⊞ Jays Antiques and Collectables
Contact Mrs J Alba
✉ **121a Fore Street, North Petherton, Bridgwater, Somerset, TA6 6SA** 🅿
☎ 01278 662688
Est. 1994 *Stock size* Medium
Stock China, glass, clocks
Open Mon 10am–1pm Tues–Sat 10am–4.30pm closed Wed
Fairs Tailsman Fairs, Bristol

PORLOCK

⊞ Magpie Antiques & Collectables
Contact Glenys Battams
✉ **High Street, Porlock, Somerset, TA24 8PT** 🅿
☎ 01643 862775/01271 850669
Ⓜ 07721 679020
Est. 1980 *Stock size* Medium
Stock Antique jewellery, silver, scent bottles, objects of virtue
Open Telephone call advisable
Fairs NEC, Westpoint
Services Valuations, restorations

QUEEN CAMEL

⊞ Steven Ferdinando (PBFA)
Contact Mr Steven Ferdinando
✉ **The Old Vicarage, Queen Camel, Yeovil, Somerset, BA22 7NG** 🅿
☎ 01935 850210 🅕 01935 850210
Est. 1978 *Stock size* Medium
Stock Antiquarian and second-hand books
Open Visitors welcome by appointment
Fairs PBFA
Services Valuations, book binding and book search

RADSTOCK

⊞ Notts Pine
Contact Jeff Nott
✉ **Old Redhouse Farm, Stratton on the Fosse, Radstock, Bath, Somerset, BA3 4QE** 🅿
☎ 01761 419911
Est. 1986 *Stock size* Medium
Stock Antique pine furniture
Open Mon–Fri 9am–6pm

SHEPTON MALLET

⊞ Edward Marnier Antiques (BABAADA)
Contact Mr E Marnier
✉ **Old Bowlish House, Forum Lane, Bowlish, Shepton Mallet, Somerset, BA4 5JA** 🅿
☎ 01749 343340
Ⓜ 07785 110122
Ⓔ emarnier@ukonline.co.uk
Est. 1989 *Stock size* Medium

Stock 17th–20thC furniture, pictures, mirrors, interesting items, antique rugs, carpets
Open Mon–Sun 9am–6pm or by appointment
Fairs Olympia, Bath, Battersea
Services Valuations

MJM's
Contact Miranda Powell
✉ **F Block, Anglo Trading Estate, Commercial Road, Shepton Mallet, Somerset, BA4 5BY** Ⓟ
☎ 01749 344881
Ⓜ Antiques enquiries 07774 935079 Reclamation enquiries 07976 361948
Est. 1993 *Stock size* Large
No. of dealers 17
Stock General and architectural antiques, period bathrooms and collectables
Open Mon–Sat 10.30am–4.30pm

Parkways Antiques
Contact Pauline Brereton
✉ **31 High Street, Shepton Mallet, Somerset, BA4 5AQ** Ⓟ
☎ 01749 345065
Est. 1972 *Stock size* Small
Stock Period and Victorian furniture, reproduction pine
Open Mon–Fri 10am–4pm closed Wed
Services Reproduction pine made to order

Pennard House Antiques (BABAADA, LAPADA)
Contact Martin Dearden
✉ **East Pennard, Shepton Mallet, Somerset, BA4 6TP** Ⓟ
☎ 01749 860731 Ⓕ 01749 860732
Ⓜ 07802 243569
Ⓔ pennardantiques@ukonline.co.uk
Est. 1979 *Stock size* Large
Stock French and English country furniture, decorative items
Open Mon–Sat 9.30am–5.30pm or by appointment
Fairs Bath Decorative and Antiques Fair Battersea Decorative and Textile Fair
Services Restorations, shipping and deliveries

SOMERTON

John Gardiner
Contact Mr John Gardiner
✉ **Monteclefe House, Kirkham Street, Somerton, Somerset, TA11 7NL** Ⓟ
☎ 01458 272238 Ⓕ 01458 274329
Ⓜ 07831 274427
Est. 1968 *Stock size* Medium
Stock General antiques, decorative items
Open By appointment
Services Workshop facilities

Knole Barometers
Contact David Crawshaw
✉ **Bingham House, West Street, Somerton, Somerset, TA11 7PS** Ⓟ
☎ 01458 241015 Ⓕ 01458 241706
Ⓜ 07785 364567
Ⓔ dccops@btconnect.com
Est. 1997 *Stock size* Medium
Stock Barometers, scientific instruments
Open Mon–Fri 9am–5pm
Services Valuations, restorations

London Cigarette Card Company Ltd
Contact Mr Laker
✉ **West Street, Somerton, Somerset, TA11 6QP** Ⓟ
☎ 01458 273452 Ⓕ 01458 273515
Ⓔ cards@londoncigcard.co.uk
Ⓦ www.londoncigcard.co.uk
Est. 1927 *Stock size* Large
Stock Cigarette cards. Publishes catalogues, card collectors magazines, trade cards
Open Mon–Sat 9.30am–5pm closed Wed Sat pm
Services Postal auctions

Simon's Books
Contact Mr B Ives
✉ **Broad Street, Somerton, Somerset, TA11 7NH** Ⓟ
☎ 01458 272313
Est. 1979 *Stock size* Medium
Stock General antiquarian and second-hand books
Open Mon–Sat 10am–4.30pm

Somerton Antique Centre
Contact Maurice Waite
✉ **Market Place, Somerton, Somerset, TA11 7NB** Ⓟ
☎ 01458 274423
Est. 1997 *Stock size* Large
No. of dealers 42
Stock General antiques including paintings, linen, militaria, pine and oak
Open Mon–Sat 10am–5pm
Services Restorations

Westville House Antiques
Contact Derek or Margaret Stacey
✉ **Westville House, Littleton, Somerton, Somerset, TA11 6NP** Ⓟ
☎ 01458 273376 Ⓕ 01458 273376
Ⓔ antique@westville.co.uk
Ⓦ www.westville.co.uk
Est. 1986 *Stock size* Large
Stock Antique country, pine, oak and mahogany furniture
Open Mon–Sat 9am–5.30pm or by appointment

SPARKFORD

Bonhams & Brooks
Contact Mike Penn
✉ **The Haynes Motor Museum, Sparkford, Nr Yeovil, Somerset, BA22 7UI**
☎ 01963 440804 Ⓕ 01963 441004
Ⓦ www.bonhams.com
Open Mon–Fri 9am–5pm
Sales Regional Representative for Somerset

STOKE SUB HAMDON

R G Watkins (PBFA)
Contact Mr R G Watkins
✉ **9 North Street Workshops, Stoke Sub Hamdon, Somerset, TA14 6QR** Ⓟ
☎ 01935 822891 Ⓕ 01935 822891
Ⓔ rgw@eurobell.co.uk
Ⓦ www.rgw.eurobell.co.uk
Est. 1985 *Stock size* Small
Stock Antiquarian books, prints, portraits. Books on art and antiques a speciality
Open Fri 10am–5pm or by appointment
Fairs PBFA
Services Valuations

TAUNTON

The Bookshop
Contact Sarah Allen
✉ **13a Paul Street, Taunton, Somerset, TA1 3PF** Ⓟ
☎ 01823 326963 Ⓕ 01458 241007
Ⓜ 07971 245301
Est. 1997 *Stock size* Medium
Stock Rare and second-hand books
Open Mon Tues Fri Sat 10am–4.30pm Thurs noon–4.30pm
Services Book search

Greenslade Taylor Hunt (SOFAA)
Contact Stuart Triggol
Magdalene House, Church Square, Taunton, Somerset, TA1 1SB
01823 332525 01823 353120
maghouse@dircom.co.uk
www.auction-net.co.uk
Est. 1843
Open Mon–Fri 9am–5pm
Sales Monthly fine art sales last Thurs 10am, viewing Tues 9.30am–4.30pm Wed 9.30am–7.30pm. Weekly household sale Wed 10am, viewing Tues 2.30–5pm. Also specialist clocks, silver, jewellery, books, collectors' sales. Phone for details
Frequency Monthly
Catalogues Yes

Hallidays (LAPADA)
Contact James Halliday
6 St James Street, Taunton, Somerset, TA1 1JH
01823 324073 01823 324073
Est. 1987 *Stock size* Medium
Stock 18th–19thC furniture, upholstery, ceramics
Open Mon–Sat 9.30am–5.30pm
Services Valuations, reupholstery, furniture renovation

Lawrences Taunton Ltd (ARVA)
Contact Angela Morley
The Corfield Hall, Magdalene Street, Taunton, Somerset, TA1 1SG
01823 330567 01823 330596
enquiries.taunton@lawrences.co.uk
www.lawrences.co.uk
Est. 1975
Open Mon–Fri 9am–5pm
Sales Fortnightly general sale first and third Tues 11am (no catalogue), viewing Mon 9am–7pm Tues 9am–11am prior to sale. 4 fine art sales a year Tues 11am, viewing Sat 9.30am–12.30pm Mon 9am–7pm. Biannual collectors sale Feb and August Tues 9.30am, viewing as fine arts sale. Biannual sporting sale April and October Tues 11am, viewing as fine arts sale
Frequency Fortnightly
Catalogues Yes

O'Marley's Ghost
Contact C Harvey
8 Station Road, Taunton, Somerset, TA1 1NH
01823 334080
Est. 2000 *Stock size* Medium
Stock Antique pine furniture, garden items
Open Mon–Sat 10.30am–4.30pm closed Wed
Services Stripping

Russell Books
Contact Mr Desmond Kerr
21 Bath Place, Taunton, Somerset, TA1 4ER
01823 330887
Est. 1998 *Stock size* Medium
Stock Antiquarian and second-hand books
Open Mon–Sat 10am–5.30pm
Services Book search

Selwoods Antiques
Contact Mr J.R Selwood
Queen Anne Cottage, Mary Street, Taunton, Somerset, TA1 3PE
01823 272780
Est. 1927 *Stock size* Large
Stock Furniture
Open Mon–Sat 9.30am–5pm

Staple Grove Antiques Centre
Contact Norman Clarke
7–9 Staplegrove Road, Taunton, Somerset, TA1 1DE
01823 283050 01823 283050
Est. 2000 *Stock size* Large
No. of dealers 18
Stock Period furniture, ceramics, jewellery, stamps, collectables
Open Mon–Sat 10am–5pm Sun 11am–4pm
Services Valuations

Taunton Antiques Market
Contact Mike Spooner
25–29 Silver Street, Taunton, Somerset, TA1 3DH
020 7969 1500 020 7969 1639
Est. 1978
No. of dealers 100
Stock General antiques and collectables including specialists in most fields
Open Mon 9am–4pm including Bank Holidays

THORNBURY

Thornbury Antiques
Contact Mrs H Hill
3a High Street, Thornbury, Bristol, BS35 2AE
01454 413722
Est. 1993 *Stock size* Medium
Stock Victorian pine furniture
Open Mon–Sat 10am–5pm

TIMSBURY

Ministry of Pine
Contact Tony Lawrence or Susan Dunn
Timsbury Village Workshop, Unit 2, Timsbury Industrial Estate, Hayeswood Road, Timsbury, Bath, Somerset, BA3 1HQ
01761 472297/434938
07770 588536
ministryofpine.uk@virgin.net
www.ministryofpine.co.uk
Est. 1980 *Stock size* Large
Stock Antique pine furniture both painted and stripped
Open Mon–Fri 9am–6pm Sat Sun 10am–4pm
Services Valuations, restorations and stripping

WEDMORE

Tinkers Antiques
Contact Mrs Sharpe
The Cottage Shop, Bath Street, Cheddar, Somerset, BS28 4EB
01934 713618
Est. 1993 *Stock size* Medium
Stock Country pine furniture, jewellery, general antiques
Open Mon–Sat 10am–5pm

WELLINGTON

Junket Bargain Bygones
Contact Mr Parsons
35 Fore Street, Wellington, Somerset, TA21 8AG
01823 667665
Est. 1992 *Stock size* Large
Stock General antiques, Victorian and post-Victorian furniture, collectables
Open Mon–Sat 10am–4pm

WELLS

Alcove Antiques
Contact Nancy Alcock
1 Priest Row, Wells, Somerset, BA5 2PY

☎ 01749 672164 Ⓕ 01749 678925
Ⓜ 07885 508736
Est. 1979 *Stock size* Medium
Stock China, brass, copper, pine, Victorian–Edwardian mahogany
Open Mon–Sat 10.30am–5pm closed Wed
Services Restorations

Kym Grant Bookseller
Contact Mr K Grant
✉ **82 Southover Wells, Wells, Somerset, BA5 1UH**
☎ 01749 675618
Est. 1995 *Stock size* Small
Stock Antiquarian and second-hand books, children's annuals and books
Open By appointment
Fairs Bloomsbury (monthly)

Bernard G House Longcase Clocks
Contact Mr B G House
✉ **13 Market Place, Wells, Somerset, BA5 2RF** Ⓟ
☎ 01749 672607 Ⓕ 01749 672607
Est. 1971 *Stock size* Medium
Stock Longcase clocks, barographs, barometers, clocks, telescopes, scientific instruments
Open Mon–Sat 10am–5.30pm or by appointment
Services Repairs and restorations to clocks and barometers

Wells Auction Rooms
Contact Nick Ewing or Cynthia Peak
✉ **66–68 Southover, Wells, Somerset, BA5 1UH** Ⓟ
☎ 01749 678094/0117 973 7201
Est. 1845
Sales Sale Wed 1.30pm, viewing Tues noon–5pm day of sale from 9am
Frequency Monthly
Catalogues Yes

Wells Reclamation Company
✉ **Coxley, Wells, Somerset, BA5 1RQ** Ⓟ
☎ 01749 677087 Ⓕ 01749 671098
Ⓔ enquiries@wellsreclamation.com
Ⓦ www.wellsreclaimation.com
Est. 1984 *Stock size* Large
Stock Architectural antiques, bricks, tiles, slates, fireplaces, doors, finials, pews, etc
Open Mon–Fri 8.30am–5.30pm Sat 9am–4pm
Services Make oak studded doors to order

WESTON-SUPER-MARE

Clifton House Furniture
Contact Michael Barrett
✉ **67 Clifton Road, Weston-super-Mare, Somerset, BS23 1BW** Ⓟ
☎ 01934 625217
Est. 1987 *Stock size* Medium
Stock Furniture, mainly pine
Open Mon–Sat 10am–6pm
Services Restorations

David Hughes Antiques
Contact Mr Hughes
✉ **37 Baker Street, Weston-super-Mare, Somerset, BS23 3AD** Ⓟ
☎ 01934 628007
Ⓜ 07860 964100
Est. 1974 *Stock size* Medium
Stock General antiques, Arts and Crafts, Art Nouveau
Open Mon Sat 9am–1pm Tues Fri 9am–1pm 2–4pm
Fairs Newark, Ardingly
Services House clearances

Severn Antiques (RADS)
Contact Mr A Coles
✉ **59 Severn Road, Weston-super-Mare, Somerset, BS23 1DR** Ⓟ
☎ 01934 413118
Ⓜ 07836 688891
Est. 1970 *Stock size* Medium
Stock General
Open Mon–Fri 9am–4pm Sat 9am–2pm
Services Valuations, shipping

Sterling Books (ABA, PBFA)
Contact Mr Nisbet
✉ **43a Locking Road, Weston-super-Mare, Somerset, BS23 3DG** Ⓟ
☎ 01934 625056
Ⓔ sterling.books@talk21.com
Est. 1966 *Stock size* Large
Stock Antiquarian and second-hand books on every subject
Open Tues–Sat 10am–5.30pm Thurs 10am–1pm
Services Valuations, book binding and picture framing

Terry's Antiques and Collectables
Contact Terry
✉ **The Inshops, Regent Street, Weston-Super-Mare, Somerset, BS23 1SR** Ⓟ
☎ 01934 643374
Ⓜ 07980 408943
Est. 1986 *Stock size* Medium
Stock Victorian furniture, ceramics, silver
Open Mon–Sat 9am–5.30pm Sun 11am–5pm
Services House clearance

Richard Twort
Contact Richard Twort
✉ **14 Sand Road, Sand Bay, Weston Super Mare, Somerset, BS22 9UH** Ⓟ
☎ 01934 641900 Ⓕ 01934 641900
Ⓜ 07711 939789
Ⓔ walls@mirage-interiors.co.uk
Est. 1962 *Stock size* Medium
Stock Barographs, thermographs, rain gauges, all types of meteorological instruments
Open By appointment

WILLITON

Courtyard Antiques
Contact Liz Cain
✉ **The Courtyard Home Farm, St Audries, Williton, Taunton, Somerset, TA4 4DR** Ⓟ
☎ 01984 633701 Ⓕ 01984 633701
Est. 1995 *Stock size* Medium
Stock Country, pine, oak and elm furniture, decorative items
Open Thurs–Tues 10am–4pm
Services Restorations

WINCANTON

Green Dragon Antiques and Crafts Centre
Contact Sally Denning
✉ **24 High Street, Wincanton, Somerset, BA9 9JF** Ⓟ
☎ 01963 34111
Ⓦ www.greendragonantiques.com
Est. 1991 *Stock size* Large
Stock General antiques, jewellery, crafts
Open Mon–Sun 9am–5pm
Services Valuations, free gift wrap, jewellery repairs

⊞ **Alan and Kathy Stacey (BAFRA)**
Contact Alan Stacey
✉ **PO Box 2771, Wincanton, Somerset, BA9 9YY** 🅿
☎ 01963 33988 Ⓕ 01963 32555
Ⓔ akstacey@cwcom.net
Est. 1990 *Stock size* Medium
Stock Tortoiseshell, ivory, shagreen and mother-of-pearl tea caddies and boxes
Open By appointment
Services Valuations, restorations

WIVELISCOMBE

⊞ **Yew Tree Antiques Warehouse**
Contact N or S Nation
✉ **Old Brewery, Wiveliscombe, Taunton, Somerset, TA4 2NT** 🅿
☎ 01984 623950/623914
Stock size Large
Stock Victorian–Edwardian and French furniture, Lloyd Loom
Open Tue–Fri 11am–4.30pm Sat 10am–5pm

YEOVIL

⊞ **Phone Cards Centre (TCC)**
Contact Mr Fowle
✉ **16 Boundary Road, Houndstone, Yeovil, Somerset, BA22 8SF**
☎ 01935 431314 Ⓕ 01935 427412
Ⓔ jfowle8142@aol.com
Est. 1993 *Stock size* Medium
Stock Phone cards bought, sold and exchanged
Open By appointment
Fairs Wessex Fairs, Telephone Collectors Club Fair
Services Valuations

⊞ **Yeovil Collectors Centre**
Contact Barry Scott
✉ **16 Hendford, Yeovil, Somerset, BA20 1TE** 🅿
☎ 01935 433739 Ⓕ 01935 433739
Est. 1969 *Stock size* Small
Stock Militaria, postcards, general collectables, animals, blue-and-white, Toby jugs
Open Mon Wed–Sat 9am–5pm

WILTSHIRE

BRADFORD ON AVON

⊞ **Audley House Antiques (BABAADA)**
Contact Mr R B Brown
✉ **5 Wooley Street, Bradford on Avon, Wiltshire, BA15 1AD**
☎ 01225 862476
Est. 1993 *Stock size* Large
Stock Victorian and Edwardian furniture, silver, pictures, porcelain
Open Mon–Sat 9am–6pm Sun by appointment
Fairs Westonbirt, Arley, Snape
Services Valuations

⊞ **Avon Antiques (BADA)**
Contact Andrew Jenkins
✉ **25–27 Market Street, Bradford on Avon, Wiltshire, BA15 1LL**
☎ 01225 862052 Ⓕ 01225 868763
Est. 1963 *Stock size* Large
Stock 17th–mid19thC furniture, clocks, barometers, metalwork, needlework, treen, English furniture
Open Mon–Sat 9.30am–5.30pm
Fairs Grosvenor House Antiques Fair

⊞ **Granary Antiques (BABAADA)**
Contact Julia or Tony Chowles
✉ **The Granary, Pound Lane, Bradford on Avon, Wiltshire, BA15 1LF** 🅿
☎ 01225 867781 Ⓕ 01225 867781
Ⓔ tony@granarypine.co.uk
Est. 1987 *Stock size* Large
Stock Country pine furniture, collectables
Open Mon–Sun 10am–5pm

⊞ **Mac Humble Antiques (BADA)**
Contact Mr Humble
✉ **7–9 Woolley Street, Bradford on Avon, Wiltshire, BA15 1AD** 🅿
☎ 01225 866329 Ⓕ 01225 866329
Ⓜ 07702 501888
Ⓔ mac.humble@virgin.net
Ⓦ www.machumbleantiques.co.uk
Est. 1979 *Stock size* Small
Stock 18th–19thC furniture, needlework, samplers, metalware and decorative items
Open Mon–Fri 9am–6pm Sat 9am–1pm
Fairs Olympia (Nov), BADA Fair (March)
Services Valuations, restorations

⊞ **Moxhams Antiques (LAPADA, BABAADA)**
Contact Roger, Jill or Nick Bichard
✉ **17, 23 & 24 Silver Street, Bradford on Avon, Wiltshire, BA15 1JZ** 🅿
☎ 01225 862789 Ⓕ 01225 867844
Ⓜ 07768 960295
Ⓔ Jill@moxhams-antiques.demon.co.uk
Est. 1967 *Stock size* Large
Stock Good 17th–early 19thC mahogany and oak furniture, ceramics, tapestries and objects
Open Mon–Sat 9am–5.30pm
Fairs Olympia (June and Nov) NEC (Jan)

⊞ **No. 32**
Contact Katie Banks
✉ **32 Silver Street, Bradford on Avon, Wiltshire, BA15 1JX** 🅿
☎ 01225 862981
Est. 1996 *Stock size* Medium
Stock Antique pine, collectables
Open Tues–Sun 10am–5pm

⊞ **Roundabout Shop**
Contact Clive or Pam Freeman
✉ **1–2 Siver Street, Bradford on Avon, Wiltshire, BA15 1JX** 🅿
☎ 01225 863241
Est. 1960 *Stock size* Large
Stock Antiquarian books, literature, modern first editions, sports, art, history, travel, military. Prints of most subjects, particularly topographical and period costumes
Open Mon–Sun 9am–5.30pm half day Wed out of season
Services Cutting and mounting prints, framing

⊞ **Town & Country Antiques (BADA, BABAADA)**
Contact Mrs R Drewett
✉ **34 Market Street, Bradford on Avon, Wiltshire, BA15 1LL** 🅿
☎ 01225 867877 Ⓕ 01225 867877
Est. 1989 *Stock size* Large
Stock Fine Georgian and Regency English furniture, tea caddies and snuff shoes
Open Mon–Fri 10am–5pm Sat 10am–1pm or by appointment

BRINKWORTH

North Wilts Exporters
Contact Caroline Thornbury
Farm Hill House, The Street, Brinkworth, Swindon, Wiltshire, SN5 5AJ
01666 510876
Est. 1974 *Stock size* Large
Stock Eastern European pine, oak, and mahogany furniture
Open Mon–Sat 9am–6pm or by appointment
Fairs Newark
Services Packers and shippers

BROAD HINTON

Bookmark (PBFA)
Contact Leonora Excell or Anne Excell
Fortnight, Wick Down, Broad Hinton, Swindon, Wiltshire, SN4 9NR
01793 731693 F 01793 731782
M 07788 841305
E leonora.excell@btinternet.com
Est. 1972 *Stock size* Medium
Stock Children's and illustrated antiquarian books. Mail order business with 3–4 catalogues a year
Open By appointment
Fairs PBFA
Services Book search

CHERHILL

P A Oxley Antique Clocks & Barometers (LAPADA)
Contact Mr M Oxley
The Old Rectory, Cherhill, Calne, Wiltshire, SN11 8UX
01249 816227 F 01249 821285
E paoxley@btinternet.com
W www.british-antiqueclocks.com
Est. 1971 *Stock size* Large
Stock Antique clocks and barometers, longcase clocks a speciality
Open Mon–Sat 9.30am–5pm closed Wed or by appointment
Services Delivery and shipping

CHIPPENHAM

Atwell Martin (RICS)
Contact Paul Dunn
2 New Road, Chippenham, Wiltshire, SN15 1EJ
01249 462222 F 01249 447780
Open 9am–6pm
Sales General antiques Sat 10am, viewing 10am–5pm. Five selected antiques sales per annum
Frequency Three weekly
Catalogues Yes

Collectors Corner
Contact Karen Groves
36 The Causeway, Chippenham, Wiltshire, SN15 3DB
01249 461617/01249 446044
Est. 1990 *Stock size* Large
Stock Antiques, collectables, musical instruments
Open Mon–Sat 9am–5pm

Cross Hayes Antiques (LAPADA)
Contact David Brooks
Unit 6 Westbrook Farm, Draycot Cerne, Chippenham, Wiltshire, SN16 5LH
01249 720033 F 01249 720033
E david@crosshayes.co.uk
W www.crosshayes.co.uk
Est. 1976 *Stock size* Large
Stock Furniture
Open Mon–Sat 9am–5pm
Services Container packing service

Heirloom & Howard Ltd (BABAADA)
Contact David or Angela Howard
Manor Farm, West Yatton, Chippenham, Wiltshire, SN14 7EU
01249 783038 F 01249 783039
Est. 1973 *Stock size* Medium
Stock Chinese armorial and other porcelain, armorial paintings, coach panels, hall chairs, portrait engravings
Open Mon–Fri 10am–6pm Sat 10am–6pm or by appointment
Services Bidding at auction

CHRISTIAN MALFORD

Harley Antiques
Contact Mr Harley
The Comedy, Main Road, Christian Malford, Chippenham, Wiltshire, SN15 4BS
01249 720112 F 01249 720553
Est. 1959 *Stock size* Large
Stock General antiques including decorative and unusual items, conservatory furniture and objects
Open Mon–Sun 9am–6pm

CORSHAM

Automattic Comics
Contact Matthew Booker
Unit 2, 17 Pickwick Road, Corsham, Wiltshire, SN13 9BQ
01249 701647
E matt@automatticcomics.com
W www.automatticcomics.com
Est. 1995 *Stock size* Large
Stock American import comics, old and new action figures, *Star Wars* figures
Open Mon Tues noon–5pm Thurs–Sat 10am–5pm
Fairs NEC memorabilia (March, Nov)

Matthew Eden
Contact Mrs M Eden or Matthew Eden
Pickwick End, Corsham, Wiltshire, SN13 0JB
01249 713335 F 01249 713644
M 07899 926076
E mail@mattheweden.co.uk
W mattheweden.com
Est. 1952 *Stock size* Large
Stock General including garden furniture
Open Mon–Sat 9am–6pm
Fairs Chelsea Flower Show

DEVIZES

Henry Aldridge & Son
Contact Alan Aldridge
Unit 1, Bath Road Business Centre, Devizes, Wiltshire, SN10 1XA
01380 720199
E andrew.aldridge@virgin.net
W www.henry-aldridge.co.uk
Est. 1989
Open Mon–Fri 10am–4pm
Sales Monthly antiques sales, Bi-annual maritime and Titanic sale on Wed 6pm, preview Mon noon–4pm Tues noon–6.30pm Wed noon–6.30pm.
Catalogues Yes

Devizes Auction Centre (ARICS)
Contact Alan Aldridge
New Park Street, Devizes, Wiltshire, SN10 1DX
01380 720900 F 01380 721200
E andrew.aldridge@virgin.net
W www.henry-aldridge.co.uk
Est. 1989

Open Mon–Fri 10am–4pm
Sales Sale every Tues 10am, viewing Mon 4–7pm
Frequency Weekly
Catalogues Yes

Margaret Mead Antiques
Contact Mrs M Mead
19 Northgate Street, Devizes, Wiltshire, SN10 1JT
01380 721060/01793 533085
07740 536560
Est. 1982 *Stock size* Medium
Stock General antiques, Georgian–Edwardian furniture, clocks, china
Open Tues–Sat 10am–5pm closed Wed
Services Restorations

St Mary's Chapel Antiques (BABAADA)
Contact Richard Sanke
St Mary's Chapel, Northgate Street, Devizes, Wiltshire, SN10 1DE
01380 721399 01380 721399
richard@rsanke.freeserve.co.uk
www.st-marys-chapel-antiques.org.uk
Est. 1971 *Stock size* Large
Stock Original painted and country furniture, garden antiques and accessories
Open Mon–Sat 10am–6pm closed Wed
Fairs Bath Decorative and Antiques Fair
Services Selective restorations

DURRINGTON

Cannon Militaria
Contact Mr L Webb
21 Bulford Road, Durrington, Salisbury, Wiltshire, SP4 8DL
01980 655099
Est. 1995 *Stock size* Large
Stock Military collectables
Open Thurs Fri 9.30am–5pm Sat 9.00am–1pm
Services Valuations

LYNEHAM

Pillars Antiques
Contact Mr K Clifford
10 The Banks, Lyneham, Chippenham, Wiltshire, SN15 4NS
01249 890632
Est. 1986 *Stock size* Large
Stock Old pine, 1940s and mahogany furniture, bric-a-brac
Open Mon–Sat 10am–5pm Sun 11am–5pm Wed by appointment closed Thurs

MALMESBURY

Athelstan's Attic
Contact Tim Harvey
The Cross Hayes, Malmesbury, Wiltshire, SN16 9AU
01666 825544/822678
07771 865318
Est. 1997 *Stock size* Large
Stock General house clearance items
Open Mon Wed Fri Sat 9.30am–4.30pm
Services House clearance

Andrew Britten Antiques
Contact Mr T M Tyler
48 High Street, Malmesbury, Wiltshire, SN16 9AT
01666 823376 01666 825563
maidolph@aol.com
Est. 1974 *Stock size* Small
Stock Small items of furniture, decorative accessories
Open Mon–Sat 9am–5.30pm
Services Valuations

Hilditch Auction (NAVA)
Contact Mr Hilditch
Gloucester Road Trading Estate, Malmesbury, Wiltshire, SN16 9JT
01666 822577 01666 825597
sales@hilditchauctions.co.uk
www.hilditchauctions.co.uk
Est. 1990
Open Mon–Fri 8.30am–5pm
Sales General household sale last Sat 10am every month, viewing Fri 10am–7pm, call for other dates
Frequency Monthly
Catalogues Yes

Rene Nicholls
Contact Mrs I Nicholls
56 High Street, Malmesbury, Wiltshire, SN16 9AT
01666 823089
Est. 1979 *Stock size* Medium
Stock English pottery and porcelain
Open Mon–Sat 9.30am–6pm or by appointment
Services Valuations, restorations

Sambourne House Antiques
Contact Tim or Kim Cove
Minety, Malmesbury, Wiltshire, SN16 9RQ
01666 860288 01666 860288
tkcove34@globalnet.co.uk
www.sambourne-pine.co.uk
Est. 1986 *Stock size* Large
Stock Antique Continental pine
Open Mon–Sun 9am–5pm
Services Hand-built kitchens, stripping

MANINGFORD BRUCE

Indigo
Contact Marion Bender or Richard Lightbown
Dairy Barn, Maningford Bruce, Wiltshire, SN9 6JW
01672 564722 01672 564733
07867 982233
indigo_uk@compuserve.com
Est. 1982 *Stock size* Large
Stock Antique Indian and Chinese furniture
Trade only Yes
Open By appointment
Fairs House and Garden fair
Services Restorations

MARLBOROUGH

Brocante Antiques Centre
Contact Peter Randall
6 London Road, Marlborough, Wiltshire, SN8 1PH
01672 516512 01672 516512
Est. 1995 *Stock size* Large
No. of dealers 20
Stock General antiques and collectables
Open Mon–Sat 10am–5pm
Services Restorations, valuations, pine stripping

Eureka Antiques
Contact Mr Newman
5 London Road, Marlborough, Wiltshire, SN8 1PH
01672 512072
Est. 1979 *Stock size* Medium
Stock Antique pots and furniture
Open Mon–Sun 9am–6pm

Katharine House Gallery (PBFA)
Contact Christopher Gange
Katharine House, The Parade, Marlborough, Wiltshire, SN8 1NE
01672 514040

WEST COUNTRY

Est. 1983 *Stock size* Medium
Stock Antiquarian and second-hand books, 20thC British pictures, general antiques and antiquities
Open Mon–Sat 10am–5.30pm
Fairs PBFA (Russell Hotel)

The Marlborough Parade Antique Centre
Contact Terry Page
The Parade, Marlborough, Wiltshire, SN8 1NE
01672 515331
Est. 1985 *Stock size* Large
Stock Small items, general antiques, very good quality
Open Mon–Sun 10am–5pm

The Rope Works
Contact Richard Nadin or Patrick Macintosh
The House (1860–1925), Katharine House Yard, Kennet Place, Marlborough, Wiltshire, SN8 1NQ
01672 512111
Est. 2000 *Stock size* Large
Stock 1600–1970 furniture, mirrors and lighting
Open Mon–Sat 10am–4pm or by appointment
Services Valuations

Nick Wheatley
Contact Nick Wheatley
The House (1860–1925), Katharine House Yard, Kennet Place, Marlborough, Wiltshire, SN8 1NQ
01672 512111
nick@thehouse1860–1925.com
www.thehouse1860–1925.com
Est. 1999 *Stock size* Large
Stock Furniture and accessories of the Arts and Crafts movement
Open Mon–Sat 10am–4pm or by appointment
Services Valuations, restorations, interior design and furnishing

D P White
Contact Mr White
59 High Street, Ramsbury, Marlborough, Wiltshire, SN8 2QN
01672 520261
Est. 1969 *Stock size* Large
Stock Victorian oil lamps, oil lamp spares (old and new stocked), brass, copper, furniture, clocks
Open Tues–Sat 10am–1pm 2–5pm closed Wed or by appointment
Services Longcase clock restoration

MELKSHAM

Peter Campbell Antiques (BABAADA)
Contact Mr P Campbell
59 Bath Road, Atworth, Melksham, Wiltshire, SN12 8JY
01225 709742
Est. 1976 *Stock size* Medium
Stock Country furniture, decorative items
Open Mon–Sat 10am–5pm Thurs and Sun by appointment

Dann Antiques Ltd (BABAADA)
Contact Gary Low
Unit S1, New Broughton Road, Melksham, Wiltshire, SN12 8BS
01225 707329 F 01225 790120
113665.1341@compuserve.com
Est. 1984 *Stock size* Large
Stock English mahogany furniture, furniture accessories
Open Mon–Fri 8.30am–5.30pm Sat 9am–1pm or by appointment
Services Restorations

Jaffray Antiques (BABAADA)
Contact Mrs J Carter
16 The Market Place, Melksham, Wiltshire, SN12 6EX
01225 702269 F 01225 790413
jaffray.antiques@talk21.com
Est. 1955 *Stock size* Large
Stock 18th–19thC furniture, tallboys, desks, linen presses, bamboo, dining tables, chests-of-drawers and Staffordshire, metalware
Open Mon–Fri 9am–5pm or by appointment

King Street Curios
Contact Lizzie Board
8–10 King Street, Melksham, Wiltshire, SN12 6HD
01225 790623
Est. 1987 *Stock size* Large
Stock General antiques, collectables
Open Mon–Sat 10am–5pm
Fairs Shepton Mallet, Royal Fairs, Walcot Street Antique Market

Polly's Parlour
Contact Pauline Hart
2–4 King Street, Melksham, Wiltshire, SN12 6HD
01225 706418
Est. 1999 *Stock size* Large
Stock General antiques, collectables, decorative items
Open Mon–Sat and Bank Holidays 10am–4.30pm
Services View by appointment

MERE

Finan and Co
Contact Robert Finan
The Square, Mere, Wiltshire, BA12 6DJ
01747 861411 F 01747 861411
enquiries@finan&co.co.uk
www.finanandco.co.uk
Est. 1997
Open Tues Thurs Sat 10am–6pm or by appointment
Sales Antiques sale Spring and Autumn Sat, viewing Thurs Fri 10am–7pm Sat 9–11am prior to sale. General monthly sales in conjunction with other auction houses
Frequency Biannual
Catalogues Yes

NETHERHAMPTON

Victor Mahy (BADA)
Contact John H Parnaby
Netherhampton House, Netherhampton, Salisbury, Wiltshire, SP2 8PU
01722 743131 F 01722 743042
johnparnaby@netherhamptonhouse.co.uk
www.netherhamptonhouse.co.uk
Est. 1918 *Stock size* Large
Stock 17th–18thC furniture
Open Mon–Sat 9.30am–5.30pm

NORTH WRAXALL

Delomosne & Son Ltd (BADA, BABAADA)
Contact Mr T N M Osborne
Court Close, North Wraxall, Chippenham, Wiltshire, SN14 7AD
01225 891505 F 01225 891907
timosborne@delomosne.co.uk
www.delomosne.co.uk
Est. 1905 *Stock size* Large
Stock Glass, porcelain, pottery, enamels, needlework pictures, treen, bygones, period glass lighting

Open Mon–Fri 9.30am–5.30pm or by appointment
Fairs International Ceramics Fair, Winter Olympia
Services Valuations, restorations, comission buying

PEWSEY

⊞ Rupert Gentle (BADA)
Contact Mrs Gentle
✉ **The Manor House, Milton Lilbourne, Pewsey, Wiltshire, SN9 5LQ** 🅿
☎ 01672 563344 Ⓕ 01672 563563
Est. 1976 *Stock size* Small
Stock 17th–19thC English and Continental domestic metalwork, treen, needlework
Open Mon–Sat 9am–6pm or by appointment
Fairs Grosvenor House (June), Olympia, BADA (March, Chelsea)
Services Valuations

⊞ Time Restored
Contact J H Bowler-Reed
✉ **20 High Street, Pewsey, Wiltshire, SN9 5AQ** 🅿
☎ 01672 563544
Est. 1978 *Stock size* Small
Stock Clocks, musical boxes, barometers
Open Mon–Fri 10am–6pm
Services Restorations

RAMSBURY

⊞ Heraldry Today (ABA)
Contact Mrs Henry
✉ **Parliament Piece, Ramsbury, Marlborough, Wiltshire, SN8 2QH** 🅿
☎ 01672 520617 Ⓕ 01672 520183
Ⓔ heraldry@heraldrytoday.co.uk
Ⓦ www.heraldrytoday.co.uk
Est. 1954 *Stock size* Large
Stock Antiquarian books on heraldry, geneaology and peerage
Open Mon–Fri 9.30am–4.30pm

SALISBURY

⊞ The Antiques Market
✉ **37 Catherine Street, Salisbury, Wiltshire, SP1 2DH** 🅿
☎ 01722 326033
Est. 1977 *Stock size* Large
Stock General antiques
Open Mon–Sat 9.30am–5pm

⊞ Robert Bradley Antiques
Contact Mr R Bradley
✉ **71 Brown Street, Salisbury, Wiltshire, SP1 2BA**
☎ 01722 333677 Ⓕ 01722 339922
Est. 1970 *Stock size* Medium
Stock 17th–18thC furniture
Open Mon–Fri 9.30am–5.30pm

⊞ Castle Galleries (OMRS)
Contact John Lodge
✉ **81 Castle Street, Salisbury, Wiltshire, SP1 3SP** 🅿
☎ 01722 333734 Ⓕ 01722 333734
Ⓜ 07971 833280
Ⓔ johnlodge@bun.com
Est. 1971 *Stock size* Medium
Stock Coins, medals, small items, jewellery
Open Tues Thurs Fri 9am–5pm Sat 9am–1pm
Services Valuations

⊞ Fisherton Antiques Market
Contact Nigel Roberts
✉ **53 Fisherton Street, Salisbury, Wiltshire, SP2 7SU** 🅿
☎ 01722 422147
Est. 1997 *Stock size* Small
Stock Victorian–Edwardian furniture, jewellery, modern and collectables
Open Mon–Sat 9.30am–5pm

⊞ Jonathan Green Antiques
Contact Jonathan Green
✉ **The Antiques Market, 37 Catherine Street, Salisbury, Wiltshire, SP1 2DH** 🅿
☎ 01722 332635 Ⓕ 01722 332635
Est. 1979 *Stock size* Medium
Stock Silver, silver plate and decorative items
Open Mon–Sat 10am–5pm

⊞ John & Judith Head Barn Book Supply (ABA)
Contact Mr or Mrs Head
✉ **88 Crane Street, Salisbury, Wiltshire, SP1 2QD**
☎ 01722 327767 Ⓕ 01722 339888
Ⓔ info@johnandjudithhead.co.uk
Ⓦ www.johnandjudithhead.co.uk
Est. 1958 *Stock size* Large
Stock Antiquarian books on field sports
Open Mon–Fri 9.30am–5pm
Fairs Badminton Horse Trials, CLA Game Fair

⊞ Myriad
Contact Karen Montlake
✉ **48–54 Milford Street, Salisbury, Wiltshire, SP1 2BP** 🅿
☎ 01722 413595/718203
Ⓕ 01722 416395
Ⓔ enquiries@myriad-antiques.co.uk
Ⓦ www.myriad-antiques.co.uk
Est. 1994 *Stock size* Large
Stock Georgian–Victorian furniture in pine, mahogany oak. Lamps, clocks, mirrors, rugs
Open Mon–Sat 9.30am–5pm Sun by appointment
Services Stripping, collection and delivery within 80 miles, antique search

⊞ Pennyfarthing Antiques
Contact Mr J M Scott
✉ **52–54 Winchester Street, Salisbury, Wiltshire, SP1 1HG** 🅿
☎ 01722 505955
Ⓜ 07778 300316
Est. 1993 *Stock size* Medium
Stock Country furniture
Open Mon–Sat 9am–5.30pm Sun 11am–4pm
Services Restorations

⊞ Steven Shell
Contact Andrew Piggott
✉ **Old Sarum Airfield, Salisbury, Wiltshire, SP4 6BJ** 🅿
☎ 01722 320120 Ⓕ 01722 328828
Stock size Small
Stock Indonesian furniture, accessories
Trade only Yes
Open Mon–Fri 8am–5pm

⊞ Trevan's Old Books
Contact John Cocking
✉ **30 Catherine Street, Salisbury, Wiltshire, SP1 2DA** 🅿
☎ 01722 325818 Ⓕ 01722 341181
Ⓔ john.cocking@virgin.net
Ⓦ www.abebooks.com/trevan/home
Est. 1994 *Stock size* Large
Stock General bookseller with some antiquarian
Open Mon–Sat 9.30am–5.30pm
Services Full Internet book search

⊞ Chris Watts Antiques (LAPADA)
Contact Mr C Watts
✉ **Salisbury Antiques Warehouse, 94 Wilton Road, Salisbury, Wiltshire, SP2 7JJ** 🅿
☎ 01722 410634 Ⓕ 01722 410635
Ⓔ antiques@interalpha.co.uk
Est. 1965 *Stock size* Large

Stock 18th–19thC furniture, paintings, clocks, bronzes, barometers
Open Mon–Fri 9am–5.30pm first Sat every month 10am–4.30pm or by appointment for trade

Woolley and Wallis Salisbury Salerooms Ltd (SOFAA)
Contact Sue McArthur
51–61 Castle Street, Salisbury, Wiltshire, SP1 3SU P
☎ 01722 424500 F 01722 424508
E enquiries@woolleyandwallace.co.uk
W http://woolley.i-collector.com
Est. 1884
Open Mon–Fri 9am–5.30pm Sat 9am–noon
Sales Household sales generally fortnightly on Fri at 10am, previews Thurs 10am–7pm. 30 specialist sales a year including furniture, ceramics, rugs and textiles, silver and jewellery, wine, books and maps, paintings
Catalogues Yes

SWINDON

Antiques and All Pine
Contact Mr or Mrs Brown
11 Newport Street, Swindon, Wiltshire, SN1 3DX P
☎ 01793 520259
Est. 1978 *Stock size* Large
Stock Antique and reproduction pine, reproduction brass and iron beds, old lace, linen and costume jewellery
Open Tues–Sat 10am–5.30pm Mon 10am–4pm closed Wed Sun

Allan Smith
Contact Mr A Smith
Amity Cottage, 162 Beechcroft Road, Upper Stratton, Swindon, Wiltshire, SN2 7QE P
☎ 01793 822977 F 01793 822977
M 07778 834342
E allansmithclocks@lineone.net
W www.allan-smith-antique-clocks.co.uk
Est. 1988 *Stock size* Large
Stock Decorative, unusual, good quality clocks including automata, Moonphase, painted dial, 30 hour, 8 day etc in mahogany, lacquer, walnut and marquetry. Mostly English longcase and bracket clocks. 50–60 fully restored longcases
Open By appointment any time
Services Valuations and clockfinder service

Swindon Auction Rooms
Contact Mrs H Burgin
The Planks, Old Town, Swindon, Wiltshire, SN3 1QP P
☎ 01793 615915
Est. 1959
Open Mon–Fri 9am–5pm
Sales Periodic antique sales
Frequency Periodic

John Williams (PBFA)
Contact Mr Williams
93 Goddard Avenue, Swindon, Wiltshire, SN1 4HT P
☎ 01793 533313
E john.williams24@virgin.net
W www.jwbooks.com
Est. 1994 *Stock size* Small
Stock Antiquarian and second-hand children's and illustrated books. Three catalogues a year
Open By appointment
Fairs PBFA

Dominic Winter Book Auctions
Contact Admin Office
The Old School, Maxwell Street, Swindon, Wiltshire, SN1 5DR P
☎ 01793 611340 F 01793 491727
E info@dominicwinter.co.uk
W www.dominicwinter.co.uk
Est. 1988
Open Mon–Fri 9.30am–5.30pm
Sales General book sale Wed 11am, viewing day prior to sale 10am–7pm. Specialist single category sale Thurs 11am, viewing day prior to sale 10am–7pm
Frequency 5 weeks
Catalogues Yes

WARMINSTER

Cassidy Antiques and Restorations (BABAADA)
Contact Matthew Cassidy
7 Silver Street, Warminster, Wiltshire, BA12 8PS P
☎ 01985 213313 F 01985 213313
M 07050 206806
E matt@cassidy166.freeserve.co.uk
Est. 1994 *Stock size* Medium
Stock Georgian–Victorian furniture
Open Mon–Fri 9am–5pm Sat 10am–4pm
Services Restorations

Choice Antiques
Contact Avril Bailey
4 Silver Street, Warminster, Wiltshire, BA12 8PS P
☎ 01985 218924
Est. 1987 *Stock size* Medium
Stock Small, the unusual, furniture, decorative objects
Open Mon–Sat 10am–5.30pm
Services Valuations, shipping

Annabelle Giltsoff (BABAADA)
Contact Anabelle Giltsoff
10 Silver Street, Warminster, Wiltshire, BA12 8PS P
☎ 01985 218188
Est. 1984 *Stock size* Medium
Stock Paintings and frames
Open Mon–Sat 9.30am–1pm 2–5pm
Fairs Shepton Mallet, Newark, NEC (June)
Services Picture restoration and gilding

Isabella Antiques (BABAADA)
Contact Mr B W Semke
11 Silver Street, Warminster, Wiltshire, BA12 8PS P
☎ 01985 218933
Est. 1990 *Stock size* Medium
Stock 18th–19thC mahogany furniture, chests-of-drawers a speciality
Open Mon–Sat 10am–5pm

Obelisk Antiques (LAPADA, BABAADA)
Contact Mr P Tanswell
2 Silver Street, Warminster, Wiltshire, BA12 8PS P
☎ 01985 846646 F 01985 219901
M 07718 630673
E all@obelisk-antiques.freeserve.co.uk
Est. 1979 *Stock size* Large
Stock 18th–19thC French, English and Continental furniture
Open Mon–Sat 10am–1pm 2–5.30pm

Warminster Antique Centre (BABAADA)
Contact Mr P Walton
6 Silver Street, Warminster, Wiltshire, BA12 8PT P
☎ 01985 847269
M 07860 584193
Est. 1993 *Stock size* Large

William Preist, Bristol. Recorded apprenticed 1751, died 1793. Classic Cuban mahogany Bristol case, 12in breakarch brass dial with moonphases and "high water at Bristol key", 8-day hourly (rack) striking. 94.5in (240cm).

Allan Smith

LONGCASE CLOCKS

'Amity Cottage', 162 Beechcroft Road,
Upper Stratton, Swindon, Wiltshire SN2 7QE
PHONE/FAX: (01793) 822977 · MOBILE: 07778 834342
Website: www.allan-smith-antique-clocks.co.uk
Email: allansmithclocks@lineone.net

QUALITY **MOONPHASE** LONGCASE CLOCKS A **SPECIALITY**

Open any day or evening by appointment

I try to maintain stocks which are decorative, unusual, of good quality, proportions and originality. I can usually offer automata, moonphase, painted dial, brass dial, 30-hour, 8-day, London and provincial examples in oak, mahogany, lacquer, walnut and marquetry. From circa 1700 to circa 1840. All properly and sympathetically restored to very high standards. 50+ good examples usually in stock.

Colour brochure available on request
Worldwide shipping
Clockfinder service
Insurance valuations
Fine clocks always wanted
12 Months Written Guarantee

FREE UK DELIVERY & SETTING UP
(Less than 10 minutes from M4 junction 15)

Richard Birch, Birmingham. Recorded 1776-87. Exceptional quality quarter sawn oak case, 13in breakarch early painted dial with moonphases to arch, 8-day hourly (rack) striking. 95in (241cm).

No. of dealers 15
Stock Wide range of antiques and collectable items, furniture, clocks, paintings, models, linens, fabrics, etc
Open Mon–Sat 10am–5pm
Services Valuations

WESTBURY

⊞ Ray Coggins Antiques
Contact Mr R Coggins
✉ 1 Fore Street, Westbury, Wiltshire, BA13 3AU P
☎ 01373 826574 F 01373 827996
Est. 1974 *Stock size* Large
Stock Antique, country and decorative furniture, architectural antiques
Open Mon–Fri 9am–5pm

WILTON

⊞ Bay Tree Antiques
Contact Mrs J D Waymouth
✉ 26 North Street, Wilton, Wiltshire, SP2 0HJ P
☎ 01722 743392 F 01722 743392
Est. 1997 *Stock size* Medium
Stock Period furniture, decorative furniture and items
Open Mon–Sat 9am–5.30pm
Fairs Battersea Decorartive

⊞ Carol Musselwhite Antiques
Contact Mrs C Musselwhite
✉ 6 West St, Wilton, Salisbury, Wiltshire, SP2 0DF P
☎ 01722 742573
E carolmusselwhite@hotmail.com
Est. 1990 *Stock size* Large
Stock China, glass, linen, lace, out-of-production Derby
Open Tues–Sat 10am–5pm

WOOTON BASSETT

⊞ Tubbjoys Antiques
Contact Mr Tubb
✉ 118 High Street, Wooton Bassett, Swindon, Wiltshire, SN4 7AU P
☎ 01793 849499
E bridgett@tubbjoys.freeserve.co.uk
W www.tubbjoys.freeserve.co.uk
Est. 1992 *Stock size* Large
Stock Stylish 1950s–1980s items
Open Fri Sat 10am–5pm or by appointment
Services Lectures on 1950s and 1960s collecting and the grade 2 listed house, coffee shop

EAST

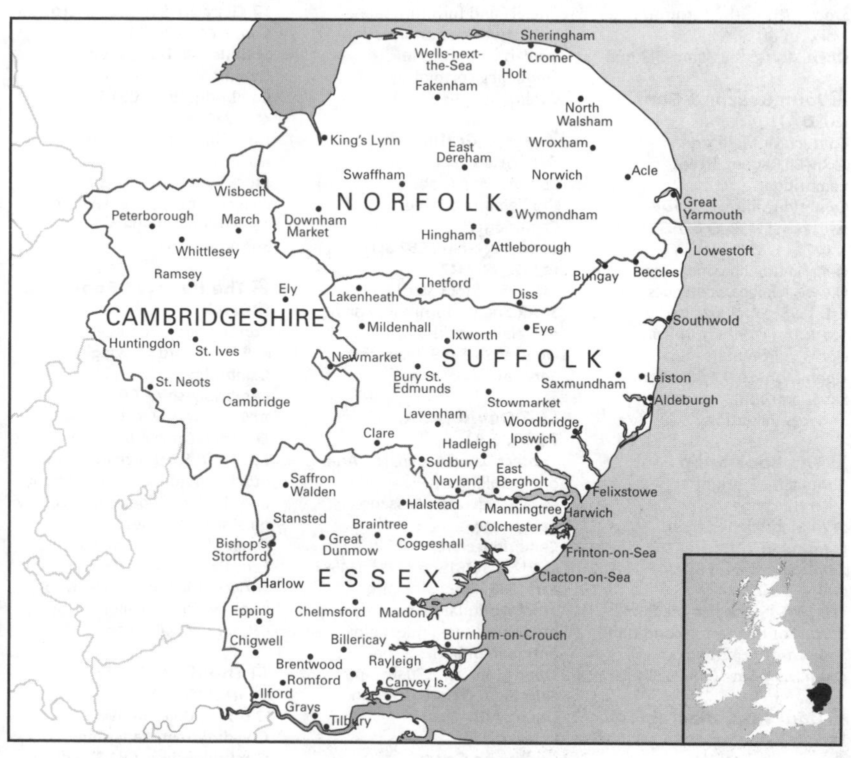

CAMBRIDGESHIRE

BALSHAM

⊞ Ward-Thomas Antiques
Contact Mr C R F Ward-Thomas
✉ **The Barn, 7 High Street, Balsham, Cambridge, Cambridgeshire, CB1 6DJ** Ⓟ
☎ 01223 892431 Ⓕ 01223 892367
Ⓔ ward-thomas@freecom.uk.com
Est. 1997 *Stock size* Large
Stock Continental pine furniture, furniture accessories
Trade only Yes
Open Mon–Fri 9am–5pm Sat 10am–5pm Sun 10am–4pm
Fairs Newark, Kempton Park
Services Restorations, mail orders

BARTON

⊞ Bagatelle Antiques
Contact Mr Martyn Jeffrey
✉ **Burwash Manor Barns, New Road, Barton, Cambridge, Cambridgeshire, CB3 7AY** Ⓟ
☎ 01223 264400 Ⓕ 01223 264445
Ⓜ 07714 104516
Ⓔ martyn@bagatelle-antiques.co.uk
Ⓦ www.bagatelle-antiques.co.uk
Est. 1998 *Stock size* Medium
Stock General antiques, decorative items, garden items
Open Mon–Fri 9am–5pm Sat 2–5pm
Services Restorations

BURWELL

⊞ Antiques Emporium
Contact Mr Stephen Hunt
✉ **59 High Street, Burwell, Cambridge, Cambridgeshire, CB5 0HD** Ⓟ
☎ 01638 741155
Est. 1994 *Stock size* Medium
Stock General antiques
Open Mon–Sat 10.30am–5pm Sun 11am–5pm closed Wed Thurs
Fairs Rowley Mile, Kempton
Services Restorations

⊞ Peter Norman Antiques
Contact Mr Tony Marpole
✉ **55 North Street, Burwell, Cambridge, Cambridgeshire, CB5 0BA** Ⓟ
☎ 01638 616914
Est. 1979 *Stock size* Medium
Stock 18th–19thC furniture, Oriental rugs, clocks, pictures, prints
Open Mon–Sat 9am–5.30pm
Fairs Stafford, Newmarket
Services Restorations

CAMBRIDGE

⊞ Jess Applin (BADA)
Contact Mr J Applin
✉ **8 Lensfield Road, Cambridge, Cambridgeshire, CB2 1EG** Ⓟ
☎ 01223 315168
Est. 1975 *Stock size* Medium

Stock 17th–19thC furniture, works of art
Open Mon–Sat 9.30am–5.30pm

John Beazor & Sons Ltd (BADA)
Contact Mr M Beazor
78–80 Regent Street, Cambridge, Cambridgeshire, CB2 1DP
☎ 01223 355178 Ⓕ 01223 355183
Ⓜ 07774 123379
Ⓔ martin@johnbeazorantiques.co.uk
Ⓦ www.johnbeazorantiques.co.uk
Est. 1875 *Stock size* Large
Stock 18th–19thC furniture, clocks, barometers
Open Mon–Fri 9.15am–5pm Sat 10am–4pm
Services Valuations

The Book Shop
Contact Mr P Bright or Mr H Hardinge
24 Magdalene Street, Cambridge, Cambridgeshire, CB3 OAF
☎ 01223 362457
Est. 1996 *Stock size* Medium
Stock Antiquarian, second-hand, and out-of-print books
Open Mon–Sat 10am–5.30pm

Books & Collectables Ltd
Contact Mr A Doyle
Unit 7–8, Railway Arches, Coldhams Road, Cambridge, Cambridgeshire, CB1 3EW Ⓟ
☎ 01223 412845 Ⓕ 01223 412845
Ⓜ 07703 795206
Ⓦ www.books&collectables.com
Est. 1996 *Stock size* Large
Stock 16thC–modern books, comics, toys, postcards, cigarette cards, records, pop memorabilia, magazines, china, furniture
Open Mon–Sat 9.30am–5pm Sun 10am–4pm
Services Valuations, shipping

Cheffins
Contact J G Law, C B Ashton or R Haywood
2 Clifton Road, Cambridge, Cambridgeshire, CB1 4BW Ⓟ
☎ 01223 213343 Ⓕ 01223 413396
Ⓔ fine.art@cheffins.co.uk
Ⓦ www.cheffins.co.uk
Est. 1824
Open Mon–Fri 9am–5pm
Sales 45 sales a year of antiques and later furnishings, specialist fine art and furniture sales. Catalogues and information available on website
Frequency Fortnightly
Catalogues Yes

Peter Crabbe Antiques
Contact Mr P Crabbe
3 Pembroke Street, Cambridge, Cambridgeshire, CB2 3QY
☎ 01223 357117
Est. 1988 *Stock size* Large
Stock English furniture, Asian porcelain, works of art
Open Mon–Sat 9.30am–5pm
Services Valuations

G David (ABA, PBFA, BA)
Contact David Asplin, N T Adams or B L Collings
16 St Edward's Passage, Cambridge, Cambridgeshire, CB2 3PJ
☎ 01223 354619 Ⓕ 01223 324663
Est. 1896 *Stock size* Large
Stock Antiquarian books, prints, publishers' remainders, fine antiquarian books a speciality
Open Mon–Sat 9.30am–5pm
Fairs PBFA Oxford, London (June), ABA (Nov)

Gabor Cossa Antiques
Contact David Theobald
34 Trumpington Street, Cambridge, Cambridgeshire, CB2 1QY Ⓟ
☎ 01223 356049
Est. 1947 *Stock size* Large
Stock 18th–19thC ceramics, small items
Open Mon–Sat 10am–5.30pm

Granta Coins, Collectables and Antiquities (ADPS, SDS)
Contact Mr Alan Fordham
23 Magdalene Street, Cambridge, Cambridgeshire, CB3 0AF Ⓟ
☎ 01223 361662 Ⓕ 01223 361662
Ⓜ 07713 513813
Ⓔ coingranta@aol.com
Ⓦ www.grantacoins.golinq.com
Est. 1978 *Stock size* Large
Stock Pre-Roman–modern coins
Open Mon–Sat 10am–5pm
Services Valuations, appraisals, probate

Gwydir Street Antiques
Contact Mrs P Gibb
Units 1–2, Dales Brewery, Gwydir Street, Cambridge, Cambridgeshire, CB1 2LJ Ⓟ
☎ 01223 356391
Est. 1987 *Stock size* Medium
No. of dealers 10
Stock Furniture, bric-a-brac, collectables, decorative items
Open Mon–Sat 10am–5pm Sun 11am–5pm

The Haunted Bookshop (PBFA)
Contact Mrs Sarah Key
9 St Edward's Passage, Cambridge, Cambridgeshire, CB2 3PJ
☎ 01223 312913 Ⓕ 08700 569392
Ⓔ sarahkey@hauntedbooks.demon.co.uk
Est. 1987 *Stock size* Medium
Stock Antiquarian, second-hand, and children's books, particularly girls' school stories
Open Mon–Sat 10am–5pm
Fairs PBFA
Services Mail order worldwide, book search for children's titles, catalogues, valuations

The Hive
Contact Mrs B Burch
Unit 3, Dales Brewery, Gwydir Street, Cambridge, Cambridgeshire, CB1 2LG Ⓟ
☎ 01223 300269
Est. 1987
No. of dealers 10
Stock Antique pine, kitchenware, collectables, period lighting, pictures, Victorian–Edwardian furniture, bric-a-brac
Open Mon–Sat 10am–5pm Sun 11am–5pm Wed 10am–7pm
Services Commissions undertaken

La Belle Epoque
Contact Mrs C Keverne
55a Hills Road, Cambridge, Cambridgeshire, CB2 1NT Ⓟ
☎ 01223 506688
Est. 1986 *Stock size* Medium
Stock Period lighting, small items
Open Tues–Sat 11am–5pm

The Old Chemist Shop Antique Centre
Contact Mrs J Tucker
206 Mill Road, Cambridge, Cambridgeshire, CB1 3NF Ⓟ
☎ 01223 247324
Est. 1996 *Stock size* Large

Stock General antiques, collectables
Open Mon–Fri 10am–5pm Sat 10am–5.30pm
Services Clock repair, house clearance

Pembroke Antiques
Contact K N Galey
7 Pembroke Street, Cambridge, Cambridgeshire, CB2 3QY
01223 363246
Est. 1984 ***Stock size*** Medium
Stock Furniture, smalls, glass, silver, jewellery
Open Tues–Sat 10am–4pm
Services Valuations

Phillips International Auctioneers and Valuers
17 Emmanuel Road, Cambridge, Cambridgeshire, CB1 1JW
01223 366523 01223 300208
www.phillips-auction.com
Sales Regional Office. Telephone for details

Those Were The Days
Contact Julia or Richard Henderson
91 & 93 Mill Road, Cambridge, Cambridgeshire, CB1 2AW
Est. 1991 ***Stock size*** Large
No. of dealers 10
Stock Furniture, lighting, fireplaces
Open Mon–Sat 9.30am–5.30pm Sun 11am–5pm

Ken Trotman Ltd (PBFA)
Contact Mr or Mrs Brown
Unit 11, The Old Maltings, 135 Ditton Walk, Cambridge, Cambridgeshire, CB5 8PY
01223 211030 01223 212317
trotman@netcomuk.co.uk
www.kentrotman.ltd.uk
Est. 1950 ***Stock size*** Large
Stock Antiquarian and new books on military history. Catalogues available
Open By appointment

Valued History
Contact Mr Paul Murawski
13 Benet Street, Cambridge, Cambridgeshire, CB2 3PT
01223 319319 01223 319319
murawski@pmurawski.fsnet.co.uk
www.historyforsale.co.uk
Est. 1996 ***Stock size*** Medium
Stock Coins, antiquities
Open Tues–Sat 10am–5pm
Services Valuations

Willroy Antiques Centre
Contact Mr Roy Williams
Unit 5, Dales Brewery, Gwydir Street, Cambridge, Cambridgeshire, CB1 2LJ
01223 311687 01480 352853
07930 193830
rwill61359@aol.com
Est. 1985 ***Stock size*** Large
No. of dealers 6
Stock General antiques
Open Mon–Sat 10am–5pm Sun noon–4pm
Services Restorations

CHATTERIS

James Fuller and Son
Contact Steven Fuller
51 Huntingdon Road, Chatteris, Cambridgeshire, PE16 6JE
01354 692740
Est. 1919 ***Stock size*** Large
Stock Telephone and letter boxes
Open Mon–Fri 8am–12.30pm 1.30pm–5pm

CHITTERING

Simon & Penny Rumble Antiques
Contact Mrs P Rumble
Causeway End Farmhouse, School Lane, Chittering, Cambridge, Cambridgeshire, CB5 9PW
01223 861831
07778 917300
penny@therumbles.freeserve.co.uk
Est. 1980 ***Stock size*** Small
Stock Early oak, country furniture, woodcarving
Open By appointment
Fairs NEC

COMBERTON

Comberton Antiques
Contact Mrs McEvoy
5A West Street, Comberton, Cambridgeshire, CB3 7DS
01223 262674
dewisem@free4all.co.uk
www.comberton_antiques.co.uk
Est. 1984 ***Stock size*** Large
Stock General furniture, Continental pine
Open Fri Sat Mon 10am–5pm Sun 2–5pm
Fairs Newark, Ardingly
Services Shipping

DUXFORD

Riro D Mooney
Contact Mr R Mooney
Mill Lane, Duxford, Cambridgeshire, CB2 4PS
01223 832252
Est. 1946 ***Stock size*** Large
Stock Victorian–Edwardian furniture
Open Mon–Sat 9am–6.30pm Sun 10am–noon 2.30–5pm
Services Restoration

ELY

Cloisters Antiques (PBFA)
Contact Barry Lonsdale
1a Lynn Road, Ely, Cambridgeshire, CB7 4EG
01353 668558
07767 881677
info@cloistersantiques.co.uk
www.cloistersantiques.co.uk
Est. 1997 ***Stock size*** Medium
Stock General clocks, china, second-hand and antiquarian books, mainly smalls
Open Mon–Sat 10.30am–4.30pm Sun 12.30–4.30pm closed Tues
Services Valuations

Mrs Mills' Antiques Etc.
Contact Mrs M Mills
1a St Mary's Street, Ely, Cambridgeshire, CB7 4ER
01353 664268
Est. 1968 ***Stock size*** Large
Stock Porcelain, silver, jewellery
Open Mon–Sat 10am–5pm closed Tues
Fairs Heritage Grosvenor Square

Waterside Antiques
Contact Mr G Peters
The Wharf, Waterside, Ely, Cambridgeshire, CB7 4AU
01353 667066
Est. 1985
No. of dealers 68
Stock Furniture, collectables
Open Mon–Sat 9.30am–5.30pm Sun 11.30am–5.30pm
Services Valuations, clearances

FORDHAM

Phoenix Antiques
Contact Mr K Bycroft
Homelands, 1 Carter Street, Fordham, Ely, Cambridgeshire, CB7 5NG
01638 720363
Est. 1966 *Stock size* Medium
Stock Everything for a European interior prior to 1750
Open By appointment only
Services Valuations

GODMANCHESTER

The Bookshop Godmanchester (BA)
Contact J H or D L Lewis
11 Post Street, Godmanchester, Huntingdon, Cambridgeshire, PE18 8BA
01480 455020 F 01480 434619
Est. 1977 *Stock size* Large
Stock Antiquarian, second-hand, new books, children's books a speciality
Open Tues–Sat 9.30am–1pm 2–5.30pm
Services Book search

GREAT SHELFORD

The Store
Contact Mr Lambourn-Brown
134 Cambridge Road, Great Shelford, Cambridge, Cambridgeshire, CB2 5JU
01223 841070
Est. 1999 *Stock size* Large
Stock Architectural antiques, furniture, ephemera, collectables, bygones, rural artefacts, decorative items
Open Tues–Sat 10am–4pm Sun 11am–4pm
Fairs Newark
Services House clearance, restorations

HADDENHAM

Hereward Books (PBFA)
Contact Mr R Pratt
17 High Street, Haddenham, Ely, Cambridgeshire, CB6 3XA
01353 740821 F 01353 741721
E sales@hereward-books.co.uk
W www.hereward-books.co.uk
Est. 1984 *Stock size* Medium
Stock Rare and collectable books, specializing in field sports and fishing
Open Mon Tues Thurs 10am–4pm Fri Sat 10am–1pm
Fairs PBFA Russell Hotel, CLA Game Fair

Ludovic Potts Antiques (BAFRA)
Contact Mr Ludovic Potts
Unit 1–1a, Station Road, Haddenham, Ely, Cambridgeshire, CB6 3XD
01353 741537 F 01353 741822
M 07889 341671
E mail@restorers.co.uk
W www.restorers.co.uk
Est. 2001 *Stock size* Small
Stock Polished wood furniture, upholstered chairs, sofas, soft furnishings, porcelain, gilt mirrors
Open By appointment
Services Restorations

HUNTINGDON

Huntingdon Trading Post
Contact Mr John De'Ath
1 St Mary's Street, Huntingdon, Cambridgeshire, PE29 3PE
01480 450998 F 01480 431142
E j.death@ntlworld.com
W www.huntingdontradingpost.co.uk
Est. 2001 *Stock size* Large
No. of dealers 35
Stock General antiques, furniture, clocks, collectables, brass ware, pictures
Open Mon–Sat 9am–5pm Sun 10am–2pm

IMPINGTON

Woodcock House Antiques
Contact Mr A M Peat
83–85 Station Road, Impington, Cambridge, Cambridgeshire, CB4 9NP
01223 232858
Est. 1978 *Stock size* Large
Stock Late 19thC decorative furniture, Aesthetic items, smalls, furniture
Open Mon–Fri 10am–5pm or by appointment
Fairs Grosvenor House
Services Valuations

LITTLE DOWNHAM

Rowley Fine Art
Contact Michelle Dobson
The Old Bishop's Palace, Little Downham, Ely, Cambridgeshire, CB6 2TD
01353 699177 F 01353 699088
E mail@rowleyfineart.com
W www.rowleyfineart.com
Est. 2001
Open Mon–Fri 9am–5pm
Sales Fine art and antiques sale every 6 weeks at Tattersalls, Newmarket
Frequency 6 weekly
Catalogues Yes

MARCH

Fagins
Contact Mrs P Humby
9 Station Road, March, Cambridgeshire, PE15 0JL
01354 656445
Est. 1998 *Stock size* Medium
Stock General antiques, furniture, collectables
Open Mon–Sat 10am–5pm closed Tues

MARKET DEEPING

Market Deeping Antiques & Craft Centre
Contact John Strutt
50–56 High Street, Market Deeping, Peterborough, Cambridgeshire, PE6 8EB
01778 380238
Est. 1995 *Stock size* Large
Stock General antiques, collectables, crafts
Open Mon–Sat 10am–5pm Sun 11am–5pm

OUNDLE

Goldsmiths Howard
Contact Mr Ian Goldsmith
15 Market Place, Oundle, Peterborough, Cambridgeshire, PE8 4BA
01832 272349 F 01832 275000
E goldsmithshoward@goldsmithshoward.co.uk
W www.goldsmithshoward.co.uk
Est. 1964
Open Mon–Fri 9am–6.30pm Sat 9am–4pm Sun 11am–3pm
Sales Antiques sales Sat 10.30am, viewing Fri 2.30–6pm and sale day 9–10.30am. Sale room is at South Road, Oundle
Frequency Bi-monthly
Catalogues Yes

PETERBOROUGH

Antiques & Curios Shop
Contact Mr M Mason
249 Lincoln Road, Millfield, Peterborough, Cambridgeshire, PE1 2PL
01733 314948
07974 548873
Est. 1989 *Stock size* Medium
Stock Mahogany, oak, pine, and country furniture, fireplaces
Open Mon–Sat 10am–5pm
Fairs Newark, RAF Swinderby
Services Restorations

Cards 'N' Collectables
Contact Colin Dorman
25 Misterton, Orton Goldhay, Peterborough, Cambridgeshire, PE2 5SZ
01733 232272
www.cards-n-collectables.com
Est. 2000
Stock Trading cards, collectable card games, action figures, movie memorabilia
Open Mon 10am–4pm Tues–Sat 10am–6pm Sun noon–4pm

T V Coles
Contact Mr T V Coles
981 Lincoln Road, Peterborough, Cambridgeshire, PE4 6AH
01733 577268
Est. 1980 *Stock size* Medium
Stock Antiquarian, out-of-print, and second-hand books, militaria, ephemera, postcards
Open Mon–Sat 9am–4.30pm

Fitzwilliam Antiques Centre
Contact Mr Paul Stafford
20–22 Fitzwilliam Street, Peterborough, Cambridgeshire, PE1 2RX
01733 566346 F 01733 565415
Est. 1990 *Stock size* Large
No. of dealers 20
Stock General antiques, collectables
Open Mon–Sat 10am–5pm
Services Valuations, restorations, repairs

Old Soke Books
Contact Peter or Linda Clay
68 Burghley Road, Peterborough, Cambridgeshire, PE1 2QE
01733 564147
Est. 1984 *Stock size* Small
Stock Antiquarian books, small antiques, pictures, prints, maps
Open By appointment only
Services Valuations

RAMSEY

Abbey Antiques
Contact Mr J Smith
63 Great Whyte, Ramsey, Cambridgeshire, PE26 1HL
01487 814753
Est. 1979 *Stock size* Medium
Stock General antiques, collectables. Mabel Lucie Attwell Museum and Collectors' Club
Open Tues–Sun 10am–5pm
Fairs Alexandra Palace,
Services Valuations

Antique Barometers
Contact William Rae
Wingfield, 26 Biggin Lane, Ramsey, Cambridgeshire, PE26 1NB
01487 814060 F 01487 814060
antiquebarometers@talk21.com
Est. 1996 *Stock size* Medium
Stock Early stick and wheel barometers, barographs
Open By appointment
Fairs Hinchingbrook House, Putteridge Bury House
Services Valuations, restorations

SOHAM

Burwell Auctions
Contact Mr N Reed-Herbert
The Church Hall, High Street, Soham, Ely, Cambridgeshire, CB7 5HD
01353 727100 F 01353 727101
Est. 1984
Open By appointment
Sales General antiques sale viewing day prior to sale 9am–5pm and day of sale 9am–10.30am or by appointment
Frequency Variable
Catalogues Yes

ST IVES

Hyperion Antique Centre (ICOM)
Contact Colin Gunter
Station Road, St Ives, Huntingdon, Cambridgeshire, PE27 5BH
01480 464114 F 01480 497552
07788 486590
hyperion_auctions@hotmail.com
Est. 1995 *Stock size* Large
No. of dealers 20
Stock A wide range of stock from £5 to £3,000
Open Mon–Sat 9.30am–5pm

Hyperion Auction Centre (ICOM)
Contact Mrs Pat Bernard or Mr Colin Gunter
Station Road, St Ives, Huntingdon, Cambridgeshire, PE17 4BH
01480 464140 F 01480 497552
07788 486590
hyperion-auctions@hotmail.com
www.hyperion-auctions.co.uk
Est. 1995
Open Mon–Sat 9.30am–5pm
Sales General antiques sale 2nd Mon monthly 10.30am, viewing Sat prior 9.30am–5pm Mon 9.30–10.30am
Frequency Monthly
Catalogues Yes

Quay Court Antiques
Contact Mr M Knight
Bull Lane, Bridge Street, St Ives, Huntingdon, Cambridgeshire, PE17 4AZ
01480 468295
michaelknight@compuserve.com
Est. 1972 *Stock size* Medium
Stock Pottery, porcelain, pictures, jewellery
Open Mon 11am–2pm Wed 10.30am–3pm Fri 11am–2pm Sat 11am–4pm
Services Valuations, lectures to antiques clubs

ST NEOTS

Brentside Programmes
Contact Mr Chris Ward
1 Dial Close, Little Paxton, St Neots, Huntingdon, Cambridgeshire, PE19 4QN
01480 474682 F 01480 370650
sales@brentside.co.uk
www.brentside.co.uk
Est. 1974 *Stock size* Medium
Stock Football memorabilia, mostly mail order
Open Mon–Fri 9am–5pm

Peggy's Pandora
Contact Mr B George
10 Crosskeys Mews, Market Square, St Neots, Huntingdon, Cambridgeshire, PE19 2AR
01480 403580
Est. 1991 *Stock size* Medium

Stock Postcards, medals, coins, toys, small items
Open Mon–Sat 9am–5pm

WARBOYS

Warboys Antiques
Contact Mr J Lambden
The Old Church School, High Street, Warboys, Cambridgeshire, PE28 2SX
01487 823686 Ⓕ 01487 496296
Ⓜ 07831 274774
Ⓔ john.lambden@virgin.net
Est. 1985 *Stock size* Large
Stock Collectables, advertising, tins, decorative items, sporting collectables
Open Tues–Sat 11am–5pm
Fairs Alexandra Palace Antique and Collectables Fair
Services Valuations

WHITTLESEY

Pinestrip
Contact Kent or Adele Griffin
Gildenburgh Waters, Eastrea Road, Whittlesey, Peterborough, Cambridgeshire, PE7 2AR
01733 351199 Ⓕ 01733 840076
Ⓜ 07960 279032
Ⓦ www.pinestrip-pine.co.uk
Est. 1992 *Stock size* Medium
Stock Antique Continental pine furniture
Open Mon–Fri 9am–5pm Sat 9am–3pm
Services Pine stripping

WISBECH

Steve Carpenter
Contact Mr S Carpenter
96 Norfolk Street, Wisbech, Cambridgeshire, PE13 2LF
01945 588411 Ⓕ 01945 588411
Ⓜ 07939 112569
Est. 1997 *Stock size* Medium
Stock 18th–19thC country furniture, longcase clocks, quality smalls
Open Mon–Sat 9am–5pm closed Wed

Peter A Crofts (BADA)
Contact Mr P A Crofts
117 High Road, Wisbech, Cambridgeshire, PE14 0DN
01945 584614
Ⓜ 07803 740972
Ⓔ crofts@bigwig.net
Est. 1949 *Stock size* Large
Stock General antiques, furniture, silver, china
Open Sun–Fri 8am–4.30pm or by appointment
Services Valuations

Granny's Cupboard Antiques
Contact Mr R J Robbs
34 Old Market, Wisbech, Cambridgeshire, PE13 1NF
01945 589606/870730
Ⓜ 07721 616154
Est. 1985 *Stock size* Medium
Stock Victorian–Edwardian china, glass and furniture to 1950s
Open Tues Thurs 10.30am–4pm Sat 10.30am–3pm
Fairs The Maltings, Ely

Grounds & Co
Contact Mr R Barnwell
2 Nene Quay, Wisbech, Cambridgeshire, PE13 1AQ
01945 585041 Ⓕ 01945 474255
Ⓜ 07885 431520
Est. 1792
Open Mon–Fri 9am–5pm Sat 9am–4pm
Sales Antiques and collectors' sales 3 a year. Phone for details
Catalogues Yes

Maxey & Son
Contact Mr Martin Allen
Auction Hall, Cattle Market Chase, Wisbech, Cambridgeshire, PE13 1RD
01945 584609 Ⓕ 01945 589440
Est. 1856
Open Mon–Fri 9am–5pm Sat 9am–noon
Sales Antiques sales 2–4 a year. Phone for details
Catalogues No

ESSEX

BARKING

Collectors' Corner
Contact Mrs S Lee
401a Ripple Road, Barking, Essex, IG11 9RB
020 8591 4441
Est. 1999 *Stock size* Large
Stock General antiques, small items, china, glass, jewellery
Open Mon–Fri 9.30am–5.30pm
Services House clearance

BATTLESBRIDGE

Battlesbridge Antiques Centre
Contact Mr Jim Gallie
Hawk Hill, Battlesbridge, Wickford, Essex, SS11 7RE
01268 575000 Ⓕ 01268 575001
Ⓔ jim.gallie@virgin.net
Ⓦ www.battlesbridge.com
Est. 1969 *Stock size* Large
No. of dealers 80
Stock General antiques, collectables
Open Mon–Sun 10am–5.30pm
Services Valuations

The Bones Lane Antiques Centre
Contact Mr Pettitt
The Green, Chelmsford Road, Battlesbridge, Wickford, Essex, SS11 7RJ
01268 763500 Ⓕ 01268 763500
Est. 1969 *Stock size* Medium
No. of dealers 12
Stock Gas, oil and early electric lighting, gramophones
Open Tues–Sun 10am–4.30pm closed Thurs
Services Restorations of lighting and gramophones

Bridgebarn Antiques (EADA)
Contact Mr Pettitt
The Bones Lane Antiques Centre, The Green, Chelmsford Road, Battlesbridge, Wickford, Essex, SS11 7RJ
01268 763500 Ⓕ 01268 763500
Est. 1969 *Stock size* Medium
Stock Gas, oil and early electric lighting, gramophones
Open Tues–Sun 10am–4.30pm closed Thurs
Services Restorations of lighting and gramophones

Cottage Antiques
Contact Mr R Jarman
The Old Granary, Battlesbridge Antique Centre, Battlesbridge, Wickford, Essex, SS11 7RE
01268 764138 Ⓕ 01268 764138
Ⓜ 07958 618629
Ⓔ bob@cottageantiquefurniture.com
Ⓦ www.cottageantiquefurniture.com
Est. 1998 *Stock size* Large
Stock Georgian–Edwardian items, mainly furniture, collectables

Open Mon–Sun 10am–5.30pm
Services Furniture restoration, French polishing, furniture search

Phoenix Fireplaces
Contact John or Cris
Hawk Hill, Batttlesbridge, Essex, SS11 7RE
01268 768844 Ⓕ 01268 768844
Ⓜ 07956 556442
Ⓦ www.phoenix-fireplaces.co.uk
Est. 1991 *Stock size* Large
Stock Fireplaces
Open Mon–Sun 10am–5.30pm

BAYTHORN END

Swan Antiques
Contact Mr K Mercado
Baythorn End, Clare (between Clare and Haverhill), Essex, CO9 4AF
01440 785306
Ⓜ 07850 426420
Est. 1993 *Stock size* Large
Stock Georgian–Edwardian furniture, fireplaces, firebacks, surrounds, pine furniture, glass, smalls
Open Mon–Sun 10am–5.30pm
Fairs Newark

BENFLEET

E J & C A Brooks (BNTA, IBNS)
Contact Mr E J Brooks
44 Kiln Road, Thundersley, Benfleet, Essex, SS7 1TB
01268 753835
Ⓜ 07850 262629
Est. 1974 *Stock size* Large
Stock Coins, English and foreign bank notes
Open By appointment
Fairs York, Birmingham, Cumberland Hotel
Services Free valuations

BRENTWOOD

Le-Potier
Contact Mr S Hall
42 King's Road, Brentwood, Essex, CM14 4DW
01277 216310
Est. 1985 *Stock size* Small
Stock Collectables
Open Tues–Sun 10am–5pm closed Thurs
Services China restoration

BROOMFIELD

The Cottage Collection
Contact Mr I Honeywood
93 Main Road, Broomfield, Chelmsford, Essex, CM1 7DQ
01245 442013
Ⓜ 07741 448025
Est. 1994 *Stock size* Medium
Stock Antique pine furniture, ceramics, brass, pictures
Open Sun–Sat 11am–5pm
Services Free delivery

Hutchison Antiques and Interiors (EADA)
Contact Mr Gavin Hutchinson
163 Main Road, Broomfield, Chelmsford, Essex, CM1 7DJ
01245 441184 Ⓕ 01245 441184
Est. 1984 *Stock size* Large
Stock Period furniture, paintings, decorative items
Open Tues–Sat 11am–5pm
Fairs NEC
Services Restorations, interior design service

CHELMSFORD

Chelmsford Coin Centre
Contact Mr D Drury
219 Springfield Road, Chelmsford, Essex, CM2 6JS
01245 261278
Est. 1968 *Stock size* Medium
Stock Ancient and modern coins, medals
Open By appointment

Cooper Hirst Auctions
Contact Mr R L C Hirst FRICS
The Granary Saleroom, Victoria Road, Chelmsford, Essex, CM2 6LH
01245 260535 Ⓕ 01245 345185
Est. 1950
Open Mon–Fri 9am–5pm
Sales Regular antiques sales and sales of household effects, furniture, electrical goods, machinery, tools. Phone for details
Catalogues Yes

S H Rowland
Contact Mr S H Rowland
42 Mildmay Road, Chelmsford, Essex, CM2 0DZ
01245 354251 Ⓕ 01245 344466
Est. 1946
Open Mon–Fri 9am–5.30pm
Sales Lesser-quality goods alternate weeks, antiques 2–3 a year on Wed, viewing Tues 9am–4.30pm Wed 9–10am
Frequency 2 weeks
Catalogues Yes

CHIPPING ONGAR

Garners (EADA)
Contact Nick Garner
The Barn (Next to the Two Brewers), Greensted Road, Chipping Ongar, Essex, CM5 9HD
01245 261863
Ⓜ 07970 206682
Ⓔ nickgarner@btinternet.com
Ⓦ www.ngarners.co.uk
Est. 1998 *Stock size* Large
Stock Studio and art pottery, Sally Tuffin, Dennis chinaworks, Lise Moorcroft, Dean Sherwin, Roger Cockram, Highland stoneware, Dartington pottery, Alexandra Copeland, general antiques
Open Sat Sun 10am–4pm
Services Valuations

CLACTON-ON-SEA

Jade Antiques
Contact Mrs J Ellis
Suffolk House, High Street, Thorpe Le Soken, Clacton-on-Sea, Essex, CO16 0EA
01255 860040
Ⓜ 07747 730852
Est. 1984 *Stock size* Small
Stock Fine porcelain, small furniture
Open Wed–Sat 10am–5pm

COGGESHALL

Argentum Antiques
Contact Mrs Dianne Carr
1 Church Street, Coggeshall, Essex, CO6 1TU
01376 561365
Est. 1994 *Stock size* Medium
Stock Early oak furniture, silver, decorative items
Open Mon–Sat 10.30am–5pm closed Wed Sun

English Rose Antiques
Contact Mr M Barrett
7 Church Street, Coggeshall, Essex, CO6 1TU
01376 562683 Ⓕ 01376 563450
Ⓜ 07770 880790
Ⓔ englishroseantiques@hotmail.com
Est. 1983 *Stock size* Large

Stock Antiquea and country pine furniture
Open Mon–Sun 10am–5.30pm
Fairs Ardingly, Newark
Services Stripping, finishing

Lion House Antiques Ltd (EADA)
Contact Mr P Young
10 East Street, Coggeshall, Colchester, Essex, CO6 1SH
01376 563282
07802 955829
lionpy@aol.com
Est. 1991 *Stock size* Large
Stock 17th–19thC English furniture, chairs, oak farmhouse tables
Open Mon–Sat 10am–5pm Sun by appointment
Fairs Newark, DMG fairs, Arthur Swallow fairs
Services Valuations, restorations, house clearance

Partners in Pine
Contact Mr W T Newton
63–65 West Street, Coggeshall, Colchester, Essex, CO6 1NS
01376 561972
Est. 1983 *Stock size* Medium
Stock Victorian pine furniture
Open Mon–Sun 10am–6pm closed Wed

COLCHESTER

Alphabets
Contact Mr Briggs
13 Trinity, Colchester, Essex, CO1 1JN
01206 572751
Est. 1974 *Stock size* Medium
Stock Antiquarian and second-hand books
Open Mon–Sat 10am–5pm closed Thurs

S Bond & Son
Contact Mr R Bond
Olivers Orchard, Olivers Lane, Colchester, Essex, CO2 0HH
01206 331175 F 01206 579859
07710 823800
bondandsonantiques@hotmail.com
Est. 1840 *Stock size* Medium
Stock 18th–19thC mahogany furniture, paintings
Trade only Yes
Open By appointment
Fairs Newark, Ardingly
Services Valuations, restorations

Bonhams & Brooks
Contact David Hawtin
Venus Cottage, Ford Street, Aldham, Colchester, Essex, CO6 3PH
01206 241280 F 01206 241280
Open Mon–Fri 9am–5pm
Sales Regional Representative for East Anglia

Elizabeth Cannon Antiques
Contact Mrs E Cannon
85 Crouch Street, Colchester, Essex, CO3 3EZ
01206 575817
Est. 1978 *Stock size* Large
Stock Antique glass, jewellery, silver, porcelain, furniture
Open Mon–Sat 9.30am–5.30pm

The Castle Book Shop (PBFA)
Contact Mr R Green
40 Osborne Street, Colchester, Essex, CO2 7DB
01206 577520 F 01206 577520
Est. 1947 *Stock size* Large
Stock Antiquarian and second-hand books, East Anglia, archaeology, modern first editions, maps, prints
Open Mon–Sat 9am–5pm
Fairs PBFA
Services Book search

Colton Antiques
Contact Mr G Colton
Station Road, Colchester, Essex, CO5 9NP
01376 571504
Est. 1992 *Stock size* Small
Stock 18th–19thC furniture, Georgian, decorative furniture
Open Mon–Sat 8am–5pm
Services Restorations

G K R Bonds Ltd (IBSS)
Contact Hazel Fisher
Unit 4, Park Farm, Inworth, Colchester, Essex, CO5 9SH
01376 571711 F 01376 570125
Est. 1979 *Stock size* Large
Stock Old bonds, share certificates
Open Mail order only
Services Valuations, annual and quarterly lists

Mill Antiques
Contact David Illingsworth
10 East Street, Colchester, Essex, CO1 2TX
01206 500996
Stock size Large
Stock Victorian, Edwardian mahogany furniture
Open Mon–Sat 10am–5pm

Reeman, Dansie, Howe & Son
Contact Mr J Grinter
12 Headgate, Colchester, Essex, CO3 3BT
01206 574271 F 01206 578213
auctions@reemans.com
Est. 1881
Open Mon–Fri 9am–5.30pm
Sales Antiques and general sales Wed 10am, viewing Tues 9am–7pm Wed 9am–10pm. Also weekly household goods sales
Frequency 6–8 weeks
Catalogues Yes

Revival
Contact Mrs B Addison
23b Drury Road, Colchester, Essex, CO2 7UY
01206 506162
Est. 1999 *Stock size* Large
Stock Architectural salvage, furniture, decorative curios
Open Tues–Sat 10am–4pm

Shipwreck Centre
Contact Mr M K Kettle
22e Marshes Yard, Victoria Place, Brightlingsea, Colchester, Essex, CO7 0BX
01206 307307
www.sos.uk.com
Est. 1995 *Stock size* Large
No. of dealers 15
Stock Collectables, furniture, books, arts, crafts
Open Mon–Sun 10am–5pm
Services House clearance

Stanfords
Contact Mr David Lord
11 East Hill, Colchester, Essex, CO1 2QX
01206 868070 F 01206 869590
Est. 1995
Open Mon–Fri 9am–5.30pm
Sales General goods Tues 10am, antique furniture, collectables quarterly Tues 11am, viewing Sat 9am–1pm Mon noon–7pm Tues 9–10am
Frequency Weekly
Catalogues Yes

DANBURY

Danbury Antiques (EADA)
Contact Mrs Southgate

✉ Eves Corner, Danbury, Chelmsford, Essex, CM3 4QF P
☎ 01245 223035 F 01245 222740
M 07711 704652
Est. 1979 *Stock size* Large
Stock Jewellery, silver, ceramics, porcelain, furniture
Open Tues–Sat 10am–5pm Wed 10am–1pm Sun 10.30am–1pm
Fairs Furze Hill
Services Restorations

DOVERCOURT

Mayflower Antiques (ADA)
Contact Mr John Odgers
✉ 105 High Street, Dovercourt, Harwich, Essex, CO12 3AP P
☎ 01255 504079
M 07860 843569
E mayflower@ukshells.co.uk
Est. 1970 *Stock size* Medium
Stock Music boxes, scientific instruments, clocks, marine items
Open By appointment
Fairs Newark, Ardingly

EPPING

Old Barn Antiques
Contact Mr T Quick
✉ Hayleys Manor, Epping Upland, Epping, Essex, CM16 6PQ P
☎ 01992 579007 F 01992 579008
Est. 1974 *Stock size* Large
Stock 1850–present day furniture
Open Mon–Fri 9am–5pm or by appointment
Services Container packing

FINCHINGFIELD

Finchingfield Antiques Centre
Contact Mr Peter Curry
✉ The Green, Finchingfield, Braintree, Essex, CM7 4JX P
☎ 01371 810258 F 01371 810258
E prospectfinch@aol.com
Est. 1996 *Stock size* Large
No. of dealers 45
Stock Furniture, silver, porcelain, antiquarian books, jewellery, collectables
Open Mon–Sun 10am–5.30pm

FRINTON-ON-SEA

Dickens Curios
Contact Miss M Wilsher
✉ 151 Connaught Avenue, Frinton-on-Sea, Essex, CO13 9AH P
☎ 01255 674134
Est. 1970 *Stock size* Large
Stock Antiques, china, glass, pewter, copper, jewellery
Open Mon Fri 11am–1pm 2.15–5.30pm Tues Thurs 9.45am–1pm 2.15–5.30pm Sat 9.45am–5pm closed Wed pm
Services Buying from public

No 24 of Frinton
Contact Mr C Pereira
✉ 24 Connaught Avenue, Frinton-on-Sea, Essex, CO13 9PR P
☎ 01255 670505
Est. 1993 *Stock size* Large
Stock Art Deco, general antiques, original prints
Open Mon–Sat 10am–5pm Sun 2–4pm closed Wed

Phoenix Trading
Contact Mr Tom Sheldon
✉ 130 Connaught Avenue, Frinton-on-Sea, Essex, CO13 9AD P
☎ 01255 851094 F 01255 851094
Est. 1996 *Stock size* Large
Stock Antique pine
Open Tues–Sat 10am–4pm
Services Restorations, stripping, cabinet makers

GRAYS

Atticus Books
Contact Mr R Drake
✉ 8 London Road, Grays, Essex, RM17 5XY P
☎ 01375 371200
M 07809 024845
Est. 1983 *Stock size* Large
Stock Antiquarian, out-of-print, second-hand books
Open Thurs–Sat 9am–4pm
Services Book search

GREAT BADDOW

The Antique Brass Bedstead Co Ltd
Contact Mr I Rabin
✉ The Bringey, Church Street, Great Baddow, Chelmsford, Essex, CM2 7JW P
☎ 01245 471137
Est. 1978 *Stock size* Large
Stock Victorian brass and iron bedsteads
Open Mon–Sat 10am–5pm Sun 11am–5pm
Services Restorations

Baddow Antique Centre (EADA)
✉ The Bringey, Church Street, Great Baddow, Chelmsford, Essex, CM2 7JW P
☎ 01245 476159
Est. 1974 *Stock size* Large
No. of dealers 20+
Stock 18th–20thC furniture, silver, glass, porcelain, paintings, Victorian brass and iron bedsteads
Open Mon–Sat 10am–5pm Sun 11am–5pm
Services Valuations, restorations

GREAT CHESTERFORD

C & J Mortimer & Son
Contact Mr C Mortimer
✉ School Street, Great Chesterford, Saffron Walden, Essex, CB10 1NN P
☎ 01799 530261
Est. 1964 *Stock size* Medium
Stock Oak furniture
Open Thurs Sat 2.30–5pm or by appointment
Services Restorations

GREAT DUNMOW

Memories (EADA)
Contact Peter Berriman
✉ 11a Market Place, Great Dunmow, Essex, CM6 1AX P
☎ 01371 872331 F 01371 872331
M 07774 937001
Est. 2000 *Stock size* Small
Stock General antiques, Victorian–Edwardian furniture, 18th–19thC clocks, 19th–20thC ceramics
Open Mon–Sat 9.30am–5pm
Fairs Brentwood
Services House clearance, reupholstery, repolishing

F B Neill
Contact Mr F B Neill
✉ Ivydene, Chelmsford Road, White Roding, Great Dunmow, Essex, CM6 1RG P
☎ 01279 876376
Est. 1975 *Stock size* Medium
Stock Antique furniture
Open By appointment

Clive Smith
Contact Mr C Smith
Brick House, North Street, Great Dunmow, Essex, CM6 1BA
01371 873171 01371 873171
clivesmith@route56.co.uk
Est. 1975 *Stock size* Small
Stock Antiquarian books, British Isles, topography, military, natural history
Trade only Yes
Open Mail order or by appointment

Trembath Welch (NAVA)
Contact Mr E Crichton
The Old Town Hall, Great Dunmow, Essex, CM6 1AU
01371 873014 01371 878239
07931 634342
trembath@netcom.co.uk
www.trembathwelch.co.uk
Est. 1886
Open Mon–Fri 9am–5.30pm
Sales Chequers Lane, Great Dunmow, fine art and antiques sales quarterly, general sales every 2 weeks. Phone for details
Frequency Quarterly
Catalogues Yes

GREAT WALTHAM

Mollie Webster
Contact Scott Saunders
The Stores, Great Waltham, Chelmsford, Essex, CM3 1DE
01245 360277
Est. 1975 *Stock size* Large
Stock English antique and period pine furniture
Open Wed–Sat 10am–5pm Sun 11am–4pm
Services Deliveries

HALSTEAD

The Antique Bed Shop
Contact Mrs V McGregor
Napier House, Head Street, Halstead, Essex, CO9 2BT
01787 477346 01787 478757
07801 626047
Est. 1976 *Stock size* Large
Stock Antique wooden beds
Open Thurs–Sat 9am–5pm or by appointment
Services Free delivery

Appleton's Allsorts
Contact Barry Appleton
9 Head Street, Halstead, Essex, CO9 2AT
01787 476273
07715 035934
Est. 1997 *Stock size* Large
Stock General antiques, second-hand items
Open Mon–Sat 9am–5pm closed Wed
Services Stripping, house clearance

Townsford Mill Antiques Centre
Contact Mr M Stuckey
The Causeway, Halstead, Essex, CO9 1ET
01787 474451 01787 473893
stackley@townsford.freeserve.co.uk
www.townsford.freeserve.co.uk
Est. 1987 *Stock size* Large
No. of dealers 80
Stock Antiques, collectables, furniture, silver, porcelain, lace, copper, Beswick, Royal Doulton, kitchenware
Open Mon–Sat 10am–5pm Sun Bank Holidays 11am–5pm
Services Tea room

HARLOW

West Essex Antiques
Contact Mr C Dovaston
Stone Hall, Down Hall Road, Matching Green, Harlow, Essex, CM17 0RA
01279 730609 01279 730609
chris@essexantiques.co.uk
www.essexantiques.co.uk
Est. 1975 *Stock size* Large
Stock Furniture
Open Mon–Fri 9am–5pm or by appointment

HARWICH

Harwich International Antique Centre
Contact Mr Hans Scholz
19 King's Quay Street, Harwich, Essex, CO12 3ER
01255 554719 01255 554719
info@antiques-access-agency.com
www.antiques-access-agency.com
Est. 1996 *Stock size* Large
No. of dealers 45
Stock A wide range of antiques, collectables and decorative items
Open Tues–Sat 10am–5pm Sun 1–5pm

HIGH EASTER

Antique Workshop
Contact Mr Haldane
Haydens Farm, High Easter, Chelmsford, Essex, CM1 4QU
01245 231770 07867 533093
Est. 1989 *Stock size* Small
Stock Victorian–Edwardian furniture
Open By appointment
Services Trade restorations

HOLLAND-ON-SEA

Bookworm
Contact Mr A Durrant
100 Kings Avenue, Holland-on-Sea, Essex, CO15 5EP
01255 815984 01255 815984
andy@adr-comms.demon.co.uk
www.adr-comms.demon.co.uk
Est. 1995 *Stock size* Medium
Stock Antiquarian and general second-hand books, fiction, modern first editions
Open Mon–Sat 9am–5pm Bank Holidays 10am–4pm
Services Free book search

ILFORD

Goodwins
Contact Mr C E Goodwin
32 Cameron Road, Ilford, Essex, IG3 8LB
020 8590 4560
Est. 1964 *Stock size* Small
Stock General antiques
Open Mon–Sat 9am–6pm

INGATESTONE

Hutchison Antiques and Interiors (EADA)
Contact Mr Gavin Hutchison
60 High Street, Ingatestone, Essex, CM4 9DW
01277 353361 01277 353361
Est. 1984 *Stock size* Large
Stock Furniture, paintings, antique and contemporary lamps
Open Mon–Sat 10am–5pm closed Wed
Fairs NEC
Services Valuations, interior design service

Jericho Cottage (EADA)
Contact Judy Wood
The Duckpond Green, Blackmore, Ingatestone, Essex, CM4 0RR

EAST

☎ 01277 821031
Est. 1994 *Stock size* Large
Stock General antiques, small furniture, collectables, ceramics, blue and white china, prints, mirrors, small silver plate etc
Open Wed–Sun 11am–5pm
Services Valuations, restoration advice

Kendons
Contact Ms Hilary O'Connor
122a High Street, Ingatestone, Essex, CM4 0BA P
☎ 01277 353625 M 07778 392699
E hilary@kendons.co.uk
W www.kendons.co.uk
Est. 1978 *Stock size* Medium
Stock Coins, medals, small collectables, stamps, old gold and silver
Open Mon Thurs–Sat 9.30am–5pm
Fairs Alexandra Palace, Sandown Park
Services Valuations

KELVEDON

G T Ratcliff Ltd
Contact Fiona Campbell
Brick House, Braxted Road, Kelvedon, Essex, CO5 9BS P
☎ 01376 570234
Est. 1947 *Stock size* Medium
Stock English lacquer, decorative furniture
Open Mon–Fri 9am–5pm
Sat Sun by appointment

LEIGH-ON-SEA

Astoria Art Deco
Contact Mr or Mrs R Taylor
80 Rectory Grove, Leigh-on-Sea, Essex, SS9 2HJ P
☎ 01702 471800
M 07711 332148
E astoriaartdeco@aol.com
Est. 1987 *Stock size* Large
Stock Furniture, mirrors, lighting
Open Tues–Sat 10.30am–5pm closed Mon Wed
Fairs Battersea, Hove
Services Polishing, upholstery

Castle Antiques
Contact Mrs Barbara Gair
PO Box 1911, Leigh-on-Sea, Essex, SS9 1JG
☎ 01702 711390 F 01702 475732
M 07973 674355
E castle@enterprise.net
W www.castle-antiques.com
Est. 1979 *Stock size* Large
Stock 19thC Staffordshire figures, ironstone wares, tribal artefacts, good taxidermy
Trade only Yes
Open By appointment
Fairs NEC, Newark
Services Valuations

Chalkwell Auctions Ltd (EADA)
Contact Trevor or David
The Arlington Rooms, Leigh-on-Sea, Essex, SS0 8NU
☎ 01702 710383 F 01702 710383
Est. 1990
Sales Antiques and collectables sale monthly, normally 2nd Wed, 6.30pm, viewing 4.30pm
Frequency Monthly
Catalogues Yes

Deja Vu Antiques
Contact Mr S Lewis
876 London Road, Leigh-on-Sea, Essex, SS9 3NQ P
☎ 01702 470829
E info@deja-vu-antiques.co.uk
W www.deja-vu-antiques.co.uk
Est. 1994 *Stock size* Large
Stock 18th–19thC French furniture
Open Mon–Sat 9.30am–5.30pm
Sun 10.30am–2pm
Services Restorations

Drizen Coins
Contact Mr Harry Drizen
1 Hawthorns, Leigh-on-Sea, Essex, SS9 4JT P
☎ 01702 521094
Est. 1961 *Stock size* Medium
Stock Coins, tokens, medallions, medals
Open Mon–Sat 9am–9pm

Christopher Mayes
Contact Mr C Mayes
75 Glendale Gardens, Leigh-on-Sea, Essex, SS9 2BG P
☎ 01702 472133 F 01702 713927
M 07989 236735
E artbooks@btinternet.com
W www.artbooks.btinternet.co.uk
Est. 1996 *Stock size* Medium
Stock Visual art books
Open Mon–Sat 10am–5pm
Fairs National Book Fairs
Services Book search for visual arts subjects

Othellos
Contact Mr F Bush or Mrs M Layzell
1376 London Road, Leigh-on-Sea, Essex, SS9 2UH P
☎ 01702 473334
M 07710 764175
Est. 1999 *Stock size* Large
Stock Antiquarian and second-hand books
Open Mon–Wed noon–7.30pm
Thurs Fri noon–9.30pm
Sat 10am–5.30pm

Pall Mall Antiques (EADA)
Contact Jo or Ray Webb
104c–d Elm Road, Leigh-on-Sea, Essex, SS9 1SQ P
☎ 01702 477235
M 07970 494122
E info@pallmallantiques.co.uk
W www.pallmallantiques.co.uk
Est. 1974 *Stock size* Large
Stock Glass, silver, metalware, china, collectables
Open Mon–Sat 10am–5pm closed Wed
Fairs Newark
Services Restoration

Paris Antiques (EADA)
Contact N Rodgers
96 The Broadway, Leigh-on-Sea, Essex, SS9 1A3 P
☎ 01702 712832 F 01702 712832
E enquiries@parisantiques.freeserve.co.uk
Est. 1983 *Stock size* Large
Stock 18th–early 20thC furniture, Art Nouveau
Open Mon–Fri 9.30am–5pm
Sat 9.30am–6pm closed Wed
Services Valuations

Recollect
Contact Mrs C Willmott
52 Rectory Grove, Leigh-on-Sea, Essex, SS9 2HJ
☎ 01702 478415
M 07790 475462
E wrecollect@aol.com
Est. 1998 *Stock size* Large
Stock Victorian–20thC, Art Deco, contemporary designer furniture
Open Mon–Sat 10am–5pm
Wed 10am–1pm
Fairs Brentwood

⊞ John Stacey & Son
Contact Mr P J Stacey
⊠ **86–90 Pall Mall, Leigh-on-Sea, Essex, SS9 1RG** 🅿
☎ 01702 477051 Ⓕ 01702 470141
Ⓔ jstacey@easynet.co.uk
Ⓦ www.jstacey.com
Est. 1946 *Stock size* Medium
Stock Victorian–Edwardian furniture, clocks, ceramics
Open Mon–Fri 9am–5.30pm Sat 9am–1pm
Fairs Newark, Ardingly
Services Adult education courses, valuations, house clearance

John Stacey & Son (Leigh Auction Rooms)
Contact Mr P J Stacey
⊠ **86–90 Pall Mall, Leigh-on-Sea, Essex, SS9 1RG** 🅿
☎ 01702 477051 Ⓕ 01702 470141
Ⓔ jstacey@easynet.co.uk
Est. 1962
Open Mon–Fri 9am–5.30pm Sat 9am–1pm
Sales General antiques sales Tues 10.30am, viewing Sat Mon 10am–4pm Sun 10am–2pm. Occasional collectors' sale
Frequency 3 weeks
Catalogues Yes

⊞ J Streamer
Contact Mrs J Streamer
⊠ **86 Broadway, Leigh-on-Sea, Essex, SS9 1AE**
☎ 01702 472895
Est. 1963 *Stock size* Medium
Stock Jewellery, silver, small furniture, art items
Open Mon–Sat 9am–5pm closed Wed
Services Jewellery repair

⊞ J Streamer
Contact Mrs J Streamer
⊠ **212 Leigh Road, Leigh-on-Sea, Essex, SS9 1BS** 🅿
☎ 01702 472895
Est. 1963 *Stock size* Medium
Stock Objets d'art, small furniture
Open Mon–Sat 9am–5pm closed Wed

⊞ Tillys Antiques
Contact Mr S T Austen or R J Austen
⊠ **1801 London Road, Leigh-on-Sea, Essex, SS9 2ST** 🅿
☎ 01702 557170
Ⓜ 07803 866318
Est. 1972 *Stock size* Large
Stock General antiques, furniture, antique dolls
Open Mon–Sat 9am–4.30pm closed Wed
Services Valuations, restorations

LITTLE WALTHAM

⊞ Collectors' Corner
Contact Mr P Workman or Alasdair MacInnes
⊠ **100 The Street, Little Waltham, Chelmsford, Essex, CM3 3NT** 🅿
☎ 01245 361166 Ⓕ 01245 361166
Est. 1987 *Stock size* Large
Stock Paper collectables, postcards, cigarette cards, ephemera, books
Open Mon–Sun 9am–6pm
Services Picture framing

MALDON

⊞ All Books
Contact Mr K Peggs
⊠ **2 Mill Road, Maldon, Essex, CM9 5HZ** 🅿
☎ 01621 856214
Ⓦ www.collect-hobbies.co.uk
Est. 1975 *Stock size* Large
Stock Antiquarian and second-hand books, especially sailing and maritime history
Open Mon–Sat 10am–5pm Sun 1.30–5pm
Services Valuations

⊞ The Antique Rooms (RADS)
Contact Mrs Ellen Hedley
⊠ **63d High Street, Maldon, Essex, CM9 5EB** 🅿
☎ 01621 856985
Est. 1977 *Stock size* Large
Stock 19th–20thC general antiques
Open Mon–Sat 10am–4pm closed Wed
Services Scandinavian spoken

⊞ Clive Beardall (BAFRA, EADA)
Contact Mr Clive Beardall
⊠ **104b High Street, Maldon, Essex, CM9 5ET** 🅿
☎ 01621 857890 Ⓕ 01621 850753
Ⓔ info@clivebeardall.co.uk
Ⓦ www.clivebeardall.co.uk
Est. 1982 *Stock size* Small
Stock 18th–20thC furniture
Open Mon–Fri 8am–5.30pm Sat 9am–4pm
Services Valuations, restorations

⊞ Mulberry House of Maldon
Contact Mr A Hunwicks
⊠ **20A High Street, Maldon, Essex, CM9 5PJ** 🅿
☎ 01621 858395
Est. 1980 *Stock size* Large
Stock Collectables
Open Mon–Sat 9.30am–5pm
Fairs Antiques for Everyone, International Gift Fair
Services Mail order

MANNINGTREE

⊞ Antiques (BAFRA)
Contact Mrs A Patterson
⊠ **49 High Street, Manningtree, Essex, CO11 1AH** 🅿
☎ 01206 396170
Est. 1977 *Stock size* Medium
Stock General antiques, furniture, glass, silver, porcelain, pictures, mirrors
Open Mon–Sat 10am–1pm 2–5pm
Services Restorations

NEWPORT

⊞ Brown House Antiques
Contact Brian Hodgkinson
⊠ **The Brown House, High Street, Newport, Saffron Walden, Essex, CB11 3QY** 🅿
☎ 01799 540238
Est. 1966 *Stock size* Medium
Stock Mainly 19thC pine and country furniture
Open Mon–Sat 10am–5.30pm

⊞ Omega Decorative Arts
Contact Mr Tony Phillips or Mrs Sybil Hooper
⊠ **High Street, Newport, Saffron Walden, Essex, CB11 3PF** 🅿
☎ 01799 540720
Est. 1985 *Stock size* Medium
Stock 1860–1960, Art Deco, Arts and Crafts
Open Mon–Sat 10am–6pm closed Thurs
Services Restorations

RAYLEIGH

⊞ F G Bruschweiler Antiques Ltd (LAPADA)
Contact Mrs K Gelsthorpe

✉ **41–67 Lower Lambricks, Rayleigh, Essex, SS6 8DA** 🅿
☎ 01268 773761/773932
Ⓕ 01268 773318
Ⓔ fred@fgbruschweiler.demon.co.uk
Ⓔ fbruschweiler@virgin.net
Ⓦ www.business.virgin.net/f.bruschweiler
Est. 1960 *Stock size* Large
Stock General antique furniture, public house bars
Open Mon–Fri 8.30am–5pm
Services Restorations

ROMFORD

⊞ Carey's Bookshop
Contact Mr Robert Carey
✉ **91 High Road, Chadwell Heath, Romford, Essex, RM6 6PB** 🅿
☎ 020 8597 4165
Est. 1985 *Stock size* Medium
Stock Antiquarian and second-hand books, especially sci-fi and crime
Open Tues–Sat 10am–5pm

⊞ Off World
Contact Mr Mark Woollard
✉ **Romford Shopping Hall, Market Place, Romford, Essex, RM1 3AT** 🅿
☎ 01708 765633
Est. 1995 *Stock size* Large
Stock Antique toys, collectables, *Star Wars* a speciality
Open Mon–Sat 9am–5.30pm
Fairs Luton

SAFFRON WALDEN

⊞ Bush Antiques (EADA)
Contact Mrs J M Hosford
✉ **26–28 Church Street, Saffron Walden, Essex, CB10 1JQ**
☎ 01799 523277
Est. 1960 *Stock size* Medium
Stock Country furniture, copper, brass, treen, ceramics, glass
Open Mon–Sat 11am–4.30pm closed Thurs

⌂ Debden Antiques (EADA)
Contact Mr Edward Norman
✉ **Debden, Saffron Walden, Essex, CB11 3JY** 🅿
☎ 01799 543007 Ⓕ 01799 542482
Ⓔ info@debden-antiques.co.uk
Ⓦ www.debden-antiques.co.uk
Est. 1999 *Stock size* Large
No. of dealers 30
Stock 17th–19thC furniture, paintings, jewellery, silver, glass, rugs, garden ornaments, furniture
Open Mon–Sat 9am–6pm Sun 11am–4pm
Services Valuations, restorations, shipping

⊞ Ickleton Antiques
Contact Mr B Arbury
✉ **4 Gold Street, Saffron Walden, Essex, CB10 1EJ**
☎ 01799 513114
Est. 1995 *Stock size* Medium
Stock Militaria, postcards, collectables WWI, WWII
Open Mon–Fri 10am–4pm Sat 10am–5pm

⊞ Lankester Antiques & Books
Contact Mr P Lankester
✉ **The Old Sun Inn, Church Street, Saffron Walden, Essex, CB10 1JW**
☎ 01799 522685
Est. 1967 *Stock size* Large
Stock General antiques, antiquarian and second-hand books
Open Mon–Sat 9.30am–5.30pm

⊞ Market Row Antiques & Collectables
Contact Mr P Bowyer or Mr D Miller
✉ **14 Market Row, Saffron Waldon, Essex, CB10 1HB**
☎ 01799 516131
Ⓜ 07759 493613
Est. 1994 *Stock size* Small
Stock General antiques, clocks, barometers
Open Mon–Wed Fri Sat 10am–5pm Thurs 2–5pm
Fairs London and Birmingham clock fairs
Services Clock and watch repairs

⊞ T Reed & Son
Contact Meg Reed
✉ **22 Castle Street, Saffron Walden, Essex, CB10 1BJ** 🅿
☎ 01799 522363
Est. 1881 *Stock size* Small
Stock Country antiques
Open Tues Sat 10am–1pm 2–5pm

⌂ Saffron Walden Antiques Centre
Contact Mr P Rowell or Mrs J Rowell
✉ **1 Market Row, Saffron Walden, Essex, CB10 1HA** 🅿
☎ 01799 524534 Ⓕ 01799 524703
Ⓦ www.saffronwaldenantiquescentre.com
Est. 1997 *Stock size* Large
No. of dealers 40
Stock Huge range of antiques, collectables, bygones, furniture, silver, jewellery, porcelain, lighting, pictures, sporting memorabilia
Open Mon–Fri 10am–5.30pm Sat 9am–5.30pm Sun 11am–5pm

Saffron Walden Auctions
Contact Mr C Bazley
✉ **1 Market Street, Saffron Walden, Essex, CB10 1JB**
☎ 01799 513281 Ⓕ 01799 513334
Est. 1905
Open Mon–Fri 9am–5pm
Sales General auction Tues 10am, viewing Mon 9am–5pm. Antiques and collectables every 2 months Fri 10.30am, viewing Thurs
Frequency Weekly
Catalogues Yes

SIBLE HEDINGHAM

⊞ Hedingham Antiques (EADA)
Contact Mrs P Patterson
✉ **100 Swan Street, Sible Hedingham, Halstead, Essex, CO9 3HP** 🅿
☎ 01787 460360 Ⓕ 01787 469109
Ⓔ patriciapatterson@totalise.co.uk
Est. 1980 *Stock size* Medium
Stock Silver, silver plate, china, glass, Victorian, Art Deco, late 18thC–early 20thC furniture
Open Mon–Fri 10am–5pm Sat 10am–4pm
Services Silver and furniture restoration

⊞ Lennard Antiques (LAPADA)
Contact G Pinn
✉ **124 Swan Street, Sible Hedingham, Halstead, Essex, CO9 3HP** 🅿
☎ 01787 461127
Est. 1969 *Stock size* Medium
Stock Oak and country furniture, Delftware
Open Mon–Sat 9.30am–6pm
Fairs Olympia, Chelsea Spring and Autumn, Kensington

W A Pinn & Sons (LAPADA, BADA)
Contact Mr J Pinn or Mr K Pinn
124 Swan Street, Sible Hedingham, Halstead, Essex, CO9 3HP
01787 461127
Est. 1969 *Stock size* Medium
Stock 17th–early 19thC furniture, accessories
Open Mon–Sat 9.30am–6pm
Fairs Olympia, Chelsea Spring and Autumn, Kensington

SOUTHEND-ON-SEA

Curio City
Contact Carol or Matt
333–335 Chartwell Square, Victoria Plaza, Southend-on-Sea, Essex, SS2 5SP
01702 611350
Est. 1998 *Stock size* Large
Stock Wide range of antiques, collectables
Open Mon–Fri 10am–5pm Sat 9am–5pm
Services Café

Dealers
Contact Gary Bell
659 London Road, Southend-on-Sea, Essex, SS0 9PD
01702 300052 01702 300050
www.les-and-gary.co.uk
Est. 1977 *Stock size* Large
Stock General antiques
Open Mon–Sun 9am–5pm

Lonsdale Antiques
Contact Mrs H Clark
86 Lonsdale Road, Southend-on-Sea, Essex, SS2 4LR
01702 462643
07899 771989
Est. 1980 *Stock size* Large
Stock General antiques, porcelain, small furniture, ceramics, gold and silver jewellery, costume jewellery, pictures
Open Mon–Sat 9.30am–5.30pm closed Wed
Fairs Essex, Enfield Middlesex

David Morton
Contact Mr D Morton
Rear of 61–69 Princes Street, Southend-on-Sea, Essex, SS1 1PT
01702 354144
Est. 1967 *Stock size* Large
Stock 19thC furniture, general antiques
Trade only Yes
Open By appointment

R & J Coins
Contact Mr R Harvey
21b Alexandra Street, Market Place, Southend-on-Sea, Essex, SS1 1BX
01702 345995
Est. 1967 *Stock size* Medium
Stock Coins, medals, bank notes, cap badges
Open Mon–Fri 10am–4pm Wed 10am–2pm Sat 10am–3pm

STANSTED MOUNTFITCHET

Harris Antiques Stansted (BAFRA, EADA)
Contact Brian Harris
40 Lower Street, Stansted Mountfitchet, Essex, CM24 8LR
01279 812233
Est. 1956 *Stock size* Large
Stock 16th–20thC furniture, clocks, barometers, ceramics
Open Mon–Sat 9am–5pm
Fairs NEC
Services Valuations, restorations

Linden House Antiques
Contact Mr A W Sargeant
3 Silver Street, Stansted Mountfitchet, Essex, CM24 8HA
01279 812372
Est. 1962 *Stock size* Large
Stock 18th–19thC furniture, pictures
Open Mon–Sat 9.30am–5.30pm
Services Valuations

G E Sworder & Sons
Contact Mr Guy Schooling RICS
14 Cambridge Road, Stansted Mountfitchet, Essex, CM24 8BZ
01279 817778 01279 817779
auctions@sworder.co.uk
www.sworder.co.uk
Est. 1782
Open Mon–Fri 9am–5pm
Sales Victoriana and lesser-quality antiques and collectables, Thurs, no catalogue, viewing Wed 2–5pm Thurs 9–11am. Antiques and fine art sale every 5 weeks Tues 10.30am, viewing Fri 10am–5pm Sat 10am–4pm Mon 10am–5pm
Frequency Weekly
Catalogues Yes

Valmar Antiques (BADA, LAPADA, CINOA)
Contact J A & M R Orpin
Croft House Cottage, High Lane, Stansted Mountfitchet, Essex, CM24 8LQ
01279 813201 01279 816962
07831 093701
valmar-antiques@cwcom.net
Est. 1967 *Stock size* Large
Stock 18th–19thC furniture and accesssories, Arts and Crafts
Open By appointment only
Fairs Olympia BADA

STOCK

Sabine Antiques (EADA)
Contact Mrs S Sabine
38 High Street, Stock, Essex, CM4 9BW
01277 840553 01277 840553
Est. 1969 *Stock size* Small
Stock 18th–19thC furniture, silver, ceramics, clocks, general household
Open Telephone for opening times
Services Valuations, restorations, French polishing

WESTCLIFF-ON-SEA

It's About Time (EADA)
Contact Mr Pane Williams
863 London Road, Westcliff-on-Sea, Essex, SS0 9SZ
01702 472574 01702 472574
iat@clocking-in.demon.co.uk
www.clocking-in.demon.co.uk
Est. 1979 *Stock size* Medium
Stock Clocks, furniture
Open Mon–Sat 9am–5.30pm
Services Restoration

Ridgeway Antiques (EADA)
Contact Trevor or Charles
66 The Ridgeway, Westcliff-on-Sea, Essex, SS0 8NU
01702 710383 01702 710383
www.ridgeweb.co.uk
Est. 1987 *Stock size* Medium
Stock 18thC pre-war furniture, general antiques

Open 10.30am–5pm
Fairs Hallmark, Ridgeway Fairs
Services Valuations

WOODFORD GREEN

Mill Lane Antiques
Contact Mr N McArtney
29 Mill Lane, Woodford Green, Essex, IG8 0UG
☎ 020 8502 9930
Est. 1987 *Stock size* Large
Stock Georgian–Victorian furniture, lighting, ironwork, collectables
Open Tues Thurs–Sat 10am–4.30pm
Fairs Kempton Park
Services House clearance

WRITTLE

Whichcraft Jewellery (EADA)
Contact Alan Turner
54–56 The Green, Writtle, Chelmsford, Essex, CM1 3DU
☎ 01245 420183
Est. 1978 *Stock size* Large
Stock Antique and modern jewellery, small silver items
Open Tues–Sat 9.30am–5.30pm
Services Jewellery repairs and restorations

NORFOLK

ACLE

Horners Auctioneers (ISVA)
Contact Mr N Horner-Glister FRICS
Acle Salerooms, Norwich Road, Acle, Norwich, Norfolk, NR13 3BY
☎ 01493 750225 F 01493 750506
E auction@horners.co.uk
W www.horners.co.uk
Est. 1900
Open Mon–Fri 9am–1pm 2–5pm Sat 9am–noon
Sales General antiques sale Thurs 10am, viewing Wed 2–4pm
Frequency Weekly
Catalogues Yes

Ivy House Antiques
Contact Mr N L Pratt
Ivy House, The Street, Acle, Norwich, Norfolk, NR13 3BH
☎ 01493 750682
Est. 1985 *Stock size* Large
Stock General antiques, porcelain, furniture, pictures, metalware
Open Mon–Sat 9am–5pm
Services Valuations, restorations

ALDBOROUGH

Knight's Sporting Auctions
Contact Tim Knight
The Thatched Gallery, The Green, Aldborough, Norwich, Norfolk, NR11 7AA
☎ 01263 768488 F 01263 768788
E tim@knights.co.uk
W www.knights.co.uk
Est. 1993
Open Mon–Fri 9am–5pm
Sales Sporting memorabilia, especially cricket and football, varied venues and dates, telephone for details, viewing day prior to sale
Frequency Quarterly
Catalogues Yes

AYLSHAM

Keys
Contact Mr J Lines
Aylsham Salerooms, Off Palmers Lane, Aylsham, Norfolk, NR11 6JA
☎ 01263 733195 F 01263 732140
E info@gakey.co.uk
W www.aylshamsalerooms.co.uk
Est. 1953
Open Mon–Fri 9am–5pm closed 1–2pm Sat 9am–noon
Sales Weekly general sale, antique sale every 3 weeks Tues Wed. Every 2 months book sale Fri, collectors' sale Thurs, picture sales Fri. Phone for details
Frequency Every 3 weeks
Catalogues Yes

BAWDESWELL

The Norfolk Polyphon Centre
Contact Mr Norman Vince
Wood Farm, Reepham Road, Bawdeswell, Dereham, Norfolk, NR20 4RX
☎ 01362 688230 F 01362 688230
Est. 1966 *Stock size* Large
Stock Antique and new musical boxes
Open By appointment

BROOKE

Country House Antiques
Contact Mr G Searle
Green Acre, Seething, Nr Brooke, Norwich, Norfolk, NR15 1AL
☎ 01508 558144 F 01508 558144
Est. 1980 *Stock size* Medium
Stock 17th–19thC furniture
Trade only Yes
Open By appointment
Fairs Newark

BURNHAM MARKET

The Brazen Head Bookshop & Gallery
Contact David Kenyon
Greenside, Market Place, Burnham Market, King's Lynn, Norfolk, PE31 8HD
☎ 01328 730700 F 01328 730929
E brazenheadbook@aol.com
Est. 1979 *Stock size* Large
Stock Antiquarian, second-hand, and out-of-print children's books, also books concerning Nelson
Open Mon–Sat 9.30am–5pm
Services Valuations, book search

M & A Cringle
Contact Mr or Mrs Cringle
The Old Black Horse, Market Place, Burnham Market, Norfolk, PE31 8HD
☎ 01328 738456
Est. 1965 *Stock size* Small
Stock Late 18thC furniture, prints, maps, china, pottery
Open Mon–Sat 9am–1pm 2–5pm closed Wed
Services Valuations

Market House Antiques (BADA)
Contact Mr or Mrs D Maufe
Market House, Burnham Market, Norfolk, PE31 8HF
☎ 01328 738475 F 01328 730750
Est. 1976 *Stock size* Medium
Stock 18th–early 19thC furniture and works of art, mirrors, bronzes
Open By appointment or by chance
Fairs BADA March, Summer and Winter Olympias

CAISTER-ON-SEA

⊞ Readers' Dream
Contact Miss T Kemp
✉ **17a Yarmouth Road, Caister-on-Sea, Great Yarmouth, Norfolk, NR30 5DL** Ⓟ
☎ 01493 720220
Est. 1998 *Stock size* Large
Stock Antiquarian books, first editions
Open Mon–Sat 10am–5.30pm Sun 10am–2pm
Services Book search

CLEY

⊞ Fullertons Booksearch
Contact Mr Humphrey Boon
✉ **Branta, 2 Maisons Bienvenues, Cley High Street, Cley, Holt, Norfolk, NR25 7RR** Ⓟ
☎ 01420 544088 Ⓕ 01420 542445
Est. 1991
Stock Books
Open Mon–Fri 9am–5pm
Services Out-of-print book searching facility. Mail order only. No obligation

COLTISHALL

⊞ Roger Bradbury Antiques
Contact Roger Bradbury
✉ **Church Street, Coltishall, Norfolk, NR12 7DJ** Ⓟ
☎ 01603 737444 Ⓕ 01603 737018
Ⓜ 07860 372528
Est. 1967 *Stock size* Medium
Stock Chinese porcelain cargoes, 18th–19thC furniture, pictures, objets d'art

Coltishall Antique Centre
Contact Isabel Ford
✉ **7 High Street, Coltishall, Norwich, Norfolk, NR12 7AA** Ⓟ
☎ 01603 738306
Est. 1977 *Stock size* Medium
No. of dealers 8
Stock Glass, ceramics, militaria, jewellery, silver, fishing, golfing items, collectables
Open Mon–Sat 10am–4.30pm

⊞ Gwendoline Golder Antiques
Contact Mrs G Golder
✉ **Point House, 5 High Street, Coltishall, Norwich, Norfolk, NR12 7AA** Ⓟ
☎ 01603 738099
Est. 1979 *Stock size* Medium
Stock General antiques, furniture, silver, jewellery, porcelain
Open Mon–Sat 10am–1pm 2–5pm

CROMER

⊞ Bond Street Antiques (NAG, FGA)
Contact Mr M R T Jones
✉ **6 Bond Street, Cromer, Norfolk, NR27 9DA** Ⓟ
☎ 01263 513134
Est. 1970 *Stock size* Medium
Stock Silver, jewellery
Open Mon–Sat 9am–5pm
Services Valuations

⊞ Books Etc.
Contact Mr Kevin Reynor
✉ **15a Church Street, Cromer, Norfolk, NR27 9ES**
☎ 01263 515501
Ⓔ bookskcr@aol.com
Est. 1997 *Stock size* Large
Stock Antiquarian and second-hand books
Open Easter–Sept Sun–Mon 11am–4pm Winter Wed–Sat 11am–4pm

⊞ Collectors' Cabin
Contact Diana Hazell Bennington
✉ **The Kiosk, North Lodge Park Promenade, Cromer, Norfolk, NR27 9HE** Ⓟ
☎ 01263 512195 Ⓕ 01263 515961
Est. 1997 *Stock size* Large
Stock All ceramics, glass, Crown Derby
Open Tues–Sun 10am–5pm
Services Restorations

⊞ Collectors' World
Contact Mrs Irene Nockels
✉ **6 New Parade, Cromer, Norfolk, NR27 9EP** Ⓟ
☎ 01263 515330/514174
Ⓔ nockels@25nr.fsnet.co.uk
Est. 1994 *Stock size* Large
Stock Furniture, general antiques, collectables
Open Tues–Sat 10am–5pm
Fairs Norwich, The International Antique and Collectables Fair, RAF Swinderby
Services Valuations, house clearance

⊞ Little Gems Rock Shop
Contact Danny or Gail Hickling
✉ **2a Mount Street, Cromer, Norfolk, NR27 9DB** Ⓟ
☎ 01263 519519
Ⓔ littlegems@breathemail.net
Ⓦ www.littlegemsrockshop.co.uk
Est. 1998 *Stock size* Large
Stock Fossils, gemstones, crystals from around the world
Open Mon–Sat 10am–5pm Sun noon–5pm

DEREHAM

Case & Dewing
Contact John Dewing
✉ **Church Street, Dereham, Norfolk, NR19 1DJ** Ⓟ
☎ 01362 692004 Ⓕ 01362 693103
Ⓔ info@case-dewing.co.uk
Ⓦ www.case-dewing.co.uk
Est. 1900
Open Mon–Fri 9am–5.30pm Sat 9am–3.30pm
Sales General antiques and effects Tues, viewing morning of sale
Frequency 2 weeks
Catalogues No

Tyrone R Roberts
Contact T R Roberts
✉ **Matlock Grange, 16 Greenfields Road, Dereham, Norfolk, NR20 3TE** Ⓟ
☎ 01362 691267 Ⓕ 01362 691267
Ⓜ 07702 642362
Ⓔ tyroneroberts@yahoo.co.uk
Ⓦ www.tyroneroberts.co.uk
Est. 1970
Open Mon–Sun 9am–5pm or by appointment
Sales General antiques
Frequency Monthly
Catalogues Yes

⊞ Village Books
Contact Mr Jack James
✉ **20a High Street, Dereham, Norfolk, NR19 1DR** Ⓟ
☎ 01362 853066
Est. 1996 *Stock size* Large
Stock General books, maps, ephemera
Open Mon Tues Thurs Fri 9.30am–4.30pm Wed 9.30am–1pm Sat 9.30am–5pm
Services Free book search, Readers' Club, postal sales

DISS

Antique and Collectors' Centre Diss
Contact Mr D Cockaday

✉ The Works, 3 Cobbs Yard, St Nicholas Street, Diss, Norfolk, IP22 4LB 🅿
☎ 01379 644472
Est. 1999 *Stock size* Large
No. of dealers 28
Stock General antiques, 1850–1970, Art Deco china and glass, commemoratives, militaria
Open Mon–Thurs 10am–5pm Fri–Sat 9am–5pm
Services Valuations

Diss Antiques & Interiors (LAPADA, GOMC)
Contact Mr Brian Wimshurst
✉ 2–3 Market Place, Diss, Norfolk, IP22 3JT
☎ 01379 642213 Ⓕ 01379 642213
Ⓜ 07770 477368
Est. 1971 *Stock size* Medium
Stock Tudor–Edwardian furniture, ceramics, silver
Open Mon–Sat 9am–5pm
Fairs Snape
Services Valuations, restorations

Thos Wm Gaze & Son (RICS)
Contact Alan M Smith FRICS
✉ Diss Auction Rooms, Roydon Road, Diss, Norfolk, IP22 4LN 🅿
☎ 01379 650306 Ⓕ 01379 644313
Ⓔ auct@twgaze.co.uk
Ⓦ www.twgaze.com
Est. 1857
Open Sat 9am–1pm Mon–Fri 9am–5pm
Sales Weekly Fri sales of antiques and collectables, Victorian pine and shipping furniture, modern furniture and effects. Periodic Fri sales of decorative arts, modern furniture and decor 19th–20thC paintings, books, ephemera. Periodic Sat sales of toys, nostalgia, architectural salvage, statuary, rural and domestic bygones, automobilia, collectors' cars. Auction calendars available, viewing Thurs 2–8pm Fri Sat from 8.30am
Frequency Weekly
Catalogues Yes

DOWNHAM MARKET

Antiques and Gifts
Contact Mrs Addrison
✉ 47 Bridge Street, Downham Market, Norfolk, PE38 9DW 🅿
☎ 01366 387700
Est. 1998 *Stock size* Medium
Stock Victorian–Edwardian furniture, second-hand books, china, glass, smalls, general antiques
Open Mon–Sat 9am–5pm

Downham Market Antique Centre
Contact Sue Cook
✉ 43 High Street, Downham Market, Norfolk, PE38 9HF 🅿
Ⓦ terry@misuzy.fsnet.co.uk
Est. 1990 *Stock size* Large
No. of dealers 40
Stock General antiques and collectables
Open Wed–Sun 10am–4pm

Barry L Hawkins
Contact Mr B Hawkins FRICS
✉ 15 Lynn Road, Downham Market, Norfolk, PE38 9NL 🅿
☎ 01366 387180 Ⓕ 01366 386626
Ⓜ 07860 451721
Ⓔ Barry@barryhawkins.freewire.co.uk
Ⓦ www.barryhawkins.freewire.co.uk
Est. 1840
Open Mon–Fri 9am–5pm
Sales Antiques and general sale of goods Wed, viewing morning of sale 8–11am. Wine sales and Oriental carpet sales, catalogued
Frequency Monthly
Catalogues No

EAST RUDHAM

The Old Grain Stores
Contact Margaret Goodwin
✉ The Square, East Rudham, Kings Lynn, Norfolk, PE31 8RB 🅿
☎ 01485 529410 Ⓕ 01485 529410
Est. 1985
Stock General antiques and collectables
Open Thurs–Tues 10am–4pm closed Wed
Services Valuations

EAST WINCH

Holt & Company (GTA)
Contact Mr N Holt
✉ The Old Vicarage, Church Lane, East Winch, King's Lynn, Norfolk, PE32 1NQ 🅿
☎ 01553 840966 Ⓕ 01553 840616
Ⓜ 07831 431591
Ⓔ enquires@holtandcompany.co.uk
Est. 1993
Open Mon–Fri 9am–5pm
Sales Modern and antique gun sales at the Duke of York's Barracks, King's Road, London, Wed 2pm, viewing Mon 9am–8pm Tues 9am–8pm Wed 9am–12.30pm
Frequency 6 per annum
Catalogues Yes

FAKENHAM

James Beck Auctions
Contact Mr James Beck
✉ The Cornhall, Cattle Market Street, Fakenham, Norfolk, NR21 9AW 🅿
☎ 01328 851557 Ⓕ 01328 851044
Est. 1840
Open Tues 10am–1pm Thurs 10am–5pm Fri 10am–2pm
Sales General antiques sales on Thurs at 11am, specialist sales occasionally, viewing Wed 2–5pm Thurs 9–11am
Frequency Weekly
Catalogues No

Fakenham Antiques Centre
Contact Mandy Allen or Julie Hunt
✉ The Old Congregational Church, 14 Norwich Road, Fakenham, Norfolk, NR21 8AZ 🅿
☎ 01328 862941
Est. 1984 *Stock size* Large
No. of dealers 20
Stock Period furniture, antiques, curios, collectables
Open Mon–Sat 10am–4.30pm
Services Restorations

Sue Rivett Antiques
Contact Sue Rivett
✉ 6 Norwich Road, Fakenham, Norfolk, NR21 8AX 🅿
☎ 01328 862924
Est. 1969 *Stock size* Small
Stock General antiques, Victorian and pre-Victorian items
Open Mon–Sat 10am–1pm closed Wed

David Steward Antiques
Contact David Steward
✉ 8 Norwich Road, Fakenham, Norfolk, NR21 8AX 🅿
☎ 01328 853535/853214
Ⓜ 07979 496193
Est. 1980 *Stock size* Medium

Stock Furniture, clocks, ceramics, glass
Open Mon–Sat 10am–3pm closed Wed

GREAT YARMOUTH

Barry's Antiques
Contact Mr Barry Nichols
35 King Street, Great Yarmouth, Norfolk, NR30 2PN
01493 842713 F 01493 745312
M 07802 619579
Est. 1979 *Stock size* Large
Stock Jewellery, porcelain, silver
Open Mon–Sat 9.30am–4.30pm closed Thurs
Services Jewellery repair, insurance valuer and agent

Curiosity Too
Contact Mr or Mrs R Moore
163 Northgate Street, Great Yarmouth, Norfolk, NR30 1BY
01493 859690
Est. 1983 *Stock size* Medium
Stock China, glass, pictures, general antiques, small furniture
Open Mon–Fri 10am–4.30pm Sat 10.30am–3.30pm closed Thurs
Services House clearance

Garry M Emms and Co Ltd
Contact Garry Emms
Great Yarmouth Salerooms, Beevor Road, Great Yarmouth, Norfolk, NR30 3PS
01493 332668 F 01493 728290
Est. 1994
Open Thurs–Fri 10am–4pm accept goods for sale
Sales Weekly sales of antiques Wed 10am, viewing Tues 2–8pm Wed 9–10am
Frequency Weekly
Catalogues No

David Ferrow (ABA, PBFA)
Contact David Ferrow
77 Howard Street South, Great Yarmouth, Norfolk, NR30 1LN
01493 843800
Est. 1940 *Stock size* Large
Stock General antiquarian books, local topography
Open Mon–Wed Fri Sat 10am–5pm closed Bank Holidays
Services Valuations

King Street Bookshop (PBFA)
Contact Mr or Mrs C or J Read
129 King Street, Great Yarmouth, Norfolk, NR30 2PQ
01493 857733
Est. 1993 *Stock size* Medium
Stock Antiquarian and out-of-print books, maritime, general history, country life, postcards, ephemera
Open Mon–Sat 10am–5pm closed Thurs
Fairs PBFA
Services Book search

HINGHAM

Hingham Antiques
Contact Mrs C Docwra
The Fairland, Hingham, Norwich, Norfolk, NR9 4HN
01953 850838
M 07789 114629
Est. 1996 *Stock size* Large
Stock General antiques
Open Tues–Sun 10am–4pm
Fairs Newark
Services Furniture restoration, reupholstery

Mongers Architectural Salvage (SALVO)
Contact Mrs Sam Coster
15 Market Place, Hingham, Norwich, Norfolk, NR9 4AF
01953 851868 F 01953 851870
E sam@mongersofhingham.co.uk
W www.mongersofhingham.co.uk
Est. 1997 *Stock size* Large
Stock Architectural salvage
Open Mon–Sat 9.30am–5.30pm Sun 11am–2pm
Fairs Newark
Services Stripping, fireplace restoration

Past & Present
Contact Christine George
16a Fairland, Hingham, Norwich, Norfolk, NR9 4HN
01953 851471
E info@pastandpresentantiques.co.uk
W www.pastandpresentantiques.co.uk
Est. 1999 *Stock size* Large
Stock Fine art and antiques
Open Tues–Sun 10am–5pm

HOLT

Baron Art
Contact Mr A Baron
9 Chapel Yard, Albert Street, Holt, Norfolk, NR25 6HJ
01263 713906 F 01263 711670
E baronart@aol.com
Est. 1990 *Stock size* Large
Stock Art Deco, paintings
Open Mon–Sat 9am–5pm
Services Valuations

Baron Art
Contact Mr A Baron
17 Chapel Yard, Albert Street, Holt, Norfolk, NR25 6HG
01263 713430 F 01263 711670
E baronart@aol.com
Est. 1990 *Stock size* Large
Stock Art Deco, paintings, antiquarian books
Open Mon–Sat 9am–5pm
Services Valuations, framing

Cobwebs
Contact Ann Buchanan
2 Fish Hill, Holt, Norfolk, NR25 6BD
01263 711955 F 01328 829592
M 0798 00 87889
Est. 1996 *Stock size* Large
Stock Bygones, collectables, woodworking and agricultural tools
Open Mon–Fri 10.30am–5pm Sat 10.30am–6pm

Cottage Collectables
Contact Philip or Linda Morris
Fish Hill, Holt, Norfolk, NR25 6BD
01263 711707
Est. 1984 *Stock size* Large
Stock General antiques, jewellery
Open Mon–Sun 10am–5pm
Fairs Newark, The International Antique and Collectables Fair, RAF Swinderby, Peterborough and Norwich showgrounds
Services Restorations, house clearance

Simon Gough Books Ltd
Contact Mr Tristram Hull
5 Fish Hill, Holt, Norfolk, NR25 6BD
01263 712650 F 01263 712276
E tristram.hull@virgin.net
W www.simongoughbooks.com
Est. 1974 *Stock size* Large
Stock General stock, antiquarian books
Open Mon–Sat 10am–5pm
Fairs The Hilton, Olympia

Heathfield Country Pine
Contact Janet, Howard or Stephen Heathfield

✉ The Warehouse,
39 Hempstead Road, Holt,
Norfolk, NR25 6DL P
☎ 01263 711609 F 01263 711609
E info@antique-pine.net
W www.antique-pine.net
Est. 1991 *Stock size* Large
Stock Antique pine, country items
Open Mon–Sat 8am–5pm
Services Restorations

Holt Antique Centre
Contact Mr D Attfield
✉ **Albert Street, Holt, Norfolk, NR25 6HX** P
☎ 01263 712097
Est. 1982 *Stock size* Large
No. of dealers 15
Stock Antiques, collectables
Open Mon–Sun 10am–5pm

Holt Antique Gallery
Contact Mrs J Holliday
✉ **2 Shire Hall Plain, Holt, Norfolk, NR25 6HT**
☎ 01263 711991 F 01263 711991
Est. 1997 *Stock size* Large
Stock Antique furniture, china, brass
Open Mon–Sun 10am–5pm
Fairs Newark, The International Antique and Collectables Fair, RAF Swinderby

Mews Antique Emporium
Contact Mr Howard Heathfield
✉ **17 High Street, Holt, Norfolk, NR25 6BN**
☎ 01263 713224
Est. 1998 *Stock size* Large
No. of dealers 14
Stock Furniture, pictures, pottery, china
Open Mon–Sat 10am–5pm Sun 11am–4pm
Services Valuations, restorations

Past Caring
Contact Mrs Lynda Mossman
✉ **6 Chapel Yard, Albert Street, Holt, Norfolk, NR25 6HG** P
☎ 01263 713771 F 01263 680078
E pstcaring@aol.com
Est. 1987 *Stock size* Large
Stock Linen, lace, vintage clothing, accessories, costume jewellery 1800s–1950
Open Mon–Sat 11am–5pm closed Thurs
Fairs Alexandra Palace

Richard Scott Antiques
Contact Mr Richard Scott
✉ **30 High Street, Holt, Norfolk, NR25 6BH** P
☎ 01263 712479
Est. 1972 *Stock size* Large
Stock Ceramics, studio pottery, oil lamps
Open Mon–Fri 10am–5pm Sat 10am–5.30pm closed Thurs
Fairs Newark
Services Advice on valuation, restorations

Trinities
Contact Mrs Lois White
✉ **29a Bull Street, Holt, Norfolk, NR25 6HP**
☎ 01263 711606
M 07730 070290
Est. 1998 *Stock size* Large
Stock Antiques, Victorian beds fully restored, collectables, artefacts, memorabilia, antique bedsteads
Open Tues–Sat 10.30am–4pm
Fairs Newark

KING'S LYNN

The Old Curiosity Shop
Contact Mrs Wright
✉ **25 St James Street, King's Lynn, Norfolk, PE30 5DA** P
☎ 01553 766591
M 07802 348635
Est. 1984 *Stock size* Small
Stock General antiques, collectables, furniture
Open Mon–Sat 11am–5pm
Fairs Alexandra Palace, Lee Valley Park
Services Teddy bear restoration, clock, watch repairs, bead restringing

The Old Granary Antique Centre
Contact Mrs J L Waymouth
✉ **Kings Staithe Lane, King's Lynn, Norfolk, PE30 1LZ** P
☎ 01553 775509
Est. 1979 *Stock size* Medium
Stock General antiques, collectables
Open Mon–Sat 10am–5pm
Services Valuations

Roderick Richardson
Contact Mr Roderick Richardson
✉ **The Old Granary Antique Centre, Kings Staithe Lane, King's Lynn, Norfolk, PE30 1LZ** P
☎ 01553 670833 F 01553 670833
W www.coin.dealers-on-line.com/roderick
Est. 1995 *Stock size* Large
Stock English hammered and early milled gold and silver
Open Mon–Sat 10am–5pm
Fairs York Northern Fair, Midland Coin Fair, London Coin Fair

MARSHAM

Euro Antiques
Contact Mr Case Van Woerkom
✉ **1–6 Outbuildings, Grove Farm, Norwich Road, Marsham, Norwich, Norfolk, NR10 5SR** P
☎ 01263 731377 F 01263 731378
M 07771 727420
Est. 1979 *Stock size* Medium
Stock Pine, general furniture
Open Mon–Fri 9am–5pm Sat 9am–1pm
Services Leathering

Brian Watson Antique Glass (LAPADA)
Contact Brian Watson
✉ **Foxwarren Cottage, High Street, Marsham, Norwich, Norfolk, NR10 5QA** P
☎ 01263 732519 F 01263 732519
E brian.h.watson@talk21.com
Est. 1991 *Stock size* Medium
Stock Georgian–Victorian drinking glasses, decanters and other glass of the period
Open By appointment
Fairs NEC, Penman fairs
Services Valuations

MULBARTON

Junk and Disorderly
Contact Mr Tony Nash
✉ **The Dell, Birchfield Lane, Mulbarton, Norfolk, NR14 8AA** P
☎ 01603 748801
Est. 1976 *Stock size* Large
Stock General antiques
Open Sat 8am–4pm
Services House clearance, removals

NORTH WALSHAM

The Angel Bookshop (PBFA)
Contact Mr E Green
✉ **4 Aylsham Road, North Walsham, Norfolk, NR28 0BH**
☎ 01692 404054
E angelbooks@onetel.net.uk

Est. 1989 *Stock size* Medium
Stock General antiquarian books, Norfolk and natural history topics a speciality
Open Mon–Fri 9.30am–5pm Sat 9.30am–3.30pm closed Wed
Fairs PBFA
Services Book search

Eric Bates & Sons
Contact Graham or Eric Bates
Melbourne House, Bacton Road, North Walsham, Norfolk, NR28 0RA
01692 403221 F 01692 404388
M 07887 776149
E furnitureebates.fsnet.co.uk
W www.batesfurniture.co.uk
Est. 1982 *Stock size* Large
Stock General 19thC antiques, Victorian chairs
Open Mon–Fri 9am–5pm Sat 9am–4.30pm
Fairs Newark

Horners Auctioneers
Contact Mr N Horner-Glister FRICS
North Walsham Sales Rooms, Midland Road, North Walsham, Norfolk, NR28 9JR
01692 500603 F 01692 500975
E auction@horners.co.uk
W www.horners.co.uk
Est. 1993
Open Mon–Fri 9am–1pm 2–5pm Sat 9am–noon
Sales General antiques sale Fri 10am, viewing Thurs 2–8pm. House clearance
Frequency Weekly
Catalogues Yes

NORWICH

Antiques & Interiors
31–35 Elm Hill, Norwich, Norfolk, NR3 1HG
01603 622695 F 01603 632446
Est. 1996 *Stock size* Large
Stock Art Deco and other furniture, porcelain
Open Mon–Sat 10am–5pm

Black Horse Gallery (LAPADA, BADA)
Contact Mr C Risebrook
10b Wensum Street, Norwich, Norfolk, NR3 1HR
01603 612428
Est. 1989 *Stock size* Medium
Stock Complete range of antiques, collectables
Open Mon–Sat 10am–5pm
Fairs Lomax Antiques Fairs
Services Valuations

Arthur Brett & Sons (BADA)
Contact Mrs T Lotis
42 St Giles Street, Norwich, Norfolk, NR2 1LW
01603 628171 F 01603 630245
Est. 1870 *Stock size* Large
Stock 17th–18thC furniture, fine art
Open Mon–Fri 9.30am–1pm 2–5pm
Fairs Olympia

The Collectors' Shop
Contact Mr L Downham
2 Angel Road, Norwich, Norfolk, NR3 3HP
01603 765672
Est. 1975 *Stock size* Large
Stock Stamps, postcards, coins, models, small items, collectables
Open Mon–Sat 9.30am–5.30pm closed Thurs
Fairs Bloomsbury

Crowe's Antiquarian Books (PBFA)
Contact Mr Peter Crowe
75 Upper St Giles Street, Norwich, Norfolk, NR2 1AB
01603 624800
Est. 1930 *Stock size* Medium
Stock Antiquarian books including local history and prints
Open Mon–Sat 9.45am–5.15pm
Services Book binding

Deja Vu
Contact Mr V Engledew or Mr A Hawes
67–69 Magdalen Street, Norwich, Norfolk, NR3 1AA
01603 765489 F 01603 765489
Est. 1987 *Stock size* Large
Stock General antiques, furniture
Open Mon–Sun 10am–5pm
Fairs Newark, The International Antique and Collectables Fair, RAF Swinderby
Services Valuations, restorations

Clive Dennett (BNTA, IBNS)
Contact Mr C Dennett
66 St Benedict's Street, Norwich, Norfolk, NR2 4AR
01603 624315 F 01603 624315
Est. 1970 *Stock size* Large
Stock Coins, medals, banknotes, currency
Open Mon–Sat 9am–5pm closed Thurs
Fairs The Cumberland Coin Fairs

Nicholas Fowle Antiques (BADA)
Contact Mr N Fowle
Websdales Court, Bedford Street, Norwich, Norfolk, NR2 1AR
01603 219964 F 01692 630378
M 07831 218808
Est. 1995 *Stock size* Medium
Stock 18th–19thC furniture
Open Mon–Fri 9am–5.30pm Sat 9am–1pm
Fairs BADA, Olympia (Nov)
Services Valuations, restorations

Peter J Hadley (PBFA, ABA)
Contact Mr P J Hadley
29 Surrey Street, Norwich, Norfolk, NR1 3NX
01603 663411 F 01603 663411
E books@hadley.co.uk
W www.hadley.co.uk
Est. 1983 *Stock size* Medium
Stock Antiquarian books, English, architectural history, art reference, literature
Open Fri Sat 10am–6pm, telephone first during week
Fairs PBFA, ABA Chelsea
Services Valuation, catalogue every 8 weeks

John Howkins Antiques Ltd
Contact Miss J Betts
1 Dereham Road, Norwich, Norfolk, NR2 4HX
01603 627832 F 01603 666626
E howkinsantiques@clara.co.uk
Est. 1930 *Stock size* Medium
Stock Victorian–Georgian furniture
Open Mon–Fri 10am–5pm
Services Valuations

The Inventory
Contact Jonty Young or Roy Benton
97 Upper St Giles Street, Norwich, Norfolk, NR2 1AB
01603 667640 F 01603 611833
Est. 2001 *Stock size* Large
Stock Architectural antiques, paintings, shop fittings, lighting, 20thC design
Open Mon–Sat 10am–5.30pm

Leona Levine Silver Specialist (BADA)
Contact Leona Levine
35 St Giles Street, Norwich, Norfolk, NR2 1JN
01603 628709 01603 628709
Est. 1865 *Stock size* Large
Stock Silver, old Sheffield plate
Open Mon–Sat 9am–5pm closed Thurs
Services Valuations, restorations

Maddermarket Antiques (NAG)
Contact Mr T Earl
18c Lower Goat Lane, Norwich, Norfolk, NR2 1EL
01603 620610 01603 620610
Est. 1984 *Stock size* Large
Stock Antique, second-hand, modern jewellery, silverware
Open Mon–Sat 9am–5pm

The Movie Shop
Contact Mr P Cossey
11 St Gregory's Alley, Norwich, Norfolk, NR2 1ER
01603 615239
petecossey@mcmail.com
www.the-movieshop.com
Est. 1985 *Stock size* Large
Stock General antiquarian books, movie, TV, theatre and vinyl
Open Mon–Sat 10.30am–5pm
Services Valuations

Norwich Auction Rooms
Contact Mr J Sutton
The Auction Centre, Bessemer Road, Norwich, Norfolk, NR4 6DQ
01603 666502 01603 666502
Est. 1991
Open Mon–Fri 9am–5pm
Sales Monthly antiques and collectables Sun 10.30am, viewing day of sale 9am and Fri prior to sale 2–4pm. Special sales occasionally
Frequency Monthly
Catalogues Yes

Phillips International Auctioneers and Valuers
Whitefriars House, 52 Fishergate, Norwich, Norfolk, NR3 1SE
01603 616426 01603 767881
www.phillips-auction.com
Sales Regional Office. Telephone for details

St Michael at Plea Antiques and Collectors Centre
Contact Mr D Clarke
Redwell Street, Bank Plain, Norwich, Norfolk, NR2 4SN
01603 618989
Est. 1987 *Stock size* Large
Stock China, silver, toys, brass, prints, small items of furniture, books, coins, medals
Open Mon–Sat 9.30am–5pm
Services Valuations, restorations

Timgems Jewellers
Contact Tim Snelling
30 Elm Hill, Norwich, Norfolk, NR3 1HG
01603 623296 01603 666183
Est. 1969 *Stock size* Medium
Stock Antique jewellery, silverware
Open Tues–Sat 11am–4.30am
Services Valuations, restorations

Tombland Antiques Centre
Contact Bob Gale
Augustine Stewart House, 14 Tombland, Norwich, Norfolk, NR3 1HF
01603 619129
Est. 1999 *Stock size* Large
No. of dealers 40
Stock A wide range of antiques and collectables
Open Mon–Sat 10am–5pm Sun 11am–3pm
Services Valuations

Tombland Bookshop
Contact Mr J Freeman
8 Tombland, Norwich, Norfolk, NR3 1HF
01603 490000 01603 760610
tombland.bookshop@virgin.net
Est. 1973 *Stock size* Large
Stock Antiquarian books
Open Mon–Sat 9.30am–5pm

Malcolm Turner
Contact Mr M Turner
15 St Giles Street, Norwich, Norfolk, NR2 1JL
01603 627007 01603 627007
Est. 1971 *Stock size* Large
Stock Mixed porcelain, bronze figures, silver, jewellery
Open Tues–Sat 10am–5pm
Services Valuations

Tymewarp
Contact Mrs C Docwra
1 Magdalen Street, Tombland, Norwich, Norfolk, NR3 1LE
01603 616396
07789 114629
Est. 2000 *Stock size* Medium
Stock Art Deco, 20thC, Retro antiques
Open Tues–Sat 10am–4pm
Fairs Newark, Take Five, Woking

RAVENINGHAM

M D Cannell
Contact Mr M Cannell
Castell Farm, Beccles Road, Raveningham, Norfolk, NR14 6NU
01508 548406 01508 548406
07801 416355
mal@raveningham.demon.co.uk
Est. 1984 *Stock size* Large
Stock European decorative furniture, carpets, Oriental rugs
Open Fri–Mon 10am–6pm or by appointment
Fairs Newark, Bath Decorative

REEPHAM

Bonhams & Brooks
Contact James Glennie or Nicola Tyler
The Market Place, Reepham, Norwich, Norfolk, NR10 4JJ
01603 871443 01603 872973
norfolk@bonhams.com
www.bonhams.com
Est. 1793
Open Mon–Fri 9am–1pm 2–5pm
Sales Offices of regional representatives for Norfolk, Suffolk, Cambridgeshire and Essex. Sales of paintings, prints and works of art relating to East Anglia. See Head Office (London) for details
Frequency 2 per annum
Catalogues Yes

Echo Antiques
Contact Marion Stiesel
Church Hill, Reepham, Norwich, Norfolk, NR10 4JW
01603 873291
Est. 1997 *Stock size* Large
Stock General antiques, English and French furniture
Open Mon–Sat 10am–5pm closed Thurs
Services Valuations

SCRATBY

⊞ Keith Lawson Antique Clocks (BHI)
Contact Keith Lawson
✉ **Scratby Garden Centre, Beach Road, Scratby, Great Yarmouth, Norfolk, NR29 3AJ** 🅿
☎ 01493 730950 Ⓕ 01493 730658
Est. 1979
Stock Clocks
Open Mon–Sun 2–6pm
Services Valuations, restorations

SHERINGHAM

⊞ Kitty Blakes Shop
Contact Mrs J McMillan
✉ **57 Station Shop, Sheringham, Norfolk, NR26 8RG** 🅿
☎ 01263 825316
Est. 1998 *Stock size* Large
Stock General antiques, stamps, prints, old sheet music, postcards, china, collectables
Open Mon–Sat 9am–5pm
Fairs Norwich Sports Centre

⊞ Dorothy's Antiques
Contact Mrs D E Collier
✉ **23 Waterbank Road, Sheringham, Norfolk, NR26 8RB** 🅿
☎ 01263 822319
Est. 1975 *Stock size* Medium
Stock Royal Worcestershire, Royal Doulton, small furniture, collectables
Open Mon–Sun 11.15am–3.30pm

SOUTH WALSHAM

⊞ Leo Pratt and Son (LAPADA)
Contact Mr Rodney Pratt
✉ **Curiosity Shop, South Walsham, Norwich, Norfolk, NR13 6EA** 🅿
☎ 01603 270204 Ⓕ 01603 270204
Est. 1890 *Stock size* Large
Stock General antiques, furniture, clocks, china
Open Mon–Sat 9.30am–5pm
Services Valuations

STALHAM

⊞ Stalham Antique Gallery (LAPADA)
Contact Mr Mike Hicks
✉ **29 High Street, Stalham, Norwich, Norfolk, NR12 9AH** 🅿
☎ 01692 580636 Ⓕ 01692 580636
Est. 1970 *Stock size* Large
Stock Period furniture, associated items
Open Mon–Fri 9am–5pm Sat 9am–1pm or by appointment
Services Valuations, restorations

SWAFFHAM

⊞ Cranglegate Antiques
Contact Mrs R D Buckie
✉ **59 Market Place, Swaffham, Norfolk, PE37 7LE** 🅿
☎ 01760 721052
Est. 1973 *Stock size* Medium
Stock Furniture, decorative and small items
Open Tues Thurs Sat 10am–1pm 2–5.30pm
Fairs Newark

THETFORD

⊞ Thetford Antiques and Collectables
Contact Dennis Crawford
✉ **6 Market Place, Thetford, Norfolk, IP24 2AJ** 🅿
☎ 01842 755511
Ⓜ 07961 302651
Est. 1998 *Stock size* Large
Stock Furniture, Doulton, Beswick, Wedgwood china, collectables including Toby jugs, silver
Open Mon–Sat 9.30am–5pm
Services Valuations

WATTON

⊞ J C Books (PBFA)
Contact Mr J A Ball
✉ **55 High Street, Watton, Thetford, Norfolk, IP25 6AB** 🅿
☎ 01953 883488 Ⓕ 01953 883488
Ⓔ j.c.books@lineone.net
Est. 1990 *Stock size* Medium
Stock General antiquarian books, ephemera, Victorian–Edwardian theatre a speciality
Open Mon–Wed Fri Sat 10am–4.30pm Thurs 10am–1pm
Fairs PBFA
Services Book search

Watton Salerooms
Contact Mr S Roberts
✉ **Breckland House, Newgreen Business Park, Norwich Road, Watton, Thetford, Norfolk, IP25 6DU** 🅿
☎ 01953 885676 Ⓕ 01953 885676
Ⓔ watton.salerooms@eidosnet.co.uk
Ⓦ www.thesalerooms.co.uk
Est. 1989
Open Mon 8am–8pm Tues 8am–6pm Wed–Fri 10am–3pm Sat 10am–1pm
Sales 7 or 8 antiques sales yearly on Bank Holidays and Sun, viewing day before the sale 3–6pm and day of sale from 9am. Also antiques and general household Tues, viewing Mon 4–8pm and day of sale
Frequency Weekly
Catalogues No

WELLS-NEXT-THE-SEA

⊞ Church Street Antiques
Contact Mrs P Ford or Mrs L Irons
✉ **2 Church Street, Wells-next-the-Sea, Norfolk, NR23 1JA** 🅿
☎ 01328 711698
Est. 1989 *Stock size* Large
Stock Small collectables, costume jewellery, linen, lace, costume, hat pins
Open Summer Tues–Sun 10am–4pm winter Thurs–Sun 10am–4pm

Wells Antique Centre
Contact Mr Vallance
✉ **The Old Mill, Maryland, Wells-next-the-Sea, Norfolk, NR23 1LY** 🅿
☎ 01328 711433
Est. 1989 *Stock size* Medium
No. of dealers 15
Stock General antiques, copper, brass, porcelain, glass, rugs, furniture, jewellery, linen, collectables
Open Mon–Sun 10am–4pm

WROXHAM

⊞ T C S Brooke (BADA)
Contact Mr S T Brooke
✉ **The Grange, Norwich Road, Wroxham, Norwich, Norfolk, NR12 8RX** 🅿
☎ 01603 782644 Ⓕ 01603 782644
Est. 1936 *Stock size* Large
Stock General antiques, 18thC furniture, Georgian items, 18thC porcelain
Open Tues–Sat 9.15am–1pm 2.15–5.30pm
Services Valuations

⊞ Bradley Hatch Jewellers
Contact Mr Bradley Hatch
✉ **Tunstead Road, Wroxham, Norwich, Norfolk, NR12 8QG** 🅿

☎ 01603 782233 Ⓕ 01603 784679
Ⓔ sales@bradleyhatch.com
Ⓦ www.bradleyhatch.com
Est. 1994 *Stock size* Medium
Stock Jewellery, watches, silver, clocks, gifts, pocket watches
Open Mon–Sat 9am–5pm
Services Valuations, restorations, shipping

WYMONDHAM

Margaret King
Contact Margaret King
✉ **16 Market Place, Wymondham, Norfolk, NR18 0AX** Ⓟ
☎ 01953 604758
Est. 1975 *Stock size* Large
Stock General antiques, furniture, porcelain, glass, silver
Open Thurs–Sat 9am–1pm 2–4pm
Fairs Langley, Woolverstone, all Lomax Fairs

M and A C Thompson
Contact Mr A C Thompson
✉ **The Bookshop, 1 Town Green, Wymondham, Norfolk, NR18 0PN** Ⓟ
☎ 01953 602244
Est. 1981 *Stock size* Medium
Stock Antiquarian, general second-hand books
Open Mon–Fri 10.30am–4.50pm closed Wed

Wymondham Antique Centre
Contact Kay Hipperson
✉ **3 Town Green, Wymondham, Norfolk, NR18 0PN** Ⓟ
☎ 01953 604817 Ⓕ 01603 811112
Est. 1987 *Stock size* Large
Stock General antiques, china, furniture, books, pictures
Open Mon–Sun 10am–5pm
Services Valuations

SUFFOLK

ALDEBURGH

Bly Valley Antiques
Contact Mr Eric Ward
✉ **152 High Street, Aldeburgh, Suffolk, IP15 5AX** Ⓟ
☎ 01728 454508 Ⓕ 01502 675376
Ⓦ www.bly-valley-antiques.com
Est. 2000 *Stock size* Medium
Stock China, glass, pictures, furniture, antiquarian books
Open Thurs–Sat 10.30am–4.30pm

Mole Hall Antiques
Contact Mr P Weaver
✉ **102 High Street, Aldeburgh, Suffolk, IP15 5AB**
☎ 01728 452361
Est. 1981 *Stock size* Large
Stock General antiques
Open Mon–Sat 10am–5pm
Fairs Snape

BECCLES

Besley's Books (PBFA, ABA)
Contact Piers or Gaby Besley
✉ **4 Blyburgate, Beccles, Suffolk, NR34 9TA** Ⓟ
☎ 01502 715762 Ⓕ 01502 675649
Ⓔ piers@besleysbooks.demon.co.uk
Ⓦ www.besleysbooks.demon.co.uk
Est. 1970 *Stock size* Medium
Stock Antiquarian books. Gardening, natural history, art, private press a speciality
Open Mon–Sat 9.30am–5pm closed Wed
Fairs PBFA, ABA
Services Valuations, restorations, booksearch, 2 catalogues a year

Blyburgate Antiques
Contact Mrs Kate Lee
✉ **27–29 Blyburgate, Beccles, Suffolk, NR34 9TB** Ⓟ
☎ 01502 711174
Ⓔ katherine.lee@lineone.net
Est. 1997 *Stock size* Medium
Stock General antiques, furniture
Open Tues–Sat 10am–4.30pm closed Wed
Fairs Alexandra Palace
Services Valuations

Durrants Auction Rooms
Contact Mr Miles Lamdin
✉ **Gresham Road, Beccles, Suffolk, NR34 9QN**
☎ 01502 713490 Ⓕ 01502 711039
Ⓔ info@durrantsauctionrooms.com
Ⓦ www.durrantsauctionrooms.com
Est. 1853
Open Mon–Fri 9am–4pm Sat 9am–noon
Sales General antiques sales every Fri. Special sale once every 6 weeks, viewing every Thurs and sale day
Frequency Weekly
Catalogues No

Fauconberges
Contact Mr R D Howard or Mr R J Crozier
✉ **8 Smallgate, Beccles, Suffolk, NR34 9AD** Ⓟ
☎ 01502 716147
Est. 1980 *Stock size* Medium
Stock 17th–19thC furniture, pictures, glass
Open Mon–Sat 10am–5pm
Fairs Lomax, Graham Turner (Long Melford)
Services Valuations for insurance and probate, sales on commission, decanter cleaning and renovation

M & A Ratcliffe
Contact Mrs A Ratcliffe
✉ **11 Saltgate, Beccles, Suffolk, NR34 9AN** Ⓟ
☎ 01502 712776
Est. 1971 *Stock size* Medium
Stock General antiques, 18th–19thC furniture
Open Mon–Sat 10am–5pm early closing Wed

BUNGAY

Beaver Booksearch
Contact Mr N Watts
✉ **33 Hillside Road East, Bungay, Suffolk, NR35 1JU**
☎ 01986 896698 Ⓕ 01986 896698
Ⓔ beaver@booksearch.u-net.com
Ⓦ www.booksearch.u-net.com
Est. 1996 *Stock size* Small
Stock Books, bridge a speciality
Open Mail order only
Services Book search

Black Dog Antiques
Contact Mr M Button
✉ **51 Earsham Street, Bungay, Suffolk, NR35 1AF** Ⓟ
☎ 01986 895554
Est. 1985 *Stock size* Medium
Stock General, collectables, pine furniture
Open Mon–Sat 10am–5pm Sun 11am–4.30pm

Friend or Faux
Contact Jane Cudlipp or Kim Sisson
✉ **28 Earsham Street, Bungay, Suffolk, NR35 1AQ** Ⓟ
☎ 01986 896170 Ⓕ 01502 714246
Est. 1989 *Stock size* Medium
Stock Antiques, decorative objects, murals, paintings, hand-painted furniture
Open Fri–Sat 10am–5pm
Services Restorations, faux finishes

One Step Back
Contact Mrs Diane Wells
4a Earsham Street, Bungay, Suffolk, NR35 1AG
01986 896626
Est. 1998 *Stock size* Medium
Stock General antiques, furniture
Open Mon–Sat 10am–5pm closed Wed
Services Restorations

BURES

Major Iain Grahame (ABA)
Contact Major Iain Grahame
Daws Hall, Lamarsh, Bures, Suffolk, CO8 5EX
01787 269213 F 01787 269634
E majorbooks@compuserve.com
W www.iaingrahamerarebooks.com
Est. 1979 *Stock size* Medium
Stock Antiquarian books, especially sporting, natural history, Africana
Open By appointment
Fairs Olympia

BURROUGH GREEN

R E and G B Way (ABA, PBFA)
Contact Mr G Way
Brettons, Church Lane, Burrough Green, Newmarket, Suffolk, CB8 9NA
01638 507217 F 01638 508058
E waybks@msn.com
Est. 1950 *Stock size* Large
Stock Antiquarian, out-of-print, horse, hunting, racing, field-sport books
Open Mon–Sat 9am–5pm telephone to check
Fairs Russell Book Fair

BURY ST EDMUNDS

Corner Shop Antiques
Contact Mrs F G Howard
1 Guildhall Street, Bury St Edmunds, Suffolk, IP33 1PR
01284 701007
Est. 1978 *Stock size* Medium
Stock China, glass, silver, prints, Victoriana, collectables
Open Tues–Sat 10am–4pm closed Thurs
Services China restoration

Lacy Scott & Knight (SOFAA)
Contact Daniella Cassandro
10 Risbygate Street, Bury St Edmunds, Suffolk, IP33 3AA
01284 748600 F 01284 748620
E fineart@lsk.co.uk
W www.lsk.co.uk
Est. 1869
Open Mon–Fri 9am–1pm 2–5.30pm
Sales Quarterly fine art sale and model and collectors' sales. Victoriana sales every 3–4 weeks, viewing Fri 3–7pm
Frequency Monthly
Catalogues Yes

Marshall Buck and Casson
Contact Mr B Moss
The Auction Rooms, Eastgate Street, Bury St Edmunds, Suffolk, IP33 1YQ
01284 756081 F 01284 756081
M 07768 324102
Est. 1999
Open Wed 8am–8pm
Sales Mixed antiques and general sales Sat, viewing Fri 2.30–8pm and Sat 8–9am. Periodic special antiques sales
Frequency Every 3 weeks
Catalogues Yes

Peppers Period Pieces
Contact Mr M Pepper
23 Churchgate Street, Bury St Edmunds, Suffolk, IP33 1RG
01284 768786 F 01284 768786
Est. 1975 *Stock size* Small
Stock 16th–18thC English oak furniture, 15th–19thC metalware
Open Mon–Sat 10am–5pm
Services Restorations

Talisman 2
Contact Mrs S McNaught
18 Out Westgate, Bury St Edmunds, Suffolk, IP33 3NZ
01284 725712 F 01284 725712
E shirley.mcnaught@btinternet.com
Est. 1994 *Stock size* Medium
Stock Antiques, period furniture, unusual small collectables
Open Mon Wed Fri 10am–1pm 2–5pm Sat 10am–3pm

CAMPSIE ASH

Abbotts Auction Rooms
Contact Mrs Linda Coates
Campsie Ash, Woodbridge, Suffolk, IP13 0PS
01728 746323 F 01728 748173
Est. 1920
Open Mon–Sat 9am–5.30pm
Sales General auction every Mon 11am, viewing Sat 9–11am and 8.30–11am on day of sale. Special antiques auctions (9 per annum) Wed 10am, viewing Mon prior to sale 2–8pm Tues 10am–4pm and morning of sale from 8.30am
Frequency Weekly
Catalogues Yes

Ashe Antiques Warehouse
Contact Mr G Laffling
Station Road, Campsie Ash, Woodbridge, Suffolk, IP13 0PT
01728 747255 F 01728 747255
Est. 1987 *Stock size* Large
Stock 18thC oak furniture, Victorian smalls, mirrors etc
Open Mon–Sun 10.30am–5pm
Fairs The International Antique and Collectables Fair, RAF Swinderby, Newark
Services French polishing, upholstery, ceramic restoration

CAVENDISH

Cavendish Rose Antiques
Contact Toby Patterson
1 Clarks Yard, High Street, Cavendish, Sudbury, Suffolk, CO10 8AT
01787 282133 F 01787 280332
E cavrose.antiques@easicom.co
Est. 1974 *Stock size* Large
Stock 18thC–Edwardian furniture, dining tables, chairs, desks, chests-of-drawers, bookcases
Open Mon–Sat 10.30am–5pm

CLARE

Clare Antique Warehouse
Contact Leonard Edwards
The Mill, Malting Lane, Clare, Suffolk, CO10 8NW
01787 278449
E patrick@worldwideantiques.co.uk
W www.antiques-access-agency.com
Est. 1988 *Stock size* Large
No. of dealers 75
Stock General, pine, oak furniture

Open Mon–Sat 9.30am–5pm
Sun 1–5pm
Services Restorations, shipping, valuations

Dyson & Son
Contact Mr M Dyson
✉ **The Auction Rooms, Church Street, Clare, Sudbury, Suffolk, CO10 8PD** P
☎ 01787 277993 F 01787 277996
E info@dyson-auctioneers.co.uk
W www.dyson-auctioneers.co.uk
Est. 1977
Open Mon–Fri 9am–5pm
Sat 9am–1pm
Sales General antiques sales every 3 weeks Sat, 600–700 lots, viewing Fri 9am–9pm and day of sale 9–11am. A yearly calendar is available on request
Frequency Every 3 weeks
Catalogues Yes

Christina Parker Antiques
Contact Christina Parker
✉ **Church Street, Clare, Suffolk, CO10 8PD** P
☎ 01787 278570/0207 628 4545
F 0207 428 5942
E chrisparker@hotmail.com
W www.jewelpast.com
Est. 1999 *Stock size* Small
Stock Jewellery, ceramics, pictures, collectables, scent bottles, vintage clothing, textiles
Open Mon–Wed 11am–4pm
Thurs–Sat 9.30am–5pm
Fairs Newmarket

F D Salter
Contact Mr F D Salter
✉ **1–2 Church Street, Clare, Sudbury, Suffolk, CO10 8PD** P
☎ 01787 277693
Est. 1960 *Stock size* Medium
Stock 18th–19thC furniture, porcelain, glass
Open Mon–Sat 9am–5pm
closed Wed
Fairs West London, Harrogate
Services Furniture restorations

Sarah Smith Scent Bottles and Collectables
Contact Sarah Smith
✉ **2 Mortimer Place, Clare, Suffolk, CO10 8QP**
☎ 01787 277609
Est. 2001 *Stock size* Small
Stock Scent bottles, handbags, compacts, jewellery
Open By appointment

Trinder's Fine Tools (PBFA)
Contact Mr P D Trinder
✉ **Malting Lane, Clare, Sudbury, Suffolk, CO10 8NW** P
☎ 01787 277130 F 01787 277677
E peter@trindersfinetools.co.uk
W www.trindersfinetools.co.uk
Est. 1974 *Stock size* Medium
Stock Woodworking tools including British infill planes by Norris, Spiers, Mathieson, Preston, second-hand, new books on furniture and woodworking, horology, model engineering
Open Mon–Sat 10am–1pm
2–5pm Wed 10am–1pm

DEBENHAM

Debenham Antiques
Contact Simon Sodeaux or Chris Bigden
✉ **73 High Street, Debenham, Suffolk, IP14 6QS** P
☎ 01728 860707 F 01728 860333
M 07836 260650
E info@debenhamantiques.com
Est. 1974 *Stock size* Large
Stock 17th–19thC furniture, paintings
Open Mon–Sat 9.30am–5.30pm

DRINKSTONE

Denzil Grant (BADA, LAPADA)
Contact Mr D Grant
✉ **Drinkstone House, Gedding Rd, Drinkstone, Bury St Edmunds, Suffolk, IP30 9TG** P
☎ 01449 736576 F 01449 737679
M 07836 223312
E denzil@denzilgrant.com
Est. 1979 *Stock size* Medium
Stock 17th–19thC country furniture
Open By appointment
Fairs LAPADA, Olympias

EASTON

Marilyn Garrow Fine Textile Art (LAPADA, BADA)
Contact Marilyn Garrow
✉ **2 Black and White Cottages, Easton, Suffolk, IP13 0EF** P
☎ 01728 747370 F 01728 747370
M 07774 842074
E marogarrow@aol.com
Est. 1977 *Stock size* Large
Stock Textiles
Open By appointment
Fairs Olympia, LAPADA
Services Valuations

EXNING

Exning Antiques & Interiors
Contact Mrs M Tabbron
✉ **5 Oxford Street, Exning, Newmarket, Suffolk, CB8 7EW** P
☎ 01638 600073 F 01638 600015
Est. 1993 *Stock size* Small
Stock Beds, canopies, covers, drapes, mirrors, original lighting
Open Tues–Sat 10am–5pm
Fairs Newark
Services Restoring and cleaning lighting

EYE

English and Continental Antiques
Contact Mr Steven Harmer or Mr Roger Ford
✉ **1 Broad Street, Eye, Suffolk, IP23 7AF** P
☎ 01379 871199 F 01379 871199
E RFORD69484@aol.com
W www.antiquesweb.co.uk
Est. 1975 *Stock size* Medium
Stock 17th–19thC furniture
Open Tues–Sat 10am–5pm

FELIXSTOWE

Ancient and Modern Collectables Centre
Contact Mr Brian Fahey
✉ **2 Bent Hill, Felixstowe, Suffolk, IP11 7DG** P
☎ 01394 275709
Est. 1984 *Stock size* Large
Stock Antique ceramics, collectables
Open Mon–Sun 10am–4.30pm
closed Wed
Services Ceramics bought on commission

Diamond Mills & Company (FSVA)
Contact Mr N J Papworth
✉ **117 Hamilton Road, Felixstowe, Suffolk, P11 7BL** P
☎ 01394 282281 F 01394 671791
E diamondmills@easynet.co.uk
W www.diamondmills.co.uk
Est. 1908
Open Mon–Fri 9am–6pm
Sat 9am–4pm

Sales Antique sales monthly, usually Wed, phone for details, 3 special sales annually
Frequency Monthly
Catalogues Yes

Poor Richard's Books
Contact Dick Moffat
17 Orwell Road, Felixstowe, Suffolk, IP11 7EP
01394 283138
moffatsfx@aol.com
Est. 1997 *Stock size* Large
Stock General and antiquarian books. modern first editions
Open Mon–Sat 9am–5pm
Services Valuations, restorations, book search

Tea and Antiques
Contact David George
109 High Road, Old Felixstowe, Suffolk, IP11 9PS
01394 277789
Est. 2000 *Stock size* Medium
Stock Antiques, collectables, furniture
Open Thurs–Sun Bank Holidays 10am–5pm
Services Tea shop

The Treasure Chest Books (PBFA)
Contact Mr Robert Green
61 Cobbold Road, Felixstowe, Suffolk, IP11 7BH
01394 270717
Est. 1981 *Stock size* Large
Stock Antiquarian and second-hand books
Open Mon–Sat 9.30am–5.30pm

FINNINGHAM

Abington Books
Contact Mr J Haldane
Primrose Cottage, Westhorpe, Finningham, Stowmarket, Suffolk, IP14 4TW
01449 780303 01449 780202
Est. 1971 *Stock size* Medium
Stock Antiquarian books on Oriental and other carpets, classical tapestries
Open By appointment
Services Valuations, restorations, book search

FRAMLINGHAM

Richard Goodbrey Antiques
Contact Mrs M Goodbrey
29 Double Street, Framlingham, Woodbridge, Suffolk, IP13 9BN
01728 621191 01728 724626
07802 868622
merlin@zetnet.co.uk
Est. 1965 *Stock size* Large
Stock 18th–19thC Continental antiques, some English furniture, sleigh beds, painted furniture, pottery, glass
Open Sat 9am–1pm 2–5.30pm or by appointment
Fairs Newark

The Green Room
Contact Mrs J Shand Kydd
2 Church Street, Framlingham, Woodbridge, Suffolk, IP13 9BE
01728 723009
Est. 1986 *Stock size* Medium
Stock Textiles, quilts, curtains, bed covers
Open Fri Sat 11am–4.45pm

The Green Shed
Contact Mr J Mulligan
26 Fore Street, Framlingham, Woodbridge, Suffolk, IP13 9DF
01728 621069
07907 524005
Est. 1994 *Stock size* Large
Stock English furniture, French country furniture, Victoriana, objets d'art
Open Mon–Sat 9.30am–5.30pm
Fairs Newark, Ardingly, Ipswich
Services Restorations

HACHESTON

Pine and Country Furniture
Contact Mrs Joyce Hardy
Wisteria Cottage, The Street, Hacheston, Woodbridge, Suffolk, IP3 0DS
01728 746485
Est. 1962 *Stock size* Medium
Stock Antique pine furniture
Open Mon–Sat 9.30am–5.30pm Sun 10am–noon
Fairs Ardingly, Ipswich

HADLEIGH

Randolph Antiques (BADA)
Contact Mr Baden F Marston
97–99 High Street, Hadleigh, Ipswich, Suffolk, IP7 5EJ
01473 823789 01473 823867
Est. 1929 *Stock size* Medium
Stock English furniture up to 1830, also accessories
Open By appointment only

HALESWORTH

Halesworth Antiques Market
Contact Mrs Hull
3a Bridge Street, Halesworth, Suffolk, IP19 8AB
01986 875599
Est. 1994 *Stock size* Medium
No. of dealers 6
Stock Victorian china, linen, lace, pine furniture
Open Mon–Sat 10am–5pm Thurs 10am–1pm

IPSWICH

A Abbott Antiques
Contact Mr A Abbott
757 Woodbridge Road, Ipswich, Suffolk, IP4 4NE
01473 728900 01473 728900
07771 533413
abbott_antiques@hotmail.com
Est. 1974
Stock General antiques, furniture, smalls, clocks
Open Mon–Sat 9.30am–5pm closed Wed
Fairs Newark, Ardingly

Antiques and Restoration
Contact Mr R Rush
Unit 5, Penny Corner, Farthing Road, Ipswich, Suffolk, IP1 5AP
01473 464609 01473 464609
07939 220041
info@antiquesandrestoration.co.uk
www.antiquesandrestoration.co.uk
Est. 1997 *Stock size* Medium
Stock 18th–19thC furniture
Open Mon–Fri 8am–6pm Sat 8am–1.30pm
Services Restorations

Bridge Collectables
Contact A A or S J Creasey
425 Norwich Road, Ipswich, Suffolk, IP1 5DN
01473 421316
Est. 1984 *Stock size* Large
Stock Mechanical bygones, postcards, Bakelite, coins, curios, militaria
Open Mon–Sat 10am–5pm closed Wed

⊞ Claude Cox Books (ABA, PBFA)
Contact Anthony Brian Cox
✉ **3–5 Silent Street, Ipswich, Suffolk, IP11 1TF** 🅿
☎ 01473 254776 Ⓕ 01473 254776
Est. 1974 *Stock size* Large
Stock Antiquarian and second-hand books, fine printing, private press, catalogues issued, Suffolk maps and prints a speciality
Open Wed–Sat 10am–5pm or by appointment

⊞ Andrew Drake Antiques
Contact Mr A Drake
✉ **211 Spring Road, Ipswich, Suffolk, IP4 5NF** 🅿
☎ 01473 713608 Ⓕ 01473 711164
Est. 1987 *Stock size* Large
Stock General
Open Mon–Sat 9am–4.30pm closed Wed
Fairs Swinderby

⊞ Hubbard's Antiques
Contact Mr Mark Hubbard
✉ **16 St Margaret's Green, Ipswich, Suffolk, IP4 2BS** 🅿
☎ 01473 233034 Ⓕ 01473 253639
Ⓔ sales@hubbard-antiques.com
Ⓦ www.hubbard-antiques.com
Est. 1965 *Stock size* Large
Stock 18th–19thC antique furniture, decorative items, works of art
Open Mon–Sat 9am–6pm or by appointment
Services Valuations by Internet

⊞ Lockdale Coins Ltd (BNTA)
Contact Dan Daley
✉ **36 Upper Orwell Street, Ipswich, Suffolk, IP4 1HR** 🅿
☎ 01473 218588 Ⓕ 01473 218588
Ⓔ lockdale@btinternet.com
Ⓦ lockdales.co.uk
Est. 1994 *Stock size* Medium
Stock British and foreign coins, banknotes, metal detectors and accessories
Open Mon–Sat 9.30am–4.30pm
Fairs Cumberland Hotel Show, Olympia
Services Valuations, auctioneering

Lockdales
Contact Dan Daley
✉ **36 Upper Orwell Street, Ipswich, Suffolk, IP4 1HR** 🅿
☎ 01473 218588 Ⓕ 01473 218588
Ⓔ ddaley@lockdales.freeserve.co.uk
Ⓦ www.lockdales.co.uk
Est. 1996
Open Mon–Sat 9.30am–4.30pm
Sales Phone for details of sales, held alternately between Ipswich and Norwich
Frequency Bi-monthly
Catalogues Yes

⊞ Maud's Attic
Contact Mrs W Childs
✉ **25 St Peter's Street, Ipswich, Suffolk, IP1 1XF** 🅿
☎ 01473 221057 Ⓕ 01473 221056
Est. 1996 *Stock size* Large
Stock Antiques, collectables
Open Tues–Sat 10am–5pm

⊞ Merchant House Antiques
Contact Mr G Childs
✉ **27–29 St Peter's Street, Ipswich, Suffolk, IP1 1XF** 🅿
☎ 01473 221054 Ⓕ 01473 221056
Ⓜ 07768 068575
Est. 2000 *Stock size* Medium
Stock Antiques and reclamation
Open Tues–Sat 10am–5pm

Phillips Auctioneers (SOFAA)
Contact Mr Peter Turner
✉ **32 Boss Hall Road, Ipswich, Suffolk, IP1 5SD** 🅿
☎ 01473 740494 Ⓕ 01473 741091
Ⓦ www.phillips-auctions.com
Est. 1796
Open Mon–Fri 8.30am–5pm. Sat 9–noon
Sales General sales Tues every 3–4 weeks, viewing Sat 9am–noon Mon 10am–7.30pm and day of sale 9–11am. Fine art sales held quarterly Wed Thurs in Bury St Edmunds in March June Sept Dec, viewing Tues 9am–6.30pm and Wed 9–11am
Frequency Every 3–4 weeks
Catalogues Yes

⊞ The Suffolk Antique Bed Centre
Contact Mr A Sandham
✉ **273 Norwich Road, Ipswich, Suffolk, IP1 4BP** 🅿
☎ 01473 252444
Est. 1985 *Stock size* Large
Stock Brass and iron bedsteads
Open Mon–Sat 9am–5.30pm
Services Hand-made mattresses

⊞ Suffolk Sci-fi Fantasy (GOMC)
Contact Mr M Milliard
✉ **17 Norwich Road, Ipswich, Suffolk, IP1 2ET** 🅿
☎ 01473 400655 Ⓕ 01473 400656
Est. 1992 *Stock size* Large
Stock Sci-fi collectables, ephemera, collectable card games, trade cards
Open Mon–Sat 9am–6pm

⊞ E F Wall Antiques
Contact Libby Wall
✉ **Cliff Quay, Ipswich, Suffolk, IP3 0BD** 🅿
☎ 01473 225010 Ⓕ 01473 254910
Ⓜ 07885 374917
Ⓔ libbyswall@ukonline.co.uk
Est. 1979 *Stock size* Large
Stock Reproduction French polished furniture
Trade only Yes
Open Mon–Fri 7am–6pm
Fairs NEC, USA
Services Restorations

IXWORTH

⊞ E W Cousins & Son (LAPADA)
Contact Mr Robert Cousins
✉ **Old School, Thetford Road, Ixworth, Bury St Edmunds, Suffolk, IP31 2HJ** 🅿
☎ 01359 230254 Ⓕ 01359 232370
Ⓔ john@ewcousins.co.uk
Ⓦ www.ewcousins.co.uk
Est. 1920 *Stock size* Large
Stock 18th–19thC furniture
Open Mon–Fri 8.30am–5pm Sat 8.30am–1pm
Services Restorations, containers packed

KELSALE

⊞ Steven Simpson Natural History Books
Contact Mr S J Simpson
✉ **Rising Sun, Kelsale, Saxmundham, Suffolk, IP17 2QY**
☎ 01728 604777 Ⓕ 01728 604555
Ⓜ 07884 366387
Est. 1986 *Stock size* Small
Stock Antiquarian books on natural history, fish topics a speciality
Open Mail order only
Services Valuations, brokerage, publisher distributor

LAVENHAM

R G Archer Books
Contact Mr Richard Archer
7 Water Street, Lavenham, Sudbury, Suffolk, CO10 9RW
01787 247229
Est. 1970 *Stock size* Medium
Stock Second-hand, antiquarian books, especially of Suffolk and Norfolk interest
Open Mon–Sun 10am–5pm closed Wed
Services Book search

J & J Baker
Contact Mrs Joy Baker
12–14 Water Street, Lavenham, Sudbury, Suffolk, CO10 9RW
01787 247610
Est. 1970 *Stock size* Large
Stock General English antiques, furniture, porcelain
Open Mon–Sat 10am–5.30pm

One Bell
Contact Mr John Tinworth
46 High Street, Lavenham, Sudbury, Suffolk, CO10 9PY
01787 248206
Est. 1986 *Stock size* Medium
Stock Militaria, small collectables
Open Mon–Sun 11am–4.30pm closed Wed Thurs

Timbers Antiques & Collectables
Contact Mrs Ann Trodd or Brenda Preece
High Street, Lavenham, Sudbury, Suffolk, CO10 9PT
01787 247218
Est. 1996 *Stock size* Medium
Stock Antique furniture, silver, glass etc
Open Mon–Sun 10am–5pm closed Wed
Fairs Newark, Birmingham

LEISTON

Leiston Trading Post
Contact Mrs L Smith
13a High Street, Leiston, Suffolk, IP16 4EL
01728 830081
Ⓜ 0771 259 6005
Est. 1967 *Stock size* Large
Stock Shipping goods, general antiques, china, bric-a-brac
Open Mon–Sat 9.30am–1pm 2–4.30pm half day Wed
Fairs Newark
Services Valuations

Warren Antiques
Contact Mr J Warren
31 High Street, Leiston, Suffolk, IP16 4EL
01728 831414 Ⓕ 01728 831414
Ⓜ 07989 865598
Est. 1970 *Stock size* Medium
Stock Late 18thC–1930s furniture
Open Mon–Tues 9am–1pm 2–5pm Thurs–Sat 9am–12.30pm
Fairs Newark, Ardingly (DMG)
Services Restorations

LONG MELFORD

Karen Bryan Antiques
Contact Karen Bryan
Little St Mary's, Long Melford, Sudbury, Suffolk, CO10 9LQ
01787 312613 Ⓕ 01206 271727
Est. 1990 *Stock size* Medium
Stock Georgian, post-Georgian furniture, pictures, prints
Open Mon–Sat 10.30am–4.30pm closed Wed

Sandy Cooke Antiques
Contact Mr Sandy Cooke
Hall Street, Long Melford, Sudbury, Suffolk, CO10 9JQ
01787 378265 Ⓕ 01284 830935
Ⓔ sandycooke@englishfurniture.co.uk
Ⓦ www.englishfurniture.co.uk
Est. 1974 *Stock size* Large
Stock 1700–1830 English furniture
Open Mon Fri Sat 10am–5pm

Alexander Lyall Antiques
Contact Mr A J Lyall
Belmont House, Hall Street, Long Melford, Sudbury, Suffolk, CO10 9JF
01787 375434 Ⓕ 01787 311115
Ⓔ alex@lyallantiques.com
Ⓦ www.lyallantiques.com
Est. 1977 *Stock size* Medium
Stock Georgian–Victorian furniture
Open Mon–Sat 10am–5.30pm closed Bank Holidays

Magpie Antiques (LMTA)
Contact Pat Coll
Hall Street, Long Melford, Sudbury, Suffolk, CO10 9JT
01787 310581 Ⓕ 01787 310581
Ⓔ terrycoll.magpie@ic24.net
Est. 1984 *Stock size* Large
Stock Stripped old pine, country collectables
Open Tues Thurs Fri 10.30am–1pm 2.15–4.30pm Sat 11am–5pm

Melford Antiques Warehouse (LMBA)
Contact Patrick
Hall Street, Long Melford, Sudbury, Suffolk, CO10 9JB
01787 379638
Ⓔ patrick@worldwideantiques.co.uk
Ⓦ www.antiques-access-agency.com
Est. 1979 *Stock size* Large
Stock 17th–20thC furniture, decorative items, large variety of dining tables, book cases, chairs, clocks etc
Open Mon–Sat 9.30am–5pm Sun 1–5pm
Services Valuations, restorations, shipping

Noel Mercer Antiques
Contact Mr Noel Mercer
Aurora House, Hall Street, Long Melford, Suffolk, CO10 9JR
01787 311882
Est. 1991 *Stock size* Large
Stock Early English oak, walnut furniture
Open Mon–Sat 10am–5pm

Seabrook Antiques
Contact Mr John Tanner
Melford Gallery, Hall Street, Long Melford, Sudbury, Suffolk, CO10 9JF
01787 375787 Ⓕ 01787 375787
Est. 1978 *Stock size* Large
Stock 17th–19thC oak and decorative furniture
Open Mon–Sat 9.30am–5.30pm
Services Interior design

Stable Antiques
Contact Mrs P Gee
Hall Street, Long Melford, Sudbury, Suffolk, CO10 9JB
01787 310754
Est. 1980 *Stock size* Medium
Stock Victorian–1960s memorabilia
Open Mon–Sat 10am–5pm Sun 1–5pm closed Thurs

Suthburgh Antiques
Contact Mr R Alston
The Red House, Hall Street, Long Melford, Sudbury, Suffolk, CO10 9JQ P
☎ 01787 374818 F 01787 374818
Est. 1977 *Stock size* Large
Stock Early oak, walnut, Georgian, mahogany furniture, clocks, barometers, period portraits, early metalware, maps
Open By appointment
Services Valuations, restorations

Trident Antiques (LAPADA)
Contact Mr Tom McGlynn
2 Foundry House, Hall Street, Long Melford, Sudbury, Suffolk, CO10 9JR P
☎ 01787 883388 F 01787 378850
M 07860 221402
E tridentoak@aol.com
Est. 1994 *Stock size* Large
Stock Early oak, English furniture, related objects, barometers
Open Mon–Sat 10am–5.30pm
Fairs LAPADA (Jan NEC)
Services Valuations, restorations, security implanting

Tudor Antiques
Contact Mrs Denton Ford
Little St Mary's, Long Melford, Sudbury, Suffolk, CO10 9HY P
☎ 01787 375950 F 01787 375950
M 07968 201654
E sford@antiqueandsilver.demon.co.uk
W www.longmelford.co.uk
Est. 1974 *Stock size* Large
Stock Furniture, glass, silver, figurines, paintings
Open Mon–Sat 10am–5pm Sun 2–4.30pm
Services Valuations, restorations

Village Clocks
Contact Mr J Massey
Little St Mary's, Long Melford, Suffolk, CO10 0LQ P
☎ 01787 375896
Est. 1989 *Stock size* Large
Stock Antique clocks
Open Mon–Sat 10am–4pm closed Wed
Services Restorations

LOWESTOFT

Lockdales (BNTA)
Contact Dan Daley
168 London Road South, Lowestoft, Suffolk, NR33 0BB P
☎ 01502 568468 F 01502 568468
E ddaley@lockdales.freeserve.co.uk
W www.lockdales.co.uk
Est. 1998 *Stock size* Medium
Stock Gold, silver jewellery, British and world coins, banknotes, metal detectors, accessories
Open Mon–Sat 9.30am–4.30pm
Fairs Cumberland Hotel, Olympia
Services Valuations, jewellery, watch, clock repairs, auctioneering

Lockdales
Contact Jean Daley
168 London Road South, Lowestoft, Suffolk, NR33 0BB P
☎ 01502 568468 F 01502 568468
E ddaley@lockdales.freeserve.co.uk
W www.lockdales.co.uk
Est. 1996
Open Mon–Sat 9.30am–4.30pm
Sales Phone for details of sales, held alternately between Ipswich and Norwich. Coins, jewellery, medals, militaria, ephemera, autographs
Frequency Bi-monthly
Catalogues Yes

Lowestoft Auction Rooms
Contact Mr J Peyto
Pinbush Road, South Lowestoft Industrial Estate, Lowestoft, Suffolk, NR33 7NL P
☎ 01502 531532 F 01502 531241
Est. 1985
Open Mon–Fri 8am–6pm
Sales Large house sales on site
Frequency Twice monthly
Catalogues Yes

Odds and Ends
Contact Mr B Smith
127 High Street, Lowestoft, Suffolk, NR32 1HP P
☎ 01502 568569 F 01502 568569
Stock All smalls, jewellery, collectables
Open Mon–Sat 10am–5pm
Services Valuations, restoration of jewellery and watches

M G Osborne
Contact Mr M G Osborne
140 High Street, Lowestoft, Suffolk, NR33 1HR P
☎ 01502 508988
Est. 1988 *Stock size* Large
Stock General antiques
Open Mon–Sat 9.30am–4pm closed Thurs
Fairs The International Antique and Collectables Fair, RAF Swinderby

John Rolph
Contact Mr John Rolph
Manor House, Pakefield Street, Lowestoft, Suffolk, NR33 0JT P
☎ 01502 572039
Est. 1948 *Stock size* Medium
Stock 17thC–20thC, second-hand books
Open Tues–Sat 11am–1pm 2.30–5pm closed Thurs

MARLESFORD

The Antiques Warehouse
Contact John or Lesley Ball
The Old Mill, Main Road, Marlesford, Suffolk, IP3 0AQ P
☎ 01728 747438 F 01728 747627
E john@wtc-omtc.fsnet.co.uk
Est. 1989 *Stock size* Large
Stock Country furniture, mirrors, lighting, general antiques
Open Mon–Fri 9am–4.30pm Sat 10am–4.30pm

MARTLESHAM

Martlesham Antiques
Contact Mr R Frost
Thatched Roadhouse, Main Road, Martlesham, Woodbridge, Suffolk, IP12 4RJ P
☎ 01394 386732 F 01394 382959
E bob@martleshamantiques.com
Est. 1983 *Stock size* Large
Stock 18th-20thC furniture
Open Mon–Fri 9am–5pm Sat 9am–12.30pm

John Reed Antiques
Contact Mr John Reed
29 Larkrise, Martlesham Heath, Suffolk, IP5 3SA P
☎ 01473 624897
M 07860 426785
Est. 1992 *Stock size* Large
Stock Early English pottery pre-1840
Open By appointment only
Fairs NEC, Chelsea
Services Valuations, restorations, shipping

MELTON

CJC Antiques
1 Station Road, Melton, Woodbridge, Suffolk, IP12 1PT

Ⓜ 07931 433511
Ⓔ chriscolling@barclays.net
Stock Ceramics, furniture, glass, religous artefacts
Open Mon–Sat 9am–5pm
Fairs Newark, Ardingly

NAYLAND

⊞ Town and Country Prints (EADA)
Contact Mr F E Jones
✉ **Longwood Cottage, Nayland, Colchester, Suffolk, CO6 4HT** Ⓟ
☎ 01206 262483
Ⓔ jonesnayland@x-stream.co.uk
Est. 1976 ***Stock size*** Medium
Stock 18th–19thC maps, Essex and Suffolk a speciality, steel and copper engravings, woodblock illustrations, views and agricultural scenes
Open By appointment
Services Framing

NEEDHAM MARKET

⊞ Needham Market Antiques Centre
Contact Mrs Sheila Abbott
✉ **Old Town Hall, High Street, Needham Market, Suffolk, IP6 8AL** Ⓟ
☎ 01449 720773
Est. 1979 ***Stock size*** Large
Stock Antiques, collectables
Open Mon–Sat 10am–5pm
Fairs Newark (DMG)
Services Restoration of jewellery

⊞ The Tool Shop (LAPADA)
Contact Mr Tony Murland
✉ **78 High Street, Needham Market, Ipswich, Suffolk, IP6 8AW** Ⓟ
☎ 01449 722992 Ⓕ 01449 722683
Ⓔ tony@antiquetools.co.uk
Ⓦ www.antiquetools.co.uk
Est. 1991 ***Stock size*** Large
Stock Antique woodworking tools, new quality French, Japanese, American
Open Mon–Sat 10am–5pm
Fairs All major national woodworking exhibitions

NEWMARKET

⊞ Jemima Godfrey Antiques
Contact Mrs A Lanham
✉ **5 Rous Road, Newmarket, Suffolk, CB8 8DH** Ⓟ
☎ 01638 663584
Est. 1964 ***Stock size*** Small
Stock Small silver, linen, jewellery, Victorian china fairings, linen
Open Thurs Fri 10am–1pm 2pm–4.30pm

Vost's Fine Art Auctioneers & Valuers Ltd
✉ **Tattersalls, Newmarket, Suffolk, CB8 9AU** Ⓟ
☎ 01638 561313 Ⓕ 01638 560251
Ⓔ mail@vosts.com
Ⓦ www.vosts.com
Est. 1994
Open Mon–Fri 9am–5.30pm
Sales Fine art sales. Bi-annual sale of sporting art and memorabilia in April and September
Frequency Every 6–8 weeks
Catalogues Yes

ORFORD

⊞ Castle Antiques
Contact Ms S Simpkin
✉ **Market Hill, Orford, Woodbridge, Suffolk, IP12 3LH** Ⓟ
☎ 01394 450100 Ⓕ 01394 450536
Ⓔ stephanie@castle-estates.uk.com
Est. 1959 ***Stock size*** Small
Stock Furniture, lamps, pictures, glass, bric-a-brac
Open Mon–Sun 11am–4pm

PEASENHALL

⊞ Peasenhall Art & Antiques Gallery
Contact Mr M Wickens
✉ **The Street, Peasenhall, Saxmundham, Suffolk, IP17 2HJ** Ⓟ
☎ 01728 660224
Est. 1972 ***Stock size*** Large
Stock 18th–early 20thC watercolours, oil paintings, country furniture in all woods
Open Mon–Sun 9am–6pm
Services Restorations

RISBY

Past and Present
Contact Mrs Pat Fuller
✉ **The Risby Barn Complex, South Street, Risby, Bury St Edmunds, Suffolk, IP28 6QU** Ⓟ
☎ 01284 811480
Est. 1996 ***Stock size*** Large
No. of dealers 50
Stock Furniture, antique to present day, china, silver, jewellery, bric-a-brac, pictures, books, glass, pine, Victorian–Edwardian furniture, European furniture
Open Mon–Sun 9.30am–4.30pm
Services Restorations, coffee shop, garden centre

⊞ The Risby Barn Antique Centre
Contact Mr R Martin
✉ **Risby Barn, South Street, Risby, Bury St Edmunds, Suffolk, IP28 6QU** Ⓟ
☎ 01284 811126 Ⓕ 01284 810783
Ⓔ r.martin@lineone.net
Est. 1980 ***Stock size*** Large
Stock Victorian furniture, china, silver, clocks, rural bygones
Open Mon–Sat 9am–5.30pm Sun Bank Holidays 10am–5pm
Services Coffee shop

SAXMUNDHAM

⊞ Keith A Savage
Contact Mr K A Savage
✉ **35 High Street, Saxmundham, Suffolk, IP17 IAJ** Ⓟ
☎ 01728 604538/01986 872231
Est. 1992 ***Stock size*** Medium
Stock Second-hand, collectors' books, second-hand ephemera, children's books a speciality
Open Mon Sat 10.30am–1pm Tues Wed Fri 10.30am–5pm

SOUTHWOLD

⊞ Architectural Artefacts
Contact Mr B Howard or Mrs J Twist
✉ **The Rope House, Station Road, Southwold, Suffolk, IP18 6AX** Ⓟ
☎ 01502 723075 Ⓕ 01502 724346
Ⓔ aa@ropehouse.easynet.co.uk
Est. 1996 ***Stock size*** Small
Stock Stained glass, architectural antiques, taps, sinks, chimney pots
Open Mon–Fri 9am–5pm
Services Stained glass design

⊞ Cannonbury Antiques Southwold
Contact Mr David Brinsmead
✉ **Bridgefoot Corner, Reydon, Southwold, Suffolk, IP18 6NF** Ⓟ
☎ 01502 722133
Est. 1998 ***Stock size*** Medium
Stock General, furniture, decorative antiques

Open Mon–Sat 10am–5pm
Sun 11am–4pm
Services Valuations

The Emporium Antiques and Collectors Centre
Contact Mike Brown or Polly Clare
70 High Street, Southwold, Suffolk, IP18 6DN
01502 723909
enquiries@emporium-antiques.co.uk
www.emporium-antiques.co.uk
Est. 1992 *Stock size* Large
No. of dealers 35
Stock Good selection of antiques, collectables, 18th–20thC
Open Mon–Sat 10am–5pm Sun noon–4pm

Farleigh House Antiques
Contact Miss S Munday
39 High Street, Southwold, Suffolk, IP18 6AB
01502 722630
sharon.munday@btinternet.com
Est. 1996 *Stock size* Medium
Stock 19thC antiques, glass, silver, brass, copper, coins, medals
Open Open Mon–Sat 10am–5pm closed Wed
Fairs Langley School, St Andrew's Hall, Norwich
Services Valuations, restoration of jewellery

Puritan Values at the Dome
Contact Anthony Geering
St Edmunds Business Park, St Edmunds Road, Southwold, Suffolk, IP18 6BZ
01502 722211 01502 722734
07966 371676
sales@puritanvalues.com
www.puritanvalues.com
Est. 1985
Stock Arts & Crafts movement, aesthetic movement, gothic revival, important furniture
Open Mon–Sat 10am–6pm
Sun 11am–5pm
Fairs NEC, SEC
Services Valuations, restorations

T Schotte Antiques
Contact Mrs Schotte
Old Bakehouse, Blackmill Road, Southwold, Suffolk, IP18 6AQ
01502 722083
Est. 1989 *Stock size* Small
Stock Antiques, decorative items
Open Mon–Sat 10am–4pm closed Wed

S J Webster-Speakman (BADA)
Contact Mrs S J Webster-Speakman
Southwold, Suffolk
01502 722252
Est. 1968 *Stock size* Medium
Stock 18th–19thC furniture, clocks, Staffordshire animals
Open By appointment
Fairs Louise Walker, Harrogate fair, Annual Chester Antiques and Fine Art Show, Guildford, Snape
Services Restoration of clocks

SPROUGHTON

Heritage Reclamations
Contact Mr Richard Howells
1a High Street, Sproughton, Ipswich, Suffolk, IP8 3AF
01473 748519 01473 748519
heritage@reclamations.fsnet.co.uk
www.heritage-reclamations.co.uk
Est. 1985 *Stock size* Large
Stock Interior fittings, stoves, ranges, fireplaces, garden ornaments
Open Mon–Fri 9am–5pm
Sat 9.30am–5pm
Fairs Newark, Ardingly, Swinderby
Services Restorations

STOWMARKET

What-Not-Shop Antiques
Contact Mr F J Smith
28 Bury Street, Stowmarket, Suffolk, IP14 1HH
01449 613126
Est. 1979 *Stock size* Medium
Stock Jewellery, china, glass
Open Mon–Sat 9am–4.30pm
Tues 9am–1pm
Services Repairs

SUDBURY

Beckham Books (PBFA)
Contact Mrs Jenny Beckham
Chilton Mount, Newton Road, Sudbury, Suffolk, CO10 2RS
01787 373683 01787 375441
sales@beckhambooks.co.uk
www.beckhambooks.co.uk
Est. 1996 *Stock size* Small
Stock Antiquarian, theological books, bibles
Open By appointment
Fairs PBFA Fairs
Services Book search

Hobknobs Antiques and Gallery
Contact Mrs S Fletcher
16 Friars Street, Sudbury, Suffolk, CO10 2AA
01787 881360
07930 899737
Est. 1987 *Stock size* Medium
Stock General, small furniture, gallery
Open Mon–Sat 9.30am–12.45pm 1.45–5pm
Services Valuations, restorations

Napier House Antiques
Contact Mrs Veronica McGregor
3 Church Street, Sudbury, Suffolk, CO10 2BJ
01787 375280 01787 478757
07768 703406
Est. 1976 *Stock size* Large
Stock 18th–19thC mahogany furniture
Open Mon–Sat 10am–4.30pm closed Wed
Services Free delivery UK mainland

Neate Militarian & Antiques (OMRS)
Contact Gary Neate
PO Box 3794, Preston St Mary, Sudbury, Suffolk, CO10 9PX
01787 248168 01787 248363
gary@neatemedals.co.uk
www.neatemedals.co.uk
Est. 1984 *Stock size* Medium
Stock Worldwide orders, decorations, medals, with an emphasis on British material
Open Mon–Fri 9am–6pm
Fairs Brittania Medal Fair, Aldershot Medal Fair
Services Valuations, restorations, mail order catalogue

Olivers (SOFAA)
Contact Mr J Fletcher
The Sale Room, Burkitts Lane, Sudbury, Suffolk, CO10 1HB
01787 880305 01787 880305
Est. 1766
Open Mon–Fri 9am–5pm

Sales Regular sales of antiques and works of art. Victorian, later furniture, household effects fortnightly Thurs 1pm, viewing day of sale from 9am
Frequency Fortnightly
Catalogues Yes

Sasha
Contact Susan Bailey
79 Melford Road, Sudbury, Suffolk, CO10 1JT
01787 375582
07781 453250
Est. 1986 *Stock size* Medium
Stock Small furniture, ceramics, collectables, books
Open Mon–Sat 10.30am–5pm
Services Book search

Sitting Pretty Antiques
Contact Mrs S Fletcher
16 Friars Street, Sudbury, Suffolk, CO10 2AA
01787 880908/881360
07930 899737
Est. 1987 *Stock size* Large
Stock Re-upholstered period furniture, 18thC–1930s
Open Mon–Sat 9.30am–12.45pm 1.45–5pm
Services Upholstery, interior design consultations

Suffolk Rare Books
Contact Mr T Cawthorne
7 New Street, Sudbury, Suffolk, CO10 1JB
01787 372075
Est. 1975 *Stock size* Medium
Stock Antiquarian books, topography, military, history
Open Tues–Sat 10.30am–4.30pm closed Wed

WOODBRIDGE

Bagatelle
Contact Mrs N Lambert
40 Market Hill, Woodbridge, Suffolk, IP12 4LU
01394 380204
Est. 1991 *Stock size* Medium
Stock General, furniture, glass, jewellery, china
Open Mon–Sat 10am–3.30pm closed Thurs half day Wed

Blake's Books (PBFA)
Contact Mr R Green
88 The Thoroughfare, Woodbridge, Suffolk, IP12 1AL
01394 380302
Stock Antiquarian and second-hand books, Suffolk and sailing books a speciality
Open Mon–Sat 9.30am–5pm
Fairs Woodbridge Book Fair

Church Street Centre
Contact Miss M Brown
6e Church Street, Woodbridge, Suffolk, IP12 1DH
01394 388887
Est. 1994 *Stock size* Large
No. of dealers 10
Stock Wide range of items including small furniture, jewellery, china, glass, silver, ephemera, textiles, pictures, bygones, clocks, collectables
Open Mon-Sat 10am–5pm half day Wed
Services Free local delivery

Collectors Books & CD Centre
Contact Mr P J Freeman
63A The Thoroughfare, Woodbridge, Suffolk, IP12 1AH
01394 383388
Est. 1997 *Stock size* Medium
Stock Includes some antiquarian books
Open Mon–Sat 10am–5pm

Dix-Sept Antiques
Contact Miss Sophie Goodbrey
17 Station Road, Woodbridge, Suffolk, IP13 9EA
01728 621505 01728 724884
Est. 1985 *Stock size* Medium
Stock French antiques, furniture glass, pottery, textiles
Open Sat 10am–1pm 2–5.30pm or by appointment
Fairs Newark

David Gibbins (BADA)
Contact Mr David Gibbins
Market Hill, Woodbridge, Suffolk, IP12 4LU
01394 383531 01394 383531
07702 306914
dgibbins@tinyonline.co.uk
Est. 1966 *Stock size* Medium
Stock 18thC furniture, Lowestoft porcelain
Open Mon–Sat 9.30am–5pm
Fairs The West London Antiques and Fine Art Fair, Louise Walker Harrogate Fair, BADA Fair
Services Valuations, restorations

Hamilton Antiques (LAPADA)
Contact Hamilton or Rosemary Ferguson
5 Church Street, Woodbridge, Suffolk, IP12 1DH
01394 387222 01394 383832
hamiltonantiques@fsmail.net
Est. 1976 *Stock size* Large
Stock 18th–20thC furniture
Trade only Yes
Open Mon–Sat 10am–5pm

Anthony Hurst (LAPADA)
Contact Mr Christopher Hurst
13 Church Street, Woodbridge, Suffolk, IP12 1DS
01394 382500 01394 382500
Est. 1968 *Stock size* Large
Stock 18th–19thC furniture, mahogany, oak
Open Mon–Fri 9.30am–1pm 2–5.30pm half day Wed Sat 10am–1pm

Raymond Lambert
Contact Mr Raymond Lambert
24a Church Street, Woodbridge, Suffolk, IP12 1DH
01394 382380
Est. 1963 *Stock size* Medium
Stock 19thC furniture
Open Mon–Sat 9.30am–1pm 2–5pm closed Wed

Sarah Meysey-Thompson Antiques
Contact Sarah Meysey-Thompson
10 Church Street, Woodbridge, Suffolk, IP12 1DH
01394 382144
Est. 1961 *Stock size* Medium
Stock Georgian–Victorian furniture, curios, decorative pieces, textiles
Open Mon–Sat 10am–5pm
Fairs Battersea Park Decorative Antique and Textile Fair

Neal Sons & Fletcher
Contact Mr Edward Fletcher FRICS
26 Church Street, Woodbridge, Suffolk, IP12 1DP
01394 382263 01394 383030
allatnsf@aol.com
www.nsf.co.uk
Est. 1951
Open Mon–Fri 9am–5.30pm Sat 9am–4pm
Sales General monthly antiques

sales, viewing day prior to sale 2.15–4.30pm and 6.30–8pm and sale day 9.30–10.30am. Bi- or tri-annual specialist sales of period English and Continental furniture, pictures, books, carpets etc at The Theatre Street Sale Room, viewing Sat prior to sale 10am–1pm and day preceding sale 11am–4.30pm and 6.30–8pm sale day 9.30–10.30am
Frequency Monthly
Catalogues Yes

Isobel Rhodes
Contact Mrs I Rhodes
10 & 12 Market Hill, Woodbridge, Suffolk, IP12 4LS P
☎ 01394 382763
Est. 1964 *Stock size* Medium
Stock Oak, country furniture, pewter, pottery, brass
Open Mon–Sat 10am–1pm 2–5pm

Woodbridge Gallery
Contact Mr David Bethell
23 Market Hill, Woodbridge, Suffolk, IP12 4OX P
☎ 01394 386500 F 01394 386500
Est. 1998 *Stock size* Large
No. of dealers 30–35
Stock General antiques, fine art gallery
Open Mon–Sat 10am–5.30pm Wed 10am–1pm

WOOLPIT

John Heather
Contact John Heather
Old Crown, The Street, Woolpit, Bury St Edmunds, Suffolk, IP30 9SA P
☎ 01359 240297
M 07715 282600
E john.heather@libertysurf.co.uk
Est. 1946 *Stock size* Medium
Stock Late 18thC furniture
Open 7 days a week
Services Restorations

WRENTHAM

Bly Valley Antiques
Contact Mr Eric Ward
Old Reading Rooms, 7 High Street, Wrentham, Beccles, Suffolk, NR34 7HD P
☎ 01502 675376 or 01728 454508
F 01502 675376
W www.bly-valley-antiques.com
Est. 1971 *Stock size* Large
Stock China, glass, pictures, furniture, antiquarian books
Open Tues–Sat 10.30am–4.30pm

Wren House Antiques
Contact Ms V Kemp
1 High Street, Wrentham, Beccles, Suffolk, NR34 7HD P
☎ 01502 675276
M 07747 824229
Est. 1984 *Stock size* Medium
Stock Small antique furniture, collectables
Open Thurs–Sun 10.30am–5pm
Fairs Newark, Ardingly

Wrentham Antiques
Contact Mr B C Spearing
40–44 High Street, Wrentham, Beccles, Suffolk, NR34 7HB P
☎ 01502 675583 F 01502 675707
E wrentham.antiques@netcom.co.uk
W www.business.netcom.co.uk/ransom
Est. 1974 *Stock size* Large
Stock Antique furniture, clocks
Open Mon–Fri 8.30am–5pm Sat 9am–4pm
Services Valuations, shipping

YOXFORD

The Garden House Bookshop
Contact Liza Adamczewski
High Street, Yoxford, Saxmundham, Suffolk, IP17 3ER P
☎ 01728 668044
E gardenhousebooks@hotmail.com
W gardenhousebooks.co.uk
Est. 1969 *Stock size* Large
Stock Antiquarian and second-hand books, specializing in modernists, travel
Open Tues–Thurs Sat 10am–5pm winter by appointment
Services Valuations, book search

Suffolk House Antiques (BADA)
Contact Mr A Singleton
High Street, Yoxford, Saxmundham, Suffolk, IP17 3EP P
☎ 01728 668122 F 01728 668122
M 07860 521583
E andrew.singleton@suffolk-house-antiques.co.uk
W www.suffolk-house-antiques.co.uk
Est. 1991 *Stock size* Large
Stock Early English furniture, ceramics, associated works of art
Open Mon–Sat 10am–1pm 2.15–5.15pm closed Wed
Fairs BADA, Snape

HEART OF ENGLAND

BEDFORDSHIRE

AMPTHILL

⊞ Ampthill Antiques
Contact Mrs A Olney
✉ **Market Square, Church Street, Ampthill, Bedfordshire, MK45 2EH**
☎ 01525 403344
Ⓜ 07050 291011
Est. 1980 *Stock size* Large
Stock General antiques
Open Mon–Sat 11am–4pm Sun 2pm–5pm closed Wed

Ampthill Antiques Emporium
Contact Marc Legg
✉ **6 Bedford Street, Ampthill, Bedfordshire, MK45 2NB** Ⓟ
☎ 01525 402131
Ⓜ 07831 374919
Ⓔ info@ampthillantiquesemporium.co.uk
Ⓦ www.ampthillantiquesemporium.co.uk
Est. 1979 *Stock size* Large
No. of dealers 30
Stock Georgian–Edwardian furniture, smalls, shipping goods
Open Mon–Sun 10am–5pm closed Tues
Services Upholstery, valuations, shipping

⊞ Antiquarius
Contact Mr P Caldwell
✉ **107 Dunstable Street, Ampthill, Bedfordshire, MK45 2NG** Ⓟ
☎ 01525 841799
Ⓔ peter.caldwell@tesco.net
Est. 1996 *Stock size* Medium
Stock Victorian–Edwardian sitting and dining room furniture
Open Mon–Sat 10.30am–5pm Sun 1–5pm closed Tues
Services Restorations, reupholstery

⊞ House of Clocks (BHI)
Contact Mrs H Proud
✉ **102–104 Dunstable Street, Ampthill, Bedfordshire, MK45 2JP** Ⓟ
☎ 01525 403136 Ⓕ 01525 402680
Ⓔ ian@houseofclocks.co.uk
Ⓦ www.houseofclocks.co.uk
Est. 1984 *Stock size* Large
Stock Fine-quality antiques, reproduction clocks
Open Mon–Sat 9am–5pm Sun 11am–5pm
Fairs Motorcycle Museum, NEC, Brunel University
Services Restorations

⊞ David Litt Antiques
Contact Mr D Litt
✉ **The Old Telephone Exchange, Claridges Lane, Ampthill, Bedfordshire, MK45 2HU** Ⓟ
☎ 01525 404825 Ⓕ 01525 404563
Ⓜ 07802 449027
Ⓔ litt@ntlworld.com
Est. 1967 *Stock size* Large
Stock French provincial, 19thC furniture
Open Mon–Fri 7am–5pm
Fairs Battersea, Olympia
Services Restorations

⊞ Paris Antiques
Contact Mr Paul Northwood
✉ **97b Dunstable Street, Ampthill, Bedfordshire, MK45 2NG** Ⓟ
☎ 01525 840488 Ⓕ 01525 840488
Ⓜ 07802 535059
Est. 1984 *Stock size* Medium
Stock 18th–early 20thC furniture and effects
Open Tues–Sun 9.30am–5.30pm
Services Valuations, restorations

⊞ Pilgrim Antiques
Contact Mr G Lester
✉ **111 Dunstable Street, Ampthill, Bedfordshire, MK45 2NG** Ⓟ
☎ 01525 633023
Est. 1996 *Stock size* Large
Stock General antiques, Georgian–Edwardian furniture, glass, china, jewellery
Open Tues–Sun 10am–5pm closed Mon

The Pine Parlour
Contact Mrs J Barber
1 Chandos Road, Ampthill, Bedfordshire, MK45 2LF
01525 403030
Est. 1987 *Stock size* Medium
Stock Victorian–Edwardian original pine, wardrobes, dressers, chests, kitchenware, sleigh beds
Open Mon–Sun 10am–5pm

Transatlantic Antiques & Fine Art Ltd
Contact Mrs Deidre Higgins
101 Dunstable Street, Ampthill, Bedfordshire, MK45 2NG
01525 403346 01525 403346
Est. 1996 *Stock size* Large
Stock Very general 19th–early 20thC antiques including glass, silver, porcelain, decorative items, watercolours
Open Mon–Sun 10.30am–5pm

BEDFORD

Architectural Antiques
Contact Mr Paul Hoare
70 Pembroke Street, Bedford, Bedfordshire, MK40 3RQ
01234 213131 01234 309858
07977 573767
Est. 1988 *Stock size* Large
Stock Architectural antiques, period fixtures and fittings, fireplaces, doors and general salvage
Open Mon–Fri noon–5pm Sat 9am–5pm
Services Installation, restorations

The Eagle Bookshop
Contact Mr Peter Budek
103 Castle Road, Bedford, Bedfordshire, MK40 3QP
01234 269295 01234 269295
customers@eaglebookshop.co.uk
www.eaglebookshop.co.uk
Est. 1991 *Stock size* Medium
Stock General second-hand speciality books on science and mathematics
Open Mon–Sat 10am–6pm closed Wed
Services Catalogues issued

Harpur Antiques
Contact Nigel Hill
58 Harpur Street, Bedford, Bedfordshire, MK40 2QT
01234 344831 01234 344831
info@harpurjewellery.com
www.harpurjewellery.com
Est. 1981 *Stock size* Medium
Stock Antique, contemporary and new jewellery, small collectables, watches, silver
Open Mon–Sat 10am–5pm closed Thurs

Victoria House
Contact Helen Felts
70a Tavistock Road, Bedford, Bedfordshire, MK40 2RP
01234 320000
Est. 1998 *Stock size* Large
Stock Victorian–Edwardian furniture, antiques, reproduction and decorative pieces
Open Mon–Fri 11.30am–5pm Sat 11am–5pm Sun 11.30am–4.30pm closed Wed
Services Interior design

B B G Wilson Peacock
Contact Mark Baker or Simon Rowell
26 Newnham Street, Bedford, Bedfordshire, MK40 3JR
01234 266366 01234 269082
Est. 1901
Open Mon–Fri 9am–5.30pm Sat 9am–5pm
Sales General and antiques sale (no catalogue) Sat 9.30am, viewing Fri 9am–8pm Sat 8.30am prior to sale, also Thurs 11am (no catalogue), viewing Wed 9am–8pm Thurs 8.30am prior to sale. Monthly antiques and collectables sale first Fri 10.45am, viewing week before Fri 5–8pm prior to sale Thurs 9am–6pm Fri 8.30–10.45am
Frequency Weekly
Catalogues Yes

BIGGLESWADE

Old Mother Hubbards
Contact Mrs D Dynes
38 Shortmead Street, Biggleswade, Bedfordshire, SG18 0AP
01767 600959
Est. 1994 *Stock size* Large
Stock Collectables, old pine furniture, small items, china, glass
Open Mon–Sat 10am–5pm
Services Made-to-measure pine furniture, waxing

Shortmead Antiques
Contact Mr S E Sinfield
46 Shortmead Street, Biggleswade, Bedfordshire, SG18 0AP
01767 601780
Est. 1989 *Stock size* Medium
Stock Victorian–Edwardian furniture, china, silver, glass, general antiques
Open Tues–Sat 10am–4.30pm closed Thurs

Simply Oak
Contact Anna Kilgarriff or Dick Sturman
Oak Tree Farm, Potton Road, Sutton, Biggleswade, Bedfordshire, SG18 0EP
01767 601559 01767 312855
antiques@simplyoak.freeserve.co.uk
Est. 1997 *Stock size* Large
Stock Late Victorian–1930s restored oak furniture
Open Mon–Sat 10am–5pm Sun 11am–4pm
Services Restorations

BROMHAM

Paperchase
Contact Brian Moakes
77 Wingfield Road, Bromham, Bedford, Bedfordshire, MK43 8JY
01234 825942
brianmoakes@aol.com
Est. 1991
Open Mon–Fri 9am–5pm
Sales Postal auction of transport-related paper memorabilia
Frequency 6 per annum
Catalogues Yes

EGGINGTON

Robert Kirkman Ltd (ABA, PBFA)
Contact Robert Kirkman
Kings Cottage, Eggington, Leighton Buzzard, Bedfordshire, LU7 9PG
01525 210647 01525 211184
Est. 1988 *Stock size* Small
Stock Antiquarian books, specializing in English Literature, Churchill, English Bibles, sets of standard authors
Open By appointment only
Fairs ABA, PBFA
Services Restorations, book binding, shipping

LEIGHTON BUZZARD

David Ball Antiques
Contact David Ball
59 North Street, Leighton Buzzard, Bedfordshire, LU7 1EQ
01525 382954
07831 111661
Est. 1970 *Stock size* Medium
Stock Furniture, clocks, barometers, 18th–early 20thC porcelain
Open Mon–Sat 10am–5pm closed Thurs
Fairs Luton Antiques Fair, Mid Beds Antiques Fair
Services Restorations

LOWER STONDON

Dippers
Contact Mr Paul Monroe
52 Bedford Road, Lower Stondon, Henlow, Bedfordshire, SG16 6DZ
01462 811003 F 01462 819197
monroe.dippers@virgin.net
Est. 1997 *Stock size* Large
Stock Architectural antiques, antique pine furniture
Open Mon–Fri 10am–6pm Sat 10am–5pm
Fairs Swinderby, Newark
Services Restorations, stripping

Memory Lane Antiques
Contact Mrs Liz Henry RAFA RJDip
14 Bedford Road, Lower Stondon, Henlow, Bedfordshire, SG16 6EA
01462 812716
07702 715477
Est. 1998 *Stock size* Medium
Stock Furniture, silver, porcelain, crystal, collectables
Open Mon–Sun 10.30am–5pm closed Wed Thurs
Services Appraisals

LUTON

The Bear Room
Contact Mrs C Smith
68–70 Old Bedford Road, Luton, Bedfordshire, LU2 7PA
01582 487799 F 01582 615625
07977 577326
c4ro1yn@aol.com
www.thebearroom.uk.com or www.ukbears.co.uk
Est. 1998 *Stock size* Large
Stock Teddy bears, antique, Steiff, Chad Valley, Hermann, new bears
Open Tues–Sat 9am–5.30pm or by appointment
Services Steiff Club Store

Off World
Contact Mr J Woollard
141a–143a Market Hall, The Luton Arndale Centre, Luton, Bedfordshire, LU1 2TP
01582 736256
Est. 1995 *Stock size* Large
Stock Collectable toys, *Star Wars*, Transformers, comics, cards etc
Open Mon–Fri 9.30am–5.30pm Wed 9.30am–2pm

POTTON

Wesley J West & Son
Contact Mr A West
58 King Street, Potton, Sandy, Bedfordshire, SG19 2QZ
01767 260589
Est. 1931 *Stock size* Medium
Stock Georgian–Edwardian furniture
Open Mon–Fri 9am–5pm Sat 9am–noon
Services Restorations, upholstery

RAVENSDEN

Lisa Cordes Antiques
Contact Mr J E Harbridge
Struttle End, Oldways Road, Ravensden, Bedford, Bedfordshire, MK44 2RF
01234 771980 F 01234 771980
Est. 1974 *Stock size* Medium
Stock Antique furniture up to 1900
Trade only Yes
Open Mon–Sat 9am–5pm
Services Restorations, cabinet-making

SHEFFORD

S and S Timms Antiques Ltd (LAPADA)
Contact Sue Timms
2/4 High Street, Shefford, Bedfordshire, SG17 5DG
01462 851051 F 01462 817047
sstimms@highstshefford.freeserve.co.uk
Est. 1976 *Stock size* Large
Stock 18th–19thC town and country furniture
Open Mon–Fri 9.30am–5.30pm Sat Sun 11am–5pm or by appointment
Fairs Chelsea, LAPADA

SLAPTON

Nick & Janet's Antiques
Contact Janet Griffin
Bury Farm, Mill Road, Slapton, Leighton Buzzard, Bedfordshire, LU7 9BT
01525 220256 F 01525 220757
nick@nickandjanets.co.uk
www.nickandjanets.co.uk
Est. 1991 *Stock size* Large
Stock Devon, Torquay, Brannam pottery, Martin Brothers, modern Moorcroft
Open By appointment
Fairs Shepton Mallett

WILSTEAD

Manor Antiques
Contact Mrs S Bowen
The Manor House, Cotton End Road, Wilstead, Bedford, Bedfordshire, MK45 3BT
01234 740262 F 01234 740262
07831 419729
Est. 1979 *Stock size* Large
Stock 19thC furniture, mirrors, lighting
Open Mon–Sat 10am–5pm
Fairs House & Gardens, Olympia

WOBURN

Bazaar Boxes (LAPADA)
Contact Andrew Grierson, Mark Brewster
Woburn Abbey Antiques Centre, Woburn, Bedfordshire, MK17 9WA
01992 504454 F 01992 504454
07970 909204/909206
bazaarboxes@hotmail.com
Stock size Medium
Stock Tortoiseshell, ivory and mother-of-pearl tea caddies and boxes
Open 363 days a year 10am–5.30pm or by appointment
Fairs NEC, LAPADA

Collectors Carbooks
Contact Mr C Knapman
14 Bedford Street, Woburn, Bedfordshire, MK17 9QB
01525 290088 F 01525 290044
sales@collectorscarbooks.com
www.collectorscarbooks.com
Est. 1991 *Stock size* Large

Stock Rare and out-of-print, motoring and motor-racing books, magazines, posters, autographs, programmes, new car-related books
Open Mon–Sat 10am–5pm
Fairs All major historic race meetings, classic car shows
Services Free book search, International mail order

Geoffrey Hugall
Contact Mr G Hugall
Woburn Abbey Antique Centre, Woburn Abbey, Bedfordshire, MK17 9WA
☎ 020 7838 0457
Ⓜ 07973 273485
Est. 1971 *Stock size* Medium
Stock General antiques, period furniture
Open Mon–Fri 10am–5pm Sat 10am–4pm
Services Valuations

Christopher Sykes
Contact Mr C Sykes or Mrs Sally Lloyd
The Old Parsonage, Bedford Street, Woburn, Milton Keynes, Bedfordshire, MK17 9QL
☎ 01525 290259 Ⓕ 01525 290061
Ⓔ sykes.corkscrews@sykes-corkscrews.co.uk
Ⓦ www.sykes-corkscrews.co.uk
Est. 1960 *Stock size* Large
Stock Items associated with wine, speciality corkscrews
Open Mon–Sat 9am–5pm

Town Hall Antiques
Contact Mr or Mrs Groves
Market Place, Woburn, Milton Keynes, Bedfordshire, MK17 9PZ
☎ 01525 290950 Ⓕ 01525 290950
Est. 1993 *Stock size* Large
Stock Varied
Open Mon–Sat 10am–5.30pm Sun 11am–5.30pm
Fairs Newark
Services Valuations, picture framing

Woburn Abbey Antiques Centre
Contact Paul Howell,
Woburn, Bedfordshire, MK17 9WA
☎ 01525 290350 Ⓕ 01525 292102
Ⓔ antiques@woburnabbey.co.uk
Est. 1967 *Stock size* Large
No. of dealers 64
Stock Furniture (dateline 1950), porcelain, silver, paintings (dateline 1940)
Open 363 days a year 10am–5.30pm

WOBURN SANDS

Pine Love
Contact A Tracoshas
37 High Street, Woburn Sands, Bedfordshire, MK17 8RB
☎ 01908 585515 Ⓕ 01908 585515
Est. 1995 *Stock size* Medium
Stock Antique pine furniture
Open Mon–Sat 10am–5.30pm closed Wed

BUCKINGHAMSHIRE

AMERSHAM

The Amersham Auction Rooms (RICS)
Contact Pippa Ellis
125 Station Road, Amersham, Buckinghamshire, HP7 0AH
☎ 01494 729292 Ⓕ 01494 722337
Ⓔ info@amershamauctionrooms.co.uk
Ⓦ www.amershamauctionrooms.co.uk
Est. 1877
Open Mon–Fri 9am–5.30pm Sat 9–11.30am
Sales Antiques and collectors' first Thurs of month. Victorian and general furniture other Thurs weekly 10.30am, viewing Tues 2–5pm Wed 9.30am–7pm Thurs 9–10.15am
Frequency Weekly
Catalogues Yes

Martony Antiques and Collectables
Contact Mr M Bainbridge
2 Grimsdells Corner, Sycamore Road, Amersham, Buckinghamshire, HP6 5EL
☎ 01494 722666
Est. 1997 *Stock size* Medium
Stock General antiques, small collectables
Open Tues–Sat 10am–5pm
Services Picture framing

Old Amersham Auctions
Contact Mr M King
2 School Lane, Amersham, Buckinghamshire, HP7 0EL
☎ 01494 722758 Ⓕ 01494 722758
Est. 1979
Open Mon–Sat 9am–5pm
Sales General and antiques sale Sat 11am, viewing Sat 9am prior to sale. Occasional house sales, telephone for details
Frequency Fortnightly
Catalogues Yes

Pop Antiques
12 The Broadway, Amersham, Buckinghamshire, HP7 0HP
☎ 01494 434443 Ⓕ 07970 043083
Ⓜ 07768 366606
Ⓦ www.popantiques.com
Est. 2001 *Stock size* Large
Stock Late 19thC French painted furniture, mirrors
Open Mon–Sat 10am–5pm
Services Shipping

Liz Quilter
Contact Liz or Jackie Quilter
38 High Street, Amersham, Buckinghamshire, HP7 0DJ
☎ 01494 433723 Ⓕ 01494 433723
Ⓔ jackie@quilters-antiques.fsnet.co.uk
Est. 1969 *Stock size* Large
Stock Old pine collectables, copper, brass, rustic furniture
Open Mon–Sat 10am–5pm

Sundial Antiques
Contact Mr A Macdonald
19 Whielden Street, Amersham, Buckinghamshire, HP7 0HU
☎ 01494 727955
Ⓜ 07866 819314
Est. 1970 *Stock size* Medium
Stock 19thC copper and brass, small furniture, ceramics
Open Mon–Sat 9.30am–5.30pm closed Thurs
Services Antiques vouchers available

AYLESBURY

Gillian Neale Antiques (BADA)
Contact Gillian Neale
PO Box 247, Aylesbury, Buckinghamshire, HP20 1JZ
☎ 01296 423754 Ⓕ 01296 334601
Ⓔ gillianneale@btconnect.com
Ⓦ www.gilliannealeantiques.co.uk
Est. 1980 *Stock size* Large
Stock English blue printed pottery 1780–1900
Open By appointment
Fairs Olympia, BADA
Services Valuations, restorations, export, search

BEACONSFIELD

Buck House Antique Centre
Contact Mrs B Whitby
47 Wycombe End, Beaconsfield, Buckinghamshire, HP9 1LZ
01494 670714
Est. 1982 *Stock size* Medium
Stock Clocks, furniture, metalware, ceramics, general antiques
Open Mon–Sat 10am–5pm closed Wed Sun

June Elsworth Beaconsfield Ltd
Contact June Elsworth
Clover House, 16 London End, Beaconsfield, Buckinghamshire, HP9 2JH
01494 675611 F 01494 671273
Est. 1986 *Stock size* Large
Stock 18th–19thC furniture, accessories
Open Tues–Sat 10am–5.30pm

Grosvenor House Interiors
Contact Mr T Marriott
51 Wycombe End, Beaconsfield, Buckinghamshire, HP9 1LX
01494 677498 F 01494 677498
M 07747 014098
Est. 1978 *Stock size* Large
Stock 18th–19thC furniture, pictures, mirrors, clocks, fireplaces
Open Mon–Sat 10am–1pm 2–5pm closed Wed

Period Furniture Showrooms (TVADA)
Contact Mr R E W Hearne
49 London End, Beaconsfield, Buckinghamshire, HP9 2HW
01494 674112 F 01494 681046
E sales@period-furniture-showrooms.co.uk
W www.period-furniture-showrooms.co.uk
Est. 1966 *Stock size* Large
Stock Victorian–Edwardian furniture
Open Mon–Sat 9am–5.30pm
Fairs TVADA Spring
Services Restoration of furniture

Spinning Wheel
Contact Mrs Meg Royle
86 London End, Beaconsfield, Buckinghamshire, 4P9 2JD
01494 673055
Est. 1969 *Stock size* Medium
Stock 18th–19thC furniture, china, glass
Open Tues–Sat 9.30am–4.30pm closed Wed

BOURNE END

Bourne End Antiques Centre
Contact Mr Simon Shepheard
67 The Parade, Bourne End, Buckinghamshire, SL8 5SB
01628 533298
M 07776 176876
Est. 1996 *Stock size* Large
No. of dealers 40
Stock General antiques, oak, pine, mahogany, silver, jewellery
Open Mon–Sat 10am–5.30pm Sun Bank Holidays 1–5.30pm

Bourne End Auction Rooms
Contact Mr S Brown
Station Approach, Bourne End, Buckinghamshire, SL8 5QH
01628 531500 F 01628 522158
Est. 1992
Open Mon–Fri 9am–5.30pm Sat 9am–noon
Sales Weekly general sale Wed 10.30am, 1st Wed monthly antiques sale 10.30am, viewing Tues 9.30am–7pm Wed 9–10.30am
Frequency Weekly
Catalogues Yes

La Maison
Contact Mr J Pratt
Crossing Stores, Cores End Road, Bourne End, Buckinghamshire, SL8 5AL
01628 525828 F 01494 670363
M 07885 209001
Est. 1994 *Stock size* Medium
Stock French mirrors, beds, tables, gifts, garden statuary
Open Mon–Sun 10am–5pm
Services Upholstery

BUCKINGHAM

Buckingham Antiques Centre Ltd
Contact Mr P Walton
5 West Street, Buckingham, Buckinghamshire, MK18 1HL
01280 824464
M 0788 4378710
Est. 1992 *Stock size* Large
Stock General antiques, furniture, clocks, silver, china
Open Mon–Sat 9am–5pm closed Wed
Services Valuations, restorations

Happers Antiques
Contact Mr or Mrs N Goodwin
2 High Street, Buckingham, Buckinghamshire, MK18 1NT
01280 813115
Est. 1980 *Stock size* Large
Stock Country pine furniture, accessories
Open Mon–Sat 9.30am–5.30pm closed Thurs

CHALFONT ST GILES

Gallery 23 Antiques
Contact Mr F Vollaro
5 High Street, Chalfont St Giles, Buckinghamshire, HP8 4QH
01494 871512 F 01494 871512
Est. 1989 *Stock size* Large
Stock China, silver, furniture, glass, pictures, prints, clocks
Open Mon–Sat 10am–5pm
Services Valuations

CHALFONT ST PETER

White House Antiques
Contact Mrs Betty St John-White
10 Market Place, Chalfont St Peter, Buckinghamshire, SL9 9EA
01753 885878
Est. 2000 *Stock size* Medium
Stock Early porcelain, glass, silver
Open Mon–Fri 10.15am–4.15pm Sat 10.15am–2pm closed Thurs

CHESHAM

The Attic
Contact Karen Page
3 High Street, Chesham, Buckinghamshire, HP5 1BG
01494 794114
Est. 1998 *Stock size* Large
Stock Collectables, furniture, jewellery, paintings, pictures, china, pottery, clocks, brass, commemoratives
Open Mon–Sat 9.30am–5.30pm Sun 11am–5pm

Chess Antiques (LAPADA)
Contact Mr Wilder
85 Broad Street, Chesham, Buckinghamshire, HP5 3EF

☎ 01494 783043 Ⓕ 01494 791302
Ⓜ 07831 212454
Ⓔ mike_wilder44@hotmail.com
Est. 1971 *Stock size* Medium
Stock Clocks
Open Mon–Fri 9am–5.30pm
Sat 10am–5pm
Services Valuations

A E Jackson
Contact Ann Jackson
✉ **Queen Anne House, 57 Church Street, Chesham, Buckinghamshire, HP5 1HY** Ⓟ
☎ 01494 783811
Est. 1910 *Stock size* Medium
Stock Home antiques
Open Wed Fri Sat 10am–12.30pm
1.30–5pm

The Sovereign
Contact Mr Leadbeater
✉ **115 High Street, Chesham, Buckinghamshire, HP5 1DE** Ⓟ
☎ 01494 783103
Ⓜ 07961 865398
Est. 1999 *Stock size* Large
Stock Period furniture, militaria, glass, general objets d'art, textiles
Open Mon–Sat 9.30am–5.30pm
Sun 11am–4pm closed Wed
Services Valuations, restorations

Stuff & Nonsense
Contact Helen or Elaine Robb
✉ **70 Broad Street, Chesham, Buckinghamshire, HP5 3DX** Ⓟ
☎ 01494 775988/782877
Est. 1998 *Stock size* Large
No. of dealers 20
Stock Collectables, books, antiques, furniture
Open Mon–Sat 9.30am–5.30pm
Sun 11am–5.30pm

HIGH WYCOMBE

The Country Furniture Shop (LAPADA)
Contact M or V Thomas
✉ **3 Hazlemere Road, Penn, High Wycombe, Buckinghamshire, HP10 8AA** Ⓟ
☎ 01494 812244 Ⓕ 01494 812244
Ⓜ 07710 240094
Est. 1961 *Stock size* Large
Stock Victorian dining room furniture, tables, chairs, some Georgian–Edwardian
Open Mon–Sat 9.30am–5pm
closed 1–2pm Thurs 9.30am–1pm

IVER

J Felstead
Contact Mr J Felstead
✉ **32 Thorney Lane South, Iver, Buckinghamshire, SL0 9AE** Ⓟ
☎ 01753 651593
Est. 1970 *Stock size* Small
Stock Antique furniture
Open Mon–Sat 10am–5pm
Services Restorations

Yester-Year
Contact Mr P J Frost
✉ **12 High Street, Iver, Buckinghamshire, SL0 9NG** Ⓟ
☎ 01753 652072
Est. 1972 *Stock size* Medium
Stock General antiques, furniture, pictures, china, glass, metalwork
Open Mon–Sat 10am–6pm
Services Valuations, restorations, picture framing, clock repairs

LITTLE CHALFONT

Nightingale Antiques
Contact Mr L Andreou
✉ **17 Nightingale Corner, Little Chalfont, Amersham, Buckinghamshire, HP7 9PZ** Ⓟ
☎ 01494 762163
Est. 1962 *Stock size* Large
Stock General antiques
Open Tues–Sat 9.30am–5.30pm
Sun 10am–4pm closed Mon
Services Restorations, valuations, silver-plating

MARLOW

Bosleys Military Auctioneers
Contact Mr S Bosley
✉ **The White House, Marlow, Buckinghamshire, SL7 1AH** Ⓟ
☎ 01628 488188 Ⓕ 01628 488111
Ⓦ www.bosleys.co.uk
Est. 1994
Open By appointment only
Sales Militaria sales Wed noon at Court Gardens, viewing Wed 8am–noon prior to sale
Frequency Quarterly
Catalogues Yes

Coldstream Military Antiques (LAPADA)
Contact Mr S Bosley
✉ **The White House, Marlow, Buckinghamshire, SL7 1AH** Ⓟ
☎ 01628 488188 Ⓕ 01628 488111
Est. 1978 *Stock size* Large
Stock Militaria including swords, medals, pictures, campaign furniture
Open By appointment only

Glade Antiques (LAPADA)
Contact Sonia Garry
✉ **PO Box 939, Marlow, Buckinghamshire, SL7 1SR**
☎ 01628 487255 Ⓕ 01628 487255
Ⓜ 07771 552328
Ⓔ sonia@gladeantiques.com
Ⓦ www.gladeantiques.com
Stock Oriental porcelain, bronzes, jades, antiquities
Open By appointment
Fairs Olympia, LAPADA
Services Valuations

Jackdaw Antique Centres Ltd
Contact Mrs J Mayle
✉ **25 West Street, Marlow, Buckinghamshire, SL7 2LS** Ⓟ
☎ 01628 898285
Ⓔ jackdaws@freeserve.com
Est. 1999 *Stock size* Large
Stock General antiques, china, Victorian, Art Deco, silver, furniture
Open Mon–Sat 10am–5.30pm
Sun Bank Holidays noon–5pm

Marlow Antiques Centre (TVADA)
Contact Marilyn Short
✉ **35 Station Road, Marlow, Buckinghamshire, SL7 1NW** Ⓟ
☎ 01628 473223 Ⓕ 01628 478989
Ⓜ 07802 188345
Est. 1995 *Stock size* Large
No. of dealers 30
Stock 18th–20thC furniture, collectors' china, Staffordshire figures, chandeliers, silver, decorative glass, writing slopes, tea caddies, postcards, pens, cuff links, equestrian items
Open Mon–Sat 10.30am–5pm
Sun 11am–4pm
Services Restorations, shipping

NAPHILL

A and E Foster (BADA, CINOA)
Contact Stephen Foster
✉ **Little Heysham, Naphill, Buckinghamshire, HP14 4SU** Ⓟ
☎ 01494 562024 Ⓕ 01494 562024
Ⓜ 07802 895146
Est. 1970 *Stock size* Medium

Stock European works of art and sculpture
Open By appointment
Fairs Grosvenor House, Spring and Winter Olympia

NEWPORT PAGNELL

Ken's Paper Collectables (UACC, Ephemera Society)
Contact Ken Graham
29 High Street, Newport Pagnell, Buckinghamshire, MK16 8AR P
☎ 01908 210683/610003
F 01908 610003
E ken@kens.co.uk
W www.kens.co.uk
Est. 1983 *Stock size* Large
Stock Autographs, vintage magazines, posters, historic newspapers, British comics, documents, printed, written ephemera, show business memorabilia
Open Mon–Wed Fri 9.30am–5pm Sat 9.30am–4pm
Fairs Alexandra Palace, ephemera fairs, film fairs

OLNEY

Archers
Contact Mr N Carter or Katherine Haslam
19 High Street, Olney, Buckinghamshire, MK46 4EB P
☎ 01234 713050 F 01234 713050
E archersantiques@ukgateway.net
Est. 1999 *Stock size* Large
Stock Mahogany, pine, oak furniture
Open Mon–Sat 10am–5pm Sun 2–5pm closed Wed
Fairs Ardingly, Newark

Courtyard Antiques
Contact Trisha Sharp
4 Rose Court, Olney, Buckinghamshire, MK46 4BY P
☎ 01234 712200
M 07713 304704
Est. 1993 *Stock size* Medium
No. of dealers 12–15
Stock Furniture, general antiques 18th–20thC, old pine, clocks, silver, ceramics (two floors)
Open Mon–Fri 10am–4.30pm Sat 10am–5pm Sun 2–5pm closed Wed

Gilpin Antiques
Contact Mr J Swallow
100a High street, Olney, Buckinghamshire, MK46 4BE P
☎ 01234 711095 F 01234 711895
M 07808 200522
Est. 1979 *Stock size* Medium
Stock Furniture, porcelain, silver, jewellery, clocks
Open Mon–Sat 10am–1pm 2–5pm Sun 2–5pm closed Wed
Services Restorations

Market Square Antiques
Contact Helen Vella
20 Market Place, Olney, Buckinghamshire, MK46 4BA P
☎ 01234 712172
Est. 1987 *Stock size* Medium
Stock Georgian–1920s furniture, china, porcelain, silver, copper
Open Mon–Sat 10am–5pm Sun 12.30–4.30pm
Services Restorations, repairs

Robin Unsworth Antiques
Contact Robin Unsworth
1a Weston Road, Olney, Buckinghamshire, MK46 5BD P
☎ 01234 711210
Est. 1972 *Stock size* Large
Stock 18th–19thC furniture, clocks
Open Mon–Sun 10am–4pm or by appointment

PRINCES RISBOROUGH

Well Cottage Antique Centre
20–22 Bell Street, Princes Risborough, Buckinghamshire, HP27 0AD P
☎ 01844 342002
W www.nwwyell.co.uk/sites/antiquesrisborough
Est. 1984 *Stock size* Medium
Stock Furniture, early silver, general antiques
Open Mon–Sat 9.30am–5.30pm Sun 1–5pm

STONY STRATFORD

Daeron's Books
Contact Mrs A Gardner
3 Timor Court, High Street, Stony Stratford, Milton Keynes, Buckinghamshire, MK11 1EJ P
☎ 01908 568989 F 01908 262491
E books@daerons.demon.co.uk
W www.daerons.demon.co.uk
Est. 1992 *Stock size* Medium
Stock Fantasy, science fiction books, Tolkien and C S Lewis a speciality
Open Mon–Fri mornings Thurs Sun by appointment
Services Book search

Periplus Books
Contact Mr J Phillips
2 Timor Court, High Street, Stony Stratford, Milton Keynes, Buckinghamshire, MK11 1EJ P
☎ 01908 263300
Est. 1997 *Stock size* Small
Stock General second-hand, antiquarian books
Open Tues–Sat 10.30am–5pm

WADDESDON

Junk and Disorderly
Contact Mrs R Mead
74 High Street, Waddesdon, Aylesbury, Buckinghamshire, HP18 0JD P
☎ 01296 658573 F 01296 651048
Est. 1993 *Stock size* Large
Stock General antiques
Open Mon–Sun 10am–5pm

WAVENDON

Jeanne Temple Antiques
Contact Mrs Temple
Stockwell House, 1 Stockwell Lane, Wavendon, Milton Keynes, Buckinghamshire, MK17 8LS P
☎ 01908 583597 F 01908 281149
Est. 1960 *Stock size* Medium
Stock Furniture, collectable items
Open Tues–Sat 10am–5pm Sun by appointment
Fairs Luton Fair, NEC

WENDOVER

Antiques at Wendover
Contact Mrs N Gregory
The Old Post Office, 25 High Street, Wendover, Buckinghamshire, HP22 6DU P
☎ 01296 625335 F 01296 625681
M 07712 032565
Est. 1987 *Stock size* Large
No. of dealers Over 30
Stock Town and country antiques, furniture, silver, glass,

rugs, garden items, kitchenware, architectural antiques, barometers, antiquities etc
Open Mon–Sat 10am–5.30pm Sun Bank Holidays 11am–5pm
Services Restoration of caning, ceramics, metals, jewellery, furniture

⊞ Bowood Antiques (LAPADA, TVADA)
Contact Miss P Peyton-Jones
✉ **Wendover Dean Farm, Bowood Lane, Wendover, Buckinghamshire, HP22 6PY** 🅿
☎ 01296 622113 Ⓕ 01296 696598
Est. 1960 ***Stock size*** Medium
Stock General antiques, 17th–early 19thC furniture
Open By appointment

⊞ Sally Turner Antiques (LAPADA)
Contact Sally Turner
✉ **Hogarth House, High Street, Wendover, Buckinghamshire, HP22 6DU** 🅿
☎ 01296 624402 Ⓕ 01296 624402
Est. 1979 ***Stock size*** Large
Stock 18th–19thC furniture, decorative items, jewellery
Open Mon–Sat 10am–5pm closed Wed
Fairs Olympia
Services Repairs

⊞ Wendover Antiques (LAPADA)
Contact Richard or Dorli Davies
✉ **1 South Street, Wendover, Buckinghamshire, HP22 6EF** 🅿
☎ 01296 622078
Est. 1979 ***Stock size*** Large
Stock 18thC–19thC furniture, pictures, oils, watercolours, miniatures, silhouettes, silver
Open Mon–Sat 10am–5.30pm or by appointment

WINSLOW

Winslow Antique Centre
Contact Mr Taylor
✉ **15 Market Square, Winslow, Buckinghamshire, MK18 3AB** 🅿
☎ 01296 714540 Ⓕ 01296 714556
Est. 1990 ***Stock size*** Large
No. of dealers 20
Stock Country-style antique centre, Staffordshire, pottery
Open Mon–Sat 10am–5pm Sun 1–5pm closed Wed

GLOUCESTERSHIRE

ANDOVERSFORD

⊞ Julian Tatham-Losh
Contact Mr Julian Tatham-Losh
✉ **Brereton House, Andoversford, Cheltenham, Gloucestershire, GL54 4JN** 🅿
☎ 01242 820646 Ⓕ 01242 820563
Ⓔ jtlantiques@onetel.net.uk
Est. 1980 ***Stock size*** Large
Stock Majolica, Staffordshire, tea caddies, bamboo furniture, general decorative items
Trade only Yes
Open Mon–Fri 8am–6pm
Fairs NEC, Newark
Services Valuations

BARNSLEY

⊞ Denzil Verey (CADA)
Contact Denzil Verey
✉ **Barnsley House, Barnsley, Cirencester, Gloucestershire, GL7 5EE** 🅿
☎ 01285 740402 Ⓕ 01285 740628
Est. 1980 ***Stock size*** Large
Stock 18th–19thC country furniture, copper, brass, glass, lighting, kitchenware, decorative accessories
Open Mon–Fri 9.30am–5.30pm Sat 10am–5.30pm

BERKELEY

Berkeley Market
Contact Mr Keith Gardener
✉ **11 The Market Place, Berkeley, Gloucestershire, GL13 9BD** 🅿
☎ 01453 511032
Ⓜ 07802 304534
Est. 1988 ***Stock size*** Large
No. of dealers 5
Stock Bric-a-brac, period furniture, general antiques
Open Tues–Sat 9.30am–5pm or by appointment
Services Free tea or coffee to trade

⊞ Proudfoot Antiques (FATG)
Contact Peter or Penny Proudfoot
✉ **16–18 High Street, Berkeley, Gloucestershire, GL13 9BJ** 🅿
☎ 01453 811513 Ⓕ 01453 511616
Ⓜ 07802 911894
Ⓔ berkpix@aol.com
Est. 1956 ***Stock size*** Medium
Stock General antiques
Open Mon–Sun 9.30am–5.30pm
Services Valuations, picture framing

BIBURY

⊞ Mill Antiques Etc
Contact Mr B Goodall
✉ **Arlington Mill, Arlington, Bibury, Cirencester, Gloucestershire, GL7 5NL** 🅿
☎ 01285 740199
Ⓜ 07788 681998
Est. 1999 ***Stock size*** Large
Stock General antiques, gifts, souvenir collectables, exclusive tea towels
Open 7 days 9am–6pm

BISLEY

⊞ High Street Antiques
Contact Heather Ross
✉ **Bisley, Stroud, Gloucestershire, GL6 7BA** 🅿
☎ 01452 770153
Ⓜ 07703 755841
Est. 1975 ***Stock size*** Small
Stock Oriental rugs, small furniture, collectables
Open Mon–Sat 2–6pm
Fairs Malvern, Horticultural Hall, Vincent Square

BOURTON-ON-THE WATER

⊞ Aquarius Books Ltd
Contact Mr S Dumbleton
✉ **Portland House, Victoria Street, Bourton-on-the-Water, Gloucestershire, GL54 2BX** 🅿
☎ 01451 820352
Est. 1992 ***Stock size*** Large
Stock Antiquarian and second-hand books
Open Mon–Sun 9.30am–5.30pm
Services Book search

⊞ The Looking Glass
Contact Mrs A P Jones
✉ **Rear of Aquarius Bookshop, Victoria Street, Bourton-on-the-Water, Gloucestershire, GL54 2BX**
☎ 01451 810818
Est. 2001 ***Stock size*** Small
Stock Glass, small furniture, collectables, silver, pottery, china, studio pottery
Open Mon–Sun 10am–5pm

Tayler & Fletcher
Contact Mr Martin Lambert
London House, High Street, Bourton-on-the-Water, Gloucestershire, GL54 2AP
01451 821666 F 01451 820818
M 07074 821666
E lambert@tayler-and-fletcher.co.uk
Est. 1790
Open Mon–Fri 9am–5.30pm Sat 9am–12.30pm
Sales Monthly furniture sales Sat 10am, viewing Fri 1–6pm and morning of sale from 7.30am. Three fine art and antiques sales per annum Tues 10.30am, viewing Mon 1–7pm and morning of sale from 8am
Frequency Monthly
Catalogues Yes

CHALFORD

Minchinhampton Architectural Salvage Co (SALVO)
Contact Eve Guinan
Cirencester Road, Aston Down, Chalford, Stroud, Gloucestershire, GL6 8PE
01285 760886 F 01285 760838
E masco@catbrain.com
W www.catbrain.com
Est. 1983 *Stock size* Large
Stock Architectural antiques, garden ornaments, reclaimed materials, metalwork, gates, staddle stones, window frames, chimney pieces
Open Mon–Fri 9am–5pm Sat 9am–3pm
Services Valuations, garden design

CHELTENHAM

Art & Antiques (LAPADA)
Contact Mrs J Turner
16–17 Montpellier Walk, Cheltenham, Gloucestershire, GL50 1SD
01242 522939
Est. 1950 *Stock size* Large
Stock General antiques
Open Mon–Sat 9am–4pm closed Thurs
Fairs Westonbirt
Services Road shows

Bed of Roses
Contact Martin Losh
12 Prestbury Road, Cheltenham, Gloucestershire, GL52 2PW
01242 231918
Est. 1978 *Stock size* Medium
Stock Fine stripped pine
Open By appointment

Cheltenham Antique Market
Contact Mr K Shave
54 Suffolk Road, Cheltenham, Gloucestershire, GL50 2AQ
01242 529812
Est. 1979 *Stock size* Large
Stock Victorian–20thC furniture, chandeliers
Open Mon–Sat 10am–5.30pm

Cheltenham Antiques Centre
Contact Mrs M Atkinson
50 Suffolk Road, Cheltenham, Gloucestershire, GL50 2AQ
01242 573556 F 01242 224564
E maggie@antiqcentre.com
W www.antiqcentre.com
Est. 1998 *Stock size* Large
No. of dealers 20
Stock Furniture, ceramics, jewellery, glass, linen, silver, Art Deco, toys, memorabilia
Open Mon–Sat 10am–5pm

The Cotswold Auction Co Ltd
Contact Mrs Elizabeth Poole
Chapel Walk Sale Room, Chapel Walk, Cheltenham, Gloucestershire, GL50 3DS
01242 256363 F 01242 571734
E info@cotswoldauction.co.uk
W www.cotswoldauction.co.uk
Est. 1890
Open Mon–Fri 9am–5.30pm
Sales General and specialist sale Tues 11am, viewing day prior 10am–5pm day of sale 9–11am
Frequency Monthly
Catalogues Yes

Giltwood Gallery
Contact Mr Jeff Butt or Mrs Gill Butt
30 Suffolk Parade, Cheltenham, Gloucestershire, GL50 2AE
01242 512482 F 01242 512482
Est. 1994 *Stock size* Medium
Stock Georgian–Edwardian furniture, mirrors, chandeliers, pictures
Open Mon–Sat 9am–5.30pm
Services Restorations, upholstery

Greens of Cheltenham Ltd (GTLGB)
Contact Mr S Reynolds
15 Montpellier Walk, Cheltenham, Gloucestershire, GL50 1SD
01242 512088 F 01242 512088
E steve@greensofcheltenham.co.uk
Est. 1947 *Stock size* Large
Stock Jewellery, Oriental works of art, silver
Open Mon–Sat 9am–1pm 2–5pm closed Wed
Fairs Olympia (June), Miami Beach (Jan)
Services Restorations

H W Keil (Cheltenham) Ltd (BADA, LAPADA, CINOA)
Contact Miss Laura Stapleton
129–131 The Promenade, Cheltenham, Gloucestershire, GL50 1NW
01242 522509 F 01386 852069
Stock size Large
Stock Furniture, rugs
Open Mon–Sat 9.15am–12.45pm 2.15–5.30pm
Services Valuations, restorations

Latchford Antiques
Contact Mrs R Latchford
215 London Road, Charlton Kings, Cheltenham, Gloucestershire, GL52 6HY
01242 226263
Est. 1985 *Stock size* Medium
Stock Victorian pine, period furniture
Open Mon–Sat 10am–5.30pm

Mallams
Contact Robin Fisher
Grosvenor Galleries, 26 Grosvenor Street, Cheltenham, Gloucestershire, GL52 2SG
01242 235712 F 01242 241943
E cheltenham@mallams.co.uk
W www.invaluable.com/mallams
Est. 1788
Open 9am–5.30pm
Sales Antiques and general sale

Thurs 11am, viewing Tues 9am–7pm Wed prior 9am–5pm. Ceramics sales, 2 per annum Wed or Thurs 11am, viewing 2 days prior 9am–5pm. Collectors' sales, 2 per annum, Wed 11am, viewing Mon Tues prior 9am–5pm
Frequency Monthly
Catalogues Yes

Montpellier Clocks (BADA, CINOA)
Contact Toby Birch
13 Rotunda Terrace, Cheltenham, Gloucestershire, GL50 1SW
01242 242178 01242 242178
montpellier.clocks@virgin.net
www.montpellierclocks.com
Est. 1959 ***Stock size*** Medium
Stock Longcase clocks, bracket clocks, chronometers, barometers, carriage clocks
Open Mon–Sat 9am–5pm
Services Restorations, conservation (BADA qualified)

Promenade Antiques
Contact Mr B Mann
18 Promenade, Cheltenham, Gloucestershire, GL50 1LR
01242 524519
Est. 1980 ***Stock size*** Large
Stock Antique and second-hand jewellery, clocks, watches, silver, plated items, rare, interesting objects
Open Mon–Sat 9am–5pm
Fairs Malvern Antiques Fair
Services Valuations, repairs

Q & C Militaria (OMRS, RSA)
Contact Mr John Wright
22 Suffolk Road, Cheltenham, Gloucestershire, GL50 2AQ
01242 519815 01242 519815
07778 613977
john@qc-militaria.freeserve.co.uk
Est. 1994 ***Stock size*** Large
Stock Militaria
Open Tues–Sat 10am–5pm
Fairs Brittania Medal Fairs
Services Medal mounting

Replay Period Clothing
Contact Ms Ruth Lane
7 Well Walk, Cheltenham, Gloucestershire, GL50 3JX
01242 238864
Est. 1987 ***Stock size*** Large
Stock Period clothing 1800–1970, linen, lace, costume jewellery
Open Tues–Sat 10am–5pm closed 1–2pm
Fairs Chelsea Town Hall, Malvern
Services Hat decoration, clothing hiring considered

Catherine Shinn Decorative Textiles
Contact Catherine Shinn
7 Suffolk Parade, Cheltenham, Gloucestershire, GL50 2AB
01242 574546 01242 578495
Est. 1988 ***Stock size*** Large
Stock Decorative textiles, antique cushions, furnishings, accessories
Open Mon–Sat 10am–5pm
Services Advice

Struwwelpeter
Contact Mrs N Bliss
The Old School House, 175 London Road, Charlton Kings, Cheltenham, Gloucestershire, GL52 6HN
01242 230088
Est. 1996 ***Stock size*** Medium
No. of dealers 6–12
Stock Period furniture, eclectic decorative items, collectables, smalls
Open Mon–Sat 10am–5.30pm or by appointment
Services Restorations

Tapestry Antiques
Contact Mrs G Hall
33 Suffolk Parade, Cheltenham, Gloucestershire, GL50 2AE
01242 512191
Est. 1984 ***Stock size*** Large
Stock Decorative antiques, pine, beds, garden furniture, mirrors
Open Mon–Sat 10am–5.30pm
Fairs Shepton Mallet
Services Valuations

Triton Gallery
Contact Mr L Bianco
27 Suffolk Parade, Cheltenham, Gloucestershire, GL50 2AE
01242 510477
Est. 1984 ***Stock size*** Large
Stock Antique mirrors, chandeliers, paintings, Continental and English furniture
Open Mon–Sat 9am–5.30pm

Troubridge Antiques
Contact Mr I Lochhead
11 Great Norwood Street, Cheltenham, Gloucestershire, GL50 2AW
01242 226919
Est. 1974 ***Stock size*** Large
Stock Mixture of general antiques
Open Tues–Sat 10am–5pm
Services Valuations

CHIPPING CAMPDEN

Cottage Farm Antiques
Contact Tony or Ann Willmore
Cottage Farm, Aston sub Edge, Chipping Campden, Gloucestershire, GL55 6PZ
01386 438263 01386 438263
info@cottagefarmantiques.co.uk
www.cottagefarmantiques.co.uk
Est. 1986 ***Stock size*** Large
Stock Original Victorian–Edwardian furniture, mostly pine, unfitted kitchens
Open Mon–Sun 9am–5pm
Services Restorations, shipping

Draycott Books
Contact Mr R H McClement
2 Sheep Street, Chipping Campden, Gloucestershire, GL55 6DX
01386 841392
Est. 1981 ***Stock size*** Medium
Stock Second-hand and antiquarian books
Open Mon–Fri 10am–1pm 2–5pm Sat 10am–5.30pm
Services Valuations, book search

Schoolhouse Antiques
Contact Mr Hammond
The Headmaster's House, The Old School, High Street, Chipping Camden, Gloucestershire, GL55 6HB
01386 841474 01386 841367
www.schoolhouseantiques.co.uk
Est. 1969 ***Stock size*** Large
Stock 17th–19thC furniture, pictures, clocks, Victorian oils
Open Mon–Sun 9am–5pm closed Thurs Oct–Mar
Services Valuations

Swan Antiques (NAG)
Contact Mr J Stocker
High Street, Chipping Campden, Gloucestershire, GL55 6HB
01386 840759
Est. 1964 ***Stock size*** Medium

Stock Silver, furniture, jewellery, porcelain
Open Mon–Sat 10am–1pm 2–4pm closed Thurs or by appointment

CIRENCESTER

Cirencester Arcade
Contact Mr P Bird
25 Market Place, Cirencester, Gloucestershire, GL7 2NX
01285 644214
Est. 1995 *Stock size* Large
No. of dealers 60
Stock Furniture, china, glass, jewellery, coins, stamps, postcards
Open Mon–Sun 9.30am–5pm
Services Shipping, book search, clock repair

Corinum Auctions (PTA)
Contact Mr K Lawson
25 Gloucester Street, Cirencester, Gloucestershire, GL7 2DJ
01285 659057 F 01285 652047
Est. 1990
Sales Quarterly sales in Mar Jun Sep Dec selling printed ephemera, cigarette cards, books, postcards etc
Frequency Quarterly
Catalogues Yes

The Cotswold Auction Co Ltd (RICS)
Contact Elizabeth Poole
Swan Yard, West Market Place, Cirencester, Gloucestershire, GL7 2NH
01285 642420 F 01285 642400
E info@cotswoldauction.co.uk
W www.cotswoldauction.co.uk
Est. 1890
Open Mon–Fri 9am–5.30pm
Sales Held at The Bingham Hall, King Street, Cirencester. General antiques and specialist sales Fri 10am, viewing Thurs prior 10am–8pm day of sale 9–10am
Frequency Monthly
Catalogues Yes

Forum Antiques
Contact Mr Weston Mitchell
Springfield Farm, Perrott's Brook, Cirencester, Gloucestershire, GL7 7DT
01285 831821
E westie@forumants.freeserve.co.uk
Est. 1985 *Stock size* Medium
Stock 18thC and earlier veneered walnut, early oak, French Empire furniture
Open By appointment only

Hare's Antiques Ltd
Contact Allan or Jenny Hare
4 Black Jack Street, Cirencester, Gloucestershire, GL7 2AA
01285 640077 F 01285 653513
M 07860 350097/6
E hares@star.co.uk
W www.hares-antiques.com
Est. 1972 *Stock size* Large
Stock 18th–19thC English furniture
Open Mon–Sat 10am–5.30pm or by appointment
Fairs Olympia
Services Restorations, upholstery

Moore, Allen & Innocent
Contact Mrs Marjorie Williams
Norcote, Cirencester, Gloucestershire, GL7 5RH
01285 646050 F 01285 652862
E fineart@mooreallen.co.uk
W www.mooreallen.co.uk
Est. 1852
Open Mon–Fri 9am–5.30pm Sat 9am–noon
Sales Selective antiques sale quarterly Fri 10am. Sporting 6 monthly Fri 10am. Picture sale 6 monthly Fri 10am. General sale monthly Fri 9.30am, viewing, day prior 10.30am–8.00pm, sale day 9am–3pm
Frequency Twice monthly
Catalogues Yes

Original Architectural Antiques (SALVO)
Contact John Rawlinson
22 Elliot Road, Love Lane Industrial Estate, Cirencester, Gloucestershire, GL7 1YS
01285 653532 F 01285 644383
M 07774 979735
E sales@originaluk.com
W www.originaluk.com
Est. 1980 *Stock size* Large
Stock Architectural antiques, fireplaces, columns, limestone troughs, oak doors
Open Mon–Sat 9am–5pm Sun 10am–4pm
Services Valuations, restorations

Parlour Farm Antiques
Contact Mr N Grunfeld
Unit 12B, Wilkinson Road, Love Lane Industrial Estate, Cirencester, Gloucestershire, GL7 1YT
01285 885336 F 01285 885338
E info@parlourfarm.com
W www.parlourfarm.com
Est. 1994 *Stock size* Large
Stock Antique pine furniture imported from Russia, Czech Republic, Germany, smalls, kitchenware, furniture
Open Mon–Sun 10am–5pm
Fairs Newark
Services Container packing

Rankine Taylor Antiques (LAPADA, CADA, CINOA)
Contact Mrs L Taylor
34 Dollar Street, Cirencester, Gloucestershire, GL7 2AN
01285 652529
W www.cirencestergalleries.com
Est. 1969 *Stock size* Large
Stock 16th–18thC furniture, silver, glass, rare associated objects
Open Mon–Sat 9am–5.30pm
Services Small repairs

Silver Street Antiques
Contact Mr S Tarrant
9 Silver Street, Cirencester, Gloucestershire, GL7 2BJ
01285 641600 F 01285 641600
Est. 1994 *Stock size* Medium
Stock General antiques, kitchenware
Open Mon Tues Thurs–Sat 10am–5pm Wed Sun noon–5pm
Services House clearance

Specialised Postcard Auctions (PTA)
Contact Mr K Lawson
25 Gloucester Street, Cirencester, Gloucestershire, GL7 2DJ
01285 659057 F 01285 652047
Est. 1976
Open As per viewing
Sales Every 6 weeks Mon 2pm, viewing Mon–Fri prior 10am–1pm 3–7pm day of sale 10am–2pm
Frequency Every 6 weeks
Catalogues Yes

William H Stokes (BADA, CADA)
Contact Mr Peter Bontoft

✉ The Cloisters,
6–8 Dollar Street,
Cirencester,
Gloucestershire, GL7 2AJ
☎ 01285 653907 Ⓕ 01285 653907
Est. 1968 *Stock size* Medium
Stock Early oak furniture, associated items
Open Mon–Fri 9.30am–5.30pm Sat 9.30am–4.30pm

Patrick Waldron Antiques
Contact Patrick Waldron
✉ 18 Dollar Street,
Cirencester,
Gloucestershire, GL7 2AN Ⓟ
☎ 01285 652880
Est. 1994 *Stock size* Medium
Stock 18th–early 19thC English furniture
Open Mon–Sat 9.30am–6pm
Services Restorations

COLESORD

Simon Lewis Transport Books
Contact Mr S Lewis
✉ PO Box 9, Colesord,
Gloucestershire, GL16 8YF Ⓟ
☎ 01594 839369 Ⓕ 01594 839369
Ⓔ simon@simonlewis.com
Ⓦ www.simonlewis.com
Est. 1985 *Stock size* Medium
Stock 1910–1990 transport related books
Open By appointment

CUTSDEAN

Architectural Heritage (CADA)
Contact Alex Puddy
✉ Taddington Manor,
Taddington, Cutsdean,
Gloucestershire, GL54 5RY Ⓟ
☎ 01386 584414§ Ⓕ 01386 584236
Ⓔ puddy@architectural-heritage.co.uk
Ⓦ www.architectural-heritage.co.uk
Est. 1986 *Stock size* Large
Stock Garden ornaments, chimney pieces, wood wall panelling
Open Mon–Fri 9.30am–5.30pm Sat 10.30am–4.30pm
Fairs Chelsea
Services Valuations

FAIRFORD

Blenheim Antiques (CADA)
Contact Mr Neil Hurdle
✉ Acacia House,
Market Place, Fairford,
Gloucestershire, GL7 4AB Ⓟ
☎ 01285 712094
Est. 1973 *Stock size* Medium
Stock 18th–19thC town and country furniture, clocks, accessories
Open Mon–Sat 9am–6pm

Gloucester House Antiques (CADA)
Contact Mrs Chester-Master
✉ Market Place, Fairford,
Gloucestershire, GL7 4AB Ⓟ
☎ 01285 712790 Ⓕ 01285 713324
Est. 1972 *Stock size* Large
Stock English and French country furniture, farmhouse tables, chairs, 18th–19thC French faïence and pottery
Open Mon–Sat 9am–5.30pm

GLOUCESTER

Agdar
Contact Mr Alan Giles
✉ 330 Barton Street,
Gloucester, Gloucestershire,
GL1 4JJ
☎ 01452 302272 Ⓕ 01452 302272
Ⓜ 07785 278878
Est. 1984 *Stock size* Medium
Stock General antiques, pine
Open Mon–Sat 9am–3pm
Services House clearance

BK Art & Antiques (SOFAA)
Contact Mr Simon Chorley
✉ 111 Eastgate Street,
Gloucester,
Gloucestershire,
GL1 1PZ Ⓟ
☎ 01452 521267 Ⓕ 01452 300184
Ⓔ artantiques@bkonline.co.uk
Ⓦ www.bkonline.co.uk
Est. 1862
Open Mon–Fri 8.30am–5.30pm
Sales Art and antiques sales, phone for details
Frequency Every 6 weeks
Catalogues Yes

The Cotswold Auction Co Ltd
Contact Robert Short FRICS
✉ 4–6 Clarence Street,
Gloucester,
Gloucestershire, GL1 1DX
☎ 01452 521177 Ⓕ 01452 305883
Ⓔ info@cotswoldauction.co.uk
Ⓦ www.cotswoldauction.co.uk
Est. 1890
Open Mon–Fri 9am–5.30pm
Sales Antiques, collectables and general sale at St Barnabas Church Hall Tues 10am, viewing Mon 9am–9pm
Frequency Every 2 months
Catalogues Yes

The Cottage
Contact Mrs Helen Webb
✉ 55 Southgate Street,
Gloucester,
Gloucestershire, GL1 1TX
☎ 01452 526027
Est. 1998 *Stock size* Large
Stock Antiques, collectables, gifts of distinction
Open Mon–Sat 9.30am–4.30pm Wed 12.30–4.30pm
Services Repairs

Gloucester Antique Centre
Contact Mrs Wright
✉ The Historic Docks,
1 Severn Road, Gloucester,
Gloucestershire, GL1 2LE Ⓟ
☎ 01452 529716 Ⓕ 01452 307161
Ⓦ www.antiques-center.com
Est. 1990 *Stock size* Large
No. of dealers 140
Stock General antiques, collectables
Open Mon–Sat 10am–5pm Sun 1–5pm
Services Valuations, shipping, book search

M & C Cards
Contact Mr M W Cant
✉ Shop 30, The Antiques Centre,
Severn Road, Gloucester,
Gloucestershire, GL1 2LE Ⓟ
☎ 01452 506361 Ⓕ 01452 307161
Ⓔ mick@mandccards.co.uk
Ⓦ www.mandccards.co.uk
Est. 1991 *Stock size* Medium
Stock Postcards, cigarette cards, advertising collectables
Open Thurs–Mon 10am–5pm Sun 1–5pm
Fairs Cheltenham Race Course Card Fair
Services Valuations

M & C Stamps
Contact Mr M W Cant
✉ Shop 30, The Antiques Centre,
Severn Road, Gloucester,
Gloucestershire, GL1 2LE Ⓟ
☎ 01452 506361 Ⓕ 01452 307161
Ⓔ mick@mandcstamps.co.uk
Ⓦ www.mandcstamps.co.uk
Est. 1984 *Stock size* Medium

Stock Stamps, first day covers, accessories
Open Thurs–Mon 10am–5pm Sun 1–5pm
Fairs Stamp Fair Cheltenham Town Hall
Services Valuations, new issue service

⊞ W H Webber Antique Clocks
Contact W H Webber
✉ **First Floor, Gloucester Antique Centre, Historic Docks, Gloucester, Gloucestershire, GL1 2LE** 🅿
☎ 029 2070 2313 Ⓕ 029 2070 2313
Ⓜ 07909 745155
Ⓔ whwebber@tesco.net
Est. 1994 *Stock size* Medium
Stock Antique clocks, especially longcase, wall clocks
Open Mon–Sat 10am–5pm Sun 1–5pm
Fairs Margam
Services Valuations, repairs, restorations

GREET

⊞ Stephen Cook Antiques (LAPADA)
Contact Stephen Cook
✉ **The Studio, Winchcombe Pottery, Becketts Lane, Greet, Cheltenham, Gloucestershire, GL54 5NU** 🅿
☎ 01242 604770 Ⓕ 01242 609098
Ⓜ 07973 814656
Ⓔ stephen@scookantiques.com
Ⓦ www.scookantiques.com
Est. 1986 *Stock size* Medium
Stock Period oak, walnut and mahogany furniture
Open By appointment
Services Valuations, restorations

KEMPSFORD

⊞ Ximenes Rare Books Inc (ABA, PBFA)
Contact Mr Stephen Weissman
✉ **Kempsford House, Kempsford, Fairford, Gloucestershire, GL7 4ET** 🅿
☎ 01285 810640 Ⓕ 01285 810650
Ⓔ steve@ximenes.com
Est. 1965 *Stock size* Medium
Stock Rare books
Open By appointment only
Fairs Olympia (June)
Services Catalogues

LECHLADE

⊞ Corner House Antiques (LADA)
Contact Mr John Downes-Hall
✉ **The Corner, High Street, Lechlade, Gloucestershire, GL7 3AE** 🅿
☎ 01367 252007
Est. 1957 *Stock size* Large
Stock Antique silver, jewellery, country furniture, porcelain, objets d'art
Open Tues–Sat 10am–5pm or by appointment
Services Designer and silversmith, restoration of old silver

⌂ Jubilee Hall Antiques Centre
Contact Mr John Calgie
✉ **Oak Street, Lechlade, Gloucestershire, GL7 3AY** 🅿
☎ 01367 253777
Ⓔ jubileehall@hotmail.com
Est. 1997 *Stock size* Large
No. of dealers 25
Stock Furniture, objets d'art, metalware, sporting antiques
Open Mon–Sat 10am–5pm Sun 11am–5pm
Services Shipping, delivery arranged

⊞ Lechlade Arcade
Contact Mr J Dickson
✉ **5–7 High Street, Lechlade, Gloucestershire, GL7 3AD** 🅿
☎ 01367 252832
Ⓜ 07949 130875
Est. 1990 *Stock size* Large
Stock 40 rooms of china, smalls, small furniture, cast-iron, farm tools and implements, antique pistols, guns, medals, Roman artefacts
Open Mon–Sun 9am–5pm
Services House clearance

⌂ The Old Ironmongers Antiques Centre
Contact Mark Serle or Geoff Allen
✉ **5 Burford Street, Lechlade, Gloucestershire, GL7 3AP** 🅿
☎ 01367 252397
Est. 2000 *Stock size* Large
No. of dealers 40
Stock Tools, town and country furniture, gramophones, iron, copperware, architectural, French, books, gardening bygones, pot lids
Open Mon–Sun 10am–5pm
Services Restorations, shipping, book search

MINCHINHAMPTON

⊞ Mick & Fanny Wright
Contact Mr M Wright
✉ **The Trumpet, West End, Minchinhampton, Stroud, Gloucestershire, GL6 9JA**
☎ 01453 883027
Ⓔ thetrumpetantiques@hotmail.com
Est. 1979 *Stock size* Medium
Stock General antiques, more smalls than furniture, antiquarian and second-hand books, watches, clocks
Open Wed–Sat 10.30am–5.30pm
Fairs Various

MORETON-IN-MARSH

⊞ Benton Fine Art and Antiques (LAPADA)
Contact Melanie Benton
✉ **Regent House, High Street, Moreton-in-Marsh, Gloucestershire, GL56 0AX** 🅿
☎ 01608 652153 Ⓕ 01608 652153
Ⓔ bentonfineart@excite.co.uk
Est. 1972 *Stock size* Medium
Stock 19th–20thC oils and watercolours, 19th–20thC fine furniture
Open Mon–Sat 10am–5.30pm Sun 11am–5.30pm closed Tues
Fairs LAPADA London and Birmingham, NEC

⊞ Berry Antiques (LAPADA)
Contact Mr C Berry
✉ **3 High Street, Moreton-in-Marsh, Gloucestershire, GL56 0AH** 🅿
☎ 01608 652929 Ⓕ 01608 652929
Stock size Medium
Stock 18th–19thC furniture
Open Mon–Sat 10am–5.30pm Sun 11am–5pm closed Tues
Fairs LAPADA

⊞ Chandlers Antiques
Contact Ian Kellam
✉ **Chandlers Cottage, High Street, Moreton-in-Marsh, Gloucestershire, GL56 OAD** 🅿
☎ 01608 651347 Ⓕ 01608 651347
Est. 1984 *Stock size* Large
Stock All small porcelain, glass, jewellery, silver

Open By appointment
Services Valuations

Cox's Architectural Salvage Yard Ltd (SALVO)
Contact Mr P Watson
10 Fosse Way Industrial Estate, Stratford Road, Moreton-in-Marsh, Gloucestershire, GL56 9NQ P
☎ 01608 652505 F 01608 652881
E coxs@fsbdial.co.uk
W www.salvo.co.uk/coxs
Est. 1991 *Stock size* Large
Stock Architectural antiques, doors, fireplaces, Gothic- style windows
Open Mon–Sat 9am–6pm
Services Valuations, shipping

Dale House
Contact Nicholas Allen
High Street, Moreton-in-Marsh, Gloucestershire, GL56 0AD P
☎ 01608 652950 F 01608 652424
Est. 1973 *Stock size* Large
Stock 18th–early 20thC furniture, works of art
Open Mon–Sat 10am–5.30pm Sun 11am–5pm

Jeffrey Formby Antiques (LAPADA, BADA)
Contact Mr J Formby
Orchard Cottage, East Street, Moreton-in-Marsh, Gloucestershire, GL56 0LQ P
☎ 01608 650558
M 07770 755546
E jeff@formby-clocks.co.uk
W www.formby-clocks.co.uk
Est. 1994 *Stock size* Small
Stock English clocks, horological books, longcase, bracket, skeleton, lantern clocks
Open By appointment
Fairs Olympia, BADA

Jon Fox Antiques (CADA)
Contact Mr Jon Fox
High Street, Moreton-in-Marsh, Gloucestershire, GL56 OAD P
☎ 01608 650714/650325
Est. 1983 *Stock size* Large
Stock Garden antiques, furniture and country bygones
Open Mon–Fri 9.30am–5.30pm closed Tues

London House Antique Centre
Contact Mr Dudley Thompson
London House, High Street, Moreton-in-Marsh, Gloucestershire, GL56 0AH P
☎ 01608 651084
Est. 1979 *Stock size* Large
Stock General antiques, Chinese porcelain, furniture, silver, porcelain, pictures
Open Mon–Sun 10am–5pm

Oriental Gallery (LAPADA)
Contact Patricia Cater
High Barn, Longborough, Moreton-in-Marsh, Gloucestershire, GL56 0QW
☎ 01451 830944 F 01451 870126
E patriciacaterorg@aol.com
W www.patriciacater-orientalart.com
Est. 1988 *Stock size* Medium
Stock Chinese ceramics, Asian works of art
Open By appointment only
Fairs NEC

Seaford House Antiques (LAPADA)
Contact Mr or Mrs D Young
Seaford House, High Street, Moreton-in-Marsh, Gloucestershire, GL56 0AD P
☎ 01608 652423 F 01608 652423
M 07714 485632/606577
Est. 1988 *Stock size* Medium
Stock Small 18th–early 20thC furniture, porcelain, pictures, objets d'art
Open Mon–Sun 10am–5.30pm closed Tues Wed
Fairs NEC

Windsor House Antiques Centre
Contact Mr T Sutton
High Street, Moreton-in-Marsh, Gloucestershire, GL56 0AD P
☎ 01608 650993 F 01858 565438
E windsorhouse@btinternet.com
W www.windsorhouse.co.uk
Est. 1992 *Stock size* Large
No. of dealers 48
Stock High-quality general antiques, porcelain, glass, silver, clocks, paintings, furniture
Open Mon–Sat 10am–5pm Tues Sun noon–5pm
Services Shipping, delivery

Gary Wright Antiques Ltd
Contact Gary or Gill Wright
5 Fosse Way Business Park, Moreton-in-Marsh, Gloucestershire, GL56 9NQ P
☎ 01608 652007 F 01608 652007
M 07831 653843
E garywrightantiques@fsbdial.co.uk
Est. 1972 *Stock size* Large
Stock Georgian mahogany, walnut, marquetry, unusual, decorative objects, 17th–19thC good-quality furniture from £500 to £20,000
Open Mon–Sat 9.30am–5.30pm
Services Valuations, buys at auction

NEWENT

Jillings (LAPADA, CINOA, BADA)
Contact John or Doro Jillings
Croft House, 17 Church Street, Newent, Gloucestershire, GL18 1PV P
☎ 01531 822100 F 01531 822666
M 07973 830110
E clocks@jillings.com
Est. 1987 *Stock size* Medium
Stock 18th–19thC English and continental clocks
Open Fri Sat 9.30am–5pm or by appointment
Fairs BADA, LAPADA
Services Valuations, restorations, shipping

NEWNHAM ON SEVERN

Christopher Saunders (PBFA, ABA)
Contact Mr C Saunders
Kingston House, High Street, Newnham on Severn, Gloucestershire, GL14 1BB P
☎ 01594 516030 F 01594 517273
E chrisbooks@aol.com
Est. 1980 *Stock size* Large
Stock Antiquarian cricket books, memorabilia
Open By appointment
Fairs PBFA

STOW-ON-THE-WOLD

Ashton Gower Antiques (LAPADA)
Contact Chris Gower or Barry Ashton

✉ **9 Talbot Court, Market Square, Stow-on-the-Wold, Gloucestershire, GL54 1BQ** P
☎ 01451 870699 F 01451 870699
E ashtongower@aol.com
Est. 1987 *Stock size* Large
Stock Gilded mirrors, French decorative furniture, 20thC Lucite
Open Mon–Sat 10am–5pm
Services Valuations

⊞ Baggott Church Street Ltd (BADA, CADA)
Contact Mrs C Baggott
✉ **Church Street, Stow-on-the-Wold, Gloucestershire, GL54 1BB**
☎ 01451 830370 F 01451 832174
Est. 1976 *Stock size* Large
Stock English 17th–19thC furniture, paintings, objects. Annual exhibition in October
Open Mon–Sat 9.30am–5.30pm

⊞ Duncan J Baggott (LAPADA, CADA)
Contact Mrs C Baggott
✉ **Woolcomber House, Sheep Street, Stow-on-the-Wold, Gloucestershire, GL54 1AA**
☎ 01451 830662 F 01451 832174
Est. 1967 *Stock size* Large
Stock English furniture, portraits, landscape paintings, domestic metalware, fireplace accoutrements, pottery, glass, garden statuary, ornaments. Annual exhibition in October
Open Mon–Sat 9.30am–5.30pm

⊞ Bears on the Wold
Contact Mrs Eileen Evers
✉ **Sheep Street, Stow-on-the-Wold, Gloucestershire, GL54 2EN** P
☎ 01451 870133 F 01451 870133
E eileen@bearsonthewold.co.uk
W www.bearsonthewold.co.uk
Est. 1991 *Stock size* Large
Stock Old bears, Steiff, Hermann, Deans, Merrythought, Hermann Spielwaren, Leebert, Tickelpenny
Open Mon–Sat 10am–5pm Sun 11am–4pm closed Wed
Fairs Hugglets, Kensington, Teddy Bear Times, Hove

⊞ Bookbox (PBFA)
Contact Mrs C Fisher
✉ **Chantry House, Sheep Street, Stow-on-the-Wold, Gloucestershire, GL54 1AA** P
☎ 01451 831214
Est. 1977 *Stock size* Medium
Stock Antiquarian, second-hand books, 19th–20thC good literature, art, topography
Open Mon–Sat 11am–5pm closed 1–2.30pm closed Wed open only Thurs–Sat in Winter

⊞ Bryden House Clocks & Antiques (LAPADA)
Contact Mr Derek Hance
✉ **Sheep Street, Stow-on-the-Wold, Gloucestershire, GL54 1JS** P
☎ 01451 832516
M 07970 555382
E J&DHANCE@brydenhouse.fsnet.co.uk
W www.antiqnet.co.uk/brydenhouse
Est. 1991 *Stock size* Small
Stock Georgian–Victorian furniture, various clocks, barometers
Open Mon–Sat 10am–5.30pm closed Thurs
Fairs NEC
Services Clock and barometer repairs

⌂ Church Street Antiques Centre
Contact Mrs Elizabeth Niner
✉ **3–4 Church Street, Stow-on-the-Wold, Gloucestershire, GL54 1BB** P
☎ 01451 870186
Est. 1997 *Stock size* Large
No. of dealers 15
Stock General antiques, mid-17th–early 20thC, furniture, pictures, mirrors, pottery, porcelain, vintage leather goods, silver, Staffordshire animals, blue-and-white pottery, glass, lacquered furniture, copper, brass
Open Mon–Sat 9.45am–5pm

⊞ Christopher Clarke Antiques (LAPADA, CADA)
Contact Mr Simon Clarke
✉ **Fosseway, Stow-on-the-Wold, Gloucestershire, GL54 1JS** P
☎ 01451 830476 F 01451 830300
M 07971 287733
E christopherclarke@barclays.net
W www.antiques-in-england.com
Est. 1961 *Stock size* Large
Stock English furniture, works of art, animal antiques, unusual decorative items
Open Mon–Sat 9.30am–5.30pm or by appointment
Fairs Olympia (June), CADA (October)

⊞ Country Life Antiques
Contact Ann or David Rosa
✉ **Grey House, The Square, Stow-on-the-Wold, Gloucestershire, GL54 1AF** P
☎ 01451 831564 F 01451 831564
Est. 1974 *Stock size* Large
Stock Scientific instruments, decorative accessories, metalware, furniture, paintings
Open Mon–Sat 10am–5pm

⌂ Durham House Antiques Centre
Contact Mr Alan Smith
✉ **Sheep Street, Stow-on-the-Wold, Gloucestershire, GL54 1AA** P
☎ 01451 870404 F 01451 870404
E durhamhouse@compuserve.com
Est. 1994 *Stock size* Large
No. of dealers 36
Stock General antiques, silver, clocks, oak, mahogany, porcelain, Derby, Worcester, Staffordshire, Mason's, linens, prints, paintings
Open Mon–Sat 10am–5pm Sun 11am–5pm

⊞ Fosse Way Antiques (CADA)
Contact Mr M Beeston
✉ **Ross House, The Square, Stow-on-the-Wold, Gloucestershire, GL54 1AF** P
☎ 01451 830776 F 01451 830776
E furnish@fossewayantiques.com
Est. 1969 *Stock size* Large
Stock 18th–early 19thC furniture, oil paintings, small period accessories
Open Mon–Sat 10am–5pm
Services Valuations, shipping

⌂ Fox Cottage Antiques
Contact Miss Sue London
✉ **Digbeth Street, Stow-on-the-Wold, Gloucestershire, GL54 1BN** P
☎ 01451 870307
Est. 1995 *Stock size* Medium
No. of dealers 8
Stock Pottery, porcelain, glassware, silver, plated ware, small furniture, decorative items, country goods, mainly pre-1910
Open Mon–Sat 10am–5pm

⊞ Grandfather Clock Shop
Contact Mr W J Styles

✉ **The Little House, Sheep Street, Stow-on-the-Wold, Gloucestershire, GL54 1JS** Ⓟ
☎ 01451 830455 Ⓕ 01451 830455
Ⓔ info@stylesofstow.co.uk
Ⓦ www.stylesofstow.co.uk
Est. 1996 *Stock size* Large
Stock Clocks including longcase clocks, 18th–19thC furniture, 19th–20thC oil paintings and watercolours
Open Mon–Sat 10am–5pm or by appointment
Services Valuations, restorations

⊞ Keith Hockin Antiques (BADA, CADA)
Contact Mr K Hockin
✉ **The Elms, The Square, Stow-on-the-Wold, Gloucestershire, GL54 1AF** Ⓟ
☎ 01451 831058 Ⓕ 01451 831058
Ⓔ keith.hockin@talk21.com
Est. 1973 *Stock size* Medium
Stock 17th–early 18thC English oak furniture, pewter, early brass, 16th–17thC wood carvings
Open Thurs–Sat 10am–5pm closed 1–2pm or by appointment

⊞ Hungry Ghost
Contact Mrs V Kern
✉ **1 Brewery Yard, Sheep Street, Stow-on-the-Wold, Gloucestershire, GL54 1AA** Ⓟ
☎ 01451 870101
Ⓦ www.hungry-ghost.co.uk
Est. 1998 *Stock size* Large
Stock Oriental antiques, gifts, china
Open Mon–Sat 9.30am–5.30pm Sun 10am–4.30pm
Fairs Battersea

⊞ Huntington Antiques Ltd (LAPADA, CADA)
✉ **Church Street, Stow-on-the-Wold, Gloucestershire, GL54 1BE** Ⓟ
☎ 01451 830842 Ⓕ 01451 832211
Ⓔ info@huntington-antiques.com
Ⓦ www.huntington-antiques.com
Est. 1975 *Stock size* Large
Stock Early furniture and works of art, tapestries, English and Continental metalwork
Open Mon–Sat 9.30am–5.30pm
Fairs LAPADA London and Birmingham
Services Valuations, restorations, interior decoration

⊞ Roger Lamb Antiques and Works of Art (LAPADA, CADA)
Contact Roger Lamb
✉ **The Square, Stow-on-the-Wold, Gloucestershire, GL54 1AB** Ⓟ
☎ 01451 831371 Ⓕ 01451 832485
Ⓜ 07860 391959
Est. 1993 *Stock size* Medium
Stock 18th–early 19thC period furniture, decorative oils, watercolours, antique lighting, accessories
Open Mon–Sat 10am–5pm
Fairs LAPADA
Services Valuations, restorations

⊞ Simon Nutter and Thomas King-Smith
Contact Mr T M King-Smith or Mr S W Nutter
✉ **Wraggs Row, Fosseway, Stow-on-the-Wold, Gloucestershire, GL54 1JT**
☎ 01451 830658 Ⓜ 07775 864394
Est. 1975 *Stock size* Medium
Stock 18th–19thC furniture, silver, porcelain
Open Mon–Sat 9.30am–5.30pm
Fairs Westonbirt
Services Valuations

⊞ Park House Antiques
Contact Mr George Sutton
✉ **8 Park Street, Stow-on-the-Wold, Gloucestershire, GL54 1AQ** Ⓟ
☎ 01451 830159
Ⓔ teamsutton@btinternet.com
Est. 1987 *Stock size* Large
Stock Old toys, textiles, small furniture, porcelain, pottery
Open Wed–Mon 10am–4.30pm closed 1–2pm closed Tues closed all May
Services Repairs, toy museum, teddy bear repair

⊞ Priest's Antiques & Fine Arts
Contact Mr Andrew Priest
✉ **The Malt House, Digbeth Street, Stow-on-the-Wold, Gloucestershire, GL54 1BN** Ⓟ
☎ 01451 830592 Ⓕ 01451 830592
Est. 1986 *Stock size* Large
Stock 17th–early 20thC English furniture
Open Mon–Sat 10am–5pm

⊞ Michael Rowland Antiques
Contact Michael Rowland
✉ **Little Elms, The Square, Stow-on-the-Wold, Gloucestershire, GL54 1AF** Ⓟ
☎ 01451 870089
Ⓜ 07779 509753
Est. 1991 *Stock size* Medium
Stock 17th–18thC oak and fruitwood country furniture
Open Mon–Sat 10.30am–5pm

⊞ Ruskin Decorative Arts (CADA)
Contact Mr or Mrs T W Morris
✉ **5 Talbot Court, Stow-on-the-Wold, Gloucestershire, GL54 1DP** Ⓟ
☎ 01451 832254 Ⓕ 01451 832167
Est. 1989 *Stock size* Small
Stock Decorative arts 1860–1930, Arts and Crafts, Art Nouveau, Art Deco, the Cotswold Movement including the Guild of Handicraft, Gordon Russell, Gimson, the Barnsleys
Open Mon–Sat 10am–5.30pm
Fairs NEC, Antiques for Everyone
Services Valuations for insurance and probate

⊞ Samarkand Galleries (LAPADA, CADA, CINOA)
Contact Brian MacDonald
✉ **7–8 Brewery Yard, Sheep Street, Stow-on-the-Wold, Gloucestershire, GL54 1AA** Ⓟ
☎ 01451 832322 Ⓕ 01451 832322
Ⓔ mac@samarkand.co.uk
Ⓦ www.samarkand.co.uk
Est. 1979 *Stock size* Large
Stock Antique and contemporary rugs from Near East and central Asia, decorative carpets, nomadic weavings
Open Mon–Sat 10am–5.30pm
Fairs Hali Antique Textile Art Fair
Services Valuations, restorations, search

⊞ Arthur Seager Antiques
Contact Mr A Seager
✉ **50 Sheep Street, Stow-on-the-Wold, Gloucestershire, GL54 1AA** Ⓟ
☎ 01451 831605
Ⓔ arthurseager@btconnect.com
Ⓦ www.arthurseager.com
Est. 1979 *Stock size* Medium
Stock 16th–17thC objects, oak furniture, carvings
Open Thurs–Sat 10am–4pm

⊞ Stow Antiques (CADA, LAPADA, CINOA)
Contact Mrs H Hutton-Clarke

✉ **The Square, Stow-on-the-Wold, Gloucestershire, GL54 1AF** 🅿
☎ 01451 830377 Ⓕ 01451 870018
Est. 1969 *Stock size* Large
Stock 18th–19thC mahogany furniture, large tables, sets of chairs, sideboards, bookcases
Open Mon–Sat 11am–5.30pm or by appointment
Services Shipping

Tudor House
Contact Mr Peter Collingridge
✉ **Sheep Street, Stow-on-the-Wold, Gloucestershire, GL54 1AA** 🅿
☎ 01451 830021 Ⓕ 01451 830021
Est. 2001 *Stock size* Large
No. of dealers 12
Stock 18th–early 20thC furniture, clocks, watercolours, porcelain, metalware, fountain pens, garden furniture, lighting, Arts and Crafts
Open Mon–Sat 10am–5pm
Services Valuations

Vanbrugh House Antiques
Contact John or Monica Sands
✉ **Vanbrugh House, Park Street, Stow-on-the-Wold, Gloucestershire, GL54 1AQ** 🅿
☎ 01451 830797 Ⓕ 01451 830797
Est. 1978 *Stock size* Large
Stock Early fine furniture, musical boxes, early maps
Open Mon–Sat 10am–6pm
Services Valuations

STROUD

Ian Hodgkins & Co Ltd (ABA)
Contact Mr Simon Weager
✉ **Upper Vatch Mill, The Vatch, Stroud, Gloucestershire, GL6 7JY** 🅿
☎ 01453 764270 Ⓕ 01453 755233
Ⓔ i.hodgkins@dial.pipex.com
Ⓦ www.ianhodgkins.com
Est. 1974 *Stock size* Medium
Stock Antiquarian, 19thC art, literature, children's books
Open By appointment
Fairs Chelsea (Nov)

Inprint
Contact Mr Mike Goodenough
✉ **31 High Street, Stroud, Gloucestershire, GL5 1AJ** 🅿
☎ 01453 759731 Ⓕ 01453 759731
Ⓔ enquiries@inprint.co.uk
Ⓦ www.inprint.co.uk
Est. 1979 *Stock size* Medium
Stock Antiquarian, second-hand, out-of-print books on fine, applied, performing arts
Open Mon–Sat 10am–5.30pm
Services Book search

Shabby Tiger Antiques
Contact Mr S Krucker
✉ **18 Nelson Street, Stroud, Gloucestershire, GL5 2HN** 🅿
☎ 01453 759175
Est. 1975 *Stock size* Large
Stock 19thC smalls, jewellery, furniture, boxes, clocks, china, silver, plate, paintings, prints, decorative objects
Open Mon–Sat 11am–5.30pm
Services Jewellery, silver repairs

TETBURY

Philip Adler Antiques (BADA)
Contact Mr P Adler
✉ **35 Long Street, Tetbury, Gloucestershire, GL8 8AA** 🅿
☎ 01666 505759 Ⓕ 01452 770525
Ⓜ 07710 477891
Ⓔ philipadlerantiques@hotmail.com
Est. 1979 *Stock size* Large
Stock Eclectic, general stock of decorative and period antiques
Open Mon–Sat 10am–6pm and by appointment
Fairs Bath Fair (December)
Services Valuations, restorations

The Antique & Interior Centre (TADA)
Contact Linda Townsend-Bateson
✉ **Unit 1, 51 Long Street, Tetbury, Gloucestershire, GL8 8AA** 🅿
☎ 01666 505083
Est. 1995 *Stock size* Medium
No. of dealers 7
Stock Good quality furniture, porcelain, silver, pictures
Open Mon–Sat 10am–5pm Sun most Bank Holidays 1–5pm

The Antique Centre (TADA)
Contact Mrs Linda Townsend Bateman
✉ **51a Long Street, Tetbury, Gloucestershire, GL8 8AA** 🅿
☎ 01666 505083
Est. 1995 *Stock size* Large
Stock French furniture, decorative pieces, 19thC Staffordshire textiles. Georgian, Victorian, Edwardian furniture
Open Mon–Sat 10am–5pm
Sun 1–5pm

The Antiques Emporium (TADA)
✉ **The Old Chapel, Long Street, Tetbury, Gloucestershire, GL8 8AA** 🅿
☎ 01666 505281 Ⓕ 01666 505661
Est. 1993 *Stock size* Large
No. of dealers 40
Stock Fine and country furniture, brass, copper, treen, kitchenware, paintings, miniatures, silver, jewellery, decorative items, pottery, porcelain, books, glass, luggage
Open Mon–Sat 10am–5pm
Sun 1–5pm

Artique (TADA)
Contact George Bristow
✉ **Talboys House, 17 Church Street, Tetbury, Gloucestershire, GL8 8JG**
☎ 01666 503597 Ⓕ 01666 503597
Ⓜ 07836 337038
Ⓔ george@artique.demon.co.uk
Ⓦ www.artique.uk.com
Est. 1990 *Stock size* Large
Stock Central Asian artefacts, rugs, jewellery, furniture, textiles, architectural items
Open Mon Tues Wed 10am–6pm
Thurs Fri 10am–8pm
Sun noon–4pm

Ball & Claw Antiques (TADA)
Contact Mr Chris Kirkland
✉ **45 Long Street, Tetbury, Gloucestershire, GL8 8AA** 🅿
☎ 01666 502440
Ⓜ 07957 870423
Ⓦ www.antiquesportfolio.com/ballclawantiques
Est. 1994 *Stock size* Medium
Stock 17th–19thC furniture, Arts and Crafts, engravings, pictures, linens, textiles, children's antique decorative toys, general antiques
Open Mon–Sat 10am–5pm
Services Valuations

Balmuir House Antiques (LAPADA)
Contact Mr P Whittam
✉ **14 Long Street, Tetbury, Gloucestershire, GL8 8AQ** 🅿
☎ 01666 503822 Ⓕ 01666 505285
Est. 1989 *Stock size* Large
Stock 19thC furniture, paintings
Open Mon–Sat 9.30am–5.30pm

Services Restoration of furniture and paintings

⊞ The Black Sheep
Contact Mr Oliver Mcerlain
✉ **51 Long Street, Tetbury, Gloucestershire, GL8 8AA** 🅿
☎ 01666 505026
Est. 2000 ***Stock size*** Medium
Stock 18th–19thC decorative country furniture, 19thC pictures
Open Mon–Sat 10am–5pm or Sun noon–4pm

⊞ Breakspeare Antiques (LAPADA, CADA)
Contact Michael or Sylvia Breakspeare
✉ **36 & 57 Long Street, Tetbury, Gloucestershire, GL8 8AQ** 🅿
☎ 01666 503122
Ⓔ mark.breakspeare@hemscott.net
Est. 1962 ***Stock size*** Medium
Stock English period furniture, mahogany, 1750–1835, early veneered walnut, 1690–1740
Open Mon–Sat 10am–5pm

⊞ The Chest of Drawers (TADA)
Contact Mrs P Bristow
✉ **24 Long Street, Tetbury, Gloucestershire, GL8 8AQ** 🅿
☎ 01666 502105
Ⓜ 07710 292064
Est. 1969 ***Stock size*** Medium
Stock English furniture, 17thC upwards
Open Mon–Fri 9.30am–5.30pm

⊞ Coach House Bookshop
Contact Mr P M Gibbons
✉ **4 The Chipping, Tetbury, Gloucestershire, GL8 8ET** 🅿
☎ 01666 504330 Ⓕ 01666 504458
Ⓔ bookshop@tetbury.co.uk
Est. 1994 ***Stock size*** Medium
Stock Antiquarian and second-hand books, Black's colour books, prints, English period Victorian furniture
Open Mon–Sat 10am–6pm Sun 11am–5pm

⊞ Day Antiques (BADA, CADA)
Contact Mrs A or Roger Day
✉ **5 New Church Street, Tetbury, Gloucestershire, GL8 8DS** 🅿
☎ 01666 502413 Ⓕ 01666 505894
Ⓜ 07836 565763
Ⓔ dayantiques@lineone.net
Ⓦ www.dayantiques.com
Est. 1975 ***Stock size*** Medium
Stock Early oak, country furniture, related items
Open Mon–Sat 10am–5.30pm

⊞ The Decorator Source (TADA)
Contact Mr Colin Gee
✉ **39a Long Street, Tetbury, Gloucestershire, GL8 8AA** 🅿
☎ 01666 505358
Est. 1979 ***Stock size*** Large
Stock French provincial furniture, accessories, English country house furniture and objects
Open Mon–Sat 10am–5.30pm or by appointment
Services Shipping

⊞ Anne Fowler (TADA)
Contact Anne Fowler
✉ **35 Long Street, Tetbury, Gloucestershire, GL8 8AA** 🅿
☎ 01666 504043
Ⓜ 07770 754043
Est. 1995 ***Stock size*** Medium
Stock Mirrors, lustres, oil paintings, prints, linen, early garden and painted furniture, faïence, pottery, French items a speciality
Open Mon–Sat 10am–5.30pm
Fairs Bath Fair (March)
Services Interior design

⊞ Catherine Hunt (TADA)
Contact Catherine Hunt
✉ **The Antique Centre, 51A Long Street, Tetbury, Gloucestershire, GL8 8AA** 🅿
☎ 01242 227794 Ⓕ 01242 227794
Ⓜ 07976 319344
Est. 1986 ***Stock size*** Large
Stock Chinese ceramics, Ming, Qing etc, furniture, textiles from Ming onwards
Open Mon–Sun 10am–5pm or by appointment
Fairs Wilton House, Petersfield

⊞ Jester Antiques (TADA)
Contact Mr Peter Bairsto
✉ **10 Church Street, Tetbury, Gloucestershire, GL8 8JG** 🅿
☎ 01666 505125
Ⓜ 07974 2327883
Est. 1995 ***Stock size*** Medium
Stock Exciting, colourful stock of furniture, decorative items, lamps, mirrors, garden and architectural antiques, specializing in wall, mantel and longcase clocks
Open Mon–Sun 10am–5.30pm
Fairs Westonbirt, Sudeley Castle
Services Shipping

⊞ Merlin Antiques
Contact Mr Brian Smith
✉ **Shops 4 & 5, Chippingcourt Shopping Mall, Chipping Street, Tetbury, Gloucestershire, GL8 8ES** 🅿
☎ 01666 505008
Est. 1996 ***Stock size*** Large
Stock Mixed, china, pictures, Victorian–Edwardian furniture, costume jewellery, reproduction furniture, garden stoneware
Open Mon–Sat 9.30am–5pm Sun by appointment
Services Valuations, repairs, items purchased, single or house clearance

⊞ Bobbie Middleton (TADA, CADA)
Contact Bobbie Middleton
✉ **58 Long Street, Tetbury, Gloucestershire, GL8 8AQ** 🅿
☎ 01666 502761 Ⓕ 01454 238619
Ⓜ 07774 192660
Ⓔ bobbymiddleton@lineone.net
Est. 1986 ***Stock size*** Medium
Stock Classic country house furniture, mirrors, sconces, decorative accessories, 18th–19thC upholstered furniture
Open Mon–Sat 10am–5pm closed 1–2.30pm
Services Search for pieces

⊞ Morpheus Beds
Contact Mrs Betty Symes
✉ **Elgin House, 1 New Church Street, Tetbury, Gloucestershire, GL8 8DT** 🅿
☎ 01666 504068 Ⓕ 01666 503352
Ⓔ info@antique-beds.co.uk
Ⓦ www.antique-beds.co.uk
Est. 1984 ***Stock size*** Large
Stock Antique beds, bedroom furniture, accessories
Open Mon–Sat 9am–5.30pm Sun by appointment

⊞ Peter Norden Antiques (LAPADA, TADA)
Contact Mr P Norden
✉ **61 Long Street, Tetbury, Gloucestershire, GL8 8AA** 🅿
☎ 01666 503854 Ⓕ 01666 503854
Ⓜ 07778 013108
Est. 1960 ***Stock size*** Medium
Stock Early oak and country furniture, early wood carvings, pewter, brass, treen

Open Mon–Sat 10am–5.30pm or by appointment
Services Valuations

⊞ Old Mill Market Shop
Contact Maurice or Judy Green
✉ 12 Church Street, Tetbury, Gloucestershire, GL8 8JG 🅿
☎ 01666 503127
Ⓜ 07714 766237
Est. 1970 *Stock size* Medium
Stock Silver, jewellery, china, glass, pine, metalware, small furniture
Open Mon–Fri 10am–5.30pm Sat 10am–5pm closed Thurs pm

Key to Symbols

⊞ = Dealer
Antiques Centre symbol = Antiques Centre
Auction House symbol = Auction House
✉ = Address
🅿 = Parking
☎ = Telephone No.
Ⓜ = Mobile tel No.
Ⓕ = Fax No.
Ⓔ = E-mail address
Ⓦ = Website address

⊞ Porch House Antiques (TADA)
Contact Mrs L A Woodburn
✉ 42 Long Street, Tetbury, Gloucestershire, GL8 8AQ 🅿
☎ 01666 502687
Ⓜ 07712 283582
Est. 1976 *Stock size* Large
Stock 17th–20thC furniture, decorative items
Open Mon–Sat 10am–5pm

⊞ Sieff (TADA, LAPADA)
Contact Kirsty Sylvester
✉ 49 Long Street, Tetbury, Gloucestershire, GL8 8AA 🅿
☎ 01666 504477 Ⓕ 01666 504478
Ⓔ sieff@sieff.co.uk
Ⓦ www.sieff.co.uk
Est. 1984 *Stock size* Large
Stock 18th–19thC French provincial fruitwood, 20thC furniture
Open Mon–Sat 10am–5.30pm
Fairs Decorative Antique & Textile Fair

⊞ Westwood House Antiques (TADA)
Contact R Griffiths
✉ 29 Long Street, Tetbury, Gloucestershire, GL8 8AA 🅿
☎ 01666 502328 Ⓕ 01666 502328
Est. 1993 *Stock size* Large
Stock 17th–19thC oak, elm and ash country furniture, some French fruitwood, decorative pottery, pewter, treen
Open Mon–Sat 10am–5.30pm

TEWKESBURY

⊞ Berkeley Antiques
Contact Peter or Susan Dennis
✉ The Wheatsheaf, High Street, Tewkesbury, Gloucestershire, GL20 5JR 🅿
☎ 01684 292034 Ⓜ 07836 243397
Est. 1973 *Stock size* Medium
Stock 17th–19thC antique furniture, accessories to match
Open Mon–Sat 10am–5.30pm closed Thurs pm
Services Restorations

⊞ Cornell Books Ltd
Contact Mr G Cornell
✉ 93 Church Street, Tewkesbury, Gloucestershire, GL20 5RS 🅿
☎ 01684 293337 Ⓕ 01684 273959
Ⓔ gtcornell@aol.com
Est. 1996 *Stock size* Medium
Stock Antiquarian and second-hand books
Open Mon–Sat 10.30am–5pm

⊞ Gainsborough House
Contact A or B Hillson
✉ 81 Church Street, Tewkesbury, Gloucestershire, GL20 5RX 🅿
☎ 01684 293072
Est. 1962 *Stock size* Large
Stock Period furniture, porcelain, silver
Open Mon–Sat 10am–5pm closed Thurs

Tewkesbury Antiques Centre
Contact Mrs Coral Pearce
✉ Tolsey Hall, Tolsey Lane, Tewkesbury, Gloucestershire, GL20 5AE 🅿
☎ 01684 294091 Ⓕ 01531 822211
Est. 1991 *Stock size* Large
No. of dealers 10
Stock Antiques, bric-a-brac, collectables, books, records, jewellery, furniture
Open Mon–Sat 10am–5pm Sun 11am–5pm

⊞ Whatnots Antiques of Tewkesbury
Contact Mr D Lothian
✉ 24 St Mary's Lane,Tewkesbury, Gloucestershire, GL20 5SF 🅿
☎ 01684 294154
Est. 1988 *Stock size* Large
Stock General small antiques, small furniture, pictures, curios
Open Mon–Sat 11am–5pm

THORNBURY

⊞ Castle Antiques
Contact Steven Davies
✉ 2 Castle Street, Thornbury, Gloucestershire, BS35 1HB 🅿
☎ 01454 880006 Ⓕ 01454 880007
Est. 1995 *Stock size* Medium
Stock General antiques
Open Mon–Sat 10am–6pm

WINCHCOMBE

⊞ Government House Quality Antique Lighting
Contact Mr M Bailey
✉ St Georges House, High Street, Winchcombe, Gloucestershire, GL54 5LJ 🅿
☎ 01242 604562 Ⓜ 07970 430684
Est. 1980 *Stock size* Large
Stock Pre-1939 lighting
Open By appointment
Services Restorations

⊞ In Period Antiques
Contact John Edgeler
✉ Queen Anne House, High Street, Winchcombe, Gloucestershire, GL54 5LJ 🅿
☎ 01242 602319
Est. 1999 *Stock size* Medium
Stock 17th–19thC furniture, metalwork, glass, porcelain, decorative items
Open Thurs–Sat 9.30am–5pm or by appointment
Services Valuations

⊞ Newsum Antiques (CADA)
Contact Mark Newsum
✉ 2 High Street, Winchcombe, Gloucestershire, GL54 5HT
☎ 01242 603446 Ⓜ 07968 196668
Est. 1985 *Stock size* Medium
Stock Oak and country furniture, treen, Swedish metalware
Open Tues–Sat 10.30am–5pm
Fairs Battersea, NEC

⊞ Prichard Antiques (CADA)
Contact Keith or Debbie Prichard
✉ 16 High Street, Winchcombe, Gloucestershire, GL54 5LJ 🅿

☎ 01242 603566
Est. 1979 ***Stock size*** Large
Stock 17th–19thC formal and country furniture, clocks, treen, boxes, metalware, decorative items, garden furniture
Open Mon–Sat 9am–5.30pm

WOTTON-UNDER-EDGE

Bell Passage Antiques (LAPADA)
Contact Mrs D Brand
36–38 High Street, Wickwar, Wotton-under-Edge, Gloucestershire, GL12 8NP P
☎ 01454 294251
Est. 1966 ***Stock size*** Medium
Stock General antiques, furniture, glass, porcelain
Open Mon–Sat 9am–5pm closed Thurs or by appointment
Services Restorations, upholstery, caning

Wotton Auction Rooms
Contact Mr Philip Taubenheim
Tabernacle Road, Wotton-under-Edge, Gloucestershire, GL12 7EB P
☎ 01453 844733 F 01453 845448
E info@wottonauctionrooms.co.uk
W www.wottonauctionrooms.co.uk
Est. 1991
Open Mon–Fri 9am–5pm
Sales Tues smalls, Wed furniture, viewing Mon 10am–7pm Tues 9–10.30am
Frequency Monthly
Catalogues Yes

HEREFORDSHIRE

HAY-ON-WYE

Addyman Books
Contact Anne Brichto
39 Lion Street, Hay-on-Wye, Herefordshire, HR3 5AA
☎ 01497 821136 F 01497 821732
E madness@addyman-books.demon.co.uk
W www.addyman-books.co.uk
Est. 1987 ***Stock size*** Medium
Stock Antiquarian and second-hand books specializing in English literature, modern first editions
Open Mon–Sat 10am–6pm Sun 10.30am–5.30pm

C Arden Bookseller (PBFA)
Contact Mrs C Arden
Radnor House, Church Street, Hay-on-Wye, Herefordshire, HR3 5DQ P
☎ 01497 820471 F 01497 820498
E c.arden@virgin.net
W www.ardenbooks.co.uk
Est. 1992 ***Stock size*** Large
Stock Antiquarian books on natural history, gardening, botany
Open Mon–Sat 10.30am–5.30pm Sun 11am–4pm please telephone
Fairs PBFA

The Book Shop
Contact Andy Cooke
Pavement House, The Pavement, Hay-on-Wye, Herefordshire, HR3 5BU
☎ 01497 821341
Est. 1987 ***Stock size*** Large
Stock Antiquarian books, general stock
Open Mon–Sat 9am–8pm Sun 9am–5pm

Richard Booth's Bookshop Ltd
Contact Mr R G W Booth
44 Lion Street, Hay-on-Wye, Herefordshire, HR3 5AA P
☎ 01497 820322 F 01497 821150
E postmaster@richardbooth.demon.co.uk
W www.richardbooth.demon.co.uk
Est. 1969 ***Stock size*** Large
Stock Antiquarian and second-hand books
Open Mon–Sat Summer 9am–8pm Winter 9am–5.30pm Sun 11.30am–5.30pm
Services Book search

Boz Books (ABA)
Contact Peter Harries
13a Castle Street, Hay-on-Wye, Herefordshire, HR3 5DF P
☎ 01497 821277 F 01497 821277
E peter@bozbooks.demon.co.uk
W www.bozbooks.demon.co.uk
Est. 1989 ***Stock size*** Medium
Stock Antiquarian, rare, second-hand books, 19thC English literature
Open Mon–Sat 10am–5pm closed 1–2pm variable in winter
Services Book search

Bullring Antiques
Contact Mrs S Spencer
Bear Street, Hay-on-Wye, Herefordshire, HR3 5AN
☎ 01487 820467
Est. 1994 ***Stock size*** Medium
No. of dealers 6
Stock Wide general stock of good-quality antiques
Open Mon–Sat 10am–5pm Sun 11am–5pm

The Children's Bookshop
Contact Judith Gardener
Toll Cottage, Pontvaen, Hay-on-Wye, Herefordshire, HR3 5EW P
☎ 01497 821083 F 01497 821083
E judith@childrensbookshop.com
W www.childrensbookshop.com
Est. 1981 ***Stock size*** Medium
Stock 18th–20thC children's books
Open Mon–Sat 9.30am–5.30pm Sun 10am–5pm
Services Book search catalogue on website

Hancock & Monks
Contact Jerry Monks
15 Broad Street, Hay-on-Wye, Herefordshire, HR3 5DB P
☎ 01497 821784 F 01591 610778
E jerry@hancockandmonks.co.uk
W www.hancockandmonks.co.uk
Est. 1974 ***Stock size*** Medium
Stock Antiquarian books on music, antiquarian sheet music
Open Mon–Sat 11am–5pm
Services Book search

Hay Antique Market
Contact Jenny Price
6 Market Street, Hay-on-Wye, Herefordshire, HR3 5AF P
☎ 01497 820175
Est. 1989 ***Stock size*** Large
No. of dealers 17
Stock China, glass, jewellery, linen, country furniture, period furniture, rural and rustic items, period clothing, lighting, pictures, brass
Open Mon–Sat 10am–5pm Sun 11am–5pm

Hay Cinema Bookshop (PBFA)
Contact Mr Greg Coombes
The Old Cinema, Castle Street, Hay-on-Wye, Herefordshire, HR3 5DF P
☎ 01497 820071 F 01497 821900
E sales@francisedwards.demon.co.uk
W www.francisedwards.co.uk
Est. 1855 ***Stock size*** Large
Stock Antiquarian and second-hand books, leather-bound

books, art, antiques topics a speciality
Open Mon–Sat 9am–7pm Sun 11.30am–5.30pm
Fairs PBFA

Hay on Wye Booksellers
Contact Mrs J Jordan
14 High Town, Hay-on-Wye, Herefordshire, HR3 5AE
☎ 01497 820875 F 01497 847129
M 07977 141745
E madness@hay-on-wyebooks.com
W www.hay-on-wyebooks.com
Est. 1969 ***Stock size*** Large
Stock Antiquarian, second-hand cut-price new books, publishers' returns
Open Mon–Sun 9.30am–6pm

G B & P E Hebbord
Contact Mrs P Hebbord
7–8 Market Street, Hay-on-Wye, Herefordshire, HR3 5AF
☎ 01497 820413
Est. 1964 ***Stock size*** Large
Stock 18th–19thC English pottery, porcelain
Open Mon–Sat 9am–4.30pm closed Tues

Lion Fine Arts
Contact Mr Charles Spencer
19 Lion Street, Hay-on-Wye, Herefordshire, HR3 5AD
☎ 01497 821726
M 01497 821058
W www.hay-on-wye.co.uk/LionFine
Est. 1995 ***Stock size*** Medium
Stock Small antique furniture, porcelain, pottery, Georgian–early 19thC glass, old prints, treen, interesting collectables, antique books
Open Mon Thurs Sat 10am–5pm other days variable telephone beforehand
Services Restorations

Lion Street Books
Contact Mr Mark Williams
1 St John's Place, Hay-on-Wye, Herefordshire, HR3 5BN
☎ 01497 820121 F 01497 820121
E mark@boxingstuff.com
W www.boxingstuff.com
Est. 1993 ***Stock size*** Large
Stock Boxing memorabilia, books, programmes, magazines, photos
Open Mon–Sat 10am–5pm
Services Mail order catalogue

Murder & Mayhem
Contact Mr Addyman
5 Lion Street, Hay-on-Wye, Herefordshire, HR3 5AA
☎ 01497 821613 F 01497 821732
E madness@hay-on-wyebooks.com
W www.hay-on-wyebooks.com
Est. 1997 ***Stock size*** Medium
Stock Antiquarian and second-hand books, specializing in detective fiction, crime, horror
Open Mon–Sat Sun in season 10.30am–5.30

Rose's Books
Contact Mrs M Goddard
14 Broad Street, Hay-on-Wye, Herefordshire, HR3 5DB
☎ 01497 820013 F 01497 820031
E enquiry@rosesbooks.com
W www.rosesbooks.com
Est. 1984 ***Stock size*** Medium
Stock Specializing in rare, out-of-print, children's, illustrated books
Open Mon–Sun 9.30am–5pm
Services Book search, catalogues

Mark Westwood Books (ABA, PBFA)
Contact Evelyn Westwood
Grove House, High Town, Hay-on-Wye, Herefordshire, HR3 5AE
☎ 01497 820068 F 01497 821641
E books@markwestwood.demon.co.uk
Est. 1976 ***Stock size*** Medium
Stock Antique, scholarly second-hand books on most subjects, specializing in the history of science and medicine
Open Mon–Sun 10.30am–6pm
Fairs Oxford

HEREFORD

The Antique Tea Shop
Contact Miss J Cockin
5a St Peters Street, Hereford, Herefordshire, HR1 2LA
☎ 01432 342172
Est. 1990 ***Stock size*** Small
Stock Small items, pastry forks, afternoon tea knives, 1920s–1930s jewellery, French furniture, mirrors, ceramics
Open Mon–Sun 9.45am–5.30pm
Services Tea shop

Bourneville Books
Contact Mr F Nutt
95 White Cross Road, Hereford, Herefordshire, HR4 0DQ
☎ 01432 261263
Est. 1990 ***Stock size*** Medium
Stock Second-hand, collectable, antiquarian, rare books, prints, watercolours, books for decoration
Open Mon–Sat 9.30am–5.30pm
Fairs Newark

I and J L Brown Ltd
Contact Mr Simon Hilton
Whitestone Park, Whitestone, Hereford, Herefordshire, HR1 3SE
☎ 01432 851991 F 01432 851994
E enquiries@brownantiques.com
W www.brownantiques.com
Est. 1978 ***Stock size*** Large
Stock English country, French provincial furniture, largest source in UK, make reproduction furniture, especially Windsor chairs
Open Mon–Sat 9am–5.30pm or by appointment
Services Re-rushing, restoration

Hereford Antique Centre
Contact Georgina Smith
128 Widemarsh Street, Hereford, Herefordshire, HR4 9HN
☎ 01432 266242
Est. 1989 ***Stock size*** Large
No. of dealers 30–35
Stock Furniture, pictures, fireplaces, china etc
Open Mon–Sat 10am–5pm Sun noon–5pm

Hereford Map Centre (IMTA)
Contact Mr J Davey
24–25 Church Street, Hereford, Herefordshire, HR1 2LR
☎ 01432 266322 F 01432 341874
E info@themapcentre.com
W www.themapcentre.com
Est. 1984 ***Stock size*** Large
Stock Old maps of varying scales, 1:10,000, 1:2,500, 1:500, tythe maps, hand-painted, County Series maps
Open Mon–Sat 9am–5.30pm
Services Laminating, mounting

Sunderlands Sale Rooms
Contact Mr Graham Baker
Newmarket Street, Hereford, Herefordshire, HR4 9HX
☎ 01432 266894 F 01432 266901
W www.sunderlandshereford.co.uk

Est. 1868
Open Mon–Fri 9am–5.30pm
Sales General furniture sale Mon 5pm. Antiques sale every 2 months Tues 11am, viewing Mon Tues prior to sale (phone Head Office on 01432 356161 for further details)
Frequency Fortnightly
Catalogues No

⊞ Waring's Antiques
Contact Mrs E Sullivan
✉ **45–47 St Owen Street, Hereford, Herefordshire, HR1 2JB**
☎ 01432 276241
Est. 1959 *Stock size* Large
Stock General antiques, collectables, pine, both new and old
Open Mon–Sat 9am–5pm

KINGTON

⊞ Castle Hill Books
Contact Mr P Newman
✉ **12 Church Street, Kington, Herefordshire, HR5 3AZ** 🅿
☎ 01544 231195 Ⓕ 01544 231161
Ⓔ newmans@castlehill.kc3.co.uk
Est. 1989 *Stock size* Medium
Stock New, antiquarian, out-of-print, second-hand books, general stock, most subjects covered, some specialist subjects including archaeology, British and Welsh topography
Open Mon–Sat 10am–5pm closed 1–2pm
Services Book search, valuations, restorations

LEDBURY

⊞ John Nash Antiques and Interiors (LAPADA, IDDA)
Contact John Nash
✉ **17c High Street, Ledbury, Herefordshire, HR8 1DS** 🅿
☎ 01531 635714 Ⓕ 01531 635050
Ⓜ 07831 382970
Ⓦ www.johnnash.co.uk
Est. 1973 *Stock size* Medium
Stock 18th–19thC fine mahogany and walnut furniture
Open Mon–Sat 9am–5.30pm Sun by appointment
Services Valuations, restorations, interior design

H J Pugh and Co
Contact Mr Howard Pugh
✉ **Ledbury Sale Rooms, Market Street, Ledbury, Herefordshire, HR8 2AQ** 🅿
☎ 01531 631122 Ⓕ 01531 631818
Ⓔ auctions@hjpugh.com
Ⓦ www.hjpugh.com
Est. 1990
Open Mon–Fri 9am–5.30pm
Sales General antiques sale Tues 6pm, viewing Tues 10am–6pm prior to sale
Frequency Monthly
Catalogues No

⊞ Serendipity
Contact Mrs R Ford
✉ **The Tythings, Preston Court, Ledbury, Herefordshire, HR8 2LL** 🅿
☎ 01531 660245 Ⓕ 01531 660421
Ⓔ sales@serendipity-antiques.co.uk
Ⓦ www.serendipity-antiques.co.uk
Est. 1969 *Stock size* Large
Stock 18thC furniture, long dining tables, four-poster beds
Open Mon–Sat 9am–5.30pm
Fairs Olympia, Battersea
Services Restorations

⊞ Keith Smith Books
Contact Mr K Smith
✉ **78b The Homend, Ledbury, Herefordshire, HR8 1BX** 🅿
☎ 01531 635336
Ⓔ keith@ksbooks.demon.co.uk
Est. 1989 *Stock size* Medium
Stock Antiquarian, general, second-hand books, WWI poetry, needlecrafts, anything interesting
Open Mon–Sat 10am–5pm
Fairs Royal National Hotel London
Services Book search

LEOMINSTER

Brightwells
Contact Roger Williams
✉ **The Fine Art Sale Room, Ryelands Road, Leominster, Herefordshire, HR6 8NZ** 🅿
☎ 01568 611122 Ⓕ 01568 610519
Ⓔ fineart@brightwells.com
Ⓦ www.catalogs.icollector.com/brightwells
Est. 1846
Open Mon–Fri 9am–5pm
Sales Antiques sale Wed Thurs 10am, viewing Tues 9am–5pm. 5–6 ceramics sales per year Wed 11am, viewing Tues 9am–5pm
Frequency 3–4 sales per month
Catalogues Yes

⊞ Jeffery Hammond Antiques (LAPADA)
Contact Mr J Hammond
✉ **Shaftesbury House, 38 Broad Street, Leominster, Herefordshire, HR6 8BS** 🅿
☎ 01568 614876 Ⓕ 01568 614876
Ⓔ enquiries@jefferyhammondantiques.co.uk
Ⓦ www.jefferyhammondantiques.co.uk
Est. 1970 *Stock size* Medium
Stock Good quality 18th–early 19thC walnut, mahogany, rosewood furniture, some clocks, paintings, mirrors
Open Mon–Sat 9am–5.30pm or by appointment
Services Valuations for insurance, probate

Leominster Antique Centre
Contact Mr J Weston
✉ **34 Broad Street, Leominster, Herefordshire, HR6 8BS** 🅿
☎ 01568 615505
Est. 1998 *Stock size* Large
No. of dealers 35
Stock Period furniture, early porcelain, pottery, objets d'art, antiquarian books, garden furniture
Open Mon–Sat 10am–5pm. Sun 11am–4pm
Services Tea rooms, gardens

Leominster Antique Market
Contact Mrs O G Dyke
✉ **14 Broad Street, Leominster, Herefordshire, HR6 8BS** 🅿
☎ 01568 612189
Est. 1975 *Stock size* Large
No. of dealers 16
Stock Glass, china, silver, pine, furniture
Open Mon–Sat 10am–5pm April–Sept Sun 11am–3pm

Linden House Antiques
Contact Michael Clayton or Caroline Scott Mayfield
✉ **1 Drapers Lane, Leominster, Herefordshire, HR6 8ND** 🅿
Ⓜ 07790 671722
Ⓔ busca@lineone.net
Est. 1972 *Stock size* Large
No. of dealers 10

Stock Furniture, lighting, glass, silver, porcelain, paintings, early country pewter etc, collectables
Open Mon–Sat 11am–6pm
Sun by appointment
Services Valuations (free if brought to shop on Sat)

Old Merchant's House Antiques Centre
Contact Elaine Griffin
10 Corn Square, Leominster, Herefordshire, HR6 8LR
01568 616141 F 01568 616141
Est. 1997 *Stock size* Large
No. of dealers 26
Stock General antiques, collectables, antiquarian and second-hand books
Open Mon–Sat 10am–5pm
Services Re-upholstery, cabinet making

Utter Clutter
Contact Mrs L M Mackenzie
16 West Street, Leominster, Herefordshire, HR6 8ES
01568 611277
Est. 1995 *Stock size* Medium
Stock General antiques, collectables, early toys
Open Mon–Sat 10am–4.30pm

PONTRILAS

Nigel Ward & Co.
Contact Mr Nigel Ward
The Border Property Centre, Pontrilas, Herefordshire, HR2 0EH
01981 240140 F 01981 240857
Est. 1988
Open Office Hours Mon–Fri 9am–5.30pm
Sales Monthly sales, usually held at the Ewyas Harold Memorial Hall, of antique and country furniture, porcelain and collectables
Frequency monthly
Catalogues Yes

ROSS-ON-WYE

Fritz Fryer (LAPADA)
Contact Mr Fritz Fryer or Margaret Lewis
12 Brookend Street, Ross-on-Wye, Herefordshire, HR9 7EG
01989 567416 F 01989 566742
E fritz@fritzfryer.co.uk
W www.fritzfryer.co.uk
Est. 1982 *Stock size* Large
Stock Antique–1950 lighting, crystal chandeliers, gasoliers, wall lights, table lights, nickel and silver fittings, industrial and post-modern lights
Open Mon–Sat 10am–5.30pm
Services Lighting design, restorations, conversion, shipping, removals and delivery

Andy Gibbs
29 Brookend Street, Ross-on-Wye, Herefordshire, HR9 7EE
01989 566833
M 07850 354480
Est. 1993 *Stock size* Large
Stock Furniture including dining tables, chairs, reformed Gothic and Gothic revival
Open Mon–Sat 10 am–1pm 2–5.30pm
Fairs Dublin Feb
Services Valuations, restorations

W John Griffiths Antiques
Contact Mr Griffiths
30a Brookend Street, Ross-on-Wye, Herefordshire, HR9 7EE
M 07768 606507
Est. 1997 *Stock size* Medium
Stock 18th–early 20thC primarily mahogany furniture, decorative objects, pictures, paintings, prints
Open Mon–Sat 10 am–1pm 2–5.30pm

Robin Lloyd Antiques
Contact Mr R R Knightley
23–24 Brookend Street, Ross-on-Wye, Herefordshire, HR9 7EE
01989 562123 F 01989 562123
E robin@robinlloydantiques.fsnet.co.uk
Est. 1972 *Stock size* Large
Stock Welsh country furniture, longcase clocks, farmhouse tables
Open Mon–Sat 10am–5.30pm
Services Valuations

The Merchant House
Contact Mr Neil Cockman
36 High Street, Ross-on-Wye, Herefordshire, HR9 5HD
01989 563010
Est. 1998 *Stock size* Large
Stock Antique lighting, country furniture, early oak, interior furnishings, small curio items, objets d'art
Open Mon–Sat 10am–5pm

Morris Bricknell
Contact Mr Nigel Morris
Stroud House, Gloucester Road, Ross-on-Wye, Herefordshire, HR9 5BU
01989 768320 F 01989 768345
Est. 1989
Open Mon–Fri 9am–5.30pm
Sales General antiques sale Sat 10.30am at V H Whitechurch and Goodrich, viewing Sat 8.30am prior to sale. Occasional special and marquee sales (phone for details)
Frequency Monthly
Catalogues No

Ross Antiques Market
Contact Mr R Kempson
Fiveways, Ross-on-Wye, Herefordshire, HR9 7EG
01989 566700 F 01989 566700
E isabelle@french2english.co.uk
Est. 1997 *Stock size* Medium
No. of dealers 4
Stock Country pine, oak, mahogany furniture, chandeliers, some smalls
Open Tues–Sat 10am–5pm
Services Restorations, stripping

Ross Old Books and Print Shop (PBFA)
Contact Mr P Thredder
51–52 High Street, Ross-on-Wye, Herefordshire, HR9 5HH
01989 567458 F 01989 567861
E enquiries@rossoldbooks.co.uk
W www.antiqueprints.com/abebooks.com
Est. 1987 *Stock size* Medium
Stock Antique, second-hand, rare books selling for £1–£1,000, also maps
Open Mon–Sat 10am–5pm closed mid-Jan to mid-Feb
Fairs PBFA
Services Post inland and overseas

Ross-on-Wye Antique Gallery
Contact Mr Michael Aslanian
Gloucester Road, Ross-on-Wye, Herefordshire, HR9 5BU
01989 762290 F 01989 762291
Est. 1996 *Stock size* Large
No. of dealers 50
Stock Gothic-style church, period

furniture, oak, country furniture, works of art, antique books, silver, gold, jewellery, English and Continental porcelain, English and French glass, Oriental antiques, rugs, Art Deco, spoons, other cutlery, longcase clocks
Open Mon–Sat 10.30am–5pm Bank Holidays by appointment
Services Valuations

Waterfall Antiques
Contact Mr O McCarthy
2 High Street, Ross-on-Wye, Herefordshire, HR9 5HL
01989 563103
Est. 1991 *Stock size* Large
Stock Pine and country furniture
Open Mon–Sat 9.30am–4.30pm half day Wed Fri
Fairs Newark

Williams & Watkins Auctioneers Ltd
Contact Roger Garlick
Ross-on-Wye Auction Centre, Overcross, Ross-on-Wye, Herefordshire, HR9 7QF
01989 762225 F 01989 566082
Est. 1866
Open Mon–Fri 9am–5pm
Sales Wed 10am. General antiques sales, viewing Tues 1–7pm and day of sale 9–10am
Frequency monthly
Catalogues yes

HERTFORDSHIRE

ABBOTS LANGLEY

Dobson's Antiques
Contact Mr Fred W Dobson
53 High Street, Abbots Langley, Hertfordshire, WD5 0AA
01923 263186
Est. 1969 *Stock size* Medium
Stock General antiques, shipping
Open Mon–Sat 8.30am–5.30pm Tues 8.30am–1pm
Services House clearance

BALDOCK

Ralph & Bruce Moss
Contact Mr B Moss
26 Whitehorse Street, Baldock, Hertfordshire, SG7 6QQ
01462 892751 F 01462 892751
Est. 1973 *Stock size* Large
Stock 17th–early 19thC furniture, porcelain, clocks, maps, prints, silver, small items
Open Mon–Sat 9am–6pm

BARNET

Antiques Little Shop
Contact Mrs F O'Gorman
2 Bruce Road, Barnet, Hertfordshire, EN5 4LS
020 8449 9282
Est. 1996 *Stock size* Medium
Stock Furniture, collectables, Georgian–1950s
Open Wed–Sat 10am–5pm Fri 11am–5pm

Barnet Bygones
Contact Mrs M Phillips
2 Bruce Road, Barnet, Hertfordshire, EN5 4LS
020 8440 7304
Est. 1994 *Stock size* Large
No. of dealers 5
Stock Furniture, smalls, collectables
Open Wed Fri Sat 9am–5pm

C Bellinger Antiques
Contact Mr C Bellinger
91 Wood Street, Barnet, Hertfordshire, EN5 4BX
020 8449 3467
Est. 1971 *Stock size* Small
Stock General antiques
Open Thurs–Sat 10am–3pm

BERKHAMSTED

Berkhamsted Auction Rooms
Contact Mr A Harris
Middle Road, Berkhamsted, Hertfordshire, HP4 3EQ
01442 865169
Est. 1920
Open Mon–Fri 9am–4.30pm
Sales Antiques, modern furniture and effects Wed 10am, viewing day prior 10am–4pm 6–8pm
Frequency Monthly
Catalogues Yes

BOREHAMWOOD

Barnet-Cattanach Antiques (BADA, LAPADA)
Contact Mr R J Gerry
The Old Marble Works, Glenhaven Avenue, Borehamwood, Hertfordshire, WD6 1BB
020 8207 6792 F 020 8381 5889
E acattana@uk.packardbell.org
Est. 1964 *Stock size* Large
Stock 18thC period furniture, accessories
Open By appointment only
Fairs Olympia (June, Sept)
Services Restorations, carriage

The Book Exchange
Contact Mr Brian Berman
120 Shenley Road, Borehamwood, Hertfordshire, WD6 1EF
020 8236 0966 F 020 8953 6673
E dee4bee@compuserve.com
Est. 1993 *Stock size* Large
Stock General antiquarian, second-hand, some new books
Open Mon–Sat 9.30am–5.30pm
Services Book search

BUSHEY

Circa Antiques
Contact Kay Wildman
43 High Street, Bushey, Watford, Hertfordshire, WD2 1BD
020 8950 9233
E kayesley@aol.com
Est. 1969 *Stock size* Large
Stock Victorian–Edwardian furniture, china, silver, clocks
Open Mon–Sat 9.30am–5pm
Fairs NEC
Services House clearance

Country Life Antiques
Contact Mr Peter Myers
33a High Street, Bushey, Watford, Hertfordshire, WD23 1BD
020 8950 8575 F 020 8950 6982
E countrylifeantiques@busheyherts.freeserve.co.uk
W www.countrylifeantiques.co.uk
Est. 1982 *Stock size* Large
Stock Victorian pine, reproduction pine in old wood, oak furniture, limited-edition prints, watercolours, general smalls, giftware, fitted kitchens
Open Mon–Sat 9am–5pm Sun 10.30am–3.30pm
Services Worldwide shipping arranged

BUSHEY HEATH

C and B Antiques
Contact Carol Epstein
22 Brooke Way, Bushey Heath, Watford, Hertfordshire, WD23 4LG
020 8950 1844 F 020 8950 1844

Ⓜ 07831 647274
Est. 1979 *Stock size* Large
Stock 1790–1930 porcelain and small furniture
Open By appointment or at fairs
Fairs The Moat House, The Bell House, Shepton Mallet
Services Valuations

⊞ Marcel Cards (Cartophilic Society)
Contact Marcel Epstein
✉ **22 Brooke Way, Bushey Heath, Watford, Hertfordshire, WD23 4LG** Ⓟ
☎ 020 8950 1844 Ⓕ 020 8950 1844
Ⓜ 07887 648255
Est. 1991 *Stock size* Large
Stock Cigarette cards 1890–1939, new collectors' cards, tea, bubblegum cards
Open By appointment and at Marcel Fairs
Fairs Peterborough, Ardingly, Dunstable
Services Odd cards to complete sets, card search, valuations

CHESHUNT

⊞ Cheshunt Antiques
Contact Mr Peter Howard
✉ **126–128 Turners Hill, Cheshunt, Waltham Cross, Hertfordshire, EN8 9BN** Ⓟ
☎ 01992 637337
Est. 1991 *Stock size* Large
Stock Georgian–early 20thC furniture
Open Tues–Fri 10am–2pm Sat 10am–4pm
Fairs Newark
Services Restorations, French polishing

CHORLEYWOOD

⊞ Pattison's Architectural Antiques
Contact Mr T Pattison
✉ **Unit 6, Darvells Works, Common Road, Chorleywood, Rickmansworth, Hertfordshire, WD3 5LP** Ⓟ
☎ 01923 284196 Ⓕ 01923 282214
Ⓔ tony@pattant.com
Est. 1992 *Stock size* Large
Stock Doors, entrance ways, chimney pieces, lighting, stained glass, mirrors, garden statuary, other architecturally unusual items
Open Tues–Sat 9.30am–5.30pm

HEMEL HEMPSTEAD

⊞ Architectural Salvage
Contact Mr L Leadbetter
✉ **Wood Lane, Paradise Industrial Estate, Hemel Hempstead, Hertfordshire, HP2 4TL** Ⓟ
☎ 01442 219936
Est. 1998 *Stock size* Medium
Stock Victorian pews, roll-top baths, internal and external doors, stained glass, French burners, Victorian fireplaces, reclaimed bricks, tiles, floor boarding
Open Mon–Fri 8am–5pm Sat 9am–4.30pm
Services Supply and fit flooring

⊞ Bushwood Antiques (LAPADA)
Contact Mr A Bush
✉ **Stags End Equestrian Centre, Gaddesden Lane, Hemel Hempstead, Hertfordshire, HP2 6HN** Ⓟ
☎ 01582 794700 Ⓕ 01582 792299
Ⓔ antiques@bushwood.co.uk
Ⓦ www.bushwood.co.uk
Est. 1967 *Stock size* Large
Stock 18th–19thC English and Continental furniture, accessories, objets d'art
Open Mon–Fri 8.30am–4pm Sat 10am–4pm

⊞ Cherry Antiques
Contact Mr R S Cullen
✉ **101–103 High Street, Hemel Hempstead, Hertfordshire, HP1 3AH** Ⓟ
☎ 01442 264358
Est. 1981 *Stock size* Medium
Stock General antiques
Open Mon–Sat 9.30am–4.30pm Wed 9.30am–1pm
Services Valuations

⊞ Libritz Stamps
Contact Mr R Hickman
✉ **70 London Road, Apsley, Hemel Hempstead, Hertfordshire, HP3 9SD** Ⓟ
☎ 01442 242691
Est. 1967 *Stock size* Large
Stock Banknotes, stamps, coins, cigarette cards; accessories, albums, catalogues
Open Mon–Sat 10am–6pm
Services Want lists serviced

⊞ Off The Wall Antique Mini Centre
Contact Deborah Tanswell
✉ **52 High Street, Hemel Hempstead, Hertfordshire, HP1 3AF** Ⓟ
☎ 01442 218300
Est. 1998 *Stock size* Large
Stock Eccentric European antiques, collectables
Open Mon–Sat 10am–5.30pm Sun noon–4.30pm
Services Eco-friendly house clearance

HERTFORD

⊞ Beckwith and Son
Contact Mr G Gray
✉ **St Nicholas Hall, St Andrew Street, Hertford, Hertfordshire, SG14 1HZ** Ⓟ
☎ 01992 582079
Est. 1903 *Stock size* Large
Stock 17thC–1930s mahogany, pine, oak furniture, silver, glass, pictures, metalware, general antiques
Open Mon–Sat 9am–1pm 2–5.30pm
Services Restorations, valuations

⊞ Gillmark Map Gallery
Contact Mr Mark Pretlove
✉ **25 Parliament Square, Hertford, Hertfordshire, SG14 1EX** Ⓟ
☎ 01992 534444 Ⓕ 01992 554734
Ⓔ maps@gillmark.idps.co.uk
Ⓦ www.gillmark.com
Est. 1997 *Stock size* Large
Stock Antique maps, prints, second-hand books
Open Tues–Sat 10am–5pm half day Wed
Services Restorations, conservation, framing, hand colouring

⌂ Hertford Antiques
Contact Mr S Garratt
✉ **51 St Andrew Street, Hertford, Hertfordshire, SG14 1HZ** Ⓟ
☎ 01992 504504 Ⓕ 01920 460648
Est. 1994 *Stock size* Large
No. of dealers 60
Stock Everything from period furniture to jewellery
Open Mon–Sun 10am–5.30pm

⊞ Tapestry Antiques
Contact Mrs P Stokes
✉ **27 St Andrew Street, Hertford, Hertfordshire, SG14 1HZ** Ⓟ

☎ 01992 587438
Est. 1974 *Stock size* Large
Stock General 18th–19thC furniture, brass, copper, porcelain, Staffordshire figures
Open Mon–Sat 10am–5pm
Services Valuations, probate

HITCHIN

Antiques Collectables & Furniture
Contact Mr Godfrey
92 Walsworth Road, Hitchin, Hertfordshire, SG4 9SX
☎ 01462 632288
Ⓜ 07711 843032
Est. 1999 *Stock size* Medium
Stock Oil lamp spares, furniture, fixtures & fittings, collectors' reference books, polishes
Open Mon–Sat 10am–5pm Sun 11am–4pm
Services Upholstery

The Book Bug
Contact Mrs S Jevon
1 The Arcade, Hitchin, Hertfordshire, SG5 1ED
☎ 01462 431309
Est. 1984 *Stock size* Large
Stock General second-hand and antiquarian books
Open Mon–Sat 9am–5.30pm

Michael Gander
Contact Mr M Gander
10–11 Bridge Street, Hitchin, Hertfordshire, SG5 2DE
☎ 01462 432678
Ⓜ 07885 728976
Est. 1974 *Stock size* Medium
Stock Period furniture, small items
Open Wed Thurs Sat 9am–5pm or by appointment

Hanbury Antiques
Contact Mrs M D Hanbury
86 Tilehouse Street, Hitchin, Hertfordshire, SG5 2DU
☎ 01462 420487
Est. 1989 *Stock size* Medium
Stock 18thC–20thC furniture, small items
Open Mon–Sat 9am–5pm
Services Valuations

Eric T Moore (ABA)
Contact Katy Maynard-Smith
24 Bridge Street, Hitchin, Hertfordshire, SG5 2DF
☎ 01462 450497
Ⓔ eric.moore.books@virgin.net
Ⓦ www.freespace.virgin.net/eric.moore.books
Est. 1965 *Stock size* Large
Stock General, second-hand, antiquarian books, maps, loose prints
Open Mon–Fri 9.30am–5pm Wed 9.30am–12.30pm Sat 9.30am–5.30pm

Geoffrey Norman
Contact Mr G Norman
93 Walsworth Road, Hitchin, Hertfordshire, SG4 9SX
☎ 01462 421138
Est. 1995 *Stock size* Medium
Stock Collectables, furniture, books, coins, clocks, watches, general antiques
Open Mon–Sat 10am–6pm

Phillips of Hitchin Antiques Ltd (BADA)
Contact Mr J Phillips
The Manor House, 26 Bancroft, Hitchin, Hertfordshire, SG5 1JW
☎ 01462 432067 Ⓕ 01462 441368
Est. 1884 *Stock size* Medium
Stock English furniture, 1730–1830, unusual items such as campaign furniture, new and out-of-print reference books on antique furniture
Open Mon–Sat 9am–5.30pm
Services Restorations

KING'S LANGLEY

Past & Present Antiques and Collectables
Contact Sue Smith
42 High Street, King's Langley, Hertfordshire, WD4 9HT
☎ 01923 291181
Ⓜ 07740 122903
Est. 1996 *Stock size* Medium
Stock Art Deco, jewellery, 1940s–1960s, Victorian furniture
Open Tues–Sat 10am–6pm Sun 11am–5pm Nov and Dec Mon–Sat 10am–6pm Sun 11am–5pm
Services Valuations

LEAVESDEN

Peter Taylor and Son
Contact Mr P Taylor
1 Ganders Ash, Leavesden, Watford, Hertfordshire, WD25 7HE
☎ 01923 663325
Est. 1973 *Stock size* Medium
Stock Tudor and medieval history antique books, documents
Open Catalogue order

REDBOURNE

J N Antiques
Contact Mrs J Brunning
86 High Street, Redbourne, St Albans, Hertfordshire, AL3 7BD
☎ 01582 793603
Est. 1974 *Stock size* Large
Stock General antiques
Open Mon–Sat 9am–6am
Services Valuations

Tim Wharton (LAPADA)
Contact Mr T Wharton
24 High Street, Redbourne, St Albans, Hertfordshire, AL3 7LL
☎ 01582 794371 Ⓕ 01727 751973
Ⓜ 07850 622880
Ⓔ tim@timwhartonantiques.co.uk
Est. 1973 *Stock size* Large
Stock 17th–19thC oak, country furniture, some period mahogany, metalware, treen, country pictures
Open Tues Wed Fri 10am–5pm Sat 10am–4pm Thurs by appointment
Fairs LAPADA (Birmingham), Olympia

RICKMANSWORTH

Galliard Antiques
Contact Mrs E Harriman
144 High Street, Rickmansworth, Hertfordshire, WD3 1AB
☎ 01923 778087 Ⓕ 01923 778087
Ⓜ 07714 068989
Ⓔ galliardi@aol.com
Est. 1996 *Stock size* Medium
Stock General antiques, furniture, pictures, china, militaria, unusual items, coins, Roman and medieval pottery
Open Mon–Thurs Sat 9.30am–5.30pm Fri 9.30am–7pm
Services Valuations

ROYSTON

Philip Dawes Antiques
37–39 Kneesworth Street, Royston, Hertfordshire, SG8 5AB
☎ 01736 243039
Est. 1997 *Stock size* Medium

Stock General antiques, garden furniture
Open Tues–Sat 9.30am–5pm
Services Upholstery, chair caning

SAWBRIDGEWORTH

Arcane Antiques Centre (EADA)
Contact Mr Nigel Hoy or Miss Nicola Smith
The Maltings, Station Road, Sawbridgeworth, Hertfordshire, CM21 9JX
01279 600562 Ⓕ 01279 600562
Ⓜ 07957 551899
Est. 1999 ***Stock size*** Large
Stock Ceramics, glass, silver, oil paintings, watercolours, fine prints, clocks, jewellery, Georgian–Edwardian furniture
Open Tues–Fri 10am–5pm Sat Sun 11am–5pm
Services Antique furniture restoration, cabinet-making, upholstery, cabinet-lining, French polishing, glass repair, picture framing

Herts & Essex Antiques Centre
Contact Mr Michael Hall
The Maltings, Station Road, Sawbridgeworth, Hertfordshire, CM21 9JX
01279 722044
Est. 1981 ***Stock size*** Large
No. of dealers 100
Stock All sorts of antiques, collectables
Open Tues–Fri 10am–5pm Sat Sun 10.30am–6pm
Services Tea room

Riverside Antiques Centre
Contact Mr J Maynard
Unit 1, The Maltings, Station Road, Sawbridgeworth, Hertfordshire, CM21 9JX
01279 600985
Est. 1998 ***Stock size*** Large
No. of dealers 185+
Stock Probably the largest antiques centre in Hertfordshire and Essex. Antiques, collectables, furniture, etc
Open Mon–Sun 10am–5pm
Services Restoration and repair of furniture, glass, ceramics

ST ALBANS

Magic Lanterns (NMTF)
Contact J A Marsden
By George, 23 George Street, St Albans, Hertfordshire, AL3 4ES
01727 865680
Ⓔ minerva639@aol.com
Est. 1987 ***Stock size*** Large
Stock 1800–1950 antique lighting, mirrors, jewellery
Open Mon–Fri 10am–5pm Sat 10am–5.30pm Sun 1–5pm
Services Reproduction Victorian lampshades made to order, lighting consultancy for period houses

Paton Books
Contact Richard Child
34 Holywell Hill, St Albans, Hertfordshire, AL1 1DE
01727 853984 Ⓕ 01727 865764
Ⓦ www.patonbooks.co.uk
Est. 1962 ***Stock size*** Large
Stock General secondhand and antiquarian books
Open Mon–Sat 9am–6pm Sun 10am–6pm

STANDON

Grand Prix Top Gear (MIA)
Contact Mr N Grint
Unit 3, Mill End, Standon, Ware, Hertfordshire, SG11 1LR
07000 553949 Ⓕ 01279 842072
Ⓔ f1@topgear.org
Ⓦ www.topgear.org
Est. 1989 ***Stock size*** Large
Stock Memorabilia. Formula One collectables including car body parts, original team clothing, signed photos, models, caps
Open Mon–Sat 9am–6pm ring first
Fairs Autosport Show NEC, Silverstone GP
Services Mail order and trade suppliers

STEVENAGE

Ayuka Ltd
Contact Mune Ota
25 Broom Walk, Stevenage, Hertfordshire, SG1 1UU
01438 362494 Ⓕ 01438 228494
Ⓔ sales@ayuka.com
Stock size Medium
Stock Pine furniture, small oak, mahogany, other wood furniture
Trade only Yes
Open Mon–Sun 9am–8pm

TRING

John Bly (BADA)
Contact Mr Parris
The Old Billiards Room, Church Yard, Tring, Hertfordshire, WD2 3DH
01442 890802
Est. 1891 ***Stock size*** Large
Stock Georgian furniture, porcelain, silver, glass, other quality antiques
Open Tues–Sat 10am–4pm
Fairs BADA, Olympia
Services Valuations, restorations

Country Clocks
Contact Mr Terry Cartmell
3 Pendley Bridge Cottages, Tring Station, Tring, Hertfordshire, HP23 5QU
01442 825090
Est. 1976 ***Stock size*** Medium
Stock 18th–19thC wall, longcase, mantel clocks
Open Mon–Fri by appointment Sat 9am–5pm Sun 2–5pm
Services Valuations, restorations

Farrelly Antiques
Contact Mr Paul Farrelly
Rear of 50 High Street, Tring, Hertfordshire, HP23 5AG
01442 891905
Est. 1979 ***Stock size*** Medium
Stock Antique furniture up to 1900
Open Mon–Sat 10am–5pm
Services Restorations

New England House Antiques
Contact Mr S Munjee
50 High Street, Tring, Hertfordshire, HP23 5AG
01442 827262 Ⓕ 01442 827262
Est. 1992 ***Stock size*** Large
Stock Georgian–Edwardian furniture, silver, glass, paintings, clocks
Open Tues–Sat 10.30am–5pm
Services Restorations, free search and find for furniture

WATFORD

Bygone Years
Contact Mrs H Alsop
250 St Albans Road, Watford, Hertfordshire, WD2 4AX P
☎ 01923 210623 F 01923 210623
Est. 1998 *Stock size* Medium
Stock Victorian and new furniture, pine, very varied stock of interesting items
Open Mon Tues 10am–2.30am Wed 10am–1pm Thurs–Sat 9am–5.30pm or by appointment
Fairs Newark, Swinderby, Goodwood

Cards Inc
Contact Mr P Freedman
Unit 9, Woodshots Meadow, Croxley Business Park, Watford, Hertfordshire, WD1 8YU P
☎ 01923 200138 F 01923 200134
E paul@cardsinc.com
W www.cardsinc.com
Est. 1987 *Stock size* Small
Stock Collectable trading cards
Open By appointment

Collectors Corner
Contact Mr L Dronkes
Charter Place, Watford Market, Watford, Hertfordshire, WD1 2RN P
☎ 01923 248855/020 8904 0552
Est. 1968 *Stock size* Small
Stock Coins, medals, bank notes, cigarette cards, small collectables
Open Tues Fri Sat 10am–5pm
Services Valuations, medal mounting

Pine Furniture Store
Contact Mrs Sheward
304a Lower High Street, Watford, Hertfordshire, WD1 2JE P
☎ 01923 441604
Est. 1979 *Stock size* Medium
Stock Reclaimed, new, old pine furniture, pine and iron beds, mirrors
Open Tues Fri Sat 10am–5pm Sun 10am–4pm
Services Stripping

Quicktest
Contact Raffi Katz
Park House, Greenhill Crescent, Watford Business Park, Watford, Hertfordshire, WD1 8QU P
☎ 01923 220206 F 01923 239089
M 07976 831953
E info@quicktest.co.uk
W www.quicktest.co.uk
Est. 1986 *Stock size* Large
Stock Testers, magnifiers, weighing machines, jewellery boxes, hand tools
Open Mon–Thurs 8am–6pm Fri 8am–3pm
Fairs Newark, Alexandra Palace

WHEATHAMPSTEAD

Collins Antiques
Contact Mr Michael Collins
Corner House, Church Street, Wheathampstead, Hertfordshire, AL4 8AP P
☎ 01582 833111
Est. 1907 *Stock size* Medium
Stock 17th–19thC furniture, including oak and mahogany tables, chairs, chests-of-drawers
Open Mon–Sat 9am–1pm 2–5pm
Services Valuations

The Old Bakery Antiques Ltd
Contact Mr Maurice Shifrin
3 Station Road, Wheathampstead, Hertfordshire, AL4 8BU P
☎ 01582 831999 F 01582 831555
Est. 1997 *Stock size* Large
Stock Mainly Victorian–Edwardian furniture, Oriental carpets
Open Mon–Sun 10am–5pm closed Wed
Fairs Newark, Ardingly

Thomas Thorp (ABA, PBFA)
Contact Mr Jim Thorp
35–37 High Street, Wheathampstead, Hertfordshire, AL4 8BB P
☎ 01582 834757 F 01582 834757
E thorpbooks@compuserve.com
Est. 1883 *Stock size* Small
Stock General antiquarian books specializing in early printed English history, literature, modern, private press editions
Open Mail order or by appointment
Fairs Olympia (Jun), Chelsea (Nov)

WILSTONE

W J Hazle
Contact Mr W J Hazle
36 Grange Road, Wilstone, Tring, Hertfordshire, HP23 4PG
☎ 01442 890493 F 01442 890493
M 07850 474672
E all-our-yesterdays@hotmail.com
W www.allouryesterdays.co.uk
Est. 1995 *Stock size* Large
Stock Original, reproduction, modern collectors' cards
Open Mail order or by appointment

OXFORDSHIRE

ASCOTT-UNDER-WYCHWOOD

William Antiques
Contact Mr R Gripper
Manor Barn, Manor Farm, Ascott-under-Wychwood, Chipping Norton, Oxfordshire, OX7 6AL P
☎ 01993 831960 F 01993 830395
E robgripper@aol.com
Est. 1982 *Stock size* Medium
Stock Good-quality decorative antiques, Georgian–Victorian furniture
Open Mon–Fri 9am–5pm
Services Restorations

BANBURY

Comic Connections
Contact Mr Glyn Smith
56–57 George Street, Banbury, Oxfordshire, OX16 8BH
☎ 01295 268989 F 01295 268989
Est. 1994 *Stock size* Large
Stock American comic books, graphic novels, action figures, science-fiction items
Open Mon–Wed 10.30am–5pm Thurs Fri 10am–5pm Sat 9.30am–5pm
Fairs D and J Fair, NEC
Services Standing order for comics, magazines, videos

Holloways (RICS)
Contact Mr Tim Holloway
49 Parsons Street, Banbury, Oxfordshire, OX16 5PF P
☎ 01295 817777 F 01295 817701
E enquiries@hollowaysauctioneers.co.uk
W www.hollowaysauctioneers.co.uk
Open Mon–Fri 9am–5.30pm Sat 9am–noon
Sales Fortnightly general sales Mon 11am, viewing Fri 9am–5pm Sat 9am–12.30pm.

Every 2 months specialist sales Wed 11am, viewing Sat 9am–12.30pm Mon 9am–7pm Tues 9am–5pm and day of sale
Catalogues No

BICESTER

R A Barnes Antiques (LAPADA)
Contact John Langin
PO Box 82, Bicester, Oxfordshire, OX25 1RA
01844 237388
Est. 1970 *Stock size* Medium
Stock Continental glass, English and Continental porcelain, Art Nouveau, paintings, English metalware, 18th–19thC brass, Belleek, Wedgwood
Open By appointment
Fairs NEC, Little Chelsea
Services Valuations

Lisseters Antiques
Contact Mr M Lisseter
3 Kings End, Bicester, Oxfordshire, OX6 7DR
01869 252402
07801 667848
Est. 1959 *Stock size* Large
Stock Antiques, used furniture
Open Mon–Sat 9am–5pm

Mallams incorporating Messengers (NAVA)
Contact T Messenger
Pevensey House, 27 Sheep Street, Bicester, Oxfordshire, OX6 7JF
01869 252901 01869 320283
07966 501794
bicester@mallams.co.uk
www.mallams.co.uk/fineart
Est. 1788
Open Mon–Fri 10am–4pm except sale days
Sales General antiques sale 11am, viewing 8am prior to sale. Valuations service
Frequency 16 per year
Catalogues Yes

Serendipity
Contact Mr A J Slade
22 Wesley Lane, Bicester, Oxfordshire, OX6 7JW
01869 322533
Est. 1993 *Stock size* Large
Stock New, old, collectable teddy bears, dolls
Open Mon Thurs–Sat 9am–5pm
Fairs NEC, Donnington Park
Services Bear, doll restorations

BIX

Easy Strip
Contact Mr R Cane
Old Manor Farm, Bix, Henley-on-Thames, Oxfordshire, RG9 6BX
01491 577289
07785 938580
Est. 1969 *Stock size* Large
Stock Victorian doors, architectural antiques
Open By appointment
Services Stripping doors

BLEWBURY

Blewbury Antiques
Contact E or S M Richardson
London Road, Blewbury, Didcot, Oxfordshire, OX11 9NX
01235 850366
07703 787070
blewbury.ant@btclick.com
Est. 1970 *Stock size* Large
Stock General, furniture, garden ornaments, books, glass, china, clocks
Open Mon–Sun 10am–6pm closed Tues

BLOXHAM

Antiques of Bloxham
Contact Mr S Robinson
Church Street, Bloxham, Banbury, Oxfordshire, OX15 4ET
01295 721641
Est. 1996 *Stock size* Large
Stock General antiques
Open Mon–Sun 10am–4.30pm
Services Delivery, clock repairs

BURFORD

Antiques @ The George
Contact Coral Oswald
104 High Street, Burford, Oxfordshire, OX18 4QJ
01993 823319
Est. 1992 *Stock size* Large
No. of dealers 20
Stock China, glass, furniture, treen, books, pictures, rugs, carpets
Open Mon–Sat 10am–5pm Sun noon–5pm

Boxroom Antiques
Contact Mr Glyn Roberts
59 High Street, Burford, Oxfordshire, OX18 4QA
01993 824268
Est. 1998 *Stock size* Large
Stock Jewellery, silver, linen, small furniture, porcelain, glass, collectables, cutlery
Open Mon–Sun 10am–6pm

Burford Antiques Centre
Contact Mr G Viventi
The Roundabout, Cheltenham Road, Burford, Oxfordshire, OX18 4JA
01993 823227
Est. 1988 *Stock size* Large
Stock General antiques, 1930s–modern period reproduction furniture
Open Mon–Sat 10am–6pm Sun noon–5pm

Bygones
Contact Mrs Jenkins
29 Lower High Street, Burford, Oxfordshire, OX18 4RN
01993 823588 01993 704338
Est. 1986 *Stock size* Medium
Stock General collectables, curios
Open Mon–Sat 10am–1pm 2–5pm Sun noon–5pm

Jonathan Fyson Antiques (CADA)
Contact Mr J Fyson
50 High Street, Burford, Oxfordshire, OX18 4QF
01993 823204 01993 823204
jrf@jonathanfysonantiques.com
www.jonathanfysonantiques.com
Est. 1971 *Stock size* Large
Stock English and Continental furniture, brass, lighting, fireplaces, accessories, club fenders, papier mâché, tôle, treen, porcelain, glass, prints, jewellery
Open Mon–Fri 9.30am–5.30pm closed 1–2pm Sat 10am–5.30pm closed 1–2pm
Services Valuations

Gateway Antiques (CADA)
Contact Mr Paul Brown or Mr Michael Ford
Cheltenham Road, Burford, Oxfordshire, OX18 4JA
01993 823678 01993 823857
www.gatewayantiques.co.uk
Est. 1985 *Stock size* Large
Stock 17th–19thC furniture, farmhouse furniture, Arts and Crafts, decorative objects, accessories

Open Mon–Sat 10am–5.30pm Sun 2–5pm
Services Shipping worldwide, multi-lingual courier service and driver, accomodation, storage

Horseshoe Antiques
Contact Mr B Evans
97 High Street, Burford, Oxfordshire, OX18 4QA
01993 823244
07711 525383
Est. 1979 *Stock size* Medium
Stock 17th–18thC furniture, oil paintings, copper, brass, horse brasses, clocks, longcase clocks
Open Mon–Sat 9.30am–5pm

David Pickup (BADA, CADA)
Contact Mr D Pickup
115 High Street, Burford, Oxfordshire, OX18 4RG
01993 822555
Est. 1980 *Stock size* Medium
Stock Fine English furniture, emphasis on the Cotswold Arts and Crafts movement early 20thC
Open Mon–Fri 9.30am–5.30pm Sat 10.30am–4.30pm
Fairs Olympia (Spring, Nov)

Saracen Antiques Ltd
Contact Mr C Mills
Upton Downs Farm, Burford, Oxfordshire, OX18 4LY
01993 822987 01993 823701
cmills6702@aol.com
Est. 1996 *Stock size* Large
Stock Predominantly 18th–19thC English furniture
Open Mon–Sat 9am–5.30pm
Services Restorations

Manfred Schotten Antiques (CADA)
109 High Street, Burford, Oxfordshire, OX18 4RG
01993 822302 01993 822055
antiques@schotten.com
www.schotten.com
Est. 1976 *Stock size* Large
Stock Sporting antiques, library furniture, leather furniture
Open Mon–Sat 9.30am–5.30pm
Fairs Olympia

Swan Gallery (CADA, LAPADA)
Contact Mr D Pratt
127 High Street, Burford, Oxfordshire, OX18 4RE
01993 822244 01993 822244
Est. 1977 *Stock size* Large
Stock Early country, period furniture
Open Mon–Sat 10am–5.30pm

CHALGROVE

Hitchcox's Antiques
The Garth, Warpsgrove, Chalgrove, Oxford, Oxfordshire, OX44 7RW
01865 890241 01865 890241
Est. 1957 *Stock size* Large
Stock 18th–20thC English furniture
Open Mon–Sat 10am–5pm Sun 2–5pm
Services Valuations, buys at auction

CHARNEY BASSETT

Brian Davis Antiques
Contact Mr B Davis
Goosey Wick Farm, Goosey Wick, Charney Bassett, Wantage, Oxfordshire, OX12 0EY
01367 718933
Est. 1981 *Stock size* Large
Stock English and Continental period pine
Open Tues–Sat 9am–5.30pm

CHILTON

Country Markets Antiques & Collectables
Contact Mr G Vaughan
Chilton Garden Centre, Newbury Road, Chilton, Didcot, Oxfordshire, OX11 0QN
01235 835125 01235 833068
country.markets.antiques@breathmail.net
www.countrymarkets.co.uk
Est. 1989 *Stock size* Large
No. of dealers 35
Stock Furniture, glass, jewellery, cased fish, porcelain, ceramics etc
Open Mon 10.30am–5.30pm Tues–Sat 10am–5.30pm Sun Bank Holidays 10.30am–4.30pm
Services Valuations, restorations

CHINNOR

Mr Booth Antiques
Contact Mr G Booth
6 Thame Road, Chinnor, Oxfordshire, OX9 4QS
01844 354344
Est. 1994 *Stock size* Small
Stock Wide range of collectables, period furniture, mirrors, pictures
Open Sat Mon 9.30am–5.30pm
Fairs Kempton Park

CHIPPING NORTON

Antique English Windsor Chairs (BADA, CINOA, CADA)
Contact Michael Harding-Hill
9 Horse Fair, Chipping Norton, Oxfordshire, OX7 5AL
01608 643322 01608 644322
07798 653134
michael@antique-english-windsor-chairs.com
www.antique-english-windsor-chairs.com
Est. 1971 *Stock size* Large
Stock Antique English Windsor chairs 18th–19thC, sets, singles for collectors and everyday use
Open 10am–5pm Mon–Sat or by appointment
Fairs Olympia (June, Nov)

Chipping Norton Antique Centre
Contact Michael Mence
Ivy House, Middle Row, Chipping Norton, Oxfordshire, OX7 5NH
01608 644212 01608 641369
Est. 1986 *Stock size* Large
No. of dealers 15
Stock General antiques, collectables, Georgian and Edwardian furniture, china, silver, kitchenware
Open 10am–5.30pm Mon–Sun
Services Tea room

Georgian House Antiques (LAPADA)
Contact Sheila Wissinger
21 West Street, Chipping Norton, Oxfordshire, OX7 5EU
01608 641369 01608 641369
Stock size Large
Stock Period oak, mahogany, walnut furniture, paintings, chairs, farmhouse furniture
Open Mon–Sun 10am–5pm or by appointment
Services Delivery, shipping arranged

Greensleeves Books (BSA)
Contact Mrs C Seers
2 Market Street, Chipping Norton, Oxfordshire, OX7 5NQ

☎ 01608 644707 Ⓕ 01608 644707
Ⓔ greensleeves@mcmail.com
Ⓦ www.greensleevesbooks.co.uk
Est. 1981 *Stock size* Medium
Stock Rare and second-hand books, mind, body and spirit books a speciality
Open Mail order only
Services Book search, catalogues

Kellow Books
Contact Mr P Combellack
✉ **6 Market Place, Chipping Norton, Oxfordshire, OX7 5NA** Ⓟ
☎ 01608 644293
Est. 1998 *Stock size* Medium
Stock Antiquarian, rare, second-hand collectable books
Open Mon–Sat 10am–4.30pm
Services Book search

Key Antiques (BADA, CADA)
Contact Jane Riley
✉ **11 Horsefair, Chipping Norton, Oxfordshire, OX7 5AL** Ⓟ
☎ 01608 643777
Ⓜ 07860 650112
Est. 1972 *Stock size* Medium
Stock Period oak, country furniture, related objects of 17th–18thC
Open Wed–Sat 10am–5.30pm
Services Valuations of period oak, metalware

The Quiet Woman Antiques Centre
Contact Ann Marriott
✉ **Southcombe, Chipping Norton, Oxfordshire, OX7 5QH** Ⓟ
☎ 01608 646262 Ⓕ 01608 646262
Ⓜ 07860 889524
Est. 1998 *Stock size* Large
No. of dealers 20
Stock Furniture, china, general antiques
Open Mon–Fri 10am–7pm Sat 10am–5.30pm Sun 10am–4pm
Services Coffee shop

Station Mill Antiques Centre
Contact Tracey Hewlett
✉ **Station Road, Chipping Norton, Oxfordshire, OX7 5HX** Ⓟ
☎ 01608 644563 Ⓕ 01327 860952
Ⓔ TL@stationmill.com
Ⓦ www.stationmill.com
Est. 1996 *Stock size* Large
No. of dealers 70
Stock Complete range of antiques, collectables
Open Mon–Sun 10am–5pm
Services Tea room

CHURCHILL

Clive Payne (LAPADA)
Contact Clive Payne
✉ **Unit 4, Mount Farm, Junction Road, Churchill, Chipping Norton, Oxfordshire, OX7 6NP** Ⓟ
☎ 01608 658856 Ⓕ 01608 658856
Ⓜ 07801 088363
Ⓔ clive.payne@virgin.net
Ⓦ www.clivepayne.com
Est. 1986 *Stock size* Medium
Stock 17thC–early Victorian furniture
Open Mon–Fri 9am–5pm
Services Antique furniture restoration

DEDDINGTON

Castle Antiques Ltd (LAPADA)
Contact John or Judy Vaughan
✉ **Manor Farm, Clifton, Deddington, Oxfordshire, OX15 0PA** Ⓟ
☎ 01869 338688
Est. 1972 *Stock size* Large
Stock General antiques, furniture, metalware, silver, £50–£2,000, reproduction garden furniture
Open Mon–Sat 10am–6pm Sun 10am–4pm

Deddington Antique Centre (TVADA)
Contact Mrs Brenda Haller
✉ **Laurel House, Bullring, Deddington, Banbury, Oxfordshire, OX15 0TT** Ⓟ
☎ 01869 338968 Ⓕ 01869 338916
Est. 1977 *Stock size* Large
No. of dealers 20
Stock Period furniture, silver, porcelain, oil and watercolours, jewellery, clocks etc
Open Mon–Sat 10am–5pm Sun 11am–5pm
Services Porcelain, silver and jewellery repairs

DORCHESTER

Dorchester Antiques (TVADA, LAPADA)
Contact Mrs S or Jonty Hearnden
✉ **The Barn, 3 High Street, Dorchester, Oxfordshire, OX10 7HH** Ⓟ
☎ 01865 341373 Ⓕ 01865 341373
Est. 1992
Stock Georgian furniture, interesting country pieces
Open Tues–Sat 10am–5pm
Fairs TVADA
Services Finding service

Hallidays (Fine Antiques) Ltd (LAPADA, CINOA, TVADA)
Contact Mr E M Reily Collins
High Street, Dorchester, Oxfordshire, OX10 7HL P
☎ 01865 340028 F 01865 341149
E antiques@hallidays.com
W www.hallidays.com
Est. 1942 *Stock size* Large
Stock 17th–19thC English furniture, decorative items, paintings
Open Mon–Fri 9am–5pm Sat 10am–4pm
Fairs Olympia, LAPADA (Jan)
Services Shipping

EAST HAGBOURNE

Craig Barfoot Clocks
Contact Craig Barfoot
Tudor House, East Hagbourne, Oxfordshire, OX11 9LR P
☎ 01235 818968 F 01235 818968
M 07710 858158
Est. 1991 *Stock size* Medium
Stock Longcase, organ, and musical clocks
Open By appointment
Services Restorations, buys at auction

E M Lawson and Co (ABA, ILAB)
Contact Mr J Lawson
Kingsholm, Main Road, East Hagbourne, Didcot, Oxfordshire, OX11 9LN P
☎ 01235 812033
Est. 1919 *Stock size* Small
Stock Rare and antiquarian books, early English literature, science, medicine, economics, travel
Open Mon–Fri 9am–6pm or by appointment

FARINGDON

Faringdon Antiques Centre
Contact Christine Lloyd
35 Marlborough Street, Faringdon, Oxfordshire, SN7 7JL P
☎ 01367 243650
Est. 1993 *Stock size* Large
No. of dealers 15
Stock Mahogany, walnut, pine, French furniture, small and decorative items
Open Tues–Sun Bank Holidays 10am–5pm
Services Restoration of furniture, clocks, porcelain, china, pine stripping, framing, valuations

HENLEY-ON-THAMES

Bonhams & Brooks
Contact Arabella Elwes
The Coach House, 66 Northfield End, Henley-on-Thames, Oxfordshire, RG9 2BE P
☎ Freephone 0800 435454 F 01494 413637
E oxfordshire@bonhams.com
W www.bonhams.com
Open Mon Fri 9am–5pm 1st Sat of month 10am–1pm
Sales Area office for Thames Valley, Oxfordshire, Berkshire, Buckinghamshire, Warwickshire, Northamptonshire, Gloucestershire, Hertfordshire and Bedfordshire. See Head Office (London) for details
Frequency Phone for details

Bromlea and Jonkers (ABA, PBFA)
Contact Mr M Johnstone
24 Hart Street, Henley-on-Thames, Oxfordshire, RG9 2AU
☎ 01491 576427 F 01491 573805
E bromlea.jonkers@bjbooks.co.uk
W www.bjbooks.co.uk
Est. 1990 *Stock size* Medium
Stock Antiquarian literature, 19th–20thC first editions, illustrated and children's books
Open Mon–Sat 10am–5.30pm
Fairs Olympia

The Country Seat (TVADA, LAPADA)
Contact William Clegg
Huntercombe Manor Barn, Henley-on-Thames, Oxfordshire, RG9 5RY P
☎ 01491 641349 F 01491 641533
E ferry&clegg@thecountryseat.com
W www.thecountryseat.com
Est. 1971 *Stock size* Large
Stock Furniture designed by architects 17th–20thC, post-war furniture, art pottery, metalwork, Whitefriars glass
Open 9am–5pm
Fairs TVADA, 20thC Olympia

The Ferret (Friday Street Antiques Centre)
Contact Mrs D Etherington
4 Friday Street, Henley-on-Thames, Oxfordshire, RG9 1AH P
☎ 01491 574104 F 01491 641039
Est. 1984 *Stock size* Medium
No. of dealers 6
Stock Jewellery, silver, furniture, china, books, collectables, interesting items
Open Mon–Sat 10am–5.30pm Sun noon–5.30pm

Henley Antique Centre
Contact Mr D Shepherd
2–4 Reading Road, Henley-on-Thames, Oxfordshire, RG9 1AG P
☎ 01491 411468
Est. 1999 *Stock size* Large
No. of dealers 48
Stock Furniture, glass, china, silver, coins, scientific instruments, tools
Open Mon–Sat 10am–5.30pm Sun noon–5.30pm

Jackdaw Antique Centres Ltd
Contact Mrs J Mayle
5 Reading Road, Henley-on-Thames, Oxfordshire, RG9 0AS
☎ 01491 572289
Est. 1998 *Stock size* Large
Stock Furniture, ceramics, glass, collectables, general antiques
Open Mon–Sat 10am–5.30pm Sun Bank Holidays noon–5pm

Simmons & Sons (RICS)
Contact Mr S Jones or Mrs E Latham
32 Bell Street, Henley-on-Thames, Oxfordshire, RG9 2BH P
☎ 01491 571111 F 01491 579833
E auctions@simmonsandsons.com
W www.simmonsandsons.com
Est. 1802
Open Mon–Fri 9am–5.30pm Sat 9am–noon
Sales 8 sales of general antiques per annum, valuations
Frequency 8 per annum
Catalogues Yes

Tudor House Antiques and Collectables
Contact Mr D Potter
49 Duke Street, Henley-on-Thames, Oxfordshire, RG9 1UR P
☎ 01491 573680
M 07709 987892

Est. 1996 *Stock size* Large
Stock General antiques, collectables
Open Mon–Sun 10am–5pm
Services Valuations, house clearance

Ways Bookshop (ABA)
Contact Diana Cook
54b Friday Street, Henley-on-Thames, Oxfordshire, RG9 1AH P
01491 576663 F 01491 576663
Est. 1977 *Stock size* Medium
Stock Rare and second-hand books bought and sold
Open Mon–Sat 10am–5.30pm
Services Book search, bookbinding, valuations

The Worm Hole Antique Centre
Contact Mr Doug Shephard
8 Greys Road, Henley-on-Thames, Oxfordshire, RG9 1RY P
01491 413333
Est. 1998 *Stock size* Large
No. of dealers 13
Stock Furniture, collectors' items
Open Mon–Sat 10am–5pm Sun noon–5pm

LONG HANBOROUGH

Hanborough Antiques
Contact Mrs S Holifield or Mrs L Pearce
125a–127 Main Road, Long Hanborough, Witney, Oxfordshire, OX8 8JX P
01993 882767
Est. 1997 *Stock size* Medium
Stock Pine, smalls, olive pots, Islamic and Turkish rugs, new garden pots
Open Tues–Sat 11am–5pm Sun Summer 1–4pm

MIDDLE ASTON

Cotswold Pine
Contact Mr Bob Prancks
The Poultry Unit, Middle Aston, Bicester, Oxfordshire, OX25 5QL P
01869 340963
Est. 1972 *Stock size* Large
Stock General antique furniture including mahogany, oak, pine
Open Mon–Fri 9am–7pm Sat 9am–6pm Sun 10am–4.30pm
Services Restorations, stripping

NETTLEBED

Nettlebed Antique Merchants (TVADA)
Contact Mr W Bicknell
1 High Street, Nettlebed, Henley-on-Thames, Oxfordshire, RG9 5DA P
01491 642062 F 01491 628811
M 07770 554559
E willow.bick.antiques@lineone.net
W www.nettlebedantiques.co.uk
Est. 1980 *Stock size* Large
Stock 17thC–late 20thC from the fine to the funky, architectural, garden items
Open Mon–Sat 10am–5.30pm Sun 11am–4pm or by appointment
Fairs TVADA (Spring, Autumn)
Services Upholstery, restorations, finding service, copying and making furniture

NORTHMOOR

Soames Country Auctioneers
Contact Gary Martin Soame
Pinnocks Farm, Northmoor, Witney, Oxfordshire, OX8 1AY P
01865 300626 F 01865 300432
E soame@msn.com
Est. 1991
Open Telephone Mon–Fri 9am–5.30pm
Sales General antiques sales
Frequency Monthly
Catalogues Yes

OXFORD

Antiques on High Ltd (TVADA)
Contact Mr P Lipson or Mrs S Young
85 High Street, Oxford, Oxfordshire, OX1 4BG
01865 251075
Est. 1997 *Stock size* Large
No. of dealers 38
Stock Smalls, collectables
Open Mon–Sat 10am–5pm Sun Bank Holidays 11am–5pm
Services Repairs

Barclay Antiques
Contact Mr Colin Barclay
107 Windmill Road, Headington, Oxford, Oxfordshire, OX3 7BT P
01865 769551
Est. 1980 *Stock size* Large
Stock China, glass, silver, bronzes, lighting
Open Mon–Sat 10am–5.30pm closed Wed
Services Repairs to lighting

Blackwell's Rare Books (ABA, PBFA)
Contact Mr P Brown
48–51 Broad Street, Oxford, Oxfordshire, OX1 3BQ P
01865 333555 F 01865 794143
E rarebooks@blackwellsbookshops.co.uk
W www.rarebooks.blackwell.co.uk
Est. 1879 *Stock size* Large
Stock Modern first editions, private press books, antiquarian English literature, juvenilia, general antiquarian books
Open Mon Wed–Sat 9am–6pm Tues 9.30am–6pm
Fairs Olympia, Chelsea Book Fair, 1 American fair per year east or west coast
Services Shipping, book search

Robert Clark (PBFA, ABA)
Contact Mr R Clark
6a King Street, Jericho, Oxford, Oxfordshire, OX2 6DF P
01865 552154 F 01865 552154
E rclark@rarebooks.u-net.com
Est. 1984 *Stock size* Medium
Stock English 17thC books, English literature, history, theology
Open By appointment
Fairs PBFA, ABA
Services Valuations

Reginald Davis (Oxford) Ltd (BADA, NAG)
Contact David Marcus
34 High Street, Oxford, Oxfordshire, OX1 4AN
01865 248347 F 01865 200915
E davisr@mail.globalnet.co.uk
Est. 1966 *Stock size* Large
Stock Jewellery, silver, old Sheffield plate
Open Tues–Fri 9am–5pm Sat 10am–6pm
Services Valuations, repairs, restorations

Jericho Books (PBFA)
Contact Mr F Stringer
48 Walton Street, Oxford, Oxfordshire, OX2 6AD P
01865 511992
M 07870 1315166
E shop@jerichobooks.com

Ⓦ www.jerichobooks.com
Est. 1996 *Stock size* Medium
Stock Rare and second-hand books
Open Mon–Sun 10am–6.30pm
Services Book search

Roger Little Antique Pottery (English Ceramic Circle)
Contact Roger Little
White Lodge, Osler Road, Headington, Oxford, Oxfordshire, OX3 9BJ P
☎ 01865 762317 Ⓕ 01865 741595
Ⓔ rogerlittle1@excite.co.uk
Est. 1985 *Stock size* Medium
Stock English and Continental pottery, tiles, 1650–1800
Open By appointment only
Fairs NEC
Services Valuations

Magna Gallery
Contact Martin Blant
41 High Street, Oxford, Oxfordshire, OX1 4AP P
☎ 01865 245805 Ⓕ 01285 750753
Ⓔ info@magna-gallery.com
Ⓦ www.magna-gallery.com
Est. 1969 *Stock size* Medium
Stock Maps, prints, books
Open Mon–Sat 10.30am–6pm Jun–Aug Dec Sun 11am–4pm
Services Valuations

Mallams
Contact Mr B Lloyd
Bocardo House, St Michael's Street, Oxford, Oxfordshire, OX1 2DR P
☎ 01865 241358 Ⓕ 01865 725483
Ⓔ oxford@mallams.co.uk
Ⓦ www.mallams.co.uk
Est. 1788
Open 9am–5.30pm
Sales Monthly fine antiques sales Wed 11am, viewing Sat 9am–1pm Mon Tues 9am–5pm. Jewellery and silver sales Apr Jun Nov. Antique books and pictures Apr Oct Dec
Catalogues Yes

Oxford Furniture Warehouse
Contact F & P K Mitchell
272 Abingdon Road, Oxford, Oxfordshire, OX1 4TA P
☎ 01865 202221 Ⓕ 01865 202221
Ⓔ oxfurniture@aol.com
Ⓦ www.oxford-furniture.co.uk
Est. 1992 *Stock size* Large
Stock Old pine, oak and general furniture, some Continental furniture
Open Mon–Sat 10am–5.30pm Sun 11am–4.30pm

Payne and Son (Goldsmiths) Ltd (BADA, NAG)
Contact Judy Payne or David Thornton
131 High Street, Oxford, Oxfordshire, OX1 4DH P
☎ 01865 243787 Ⓕ 01865 793241
Ⓔ silver@payneandson.co.uk
Ⓦ www.payneandson.co.uk
Est. 1790 *Stock size* Large
Stock 17thC–present day silver including Arts and Crafts and contemporary designs
Open Mon–Sat 9am–5pm
Fairs BADA Chelsea, Olympia
Services Restorations

St Clements Antiques
Contact Mr G Power
93 St Clements Street, Oxford, Oxfordshire, OX4 1AR P
☎ 01865 727010 Ⓕ 01865 864690
Ⓔ s_c_antiques@hotmail.com
Est. 1999 *Stock size* Medium
Stock Town and country pieces from home and abroad
Open Mon–Sat 10.30am–5pm
Services Valuations

Unsworths Booksellers Ltd (ABA, PBFA, BA)
Contact Ms Antigone Blair
15 Turl Street, Oxford, Oxfordshire, OX1 3DQ P
☎ 01865 727928 Ⓕ 01865 727206
Ⓔ books@unsworths.com
Ⓦ www.unsworths.com
Est. 1986 *Stock size* Medium
Stock Antiquarian, second-hand, remaindered books on humanities
Open Mon–Sat 10am–6pm Sun noon–4pm
Fairs See website for details

ROTHERFIELD GREYS

The Old French Mirror Company (TVADA)
Contact Bridget de Breanski
The Nightingales, Greys Green, Rotherfield Greys, Henley-on-Thames, Oxfordshire, RG9 4QQ P
☎ 01491 629913 Ⓕ 01491 629913
Ⓔ bridget@frenchmirrors.co.uk
Ⓦ www.frenchmirrors.co.uk
Est. 1999 *Stock size* Large
Stock Decorative gilded and painted French mirrors, 1720–1920
Open By appointment
Fairs TVADA
Services Shipping, restorations, re-gilding

STANDLAKE

Manor Farm Antiques
Contact Charles Gower
159 Abingdon Road, Standlake, Witney, Oxfordshire, OX8 7RL P
☎ 01865 300303 Ⓕ 01865 300153
Est. 1964 *Stock size* Large
Stock Brass, iron, wooden bedsteads
Open Mon–Sat 10am–5pm

STEVENTON

Bennett and Kerr Books (PBFA, ABA)
Contact Mr E Bennett
Millhill Warehouse, Church Lane, Steventon, Abingdon, Oxfordshire, OX13 6SW P
☎ 01235 820604
Ⓔ bennett_kerr@compuserve.com
Est. 1982 *Stock size* Medium
Stock Antique, scholarly books on Middle Ages, Renaissance, medieval studies
Open By appointment
Fairs PBFA, Oxford
Services Catalogues issued

TETSWORTH

A D Antiques
Contact Alison Davey
The Swan at Tetsworth, High Street, Tetsworth, Thames, Oxfordshire, OX9 7AB
Ⓜ 07939 508171
Ⓔ alison@adantiques.freeserve.co.uk
Ⓦ www.adantiques.com
Est. 1997 *Stock size* Medium
Stock Decorative arts, ceramics, metalware
Open By appointment
Fairs NEC, Bingley Hall

Gillian Gould Antiques
Contact Gill Gould
The Swan at Tetsworth, High Street, Tetsworth, Oxfordshire, OX9 7AB P
☎ 020 7419 0500 Ⓕ 020 7419 0400
Ⓜ 07831 150060
Ⓔ gillgould@dealwith.com
Est. 1989 *Stock size* Small

Stock Scientific, marine, general gifts
Open By appointment only
Services Valuations, restorations

The Swan at Tetsworth (TVADA)
Contact Elizabeth Fell
High Street, Tetsworth, Thame, Oxfordshire, OX9 7AB P
☎ 01844 281777 F 01844 281770
E antiques@theswan.co.uk
W www.theswan.co.uk
Est. 1994 *Stock size* Large
No. of dealers 80
Stock 80 dealers in historic Elizabethan coaching inn
Open Mon–Sun 10am–6pm
Services Renowned restaurant, delivery arranged, events, shipping

THAME

Rosemary & Time
Contact Mr Tom Fletcher
42 Park Street, Thame, Oxfordshire, OX9 3HR P
☎ 01844 216923
Est. 1983 *Stock size* Large
Stock Clocks
Open Tues–Sat 9am–5.30pm
Services Restorations, repairs

WALLINGFORD

Alicia Antiques
Contact Mrs A Collins
Lamb Arcade, High Street, Wallingford, Oxfordshire, OX10 0BS P
☎ 01491 833737
Est. 1979 *Stock size* Medium
Stock Silver, plate, glass, small furniture
Open Mon–Sat 10am–5pm
Services Silver repairs

Bonhams & Brooks
Contact Tony Guy
Moat Cottage, Brightwell cum Sotwell, Wallingford, Oxfordshire, OX10 0RP
☎ 01491 838846 F 01491 839733
W www.bonhams.com
Open Mon–Fri 9am–5pm
Sales Regional Representative for Oxfordshire

M & J De Albuquerque
Contact Ms J De Albuquerque
12 High Street, Wallingford, Oxfordshire, OX10 0BP P
☎ 01491 832322 F 01491 832322
E janede@lineone.net
Est. 1982 *Stock size* Medium
Stock 18th–19thC French and English furniture, objects of the period
Open Mon–Sat 9.30am–5.30pm
Fairs Olympia, NEC, Newark, Ardingly
Services Restorations, framing, gilding

Toby English Antique & Secondhand Books (PBFA)
Contact Mr T English
10 St Mary's Street, Wallingford, Oxfordshire, OX10 0EL P
☎ 01491 836389 F 01491 836389
E toby@tobyenglish.com
W www.tobyenglish.com
Est. 1984 *Stock size* Large
Stock Art, architectural, Renaissance literature, large general stock
Open Mon–Sat 9.30am–5pm
Fairs PBFA
Services Book search, valuations, catalogues issued

The Lamb Arcade (TVADA)
Contact Mrs P Hayward
83 High Street, Wallingford, Oxfordshire, OX10 0BX P
☎ 01491 835166 F 01491 824247
E pdhayward@netscapeonline.co.uk
W thelambarcade.co.uk
Est. 1979 *Stock size* Large
No. of dealers 39
Stock Everything from period furniture to small items
Open Mon–Fri 10am–5pm Sat 10am–5.30pm

O'Donnell Antiques
Contact Lin O'Donnell
26 High Street, Wallingford, Oxfordshire, OX10 0BU P
☎ 01491 839332
Est. 1974 *Stock size* Large
Stock General antiques, Georgian–early 20thC furniture, taxidermy, rugs, English pine, Oriental items
Open Mon–Sat 9.30am–5pm

Otter Antiques
Contact Mr P Otter
20 High Street, Wallingford, Oxfordshire, OX10 0BP P
☎ 01491 825544 F 01865 407396
W www.otterantiques.co.uk
Est. 1994 *Stock size* Medium
Stock 18th–19thC boxes, period furniture
Open Mon–Sat 9.30am–5pm Sun 10.30am–5pm
Services Restoration of boxes

Summers Davis Antiques Ltd (TVADA, LAPADA)
Contact Mr J Driver-Jones
Calleva House, 6 High Street, Wallingford, Oxfordshire, OX10 0BP P
☎ 01491 836284 F 01491 833443
E summersdavisantiques@msn.com
W www.sd-antique-furniture.com
Est. 1915 *Stock size* Large
Stock 11 showrooms. 17th–19thC English and Continental furniture
Open Mon–Fri 9am–5.30pm Sat 9am–5pm Sun 11am–5pm
Fairs TVADA, Radley

Tooley, Adams and Co (IMCOS, ABA)
Contact Steve Luck
PO Box 174, Wallingford, Oxfordshire, OX10 0RY P
☎ 01491 838298 F 01491 834616
E steve@tooleys.co.uk
W www.tooleys.co.uk
Est. 1982 *Stock size* Large
Stock Antiquarian maps, atlases
Open By appointment
Fairs IMCoS, Bonnington Map Fair (monthly)
Services Valuations

WESTON ON THE GREEN

Julie Strachey (TVADA)
Contact Julie Strachey
Southfield Farm, North Lane, Weston on the Green, Oxfordshire, OX6 8RG P
☎ 01869 350833
M 07711 249939
Est. 1972 *Stock size* Large
Stock 2 large barns. Antique farm and country furniture in pine, oak etc, ironwork, interesting pieces for the garden
Open Mon–Sat 10am–5pm
Fairs TVADA, NEC
Services Storage, delivery, shipping

WHEATLEY

Country Collections
Contact Mrs A Descenclos

✉ **47 High Street, Wheatley, Oxford, Oxfordshire, OX33 1XX** P
☎ 01865 875701
Est. 1992 *Stock size* Medium
Stock Small items, furniture, general antiques
Open Mon–Sat 10am–4.30pm closed Wed pm

WITNEY

Church Green Books (PBFA)

Contact Margaret or Roger Barnes
✉ **46 Market Square, Witney, Oxfordshire, OX8 6AL** P
☎ 01993 700822
ⓔ books@churchgreen.co.uk
ⓦ www.churchgreen.co.uk
Est. 1995 *Stock size* Medium
Stock General second-hand and antiquarian books, books on bellringing a speciality
Open Mon–Sat 10am–4pm
Services Book search

Colin Greenway Antiques (CADA)

Contact Jean Greenway
✉ **90 Corn Street, Witney, Oxfordshire, OX8 7BU** P
☎ 01993 705026 ⓕ 01993 705026
ⓜ 07831 585014
Est. 1974 *Stock size* Medium
Stock 17th–early 20thC furniture, general antiques, interesting, unusual items
Open Mon–Fri 9.30am–5.30pm Sat 10am–4pm
Services Valuations

W R Harvey & Co (Antiques) Ltd (BADA, CADA)

Contact Mr A D Harvey
✉ **86 Corn Street, Witney, Oxfordshire, OX8 7BU** P
☎ 01993 706501 ⓕ 01993 706601
ⓔ antiques@wrharvey.co.uk
ⓦ www.wrharvey.co.uk
Est. 1950 *Stock size* Large
Stock Important stock of English furniture, clocks, pictures, mirrors, works of art, 1680–1830
Open Mon–Sat 9.30am–5.30pm
Fairs Chelsea Spring & Autumn Fair, BADA, Olympia (June)
Services Valuations, restorations

Teddy Bears of Witney

Contact Ian Pout
✉ **99 High Street, Witney, Oxfordshire, OX8 6LY** P
☎ 01993 702616 ⓕ 01993 702344
Est. 1985 *Stock size* Large
Stock Steiff, Merrythought, Deans, Hermann, artists' bears
Open Mon–Fri 9.30am– 5.30pm Sat 9.30am–5pm Sun 10.30am–4.30pm
Fairs San Diego, Hennef
Services Valuations

Witney Antiques (BADA, LAPADA, CADA)

Contact Mrs C J Jarrett
✉ **96–100 Corn Street, Witney, Oxfordshire, OX8 7BU** P
☎ 01993 703902 ⓕ 01993 779852
ⓔ witneyantiques@community.co.uk
ⓦ www.witneyantiques.com
Est. 1963 *Stock size* Large
Stock 17th–early 19thC furniture, clocks, works of art, needleworks, probably the largest selection of samplers in the UK
Open Mon–Sat 10am–5pm
Fairs Grosvenor House, BADA
Services Restorations, catalogues

WOODSTOCK

Chris Baylis Country Chairs (TVADA)

Contact Mr C Baylis
✉ **16 Oxford Street, Woodstock, Oxfordshire, OX20 1TS** P
☎ 01993 813887 ⓕ 01993 812379
ⓔ rwood@mcmail.com
ⓦ www.realwoodfurniture.co.uk
Est. 1979 *Stock size* Large
Stock English country chairs 1780–present day. Windsors, rush-seated ladder and spindleback chairs, kitchen chairs etc
Open Tues–Sat 10.30am–5.30pm Sun 11am–5pm

Bees Antiques (TVADA)

Contact Mr J Bateman
✉ **30 High Street, Woodstock, Oxfordshire, OX20 1TG** P
☎ 01993 811062
Est. 1989 *Stock size* Medium
Stock Fine 18th–19thC British and Continental ceramics, glass, jewellery, decorative furniture, metalware
Open Mon–Sat 10am–1pm 1.30–5pm Sun 11am–5pm closed Tues or by appointment
Services Valuations for ceramics, glass, jewellery

The Chair Set

Contact Allan James
✉ **18 Market Place, Woodstock, Oxfordshire, OX20 1TA** P
☎ 01428 707301 ⓕ 01428 707301
ⓔ allan.james@antiquesofwoodstock.com
ⓦ www.antiquesofwoodstock.com
Est. 1985 *Stock size* Large
Stock 18th–19thC sets of chairs and dining room antiques
Open Mon–Sun 10.30am–5.30pm
Services Valuations, search

Span Antiques (TVADA)

Contact Mrs B Johnson or Miss R Mobey
✉ **6 Market Place, Woodstock, Oxfordshire, OX20 1TA** P
☎ 01993 811332
Est. 1978 *Stock size* Medium
No. of dealers 10
Stock An interesting variety of silver, decorative textiles, furniture, 19th–20thC pictures, Art Deco, Art Nouveau, porcelain, books
Open Mon–Sat 10am–5pm Sun 1pm–5pm

The Woodstock Bookshop (PBFA)

Contact Mr Mark Wratten
✉ **3 Market Place, Woodstock, Oxfordshire, OX20 1SY** P
☎ 01993 811005 ⓕ 01993 811005
ⓔ markwrat@dircon.co.uk
Est. 1989 *Stock size* Small
Stock Antiquarian and second-hand books on literature, travel, topography, art, history of art, prints
Open Mon–Sun 10am–5pm closed 1–2pm
Fairs PBFA

YARNTON

Yarnton Antique Centre

Contact Mr M Dunseath
✉ **within Yarnton Nurseries, Sandy Lane, off A44, Yarnton, Kidlington, Oxfordshire, OX5 1PA** P
☎ 01865 379600
Est. 1998 *Stock size* Large
No. of dealers 45 (21 cabinets)
Stock Furniture, silver, china, brass, books, jewellery, lighting, decorative items
Open Mon–Sun 10am–4.30pm

MIDLANDS

DERBYSHIRE

ALFRETON

Alfreton Antique Centre
Contact Helen Dixon
11 King Street, Alfreton, Derbyshire, DE55 7AF P
☎ 01773 520781
Ⓜ 07970 786968
Ⓔ alfretonantiques@supanet.com
Ⓦ www.alfretonantiques.supanet.com
Est. 1996 *Stock size* Large
No. of dealers 35
Stock General antiques, collectables, furniture, clocks, silver, militaria, books, postcards, lighting
Open Mon–Sat 10am–4.30pm Sun 11am–4.30pm
Services Derby replacement service

Curiosity Shop
Contact Kenneth Allsop
37 King Street, Alfreton, Derbyshire, DE55 7BY P
☎ 01773 832429
Ⓜ 07932 7674663
Est. 1974 *Stock size* Medium
Stock General antiques
Open Mon–Sat 9.30am–5pm

ALPORT

Peter Bunting (LAPADA, BADA, CINOA)
Contact Mr P Bunting
Harthill Hall, Alport, Bakewell, Derbyshire, DE45 1LH P
☎ 01629 636203 Ⓕ 01629 636190
Ⓜ 07860 540870
Est. 1975
Stock English oak and country furniture, tapestries, portraits
Open By appointment
Fairs Olympia, NEC

ASHBOURNE

Ashbourne Antiques Ltd
Contact Robert Allsebrook
Blake House Farm, Shirely, Ashbourne, Derbyshire, DE6 3AS P
☎ 01332 290280
Ⓜ 07970 094883
Est. 1975 *Stock size* Large
Stock 18th–20thC furniture
Open By appointment
Services Restorations, shipping

M G Bassett
Contact Mrs G Bassett or Mr M Bassett
38 Church Street, Ashbourne, Derbyshire, DE6 1AJ
☎ 01335 300061/347750 (workshop) Ⓕ 01335 300061
Ⓔ mgbassett@aol.com
Est. 1979 *Stock size* Large

Stock General antiques
Open Mon–Sat 10am–5pm
closed Wed

Daniel Charles Antiques
Contact Keith Phillips-Moul
33 Church Street, Ashbourne, Derbyshire, DE6 1AE
01335 300002 F 01335 348200
E keith@danielcharlesantiques.com
W www.danielcharlesantiques.com
Est. 2000 *Stock size* Medium
Stock 17th–20thC furniture, paintings, chandeliers, decorative items
Open Mon–Sat 10am–5pm
closed Wed
Services Restorations

Pamela Elsom Antiques (LAPADA)
Contact Mrs P Elsom
5 Church Street, Ashbourne, Derbyshire, DE6 1AE
01335 343468/344311
Est. 1965 *Stock size* Medium
Stock General antiques
Open Thurs–Sat 10am–5pm
Services Valuations

Hotspur & Nimrod
Contact Mrs Jarrett
14 Church Street, Ashbourne, Derbyshire, DE6 1AE
01335 342518
M 07718 634605
W www.hotspurandnimrodantiques.co.uk
Est. 1997 *Stock size* Medium
Stock General antiques
Open Mon–Sat 10am–5pm
Sun noon–4pm
Services Coffee shop

J H S Antiques (LAPADA, CINOA, Pewter Society, Metalware Society)
Contact Mr J H Snodin
41a Church Street, Ashbourne, Derbyshire, DE6 1AJ
01335 347733
M 07768 828536
W www.antiques-atlas.com/jhs.htm
Est. 1970 *Stock size* Medium
Stock Period oak, metalware, carving, treen
Open Tues–Sat 10am–5pm
closed Wed

Prestwood Antiques
Contact Mr Chris Ball
39 Church Street, Ashbourne, Derbyshire, DE6 1AJ
01335 342198 F 01335 342198
M 07976 767629
Est. 1989 *Stock size* Large
Stock General antiques
Open Mon–Sat 10am–5pm
closed Wed
Services Restorations

Rose Antiques
Contact Mrs G Rose
37 Church Street, Ashbourne, Derbyshire, DE6 1AE
01335 343822 F 01335 343822
Est. 1984 *Stock size* Medium
Stock General antiques
Open Mon–Sat 10am–5pm
closed Wed

Spurrier-Smith Antiques (LAPADA, CINOA)
Contact Mr I Spurrier-Smith
28b & 39 Church Street, Ashbourne, Derbyshire, DE6 1AE
01335 343669 F 01335 342198
M 07831 454603
Est. 1974 *Stock size* Large
Stock General antiques, furniture, decorative items
Open Mon–Sat 10am–5pm
closed Wed
Services Valuations, restorations

Top Drawer Antiques
Contact Justin Flint
30 Church Street, Ashbourne, Derbyshire, DE6 1AE
F 01335 342198
M 07966 133171
E sarah@topdrawerantiques.freeserve.co.uk
Est. 1990 *Stock size* Large
Stock General antiques, pine, kitchenware, decorative items
Open Mon–Sat 10am–5pm
closed Wed or by appointment
Services Restorations

Watson & Watson
Contact Mrs Lucie-Clare Watson
29 Church Street, Ashbourne, Derbyshire, DE6 1AE
01335 345796 F 01335 345628
E info@watson-watson.co.uk
W www.watson-watson.co.uk
Est. 1994 *Stock size* Medium
Stock 18th–19thC French country furniture
Open Mon–Sat 10am–5pm
Services Interior design

BAKEWELL

Chappells & The Antiques Centre, Bakewell (BADA, LAPADA)
Contact Mrs J Chappell
King Street, Bakewell, Derbyshire, DE45 1DZ
01629 812496 F 01629 814531
E bacc@chappells-antiques.co.uk
W www.chappells-antiques.co.uk
Est. 1992 *Stock size* Large
No. of dealers 30
Stock 17th–20thC items
Open Mon–Sat 10am–5pm
Sun 11am–5pm
Services Restoration, valuation for sale, wedding lists, finance

J Dickinson
The Bakewell Antiques Centre, King Street, Bakewell, Derbyshire, DE45 1DZ
01246 551370
M 07885 174890
Est. 1995
Stock Antique maps, 16th–19thC prints, Derbyshire books and related items
Open By appointment only
Fairs NEC
Services Valuations, restorations

G W Ford & Son Ltd (LAPADA)
Contact Mr I Thomson
Stand 2, Bakewell Antiques Centre, King Street, Bakewell, Derbyshire, DE45 1DZ
01246 410512 F 01246 419223
M 07702 063467
E enquiries@gwfordantiques.co.uk
W www.gwfordantiques.co.uk
Est. 1890 *Stock size* Small
Stock 18th–19thC mahogany, country furniture, 19thC–early 20thC sculpture, silver, Sheffield plate, treen, decorative items
Open Mon–Sat 10am–5pm
Sun 11am–5pm
Services Restorations

Ganymede Antiques
Contact Keith Petts
Bakewell Antiques Centre, King Street, Bakewell, Derbyshire, DE45 1DZ
0114 266 5015

MIDLANDS

DERBYSHIRE • BAMFORD

Ⓔ ganymede@talk21.com
Est. 1992 *Stock size* Medium
Stock Scientific instruments, clocks, silver, metalwork
Open Mon–Sat 10am–5pm Sun 11am–5pm
Fairs International Antique Scientific & Medical Instrument Fair
Services Valuations, restorations

⊞ Martin and Dorothy Harper Antiques (LAPADA)
Contact Martin or Dorothy Harper
✉ **King Street, Bakewell, Derbyshire, DE45 1DZ** Ⓟ
☎ 01629 814757
Ⓜ 07885 347134
Est. 1971 *Stock size* Medium
Stock 18th–early 20thC furniture, metalware, decorative items
Open Tues Wed Fri Sat 10am–5pm or by appointment
Services Valuations

⊞ Lewis Antiques
Contact Les Lewis
✉ **King Street, Bakewell, Derbyshire, DE5 1DZ** Ⓟ
☎ 01629 813141 Ⓕ 01246 234578
Ⓔ Les@lewisantiques.co.uk
Ⓦ www.lewisantiques.co.uk
Est. 1974 *Stock size* Small
Stock General antiques, 18th–19thC furniture and clocks
Open Mon–Sat 10am–5pm closed Thurs
Services Valuations, restorations

⊞ Thornbridge Antiques (LAPADA)
Contact Mrs Caroline Taylor
✉ **King Street, Bakewell, Derbyshire, DE45 1DZ** Ⓟ
☎ 01629 814224 Ⓕ 01629 814224
Est. 1998 *Stock size* Large
Stock General antiques
Open Mon–Sat 10am–5pm Sun 11am–4pm

BAMFORD

⊞ High Peak Antiques
Contact Pat Infanti
✉ **High Peak Garden Centre, Sickleholme, Bamford, Derbyshire, S33 0AH** Ⓟ
☎ 01433 659595
Ⓜ 07967 862093
Est. 1998 *Stock size* Large
Stock Sports memorabilia, Flemish furniture, books, Victoriana, jewellery, Moorcroft, toys, garden items, kitchenware
Open Mon–Sun 10am–5pm

BARLOW

⊞ Hackney House Antiques
Contact Mrs J M Gorman
✉ **Hackney House, Hackney Lane, Barlow, Dronfield, Derbyshire, S18 7TF** Ⓟ
☎ 0114 289 0248
Est. 1981 *Stock size* Medium
Stock Georgian–Edwardian furniture, silver, pictures, porcelain, glass, clocks
Open Tues–Sun 9am–6pm

BELPER

⊞ Derwentside Antiques
Contact Mr M J Adams
✉ **Derwent Street, Belper, Derbyshire, DE56 1WN** Ⓟ
☎ 01773 828008 Ⓕ 01773 828983
Ⓦ www.derwentsideantiques.co.uk
Est. 1994 *Stock size* Large
Stock General antiques
Open Mon–Sun 8am–5.30pm
Fairs Newark, Swinderby
Services Architectural salvage

⊞ Sweetings Antiques Belper
Contact Mr or Mrs Sweeting
✉ **1–1a The Butts, Belper, Derbyshire, DE56 1HX** Ⓟ
☎ 01773 825930 Ⓕ 01773 822780
Ⓜ 07973 658640
Est. 1972 *Stock size* Large
Stock General antiques, country pine furniture, home accessories
Open Mon–Sat 9.30am–5.30pm Sun 11am–4.30pm
Services Restorations and pine stripping

BRADWELL

Bradwell Antiques Centre
Contact Mr N Cottam
✉ **Newburgh Hall, Netherside, Bradwell, Derbyshire, S33 9JL** Ⓟ
☎ 01433 621000 Ⓕ 01433 621000
Ⓔ nick@bradwellantiques.com
Ⓦ www.bradwellantiques.com
Est. 2000 *Stock size* Large
No. of dealers 28
Stock Furniture, paintings, general antiques, collectables
Open Mon–Sat 10am–5pm Sun 11am–5pm
Services Licensed café, bar, booksearch, restoration

BUXTON

⊞ Antiques Warehouse
Contact Nigel Thompson
✉ **25 Lighthouse Road, Buxton, Derbyshire, SK17 7BJ** Ⓟ
☎ 01298 72967 Ⓕ 01298 22603
Ⓜ 07947 050552
Est. 1979 *Stock size* Large
Stock General antiques
Open Mon–Fri 10am–3pm Sat 10am–4pm Sun by appointment
Services Valuations, restorations

⊞ Back to Front
Contact Miss Simone Jordan-Lomas
✉ **9–11 Market Street, Buxton, Derbyshire, SK17 6JY** Ⓟ
☎ 01298 23969
Est. 1974 *Stock size* Large
Stock Antique textiles
Open Mon–Sun 10am–8pm
Fairs Newark, The International Antique and Collectables Fair at RAF Swinderby
Services Seminars and valuations

⊞ A & A Needham
Contact Ann Needham
✉ **8 Cavendish Circus, Buxton, Derbyshire, SK17 6AT** Ⓟ
☎ 01298 24546
Ⓜ 07941 436931
Est. 1953 *Stock size* Small
Stock French, Dutch, English furniture, paintings, bronzes, works of art
Open Mon–Sat 9am–5pm
Fairs Buxton Fair, Chester

⊞ What Now Antiques
Contact Mrs L Carruthers
✉ **Unit 8, Cavendish Arcade, The Crescent, Buxton, Derbyshire, SK17 6BQ** Ⓟ
☎ 01298 27178
Est. 1987 *Stock size* Medium
Stock General 19th–20thC antiques
Open Tues–Sat 10am–5pm Sun 1–4pm
Services Valuations, restorations

CASTLE DONNINGTON

⊞ The Gallery Book Shop
Contact Mrs J Ethelston

17 Borough Street, Castle Donnington, Derbyshire, DE74 2LA
01332 814391
Est. 2000 *Stock size* Medium
Stock Antiquarian and collectable books, prints
Open Mon–Fri 9am–4.30pm Sat 9am–1pm closed Wed
Services Picture framing

CASTLETOL

Hawkridge Books
Contact Irene or Joe Tierney
Crucu Barn, Cross Street, Castletol, Derbyshire, S33 8WH
01433 621999
www.hawkridge.co.uk
Est. 1995 *Stock size* Large
Stock Antiquarian, rare and second-hand books, and ornithology
Open Mon–Fri 10am–5pm Sat 10am–5.30pm Sun noon–5.30pm

CHESTERFIELD

Caroline Hartley Books
Contact Caroline Hartley
2 Hoole Street, Hasland, Chesterfield, Derbyshire, S41 0AR
01246 558481 01246 558481
carohartley@aol.com
www.abebooks.com
Est. 1984 *Stock size* Small
Stock Antiquarian, rare and second-hand books
Open Internet only
Fairs The London Book Fairs

Haslam Antiques
Contact Neil Haslam
414 Chatsworth Road, Chesterfield, Derbyshire, S40 3BG
01246 853672
07767 416148
neilandcynthia@haslamantiques.fsnet.co.uk
Est. 1989 *Stock size* Small
Stock General antiques, period and decorative
Open Thurs–Sat 9am–5pm or by appointment
Services Valuations, restorations, interior design, antiques butler service

Ian Morris
Contact Mr I Morris
479 Chatsworth Road, Chesterfield, Derbyshire, S40 3AD
01246 235120
Est. 1974 *Stock size* Medium
Stock General antiques
Open Mon–Sat 9am–5pm

Marlene Rutherford Antiques
Contact Mrs M Rutherford
401 Sheffield Road, Whittington Moor, Chesterfield, Derbyshire, S41 8LS
01246 450209
07885 665440
Est. 1984 *Stock size* Large
Stock General antiques, upholstered furniture, oil lamps, clocks
Open Mon Tues Fri Sat 1–4pm Thurs 10am–4pm

CROMFORD

Antiques Loft
Contact Brendan Rogerson
Market Place, Cromford, Matlock, Derbyshire, DE4 3QH
01629 826565
Est. 1993 *Stock size* Large
Stock Victorian pine, shipping furniture
Open By appointment
Fairs Swinderby, Newark

DALE ABBEY

Flourish Farm Antiques
Contact Mrs J Mumford
Flourish Farm, Dale Abbey, Derbyshire, DE7 4PQ
01332 667820
07970 055151
Est. 1995 *Stock size* Medium
Stock Antique pine furniture, fireplaces, doors
Open Tues–Sat 10am–5pm Sun 11am–4pm
Fairs Newark
Services Stripping

DERBY

Antiques & Curios
Contact Mr McCann
8 Ashbourne Road, Derby, Derbyshire, DE22 3AA
01332 363330
Est. 2001 *Stock size* Small
Stock Furniture, ceramics,
Open Mon–Sat 10am–5pm

Derventio Books
Contact Ian Briddon
20 Monk Street, Derby, Derbyshire, DE22 3QB
01322 343538
spikeyclare@zoom.co.uk
www.derventio-books.co.uk
Est. 1996 *Stock size* Medium
Stock Antiquarian and second-hand books, antiquarian topographical prints, Derbyshire books a speciality
Open Mon–Sat 10.15am–5pm
Services Online catalogue

Finishing Touches
Contact Lynne Robertson
224 Uttoxeter Old Road, Derby, Derbyshire, DE1 1NF
01332 721717
www.derbyantiques.co.uk
Est. 1994 *Stock size* Medium
Stock Georgian and Victorian fireplaces and fire surrounds, pine doors, locks, handles, window catches
Open Tues–Sat 10am–5.30pm

Friargate Antiques Company
Contact Glyn or Daryl Richards
120 Friargate, Derby, Derbyshire, DE1 1EX
01332 297966 01332 297966
07976 929456
daryl@friargateantiques.demon.co.uk
www.friargateantiques.co.uk
Est. 1978 *Stock size* Large
Stock General antiques including Royal Crown Derby
Open Mon–Fri 10am–4pm Sat 10am–5pm
Fairs Newark
Services Valuations, restorations

Friargate Pine Co Ltd
Contact John Marianszi
Old Pump House, Stafford Street, Derby, Derbyshire, DE1 1JL
01332 341215 01332 341215
enquiries@friargatepine.co.uk
www.friargatepine.co.uk
Est. 1984 *Stock size* Medium
Stock Antique, reproduction pine
Open Mon–Sat 9am–5pm
Services Made to measure

Neales Auctioneers (ARVA, SOFAA)
Contact Mr J Lewis
Becket Street, Derby, Derbyshire, DE1 1HU

☎ 01332 203601 Ⓕ 01332 295543
Ⓔ derby@neales.co.uk
Ⓦ www.neales.co.uk
Est. 1840
Open Mon–Fri 9am–5.30pm
Sales Victorian and later sales fortnightly, quarterly antique furniture and effects sales
Frequency Fortnightly
Catalogues Yes

⊞ Rummages
Contact Mr P Lyttel
✉ **2 Monk Street, Derby, Derbyshire, DE22 3QB**
☎ 01332 200590
Est. 1994 *Stock size* Small
Stock General antiques
Open Mon–Sat 9am–5pm

DUFFIELD

⊞ Wayside Antiques
Contact Brian Harding
✉ **62 Town Street, Duffield, Belper, Derbyshire, DE56 4GG** Ⓟ
☎ 01332 840346
Est. 1976
Stock 18th–19thC furniture
Open Mon–Sat 10am–6pm
Services Valuations

GLOSSOP

⊞ The Chair Shop
Contact Louise Jannetta
✉ **53 High Street East, Glossop, Derbyshire, SK13 8PN** Ⓟ
☎ 01457 856389
Est. 1994 *Stock size* Medium
Stock Upholstered chairs, antique soft furnishings
Open Mon–Sat 9am–5pm
Services Restorations

⊞ Chapel Antiques
Contact Mr Norman Pogsom
✉ **126 Brookfield, Glossop, Derbyshire, SK13 6JE** Ⓟ
☎ 01457 866711
Est. 1984 *Stock size* Medium
Stock Clocks, barometers, pottery, general antiques
Open Thurs–Sun 10am–5pm

⊞ Cornish Connection
Contact Janet Winterbottom
✉ **PO Box 18, Glossop, Derbyshire, SK13 8FA**
☎ 01457 864833 Ⓕ 01457 857703
Ⓔ cornishconnection@tesco.net
Est. 1996 *Stock size* Medium
Stock Old and new Cornish collectables, limited editions
Open By appointment Mon–Thurs 9.30am–4.30pm
Services Mail order only

⊞ Cottage Antiques
Contact Mrs J Shapter
✉ **Unit 13, Brookfield, Glossop, Derbyshire, SK13 6JF** Ⓟ
☎ 01457 860092
Est. 1979 *Stock size* Large
Stock General antiques
Open Thurs–Sun Bank Holidays 10am–5pm
Services Valuations, restorations, house clearance

⊞ Derbyshire Clocks
Contact Terry or Judith Lees
✉ **104 High Street West, Glossop, Derbyshire, SK13 8BB** Ⓟ
☎ 01457 862677
Est. 1971 *Stock size* Medium
Stock Clocks, barometers and other related items. Pre-1880 longcase and wall clocks
Open Thurs–Sat 9am–5pm Sun noon–4.30pm
Services Restorations

Glossop Antique Centre
Contact Mr A R Mays
✉ **Brookfield, Glossop, Derbyshire, SK13 6JE** Ⓟ
☎ 01457 863904
No. of dealers 11
Stock General antiques
Open Thurs–Sun 10am–5pm
Services Valuations, restorations, café

HAYFIELD

⊞ Paul Pickford Antiques
Contact Paul Pickford
✉ **Top of the Town, Hayfield, High Peak, Derbyshire, SK22 2JE** Ⓟ
☎ 01663 747276/743356
Ⓜ 07885 952236
Ⓔ paul@pickfordantiques.co.uk
Ⓦ www.pickfordantiques.co.uk
Est. 1974 *Stock size* Medium
Stock General antiques, furniture, stripped pine, light fittings
Open Tues Thurs Sat 11am–4pm Sun 1–5pm

HEANOR

Heanor Antiques Centre
Contact Jane Richards
✉ **Church Square, 1–2 Ilkeston Road, Heanor, Derbyshire, DE75 7AE** Ⓟ
☎ 01773 531181
Est. 1997 *Stock size* Large
No. of dealers 150
Stock General antiques, small collectable items
Open Mon–Sun 10.30am–4.30pm

MATLOCK

Antique Centre
Contact Margaret O'Reilly or Keith Allsop
190 South Parade, Matlock Bath, Derbyshire, DE4 3NR P
01629 582712
Est. 1970 *Stock size* Large
Stock Georgian–Edwardian furniture, upholstered furniture
Open Mon–Sun 10am–5pm or later

R F Barrett Rare Books
Contact Mr R Barrett
87 Dale Road, Matlock, Derbyshire, DE4 3LU P
01629 57644
RFBarrett@gas.com
Est. 1979 *Stock size* Medium
Stock Antique, rare and second-hand books
Open Mon–Sun 10am–5pm

Country Cottage Antiques
Contact Barbara or Sally Powell
69 Matlock Green, Matlock, Derbyshire, DE43BT P
01629 57109/582762
07974 954956
Est. 1983 *Stock size* Medium
Stock General antiques, upholstered chairs
Open Tues–Fri 1–5pm Wed 2–5pm Sat 11am–4.30pm or by appointment
Fairs Buxton
Services Upholstery and removals

Matlock Antiques & Collectables
Contact Miss Wendy Shirley
7 Dale Road, Matlock, Derbyshire, DE4 3LT P
01629 760808 01629 760808
www.matlock-antiques-collectables.cwc.net
Est. 1996 *Stock size* Large
No. of dealers 70+
Stock General antiques, collectables
Open Mon–Sun 10am–5pm
Services Delivery, riverside café

Noel Wheatcroft & Son (FNAVA)
Contact Mrs J Kinnear
Matlock Auction Gallery, The Old Picture Palace, Dale Road, Matlock, Derbyshire, DE4 3LT
01629 57460 01629 57956
mag@wheatcroft-noel.co.uk
www.wheatcroft-noel.co.uk
Est. 1923
Open Mon–Fri 10am–4pm closed Thurs
Sales Phone for sale details
Frequency Monthly
Catalogues Yes

NEW MILLS

Michael Allcroft Antiques
Contact Michael Allcroft
203 Buxton Road, Newtown, New Mills, Nr Stockport, SK12 2RA P
01663 744014 01663 744014
07798 781642
Est. 1986 *Stock size* Large
Stock General antiques
Open Mon–Wed noon–5pm Thurs 11am–5.30pm Sat 9am–noon
Fairs Newark

OCKBROOK

The Good Olde Days
Contact Mr S Potter
6 Flood Street, Ockbrook, Derby, Derbyshire, DE72 3RF P
01332 544244
Est. 1995 *Stock size* Large
Stock General antiques
Open Tues–Sat 10am–5pm Wed noon–5pm
Fairs Newark, Cheltenham, Kettering
Services Valuations

RIDDINGS

South Street Trading Co
Contact Mr R Evison
31 South Street, Riddings, Alfreton, Derbyshire, DE55 4EJ P
01773 541527 01773 541527
07713 514320
raevison@aol.com
www.steammodels.uk.com
Est. 1990 *Stock size* Large
Stock Old and new live steam models
Open Mon–Fri 9am–5pm

RIPLEY

A A Ambergate Antiques
Contact Mr C Lawrence
8 Derby Road, Ripley, Derbyshire, DE5 3HR P
01773 745201
07885 327753
Est. 1971 *Stock size* Large
Stock Edwardian bedroom furniture
Open Mon–Sat 9.30am–4.30pm
Services Valuations, restorations

Memory Lane Antiques
Contact Jim Cullen
Nottingham Road, Ripley, Derbyshire, DE5 3AS P
01773 570184
07703 115626
JamesGC1@aol.com
Est. 1993 *Stock size* Large
No. of dealers 40
Stock General antiques, collectables, shipping goods, kitchenware, Denby
Open Mon–Sun 10.30am–4pm only closed Christmas Day
Services Valuations, talks, house clearance

Wartime Wardrobe
Contact Mr Barry Draycott
193 Church Street, Waingroves, Ripley, Derbyshire, DE5 9TF P
01773 744427 01773 744427
07966 450726
Est. 1995 *Stock size* Medium
Stock Military and civilian 1940s vintage clothing, general militaria
Open Any time by appointment
Fairs Most major military shows throughout the UK
Services Valuations, advice

SHARDLOW

Shardlow Antiques Warehouse
Contact N J Critchlow
24 The Wharf, Shardlow, Derbyshire, DE72 2GH P
01332 792899/662899 01322 662899
Est. 1985 *Stock size* Large
Stock 18th–20thC furniture
Open Mon–Sat 11am–5pm Sun noon–5pm closed Fri
Fairs Newark
Services Part house clearance

MIDLANDS

DERBYSHIRE • WHALEY BRIDGE

WHALEY BRIDGE

Nimbus Antiques
Contact Mr H C Brobbin
14 Chapel Road, Whaley Bridge, High Peak, Derbyshire, SK23 7JZ
☎ 01663 734248 Ⓕ 01663 734248
Est. 1979 *Stock size* Large
Stock General antiques, Georgian–Victorian furniture and clocks
Open Mon–Fri 9am–5.30pm Sat 10am–5.30pm Sun 2–5.30pm

LEICESTERSHIRE

ASHBY DE LA ZOUCH

Affordable Antiques
Contact Mrs J Sidwells
The Old Forge, North Street, Ashby de la Zouch, Leicestershire, LE65 1HS
☎ 01530 413744
Ⓜ 07966 424861
Est. 1994 *Stock size* Medium
Stock Pre-1950s furniture and effects
Open Mon–Sat 10am–5pm closed Wed
Fairs Newark, Swinderby
Services Pine, oak stripping

COALVILLE

Keystone Antiques (LAPADA)
Contact Miss H McPherson
9 Ashby Road, Coalville, Leicestershire, LE67 3LF
☎ 01530 835966
Ⓔ heathermcp@webleicester.co.uk
Est. 1980 *Stock size* Medium
Stock General antiques, jewellery, silver, small collectables
Open Mon–Fri 10am–5pm Sat 10am–4.30pm closed Wed
Fairs NEC
Services Valuations

EAST LEAKE

Booklore (SOBB)
Contact Mr R Corbett
4 Brookside, East Leake, Loughborough, Leicestershire, LE12 6PB
☎ 01509 852044 Ⓕ 01509 852044
Est. 1994 *Stock size* Medium
Stock Antiquarian and collectable books, maps
Open Mon–Sat 9.30am–5.30pm Wed 9.30am–1.30pm
Fairs Buxton Book Fair, Bloomsbury
Services Restorations, binding

GREAT GLAN

Sitting Pretty
Contact Mrs J Jones-Fenleigh
45a Main Street, Great Glan, Leicestershire, LE8 9EH
☎ 01162 593711
Est. 1979 *Stock size* Medium
Stock Antique furniture
Open Thurs–Sat 10am–6pm
Services Upholstery restoration

GRIMSTON

Ancient and Oriental Ltd (ADA)
Contact Mr Alex Szolin
Park View, Grimston, Melton Mowbray, Leicestershire, LE14 3BZ
☎ 01664 812044
Ⓔ alex@antiquities.co.uk
Ⓦ www.antiquities.co.uk
Est. 1992
Stock Ancient art and items of archaeological interest from major world cultures, ancient–medieval
Open Mon–Sun 8am–8pm or by appointment
Services Mail order, catalogues and website

HINCKLEY

House Things Antiques
Contact P Robertson
44 Mansion Street, Trinity Lane, Hinckley, Leicestershire, LE10 0AU
☎ 01455 618518
Est. 1979 *Stock size* Medium
Stock General antiques
Open Mon–Sat 10am–6pm closed Tues
Fairs The International Antique and Collectables Fair at RAF Swinderby
Services Valuations, restorations

Magpie Antiques & Collectables
Contact Michelle Johnston
126 Castle Street, Hinckley, Leicestershire, LE10 1DD
☎ 01455 891819
Ⓜ 07713 099744
Est. 1983 *Stock size* Medium
Stock Antique furniture, collectables, pre-1950s ephemera and effects
Open Mon–Sat 9am–5pm

HOBY

Withers of Leicester
Contact Simon Frings
The Old Rutland, 6 Regent Road, Hoby, Leicestershire, LE14 3DU
☎ 01664 434803
Ⓜ 07836 526595
Est. 1860 *Stock size* Medium
Stock 17th–early 20thC furniture
Open Mon–Sat prior telephone call advisable
Services Valuations, restorations

KIBWORTH

Kibworth Pine Co
Contact Mrs Burdett
16 Harcourt Estate, Kibworth, Leicestershire, LE8 0NE
☎ 0116 279 3475
Ⓦ www.kibworthpinecompany.com
Est. 1981 *Stock size* Large
Stock Antique pine furniture
Open Tues–Sat 9.30am–5,30pm Sun noon–4pm

LEICESTER

Betty's Antiques
Contact Mr A Smith
9 Knighton Fields Road West, Leicester, Leicestershire, LE2 6LH
☎ 0116 283 9048
Est. 1983 *Stock size* Small
Stock General antiques
Open Mon–Sat 10am–5pm

The Black Cat Bookshop
Contact Mr P Woolley
36–39 Silver Arcade, Leicester, Leicestershire, LE1 5FB
☎ 01162 512756 Ⓕ 01162 813545
Ⓔ blackcatuk@aol.com
Ⓦ www.blackcatbookshop.com
Est. 1987 *Stock size* Large
Stock Antiquarian, rare and second-hand books, British comics, magazines, printed ephemera
Open Mon–Sat 9.30am–5pm
Services Worldwide mail order, book search, catalogues

Churchgate Auctions Ltd
Contact Mr D Dearman

✉ 66 Churchgate, Leicester, Leicestershire, LE1 4AL P
☎ 01162 621416 F 01162 517711
E info@churchgateauc.co.uk
W www.churchgateauctions.co.uk
Est. 1966
Open Mon–Fri 8.30am–6pm
Sat 8.30am–noon
Sales General and antiques sales Tues Fri 10am
Frequency Twice weekly
Catalogues Yes

Clarendon Books (PBFA)
Contact Mr J Smith
✉ **144 Clarenden Park Road, Leicester, Leicestershire, LE2 3AE** P
☎ 01162 701856 F 01162 709020
M 07710 683996
E clarendonbooks@aol.com
Est. 1986 *Stock size* Medium
Stock Antiquarian, rare and second-hand books
Open Mon–Sat 10am–5pm
Fairs PBFA

Corry's Antiques (LAPADA)
Contact Mrs E I Corry
✉ **26 Francis Street, Stoneygate, Leicester, Leicestershire, LE2 2BD** P
☎ 01162 703794 F 01162 703794
W www.corrys-antiques.com
Est. 1964 *Stock size* Large
Stock General antiques, clocks, mirrors
Open Mon–Sat 10am–5pm
Fairs LAPADA
Services Restorations

Glory Hole Antiques
✉ **69 High Street, East Shilton, Leicester, Leicestershire, LE9 7DH** P
☎ 01455 847922
M 07710 101364
E mark@thegloryhole.co.uk
W www.thegloryhole.co.uk
Est. 1994 *Stock size* Large
Stock General antiques, Victorian–Edwardian items
Open Mon–Sat 10am–5.30pm
Fairs Newark, Ardingly
Services Valuations, restorations, stripping, shipping

John Hardy Antiques
Contact John Hardy
✉ **91 London Road, Oadby, Leicester, Leicestershire, LE2 5DP** P
☎ 01162 7128622
Est. 1969 *Stock size* Medium
Stock General antiques
Open Mon–Sat 10am–6pm

Heathcote Ball and Co Fine Art Auctioneers & Valuers
Contact James Lees
✉ **Castle Auction Rooms, 78 St Nicholas Circle, Leicester, Leicestershire, LE1 5NW** P
☎ 01162 536789 F 01162 538517
E heathcote-ball@clara.co.uk
W www.heathcote-ball.clara.co.uk
Est. 1974
Open Mon–Fri 9am–1pm 2–5.30pm
Sales General antiques and fine art sales (phone for details)
Frequency 5 to 6 weeks
Catalogues Yes

Letty's Antiques
Contact Mr Dubberley
✉ **6 Rutland Street, Leicester, Leicestershire, LE1 1RA**
☎ 01162 626435
M 07050 163532
Est. 1952 *Stock size* Small
Stock General antiques, jewellery and silver
Open Mon–Sat 9.30am–4.45pm closed Thurs except Nov Dec
Services Free verbal valuations

Oxford Street Antique Centre
Contact Mr P Giles
✉ **16–26 Oxford Street, Leicester, Leicestershire, LE1 5XU** P
☎ 0116 2553006 F 0116 2555863
Est. 1987 *Stock size* Large
Stock Victorian–present-day furniture
Open Mon–Fri 10am–5.30pm Sat 10am–5pm Sun 2–5pm
Services Export, container packing

Retrobuy
Contact Mr Mark Williamson
✉ **62 Silver Arcade, Leicester, Leicestershire, LE1 5FB**
☎ 0116 242 5949 F 0116 242 5949
E retrobuy@ntlworld.com
W www.retrobuy.co.uk
Est. 1997 *Stock size* Large
Stock Retro toys, clothes, arcade, home, music, records
Open Mon–Sat noon–5pm
Fairs NEC, Donnington
Services Valuations, Mail order

The Rug Gallery
Contact Mr R Short
✉ **50 Montague Road, Leicester, Leicestershire, LE2 1TH**
☎ 01162 700085 F 01162 700113
Est. 1987 *Stock size* Large
Stock Old and new Oriental rugs and kilims, antique Oriental furniture
Open Fri Sat 10am–4pm or by appointment

MIDLANDS

LEICESTERSHIRE • LOUGHBOROUGH

Treasure Trove Books
Contact Linda Sharman
21 Mayfield Road, Leicester, Leicestershire, LE2 1SR
0116 2755933
Est. 1993
Stock Second-hand books, records (pop and classical), CDs, tapes
Open Mon–Sat 9.30am–5.30pm
Fairs Leicestershire, Missing Book Fair

Warner Auctions Ltd
Contact Amanda Harding
52 Sanvey Gate, Leicester, Leicestershire, LE1 4BQ
01162 512510 Ⓕ 01162 510204
Ⓔ enquiries@warnerauctions.co.uk
Ⓦ www.warnerauctions.co.uk
Est. 1846
Open Mon–Fri 9am–5.30pm
Sales General sale Wed 10.30am, viewing Tues noon–6pm Wed 9–10.30am prior to sale. Antiques and fine art sale quarterly Wed 11am, viewing Tues 9am–5pm Wed 9–11am prior to sale, also occasional books and collectors' sales
Frequency Fortnightly
Catalogues Yes

West End Antiques
Contact Mrs C Vaughan
1 Lothair Road, Aylestone Road, Leicester, Leicestershire, LE2 7QE
0116 2440086
Est. 1985 *Stock size* Medium
Stock General antiques
Open Tues–Sat 10am–4.30pm
Fairs Donnington

LOUGHBOROUGH

Malcolm Hornsby
Contact Mr Malcolm Hornsby
41 Church Gate, Loughborough, Leicestershire, LE11 1UE
01509 269860 Ⓕ 01509 269860
Ⓔ hornsby@webleicester.co.uk
Est. 1969 *Stock size* Large
Stock Antiquarian, rare and second-hand books, Eastern Mediterranean travel books a speciality
Open Mon–Sat 9.30am–5.30pm

Loughborough Antiques Centre
Contact Richard or Carol Wesley
50 Market Street, Loughborough, Leicestershire, LE11 3ER
01509 239931
Est. 1979 *Stock size* Medium
Stock General antiques, jewellery, clocks
Open Tues Thurs–Sat 10am–5pm
Fairs NEC, Newark
Services Valuations

LUBENHAM

Oaktree Antiques
Contact Gillian Abraham
The Drapers House, Main Street, Lubenham, Market Harborough, Leicestershire, LE16 9TF
01858 410041
Ⓦ www.oaktreeantiques.co.uk
Stock size Large
Stock Town and country 17th–19thC furniture, longcase clocks, works of art
Open Wed–Sun 10am–6pm

MARKET BOSWORTH

Bosworth Antiques
Contact Mr J H Thorp
12 Main Street, Market Bosworth, Leicestershire, CV13 0JW
01455 292134
Est. 1986 *Stock size* Medium
Stock General antiques and collectables
Open Mon–Sat 10am–5pm closed Tues
Services Valuations

Corner Cottage Antiques
Contact Jill or Bob Roberts
7 Market Place, Market Bosworth, Leicestershire, CV13 0LF
01455 290344/285583
Ⓜ 07909 920903
Est. 1974 *Stock size* Large
Stock 18th–early 20thC furniture, silver, porcelain, copper, brass, glass, oil lamps
Open Tues–Sat 10am–5pm
Fairs Newark

MARKET HARBOROUGH

Aquarius Books
Contact Mr R Lack
17 St Marys Road, Market Harborough, Leicestershire, LE16 7DS
01858 431060
Ⓦ www.aquariusbooks.co.uk
Est. 1989 *Stock size* Medium
Stock Antiquarian, rare and second-hand books
Open Mon–Sat 10am–4pm

Gildings
Contact John Gilding
Roman Way, Market Harborough, Leicestershire, LE16 7PQ
01858 410414 Ⓕ 01858 432956
Ⓔ sales@gildings.co.uk
Ⓦ www.gildings.co.uk
Est. 1980
Open Mon–Fri 9am–5pm
Sales Regular fine art, antiques, specialist sales, weekly Victoriana and collectables sales
Frequency Monthly
Catalogues Yes

Richard Kimbell Ltd
Contact Mrs Jane Armstrong Wade
Rockingham Road, Market Harborough, Leicestershire, LE16 7QE
01858 433444 Ⓕ 01858 461301
Ⓔ sallyd@richard-kimbellatq.co.uk
Est. 1969 *Stock size* Medium
Stock Country furniture
Open Mon–Sat 9am–6pm Sun 11am–5pm

Mosstique
Contact Mrs Andre C Moss
6 Adam & Eve Street, Market Harborough, Leicestershire, LE16 7LT
01858 469448 Ⓕ 01604 882399
Ⓜ 07889 365423
Ⓔ mossfairs@hotmail.com
Est. 1995 *Stock size* Medium
No. of dealers 6
Stock Collectables, furniture, books, ephemera, militaria, commemoratives, postcards, cigarette cards
Open Mon–Sun 10am–4pm

Phillips International Auctioneers and Valuers
34 High Street, Market Harborough, Leicestershire, LE16 7NL
01858 438900 Ⓕ 01858 438909
Ⓦ www.phillips-auction.com
Sales Regional Office (Telephone for details)

MELTON MOWBRAY

⊞ Flagstones Pine and Country Furniture
Contact Julie Adcock
✉ **24 Burton Street, Melton Mowbray, Leicestershire, LE13 1AF** P
☎ 01664 566438
Ⓜ 07971 299206
Est. 1984 *Stock size* Medium
Stock Pine and country furniture, old and reproduction lighting, accessories
Open Mon–Sat 9.30am–5.15pm Sun 10.30am–3.30pm
Services Stripping service, custom built furniture

⊞ Lotties
Contact Mr M Allen
✉ **33 High Street, Melton Mowbray, Leicestershire, LE13 0TR** P
☎ 01664 560056
Ⓜ 07970 400551
Est. 1991 *Stock size* Medium
Stock General antiques, collectables
Open Tues–Sat 9.30am–5pm
Fairs Newark, Donnington Park

⊞ Parkside Antiques
Contact Marylyn Gordon
✉ **25 Leicester Street, Melton Mowbray, Leicestershire, LE13 0PP** P
☎ 01664 560446 Ⓕ 01664 560446
Ⓜ 07773 176727
Est. 1996 *Stock size* Medium
Stock General antiques
Open Tues Fri Sat 9.30am–5pm or by appointment
Fairs Ardingly, Newark

NARBOROUGH

⊞ Ken Smith Antiques Ltd (LAPADA)
Contact Mr K Smith
✉ **215–217 Leicester Road, Narborough, Leicester, Leicestershire, LE9 5BE** P
☎ 0116 286 2341
Ⓔ KSL@kensmithltd.co.uk
Ⓦ www.kensmithltd.co.uk
Est. 1888 *Stock size* Medium
Stock General antiques, furniture and collectables
Open Mon–Sat 9.30am–5pm
Fairs Newark

OSGATHORPE

⊞ David E Burrows Antiques (LAPADA)
Contact Mr David Burrows
✉ **Manor House Farm, Osgathorpe, Nr Loughborough, Leicestershire, LE12 9SY** P
☎ 01530 222218 Ⓕ 01530 223139
Ⓔ david.burrows2@virgin.net
Est. 1970 *Stock size* Large
Stock Pine, oak, mahogany and walnut furniture, clocks, pictures
Trade only Yes
Open By appointment
Services Valuations, shipping

🔨 David Stanley Auctions
Contact David Stanley
✉ **Stordon Grange, Osgathorpe, Loughborough, Leicestershire, LE12 9SR** P
☎ 01530 222320 Ⓕ 01530 222523
Ⓔ auctions@davidstanley.com
Ⓦ www.davidstanley.com
Est. 1979
Open Mon–Sat 8am–5pm
Sales Antique woodwork tools (phone for details)
Frequency Bi-monthly
Catalogues Yes

QUENIBOROUGH

⊞ J Green & Son
Contact Mr R Green
✉ **1 Coppice Lane, Queniborough, Leicestershire, LE7 3DR** P
☎ 01162 606682 Ⓕ 01162 606682
Ⓜ 07860 513121
Est. 1949 *Stock size* Medium
Stock Georgian and period furniture
Open By appointment

SEAGRAVE

🔨 Miller Services
Contact Robert Miller
✉ **43–45 Swan Street, Seagrave, Leicestershire, LE12 7NN** P
☎ 01509 812037 Ⓕ 01509 812037
Est. 1986
Open Mon–Fri 9am–5pm Sat 10am–12.30pm
Sales Antiques and jewellery sales, Seagrave Village Hall, Sun 12.30pm, viewing 10am
Frequency Monthly
Catalogues Yes

SWINFORD

⊞ Old Timers (BHI)
Contact Mr M Harris
✉ **High Street, Swinford, Lutterworth, Leicestershire, LE17 6BL** P
☎ 01788 860311 Ⓕ 01788 860311
Ⓜ 07836 505111
Ⓦ www.old-timers.co.uk
Est. 1993 *Stock size* Medium
Stock Antique clocks including longcase, furniture
Open Mon–Sat 9am–5pm Sun 10am–1.30pm advised to call first
Services Valuations, restorations

WOODHOUSE EAVES

⊞ Paddock Antiques
Contact Carole Bray
✉ **The Old Smithy, Brand Hill, Woodhouse Eaves, Loughborough, Leicestershire, LE1 5SS** P
☎ 01509 890264
Ⓜ 07860 785325
Est. 1974 *Stock size* Large
Stock Porcelain, small furniture
Open Tues Fri Sat 9.30am–5.30pm
Fairs NEC, Shepton Mallet
Services Valuations, restorations

WYMESWOLD

⊞ N F Bryan-Peach Antiques
Contact Mr N Bryan-Peach
✉ **28 Far Street, Wymeswold, Loughborough, Leicestershire, LE12 6TZ** P
☎ 01509 880425 Ⓕ 01509 880425
Ⓜ 07860 559590
Ⓔ norm@bryanpeach.demon.co.uk
Ⓦ www.country-focus.co.uk/antiques
Est. 1974 *Stock size* Medium
Stock 18th–19thC furniture, clocks, barometers
Open Mon–Sat 9.30am–5pm closed Thurs
Services Valuations, restorations

WYMONDHAM

⊞ The Old Bakery Antiques
Contact Mrs T Bryan
✉ **The Old Bakery, Main Street, Wymondham, Melton Mowbray, Leicestershire, LE14 2AG** P
☎ 01572 787472

MIDLANDS

NORTHAMPTONSHIRE • BRACKLEY

Est. 1990 *Stock size* Medium
Stock Antique kitchenware, pine, stained glass, door hardware, chimney pots, tiles, decorative items, garden items, architectural antiques
Open Mon–Sat 10am–5.30pm closed Thurs

NORTHAMPTONSHIRE

BRACKLEY

Brackley Antiques
Contact Mrs B H Nutting
69 High Street, Brackley, Northamptonshire, NN13 7BW P
☎ 01280 703362 F 01280 703362
M 07761 443726
Est. 1979 *Stock size* Medium
Stock General antiques
Open Mon–Sat 10am–6pm Wed by appointment
Services Traditional upholstery

The Brackley Antique Cellar
Contact Debby Perry
Drayman's Walk, Brackley, Northamptonshire, NN13 6BE P
☎ 01280 701393 F 01280 841851
Est. 2000 *Stock size* Large
No. of dealers 102
Stock General antiques, smalls, collectables, furniture, militaria
Open Mon–Sun 10am–5pm
Services Valuations, restorations, tea room

Juno Antiques
4 Bridge Street, Brackley, Northamptonshire, NN13 7EP
☎ 01280 700639
Est. 1983 *Stock size* Medium
Stock General antiques
Open Mon–Sat 10am–1pm 2–5pm closed Wed

DESBOROUGH

Richard Kimbell Ltd
Contact Fiona Kimbell
Old Bus Station, Harborough Road, Desborough, Northamptonshire, NN14 2QX P
☎ 01536 762093 F 01536 763263
E sallyd@richard-kimbellatq.co.uk
Est. 1969 *Stock size* Large
Stock Country furniture, old-wood reproduction furniture, smalls
Open Mon–Fri 7.30am–5.30pm

FINEDON

Antiques en France
Contact Mr K Day
3 Church Street, Finedon, Wellingborough, Northamptonshire, NN9 5NA P
☎ 01933 682515 F 01933 682951
E kenday@btinternet.com
Est. 1994 *Stock size* Large
Stock General French and English decorative furniture
Open Mon–Sat 9.30am–5.30pm Sun by appointment
Services Valuations, shipping

Aspidistra Antiques (RADS)
Contact Patricia Moss
51 High Street, Finedon, Wellingborough, Northamptonshire, NN9 9JN P
☎ 01933 680196 F 01933 682552
M 07768 071948
E aspidistra@patandgeoff.demon.co.uk
W www.aspidistra.antiques.com
Est. 1994 *Stock size* Medium
No. of dealers 6
Stock Specialist in decorative arts, good selection of smalls and furniture, 1960s–1970s items

Open Mon–Sat 10am–5pm
Sun 11am–5pm
Services Valuations, commission sales, restoration

Simon Banks Antiques
Contact Mr S Banks
28 Church Street, Finedon, Wellingborough, Northamptonshire, NN9 5NA P
01933 680371
07976 787539
Est. 1984 *Stock size* Large
Stock General antiques, dining room furniture, clocks, silver, silver plate, pottery, porcelain
Open Mon–Fri 10am–5.30pm Sat 10am–5.30pm Sun 11am–4.30pm
Services Valuations

Robert Cheney Antiques
Contact Robert Cheney
11–13 High Street, Finedon, Wellingborough, Northamptonshire, NN9 5JN P
01933 681048
07939 373901
Est. 1992 *Stock size* Medium
Stock General antiques
Open Mon–Sat 9am–5pm
Sun 11am–4pm
Services Valuations and house clearances

E K Antiques
Contact E Kubacki
37 High Street, Finedon, Wellingborough, Northamptonshire, NN9 5JN P
01933 681882
07711 245530
Est. 1991 *Stock size* Medium
Stock General antiques
Open Mon–Sat 9.30am–5pm
Sun 11am–4pm
Fairs Hinchingbrooke, Hunts
Services Valuations, restorations, house clearance

Finedon Antiques Ltd (LAPADA)
Contact Roy Kirkpatrick, Michael Chapman or Stephen Burnett
11–25 Bell Hill, Finedon, Wellingborough, Northamptonshire, NN9 5ND P
01933 681260/682210
01933 682210
sales@finedonantiques.com
www.finedonantiques.com
Est. 1972 *Stock size* Large
No. of dealers 35
Stock 18th–19thC English and French furniture, pottery, porcelain, decorative items
Open Mon–Sat 9am–5.30pm
Sun 11am–5pm
Services Valuations, restorations

Village Antiques
Contact John Kerti
59 High Street, Finedon, Northamptonshire, NN9 5JN P
01933 681522
07951 071896
Est. 2000 *Stock size* Small
Stock Furniture
Open Mon–Sun 9am–6pm

FLORE

Richard Sear
Contact Mr Richard Sear
The Huntershields, The Avenue, Flore, Northampton, Northamptonshire, NN7 4LZ P
01327 340718 01327 349263
Est. 1964 *Stock size* Medium
Stock General antiques, 17th–19thC metalwork, replicas, decorative items
Open Mon–Fri 10am–6pm Sat Sun by appointment
Fairs Newark, Stoneleigh
Services Valuations

GUILSBOROUGH

Nick Goodwin Exports
Contact Mr N Goodwin
The Firs, Nortoft, Guilsborough, Northamptonshire, NN6 8QB P
01604 740234 01604 740827
Est. 1974 *Stock size* Medium
Stock General antiques
Open By appointment
Fairs Ardingly, Swinderby
Services Packing, shipping

HARPOLE

Inglenook Antiques
Contact Tony or Pamela Havard
23 High Street, Harpole, Northamptonshire, NN7 4DH P
01604 830007
Est. 1971 *Stock size* Small
Stock Small country items, copper, brass, Victoriana, general antiques
Open Mon–Sat 9am–6.30pm
Services Longcase clock restoration

IRTHLINGBOROUGH

Hock & Dough Antiques
Contact Brian F Knight
82 High Street, Irthlingborough, Northamptonshire, NN7 4DH P
01933 650109
Est. 1919 *Stock size* Small
Stock Silver, general antiques
Open By appointment
Services Valuations, restorations

KETTERING

John Roe Antiques
Contact Mr John Roe
Furnace Site, Kettering Road, Kettering, Northamptonshire, NN14 3JW P
01832 732937 01832 732937
Est. 1969 *Stock size* Large
Stock General antique furniture
Open Mon–Fri 9am–6pm Sat 10am–5pm Sun by appointment
Fairs Newark
Services Shipping, packing

NORTHAMPTON

The Collectors Shop
Contact Mr V Hart
Northampton Indoor Market, Bradshaw Street, Northampton, Northamptonshire, NN1 2BL
01604 644932
07801 923029
collectors@hart1968.freeserve.co.uk
Est. 1997 *Stock size* Medium
Stock Antiques and collectables
Open Wed Fri Sat 8am–4pm
Fairs Newark

Laila Gray Antiques
Contact Ms L Gray
25 Welford Road, Northampton, Northamptonshire, NN2 8AQ P
01604 715277 01604 715277
Est. 1984 *Stock size* Medium
Stock Antique pine furniture
Open By appointment
Fairs Newark, Swinderby
Services Restorations, stripping

Legends
Contact Paul Edwards
4 Victoria Road, Northampton, Northamptonshire, NN1 5ED P
01604 473133 01604 473881
legends@myth-and-magic.co.uk
www.myth-and-magic.co.uk
Est. 1996 *Stock size* Large

Stock Tudor mint, pewter, Myth and Magic crystal figures
Open Mon–Sat 10am–5pm
Services Valuations for insurance, mail order worldwide

Merry's Auctions
Contact Mrs Denise Cowling FGA
Northampton Auction & Sales Centre, Liliput Road, Brackmills, Northampton, Northamptonshire, NN4 7BY P
☎ 01604 769990 F 01604 763155
M 0781 800 3786
E denise@northantsauctions,co.uk
W www.northantsauctions.com
Est. 1815
Open Mon–Fri 9am–5pm or by appointment
Sales Bi-monthly antique, fine art and collectables sale. Victorian, later and general antiques sale twice per month. Bar and cafeteria
Catalogues Yes

Giuseppe Miceli (OMRS)
Contact Mr Guiseppe Miceli
173 Wellingborough Road, Northampton, Northamptonshire, NN1 4DX P
☎ 01604 639776
Est. 1969 *Stock size* Medium
Stock Coins, medals
Open Mon–Sat 9am–5.30pm
Services Valuations

The Old Brigade
Contact Mr S Wilson
10a Harborough Road, Kingsthorpe, Northampton, Northamptonshire, NN2 7AZ P
☎ 01604 719389 F 01604 712489
Est. 1985 *Stock size* Medium
Stock 1850–1945 militaria, Third Reich items
Open Mon–Sat 10.30am–5pm but by appointment only
Services Valuations

POTTERSPURY

Reindeer Antiques Ltd (LAPADA, BADA)
Contact John Butterworth or Nicholas Fuller
43 Watling Street, Potterspury, Northamptonshire, NN12 7QD P
☎ 01908 542407/542200
F 01908 542121
M 07711 446221
E nicholas@reindeerantiques.co.uk
W www.reindeerantiques.co.uk
Est. 1969 *Stock size* Large
Stock 17th–19thC fine English furniture
Open Mon–Fri 9am–6pm Sat 10am–5pm Sun by appointment
Fairs BADA, LAPADA
Services Valuations, restorations

Tillmans Antiques
Contact Nick Tillman
Wakefield Country Courtyard, Wakefield Farm, Potterspury, Northamptonshire, NN12 7QX P
☎ 01327 811882
M 07711 570798
E nick_tillman@lineone.net
Est. 1999 *Stock size* Medium
No. of dealers 17
Stock Porcelain, silver, glass, small range of furniture, pictures
Open Wed–Sat 10am–5pm Sun and Bank Holidays 10.30am–4.30pm

RUSHDEN

Magpies
Contact Mr J E Ward
1 East Grove, Rushden, Northamptonshire, NN10 0AP P
☎ 01933 411404
Est. 1994 *Stock size* Medium
Stock General antiques
Open Mon–Sat 10am–5pm Sun noon–4pm

D W Sherwood Ltd
Contact Mrs S Sherwood
59 Little Street, Rushden, Northamptonshire, NN10 0LS P
☎ 01933 353265
Est. 1959 *Stock size* Large
Stock General antiques, paintings, clocks, furniture, prints, maps, glass, china, lace bobbins
Open Tues–Sat 11am–5pm closed Thurs
Services Valuations

THRAPSTON

Southam & Sons (RICS)
Contact Mr N Croskell
Corn Exchange, High Street, Thrapston, Kettering, Northamptonshire, NN14 4JJ P
☎ 01832 734486 F 01832 732409
Est. 1900
Open Mon–Fri 9am–5pm
Sales Antiques, sporting memorabilia, guns, household
Frequency Monthly
Catalogues Yes

TOWCESTER

Ron Green
Contact Mr M Green
227 & 239 Watling Street West, Towcester, Northamptonshire, NN12 6DD P
☎ 01327 350387 F 01327 350615
M 07885 436363
E ron@green227.freeserve.co.uk
Est. 1954 *Stock size* Medium
Stock General antiques, furniture, paintings, decorative items
Open Mon–Sat 8.30am–5.30pm Sun by appointment
Services Valuations for probate and insurance

R J K Nicholas
Contact Mr R Nicholas
161 Watling Street, Towcester, Northamptonshire, NN12 6BX P
☎ 01327 350639
Est. 1969 *Stock size* Medium
Stock Glass, prints, silver
Open Mon–Sat 9.30am–5pm
Fairs NEC

WEEDON

Heart of England Antiques
Contact Mrs Myra Wain
23 High Street, Weedon, Northamptonshire, NN7 4QD P
☎ 01327 341928 F 01327 342524
E myra.wain@btinternet.com
W www.everythingantique.co.uk
Est. 1991 *Stock size* Medium
Stock Antique French pine and decorative items
Open Mon–Sun 9am–5pm or by appointment

Helios and Co
Contact Mr B Walters
25–27 High Street, Weedon, Northamptonshire, NN7 4QD P
☎ 01327 340264 F 01327 342235
Est. 1976 *Stock size* Large
Stock General antiques, reproduction 18thC-style oak furniture
Open Tues–Sat 9.30am–5.30pm Sun 10.30am–4pm Mon 1.30–4.30pm
Services Valuations, restorations

Shabby Genteel
Contact Mrs N Hesketh
29A High Street, Weedon, Northamptonshire, NN7 4QD
☎ 01327 342139/340218

Est. 1994 *Stock size* Medium
Stock General antiques, collectables
Open Mon–Fri 11am–4pm Sat Sun 11am–5pm
Services Free local delivery

Streeton Antiques Ltd
Contact Les Streeton
Watling Street, Weedon, Northamptonshire, NN7 4QG
01327 340999 F 01327 342234
www.streetons.com
Est. 1986 *Stock size* Large
Stock Pine furniture
Open Mon–Sat 9am–5pm

The Village Market Antiques
Contact Mrs M Howard
62 High Street, Weedon, Northamptonshire, NN7 4QD
01327 342015
Est. 1981 *Stock size* Large
No. of dealers 40
Stock General antiques
Open Mon–Fri 9.30am–5.15pm Sat 10 am–5.15pm Sun Bank Holidays 10.30am–5.15pm

Weedon Antiques
Contact Nick Tillman
23 High Street, Weedon, Northamptonshire, NN7 4QD
01327 349777
M 07711 570798
E nick_tillman@lineone.net
Est. 2000 *Stock size* Large
No. of dealers 21
Stock Porcelain, silver, glass, small range of furniture, pictures
Open Wed–Sat 10am–5pm Sun 10.30am–4.30pm

WELLINGBOROUGH

Wilfords
Contact Mr S Wilford
76 Midland Road, Wellingborough, Northamptonshire, NN8 1NB
01933 222760 F 01933 271796
Est. 1934
Open Mon–Fri 8am–5pm Sat 8am–11am
Sales General antiques, weekly on Thurs 9.30am
Frequency Weekly
Catalogues No

WEST HADDON

Barber Antiques
Contact Miss A Barber
8 High Street, West Haddon, Northampton, Northamptonshire, NN6 7AP
01788 510315 F 01788 510315
E ali@barberantiques.freeserve.co.uk
W www.barberantiques.co.uk
Est. 1992 *Stock size* Large
Stock General antiques, furniture, ceramics, glass, silver
Open Tues–Sat 10am–5pm
Services Valuations, restorations

Paul Hopwell Antiques (BADA, LAPADA)
Contact Mr or Mrs P Hopwell
30 High Street, West Haddon, Northampton, Northamptonshire, NN6 7AP
01788 510636 F 01788 510044
E paulhopwell@antiqueoak.co.uk
W www.antiqueoak.co.uk
Est. 1969 *Stock size* Large
Stock 17th–18thC English oak furniture, metalware, treen, Delftware
Open Mon–Sat 10am–6pm Sun by appointment
Fairs Olympia, Chelsea, NEC
Services Valuations, restorations

Mark Seabrook Antiques
Contact Mr M Seabrook
9 West End, West Haddon, Northampton, Northamptonshire, NN6 7AY
01788 510772
M 07770 721931
Est. 1996 *Stock size* Medium
Stock Early English Oak, country furniture, metalware
Open Mon–Sat 10.30am–5.30pm Tues 1–5.30pm
Fairs NEC, Snape
Services Valuations, restorations

WESTON FAVELL

Discovery Antiques
Contact Mrs M Eales
1a Park Way, Weston Favell, Northampton, Northamptonshire, NN3 3BS
01604 401116
M 07712 309929
Est. 1996 *Stock size* Medium
Stock Antique furniture, china, collectables
Open Mon–Sat 10am–5pm
Fairs Newark
Services Valuations, restorations

NOTTINGHAMSHIRE

BALDERTON

The Blacksmiths Forge
Contact Mr or Mrs K Sheppard
74 Main Street, Balderton, Newark, Nottinghamshire, NG24 3NP
01636 700008
Est. 1984 *Stock size* Medium
Stock Antique fireplaces
Open By appointment
Fairs Swinderby
Services Restorations

BEESTON

Turner Violins
Contact Johanna or Monique
1–5 Lily Grove, Beeston, Nottinghamshire, NG9 1QL
0115 9430333 F 0115 943 0444
E turnerviolins@compuserve.com
W www.turnerviolins.co.uk
Est. 1980
Stock Violins, double basses, violas, cellos, bows
Open Mon–Fri 9am–6pm, Sat 9am–5pm
Services Valuations, restorations, part exchange

BUDBY

Dukeries Antiques Centre
Contact John Coupe
Thoresby Park, Budby, Nottinghamshire, NG22 9EX
01623 822252 F 01623 822209
M 07836 635312
E dukeriesantiques@aol.com
Est. 2001 *Stock size* Large
No. of dealers 18
Stock Antique furniture, paintings, porcelain, glass, silver
Open Mon–Sun 10am–5pm
Services Valuations, restorations

DUNHAM ON TRENT

R G Antiques
Contact Mr R G Barnett
Main Street, Dunham on Trent, Newark, Nottinghamshire, NG22 0TY
01777 228312 F 01777 228312
Est. 1979 *Stock size* Medium
Stock General antiques
Open Mon–Sun 10am–6pm
Fairs Newark
Services Valuations

MIDLANDS

NOTTINGHAMSHIRE • EASTWOOD

EASTWOOD

Millennium Collectables
Contact Mrs Carol Hadwick
PO Box 146, 68 Nottingham Road, Eastwood, Nottingham, Nottinghamshire, NG16 3SP
☎ 01773 535333 Ⓕ 01773 535374
Est. 1997 *Stock size* Large
Stock Royal Doulton, special commissions, advertising-related memorabilia
Open Mail order only

FARNSFIELD

A B Period Pine
Contact Alan Baker
The Barn, 38 Main Street, Farnsfield, Newark, Nottinghamshire, NG22 8EA P
☎ 01623 882288 Ⓕ 01623 882288
Ⓔ alan@abperiodpine.fsnet.co.uk
Ⓦ www.periodpine.co.uk
Est. 1998 *Stock size* Large
Stock Pine
Open Mon–Fri 10am–3pm Sat 10am–5pm closed Wed
Services Farmhouse and painted pine kitchens

GOTHAM

T Vennett-Smith Auctioneers and Valuers
Contact T or M A Vennett-Smith
11 Nottingham Road, Gotham, Nottingham, Nottinghamshire, NE11 0HE P
☎ 0115 983 0541 Ⓕ 0115 983 0114
Ⓔ info@vennett-smith.com
Ⓦ www.vennett-smith.com
Est. 1989
Open Mon–Fri 9am–5.30pm
Sales Autographs, postcards, cigarette cards, 5 sales per year, 2 postal auctions
Frequency 5 per annum
Catalogues Yes

HOCKLEY

Retrospect
Contact Mr Duffy
17 Heathcote Street, Hockley, Nottinghamshire, NG1 3AQ P
☎ 0115 956 1182
Est. 1993 *Stock size* Small
Stock Decorative arts, 1880–1980
Open Wed–Sun 9am–5pm

KIRKBY IN ASHFIELD

Kyrios Books
Contact Mr K Parr
11 Kingsway, Kirkby in Ashfield, Nottingham, Nottinghamshire, NG17 7BB P
☎ 01623 452556
Ⓔ kyriosbooks@barclays.net
Ⓦ www.churchnet.org.uk/kyrios/
Est. 1989 *Stock size* Large
Stock Rare and second-hand books, religion and philosophy a speciality
Open Mon Tues Thur Fri 10.30am–noon Sat 10am–1pm or by appointment
Services Mail order. Bi-monthly Catalogue

LANGFORD

T Baker
Contact Mr T Baker
Langford House Farm, Langford, Newark, Nottinghamshire, NG23 7RR P
☎ 01636 704026
Est. 1966 *Stock size* Medium
Stock Period and Victorian furniture
Open Mon–Fri 8am–5pm or by appointment
Fairs Newark

MANSFIELD

Antiques & Clock Shop (BWCG)
Contact Mr Tom Matthews
34a Bancroft Lane, Mansfield, Nottinghamshire, NG18 5LQ P
☎ 01623 476097
Ⓜ 07808 693559
Est. 1974 *Stock size* Large
Stock General antiques
Open Mon–Fri 8.30am–5pm Sat 8.30am–3pm
Fairs Birmingham Clock Fair
Services Valuations, restorations of clocks and jewellery

Fair Deal Antiques
Contact Mr Low
138 Chesterfield Road North, Mansfield, Nottinghamshire, NE19 7PE P
☎ 01623 653768
Est. 1979 *Stock size* Large
Stock General antiques
Open Mon–Sun 8am–6pm or by appointment
Services Container packing

Mansfield Antique Centre
Contact Dave Buckinger
185 Yorke Street, Mansfield Woodhouse, Mansfield, Nottinghamshire, NG19 2NJ P
☎ 01623 661122 Ⓕ 01623 631738

Est. 1992 *Stock size* Medium
Stock General antiques
Open Thurs–Sun 10am–5.30pm

NEWARK

Castlegate Antique Centre
Contact John Dench
55 Castle Gate, Newark, Nottinghamshire, NG24 1BE
01636 700076 01636 700144
Est. 1983 *Stock size* Large
No. of dealers 9
Stock General antiques
Open Mon–Sat 9.30am–5.30pm
Services Valuations, restorations

Gallerie
Contact Gillian Jennison
1 Bar Gate, Newark, Nottinghamshire, NG24 1ES
01636 705400
Est. 2000 *Stock size* Small
Stock French antiques
Open Wed–Sat 10am–5pm

Lawrence Books
Contact Mr A Lawrence
Newark Antique Centre, Lombard Street, Newark, Nottinghamshire, NG24 1XR
01636 605865/701619
arthurlawrence@totalise.co.uk
Est. 1987 *Stock size* Small
Stock Antiquarian, rare and second-hand books
Open Mon–Sat 9.30am–5pm Sun 11am–4pm
Services Valuations

R R Limb Antiques
Contact Mr R Limb
31/35 North Gate, Newark, Nottinghamshire, NG24 1HD
01636 674546
Est. 1955 *Stock size* Large
Stock General antiques, piano exporters
Open By appointment
Fairs Newark, Swinderby

M B G Antiques (BGA)
Contact Margaret Begley-Gray DGA
41b Castlegate, Newark, Nottinghamshire, NG24 1BE
01636 704442 01616 679586
07702 209808
Est. 1982 *Stock size* Medium
Stock Period jewellery, quality pictures, general antiques, diamond rings
Open Wed–Sat 11am–4pm
Fairs NEC, Newark
Services Valuations, picture search

Newark Antiques Centre
Contact Mr M Tinsley
Regent House, Lombard Street, Newark, Nottinghamshire, NG24 1XP
01636 605504 01636 605101
07931 109860
Est. 1988 *Stock size* Large
No. of dealers 101
Stock General antiques
Open Mon–Sat 9.30am–5pm Sun Bank Holidays 11am–4pm
Services Valuations, upholstery, clock repairs, specialist book service

Newark Antiques Warehouse Ltd
Contact Nick Mellors
Kelham Road, Newark, Nottinghamshire, NG24 1BX
01636 674869 01636 612933
07974 429185
enquiries@newarkantiques.co.uk
www.newarkantiques.co.uk
Est. 1984 *Stock size* Large
No. of dealers Approximately 80
Stock Good furniture, collectables, smalls
Open Mon–Fri 8.30am–5.30pm Sat 9.30am–4pm Sun at Newark Antiques Fair 9am–7pm
Services Valuations

No 1 Castlegate Antiques
1–3 Castlegate, Newark, Nottinghamshire, NG24 1AZ
01636 701877
Est. 1974 *Stock size* Large
No. of dealers 10
Stock 18th–19thC antique furniture, clocks, barometers, decorative items
Open Mon–Fri 9.30am–5pm Sat 9.30am–5.30pm
Services Valuations, restorations of clocks and barometers

Pearman Antiques & Interiors
Contact Jan Parnham
9 Castle Gate, Newark, Nottinghamshire, NG24 1AZ
01636 679158/01949 837693
Est. 2001 *Stock size* Medium
Stock Oak, mahogany furniture
Open Wed–Sat 10am–4pm

Portland Antiques
Contact Colin Duckworth
20 Portland Street, Newark, Nottinghamshire, NG24 4XG
01636 701478
Est. 1969 *Stock size* Large
Stock General antiques
Open Tues Wed Fri Sat 9.30am–4.30pm

Tudor Rose Antiques Centre
Contact Mrs C Rose
12–13 Market Place, Newark, Nottinghamshire, NG24 1DU
01636 610311
07970 972191
Est. 1979 *Stock size* Large
No. of dealers 30
Stock Small collectable antiques, antique furniture, silver, metalware, treen, country items
Open Mon–Sat 10am–5pm Sun prior to Newark Antiques Fair noon–5pm
Services Valuations

NOTTINGHAM

Acanthus Antiques & Collectables
Contact Trak or Sandra Smith
164 Derby Road, Nottingham, Nottinghamshire, NG7 1LR
0115 978 3994 0115 982 2137
trak.e.smith@talk21.com
www.acanthusantiques.co.uk
Est. 1979 *Stock size* Medium
Stock General antiques
Open Tues–Fri 10am–3pm Sat noon–4pm Sun by appointment
Fairs Newark, Swinderby
Services Valuations, lectures and teaching

Antiques Across the World (LAPADA)
Contact Mr Rimes
James Alexander Buildings, London Road, Manvers Street, Nottingham, Nottinghamshire, NG2 3AE
0115 979 9199 0115 958 8314
07785 777787
tonyrimes@btinternet.com
Est. 1992 *Stock size* Large
Stock Georgian–Edwardian furniture
Open Mon–Fri 9am–5pm Sat 10am–2pm
Fairs Newark
Services Valuations, courier service, antique finder service

MIDLANDS

NOTTINGHAMSHIRE • NOTTINGHAM

The Autograph Collectors Gallery
Contact Mr or Mrs G Clipson
7 Jessops Lane, Gedling, Nottingham, Nottinghamshire, NG4 4BQ
☎ 0115 961 2956/987 6578
Ⓕ 0115 961 2956
Ⓔ graham.clipson@btinternet.com
Ⓔ postmaster@autograph-gallery.co.uk
Ⓦ www.autograph-gallery.co.uk
Est. 1990 *Stock size* Large
Stock Signed photographs, documents, letters
Open Telephone 9am–8pm
Services Mail order only

Bonhams & Brooks
Contact John Knight
57 Mansfield Road, Nottingham, Nottinghamshire, NG1 3FL Ⓟ
☎ 0115 947 4414 Ⓕ 0115 947 4885
Ⓔ midlands@bonhams.com
Ⓦ www.bonhams.com
Open Mon–Fri 9am–5.30pm
Sales Regional representative for Midlands, Derbyshire, Nottinghamshire and Cheshire, see head office (London) for details

Castle Antiques
Contact Mr L Adamson
78 Derby Road, Nottingham, Nottinghamshire, NG1 5FD Ⓟ
☎ 0115 947 3913
Est. 1979 *Stock size* Medium
Stock General antiques, pictures, maps, prints
Open Mon–Sat 9.30am–5pm

Cathay Oriental Antiques
Contact Jenny Bu
74 Derby Road, Nottingham, Nottinghamshire, NG1 5FD Ⓟ
☎ 0115 988 1216
Ⓔ paulshum@hotmail.com
Est. 2000 *Stock size* Medium
Stock Furniture, porcelain, ceramic, pottery, Chinese folk art
Open Mon–Sat 10am–5pm

Collectors World
Contact Mr M Ray
188 Wollaton Road, Wollaton, Nottingham, Nottinghamshire, NG8 1HJ Ⓟ
☎ 0115 928 0347 Ⓕ 0115 928 0347
Est. 1991 *Stock size* Large
Stock Coins, banknotes, cigarette cards, postcards
Open Tues–Sat 10.30am–5pm
Fairs Newark, specialist
Services Valuations, currency exchange, framing

Dutton & Smith Medal Collectors
Contact Mr A Dutton
Room 143, 48 Derby Road, Nottingham, Nottinghamshire, NG1 5FQ Ⓟ
☎ 0115 987 6949 Ⓕ 0115 982 2137
Ⓔ duttonf@019.mbe.uk.com
Ⓦ www.acanthusantiques.co.uk
Est. 1991 *Stock size* Medium
Stock Campaign medals
Open By appointment
Fairs Newark, Swinderby
Services Valuations

Fourways Antiques
Contact Mr Peter Key
38 Owen Avenue, Nottingham, Nottinghamshire, NG10 2FS Ⓟ
☎ 0115 972 1830
Ⓜ 07850 973889
Est. 1974 *Stock size* Medium
Stock General antiques
Open By appointment
Fairs Newark, Swinderby

Gatehouse Workshops
Contact Mr S J Waine
163 Castle Boulevard, Nottingham, Nottinghamshire, NG7 1FS Ⓟ
☎ 0115 948 3954 Ⓕ 0115 948 3954
Ⓦ www.gatehouseworkshops.co.uk
Est. 1979 *Stock size* Medium
Stock Architectural antiques, stained glass
Open Mon–Fri 9.30am–4pm Sat 9am–5pm
Services Pine stripping

Hallam Antique and Diamond Jewellery
Contact Stuart Thexton
Kings Walk Corner, 30 Upper Parliament Street, Nottingham, Nottinghamshire, NG1 2AG Ⓟ
☎ 0115 941 1276
Est. 1998 *Stock size* Medium
Stock Range of dining room pieces, condiment sets, watches
Open Mon–Sat 9am–5.30pm
Services Valuations, watch repair

Harlequin Antiques
Contact Peter Hinchley
79 Mansfield Road, Nottingham, Nottinghamshire, NG5 6BH Ⓟ
☎ 0115 967 4590
Ⓔ sales@antiquepine.net
Ⓦ www.antiquepine.net
Est. 1993 *Stock size* Large
Stock Antique pine furniture
Open Mon–Fri 9.30am–5pm Sat 9am–5pm or by appointment
Fairs Newark
Services Restorations of all period furniture

Andy Holmes (PBFA)
82 Highbury Avenue, Bulwell, Nottingham, Nottinghamshire, NG6 9DB Ⓟ
☎ 0115 979 5603 Ⓕ 0115 979 5616
Ⓔ holmesbook@aol.com
Est. 1996 *Stock size* Large
Stock Antiquarian, rare and second-hand books, 19thC travel, gypsies, folklore and general topics
Open By appointment only
Fairs London Royal National, Buxton
Services Valuations, book search

D D & A Ingle (ORMS, FSE)
Contact Mr D Ingle
380 Carlton Hill, Carlton, Nottingham, Nottinghamshire, NG4 1JA Ⓟ
☎ 0115 987 3325 Ⓕ 0115 987 3325
Ⓔ ddaingle@talk21.com
Est. 1968 *Stock size* Medium
Stock General antiques
Open Mon–Sat 9am–5pm
Services Valuations

Ivory Gate Antiques
Contact Mr B Orridge
106 Derby Road, Nottingham, Nottinghamshire, NG1 5FB Ⓟ
☎ 0115 947 3054
Ⓔ ivorygateantiques@hotmail.com
Est. 1979 *Stock size* Large
Stock General antiques
Open Mon–Sat 9.45am–4.45pm
Fairs Newark, Swinderby
Services Restoration of furniture

Jeremy & Westerman
Contact Geoff Blore
203 Mansfield Road, Nottingham, Nottinghamshire, NG1 3FF
☎ 0115 947 4522
Est. 1981 *Stock size* Medium

Stock Antique and second-hand books
Open Mon–Sat 11am–5pm
Fairs H & D Book Fairs

Arthur Johnson & Sons
Contact Mr R Hannersley
✉ **Nottingham Auction Centre, Meadow Lane, Nottingham, Nottinghamshire, NG2 3GY** P
☎ 0115 986 9128 F 0115 986 2139
Est. 1899
Open Mon–Fri 9am–5pm closed lunch
Sales Antique and export furniture Sat 10am, viewing Fri 2–6.45pm Sat from 9am
Frequency Weekly
Catalogues Yes

Lights, Camera, Action (UACC)
Contact Mr N Straw
✉ **36 Cyril Avenue, Nottingham, Nottinghamshire, NG8 5BA** P
☎ 0115 913 1116 F 0115 913 1116
M 0797 034 2363
Est. 1998 ***Stock size*** Large
Stock Collectors' items, autographs, Titanic memorabilia
Open By appointment
Fairs NEC, Olympia, Newark
Services Valuations

Michael D Long Ltd (GTA, BACA Award Winner 2001)
Contact Mr M D Long
✉ **96–98 Derby Road, Nottingham, Nottinghamshire, NG1 5FB** P
☎ 0115 941 3307 F 0115 941 4199
E sales@michaeldlong.com
W www.michaeldlong.com
Est. 1964 ***Stock size*** Large
Stock Fine antique arms and armour
Open Mon–Fri 9.30am–5.15pm Sat 10am–4pm
Fairs London Arms Fair, Birmingham, Nottingham
Services Valuations

Luna
Contact Paul Rose
✉ **23 George Street, Nottingham, Nottinghamshire, NG1 3BH** P
☎ 0115 924 3267
E info@luna-online.co.uk
W www.luna-online.co.uk
Est. 1993 ***Stock size*** Medium
Stock 1950s–1970s objects for the home
Open Mon–Sat 10.30am–5.30pm
Fairs Newark
Services Sourcing items, hire

Mellors & Kirk (RICS)
Contact Nigel Kirk or Martha Parvin
✉ **The Auction House, Nottingham, Nottinghamshire, NG7 2NL** P
☎ 0115 979 0000 F 0115 978 1111
E mellkirk@dircon.co.uk
W www.mellors-kirk.co.uk
Est. 1993
Open Mon–Fri 8.30am–5pm Sat 9am–noon
Sales Weekly general sale on Tues. Fine art sale every six weeks
Frequency Six weekly
Catalogues yes

N S E Medal Department (ORMS)
Contact Dennis Henson
✉ **97 Derby Road, Nottingham, Nottinghamshire, NG1 5BB** P
☎ 0115 950 1882
E nsemed@totalserve.com
Est. 1974 ***Stock size*** Large
Stock Antique coins and medals, cap badges
Open Mon–Sat 9am–3.30pm
Services Valuations

Neales Auctioneers (SOFAA, ARVA)
Contact Bruce Fearn
✉ **192 Mansfield Road, Nottingham, Nottinghamshire, NG1 3HU** P
☎ 0115 962 4141 F 0115 985 6890
E fineart@neales.co.uk
W www.neales.co.uk
Est. 1840
Open Mon–Fri 9am–5.30pm Sat 9am–12.30pm
Sales Specialist antique and fine art sales every 2–3 months plus general antiques and later sales
Frequency Weekly
Catalogues Yes

Nottingham Coin Centre
Contact Mr P Muir
✉ **28 Alfreton Road, Nottingham, Nottinghamshire, NG7 3NG**
☎ 0115 942 42777
Est. 1987 ***Stock size*** Medium
Stock Coins, medals, collectables
Open Mon–Sat 10am–2pm
Services Valuations

P & P Antiques
Contact Mr J Pollard
✉ **Nottingham Auction Centre, Gregory Street, Nottingham, Nottinghamshire, NG7 2NL** P
☎ 0115 924 4447 F 0115 978 3135
E no1export@aol.com
Est. 1994 ***Stock size*** Large
Stock General antiques, shipping goods
Open Mon–Fri 9am–5pm
Services Courier, shipping containers

Pegasus Antiques (NAG)
Contact Pat or John Clewer
✉ **62 Derby Road, Nottingham, Nottinghamshire, NG1 5FD** P
☎ 0115 947 4220
Est. 1979 ***Stock size*** Medium
Stock General antiques, 18th–19thC furniture
Open Mon–Sat 9.30am–5pm
Services Stockist of Libero, waxes and restoration products

David & Carole Potter (LAPADA)
Contact Mr or Mrs D Potter
✉ **76 Derby Road, Nottingham, Nottinghamshire, NG1 5FD** P
☎ 0115 941 7911
M 07973 689962
Est. 1966 ***Stock size*** Medium
Stock General antiques, 18th–19thC furniture, quality decorative items
Open By appointment only
Fairs NEC, Olympia
Services Valuations

John Priestley
Contact Mr John Priestley
✉ **48–50 Avenue B, Sneinton Market, Nottingham, Nottinghamshire, NG1 1DU** P
☎ 0115 910 3393
Est. 1989 ***Stock size*** Large
Stock Autographs, football programmes, postcards
Open Mon–Fri 10.30am–4.30pm
Fairs Glascow, NEC
Services Valuations

John Pye & Sons Ltd (NAVA)
Contact Adam Pye FNAVA
✉ **James Shipstone House, Radford Road, Nottingham, Nottinghamshire, NG7 7EA**
☎ 0115 970 6060 F 0115 942 0100
E ap@johnpye.co.uk.
W www.johnpye.co.uk

MIDLANDS

NOTTINGHAMSHIRE • RETFORD

Est. 1969
Open Mon–Fri 8am–4.30pm
Sales General
Frequency Fortnightly
Catalogues No

Top Hat Antique Centre
Contact Mrs J Wallis
70–72 Derby Road, Nottingham, Nottinghamshire, NG1 5FD
0115 941 9143
sylvia@artdeco-fairs.co.uk
www.tophat-antiques.co.uk
Est. 1979 *Stock size* Large
No. of dealers 15
Stock General antiques
Open Mon–Sat 9.30am–5pm

RETFORD

Lynn Guest Antiques
Contact Lynn Guest
15 Mill Lane, Rockley, Retford, Nottinghamshire, DN22 0QP
01777 838498
Est. 1979 *Stock size* Medium
Stock General antiques and collectables
Open Mon–Fri 9am–6pm or by appointment
Fairs Newark
Services Valuations, house clearance

Phillips International Auctioneers and Valuers
20 The Square, Retford, Nottinghamshire, DN22 6XE
01777 708633 F 01777 706724
www.phillips-auction.com
Sales Regional Office. Ring for details

SANDIACRE

The Glory Hole
Contact Mr or Mrs C Reid
14 Station Road, Sandiacre, Nottingham, Nottinghamshire, NG10 5BG
0115 939 4081 F 0115 939 4085
Est. 1984 *Stock size* Medium
Stock Antique furniture, fireplaces
Open Mon–Sat 9.30am–5.30pm
Services Restorations

SOUTHWELL

Strouds of Southwell Antiques
Contact Mr V Stroud
3/7 Church Street, Southwell, Nottinghamshire, NG25 0HQ
01636 815001 F 01636 815001
Est. 1969 *Stock size* Large
Stock Antique fine period furniture
Open Mon–Sat 9.30am–5pm or by appointment
Services Valuations, restorations

SUTTON-IN-ASHFIELD

Carol's Curiosity Shop
Contact Mrs C Wilcockson
33 High Street, Station Hill, Sutton-in-Ashfield, Nottinghamshire, NG17 3GG
01623 555903
Est. 1998 *Stock size* Medium
Stock General antiques
Open Mon 10am–4pm Tues 9am–5pm Wed 10am–1pm Thurs Fri 9am–5.30pm Sat 9am–4pm
Fairs Newark, Swinderby

C B Sheppard & Son
Contact Mr B Sheppard
The Auction Gallery, 87 Chatworth Street, Sutton-in-Ashfield, Nottinghamshire, NG17 4GG
01623 556310 (sale rooms) 01773 872419 (office)
Est. 1951
Open Auction Gallery Fri 10am–4pm Office 9am–5pm
Sales General antiques
Frequency Monthly
Catalogues Yes

Yesterday and Today
Contact Mr J Turner
82 Station Road, Sutton-in-Ashfield, Nottinghamshire, NG17 5HB
01623 442215
07957 552753
Est. 1984 *Stock size* Medium
Stock Collectables, 1920s and 1930s oak furniture
Open Mon–Sat 9am–5pm
Fairs Newark, Swinderby

WEST BRIDGFORD

Bridgford Antiques
Contact Joe Domeika
2a Rushworth Avenue, West Bridgford, Nottingham, Nottinghamshire, NG2 7LF
0115 982 1835
Est. 1974 *Stock size* Medium
Stock General antiques and collectables
Open Mon–Sat 10am–5pm
Fairs Newark, Swinderby

Joan Cotton
Contact Mrs Joan Cotton
5 Davies Road, West Bridgford, Nottingham, Nottinghamshire, NG2 5JE
0115 981 3043
Est. 1964 *Stock size* Medium
Stock General antiques except furniture
Open Mon–Sat 9am–4pm closed Wed Sun
Fairs Newark

RUTLAND

MANTON

David Smith Antiques
Contact Mr D Smith
20 St Mary's Road, Manton, Oakham, Rutland, LE15 8SY
01572 737244/737607
Est. 1952 *Stock size* Medium
Stock General antiques
Open Mon–Sat 9am–5pm or by appointment
Fairs Kettering
Services Valuations, restorations

OAKHAM

Decorum Antiques and Linens
Contact Mrs G Flach
18 Church Street, Oakham, Rutland, LE15 6AA
01572 771775
Est. 1996 *Stock size* Medium
Stock General antiques
Open Tues Wed Fri 10am–5pm Sat 9am–5pm
Services Valuations, restorations

Swans Antiques and Interiors
Contact Mr Peter Jones
17 Mill Street, Oakham, Rutland, LE15 6EA
01572 724364 F 01572 755094
07860 304084
swansoakham@hotmail.com
swansofoakham.co.uk
Est. 1986 *Stock size* Large
Stock Antique beds, English and French decorative furniture
Open Mon–Sat 9am–5.30pm Sun 2–5pm
Fairs Newark
Services Valuations, restorations

Treedale Antiques
Contact Mr G Warren
10b Mill Street, Oakham, Rutland, LE15 6EA
01572 757521 01572 757521
Est. 1968 *Stock size* Medium
Stock 17th–18thC furniture, specializing in walnut and oak
Open Mon–Sat 9am–5.30pm Sun 2–5pm
Services Restorations

UPPINGHAM

Clutter Antiques
Contact Maureen Sumner
14 Orange Street, Uppingham, Oakham, Rutland, LE15 9SQ
01572 823745/717243
01162 697729
cfi@sumnerlikeithot.fsnet.co.uk
Est. 1982 *Stock size* Medium
Stock Victorian kitchen and parlour clutter, textiles, linens, treen, glass, china
Open Mon–Fri 10am–5pm Sat 10am–6pm or by appointment

John Garner Antiques
Contact John Garner
51 & 53 High Street East, Uppingham, Oakham, Rutland, LE15 9PY
01572 823607 01572 821654
07850 596556
www.johngarnerantiques.com
Est. 1966 *Stock size* Large
Stock General antiques, 18th–19thC furniture and paintings, garden statuary, clocks, bronzes, sports prints
Open Mon–Sat 9am–5.30pm
Services Valuations, restorations

Goldmark Books
Contact Emma Beanland
14 Orange Street, Uppingham, Oakham, Rutland, LE15 9SQ
01572 822694 01572 821503
Mike@mgoldmark.freeserve.co.uk
Est. 1974 *Stock size* Large
Stock General stock including antiquarian and second-hand books, art and poetry a speciality
Open Mon–Sat 9.30am–5.30pm Sun 2.30–5.30pm
Services Book search

Tattersalls
Contact Mrs J Tattersall
14b Orange Street, Uppingham, Oakham, Rutland, LE14 2AG
01572 821171
Est. 1985 *Stock size* Medium
Stock Antique and old Persian rugs
Open Tues–Sat 9.30am–5pm
Services Restorations

Woodmans House
Contact Mr or Mrs J Collie
35 High Street, Uppingham, Oakham, Rutland, LE15 9PY
01572 821799
woodmanshouse@aol.com
www.woodmanshouse-antiques.co.uk
Est. 1992 *Stock size* Medium
Stock Georgian furniture
Open Mon–Sat 9.30am–5pm or Sun by appointment
Fairs NEC, Olympia
Services Valuations, restorations, reference library

SHROPSHIRE

ATCHAM

Mytton Antiques
Contact M A Nares
Norton Crossroads, Atcham, Shrewsbury, Shropshire, SY4 4UH
01952 740229 01952 461154
07860 575639
nares@myttonantiques.freeserve.co.uk
Est. 1979 *Stock size* Medium
Stock 18th–19thC furniture and smalls, longcase clocks, country furniture, restoration materials
Open Mon–Sat 10am–5pm or by appointment
Services Valuations, restoration, shipping, courier service

BISHOPS CASTLE

Autolycus
Contact Mr David Wilkinson
Porch House, High Street, Bishops Castle, Shropshire, SY9 5BE
01588 630078 01588 638686
autolycusbc@aol.com
www.booksonline.uk.com
Est. 1996 *Stock size* Medium
Stock Antiquarian and quality second-hand books, specializing in modern first editions, illustrated, childrens, travel, topography, fine sporting prints and pictures
Open Mon–Fri 11am–4.30pm Sat 10.30am–5pm

Decorative Antiques
Contact Richard Moulson
47 Church Street, Bishops Castle, Shropshire, SY9 5AD
01588 638851 01588 638851
enquiries@decorative-antiques.co.uk
www.decorative-antiques.co.uk
Est. 1996 *Stock size* Small
Stock Art Deco, 1860–1960, Arts and Crafts, pottery, glass, jewellery, metalware
Open Most days 10am–6pm
Fairs Warwick, Chester Art Deco
Services Identification and informal valuations

BRIDGNORTH

The Book Passage
Contact Mr David Lamont
57a High Street, Bridgnorth, Shropshire, WV16 4DX
01746 768767
Est. 1999 *Stock size* Large
Stock Antiquarian and second-hand books
Open Mon–Sat 9am–5.30pm

Bookstack
Contact Mrs E Anderson
The Harp Yard, St Leonards Close, Bridgnorth, Shropshire, WV16 4EJ
01746 767089 01746 768008
Est. 1992 *Stock size* Small
Stock Antiquarian and second-hand books
Open Mon–Fri 9am–5pm
Services Restorations, bookbinding

Bridgnorth Antiques Centre
Contact Mr Richard Lewis
Whitburn Street, Bridgnorth, Shropshire, WV16 4QP
01746 768055
antiquesrl@fsb.com
www.as4uk.com
Est. 1994 *Stock size* Large
No. of dealers 19 (6 rooms)
Stock Late Victorian–Edwardian and 1930s furniture, collectables
Open Mon–Sat 10am–5.30pm Sun 10.30am–4.30pm
Services Clock repairs

English Heritage
Contact Mrs M Wainwright
2 Whitburn Street, Bridgnorth, Shropshire, WV16 4QN

☎ 01746 762097
Est. 1988 *Stock size* Medium
Stock General antiques, giftware, medals, coins and silverware
Open Mon–Sat 10am–5pm closed Thurs

Malthouse Antiques
Contact Mrs Susan Mantle
✉ 6 Underhill Street, Bridgnorth, Shropshire, WV16 4BB P
☎ 01746 763054 F 01746 763054
Est. 1979 *Stock size* Large
Stock Victorian–Edwardian furniture, smalls
Open Mon–Sat 10am–6pm Sun 2–5pm closed Wed
Services Restorations

Old Mill Antique Centre
Contact Mr Dennis Ridgeway
✉ 48 Mill Street, Bridgnorth, Shropshire, WV15 5AG P
☎ 01746 768778 F 01746 768944
Est. 1996 *Stock size* Large
No. of dealers 90
Stock Complete range of antiques and collectables
Open Mon–Sun 10am–5pm
Services Restaurant

Perry & Phillips
Contact Dennis Ridgeway
✉ Old Mill Auction Rooms, Mill Street, Bridgnorth, Shropshire, WV1 5AG P
☎ 01746 762248 F 01746 768944
E sales@perryandphillips.co.uk
W www.perryandphillips.co.uk
Est. 1835
Open Mon–Fri 9am–5pm
Sales General antiques sales Tues 10.30am, viewing Sat–Mon 10am–5pm, occasional special sales
Frequency Monthly
Catalogues Yes

BURLTON

North Shropshire Reclamation and Antique Salvage (SALVO)
Contact Mrs J Powell
✉ Wackley Lodge Farm, Wackley, Burlton, Shrewsbury, Shropshire, SY4 5TD P
☎ 01939 270719 F 01939 270895
M 07802 315038
Est. 1997 *Stock size* Large
Stock Garden statuary, bricks, baths, hand basins, tiles, doors, architectural salvage of all types
Open Mon–Fri 9am–6pm Sat Sun 9am–5.30pm
Services Paint stripping

CHURCH STRETTON

Church Stretton Books (PBFA)
Contact Mr Roger Toon
✉ Victoria House, 48 High Street, Church Stretton, Shropshire, SY6 6BX P
☎ 01694 724337 F 01694 724337
E csbooks@btinternet.com
W www.abebooks.com
Est. 1994 *Stock size* Medium
Stock High-quality second-hand and antiquarian books, Malcolm Saville books a speciality
Open Mon–Sat 10am–5pm Wed 10am–1pm
Fairs Bloomsbury

Cobwebs Antiques & Collectables
Contact Mr S Thomas
✉ 13–15 High Street, Church Stretton, Shropshire, SY6 6BU P
☎ 01694 723090
M 07970 358404
E steven.thomas1@virgin.net
Est. 1994 *Stock size* Large
Stock General antiques and collectables, 1800s–1930s furniture
Open Mon–Sun 10am–5pm
Fairs Newark, Stafford

Longmynd Antiques
Contact Mr James Coomber or David Coomber
✉ Crossways, Church Stretton, Shropshire, SY6 6PG P
☎ 01694 724474 F 01694 724474
E antiques@longmynduk.freeserve.co.uk
W www.longmynd.freeserve.co.uk
Est. 1994 *Stock size* Large
Stock 17th–19thC country oak and mahogany furniture
Open Mon–Sat 10.30am–5pm

Old Post Office Antiques
Contact Mr A Walker
✉ 46 Sandford Avenue, Church Stretton, Shropshire, SY6 6BH P
☎ 01694 724491
F 01694 724491
Est. 1998 *Stock size* Large
Stock Jewellery, Halcyon Days, Steiff bears
Open Mon–Sat 10am–5pm

The Snooker Room
Contact Mr A Walker
✉ 46a Sandford Avenue, Church Stretton, Shropshire, SY6 6BH P
☎ 01694 724491 F 01694 724491
M 07790 906570
Est. 1939 *Stock size* Large
Stock Snooker tables, lighting, accessories
Open Mon–Sat 10am–5pm
Fairs Olympia

Stretton Antiques Market
Contact Terry or Lisa Elvins
✉ 36 Sandford Avenue, Church Stretton, Shropshire, SY6 6BH P
☎ 01694 723718 F 01694 723718
Est. 1985 *Stock size* Large
No. of dealers 60
Stock Wide range of antiques and collectables
Open Mon–Sat 9.30am–5.30pm Sun 10.30am–4.30pm

COSFORD

Hall & Lloyd
Contact Mr C Sidebottom
✉ Cosford Auction Rooms, Long Lane, Cosford, Shropshire, TF11 8PJ P
☎ 01902 375555 F 01902 375566
Est. 1882
Open Mon–Fri 9am–5.30pm
Sales Victorian–Edwardian shipping and contemporary furniture, collectables Sat 10am, viewing Fri 10am–6pm. Also fine art every six weeks
Frequency Fortnightly
Catalogues Yes

CRAVEN ARMS

Marine
Contact Mark Jarrold
✉ Lower House Farm, Middlehope, Craven Arms, Shropshire, SY7 9JT P
☎ 01584 841210 F 01584 841210
M 07776 193193
E markjarrold@btinternet.com
Est. 1989
Stock Binoculars, ships' models, navigational instruments, chronometers, clocks, optical equipment

Open By appointment
Fairs Birmingham International Arms Fair
Services Valuations, restorations

Portcullis Furniture
Contact Mr John Cox or Mrs Sally Allen
Ludlow Road, Craven Arms, Shropshire, SY7 9QL
01588 672263 F 01588 673321
M 07966 188364
Est. 1995 *Stock size* Large
Stock Antique, reproduction and new furniture, copper, brass, silver, china, clocks
Open Mon–Sat 10am–5.30pm Sun 10.30am–4.30pm
Fairs Newark
Services Shipping

DITTON PRIORS

Priors Reclamation (SALVO)
Contact Miss V Bale
Unit 2a, Ditton Priors Industrial Estate, Ditton Priors, Bridgnorth, Shropshire, WV16 6SS
01746 712450 F 01746 712450
M 07976 638555
E v.bale@btinternet.co.uk
W www.priorsrec.co.uk
Est. 1998 *Stock size* Large
Stock Doors, pine and oak, antique items for the garden
Open By appointment at any time

ELLESMERE

Bowen, Son & Watson
Contact Mr Eddie Bowen
Wharf Road, Ellesmere, Shropshire, SY12 0EJ
01691 622534 F 01691 623603
E bsw.ellesmere@virgin.net
W www.bowensonandwatson.co.uk
Est. 1869
Open Mon–Fri 9am–5pm Sat 9am–noon
Sales Antique and household goods monthly Tues 11am, viewing Mon 9am–5pm Tues 9–11am
Frequency Monthly
Catalogues No

IRONBRIDGE

Bears on the Square
Contact Margaret Phillips
2 The Square, Ironbridge, Telford, Shropshire, TF8 7AQ
01952 433924 F 01952 433926
E bernie@bearsonthesquare.com
W www.bearsonthesquare.com
Est. 1991 *Stock size* Large
Stock Steiff, Deans, Hermann, Spielwaren, Artist, and second-hand bears, country life
Open Mon–Sun 10am–5pm
Services Worldwide mail order

Tudor House Antiques
Contact Mr Peter Whitelaw
11 Tontine Hill, Ironbridge, Telford, Shropshire, TF8 7AL
01952 433783
E tudoriron@aol.com
W www.tudorhouse.co.uk
Est. 1964 *Stock size* Large
Stock Coalport, Caughley, general English ceramics
Open Mon–Sat 10am–5pm Sun by appointment
Services Valuations

LONGNOR

Oriental & African Books
Contact Mr Paul Wilson
The Corbett Rooms, Longnor Hall, Longnor, Shrewsbury, Shropshire, SY5 7PZ
01743 718367 F 01743 354699
E abumoya@dial.pipex.com
W www.africana.co.uk
Est. 1982 *Stock size* Medium
Stock Rare, antiquarian and out-of-print books on Africa and the Middle East
Open By appointment

LUDLOW

Bayliss Antiques
Contact Mr A B Bayliss
22–24 Old Street, Ludlow, Shropshire, SY8 1NP
01584 873634 F 01584 873634
M 07831 672211
Est. 1968 *Stock size* Medium
Stock Oak and mahogany furniture paintings
Open Mon–Sat 9am–6pm or by appointment
Fairs Bailey Fairs, NEC
Services Valuations

R G Cave & Sons Ltd (LAPADA, BADA)
Contact Mr R G Cave or John Cave
17 Broad Street, Ludlow, Shropshire, SY8 1NG
01584 873568 F 01584 875050
Est. 1965 *Stock size* Medium
Stock Period furniture, metalwork, works of art
Open Mon–Sat 9.30am–5.30pm
Services Valuations for probate and insurance

Claymore Antiques
Contact Sean A Slater
18 Broad Street, Ludlow, Shropshire, SY8 1NG
01584 875851 F 01885 400616
Est. 1996 *Stock size* Large
Stock Georgian–Edwardian English furniture, collectables
Open Mon–Sat 10am–5.30pm
Services UK mainland delivery

John M Clegg
Contact Mr J Clegg
12 Old Street, Ludlow, Shropshire, SY8 1NP
01584 873176
Est. 1974 *Stock size* Large
Stock Period oak, mahogany furniture and associated items
Open Mon–Fri 8.30am–5pm Sat 10.30am–5pm

Corve Street Antiques
Contact Mr Jones or Mr Mcavoy
141a Corve Street, Ludlow, Shropshire, SY8 2PG
01584 879100
Est. 2001 *Stock size* Medium
Stock Longcase clocks, oak country, mahogany furniture, copper, brass, pictures
Open Mon–Sat 10am–5pm
Services Valuations

Garrard Antiques
Contact Mrs C Garrard
139a Corve Street, Ludlow, Shropshire, SY8 2PG
01584 876727 F 01584 781277
M 07971 588063
Est. 1985 *Stock size* Large
Stock Period pine, oak and country furniture, pottery, porcelain, glass, treen, books, collectables
Open Mon–Fri 10am–1pm 2–5pm Sat 10am–5pm

Leon Jones
Contact Mr L Jones
Mitre House Antiques, Corve Bridge, Ludlow, Shropshire, SY8 1DY

☎ 01584 872138
Ⓜ 07976 549013
Est. 1972 *Stock size* Large
Stock Country furniture, mahogany, clocks
Open Mon–Sat 9am–5pm
Fairs Newark, Ardingly

Little Paws
Contact Mr Martin Rees-Evans
4 Castle Street, Ludlow, Shropshire, SY8 1AT
☎ 01584 875286
Est. 1992 *Stock size* Medium
Stock Traditional teddy bears, dolls
Open Mon–Sat 10am–5pm

Ludlow Antique Beds & Fireplaces
Contact Mr G Jones or Mrs S Small
142 Corve Street, Ludlow, Shropshire, SY8 2PG
☎ 01584 875506
Est. 1987 *Stock size* Medium
Stock Victorian and Edwardian original fireplaces, brass, iron and wooden beds of all sizes, country furniture, garden furniture
Open Mon and Fri 11am–4pm Sat 11am–5pm

McCartneys
Contact Mr N Carter or Miss Mary-Jane Hughes
The Ox Pasture, Overton Road, Ludlow, Shropshire, SY8 4AA
☎ 01584 872251 Ⓕ 01584 875727
Ⓔ fineart@mccartneys.co.uk
Ⓦ www.maccartneys.co.uk
Est. 1874
Open Mon–Fri 9am–5.30pm
Sales Fine art, antiques and household effects Fri 10.30am, viewing Thurs 2–8pm day of sale 9–10.30am. Occasional specialist sales
Frequency Monthly
Catalogues Yes

K W Swift
Contact Mr K W Swift
56 Mill Street, Ludlow, Shropshire, SY8 1BB
☎ 01584 878571 Ⓕ 01746 714407
Ⓔ ken@kwswift.demon.co.uk
Est. 1989 *Stock size* Medium
No. of dealers 20
Stock Book market, total circa 5,000 volumes (frequently changed)
Open Mon–Sat 10am–5pm
Services Mounting, framing

M & R Taylor Antiques
Contact Michael Taylor
1 Pepper Lane, Ludlow, Shropshire, SY8 1PX
☎ 01584 874169 Ⓕ 01584 874169
Est. 1977 *Stock size* Small
Stock Furniture, copper, brass
Open Mon–Sat 10am–4pm closed Thurs

Teme Valley Antiques (NAG, Sothebys.com associates)
Contact Mr C Harvey
1 The Bull Ring, Ludlow, Shropshire, SY8 1AD
☎ 01584 874686
Ⓜ 07710 230038
Ⓔ christopher-harvey@lineone.net
Est. 1979 *Stock size* Large
Stock Silver, porcelain, jewellery, small furniture, pictures related to porcelain artists
Open Mon–Sat 10am–5pm Sun by appointment
Services Valuations

MARKET DRAYTON

Deppner Antiques
Contact Mr J Deppner
Towers Lawn, Cheshire Street, Market Drayton, Shropshire, TF9 3EB
☎ 01630 654111
Ⓜ 07974 020642
Est. 1987 *Stock size* Medium
Stock Stripped pine furniture, French antiques
Open Mon Wed Fri Sat 9am–5.30pm
Fairs Newark, Ardingly
Services Courier service for Newark and Ardingly fairs and at all other times, pine stripping

Kev 'n' Di's Antiques
Contact Mr K Williams
Country Needs, Rosehill Road, Market Drayton, Shropshire, TF9 2JU
☎ 01630 638320 Ⓕ 01630 638658
Ⓜ 07976 547174
Ⓔ Kev.and.Dianas.Antiques@tinyworld.co.uk
Est. 1980 *Stock size* Large
Stock Edwardian and Victorian shipping furniture, memorabilia, kitchenware, pine, enamel, four-poster beds, house clearance
Open Mon–Sat 8.30am–6pm Sun 1–5pm open to trade
Fairs Swinderby, Newark
Services Valuations, light restorations, courier service

MUCH WENLOCK

Cruck House Antiques
Contact Mrs B Roderick Smith
23 Barrow Street, Much Wenlock, Shropshire, TF13 6EN
☎ 01952 727165 Ⓕ 01952 727165
Est. 1984 *Stock size* Medium
Stock Silver, pictures, small furniture, collectables
Open Mon–Sat 10am–5pm

John King (BADA)
Contact Mr J King
Raynalds Mansion, Much Wenlock, Shropshire, TF13 6AE
☎ 01952 727456 Ⓕ 01952 727456
Est. 1967 *Stock size* Large
Stock Period furniture and associated items
Open By appointment only
Fairs Olympia (June)

Myra's Antiques
Contact Myra Mullard
5 High Street, Much Wenlock, Shropshire, TF13 6AA
☎ 01952 727596
Ⓜ 07961 832357
Ⓔ Paul@pmullard.freeserve.co.uk
Est. 1997 *Stock size* Large
Stock Collectables, small pieces of furniture, mirrors, Carlton ware
Open Tues–Sat 10am–4pm closed Wed
Services Restorations, re-polishing

NEWPORT

Davies, White & Perry
Contact Mr J P Davies
45–47 High Street, Newport, Shropshire, TF10 7AT
☎ 01952 811003 Ⓕ 01952 811439
Ⓔ newport@davieswhiteperry.co.uk
Ⓦ www.davieswhiteperry.co.uk
Est. 1806
Open Mon–Fri 8.15am–5pm Sat 9am–4pm closed noon–2pm Sun 11am–4pm

Sales Occasional antiques sales on site
Catalogues Yes

NORBURY

Brook Farm Antiques
Contact Mr Tucker or Mr James
Brook Farm, Gauntons Bank, Norbury, Shropshire, SY13 4HY
01948 666043
07754 418777
Est. 1983 *Stock size* Medium
Stock Victorian–Edwardian dining room tables
Open Mon–Sun 9am–5pm
Fairs Stafford Bingley Hall, DMG Shepton Mallett
Services Restorations

OSWESTRY

Arcadia
Contact Joyce or Rod Whitehead
6 Upper Brook Street, Oswestry, Shropshire, SY10 2TB
01691 655622
Est. 1997 *Stock size* Large
Stock Antique and contemporary works of art, ceramics, pictures, books, textiles, designer jewellery, small furniture
Open Mon–Sat 9.30am–5.30pm or by appointment
Services Home decoration

Bookworld
Contact Mr J Cranwell
32 Beatrice Street, Oswestry, Shropshire, SY11 1QG
01691 657112 F 01691 657112
bookworld@tgal.co.uk
www.tgal.co.uk/bookworld
Est. 1995 *Stock size* Medium
Stock Antiquarian and second-hand books
Open Mon–Sat 9am–5.30pm
Services Book search

Judith Charles Antiques & Collectables
Contact Judith Charles
67 Beatrice Street, Oswestry, Shropshire, SY11 1QT
01691 653524 F 01691 624416
07855 253617
Est. 2001 *Stock size* Large
Stock Royal Doulton, china, porcelain, small items, furniture, Beswick, Royal Albert, Sadler, jewellery
Open Mon–Fri 10am–3pm
Sat 10am–5pm
Fairs Ellesmere
Services Valuations

PREES HEATH

Whitchurch Antique Centre
Contact Mr John Simcox
Heath Road, Prees Heath, Whitchurch, Shropshire, SY13 2AD
01948 662626 F 01948 662604
www.whitchurchantiques.co.uk
Est. 1979 *Stock size* Large
Stock French and English furniture
Open Mon–Sun 9am–5pm
Services Packing, shipping

SHERIFFHALES

Corner Farm Antiques
Contact Mr Tim Dams
Weston Heath, Sheriffhales, Shropshire, TF11 8RY
01952 691543 F 01952 691543
07971 578585
www.1cfa.co.uk
Est. 1995 *Stock size* Large
Stock Georgian–Victorian and dining furniture, clocks, barometers, longcase clocks, collectables
Open Mon–Sun 10am–5pm
Services Restorations, clock repairs, valuations

SHIFNAL

Davies, White & Perry
Contact Mr J P Davies
18 Market Place, Shifnal, Shropshire, TF11 9AZ
01952 460523
Est. 1806
Open Mon–Fri 9am–5pm closed 1pm–2pm Sat 9am–noon
Sales Occasional antiques sales on site
Catalogues Yes

SHREWSBURY

Bear Steps Antiques
Contact John or Sally Wyatt
2 Bear Steps, Fish Street, Shrewsbury, Shropshire, SY1 1UR
01743 344298
07720 675813
www.bear-steps-antiques.co.uk
Est. 1990 *Stock size* Large
Stock 18th–early 19thC English porcelain
Open Mon–Sat 9am–5pm
Fairs NEC Antiques for Everyone

Candle Lane Books
Contact Mr J Thornhill
28 Princess Street, Shrewsbury, Shropshire, SY1 1LW
01743 365301 F 01952 771127
Est. 1965 *Stock size* Large
Stock Antiquarian and second-hand books
Open Mon–Sat 9.30am–1pm 2–4.45pm

Collectors Gallery (IBNS, IBASS, ANA, BNTA)
Contact Mr Veissid
Castle Hall, Castle Gates, Shrewsbury, Shropshire, SY1 2AD
01743 272140 F 01743 366041
m.veissid@btinternet.com
www.collectors-gallery.co.uk
Est. 1976 *Stock size* Medium
Stock Coins, medals, stamps, bank notes, postcards, bonds and shares
Open Mon–Sat 9am–5.30pm
Services Mail order

Collectors Place
Contact Mr Keith Jones
29a Princess Street, Shrewsbury, Shropshire, SY1 1LW
01743 246150
Est. 1996 *Stock size* Large
Stock Antique bottles, pot lids, Wade, Beswick, Carlton ware, Art Deco, collectables
Open Wed–Fri 10am–4pm
Sat 9.30am–5pm
Fairs The Antique Bottle Fair
Services Valuations on bottles

Deborah Paul
Contact Debbie or Paul
23 Belle Vue Road, Shrewsbury, Shropshire, SY3 7LN
01743 357696
07890 926530
pgurden@aol.com
Est. 2000 *Stock size* Medium
Stock Decorative and period furniture
Open Mon–Sat 10am–5pm or by appointment
Services Clock restorer on site

MIDLANDS

SHROPSHIRE • STANTON UPON HINE HEATH

⊞ Sue Dyer Antiques
Contact Mrs S Dyer
✉ 9 St Johns Hill, Shrewsbury, Shropshire, SY1 1JD Ⓟ
☎ 01743 350358
Ⓜ 07808 185612
Ⓔ suedyer@suedyerantiques.co.uk
Ⓦ www.suedyerantiques.co.uk
Est. 1972 *Stock size* Medium
Stock Small silver collectables, Victorian and Edwardian cutlery, small furniture, Victorian glass, lamps, unusual items
Open Mon–Sat 9.45am–5.30pm
Services Advice on repairs

⊞ Expressions
Contact Mrs J Griffiths
✉ 17 Princess Street, Shrewsbury, Shropshire, SY1 1LP Ⓟ
☎ 01743 351731
Est. 1991 *Stock size* Medium
Stock Art Deco, furniture, pictures, glass, ceramics
Open Mon–Sat 10am–4pm

Halls Fine Art Auctions (ARVA)
Contact Mr Richard Allen or Jeremy Lamond
✉ Welsh Bridge, Shrewsbury, Shropshire, SY3 8LA Ⓟ
☎ 01743 231212 Ⓕ 01743 271014
Ⓔ fineart@halls-auctioneers.ltd.uk
Ⓦ www.halls-auctioneers.ltd.uk
Est. 1865
Open 9am–5pm
Sales Antiques sales every 6 weeks, general and collectors sales every Fri 10.30am, viewing Thurs 9.30am–7pm
Frequency Every 6 weeks
Catalogues Yes

⊞ Hutton Antiques
Contact Mrs C Brookfield
✉ 18 Princess Street, Shrewsbury, Shropshire, SY1 1LP Ⓟ
☎ 01743 245810
Est. 1979 *Stock size* Medium
Stock Silver, porcelain and small furniture
Open Tues–Sat 9.30am–4pm

⊞ The Little Gem (NAG)
Contact Mrs M A Bowdler
✉ 18 St Marys Street, Shrewsbury, Shropshire, SY1 1ED Ⓟ
☎ 01743 352085 Ⓕ 01743 352085
Ⓔ mbowdler@littlegem.freeserve.co.uk
Ⓦ www.thelittlegem.co.uk
Est. 1960 *Stock size* Medium
Stock Antique and second-hand jewellery, modern Waterford crystal, lighting, handmade jewellery
Open Mon–Sat 9am–5.30pm closed Thurs except Dec
Services Jewellery and watch repair

⊞ F C Manser & Son Ltd (LAPADA)
Contact Paul Manser
✉ 53–54 Wyle Cop, Shrewsbury, Shropshire, SY1 1XJ Ⓟ
☎ 01743 351120 Ⓕ 01743 271047
Ⓔ mansers@theantiquedealers.com
Ⓦ www.theantiquedealers.com
Est. 1944 *Stock size* Large
Stock Antiques, furniture, porcelain, glassware, jewellery
Open Mon–Thurs 9am–5.30pm Fri Sat 9am–5pm
Fairs LAPADA – NEC
Services Valuations, restorations

Princess Antique Centre
Contact Mr John Langford
✉ 14a The Square, Shrewsbury, Shropshire, SY1 1LH
☎ 01743 343701
Est. 1984 *Stock size* Large
No. of dealers 100
Stock Complete range of antiques and collectables
Open Mon–Sat 9.30am–5.15pm

⊞ Quayside Antiques
Contact Mr Chris Winter
✉ 9 Frankwell, Shrewsbury, Shropshire, SY3 8JY Ⓟ
☎ 01743 360490/01948 830363
Ⓜ 07715 612111
Est. 1974 *Stock size* Large
Stock Victorian and Edwardian mahogany furniture, large tables, sets of chairs
Open Tues–Sat 10am–4pm closed Thurs
Fairs NEC, Shepton Mallet
Services Restorations

⊞ Remains To Be Seen
Contact Mr Moseley or Ms Roberts
✉ 62 Wyle Cop, Shrewsbury, Shropshire, SY1 1UX Ⓟ
☎ 01743 361560
Ⓜ 07715 597137
Est. 1991 *Stock size* Medium
Stock Arts & Crafts, Art Nouveau, Gothic revival
Open Mon–Fri 10am–5pm Sat 10am–6pm

Shrewsbury Antique Centre
Contact Mr John Langford
✉ 15 Princess House, The Square, Shrewsbury, Shropshire, SY1 1JZ Ⓟ
☎ 01743 247704
Est. 1984 *Stock size* Large
No. of dealers 70
Stock Wide range of stock
Open Mon–Sat 9.30am–5.15pm

Shrewsbury Antique Market
Contact Mr W Williams
✉ Frankwell Quay Warehouse, Frankwell, Shrewsbury, Shropshire, SY3 8LG Ⓟ
☎ 01743 350916
Est. 1979 *Stock size* Medium
No. of dealers 45
Stock Antique and period collectables
Open Mon–Sat 9.30am–5pm

⊞ Shrewsbury Clock Shop (BHI)
Contact Mr A Donnelly
✉ The Clock Shop, 7 The Parade, St Marys Place, Shrewsbury, Shropshire, SY1 1DL Ⓟ
☎ 01743 361388 Ⓕ 01743 361388
Ⓔ clockshopshrewsbury@hotmail.com
Est. 1987 *Stock size* Medium
Stock Clocks, especially longcase and barometers
Open By appointment
Fairs NEC Spring
Services Clock and barometer repairs and restorations

STANTON UPON HINE HEATH

⊞ Marcus Moore Antiques
Contact Mr M Moore
✉ Booley House, Booley, Stanton upon Hine Heath, Shrewsbury, Shropshire, SY4 4LY Ⓟ
☎ 01939 200333 Ⓕ 01939 200333
Ⓜ 07976 228122
Ⓔ mooreantiques@aol.com
Ⓦ www.marcusmoore-antiques.com
Est. 1980 *Stock size* Large
Stock Georgian–Victorian oak, country, and mahogany furniture and associated items

Open By appointment any time
Services Restorations, upholstery, search, courier

WALL UNDER HEYWOOD

Mullock & Madeley (RICS, ISVA)

Contact John Mullock or Paul Madeley
The Old Shippon, Wall under Heywood, Church Stretton, Shropshire, SY6 7DS
01694 771771 01694 771772
info@mullockmadeley.co.uk
www.mullockmadeley.co.uk
Est. 1997
Open Mon–Fri 9am–5pm
Sales Sporting memorabilia, vintage fishing tackle. Sales held London, Ludlow Race Course, Kempton Park, Solihull
Frequency Every 3 months

WELLINGTON

Bernie Pugh at Oddfellows Corner

Contact Mr B Pugh
120 High Street, Wellington, Telford, Shropshire, TF1 1JU
01952 256184 01952 277888
Est. 1979 *Stock size* Large
Stock Antiques, architectural, country effects, collectors' items, salvage
Open Wed–Fri 4–8pm Sat Sun 2–8pm
Fairs Newark, Epsom
Services Courier service

WEM

The Deermoss Gallery

Contact Colin C Moodley
The Old School, Edstaton, Wem, Shrewsbury, Shropshire, SY4 5RJ
01948 880984 01948 880984
colin.moodley@pipemedia.co.uk
Est. 1989 *Stock size* Large
Stock Pre-1920 antiques and curios
Open Thurs Fri Sat 10am–5pm
Services Framing, shipping and packing

Heritage Antiques

Contact M Nelms
Unit 2, Trench Farm, Tilley Green, Wem, Shropshire, SY4 5PJ
01939 235416
www.heritageantiques.co.uk
Est. 1988 *Stock size* Medium
Stock Regency–Edwardian furniture and collectables
Open Mon–Fri 9am–5pm Sat by appointment
Services Restorations

STAFFORDSHIRE

ALREWAS

Poley Antiques

Contact Mr D Poley
5 Main Street, Alrewas, Burton-on-Trent, Staffordshire, DE13 7AA
01283 791151 01283 791151
07976 676228
dennis.poley@which.net
Est. 1977 *Stock size* Medium
Stock Ceramics, small furniture, silver, brass, copper items
Open Thurs–Sat 10am–5.30pm
Fairs Alexandra Palace, Newark, NEC
Services Valuations

BASFORD

The Pottery Buying Centre

Contact Mr P Hume
535 Etruria Road, Basford, Stoke-on-Trent, Staffordshire, ST5 0PN
01782 635453
07971 711612
Est. 1997 *Stock size* Medium
Stock Fine ceramics, collectables, Doulton, Moorcroft, Beswick, small furniture
Open Mon–Sat 10am–4pm
Services Valuations, restorations of ceramics

BREWOOD

David & Paula Whitfield

Contact David or Paula Whitfield
Passiflora, 25 Stafford Street, Brewood, Staffordshire, ST19 9DX
01902 851557
paula.whitfield@ukonline.co.uk
Est. 1988 *Stock size* Large
Stock Antiques and collectables dating back to Victorian times, glass, china, pottery, copper, brass, cast-iron, curios, leather, ephemera, postcards, children's books, bric-a-brac, garden statuary, small furniture, decorative items including Mabel Lucie Attwell
Open By appointment
Fairs Stafford Bingley Hall, West Midlands Fairs
Services Valuations and house clearance

BURSLEM

H Chesters & Sons

Contact Mr H Chesters
196 Waterloo Road, Burslem, Stoke-on-Trent, Staffordshire, ST6 3HQ
01782 822344
Est. 1912
Open Mon–Fri 10am–5pm telephone service 7am–noon
Sales Fine antiques sales, 2 per annum, Feb and Sept, viewing advertised locally
Catalogues Yes

Top of the Hill Antiques

Contact Mr A Phillips
12/14–14a Mile Street, Burslem, Stoke-on-Trent, Staffordshire, ST6 2AF
01782 834506 01782 834506
ceramic.search@mcmail.com
www.ceramic-search.mcmail.com
Est. 1995 *Stock size* Large
Stock Staffordshire ceramics, general antiques, collectables, antique and reproduction beds
Open Mon–Sat 9.30am–5pm
Fairs Specialist Doulton and Beswick fairs
Services Valuations, restorations, ceramic search service

BURTON-ON-TRENT

Burton Antiques

Contact Mr M Rodgers
1–2 Horninglow Road, Burton-on-Trent, Staffordshire, DE14 2PR
01283 542331
Est. 1978 *Stock size* Medium
Stock Antique pine and other antique furniture, shipping
Open Mon–Sat 9am–5pm Sun 11am–4pm
Services Valuations and pine stripping

Byrkley Books Ltd

Contact Mrs P Tebbett
159 Station Street, Burton-on-Trent, Staffordshire, DE14 1BE
01283 565900

Est. 1963 *Stock size* Medium
Stock Antiquarian, second-hand and remainder books, horse racing a speciality
Open Mon–Fri 9.30am–5pm
Sat 9am–5pm

Martin Gilbert Antiques
Contact Mr M Gilbert
Unit 3, Manor Trading Estate, Hawkins Lane, Burton-on-Trent, Staffordshire, DE14 1QX
☎ 01283 517717
mgilbert10@aol.com
Est. 1987 *Stock size* Medium
Stock Georgian and Victorian mahogany and oak furniture, fully restored
Open Mon–Fri 8.30am–5pm or by appointment
Fairs Newark

Roy C Harris (LAPADA)
Contact Roy Harris,
Burton-on-Trent, Staffordshire
☎ 01283 520355
rchclocks@aol.com
Est. 1983 *Stock size* Medium
Stock Longcase clocks, bracket, mantel and wall clocks
Open By appointment
Fairs NEC
Services Valuations, restorations, shipping

One Off
Contact Mr P Walton
35 Outwoods Street, Burton-on-Trent, Staffordshire, DE14 2PL
☎ 01283 563565
Est. 1989 *Stock size* Small
Stock Hand-painted furniture of all types
Open Mon–Sat 9am–6pm

Richard Winterton Auctioneers and Valuers
Contact Mr A Rathbone or Mr R Winterton
School House Auction Rooms, Hawkins Lane, Burton-on-Trent, Staffordshire, DE14 1PT
☎ 01283 511224 F 01283 568650
richard.winterton@btinternet.com
www.icollector.com
Est. 1864
Open Mon–Fri 9am–5pm
Tues 9am–7.30pm
Sales Monthly sales of specialist antiques and collectables, and of Victorian and later furniture and effects
Frequency One per month
Catalogues Yes

CHEADLE

Country Pine Trading Co
Contact Mr S Beard
Unit D, The Green, Cheadle, Staffordshire, ST10 1PH
☎ 01538 756894 F 01538 750244
M 07959 585133
www.countrypinetrading.co.uk
Est. 1974 *Stock size* Large
Stock Country pine and antique pine furniture
Open Mon–Fri 8am–5pm
Sat 8am–1pm or by appointment
Fairs Newark
Services Restorations and pine stripping

COBRIDGE

Potteries Antique Centre
Contact Ms K Ware
271 Waterloo Road, Cobridge, Stoke-on-Trent, Staffordshire, ST6 3HR
☎ 01782 201455 F 01782 201518
www@potteriesantiquecentre.com
www.potteriesantiquecentre.com
Est. 1990 *Stock size* Large
Stock Wedgwood, Doulton, Beswick, Moorcroft, Crown Devon, Coalport, Minton, Clarice Cliff, Crown Derby, Wade, Shelley, Carlton ware
Open Mon–Sat 9am–5.30pm
Sun 10am–4pm
Fairs Newark, Ardingly
Services Valuations

Potteries Specialist Auctions
Contact Stella M Ashbrook
271 Waterloo Road, Cobridge, Stoke-on-Trent, Staffordshire, ST6 3HR
☎ 01782 286622 F 01782 213777
www.potteriesauctions.com
Est. 1986
Open Mon–Fri 9am–5pm
Sales Mainly British 20thC pottery, last Sat of each month 11.30am, viewing Fri prior 9am–7pm day of sale from 9am
Frequency Monthly
Catalogues Yes

ECCLESHALL

Cottage Collectibles
Contact Mrs S Kettle
Off Castle Street, Eccleshall, Staffordshire
☎ 01785 850210 F 01785 850757
M 07967 713512
sheila@cottagecollectibles.co.uk
www.cottagecollectibles.co.uk
Est. 1995 *Stock size* Medium
Stock English and Continental country antiques, kitchenware, pine furniture, garden and dairy tools
Open By appointment only
Fairs Shepton Mallet, NEC
Services Restorations, antiques learning holidays

Worldwide Arms Ltd (GTA)
Contact Mrs Marita Rawlins
PO Box 5, Eccleshall, Staffordshire, ST21 6SN
☎ 01785 851515 F 01785 850035
sales@worldwidearms.com
www.worldwidearms.com
Est. 1974 *Stock size* Large
Stock From medieval armour to deactivated machine guns
Open Telephone sales 9am–5.30pm
Fairs Many in UK and Germany
Services Mail order only, 3 colour catalogues annually

HANFORD

Bonhams & Brooks
Contact Chris Shenton
Unit 1, Wilson Road, Hanford, Staffordshire, ST4 4QQ
☎ 01782 643159 F 01782 643159
Open Mon–Fri 9am–5pm
Sales Regional Representative for Cheshire and Staffordshire

HANLEY

Louis Taylor Fine Art Auctioneers (ASVA, ARICS)
Contact Mr C Hillier
Britannia House, 10 Town Road, Hanley, Stoke-on-Trent, Staffordshire, ST1 2QG
☎ 01782 214111 F 01782 215283
Est. 1877
Open Mon–Fri 9am–5pm closed 1–2pm
Sales Quarterly 2-day fine art sales Mon Tues 10am, viewing

Thurs 10am–7pm Fri 10am–4pm day of sale from 9am, specialist Doulton and Beswick quarterly, viewing as for fine art. General and Victoriana every two weeks Mon 10am, viewing Fri 10am–4pm Sat 9am–noon
Frequency Fortnightly
Catalogues Yes

⊞ The Tinder Box
Contact Mrs P Yarwood
✉ **61 Lichfield Street, Hanley, Stoke-on-Trent, Staffordshire, ST1 3EA** P
☎ 01782 261368 F 01782 261368
M 07946 445659
Est. 1969 *Stock size* Large
Stock Jewellery, pottery, silver, lamps, spares for oil lamps
Open Mon–Sat 9.30am–6.30pm
Services Valuations, restorations

HARRISEAHEAD

⊞ David J Cope
Contact Mr D Cope
✉ **Fox Earth, Harriseahead Lane, Harriseahead, Stoke-on-Trent, Staffordshire, ST7 4RF** P
☎ 01782 511926 F 01782 516931
M 07712 880695
Est. 1979 *Stock size* Medium
Stock Moorcroft, Royal Worcester, Royal Doulton and porcelain
Open Mon–Sun 10am–5pm
Fairs Newark
Services Valuations

HARTSHILL

⊞ Antiquities of Hartshill
Contact Mrs J Brunetti
✉ **311 Hartshill Road, Hartshill, Stoke-on-Trent, Staffordshire, ST4 7NR** P
☎ 01782 620222
Est. 1996 *Stock size* Large
Stock Wide range of antiquities including furniture, china, dolls, porcelain
Open Mon–Sat 10am–4.30pm
Services Valuations, Hummel figures found

⊞ Checkley Interiors
Contact Mr S Clegg
✉ **493–495 Hartshill Road, Hartshill, Stoke-on-Trent, Staffordshire, ST4 6AA** P
☎ 01782 717522 F 01782 717522
Est. 1998 *Stock size* Medium
Stock Victorian and Edwardian upholstered and occasional furniture
Open Mon–Sat 9.30am–5pm closed Thurs
Services Restorations, upholstery, room interior service

LEEK

⊞ The Antique Store
Contact Mrs J Hopwood
✉ **1 Clerk Bank, Leek, Staffordshire, ST13 5HE** P
☎ 01538 386555 F 01782 570119
Est. 1999 *Stock size* Medium
Stock Painted furniture, decorative items, garden items, architectural antiques, French items, ecclesiastical items
Open Mon–Sat 10am–5pm

⊞ Antiques Within
Contact Mr R Hicks or Mrs K Hicks
✉ **Ground Floor, Compton Mill, Compton, Leek, Staffordshire, ST13 5NJ** P
☎ 01538 387848 F 01538 387848
E antiques.within@virgin.net
W www.antiques-within.com
Est. 1994 *Stock size* Large
Stock Pine, oak, mahogany and Continental furniture, brass, copper, mirrors, collectables and furniture
Open Mon–Sat 10am–5.30pm
Fairs Newark, Swinderby and Ardingly
Services Shipping

⊞ Anvil Antiques
Contact Mrs Lynn Davis
✉ **Cross Street Mill, Cross Street, Leek, Staffordshire, ST13 6BL** P
☎ 01538 371657 F 01538 385118
Est. 1975 *Stock size* Medium
Stock Reproduction and old pine furniture, Old French dark-wood furniture
Open Mon–Fri 9am–5pm Sat 10am–5pm Sun by appointment
Services Restorations

Bury & Hilton
Contact John Hilton
✉ **6 Market Street, Leek, Staffordshire, ST13 6HZ** P
☎ 01538 383344 F 01538 371314
Est. 1887
Open Mon–Fri 9am–5.30pm
Sales Antiques sales, 1st Thurs monthly, special antiques sales April and October.
Frequency Monthly
Catalogues Yes

⊞ Sylvia Chapman Antiques
Contact Mrs S Chapman
✉ **56 St Edward Street, Leek, Staffordshire, ST13 5DL** P
☎ 01538 399116
Est. 1983 *Stock size* Medium
Stock Quality furniture, porcelain, pottery, decorative items, oil lamps, Victorian coloured glass
Open Mon–Sat 11am–5.30pm closed Thurs

Compton Mill Antique Emporium
Contact Mrs S K Butler
✉ **Compton Mill, Compton, Leek, Staffordshire, ST13 5NJ** P
☎ 01538 373396 F 01538 399092
E kelly@comptonmill.fsnet.co.uk
W www.comptonmill.com
Est. 1996 *Stock size* Large
No. of dealers 25
Stock Wide range of antiques
Open Mon–Sat 10am–5.30pm Sun 1–5pm
Services Pine furniture made from reclaimed timber

⊞ Cornerhouse Antiques
Contact Ms H Balmer
✉ **2 Brook Street, Leek, Staffordshire, ST13 5JE** P
☎ 01538 399901 F 01538 399901
M 07973 189468
Est. 1996 *Stock size* Medium
Stock Georgian, Victorian, pine and mahogany furniture, brass, copper, iron, steel, kitchenware, country items, 1920s antiques
Open Mon–Sat 10am–5pm
Fairs Stafford Bowmans, Swinderby, Newark
Services Metal polishing

⊞ Decorative Antiques
Contact Ms J Smith-Gamble
✉ **60b St Edward Street, Leek, Staffordshire, ST13 5DL** P
☎ 01538 372202 F 01538 381939
M 07887 637945
E decant@decant.fsnet.co.uk
Est. 1998 *Stock size* Medium
Stock 19th–early 20thC English and European decorative antiques, soft furnishings, lighting, tapestries
Open Mon–Sat 10am–5pm

MIDLANDS

STAFFORDSHIRE • LICHFIELD

K Grosvenor
Contact Mr K Grosvenor
71 St Edward Street, Leek, Staffordshire, ST13 5DH
01538 385669 01538 385669
keith.grosvenor@virgin.net
Est. 1970 *Stock size* Large
Stock Clocks, barometers, scientific instruments
Open Mon–Sat 9am–4pm or by appointment
Services Restorations, repairs of clocks

Roger Haynes Antique Finder
Contact Mr R Haynes
31 Compton, Leek, Staffordshire, ST13 5NJ
01538 385161 01538 385161
Est. 1959 *Stock size* Large
Stock Decorative English and French items, pine and country small items, collectables
Trade only Yes
Open By appointment only
Services Export trade

Stephen Hibberts Antiques
Contact Mr S Hibbert
24 St Edward Street, Leek, Staffordshire, ST13 5DL
01538 381274
07768 835032
Est. 1984 *Stock size* Large
Stock Lalique, Gallé tapestries, carved furniture, chandeliers, carpets, beds, furniture, clocks
Open Mon–Sat 10am–5.30pm
Services Valuations

Johnsons
Contact Mr P Johnson
120 Mill Street, Leek, Staffordshire, ST13 8HA
01538 386745 01538 386745
07714 288765
Est. 1976 *Stock size* Medium
Stock English and French country furniture, decorative accessories, unique objects
Open Mon–Fri 8am–5pm
Sat Sun by appointment
Services Suppliers to export market

Jonathan Charles Antiques
Contact Mr J Heath
6 Broad Street, Leek, Staffordshire, ST13 5NS
01538 381883/385922 (workshops)
Est. 1999 *Stock size* Medium
Stock Pine furniture, country furniture, iron and brass bedsteads, collectables
Open Mon–Sat 11am–5pm
Services One-off pieces made to measure

Leek Antiques Centre (Barclay House)
Contact Mr P Lumley
4–6 Brook Street, Leek, Staffordshire, ST13 5JE
01538 398475
07721 413095
Est. 1969 *Stock size* Large
No. of dealers 7–8
Stock Wide range of antiques including dining tables, sets of chairs, bedroom furniture, chests-of-drawers, pottery, watercolours, oil paintings, pine
Open Mon–Sat 10am–5pm
Services Restoration, polishing and upholstery

Leek Old Books
Contact Bruce Richardson
1 King Street, Leek, Staffordshire, ST13 5NW
01538 399033 01538 399696
sally@picturebook.fsnet.co.uk
Est. 1987 *Stock size* Medium
Stock Antiquarian and second-hand books on ornithology, natural history, local history, military and transport history
Trade only Yes
Open Tues Wed Fri 9.30am–5pm
Sat 9am–5pm
Services Publishing local history books

Molland Antique Mirrors
Contact John Molland
2 Duke Street, Leek, Staffordshire, ST13 5NH
01538 372553 01538 372553
07774 226042
sales@mollandmirrors.co.uk
www.mollandmirrors.co.uk
Est. 1988 *Stock size* Large
Stock 19thC French and English mirrors
Open Mon–Sat 8am–5pm
Fairs NEC
Services Export packing

Odeon Designs Ltd (Lighting Association)
Contact Mr S Ford
78 St Edward Street, Leek, Staffordshire, ST13 5DL
01538 387188 01538 387188
07973 317961
odeonantiques@hotmail.com
www.odeonantiques.co.uk
Est. 1993 *Stock size* Large
Stock Pine furniture, antique and reproduction lighting, small decorative objects
Open Mon–Sat 10am–5pm
Services Valuations, restorations of lighting

Roberts & Mudd Antiques
Contact Mr C Mudd
Britannia Works, Britannia Street, Leek, Staffordshire, ST13 5EL
01538 371284 01538 371284
robertsmudd@compuserve.com
www.robertsandmudd.com
Est. 1993 *Stock size* Large
Stock French, pine and country furniture, decorative items
Open Mon–Fri 8am–6pm
Sat 9am–noon
Services Restorations

Simpsons
Contact Mr M Simpson
39 St Edward Street, Leek, Staffordshire, ST13 5DH
01538 371515 01538 371515
Est. 1989 *Stock size* Medium
Stock Original decorative, painted and pine furniture for home and garden
Open Mon–Sat 10am–5pm
Thurs 11am–4pm

LICHFIELD

Cathedral Gallery
Contact Mrs R Thompson-Yates
22 Dam Street, Lichfield, Staffordshire, WS13 6AA
01543 253115
Est. 1984 *Stock size* Large
Stock Antique maps, prints
Open Mon–Sat 9.30am–5pm closed Wed
Services Valuations, restorations, framing, colouring

Cordelia & Perdy's Antique Shop
Contact Mrs Perdy Mellor
53 Tamworth Street, Lichfield, Staffordshire, WS13 6JW
01543 263223
Est. 1974 *Stock size* Medium
Stock Wide range of antiques

including furniture, porcelain and collectables
Open Tues Thurs–Sat 10am–4pm

Curborough Hall Farm Antiques Centre (ADA)
Contact Mr J Finnemore
Unit 10, Curborough Hall Farm, Watery Lane, Lichfield, Staffordshire, WS13 7SE
01543 417100
07885 285053
Est. 1995 *Stock size* Large
No. of dealers 31
Stock Furniture, china, collectables, jewellery, books, linen, pictures
Open Tues–Sun Bank Holidays 10.30am–5pm
Services Restaurant

The Essence of Time (BHI)
Contact Malcolm Hinton
Unit 2, Curborough Antiques and Lichfield Craft Centre, Curborough Hall Farm, Watery Lane, Off Eastern Avenue Bypass, Lichfield, Staffordshire, WS13 8ES
01902 764900 (evenings)
07944 245064 (any time)
Est. 1990 *Stock size* Large
Stock Longcase, Vienna, wall, mantel and novelty clocks
Open Wed–Sun 10.45am–5pm

James A Jordan (BHI)
Contact Mr J Jordan
7 The Corn Exchange, Conduit Street, Lichfield, Staffordshire, WS13 6JR
01543 416221
Est. 1988 *Stock size* Large
Stock Jewellery, watches, clocks, silver
Open Mon–Sat 9am–5pm closed Wed
Services Watch, clock and barometer repairs

Milestone Antiques (LAPADA)
Contact Humphrey and Elsa Crawshaw
5 Main Street, Whittington, Lichfield, Staffordshire, WS14 9JU
01543 432248
Est. 1988 *Stock size* Medium
Stock Georgian–early Victorian traditional English furniture, 19thC English porcelain including Coalport, decorative items
Open Thurs–Sat 10am–6pm Sun 11am–3pm or by appointment

Royden Smith
Contact Mr R Smith
Church View House, Farewell Lane, Burntwood, Lichfield, Staffordshire, WS7 9DP
01543 682217
Est. 1973 *Stock size* Large
Stock Antiquarian, second-hand books
Open Sat 10am–4.30pm Sun 11am–4.30pm or by appointment
Services Valuations

The Staffs Bookshop
Contact Mr P Stockham
4 & 6 Dam Street, Lichfield, Staffordshire, WS13 6AA
01543 264093
Est. 1930 *Stock size* Large
Stock Children's, antiquarian, second-hand and new books, Samuel Johnson, 18thC literature
Open Mon–Sat 9.30am–5pm
Services Valuations

Wintertons Ltd (SOFAA)
Contact Mrs Sally Oldham
Lichfield Auction Centre, Fradley Park, Lichfield, Staffordshire, WS13 8NF
01543 263256 01543 415348
enquiries@wintertons.co.uk
Est. 1864
Open Mon–Fri 9am–5.30pm
Sales Victorian and general sales, every 2 or 3 weeks Thurs 10.30am, viewing Wed 1–7pm. Bi-monthly 2-day fine art sale, Wed Thurs 10.30am, viewing Tues noon–8pm and day of sale
Frequency Bi-monthly
Catalogues Yes

NEWCASTLE-UNDER-LYME

Richard Midwinter Antiques
Contact Mr R Midwinter
31 Bridge Street, Newcastle-under-Lyme, Staffordshire, ST5 2RY
01782 712483/01630 672289
01630 672289
07830 617361
antiques@midwinter.fslife.co.uk
Est. 1972 *Stock size* Medium
Stock 16th–19thC oak, mahogany and walnut furniture
Open By appointment
Fairs Olympia
Services Restorations

Windsor House Antiques (BACA Award Winner 2001)
Contact Miss Shelagh Teahan or Mr Paul Barker
5a King Street, Newcastle-under-Lyme, Staffordshire, ST5 1EH
01782 633111
07946 761081
windsorantiques@clara.net
www.windsorantiques.clara.net
Est. 1997 *Stock size* Large
Stock Wide range of antiques including furniture, silver, glass, ceramics, linen, pictures, kitchenware
Open Mon–Sat 10am–5pm
Fairs West Midland – Staffordshire, Bingley Hall
Services House clearances, coffee shop

PENKRIDGE

Golden Oldies
Contact Mr Knowles
5 Crown Bridge, Penkridge, Staffordshire, ST19 5AA
01785 714722
Est. 1973 *Stock size* Large
Stock Antique and reproduction stock mainly furniture and general antiques
Open Mon–Sat 9.30am–5.30pm
Fairs Newark

POLESWORTH

G & J Chesters (PBFA)
Contact Mr G Chesters
14 Market Street, Polesworth, Tamworth, Staffordshire, B78 1HW
01827 894743
gandjchesters@bun.com
Est. 1970 *Stock size* Large
Stock Antiquarian and second-hand books, maps, prints
Open Mon–Sat 9.30am–5.30pm Wed 9.30am–9pm
Fairs NEC Antiques for Everyone fairs

MIDLANDS

STAFFORDSHIRE • RUGELEY

RUGELEY

Rugeley Antique Centre
Contact Mrs M Edwards
161 Main Road, Brereton, Rugeley, Staffordshire, WS15 1DX
01889 577166
info@rugeleyantiquecentre.co.uk
www.rugeleyantiquecentre.co.uk
Est. 1980 *Stock size* Large
No. of dealers 35
Stock Antiques and collectables
Open Mon–Sat 9am–5pm Sun Bank Holidays noon–4.30pm
Services Small parcel shipping

STAFFORD

Browse Antiques
Contact Mrs V Barnes
127 Lichfield Road, Stafford, Staffordshire, ST17 4LF
01785 241097 F 01785 212374
sales@browse-antiques.freeserve.co.uk
www.browse-antiques.freeserve.co.uk
Est. 1982 *Stock size* Large
Stock Antiques, quality second-hand and reproduction furniture, collectables, giftware
Open Mon–Sat 10am–5pm Sun noon–4pm closed Wed
Fairs Newark
Services Stripping, re-finishing, bookcases made to order

Windmill Antiques
Contact Mr I Kettlewell
9 Castle Hill, Broad Eye, Stafford, Staffordshire, ST16 2QB
01785 228505 F 01785 228505
Est. 1992 *Stock size* Large
Stock Antiques, jewellery, decorative items
Open Mon–Sat 10am–5pm
Services Valuations, barometer and ceramic restoration

STOKE-ON-TRENT

Wooden Heart
Contact Mrs Y Quirke
51 Stoke Road, Shelton, Stoke-on-Trent, Staffordshire, ST4 2QH
01782 411437
Est. 1995 *Stock size* Large
Stock Victorian–Edwardian mahogany furniture and decorative items
Open Mon–Fri 8.30am–5pm Sat 10.30am–3.30pm
Services Restorations

Abacus Gallery
Contact Mr D Mycock
56 & 58 Millrise Road, Milton, Stoke-on-Trent, Staffordshire, ST2 7BW
01782 543005
Est. 1980 *Stock size* Small
Stock Antiquarian and second-hand books, prints, engravings, local history a speciality
Open Mon–Fri 9am–5pm Sat 9am–4pm
Fairs Buxton Book Fair

Ann's Antiques
Contact Mrs A Byatte
26 Leek Road, Stockton Brook, Stoke-on-Trent, Staffordshire, ST9 9NN
01782 503991
Est. 1969 *Stock size* Large
Stock Victorian–Edwardian furniture, cranberry glass, Victorian oil lamps, jewellery, pottery, porcelain, rocking horses, dolls' houses
Open Fri Sat 10am–5pm or by appointment

Ceramics International
Contact Christine Cope
Unit 1, Canal Lane, Tumstall, Stoke-on-Trent, Staffordshire, ST6 4NZ
01782 575545 F 01782 814447
theoldchintzcompany@compuserve.com
Est. 1996 *Stock size* Large
Stock English, imported ceramics, Worcester, Wedgwood, Moorcroft, chintz, flow blue
Trade only Yes
Open Mon–Fri 9am–5.30pm

On the Hill Antiques
Contact Ms Sue Bird
450 Hartshill Road, Stoke-on-Trent, Staffordshire, ST4 7PL
01782 252249 F 01782 252249
M 07932 726035
Est. 1996 *Stock size* Large
Stock 1930s oak furniture, pottery, collectables
Open Mon–Sat 9am–5pm
Fairs Bingley, Staffordshire
Services Valuations

STONE

Hallahan
Contact Hilary Jeffries
13 Station Road, Stone, Staffordshire, ST15 8JP
01785 815187 F 01785 815187
Est. 1995 *Stock size* Large
Stock 1960s–70s collectables, antiques, upholstered furniture, antiquarian books, jewellery
Open Mon–Sat 9.30am–5pm closed Wed
Services Upholstery

SWADLINCOTE

Armstrongs Auctions (ISVA)
Contact Mr J Walker FRICS
Midland Road, Swadlincote, Burton-on-Trent, Staffordshire, DE11 0AH
01283 217772 F 01283 550467
Est. 1930
Open Mon–Fri 2.30–4.30pm
Sales Antiques and collectors' auctions last Wed of March, June, Sept, Nov 11am. General household auctions most Wed 11am, viewing Mon Tues 2–4pm Wed 9–11am

TAMWORTH

Aldergate Antiques
Contact Mr Mike Foster
George Street, Tamworth, Staffordshire, B79 7LQ
01827 62164
aldergate.antiques@virgin.net
Est. 1998 *Stock size* Medium
Stock Ceramics, silver, ivory, smalls
Open By appointment
Fairs Malvern Fair, Donnington, NEC

TUTBURY

The Clock Shop (MBHI)
Contact Ms A James
1 High Street, Tutbury, Burton-on-Trent, Staffordshire, DE13 9LP
01283 814596 F 01283 814594
M 07710 161949
sales@antique-clocks-watches.co.uk
www.antique-clocks-watches.co.uk
Est. 1987 *Stock size* Large
Stock Antique clocks, longcase clocks and watches

Open Mon–Sat 10am–5pm
Services Valuations, restorations and repairs

The Old Chapel Antiques & Collectables Centre (OCS)
Contact Mr R Clarke
High Street, Tutbury, Burton-on-Trent, Staffordshire, DE13 9LP
01283 815255
Est. 1996 *Stock size* Large
No. of dealers 26
Stock Wide range of antiques and collectables
Open Mon–Sun 10am–5pm

Tutbury Mill Antique Centre
Contact Mrs L Carlin
Tutbury Mill Mews, Lower High Street, Tutbury, Burton-on-Trent, Staffordshire, DE13 9LU
01283 520074
07973 153246
www.antiquesplus.co.uk
Est. 1995 *Stock size* Large
No. of dealers 25
Stock Wide range of antiques and collectables
Open Mon–Sat 10.00am–5.30pm, Sun noon–5pm

UTTOXETER

Lion Antiques Centre
Contact Mrs Vicky Jacques
8 Market Place, Uttoxeter, Staffordshire, ST14 8HP
01889 567717 F 01889 567717
Est. 1999 *Stock size* Large
No. of dealers 28+
Stock Wide range of antiques
Open Mon–Sat 10am–5pm Sun 1–5pm
Services Sourcing service, design

Mouse Mill Antique Centre
Contact Mrs De Ville
The Old Warehouse, Market Street, Uttoxeter, Staffordshire, ST14 8JA
01889 565032
Est. 1999 *Stock size* Large
No. of dealers 10
Stock General antiques, collectables, Arts & Crafts, Art Deco, Victoriana
Open Mon–Sat 10am–5pm

YOXALL

H W Heron & Son Ltd (LAPADA)
Contact Mrs J Heron
The Antique Shop, King Street, Yoxall, Burton-on-Trent, Staffordshire, DE13 8NF
01543 472266 F 01543 473800
E hwheron@btinternet.com
Est. 1949 *Stock size* Medium
Stock Period furniture, ceramics, objects, paintings
Open Mon–Fri 9am–6pm Sat 9am–5.30pm Sun 2–6pm
Fairs Newark
Services Valuations

WARWICKSHIRE

ALCESTER

Malthouse Antiques Centre
Contact Pat Alcock
4 Market Place, Alcester, Warwickshire, B49 5AE
01789 764032
Est. 1984 *Stock size* Large
No. of dealers 15–20
Stock 18th–early 20thC furniture, ceramics, silver, collectables etc
Open Mon–Sat 10am–5pm, Sun 1–4pm

Justin Neales Antiques & Interiors
Contact Mr Justin Neales
3 Evesham Street, Alcester, Warwickshire, B49 5DS
01789 766699
www.justinnealesantiques.co.uk
Est. 1987 *Stock size* Large
Stock Georgian, Victorian and Edwardian furniture, painted furniture, tapestry, cushions, mirrors, silver picture frames
Open Mon–Fri 9am–5pm Sat 10am–5pm
Services Restorations, reupholstery

BIDFORD ON AVON

Bidford Antique Centre
Contact Mr B Owen
Warwick House, 94–96 High Street, Bidford on Avon, Alcester, Warwickshire, B50 4AF
01789 773680
Est. 1974 *Stock size* Large
No. of dealers 6
Stock General antiques and collectables
Open Tues–Sat 10am–5pm

BRINKLOW

Annie's Attic
Contact Ann Wilson
19a Broad Street, Brinklow, Warwickshire, CV23 0LS
01788 833094
Est. 1998 *Stock size* Medium
Stock Clocks, small furniture, metalwork, oil lamps, old and interesting objects
Open Fri Sat 11am–5pm Sun 11am–4pm also some Wed
Services Clock restoration

Christopher Peters Antiques
Contact Mr C Peters
19 Broad Street, Brinklow, Rugby, Warwickshire, CV23 0LF
01788 832673 F 01788 832673
E enquiries@christopherpetersantiques.co.uk
www.christopherpetersantiques.co.uk
Est. 1985 *Stock size* Large
Stock 17th–19thC painted fruitwood and country furniture
Open Tues–Sat 10am–5.30pm
Fairs NEC (Spring, Summer)

The Victorian Ironmonger
Contact Mr D Thompson
The Old Garage, 70 Broad Street, Brinklow, Rugby, Warwickshire, CV23 0LN
01788 832292
Est. 1993 *Stock size* Large
Stock Original Victorian ironmongery, fireplaces, doors, house fittings
Open Fri–Sat 10am–5pm Sun 11am–4pm

DUNCHURCH

Dunchurch Antiques Centre
Contact Graham Sutherland
16a Daventry Road, Dunchurch, Rugby, Warwickshire, CV22 6NS
01788 522450
Est. 1999 *Stock size* Medium
No. of dealers 10
Stock General antiques, collectables, antiquarian books
Open Mon–Sun 10am–5pm

MIDLANDS

WARWICKSHIRE • HATTON

Now & Then
Contact Mike Best
6 The Green, Dunchurch, Rugby, Warwickshire, CV22 6NX
01788 811211
07711 248951
Est. 2001 *Stock size* Large
Stock General antiques
Open Mon–Sun 10am–5pm

HATTON

The Stables Antique Centre
Contact Mr John Colledge
Hatton Country World, Dark Lane, Hatton, Warwick, Warwickshire, CV35 8XA
01926 842405 F 01926 842023
Est. 1992 *Stock size* Large
No. of dealers 25
Stock Old clocks, furniture, curios, china etc
Open Mon–Sun 10am–5pm
Services Craft centre, café, bar, clock repairs

ILMINGTON

Peter Finer (BADA)
Contact Peter Finer or Nickki Eden
The Old Rectory, Ilmington, Shipston-on-Stour, Warwickshire, CV36 4JQ
01608 682267 F 01608 682575
pf@peterfiner.com
www.peterfiner.com
Stock size Large
Stock Arms, armour and related objects
Open Strictly by appointment
Fairs New York, Texas
Services Restorations

KENILWORTH

Aspidistra
Contact Jenny Young
84 Warwick Road, Kenilworth, Warwickshire, CV8 1HP
01926 864308 F 01926 777224
Est. 1991 *Stock size* Medium
Stock Antiques, Art Deco, antique and modern silver
Open Mon–Sat 10am–5pm

Paull's of Kenilworth (LAPADA, BADA, CINOA)
Contact Janice Paull
Beehive House, 125 Warwick Road, Kenilworth, Warwickshire, CV8 1HU
01926 851311 F 01926 851311
07831 691254
janicepaull@btinternet.com
www.masonsironstone.com
Est. 1964 *Stock size* Large
Stock Mason's ironstone, 18th–19thC pottery, Le Bond oval prints
Open Tues–Fri 10am–4pm
Fairs Olympia – USA (Feb, June, Nov), BADA Duke of York's, NEC (April, Aug, Nov)
Services Valuations

LEAMINGTON SPA

Kings Cottage Antiques (LAPADA)
Contact Mr A Jackson
4 Windsor Street, Leamington Spa, Warwickshire, CV32 5EB
01926 422927 F 01926 422927
Est. 1993
Stock Early oak and country furniture
Open Mon–Fri 9am–5pm
Sat by appointment

BBG Locke & England
Contact Nicola Ellis
18 Guy Street, Leamington Spa, Warwickshire, CV32 4RT
01926 889100 F 01926 470608
info@leauction.co.uk
www.leauction.co.uk
Open 9am–1pm 2–5.30pm
Sales Household and Victoriana auctions weekly, antiques and fine art auctions monthly
Frequency Weekly
Catalogues Yes

The Old Pine House
Contact Keith Platt
16 Warwick Street, Leamington Spa, Warwickshire, CV32 5LL
01926 470477 F 01926 470477
Est. 1993 *Stock size* Large
Stock Victorian stripped pine
Open Tues–Fri 10am–5.30pm
Sat 9am–5.30pm evenings by appointment

Portland Books
Contact Mr Martyn Davies
7 Campion Terrace, Leamington Spa, Warwickshire, CV32 4SU
01926 888776 F 01926 888775
martyn@portlandbooks.freeserve.co.uk
www.portlandbooks.com
Est. 1974 *Stock size* Large
Stock Antiquarian and second-hand books, Warwickshire history a speciality
Open Thurs–Sat 9.30am–6pm or by appointment
Services Valuations, book search

Yesterdays
Contact Mrs Shona Caldwell
21 Portland Street, Leamington Spa, Warwickshire, CV32 5EZ
01926 450238
Est. 1985 *Stock size* Medium
Stock General antiques shop, period furniture, pictures, bric-a-brac
Open Tues Wed Fri Sat 10am–5pm

LONG MARSTON

Barn Antique Centre
Contact Bev and Graham Simpson
Station Road, Long Marston, Stratford-upon-Avon, Warwickshire, CV37 8RB
01789 721399 F 01789 721390
barnantiques@aol.com
www.barnantique.com
Est. 1978 *Stock size* Large
No. of dealers 30+
Stock Huge barn full of antiques and collectables.13,000+ sq ft
Open Mon–Sun 10am–5pm
Services Licensed French restaurant

MIDDLETON

Middleton Hall Antiques (BAFRA)
Contact Mr S Herberholz
Middleton Hall, Middleton, Tamworth, Warwickshire, B78 2AE
01827 282858
07973 151681
Est. 1997 *Stock size* Small
Stock 18th–19thC furniture, porcelain
Open Wed–Sun 11am–5pm

NUNEATON

The Granary Antiques
Contact Gordon Stockdale
Hoar Park, Craft Village, Ansley, Nuneaton, Warwickshire, CV10 0QU

☎ 024 7639 5551 ⓕ 024 7639 4433
ⓔ jl@hpcv.freeserve.co.uk
ⓦ www.hpcv.freeserve.co.uk
Est. 1996 *Stock size* Large
Stock General antiques, pine, kitchenware, Edwardian furniture, porcelain and Mason's ironstone in a 17thC converted building
Open Tues–Sun 10am–5pm
Services Restaurant on premises

G Payne Antiques
Contact Mr G Payne
✉ **25 Watling Street, Nuneaton, Warwickshire, CV11 6JJ** Ⓟ
☎ 024 7632 5178
ⓜ 07836 754489
Est. 1991 *Stock size* Medium
Stock Mahogany and oak furniture
Open Mon–Sat 8am–6pm

RUGBY

272 Antiques
Contact Sue Walters
✉ **272 Hillmorton Road, Rugby, Warwickshire, CV22 5BW** Ⓟ
☎ 01788 541818 ⓕ 01788 541818
Est. 2001 *Stock size* Small
Stock French country and English pine furniture
Open Wed–Sat 10.30am–5pm
Services Restorations, pine stripping

The Rugby Salerooms
Contact Mrs M or Miss L Seaman
✉ **16–18 Albert Street, Rugby, Warwickshire, CV21 2RS** Ⓟ
☎ 01788 542367/543445
Est. 1979
Sales Weekly auction of antiques and general household goods. Held at 6 Payne's Lane, Rugby on Mondays at 7pm. Viewing Sun 11am–3pm Mon noon–7pm
Frequency Weekly
Catalogues Yes

M G Seaman
Contact Mrs M Seaman
✉ **16–18 Albert Street, Rugby, Warwickshire, CV21 2RS** Ⓟ
☎ 01788 560998 ⓕ 01788 570425
Est. 1979 *Stock size* Large
Stock 1920s–1960s antiques, glass, china, clothing, accessories, jewellery
Open Mon–Sat 9am–5pm closed Wed

SHENTON

Whitemoors Antique Centre
Contact Mr Colin Wightman
✉ **Main Street, Shenton, Warwickshire, CV13 6BZ** Ⓟ
☎ 01455 212250
Est. 1993 *Stock size* Large
No. of dealers 15
Stock Furniture, pottery, clocks, bric-a-brac, paperweights
Open Mon–Sun summer 11am–5pm winter 11am–4pm

SHIPSTON-ON-STOUR

Church Street Gallery
Contact Mr Robert Field
✉ **24 Church Street, Shipston-on-Stour, Warwickshire, CV36 4AP** Ⓟ
☎ 01608 662431 ⓕ 01608 662431
ⓦ www.churchstreetgallery.co.uk
Est. 1979 *Stock size* Large
Stock Antique maps and prints, late 19th–early 20thC watercolours, oils, furniture, bric-a-brac
Open Mon–Fri 9.30am–6pm Thurs 9.30am–1pm Sat 10am–5.30pm
Services Picture framing and restoration

Pine & Country Antiques
Contact Mr C Harvey
✉ **28 Church Street, Shipston-on-Stour, Warwickshire, CV36 4AP** Ⓟ
☎ 01608 662168 ⓕ 01608 662168
Est. 1973 *Stock size* Large
Stock General range of antiques, decorative items, French oak and mahogany furniture
Open Mon–Sat 9am–5.30pm or by appointment

Pine and Things
Contact Mr R Wood
✉ **Portobello Farm, Campden Road, Shipston-on-Stour, Warwickshire, CV36 4PY** Ⓟ
☎ 01608 663849 ⓕ 01608 663849
ⓔ richard@pineandthings.freeserve.co.uk
ⓦ www.pineandthings.net
Est. 1991 *Stock size* Large
Stock Victorian and earlier pine furniture
Open Mon–Sat 9am–5pm

SNITTERFIELD

Phillips Brothers (NAVA)
Contact Robin Phillips
✉ **The Sale Room, Bearley Road, Snitterfield, Stratford-upon-Avon, Warwickshire, CV37 0EZ** Ⓟ
☎ 01789 731114 ⓕ 01789 731114
Est. 1980
Open Mon–Fri 9.30am–5pm
Sales General and antiques sales Sat 10am, viewing from 9am. Occasional antique sales Sat, viewing 9am
Frequency Fortnightly
Catalogues Yes

STRATFORD-UPON-AVON

Alscot Bathroom Company (SALVO)
Contact Mr Cockroft
✉ **The Stable Yard, Alscot Park, Stratford-upon-Avon, Warwickshire, CV37 8BL** Ⓟ
☎ 0121 709 1901
Est. 1960 *Stock size* Large
Stock Victorian–Edwardian sanitary ware, Art Deco, roll-top baths
Open Mon–Fri 9.30am–5pm Sat 9.30am–2.30pm
Services Restorations

Arbour Antiques Ltd
Contact Mr R J Wigington
✉ **Poets Arbour, Sheep Street, Stratford-upon-Avon, Warwickshire, CV37 6EF**
☎ 01789 293453
Est. 1954 *Stock size* Large
Stock 17th–18thC arms and armour
Open Mon–Fri 9am–5pm

Steven B Bruce Auctioneers Ltd (NAVA, ANAEA)
Contact Mr S Bruce
✉ **Estate House, Meer Street, Stratford-upon-Avon, Warwickshire, CV37 6QB**
☎ 01789 296689 ⓕ 01789 293905
ⓜ 07778 595952
ⓔ stevenbruce@hotmail.com
ⓦ www.antiquesvaluers.co.uk
Est. 1995
Open Mon–Fri 9.30am–5.30pm Sat by appointment
Sales Antiques sales Sat 11am, viewing Fri 10am–7pm

MIDLANDS

WARWICKSHIRE • TIDDINGTON

Sat 9–11am. Held at local venues. Occasional specialist sales
Frequency Monthly
Catalogues Yes

Thomas Crapper & Co (SALVO, Institute of Plumbing)
Stable Yard, Alscot Park, Stratford-upon-Avon, Warwickshire, CV37 8BL
01789 450522 01789 450523
wc@thomas-crapper.co.uk
www.thomas-crapper.co.uk
Est. 1861 *Stock size* Medium
Stock Victorian–Edwardian and unusual bathroom fittings. Art Deco and coloured 1930s bathrooms
Open Mon–Fri 9am–5.30pm or by appointment
Services Restorations, catalogues (£4)

Goodbye To All That
Contact Mr Briggs
Ely Street, Stratford-upon-Avon, Warwickshire, CV37 6LN
01789 204180
Est. 1999 *Stock size* Small
Stock Firearms, scientific instruments
Open Mon–Sun 10am–5.30pm

Pickwick Gallery
Contact Mr H D Dankenbring
32 Henley Street, Stratford-upon-Avon, Warwickshire, CV37 6QW
01789 294861
meridienmaps@btinternet.com
Est. 1986 *Stock size* Medium
Stock Antique maps, sporting prints, 1600–1880
Open Mon–Sat 10am–5pm Sun Bank Holidays 11am–4.30pm

Riverside Antiques
Contact Mr Richard Monk
60 Ely Street, Stratford-upon-Avon, Warwickshire, CV37 6LN
01789 262090
07931 512325
Est. 1996 *Stock size* Medium
Stock Clarice Cliff, antique and designer jewellery
Open Mon–Sun Oct–Mar 10am–5pm Jun–Sept 10am–5.30pm
Services Rings designed and made

Stratford Antiques and Interiors
Contact Mr or Mrs Kerr
Dodwell Trading Estate, Evesham Road, Stratford-upon-Avon, Warwickshire, CV37 9SY
01789 297729 01789 297710
info@stratfordantiques.co.uk
www.stratfordantiques.co.uk
Est. 1995 *Stock size* Large
No. of dealers 20
Stock A wide range of antiques and collectables, home furnishings and decorative items
Open Mon–Sun 10am–5pm

Stratford Antiques Centre
Contact Mr Mike Conway
59–60 Ely Street, Stratford-upon-Avon, Warwickshire, CV37 6LN
01789 204180
Est. 1981 *Stock size* Large
No. of dealers 50
Stock Wide range of antiques and collectables. One of the largest antiques markets in the Midlands
Open Mon–Sun summer 10am–5.30pm winter 10am–5pm
Services Restaurant

Robert Vaughan Antiquarian Booksellers (ABA, PBFA)
Contact Mrs Colleen Vaughan
20 Chapel Street, Stratford-upon-Avon, Warwickshire, CV37 6EP
01789 205312
Est. 1953 *Stock size* Large
Stock Fine and first editions of English literature, theatre, related subjects, Shakespeare
Open Mon–Sat 9.30am–5.30pm
Services Valuations, search

TIDDINGTON

Bigwood Auctioneers Ltd (SOFAA)
Contact Mr C Ironmonger
The Old School, Tiddington, Stratford-upon-Avon, Warwickshire, CV37 7AW
01789 269415 01789 294168
sales@bigwoodauctioneers.co.uk
www.bigwoodauctioneers.co.uk
Est. 1849
Open Mon–Fri 9am–5.30pm closed 12.45–2pm Sat 9am–noon
Sales Quarterly fine furniture and works of art, monthly antiques and collectables, monthly furniture (Mar Sept) sporting memorabilia (Mar Aug Sept Dec) wine sales (April Oct) collectables, games, toys, viewing 9am–8pm
Frequency 45 per annum
Catalogues Yes

WARWICK

Apollo Antiques Ltd (LAPADA, CINOA)
Contact Roger Mynott
The Saltisford, Warwick, Warwickshire, CV34 4TD
01926 494746/494666
01926 401477
mynott@apolloantiques.com
www.apolloantiques.com
Est. 1968 *Stock size* Large
Stock English 18th–19thC furniture, sculpture, paintings, decorative items, arts and crafts, Gothic revival
Open Mon–Fri 9am–6pm Sat 9.30am–12.30pm
Services Free delivery service to London

W J Casey Antiques (LAPADA, CINOA)
Contact Mr Bill Casey
9 High Street, Warwick, Warwickshire, CV34 4AP
01926 499199
07771 920475 *Stock size* Large
Stock 18th–19thC furniture, especially dining room furniture
Open Mon–Sat 10am–5pm or by appointment

Castle Antiques
Contact Julia Reynolds
24 Swan Street, Warwick, Warwickshire, CV34 4BJ
01926 401511
Est. 1998 *Stock size* Large
Stock Victorian–Edwardian furniture, small items
Open Mon–Sat 10am–5pm
Services Restorations

Dorridge Antiques
Contact Mrs P Spencer
Warwick Antique Centre, 22–24 High Street, Warwick, Warwickshire, CV34 4AP
01926 499857
Est. 1981 *Stock size* Medium
Stock Silver, jewellery
Open Mon–Sat 10am–5pm

Emscote Antiques
Contact Mr Paul Hannan
152 Emscote Road, Warwick, Warwickshire, CV34 5QN
01926 407979
Est. 1994 *Stock size* Medium
Stock Original and reproduction painted pine furniture
Open Thurs–Sat 10am–5pm
Fairs Newark, Ardingly
Services Pine stripping

English Antiques
Contact Mrs Jean Fair
3 High Street, Warwick, Warwickshire, CV34 4AP
01926 408656 F 01926 408656
M 07802 419536
Est. 1957 *Stock size* Large
Stock 18th–19thC furniture, decorative items
Open Mon–Sat 10am–5.30pm or by appointment

Entente Cordiale
Contact Carol Robson
9 High Street, Warwick, Warwickshire, CV34 4AP
01926 403733 F 01905 754129
Est. 2000 *Stock size* Small
Stock Mixture of English and French generally small furniture
Open Mon–Sat

John Goodwin & Sons
Contact Mr Neil Goodwin
22–24 High Street, Warwick, Warwickshire, CV34
01926 853332
Est. 1969 *Stock size* Large
Stock General antiques, furniture, pictures, collectables
Open Mon–Sat 8.30am–5.30pm

Keith Gormley Antiques
Contact Mr Keith Gormley
56 West Street, Warwick, Warwickshire, CV34 6AW
01926 419880
M 07866 314504
Est. 1996 *Stock size* Large
Stock Period and decorative furniture, accessories
Open Mon–Fri 10am–5pm

Russell Lane Antiques
Contact Mr Lane
2–4 High Street, Warwick, Warwickshire, CV34 4AP
01926 494494 F 01926 492972
E russell.laneantiques@virgin.net
Est. 1974 *Stock size* Large
Stock Antique jewellery and silver. Official jewellers to the Royal Show
Open Mon–Sat 10am–5pm
Services Replacement insurance claims

Patrick & Gillian Morley (LAPADA)
Contact Mr P Morley
62 West Street, Warwick, Warwickshire, CV34 6AW
01926 494464
M 07768 835040
Est. 1969 *Stock size* Large
Stock Period decorative and unusual furniture, works of art
Open Mon–Fri 9.15am–5.30pm or by appointment

Patrick & Gillian Morley (LAPADA)
Contact Mr P Morley
Unit 7, Cape Industrial Estate, Cattell Road, Warwick, Warwickshire, CV34 4JN
01926 498849
M 07768 835040
Est. 2000 *Stock size* Large
Stock Period decorative and unusual furniture, works of art
Open Mon–Fri 9.15am–5.30pm or by appointment

Quinneys of Warwick
Contact James Reeve
9 Church Street, Warwick, Warwickshire, CV34 4AB
01926 498113 F 01926 498113
Est. 1865 *Stock size* Large
Stock 17th–19thC English furniture
Open Mon–Fri 9.30am–5.30pm Sat 9.30am–1pm
Services Restorations

Don Spencer Antiques
Contact Don Spencer
36a Market Place, Warwick, Warwickshire, CV34 4SH
01926 407989 F 01564 775470
M 07836 525755
E antiques@btinternet.com
W www.antique-desks.co.uk
Est. 1974 *Stock size* Large
Stock Old desks, oak, mahogany, walnut, Victorian, Edwardian, roll-top, writing tables, desk chairs
Open Mon–Sat 10am–5pm
Services Free delivery anywhere in the UK

Summersons
Contact Mr Peter Lightfoot
172 Emscote Road, Warwick, Warwickshire, CV34 5QN
01926 400630 F 01926 400630
E clocks@summersons.com
W www.summersons.com
Est. 1979 *Stock size* Medium
Stock Clocks, barometers
Open Mon–Fri 9am–5pm Sat 10am–1pm
Services Restorations, repairs of clocks and barometers, sales of materials for restoration

Tango Art Deco & Antiques
Contact Jenny and Martin Wills
46 Brook Sreet, Warwick, Warwickshire, CV34 4BL
01926 496999 F 0121 704 4969
M 07889 046969
E info@tango-artdeco.co.uk
W www.tango-artdeco.co.uk
Est. 1987 *Stock size* Large
Stock Art Deco ceramics, furniture and accessories, Clarice Cliff, Susie Cooper
Open Thurs–Sat 10am–5pm
Fairs NEC

The Tao Antiques
Contact Mr A Ross
59 Smith Street, Warwick, Warwickshire, CV34 4HU
01926 411772
Est. 1964 *Stock size* Medium
Stock Victorian furniture, copper, brass, china, general antiques
Open Mon–Sat 2pm–6pm

Vintage Antiques Centre (WADA)
Contact Mr Peters Sellors
36 Market Place, Warwick, Warwickshire, CV34 4SH
01926 491527
E vintage@globalnet.co.uk
Est. 1979 *Stock size* Large
No. of dealers 20
Stock Victorian glass, 19thC ceramics, 20thC collectables, 1950s, smalls
Open Mon–Sat 10am–5.30pm Sun 11.30am–4.30pm

Warwick Antique Centre
Contact Mr P Viola
22–24 High Street, Warwick, Warwickshire, CV34 4AT
01926 491382
Est. 1971 *Stock size* Large
No. of dealers Over 30

Stock General antiques, collectables
Open Mon–Sat 10am–5pm
Services Valuations

Warwick Antiques
Contact Mr M Morrison
16–18 High Street, Warwick, Warwickshire, CV34 4AP
01926 492482 01926 492482
antiques@warwick492482.freeserve.co.uk
Est. 1965 *Stock size* Large
Stock General antiques
Open Mon–Sat 10am–5pm

John Williams Antique & Collectables
Contact Mr John Williams
Warwick Antiques Centre, 22–24 High Street, Warwick, Warwickshire, CV34 4AP
01926 419966
Est. 1981 *Stock size* Medium
Stock Cameras, toys, tools, collectables, militaria, porcelain
Open Mon–Sat 10am–4.30pm
Fairs Alexandra Palace, Birmingham Rag Market, NEC, Motorcycle Museum – Birmingham
Services Valuations

WOOTTON WAWEN

Le Grenier
Contact Joyce Ellis
Yew Tree Farm, Stratford Road, Wootton Wawen, Stratford-upon-Avon, Warwickshire, B95 6BY
01564 795401 01564 795401
07712 126048
Est. 1989 *Stock size* Medium
Stock French country furniture, fine period furniture
Open Tues–Sun 9am–5.30pm
Services Restorations for painted furniture, pen work general restoration

WEST MIDLANDS

BARNT GREEN

Barnt Green Antiques
Contact Neville Slater
93 Hewell Road, Barnt Green, Birmingham, West Midlands, B45 8NL
0121 445 4942 0121 445 4942
Est. 1977 *Stock size* Medium
Stock Furniture, clocks
Open Mon–Fri 9am–5.30pm
Sat 9am–1pm
Services Valuations, restorations

BIRMINGHAM

Acme Toy Company
Contact Mr P Hall
17 Station Road, Erdington, Birmingham, West Midlands, B23 6UB
0121 384 8835
www.solnet.co.uk/acme
Est. 1995 *Stock size* Medium
Stock Antique and collectable toys – TV, Sci-Fi, Action Man
Open Mon–Thurs 11am–3pm
Fri Sat 11am–5pm
Fairs D & G Fairs

Biddle & Webb Ltd
Contact Mr Thornton
Icknield Square, Ladywood, Middleway, Birmingham, West Midlands, B16 0PP
0121 455 8042 0121 454 9615
antiques@biddleandwebb.freeserve.co.uk
Est. 1955
Open Mon–Fri 9am–5pm
Sales Pictures and prints 11am 1st Fri of month, viewing Sat prior 9am–noon Wed Thur 10am–4pm. Antiques and later furnishings, porcelain, glass sale 2nd Fri, viewing as previously. Toys or Decorative Art 3rd Fri. Jewellery 4th Fri.
Catalogues Yes

The Birmingham Antique Centre
Contact Mr Baldock
1407 Pershore Road, Stirchley, Birmingham, West Midlands, B30 2JR
0121 459 4587 0121 689 6565
Est. 1994 *Stock size* Large
No. of dealers 65+
Stock Antique furniture, second-hand furniture, bric-a-brac
Open Mon–Sat 9am–5.30pm
Sun 10am–5pm
Services Valuations, house clearance

Birmingham Coins
Contact Mr D Harris
30 Shaftmoor Lane, Acocks Green, Birmingham, West Midlands, B27 7RS
0121 707 2808 0121 707 2808
Est. 1996 *Stock size* Large
Stock General, world and British coins and bank notes, collectors' models, medals
Open Tues Thurs Fri 10.30am–5pm

Cambridge House Antiques
Contact Mr T McIntosh
168 Gravelly Lane, Birmingham, West Midlands, B23 5SN
0121 386 1346
Est. 1998 *Stock size* Large
Stock General antiques
Open Mon–Sat 10am–5.30pm
Fairs Newark, Birmingham Rag Market

Chesterfield Antiques
Contact Mrs Mara Cirjanic
181 Gravelly Lane, Birmingham, West Midlands, B23 5SG
0121 373 3876
Est. 1974 *Stock size* Large
Stock Victorian, Edwardian and 1930s furniture and sets of chairs
Open Mon–Sat 9.30am–5.30pm

Cross's Curios
Contact Mrs Valerie Cross
928 Pershore Road, Selly Park, Birmingham, West Midlands, B29 7PU
0121 415 4866
07961 841492
Est. 1970 *Stock size* Medium
Stock General antiques and old toys
Open Tues–Sat 10.30am–5pm closed Wed or by appointment
Services Valuations

Fellows & Sons
Contact Mr S Whittaker
Augusta House, 19 Augusta Street, Birmingham, West Midlands, B18 6JA
0121 212 2131 0121 212 1249
info@fellows.co.uk
www.fellows.co.uk
Est. 1876
Open Mon–Thurs 9am–5pm
Fri 9am–4pm
Sales 5 antique furniture, porcelain, pictures, clocks and collectables sales per annum. Also general furniture and household contents sales. Fortnightly sales of jewellery and watches from pawnbrokers nationwide. 8 antique and

modern jewellery, watches and silver sales per annum
Catalogues Yes

Format Coins (IAPN, BNTA)
Contact Mr D Vice
18–19 Bennetts Hill, Birmingham, West Midlands, B2 5QJ
0121 643 2058 0121 643 2210
Est. 1970 *Stock size* Medium
Stock Coins, medallions, bank notes.
Open Mon–Fri 9.30am–5pm
Fairs London Coinex

J Girvan Antiques
Contact Mr J Girvan
46 Poplar Road, Kings Heath, Birmingham, West Midlands, B14 7AG
0121 443 2538
girvanantiques@aol.com
Est. 1974 *Stock size* Medium
Stock Pre-1920s decorative items, French beds a speciality
Open Mon–Sat 10am–6pm or by appointment
Fairs Newark, Stoneleigh

Lindsay Architectural Antiques
Contact Mr G Lindsay
57 Hugh Road, Birmingham, West Midlands, B10 9AL
0121 772 5766 0121 785 0634
07966 221632
glindsay@zoom.co.uk
www.authenticfireplaces.co.uk
Est. 1996 *Stock size* Large
Stock Architectural salvage, fireplaces, quarry tiles, wrought-iron gates etc
Open Mon–Sat 10am–5pm Sun 10am–4pm
Fairs Newark, Swinderby
Services Restoration and fitting service

MDS Ltd
Contact Mr R Wootton
14–16 Stechford Trading Estate, Lyndon Road, Stechford, Birmingham, West Midlands, B33 8BU
0121 783 9274 0121 783 9274
07836 649064
Est. 1969 *Stock size* Medium
Stock Architectural antiques
Open Mon–Sun 8am–6pm

Midland Football Programme Shop
Contact Mr John Garrad
253a Oxhill Road, Birmingham, West Midlands, B21 8ED
0121 551 1683 0121 551 1683
Est. 1976 *Stock size* Medium
Stock Football programmes, memorabilia
Open Tues–Sat 10am–4.15pm
Services Catalogue available

Moseley Emporium
Contact Miss G Dorney
116 Alcester Road, Moseley, Birmingham, West Midlands, B13 3EF
0121 449 3441
07973 156902
Est. 1993 *Stock size* Large
Stock Victorian, Edwardian and period furniture, architectural antiques
Open Mon–Sat 9.30am–6pm
Services Restoration

Raven Reclaim & Architectural Salvage Ltd
Contact Mr M Coughlan
453 Stockfield Road, Yardley, Birmingham, West Midlands, B25 8JH
0121 765 4840
Est. 1979 *Stock size* Medium
Stock Architectural antiques
Open Mon–Sat 8am–5.30pm

Roberts Korner
Contact Mr G Roberts
2a Katie Road, Selly Oak, Birmingham, West Midlands, B29 6JG
0121 246 2662 0121 246 2662
07074 555055
roberts_korner@lineone.net
Est. 1998 *Stock size* Medium
Stock Furniture, collectables
Open Mon–Sun noon–8pm
Services Restorations

Weller & Dufty Ltd (GTA)
Contact Mr W Farmer
141 Bromsgrove Street, Birmingham, West Midlands, B5 6RQ
0121 692 1414 0121 622 5605
wellerdufty@freewire.co.uk
www.wellerandddufty.co.uk
Est. 1835
Open Mon–Fri 9am–4.45pm
Sales Fine art and antiques
Frequency 6–8 per annum
Catalogues Yes

Stephen Wycherley (PBFA)
Contact Mr S Wycherley
508 Bristol Road, Selly Oak, Birmingham, West Midlands, B29 6BD
0121 471 1006
Est. 1971 *Stock size* Large
Stock Traditional general second-hand and antiquarian bookshop
Open Mon–Sat 10am–5pm closed Wed Jul Aug Thurs–Sat 10am–5pm
Fairs PBFA
Services Valuations

BRIERLEY HILL

Cast Offs
Contact Mr Terence Young
Moor Street Industrial Estate, Moor Street, Brierley Hill, West Midlands, DY5 3EH
01384 486456
0771 1661135
Est. 1996 *Stock size* Medium
Stock Quarry tiles, pavors, cast-iron fireplaces, troughs, baths, radiators, sinks, taps, doors, furniture, chimney pots, gates, fencing bricks
Open Mon–Fri 9am–5pm Sat 9am–2pm

COVENTRY

Duncan M Allsop (ABA)
Contact Mr D Allsop
68 Smith Street, Coventry, West Midlands, CV6 5EL
01926 493266 01926 493266
duncan@allsop-books.freeserve.co.uk
www.allsop-books.freeserve.co.uk
Est. 1966 *Stock size* Medium
Stock Varied stock of books including antiquarian, fine bindings and modern books
Open Mon–Sat 9.30am–5.30pm
Fairs Royal National

Armstrong's Books & Collectables
Contact Mr Colin Armstrong
178 Albany Road, Coventry, West Midlands, CV5 6NG
024 7671 4344
Est. 1983 *Stock size* Medium
Stock General second-hand books, special sci-fi comics,

annuals, magazines, posters, postcards, advertisements
Open Tues–Sat 10am–5.30pm

The Bookshop
Contact Mr A R Price
173 Walsgrave Road, Coventry, West Midlands, CV2 4HH
024 7645 5669
Est. 1990 *Stock size* Medium
Stock Antiquarian and second-hand books on all subjects
Open Mon–Sat 9am–5pm
Services Valuations

Cobwebs
Contact Mr R Clutterbuck
58 Far Gosford Street, Coventry, West Midlands, CV1 5DZ
024 7622 2032
Est. 1988 *Stock size* Large
Stock Victorian furniture and antiques, modern wares
Open Mon–Sat 9.30am–5pm
Fairs Newark, Towcester

Earlsdon Antiques
Contact Mrs V Kemp
35 Hearsall Lane, Coventry, West Midlands, CV5 6HF
024 7667 5456
Est. 1984 *Stock size* Medium
Stock General antiques and collectables
Open Fri Sat noon–5pm

Nicholas Green Antiques
Contact Mr N Green
Binley Common Farm, Rugby Road, Binley, Coventry, West Midlands, CV3 2AW
024 7645 3878 F 024 7644 5847
Est. 1969 *Stock size* Large
No. of dealers 10
Stock Victorian, shipping furniture
Open Mon–Sat 9.30am–5.30pm Sun 10am–4.30pm
Services Valuations, container storage

Luckmans Antiques
Contact Mr K Harris
40 Far Gosford Street, Coventry, West Midlands, CV1 5DW
024 7622 3842
E luckmans@luckmansantiques.co.uk
W www.luckmansantiques.co.uk
Est. 1890 *Stock size* Small
Stock Bric-a-brac, books, medals, cigarette cards, postcards
Open Mon–Sat noon–6pm closed Tues

Warwick Auctions (NAVA)
Contact Mr R Beaumont
3 Queen Victoria Road, Coventry, West Midlands, CV1 3JS
024 7622 3377 F 024 7622 0044
W www.warwickauctions.com
Est. 1947
Open Mon–Fri 9am–5pm
Sales General household goods Wed 10am, viewing Tues 9am–4.30pm Wed 9–10am. Antiques and collectables sales first Wed of each month, except Jan
Frequency Weekly
Catalogues Yes

CRADLEY HEATH

R & L Furnishings
Contact Mr R Randall
244 Halesowen Road, Old Hill, Cradley Heath, West Midlands, B64 6NH
01384 410077
Est. 1980 *Stock size* Medium
Stock Antique furniture, bric-a-brac
Open Mon–Sat 10.30am–5.30pm closed Wed
Services House clearance

Yesterdays Treasures
Contact Mrs Christine Tildesley
205 Halesowen Road, Old Hill, Cradley Heath, West Midlands, B64 6HE
01384 413768 F 01384 413768
Est. 1994 *Stock size* Large
Stock General antiques and collectables
Open Mon–Fri 9.30am–5pm Sat 10am–5pm

HALESOWEN

Anvil Books
Contact Mr J K Maddison
52 Summer Hill, Halesowen, West Midlands, B63 3BU
0121 550 0600
E jkm@anvilbookshalesowen.co.uk
W www.anvilbookshalesowen.co.uk
Est. 1997 *Stock size* Small
Stock General second-hand and antiquarian books, local history, transport and maritime topics specialities
Open Mon–Sat 10am–5pm
Fairs Kinver Book Fair, Waverley Fairs
Services Book search

Tudor House Antiques
Contact Mr D J Taylor
68 Long Lane, Halesowen, West Midlands, B62 9LS
0121 561 5563
Est. 1991 *Stock size* Medium
Stock Architectural antiques, stripped pine furniture
Open Tues–Sat 9.30am–5pm
Services Restorations, stripping

KINGSWINFORD

Unicorn Antiques & Reproductions
Contact Mrs J Vaughan
29 High Street, Wall Heath, Kingswinford, West Midlands, DY6 0JA
01384 288122
Est. 1998 *Stock size* Large
Stock Collectables, Edwardian furniture, glass, Doulton, general antiques
Open Tues Wed Fri Sat 10.15am–4.15pm or by appointment
Services Restorations

OLDBURY

The Glory Hole
Contact Mr Colin Dickens
431 Moat Road, Oldbury, West Midlands, B68 8EJ
0121 544 1888
Est. 1989 *Stock size* Medium
Stock Quality second-hand furniture, antiques and collectables
Open Mon–Sat 9.30am–5.30pm
Fairs Newark, Stoneleigh
Services House clearance

S R Furnishings
Contact Mr S Wilder
18 Stanley Road, Oldbury, West Midlands, B68 0DY
0121 422 9788 F 0121 585 5611
Est. 1975 *Stock size* Large
Stock General antiques, shipping furniture, silver, china
Open Mon–Sat 9.30am–5.30pm
Fairs Stafford

Warley Antique Centre
Contact Mrs Hamilton
146 Pottery Road, Warley Woods, Oldbury, West Midlands, B68 9HD
0121 434 3813
Est. 1989 *Stock size* Medium
No. of dealers 40
Stock 19th–20thC furniture and collectables
Open Mon–Sat 10am–5pm
Services Valuations, jewellery repairs

SOLIHULL

Dorridge Antiques & Collectables Centre
Contact Miss Swift or Mr Kentish
7 Forest Court, Dorridge, Solihull, West Midlands, B93 8HN
01564 779336/01574 779768
Est. 1996 *Stock size* Large
Stock Guns, swords, brass ware, furniture, ceramics, paintings, prints, jewellery, silver, bric-a-brac
Open Mon–Sat 11am–6pm Wed 11am–7pm
Services Valuation & restoration advice

Phillips International Auctioneers and Valuers
The Old House, Station Road, Knowle, Solihull, West Midlands, B93 0HT
01564 776151 F 01564 778069
www.phillips-auction.com
Sales Regional Saleroom. Ring for details

Yoxall Antiques & Fine Arts
Contact Mr Paul Burrows
68 Yoxall Road, Solihull, West Midlands, B90 3RP
0121 744 1744
M 07860 168078
www.yoxall.co.uk
Est. 1988 *Stock size* Large
Stock Period furniture, quality porcelain, glassware, clocks, barometers
Open Mon–Sat 9.30am–5pm closed Wed or by appointment
Fairs Shepton Mallet, NEC
Services Restorations

STOURBRIDGE

Crown Furnishers
Contact Mr C Cartwright
Unit 97 Crown Centre, Crown Lane, Stourbridge, West Midlands, DY8 1YD
01384 441488
Est. 1995 *Stock size* Large
Stock Antique furniture and collectables
Fairs Malvern

Memory Lane Antiques
Contact Mr Paul Jones
129 Brettell Lane, Stourbridge, West Midlands, DY8 4BA
01384 370348
M 07801 139949
Est. 1989 *Stock size* Large
Stock Country furniture, architectural antiques
Open Mon–Sat 10am–6pm
Fairs Newark, Ardingly

Pickwicks Antiques
Contact Mrs J Smith
35 Audnam, Amblecote, Stourbridge, West Midlands, DY8 4AG
01384 443404/79335
Est. 1987 *Stock size* Medium
Stock Antiques, Victorian and Edwardian furniture, textiles etc
Open Mon–Sat 10am–5pm
Fairs Stafford, Bowmans

Walton & Hipkiss
Contact Mr J Carter
111 Worcester Street, Hayley, Stourbridge, West Midlands, DY9 0NE
01562 886688 F 01562 886655
E walton-hipkiss&stour@lineone.net
www.walton-hipkiss.co.uk
Est. 1929
Open Mon–Fri 9am–5.30pm Sat 9am–4pm
Sales General antiques occasionally Sat 10.30am, viewing Fri 6–8pm Sat 8.30am–10.30am, phone for details
Catalogues Yes

SUTTON COLDFIELD

Acres Fine Art Auctioneers & Valuers
Contact Mr I Kettlewell
28 Beeches Walk, Sutton Coldfield, West Midlands, B73 6HN
0121 355 1133 F 0121 354 5251
Est. 1992
Open Mon–Sat 9am–5.30pm
Sales Antiques sales. Telephone for details
Frequency Quarterly
Catalogues Yes

Thomas Coulborn and Sons (BADA, CINOA)
Contact Jonathan Coulborn
Vesey Manor, 64 Birmingham Road, Sutton Coldfield, West Midlands, B72 1QP
0121 354 3974 F 0121 354 4614
M 07941 252299
E jc@coulborn.com
www.coulborn.com
Est. 1940 *Stock size* Large
Stock 18thC furniture and works of art, 19th–20thC paintings and watercolours
Open Mon–Sat 9.15am–1pm 2–5.30pm
Services Valuations

H & R L Parry Ltd
Contact Mrs Rachel Parry
23 Maney Corner, Sutton Coldfield, West Midlands, B72 1QL
0121 354 1178
Est. 1942 *Stock size* Medium
Stock Silver, jewellery, porcelain
Open Mon–Sat 9.30am–5pm closed Wed
Services Valuations

S & J Antiques
Contact Mr Steve Dowling
431 Birmingham Road, Wylde Green, Sutton Coldfield, West Midlands, B72 1AX
0121 384 1595
Est. 1988 *Stock size* Large
Stock Silver, silver plate, oak, period and stripped pine furniture, coins
Open Mon–Sat 10am–5.30pm
Fairs Birmingham Rag Market, Newark
Services Restorations, re-plating

WALSALL

Collectors Centre
Contact Mr Tom Moran
66 Bridge Street, Walsall, West Midlands, WS1 1JG
01922 625518
Est. 1979 *Stock size* Large
Stock Coins, medals, militaria, postcards, cigarette cards, toys, antique jewellery

Open Mon–Sat 9am–5pm
Thurs 9am–1pm
Services Valuations

WEDNESBURY

⊞ Abacus
Contact Mr Lambert
✉ 37 Lower High Street, Wednesbury, West Midlands, WS10 7AQ 🅿
☎ 0121 502 4622
Est. 1988 ***Stock size*** Medium
Stock General second-hand and antiquarian books
Open Mon–Sat 9am–2pm closed Wed
Services Book search

WOLVERHAMPTON

⊞ Antiquities
Contact Mrs M Konczyk
✉ 75–76 Dudley Road, Wolverhampton, West Midlands, WV2 3BY 🅿
☎ 01902 459800
Est. 1968 ***Stock size*** Large
Stock General antiques
Open Mon–Sat 10.30am–5pm

⊞ Bookstack
Contact Mrs E Anderton
✉ 53 Bath Road, Wolverhampton, West Midlands, WV1 4EL 🅿
☎ 01902 421055 Ⓕ 01902 421055
Ⓔ bookstack@ntl.com
Est. 1975 ***Stock size*** Large
Stock Antiquarian and second-hand books
Open Tues–Sat 10am–5pm
Services Book search

⊞ Doveridge House Antiques (BADA, LAPADA, CINOA)
Contact Commander Harry Bain
✉ PO Box 1856, Wolverhampton, West Midlands, WV3 9XH 🅿
☎ 01902 312211
Est. 1976 ***Stock size*** Large
Stock Fine antique furniture, lamps, paintings, silver, decorative objects
Open By appointment
Fairs NEC (Spring Autumn pre-Christmas)
Services Customer advice

⊞ Lamb Antique Fine Arts & Craft Originals (LAPADA)
Contact Beris or Cheryl Lamb
✉ 77 Fancourt Avenue, Penn, Wolverhampton, West Midlands, WV4 4HZ 🅿
☎ 01902 338150 Ⓕ 01902 830805
Ⓜ 07850 406907
Ⓔ berislamb.artscrafts@virgin.net
Ⓦ www.antiques-originals.com
Est. 1985 ***Stock size*** Medium
Stock Arts and Crafts, pottery, pewter, prints, silver, glass, jewellery, copper, furniture
Open By appointment only
Fairs Bowman Fairs, NEC

⊞ Newhampton Road Antiques
Contact Mr R G Hill
✉ 184–184a Newhampton Road East, Wolverhampton, West Midlands, WV1 4PQ 🅿
☎ 01902 334363/712583
Est. 1985 ***Stock size*** Large
Stock Antiques and collectables
Open Mon–Sat 9.30am–3.30pm
Fairs Newark, Stoneleigh
Services House clearance

⊞ No. 9 Antiques
Contact Miss C Weaver
✉ 9 Upper Green, Tettenhall, Wolverhampton, West Midlands, WV6 8QQ 🅿
☎ 01902 755333
Est. 1995 ***Stock size*** Medium
Stock 19thC furniture, porcelain, silver, watercolours
Open Wed–Fri 10am–6pm
Sat 9am–5.30pm

⊞ Martin Quick Antiques (LAPADA)
Contact Mr C Quick
✉ 323 Tettenhall Road, Wolverhampton, West Midlands, WV6 0JZ 🅿
☎ 01902 754703 Ⓕ 01902 756889
Ⓜ 07774 124859
Ⓔ mqantiques@hotmail.com
Est. 1970 ***Stock size*** Large
Stock Georgian–Victorian and later furniture, French furniture
Open Mon–Fri 9am–5.30pm
Sat 9am–2pm
Fairs Newark
Services Valuations

⊞ Martin Taylor Antiques (LAPADA)
Contact Mr Martin Taylor
✉ 140b Tettenhall Road, Wolverhampton, West Midlands, WV6 0BQ 🅿
☎ 01902 751166 Ⓕ 01902 746502
Ⓜ 07836 636524
Ⓔ enquiries@mtaylor-antiques.co.uk
Ⓦ www.mtaylor-antiques.co.uk
Est. 1976 ***Stock size*** Large
Stock Furniture c1800–1930
Open Mon–Fri 8.30am–5.30pm
Sat 9.30am–4pm
Fairs NEC
Services Search, restoration and delivery

Walker, Barnett & Hill
Contact Christopher Sidebottom
✉ 1 Clarence Street, Wolverhampton, West Midlands, WV1 4JE 🅿
☎ 01902 773531/375555 (Cosford)
Ⓕ 01902 712940
Ⓦ www.thesaurus.co.uk/wbh
Est. 1780
Open Mon–Fri 9am–5pm
Sales Monthly fine art and antiques sales, specialist sales of ceramics, jewellery and silver, mirrors and lighting, books and prints. Fortnightly antique and contemporary furniture sales at Cosford Auction Rooms
Frequency Monthly
Catalogues Yes

⊞ West Midlands Collectors Centre
Contact Mr S Moran
✉ 9 Heatin House, Salop Street, Wolverhampton, West Midlands, WV3 0SQ 🅿
☎ 01902 772570
Est. 1983 ***Stock size*** Small
Stock Stamps, coins, medals, bank notes, curios
Open Mon–Sat 9.30am–5pm

⊞ Wood 'n' Things
Contact Mrs K Carter
✉ 388 Penn Road, Wolverhampton, West Midlands, WV4 4DF 🅿
☎ 01902 333324
Est. 1983 ***Stock size*** Medium
Stock Antiques, collectables, Victorian–Edwardian and 1920s furniture
Open Mon Wed 10am–1pm
Tues Thurs–Sat 10am–5pm
Services Restorations

⊞ Woodward Antique Clocks Ltd (LAPADA)
Contact Patricia Woodward
✉ 14 High Street, Tettenhall, Wolverhampton, West Midlands, WV6 8QT 🅿
☎ 01902 745608 Ⓕ 01902 743565
Ⓔ woodwardclocks@bun.com

Ⓦ www.antiqnet.co.uk/woodward
Est. 1993 *Stock size* Large
Stock Antique clocks, decorative French mantel clocks, longcase, bracket, carriage and wall clocks
Open Wed–Sat 11am–5.30pm
Fairs NEC
Services Valuations, restorations

WORCESTERSHIRE

BEWDLEY

Antiques Unlimited
Contact Mr M Mayall
44 Load Street, Bewdley, Worcestershire, DY12 2AP Ⓟ
☎ 01299 401431
Ⓜ 07968 050439
Est. 1998 *Stock size* Medium
Stock 18th–19thC decorative furniture, decorative items
Open Tues–Sat 10.30am–5.30pm closed Wed
Services Restorations

Bewdley Antiques
Contact Mrs A Hamilton
62a Load Street, Bewdley, Worcestershire, DY12 2AP Ⓟ
☎ 01299 405636 Ⓕ 01299 841568
Est. 1999 *Stock size* Medium
No. of dealers 30
Stock 19th–20thC furniture, collectables, small decorative pieces
Open Mon–Sat 10am–5.30pm Sun 11am–4.30pm
Services Valuations, picture framing, jewellery repairs

Gerard Guy Antiques
Contact Mr C Mason
The Old Post Office, 24 Kidderminster Road, Bewdley, Worcestershire, DY12 1AG Ⓟ
☎ 01299 400032
Est. 1990 *Stock size* Large
Stock Pine and oak Victorian furniture, mirrors, prints, collectables etc
Open Mon–Sat 11am–4pm
Services Restorations

BROADWAY

Fenwick & Fenwick Antiques (CADA)
Contact Mr G Fenwick
88–90 High Street, Broadway, Worcestershire, WR12 7AJ Ⓟ
☎ 01386 853227/841724
Ⓕ 01386 858504
Est. 1980 *Stock size* Large
Stock 17th–early 19thC oak, mahogany, walnut furniture and works of art. Treen, boxes, pewter, lace bobbins, Chinese porcelain, corkscrews, early metalware
Open Mon–Sat 10am–6pm

Gallimaufry
Contact Chris Stone
51a High Street, Broadway, Worcestershire, WR12 7DP Ⓟ
☎ 01386 852898
Est. 1992 *Stock size* Medium
Stock China, glass, furniture, pictures, collectables
Open Mon–Sat 10am–5pm Sun 11am–5pm

Howards of Broadway
Contact Robert Light
27a High Street, Broadway, Worcestershire, WR12 7DP Ⓟ
☎ 01386 858924
Ⓜ 07850 066312
Est. 1989 *Stock size* Medium
Stock Antique and modern silver and jewellery
Open Mon–Sat 10am–5.30pm
Services Valuations, restorations

H W Keil Ltd (BADA, CADA)
Contact Mr Keil
Tudor House, Broadway, Worcestershire, WR12 7DB Ⓟ
☎ 01386 852408 Ⓕ 01386 852069
Ⓔ info@hwkeil.co.uk
Ⓦ www.hwkeil.co.uk
Est. 1932 *Stock size* Large
Stock Early 17th–early 19thC furniture, works of art
Open Mon–Sat 9.15am–1.15pm 2.15–5.30pm
Services Restorations

John Noott Galleries (BADA, LAPADA, CADA)
Contact Kathryn Plume
High Street, Broadway, Worcestershire, WR12 7DP Ⓟ
☎ 01386 854868 Ⓕ 01386 854919
Ⓔ info@john-noott.com
Ⓦ www.john-noott.com
Est. 1972 *Stock size* Large
Stock 19th–early 20thC oils and watercolours
Open Mon–Sat 10am–1pm 2pm–5pm
Fairs NEC, Harrogate
Services Valuations, restorations, shipping

BROMSGROVE

Adrian Jennings Antiques
Contact Mr A Jennings
144 New Road, Astonfields, Nr Bromsgrove, B60 2LE Ⓟ
☎ 01527 835300 Ⓕ 01527 835300
Ⓜ 07802 251423
Ⓔ adrian.j@talk21.com
Ⓦ www.adrianjenningsantiques.co.uk
Est. 1992 *Stock size* Medium
Stock 18th–20thC furniture, decorative items for home and garden, country oak furniture
Open Wed 8.30am–12.30pm Fri–Sat 10.30am–5.30pm or by appointment
Fairs Stafford
Services Valuations for insurance and probate

Worcester Medal Service Ltd
Contact Mrs K McDermott
56 Broad Street, Sidemoor, Bromsgrove, Worcestershire, B61 8LL Ⓟ
☎ 01527 835375 Ⓕ 01527 576798
Ⓔ wms@worcmedals.com
Ⓦ www.worcmedals.com
Est. 1988 *Stock size* Large
Stock Medals and medal mountings
Open Mon–Fri 9am–5pm Thurs 9am–noon Sat 9–11.30am
Services Suppliers of specialist cases

CLEOBURY MORTIMER

M & M Baldwin
Contact Dr M Baldwin
24 High Street, Cleobury Mortimer, Kidderminster, DY14 8BY Ⓟ
☎ 01299 270110 Ⓕ 01299 270110
Ⓔ mb@mbaldwin.free-online.co.uk
Est. 1978 *Stock size* Medium
Stock Second-hand and antiquarian books, books on transport, industrial history and WWII intelligence and codebreaking a speciality
Open Wed 2–6pm Fri (Easter–October) 10am–6pm Sat 10am–1pm 2pm–6pm or by appointment
Services Book search, valuations

MIDLANDS

WORCESTERSHIRE • DROITWICH SPA

DROITWICH SPA

Robert Belcher Antiques
Contact Mr R Belcher
128 Worcester Road, Droitwich Spa, Worcestershire, WR9 8AN
01905 772320
Est. 1984 *Stock size* Large
Stock Georgian–Edwardian furniture, ceramics, silver, glass, pictures etc
Open Tues–Sat 9.30am–5.30pm
Fairs NEC
Services Furniture restoration, picture framing

EVESHAM

Bookworms of Evesham (PBFA)
Contact Mr T Sims
81 Port Street, Evesham, Worcestershire, WR11 3LF
01386 45509
Est. 1971 *Stock size* Medium
Stock Second-hand and antiquarian books on most subjects, Gloucestershire and Worcestershire topics specialities
Open Tues–Sat 10am–5pm
Fairs Churchdown, Gloucestershire Book Fair (1st Sunday of each month)

FLADBURY

The Hayloft Antiques
Contact Mrs S Pryse-Jones
Craycombe Farm, Old Worcester Road, Fladbury, Evesham, Worcestershire, WR10 2QS
01386 861166
Est. 1994 *Stock size* Medium
No. of dealers 9
Stock Antique furniture, stripped pine, collectables, china, glass, paintings, prints, books, linen, textiles
Open Mon–Sun summer 10.30am–5pm winter 10.30am–4pm
Services Pine stripping, French polishing, Furniture restoration

KIDDERMINSTER

The Antique Centre
Contact Mrs V Bentley
5–8 Lion Street, Kidderminster, Worcestershire, DY10 1PT
01562 740389 F 01562 740389
Est. 1980 *Stock size* Large
No. of dealers 12
Stock Furniture, china, glass, silver, jewellery, architectural salvage, cast-iron fireplaces, surrounds, tiles, books
Open Mon–Sat 10am–5.30pm
Services Jewellery and clock repairs, furniture and door stripping, furniture restoration

BBM Jewellery, Coins & Antiques (BJA)
Contact Mr W V Crook
9 Lion Street, Kidderminster, Worcestershire, DY10 1PT
01562 744118 F 01562 825954
E williamvcrook@aol.com
Est. 1980 *Stock size* Large
Stock Antique and second-hand jewellery, coins, medals, porcelain, silver
Open Mon–Sat 10am–5pm closed Tues
Services Valuations, restorations and repairs

Gemini Antiques & Gallery
Contact Mr D Southern
152 Offmore Road, Kidderminster, Worcestershire, DY10 1SB
01562 824109
Est. 1984 *Stock size* Large
Stock Antique furniture, glass, pictures, mirrors, porcelain
Open Mon–Sat 10am–6pm closed Wed
Services Valuations, restorations

Kidderminster Market Auctions
Contact Mr B Cooke
Wholesale Market, Comberton Hill, Kidderminster, Worcestershire, DY10 1QH
01562 741303 F 01562 865495
Est. 1957
Open Mon–Fri 9am–5pm Sat 9am–1pm
Sales General antiques sale Thurs 10.30am, furniture 2.30pm, viewing Wed 4–8pm Thurs from 7am
Frequency Weekly

Phipps & Pritchard
Contact Mr A Mayall
Bank Buildings, Exchange Street, Kidderminster, Worcestershire, DY10 1BU
01562 822244 F 01562 825401
M 07970 218140
Est. 1848
Open Mon–Fri 9am–5.15pm Sat 9am–3.30pm
Sales General antiques and collectables Sat 10.30am, viewing Fri 3–6.30pm Sat from 8.30am. Sale held at Hartlebury Village Hall
Frequency Every 6 weeks
Catalogues Yes

Retro Products
Contact Adam Holden-Milner
Hoo Farm Industrial Estate, Kidderminster, Worcestershire, DY11 7RA
01562 865435 F 01562 865267
E info@retro-products.com
W www.retro-products.com
Est. 1983
Stock Antique and reproduction furniture, handles, knobs, hinges, accessories
Open Mon–Fri 9am–5.30pm

MALVERN

Carlton Antiques
Contact Mr D W Roberts
43 Worcester Road, Malvern, Worcestershire, WR14 4RB
01684 573092
E dave@carlton-antiques.com
W www.carlton-antiques.com
Est. 1991 *Stock size* Medium
Stock Furniture, ephemera, postcards, bottles, die-cast toys, second-hand books etc
Open Mon–Sun 10am–5pm

Foley Furniture
Contact Mr D W Roberts
Foley Bank, Malvern, Worcestershire, WR14
01684 891255
E dave@carlton-antiques.com
W www.carlton-antiques.com
Est. 1991 *Stock size* Medium
Stock Furniture of all periods, postcards, bottles, die-cast toys, books etc
Open Wed–Sun 10am–5pm

Great Malvern Antiques
Contact Mr R Rice or Mr L Sutton
Salisbury House, 6 Abbey Road, Malvern, Worcestershire, WR14 3HG
01684 575490
E gma@4unet.co.uk
Est. 1984 *Stock size* Medium
Stock Decorative furniture and furnishings, paintings
Trade only Yes

Open By appointment
Fairs Bath Decorative Antiques Fair, Decorative Antiques and Textiles Fair

Kimber & Son
Contact Mr E M Kimber
6 Lower Howsell Road, Malvern, Worcestershire, WR14 1EF
01684 574339
Est. 1950 *Stock size* Medium
Stock 18th–early 20thC furniture, English, European and American markets
Open Mon–Fri 9am–5.30pm Sat 9am–1pm
Fairs Newark

Philip Laney
Contact Mr P Laney
Malvern Auction Centre, Portland Road, off Victoria Road, Malvern, Worcestershire, WR14 2TA
01684 893933 01684 577948
philiplaney@compuserve.com
Est. 1969
Open Mon–Fri 9am–1pm 2–4.30pm
Sales General antiques and collectables sales
Frequency Monthly
Catalogues Yes

Lechmere Antiquarian Books
Contact Mr R Lechmere
Primswell, Evandrine, Colwall, Malvern, Worcestershire, WR13 6DT
01684 540340
Est. 1945 *Stock size* Small
Stock Antiquarian, rare and second-hand books on Hereford, Worcester, Australia
Open Mail order only
Services Mail order

The Malvern Bookshop
Contact Howard Hudson
7 Abbey Road, Malvern, Worcestershire, WR14 3ES
01684 575915 01684 575915
browse@malvern-bookshop.co.uk
Est. 1954 *Stock size* Medium
Stock Antiquarian, rare and second-hand books, books on music and sheet music a speciality
Open Mon–Sat 10am–5pm
Services Book search

Malvern Link Antiques Centre
Contact Mr R Hales
154 Worcester Road, Malvern, Worcestershire, WR14 1AA
01684 575750
Est. 1997 *Stock size* Large
No. of dealers 10
Stock China, glass, Victorian–Edwardian furniture, jewellery, mirrors, pictures etc
Open Mon–Sat 10am–5.30pm Sun 11am–5pm
Services National or international delivery

Malvern Studios (BAFRA, UKIC, LCGI, NCCR)
Contact Jeff Hall
56 Cowleigh Road, Malvern, Worcestershire, WR14 1QD
01684 574913 01684 569475
Est. 1961
Stock 18th–20thC furniture
Open Mon Tues Thurs 9am–5.15pm Fri Sat 9am–4.45pm
Services Restorations

Miscellany Antiques
Contact R S or E A Hunaban
20 Cowleigh Road, Malvern, Worcestershire, WR14 1QD
01684 566671 01684 560562
liz.hunaban@virgin.net
www.freespace.virgin.net/lizhunaban
Est. 1974 *Stock size* Medium
Stock Georgian–Edwardian furniture, some country oak, bronzes, ivories, silver, jewellery, decorative items
Open By appointment
Services Valuations, restorations

Priory Books
Contact Mr L P Kelly
Church Walk, Malvern, Worcestershire, WR14 2XH
01684 560258
Est. 1985 *Stock size* Medium
Stock Wide range of antiquarian and second-hand books
Open Tues–Sat 10am–5pm closed 1–2pm
Services Valuations, book search

Promenade Antiques & Books
Contact Mr M Seldester
41 Worcester Road, Malvern, Worcestershire, WR14 4RB
01684 566876 01684 566876
promant@bigfoot.com
Est. 1990 *Stock size* Medium
Stock Victorian–Edwardian furniture, collectables, decorative items, reproduction lamps, books
Open Mon–Sat 10am–5pm Sun noon–5pm

St James Antiques
Contact Mr Hans Van Wyngaarden
De Lys, Wells Road, Malvern, Worcestershire, WR14 4JL

MIDLANDS
WORCESTERSHIRE • PERSHORE

☎ 01684 563404
Est. 1992 *Stock size* Large
Stock Pine furniture, lighting, decorative items
Open Mon–Sat 9am–5.30pm closed Wed

PERSHORE

Coach House Books
Contact Mr P Ellingworth
✉ **17a Bridge Street, Pershore, Worcestershire, WR10 1AJ**
☎ 01386 552801/556100
Ⓕ 01386 552801
Ⓔ sue@chb.co.uk
Est. 1982 *Stock size* Large
Stock Antiquarian, rare, new and second-hand books. Picture framing, artists' materials, prints
Open Mon–Sat 9am–5pm
Services Book search

Hansen Chard Antiques (BHI)
Contact Mr P Ridler
✉ **126 High Street, Pershore, Worcestershire, WR10 1EA** Ⓟ
☎ 01386 553423
Est. 1984 *Stock size* Large
Stock Clocks, barometers, old and antique model steam engines, scientific instruments
Open Tues–Sat 10am–4.30pm closed Thurs or by appointment
Fairs Brunel Clock Fair, Birmingham Clock Fair, Haydock
Services Valuations, restorations

Lion Antiques
Contact Mrs R Mansfield
✉ **12 Bridge Street, Pershore, Worcestershire, WR10 1AT** Ⓟ
☎ 01386 555688/750214
Ⓕ 01386 555688
Ⓜ 07703 857270/0777 3530022
Ⓔ lionantiques@talk21.com
Est. 1982 *Stock size* Medium
Stock Lighting, mirrors, bed canopies, pine, oak and mahogany furniture, sculptures
Open Tues–Sat 9.30am–4.30pm, Mon Thurs by appointment

Ian K Pugh Books
Contact Mr I Pugh
✉ **40 Bridge Street, Pershore, Worcestershire, WR10 1AT** Ⓟ
☎ 01386 552681
Est. 1974 *Stock size* Medium
Stock Antiquarian, rare and second-hand books on most subjects. Antiques, fine art, horticulture and military topics specialities
Open Wed–Fri 10.30am–5pm Sat 9.30am–5pm
Services Valuations, book search

S W Antiques
Contact Mr Richard Whiteside or Mr Adrian Whiteside
✉ **Abbey Showrooms, Newlands, Pershore, Worcestershire, WR10 1BP** Ⓟ
☎ 01386 555580 Ⓕ 01386 556205
Ⓔ sw-antiques@talk21.com
Ⓦ www.sw-antiques.co.uk
Est. 1978 *Stock size* Large
Stock 19th–early 20thC furniture, antique beds
Open Mon–Sat 9am–5pm Sun 10.30am–4pm
Services Valuations, restorations

REDDITCH

Angel Antiques
Contact Mrs C Manners
✉ **211 Mount Pleasant, Redditch, Worcestershire, B97 4JG** Ⓟ
☎ 01527 545844
Est. 1989 *Stock size* Medium
Stock Georgian–Edwardian antique furniture, decorative items
Open Tues–Sat 10am–5pm closed Wed
Services Restorations

Arrow Auctions (NAVA)
Contact Mr A Reeves
✉ **Bartleet Road, Washford, Redditch, Worcestershire, B98 0DG** Ⓟ
☎ 01527 517707 Ⓕ 01527 510924
Ⓔ enquiries@arrowauctions.co.uk
Ⓦ www.arrowauctions.co.uk
Est. 1982
Open Mon–Fri 8.30am–5pm
Sales General household sale every Tues 6pm, viewing from 9am. Specialist bi-annual fine art sales Tues 11am. Free valuations. Removal, collection and storage facilities available. On-site restaurant
Frequency Weekly
Catalogues Yes

TENBURY WELLS

Antiques & Anything
Contact Mr S Deakin
✉ **13 Teme Street, Tenbury Wells, Worcestershire, WR15 8BB** Ⓟ
☎ 01584 810830
Ⓜ 07971 869256/07977 579278
Est. 1999 *Stock size* Medium
Stock Furniture, porcelain, china, decorative items, collectables
Open Mon–Sat 9am–5pm Sun 11am–4pm

UPTON-UPON-SEVERN

Boar's Nest Trading
Contact Mr G Smith
✉ **37a–37b Old Street, Upton-upon-Severn, Worcester, Worcestershire, WR8 0HN** Ⓟ
☎ 01684 592540
Ⓜ 07881 797443
Est. 1992 *Stock size* Large
Stock Second-hand and antiquarian books, non-fiction a speciality
Open Mon–Sun 10.30am–6pm
Services Valuations

WHITBOURNE

Juro Farm and Garden Antiques
Contact Mr R Hughes
✉ **Whitbourne, Worcester, Worcestershire, WR6 5SF** Ⓟ
☎ 01886 821261 Ⓕ 01886 821261
Ⓔ roy@juro.co.uk
Ⓦ www.juro.co.uk
Est. 1991 *Stock size* Large
Stock Garden antiques, staddle stones, troughs, cider mills, statuary, farming and garden implements
Open Mon–Sat 9am–5pm
Fairs Newark, Hampton Court, Malvern Spring Garden Show
Services Valuations

WORCESTER

Antiques & Curios
Contact Mr B Inett
✉ **50 Upper Tything, Worcester, Worcestershire, WR1 1JZ** Ⓟ
☎ 01905 25412 Ⓕ 01905 25412
Est. 1980 *Stock size* Large
Stock Victorian–Edwardian furniture, mirrors, clocks, porcelain, glass, decorative items
Open Mon–Sat 9.30am–5.30pm
Services Valuations, restorations

The Antiques Warehouse
Contact Mr D Venn
✉ **74 Droitwich Road (rear), Worcester, Worcestershire, WR1 8BW** Ⓟ

☎ 01905 27493
Est. 1979 *Stock size* Large
Stock Pine furniture, Victorian interior doors, antique and reproduction fireplaces
Open Mon–Fri 8am–6pm Sat 10am–5pm
Services Restorations

The Barbers Clock
Contact Graham Gopsill
37 Droitwich Road, Worcester, Worcestershire, WR3 7LG
☎ 01905 29022
Ⓜ 07710 486598
Est. 1993 *Stock size* Medium
Stock Clocks from 1840–1930, wind-up gramophones, Art Deco
Open Mon–Sat 9am–5pm Sun 2pm–5pm
Services Valuations, gramophone and clock repairs

Box Bush Antiques
Contact Mrs P Difford
43 Upper Tything, Worcester, Worcestershire, WR1 1JZ
☎ 01905 28617 Ⓕ 01905 28617
Est. 1995 *Stock size* Medium
Stock 18th–19thC pine, mahogany and walnut furniture, decorative items, silver
Open Mon–Sat 9am–5.30pm
Services Valuations, restorations, wood turning

B Browning & Son
Contact Mr A Browning
35a Wylds Lane, Worcester, Worcestershire, WR5 1DA
☎ 01905 355646
Est. 1904 *Stock size* Medium
Stock Antique and modern general household furniture
Open Mon–Sat 9am–5pm closed Thurs
Services House clearance

Bygones by the Cathedral (LAPADA, FGA)
Cathedral Square, Worcester, Worcestershire, WR1 2JD
☎ 01905 25388 Ⓕ 01905 23132
Est. 1946 *Stock size* Medium
Stock Decorative antiques, silver, jewellery, porcelain, furniture, paintings, glass, metalwork
Open Mon–Fri 9.30am–5.30pm Sat 9.30am–1pm 2–5.30pm

Bygones of Worcester (LAPADA)
Contact Gabrielle Bullock
55 Sidbury, Worcester, Worcestershire, WR1 2HU
☎ 01905 23132 Ⓕ 01905 23132
Est. 1946 *Stock size* Medium
Stock 17th–20thC furniture, paintings, bronzes, silver, porcelain
Open Mon–Sat 9.30am–1pm 2–5.30pm

Andrew Grant Fine Art Auctioneers
Contact Mr A Mackwell ARICS
St Marks Close, Worcester, Worcestershire, WR5 3DJ
☎ 01905 357547 Ⓕ 01905 763942
Ⓔ fine.arts@andrew-grant.co.uk
Ⓦ www.andrew-grant.co.uk
Est. 1980
Open Mon–Fri 9am–5.30pm
Sales Quarterly antiques and fine art sale Thurs, viewing day prior 10am–7pm. Monthly Victoriana and collectables sale Sat, viewing day prior 10am–5pm
Frequency Quarterly
Catalogues Yes

Grays Antiques
Contact Mr D Gray
29 The Tiding, Worcester, Worcestershire, WR1 1JL
☎ 01905 724456 Ⓕ 01905 723433
Ⓔ enquiries@grays-antiques.com
Ⓦ www.grays-antiques.com
Est. 1984 *Stock size* Large
Stock Early 19th–early 20thC furniture and furnishings and decorative items including chandeliers
Open Mon–Sat 8.30am–5.30pm
Services Valuations, restorations

Heirlooms
Contact Mrs L Rumford
46 Upper Tything, Worcester, Worcestershire, WR1 1JZ
☎ 01905 23332
Est. 1988 *Stock size* Large
Stock Antique and old reproduction furniture, china, glass, decorative items
Open Mon–Sat 9.30am–4.30pm

P J Hughes Antiques
Contact Mr P J Hughes
3 Barbourne Road, Worcester, Worcestershire, WR1 1RS
☎ 01905 610695
Ⓜ 07774 204127
Est. 1972 *Stock size* Large
Stock Jewellery, collectables, china, silver, small furniture
Open Tues–Sat 9.30am–5pm
Fairs St Martin's Market, Birmingham
Services Valuations

M Lees & Son (LAPADA)
Contact Mr M Lees
Tower House, 1 Castle Place, Severn Street, Worcester, Worcestershire, WR1 2NB
☎ 01905 26620 Ⓕ 01905 26620
Ⓜ 07860 826218
Est. 1974 *Stock size* Medium
Stock Period furniture, china, pictures, decorative items, mirrors
Open Mon–Fri 9.30am–4.45pm Thurs 9.30am–12.45pm Sat 10.30am–4pm
Services Valuations

The Old Toll House
Contact Mr D Askew
1 Droitwich Road, Worcester, Worcestershire, WR3 7LG
☎ 01905 20608
Ⓔ derek@theoldtollhouse.freeserve.co.uk
Est. 1980 *Stock size* Medium
Stock Pine furniture, reclaimed wooden doors, pottery, porcelain, glass
Open Mon–Sat 10am–6pm
Services Restorations, stripping

Round the Bend
Contact Gabrielle Bullock FGA
1 Deansway, Worcester, Worcestershire, WR1 2JD
☎ 01905 616516
Est. 1992 *Stock size* Medium
Stock Eccentricities
Open Mon–Sat 10am–5.30pm

Philip Serrell FSVA
Contact P Serrell
Sansome House, 6 Sansome Walk, Worcester, Worcestershire, WR1 1LH
☎ 01905 26200 Ⓕ 01905 21202
Ⓔ serrell.auctions@virgin.net
Ⓦ www.serrell.com

MIDLANDS
WORCESTERSHIRE • WORCESTER

Open Mon–Fri 9am–5pm closed 1–2pm
Sales General and fine art sales at the Malvern Sale Room, Malvern
Frequency Fortnightly
Catalogues Yes

Tything Antiques Centre
Contact Mr or Mrs Shuckburgh
39 The Tything, Worcester, Worcestershire, WR1 1JL
01905 723322
Est. 1994 *Stock size* Large
No. of dealers 12
Stock General antiques
Open Mon–Sat 10am–5.30pm

Worcester Antiques Centre
Contact Mr S Zacaroli
Unit 15, Reindeer Court, Mealcheapen Street, Worcester, Worcestershire, WR1 4DS
01905 610680
Est. 1991 *Stock size* Large
No. of dealers 45
Stock Porcelain,early Worcester, furniture, silver, jewellery, Art Nouveau, Arts and Crafts

YORKS & LINCS

EAST RIDING OF YORKSHIRE

BEVERLEY

⊞ Hawley Antiques (LAPADA)
Contact John Hawley
✉ **5 North Bar Within, Beverley, East Riding of Yorkshire, HU17 8AP** 🅿
☎ 01482 868193 Ⓕ 01482 874672
Ⓜ 07850 225805
Ⓔ antiques@hawleys.org.uk
Ⓦ www.hawleys.org.uk
Est. 1966 *Stock size* Medium
Stock General antiques, mainly Georgian–Victorian
Open Mon–Fri 10am–4pm Sat 9.30am–5pm
Fairs Newark
Services Valuations, restorations

⊞ Time and Motion (BHI)
Contact Mr P Lancaster
✉ **1 Beckside, Beverley, East Riding of Yorkshire, HU17 0PB** 🅿
☎ 01482 881574
Est. 1984 *Stock size* Large
Stock Antique clocks and barometers
Open Mon–Wed Fri Sat 10am–5pm
Services Valuations, restorations

BRIDLINGTON

⊞ Dixons Medals (OMRS)
Contact Mr C J Dixon
✉ **23 Prospect Street, Bridlington, East Riding of Yorkshire, YO15 2AE** 🅿
☎ 01262 603348 Ⓕ 01262 606600
Ⓔ chris@dixonsmedals.co.uk
Ⓦ www.dixonsmedals.co.uk
Est. 1969 *Stock size* Large

Stock Medals from Peninsular war, Victorian campaigns, Victoria Cross–present day
Open Mon–Fri 9.30am–5pm
Fairs OMRS convention
Services Restorations to medals, catalogue, mail order worldwide, Dixons Gazette

The Emporium
Contact Mr Burdall
59 St John Street, Bridlington, East Riding of Yorkshire, YO16 7NN P
☎ 01262 677560
Ⓜ 07779 200335
Est. 1979 *Stock size* Large
Stock Sanitary ware, doors, radiators, pine furniture, cast-iron fires, French stoves, brass ware, reclaimed timber etc
Open Tues–Sat 10am–5.30pm or by appointment
Services Valuations, restorations, stripping

The Georgian Rooms
Contact David Rothwell
56 High Street, Bridlington, East Riding of Yorkshire, YO16 4QA P
☎ 01262 608600
Est. 2000 *Stock size* Large
No. of dealers 15
Stock General antiques, silver, jewellery, furniture, paintings
Open Mon–Sat 10am–5pm

Michael James Antiques & Curios
Contact Mr M James
45 High Street, Bridlington, East Riding of Yorkshire, YO16 4PR P
☎ 01262 401909
Ⓜ 07977 327364
Est. 1992 *Stock size* Medium
Stock Pre-war shipping furniture, decorative items
Open Mon–Sat 9am–5pm

The Magpie's Nest
Contact Ms R Szpakowski
92 St John Street, Bridlington, East Riding of Yorkshire, YO16 7JS P
☎ 01262 400533
Ⓜ 07721 090414
Est. 1994 *Stock size* Medium
Stock Antiques, bric-a-brac, collectables
Open Fri–Sat 10am–5pm
Fairs Wetherby, Harrogate, Swinderby

BROUGH

Lincoln House Antiques (LAPADA)
Contact Mr J Daggett
51 Market Place, South Cave, Brough, East Riding of Yorkshire, HU15 2BS P
☎ 01430 424623
Ⓜ 07764 273695
Est. 1993 *Stock size* Medium
Stock Georgian–Edwardian furniture, porcelain, pictures, clocks
Open Mon–Sat 10am–5pm closed Wed or by appointment
Fairs Burleys, Harrogate
Services Valuations

Pennyfarthing Antiques
Contact Mrs C Dennett
Albion House, 18 Westgate, North Cave, Brough, East Riding of Yorkshire, HU15 2NJ P
☎ 01430 422958
Est. 1989 *Stock size* Medium
Stock Brass and iron beds, sofas, silver, decorative items, furniture, porcelain
Open Mon–Sat 9.30am–6pm
Fairs Newark
Services Valuations

DRIFFIELD

The Crested China Co
Contact Mr David Taylor
Station House, Railway Station, Driffield, East Riding of Yorkshire, YO25 6PX P
☎ 01377 255002/257042
Ⓔ dt@thecrestedchinacompany.com
Ⓦ www.thecrestedchinacompany.com
Est. 1980 *Stock size* Large
Stock Goss and Crested china
Open Mon–Fri 9am–5pm or by appointment
Fairs Goss Collectors Club Fairs
Services Mail order, bi-monthly catalogue

Dee, Atkinson and Harrison
Contact Owen Nisbet or Helen Pickering
The Exchange, Driffield, East Riding of Yorkshire, YO25 6LD P
☎ 01377 253151 Ⓕ 01377 241041
Ⓔ driffield@dee.atkinson.harrison.co.uk
Ⓦ www.dee.atkinson.harrison.co.uk
Est. 1880
Open 9am–5.30pm
Sales 6 Antique and collectors' sales per annum, 2 collectors' sports and toy sales per annum, fortnightly 19thC and modern sales
Catalogues Yes

Smith & Smith Designs, Antique Pine and Country Furniture
Contact Mr D Smith
58a Middle Street North, Driffield, East Riding of Yorkshire, YO25 6SU P
☎ 01377 256321 Ⓕ 01377 256070
Ⓜ 07941 034446
Ⓔ shop@pine-on-line.co.uk
Ⓦ www.pine-on-line.co.uk
Est. 1976 *Stock size* Medium
Stock Antique and reproduction pine furniture, other period furniture, decorative items, lighting, water features
Open Mon–Sat 9.30am–5.30pm
Services Restorations

GOOLE

Arcadia Antiques Centre
Contact Mr Martin Spavin
10–14 The Arcade, Goole, East Riding of Yorkshire, DN14 5QT P
☎ 01405 720549
Ⓜ 07775 557499
Est. 1991 *Stock size* Medium
No. of dealers 20
Stock Collectables, costume jewellery, pictures, furniture etc
Open Mon–Sat 10am–5pm Sun by appointment

Clegg & Son
Contact Mr C Clegg
68 Aire Street, Goole, East Riding of Yorkshire, DN14 5QE P
☎ 01405 763140 Ⓕ 01405 764235
Ⓔ gooleoffice@cleggandson.co.uk
Ⓦ www.cleggandson.co.uk
Est. 1895
Open Mon–Fri 9am–5pm
Sales Antiques and household sale Sat am, viewing day of sale 9am–sale. Held at St Mary's Church Hall, Goole
Frequency Every other month
Catalogues Yes

HORNSEA

Harvatt Antiques
Contact Robert Harvatt

✉ 1 Willow Drive, Hornsea, East Riding of Yorkshire, HU18 1DA 🅿
☎ 01964 533362 Ⓕ 01964 533362
Ⓦ www.harvattsantiques.com
Est. 1984 *Stock size* Medium
Stock General antiques, clocks
Open Mon–Sat 9am–5pm
Services Clock repairs

Second Time Around
Contact Mr T Brown
✉ 61–61a Southgate, Hornsea, East Riding of Yorkshire, HU18 1AL
☎ 01964 532037
Est. 1981 *Stock size* Large
Stock General antiques, furniture, pottery, collectables, china etc
Open Mon–Sat 10am–4.30pm closed Wed
Services Restorations, upholstery

HOWDEN

Kemp Booksellers (ABA, PBFA, BA)
Contact Mike Kemp
✉ 5–7 Vicar Lane, Howden, East Riding of Yorkshire, DN14 7BP 🅿
☎ 01430 432071 Ⓕ 01430 431666
Ⓔ kemp.books@dial.pipex.com
Ⓦ www.kempbooksellers.co.uk
Est. 1979 *Stock size* Medium
Stock Mervyn Peake, modern first editions, Yorkshire and Lincolnshire topography
Open Mon–Sat 9am–5pm
Fairs ABA, PBFA, BA

HULL

Anderson Antiques (UK) Ltd
Contact Mr Anderson
✉ Anderson Wharf, Wincomlee, Hull, East Riding of Yorkshire, HU2 8AH 🅿
☎ 01482 609691
Ⓦ www.andersonantiques.com
Est. 1972 *Stock size* Large
Stock General antiques and collectables
Open Mon–Sun 9am–5pm
Services Valuations

David Hakeney Antiques
Contact David Hakeney
✉ PO Box 65, Hull, East Riding of Yorkshire, HU10 7XT 🅿
☎ 01482 651177
Ⓜ 07860 507774
Est. 1970 *Stock size* Medium
Stock General antiques, quality items
Open By appointment
Services Restorations

Imperial Antiques
Contact M Langton
✉ 397 Hessle Road, Hull, East Riding of Yorkshire, HU3 4EH 🅿
☎ 01482 327439
Est. 1980 *Stock size* Medium
Stock Pine furniture
Open Mon–Sat 9am–5pm

Kilnsea Antiques
Contact Tony Smith
✉ The Old Barn, Kilnsea Road, Hull, East Riding of Yorkshire, HU12 0UB 🅿
☎ 01964 650311
Ⓦ tony@smithantiques.freeserve.co.uk
Est. 1981 *Stock size* Medium
Stock Furniture and collectables from the late 1800s
Open Tues–Sun 10am–5pm

Mill Antiques
Contact John Mills
✉ 388–390 Beverley Road, Hull, East Riding of Yorkshire, HU5 1LN 🅿
☎ 01482 342248
Ⓔ john@millantiques.co.uk
Est. 1971 *Stock size* Medium
Stock Antique pine, brass beds, cast-iron fireplaces, architectural
Open Mon–Sat 9am–5pm
Services Valuations, pine stripping

Pine-Apple Antiques
Contact Diane Todd
✉ 321–327 Beverley Road, Hull, East Riding of Yorkshire, HU5 1LD 🅿
☎ 01482 441384 Ⓕ 01482 441073
Ⓜ 07860 874480
Ⓔ diane@pineapple.co.uk
Ⓦ www.pine-apple.co.uk
Est. 1981 *Stock size* Large
Stock Architectural antiques, pine, lighting, clocks, pottery, curios, fireplaces
Open Mon–Sat 9am–5.30pm Sun 11am–4pm

MARKET WEIGHTON

R Hornsey & Sons
Contact Mr M Swan
✉ 33 High Street, Market Weighton, East Riding of Yorkshire, YO43 3AQ 🅿
☎ 01430 872551 Ⓕ 01430 871387
Ⓜ 07711 200854
Est. 1884
Open Mon–Fri 9am–5.30pm Sat 9am–noon
Sales General antiques
Frequency Periodic
Catalogues No

Mount Pleasant Antiques Centre
Contact Linda Sirrs
✉ 46 Cliffe Road, Market Weighton, East Riding of Yorkshire, YO43 3BP 🅿
☎ 01430 872872
Est. 1999 *Stock size* Large
No. of dealers 20
Stock Good-quality furniture, collectables
Open Mon–Sun 9.30am–5pm
Services Restorations, tea room

PATRINGTON

Clyde Antiques
Contact Ms S Nettleton
✉ 12a Market Place, Patrington, Hull, East Riding of Yorkshire, HU12 0RB 🅿
☎ 01964 630650
Est. 1980 *Stock size* Medium
Stock Wide range of antique stock from period furniture to collectables
Open Tues–Sat 10am–5pm closed Wed
Services Valuations

Frank Hill & Son
Contact Mr R E Ward
✉ 18 Market Place, Patrington, Hull, East Yorkshire, HU12 0RB 🅿
☎ 01964 630531 Ⓕ 01964 631203
Ⓜ 07860 123057
Est. 1926
Open Mon–Fri 9am–5pm Sat 9am–noon
Sales Antique and modern household furniture and effects quarterly, phone for details, viewing morning of sale. Held at Church Hall, Ottringham
Frequency Quarterly
Catalogues Yes

THORNTON

Abacus Fireplaces
Contact Mr J White
Common End Farm, Thornton, Melbourne, East Riding of Yorkshire, YO42 4RZ
01759 318575 01423 524999
07703 517544
abacus03@globalnet.co.uk
Est. 1969 *Stock size* Large
Stock Architectural antiques, fireplaces, fireplace furnishings
Open Mon–Sat 9am–4.30pm
Fairs Newark
Services Restorations to all antiques, custom-made castings

WITHERNSEA

Mathy's Emporium
Contact Mr M Quinn
2 Pier Road, Withernsea, East Riding of Yorkshire, HU19 2JS
01964 615739
Est. 1994 *Stock size* Large
Stock Brass, furniture, pottery, Wade, collectables
Open Mon–Sun 10am–5pm closed Wed
Services Valuations

NORTH YORKSHIRE

ALLERTON MAULEVERER

Mauleverer Antiques
Contact Ms Caroline Louise Forster
Allerton Park Castle, Allerton Mauleverer, Knaresborough, North Yorkshire, HG5 0SE
01423 340170 01423 340170
07974 255087
Est. 1984 *Stock size* Medium
Stock 1650–1850 early English oak and provincial furniture
Open By appointment only
Fairs NEC, The Northern Antique Fair, Harrogate

Mauleverer Antiques
Contact Ms Caroline Louise Forster
The Old Cottage, Shaw Lane, Farnham, Knaresborough, North Yorkshire, HG5 9JE
01423 340170 01423 340170
07974 255087
Est. 1984 *Stock size* Medium
Stock 1650–1850 early English oak and provincial furniture
Open By appointment only
Fairs NEC, The Northern Antique Fair, Harrogate

ASKRIGG

J R Hopper & Co
Contact Mr D Lambert
Wood End Countersett, Askrigg, North Yorkshire, DL8 3DE
01969 650776 01969 624319
brian.carlisle@easynet.co.uk
Est. 1886
Open Possible to contact at all times
Sales General antiques, household furnishings
Frequency Monthly
Catalogues Yes

AUSTWICK

Austwick Hall Books
Contact Michael Pearson
Townhead Lane, Austwick, Nr Settle, North Yorkshire, LA2 8BS
01524 251794
austwickhall@btinternet.com
Est. 2000 *Stock size* Medium
Stock Antiquarian, rare and second-hand books, including natural history and science
Open By appointment only
Services Book search

BEDALE

Bedale Antiques
Contact Mr or Mrs R C Stubley
2a Sussex Street, Bedale, North Yorkshire, DL8 2AJ
01677 427765
Est. 1998 *Stock size* Medium
Stock Period furniture, pottery
Open Daily 10am–4.30pm closed Sun

Bennetts Antiques & Collectables Ltd
Contact Paul Bennett
7 Market Place, Bedale, North Yorkshire, DL8 1ED
01677 427900 01677 426858
info@bennetts.uk.com
www.bennetts.uk.com
Est. 1997 *Stock size* Large
Stock Furniture, clocks, works of art, 19thC Yorkshire paintings, collectables
Open Mon–Sat 9am–5pm Sun by appointment
Services Restorations, clock repair

Bonhams & Brooks
Contact Henrietta Graham or Anthony Chisenhale-Marsh
Market Chambers, 14 Market Place, Bedale, North Yorkshire, DL8 1EQ
01677 424114 01677 424115
yorkshire@bonhams.com
www.bonhams.com
Open Mon–Fri 9am–5.30pm
Sales Regional representatives for Yorkshire and North East. See Head Office (London) for details

M W Darwin & Son
Contact Mr M W Darwin
The Dales Furniture Hall, Bridge Street, Bedale, North Yorkshire, DL8 2AD
01677 422846 01609 779072
mwdarwin1@estategazette.net
Est. 1959
Open Mon–Fri 9am–4.30pm Thurs 9am–noon
Sales General antiques sales held on Fri
Frequency Every 3 weeks
Catalogues No

Dovetail Interiors of Bedale
Contact Brian Jutsum
Bridge Street, Bedale, North Yorkshire, DL8 2AD
01677 426464 01677 426464
www.dovetailinteriors.com
Est. 1997 *Stock size* Medium
Stock Antiques, bespoke furniture, ethnic artefacts
Open Mon–Sun 10am–5pm

BILLINGHAM

Margaret Bedi Antiques and Fine Art (LAPADA)
Contact Mrs Margaret Bedi
5 Station Road, Billingham, Stockton-on-Tees, North Yorkshire, TS23 1AG
01642 782346
07860 577637
Est. 1976 *Stock size* Large
Stock Fine furniture 1660–1920, watercolours, oils
Open By appointment only
Fairs Northern Antiques Fair, Harrogate
Services Valuations, restorations

BOLTON ABBEY

Grove Country Bookshop
Contact Mr A Sharpe
The Old Post Office, Bolton Abbey, Skipton, North Yorkshire, BD23 6EX
01756 710717
Est. 1997 *Stock size* Medium
Stock Antique, rare and second-hand books, local topography a speciality
Open Tues–Sun 10.30am–4pm variable during Winter
Services Restorations, book search

BOROUGHBRIDGE

James Johnston
Contact Mr P Johnston
St James Square, Boroughbridge, North Yorkshire, YO51 9AS
01423 322382 F 01423 324735
M 07885 497825
Est. 1919
Open Mon–Fri 9am–5pm Sat 9–11am
Sales General antiques and periodic catalogue sales
Frequency Every 3 weeks
Catalogues Yes

St James House Antiques & Restoration (LAPADA)
Contact Mr John Wilson or Mr P Wilson
St James Square, Boroughbridge, North Yorkshire, YO5 9AR
01423 322508 F 01423 326690
Est. 1989 *Stock size* Medium
Stock General antiques, 18th–19thC furniture
Open Mon–Sat 9am–5.30pm or by appointment
Services Valuations, restorations

R S Wilson & Son
Contact Mr R Wilson
4 Hall Square, Boroughbridge, North Yorkshire, YO51 9AN
01423 322417 F 01423 322417
Est. 1917 *Stock size* Medium
Stock 17th–19thC furniture
Open Mon–Sat 9am–5.30pm closed Thurs

EASINGWOLD

Country House Furniture
Contact Judith O'Brien
108 Long Street, Easingwold, North Yorkshire, YO61 3HY
01347 822977
Est. 1978 *Stock size* Medium
Stock English and French period pine, country furniture, decorative items, upholstered chairs etc
Open Mon–Sat 10.30am–5pm
Fairs Galloway Fairs

Milestone Antiques
Contact Mr A Streetley
Farnley House, 101 Long Street, Easingwold, York, North Yorkshire, YO61 3HY
01347 821608
Est. 1982 *Stock size* Medium
Stock Furniture, clocks
Open Mon–Sat 9am–5.30pm Sun by appointment
Services Valuations

Vale Antiques (GADAR)
Contact J M Leach
Mooracres, North Moor, Easingwold, York, North Yorkshire, YO61 3NB
01347 821298 F 01347 821298
E chris.leach@ukonline.co.uk
Est. 1990 *Stock size* Medium
Stock Georgian–Victorian and later furniture, collectables
Open Mon–Sun 9am–5pm
Services Furniture restoration

FLAXTON

Flaxton Antique Gardens (SALVO)
Contact Tim Richardson
Glebe Farm, Flaxton, North Yorkshire, YO60 7RU
01904 468468 F 01904 468468
W www.salvo.co.uk/dealers/flaxton
Est. 1990 *Stock size* Large
Stock Garden antiques, terracotta urns, seats, Victorian edging, bird baths, troughs, sun dials
Open Mon–Sun 10am–4pm closed Tues winter times telephone call advisable
Services Valuations

GARGRAVE

Dickinson Antiques
Contact H H or A E Mardall
Estate Yard, West Street, Gargrave, North Yorkshire, BD23 3PH
01756 748257
Est. 1959 *Stock size* Medium
Stock Antique early furniture
Open Mon–Fri 9am–5.30pm or by appointment

Gargrave Gallery
Contact Mr B Herington
48 High Street, Gargrave, Skipton, North Yorkshire, BD23 1JP
01756 749641
Est. 1974 *Stock size* Medium
Stock General antiques, Georgian–Victorian furniture
Open Mon–Sat 10am–4pm

R N Myers & Son (BADA)
Contact Mrs J M Myers
Endsleigh House, High Street, Gargrave, Skipton, North Yorkshire, BD23 3LX
01756 749587 F 01756 749322
M 0780 131 0126
E rnmyersson@aol.com
Est. 1890 *Stock size* Medium
Stock Georgian furniture, works of art
Open Mon–Sat 9am–5pm or by appointment
Fairs Harrogate
Services Valuations

GREAT AYTON

Cook's Cottage Antiques
Contact E Cook
59 High Street, Great Ayton, Middlesbrough, Cleveland, North Yorkshire, TS9 6NH
01642 722821/701664
Est. 1996 *Stock size* Medium
Stock Antique furniture, pictures, ceramics
Open Wed–Sun 11am–5pm
Services Restorations

GUISBOROUGH

Curiosity Corner
Contact Mr B Wilson
47 Church Street, Guisborough, Cleveland, North Yorkshire, TS14 6HG
01287 636660

Est. 1987 *Stock size* Medium
Stock General antiques, longcase clocks
Open Mon–Sat 9am–4.30pm
Fairs Newark, Swinderby

HARROGATE

Armstrong Antiques (BADA, LAPADA)
Contact M A Armstrong
10–11 Montpellier Parade, Harrogate, North Yorkshire, HG1 2TJ
01423 506843
07802 721815
Est. 1983 *Stock size* Medium
Stock Fine 18th–19thC English furniture
Open Mon–Sat 10am–5.30pm
Fairs Olympia

Richard Axe Books
Contact Mr R Axe
12 Cheltenham Crescent, Harrogate, North Yorkshire, HG1 1DH
01423 561867 01423 561837
rja@axebooks.com
Est. 1980 *Stock size* Large
Stock Antiquarian, rare, second-hand books, Yorkshire topics a speciality
Open Mon–Sat 10am–5.30pm

Margaret Bedi's Antiques and Fine Art (LAPADA)
Contact Mrs Margaret Bedi
Corn Exchange Building, The Ginnel, Harrogate, North Yorkshire, HG1 2RB
01642 782346
07860 577637
Est. 1976 *Stock size* Large
Stock Fine furniture 1660–1920, watercolours, oils
Open By appointment only
Fairs Northern Antiques Fair, Harrogate
Services Valuations, restorations

Carlton Hollis Ltd
Contact Paul Hollis
10 Montpellier Mews, Montpellier Street, Harrogate, North Yorkshire, HG1 2TQ
01423 500216 01423 500283
Est. 2000 *Stock size* Medium
Stock Antique silver and jewellery
Open Mon–Sat 10am–5pm
Services Valuations, restorations

Crown Jewellers of Harrogate
Contact Steve Kramer
23 Commercial Street, Harrogate, North Yorkshire, HG1 1UB
01423 502000 01423 502000
sask@crownjewellers.freeserve.co.uk
www.crownjewellersharrogate.co.uk
Est. 2000 *Stock size* Medium
Stock Jewellery, porcelain, glass, silver
Open Mon–Sat 10am–5pm closed Wed
Services Valuations, jewellery repairs

John Daffern Antiques
Contact John Daffern
38 Forest Lane Head, Harrogate, North Yorkshire, HG2 7TS
01423 889832
Est. 1968 *Stock size* Medium
Stock Fine 17th–18thC furniture, clocks
Open Mon Wed Fri Sat 10.30am–5.30pm

Derbyshire Antiques Ltd
Contact Mr R Derbyshire
27 Montpellier Parade, Harrogate, North Yorkshire, HG1 2TG
01423 503115
07860 580836
Est. 1962 *Stock size* Medium
Stock Early oak pieces, associated items, Georgian furniture to 1820
Open Mon–Sat 10am–5.30pm

Dragon Antiques
Contact Mr P Broadbelt
10 Dragon Road, Harrogate, North Yorkshire, HG1 5DF
01423 562037
Est. 1964 *Stock size* Medium
Stock General antiques, ephemera, postcards
Open Mon–Sat 11am–6pm

Garth Antiques (LAPADA)
Contact Mr or Mrs J Chapman
16 Montpellier Parade, Harrogate, North Yorkshire, HG1 2TG
01423 530573
Est. 1989 *Stock size* Small
Stock General antiques
Open Mon–Sat 10am–5.30pm
Services Restorations

The Ginnel Antiques Centre
Contact Mrs P Stephenson
Corn Exchange Building, The Ginnel, Harrogate, North Yorkshire, HG1 2RB
01423 508857 01423 508857
info@theginnel.com
www.theginnel.co.uk
Est. 1986 *Stock size* Large
No. of dealers 50
Stock Quality date-lined antiques
Open Mon–Sat 9.30am–5.30pm
Services Courier service, café, licensed restaurant

Grandad's Attic
Contact Miss B F Dawson
2 Granville Road, Harrogate, North Yorkshire, HG1 1BY
01423 503003
Est. 1984 *Stock size* Medium
Stock Antique usable tools, garden tools, kitchenware
Open Thurs Fri Sat 10.30am–4.30pm or by appointment
Fairs David Stanley Tools Auction

Havelocks Pine and Antiques
Contact Philip Adam
13–17 Westmoreland Street, Harrogate, North Yorkshire, HG1 5AY
01423 506721 01423 506721
07802 914419
Est. 1986 *Stock size* Large
Stock General antiques
Open Mon–Sat 10am–5pm Sun 11am–4pm
Fairs Newark
Services Restorations, pine stripping, valuations

Haworth Antiques (BWCG)
Contact Mr G White
26 Cold Bath Road, Harrogate, North Yorkshire, HG2 0NA
01423 521401
07831 692263
Est. 1969 *Stock size* Medium
Stock Small furniture, clocks
Open Tues–Sat 10am–5pm
Services Valuations, restorations

Charles Lumb & Sons Ltd (BADA)
Contact Mr A Lumb
2 Montpellier Gardens, Harrogate, North Yorkshire, HG1 2TF
01423 503776 01423 530074

Est. 1910 *Stock size* Medium
Stock 18th–19thC English furniture, works of art
Open Mon–Sat 9.30am–6pm closed 1–2pm

Christopher Matthews
Contact Mr C Matthews
23 Mount Street, Harrogate, North Yorkshire, HG2 8DQ
01423 871756 01423 879700
Est. 1989
Open Mon–Fri 9am–5pm
Sales Quarterly antiques auctions, phone for details

Montpellier Mews Antique Market
Contact Murray Burgess
Montpellier Street, Harrogate, North Yorkshire, HG1 2TQ
01423 530484
Est. 1987 *Stock size* Medium
No. of dealers 10
Stock General antiques, collectables, golf antiques, silver, china
Open Mon–Sat 10am–5pm

Morphets of Harrogate (SOFAA)
Contact Elizabeth Pepper-Darling
6 Albert Street, Harrogate, North Yorkshire, HG1 1JL
01423 530030 01423 500717
www.morphets.co.uk
Est. 1895
Open Mon–Fri 9am–5.30pm Wed 9am–6pm Sat 9am–noon
Sales Fine art and antiques sale quarterly Thurs 10am, viewing Tues 2–7pm Wed 10am–5pm Thurs 8.30–10am. Victorian and later furniture and effects Thurs 10am, viewing Wed 10am–7pm Thurs 8.30–10am
Catalogues Yes

Paul M Peters (LAPADA)
Contact Mr Paul Peters
15a Bower Road, Harrogate, North Yorkshire, HG1 1BE
01423 560118 01423 560118
07803 082378
Est. 1964 *Stock size* Large
Stock Chinese, Japanese, European ceramics, Oriental works of art
Open Mon–Fri 10am–5pm
Fairs Olympia

Elaine Phillips Antiques Ltd (BADA)
Contact Elaine, Colin or Louise Phillips
1–2 Royal Parade, Harrogate, North Yorkshire, HG1 2SZ
01423 569745
07710 793753
elainephillips@heliscott.co.uk
Est. 1965 *Stock size* Medium
Stock 17th–18thC oak furniture, metalware, treen, some mahogany
Open Mon–Sat 9.30am–5.30pm or by appointment
Fairs Harrogate (Apr Sept)
Services Interior design

Shieling Antiques
Contact Mrs Irene Meyler
5 Montpellier Mews, Montpellier Street, Harrogate, North Yorkshire, HG1 2TQ
01423 521884
Est. 1994 *Stock size* Small
Stock Pine and country furniture, brass, copper, decorative items for the country kitchen
Open Mon–Sat 10am–5pm

St Julien (MCG)
Contact Mr J White
4 Royal Parade, Harrogate, North Yorkshire, HG1 2S2
01423 526569 01423 524999
07703 517544
abacus03@globalnet.co.uk
Est. 1998 *Stock size* Large
Stock Antique and period lighting, door furniture, fireplaces
Open Mon–Sat 10am–5.30pm
Fairs Newark
Services Restorations, light fittings, custom-made brass castings

Tennants Auctioneers
Contact Mr N Smith
34 Montpellier Parade, Harrogate, North Yorkshire, HG1 2TG
01423 531661 01423 530990
www.tennants.co.uk
Est. 1899
Open Mon–Fri 9am–5pm Sat 9.30am–3.30pm
Sales 3 general antiques sales per month, quarterly fine art sales, 2 books and collectors' sales, 2 militaria sales per annum
Catalogues Yes

Thorntons of Harrogate (LAPADA)
Contact Mr Jason O'Hugh
1 Montpellier Gardens, Harrogate, North Yorkshire, HG1 2TF
01423 504118 01423 528400
tofh@harrogateantiques.com
www.harrogateantiques.com
Est. 1973 *Stock size* Medium
Stock 18th–19thC furniture, clocks, barometers, decorative items
Open Mon–Sat 9.30am–5.30pm or by appointment
Fairs Harrogate fair (Apr May)
Services Restorations, valuations

Walker Galleries (BADA, LAPADA, CINOA)
Contact Ian Walker
1 Crown Place, Harrogate, North Yorkshire, HG1 2RY
01423 520599 01423 536664
walkermodern@aol.com
www.walkerfineart.co.uk
Est. 1972 *Stock size* Large
Stock 20thC British paintings, French Impressionist paintings
Open Tues–Sat 9.30am–5.30pm
Fairs Olympia, BADA, Harrogate Fine Art and Antique Fair
Services Valuations, restorations

Walker Galleries (BADA, LAPADA, CINOA)
Contact Ian Walker
6 Montpellier Gardens, Harrogate, North Yorkshire, HG1 2TF
01423 567933 01423 536664
wgltd@aol.com
www.walkerfineart.co.uk
Est. 1972 *Stock size* Large
Stock 18th–20thC British and Continental watercolours and oil paintings, small furniture, bronzes
Open Mon–Sat 9.30am–5.30pm
Fairs Olympia, BADA, Harrogate Fine Art and Antique Fair
Services Valuations, restorations

Weatherell's Antiques (LAPADA)
Contact Mr J Weatherell
29–30 Montpellier Parade, Harrogate, North Yorkshire, HG1 2TG
01423 507810 01423 520005
Est. 1964 *Stock size* Large

Stock 18th–early 20thC English and Continental furniture, paintings, objets d'art
Open Mon–Sat 9am–5.30pm

Chris Wilde Antiques (LAPADA)
Contact Mr C Wilde
134 Kings Road, Harrogate, North Yorkshire, HG1 5HY P
☎ 01423 525855 F 01423 552301
M 07831 543268
E chris@harrogate.com
W www.antiques.harrogate.com
Est. 1995 *Stock size* Large
Stock Georgian–Victorian furniture, longcase clocks, pictures
Open Mon–Sat 10am–5pm
Fairs NEC Antiques for Everyone, Bailey fair, Harrogate
Services Valuations, restorations

Year Dot Interiors
Contact Lyn Pickles or Terry Kindon
4A Regent Parade, Harrogate, North Yorkshire, HG1 5AN P
☎ 01423 817007 F 01423 817007
E sales@yeardotinteriors.com
W www.yeardotinteriors.com
Est. 1970
Stock Painted, pine, oak and country furniture
Open Mon–Sat 9am–5pm

HAWES

Cellar Antiques
Contact Mr I Iveson
Bridge Street, Hawes, North Yorkshire, DL8 3QL P
☎ 01969 667224
Est. 1987 *Stock size* Medium
Stock General antiques, oak country period furniture, clocks, longcase clocks
Open Mon–Sun 10am–5pm
Services Valuations, house clearance

Sturmans Antiques (LAPADA)
Contact Mr Peter Sturman
Main Street, Hawes, North Yorkshire, DL8 3QW P
☎ 01969 667742
E sturmansantiques@tinyonline.co.uk
Est. 1984 *Stock size* Medium
Stock 18th–19thC furniture, clocks, porcelain
Open Mon–Sat 10am–5.30pm Sun 11am–5pm
Services Valuations, restorations, nationwide delivery, overseas shipping arranged

HELMSLEY

Buckingham Antiques
Contact Mrs H Wilson
17 Bridge Street, Helmsley, York, North Yorkshire
☎ 01439 771642
Est. 1997 *Stock size* Large
Stock General antiques
Open Tues–Sat 10am–4pm

Church Street Antiques
Contact Mr D Hartshorne
15 Church Street, Helmsley, York, North Yorkshire, YO62 5AD P
☎ 01439 770370 F 01439 770370
Est. 1999 *Stock size* Large
Stock General antiques
Open Mon–Sun 10.30am–5pm
Services Valuations

Helmsley Antiquarian & Secondhand Books
Contact Mr M Moorby
Old Fire Station, Borogate, Helmsley, North Yorkshire, YO62 5BN P
☎ 01439 770014
Est. 1985 *Stock size* Medium
Stock Antiquarian, rare and second-hand books, Yorkshire topography a speciality
Open Mon–Sat 10am–5pm Sun noon–5pm

Westway Pine
Contact Mr J Dzierzek
Carlton Lane, Helmsley, North Yorkshire, YO62 5HB P
☎ 01439 771399 F 01439 770172
E derzie@supanet.co.uk
Est. 1987 *Stock size* Large
Stock Pine
Open Mon–Fri 9am–5pm Sat 10am–5pm
Services Valuations, restorations

York Cottage Antiques (LAPADA)
Contact G or E M Thornley
7 Church Street, Helmsley, North Yorkshire, YO62 5AD P
☎ 01439 770833
Est. 1965 *Stock size* Medium
Stock Early oak and country furniture, metalware, pewter, blue-and-white pottery, maps, prints
Open Fri Sat 10am–4pm or by appointment

HEMINGBOROUGH

Bonhams & Brooks
Contact Stewart Skilbeck
The Villa, Main Street, Hemingborough, North Yorkshire, YO8 7QF
☎ 01757 638894 F 01757 638894
W www.bonhams.com
Open Mon–Fri 9am–5pm
Sales Regional Representative for Northern counties and Scotland

KILLINGHALL

Thompson Auctioneers
Contact Mr B D Thompson
The Dales Salesroom, Levens Hall Park, Lund Lane, Killinghall, Harrogate, North Yorkshire, HG3 2BG P
☎ 01423 709086 F 01423 709085
E thompsonsauctions@excite.co.uk
W thompsonsauctioneers.co.uk
Est. 1989
Open Mon–Fri 9am–5pm Sat 9.30am–noon closed Thurs pm
Sales General antiques Fri 1pm quarterly antiques and collectables sale
Frequency Weekly
Catalogues No

KNARESBOROUGH

H & L Bowkett
Contact Mr E Starkie
9 Abbey Road, Knaresborough, North Yorkshire, HE5 8HY P
☎ 01423 866112
E barbara@rivermidd.freeserve.co.uk
Est. 1974 *Stock size* Medium
Stock General antiques
Open Mon–Sat 9am–6pm

John Thompson Antiques (LAPADA)
Contact Mr J Thompson
Swadforth House, Gracious Street, Knaresborough, North Yorkshire, HG5 8DT P
☎ 01423 864698 F 01423 864698
M 07831 899948
Est. 1967 *Stock size* Medium
Stock Fine 18th–19thC furniture, related decorative objects

Open Mon–Sat 9am–5.30pm or by appointment
Fairs Olympia

Thornton & Linley
Contact Mr I A Thornton
2–4 Jockey Lane, High Street, Knaresborough, North Yorkshire, HG5 0HG
01423 862271 F 01423 862271
Est. 1909
Open Tues–Fri 9am–5pm closed 1–2pm
Sales General antiques
Frequency Periodic
Catalogues Yes

LEALHOLM

Stepping Stones
Contact Mrs J Davies
Lealholm, Whitby, North Yorkshire, YO21 2AJ
01947 897382
Est. 1974 *Stock size* Medium
Stock General antiques, books
Open Daily 10am–5pm
Services Bed and breakfast

LEYBURN

Tennants Auctioneers (BACA Award Winner 2001)
Contact Mr Rodney Tennant
The Auction Centre, Leyburn, North Yorkshire, DL8 5SG
01969 623780 F 01969 624281
E enquiry@tennants-ltd.co.uk
W www.tennants.co.uk
Open Mon–Fri 9am–5pm
Sales General sales Sat 9.30am 3–4 per month, viewing day prior 9am–7pm. 3 fine art sales per annum, 2 book sales and collectors' sales per annum
Catalogues Yes

MALTON

Boulton & Cooper Fine Art (SOFAA)
Contact Mr A McMillan
Forsyth House, Market Place, Malton, North Yorkshire, YO17 7LR
01653 696151 F 01653 600311
Est. 1801
Open Mon–Fri 9am–5.30pm Sat by appointment
Sales General antiques
Frequency Alternate months
Catalogues Yes

Cundalls
Contact Mr F Dimmey
15 Market Place, Malton, North Yorkshire, YO17 7LP
01653 697820 F 01653 698305
W www.cundalls.co.uk
Est. 1860
Open Mon–Fri 9am–5.30pm
Sales General antiques, phone for details
Frequency 8–10 per annum
Catalogues Yes

Magpie Antiques
Contact Mrs G Warren
9–13 The Shambles, Malton, North Yorkshire, YO17 7LZ
01653 691880/658335
M 07714 230224
Est. 1987 *Stock size* Medium
Stock General antiques, kitchenware, small collectables
Open Mon–Sat 10am–4pm closed Thurs
Fairs Newark
Services Will buy to order bric-a-brac to decorate pubs, shops etc

Malton Antique Market
Contact Mrs Cleverly
2 Old Maltongate, Malton, North Yorkshire, YO17 7EG
01653 692732
Est. 1970 *Stock size* Medium
Stock 18th–19thC furniture, glass, silver, brass, copper, china
Open Mon–Sat 10am–4pm closed Thurs

Matthew Maw
Contact Mr M Maw
18 Castlegate, Malton, North Yorkshire, YO17 7DT
01653 694638 F 01653 694638
Stock size Medium
Stock General antiques
Open Mon–Sat 9am–5pm

Old Talbot Gallery
Contact Mrs C Bull
Old Talbot Gallery, 9 Market Street, Malton, North Yorkshire, YO17 7LY
01653 696142
Est. 1981 *Stock size* Medium
Stock Books, prints, pictures, maps
Open Please telephone
Services Valuations, restorations

MASHAM

Aura Antiques
Silver Street, Masham, North Yorkshire, HE4 4DX
01765 689315
E robert@aura-antiques.co.uk
W www.aura-antiques.co.uk
Est. 1986 *Stock size* Medium
Stock Georgian, Regency, mahogany and oak furniture
Open Mon–Sat 10am–4.30pm
Services Delivery throughout UK

MIDDLEHAM

Castle Antiques
Contact Mr D Jarvill or Mrs J Jarvill
34 Market Place, Middleham, North Yorkshire, DL8 4QW
01969 624655
Est. 1992 *Stock size* Large
No. of dealers 20
Stock Furniture, art pottery, porcelain, glassware, blue-and-white, pictures, prints, clocks, scientific instruments, lamps, jewellery, books, general antiques, collectors' items
Open Wed–Mon 10am–5.30pm Tues by appointment

Middleham Antiques
Contact Mr Mike Pitman
The Corner Shop, Kirkgate, Middleham, North Yorkshire, DL8 4PF
01969 622982 F 01969 622982
Est. 1986 *Stock size* Small
Stock Pre-1830 oak and country furniture, longcase clocks, curios etc
Open Most days 10am–5.30pm Wed by appointment. Call before visiting recommended

NORTHALLERTON

Northallerton Auctions Ltd
Contact Mr P Richardson
Applegarth Sales Rooms, Romanby Road, Northallerton, North Yorkshire, DL7 8LZ
01609 772034 F 01609 778786
Open Mon–Sat 9am–5pm
Sales General antiques Fri 1pm fortnightly
Frequency Fortnightly
Catalogues Yes

YORKS & LINCS

NORTON

Northern Antiques Co
Contact Mrs Ashby-Arnold
2 Parliament Street, Scarborough Road, Norton, Malton, North Yorkshire, YO17 9HE P
01653 697520 01653 690056
Est. 1990 *Stock size* Medium
Stock Georgian–Victorian furniture, decorative accessories
Open Mon–Fri 9am–5pm closed 1–2pm Sat 9.30am–12.30pm

PATELEY BRIDGE

H S C Fine Arts & Antiques
Contact David Hinchliffe
45 High Street, Pateley Bridge, North Yorkshire, HG3 5LB P
01423 712218
Est. 1997 *Stock size* Medium
Stock Small furniture, silver, jewellery, porcelain, Royal Worcester, pictures
Open Fri Sat 10.30am–4.30pm or by appointment

Brian Loomes (BACA Award Winner 2001)
Contact Brian Loomes
Calf Haugh Farm, Pateley Bridge, Harrogate, North Yorkshire, HG3 5HW P
01423 711163
brianloomes@antiqueclocks.freeserve.co.uk
www.brianloomes.com
Est. 1966 *Stock size* Large
Stock British clocks
Open By appointment
Services Restoration, valuation, author of books on subject

Needfull Things Ltd
Contact Rebecca Hinchliffe
off High Street, Pateley Bridge, North Yorkshire, HG3 5AW P
01423 712851 01423 712851
Est. 1999 *Stock size* Medium
Stock Jewellery, glassware, ceramics
Open Sun Wed Thurs 10am–4pm or by appointment

Pateley Bridge Antiques
Contact Mr André Gora
35 High Street, Pateley Bridge, North Yorkshire, HG3 5JZ P
01423 711004
info@earlyoak.co.uk
www.earlyoak.co.uk
Est. 1994 *Stock size* Large
Stock Oak and country furniture, samplers, Delft, pewter, 17thC oak furniture a speciality
Open Mon–Fri 10am–5.30pm Sat 11am–5pm
Fairs Newark

PICKERING

Country Collector
Contact G or M Berney
11–12 Birdgate, Pickering, North Yorkshire, YO18 7AL
01751 477481
Est. 1992 *Stock size* Medium
Stock Ceramics, blue-and-white china, glass, silver, metalware, collectables, antiquities
Open Mon–Sat 10am–5pm closed Wed
Services Valuations

Inch's Books (PBFA, ABA)
Contact Mr P Inch
6 Westgate, Pickering, North Yorkshire, YO18 8BA P
01751 474928 01751 475939
inchs.books@dial.pipex.com
www.inchsbooks.co.uk
Est. 1982 *Stock size* Medium
Stock Antique and second-hand books
Open By appointment
Fairs ABA Chelsea, PBFA June fair
Services Mail order, catalogues (8 per year)

Pickering Antique Centre
Contact Mrs C Vance
Southgate, Pickering, North Yorkshire, YO18 8BN P
01751 477210 01751 477210
sales@pickantiques.freeserve.co.uk
Est. 1998 *Stock size* Large
No. of dealers 32
Stock General antiques, books, postcards, pictures
Open Mon–Sun 10am–5pm
Services Valuations, metal restoration service

C H & D M Reynolds
Contact Mr C Reynolds
The Curiosity Shop, 122 Eastgate, Pickering, North Yorkshire, YO18 7DW P
01751 472785
07714 355676
Est. 1949 *Stock size* Large
Stock General antiques including furniture, curios
Open Mon–Sat 9.30am–5.30pm Sun by appointment
Services Valuations

Stable Antiques
Contact Mrs Y Kitching-Walker
Pickering Antique Centre, Southgate, Pickering, North Yorkshire, YO18 8BN P

☎ 01751 477210
Est. 1998 *Stock size* Large
Stock General antiques
Open Mon–Sun 10am–5pm
Services Valuations

RICHMOND

Recollections
Contact Mrs J M Farquhar
35 Market Road, Richmond, North Yorkshire, DL10 4QG
☎ 01748 823568
Est. 1998 *Stock size* Medium
Stock General antiques
Open Mon–Sat 9.30am–4.30pm Sun noon–4pm
Fairs Newark
Services Valuations

Vokes Books Ltd (PBFA)
43 Bargate, Richmond, North Yorkshire, DL10 4QY
☎ 01748 824946 Ⓕ 01748 824946
Ⓜ 07790 793823
Ⓔ vokes-vokesbooksltd@tinyworld.co.uk
Stock size Medium
Stock Antiquarian, rare, and second-hand books, including military, north of England topography, travel, gardening, horticulture, natural history
Open By appointment
Services Valuations, booksearch

York House (Antiques)
Contact Mrs C Swift
60 Market Place, Richmond, North Yorkshire, DL10 4JQ
☎ 01748 850338 Ⓕ 01748 850578
Ⓜ 07711 307045
Est. 1997 *Stock size* Medium
Stock Pine, general antiques
Open Mon–Sat 9.30am–5.30pm Sun noon–4pm
Fairs Newark, Swinderby
Services Restorations, pine stripping

RIPON

Crown Auctions
Contact Mr C. Hanby
The Old Sale Room, St Wilfrid's Road, Ripon, North Yorkshire, HG4 2AR
☎ 01765 600111
Ⓜ 07779 224474
Est. 1994
Open Mon–Fri 9–10.30am Sat 10–11.30am

Hornsey's of Ripon
Contact Bruce, Susan or Daniel Hornsey
3 Kirkgate, Ripon, North Yorkshire, HG4 1PA
☎ 01765 602878 Ⓕ 01765 601692
Ⓔ daniel@rarebooks.freeserve.co.uk
Est. 1974 *Stock size* Large
Stock Antiques, collectables, rare books, fine linen, lace
Open Mon–Sat 9am–5.30pm or by appointment
Services Valuations

Hug & Plum
Contact Mr B M Plummer or Miss S A Hugill
5 Kirkgate, Ripon, North Yorkshire, HG4 1PA
☎ 01765 690428 Ⓕ 01765 601739
Ⓔ BPBAZZI@aol.com
Est. 1996 *Stock size* Medium
Stock General antiques, collectables
Open Mon–Sat 10am–4.30pm
Fairs Swinderby, Harrogate
Services House clearance, valuations, restorations

Sigma Antiques
Contact Mr David Thomson
The Old Opera House, Water Skellgate, Ripon, North Yorkshire, HG4 1BH
☎ 01765 603163 Ⓕ 01765 603163
Est. 1964 *Stock size* Large
Stock General antiques
Open Mon–Sat 9am–5.30pm

Skellgate Curios
Contact Mrs J Wayne
2 Low Skellgate, Ripon, North Yorkshire, HG4 1BE
☎ 01765 601290
Est. 1975 *Stock size* Medium
Stock General antiques
Open Mon–Sat 11am–5pm closed Wed

ROBIN HOOD'S BAY

John Gilbert Antiques
King Street, Robin Hood's Bay, Whitby, North Yorkshire, YO22 4SY
☎ 01947 880528
Est. 1990 *Stock size* Medium
Stock 18th–19thC oak, country furniture
Open Sat 10am–1pm Sun 10am–5pm or by appointment
Services Valuations, restorations

SALTBURN-BY-THE-SEA

Anderson Antiques
Contact Mrs K Anderson
20 Milton Street, Saltburn-by-the-Sea, Cleveland, North Yorkshire, TS12 1DG
☎ 01287 624810 Ⓕ 01287 625349
Ⓜ 07798 587622
Ⓔ andersak@fsbdial.co.uk
Est. 1996 *Stock size* Medium
Stock Furniture, pictures, porcelain, jewellery, clocks, linen
Open Mon–Sat 10am–5pm closed Wed
Fairs Newark, Swinderby, Harrogate, Edinburgh
Services Valuations

J C Simmons & Son
Contact Mr G Aked
Saltburn Salerooms, Diamond Street, Saltburn-by-the Sea, North Yorkshire, TS12 1EB
☎ 01287 622366
Est. 1949
Open Viewing Mon–Sat 10am–4pm
Sales General antiques
Frequency Periodic
Catalogues Yes

Jösef Thompson
Contact Jösef Thompson
Saltburn Bookshop, 3 Amber Street, Saltburn-by-the-Sea, Cleveland, North Yorkshire, TS12 1DT
☎ 01287 623335
Est. 1977 *Stock size* Large
Stock Second-hand books
Open March–Oct Mon–Sat 11am–5pm Nov–Feb Mon–Sat 11am–5pm closed 1–2pm Sun in August 2–4pm
Services Book search

SCARBOROUGH

Antique and Collector's Centre (PTA)
Contact Colin Spink
35 St Nicholas Cliff, Scarborough, North Yorkshire, YO11 2ES
☎ 01723 365221
Ⓜ 07730 202405
Ⓔ spink@collectors.demon.co.uk
Ⓦ www.collectors.demon.co.uk
Est. 1965 *Stock size* Medium
Stock General antiques, cigarette cards, jewellery, ephemera

coins, postcards, antiques, commemorative ware, etc
Open Mon–Sat 10am–4.30pm
Services Valuations

Bar Bookstore (The Antiquary Ltd) (PBFA)
Contact Mr M Chaddock
4 Swan Hill Road, Scarborough, North Yorkshire, YO11 1BW
01723 500141
antiquary@btinternet.com
Est. 1976 *Stock size* Medium
Stock Antiquarian, rare, and second-hand books
Open Tues–Sat 10.30am–5pm
Fairs York, Harrogate, Darlington
Services Valuations, book search

Bar Street Antiques
Contact Mr D Lowe
40 Bar Street, Scarborough, North Yorkshire, YO11 2HT
01723 376447
Est. 1998 *Stock size* Medium
Stock General antiques
Open Mon–Sat 10am–5pm

David Duggleby Fine Art
Contact Jane Duggleby
The Vine Street Salerooms, Scarborough, North Yorkshire, YO11 1XN
01723 507111 01723 507222
auctions@davidduggleby.com
www.davidduggleby.com
Est. 1996
Open Mon–Fri 8.30am–5pm
Sales Fortnightly 500-lot house contents and Victoriana sales, 700 lots of fine art and antiques every 8 weeks
Catalogues Yes

Allen Reed
Contact Mr A Reed
109 Fallsgrave Road, Scarborough, North Yorkshire, YO12 5EG
01723 360251
Est. 1999 *Stock size* Large
Stock General antiques
Open Mon–Sat 11am–4pm

Allen Reed
Contact Mr A Reed
188–190 Victoria Road, Scarborough, North Yorkshire, YO12 5EG
01723 360251
Est. 1969 *Stock size* Large
Stock General antiques
Open Mon–Sat 11am–4pm

Charles Smith & Son
54 Ramshill Road, Scarborough, North Yorkshire, YO11 2QG
01723 500378
charlessmith@btinternet.com
Est. 1984 *Stock size* Large
Stock General antiques, 19thC watercolours
Open Mon–Sat 9am–5pm
Services Valuations, restorations

Ward Price Ltd (ASVA)
Contact Mr I Smith
Royal Auction Rooms, 14–15 Queen Street, Scarborough, North Yorkshire, YO11 1HA
01723 353581 01723 369926
www.wardprice.co.uk
Est. 1901
Open Mon–Fri 9am–5pm Sat 10am–2pm
Sales General antiques
Frequency Alternate months
Catalogues Yes

SESSAY

Potterton Books
Contact Mrs Clare Jameson
The Old Rectory, Sessay, Nr Thirsk, North Yorkshire, YO7 3L2
01845 501218 01845 501439
enquiries@pottertonbooks.sagehost.co.uk
www.pottertonbooks.co.uk
Est. 1982
Stock Fine and decorative arts books
Open Mon–Fri 9am–5pm
Fairs Fine Art Olympia, Decorex International
Services Book search

SETTLE

Nanette Midgley
Contact Mr or Mrs J Midgley
Roundabout, 41 Duke Street, Settle, North Yorkshire, BD24 9DJ
01729 823324
midglui@aol.com
Est. 1953 *Stock size* Small
Stock 18th–19thC pottery, porcelain
Open Tues Fri Sat 11am–12.30pm 2–5.30pm
Services Valuations

Mary Milnthorpe & Daughters
Contact Miss Judith Milnthorpe
Market Place, Settle, North Yorkshire, BD24 9DX
01729 822331 01729 823062
Est. 1959 *Stock size* Medium
Stock Antique jewellery, silver
Open Mon–Sat 9.30am–5pm closed Wed
Services Valuations, repairs

Nanbooks
Contact Mr or Mrs J L Midgley
Roundabout, 41 Duke Street, Settle, North Yorkshire, BD24 9DJ
01729 823324
crackpot.midgley@ukonline.co.uk
Est. 1955 *Stock size* Medium
Stock English and Continental glass, ceramics
Open Tues Fri Sat 11am–5pm closed 12.30–2pm or by appointment

Anderson Slater
Contact K C Slater
Duke Street, Settle, North Yorkshire, BD24 9DW
01729 822051
Est. 1959 *Stock size* Large
Stock 18th–19thC oak, mahogany furniture
Open Mon–Sat 10am–5pm
Services Valuations, restorations, interior designs

Thistlethwaite Antiques
Contact Mr E C Thistlethwaite
Market Square, Settle, North Yorkshire, BD24 9EF
01729 822460
Est. 1978 *Stock size* Medium
Stock 18th–19thC country furniture, metalware
Open Mon–Sat 9am–5pm closed Wed

SHERBURN-IN-ELMET

The Glass-House
Contact Sara Qualter
Low Street Farm, Sherburn-in-Elmet, North Yorkshire, LS25 6BB
01977 689119 01977 682673
07890 134063
theglasshouse@ic24.net

Est. 2001 *Stock size* Medium
Stock Antiques and collectables, oak and country furniture, pine, 20thC design
Open Tues–Sun 9am–5pm
Fairs Swinderby, Newark
Services Shipping

SKIPTON

Cherub Antiques
Contact G or V Hutchinson
2 Albert Street, Skipton, North Yorkshire, BD23 1JD
☎ 01756 700899
Ⓜ 07771 858022
Ⓔ mail@cherubantiques.co.uk
Ⓦ www.cherubantiques.co.uk
Est. 1997 *Stock size* Medium
Stock General antiques, collectables, textiles, small furniture
Open Mon–Sat 10.30am–4.30pm closed Tues
Services China restorations

Corn Mill Antiques
Contact Mr or Mrs Hawkridge
High Corn Mill, Chapel Hill, Skipton, North Yorkshire, BD23 1NL
☎ 01756 792440
Est. 1983 *Stock size* Medium
Stock Georgian–Edwardian furniture, porcelain, pictures etc
Open Mon Thurs Fri Sat 10am–4pm

Skipton Antiques & Collectors Centre
Contact Ann Hall
The Old Foundry, Cavendish Street, Skipton, North Yorkshire, BD23 2AB
☎ 01756 797667
Est. 1995 *Stock size* Large
No. of dealers 30
Stock General antiques and collectables, Art Deco, clocks, books, ceramics, pine, etc
Open Mon–Sat 10.30am–4pm Sun 11am–4pm

SLINGSBY

Tony Popek Antiques
Contact Mr E Popek
West View, Railway St, Slingsby, York, North Yorkshire, YO62 24A
☎ 01653 628533
Est. 1989 *Stock size* Medium
Stock General antiques
Open Tues Fri Sat 10am–5pm or by appointment
Fairs Harrogate

SPOFFORTH

Nicholas Merchant
Contact Mr N Merchant
11 High Street, Spofforth, Harrogate, North Yorkshire, HG3 1BQ
☎ 01937 591022 Ⓕ 01937 591033
Ⓔ merchantn@btconnect.com
Est. 1989 *Stock size* Small
Stock Antique and collectors' books, decorative, fine arts, reference books a speciality
Open By appointment
Services Valuations, mail order, out-of-print search

STOCKTON-ON-TEES

Paraphernalia
Contact Mrs R Thomas
12 Harland Place, High Street, Norton, Stockton-on-Tees, North Yorkshire, TS20 1AL
☎ 01642 535940
Est. 1984 *Stock size* Large
Stock General antiques
Open Mon–Sat 9.30–5pm
Services Restorations, repairs, Victorian-style tea rooms

STOKESLEY

Fiddlesticks
Contact Mr Bennett
1 Bridge Road, Stokesley, Middlesbrough, North Yorkshire, TS9 5AA
☎ 01642 713247
Ⓜ 07947 108174
Est. 1991 *Stock size* Medium
Stock Victorian–Edwardian furniture, pine, smalls
Open Mon–Sat 10.30am–5pm
Services Restorations,

Lithgow & Partners
Contact Richard Storry
The Auction Houses, Station Road, Stokesley, North Yorkshire, TS9 7AB
☎ 01642 710158 Ⓕ 01642 712641
Ⓔ lithglow.auctions@oxynet.co.uk
Est. 1868
Open Mon–Fri 9am–5pm
Sales Weekly sale Wed, viewing Tues noon–4pm
Frequency Weekly
Catalogues Yes

Mantle Antiques
Contact Mr Derek Bushby
23 College Square, Stokesley, North Yorkshire, TS9 5DN
☎ 01642 714313
Ⓜ 07713 155772
Est. 1973 *Stock size* Medium
Stock Victorian furniture, architectural antiques
Open Tues Thurs Fri Sat 10am–4pm

STRENSALL

Bonhams & Brooks
Contact Michael Smith
The Laurels, Brecks Lane, Strensall, Nr York, North Yorkshire, YO3 5UZ
☎ 01904 491195
Ⓦ www.bonhams.com
Open Mon–Fri 9am–5pm
Sales Regional Representative for Yorkshire

TADCASTER

Scarthingwell Antiques
Contact Mr B Brier
Scarthingwell Centre, Scarthingwell Farm, Tadcaster, North Yorkshire, LS24 9PG
☎ 01937 557877 Ⓕ 01937 558084
Est. 1989 *Stock size* Large
Stock General antiques
Open Mon–Sun 10am–5pm closed Sat

Scarthingwell Auction Centre
Contact John Griffiths or Christine Bridge
Scarthingwell, Tadcaster, North Yorkshire, LS24 9PG
☎ 01937 557955 Ⓕ 01937 557955
Ⓜ 07778 520463
Est. 1990
Open Mon–Fri 10am–5pm
Sales Antiques and general sales 6pm Mon Tues every 2–3 weeks, viewing Sun prior to sale noon–5pm Mon 2pm Tues 4pm

THIRSK

The Book & Stamp Shop
Contact Mr R O'Brien
7 Westgate, Thirsk, North Yorkshire, YO7 1QR
☎ 01845 524615
Est. 1995 *Stock size* Medium
Stock Antiquarian, rare, and second-hand books, prints,

British and Commonwealth stamps
Open Mon–Sat 10.30am–4.30pm closed Wed
Services Valuations, bookbinding

Hambleton Books
Contact Mr T F Parr
43 Market Place, Thirsk, North Yorkshire, YO7 1HA
01845 522343
hambooks@btinternet.com
Est. 1979 *Stock size* Medium
Stock Antique, rare, second-hand books, books on cricket a speciality
Open Mon–Sat 9am–5.30pm Sun 10am–4pm

Millgate Antiques
Contact Tim Parvin
Abel Grange, Newsham Road, Thirsk, North Yorkshire, YO7 4DB
01845 523878 F 01845 523878
M 07966 251609
babs.jenkins@btinternet.com
Est. 1991 *Stock size* Large
Stock Pine furniture, panelled doors
Open Mon–Sat 8.30am–5pm
Fairs Newark, Swinderbury
Services Stripping, restoration

Millgate Pine & Antiques
Contact Tim Parvin
12 Millgate, Thirsk, North Yorkshire, YO7 1AA
01845 523878 F 01845 523878
M 07966 251609
babs.jenkins@btinternet.com
Est. 1991 *Stock size* Large
Stock Pine furniture, panelled doors
Open Mon–Sat 8.30am–5pm
Fairs Newark, Swinderbury
Services Stripping

THORNTON-LE-DALE

Cobweb Books
Contact Mr Robin Buckler
Ye Olde Corner Shoppe, 1 Pickering Road, Thornton-le-Dale, North Yorkshire, YO18 7LE
01751 476638
sales@cobwebbooks.co.uk
www.cobwebbooks.co.uk
Est. 1991 *Stock size* Medium
Stock Antiquarian, rare, second-hand books
Open Tues–Sun 10am–5pm
Fairs Royal National Hotel Book Fair, London
Services Book search

Stable Antiques
Contact Mrs Y Kitching-Walker
4 Pickering Road, Thornton-le-Dale, Pickering, North Yorkshire, YO18 7LG
01751 474332/474435
yvonne@stable-antiques.co.uk
www.stable-antiques.co.uk
Est. 1987 *Stock size* Large
Stock Porcelain
Open Mon–Sun 2–5pm or by appointment
Services Valuations

TOCKWITH

Tomlinson Antiques (LAPADA, CINOA)
Contact Mike Grant
Moorside, Tockwith, North Yorkshire, YO26 7QG
01423 358833 F 01423 358188
info@tomlinsonfurniture.com
antique-furniture.co.uk
Est. 1977 *Stock size* Large
Stock Quality Georgian–pre-war furniture, china, silver, silver plate, longcase clocks, rugs
Open Mon–Sat 9am–4.30pm Sun 10am–4pm
Services Restorations, shipping

UPPER POPPLETON

D Wombell & Son
Contact Mr W Rice
Northminster Business Park, Upper Poppleton, York, North Yorkshire, YO41 4AR
01904 790777 F 01904 798018
www.invaluable.com/wombell
Est. 1984
Open Mon–Fri 10am–5pm
Sales General antiques monthly
Frequency Monthly
Catalogues Yes

WHITBY

Abbey Antiques
Contact Mr A L Barsby
4–5 Grape Lane, Whitby, North Yorkshire, YO22 4DD
01947 821424
Est. 1996 *Stock size* Large
Stock General antiques, collectables
Open Flexible, please telephone

Clewlow Antiques (PBFA)
Contact Mr A Clewlow
Sandringham House, 6–8 Skinner Street, Whitby, North Yorkshire, YO21 3AJ
01947 821655
fiona.clewlow@virgin.net
www.members.ebay.com/abcutme/gonzostuff
Est. 1977 *Stock size* Large
Stock General antiques
Open Summer Mon–Sat 10am–5pm winter Sat 10am–5pm

Curio Corner
Contact Mr A L Barsby
7 Market Plate, Whitby, North Yorkshire, YO22 4DD
01947 821424
Est. 1969 *Stock size* Small
Stock General antiques, collectables
Open Mon–Sun 10am–5pm or by appointment

Endeavour Books
Contact Mrs L Allison
1 Grape Lane, Whitby, North Yorkshire, YO22 4BA
01947 821331
linda@enbooks.co.uk
www.enbooks.co.uk
Est. 1989 *Stock size* Medium
Stock Rare and second-hand books
Open Mon–Sun summer 10am–8pm winter 10.30am–5pm

Eskdale Antiques
Contact Mr P Smith
85 Church Street, Whitby, North Yorkshire, YO22 4BH
01947 600512
M 07813 589117
Est. 1982 *Stock size* Medium
Stock Antique china, collectables
Open Daily 10.30am–5pm

Eskdale Antiques
Contact Mr P Smith
164 Coach Road, Whitby, North Yorkshire, YO22 5EQ
01947 810297
M 07813 589117
Est. 1979 *Stock size* Medium
Stock Antique stripped pine, garden ornaments
Open Daily 9.30am–5pm

Picfair Antiques
Contact Mr J Robertson
67 Haggersgate, Whitby, North Yorkshire, YO21 3PP

☎ 01947 602483
Ⓔ picfair@amserve.net
Ⓦ picfair.com
Est. 1987 *Stock size* Medium
Stock General antiques including glass, costume jewellery, porcelain
Open Mon–Sun noon–6pm
Services Valuations, advice to collectors

Quarter Deck Antiques
Contact Mr M B Taylor
✉ **8 Silver Street, Whitby, North Yorkshire, YO21 3BU** Ⓟ
☎ 01947 820220
Est. 1982 *Stock size* Large
Stock General antiques, furniture, bric-a-brac, antiquities
Open Mon–Sun 8.30am–4.30pm

Venus Trading
Contact Mr Tim Ruff
✉ **4 Sandgate, Whitby, North Yorkshire, YO22 4DB** Ⓟ
☎ 01947 601221
Est. 1976 *Stock size* Large
Stock Victorian–Edwardian furniture, fireplaces
Open Mon–Sun 9am–6pm

WHIXLEY

Garth Antiques (LAPADA)
Contact Mr or Mrs J Chapman
✉ **The Old School, Franks Lane, Whixley, North Yorkshire, YO26 8AP** Ⓟ
☎ 01423 331055 Ⓕ 01423 331733
Est. 1978 *Stock size* Medium
Stock General antiques
Open Tues–Sat 10am–5pm
Services Restorations

YARM

Arts & Memorabilia
Contact J E or M H Parker
✉ **111 High Street, Yarm, Cleveland, North Yorkshire, TS15 9BB**
☎ 01642 787178
Est. 1987 *Stock size* Medium
Stock General antiques
Open Mon–Sat 10am–5.30pm

Farthing
Contact Shirley Smith or Sybil Watson
✉ **63 High Street, Yarm, Cleveland, North Yorkshire, TS15 9BH** Ⓟ
☎ 01642 785881
Est. 1977 *Stock size* Medium
Stock General antiques, gifts
Open Mon–Sat 9.30am–5.30pm
Services Picture framing

Ruby Snowden Antiques
Contact Ruby Snowden
✉ **Glenisle House, 10 High Street, Yarm, Cleveland, North Yorkshire, TS15 9AE** Ⓟ
☎ 01642 801188/830246
Est. 1976 *Stock size* Medium
Stock Georgian–Edwardian furniture, porcelain, smalls, copper, brass, local prints, pictures
Open Wed–Sat 9.30am–5pm

YORK

Advena Antiques & Fairs
Contact Mr A White
✉ **Stonegate Antique Centre, 41 Stonegate, York, North Yorkshire, YO1 8AW**
☎ 01904 668785
Ⓜ 07713 150510
Est. 1992 *Stock size* Medium
Stock Antique silver, jewellery
Open Mon–Sat 9am–6pm Sun 10am–4pm
Services Valuations, repairs

Ancient World (ADA)
Contact John Moor
✉ **16 High Petergate, York, North Yorkshire, YO1 7EH** Ⓟ
☎ 01904 624062
Est. 1975 *Stock size* Medium
Stock Ancient coins, antiquities
Open Mon–Sun 10am–5pm
Fairs ADA
Services Valuations for probate etc

Margaret Bedi Antiques and Fine Art (LAPADA)
Contact Mrs Margaret Bedi
✉ **The Red House Antique Centre, Duncombe Place, York, North Yorkshire, YO1 2EF** Ⓟ
☎ 01642 782346
Ⓜ 07860 577637
Est. 1976 *Stock size* Large
Stock Fine furniture 1660–1920, watercolours, oils
Open By appointment only
Fairs Northern Antiques Fair, Harrogate
Services Valuations, restorations

Bishopgate Antiques
Contact Mr R Weatherill
✉ **23–24 Bishopgate, York, North Yorkshire, YO23 1JH** Ⓟ
☎ 01904 623893 Ⓕ 01904 626511
Est. 1965 *Stock size* Medium
Stock General antiques
Open Mon–Sat 9.15am–6pm Sun noon–5pm

Barbara Cattle (BADA)
Contact Mr Richard Pool
✉ **45 Stonegate, York, North Yorkshire, YO1 8AW**
☎ 01904 623862
Ⓔ info@hl-brown.co.uk
Stock Jewellery, silver, old Sheffield plate
Open Mon–Sat 9am–5.30pm
Services Valuations, repairs, restorations

Cavendish Antiques & Collectors Centre (BSSA)
Contact A Gilberthorpe
✉ **44 Stonegate, York, North Yorkshire, YO1 8AS**
☎ 01904 621666 Ⓕ 01904 644400
Ⓦ www.yorkantiquescentre.co.uk
Est. 1999 *Stock size* Large
No. of dealers 60
Stock General antiques
Open Mon–Sun 9am–6pm

Collectors Corner
Contact Mr K Richards
✉ **16 George Hudson Street, York, North Yorkshire, YO1 6WR** Ⓟ
☎ 01904 628789 Ⓕ 01904 628789
Ⓔ enquiries@railcollector.demon.co.uk
Est. 1998 *Stock size* Large
Stock Railway antiquities, memorabilia
Open Mon–Sat 9.30am–5.30pm
Fairs Sheffield, Malton, Kidlington
Services Valuations

Jack Duncan
Contact Mr Jack Duncan
✉ **36 Fossgate, York, North Yorkshire, YO1 9TF** Ⓟ
☎ 01904 641389 Ⓕ 01904 672184
Est. 1984 *Stock size* Medium
Stock Antique, scholarly, and second-hand books, English literature a speciality
Open Mon–Sat 10am–5.30pm

Mike Fineron Cigarette Cards & Postcards
Contact Mike Fineron
28 The Pastures, Dringhouses, York, North Yorkshire, YO24 2JE
01904 703911
Est. 1997 *Stock size* Medium
Stock Cigarette cards, postcards, Yorkshire postcards a speciality
Open By appointment
Fairs Pudsey, Chester Le Street
Services Valuations, postal service

French House Antiques
Contact Steve
74 Micklegate, York, North Yorkshire, YO1 6LF
01904 624465 F 01904 629965
E info@thefrenchhouse.co.uk
W www.thefrenchhouse.co.uk
Est. 1995 *Stock size* Large
Stock Antique French furniture
Open Mon–Sat 9.30am–5.30pm
Services Restorations

Harpers Jewellers Ltd
Contact Jonathan Scatchard
2–6 Minster Gates, York, North Yorkshire, YO1 7HL
01904 632634 F 01904 673370
E harplist@aol.com
W www.vintage-watches.co.uk
Est. 1990 *Stock size* Large
Stock Jewellery
Open Mon–Sat 9am–5.30pm
Services Valuations

Hudsons of York
Contact Mr I Hudson
8 The Stonebow, York, North Yorkshire, YO1 7NY
01904 643131 F 01904 643132
M 07050 136828
E enq@hudsonsofyork.com
W www.hudsonsofyork.com
Est. 1997 *Stock size* Large
Stock General antiques, European and oak furniture
Open Mon–Sat 9.30am–5pm Sun 11am–4pm
Fairs Newark, Swinderby

Hunts Pine (GADAR)
Contact Mr W Dougherty
Unit 6a, Victoria Farm, Water Lane, York, North Yorkshire, YO30 6PQ
01904 690561 F 01904 690561
Est. 1995 *Stock size* Medium
Stock Antique pine furniture
Open Mon–Fri 9am–5.30pm Sat 9am–2pm
Fairs Newark
Services Stripping

Laurel Bank Antiques
Contact Mr K Lamb
52 Clarence Street, York, North Yorkshire, YO31 7EW
01904 676030 F 01904 438700
Est. 1997 *Stock size* Medium
Stock General antiques, collectables, Georgian–Edwardian furniture, longcase, wall and mantel clocks
Open Mon–Sat 10am–5pm closed Tues Sun
Services Restorations, French polishing

Minster Antiques
Contact Mr M Tanner
24 Goodramgate, York, North Yorkshire, YO1 7LG
01904 655481
Est. 1982 *Stock size* Medium
Stock General antiques
Open Mon–Sat 10am–5pm
Fairs Newark

Minstergate Bookshop (PBFA)
Contact Mr N Wallace
8 Minster Gates, York, North Yorkshire
01904 621812 F 01904 622960
E rarebooks@minstergatebooks.co.uk
W www.minstergatebooks.co.uk
Est. 1977 *Stock size* Medium
Stock Books, children's and illustrated a speciality
Open Mon–Sun 10am–5.30pm
Services Valuations, book search

The Mulberry Bush Antique Shop
Contact Mr P A Young
36 Goodramgate, York, North Yorkshire, YO1 7LF
01904 638842 F 01904 468665
E mulberryan@aol.com
W www.yorkantiques.co.uk
Est. 1994 *Stock size* Medium
Stock General antiques, watercolours, oils, clocks
Open Mon–Sat 9.30am–5pm
Services Clock and furniture restorations, valuations

Janette Ray Rare Books (PBFA ABA)
Contact Miss J Ray
8 Bootham, York, North Yorkshire, YO30 7BL
01904 623088 F 01904 625528
E books@janetteray.co.uk
W www.janetteray.co.uk
Est. 1995 *Stock size* Medium
Stock Architectural and decorative arts, rare and second-hand books, landscape design, gardens, specializing in 19thC Arts and Crafts, Art Deco, Modernism
Open Fri–Sat 10am–5pm other times by appointment
Fairs York PBFA, London PBFA
Services Book search, valuations

The Red House Antique Centre
Contact Mrs P Stephenson
Duncombe Place, York, North Yorkshire, YO1 2EF
01904 637000 F 01904 637000
W www.redhouseyork.co.uk
Est. 1999
No. of dealers 60
Stock Date-lined stock
Open Mon–Wed 9.30am–5.30pm Thurs–Sat 9.30am–8pm Sun 10.30am–5.30pm
Services Antiques and arts lecture programmes, café and restaurant, antiques parties, courier service

John Simpson (ASVA)
Contact Mr John Simpson
4 Forest Grove, York, North Yorkshire, YO3 0BL
01904 424797
Est. 1984
Open By appointment
Sales General antiques
Frequency Quarterly
Catalogues Yes

J Smith (BNTA)
Contact Mr J Smith
47 Shambles, York, North Yorkshire, YO1 7LX
01904 654769 F 01904 677988
Est. 1963 *Stock size* Large
Stock Coins, stamps, medals
Open Mon–Sat 9am–4.30pm
Services Valuations

Ken Spelman (ABA, PBPA, ILAB)
Contact P Miller or A Fothergill
70 Micklegate, York, North Yorkshire, YO1 6LF
01904 624414 F 01904 626276
E rarebooks@kenspelman.com
W www.kenspelman.com
Stock size Large

Stock Antique, rare, second-hand books
Open Mon–Sat 9am–5.30pm
Fairs Olympia
Services Valuations, restorations, catalogues

Stable Antiques
Contact Mrs Y Kitching-Walker
Cabinet 2, Stonegate Antiques Centre, 41 Stonegate, York, North Yorkshire, YO1 8AW
☎ 01904 613888
Est. 1996 *Stock size* Medium
Stock General antiques, porcelain
Open Mon–Sun 8.30am–5.30pm
Services Valuations

Stonegate Antiques Centre (BSSA)
Contact Mr Gilberthorpe
41 Stonegate, York, North Yorkshire, YO1 8AW
☎ 01904 613888 F 01904 644400
W www.yorkantiquescentre.co.uk
Est. 1996 *Stock size* Large
No. of dealers 120
Stock General antiques
Open Mon–Sun 9am–6pm
Services Café

Taikoo Books Ltd
Contact Mr David Chilton
46 Bootham, York, North Yorkshire, YO30 7BZ P
☎ 01904 641213
Est. 1978 *Stock size* Medium
Stock Books on Africa and the Orient
Open Mon–Fri 10am–5pm or by appointment

York Antiques Centre
Contact Mr S Revere
2 Lendal, York, North Yorkshire, YO1 8AA
☎ 01904 641445
Est. 1984 *Stock size* Large
No. of dealers 15
Stock General antiques
Open Mon–Sat 10am–5pm

York Vale Antiques (GADAR)
Contact Mr W Dougherty
Unit 6a, Victoria Farm, Water Lane, York, North Yorkshire, YO30 6PQ P
☎ 01904 690561 F 01904 690561
Est. 1995 *Stock size* Medium
Stock General antique furniture
Open Mon–Fri 9am–5.30pm Sat 9am–2pm
Fairs Newark
Services Restorations, repairs

SOUTH YORKSHIRE

BARNSLEY

BBR Auctions
Contact Mr Alan Blakeman
Elsecar Heritage Centre, Barnsley, South Yorkshire, S74 8HJ P
☎ 01226 745156 F 01226 361561
E sales@bbrauctions.co.uk
W www.bbrauction.co.uk
Est. 1979
Open Mon–Fri 9am–4pm
Sales Antique bottles and pot lids, 3 per annum. Antique advertising every 6 months. Doulton, Beswick and 20thC pottery, 2 per annum. Kitchenware, 2 per annum. Breweriana and pub jugs, 2 per annum. All sales Sun 11am, viewing full week prior 9am–5pm
Catalogues Yes

BAWTRY

Peter Young Auctioneers
Contact Mr P Young
Doncaster Road, Bawtry, Doncaster, South Yorkshire, DN10 6NQ P
☎ 01302 711770 F 01302 711770
M 07801 079818
E auction@auction.demon.co.uk
W www.auction.demon.co.uk
Est. 1961
Open Mon–Fri 9.30am–5.30pm
Sales Antiques and collectables Sat 10am, viewing Fri 4–9pm Sat 9–10am. Quarterly antiques and collectables sales. Held at Lord Barnby Memorial Hall, Blyth
Frequency Every month
Catalogues Yes

BENTLEY

Phoenix Trading Company – South Yorkshire
Contact John A Hallam
127–129 Askern Road, Bentley, Doncaster, South Yorkshire, DN5 0JH P
☎ 01302 872547 F 01302 875735
M 07801 631072
E JHallamPTC@aol.com
Est. 1995 *Stock size* Large
Stock Georgian–Victorian furniture, shipping items, brass, copper, ceramics, silver, curios
Open Mon–Sat 9am–5pm
Fairs Newark, Harrogate
Services Restorations, repairs, valuations

BIRDWELL

Birdwell Lodge Craft & Antiques Centre
Contact Mrs C Vaines
Pilley Lane, Birdwell, Barnsley, South Yorkshire, S70 5UD P
☎ 01226 743489
M 07714 353481
Est. 1998 *Stock size* Large
Stock Crafts, new hand-painted, stained glass, dolls' houses, dolls' furniture, antique jewellery, pottery, furniture, paintings
Open Mon 1pm–4pm Tues–Sun 11am–4pm closed Fri
Services Painting classes, sugar craft, coffee shop

CAWTHORNE

Cawthorne Antiques Centre
Contact Mr P Gates
2 Church Street, Cawthorne Village, Barnsley, South Yorkshire, S75 4HP P
☎ 01226 792237
Est. 1997 *Stock size* Large
No. of dealers 50
Stock Wide range of antique stock, collectables
Open Mon–Sat 10am–4pm Sun 10.30am–4.30pm closed Wed
Services Tea room

Madalyn S Jones (PBFA)
Contact Ms M S Jones
Unit 14, Cawthorne Antiques Centre, Cawthorne Village, Nr Cannon Hall, Cawthorne, South Yorkshire, S75 4HP P
☎ 01226 792237
Est. 1979 *Stock size* Small
Stock Antiquarian, rare, second-hand books
Trade only Yes
Open Tues–Sat 10am–4pm Sun 10.30am–4.30pm

Fairs PBFA
Services Out-of-print search, valuations, occasional sculpture catalogues

DONCASTER

Harrison Sales
Contact Mr F Harrison
3 Carr Hill, Balby, Doncaster, South Yorkshire, DN4 8BS P
☎ 01302 769400 F 01302 812958
Est. 1995
Open Mon–Sat 9am–6pm
Sales Antiques sale last Sat of the month 11am, viewing day prior noon–7pm Sat 9am–11am. Weekly general sale Sat noon, viewing Fri 4–7pm Sat 9am–noon
Frequency Monthly
Catalogues Yes

ECCLESFIELD

Any Old Iron
Contact Miss Leigh Bell
10 Town End Road, Ecclesfield, Sheffield, South Yorkshire, S35 9YY P
☎ 0114 257 7117
M 07971 522448
Est. 1996 *Stock size* Large
Stock Victorian cast-iron fireplaces
Open Thurs–Sun 10am–5pm
Fairs Swinderby, Newark
Services Restorations

Courthouse Antiques Centre
Contact Mrs S M Grayson
2–6 Town End Road, Ecclesfield, Sheffield, South Yorkshire, S35 9YY P
☎ 0114 257 0641
Est. 1994 *Stock size* Large
No. of dealers 35
Stock Town and country furniture, jewellery, kitchenware, clocks, textiles, decorative items, French furniture, mirrors, lighting
Open Mon–Sat 10.30am–5pm Sun 11.30am–5pm

GREAT HOUGHTON

Farmhouse Antiques
Contact Mrs A Calvert
7 High Street, Great Houghton, Barnsley, South Yorkshire, S72 0AA P
☎ 01226 754057
Est. 1992 *Stock size* Small
Stock 19th–20thC decorative furniture, associated objects, Art Deco, Susie Cooper
Open Mon Sat 10am–noon 1–5pm or by appointment
Fairs NEC
Services Free advice on values and laying out of rooms on premises

KILLAMARSH

Havenplan Ltd
Contact Mrs M Buckle
The Old Station, Station Road, Killamarsh, Sheffield, South Yorkshire, S21 1EN P
☎ 0114 248 9972 F 0114 248 9972
M 07720 635889
Est. 1972 *Stock size* Large
Stock Mainly Victorian pine furniture, architectural items, panelling, doors, fireplaces, troughs, gates, lighting
Open Tues–Sat 10am–3pm
Services Prop hire

PARKGATE

John Shaw Antiques Ltd
Contact Ms D Ellis
The Old Methodist Chapel, Broad Street, Parkgate, Rotherham, South Yorkshire, S62 6DL P
☎ 01709 522340 F 01709 528593
Est. 1969 *Stock size* Large
Stock Wide range of Victorian–Edwardian furniture, clocks, pictures, mirrors etc
Open Mon–Fri 9am–5pm Sat 9.30am–5pm
Services Valuations Sat 10am–noon

PENISTONE

Penistone Pine & Antiques
Contact Mr P W Lucas
Unit 2–3, Sheffield Road, Penistone, Sheffield, South Yorkshire, S36 6HG P
☎ 01226 370018
Est. 1985 *Stock size* Large
Stock Antique, original Victorian pine furniture
Open Mon–Sat 9am–5pm
Services Restorations, stripping

ROTHERHAM

Roger Appleyard Ltd (LAPADA)
Contact Roger Appleyard
Fitzwilliam Road, Eastwood Trading Estate, Rotherham, South Yorkshire, S65 1SL P
☎ 01709 367670 F 01709 829395
E apple.antiques@dial.pipex.com
Est. 1971 *Stock size* Large
Stock Turn-of-the-century and shipping furniture
Trade only Yes
Open Mon–Fri 8am–5pm
Services Shipping

SHEFFIELD

Abbeydale Antiques
Contact Mr D Barks
639 Abbeydale Road, Sheffield, South Yorkshire, S7 1TB P
☎ 0114 255 5646 F 0114 255 2555
Est. 1974 *Stock size* Large
Stock 1950s furniture
Open By appointment

Acorn Antiques
Contact Mr B Priest
298 Abbeydale Road, Sheffield, South Yorkshire, S7 1FL P
☎ 0114 255 5348 F 0114 225 5348
E info@acornantique.co.uk
Est. 1988 *Stock size* Large
Stock General antiques, small furniture, collectables
Open Mon–Sat 10am–6pm

Antics
Contact Bronwen Stone
224 Abbeydale Road, Sheffield, South Yorkshire, S7 1FL P
☎ 0114 255 1664 F 0114 250 8480
M 07812 517331
E anticantiques@hotmail.com
Est. 1997 *Stock size* Large
Stock Furniture, fireplaces, dressers, oil paintings, old French enamelled fires, soft furnishings, contemporary design
Open Mon–Sat 10am–5pm Sun by appointment
Fairs Newark
Services Advice on furniture renovation, reupholstery

Banners Collectors & Antiques Centre
Contact Miss S Bates
Banners Business Centre, Attercliffe Road, Sheffield, South Yorkshire, S9 3QS
0114 244 0742
Est. 1997 *Stock size* Large
No. of dealers 40
Stock Wide range of antiques, collectables, Wade, Beanies, McDonald's, clocks etc
Open Mon–Sat 10am–5pm Sun 11am–5pm
Services Lists of goods wanted, deliveries, all collectables bought

Barmouth Court Antique Centre
Contact Mr M J Taylor
Abbeydale, Sheffield, South Yorkshire, S7 2DH
0114 255 2711
07970 437248
Est. 1999 *Stock size* Large
No. of dealers 60
Stock Complete range of antiques, Art Deco, collectables
Open Mon–Sat 10am–5pm Sun 11am–4pm
Services Valuations

Beech House
Contact Mr M Beech
361 Abbeydale Road, Sheffield, South Yorkshire, S7 1FS
0114 250 1004 0114 250 1004
beech.house@lineone.net
Est. 1996 *Stock size* Medium
Stock Rustic country pine furniture, cupboards, tables, dressers, chairs, fine art
Open Mon–Sat 10am–5pm closed Thurs or by appointment
Fairs Newark, Swinderby

Calico by Carol Anne
Contact Mrs C Slack
35 Abbey Lane, Sheffield, South Yorkshire, S8 0BJ
0114 249 3131
www.woodseats.com
Est. 1991 *Stock size* Large
Stock Antique and reproduction giftware, decorative items, Tiffany lamps
Open Mon–Sat 10am–4.30pm

Chapel Antiques Centre
Contact Miss K Sleath
99 Broadfield Road, Sheffield, South Yorkshire, S8 0XQ
0114 258 8288 0114 258 8288
Est. 1997 *Stock size* Large
No. of dealers 20
Stock Wide range of antique stock including French beds, textiles, trimmings
Open Mon–Sat 10am–5pm Sun Bank Holidays 11am–5pm
Services Restorations, upholstery, finding service

Cobwebs
Contact Mrs S Sleath
208 Whitham Road, Sheffield, South Yorkshire, S10 2SS
0114 268 1923
07836 765695
Est. 1979 *Stock size* Medium
Stock Wide range of French decorative items, small furniture etc
Open Mon Wed Fri Sat 10am–5pm
Fairs Sheffield City Fairs

A E Dowse & Son (NAVA)
Contact Michael Dowse ANAVA
Cornwall Galleries, Scotland Street, Sheffield, South Yorkshire, S3 7DE
0114 272 5858 0114 249 0550
www.aedowseandson.com
Est. 1915
Open Mon–Fri 9.30am–4pm
Sales Antiques and collectables monthly. Fine art and antiques quarterly Wed 11am. Die-cast, tinplate and collectors' toys quarterly Sat 11am, viewing for Wed sales Mon 4–7pm Tues 10am–7pm Wed 9–11am, viewing for Sat sales Fri 2.30–7.30pm Sat 9.30am–11am
Frequency Monthly
Catalogues Yes

E L R Auctions Ltd
Contact Liz Dashper
The Nichols Building, Shalesmoor, Sheffield, South Yorkshire, S3 8UJ
0114 281 6161 0114 281 6162
liz.dashper@virgin.net
www.elrauctions.com
Est. 1840
Open Mon–Fri 9am–5pm
Sales Quarterly antiques Fri 10.30am, viewing Wed 2–7.30pm Thurs 9am–7.30pm Fri 8.30am–sale. Antiques and collectables Fri 11am, viewing Thurs 10am–6.30pm Fri 9–11am
Frequency Fortnightly
Catalogues Yes

Filibuster & Booth Ltd
Contact Mr A Booth
158 Devonshire Street, Sheffield, South Yorkshire, S3 7SG
0114 275 2311
Stock Unusual, eclectic mixture of genuine things
Open Please telephone, times irregular
Services Valuations

Just Military Ltd
Contact Mr T Smith
701 Abbeydale Road, Sheffield, South Yorkshire, S7 2BE
0114 255 0536
Est. 1994 *Stock size* Large
Stock Militaria, WWI–Falklands. 1940s clothing, memorabilia, uniforms etc
Open Mon–Fri 10am–4.30pm Sat 10am–5pm
Services Medal mounting, uniform hire

Nichols Antique Centre
Contact Mr T Vickers
Nichols Building, Shalesmoor, Sheffield, South Yorkshire, S3 8UJ
0114 281 2811 0114 281 2812
Est. 1994 *Stock size* Large
No. of dealers 65
Stock Wide range of antique stock, specializing in Victorian furniture
Open Mon–Sun 10.30am–5pm
Services In-house auctioneers, French polishing

Paraphenalia
Contact W K Keller
66–68 Abbeydale Road, Sheffield, South Yorkshire, S7 1FD
0114 255 0203
Est. 1969 *Stock size* Large
Stock Large range of antique stock including porcelain, glass, light fittings, brass, iron beds, chimney pots, kitchenware
Open Mon–Sat 9.30am–5pm

Phillips International Auctioneers and Valuers
9 Paradise Square, Sheffield, South Yorkshire, S1 2DE
0114 272 8728 0114 275 0580
www.phillips-auction.com
Sales Regional Saleroom. Telephone for details

Renishaw Antique & Pine Centre
Contact Mr B Findley
32 Main Road, Sheffield, South Yorkshire, S21 3UT P
☎ 01246 435521
Est. 1988 *Stock size* Medium
Stock Victorian–Edwardian and 1930s furniture, pine, architectural items
Open Mon–Fri 8am–1pm Sun 11am–2pm

N P and A Salt Antiques (LAPADA)
Contact Mrs Annette Salt
Barmouth Court Antiques Centre, Barmouth Road, Sheffield, South Yorkshire, S7 2DH P
☎ 0114 2552711 F 0114 2582672
M 07801 101363
Est. 2000 *Stock size* Large
Stock General antiques, collectables, furniture, jewellery, toys
Open Mon–Sat 10am–5pm Sun 11am–4pm
Services Restorations

Sheffield Antiques Emporium
Contact Mr S Sleath
15–19 Clyde Road, Sheffield, South Yorkshire, S8 0YD P
☎ 0114 258 4863 F 0114 255 5609
Est. 1994 *Stock size* Large
No. of dealers 50
Stock Wide range of antique stock
Open Mon–Sat 10am–5pm Sun 11am–5pm

Michael J Taylor Antiques
Contact Michael Taylor
Barmouth Court Antiques Centre, Barmouth Road, Sheffield, South Yorkshire, S7 2DH P
☎ 01226 340595
M 07970 437248
Est. 1995 *Stock size* Large
Stock Georgian–Edwardian furniture, porcelain
Open Mon–Sat 10am–5pm Sun 11am–4pm
Services Valuations

Tilleys Vintage Magazine Shop
Contact Mr A Tilley
281 Shoreham Street, Sheffield, South Yorkshire, S1 4SS P
☎ 0114 275 2442 F 0114 275 2442
M 07939 066872
E tilleys281@aol.com
W www.tilleysmagazines.com
Est. 1978 *Stock size* Large
Stock Antique, rare, second-hand books, magazines
Open Mon 1.30–4.30pm Tues–Fri 10am–4.30pm Sat 10am–1.30pm 3.15–4.30pm

Top Hat Antique Centre
Contact Mr R Crabtree
529 Ecclesall Road, Sheffield, South Yorkshire, S11 8PR P
☎ 0114 266 6876
M 07946 277814
Est. 1992 *Stock size* Large
Stock Collectables, porcelain, clocks, furniture, nautical items, spelter, bronzes etc
Open Mon–Fri 10am–4pm Sat 10am–5pm closed Thurs noon–4pm
Services Valuations, re-caning, French polishing, clock and barometer repairs

Vision Thing
Contact Miss Jin Brook
368 Abbeydale Road, Sheffield, South Yorkshire, S7 1FH P
☎ 0114 255 5896 F 0114 255 5896
M 07714 207797
E webmaster@sheffieldscene.co.uk
W www.sheffieldscene.co.uk.
Est. 1984 *Stock size* Large
Stock Period interiors 1840–1960 chenilles, linen, quilts, cushions etc, decorative items, period clothing
Open Thurs Fri Sat 10am–5.30pm Wed 1–5pm or by appointment
Fairs Swinderby
Services Theatrical costumes made

Paul Ward Antiques
Contact Paul or Christine Ward
Owl House, 8 Burnell Road, Sheffield, South Yorkshire, S6 2AX P
☎ 0114 233 5980 F 0114 233 5980
M 07702 309000
Est. 1977 *Stock size* Large
Stock Country chairs
Trade only Yes
Open By appointment only

Y S F Books Ltd
Contact Mr R Eldridge or Mrs J Eldridge
365 Sharrowvale Road, Sheffield, South Yorkshire, S11 8ZG P
☎ 0114 268 0687
E ysf@globalnet.co.uk
W www.ysfbooks.com
Est. 1986 *Stock size* Large
Stock General range of antiquarian, rare, and second-hand books
Open Mon–Sat 9am–5pm

THURCROFT

Wilkinson & Beighton
Contact Miss S Lally
Woodhouse Green, Thurcroft, Rotherham, South Yorkshire, S66 9AQ P
☎ 01709 700005 F 01709 700244
E wb.auctioneers@virgin.net
W www.wb-auctioneers.co.uk
Est. 1987
Open Mon–Fri 9am–5pm
Sales Antiques and general Sun 11am, viewing Fri prior 2–5pm Sun 9–11am. Quarterly fine art sales Sun 11am, see press for details
Frequency Fortnightly
Catalogues Yes

WADWORTH

Whittontique Curios & Collectables
Contact M Leaney
1 Main Street, Wadworth, Doncaster, South Yorkshire, DH9 11AY P
☎ 01302 850339 F 0870 131 4197
M 07808 755444
E m.leaney@talk21.co.uk
W www.whittontique.co.uk
Est. 1994 *Stock size* Small
Stock Pottery, porcelain, clocks, curios, collectables
Open By appointment
Fairs Newark, Ardingly, Harrogate

WENTWORTH

Holly Farm Antiques
Contact Mrs L Hardwick
Holly Farm, Harley, Wentworth, Rotherham, South Yorkshire, S62 7UD P
☎ 01226 744077
Est. 1989 *Stock size* Medium
Stock Porcelain, Coalport,

Worcester, Rockingham, silver, silver plate, jewellery, mirrors, furniture, lamps etc
Open Sat Sun 10am–5pm weekdays by appointment
Services Valuations

WEST YORKSHIRE

ABERFORD

Aberford Country Furniture
Contact J W H Long
Hicklam House, Aberford, Leeds, West Yorkshire, LS25 3DP P
☎ 0113 281 3209 F 0113 281 3121
M 07712 657867
E johnwhlong@aol.com
W www.aberfordpine.co.uk
Est. 1973 *Stock size* Medium
Stock Oak and pine country furniture
Open Tues–Sat 9am–5.30pm Sun 10am–5.30pm
Services Restorations

BAILDON

The Baildon Furniture Co
Contact Mr R Parker
Spring Mills, Otley Road, Baildon, Bradford, West Yorkshire, BD17 6AD P
☎ 01274 414345 F 01274 414345
E baildonfurniture@aol.com
Est. 1974 *Stock size* Large
Stock General antique furniture
Open Mon–Sat 10.30am–4.30pm
Services Valuations, restorations

Browgate Antiques
Contact Mrs D Shaw
13 Browgate, Baildon, Shipley, West Yorkshire, BD17 6BP P
☎ 01274 597494
Est. 1995 *Stock size* Medium
Stock Georgian–Victorian furniture, clocks, porcelain
Open Mon–Sun 10.30am–5pm closed Thurs
Services Valuations

BATLEY

Batley Auction House
Contact Mr K Tuckwell
8–10 Station Road, Batley, West Yorkshire, WF17 5SU P
☎ 01924 472301 F 01924 472301
E angie@jessops.10@freeserve.co.uk
W www.batley/antiques.webjump.com
Est. 1996
Open Mon–Sat 8am–4pm Sun 10am–4pm
Sales General antiques, fine arts last Mon of each month
Frequency Monthly
Catalogues Yes

Jessops Antique Village
Contact Mr K Tuckwell
8–10 Station Road, Batley, West Yorkshire, WF17 5SU P
☎ 01924 478002 F 01924 472301
E angie@jessops.10@freeserve.co.uk
W www.batley/antiques.webjump.com
Est. 1996 *Stock size* Large
No. of dealers 40
Stock General antiques, collectables
Services Valuations, restorations, restaurant

Tansu
Contact Mr N Hall or Mr C Battye
Red Brick Mill, 218 Bradford Road, Batley Carr, Batley, West Yorkshire, WF17 6JF P
☎ 01924 460044 F 01924 462844
E tansu@uktansu.co.uk
W www.tansu.co.uk
Est. 1992 *Stock size* Large
Stock Japanese antique furniture
Open Mon–Sat 9.30am–5.30pm Sun 11am–5pm
Fairs NEC Antiques for Everyone, BBC Good Homes
Services Storage, restorations, valuations, customer pickup service from airports and train stations

Dale Wood & Co
Contact Mr Dale Wood
20 Station Road, Batley, West Yorkshire, WF17 5SU P
☎ 01924 479439 F 01924 472291
M 07711 645236
Est. 1989
Open Mon–Fri 9am–5pm
Sales General antiques and general furnishings
Frequency Fortnightly
Catalogues Yes

BINGLEY

Antique Interiors
Contact Mrs L Dickens
16 Mornington Road, Bingley, West Yorkshire, BD16 4NJ P
☎ 01274 568024 F 01274 568024
Est. 1993 *Stock size* Medium
Stock Victorian–Edwardian furniture, china, glass
Open Mon–Sat 10am–6pm Sun noon–6pm
Services Restorations

BRADFORD

Cottingly Antiques
Contact Mr P Nobbs
286 Keighley Road, Bradford, West Yorkshire, BD9 4LH P
☎ 01274 545829
Est. 1979 *Stock size* Medium
Stock General antiques, pine furniture
Open Tues–Sat 9am–4.30pm
Services Restorations

de Rome
Contact Mr S Le Blancq
12 New John Street, Bradford, West Yorkshire, BD1 2QY
☎ 01274 734116 F 01274 729970
W www.deromes.co.uk
Est. 1948
Open Mon–Fri 9am–5.15pm
Sales General antiques
Frequency Periodic
Catalogues Yes

Windle & Co
Contact Mr A Windle
535 Great Horton Road, Bradford, West Yorkshire, BD7 4EG P
☎ 01274 572998 F 01274 572998
Est. 1971
Open Mon–Thurs 9.15am–5.30pm Fri 9.15am–noon
Sales General antiques sales Wed 6.30pm
Frequency Weekly

BRAMHAM

Priory Furnishing
Contact Mr or Mrs J Furniss
The Biggin', Bramham Park, Bramham, West Yorkshire, LS2 3 6LR P
☎ 01937 843259 F 01937 843259
E jeanette@priory-oak-furniture.in2home.co.uk
Est. 1992 *Stock size* Large
Stock 17th–18thC oak, mahogany, walnut furniture
Open Tues–Sun 10am–5pm
Services Valuations

BURLEY IN WHARFEDALE

Beacon Antiques
Contact L Cousins
128 Main Street, Burley in Wharfedale, West Yorkshire, LS29 7JP
☎ 01943 864095
Ⓜ 07887 812858
Ⓔ les@beacon-antiques.co.uk
Ⓦ beacon-antiques.co.uk
Est. 1994 *Stock size* Medium
Stock Porcelain, silver, small Georgian–Edwardian furniture
Open Tues Wed 12.30–4.30pm Thurs Fri 10.30am–4.30pm Sat 9.30am–1pm
Fairs Harrogate, Stafford

BURTON SALMON

Old Hall Antiques
Contact Mr J Fenteman
21 Main Street, Burton Salmon, Leeds, West Yorkshire, LS25 5JS
☎ 01977 607778
Est. 1998 *Stock size* Large
Stock Antique oak and country furniture
Open Tues–Sun 10am–5pm

CROSS HILLS

Heathcote Antiques
Contact Mr M Webster
Skipton Road Junction Crossroads, Cross Hills, Keighley, West Yorkshire, BD20 7DS
☎ 01535 635250/635703
Ⓕ 01535 637205
Ⓜ 07836 259640
Est. 1974 *Stock size* Large
Stock General antiques, original English unstripped pine, pottery, porcelain
Open Wed Thurs Fri Sat 10am–5.30pm Sun 12.30–4.30pm

DENBY DALE

Worlds Apart
Contact Mrs Sharon Dawson
Unit 6A, Springfield Mill, Norman Road, Denby Dale, Huddersfield, West Yorkshire, HD8 8TH
☎ 01484 866713
Ⓜ 07801 349960
Ⓔ shaz@chris216.fsnet.co.uk
Est. 1995 *Stock size* Large
Stock Antiques, collectables
Open Mon–Sat 10am–5pm Sun noon–5pm

DEWSBURY

Collectors Corner
Contact Mr Tranter
246 Lees Hall Road, Dewsbury, West Yorkshire, WF12 9HF
☎ 01924 464111 Ⓕ 01924 464111
Est. 1995 *Stock size* Medium
Stock General collectables
Open Mon–Fri 9.30am–3.30pm Sat 9am–noon
Fairs Newark, Leeds
Services Valuations

FAIRBURN

Fairburn Books (PBFA)
Contact Elaine Lonsdale
8 Manor Court, Fairburn, Knottingley, West Yorkshire, WF11 9NY
☎ 01977 678193
Ⓜ 07710 480581
Ⓔ elaine.lonsdale@barclays.net.
Est. 1987 *Stock size* Medium
Stock Antique, rare, second-hand books, literature, social history, bindings, local topography a speciality
Open Daily by appointment
Fairs PBFA, Kemswell Antiques Centre
Services Book binding, repairs, restorations, valuations

FEATHERSTONE

A645 Trading Post
Contact Mr G Thomas
Chapel Works, Wakefield Road, Featherstone, Pontefract, West Yorkshire, WF7 5HL
☎ 01977 695255
Est. 1982 *Stock size* Large
Stock Furniture, collectables, books, die-cast toys, ceramics
Open Mon–Sat 10am–5pm Sun 11am–5pm closed Wed

GREETLAND

West Vale Trading Post
Contact Mr T Gresty
61–63 Saddleworth Road, Greetland, West Vale, Halifax, West Yorkshire, HX4 8AG
☎ 01422 311630 Ⓕ 01422 311630
Est. 1989 *Stock size* Large
Stock General antiques, second-hand items
Open Wed–Sat 9am–5pm
Fairs Newark

HALIFAX

Antiquary Antiques
Contact Mrs B Hardy
231 King Cross Road, King Cross, Halifax, West Yorkshire, HX1 3JL
☎ 01422 341770
Est. 1990 *Stock size* Medium
Stock General antiques, Victorian furniture
Open Mon–Sat 10am–4.30pm closed Wed
Services Valuations

Collectors Old Toy Shop
Contact Simon Haley
89 Northgate, Halifax, West Yorkshire, HX1 1XF
☎ 01422 822148/360434
Ⓔ collectorsoldtoy@aol.com
Est. 1983 *Stock size* Medium
Stock Dinky, Corgi, die-casts, tin-plate toys, railways, money boxes
Open Mon–Sat 10.30am–4.30pm closed Thurs
Fairs Sandown Park, Harrogate International
Services Insurance valuations

Halifax Antique Centre
Contact Mr M Carroll
Queens Road, Halifax, West Yorkshire, HX1 4LR
☎ 01422 366657 Ⓕ 01422 369293
Ⓔ info@halifaxantiques.co.uk
Ⓦ www.halifaxantiques.co.uk
Est. 1981 *Stock size* Large
No. of dealers 30
Stock French and English furniture, Art Deco, costume, kitchenware, collectables
Open Tues–Sat 10am–5pm
Services Valuations, restorations, café

Muir Hewitt
Contact Mr M Hewitt
Halifax Antiques Centre, Queens Road, Gibbet Street, Halifax, West Yorkshire, HX1 4LR
☎ 01422 347377 Ⓕ 01422 347377
Ⓔ muir.hewitt@virgin.net
Ⓦ www.muir-hewitt.com/hewitt
Est. 1982 *Stock size* Large
Stock Art Deco ceramics, furniture, lighting etc
Open Tues–Sat 10am–5pm closed

Sun Mon, please telephone for seasonal time changes
Fairs Chester, Leeds Art Deco fairs
Services Valuations

⊞ Holmfirth Antiques
Contact Ken Priestley
✉ **Halifax Antiques Centre, Queens Road, Gibbet Street, Halifax, West Yorkshire, HX1 4LR** P
☎ 01484 686854 F 01484 686854
M 07973 533478
E kenpriestley@fonograf.demon.co.uk
W www.fonograf.demon.co.uk
Est. 1988 *Stock size* Medium
Stock Mechanical music, gramophones, phonographs
Open Tues–Sat 10am–5pm
Services Valuations, restorations, mail order

HAWORTH

⊞ Bingley Antiques
Contact J B or J Poole
✉ **Springfield Farm Estate, Flappit, Haworth, Keighley, West Yorkshire, BD21 5PT** P
☎ 01535 646666 F 01535 646666
E john@bingley-antiques.co.uk
W www.bingley-antiques.co.uk
Est. 1969 *Stock size* Large
Stock General antiques, see website
Open Tues–Fri 8.30am–5pm Sat 9.30am–5pm
Services Valuations

⊞ Yorkshire Relics
Contact Miss C Mettam or Mr S Ferguson
✉ **11 Main Street, Haworth, West Yorkshire, BD22 8DA** P
☎ 01535 642218 F 01535 642218
M 07971 701278/07974 531618
Est. 1987 *Stock size* Large
Stock Antiquarian and collectable books, records
Open Mon–Sun
Services Vintage-period packaging for hire for film, TV etc

HEBDEN BRIDGE

⊞ Cornucopia
Contact Mrs C Nassor
✉ **13 West End, Hebden Bridge, West Yorkshire, HX7 8JP** P
☎ 01422 844497
Est. 1974 *Stock size* Medium
Stock General antiques
Open Thurs–Fri Sun noon–5pm Sat 11am–5pm
Fairs Newark, Nottinghamshire

⊞ Re-Collections
Contact Mr A Cooper
✉ **24 Market Street, Hebden Bridge, West Yorkshire, HX7 6AA** P
☎ 01422 845764 F 01422 845764
M 07979 404757
E ae.cooper@talk21.com
Est. 1989 *Stock size* Medium
Stock Wide range of general antiques, furniture
Open Mon–Fri 10.30am–4pm Sat 11am–4.30pm Sun noon–5pm
Fairs Newark

⊞ G J Saville (LAPADA, BADA)
Contact Graham Saville
✉ **Foster Clough, Hebden Bridge, West Yorkshire, HX7 5QZ** P
☎ 01422 882808 F 01422 882808
M 07889 750711
E g.j.saville@btinternet.com
Est. 1968 *Stock size* Large

Stock 1750–1830 caricatures, caricature reference books
Open By appointment
Fairs Olympia, BADA
Services Valuations

Weather House Antiques (BADA, LAPADA)
Contact Kym Walker
Foster Clough, Hebden Bridge, West Yorkshire, HX7 5QZ P
01422 882808/886961 (workshop) F 01422 882808
M 07889 750711
E kymwalker@btinternet.com
Est. 1986
Stock Barometers, weather instruments
Open By appointment only
Fairs Olympia, BADA
Services Restorations

HOLMFIRTH

Old Friendship Antiques
Contact Mr C J Dobson
77 Dunford Road, Holmfirth, Huddersfield, West Yorkshire, HD7 1DT P
01484 682129
Est. 1984 *Stock size* Large
Stock Antique furniture, old pine, clocks
Open Mon–Fri 9.30am–5.30pm Sat 9am–4pm Sun 2–4pm
Fairs Newark
Services Pine stripping

William Sykes & Son
Contact Mr R Dixon
Sude Hill Saleroom, New Mill, 38 Huddersfield Road, Holmfirth, Huddersfield, West Yorkshire, HD7 1JH P
01484 683543 F 01484 683543
Est. 1866
Open Mon–Fri 9am–5.15pm Sat 9am–2pm Sun 11am–2pm
Sales General antiques every 3rd Friday
Frequency Every 3 weeks

Upperbridge Antiques
Contact Mr I Ridings
9 Huddersfield Road, Holmfirth, Huddersfield, West Yorkshire, HD7 1JR
01484 687200
Est. 1987 *Stock size* Medium
Stock General antiques
Open Wed–Sat 1–5pm Sun 2–5pm
Fairs Newark, Swinderby

HORBURY

Horbury Antique Workshop
Contact Mr J R Smithson
17 High Street, Horbury, Wakefield, West Yorkshire, WF4 5AB P
01924 271911
Est. 1997 *Stock size* Medium
Stock General antiques, Victorian–Edwardian furniture
Open Mon–Sat 9am–5pm
Services Restorations

John Walsh & Co.
Contact Mr J Walsh
55 Jenkin Road, Horbury, Wakefield, West Yorkshire, WF4 6DP P
01924 264030 F 01924 267758
M 07976 241587
E auctions@john-walsh.co.uk
W www.john-walsh.co.uk
Est. 1989
Open Mon–Fri 9am–6pm
Sales General antiques
Frequency Alternate months
Catalogues Yes

HUDDERSFIELD

Christopher J L Dawes
Contact Mr C Dawes
26 Lidget Street, Lindley, Huddersfield, West Yorkshire, HD3 3JP P
01484 649515
Est. 1999 *Stock size* Small
Stock General antiques, porcelain, glass, silver
Open Tues–Sat 10am–5pm closed Wed
Fairs Mytholmroyd, West Yorkshire

Huddersfield Picture Framing Co.
Contact Miss P Ward
Cloth Hall Street, Huddersfield, West Yorkshire, HD1 2EG P
01484 546075
Est. 1979 *Stock size* Medium
Stock Paintings, prints, swept frames, ovals, circles, mouldings etc
Open Mon Tues Thurs Fri 9am–5pm Wed 9am–1pm Sat 9am–4pm
Services Restorations, framing

Pat's Antique and Reproduction Pine Furniture and Gift Shop
Contact Pat or Jonathan Marsden
29–37 Beast Market, Huddersfield, West Yorkshire, HD1 1QF P
01484 430830 F 01484 431231
Est. 1987 *Stock size* Large
Stock Antique and reproduction pine furniture
Open Mon–Fri 10am–6pm Sat 10am–5.30pm Sun 11am–5pm
Services Furniture custom made to size, gift shop

Serendipity
Contact Mr Franco
1 Bridge Street, Huddersfield, West Yorkshire, HD4 6EL P
01484 428223
Est. 1988 *Stock size* Medium
Stock Situated in a Georgian coach house, selling general antiques, pine, porcelain, Victorian–Edwardian furniture
Open Wed–Sat 10.30am–5pm
Services Valuations, restorations

ILKLEY

Coopers of Ilkley (LAPADA)
Contact Charles Cooper
46–50 Leeds Road, Ilkley, West Yorkshire, LS29 8EQ P
01943 608020 F 01943 604321
E enquiries@coopersantiquesilkley
W www.coopersantiquesilkley
Stock size Medium
Stock Period and Victorian furniture
Open Mon–Fri 9am–1pm 2pm–5.30pm Sat 9am–5.30pm
Services Restorations

The Grove Bookshop (PBFA)
Contact Mr A Sharpe
10 The Grove, Ilkley, West Yorkshire, LS29 9EG P
01943 609335 F 01943 817086
E antiquarian@grovebookshop.co.uk
W www.grovebookshop.co.uk
Est. 1976 *Stock size* Medium
Stock Antiquarian, rare, and collectable books, specializing in Yorkshire topography, angling, field sports, literature
Open Mon–Sat 9am–5.30pm

Andrew Hartley Fine Arts (ISVA)
Contact Mr A D Hartley
Victoria Hall, Little Lane, Ilkley, West Yorkshire, LS29 8EA
01943 816363 F 01943 817610
E ahartley.finearts@talk21.com
Est. 1906
Open Mon–Fri 9am–5.30pm Sat 9am–12.30pm
Sales General antiques
Frequency Alternate months
Catalogues Yes

KEIGHLEY

Revival
Contact Peter Pryimuk
104–106 South Street, Keighley, West Yorkshire, BD21 1EH
01535 606837
Est. 1987 *Stock size* Medium
Stock General antiques, architectural items, pine, bric-a-brac
Open Mon–Sat 10am–5pm telephone call advisable

LEEDS

Abbey Auctions
Contact John Midgely
11 Morris Lane, Kirkstall, Leeds, West Yorkshire, LS5 3JT
0113 275 8787
Open Mon–Fri 8am–5pm Sat 8am–noon
Sales General antiques sales Tues 10am
Frequency Weekly
Catalogues No

Aquarius Antiques
Contact Peter McGlade
Abbey Mills, Abbey Road, Leeds, West Yorkshire, LS5 3HP
0113 278 9216
Est. 1979 *Stock size* Medium
Stock General antiques, Georgian–Victorian furniture
Open Mon–Sat 9am–5pm
Services Repairs, restorations

Cottage Antiques
Contact Mr D Atkinson
78 Otley Road, Leeds, West Yorkshire, LS6 4BA
0113 2955125
Est. 1993 *Stock size* Medium
Stock General antiques
Open Mon Thurs 11am–4pm Tues Wed Fri Sat 10am–5pm
Fairs Newark, Ardingly
Services Valuations, French polishing

Headrow Antiques
Contact Pat Cooper or Sally Hurrell
Level 3, The Headrow Shopping Centre, The Headrow, Leeds, West Yorkshire, LS1 6JE
0113 245 5344
Est. 1992 *Stock size* Large
No. of dealers 20
Stock General antiques
Open Mon–Sat 10am–5pm Nov Dec Thurs 10am–8pm Sun 11am–5pm

Leeds Antique Centre
Contact Mr A Brook
16 Globe Road, Leeds, West Yorkshire, LS11 5QG
0113 2423194
Est. 1989 *Stock size* Large
No. of dealers 16
Stock General antiques
Open Tues–Sat 10am–5pm Sun 11am–5pm

Phillips International Auctioneers and Valuers (SOFAA)
Contact Miss M Minshull
Hepper House, 17a East Parade, Leeds, West Yorkshire, LS1 2BH
0113 244 8011 F 0113 242 9875
E minshull@philmail.demon.co.uk
W www.phillips-auctions.com
Est. 1796
Open Mon–Fri 8.30am–5pm Sat 9am–noon by appointment
Sales General antiques and fine specialist sales 3–4 per month. Regional saleroom. Telephone for details
Catalogues Yes

Swiss Cottage Furniture
Contact Mr J Howorth
85 Westfield Crescent, Burley, Leeds, West Yorkshire, LS3 1DJ
0113 242 9994
W www.swisscottageantiques.com
Est. 1987 *Stock size* Large
Stock General antiques, salvage yard
Open Mon–Sat 10am–5pm Sun 1–5pm closed Tues
Fairs Newark

Woodstock Antiques
Contact Mr R J Link
134 Woodhouse Street, Leeds, West Yorkshire, LS6 2JN
0113 246 1296
Est. 1990 *Stock size* Medium
Stock General antiques
Open Mon–Sat 10am–5pm
Fairs Newark

Works of Iron
Contact Mr G Higgins
Beaver Works, 36 Whitehouse Street, Leeds, West Yorkshire, LS10 1AD
0113 234 0555 F 0113 234 2555
Est. 1985 *Stock size* Large
Stock Antique beds
Open Daily 11am–5pm
Services Valuations, restorations

Year Dot
Contact Mr A Glithro
16 Market Street Arcade, Leeds, West Yorkshire, LS1 6DH
0113 246 0860
Est. 1977 *Stock size* Medium
Stock General antiques, jewellery
Open Mon–Sat 9.30am–5pm
Fairs Newark

LEPTON

K L M & Co
Contact Mr K L Millington
Wakefield Road, Lepton, West Yorkshire, HD8 0EL
01484 607763 F 01484 607763
M 07860 671547
Est. 1981 *Stock size* Large
Stock Antiques, 1940s furniture
Open Mon–Sat 10.30am–5pm

LUDDENDENFOOT

Calder Valley Auctioneers (RICS)
Contact Mr I Peace
Fairlea Mill, Ellenholme Road, Luddendenfoot, Halifax, West Yorkshire, HX2 6EP
01422 8886648
Est. 1995
Open By appointment
Sales General antiques Thurs view day prior 2–7pm and morning of sale
Frequency Monthly
Catalogues Yes

MENSTON

⊞ J Hanlon Antiques
Contact Mrs J Hanlon
✉ **101 Bradford Road, Menston, Ilkley, West Yorkshire, LS29 6BU** P
☎ 01943 877634
Est. 1974 *Stock size* Medium
Stock Small collectables, textiles, jewellery, silver
Open Mon Thurs–Sat 2.30–5pm
Fairs Newark

⊞ Park Antiques
Contact Mr or Mrs Roe
✉ **2 North View, Main Street, Menston, Ilkley, West Yorkshire, LS29 6JU** P
☎ 01943 872392 F 01943 878004
M 07801 624530
E parkantiques@nr-ilkley.demon.co.uk
Est. 1975 *Stock size* Medium
Stock Fine-quality 19thC rosewood, walnut and mahogany furniture
Open Wed–Sat 10am–6pm Sun 10am–5pm
Services Upholstery

OTLEY

⊞ Mayfair Antiques
Contact Mr I Hughes
✉ **26 Cross Green, Otley, West Yorkshire, LS21 1HD** P
☎ 01943 463380 F 01943 463380
M 07802 740012
E ivor@frantique.fsnet.co.uk
W www.frantique.co.uk
Est. 1998 *Stock size* Large
Stock Continental decorative arts, including faïence, kitchen antiques, clocks, bronzes, stoves, metalware, architectural, enamelware
Open Mon–Sat 10am–6pm closed Sun Wed
Services Anglo-French antiques press relations

Wharfdale Farmers Auction Mart Ltd
Contact Mr E Sherwin
✉ **Leeds Road, Otley, West Yorkshire, LS21 3BD** P
☎ 01943 462172 F 01943 461135
E wfamotley1@mcmail.com
Est. 1893
Open Mon–Fri 9am–5pm
Sales General antiques
Frequency Periodic
Catalogues No

PONTEFRACT

⊞ Wards Collectables
Contact Mrs S Ward
✉ **53 South Avenue, Pontefract, West Yorkshire, WF8 4EW** P
☎ 01977 703970
Est. 1989 *Stock size* Small
Stock General antiques, collectables
Open By appointment
Fairs Newark

PUDSEY

⊞ Geary Antiques
Contact Mr J A Geary
✉ **114 Richardshaw Lane, Pudsey, Leeds, West Yorkshire, LS28 6BN** P
☎ 0113 256 4122
M 07802 441245
E jag@t-nlbi.demon.co.uk
Est. 1933 *Stock size* Large
Stock General antique English furniture
Open Mon–Sat 10am–5.30pm Sun noon–4pm
Services Restorations, interior design, furnishing fabrics, wallpapers

SALTAIRE

⊞ Mick Burt (Antique Pine)
Contact Andrew Draper
✉ **The Victoria Centre, 3–4 Victoria Road, Saltaire, Shipley, West Yorkshire, BD18 3LA** P
☎ 01274 530611 F 01274 533722
Est. 1994 *Stock size* Medium
Stock Restored antique pine furniture
Open Wed–Sun 10am–5pm
Services Restorations

⊞ Harwood Antiques
Contact Mr R Harwood
✉ **The Victoria Centre, 3–4 Victoria Road, Saltaire, Shipley, West Yorkshire, BD18 3LA** P
☎ 01274 874138
M 07885 137573
Est. 1974 *Stock size* Medium
Stock Antique furniture, clocks
Open Wed–Sun 10.30am–5.30pm
Services Valuations

⊞ John Lewis
✉ **The Victoria Centre, 3–4 Victoria Road, Saltaire, Shipley, West Yorkshire, BD18 3LA** P
☎ 01274 533722 F 01274 530611
Est. 1988 *Stock size* Large
Stock Burmantofts art pottery
Open Tues–Sun 10.30am–5.30pm
Fairs NEC, Alexandra Palace

⊞ Swan Antiques
Contact Mrs B Harwood
✉ **The Victoria Centre, 3–4 Victoria Road, Saltaire, Shipley, West Yorkshire, BD18 3LA** P
☎ 01274 533722
Est. 1998 *Stock size* Small
Stock General antiques, country furniture
Open Wed–Sun 10.30am–5.30pm

The Victoria Centre
Contact Mr Andrew Draper
✉ **3–4 Victoria Road, Saltaire, Shipley, West Yorkshire, BD18 3LA** P
☎ 01274 533722 F 01274 533722
E info@victoriacentre.co.uk
W www.victoriacentre.co.uk
Est. 1994 *Stock size* Large
No. of dealers 50
Stock General antiques, furniture, fine art and collectables
Open Wed–Sun 10.30am–5.30pm
Services Valuations, restorations

SHERBURN-IN-ELMET

Malcolms No1 Auctioneers & Valuers
Contact Mr M Dowson
✉ **The Chestnuts, 16 Park Avenue, Sherburn-in-Elmet, Leeds, West Yorkshire, LS25 6EF** P
☎ 01977 684971 F 01977 681046
M 07774 130784
Est. 1980
Open Mon–Fri 9am–5pm
Sales Antiques and collectables, named ceramics (all periods), 6 weekly Mon 6.30pm, viewing Sun 1–6pm Mon all day. Venue Trustees Hall, High Street, Boston Spa, Wetherby, North Yorkshire
Frequency 6 weekly
Catalogues Yes

SHIPLEY

⊞ Victoria Antiques
Contact Mr Andrew Draper
✉ **27–31 Atkinson Street, Shipley, West Yorkshire, BD18 3QS** 🅿
☎ 01274 533722 Ⓕ 01274 533722
Ⓔ info@victoriacentre.co.uk
Ⓦ www.victoriacentre.co.uk
Est. 1994 *Stock size* Large
Stock Furniture, including pine
Open Mon–Sun 10am–4.30pm
Services Valuations, restorations

SOWERBY BRIDGE

⊞ Old Cawsey Antiques
Contact Miss S Stirrup
✉ **22 Wharf Street, Sowerby Bridge, West Yorkshire, HX6 2AE** 🅿
☎ 01422 832140
Ⓜ 07711 519545
Est. 1989 *Stock size* Medium
Stock Early oak, country furniture, accessories
Open Tues–Sat 10am–4.30pm

⊞ Talking Points Antiques
Contact Mr Paul Austwick
✉ **66 West Street, Sowerby Bridge, West Yorkshire, HX6 3AP** 🅿
☎ 01422 834126
Ⓔ tpagrams@aol.com
Est. 1985
Stock General antiques
Open Thurs Fri Sat 10.30am–5.30pm and by appointment
Fairs NEC Vintage Communications Fair, Blackpool Vintage Technology Fair

WAKEFIELD

⊞ The Old Vicarage Bookshop
Contact Mr J Longfellow
✉ **24 Zetland Street, Wakefield, West Yorkshire, WF1 1QT**
☎ 01924 380432
Ⓔ vicarage.books@virgin.net
Est. 1987 *Stock size* Large
Stock Antique, rare, second-hand books
Open Daily 10.30am–5pm closed Wed Sun
Services Valuations

⊞ D Turner Antiques
Contact Miss D Turner
✉ **574 Leeds Road, Outwood, Wakefield, West Yorkshire, WS1 2DT**
☎ 01924 835942
Est. 1987 *Stock size* Small
Stock General antiques
Open Mon–Sat 11am–5pm closed Thurs
Services Valuations, house clearance

LINCOLNSHIRE

ALLINGTON

⊞ Garth Vincent Antique Arms and Armour (LAPADA)
Contact Garth Vincent
✉ **The Old Manor House, Allington, Nr Grantham, Lincolnshire, NG32 2DH** 🅿
☎ 01400 281358 Ⓕ 01400 282658
Ⓜ 077285 352151
Ⓔ garthvincent@compuserve.com
Ⓦ www.guns.co.uk
Est. 1980 *Stock size* Large
Stock International guns, swords, helmets, reproduction arms and armour
Open By appointment only
Fairs Birmingham and London Arms Fairs
Services Valuations

AYLESBY

⊞ Robin Fowler Period Clocks (LAPADA)
Contact Mr R Fowler
✉ **Washingdales, Washingdales Lane, Aylesby, Grimsby, Lincolnshire, DN37 7LH** 🅿
☎ 01472 751335 Ⓕ 01472 751335
Ⓜ 07949 141891
Ⓔ periodclocks@washingdales.fsnet.co.uk
Est. 1968 *Stock size* Large
Stock Antique clocks, barometers, scientific instruments
Open By appointment
Fairs LAPADA, Bailey, Galloway
Services Valuations, restorations

BARTON UPON HUMBER

⊞ Ken Mannion Fossils
Contact Mr K Mannion
✉ **59 Barrow Road, Barton upon Humber, Lincolnshire, DN18 6AE** 🅿
☎ 01652 634827 Ⓕ 01652 660700
Ⓔ kenmannion@kenmannion.co.uk
Ⓦ www.kenmannion.co.uk
Est. 1980 *Stock size* Medium
Stock Fossils, meteorites, artefacts
Open By appointment
Services Valuations, restorations

BELTON

⊞ Richard Ellory
Contact Richard Ellory
✉ **Unit 5, Sandtoft Industrial Estate, Sandtoft Road, Belton, Lincolnshire, DN9 1PN** 🅿
☎ 01427 874064 Ⓕ 01427 873626
Ⓔ richard@ellory.fsnet.co.uk
Est. 1981 *Stock size* Medium
Stock English pine
Open Mon–Sat 8am–4.30pm Sun 10am–4pm

BOSTON

⊞ Antique Workshop Ltd
Contact Mr Murphy
✉ **4a Pulverstoft Lane, Boston, Lincolnshire, PE21 8TA** 🅿
☎ 01205 368692
Est. 1967 *Stock size* Large
Stock General antique furniture
Open Mon–Sat 8am–5pm
Services Restorations

⊞ Tony Coda Antiques
Contact Mr T Coda
✉ **121 High Street, Boston, Lincolnshire, PE21 8TJ** 🅿
☎ 01205 352754
Ⓜ 07979 943084
Est. 1966 *Stock size* Medium
Stock General antiques, clocks, silver, paintings
Open Mon–Sat 9.30am–5pm closed Wed
Fairs Newark, The International Antique and Collectables Fair at RAF Swinderby
Services Valuations

⊞ Junktion Antiques
Contact Mr Jack Rundle
✉ **The Old Railway Station, Main Road, New Bolingbroke, Boston, Lincolnshire, PE22 7LN** 🅿
☎ 01205 480068 Ⓕ 01205 480132
Ⓜ 07836 345491
Est. 1983 *Stock size* Large
Stock Early toys, advertising,

bygones, architectural and mechanical antiques 1880–1960
Open Wed Thurs Sat 10am–5pm
Fairs Newark, The International Antique and Collectables Fair at RAF Swinderby

⊞ Pennyfarthing Antiques
Contact Mr Hale
✉ **1 Red Lion Street, Boston, Lincolnshire, PE21 6NY** 🅿
☎ 01205 362988
Est. 2000 *Stock size* Medium
Stock General antiques
Open Tues Wed Fri Sat 10am–4.30pm

BOURNE

⊞ Antique and Second Hand Traders
Contact Mr C Thompson
✉ **39 West Street, Bourne, Lincolnshire, PE10 9N3** 🅿
☎ 01778 394700 ⓕ 01778 394700
ⓜ 07958 941728
Est. 1969 *Stock size* Large
Stock General antiques
Open Mon–Sat 10am–5pm closed Wed Thurs
Fairs Newark, Ardingly
Services House clearance, removals

BRIGG

DDM Auction Rooms
Contact Mr R Horner
✉ **Old Courts Road, Brigg, North Lincolnshire, DN20 8JJ** 🅿
☎ 01652 650172 ⓕ 01652 650085
ⓜ 07970 126311
ⓔ sales@ddmauctionrooms.co.uk
ⓦ www.ddmgroup.co.uk
Est. 1884
Open Mon–Fri 9am–5.30pm
Sales Fine art and collectables sale every 6 weeks Tues Wed 9.30am. Fortnightly sale of general, household and shipping Sat 9.30am, ring for details, viewing day prior 2–7pm day of sale from 8.30am
Frequency Every 6 weeks
Catalogues Yes

CLEETHORPES

⊞ Cleethorpes Collectables
Contact Mr A Dalton
✉ **34 Alexandra Road, Cleethorpes, Lincolnshire, DN35 8LF** 🅿
☎ 01472 291952 ⓕ 01472 291952
Est. 1999 *Stock size* Large
Stock General antiques, collectables, curios
Open Mon–Sun 10am–5pm
Services Valuations

⊞ Yesterdays Antiques
Contact Mr N Bishop
✉ **86 Grimsby Road, Cleethorpes, Lincolnshire, DN35 7DP** 🅿
☎ 01472 343020
ⓔ n.bishop2@ntlworld.com
ⓦ yesterdaysantiques.org.uk
Est. 1987 *Stock size* Large
Stock General antiques, fireplaces a speciality
Open Mon–Sat 9am–5pm or by appointment
Services Valuations, restorations, polishing

EPWORTH

⊞ Ellory & Chaffer
Contact Mr R Ellory
✉ **25a Burnham Road, Epworth, Lincolnshire, DN9 1BX** 🅿
☎ 01427 874064 ⓕ 01427 874064
Est. 1985 *Stock size* Medium
Stock Antique English reproduction pine furniture
Open Mon–Fri 8am–4.30pm Sat 8am–noon
Services Restorations, stripping

GAINSBOROUGH

Drewery and Wheeldon
Contact Mr M G Tomson
✉ **124 Trinity Street, Gainsborough, Lincolnshire, DN21 1JD** 🅿
☎ 01427 616118 ⓕ 01427 811020
ⓔ auctions@drewery-&-wheeldon.co.uk
Est. 1879
Open Mon–Fri 9am–5.30pm Sat 9am–12.30pm
Sales General antiques sale phone for details
Frequency Periodic
Catalogues Yes

⊞ Trevor Moss Antiques
Contact Mr T Moss
✉ **Building 1, Room 2, Caenby Corner Estate, Gainsborough, Lincolnshire, DN21 5TW** 🅿
☎ 01427 667767 ⓕ 01427 614506
ⓔ info@tsmossantiques.co.uk
ⓦ www.tsmossantiques.co.uk
Est. 1985 *Stock size* Large
Stock General antiques
Open Mon–Sun 10am–5pm
Fairs Newark, Swinderby
Services Restorations

Pilgrims Antiques Centre
Contact Mr M Wallis
✉ **66a Church Street, Gainsborough, Lincolnshire, DN21 2JR** 🅿
☎ 01427 810897 ⓕ 01427 810897
Est. 1985 *Stock size* Large
No. of dealers 8
Stock General antiques
Open Tues–Sat 10am–4.30pm closed Wed

⊞ R M Antiques
Contact Mr R Maclennan
✉ **4a Tennyson Street, Gainsborough, Lincolnshire, DN21 2GJ** 🅿
☎ 01427 810624 ⓕ 01427 810624
Est. 1984 *Stock size* Large
Stock General antiques
Trade only Yes
Open Mon–Sat 9am–3pm
Services Export

GRANTHAM

Golding, Young & Co (NAVA)
Contact Mr Colin Young
✉ **The Grantham Auction Rooms, Old Wharf Road, Grantham, Lincolnshire, NG31 7AA** 🅿
☎ 01476 565118 ⓕ 01476 561475
ⓔ goldingyoung@compuserve.com
ⓦ www.goldingyoung.co.uk
Est. 1900
Open Mon–Fri 9am–5pm closed 1–2pm
Sales Fortnightly general antiques sale, bi-monthly antiques and fine art sale
Frequency Fortnightly
Catalogues Yes

⊞ Grantham Clocks
Contact M R Conder
✉ **30 Lodge Way, Grantham, Lincolnshire, NE31 8DD** 🅿
☎ 01476 561784
Est. 1987 *Stock size* Medium
Stock Clocks
Open By appointment
Services Valuations, restorations

⊞ Grantham Furniture Emporium
Contact K or J E Hamilton

✉ 4–6 Wharf Road, Grantham, Lincolnshire, NG31 6BA P
☎ 01476 562967
Ⓜ 07710 483865
Est. 1976 *Stock size* Large
Stock Victorian–Edwardian furniture, 1920s shipping
Open Tues–Sun 11am–4pm closed Wed

Harlequin Antiques
Contact Tony or Sandra Marshall
✉ 46 Swinegate, Grantham, Lincolnshire, NG31 6RL
☎ 01476 563346
Est. 1995 *Stock size* Medium
Stock General antiques
Open Mon–Sat 9am–5pm
Services Valuations

Notions Antiques
Contact Mr or Mrs L Checkley
✉ 2A Market Place, Grantham, Lincolnshire, NG31 6LQ P
☎ 01476 563603
Ⓜ 07974 683120
Ⓔ scheckley@fsbdial.co.uk
Est. 1984 *Stock size* Medium
Stock General antiques
Open Mon–Fri 10am–5pm Sat 9.30am–5pm
Fairs Newark, Ardingly

Pinfold-Wilkinson Antiques (BHI, AHS)
Contact Mr M Wilkinson
✉ The Tyme House, 1 Blue Court, Guildhall Street, Grantham, Lincolnshire, NG31 6NJ P
☎ 01476 560400 Ⓕ 01476 568791
Ⓜ 07966 154590
Est. 1935 *Stock size* Small
Stock Clocks, watches, jewellery
Open Mon–Sat 10am–4.30pm
Services Valuations, restorations

Marilyn Swain Auctions (SOFAA)
Contact John Munroe
✉ The Old Barracks, Sandon Road, Grantham, Lincolnshire, NG31 9AS P
☎ 01476 568861 Ⓕ 01476 576100
Ⓔ swain.auctions@virgin.net
Est. 1991
Open Mon–Fri 9am–5.30pm
Sales General antiques
Frequency Fortnightly
Catalogues Yes

GRIMSBY

Bell Antiques
Contact Mr Victor Hawkey
✉ 68 Harold Road, Grimsby, Lincolnshire, DN32 7NQ P
☎ 01472 695110
Est. 1964 *Stock size* Large
Stock Clocks, music boxes
Open By appointment
Services Valuations

Jackson, Green & Preston
Contact Mr D Arliss
✉ New Cartergate, Grimsby, Lincolnshire, DN31 1RB P
☎ 01472 311115 Ⓕ 01472 311114
Ⓔ auction@jacksongreenpreston.co.uk
Ⓦ www.jacksongreenpreston.co.uk
Est. 1920
Open By appointment
Sales General household and antiques
Frequency Weekly
Catalogues No

HEMSWELL CLIFF

Advena Antiques & Fairs
Contact Alan White
✉ Building II, Hemswell Antique Centre, Hemswell Cliff, Gainsborough, Lincolnshire, DN21 5TJ P
☎ 01427 668389
Ⓜ 07713 150510
Est. 1992 *Stock size* Large
Stock Antique silver, jewellery, silver plate
Open Mon–Sun 10am–5pm
Services Valuations, repairs

Astra House Antique Centre
Contact Mr M J Frith
✉ Old RAF Hemswell, Nr Caenby Corner, Gainsborough, Lincolnshire, DN21 5TL P
☎ 01427 668312 Ⓕ 01427 668312
Ⓔ astraantiqueshemswell@btinternet.com
Est. 1992 *Stock size* Large
No. of dealers 50
Stock General antiques and collectables including second-hand items
Open Mon–Sun 10am–5pm
Services Shipping

Barleycorn Antiques
Contact Shirley or John Wheat
✉ Hemswell Antiques Centre, Caenby Corner Estate, Hemswell Cliff, Gainsborough, Lincolnshire, DN21 5TW P
☎ 01427 668789
Ⓜ 07850 673965
Ⓦ www.barleycorn-antiques.co.uk
Est. 1982
Stock Furniture, brass, lighting, ceramics, clocks,
Open Mon–Sun 10am–5pm

Guardroom Antiques
Contact Mr C Lambert
✉ RAF Station Hemswell, Gainsborough, Lincolnshire, DN21 5TU P
☎ 01427 667113
Est. 1993 *Stock size* Large
No. of dealers 50
Stock General antiques including Victorian and Georgian furniture
Open Mon–Sun 10am–5pm

Hemswell Antique Centres
Contact Robert Miller
✉ Caenby Corner Estate, Hemswell Cliff, Gainsborough, Lincolnshire, DN21 5TJ P
☎ 01427 668389 Ⓕ 01427 668935
Ⓔ info@hemswell-antiques.com
Ⓦ www.hemswell-antiques.com
Est. 1989 *Stock size* Large
No. of dealers 270
Stock General antiques
Open Daily 10am–5pm
Services Furniture restoration

Second Time Around
Contact Mr G Powis
✉ Hemswell Antique Centre, Caenby Corner Estate, Hemswell Cliff, Gainsborough, Lincolnshire, DN21 5TN P
☎ 01522 543167 or 01427 668389
Ⓜ 07860 679495
Est. 1984 *Stock size* Large
Stock Period longcase clocks, other 17th–mid 20thC clocks
Open Mon–Sun 10am–5pm
Services Valuations, restorations

Janie & Skip Smithson
Contact Janie or Skip Smithson
✉ Hemswell Antique Centre, Hemswell Cliff, Caenby Corner, Gainsborough, Lincolnshire DN21 5TJ
☎ 01754 810265 Ⓕ 01754 810265
Ⓜ 07831 399180
Est. 1987 *Stock size* Large
Stock Kitchen and dairy antiques
Open Mon–Sun 10am–5pm
Fairs NEC, Alexandra Palace
Services Shipping

HOLBEACH

P J Cassidy
Contact Mr P Cassidy
1 Boston Road, Holbeach, Spalding, Lincolnshire, PE12 7LR P
☎ 01406 426322
Ⓔ bookscass@aol.com
Est. 1974 *Stock size* Large
Stock Antiquarian books, maps, prints, and Lincolnshire topography
Open Mon–Sat 10am–6pm
Services Framing

HOLTON LE CLAY

C A Johnson
Contact Mr C A Johnson
32 Pinfold Lane, Holton Le Clay, Grimsby, Lincolnshire, DN36 5DH P
☎ 01472 822406 Ⓕ 01472 822406
Est. 1979 *Stock size* Medium
Stock General antiques
Open By appointment
Fairs Newark
Services Valuations

HORNCASTLE

G Baker Antiques
Contact Mr or Mrs G Baker
16 South Street, Horncastle, Lincolnshire, LN9 6DX P
☎ 01507 526553
Ⓜ 07767 216264
Est. 1973 *Stock size* Medium
Stock Period and general furniture
Open Mon–Sat 9am–5pm or by appointment
Fairs Newark, Swinderby
Services Restorations

Clare Boam
Contact Clare Boam
22–38 North Street, Horncastle, Lincolnshire, LN9 5DX P
☎ 01507 522381 Ⓕ 01507 524202
Ⓔ clareboam@btconnect.com
Ⓦ www.greatexpectationshorncastle.co.uk
Est. 1976 *Stock size* Large
Stock General antiques and collectables
Open Mon–Sat 9am–5pm Sun 2–4.30pm

Great Expectations
Contact Miss M C Boam
37–43 East Street, Horncastle, Lincolnshire, LN9 6AZ P
☎ 01507 524202 Ⓕ 01507 524202
Ⓔ clareboam@btconnect.com
Ⓦ www.greatexpectationshorncastle.co.uk
Est. 1996 *Stock size* Large
No. of dealers 60
Stock General antiques
Open Mon–Sat 9am–5pm Sun 1–4.30pm and Bank Holidays

Horncastle Antique Centre
Contact Mrs P Sims or Mr D Sims
26 Bridge Street, Horncastle, Lincolnshire, LN9 3H2 P
☎ 01507 527777/525898
Ⓕ 01507 527777
Ⓦ www.freeshop.co.uk/antiques
Est. 1976 *Stock size* Large
Stock General antiques and collectables
Open Mon–Sat 9.30am–5pm Sun 1–5pm
Services Valuations, restorations, shipping

Lindsay Court Architectural
Contact Mr Lindsay White
Lindsay Court, Horncastle, Lincolnshire, LN9 5DH P
☎ 01507 527794 Ⓕ 01507 526670
Ⓜ 07768 396117
Ⓔ lndsy150@netscapeonline.co.uk
Ⓦ www.1starchitectural.co.uk
Est. 1987 *Stock size* Large
Stock Architectural antiques, stoneware, garden statuary, reclamations
Open Mon–Sat 10am–4pm Sun 12.30–4pm or by appointment
Fairs Newark
Services Export, container packing

North Street Antiques & Interiors
Contact Mrs Vivien Hallberg
48 North Street, Horncastle, Lincolnshire, LN9 5DX P
☎ 01507 525835 Ⓕ 01507 525835
Ⓜ 07714 920196
Est. 1984 *Stock size* Medium
Stock General antiques
Open Mon–Sat 10am–4.30pm or by appointment
Fairs Newark, Lincoln
Services Restorations,sourcing

Alan Read
Contact Mr A Read
60–62 West Street, Horncastle, Lincolnshire, LN9 5AD P
☎ 01507 524324/525548
Ⓕ 01507 525548
Ⓜ 07778 873838 *Stock size* Large
Stock 17th–18thC English furniture and decorative items
Open Tues–Sat 10am–4.30pm closed Wed or by appointment 7 days a week
Services Valuations, bespoke replicas made

Seaview Antiques
Contact Mr M Chalk
Stanhope Road, Horncastle, Lincolnshire, LN9 5DG P
☎ 01507 524524
Ⓔ tracey@seaviewantiques.co.uk
Ⓦ www.seaviewantiques.co.uk
Est. 1972 *Stock size* Large
Stock General antiques
Open Mon–Sat 9am–5pm
Fairs Newark

KIRTON

Kirton Antiques (LAPADA)
Contact Alan Marshall
3 High Street, Kirton, Lincolnshire, PE20 1DR P
☎ 01205 722595 Ⓕ 01205 722895
Ⓜ 07860 531600
Ⓔ alan.marshall@modcomp.net
Est. 1973 *Stock size* Large
Stock General antiques including period furniture
Open Mon–Fri 8am–5pm Sat 8.30am–noon or by appointment
Services Valuations, property hire

LINCOLN

Eric A Bird Jewellers (BHI)
Contact Mr S Thompson
1 St Mary's Street, Lincoln, Lincolnshire, LN5 7EQ
☎ 01522 520977 Ⓕ 01522 560586
Ⓦ www.eric-a-bird.co.uk
Est. 1959 *Stock size* Medium
Stock Antique and modern clocks, pocket watches
Open Mon–Sat 9am–5pm
Services Valuations, restorations and repairs

Rebecca Calvert Antiques (LAPADA)
Contact Rebecca Calvert
6–7 Castle Hill, Lincoln, Lincolnshire, LN1 3AA
01522 530044 01522 530044
07770 978501
Est. 1992 *Stock size* Medium
Stock English oak furniture and associated objects
Open Mon–Sat 10am–5.30pm
Fairs NEC, LAPADA
Services Valuations, restorations

C & K Dring
Contact Mr C Dring
111 High Street, Lincoln, Lincolnshire, LN5 7PY
01522 540733
Est. 1977 *Stock size* Medium
Stock Victorian and Edwardian inlaid furniture, clocks, music boxes, tinplate toys
Open Mon–Sat 10am–5pm closed Wed
Fairs Newark, Swinderby
Services Valuations, restorations

David J Hansord and Son (BADA, BACA Award Winner 2001)
Contact John Hansord
6–7 Castle Hill, Lincoln, Lincolnshire, LN1 3AA
01522 530044 01522 530044
07831 183511
Est. 1972 *Stock size* Large
Stock 18thC English furniture, works of art and objects
Open Mon–Sat 10am–5.30pm
Fairs Olympia
Services Valuations, restorations

Harlequin Gallery (PBFA)
Contact Mrs Anna Cockram
20–22 Steep Hill, Lincoln, Lincolnshire, LN2 1LT
01522 522589
harlequin@acockram.fsbusiness.co.uk
Est. 1964 *Stock size* Large
Stock Antiquarian and second-hand books, maps, prints
Open Mon–Sat 10.30am–5.45pm Wed 11am–4.30pm
Services Valuations, antique globe restoration

Dorrian Lamberts
Contact Mr R Lambert
64–65 Steep Hill, Lincoln, Lincolnshire, LN2 1LR
01522 545916
Est. 1984 *Stock size* Medium
Stock General antiques
Open Mon–Sat 10am–5pm
Fairs Newark, Swinderby
Services Valuations

Thomas Mawer & Son Ltd
Contact Mr J C Slingsby
Dunston House, Portland Street, Lincoln, Lincolnshire, LN5 7NN
01522 524984
mawer.thos@lineone.net
Est. 1864
Open Mon–Fri 9am–5pm
Sales General antiques
Frequency Quarterly

Whatnots
Contact Mr D Fowler
Cobb Hall, St Pauls Lane, Bailgate, Lincoln, Lincolnshire, LN1 3AX
01522 544723
07931 988974
Est. 1996 *Stock size* Medium
Stock General antiques, collectables
Open Mon–Sun 10am–5pm

LONG SUTTON

Chapel Emporium
Contact Miss B Hill or Miss Jennifer Beck
London Road, Long Sutton, Spalding, Lincolnshire, PE12 9EA
01406 364808
Est. 1983 *Stock size* Large
Stock General antiques
Open Mon–Sun 10am–5pm
Services Restorations

Long Sutton Antique and Craft Centre
Contact Ms G Shergold
72–74 London Road, Long Sutton, Spalding, Lincolnshire, PE12 9EB
01406 362991
Est. 1998 *Stock size* Large
No. of dealers 64
Stock General antiques, collectables and craft centre
Open Mon–Sat 10.30am–5.30pm Sun 11am–5pm

LOUTH

The Old Maltings Antique Centre
Contact Mr Norman Coffey
Aswell Street, Louth, Lincolnshire, LN11 9HP
01507 608257
margaret@eastcoast88.freeserve.co.uk
Est. 1979 *Stock size* Large
No. of dealers 20
Stock General antiques, collectables, Victorian–Edwardian furniture
Open Mon–Sat 10am–4.30pm
Services Valuations, restorations

John Taylor's
Contact Mrs A Laverack
The Wool Mart, Kidgate, Louth, Lincolnshire, LN11 9EZ
01507 611107 01507 601280
johntaylors@btconnect.com
www.johntaylors.com
Est. 1869
Open Mon–Fri 9am–5.15pm Sat 9am–2pm
Sales General antiques
Frequency Monthly
Catalogues Yes

MARKET DEEPING

Portland House Antiques
Contact Mr Cree
23 Church Street, Market Deeping, Lincolnshire, PE6 8AN
01778 347129
Est. 1971 *Stock size* Large
Stock 18th–early 19thC furniture, pictures and clocks
Open Sat 10am–4pm or by appointment
Services Valuations

NETTLEHAM

Autumn Leaves
Contact Mrs Susan Young
Unit 2 Co-op Building, 19 The Green, Nettleham, Lincoln, Lincolnshire, LN2 2NR
01522 750779
leaves@uk.packardbell.org
www.abebooks.com/home/autumn leaves
Est. 1997 *Stock size* Medium
Stock Second-hand books on all subjects
Open Tues–Thurs 9.15am–4pm Fri 9.15am–5pm Sat 9.15am–12.30pm
Services Book search

⊞ Homme de Quimper
Contact Mr S Toogood
✉ **Hillstead, 11 Church Street, Nettleham, Lincoln, Lincolnshire, LN2 2PD** 🅿
☎ 01522 753753
Ⓜ 07831 773622
Ⓔ steve.toogood@ntlworld.com
Ⓦ www.hommedequimper.co.uk
Est. 1996 *Stock size* Medium
Stock Antique French pottery, Quimper
Open Mon–Sun 9am–6pm
Services Valuations, restorations

⊞ Juke Box World
Contact Mr S Toogood
✉ **Hillstead, 11 Church Street, Nettleham, Lincoln, Lincolnshire, LN2 2PD** 🅿
☎ 01522 753753
Ⓔ steve.toogood@tesco.net
Est. 1985 *Stock size* Medium
Stock 20thC juke boxes
Open Mon–Sun 9am–6pm
Fairs Ascot Racecourse, Copthorne
Services Valuations, restorations

SCUNTHORPE

Canter & Francis (NAEA)
Contact Mr S J Francis, NAEA
✉ **41 Oswald Road, Scunthorpe, Lincolnshire, DN15 7PN** 🅿
☎ 01724 858855 Ⓕ 01724 858855
Est. 1947
Open Mon–Fri 9am–5pm
Sales General antiques
Frequency Periodic
Catalogues No

SOUTH HYKEHAM

Naylors Auctions
Contact Mr R Phillips
✉ **The Hall, Meadow Lane, South Hykeham, Lincoln, Lincolnshire, LN6 9PF** 🅿
☎ 01522 696496 Ⓕ 01522 696496
Ⓜ 07778 604401
Ⓔ raymondphillips@oden.org.uk
Ⓦ www.countrysales.co.uk
Est. 1979
Open By appointment
Sales General antiques
Frequency Monthly
Catalogues No

SPALDING

A P Sales
Contact Alan Porter
✉ **23a High Street, Spalding, Lincolnshire, PE11 1TX** 🅿
☎ 01775 762795 Ⓕ 01775 712091
Ⓔ auctions@apsales.co.uk
Ⓦ www.apsales.co.uk
Est. 1983
Open Mon–Fri 9am–5pm or by appointment
Sales Monthly antiques and collectables sale 3rd Fri (phone for details), general antiques sales every Sat and Tues
Frequency Monthly
Catalogues Yes

R Longstaff & Co
Contact Mr J A Smith
✉ **5 New Road, Spalding, Lincolnshire, PE11 3YZ** 🅿
☎ 01775 766766 Ⓕ 01775 762289
Ⓔ admin@longstaff.com
Ⓦ www.longstaff.com
Est. 1770
Open Mon–Fri 9am–6pm Sat 9am–3pm Sun 11am–3pm
Sales General antiques, house clearance
Frequency Bi-monthly
Catalogues No

Munton & Russell (ISVA)
Contact Mr James Smith
✉ **16 Sheep Market, Spalding, Lincolnshire, PE11 1BE** 🅿
☎ 01775 722475 Ⓕ 01775 769958
Est. 1964
Open Mon–Fri 9am–6pm
Sales General antiques.
Frequency Periodic
Catalogues No

⊞ Penman Clockcare (BWCG)
Contact Mr M Strutt
✉ **Unit 5, Pied Calf Yard, Spalding, Lincolnshire, PE11 1BE** 🅿
☎ 01775 714900
Ⓜ 07940 911167
Ⓔ strutt@clara.net
Ⓦ www.antique-clockrepairs.co.uk
Est. 1997 *Stock size* Medium
Stock Antique clocks
Open Mon–Sat 9am–5pm
Services Restorations, full repair service, home visits

⊞ Spalding Antiques
Contact Mr John Mumford
✉ **1 Abbey Path, Spalding, Lincolnshire, PE11 1AY**
☎ 01775 713185
Est. 1987 *Stock size* Medium
Stock General antiques, clocks, watches
Open Mon–Sat 10am–5pm

STAMFORD

⊞ Robert Loomes Clock Restoration (BWCG MBHI)
Contact Mr R Loomes
✉ **3 St Leonards Street, Stamford, Lincolnshire, PE9 2HU** 🅿
☎ 01780 481319
Ⓦ www.dialrestorer.co.uk
Est. 1987 *Stock size* Small
Stock Clocks
Open Mon–Fri 9am–5pm or by appointment
Services Restorations

⊞ Graham Pickett Antiques
Contact Mrs H Pickett
✉ **7 High Steet, St Martins, Stamford, Lincolnshire, PE9 2LF** 🅿
☎ 01780 481064
Ⓜ 07710 936948
Ⓔ graham@pickettantiques.demon.co.uk
Ⓦ www.pickettantiques.demon.co.uk
Est. 1987 *Stock size* Medium
Stock English and French provincial furniture, beds
Open Mon–Sat 10am–5.30pm Sun 11.30am–4pm
Fairs Newark

⊞ St Georges Antiques
Contact Mr G Burns
✉ **1 St Georges Square, Stamford, Lincolnshire, PE9 2BN** 🅿
☎ 01780 754117
Ⓜ 07779 528713
Est. 1974 *Stock size* Large
Stock General antiques, furniture
Trade only Yes
Open Mon–Fri 9am–1pm 2–4.30pm

St Martins Antique Centre
Contact Mr P Light
✉ **23a High Street, St Martins, Stamford, Lincolnshire, PE9 2LF** 🅿
☎ 01780 481158 Ⓕ 01780 481158
Ⓔ peter@st-martins-antiques.co.uk
Ⓦ www.st-martins-antiques.co.uk
Est. 1992 *Stock size* Large
No. of dealers 58+
Stock General antiques, collectables, objets d'art, 20thC items

Open Mon–Sat 10am–5pm
Sun 10.30am–5pm
Services Restorations, shipping

St Mary's Books & Prints
Contact Mr Tyers
9 St Mary's Hill, Stamford, Lincolnshire, PE9 2DP
☎ 01780 763033 Ⓕ 01780 763033
Ⓔ info@stmarysbookscom
Ⓦ www.stmarysbooks.com
Est. 1971 *Stock size* Large
Stock Antiquarian, rare and second-hand books, Wisden's Cricket Almanac a speciality
Open Mon–Sun 8am–6.30pm
Services Valuations, restorations and book search

St Paul's Street Bookshop (PBFA)
Contact Mr J Blessett
7 St Paul's Street, Stamford, Lincolnshire, PE9 2BE
☎ 01780 482748/343175
Ⓕ 01778 38053
Ⓔ jimblessett@aol.com
Est. 1978 *Stock size* Medium
Stock Antiquarian, rare and second-hand books, specializing in motoring books
Open Mon–Sat 10am–5pm closed Wed
Services Valuations

Staniland Booksellers (PBFA)
Contact Mr V Ketchum
4–5 St Georges Street, Stamford, Lincolnshire, PE9 2BJ
☎ 01780 755800 Ⓕ 01780 755800
Ⓔ stanilandbooksellers@btinternet.com
Est. 1972 *Stock size* Large
Stock Antiquarian, rare and second-hand scholarly books, architecture, applied art, philosophy, music, history, literature
Open Mon–Sat 10am–5pm
Fairs London Book Fairs
Services Valuations, probate and insurance valuations

Andrew Thomas
Contact Mr A Thomas
Old Granary, 10 North Street, Stamford, Lincolnshire, PE9 1EH Ⓟ
☎ 01780 762236 Ⓕ 01780 762236
Est. 1969 *Stock size* Large
Stock General antiques and antique painted furniture
Open Mon–Sat 9am–6pm

Undercover Books
Contact Mr T Dobson
30 Scotgate, Stamford, Lincolnshire, PE9 2YQ Ⓟ
☎ 01780 480989 Ⓕ 01780 763963
Ⓔ undercoverbooks@btinternet.com
Ⓦ www.abebooks.com/home/tonydodson/
Est. 1989 *Stock size* Large
Stock Antiquarian, rare and second-hand books, law enforcement a speciality
Open Tues–Sat 10am–5pm

Vaughan Antiques (LAPADA)
Contact Mr B Vaughan
45 Broad Street, Stamford, Lincolnshire, PE9 1PA Ⓟ
☎ 01780 765888 Ⓕ 01778 342053
Ⓜ 07712 657414
Est. 1994 *Stock size* Large
Stock English furniture, clocks, decorative items, 18th–19thC furniture a speciality
Open Mon–Sat 10am–5pm
Fairs NEC

STICKNEY

B & B Antiques
Main Road, Stickney, Boston, Lincolnshire, PE22 8AD Ⓟ
☎ 01205 480204
Stock General antiques
Open By appointment

SUTTON BRIDGE

Old Barn Antiques
Contact Mr S Jackson
48–50 Bridge Road, Sutton Bridge, Spalding, Lincolnshire, PE12 9UA Ⓟ
☎ 01406 359123/350435 (warehouse)
Ⓕ 01406 359158
Ⓜ 07956 677228
Est. 1983 *Stock size* Large
Stock Victorian, Edwardian and 1920s furniture
Open Mon–Fri 9am–5pm Sat 10am–5pm Sun 11am–4pm
Fairs Newark
Services Containers packed

Old Barn Antiques
Contact Mr S Jackson
220 New Road, Sutton Bridge, Spalding, Lincolnshire, PE12 9QE Ⓟ
☎ 01406 350435 Ⓕ 01406 359158
Ⓜ 07956 677228
Est. 1984 *Stock size* Large
Stock Victorian–Edwardian and 1920s furniture
Trade only Yes
Open Mon–Fri 8.30am–5.30pm and by appointment
Fairs Newark
Services Containers packed

SWINDERBY

Graham the Hat
Contact Graham Rodwell
Newark Road, Swinderby, Lincolnshire, LN6 9HN
☎ 01493 650217 Ⓕ 01493 650217
Ⓜ 07899 892337
Ⓔ graham@grahamthehat.com
Ⓦ www.grahamthehat.com
Est. 1997 *Stock size* Large
Stock Collectables
Open By appointment
Fairs Swinderby, Ardingly
Services Trade prices on request

TATTERSHALL

Wayside Antiques
Contact Mr G Ball
10 Market Place, Tattershall, Lincolnshire, LN4 4LQ Ⓟ
☎ 01526 342436
Est. 1972 *Stock size* Medium
Stock General antiques
Open By appointment

WAINFLEET

Ann-Tiques
Contact Mrs M Bark
40 High Street, Wainfleet, Lincolnshire, PE24 43H Ⓟ
☎ 01754 880770
Est. 1981 *Stock size* Medium
Stock General antiques
Open Tues–Sat 10am–12.30pm 1.30–4pm closed Thurs
Fairs Swinderby
Services Repair of clocks and jewellery

Naylor's Auctions (RICS, ISVA, NAEA,)
Contact Mr Ian Naylor
20 St Johns Street, Wainfleet, Skegness, Lincolnshire, PE24 4DJ Ⓟ
☎ 01754 881210 Ⓕ 01754 881210
Ⓜ 07989 372671
Ⓔ raymondphillips@oden.org.uk
Est. 1994
Open By appointment

Sales General antiques, weekly, monthly, periodic
Frequency Weekly
Catalogues No

WALESBY

⊞ Lincolnshire Antiques and Fine Art
Contact Mr N J Rhodes
⊠ **1 White House, Walesby, Market Rasen, Lincolnshire, LN8 3UW** 🅿
☎ 01673 838278
Ⓜ 07950 271898
Est. 1979
Stock Quality 17th–19thC oil paintings and furniture
Open By appointment only

WOODHALL SPA

⊞ M & J Antiques
Contact Mr J Goodyear
⊠ **Tattershall Road, Woodhall Spa, Lincolnshire, LN10 6QJ**
☎ 01526 352140
Stock General antiques
Open Flexible

⊞ Underwood Hall Antiques
Contact G Underwood
⊠ **5 The Broadway, Woodhall Spa, Lincolnshire, LN10 6ST** 🅿
☎ 01526 353815
Est. 1974 *Stock size* Medium
Stock Small furniture, 19th–20thC pottery, porcelain, silver, jewellery, postcards
Open Mon–Sat 10.30am–4.30pm Sun 1–4pm or by appointment
Fairs Newark
Services Valuations

⊞ VOC Antiques (LAPADA)
Contact David Leyland
⊠ **27 Witham Road, Woodhall Spa, Lincolnshire, LN10 6RW** 🅿
☎ 01526 352753 Ⓕ 01526 352753
Ⓔ djleyland@tinyworld.co.uk
Est. 1975 *Stock size* Medium
Stock Georgian–Victorian furniture, brass, copper, general antiques
Open Mon–Sat 9.30am–5.30pm Sun 2pm–5pm
Services Valuations, restorations

NORTH EAST

CO DURHAM

BARNARD CASTLE

⊞ Edward Barrington-Doulby
Contact Mike or Fiona
✉ **23 The Bank, Barnard Castle, Co Durham, DL12 8PH** Ⓟ
☎ 01833 630500
Est. 1994
Stock Furniture, smalls, ironmongery
Open Mon–Sat 11am–5pm Sun 1–5pm closed Tues Thurs

⊞ Farmhouse Antiques
Contact Mr or Mrs Robson
✉ **27 Newgate, Barnard Castle, Co Durham, DL12 8NJ** Ⓟ
☎ 01833 638700
Est. 1975
Stock Fireplaces, Durham quilts, glass, silver
Open Mon–Fri 10am–5.30pm Sat 10am–6pm Sun 1.30–5pm
Fairs Birmingham Glass Fair, Newark
Services Fireplace restoration

⊞ James Hardy Antiques Ltd
Contact Alan Hardy or Amanda Longstaff
✉ **12 The Bank, Barnard Castle, Co Durham, DL12 8PQ** Ⓟ
☎ 01833 695135 Ⓕ 01833 695135
Ⓜ 07710 162003
Ⓔ alan@jameshardyantiques.co.uk
Ⓦ www.jameshardyantiques.co.uk
Est. 1993
Stock 18th–19thC furniture, silver, porcelain, metalware
Open Mon–Sat 10am–5pm closed Thurs
Fairs Harrogate
Services Restorations of silver and furniture

⊞ Kingsley & Co
Contact Anthony Kelton
✉ **13 The Bank, Barnard Castle, Co Durham, DL12 8PH** Ⓟ
☎ 01833 630522
Ⓦ www.kingsleyantiques.co.uk
Est. 2000
Stock Furniture, smalls, Asian works of art
Open Mon–Sat 10.30am–5.30pm closed Thurs
Services Valuations, restorations

BISHOP AUCKLAND

⊞ Eden House Antiques
Contact Chris Metcalfe
✉ **10 Staindrop Road, West Auckland, Bishop Auckland, Co Durham, DL14 9JX** Ⓟ
☎ 01388 833013
Ⓔ chrismetcalfe01@genie.co.uk
Est. 1977 *Stock size* Medium
Stock Furniture, clocks, china, pottery
Open Mon–Sun 10am–6pm
Services Valuations, restorations

G H Edkins and Son
✉ **Auckland Auction Rooms, 58 Kingsway, Bishop Auckland, Co Durham, DL14 7JF** Ⓟ
☎ 01388 603095 Ⓕ 01388 661239
Est. 1907
Open Mon–Fri 9.30am–4.30pm
Sales General antiques household sale every Thurs, viewing Wed 10am–noon 2–5pm
Frequency Fortnightly
Catalogues No

⊞ Something Different
Contact Mr Peter Reeves or Mr Melvin Holmes
✉ **34a Maude Terrace, St Helen Auckland, Bishop Auckland, Co Durham, DL14 9BD** Ⓟ
☎ 01388 664366
Ⓜ 07794 9656313
Est. 1980 *Stock size* Large
Stock Memorabilia, militaria, furniture, clocks, collectables, silver, lights, decorative items, carpets, rugs
Open Mon–Sat 9.30am–5.30pm Sun 10am–5pm
Services Valuations, clock restorations, delivery

CONSETT

⊞ Harry Raine
Contact Mr N C Raine
✉ **Kelvinside House, 91 Villa Real Road, Consett, Co Durham, DH8 6BL** Ⓟ
☎ 01207 503935
Ⓜ 07802 667173
Est. 1965

Stock General antiques
Trade only Yes
Open By appointment only

⊞ Westend Antiques & Jewellery
Contact Peter Ray
✉ **63 Middle Street, Consett, Co Durham, DH8 5QG** 🅿
☎ 01207 582228 Ⓕ 01207 582228
Stock Jewellery, general antiques, bric-a-brac
Open Mon–Sat 9am–5pm
Fairs Newark
Services Valuations, restorations

DARLINGTON

⊞ Collectables
Contact Mr Ken Bradley
✉ **154 Gladstone Street, Darlington, Co Durham, DL3 6LD** 🅿
☎ 01325 351195
Ⓜ 07968 941588
Est. 1980
Stock Furniture, paintings, architectural items, objets d'art
Open Mon–Sat 10am–5pm
Fairs Ardingly, Swinderby
Services Valuations

⊞ Decorative Antiques
Contact Mr Watt
✉ **12 King Street, Darlington, Co Durham, DL3 6JH** 🅿
☎ 01325 361575
Est. 1990
Stock Furniture, bric-a-brac, architectural
Open Mon–Sat 9am–5pm
Fairs Newark
Services Restorations

Hunts Auctioneers
Contact Mr Thornton or Mr Windsor
✉ **Four Riggs, Darlington, Co Durham, DL3 6TL** 🅿
☎ 01325 352328 Ⓕ 01325 352328
Ⓜ 07710 376166
Est. 1960
Open Mon–Fri 9am–5pm
Sales General sales fortnightly Mon 6pm. Viewing all day Mon from 9am. Periodic antique sales
Catalogues No

⊞ Look 'N' Hear
Contact Michael Geall
✉ **57 Bondgate, Darlington, Co Durham, DL3 7JJ** 🅿
☎ 01325 360654
Est. 1993 *Stock size* Large
Stock Postcards, cigarette cards, stamps, prints, documents
Open Mon–Sat 9.30am–4.30pm Wed 9.30am–3pm
Services Approval for postcards

⊞ Alan Ramsey Antiques (LAPADA)
Contact Mr A Ramsey
✉ **Dudley Road, Darlington, Co Durham, DL1 4GG** 🅿
☎ 01325 361679/01642 711311
Ⓕ 01325 469739
Est. 1970 *Stock size* Large
Stock Georgian–Edwardian furniture, clocks
Open Mon Tue Thurs Fri 9.30am–4pm or by appointment

⊞ Tango Curios
✉ **3a Houndgate, Darlington, Co Durham, DL1 5RL** 🅿
☎ 01325 465768
Ⓜ 07977 979770
Est. 1986 *Stock size* Large
Stock 20thC Decorative Arts, glass, ceramics, metalware, pictures
Open Mon 10am–1pm 2–5pm Fri 10am–1pm 2–5pm Sat 10am–5pm
Fairs Antiques for Everyone, Loughborough Art Deco Antiques Fair
Services Valuations

DURHAM

⊞ Finley's Finds
Contact Mr B Finley
✉ **23 Flambard Road, Durham, Co Durham, DH1 5HY** 🅿
☎ 0191 384 1643
Est. 1995
Stock Furniture, china, jewellery
Open Mon–Fri 9am–5pm
Fairs Newark, Swinderby
Services Valuations, house clearance

⊞ Old & Gold
Contact Pam Tracey
✉ **88 Claypath, Durham, Co Durham, DH1 1LG** 🅿
☎ 0191 386 0728
Ⓜ 07831 362252
Ⓔ pampaul@traceyppt.freeserve.co.uk
Est. 1989 *Stock size* Medium
Stock General antiques
Open Mon–Fri 10am–4.30pm Sat 10am–2pm closed Wed
Fairs Newark
Services Jewellery repairs

FIR TREE

⊞ Old School House Antiques and Tea Room
Contact Peter Ditchfield
✉ **Old School House, Fir Tree, Co Durham, DL15 8DG** 🅿
☎ 01388 765699/766919
Est. 1994 *Stock size* Medium
Stock General antiques, Georgian–Edwardian furniture
Open Wed–Sat 11am–5pm Sun 1–5.30pm
Services Tea room

MIDDLETON IN TEESDALE

⊞ Brown's Antiques & Collectables
Contact JR or V Brown
✉ **13 Chapel Row, Middleton in Teesdale, Co Durham, DL12 0SN** 🅿
☎ 01833 640276
Ⓔ antiques@13chapelrow.freeserve.co.uk
Ⓦ www.browns-antiques.co.uk
Est. 1991 *Stock size* Medium
Stock Antique furniture, ceramics, metalware, kitchenware
Open Mon–Sat 10am–5pm

NORTHUMBERLAND

ALNWICK

⊞ Barter Books
Contact Stuart Manley
✉ **Alnwick Station, Alnwick, Northumberland, NE66 2NP** 🅿
☎ 01665 604888 Ⓕ 01665 604444
Ⓔ bb@barterbooks.co.uk
Ⓦ www.barterbooks.co.uk
Est. 1991 *Stock size* Large
Stock Antiquarian and second-hand books, records, CDs, videos
Open Summer Mon–Sun 9am–7pm winter Mon–Sun 9am–5pm Thurs 9am–7pm
Services Book search, valuations

⊞ John Smith of Alnwick Ltd
Contact Mr P Smith
✉ **West Cawledge Park Gallery, Alnwick, Northumberland, NE66 2HJ** 🅿
☎ 01665 604363
Est. 1972 *Stock size* Medium
Stock Country and general antiques, rugs, pictures, furniture
Open Mon–Sun 9am–5pm

Tamblyn Antiques
Contact Professor Hirst
12 Bondgate Without, Alnwick, Northumberland, NE66 1PP
01665 603024
profbehirst@tamblyn.freeserve.co.uk
Est. 1981 *Stock size* Medium
Stock Small period furniture, ceramics, Finnish, Swedish and Dutch glass
Open Mon–Sat 9.30am–4.30pm
Services Valuations

BERWICK-UPON-TWEED

Leslies Mount Road Auction Galleries
Contact Miss A Watson
Mount Road, Tweedmouth, Berwick-upon-Tweed, Northumberland, TD15 2BA
01289 304635 F 01289 304635
auctionhouse@rocketmail.com.
Est. 1995
Open Mon–Fri 10am–5pm
Sales General antiques auction Mon 10.30am, viewing Sat 11.30am–6pm Sun 1–5pm Mon 9.30–10.30am
Frequency Monthly
Catalogues Yes

James E McDougall
Contact James E McDougall MRICS
St Duthus, 6 Palace Street East, Berwick-upon-Tweed, Northumberland, TD15 1HT
01289 330791
james.mcdougall@caucasian-rugs.co.uk
www.caucasian-rugs.co.uk
Est. 1989 *Stock size* Small
Stock Antique carpets and rugs
Open By appointment
Services Valuations

CHATTON

Jim Railton
Contact Jim Railton
Nursery House, Chatton, Alnwick, Northumberland, NE66 5PY
01668 215323 F 01668 215400
M 07774 241111
jimrailton@virgin.net
Est. 1993
Open Mon–Sat 9am–5pm or by appointment
Sales General antiques sale, specializing in country house sales at historic properties
Frequency 4 per annum
Catalogues Yes

CORBRIDGE

Judith Michael
Contact Gillian Anderson or Judith Troldahl
20a Watling Street, Corbridge, Northumberland, NE45 5AH
01434 633165 F 01434 633165
jma@supanet.com
www.judithmichael.co.uk
Est. 1989 *Stock size* Medium
Stock General antiques, decorative items, jewellery, small furniture, glass, china, gardening section
Open Mon–Sat 10am–5pm Sun noon–4pm
Services Interior design

FORD

Latto Books
Contact Mr A Latto
West Lodge, Ford, Berwick-upon-Tweed, Northumberland, TD15 2PX
01890 820702
M 07714 293644
Est. 1980 *Stock size* Medium
Stock Antiquarian, rare and second-hand books, specializing in Mary Queen of Scots, Scottish borders, Northumberland, Robert Burns and jazz
Open By appointment
Services Catalogues, mail order

HEXHAM

Boadens Antiques
Contact Christopher Boaden
29–30 Market Place, Hexham, Northumberland, NE46 3PB
01434 603187 F 01434 603474
antiques@boadens.fsnet.co.uk
Est. 1948 *Stock size* Large
Stock General antiques, furniture, silver, china, jewellery
Open Mon–Sat 9am–5pm
Services Valuations

Hedley's of Hexham
Contact Mrs P Torday
3 St Marys Chare, Hexham, Northumberland, NE46 1NQ
01434 602317 F 01434 230740
Est. 1809 *Stock size* Medium
Stock General antiques, furniture, collectables, china, rugs, Moorcroft
Open Mon 10am–4pm Tues–Sat 9.30am–5pm
Services Restorations of furniture

Hencotes Books and Prints (PBFA)
Contact Mrs P Pearce
8 Hencotes, Hexham, Northumberland, NE46 2EJ
01434 605971
Est. 1992 *Stock size* Medium
Stock Antiquarian and second-hand books, specializing in local history, literature, children's books, gardening, cookery
Open Mon–Sat 10.30am–5pm closed Thurs
Fairs Local PBFA, Durham, Newcastle
Services Booksearch

Hexham and Northern Mart
Contact Mr Brian Rogerson
Mart Office, Tyne Green, Hexham, Northumberland, NE46 3SG
01434 605444/01669 620392 (Rothbury)
furniture@hexhammart.co.uk
www.hexhammart.co.uk
Est. 1850
Open Mon–Fri 9am–5pm
Sales House clearances, antiques sales (held at Rothbury), viewing 2 days prior to sale
Frequency Every 2 or 3 months
Catalogues No

Hexham Antiques
Contact John and Dorothy Latham
6 Rear Battle Hill, Hexham, Northumberland, NE46 1BB
01434 603851
Est. 1978 *Stock size* Large
Stock General antiques, collectables, pictures, bric-a-brac
Open Mon Tues Fri Sat 10.30am–4pm
Services Picture framing, valuations, house clearance

O'Neil's Old Warehouse Antiques
Contact Neil Perry
45 Hallstile Bank, Hexham, Northumberland, NE46 3PQ
01434 600510
M 07801 818966
Est. 1989 *Stock size* Large

NORTH EAST

Stock Georgian, Victorian, pine and country furniture
Open Mon–Fri 10am–4pm
Sat 9am–5pm
Fairs Newark

Pine Workshop (ADA)
Contact John Askell
28 Priestpopple, Hexham, Northumberland, NE46 1PQ
☎ 01434 601121
Est. 1987 *Stock size* Medium
Stock Antique pine and oak
Open Mon–Sat 9am–5pm

Priestpopple Books
Contact Mr J B Patterson
9B Priestpopple, Hexham, Northumberland, NE46 1PF
☎ 01434 607773
priestpopple.books@tinyworld.co.uk
Est. 1998 *Stock size* Large
Stock Antiquarian books, general antiques, militaria, music, entertainment, art
Open Mon–Sat 9am–5pm
Services Valuations, restorations

MORPETH

Grove Antiques
Contact Lorna Gates
Green Tiles, Main Street, Red Row, Morpeth, Northumberland, NE61 5AD
☎ 01670 760330
07710 342965
northumbrian@btinternet.com
Est. 1986 *Stock size* Medium
Stock General antiques
Trade only Yes
Open By appointment
Fairs International Antique and Collectables Fair RAF Swinderby

Louis Johnson
Contact John Hayes
63 Bridge Street, Morpeth, Northumberland, NE61 1PQ
☎ 01670 513025 01670 503267
lj@lj-estates.fsbusiness.co.uk
Est. 1955
Open Mon–Fri 9am–5pm
Sales General antiques, cars and motorcycles on Sat, viewing 2 days prior to sale. Advisable to call for details
Frequency Monthly
Catalogues Yes

Pottery Bank Antiques
Contact Mr Everitt
43 Bullers Green, Morpeth, Northumberland, NE61 1DF
☎ 01670 516160
apope@morpethnet.co.uk
www.morpethnet.co.uk
Est. 1977 *Stock size* Medium
Stock General antiques, furniture, silver
Open Mon–Sat 11.30am–5.30pm or by appointment

ROTHBURY

Golfark International
Contact Michael Arkle
5 Tollgate Crescent, Rothbury, Northumberland, NE65 7RE
☎ 01669 620487 01669 620487
07710 693860
Est. 1997 *Stock size* Small
Stock Old golf clubs, bags and balls, sporting antiques, golfing memorabilia
Open By appointment

SCREMERSTON

Woodside Reclamation (SALVO)
Contact Keith Allan
Woodside, Scremerston, Berwick-upon-Tweed, Northumberland, TD15 2SY
☎ 01289 331211/302658
01289 330274
Est. 1990 *Stock size* Medium
Stock Fireplaces, antique baths, bathroom ware, doors, timber, beams, flooring
Open Mon–Sat 9am–5pm
Sun 11am–4pm
Services Furniture and door stripping, restoration

WOOLER

Hamish Dunn Antiques
Contact Mr Dunn
17 High Street, Wooler, Northumberland, NE71 6BU
☎ 01668 281341 01668 281341
07773 756776
hamishdunn@wooler20.freeserve.co.uk
Est. 1986 *Stock size* Medium
Stock General antiques, second-hand and antiquarian books
Open Mon–Sat 9am–4.30pm

James Miller (LAPADA)
Contact James Miller
1–5 Church Street, Wooler, Northumberland, NE71 6BZ
☎ 01668 281500 01668 282383
www.millersantiquesofwooler.com
Est. 1947 *Stock size* Large
Stock Georgian and Victorian furniture
Open Mon–Fri 9.30am–5pm

TYNE AND WEAR

EAST BOLDEN

Bolden Auction Galleries
Contact Mr Hodges
Front Street, East Bolden, Tyne and Wear, NE36 0SJ
☎ 0191 537 2630 0191 536 3875
Est. 1981
Sales General antiques sales Wed 10am, viewing Tues 2–6pm, 4 antiques sales annually, 2 collectors toy and 20thC modern design sales annually
Frequency Weekly
Catalogues Yes

GATESHEAD

Mulroys Antiques
Contact Miss J Mulroy
24 The Boulevard, Metro Centre, Gateshead, Tyne and Wear, NE11 9YL
☎ 0191 461 1211 0191 461 1211
Est. 1959 *Stock size* Large
Stock General antiques and period jewellery
Open Mon–Fri 10am–8pm
Thurs 10am–9pm Sat 9am–7pm
Sun 11am–5pm
Fairs Newark, Swinderby
Services Valuations, restorations

GOSFORTH

Anna Harrison Antiques (LAPADA)
Contact Mr or Mrs Harrison
Harewood House, 49 Great North Road, Gosforth, Newcastle-upon-Tyne, Tyne and Wear, NE3 2DG
☎ 0191 284 3202 0191 284 3202
annaharrisonantiques@ukgateway.net
Est. 1976 *Stock size* Large
Stock Early porcelain, Georgian–Edwardian furniture, dining and lounge furniture
Open Mon–Fri 8am–5pm Sat 10am–5pm or by appointment
Fairs Galloways Fairs, Bailey Fairs
Services Restorations

O'Neil's Antiques Gosforth
Contact Neil Perry

✉ **23 Station Road, South Gosforth, Tyne and Wear, NE3 1QD** P
☎ 01434 600510
Ⓜ 07801 818966
Est. 2000 *Stock size* Large
Stock Georgian–Victorian, pine and country furniture
Open Mon–Fri 10am–4pm Sat 9am–5pm
Fairs Newark

NEWCASTLE-UPON-TYNE

Acquisitions Antique & Handmade Furniture
Contact Mr J Maughan
✉ **57b Sanderson Road, Newcastle-upon-Tyne, Tyne and Wear, NE2 2DZ** P
☎ 0191 281 6690 Ⓕ 0191 281 6690
Ⓜ 07930 558823
Ⓔ acqpine@aol.com
Est. 1979 *Stock size* Medium
Stock Antique furniture, hand-made furniture to order
Open Mon–Fri 9.30am–4pm Sat 10am–2pm
Services Restorations

Aladdins Architectural Antiques (SALVO)
Contact Mr D Crowley
✉ **626 Welbeck Road, Walker, Newcastle-upon-Tyne, Tyne and Wear, NE6 1DJ** P
☎ 0191 262 7373
Ⓜ 07762 527640
Est. 1976 *Stock size* Large
Stock General antiques
Open Mon–Sat 10am–6pm
Services Valuations, restorations

Anderson & Garland (SOFAA)
Contact Mr A McCoull
✉ **Marlborough House, Marlborough Crescent, Newcastle-upon-Tyne, Tyne and Wear, NE1 4EE**
☎ 0191 232 6278 Ⓕ 0191 261 8665
Ⓔ garland@compuserve.com
Ⓦ www.auction-net.co.uk
Est. 1840
Open Mon–Fri 9am–5.30pm
Sales Fine art sales every 3 months, general antiques sales fortnightly
Frequency Fortnightly
Catalogues Yes

Antique Centre
Contact Mr C Parkin
✉ **2nd Floor, 142 Northumberland Street, Newcastle-upon-Tyne, Tyne and Wear, NE1 7DG**
☎ 0191 232 9832
Ⓔ timeantiques@zoom.co.uk
Ⓦ www.timeantiques.co.uk
Est. 1983 *Stock size* Large
No. of dealers 13
Stock General antiques
Open Mon–Sat 10am–5pm
Services Tea rooms, jewellery and clock repairs

Antiques at H & S Collectables
Contact Mrs Shorrick
✉ **1 Ashburton Road, Corner Salters Road, Newcastle-upon-Tyne, Tyne and Wear, NE3 4XN** P
☎ 0191 284 6626
Est. 1987 *Stock size* Large
Stock General antiques, curios, Victoriana, silver, Tyneside Maling pottery 1817–1963
Open Mon–Sat 10am–5pm
Fairs Colin Caygil
Services Valuations

Big Lamp Antiques
Contact Mr D H M Ching
✉ **301 Westgate Road, Newcastle-upon-Tyne, Tyne and Wear, NE4 6AJ** P
☎ 0191 222 1442
Est. 1987 *Stock size* Medium
Stock General antiques
Open Mon–Sat 9am–5pm
Fairs Newark
Services Valuations, restorations

B J Coltman Antiques
Contact B J Coltman
✉ **80 Meldon Terrace, Heaton, Newcastle-upon-Tyne, Tyne and Wear, NE6 5XP** P
☎ 0191 224 5209
Ⓔ inquiries@coltmanantiques.co.uk
Ⓦ www.coltmanantiques.co.uk
Est. 1993 *Stock size* Medium
Stock General antiques
Open Mon–Fri 9am–5pm
Fairs Newark
Services Restorations

Corbitt's (ASDA, APS, BPA)
Contact Mr D McMonaghe
✉ **5 Mosley Street, Newcastle-upon-Tyne, Tyne and Wear, NE1 1YE**
☎ 0191 2327268 Ⓕ 0191 2614130
Ⓔ info@corbitts.com
Ⓦ www.corbitts.com
Est. 1964 *Stock size* Medium
Stock Antiques, coins, stamps, medals, ephemera
Open Mon–Fri 9am–5pm Sat 9.30am–4pm
Services Valuations

Corbitt's
Contact Mr D McMonaghe
✉ **5 Mosley Street, Newcastle-upon-Tyne, Tyne and Wear, NE1 1YE**
☎ 0191 2327268 Ⓕ 0191 2614130
Ⓔ info@corbitts.com
Ⓦ www.corbitts.com
Est. 1964
Open Mon–Fri 9am–5pm
Sales Antique coins, medals, 3 per year. Stamps, history 4 per year. Cigarette cards, ephemera 2 per year
Catalogues Yes

Cradlewell Antiques
Contact Mr S Bardy
✉ **4 Churchill Gardens, Jesmond, Newcastle-upon-Tyne, Tyne and Wear, NE2 1HB**
☎ 0191 212 1500
Ⓦ www.cradlewell.co.uk
Est. 1979 *Stock size* Medium
Stock General antiques, 20thC design classics
Open Thurs–Sat 11am–5pm Sun noon–4pm
Fairs Newark

Dog Leap Antiques
Contact Mr N MacDonald
✉ **61 The Side, Newcastle-upon-Tyne, Tyne and Wear, NE1 3JE** P
☎ 0191 232 7269
Est. 1969 *Stock size* Medium
Stock Antiquarian prints and reproductions
Open Mon–Fri 9.15am–5pm Sat 9am–1pm

Owen Humble (LAPADA)
Contact Mr M Humble
✉ **11–12 Clayton Road, Jesmond, Newcastle-upon-Tyne, Tyne and Wear, NE2 4RP** P
☎ 0191 281 9076 Ⓕ 0191 281 9076
Ⓜ 07836 261107
Ⓔ antiques@owenhumble.fsnet.co.uk
Est. 1959 *Stock size* Large
Stock General antiques

Open Mon–Sat 9am–5pm or by appointment
Fairs LAPADA, NEC, Harrogate Antique and Fine Art Fair
Services Valuations, restorations, trade warehouse

Intercoin
Contact Mr Brian
103 Clayton Street, Newcastle-upon-Tyne, Tyne and Wear, NE1 5PZ
0191 232 2064
Est. 1964 *Stock size* Large
Stock Coins, medals, bank notes
Open Mon–Sat 9.30am–4.30pm
Services Valuations

Little Theatre Antiques Centre
Contact Mr J Bell
Fern Avenue, Jesmond, Newcastle-upon-Tyne, Tyne and Wear, NE2 2RA
0191 2094321
john@bennett-bell.demon.co.uk
www.bennett-bell.demon.co.uk
Est. 1993 *Stock size* Large
No. of dealers 13
Stock General antiques
Open Mon–Sat 10am–5.30pm

Thomas N Miller Auctioneers
Contact Mr A Scott
Algernon Road, Byker, Newcastle-upon-Tyne, Tyne and Wear, NE6 2UZ
0191 265 8080 0191 265 5050
millerlot1@aol.com
Est. 1902
Open Mon–Fri 8.30am–5pm
Sales General antiques, later furniture, viewing Sun 10am–noon Mon Tues 9.30am–4pm
Frequency Weekly
Catalogues Yes

Oxfam Books
Contact Mr A Chadwin
17 Ridley Place, Newcastle-Upon-Tyne, Tyne and Wear, NE1 8JQ
0191 232 2476
Est. 1998 *Stock size* Medium
Stock General and antiquarian books
Open Mon Wed–Fri 9.30am–5.30pm Sat 10am–5.30pm

Phillips International Auctioneers and Valuers
30–32 Grey Street, Newcastle-upon-Tyne, Tyne and Wear, NE1 6AE
0191 233 9930 0191 233 9933
www.phillips-auction.com
Sales Regional Office. Ring for details

Phoenix Design & Antiques
Contact Mrs M Ryle
The Old Monastery, Blackfriars, Newcastle-upon-Tyne, Tyne and Wear, NE1 4XN
0191 230 3804
Est. 1984 *Stock size* Small
Stock General antiques
Open Mon–Fri 11.30am–4.30pm Sat 10.30am–5pm

Shiners Snobs Knobs (SALVO)
Contact Mr Barry Lawson
81 Fern Avenue, Jesmond, Newcastle-Upon-Tyne, Tyne and Wear, NE2 2RA
0191 281 6474 0191 281 9041
07966 155350
Est. 1983 *Stock size* Large
Stock Internal fittings, doors, fireplaces, antique beds
Open Tues–Sat 10am–5.30pm
Services Polishing

Graham Smith Antiques (LAPADA)
Contact Mr Graham Smith
83 Fern Avenue, Jesmond, Newcastle-Upon-Tyne, Tyne and Wear, NE2 2RA
0191 281 5065 0191 281 5072
gsmithantiques@aol.com
Est. 1973 *Stock size* Medium
Stock Furniture, clocks, smalls
Open Mon–Sat 10am–5pm

Frank Smith Maritime Aviation Books (PBFA)
100 Heaton Road, Newcastle-upon-Tyne, Tyne and Wear, NE6 5HL
0191 265 6333 0191 224 2620
books@franksmith.freeserve.co.uk
Est. 1981 *Stock size* Medium
Stock Antiquarian, rare and out-of-print books, maritime and aviation
Open Mon–Fri 10am–4pm Sat 10am–1pm
Fairs Occasional PBFA
Services Free monthly catalogues on maritime and aviation

Robert D Steedman (ABA)
Contact Mr D Steedman
9 Grey Street, Newcastle-upon-Tyne, Tyne and Wear, NE1 6EE
0191 2326561
Est. 1907 *Stock size* Medium
Stock General antiquarian
Open Mon–Fri 9am–5pm Sat 9am–12.30pm
Fairs Olympia

Turnburrys Ltd (SALVO)
257 Jesmond Road, Newcastle-upon-Tyne, Tyne and Wear, NE2 1LB
0191 281 1770 0191 240 2569
info@turnburrys.co.uk
www.turnburrys.co.uk
Est. 1996 *Stock size* Medium
Stock Architectural antiques, fireplaces, doors, radiators, baths, mirrors, bespoke doors, etched and stained glass, chandeliers
Open Mon–Sat 9am–6pm Sun 11am–3pm
Services Valuations, restorations

NORTH SHIELDS

Chimney Pieces
Contact Mr T Chester
98a Howard Street, North Shields, Tyne and Wear, NE30 1NA
0191 2572118
www.chimneypieces.com
Est. 1985 *Stock size* Medium
Stock Antique chimney pieces, architectural antiques, fireplaces in marble and wood
Open Mon–Sat 10am–5pm
Fairs Newark
Services Restorations

The Clock Shop
Contact Mr G Ball
1a John Street, Cullercoates, North Shields, Tyne and Wear, NE30 4PL
0191 290 1212
07808 231306
Est. 1997 *Stock size* Medium
Stock General antiques
Open Mon–Sat 10am–5pm
Fairs Swinderby, Newark
Services Valuations, restorations, clock repairs

Keel Row Books
Contact Bob and Brenda Cook
✉ **11 Fenwick Terrace, Preston Road, North Shields, Tyne and Wear, NE29 0LU**
☎ 0191 2960664/2873914
Est. 1980 *Stock size* Large
Stock General antiquarian books. Children's, military, mountaineering, local history, cinema a speciality
Open Mon–Sat 10.30am–5pm closed Wed

Tynemouth Architectural Salvage (SALVO)
Contact Mr Robin Archer
✉ **28 Tynemouth Road, North Shields, Tyne and Wear, NE30 4AA**
☎ 0191 296 6070 Ⓕ 0191 296 6097
Ⓔ robin@tynemoutharchitecturalsalvage.com
Ⓦ www.tynemoutharchitecturalsalvage.com
Stock size Large
Stock Architectural antiques
Open Mon–Fri 10am–6pm Sat 10am–5pm
Fairs Newark
Services Door stripping, bath restorations

SOUTH SHIELDS

The Curiosity Shop
Contact Mr G Davies
✉ **16 Frederick Street, South Shields, Tyne and Wear, NE33 5EA**
☎ 0191 456 5560 Ⓕ 0191 427 7597
Ⓜ 07860 219949
Est. 1969 *Stock size* Medium
Stock General antiques, Royal Doulton
Open Mon–Sat 9am–5pm closed Wed
Fairs Newark

De-Ja-Vu
Contact Mr J Atkinson
✉ **2 Imeary Street, South Shields, Tyne and Wear, NE33 4EG**
☎ 0191 425 0031
Est. 1998 *Stock size* Small
Stock General antiques
Open Mon–Sat 10am–5pm

SUNDERLAND

Peter Smith Antiques (LAPADA)
Contact Mrs Smith
✉ **12–14 Borough Road, Sunderland, Tyne and Wear, S01 1EP**
☎ 0191 567 3537/514 0008
Ⓕ 0191 514 2286
Ⓜ 07802 273372
Ⓔ petersmithantiques@btinternet.com
Ⓦ www.petersmithantiques.co.uk
Est. 1968 *Stock size* Large
Stock General antiques
Open Mon–Fri 9.30am–4.30pm Sat 10am–1pm or by appointment
Services Valuations

TYNEMOUTH

Coast Antiques
Contact Mrs Dorothy Wadge or Mr Alex Beacham
✉ **10 Front Street, Tynemouth, Tyne and Wear, NE30 4RG**
☎ 0191 296 0700 Ⓕ 0191 296 0700
Ⓜ 07977 780248
Est. 1989 *Stock size* Medium
Stock Victorian–Edwardian furniture and associated items
Open Mon–Sat 10.30am–4.30pm Sun noon–4pm or by appointment
Services Interest-free credit, free local delivery

Curio Corner
Contact Mrs S Welton
✉ **Units 5 & 6, Land of Green Ginger, Front Street, Tynemouth, North Shields, Tyne and Wear, NE30 4BP**
☎ 0191 296 3316 Ⓕ 0191 296 3319
Ⓜ 07831 339906
Ⓦ www.curiocorner.com.uk
Est. 1988 *Stock size* Large
Stock General antique furniture
Open Mon–Sat 11am–4.30pm
Fairs Newark
Services Restorations

Ian Sharp Antiques (LAPADA)
Contact Mr Ian Sharp
✉ **23 Front Street, Tynemouth, North Shields, Tyne and Wear, NE30 4DX**
☎ 0191 296 0656 Ⓕ 0191 296 0656
Ⓜ 07850 023689
Ⓔ iansharp@sharpantiques.demon.co.uk
Ⓦ www.sharpantiques.demon.co.uk
Est. 1988 *Stock size* Medium
Stock Georgian–Edwardian furniture, pottery
Open Mon–Sat 10am–1pm 1.30–5.30pm or by appointment
Fairs Newark

WHITLEY BAY

Bay Books
Contact Mr J Cairns
✉ **10A Norham Road, Whitley Bay, Tyne and Wear, NE16 2SB**
☎ 0191 251 4448
Est. 1989 *Stock size* Medium
Stock Quality second-hand books, records, cassettes, CDs
Open Mon–Thurs 11am–4pm Fri Sat 11am–5pm
Fairs Tynemouth Station
Services Book search

Olivers Bookshop
Contact Mr J Oliver
✉ **48a Whitley Road, Whitley Bay, Tyne and Wear, NE26 2NF**
☎ 0191 251 3552
Est. 1986 *Stock size* Medium
Stock Antiquarian, rare and second-hand books
Open Mon Thurs Fri Sat 11am–5pm
Fairs Tynemouth Book Fair

Treasure Chest Antiques
Contact Mr J Rain
✉ **2a–4 Norham Road, Whitley Bay, Tyne and Wear, NE26 2SB**
☎ 0191 251 2052
Ⓜ 07808 966611
Est. 1969 *Stock size* Medium
Stock General antiques
Open Mon–Sat 10.30am–4pm closed 1–2pm

NORTH WEST

CHESHIRE

ALDERLEY EDGE

⊞ Anthony Baker (LAPADA)
Contact Ms A Price
✉ **14 London Road, Alderley Edge, Cheshire, SK9 7JS** 🅿
☎ 01625 582674
Est. 1976 *Stock size* Medium
Stock Wide range of antique stock including 18th–19thC furniture, barometers and collectors' items
Open Tues–Sat 10am–5.30pm closed Wed

ALSAGER

⊞ Trash 'n' Treasure
Contact George G Ogden
✉ **48 Sandbach Road South, Alsager, Cheshire, ST7 2LP** 🅿
☎ 01270 873246/872972
Est. 1962 *Stock size* Medium
Stock Furniture, ceramics, pictures
Open Tues–Sat 10am–4pm closed Wed
Services Valuations

BEESTON

⊞ Beeston Reclamations
Contact Mr D Malam
✉ **The Old Coal Yard, Whitchurch Road, Beeston, Tarporley, Cheshire, CW6 9NW** 🅿
☎ 01829 260299
Ⓜ 07721 424400
Est. 1998 *Stock size* Large
Stock Garden statuary, bricks, slates, oak beams, pine beams, floor boards, York stone, fireplaces, block flooring
Open Mon–Sat 8am–5pm
Services Valuations, restorations

Wright-Manley
Contact Mr W T Witter
✉ **Beeston Castle Salerooms, Beeston Castle, Tarporley, Cheshire, CW6 9NJ** 🅿
☎ 01829 262150 Ⓕ 01829 262150
Ⓔ wtwitter@wrightmanley.co.uk
Ⓦ www.wrightmanley.co.uk
Est. 1861
Open Mon–Fri 8.30am–5pm
Sales Victoriana 1st and 3rd Wed of month 10.30am, viewing Tues 10am–7pm. Quarterly Fine Art sale (phone for details)
Frequency Fortnightly
Catalogues Yes

BELGRAVE

⊞ Antique Garden
Contact Maria Hopwood
✉ **Grosvenor Garden Centre, Wrexham Road, Belgrave, Chester, Cheshire, CH4 9EB** 🅿
☎ 01244 629191
Ⓜ 07976 539990
Est. 1991 *Stock size* Medium
Stock Garden items
Open Mon–Sun 10am–4.30pm
Services Valuations, shipping

CHESTER

⊞ Adams Antiques of Chester (LAPADA)
Contact Mr B Adams
✉ **65 Watergate Row, Chester, Cheshire, CH1 2LE** 🅿
☎ 01244 319421
Est. 1975 *Stock size* Medium
Stock 18th–19thC furniture,

clocks, glass, 19th–early 20thC small silver, mechanical devices, lighting
Open Mon–Sat 10am–5pm
Services Valuations, restorations, export service

⊞ Antique Scientific Instruments
Contact Charles Tomlinson
✉ **28 Chester, Cheshire**
☎ 01244 318395 Ⓕ 01244 318395
Ⓔ charles.tomlinson@lineone.net
Ⓦ www.lineone.net/~charles.tomlinson
Est. 1980
Stock Slide rules, calculators, early scientific instruments and drawing equipment
Open By appointment
Services Valuations

⊞ The Antique Shop
Contact Peter Thornber
✉ **40 Watergate Street, Chester, Cheshire, CH1 2LA**
☎ 01244 316286
Est. 1987 *Stock size* Medium
Stock Small items, mainly brass, copper, pewter
Open Mon–Sat Sun from Easter to Christmas 10am–5.30pm
Services Metal repair, restoration, polishing

⊞ Ask Simon
Contact Mr S Cleveland
✉ **25 Christleton Road, Chester, Cheshire, CH3 5UF** Ⓟ
☎ 01244 320704
Ⓜ 07815 559431 *Stock size* Large
Stock Decorative antiques, domestic paraphernalia, sporting and farming items, pictures, collectables, furniture
Open Mon–Sat 10am–5pm
Fairs Newark, Ardingly

⊞ Borg's Antiques
Contact Mr R Borg
✉ **14 and 26 Christleton Road, Chester, Cheshire, CH3 5UG** Ⓟ
☎ 01244 400023
Ⓜ 07939 227165
Est. 1991 *Stock size* Medium
Stock Silver, furniture, porcelain, Royal Doulton, small decorative items etc
Open Mon–Sat 10am–5.30pm Sun 11am–4pm
Fairs Swinderby, Newark

⊞ Bowstead Antiques (LAPADA)
Contact Olwyn Bowstead
✉ **59–61 Watergate Row South, Chester, Cheshire, CH1 2LE** Ⓟ
☎ 01244 342300
Est. 1981 *Stock size* Medium
Stock 18th–19thC town and country furniture, oil paintings, metalware
Open Mon–Sat 10am–6pm
Fairs NEC
Services Valuations

⊞ Cestrian Antiques
Contact Mr Malcolm Tice
✉ **28 Watergate Street, Chester, Cheshire, CH1 2LA** Ⓟ
☎ 01244 400444
Est. 1993 *Stock size* Large
Stock Small items of furniture, oak coffers, boxes, silver, glass, ceramics, longcase clocks, mantel clocks, wall clocks, pictures, lighting
Open Mon–Sat 10am–5.30pm or by appointment Sun eves
Services Valuations

⊞ Chester Antique Furniture Cave
Contact Mrs L Jones or G A Hadley
✉ **Congregational Church, 97a Christleton Road, Boughton, Chester, Cheshire, CH3 5UQ** Ⓟ
☎ 01244 314798 Ⓕ 01829 782330
Ⓜ 07710 622749
Ⓔ www.netcentral.co.uk/chester/cave
Est. 1984 *Stock size* Large
Stock Furniture of all periods and types including large dining tables, desks, bureaux, chairs etc
Open Mon–Sat 10am–5pm

⊞ D K R Refurbishers
Contact Mr D Wisinger
✉ **26b High Street, Saltney, Chester, Cheshire, CH4 8SE** Ⓟ
☎ 01244 680290
Est. 1984 *Stock size* Large
Stock Original pine and oak furniture
Open Mon–Sat 10am–4.30pm Sun 2–4pm
Services Valuations, restorations

⊞ Deja Vu Antiques
Contact Mr I Jones
✉ **23 Grosvenor Street, Chester, Cheshire, CH1 2DD** Ⓟ
☎ 01244 315625
Ⓜ 07772 691939
Ⓔ dejavuantiques@lineone.net
Ⓦ www.lineone.net/~dajuantiques
Est. 1984 *Stock size* Medium
Stock Antique telephones, Art Deco, pine furniture
Open Mon–Sat 9.30am–4.30pm
Fairs Chester, Leeds and Loughborough Art Deco fairs
Services Valuations, restorations, repairs, mail order service

⊞ Dollectable
Contact Mo Harding
✉ **53 Lower Bridge Street, Chester, Cheshire, CH1 1RS**
☎ 01244 344888/679195
Ⓕ 01244 679469
Est. 1972 *Stock size* Large
Stock Antique dolls
Open Fri noon–5pm Sat 10am–5pm
Fairs Kensington, Chelsea, Newark
Services Valuations, restorations

⊞ Farmhouse Antiques
Contact Ms K Appleby
✉ **23 Christleton Road, Boughton, Chester, Cheshire, CH3 5UF** Ⓟ
☎ 01244 322478 Ⓕ 01244 322478
Est. 1973 *Stock size* Large
Stock Wide range of antiques, country furniture, collectables, longcase and other clocks
Open Mon–Sat 9am–5pm

Halls Fine Art (Chester) Ltd (ARVA)
Contact Mr A Byrne
✉ **Booth Mansion, 30 Watergate Street, Chester, Cheshire, CH1 2LA** Ⓟ
☎ 01244 312300 Ⓕ 01244 312112
Ⓔ fineart@halls-auctioneers.ltd.uk
Ⓦ www.halls-auctioneers.ltd.uk
Est. 1999
Open Mon–Fri 9am–5.30pm
Sales Fortnightly general sales Wed 11am, viewing day prior noon–7pm. Quarterly antiques sales Fri 11am, viewing 2 days prior. Bi-annual wine sales and collectors' models, toys, scientific instruments and juvenilia sales three times a year
Catalogues Yes

⊞ Uri Jacobi Oriental Carpet Gallery (LAPADA)
Contact Uri Jacobi
✉ **55–57 Watergate Row, Chester, Cheshire, CH1 2LE** Ⓟ
☎ 01244 311300 Ⓕ 01244 311300
Ⓜ 07973 760722
Ⓔ urijacobi@aol.com
Ⓦ www.urijacobi.co.uk

Est. 1994 *Stock size* Medium
Stock Contemporary and antique carpets, rugs and tapestries
Open Mon–Sat 9am–5pm
Fairs NEC, LAPADA
Services Valuations, restorations, cleaning

⊞ K D Antiques
Contact Mrs D Gillett
✉ **11 City Walls, Chester, Cheshire, CH1 1LD**
☎ 01244 314208
Est. 1997 *Stock size* Medium
Stock Boxes, Staffordshire figures, prints, collectables, glass
Open Mon–Sat 10am–5pm
Fairs Welsh circuit, Manchester G-Mex

⊞ Kayes (LAPADA, NAG)
Contact Mr Nick Kaye
✉ **9 St Michaels Row, Chester, Cheshire, CH1 1EF** 🅿
☎ 01244 327149/343638
Ⓕ 01244 318404
Ⓔ kayesgem@globalnet.co.uk
Ⓦ www.kayeschester.com
Est. 1949 *Stock size* Large
Stock Second-hand, antique and new jewellery and silver
Open Mon–Sat 9.30am–5pm
Services Valuations, restorations

⊞ Made of Honour
Contact Mr Eric Jones
✉ **11 City Walls, Chester, Cheshire, CH1 1LD**
☎ 01244 314208
Ⓔ eric.antiques@virginnet.co.uk
Est. 1969 *Stock size* Medium
Stock 18th–19thC British pottery and porcelain, decorative items, boxes, caddies, Staffordshire figures
Open Mon–Sat 10am–5pm
Fairs Welsh circuit, Anglesey
Services Talks, lectures

⊞ McLarens Antiques & Interiors
Contact Sara Ewing
✉ **Boughton House, 38 Christleton Road, Chester, Cheshire, CH3 5UE** 🅿
☎ 01244 320774 Ⓕ 01244 314774
Est. 1983 *Stock size* Large
Stock French and Italian furniture, European and reclaimed pine
Open Mon–Sat 10am–6pm Sun 11am–5pm

⊞ Melody's Antique Galleries (LAPADA)
Contact G Melody
✉ **32 City Road, Chester, Cheshire, CH1 3AE** 🅿
☎ 01244 660204
Ⓔ george.melody@btinternet.com
Est. 1977 *Stock size* Large
Stock 17th–20thC furniture, varied small items, paintings
Open Mon–Sat 10am–5.30pm or by appointment
Fairs Newark
Services Valuations, shipping, nationwide delivery

⊞ Moor Hall Antiques
Contact John Murphy
✉ **27 Watergate Row, Chester, Cheshire, CH1 2LE**
☎ 01244 340095
Est. 1993 *Stock size* Medium
Stock 18th–19thC British furniture
Open Mon–Sat 10.00am–5pm

More Books
Contact Sue Morley
64 Lower Bridge Street, Chester, Cheshire, CH1 1RU
01244 310021 F 01244 310021
E sales@morebooks.co.uk
W www.morebooks.co.uk
Est. 1995 *Stock size* Medium
Stock Rare and second-hand books, stock of local Welsh history
Open Mon–Sat Sun in summer 9.30am–5.30pm

O'Keeffe Antiques
Contact Mr D O'Keeffe
2 Christleton Road, Chester, Cheshire, CH3 5UG
01244 311279
Est. 1998 *Stock size* Large
Stock Antique lighting, architectural antiques
Open Tues–Sat 10am–5pm

Objets d'Art
Contact Martin or Sonja De Rooy
67–71 Watergate Row, Chester, Cheshire, CH1 2LE
01244 312211 F 01244 400880
Est. 1998 *Stock size* Large
Stock Clocks, furniture, quality decorative items
Open Mon–Sat 10am–5pm
Services Restorations

The Old Warehouse Antiques
Contact Mrs U O'Donnell
7–9 Delamere Street, Chester, Cheshire, CH1 4DS
01244 383942
M 07790 533850
Est. 1989 *Stock size* Large
Stock Victorian–Edwardian furniture, beds, soft furnishings
Open Mon–Sat 10am–5.30pm
Services Valuations

Phillips International Auctioneers and Valuers
New House, 150 Christleton Road, Chester, Cheshire, CH3 5TD
01244 313936 F 01244 340028
W www.phillips-auction.com
Sales Regional Saleroom. Ring for details

Richmond Galleries
Contact Mrs M Armitage
Watergate Buildings, New Crane Street, Chester, Cheshire, CH1 4JE
01244 317602 F 01244 317602
Est. 1974 *Stock size* Large
Stock New and old country pine furniture, decorative items
Open Mon–Sat 9.30am–5pm

Saltney Restoration Services
Contact Mr J Moore
50 St Marks Road, Chester, Cheshire, CH4 8DQ
01244 312529 F 01244 312529
M 07713 823383
Est. 1967 *Stock size* Small
Stock Lighting, sanitary ware, furniture, ironware
Open By appointment
Services Restorations

Second Time Around
Contact Graham Shacklady
Staff Yard, 34 Spital Walk, Boughton, Cheshire, CH3 5DB
01244 316439 F 01244 322042
Est. 1979 *Stock size* Large
Stock Georgian–Edwardian furniture
Services Packing, courier, export

Second Time Around
Contact Graham Shacklady
6 Christleton Road, Boughton, Chester, Cheshire, CH3 5UG
01244 316394 F 01244 322042
Est. 1979 *Stock size* Large
Stock Georgian–Edwardian furniture
Open Mon–Sat 9am–5pm
Fairs Newark
Services Packing, courier, export

Stothert Old Books (PBFA)
Contact Mr A Checkley
4 Nicholas Street, Chester, Cheshire, CH1 2NX
01244 340756
M 07778 137461
Est. 1998 *Stock size* Large
Stock Wide range of antiquarian and second-hand books including local history, topography, natural history, good illustrated books etc
Open Mon–Sat 10am–5pm
Fairs PBFA, North West Book Fairs
Services Valuations, book search

Watergate Antiques
Contact Mr A Shindler
56 Watergate Street, Chester, Cheshire, CH1 2LD
01244 344516 F 01244 320350
E watergate.antiques@themail.co.uk
Est. 1968 *Stock size* Large
Stock Silver, silver plate, ceramics
Open Mon–Sat 9.30am–5pm
Fairs Newark
Services Restorations, repairs

Wheatsheaf Antiques Centre
Contact Jeremy Marks
57 Christleton Road, Boughton, Chester, Cheshire, CH3 5UF
01244 403743 F 01244 351713
E info@antiqueslineuk.com
W www.antiqueslineuk.com
Stock size Large
Stock General antiques 1600–1930s
Open Mon–Sat 11am–4pm Sun noon–4pm or by appointment
Services Shipping

CONGLETON

Pine Too
Contact Joan Tryon
8–10 Rood Hill, Congleton, Cheshire, CW12 1LG
01260 279228 F 01260 279228
M 07808 808980
E abletocane_uk@yahoo.co.uk
W www.touristnetuk.co.uk
Est. 1974 *Stock size* Medium
Stock Antique and reproduction pine, decorative antiques, bergère furniture
Open Mon–Sat 9.30am–5.30pm
Fairs Cheshire
Services Re-caning bergère furniture

Whittaker & Biggs (RICS)
Contact Mr J Robinson
The Auction Room, Macclesfield Road, Congleton, Cheshire, CW12 1NS
01260 279858 F 01260 271629
W www.whittakerandbiggs.co.uk
Est. 1931
Open Mon–Fri 9am–5pm
Sales General household furniture and effects 1st Sat of month and 2nd and 4th Fri 10am. Antiques, reproduction and collectables auction 3rd Fri 4.30pm, viewing evening prior 5–7pm
Frequency Weekly
Catalogues Yes

CREWE

Antique & Country Pine
Contact Mr S Blackhurst
102 Edleston Road, Crewe, Cheshire, CW2 7HD
01270 258617
Est. 1990 *Stock size* Small
Stock English and Continental original and stripped pine, hand-made reproductions
Open Mon–Sat 9.30am–5.30pm closed Wed
Services Restorations

The Buying Centre
Contact Mr D Lunt
60 Nantwich Road, Crewe, Cheshire, CW2 6AL P
01270 258241 F 01270 258241
M 07711 098070
Est. 1994 *Stock size* Medium
Stock Furniture, clocks, watches, jewellery
Open By appointment
Services Valuations, restorations

Cheshire Cast Company
Contact Mr D Davis
17 Crewe Hall, Weston Road, Crewe, Cheshire, CW1 6UV P
01270 873111 F 01270 873222
Est. 1994 *Stock size* Large
Stock Original cast-iron radiators
Open By appointment
Services Refurbishing and rebuilding original cast-iron radiators

Copnal Books
Contact Mr P Ollerhead
18 Meredith Street, Crewe, Cheshire, CW1 2PW P
01270 580470
Est. 1982 *Stock size* Medium
Stock Wide variety of second-hand and antiquarian books
Open Mon Fri Sat 9.30am–5pm or by appointment
Services Valuations

J D Luffman
Contact Mr J D Luffman
Bank House, 13 Bradeley Road, Haslington, Crewe, Cheshire, CW1 5PW P
01270 500199 F 01270 500199
M 07836 592898
Est. 1970 *Stock size* Medium
Stock Clocks, country furniture, militaria, musical boxes
Open By appointment

CUDDINGTON

www.horsebrass.co.uk
Contact Diane Wilkinson
Cuddington Lane, Cuddington, Northwich, Cheshire, CW8 2SY P
01606 882555 F 01606 882555
E brasses@horsebrass.co.uk
W www.horsebrass.co.uk
Stock size Large
Stock Horse brasses
Open By appointment only
Fairs DMG, Antiques for Everyone
Services Valuations

DAVENHAM

Davenham Antiques Centre & Tea Room
Contact Mr G Maxwell
461 London Road, Davenham, Northwich, Cheshire, CW9 8NA P
01606 44350 F 01606 782317
E maxwells@connectfree.co.uk
W www.antiques-atlas.com/davenham.htm
Est. 1984 *Stock size* Large
No. of dealers 15
Stock Wide range of antiques including furniture, collectables, china, silver, books
Open Mon–Sat 10am–5pm Sun 11am–5pm closed Wed
Services Tea room

DISLEY

Crescent Antiques
Contact Mr J Cooper
7 Buxton Road, Disley, Stockport, Cheshire, SK12 2DZ P
01663 765677
Est. 1972 *Stock size* Medium
Stock Wide range of furniture, silver, porcelain
Open Mon–Sun 10am–5.30pm
Services Valuations

Mill Farm Antiques
Contact Mr S Berry
50–54 Market Street, Disley, Stockport, Cheshire, SK12 2DT P
01663 764045 F 01663 762690
Est. 1971 *Stock size* Medium
Stock Longcase and other clocks, general antiques, mechanical music
Open Mon–Sat 9am–6pm Sun noon–6pm
Services Valuations, clock restorations, mechanical music, barometers

FARNDON

Derek & Tina Rayment Antiques (BADA, LAPADA, CINOA)
Contact Derek or Tina Rayment
Orchard House, Barton Road, Barton, Farndon, Cheshire, SY14 7HT P
01829 270429 F 01829 270893
M 07860 666629 or 07702 922410
E raymentantiques@aol.com
Est. 1960 *Stock size* Large
Stock Antique barometers
Open By appointment
Fairs Olympia, Chelsea, LAPADA, NEC (Jan)
Services Restorations, repairs

GREAT BARROW

Iain Campbell (PBFA)
Contact Iain Campbell
1d Barrowmore Trading Estate, Village Road, Great Barrow, Chester, Cheshire, CH3 7JA P
01829 741499
Est. 1970
Stock Antiquarian and second-hand books (mainly 19thC), maps, prints, ephemera, drawings, watercolours
Open By appointment
Fairs PBFA, Newark, Ephemera Society

HALEBARNS

Cottage Antiques
Contact Joy or John Gholam
Hasty Lane, Halebarns, Ringway, Altrincham, Cheshire, WA15 8UT P
0161 980 7961
Est. 1975 *Stock size* Medium
Stock General antiques, oak, mahogany furniture, brass, copper, paintings, ceramics
Open Mon–Sat 9am–5pm or by appointment
Services Valuations

HATTON

H & H Classic Auctions Ltd
Contact Simon Hope or Mark Hamilton
Whitegate Farm, Hatton Lane, Hatton, Cheshire, WA4 4BZ P
01925 730630 F 01925 730830
E info@classic-auctions.co.uk
W www.classic-auctions.co.uk

Est. 1993
Open Mon–Fri 9am–5pm
Sales Vintage and classic car sales 6 per annum, Wed 1pm, viewing day prior 2–7pm. Vintage and classic motorbike sales 2 per annum, Tues noon, viewing day prior 2–7pm. Held at the Pavilion Gardens, Buxton
Catalogues Yes

HELSBY

⊞ Sweetbriar Gallery Ltd (Paperweight Collectors Association)
Contact Anne Metcalfe
✉ **Sweetbriar House, 106 Robin Hood Lane, Helsby, Cheshire, WA6 9NH** 🅿
☎ 01928 723851 Ⓕ 01928 723153
Ⓜ 07860 907532
Ⓔ sweetbr@globalnet.co.uk
Ⓦ www.sweetbriar.co.uk
Est. 1988 *Stock size* Large
Stock Paperweights
Open Mon–Fri 9am–5pm
Fairs The Glass Fairs, DMG Fairs
Services Valuations

HUNTINGTON

⊞ Huntington Antiques
Contact Mrs Gregson
✉ **53 Chester Road, Huntington, Cheshire, CH3 6BS** 🅿
☎ 01244 324162
Est. 1994 *Stock size* Small
Stock Furniture, clocks, paintings
Open Mon–Fri 9am–5.30pm
Services Restorations

KNUTSFORD

⊞ Coppelia Antiques
Contact Mr K R Clements
✉ **Holford Lodge, Plumley Moor Road, Knutsford, Cheshire, WA16 9RS** 🅿
☎ 01565 722197 Ⓕ 01565 722744
Ⓦ www.coppeliaantiques.com
Est. 1976 *Stock size* Large
Stock Large collection of longcase clocks, fine Georgian furniture
Open Mon–Sun 10am–6pm or by appointment
Fairs Buxton (May)
Services Shipping

⊞ King Street Antiques
Contact Mrs E L MacDougal
✉ **1 King Street, Knutsford, Cheshire, WA16 6DW** 🅿
☎ 01565 750387
Est. 1993 *Stock size* Small
Stock Furniture, porcelain, silver
Open Tues–Fri 10.30am–5pm Sat 10am–5pm closed Wed
Services Valuations

⊞ The Lemon Tree
Contact Mr S Nelson
✉ **103 King Street, Knutsford, Cheshire, WA16 6EQ** 🅿
☎ 01565 751101 Ⓕ 01565 751101
Est. 1997 *Stock size* Medium
Stock English country furniture in satin walnut, stripped pine
Open Mon–Sat 10am–5.30pm Sun noon–5pm

Frank R Marshall & Co
Contact Mr A Partridge
✉ **Marshall House, Church Hill, Knutsford, Cheshire, WA16 6DH** 🅿
☎ 01565 653284 Ⓕ 01565 652341
Ⓜ 07808 483435
Ⓔ antiques@frankmarshall.co.uk
Ⓦ www.antiques@frankmarshall.co.uk
Est. 1969
Open Mon–Fri 9am–5.30pm closed noon–1pm
Sales General antiques and collectors' sales, 5 per annum, Tues 10am. Fortnightly household sales Tues 10am, viewing Mon 9am-6.30pm
Frequency Fortnightly
Catalogues Yes

⊞ Past & Presents
Contact Lindsey Bowman
✉ **35 King Street, Knutsford, Cheshire, WA16 6DW** 🅿
☎ 01565 653599 Ⓕ 01565 653599
Est. 1997 *Stock size* Large
Stock General antiques, model ships, extensive range of clocks, collectables, furniture
Open Mon–Sat 10.30am–5.30pm Sun 1.30–5.30pm or by appointment
Services Clock and furniture restoration

LYMM

⊞ Baron Antiques (LAPADA)
Contact Mrs Roberts
✉ **Port of Willow Pool, Burford Lane, Lymm, Cheshire, WA13 0SH** 🅿
☎ 01925 757827 Ⓕ 01925 758101
Est. 1964 *Stock size* Medium
Stock Architectural antiques, decorative arts, reclamations and general antiques
Open Mon–Sun 9am–6pm
Fairs Newark, Ardingly
Services Tea shop

⊞ Reflections (AMU)
Contact Mr John Sprague
✉ **11 The Cross, Lymm, Cheshire, WA13 0HR** 🅿
☎ 01925 753555/757331
Est. 1995 *Stock size* Large
Stock Furniture, china, glass, bric-a-brac, 1850s–1950s
Open Tues–Sat 9.30am–5pm Sun by appointment
Services Polishing, traditional upholstery

MACCLESFIELD

⊞ Churchills Auction Room
Contact Mr P Ginsberg
✉ **Union Street, Macclesfield, Cheshire, SK11 6QG** 🅿
☎ 01625 420088
Est. 1997 *Stock size* Large
Stock Antique, new and reproduction furniture, pianos, clocks, collectables, china, glass
Open Mon–Sun 11am–5pm
Services Valuations, restorations, occasional auctions

⊞ Gatehouse Antiques
Contact Mr W Livesley
✉ **72 Chestergate, Macclesfield, Cheshire, SK11 6DY** 🅿
☎ 01625 426476 Ⓕ 01625 426476
Est. 1974 *Stock size* Large
Stock Wide range of antiques including 18th–20thC furniture, jewellery, silver, glass
Open Mon Tues Thurs Fri 9am–5pm Wed 9am–1pm Sat 10am–5pm
Services Valuations, restorations, repairs

⊞ D Hill
Contact Mr D Hill
✉ **Unit 47, Market Hall, Grosvenor Centre, Macclesfield, Cheshire, SK11 6AR** 🅿
☎ 01625 420777
Ⓜ 07711 855937
Ⓔ hillsantiques@tinyworld.co.uk
Est. 1969 *Stock size* Large
Stock Collectables, brass, copper, militaria, jewellery, stamps, cigarette cards etc

Open Mon–Sat 9am–5.30pm
Services Valuations, jewellery repairs

Mereside Books
Contact Ms S Laithwaite
75 Chestergate, Macclesfield, Cheshire, SK11 6DG P
01625 425352
Est. 1996 *Stock size* Small
Stock Antiquarian and second-hand books, local history and illustrated books specialities
Open Wed–Sat 10am–5pm
Fairs Cheshire, Buxton
Services Book search

NANTWICH

Adams Antiques (BADA, LAPADA)
Contact Mrs Sandy Summers
Churche's Mansion, 150 Hospital Street, Nantwich, Cheshire, CW5 5RY P
01270 625643 F 01270 625643
M 07901 855200
E sandy@0800260.com
Est. 1970 *Stock size* Large
Stock Early oak, walnut and country furniture, Welsh dressers, Mason's ironstone, longcase clocks
Open 10am–6pm
Fairs NEC, BADA
Services Valuations, restorations, vetting

Antiques Traders of Nantwich
Contact Jonathan Coupe
The Manor House, 7 Beam Street, Nantwich, Cheshire, CW5 5LR P
01270 611125
M 07973 686378
E antiquetraders@hotmail.com
W www.antique-traders. co.uk
Est. 1990 *Stock size* Small
Stock Antique furniture
Open Mon–Fri 10am–5pm Sat 9am–5pm
Services House clearance

Barn Antiques
Contact Mr Brian Lee
8 The Cocoa Yard, Pillory Street, Nantwich, Cheshire, CW5 5BL P
01270 627770
Est. 1993 *Stock size* Medium
Stock Wide range of china, small furniture, copper, brass, collectables including Carlton Ware, Beswick
Open Mon Tues 10am–4pm Thurs Fri 9.30am–4.30pm Sat 9.30am–5pm closed 12.30–1.30pm

Bonhams & Brooks
Contact Andrew Turner
8 Pall Mall, Nantwich, Cheshire, CW5 5BN
01270 624127
E info@bonhams.com
W www.bonhams.com
Sales Regional representative for Wales and Border Counties. See Head Office (London) for details

Chapel Antiques
Contact Mrs D Atkin
47 Hospital Street, Nantwich, Cheshire, CW5 5RL P
01270 629508
Est. 1983 *Stock size* Medium
Stock Georgian–Victorian furniture, decorative items, mirrors
Open Tues–Sat 9.30am–5.30pm
Services Furniture restoration

Clock Corner (BHI)
Contact Mr M Green
176 Audlem Road, Nantwich, Cheshire, CW5 7QJ P
01270 624481
E clocks.corner@virginnet
W clockscorner.com
Est. 1975 *Stock size* Large
Stock Antique clocks of all types – bracket, Vienna, longcase, mantel etc
Open By appointment
Services Valuations

Dagfields Crafts & Antiques Centre
Contact Mr I Bennion
Dagfields Farm, Walgherton, Nantwich, Cheshire, CW5 7LG P
01270 841336 F 01270 842604
E ian@dagfields.co.uk
W www.dagfields.co.uk
Est. 1989 *Stock size* Large
No. of dealers 150 and 25 workshops
Stock Collectables and furniture of all periods
Open Mon–Sun 10am–5pm
Services 2 restaurants

Roderick Gibson
Contact Mrs R Gibson
70–72 Hospital Street, Nantwich, Cheshire, CW5 5RP P
01270 625301 F 01270 629603
E antiques@sfc.co.uk
W www.sfc.co.uk/antiques
Est. 1975 *Stock size* Medium
Stock Antique and reproduction furniture, small collectables
Open Mon–Sat 9am–5pm
Services Valuations, probate service

Love Lane Antiques
Contact Mary Simon
Love Lane, Nantwich, Cheshire, CW5 5BH P
01270 626239
Est. 1979 *Stock size* Medium
Stock General antiques
Open Mon–Sat 10am–5pm closed Wed

Nantwich Antiques
Contact Dr Coupe
The Manor House, 7 Beam Street, Nantwich, Cheshire, CW5 5LR P
01270 611125 F 01270 610637
E tony@indianfurniture.co.uk
W www.indianfurniture.co.uk
Est. 1979 *Stock size* Large
Stock Period and reproduction furniture, Oriental rugs, silver, prints, paintings, jewellery, Indian furniture
Open Mon–Fri 10am–5pm Sat 9am–5pm
Fairs Many nationwide
Services Valuations, restorations

Peter Wilson (SOFAA)
Contact Mr D Morgan-Wynne
Victoria Gallery, Market Street, Nantwich, Cheshire, CW5 5DG P
01270 623878 F 01270 610508
E auctions@peterwilson.co.uk
W www.peterwilson.co.uk
Est. 1955
Open Mon–Fri 9am–5.30pm Sat 9.30am–noon
Sales 2-day sales, 5 per annum, Wed Thurs 10.30am, viewing Sun prior 2–4pm Mon Tues 10am–4pm. Uncatalogued fast weekly sale Thurs 11am, viewing Wed 10am–4pm
Frequency 40 per annum
Catalogues Yes

POYNTON

Recollections
Contact Angela Smith
69 Park Lane, Poynton, Stockport, Cheshire, SK12 1RD P
01625 859373

Ⓜ 07778 993307
Est. 1984 *Stock size* Medium
Stock Costume jewellery, decorative china, glass, antique and pre-war furniture
Open Mon–Sat 10am–5pm

SANDBACH

Andrew Hilditch & Son Ltd
Contact Mr T Spencer Andrew
✉ **Hanover House, 1a The Square, Sandbach, Cheshire, CW11 1AP** Ⓟ
☎ 01270 767246 Ⓕ 01270 767246
Est. 1866
Open Mon–Fri 9am–5pm closed 12.30–2pm
Sales Quarterly general antiques Wed 10.30am, viewing Mon 10.30am–3pm Tues 10am–3.30pm and 7–8.30pm. General sale weekly, Wed 10am, viewing Tues 10.30am–3.30pm
Catalogues Yes

Saxon Cross Antiques Emporium
Contact John Jones
✉ **Town Mill, High Street, Sandbach, Cheshire, CW11 1AH** Ⓟ
☎ 01270 753005 Ⓕ 01270 753005
Ⓦ www.saxonantique.co.uk
Est. 1999 *Stock size* Large
No. of dealers 32
Stock Fine antiques from 17th–20thC, porcelain, silver, collectables
Open Tues–Sat 10am–5pm Sun 11am–4pm

STOCKTON HEATH

Bridge Antiques
Contact Mrs N White
✉ **123 Fairfield Road, Stockton Heath, Warrington, Cheshire, WA4 2BU** Ⓟ
☎ 01925 486365
Est. 1999 *Stock size* Medium
Stock Old and new pine furniture and other furniture, decorative items
Open Mon–Sat 10am–5pm

STRETTON

Harlequin Antiques
Contact Bernard Snagg
✉ **Roadside Farm, London Road, Stretton, Cheshire, WA4 5PG** Ⓟ
☎ 01925 730031/730781
Est. 1997 *Stock size* Large
Stock Victorian pine, oak, mahogany furniture
Open Tues–Sun 10am–6pm

TARPORLEY

Tarporley Antique Centre
Contact Peter Wright
✉ **76 High Street, Tarporley, Cheshire, CW6 0AT** Ⓟ
☎ 01829 733919
Est. 1991 *Stock size* Large
No. of dealers 9
Stock Pictures, small items of furniture, brass, copper, glass, books
Open Mon–Sat 10am–5pm Sun 11am–4pm

TATTENHALL

Great Northern Architectural Antiques Co Ltd
Contact Mrs J Devoy
✉ **New Russia Hall, Chester Road, Tattenhall, Chester, Cheshire, CH3 9AH** Ⓟ
☎ 01829 770796 Ⓕ 01829 770971
Ⓔ gnaacoltd@enterprise.net
Est. 1990 *Stock size* Large
Stock Stone, church exteriors, fireplaces, doors, brass ware, sanitary ware, pews, statuary etc
Open Mon–Sun 9.30am–5pm or by appointment
Services Valuations, restorations

WARRINGTON

Rocking Chair Antiques
Contact Michael Barratt
✉ **Unit 3, St Peters Way, Warrington, Cheshire, WA2 7BL** Ⓟ
☎ 01925 652409 Ⓕ 01925 652409
Est. 1976 *Stock size* Large
Stock Victorian–Edwardian bedroom and dining room furniture
Open Mon–Fri 8am–5pm Sat 10am–4pm
Fairs Swinderby
Services Valuations

WAVERTON

Antique Exporters of Chester
Contact Mike Kilgannon
✉ **Guy Lane Farm, Guy Lane, Waverton, Chester, Cheshire, CH3 7RZ** Ⓟ
☎ 01829 741001/01244 570069
Est. 1969 *Stock size* Large
Stock 1700–1930s furniture
Open Mon–Sun 9am–7pm
Services Restorations, shipping

White House Antiques & Stripped Pine
Contact Mrs E Rideal
✉ **The White House, Whitchurch Road, Waverton, Chester, Cheshire, CH3 7PB** Ⓟ
☎ 01244 335063 Ⓕ 01244 335098
Ⓔ rideal@whitehousescientifics.com
Est. 1979 *Stock size* Large
Stock German and English stripped pine furniture of all types
Open Mon–Sat 10am–5pm

WILMSLOW

The Old Sofa Warehouse
Contact Ms G Hargreaves-Jones or Mr R F M Jackson
✉ **Unit 1, 3 Hawthorn Lane, Wilmslow, Cheshire, SK9 1AA** Ⓟ
☎ 01625 536397
Ⓜ 07803 497938
Est. 1994 *Stock size* Large
Stock Victorian, Edwardian and later furniture, sofas, winged armchairs, chaise longues etc
Open Thurs Fri 10am–5pm Sat 10.30am–5pm or by appointment
Services Upholstery, designer fabrics

Wilmslow Antiques
Contact Mr M Dale
✉ **5 Church Street, Wilmslow, Cheshire, SK9 1AX** Ⓟ
☎ 01625 540472
Ⓔ pmdale99@aol.com
Est. 1996 *Stock size* Large
No. of dealers 20
Stock Wide range of stock including furniture, silver, copper, brass, pottery, china, pictures
Open Mon–Sat 10am–5pm

CUMBRIA

ALSTON

Alston Antiques
Contact Mrs J Bell
10 Front Street, Alston, Cumbria, CA9 3HU
01434 382129
07778 624021
Est. 1974 *Stock size* Large
Stock Wide range of antiques, furniture, clocks, barometers, china, textiles etc
Open Mon–Sat 10am–5pm Sun 1–5pm closed Tues
Fairs Newark

APPLEBY-IN-WESTMORLAND

Bridge End Antiques
Contact Mrs S Murton
3 Bridge End, The Sands, Appleby-in-Westmorland, Cumbria, CA16 6XL
017683 520502
Est. 1979 *Stock size* Large
Stock General antiques and decorative items, collectables, small items of furniture
Open Mon–Sat 9am–5pm

Barry McKay Rare Books (PBFA)
Contact Mr B McKay
Kingstone House, Battlebarrow, Appleby-in-Westmorland, Cumbria, CA16 6XT
017683 52282 017683 52946
barry.mckay@britishlibrary.net
Est. 1986 *Stock size* Medium
Stock Antiquarian, second-hand and new books, specializing in all aspects of book production and distribution, some books on Cumbria and the North
Open Mon–Sat 10am–4pm preferably by appointment
Services Book search, catalogue

BARROW-IN-FURNESS

P J Cassells
Contact Mr P J Cassells
138 Cavendish Street, Barrow-in-Furness, Cumbria, LA14 1DJ
01229 834747
07788 905324
Est. 1993 *Stock size* Large
Stock Edwardian–Victorian furniture, longcase clocks
Open Mon–Sat 10am–4pm
Fairs Newark, Swinderby
Services Valuations

BOWNESS-ON-WINDERMERE

The White Elephant
Contact Mrs J Moore
66 Quarry Rigg, Bowness-on-Windermere, Windermere, Cumbria, LA23 3DO
01539 446962 01539 446962
mooredsr@paveyarkfreeserve.co.uk
Est. 1989 *Stock size* Large
Stock General range of antiques, furniture, porcelain, pewter, mahogany furniture
Open Mon–Sun 10am–5pm

BRAMPTON

Something Old, Something New
Contact Mrs J Potts
46 Main Street, Brampton, Cumbria, CA8 1SB
0169 7741740
Est. 1979 *Stock size* Large
Stock Victorian pine furniture, country items, French decorative furniture
Open Mon–Sat 10am–4.30pm

Watsons Antiques
Contact Mr M Watson
40 Front Street, Brampton, Cumbria, CA8 1NG
01697 741066
enquiries@watsonline-ltd.co.uk
www.watsonline-ltd.co.uk
Est. 1987 *Stock size* Large
Stock Linen, lace, badges, medals, china, glass etc
Open Internet only
Services House clearance

CANONBIE

John Mann Fine Antique Clocks (BHI, AHS)
Contact John Mann
The Clock Showrooms, Canonbie, Carlisle, Cumbria, DG14 0SY
01387 371337 01387 371337
07850 606147
jmannclock@aol.com
www.johnmannantiqueclocks.co.uk
Est. 1987 *Stock size* Large
Stock Fine antique clocks
Open By appointment
Services Restoration, delivery, shipping, valuations

CARLISLE

Bookcase
Contact Mr S Matthews
17 Castle Street, Carlisle, Cumbria, CA3 8TP
01228 544560 01228 544560
Est. 1978 *Stock size* Large
Stock Antiquarian, rare and second-hand books, classical CDs and LPs, art gallery
Open Mon–Sat 10am–5pm
Services Book search, repairs, valuations

Carlisle Antique Centre
Contact Mrs W Mitton
Cecil Hall, 40a Cecil Street, Carlisle, Cumbria, CA1 1NT
01228 536910 01228 536910
wendymitton@aol.com
Est. 1986 *Stock size* Large
No. of dealers 6
Stock Wide range of antiques, clocks, watches, jewellery, silver, porcelain
Open Mon–Sat 9am–5pm
Services Restaurant

J W Clements
Contact Mrs J Morgan
19 Fisher Street, Carlisle, Cumbria, CA3 8RF
01228 525565
clements.antiques@btinternet.com
www.clements-antiques.co.uk
Est. 1887 *Stock size* Medium
Stock General antiques
Open Mon–Sat 9.30am–5pm closed Thurs

Cumbria Auction Rooms (NAVA)
Contact Howard Naylor
12 Lowther Street, Carlisle, Cumbria, CA3 8DA
01228 525259 01228 597183
www.invaluable.com/cumbria
Est. 1880
Open Mon–Fri 9am–5pm Sat 9am–noon
Sales Weekly sale of Victorian and later furniture and effects Mon. Quarterly antiques and works-of-art sales Mon 10am, view Fri 9am–5pm Sat 9am–noon
Frequency Weekly
Catalogues Yes

The Eddie Stobart Fan Club Shop
Contact Mrs G Collins
27 Castle Street, Carlisle, Cumbria, CA3 8TP
01228 515166 01228 590955
Est. 1996 *Stock size* Medium
Stock Eddie Stobart collection, die-cast models, clothing, ceramics, pens, mugs, limited editions
Open Mon–Sat 9am–5.30pm

Eddie Stobart Promotions Ltd
Contact Ms Debbie Rodgers
Kingstown Industrial Estate, Carlisle, Cumbria, CA3 0EH
01228 514151 01228 515158
promotions@eddiestobart.co.uk
Est. 1993 *Stock size* Large
Stock Eddie Stobart collection, die-cast models, clothing, ceramics, pens, limited editions
Open Mon–Fri 8.30am–5.30pm
Services Mail order service with catalogue

Phillips International Auctioneers and Valuers
48 Cecil Street, Carlisle, Cumbria, CA1 1NT
01228 542422 01228 590106
www.phillips-auction.com
Sales Regional Office. Ring for details

Souvenir Antiques
Contact Mr J Higham
4 Kinmont Arcade, Fisher Street, Carlisle, Cumbria, CA3 8RF
01228 401281 01228 401281
cumbriamaps@fsnet.co.uk
Est. 1986 *Stock size* Large
Stock Wide range of antiques and collectables, Roman and medieval coins, local maps, prints
Open Mon–Sat 10am–5pm

St Nicholas Galleries Ltd
Contact Mr C Carruthers
39 Bank Street, Carlisle, Cumbria, CA3 8HJ
01228 544459 01228 511015
Est. 1975 *Stock size* Medium
Stock Late Victorian and Edwardian furniture, watercolours, silver, silver plate, Doulton figures, Rolex and Omega watches, diamond and other jewellery
Open Tues–Sat 10am–5pm
Services Jewellery repairs

Thomson, Roddick & Laurie Auctioneers (RICS, ISVA)
19 Crosby Street, Carlisle, Cumbria, CA1 1DQ
01228 528939 01228 592128
Est. 1880
Sales 6 Antiques and collectors' sales per annum plus specialist sales of pictures, books etc
Frequency 6 per annum
Catalogues Yes

COCKERMOUTH

CG's Curiosity Shop
Contact Corrine Ritchie or Colin Graham
Cocker Bridge, 43 Market Place, Cockermouth, Cumbria, CA13 9LT
01900 824418/01697 321108
07712 206786
cgcuriosity@hotmail.com
Est. 1987 *Stock size* Large
Stock Unusual items, pictures, militaria, furniture, porcelain, glass, books, records
Open Mon–Sat 10am–12.45pm 1.45–5pm
Fairs Newark, Swinderby
Services Restorations, house clearance

Cockermouth Antiques
Contact Ms E Bell
5 Station Street, Cockermouth, Cumbria, CA13 9QW
01900 826746
elainebell@aol.com
Est. 1984 *Stock size* Large
Stock Large range of antiques, ceramics, glass, metalware, silver, jewellery, books, pictures, fireplaces
Open Mon–Sat 10am–5pm closed 1–2pm

Cockermouth Antiques & Craft Market
Contact Mrs P Gilbert
The Old Courthouse, Main Street, Cockermouth, Cumbria, CA13 9LU
01900 824346
Est. 1978 *Stock size* Large
No. of dealers 4
Stock Wide range of antiques including jewellery, china, glass, postcards, books, ephemera
Open Mon–Sat 10am–5pm
Services Pine stripping and French polishing

Mitchell's Auction Company (ISVA)
Contact Mr M Wise or Mr R Harrison ASVA
The Furniture Hall, 47 Station Road, Cockermouth, Cumbria, CA13 9PZ
01900 827800 01900 828073
MFineart@aol.com
www.mitchellsauction.co.uk
Est. 1873
Open Mon–Fri 9am–5pm
Sales 5 Fine Art sales per annum every 10 weeks Thurs and Fri 9.30am, viewing Tues 11am–5pm Wed 10am–7pm
Frequency Weekly
Catalogues Yes

GRANGE-OVER-SANDS

Anthemion (BADA, LAPADA)
Contact Jonathan Wood
Cartmel, Grange-over-Sands, Cumbria, LA11 6QD
015395 36295 015395 35356
07768 443757
Est. 1989 *Stock size* Large
Stock Georgian furniture, decorative items
Open Mon–Sun 10am–5pm
Fairs BADA, LAPADA, Olympia (June)

Gedyes Auctioneers & Estate Agents (NAEA)
Contact Mr N Gedyes
The Auction Centre, Main Street, Grange-over-Sands, Cumbria, LA11 6AB
015395 33366 015395 33366
07740 174537
gedyes@aol.com
Est. 1968
Open Mon–Fri 9am–noon
Sales General and antiques sales Fri 10am, viewing Thurs 1–6pm
Frequency Monthly
Catalogues No

Norman Kerr (PBFA)
Contact Mrs H Kerr
Priory Barn, Priest Lane, Cartmel, Grange-over-Sands, Cumbria, LA11 6PX
015395 36247
Est. 1933 *Stock size* Medium

Stock Second-hand and antiquarian books concerning art, architecture, travel, natural history, sport
Open By appointment only
Services Valuations

⊞ Utopia Antiques Ltd
Contact Mrs J Wilkinson
✉ **Yew Tree Barn, High Newton, Grange-over-Sands, Cumbria, LA11 6JP** 🅿
☎ 015395 30065 Ⓕ 015242 71867
Est. 1993 *Stock size* Large
Stock Pine and country furniture, Indian imports, handicrafts, furniture, fabrics, silver
Open Mon–Sat 10am–5pm Sun 11am–5pm
Services Bespoke furniture, hand-built kitchens

GRASMERE

⊞ Lakes Craft & Antiques Gallery
Contact Joe or Sandra Arthy
✉ **3 Oakbank, Broadgate, Grasmere, Ambleside, Cumbria, LA22 9TA** 🅿
☎ 015394 35037 Ⓕ 015394 44271
Ⓔ allbooks@globalnet.co.uk
Est. 1991 *Stock size* Medium
Stock Antiques, craft and gift items, china, silver, jewellery, small furniture, antiquarian books, postcards, cameras etc
Open Mon–Sun March–Nov 9.30am–6pm winter 10am–4pm

GREAT SALKELD

⊞ G K Hadfield (BHI)
Contact G K Hadfield
✉ **Beck Bank, Great Salkeld, Penrith, Cumbria, CA11 9LN** 🅿
☎ 01768 870111 Ⓕ 01768 870111
Ⓜ 07968 775694
Ⓔ gkhadfield@dial.pipex.com
Est. 1966 *Stock size* Large
Stock Clocks, horological books, clock restoration materials
Open Mon–Sat 9am–5pm or by appointment
Fairs Specialist clock fairs
Services Valuations, restorations

GREYSTOKE

⊞ Roadside Antiques
Contact Mrs K Sealby
✉ **Watsons Farm, Greystoke Gill, Greystoke, Penrith, Cumbria, CA11 0UQ** 🅿
☎ 017684 83279
Est. 1988 *Stock size* Large
Stock Antique ceramics, glass, Staffordshire figures, longcase clocks, Victorian–Edwardian furniture, silver, jewellery
Open Mon–Sun 10am–6pm

KENDAL

⊞ Below Stairs
Contact Mr S Ritchie
✉ **125 Stricklandgate, Kendal, Cumbria, LA9 4RF** 🅿
☎ 01539 741278
Ⓜ 07780 818915
Est. 1982 *Stock size* Medium
Stock Late 1800s–early 1900s brass, copper, porcelain, coloured glass, silver
Open Mon–Sat 10am–4pm

⊞ Dower House Antiques
Contact Mrs J H Blakemore
✉ **40 Kirkland, Kendal, Cumbria, LA9 5AD** 🅿
☎ 01539 722778
Est. 1959 *Stock size* Small
Stock 18th–19thC pottery, porcelain, furniture, pictures
Open By appointment
Services Valuations

⊞ Granary Collectables
Contact Mr B Cross
✉ **29 Allhallows Lane, Kendal, Cumbria, LA9 4JH** 🅿
☎ 01539 740770
Est. 1998 *Stock size* Medium
Stock Kitchenware, advertising, stoneware, pottery, collectables, pictures
Open Tues–Sat 10am–4.30pm

⊞ Kendal Studio Pottery Antiques
Contact Mr R Aindow
✉ **2–3 Wildman Street, Kendal, Cumbria, LA9 6EN** 🅿
☎ 01539 723291
Est. 1953 *Stock size* Medium
Stock Oak furniture, art pottery, maps, prints
Open 10.30am–4.30pm usually or by appointment

⊞ Lakeland Architectural Antiques
Contact Mr G Fairclough
✉ **146 Highgate, Kendal, Cumbria, LA9 4HW** 🅿
☎ 01539 737147 Ⓕ 01539 737147
Ⓔ gordonfairclough@cs.com
Ⓦ www.architecturalantiques.co.uk
Est. 1987 *Stock size* Medium
Stock Fireplaces, mirrors, lighting
Open Mon–Sat 10am–5pm
Services Valuations

⊞ The Lion's Den
Contact Mrs L Marwood
✉ **28c Finkle Street, Kendal, Cumbria, LA9 4AB** 🅿
☎ 01539 720660
Est. 1998 *Stock size* Large
Stock Antique and reproduction jewellery, clocks, pottery etc
Open Mon–Sat 10am–5pm closed Wed
Services Hand-made gold jewellery

⊞ Shambles Antiques
Contact Mr John or Mrs Janet Smyth
✉ **17–19 New Shambles, off Market Place, Kendal, Cumbria, LA9 4TS** 🅿
☎ 01539 729947
Ⓜ 07710 245059
Ⓔ j&jsmyth@shamblesantiques.demon.co.uk
Est. 1991 *Stock size* Medium
Stock Ceramics, glass, objects of virtue
Open Tues–Sat 10am–5pm
Services Valuations

⊞ John Smyth Antiques
Contact J Smyth
✉ **16 New Shambles, off Market Place, Kendal, Cumbria, LA9 4TS** 🅿
☎ 01539 729947
Ⓔ j&jsmyth@shamblesantiques.demon.co.uk
Ⓦ www.shamblesantiques.demon.co.uk
Est. 1992 *Stock size* Small
Stock Furniture, paintings, works of art
Open Tues–Sat 10am–5pm
Services Valuations

⊞ Thomond Antiques
Contact Mr D Masters
✉ **33 Allhallows Lane, Kendal, Cumbria, LA9 4JH** 🅿
☎ 01539 736720
Ⓔ thomondantiques@aol.com
Est. 1998 *Stock size* Medium
Stock China, glass, silver plate, 18th–20thC ceramics
Open Mon–Sat 10am–4.30pm
Services Valuations

KESWICK

Cat in the Window Antiques
Contact Mrs E Fell
29 Station Road, Keswick, Cumbria, CA12 5HH
0798 9217088
Est. 1988 *Stock size* Medium
Stock Small furniture, porcelain, pewter, copper, treen, pictures, 1930s Chintz porcelain
Open Tues–Sat 10.30am–4.30pm closed Wed
Fairs Carlisle, Moota Cockermouth
Services Valuations, bidding at sales

Keswick Bookshop (PBFA)
Contact Ms J Kinnaird
4 Station Street, Keswick, Cumbria, CA12 5HT
017687 75535
Est. 1994 *Stock size* Medium
Stock Antiquarian and second-hand books, maps, prints
Open Mon–Sat Easter–Oct 10.30am–5pm winter Sat 10.30am–5pm advisable to phone

Keswick Collectables
Contact Mr M Stainton or David Lomas
18 St Johns Street, Keswick, Cumbria, CA12 5AS
01768 774928
Est. 1997 *Stock size* Medium
Stock Collectables, stamps, books, records, Victoriana, Beatles memorabilia
Open Mon–Sat 10am–6pm Sun noon–6pm
Services Postal service

Lakes Antiques & Collectables
Contact Mrs B Wren
5 St Johns Street, Keswick, Cumbria, CA12 5AP
01768 775855
Est. 1992 *Stock size* Medium
Stock Collectables, china, glass, jewellery, hat pins etc
Open Mon–Sat 10am–5pm
Fairs Newark
Services Valuations

John Young & Son Antiques (LAPADA)
Contact Mr J Young
12–14 Main Street, Keswick, Cumbria, CA12 5JD
017687 73434 F 017687 73306
www.john-young-antiques.co.uk
Est. 1890 *Stock size* Large
Stock Fine selection of 17th–19thC oak and mahogany furniture, longcase clocks
Open Mon–Sat 9.30am–5pm advisable to ring Wed

KIRKBY STEPHEN

The Book House (PBFA)
Contact Mr C Irwin
Ravenstonedale, Kirkby Stephen, Cumbria, CA17 4NQ
015396 23634 F 015396 23434
mail@thebookhouse.co.uk
www.thebookhouse.co.uk
Est. 1984 *Stock size* Medium
Stock Wide range of general books including history of technology, gardening literature, children's and language books
Open Mon–Sat 9am–5pm closed Tues
Fairs PBFA
Services Catalogues issued

Haughey Antiques (LAPADA)
Contact D M Haughey
30 Market Street, Kirkby Stephen, Cumbria, CA17 4QW
017683 71302 F 017683 72423
Est. 1969 *Stock size* Large
Stock 17th–19thC furniture, decorative items
Open Mon–Sat 10am–5pm or by appointment
Fairs Olympia (June, Nov), LAPADA Birmingham
Services Valuations, restorations

David Hill
Contact Mr D Hill
36 Market Square, Kirkby Stephen, Cumbria, CA17 4QT
01768 371598
Est. 1966 *Stock size* Medium
Stock Small antiques, kitchenware, collectables, metalware
Open Mon–Fri Sat 9.30am–4pm

LONG MARTON

Ben Eggleston
Contact Ben Eggleston
The Dovecote, Long Marton, Nr Appleby, Cumbria, CA16 6BJ
01768 361849 F 01768 361849
Est. 1974 *Stock size* Large
Stock Pine furniture still in the paint
Trade only Yes
Open By appointment
Fairs Newark

LONGTOWN

T Potts
Contact Mr T Potts
Scaurbank House, Netherby Road, Longtown, Carlisle, Cumbria, CA6 5NX
01228 791513
07702 449770
Est. 1974 *Stock size* Large
Stock Period furniture
Open By appointment
Services Valuations

NEWBY BRIDGE

Townhead Antiques (LAPADA)
Contact Mr C P Townley
Townhead, Newby Bridge, Cumbria, LA12 8NP
01539 531321 F 01539 530019
townhead@aol.com
www.townhead.com
Est. 1960 *Stock size* Large
Stock Wide variety of antiques, including oak, mahogany, walnut, rosewood furniture, porcelain, glass, brass, silver etc
Open Mon–Sat 10am–5pm eves and Sun by appointment
Services Valuations

PENRITH

Antiques of Penrith
Contact Mrs S Tiffin
4 Corney Square, Penrith, Cumbria, CA11 7PX
01768 862801
Est. 1953 *Stock size* Large
Stock Varied stock of furniture, decorative items, collectables
Open Mon–Fri 10am–5pm closed noon–1.30pm Sat 10am–1pm closed Wed

Brunswick Antiques
Contact Mr Martin Hodgson
8 Brunswick Road, Penrith, Cumbria, CA11 7LU
01768 899338
Est. 1987 *Stock size* Small
Stock 18th–19thC clocks, furniture, glass, ceramics, collectables

Open Mon–Sat 10am–5pm closed Wed
Services Clock repairs

Penrith Farmers' & Kidd's Plc
Contact Mr M Huddleston
Skirsgill Saleroom, Skirsgill, Penrith, Cumbria, CA11 0DN
01768 890781 F 01768 895058
E penrith.farmers@virgin.net
W www.i-collector.com
Est. 1876
Open Mon–Fri 9am–5pm Tues 9am–6pm
Sales Victoriana sale monthly Wed 9.30am, household and effects sale weekly Wed 9.30am, viewing day prior 3.30–6pm day of sale from 8.30am. Quarterly catalogue sale of antiques and collectors' items Wed 10.30am, viewing Mon 10am–5pm Tues 10am–7pm day of sale from 8.30am
Frequency Weekly
Catalogues Yes

RAUGHTON HEAD

Cumbria Architectural Salvage (SALVO)
Contact Mr R Temple
Birkshill, Raughton Head, Carlisle, Cumbria, CA5 7DH
016974 76420 F 016974 76420
M 07703 881170
Est. 1986 *Stock size* Small
Stock Fireplaces, sanitary ware, oak beams, sandstone flags, doors, radiators, kitchen ranges
Open Mon–Fri 9am–5pm Sat 9am–noon
Services Fireplace restoration

SEDBERGH

R F G Hollett & Son (ABA)
Contact Mr C G Hollett
6 Finkle Street, Sedbergh, Cumbria, LA10 5BZ
01539 620298 F 01539 621396
E hollett@sedbergh.demon.co.uk
W www.holletts-rarebooks.co.uk
Est. 1960 *Stock size* Large
Stock Wide selection of antiquarian books including natural history, travel, topography of Northern England
Open Wed–Sat 10am–5pm
Services Valuations, catalogues

Stable Antiques
Contact Mrs S Thulby
16 Back Lane, Sedbergh, Cumbria, LA10 5AQ
015396 20251
W www.ourworld.compuserve.co/homepages/sedbergh
Est. 1968 *Stock size* Small
Stock Small antiques, tools, treen, silver, small items of furniture
Open Mon–Sat 10am–6pm Sun by appointment
Services Search, valuations

Avril Whittle, Bookseller
Contact Mrs A Whittle
Swarth Gill House, Garsdale, Sedbergh, Cumbria, LA10 5PD
01539 620026 F 01539 621770
E whittray@aol.com
Est. 1980 *Stock size* Medium
Stock Scarce, out-of-print and antiquarian books on art, craft and design
Open By appointment
Fairs Northumberland Lacemakers, Embroiders Guild
Services Book search, catalogue, valuations

Avril Whittle, Bookseller
Contact Mrs A Whittle
Whittle's Warehouse, Rear 7–9, Bainbridge Road, Sedbergh, Cumbria, LA10 5AU
01539 620026 F 01539 621770
E whittray@aol.com
Est. 1980 *Stock size* Medium
Stock Scarce, out-of-print and antiquarian books on art, craft and design
Open By appointment
Fairs Northumberland Lacemakers, Embroiders Guild
Services Book search, catalogue, valuations

SHAP

David A H Grayling (PBFA)
Verdun House, Shap, Penrith, Cumbria, CA10 3NG
01931 715282 F 01931 715282
E graylingbook@fsbdial.co.uk
Est. 1972 *Stock size* Medium
Stock Rare, out-of-print and new books on big game, deer, shooting, angling, hunting and natural history
Open By appointment only
Fairs Game fairs
Services Book search, catalogue, mail order, valuations, fine binding

SKELTON

The Pen & Pencil Gallery
Contact Mrs J Marshall
Church House, Skelton, Penrith, Cumbria, CA11 9TE
01768 484300 F 01768 484300
M 07787 613780
E ppgallery@aol.com
Est. 1995 *Stock size* Large
Stock Vintage and modern fountain pens, writing equipment, pencils, dip pens, inkwells
Open By appointment
Fairs London, Northern, USA pen shows
Services Valuations, repairs

STAVELEY

Staveley Antiques
Contact Mr J Corry
27 Main Street, Staveley, Kendal, Cumbria, LA8 9LU
01539 821393
Est. 1990 *Stock size* Large
Stock Brass and iron beds, French wooden beds, lighting, metalware
Open Mon–Sat 10am–5pm
Services Metalware restoration

THURSBY

Maurice Dodd Books (PBFA)
Contact Mr R McRoberts
Greenwood House, Thursby, Carlisle, Cumbria, CA5 6NU
01228 710456 F 01228 710456
E doddbook@globalnet.co.uk
Est. 1946 *Stock size* Medium
Stock Antiquarian books including topography, poetry, Lake District topics
Open By appointment only
Fairs Russell Hotel
Services Valuations

ULVERSTON

Brogden Books
Contact Mr I Chapman
11 Brogden Street, Ulverston, Cumbria, LA12 7AH
01229 588222
W brogdenbooks.co.uk

Est. 1998 *Stock size* Medium
Stock Antiquarian and second-hand books
Open Mon–Sat 10am–5pm closed Wed
Services Valuations

⊞ Elizabeth & Son
Contact Mr J Bevins
✉ **Market Hall, New Market Street, Ulverston, Cumbria, LA12 7LJ** 🅿
☎ 01229 582763
Est. 1961 *Stock size* Small
Stock Late 1800–1900s china, glass, jewellery, books
Open Mon–Sat 9am–5pm closed Wed
Services Valuations

WHITEHAVEN

⊞ Michael Moon (PBFA)
Contact Mr M Moon
✉ **19 Lowther Street, Whitehaven, Cumbria, CA28 7AL** 🅿
☎ 01946 599010 Ⓕ 01946 599010
Est. 1970 *Stock size* Large
Stock Rare, second-hand, antiquarian books on cinema, history, local history
Open Mon–Sat 9am–5pm
Services Valuations, book search, catalogues (2–3 a year)

WINDERMERE

⊞ The Birdcage Antiques
Contact Mrs T Griffiths
✉ **College Road, Windermere, Cumbria, LA23 1BX** 🅿
☎ 015394 45063
Est. 1983 *Stock size* Small
Stock 19thC items, country bygones, metalware, lighting, small items of furniture
Open Wed Fri Sat 10am–5pm closed 1–2pm

⊞ Serpentine Antiques
Contact Mrs M Worsley
✉ **30 Main Road, Windermere, Cumbria, LA23 1DY** 🅿
☎ 01539 442189
Ⓔ mworsley@fsb.co.uk
Est. 1974 *Stock size* Medium
Stock Furniture, collectables, china, glass, pictures, jewellery
Open Mon–Sat 9.30am–5.30pm Sun by appointment

WORKINGTON

⊞ Castle Antiques
Contact Mr K Wallace
✉ **18 Pow Street, Workington, Cumbria, CA14 3AG** 🅿
☎ 01900 607499
Est. 1997 *Stock size* Medium
Stock Collectors' items, curios, furniture, pictures. Publisher of local history books
Open Mon–Sat 9am–5pm
Fairs Charnock Richard, Newark
Services Valuations

GREATER MANCHESTER

ALTRINCHAM

⊞ Abacus Books
Contact Mr C Lawton
✉ **24 Regent Road, Altrincham, Cheshire, WA14 1RP** 🅿
☎ 0161 928 5108
Est. 1979 *Stock size* Medium
Stock Antiquarian and second-hand books. Arts, gardening and crafts books a speciality
Open Mon–Fri 10am–5pm closed Wed pm
Services Valuations

⊞ Altrincham Antiques
Contact The Owner
✉ **The Courtyard, 21–23 Tipping Street, Altrincham, Cheshire, WA14 2EZ** 🅿
☎ 0161 941 3554
Ⓜ 07836 316366
Est. 1868 *Stock size* Medium
Stock Wide range of general antiques
Open By appointment 7 days a week
Fairs Newark, Swinderby
Services Courier, finder, prop hire, photography

Patrick Cheyne Auctions (FSVA)
Contact Mr P Cheyne
✉ **38 Hale Road, Altrincham, Cheshire, WA14 2EX** 🅿
☎ 0161 941 4879 Ⓕ 0161 941 4879
Est. 1982
Open Mon–Fri 10am–5.30pm
Sales Every 2 months Fri 10.30am, viewing Thurs 2–4.30pm 6–8pm Fri 9–10.30am. Held at St Peters Assembly Rooms, Hale
Frequency Every 2 months
Catalogues Yes

⊞ Church Street Antiques Ltd (LAPADA)
Contact Mr A Smalley
✉ **4–4a Old Market Place, Altrincham, Cheshire, WA14 4NP** 🅿
☎ 0161 929 5196 Ⓕ 0161 929 5196
Ⓜ 07768 318661
Ⓔ sales@churchstreetantiques.com
Ⓦ www.churchstreetantiques.com
Est. 1992 *Stock size* Large
Stock Fine Georgian and Victorian furniture, art, objets d'art, carpets, decorative items
Open Mon–Sat 10am–5pm Sun noon–4pm
Fairs Baileys, Coopers
Services Valuations, restorations

⊞ Squires Antiques
Contact Mrs V Phillips
✉ **25 Regent Road, Altrincham, Cheshire, WA14 1RX** 🅿
☎ 0161 928 0749
Ⓜ 07831 682229
Est. 1977 *Stock size* Large
Stock Silver, jewellery, porcelain, brass, copper, lighting, small fine furniture
Open Tues–Sat 10am–5pm closed Wed
Services Valuations

ASTLEY BRIDGE

⊞ Alpine Antiques
Contact Mr B Carney
✉ **15 Sharples Avenue, Astley Bridge, Bolton, Lancashire, BL1 7HB** 🅿
☎ 01204 303364 Ⓕ 01204 303364
Ⓔ maybern@alpineantiques.co.uk
Ⓦ www.alpineantiques.co.uk
Est. 1974 *Stock size* Medium
Stock Silver, glass, porcelain, collectables etc
Open Mon–Sat 9.30am–5pm
Fairs Chester
Services Valuations

⊞ Red Rose Cricket Books
Contact Mr M Tebay
✉ **196 Belmont Road, Astley Bridge, Bolton, Lancashire, BL1 7AR** 🅿
☎ 01204 596118 Ⓕ 01204 597070
Ⓔ redrosebooks@btinternet.com
Ⓦ www.redrosebooks.co.uk
Est. 1993 *Stock size* Small

Stock Antiquarian and second-hand books and prints on cricket
Open By appointment
Services Catalogues (5 per annum)

ATHERTON

The Emporium
Contact Mr G Wilson
486 Blackburn Road, Atherton, Bolton, Lancashire, BL1 8PE
01204 303090 F 01204 302299
Est. 1989 *Stock size* Large
Stock Wide variety of second-hand Victorian–Edwardian furniture, china, collectables, glass etc
Open Mon–Sat 9.30am–5pm Sun 11am–4pm
Services Valuations

BOLTON

Bolton Antique Centre
Contact Mr G Roberts
96 Great Moor Street, Bolton, Lancashire, BL3 6DS
01204 362694
M 0780 9012306
Est. 1992 *Stock size* Medium
No. of dealers 20
Stock Quality antique furniture, paintings, china, silver, Art Deco, collectables
Open Mon–Sat 10am–4.30pm
Services Valuations

Bolton Pianos & Antique Export
Contact Frank Sotgiu
Victoria Buildings, Hanover Street, Bolton, Lancashire, BL1 4TG
01204 362036 F 01204 380355
W www.antica.co.uk
Est. 1983 *Stock size* Large
Stock Georgian– Edwardian furniture for export
Open Mon–Sat 9am–5pm
Services Shipping

Bonhams & Brooks
Contact Alan Whitehead
PO Box 107, Bolton, Lancashire, BL1 5SA
01204 364646 F 01204 521085
W www.bonhams.com
Open Mon–Fri 9am–5pm by appointment
Sales Regional Representative for Lancashire and Cumbria

B J Dawson (BNTA)
Contact Mr P Dawson
52 St Helens Road, Bolton, Lancashire, BL3 3NN
01204 63732 F 01204 63732
M 07801 537412
E dawsoncoins@btconnect.com
W historycoin.com
Est. 1966 *Stock size* Large
Stock Ancient coins – Greek, Roman, Byzantine, medallions, old English coins
Open Mon–Fri 9am–5pm Sat 9am–noon
Fairs London Coin Fair
Services Valuations, lists, medal mounting

Ironchurch Antique Centre
Contact Mr P Wilkinson
Iron Church, Blackburn Road, Bolton, Lancashire, BL1 8DR
01204 383616
Est. 1993 *Stock size* Large
No. of dealers 20
Stock Situated in an old church, offering antiques, furniture, pottery, porcelain, clocks, paintings
Open Mon–Sun 10am–5pm

G Oakes & Son
Contact Mr S Hughes
160–162 Blackburn Road, Bolton, Lancashire, BL1 8DR
01204 526587
M 07774 284609
E ycs12@dial.pipex.com
W www.Antique-DealerUK.com
Est. 1959 *Stock size* Large
Stock Antiques, 1700s–1920s furniture, shipping furniture
Open Tues–Sat noon–5pm or by appointment
Services Shipping

Olde Mill Antiques
Contact Paul Morris
Grecian Mill, Fletcher Street, Bolton, Lancashire, BL3 6NG
0800 542 5756/01204 528678
Est. 1980 *Stock size* Large
Stock Georgian–Victorian and shipping furniture
Open Mon–Fri 9am–5.30pm Sat Sun 9.30am–4pm

Park Galleries Antiques
Contact Mrs S Hunt
167 Mayor Street, Bolton, Lancashire, BL1 4SJ
01204 529827/0161 764 5853
Est. 1964 *Stock size* Medium
Stock 18th–early 20thC furniture, porcelain, decorative items, metalware, glass, pictures
Open Thurs–Sat 11am–4pm or by appointment
Services Restorations of most kinds

BOWDON

English Garden Antiques
Contact Bill Seddon
The White Cottage, Church Brow, Bowdon, Altrincham, Cheshire, WA14 2SF
0161 929 8081 F 0161 928 0854
E bill@english-garden-antiques.co.uk
W www.english-garden-antiques.co.uk
Est. 1996 *Stock size* Large.
Stock English garden antiques including stone troughs, sundials, bird baths, cast-iron urns, staddle stones, gargoyles
Open 10am–5pm confirm by phone
Services Valuations, restorations, repair

Richmond Antiques
Contact Mr J Freeman
The Hollies, Richmond Road, Bowdon, Altrincham, Cheshire, WA14 2TT
0161 928 1229 F 0161 233 0431
M 07720 416055
E info@richmondantiques.com
W www.richmondantiques.com
Est. 1993 *Stock size* Large
Stock Decorative furniture, chandeliers, mirrors including 19thC French and English
Open Tues–Sat noon–6pm or by appointment
Services Valuations, restorations

BREDBURY

The Old Curiosity Shop
Contact Mrs S Crook
123 Stockport Road West, Bredbury, Stockport, Greater Manchester, SK6 2AN
0161 494 9469
Est. 1983 *Stock size* Large
Stock 1920s furniture, barley twist a speciality, brass, clocks, pottery
Open Mon–Sat 10am–6pm Sun noon–5pm closed Wed
Services Hand stripping service

BROMLEY CROSS

⊞ Drop Dial Antiques
Contact Irene Roberts
✉ **Last Drop Village, Hospital Road, Bromley Cross, Bolton, Lancashire, BL7 9PZ** 🅿
☎ 01204 307186
Est. 1974 *Stock size* Medium
Stock Clocks, barometers, boxes, small items of furniture
Open Tues–Sun 12.30–4.30pm closed Fri Mon
Fairs Ripley Castle, Stoneyhurst (Galloway Fairs)
Services Clock and barometer restoration

⊞ Ellis & Wedge Books
Contact Siri Ellis
✉ **Last Drop Village, Hospital Road, Bromley Cross, Bolton, Lancashire, BL7 9PZ** 🅿
☎ 01204 597511
Est. 1998 *Stock size* Medium
Stock Antiquarian, second-hand and illustrated, local interest books and children's
Open Mon–Fri noon–5pm Sat Sun 10am–5pm
Fairs Buxton, Pudsey
Services Free book search

BURY

⊞ Newtons of Bury
Contact Mr Glen Wild
✉ **151 The Rock, Bury, Lancashire, BL9 0ND** 🅿
☎ 0161 764 1863 ❺ 0161 761 7129
Est. 1989 *Stock size* Medium
Stock Antiques, furniture, china etc
Open Mon–Sat 9am–5pm Sun noon–4pm
Services House clearance

CHEADLE HULME

John Arnold & Co
Contact Mr W Bradshaw
✉ **Central Salerooms, 15 Station Road, Cheadle Hulme, Cheshire, SK8 5AF** 🅿
☎ 0161 485 2777 ❺ 0161 485 3777
Est. 1865
Open Mon–Fri 10am–4pm
Sales Antiques and general sale Wed 11am, viewing day prior 11am–4pm day of sale 10–11am
Frequency Weekly
Catalogues No

Dockree's Fine Art Auctioneers & Valuers (RICS, ISVA)
Contact Mr David Dockree
✉ **Redwood Suite, Clemence House, Mellor Road, Cheadle Hulme, Cheshire, SK8 5AT** 🅿
☎ 0161 485 1258
Ⓦ www.thesaurus.co.uk./dockrees
Est. 1990
Open Mon–Fri 9am–5pm
Sales Antiques and works of art sales
Frequency 4–6 a year
Catalogues Yes

⊞ David Lloyd
Contact David Lloyd
✉ **10 Ravenoak Road, Cheadle Hulme, Cheshire, SK8 7DL** 🅿
☎ 0161 486 6368
Ⓜ 07711 948403
Ⓔ dloyd@onetel.net.uk
Est. 1991 *Stock size* Medium
Stock 18th–20thC silver, silver plate, flatware
Open By appointment only
Fairs Newark, Staffordshire
Services Matching flatware for canteens

DUNHAM MASSEY

⊞ Village Farm Antiques
Contact Mr C Thomason
✉ **Village Farm, Station Road, Dunham Massey, Altrincham, Cheshire, WA14 5SA** 🅿
☎ 0161 929 4468
Ⓜ 07977 139708
Ⓦ villagefarmantiques.co.uk
Est. 1987 *Stock size* Large
Stock Wide range of stock including pine furniture, architectural antiques, fireplaces, chaise longues etc
Open Mon–Sun 9am–5pm
Fairs Newark, Swinderby
Services Wood stripping, upholstery

ECCLES

Stephen Shawcross & Son
Contact Mr J. McInnes
✉ **103 Church Street, Eccles, Lancashire, M30 0EJ** 🅿
☎ 0161 789 3537 ❺ 0161 787 8461
Est. 1870
Open Mon–Sat 9am–5pm closed Wed

FAILSWORTH

⊞ Failsworth Mill Antiques
Contact Mr I Macdonald
✉ **Failsworth Mill, Ashton Road West, Failsworth, Manchester, Lancashire, M35 0SD** 🅿
☎ 0161 684 7440 ❺ 0161 681 7111
Est. 1993 *Stock size* Large
Stock Furniture, small collectables etc in one of the largest warehouses in North England
Open Mon–Fri 9am–5pm Sun 10am–4pm closed Bank Holidays
Services Restorations, export

The New Cavern Antiques & Collectors' Centre
Contact Mr Peter Stanley
✉ **Failsworth Mill, Ashton Road West, Failsworth, Manchester, Lancashire, M35 0FD** 🅿
☎ 0161 684 7802 ❺ 0161 628 5999
Est. 1997 *Stock size* Large
No. of dealers 40+
Stock Antiques, collectables, furniture
Open Mon–Sun 10am–4.30pm closed Sat
Services Shipping, valuations

⊞ R J O'Brien & Son Antiques Ltd
Contact Mr R O'Brien
✉ **Failsworth Mill, Ashton Road West, Failsworth, Manchester, Lancashire, M35 0FD** 🅿
☎ 0161 688 4414 ❺ 0161 688 4414
Ⓔ obantiques@btinternet.com
Ⓦ www.antique-exports.com
Est. 1972 *Stock size* Large
Stock Antique furniture
Open Mon–Fri 9am–5pm or by appointment
Services Container and courier service

T L H & Company
Contact Mr Thomas Higham
✉ **Unit 5, Victory Industrial Estate, Mill Street, Failsworth, Manchester, Lancashire, M35 0BJ** 🅿
☎ 0161 688 9099 ❺ 0161 688 9050
Ⓔ tlh@auctions1.freeserve.co.uk
Est. 1994
Open Mon–Sat 9am–5.30pm
Sales Weekly sales Tues 10am, viewing Mon 2–5.30pm

Tues 9–10am
Frequency Weekly
Catalogues Yes

HALE

⊞ Affordable Antiques
Contact Mr J Freeman
✉ **25 Stamford Park Road, Hale, Altrincham, Cheshire, WA15 9EL** 🅿
☎ 0161 929 0700
Ⓜ 07808 886982
Ⓔ affordableantiques@hotmail.com
Est. 1999 *Stock size* Large
Stock Wide range of antique furniture, mirrors, distressed and painted furniture
Open Mon–Sat 9am–6pm Sun noon–4.30pm
Services Restorations

⊞ French Country Style
Contact Margaret Ernstone
✉ **61 Stamford Park Road, Hale, Altrincham, Cheshire, WA15 9EZ** 🅿
☎ 0161 927 9041 Ⓕ 0161 980 8949
Est. 2000 *Stock size* medium
Stock French decorative items, furniture, lighting, mirrors
Open Tues–Sat 10am–5pm or by appointment
Services Restorations

⊞ Porcupine
Contact Ms V Martin
✉ **110 Ashley Road, Hale, Altrincham, Cheshire, WA14 2UN**
☎ 0161 928 4421
Est. 1982 *Stock size* Medium
Stock Antique pine, pottery
Open Mon–Sat 9.30am–5.30pm

HAZEL GROVE

A F Brock & Co Ltd
Contact Mr A F Brock or Mrs W Jensen
✉ **269 London Road, Hazel Grove, Stockport, Cheshire, SK7 4PL** 🅿
☎ 0161 456 5050 Ⓕ 0161 456 5112
Ⓔ info@afbrock.co.uk
Ⓦ www.afbrock.co.uk
Est. 1969
Open Mon–Sat 9am–5pm Wed 9am–1pm
Sales 8 Coins, jewellery and antiques sales per year, phone for details of sale. Specialist coin and banknote sales held periodically at the Acton Court Hotel, Stockport
Frequency 8 per year
Catalogues Yes

HEYWOOD

⊞ Heywood Antiques
Contact Mr Norman Marsh
✉ **5 Manchester Road, Heywood, Lancashire, OL10 2DZ** 🅿
☎ 01706 621281
Est. 1989 *Stock size* Medium
Stock Late Victorian–Edwardian furniture, clocks
Open Mon–Sat 9.30am–5pm closed Tues
Fairs Newark, Camelot
Services Clock repairs, restorations

HOLLINGWORTH

⊞ Annatique
Contact Mr G MacKay
✉ **3 Wooley Lane, Hollingworth, Hyde, Cheshire, SK14 8NW** 🅿
☎ 01457 852960
Est. 1977 *Stock size* Large
Stock Small furniture, clocks, lighting, mirrors, collectables
Open Thurs–Sat noon–6pm
Services Clock repairs

HORWICH

⊞ Stag's Head Antiques
Contact Mr George Bush
✉ **165 Chorley New Road, Horwich, Bolton, Lancashire, BL6 5QE** 🅿
☎ 01204 690962
Est. 1969 *Stock size* Medium
Stock General antiques mainly small furniture and bric-a-brac
Open Mon–Sat 10.30am–5pm closed 12.30–1.30pm

⊞ The Toy Shop
Contact Mr D Brandwood
✉ **138a Wright Street, Horwich, Bolton, Lancashire, BL6 7HU** 🅿
☎ 01204 669782 Ⓕ 01204 669782
Est. 1972 *Stock size* Large
Stock Collectable toys, Dinky, Corgi, Hornby, Triang, Matchbox etc
Open Mon Thurs Fri 9.30am–5pm Tues Sat 9.30am–2pm
Services Valuations

LITTLEBOROUGH

⊞ George Kelsall (PBFA)
Contact Mr G Kelsall
✉ **22 Church Street, Littleborough, Lancashire, OL15 9AA** 🅿
☎ 01706 370244
Est. 1979 *Stock size* Large
Stock Mainly second-hand, modern and antiquarian books on art, history, reference, topography of Northern England, industrial history, transport, social history
Open Mon–Sat 10am–5pm Tues 1–5pm
Fairs PBFA (Lancashire, York)

⊞ Nostalgia
Contact Mr Philip Sunderland
✉ **24 Church Street, Littleborough, Lancashire, OL15 9AA** 🅿
☎ 01706 377325 Ⓜ 07711 503 755
Est. 1994 *Stock size* Medium
Stock General antiques, furniture, lighting, Victorian fireplaces
Open Mon–Sat 10.30am–5.30pm

MANCHESTER

Capes, Dunn & Co (ISVA)
Contact Alison Lakin
✉ **38 Charles Street, Manchester, M1 7DB** 🅿
☎ 0161 273 1911 Ⓕ 0161 273 3474
Ⓔ capesdunn@compuserve.com
Ⓦ www.ukauctioneers.com
Est. 1826
Open Mon–Fri 9am–5pm
Sales Victorian and later period furniture and effects Mon noon, viewing from 10am day of sale. Specialist sales most Tues noon, viewing Mon 10am–4pm Tues 10–noon
Frequency Twice fortnightly
Catalogues Yes

⊞ Carl Ross Fireplaces
Contact Carl Ross
✉ **1026–1028 Stockport Road, Manchester, M19 3WX** 🅿
☎ 0161 224 2550
Est. 1991 *Stock size* Large
Stock Fireplaces and accessories
Open Mon– 9.30am–4pm

⊞ Didsbury Antiques
Contact Mr Alan Willis

✉ **85 School Lane, Manchester, M20 6WN** Ⓟ
☎ 0161 434 7487
Est. 1979 *Stock size* Medium
Stock General antiques
Open Mon–Sat 10am–5pm
Fairs Newark
Services Valuations, house clearance

Dollies Bear-Gere Ltd
Contact Robin Cottrill
✉ **61 Festival Village, The Trafford Centre, Manchester, M17 8FS** Ⓟ
☎ 0161 202 9800 Ⓕ 0161 749 9955
Est. 1998 *Stock size* Large
Stock New and second-hand Steiff and collectable bears, dolls
Open Mon–Fri 10am–10pm Sat 9am–7pm Sun noon–6pm

Dollies Bear-Gere Ltd
Contact Susan Cottrill
✉ **113 Regents Crescent, The Trafford Centre, Manchester, M17 8AR** Ⓟ
☎ 0161 749 9898 Ⓕ 0161 749 9955
Est. 1998 *Stock size* Large
Stock New and second-hand Steiff and collectable bears, dolls
Open Mon–Fri 10am–10pm Sat 9am–7pm Sun noon–6pm

Empire Exchange
Contact Mr David Ireland
✉ **62 Charles Street, Manchester, M1 7DF** Ⓟ
☎ 0161 236 4445 Ⓕ 0161 273 5007
Ⓔ empire@globalnet.co.uk
Ⓦ www.empir-uk.com
Est. 1986 *Stock size* Large
Stock Collectors' items, old and new books, toys, football memorabilia, dolls, teddy bears, jewellery, militaria
Open Mon–Sun 9am–7.30pm
Services Valuations

Forest Books of Cheshire
Contact Mrs I Mottershead
✉ **The Ginnel Gallery, 18–22 Lloyd Street, Manchester, M2 5WA**
☎ 0161 834 0747
Est. 1998 *Stock size* Large
Stock Antiquarian, rare, second-hand, new books, pictures, prints
Open Mon–Sat 10am–5.30pm
Fairs Buxton Book Fair

Ginnell Gallery
Contact Mr J K Mottershead
✉ **The Ginnell, 18–22 Lloyd Street, Manchester, M2 5WA** Ⓟ
☎ 0161 833 9037 Ⓕ 0161 833 9037
Ⓦ www.antiques-atlas.com/ginnell.htm
Est. 1980 *Stock size* Large
No. of dealers 30
Stock General antiques, decorative arts (1900–present day), antiquarian and second-hand books
Open Mon–Sat 9.30am–5.30pm
Services Café, bar

Levenshulme Antiques Village
Contact Mr Tony Warburton
✉ **965 Stockport Road, Manchester, M19 3NP** Ⓟ
☎ 0161 256 4644
Est. 1979
No. of dealers 20
Stock Furniture dealers situated in Old Town Hall
Open Mon–Sat 10am–5.30pm Sun 11am–4pm
Services Restoration, wood stripping

Malik Antiques
Contact Miss C Malik
✉ **10–12 Slade Lane, Manchester, M13 0QE** Ⓟ
☎ 0161 225 4431 Ⓕ 0161 225 4431
Est. 1985 *Stock size* Large
Stock Antique furniture, porcelain, architectural items, garden furniture
Open Mon–Fri 10am–6pm Sat by appointment

Secondhand & Rare Books
Contact Mr E Hopkinson
✉ **1 Church Street, Manchester, M4 1PN** Ⓟ
☎ 0161 834 5964/01625 861608
Est. 1972 *Stock size* Medium
Stock Antiquarian and second-hand books, some topography and special interest
Open Mon–Sat noon–4pm

Select
Contact Mr Abushal
✉ **276a Claremont Road, Manchester, M14 4TS** Ⓟ
☎ 0161 226 1152 Ⓕ 0161 226 1152
Est. 1994 *Stock size* Medium
Stock General antiques, mostly furniture
Open Mon–Sat 10am–5pm

MARPLE BRIDGE

Townhouse Antiques
Contact Mr Paul Buxcey
✉ **21 Town Street, Marple Bridge, Stockport, Cheshire, SK6 5AA** Ⓟ
☎ 0161 427 2228
Est. 1985 *Stock size* Medium
Stock Stripped pine furniture, carved wood, brass, iron beds, decorative antiques
Open Mon–Sat 10am–6pm

Vogue Antiques
Contact Mrs J Husband
✉ **80a Lower Fold, Marple Bridge, Stockport, Cheshire, SK6 5DU** Ⓟ
☎ 0161 427 1070
Est. 1995 *Stock size* Medium
Stock French country provincial furniture, lighting, mirrors, decorative items
Open Wed–Sat 10.30am–4.30pm
Services Restorations

OLDHAM

The Collectors Centre
Contact Mr I Thorogood
✉ **12a Waterloo Street, Oldham, Lancashire, OL1 1SQ** Ⓟ
☎ 0161 624 1365
Est. 1991 *Stock size* Large
No. of dealers 4
Stock Broad range of collectables – records, pop memorabilia, brass, pressed and old English glass, china, pottery, silver, videos, toys, etc
Open Mon–Sat 10am–5pm closed Tues
Services Valuations

Bob Lees
Contact Mr Bob Lees
✉ **65 George Street, Oldham, Lancashire, OL1 1LX** Ⓟ
☎ 0161 628 4693
Est. 1994 *Stock size* Large
Stock General bookshop, second-hand, some antiquarian, local history
Open Mon–Sat 10.30am–6pm
Fairs North West Book Fairs, Pudsey, Cresta Court

Marks Antiques, Jewellers/Pawnbrokers
Contact Mrs Marks

16 Waterloo Street,
Oldham, Lancashire, OL1 1SQ P
☎ 0161 624 5975 F 0161 624 5975
M 07979 508495
E bmarks46@hotmail.com
Est. 1970 *Stock size* Medium
Stock Jewellery, pottery, good-quality furniture
Open Mon–Sat 9.30am–5pm closed Tues
Fairs Newark
Services Pawn broker, valuations

PRESTWICH

Family Antiques
Contact Jean Ditondo
405–407 Bury New Road, Prestwich, Manchester, M25 1AA P
☎ 0161 798 0036 F 0161 798 0036
Est. 1984 *Stock size* Large
Stock Antique furniture
Open Mon–Sat 10am–5pm
Fairs Newark, Swinderby
Services Valuations

Prestwich Antiques
Contact Mr S Harris or Mr T Finn
371 Bury New Road, Prestwich, Manchester, M25 1AW P
☎ 07946 417074 F 07946 417074
E victorianimports@btinternet.com
W www.welcome.to/victorianimports
Est. 1984 *Stock size* Large
Stock Antique four-poster beds, furniture
Open Mon–Sat 10am–5.30pm
Fairs Newark, Ardingly
Services Valuations, restorations

Victorian Imports
Contact Mr Harris
371–373 Bury New Road, Prestwich, Manchester, M25 1AW
☎ 0161 7980911
E victorianimports@btinternet.com
W www.welcome.to/victorianimports
Stock Victorian beds
Open Please telephone

Village Antiques
Contact Ruth Weidenbaum
416 Bury New Road, Prestwich, Manchester, M25 1BD P
☎ 0161 773 3612
Est. 1981 *Stock size* Medium
Stock Porcelain, pottery, glass, pewter, small furniture
Open Mon–Sun 10am–5pm half day Wed

RADCLIFFE

Partners Antiques
Contact Mr L Ditondo
Walker Street, Radcliffe, Manchester, M26 1FH P
☎ 0161 796 7095 F 0161 796 7095
E luigi.ditondo@btinternet.com
W www.luigi.ditondo@btinternet.com
Est. 1991 *Stock size* Large
Stock Victorian furniture, shipping furniture
Open Mon–Sun 9am–6pm
Fairs Newark, Ardingly
Services Container service

ROCHDALE

Antiques & Bygones
Contact Mr K Bonn
100 Drake Street, Rochdale, Lancashire, OL16 1PQ P
☎ 01706 648114
Est. 1983 *Stock size* Medium
Stock Small antique items including pottery, silver, coins, medals, jewellery, militaria, collectables
Open Wed–Sat 10am–4pm

Central Auction Rooms
Contact Terry Pickering
4 Baron Street, Rochdale, Lancashire, OL16 1SJ P
☎ 01706 646298 F 01706 646298
Est. 1919
Open Mon–Fri 9.30am–4.30pm
Sales General household sales Tues 2pm, viewing Mon 9.30am–4.30pm. Occasional antiques and small items Tues 2pm, viewing Mon 9.30am–4.30pm
Frequency Fortnightly
Catalogues Yes

Rochdale Book Company (PBFA)
Contact Mr John Worthy
399 Oldham Road, Rochdale, Lancashire, OW6 5LN P
☎ 01706 631136 F 01706 713294
Est. 1972 *Stock size* Medium
Stock General stock of antiquarian and second-hand books
Open Sat 10.30am–5.30pm weekdays by appointment
Fairs PBFA (London, Lancashire and Yorkshire)
Services Valuations

ROMILEY

Romiley Antiques & Jewellery
Contact Mr Peter Green
42 Stockport Road, Romiley, Stockport, Cheshire, SK6 3AA P
☎ 0161 494 6920
Est. 1984 *Stock size* Medium
Stock Antique and second-hand jewellery, Georgian and Victorian furniture, pottery, general antiques, clocks, barometers
Open Mon–Sat 9am–5pm closed Tues Wed
Services Valuations, house clearance

SALE

Cobwebs of Antiquities Ltd
Contact Mrs J Williams
13 Green Lane, Sale, Cheshire, M33 5PH P
☎ 0161 905 3554 F 0161 905 3554
M 07768 934381
Est. 1996 *Stock size* Large
Stock Furniture, ceramics, mirrors, decorative items, pictures, lighting
Open Mon–Sat 9.30am–5.30pm
Services Restorations

Phillips International Auctioneers and Valuers
Eaton Place, 114 Washway Road, Sale, Manchester, M33 7RF
☎ 0161 962 9237 F 0161 976 5307
W www.phillips-auction.com
Sales Regional Office. Ring for details

SALFORD

A S Antiques
Contact Audrey Sternshine
26 Broad Street, Pendleton, Salford, Greater Manchester, M6 5BY P
☎ 0161 737 5938 or 07000 ART DECO F 0161 737 6626
E as@sternshine.demon.co.uk
Est. 1973 *Stock size* Large
Stock Art Nouveau and Art Deco, bronze and bronze and ivory figures, lighting, cameo glass, pewter, ceramics, furniture, jewellery, silver and general antiques
Open Thurs–Sat 10am–5.30pm or by appointment

Services Valuations, restorations, commissions to purchase

STALYBRIDGE

Highams Auctions (NAVA)
Contact Mr M McLaughlin
Waterloo House, Waterloo Road, Stalybridge, Cheshire, SK15 2AU
☎ 0161 338 8698 Ⓕ 0161 338 4183
Ⓔ info@hyamauctions.com
Ⓦ www.highamsauctions.com
Est. 1941
Open Mon–Fri 9am–5pm
Sales General antiques sales Sat 10am, viewing Fri 1–4.30pm Sat 9–10am
Frequency Fortnightly
Catalogues Yes

STANDISH

Corner Cupboard Antiques
Contact Mrs B Calderbank
49 Preston Road, Standish, Wigan, Lancashire, WN6 0JH
☎ 01257 426454
Est. 1980 ***Stock size*** Small
Stock General antiques, furniture, old dolls, china, pottery
Open Thurs Fri 10am–4pm

STOCKPORT

Antique Furniture Warehouse
Contact Mr M Shields
Unit 3–4, Royal Oak Buildings, Cooper Street, Stockport, Cheshire, SK1 3QJ
☎ 0161 429 8590 Ⓕ 0161 480 5375
Est. 1981 ***Stock size*** Large
Stock Wide range of antiques 1700s–1940s including porcelain, English inlay furniture, decorative items, architectural antiques, credenzas, walnut and mahogany bookcases
Open Mon–Sat 9am–5pm

Bonhams & Brooks North
Contact Robert Gowland or Kevin Scott
St Thomas's Place, Stockport, Cheshire, SK1 3TZ
☎ 0161 429 8283 Ⓕ 0161 429 8285
Ⓔ manchester@bonhams.com
Ⓦ www.bonhams.com
Open Mon–Fri 9am–5.30pm
Sales National and International Salerooms. Regional Representative for Cheshire, Merseyside, Manchester and the North West
Frequency Call for details

E R Antiques Centre
Contact Mrs E Warlowton
122 Wellington Street, Stockport, Cheshire, SK1 1YH
☎ 0161 429 6646 Ⓕ 0161 480 5598
Est. 1980 ***Stock size*** Large
No. of dealers 6
Stock Glass, china, pottery, scent bottles, costume jewellery, silver plate
Open Mon–Sat noon–7pm

Flintlock Antiques
Contact Mr F Tomlinson
28–30 Bramhall Lane, Stockport, Cheshire, SK2 6HR
☎ 0161 480 9973
Est. 1968 ***Stock size*** Medium
Stock Scientific instruments, telescopes, military items, paintings, marine models, furniture
Open Mon–Fri 10am–6pm

Hole in the Wall Antiques
Contact Mr A Ledger
20 Buxton Road, Heaviley, Stockport, Cheshire, SK2 6NU
☎ 0161 476 4013 Ⓕ 0161 285 2860
Ⓔ paul@antiquesimportexport.freeserve.co.uk.
Est. 1963 ***Stock size*** Large
Stock 1850–1920 American, Georgian–Edwardian furniture
Open Mon–Sat 9.30am–5.30pm or by appointment
Fairs Newark, Ardingly
Services Courier

Imperial Antiques (LAPADA)
Contact Alfred Todd
295 Buxton Road, Great Moor, Stockport, Cheshire, SK2 7NR
☎ 0161 483 3322 Ⓕ 0161 483 3376
Ⓔ alfred@imperial antiques.com
Ⓦ imperialantiques.com
Est. 1975 ***Stock size*** Medium
Stock Oriental antiques, ceramics, carpets, lighting, silver, silver plate
Open Mon–Fri 9am–5pm
Fairs NEC
Services Valuations

Limited Editions
Contact Charles Fogg
35 King Street, Stockport, Cheshire, SK1 1XJ
☎ 0161 480 1239
Ⓔ info@ltd-editions.co.uk
Ⓦ www.ltd-editions.co.uk
Est. 1974 ***Stock size*** Large
Stock Mostly furniture, especially dining tables and chairs
Open Mon–Fri 9.45am–6pm Sat 9.30am–5.30pm
Services Restorations, joinery, polishing, upholstery

Manchester Antique Company
Contact Mr J Long
Mac House, St Thomas's Place, Stockport, Cheshire, SK1 3TZ
☎ 0161 355 5566 Ⓕ 0161 355 5588
Ⓔ sales@manchester-antique.co.uk
Ⓦ www.manchester-antique.co.uk
Est. 1969 ***Stock size*** Large
Stock General antiques, second-hand and continental European furniture
Trade only Mainly trade
Open Mon–Fri 8am–5pm Sat 10am–4pm
Fairs Newark

Nostalgia
Contact Mrs E Durrant
Holland's Mill, 61 Shaw Heath, Stockport, Cheshire, SK3 8BH
☎ 0161 477 7706 Ⓕ 0161 477 2267
Ⓔ info@nostalgiafireplaces.com
Ⓦ www.nostalgiafireplaces.com
Est. 1977 ***Stock size*** Large
Stock Antique fireplaces, 1780–1900 sanitary ware
Open Tues–Fri 10am–6pm Sat 10am–5pm

Page Antiques
Contact Dennis Page
424 Buxton Road, Stockport, Cheshire, SK2 7JQ
☎ 0161 483 9202
Ⓜ 07966 154993
Est. 1979 ***Stock size*** Medium
Stock General antiques, Georgian–Edwardian furniture
Open Mon–Sat 10am–5pm
Fairs Swinderby, Buxton
Services Valuations, exports

STRETFORD

Insitu (SALVO)
Contact Mr F Newsham
149–151 Barton Road, Stretford, Manchester, Lancashire, M32 8DP
0161 865 2110
Est. 1984 *Stock size* Large
Stock Complete range of antiques, fixtures and fittings
Open Mon–Sat 9am–5.30pm Sun 11am–5pm

WIGAN

Avaroot
Contact Mr P Prescott
53a Mesnes Street (rear), Wigan, Lancashire, WN1 1QX
01942 241500
Est. 1994 *Stock size* Large
Stock Collectables including Doulton, Beswick, books, cigarette cards, records, coins, badges, railwayana, lamps
Open Mon–Sat 10am–5pm

John Robinson Antiques
Contact Mrs E Halliwell
172–176 Manchester Road, Higher Ince, Wigan, Lancashire, WN2 2EA
01942 247773 F 01942 824964
Est. 1963 *Stock size* Large
Stock Wholesale exporters, mostly shipping furniture
Trade only Yes
Open By appointment only

Colin de Rouffignac (BNTA)
Contact Mr C de Rouffignac
57 Wigan Lane, Wigan, Lancashire, WN1 2LF
01942 237927
Est. 1970 *Stock size* Medium
Stock 18th–early 20thC furniture, early coins, medals, general antiques, paintings
Open Mon–Sat 10am–4.30pm closed Wed
Fairs Tatton
Services Valuations

Steve's World Famous Movie Store
Contact Mr S Ellison
45 Cadogan Drive, Winstanley, Wigan, Lancashire, WN3 6JH
01942 213541 F 01942 213541
E movie.store@virgin.net
W www.1st.to/moviestore
Est. 1973 *Stock size* Large
Stock Stills, posters, vinyl and CD soundtracks, books and movie magazines from 1916 onwards, other memorabilia, autographs
Open By appointment
Services Free search, mail order, valuations

Wiend Books & Collectables (PBFA)
Contact Mr P G Morris
8–10 and 12 The Wiend, Wigan, Lancashire, WN1 1PF
01942 820500 F 01942 820500
M 07976 604203
E wiendbooks@lycos.co.uk
W www.wiendbooks.co.uk
Est. 1997 *Stock size* Large
Stock General stock of antiquarian and second-hand books, printed collectables, comics, stamps, programmes, badges, Wade
Open Mon–Sat 9.30am–5pm closed Tues
Fairs PBFA
Services Valuations

WOODFORD

Maxwells of Wilmslow
Contact Mrs Blackmore
133a Woodford Road, Woodford, Cheshire, SK7 1QD
0161 439 5182 F 0161 439 5182
Est. 1989
Open Mon–Fri 9am–5pm
Sales 2 general chattels sales per month, quarterly antiques sales
Frequency 2 per month
Catalogues Yes

WORSLEY

Northern Clocks
Contact Robert or Mary Anne
Boothsband Farm, Worsley, Manchester, M28 1LL
0161 790 8414
M 07970 820258
E info@northernclocks.co.uk
W www.northernclocks.co.uk
Est. 1997 *Stock size* Medium
Stock Longcase, bracket clocks
Open Thurs–Sat 10am–5pm or by appointment
Fairs Harrogate, G-Mex
Services Valuations, restoration

G White
Contact Mr G White
273 Chorley Road, Worsley, Manchester, M27 6AZ
0161 794 3806
Est. 1964 *Stock size* Medium
Stock General antiques, period furniture, clocks, sporting equipment
Open By appointment
Services Valuations, restorations

LANCASHIRE

ACCRINGTON

Almonds House Clearances
Contact Mr E Phillips
79 Burnley Road, Accrington, Lancashire, BB5 1AG
01254 391661 M 07881 407982
Est. 1984 *Stock size* Medium
Stock Victorian to modern furniture, pottery etc
Open Mon–Sat 9am–5pm closed Wed
Services Valuations

Alpha Coins & Medals (OMRS)
Contact Mr P Darlington
10 Water Street, Accrington, Lancashire, BB5 6PX
01254 395540 F 01254 393323
Est. 1994 *Stock size* Medium
Stock Post-1800 British coins and medals
Open Mon–Sat 9.30am–5pm
Fairs Bradford Coin Show, Outwood Memorial Hall Medal Show, Wakefield
Services Medal mounting

Bohemia
Contact Mrs P Oldman
11 Warner Street, Accrington, Lancashire, BB5 1HN
01254 231119
Est. 1993 *Stock size* Large
Stock 1940s–1970s clothing and accessories
Open Tues–Sat 10.30am–5pm closed Mon Wed
Fairs Manchester Textile Fair

Revival
Contact Mr Ian Smith
34 Warner Street, Accrington, Lancashire, BB5 1HN
01254 382316
Est. 1989 *Stock size* Large
Stock Costume, textiles, jewellery from 1900–1970s
Open Mon–Sat 10.30am–5pm closed Wed or by appointment
Fairs Hammersmith Textiles
Services Costume hire

BARTON

Kopper Kettle Furniture
Contact Mr Steve Round
639 Garstang Road, Barton, Preston, Lancashire, PR3 5DQ
01772 861064
Est. 1998 *Stock size* Medium
Stock Victorian–Edwardian furniture, some reproduction
Open Mon–Sun 10.30am–5.30pm closed Fri
Services Valuations, metal polishing

BLACKBURN

Ancient and Modern (NAG, OMRS)
Contact Zac Coles
17 Newmarket Street, Blackburn, Lancashire, BB1 7DR
01254 668818 F 01254 677866
Est. 1943 *Stock size* Large
Stock Georgian–modern jewellery, watches, silver, coins, medals
Open Mon–Sat 9am–5.30pm
Fairs Miami, Bangkok
Services Valuations, restorations

Decades (Textile Association)
Contact Janet Conroy
20 Lord Street West, Blackburn, Lancashire, BB2 1JX
01254 693320
Est. 1989 *Stock size* Large
Stock Costumes, textiles, accessories, pottery, small furniture, pictures, glass, curios, collectables
Open Mon–Sat 10.30am–5pm or by appointment
Fairs Margaret Bolger Art Fairs, Hammersmith

Fieldings Antiques & Clocks
Contact Mr Andrew Fielding
149 Blackmoor Road, Blackburn, Lancashire, BB1 2LG
01254 263358
M 07973 698961
Est. 1964 *Stock size* Large
Stock Clocks (including longcase), period furniture, steam engines, vintage motorcycles
Open Mon–Fri 9am–5pm

Great Expectations
Contact Mrs C Haworth
918 Whalley New Road, Blackburn, Lancashire, BB1 9BD
01254 248261 F 01254 248261
Est. 1998 *Stock size* Medium
Stock Victorian–Edwardian furniture, pottery, pictures, glassware, general antiques
Open Mon Wed–Sat 10am–5.30pm Sun 11am–4.30pm
Services Restorations

Mitchells Lock Antiques
Contact Mr S Mitchell
76 Bolton Road, Blackburn, Lancashire, BB2 3PZ
01254 664663
Est. 1973 *Stock size* Large
Stock General antiques
Open Mon–Sat 9am–5pm
Fairs Newark, Swinderby

BLACKPOOL

Ascot Antiques
Contact Mr C Winwood
106 Holmefield Road, Blackpool, Lancashire, FY2 9RF
01253 356383
Est. 1987 *Stock size* Medium
Stock Georgian–Victorian furniture and oil paintings
Open By appointment
Fairs Hoyles, Blackpool
Services Valuations

Peter Christian
Contact Mrs Ann Christian
400–402 Waterloo Road, South Shore, Blackpool, Lancashire, FY4 4BL
01253 763268 F 01253 763268
Est. 1978 *Stock size* Medium
Stock 1860s–1920s decorative arts
Open Mon–Sat 10am–5.30pm closed Wed
Fairs Newark, Swinderby

Robinsons Timber Building Supplies Ltd
Contact Mr A Robinson
3–7 Boothley Road, Blackpool, Lancashire, FY1 3RS
01253 628826 F 01253 627812
Est. 1938 *Stock size* Large
Stock Architectural antiques, doors, floors etc, garden items
Open Mon–Fri 8am–5.30pm Sat 8am–2pm
Services Restorations of timber flooring

B Scott-Spencer
Contact Mr J Neiman
228 Church Street, Blackpool, Lancashire, FY1 3PX
01253 294489 F 01253 626977
Stock Wide range of general antiques, jewellery, stamps, collectables etc
Open Mon–Fri 10am–4pm phone for appointment
Services Valuations, repairs, buying large diamonds

BRETHERTON

The Old Corn Mill Antique Centre
Contact Mr M Fellows
64 South Road, Bretherton, Lancashire, PR5 7AG
01772 601371 F 01772 601932
Est. 1999 *Stock size* Large
No. of dealers 50
Stock Antiques and collectables
Open Mon–Sat 10.30am–5.30pm Sun 11am–5pm

BURNLEY

Brun-Lea Antiques & Furnishings
Contact Mr John Waite
Unit 1, Travis Street, Burnley, Lancashire, BB10 1DG
01282 413513 F 01282 832769
M 07860 511842
W www.antiques-atlas.com/brunlea.htm
Est. 1970 *Stock size* Large
Stock Period furniture
Open Mon–Thurs 8.30am–5.30pm Fri Sat 8.30am–4pm Sun noon–4pm

Lonesome Pine Antiques
Contact Mr P Berry
19 Bank Parade, Burnley, Lancashire, BB11 1UH
01282 428415
Est. 1987 *Stock size* Medium
Stock Antique pine furniture, period furniture, reclaimed pine furniture
Open Mon–Sat 9am–5pm
Services Bespoke furniture

BURSCOUGH

West Lancashire Antiques Export (LAPADA)
Contact Brett Griffiths
Victoria Mill, Victoria Street, Burscough, Lancashire, LN40 0SN P
☎ 01704 894634
Est. 1969 *Stock size* Large
Stock Antique furniture
Open Mon–Fri 9am–5.30pm Sat Sun 10am–5.30pm
Fairs Swinderby, Newark
Services Shipping

CHARNOCK RICHARD

Park Hall
Contact Mr David Fletcher
Exhibition Halls, Charnock Richard, Lancashire, PR7 5LP P
☎ 0161 7737001 *Stock size* Large
No. of dealers 150
Stock General antiques fair held every Sunday. £2 entrance fee
Open 5am–3pm outside stalls 8.30am–3pm

CHATBURN

T & J Brindle Antiques (LAPADA)
Contact T Brindle
6–8 Sawley Road, Chatburn, Clitheroe, Lancashire, BB7 4AS P
☎ 01200 440025 F 01200 440090
W www.antiqueweb.co.uk/tbrindle
Est. 1961 *Stock size* Large
Stock Good quality antiques
Open Mon–Fri 9am–5pm or by appointment
Fairs Olympia

CLEVELEYS

Smythe's
Contact Mr P Smythe
174 Victoria Road West, Cleveleys, Lancashire, FY5 3NE P
☎ 01253 852184 F 01253 854084
Est. 1929
Open Mon–Fri 9am–5.30pm Sat 9am–4pm
Sales General sales every 2 weeks
Frequency Antiques sales every 6 weeks
Catalogues Yes

CLITHEROE

Clitheroe Collectables
Contact Mrs J D Mulligan
13 Duck Street, Clitheroe, Lancashire, BB7 1LP P
☎ 01200 422222 F 01200 422223
Est. 1989 *Stock size* Medium
Stock Pottery, Victorian pine furniture
Open Mon–Sat 9am–5.30pm closed Wed
Services Restorations of antique pine

Past and Present Fireplaces
Contact Mr David Hollings
22 Whalley Road, Clitheroe, Lancashire, BB7 1AW P
☎ 01200 428678/445373
Est. 1987 *Stock size* Large
Stock Architectural antiques, general antiques, fireplaces a speciality
Open Mon–Sat 10.30am–5pm Sun by appointment closed Wed
Fairs Newark
Services Fitting service, fire accessories

Roundstone Books
Contact Mr J Harding
120 Lowergate, Clitheroe, Lancashire, BB7 1AG P
☎ 01200 444242
E joharbooks@aol.com
W www.roundstonebooks.co.uk
Est. 1995 *Stock size* Medium
Stock Antiquarian and second-hand books, general stock including alternative medicine, poetry, literature, children's books
Open Tues–Sat 10am–5pm closed Wed
Services Book search

COLNE

Ingleside Antiques
Contact Mr Jack Fry
13 Keighley Road, Colne, Lancashire, BB8 0LP P
☎ 01282 860046
M 07775 515014
Est. 1990 *Stock size* Medium
Stock Longcase, bracket, wall, mantel clocks, furniture
Open Mon Wed Fri Sat 10am–5pm
Services Repairs

DARWEN

Belgrave Antiques Centre
Contact Mr M Cooney
Brittania Mill, 136 Bolton Road, Darwen, Lancashire, BB3 1BZ P
☎ 01254 777714
E belgraveantiques@aol.com
Est. 1997 *Stock size* Large
No. of dealers 40
Stock Furniture, pottery, Victorian stripped pine, architectural antiques, collectables
Open Mon–Sat 9.30am–5pm Sun 10am–4.30pm
Services Stripping, shipping

Grove Antiques
Contact Mr K Cooney
Hampden Mill, Springdale, Grimshaw Street, Darwen, Lancashire, BB3 P
☎ 01254 776644
Est. 1984 *Stock size* Small
Stock Mixed stock of Edwardian furniture, bric-a-brac
Open Mon–Sat 10am–4pm
Fairs Newark, Kempton

K C Antiques (LAPADA)
Contact Mr C Davies
538 Bolton Road, Darwen, Lancashire, BB3 2JR P
☎ 01254 772252 F 01254 704267
E mickdavies@breathe.mail.net.
Est. 1970 *Stock size* Medium
Stock 18th–19thC furniture and decorative items
Open Mon–Sat 9am–5.30pm Sun 10am–4pm and by appointment
Fairs NEC, LAPADA

ECCLESTONE

Bygone Times
Contact Ged Wood
Grove Mill, The Green, Ecclestone, Chorley, Lancashire, PR7 5PD P
☎ 01257 451889 F 01257 451090
E ged.wood@virgin.net
W www.bygonetimes.co.uk
Est. 1988 *Stock size* Large
No. of dealers 250 stalls
Stock Antiques, furniture, small items, collectables, memorabilia
Open Mon–Sun 10am–6pm Wed 10am–8pm

⊞ Bygone Times International Plc
Contact Mr Charles Frankland
✉ **Grove Mill, The Green, Eccleston, Chorley, Lancashire, PR7 5PD** Ⓟ
☎ 01257 453780 Ⓕ 01257 450197
Ⓔ enquire@ebygone-times.co.uk
Ⓦ www.bygone-times.com
Est. 1987 *Stock size* Large
Stock Wide range of architectural antiques
Open Mon–Sun 10am–5pm
Fairs Plaza, LIW.

⊞ The Cutlery Chest
Contact Mr R W Metcalf
✉ **7 The Carrington Centre, The Green, Eccleston, Chorley, Lancashire, PR7 5UP** Ⓟ
☎ 01257 451281
Ⓔ Robert.W.Metcalf@btinternet.com
Est. 1989 *Stock size* Medium
Stock Silver-plated cutlery, linen, china, glass
Open Wed–Sat 10.30am–5pm
Fairs Newark, Ardingly
Services Cutlery repair and silver plating

FLEETWOOD

⊞ Pavilion
Contact Mr Edward McLaughlin
✉ **228 Dock Street, Fleetwood, Lancashire, FY7 6NU** Ⓟ
☎ 01253 778851 Ⓕ 01253 779192
Ⓔ pavilion@propitup.demon.co.uk
Est. 1984 *Stock size* Medium
Stock Decorative items for the home
Open Mon–Sat 10am–5.30pm
Fairs Newark

GARSTANG

⊞ Acanthus
Contact Mrs L Stocks
✉ **Unit 3, Thomas Court, Thomas Weind, Garstang, Preston, Lancashire, PR3 1LL** Ⓟ
☎ 01995 604780
Est. 1987 *Stock size* Medium
Stock Wide variety of stock including small furniture, china, copper, brass, pictures etc
Open Mon–Sat 10am–5pm closed Wed

GREAT HARWOOD

⊞ Benny Charlsworth's Snuff Box
Contact Naomi Walsh
✉ **51 Blackburn Road, Great Harwood, Blackburn, Lancashire, BB6 7DF** Ⓟ
☎ 01254 888550
Est. 1983 *Stock size* Large
Stock Antique furniture, paintings, pottery, costume jewellery, linen etc
Open Mon–Fri 10am–1pm 2pm–5pm Sat 9.30am–4pm closed Tues
Fairs Newark

⊞ Jean's Military Memories
Contact Mrs J South
✉ **32 Queen Street, Great Harwood, Blackburn, Lancashire, BB6 7QQ** Ⓟ
☎ 01254 877825 Ⓕ 01254 877825
Ⓜ 07710 713133
Est. 1996 *Stock size* Large
Stock Militaria, guns of all types, edged weaponry
Open Mon–Fri 9.30am–4.30pm Sat 10am–2pm or by appointment

HAPTON

⊞ Pipkins Antiques
Contact Maurice Bradley
✉ **5 The Stables, Hapton, Nr Burnley, Lancashire, BB12 7LL**
Ⓟ Ⓕ 01282 770548
Ⓜ 07778 265909
Ⓔ maurice@pipkins.fsbusiness.co.uk
Ⓦ www.olddoors.co.uk
Est. 1996 *Stock size* Large
Stock Doors, door furniture, Belfast sinks, general architectural salvage
Open By appointment

HARLE SYKE

⌂ Kings Mill Antique Centre
Contact Linda Heuer
✉ **Unit 6, Kings Mill, Queen Street, Harle Syke, Burnley, Lancashire, BB10 2HX** Ⓟ
☎ 01282 431953 Ⓕ 01282 431953
Ⓜ 07803 153752
Ⓔ antiques@kingsmill.demon.co.uk
Ⓦ www.kingsmill.demon.co.uk
Est. 1996 *Stock size* Large
No. of dealers 30
Stock Antique furniture, continental European collectables
Open Mon–Sat 10am–5pm Thurs 10am–8pm Sun 11am–5pm
Services Container service, export

HASLINGDEN

⊞ P J Brown Antiques
Contact Mrs K Brown
✉ **8 Church Street, Haslingden, Rossendale, Lancashire, BB4 5QU** Ⓟ
☎ 01706 224888 Ⓕ 01706 224888
Est. 1979 *Stock size* Medium
Stock Georgian–Edwardian furniture, small antiques, advertising items, shop fittings, old bottles, pot lids
Open Mon–Fri 10am–5.30pm Sat 10am–4pm or by appointment
Fairs Newark
Services Containers

⌂ Holden Wood Antiques Centre
Contact John Ainslough
✉ **St Stephens, Grane Road, Haslingden, Rossendale, Lancashire, BB4 4AT** Ⓟ
☎ 01706 830803
Ⓔ john@holdenwood.co.uk
Ⓦ www.holdenwood.co.uk
Est. 1996 *Stock size* Large
No. of dealers 30+
Stock Ceramics, clocks, watches, paintings, period and country furniture
Open Mon–Sun 10am–5pm
Services Valuations, restorations, tea rooms

HESKIN GREEN

⌂ Heskin Hall Antiques
Contact Mr Dennis Harrison
✉ **Wood Lane, Heskin Green, Chorley, Lancashire, PR7 5PA** Ⓟ
☎ 01257 452044 Ⓕ 01257 450690
Ⓔ heskinhallantiques@attglobal.net
Est. 1995 *Stock size* Large
No. of dealers 65
Stock A complete range of antiques and collectables
Open Mon–Sun 10am–5.30pm
Services Restorations

KIRKBY LONSDALE

⊞ Architus Antiques & Collectables
Contact Mrs J Pearson

14 Main Street, Kirkby Lonsdale, Carnforth, Lancashire, LA6 2AE
01524 272409
Est. 1994 *Stock size* Large
Stock Wide range of antiques and collectables
Open Tues–Sat 10am–5pm
Services Valuations

Beck Head Books & Gallery
Contact Mr Stuart French
10 Beck Head, Kirkby Lonsdale, Lancashire, LA6 2AY
015242 71314
Est. 1984 *Stock size* Medium
Stock Furniture and decorative arts, chairs, small antiques, pictures, prints, antiquarian, out-of-print and second-hand books, antique maps, prints, old postcards
Open Tues–Sat 10am–5pm closed Wed

LANCASTER

Anything Old & Military Collectables
Contact Mr G H Chambers
55 Scotforth Road, Lancaster, Lancashire, LA1 4SA
01524 69933
Est. 1984 *Stock size* Medium
Stock Militaria including medals, cap badges, edged weapons, uniforms, helmets, Third Reich militaria
Open Wed Sat Sun 1.30–6pm
Services Valuations, medal mounting

Atticus Bookshop
Contact Miss Tracey Mansell
26 King Street, Lancaster, Lancashire, LA1 1JY
01524 381413
trace@atticusbooks.demon.co.uk
Est. 1974 *Stock size* Medium
Stock General second-hand stock of books.
Open Mon–Sat 10am–5pm
Services Book search

G B Antiques Centre
Contact Mr Alan Blackburn
Lancaster Leisure Park, Wyresdale Road, Lancaster, Lancashire, LA1 3LA
01524 844734 F 01524 844735
Est. 1990 *Stock size* Large
No. of dealers 140
Stock Wide range of antiques, collectables
Open Mon–Sun 10am–5pm
Services Café, factory shop

Lancastrian Antiques & Co
Contact Mr S Wilkinson
70–72 Penny Street, Lancaster, Lancashire, LA1 1XF
01524 847004
info@rectorylancs.co.uk
Est. 1981 *Stock size* Medium
Stock General, period furniture, porcelain, pottery, paintings
Open Mon–Sat 10am–4.30pm closed Wed
Services Valuations

LONGRIDGE

Henry Holden & Son
Contact Mrs S MacCarthy
Central Salerooms, Towneley Road, Longridge, Preston, Lancashire, PR3 3EA
01772 783274 F 01772 783274
www.holmesandsons.co.uk
Est. 1890
Open Tues–Fri 9am–5.30pm
Sales Fortnightly on Sat, household 10am, antiques noon, viewing Fri 10am–8pm day of sale 9–10am
Frequency Fortnightly

LYTHAM ST ANNE'S

Antiques at 35
Contact Mr A Sumner
35 St Andrew's Road South, Lytham St Anne's, Lancashire, FY8 1PZ
M 07980 403516
arnold.antiques@talk21.com
Est. 1979 *Stock size* Medium
Stock General antiques
Open Tues Fri Sat 10.30am–5pm
Fairs Newark, Swinderby

Mike Mallinson
Contact Mr M Mallinson
Lot 3 Auction Hall, 3 Kingsway, Lytham St Anne's, Lancashire, FY8 1AB
01253 731600 F 01253 731614
Est. 1993
Open Mon–Fri 9am–5pm
Sales Antiques, reproductions and collectables every 3rd Wed 9.30am–2.30pm, viewing Sat 10–12am Mon 10am–6pm Tues 10am–5pm
Frequency Every 3rd Wed

The Victorian Shop
Contact Mr G O Freeman
19 Alexandria Drive, Lytham St Anne's, Lancashire, FY8 1JF
01253 725700
Est. 1974 *Stock size* Medium
Stock General antiques
Open Sat 10am–5pm or by appointment
Fairs Newark, Swinderby

Windmill Bookshop
Contact Gail Welsh
62a Preston Road, Lytham St Anne's, Lancashire, FY8 5AE
01253 732485 F 01253 732485
M 07710 378707
Est. 1993 *Stock size* Medium
Stock General stock of antiquarian and second-hand books
Open Mon–Sun 9.30am–5.30pm
Fairs Buxton, Pudsey

MORECAMBE

G Vescovi
135 Balmoral Road, Morecambe, Lancashire, LA3 1HJ
01524 416732
M 07860 784856
Est. 1970 *Stock size* Large
Stock Georgian–Edwardian furniture
Open By appointment any time

NELSON

Brittons Antiques (NAG)
Contact Mr P Walden or Glen Britton
28 Scotland Road, Nelson, Lancashire, BB9 7UU
01282 697659 F 01282 618867
info@brittons-watches.co.uk
www.brittons-watches.co.uk
Est. 1969 *Stock size* Large
Stock A large range of quality antiques, quality smalls
Open Mon–Sat 10am–5pm closed Tues
Services Valuations

Brittons Jewellers (NAG)
Contact Mr P Walden, Glen Britton or Carl Britton
34 Scotland Road, Nelson, Lancashire, BB9 7UU
01282 697659 F 01282 618867

info@brittons-watches.co.uk
www.brittons-watches.co.uk
Est. 1969 *Stock size* Large
Stock Quality second-hand wrist watches 1920s–present day, antique and quality second-hand jewellery
Open Mon–Sat 10am–5pm closed Tues
Services Watch and jewellery repairs, valuations

Brooks Antiques
Contact David & Susan Brooks
Russell Street, Nelson, Lancashire, BB9 7NL
01282 698148
Est. 1987 *Stock size* Large
Stock General antiques and collectables
Open Mon–Sat 9am–5pm closed Tues

Timbercraft
Contact Mr A J Fishwick
Bottomley Yard, Bottomley Street, Nelson, Lancashire, BB9 9SW
01282 611277 F 01282 615651
www.subnet.co.uk/timbercraft.nw
Est. 1997 *Stock size* Medium
Stock Makers of display units for antique thimbles, spoons, cabinets for medals etc
Open By appointment
Services Bespoke display units

ORMSKIRK

Browzaround
Contact Mrs P Graham
16 Derby Street West, Ormskirk, Lancashire, L39 3NH
01695 576999
Est. 1975 *Stock size* Medium
Stock Pre-war furniture, collectables and antique agricultural tools
Open Tues–Sat 10am–4pm closed Wed

Collectors' Corner
Contact Mr B Jermyn
117 Aughton Street, Ormskirk, Lancashire, L39 3BN
01695 577455
M 07710 741250
Beaniebob@fbtinternet.com
Est. 1997 *Stock size* Large
Stock Cigarette cards, Beanie Babies, dolls' houses
Open Thur–Sat 10.30am–5pm Wed 10.30am–4pm
Services Valuations

Green Lane Antiques
Contact Mr J Swift
Unit B20, Malthouse Business Centre, 48 Southport Road, Ormskirk, Lancashire, L39 1QR
01695 580731
Est. 1998 *Stock size* Large
Stock Architectural antiques, period furniture, clocks, pine etc
Open Mon–Sun 10am–4pm
Services Restorations

A Grice
Contact Mr A Grice
106 Aughton Street, Ormskirk, Lancashire, L39 3BS
01695 572007
Est. 1946
Stock Furniture
Trade only Yes
Open Mon–Sat 10am–5pm
Services Valuations, antique furniture restoration

PADIHAM

Discretion Antiques Ltd
Contact Iris Owen
37 Burnley Road, Padiham, Burnley, Lancashire, BB12 8BY
01282 775693
Est. 1992 *Stock size* Medium
Stock Small modestly-priced antiques and collectables
Open Mon–Fri 10.30am–4.45pm Sat 10.30am–12.30pm closed Tues

PRESTON

European Fine Arts & Antiques
Contact Mr Brian Beck
10 Cannon Street, Preston, Lancashire, PR1 3NR
01772 883886 F 01772 823888
M 07967 427710
info@european-fine-arts.co.uk
www.european-fine-arts.co.uk
Est. 1969 *Stock size* Large
Stock Victorian gallery, furniture, Louis XIV-style furniture
Open Mon–Sat 9.30am–5.30pm or by appointment

Fine Art Antiques
Contact Mr Mark Pedler
109 New Hall Lane, Preston, Lancashire, PR1 5PB
01772 794010
M 07798 635477
Est. 1987 *Stock size* Medium
Stock Georgian oak furniture, bracket and longcase clocks, barometers, general antiques
Open Mon–Fri 10am–4pm
Fairs Newark
Services Restorations, chandelier re-wiring

K C Antiques & K D Interiors at Samlesbury Hall
Contact Julie Robinson
The Long Gallery, Samlesbury Hall, Preston New Road, Preston, Lancashire, PR5 0UP
01254 813883
www.antique-interiors.co.uk
Est. 1990 *Stock size* Medium
Stock 18th–19thC furniture and decorative items
Open Mon–Fri 11am–4.30pm Sun 10am–4pm

Nelson Antiques
Contact Mr W Nelson
113 New Hall Lane, Preston, Lancashire, PR1 5PB
01772 794896
Est. 1969 *Stock size* Medium
Stock General antiques, small items, silver, jewellery, copper, miners' lamps, collectables
Open Mon–Sat 9.30am–5pm
Fairs Newark

The Odd Chair Company
Contact Sue Cook
The Studio, Eaves Cottage Farm, Eaves, Preston, Lancashire, PR4 0BH
01772 691777 F 01772 691888
info@theoddchaircompany.com
www.theoddchaircompany.com
Est. 1969 *Stock size* Large
Stock 19thC antique chairs, sofas, decorative furniture
Open By appointment only
Fairs Newark, Ardingly
Services Interior design

Preston Antique Centre Ltd
Contact Mr S Shalloe
The Mill, New Hall Lane, Preston, Lancashire, PR1 5UH
01772 794498 F 01772 651694
prestonantiques@hotmail.com
www.antiques-atlas.com/prestonantiques.htm
Est. 1979 *Stock size* Large
No. of dealers 43
Stock English furniture, shipping goods, comprehensive range of English, French, German and

Italian furniture, longcase clocks, small items, porcelain
Open Mon–Fri 8.30am–5.30pm Sat 10am–4pm Sun 10am–5pm

Priory Collectables
Contact Mr David Howden
7 Priory Lane, Penwortham, Preston, Lancashire, PR1 OAR
01772 752090
Est. 1989 *Stock size* Medium
Stock Cutlery, silver plate, glassware, china, Doulton, Wade, clocks etc
Open Tues Thurs Fri 1–5pm Sat 10.30am–5pm Sun by appointment

Ribble Reclamation (SALVO)
Contact Mr Joe Hindle
Ducie Place, Off New Hall Lane, Preston, Lancashire, PR1 4UJ
01772 794534 F 01772 794604
joe@ribble-reclamation.com
www.ribble-reclamation.com
Est. 1977 *Stock size* Large
Stock Garden statuary, arches, stone flags, lamp posts, fountains, architectural antiques, reclaimed building materials
Open Mon–Fri 8am–5pm Sat 8am–1pm
Fairs Holker Hall Country Garden Festival, Harrogate Spring Flower Show
Services Auctions, last Sat of April and Sept

ROSSENDALE

Fieldings Antiques & Clocks
Contact Mr Andrew Fielding
176–180 Blackburn Road, Haslingden, Rossendale, Lancashire, BB4 5HW
01706 214254
M 07973 698961
Est. 1964 *Stock size* Large
Stock Clocks (including longcase), period furniture, steam engines, vintage motorcycles
Open Mon–Fri 9am–5pm

SABDEN

Walter Aspinall Antiques
Contact Mr W Aspinall
Pendle Antiques Centre, Union Mill, Watt Street, Sabden, Clitheroe, Lancashire, BB7 9ED
01282 778642 F 01282 778643
walter.aspinall@btinternet.com
Est. 1986 *Stock size* Large
Stock General antiques 1840s–1940s, shipping furniture, collectables, leaded windows etc
Open Mon–Thurs 9am–6pm Fri 9am–5pm Sat 10am–5pm Sun 11am–5pm or by appointment
Services Restorations, café

Pendle Antiques Centre Ltd
Contact Mr Jason Billington
Union Mill, Watt Street, Sabden, Clitheroe, Lancashire, BB7 9ED
01282 776311 F 01282 777642
sales@pendleantiquescentre.co.uk
Est. 1984 *Stock size* Large
No. of dealers 15
Stock Wide range of antiques including architectural and shipping wares
Open Mon–Sat 10am–5pm Sun 11am–5pm
Services Shipping

TODMORDEN

The Border Bookshop (PBFA, BA)
Contact Mr V H Collinge
61a Halifax Road, Todmorden, Lancashire, OL14 5BB
01706 814721
collinge@borderbookshop.fs.co.uk
Est. 1979 *Stock size* Large
Stock Second-hand books, comics, story papers 1880–1965
Open Mon–Sat 10am–5pm closed Tues
Fairs PBFA
Services Book tokens

Cottage Antiques Ltd
Contact Angelica Slater
788 Rochdale Road, Walsden, Todmorden, Lancashire, OL14 7UA
01706 813612 F 01706 813612
Est. 1984 *Stock size* Large
Stock Country furniture (particularly with original paint finishes), European antiques, country collectables
Open Tues–Sun 9am–5pm
Fairs Newark
Services Stripping, polishing, paint finishes, renovations

Echoes
Contact Mrs P Oldman
650a Halifax Road, Eastwood, Todmorden, Lancashire, OL14 6DW
01706 817505
Est. 1986 *Stock size* Large
Stock Clothing, textiles, pre-1840s to late 1950s
Open Wed–Sat 11am–6pm Sun noon–5pm
Fairs Textile Fair, Manchester
Services Valuations

Fagin & Co
Contact Mr John Ratcliff
54 Burnley Road, Todmorden, Lancashire, OL14 5EY
01706 819499/814773
M 07899 774257
mrhillside@aol.com
Est. 1994 *Stock size* Medium
Stock General antiques, collectables
Open Mon–Sat 10.30am–5pm closed Tues Sun
Services Valuations, restorations

Todmorden Antique Centre
Contact Mr E Hoogeveen
Sutcliffe House, Halifax Road, Todmorden, Lancashire, OL14 5BG
01706 818040 F 01706 814344
mr.ed@freenat.co.uk
Est. 1994 *Stock size* Large
No. of dealers 30
Stock Wide range of antiques, collectables and collectors' cars
Open Mon–Fri 10am–5pm Sat 10am–4pm Sun noon–4pm

WHALLEY

As Time Goes By
Contact Mrs J Bland
3 Accrington Road, Whalley, Clitheroe, Lancashire, BB7 9TD
01254 822199 F 01254 822199
M 07989 063395
Est. 1989 *Stock size* Medium
Stock Antique and new furniture, decorative items, lighting, textiles etc
Open Tues–Sat 12.30-4.30pm by appointment
Services Upholstery

Brindle Fine Arts Ltd (LAPADA)
Contact Julian Brindle
King Street, Whalley, Lancashire, BB7 9SP

☎ 01254 825200 ℱ 01200 440090
Ⓦ www.antiqueweb.co.uk/tbrindle
Est. 1961 *Stock size* Large
Stock Good-quality antiques
Open Mon–Fri 9am–5pm
or by appointment
Fairs Olympia

⊞ Edmund Davies & Son Antiques
Contact Philip Davies
✉ **32 King Street, Whalley, Clitheroe, Lancashire, BB7 9SL** 🅿
☎ 01254 823764 ℱ 01254 823764
Ⓜ 07879 877306
Est. 1960 *Stock size* Large
Stock Longcase clocks, country furniture
Open Mon–Sat 10am–5pm
Services Clock and furniture restoration

MERSEYSIDE

BIRKENHEAD

⊞ D & T Architectural Salvage
Contact Mr Dave Lyons
✉ **106 Church Road, Birkenhead, Merseyside, CH42 0LJ** 🅿
☎ 0151 670 0058
Est. 1990 *Stock size* Large
Stock Original interior doors, fireplaces, all salvage material
Open By appointment

⊞ Mistermicawber Co. Ltd
Contact Mr Barrington
✉ **100 Woodchurch Lane, Birkenhead, Merseyside, CH42 9PD** 🅿
☎ 0151 608 5445
Ⓔ mistermicawber.co@btinternet.com
Est. 1974 *Stock size* Medium
Stock Pre-1930s furniture
Open Mon–Sat 9am–5pm closed Thurs
Services Valuations

⊞ Paraphernalia Antiques
Contact John
✉ **1 Woodchurch Road, Birkenhead, Merseyside, CH41 2XN**
☎ 0151 653 7530
Est. 1999 *Stock size* Medium
Stock Variety of Art Deco, Victorian, Edwardian furniture
Open Thurs Fri Sat 10am–5pm

BLUNDELLSANDS

⊞ Boydell Galleries (BADA, LAPADA)
Contact Paul Breen
✉ **48 Dowhills Road, Blundellsands, Liverpool, Merseyside, L23 8SW** 🅿
☎ 0151 932 9220 ℱ 0151 924 0199
Ⓔ boydellgalleries@btinternet.com
Ⓦ www.boydellgalleries.co.uk
Est. 1851 *Stock size* Medium
Stock British drawings and watercolours, early maps and prints
Open By appointment
Fairs The Watercolour Fair, Jan LAPADA

BROMBOROUGH

⊞ William Courtney & Son
Contact Beryl Courtney
✉ **896 New Chester Road, Bromborough, Wirral, Merseyside, CH62 6AU** 🅿
☎ 0151 343 9174
Est. 1891 *Stock size* Medium
Stock General antiques, furniture, Victorian art glass etc
Open Mon–Sat 10am–4pm

⊞ Full of Beans
Contact Kris Richards
✉ **Unit 34, Croft Retail Park, Dinsdale Road, Bromborough, Wirral, Merseyside, CH62 3PY** 🅿
☎ 0151 334 6999 ℱ 0151 334 0197
Ⓜ 07961 364284
Ⓦ www.fullofbeans.uk.com
Est. 1999 *Stock size* Large
Stock Beanie Babies and accessories
Open Mon–Fri 9.45am–5pm Sat 9.45am–4.30pm Sun 10.30am–4pm

HESWALL

⊞ The Antique Shop
Contact Mr C Rosenberg
✉ **120–122 Telegraph Road, Heswall, Wirral, Merseyside, CH60 0AQ** 🅿
☎ 0151 342 1053 ℱ 0151 342 1053
Est. 1961 *Stock size* Medium
Stock Victorian jewellery, silver, bric-a-brac
Open Tues–Sat 10am–5pm closed Mon Wed
Services Jewellery repairs, silver repairs, valuations

⊞ Peninsula Books (PBFA)
Contact Mr Paul Cartmill
✉ **5 The Mount, Heswall, Wirral, CH60 4RE** 🅿
☎ 0151 342 5418
Est. 1986 *Stock size* Medium
Stock Antiquarian and second-hand books
Open Tues–Sat 10.30am–5pm
Fairs York, Oxford
Services Valuations, book search

HOYLAKE

⊞ Hoylake Antique Centre
Contact Rose Meldrum
✉ **128–130 Market Street, Hoylake, Wirral, Merseyside, CH47 3BH** 🅿
☎ 0151 632 4231
Ⓜ 0771 4600128
Est. 1979 *Stock size* Medium
Stock Furniture, porcelain, pine, silver plate, lighting
Open Mon–Sat 9am–5pm closed Wed

Kingsleys Auctions Ltd
Contact Mr I McKellar
✉ **3–4 The Quadrant, Hoylake, Wirral, Merseyside, CH47 2EE** 🅿
☎ 0151 632 5821 ℱ 0151 632 5823
Ⓔ kingsleyauctions@msn.com
Est. 1972
Open Mon–Fri 9am–5pm closed 1–2pm Wed–Fri
Sales General auction sale Tues 10am, viewing Sat 9am–12.30pm Mon 9am–5pm day of sale 9–10am
Frequency Weekly
Catalogues Yes

⊞ Mansell Antiques & Collectables
Contact Mr Gary Challinor
✉ **Mulberry House, 128–130 Market Street, Hoylake, Wirral, Merseyside, CH47 3BH** 🅿
☎ 0151 632 0892 ℱ 0151 632 6137
Ⓦ www.antiquesatlas.com
Est. 1998 *Stock size* Large
Stock 20thC collectables, Art Deco, Carlton Ware, Shelley etc
Open Mon–Sat 9am–5pm closed Wed
Fairs Birmingham Rag Market, Chester Racecourse

LIVERPOOL

Abram & Mitchell
Contact Mr Crane
41 Stanhope Street, Liverpool, Merseyside, L8 5RF
0151 708 5180 Ⓕ 0151 707 2454
johncrane@cato-crane.co.uk
www.cato-crane.co.uk
Est. 1880
Open Mon–Fri 9am–5pm Sat by appointment
Sales Antiques, general and household furnishings sales every Thursday
Frequency Weekly
Catalogues No

Black Cat Antiques
Contact Mr Barry Corbitt
100a High Street, Wavetree, Liverpool, Merseyside, L15 8HQ
0151 734 1149
Est. 1969 *Stock size* Small
Stock Smalls, jewellery, ivories, miniatures, antique teddy bears
Open By appointment
Services Teddy bear repair

Cato Crane & Co
Contact Mr J Crane AMATA
6 and 33–41 Stanhope Street, Liverpool, Merseyside, L8 5RF
0151 709 5559 Ⓕ 0151 707 2454
johncrane@cato-crane.co.uk
www.cato-crane.co.uk
Est. 1986
Open Mon–Fri 9am–5pm or by appointment
Sales Auctions every Thursday including antique Victorian and 20thC furniture, collectables and decorative objects. Quality antiques and fine art auction every two months
Frequency Weekly
Catalogues Yes

Circa 1900
Contact Mr W Colquhoun
11–13 Holts Arcade, India Buildings, Water Street, Liverpool, Merseyside, L2 0RR
0151 236 1282 Ⓕ 0151 236 1282
www.merseyworld.com/circa1900
Est. 1996 *Stock size* Large
Stock Art Nouveau, classic Art Deco, applied arts
Open 10am–6pm or by appointment

Cottage Antiques
Contact Mr V Blundell
64 Moss Lane, Orrell Park, Liverpool, Merseyside, L9 8AN
0151 284 6771
Est. 1994 *Stock size* Medium
Stock Victorian–Edwardian furniture, collectables, bric-a-brac
Open Mon–Sat 10am–5pm
Fairs Newark, Ardingly

Hartley & Co
Contact Mr J Brown
12–14 Moss Street, Low Hill, Liverpool, Merseyside, L6 1HF
0151 263 6472 Ⓕ 0151 260 3417
Ⓜ 0780 398 4199
Est. 1849
Open Mon–Fri 9am–4.30pm
Sales General sales Fri 10am, viewing Thurs 9am–4.30pm Fri 9–10am. Merseyside Police lost property
Frequency Weekly
Catalogues No

Liverpool Militaria
Contact Mr Bill Tagg
15 Cheapside, Liverpool, Merseyside, L2 2DY
0151 236 4404 Ⓕ 0800 590009
Est. 1977 *Stock size* Medium
Stock General military antiques
Open Mon–Sat 10.30am–5pm closed Wed
Fairs Northern Arms & Armour, International – Birmingham

Maggs Shipping Ltd
Contact Mr R Webster
66–68 St Anne Street, Liverpool, Merseyside, L3 3DY
0151 207 2555 Ⓕ 0151 207 2555
maggsantiques@compuserve.com
Est. 1971 *Stock size* Large
Stock Restored Georgian-style furniture, country and pine furniture
Trade only Yes
Open Mon–Fri 9am–5pm
Services Restorations, packing, shipping

Mersey Collectables
Contact Mr J Foy
81 Renshaw Street, Liverpool, Merseyside, L1 2SJ
0151 708 9012
jfoy71160@aol.com
Est. 1995 *Stock size* Large
Stock Collectable toys
Open Mon–Sat 10am–5pm Sun 11am–4pm

Nothing Fancy
Contact Mr Robert M Adams
184 Derby Lane, Liverpool, Merseyside, L13 6QQ
0151 259 1661
Est. 1979 *Stock size* Large
Stock Collectables, general antiques, bric-a-brac, fireplaces, doors, wrought-iron gates
Open Mon–Sat 8am–3pm closed Thurs

Outhwaite & Litherland (SOFAA)
Contact Mr Kevin Whay
Kingsway Galleries, Fontenoy Street, Liverpool, Merseyside, L3 2BE
0151 236 6561 Ⓕ 0151 236 1070
auction@lots.uk.com
www.lots.uk.com
Est. 1907
Open Mon–Fri 9am–5pm
Sales Antiques sales 4–5 per annum Wed. Weekly general household sales Tues 10.30am, viewing Mon 9am–5pm Tues 9-10.30am. Monthly cavalcade collectors' sales 1st Tues of month or day prior to major fine art and antiques sale
Frequency Weekly
Catalogues Yes

Pilgrim's Progress
Contact Selwyn Hyams
1a–3a Bridgewater Street, Liverpool, Merseyside, L1 0AR
0151 708 7515
www.pilgrimsprogress.co.uk
Est. 1979 *Stock size* Large
Stock Five floors of mainly 19th and early 20thC furniture
Open Mon–Fri 9am–5pm Sat 1–4pm
Services Valuations, restorations

Seventeen Antiques
Contact Mr J Brake
306 Aigburth Road, Liverpool, Merseyside, L17 9PW
0151 727 1717
Ⓜ 07712 189604
Est. 1997 *Stock size* Large
Stock Antique pine furniture
Open Mon–Sat 10am–5pm closed Wed
Services Restorations, stripping

Stefani Antiques
Contact Mrs T Stefani
497 Smithdown Road, Liverpool, Merseyside, L15 5AE

☎ 0151 734 1933/733 4836
Ⓜ 07946 646395
Est. 1987 *Stock size* Large
Stock General antiques
Open Mon–Sat 10am–5pm closed Wed
Services Valuations, restorations

Turner & Sons (1787) (NAVA)
Contact Mr Kevin Davies
✉ Century Salerooms, 28–36 Roscoe Street, Liverpool, Merseyside, L1 9DW Ⓟ
☎ 0151 709 4005 Ⓕ 0151 709 4005
Ⓜ 07831 445816
Ⓔ Kevjdav@yahoo.co.uk
Est. 1787
Open Mon–Fri 9am–5pm
Sales General household, antique and commercial sales Thurs 11am, viewing Wed 9am–4.45pm Thurs 9–11am
Frequency Weekly
Catalogues No

Yazuka
Contact Mr Bill Tagg
✉ 15 Cheapside, Liverpool, Merseyside, L2 2DY Ⓟ
☎ 0151 236 4404
Est. 1985
Stock Japanese swords and fittings
Open By appointment only
Fairs International – Birmingham, Northern Arms
Services Sword polishing

SOUTHPORT

Birkdale Antiques
Contact John Napp
✉ 119a Upper Augaton Road, Southport, Merseyside, PR8 5EX Ⓟ
☎ 01704 550117
Ⓜ 07940 580107
Ⓦ www.net-traders/birkdaleantiquesint
Est. 1990 *Stock size* Medium
Stock Antique pine, English and continental European furniture 1820–1900s
Open Tues–Sat 10am–5.30pm
Fairs Newark, Ardingly
Services Restorations

Broadhursts of Southport Ltd (ABA, PBFA)
Contact Laurens Hardman
✉ 5–7 Market Street, Southport, Merseyside, PR8 1HD Ⓟ
☎ 01704 532064 Ⓕ 01704 542009
Ⓔ litereria@aol.com
Est. 1926
Stock Wide range of scarce and collectable books
Fairs Chelsea, Olympia
Services Valuations, restorations, booksearch

King Street Antiques
Contact Mr John Nolan
✉ 27–29 King Street, Southport, Merseyside, PR8 1LH Ⓟ
☎ 01704 540808
Ⓜ 07714 088388
Est. 1969 *Stock size* Large
Stock Antique furniture, interior design service
Open Mon–Sat 10am–5pm or by appointment
Services Packing, courier

Molloy's Furnishers Ltd
Contact Mr S Molloy
✉ 6–8 St James Street, Southport, Merseyside, PR8 5AE Ⓟ
☎ 01704 535204 Ⓕ 01704 548101
Ⓔ sales@molloysfurnishers.co.uk
Ⓦ www.molloysfurnishers.co.uk
Est. 1976 *Stock size* Medium
Stock Antique shipping, reproduction furniture
Open Mon–Sat 9am–5.30pm

Osiris
Contact Mr Paul Wood
✉ 104 Shakespeare Street, Southport, Merseyside, PR8 5AJ Ⓟ
☎ 01704 500991/560418
Ⓜ 07802 818500
Est. 1979 *Stock size* Medium
Stock Vintage clothing and textiles, Art Nouveau, Art Deco ceramics, glass, metalware, lighting
Open Mon–Sat 11am–5pm
Fairs Newark
Services Lectures, talks, valuations, period clothing hire

K A Parkinson Books
Contact K A or J Parkinson
✉ 359–363 Lord Street, Southport, Merseyside, PR8 1NH Ⓟ
☎ 01704 547016 Ⓕ 01704 386416
Ⓔ info@parki.com
Ⓦ www.parki.com
Est. 1972 *Stock size* Large
Stock Antiquarian and second-hand books, sheet music, maps, prints, prehistoric, ancient and medieval antiquities, natural history items, vinyl records, autographs, manuscripts
Open Mon–Sat 10am–5pm Sun noon–5pm
Services Book search

Phillips International Auctioneers and Valuers
✉ 33 Botanic Road, Churchtown, Southport, Merseyside, PR9 7NE
☎ 01704 507875 Ⓕ 01704 507877
Ⓦ www.phillips-auction.com
Sales Regional Saleroom. Ring for details

D M Regan
Contact Mr David Regan
✉ 25 Hoghton Street, Southport, Merseyside, PR9 0NS Ⓟ
☎ 01704 531266 Ⓕ 01704 546206
Est. 1983 *Stock size* Medium
Stock Coins, postcards, medals, cigarette cards, other collectables
Open Mon Wed Fri Sat 10am–5pm
Fairs Coin Fairs – Birmingham and Morely

Southport Furnishings
Contact Steven Ross
✉ 119a Portland Street, Southport, Merseyside, PR8 6RA Ⓟ
☎ 01704 533122
Ⓜ 07790 551117
Est. 1997 *Stock size* Large
Stock Victorian–Edwardian furniture
Open Mon–Sat 9am–5pm
Services Restorations

Southport Furnishings
Contact Steven Ross
✉ 4 Wesley Street, Southport, Merseyside, PR8 1BN Ⓟ
☎ 07790 551117
Est. 1997 *Stock size* Large
Stock Victorian–Edwardian furniture
Open Mon–Sat 9am–5pm
Services Restorations

The Spinning Wheel Antiques (IBNS, TPCS)
Contact Roy or Pat Bell
✉ 1 Liverpool Road, Birkdale, Southport, Merseyside, PR8 4AR Ⓟ
☎ 01704 568245 Ⓕ 01704 567613
Est. 1974 *Stock size* Medium
Stock General collectables, coins, medals, porcelain, small fine furniture, clocks, violins,

barometers, dolls, golf memorabilia etc
Open Mon–Sat 10.30am–5pm closed Tues
Fairs Most major fairs

WALLASEY

⊞ Arbiter
Contact Mr P Ferrett
✉ **10 Atherton Street, New Brighton, Wallasey, Merseyside, CH45 2NY** 🅿
☎ 0151 639 1159
Est. 1983 *Stock size* Medium
Stock Small objects, 1850–1970 decorative arts, Asian, tribal, base metal, treen, 20thC prints, Oriental, Islamic
Open Wed–Sat 1–5pm or by appointment
Services Valuations

⊞ Decade Antiques & Textiles
Contact A Duffy
✉ **62 Grove Road, Wallasey, Merseyside, CH45 3HW** 🅿
☎ 0151 638 0433/0151 639 6905
Ⓕ 0151 638 9995
Est. 1974 *Stock size* Medium
Stock Furniture, decorative items, textiles, upholstered furniture, pictures, china
Open Mon Tues Thurs 10.15am–5.30pm closed 1–2.15pm Fri Sat 10.15am–1pm or by appointment
Fairs Manchester Textile Fairs

⊞ Victoria Antiques
Contact Mr J Collier
✉ **155–157 Brighton Street, Wallasey, Merseyside, CH44 8DU** 🅿
☎ 0151 639 0080
Ⓦ www.victoriaantiques.com
Est. 1990 *Stock size* Large
Stock Victorian–Edwardian furniture, grandfather clocks
Open Mon–Sat 9.30am–5.30pm closed Wed
Services Restorations

WALES

CARMARTHENSHIRE

CAPEL IWAN

Bonhams & Brooks
Contact Mike Worthington-Williams
✉ **Glaspant Manor, Capel Iwan, Carmarthenshire, SA38 9LS**
☎ 01539 370928
www.bonhams.com
Open Mon–Fri 9am–5pm
Sales Regional Representative for Wales

CARMARTHEN

Audrey Bull Antiques
Contact Jane Bull
✉ **2a Jacksons Lane, Carmarthen, Carmarthenshire, SA31 1WD**
☎ 01267 222655
Est. 1949 *Stock size* Medium
Stock General antiques, Georgian–Edwardian furniture, antique jewellery
Open Mon–Sat 10am–5pm
Services Valuations, restorations, repairs

Cwmgwili Mill Antiques
Contact Michael Sandell
✉ **Cwmgwili Mill, Bronwydd Arms, Carmarthen, Carmarthenshire, SA33 6HX** P
☎ 01267 231500/237215
Est. 1979 *Stock size* Large
Stock General antiques
Open Mon–Fri 9am–6pm Sat 10am–6pm or by appointment
Services Repairs, restorations

Mark's Mart
Contact Mark Terry
Colonial Buildings, Little Water Street, Carmarthen, SA31 1ER
01267 236613
mterry@marksmart.f9.co.uk
Est. 1970 *Stock size* Large
Stock General antiques, mainly furniture
Open Mon–Fri 9am–5pm Sat 9am–4pm closed Thurs pm

Phillips International Auctioneers and Valuers
Napier House, Spilman Street, Carmarthen, Carmarthenshire, SA31 IJY
01267 238231 01227 222625
www.phillips-auction.com
Sales Regional Office. Ring for details

The Pot Board
Contact Nigel or Gill Batten
30 King Street, Carmarthen, Carmarthenshire, SA31 1BS
01267 236623 01267 236623
07785 924007
Gill@potboard.co.uk
www.potboard.co.uk
Est. 1980 *Stock size* Large
Stock Antique pine and country furniture, Welsh pine
Open Mon–Sat 9.30am–5.30pm

Roderick Price & Co
Contact Mr Deri Price
19–20 Lammas Street, Carmarthen, Carmarthenshire, SA31 3AL
01267 230571 01267 238422
enquiries@roderickprice.co.uk
www.roderickprice.co.uk
Open Mon–Fri 9am–5pm Sat 9am–4pm Sun 10am–noon
Sales General antiques
Frequency Occasional
Catalogues Yes

CROSS HANDS

C J C Antiques
Contact Caroline Carpenter
Llanllyan Foelgastell, Cross Hands, Carmarthenshire, SA14 7HA
01269 831096 01269 831094
antique@dircon.co.uk
www.antique.dircon.co.uk
Est. 1979 *Stock size* Large
Stock Various Victorian items etc, musical instruments
Trade only Yes
Open By appointment
Services Shipping, valuations

Welsh Country Auctions
Contact Andrew or Bethan Williams
2 Carmarthen Road, Cross Hands, Llanelli, Carmarthenshire, SA14 6JP
01269 844428 01269 844428
www.welshcountryauctions.com
Est. 1995
Open Mon–Fri 9am–5pm Sat 9am–12.30pm
Sales General antiques
Frequency Every 3 weeks
Catalogues Yes

KIDWELLY

Country Antiques (Wales) (BADA)
Contact Mr R Bebb
Castle Mill, Kidwelly, Carmarthenshire, SA17 4UU
01554 890534 01554 891705
richardbebb@countryantiqueswales.fsnet.co.uk
www.countryantiqueswales.co.uk
Est. 1969 *Stock size* Large
Stock Welsh Furniture, pottery, folk art, metalware
Open Tues–Sat 10am–5pm or by appointment
Services Valuations

Kidwelly Antiques
Contact Mr R Bebb
31 Bridge Street, Kidwelly, Carmarthenshire, SA17 4UU
01554 890328 01554 891705
Est. 1969 *Stock size* Large
Stock Georgian–Victorian furniture and accessories
Open Tues–Sat 10am–5pm or by appointment
Services Valuations

LLANDEILO

James Ash Antiques
Contact James Ash
The Warehouse, Station Road, Llandeilo, Carmarthenshire, SA19 6NG
01558 823726/822130
01558 822130
James@ashantiques.freeserve.co.uk
Est. 1976 *Stock size* Large
Stock Victorian and Welsh country furniture
Open Mon–Fri 8.30am–6pm or by appointment
Fairs Newark
Services Valuations

Jones & Llewelyn (NAEA)
Contact Mrs Ann Reece
Llandeilo Auction Rooms, 21 New Road, Llandeilo, Carmarthenshire, SA19 6DE
01558 823430 01558 822004
enquiries@jonesllewelyn.freeserve.co.uk
www.jonesllewelyn.freeserve.co.uk
Est. 1948
Open Mon–Fri 9am–5.30pm
Sales General antiques and collectables once a quarter, also property for sale
Frequency Quarterly
Catalogues Yes

Bob Jones Prytherch & Co Ltd
Contact Jonathon Morgan
50 Rhosmaen Street, Llandeilo, Carmarthenshire, SA19 6HA
01558 822468 01558 823712
property@bjpandco.s9.co.uk
www.bjpproperty.co.uk
Est. 1996
Open Mon–Fri 9am–5.30pm
Sales General antiques
Frequency Quarterly
Catalogues No

Roderick Price & Co
Contact Mr Dewi Price
85 Rhosmaen Street, Llandeilo, Carmarthenshire, SA19 2DS
01558 822280 01558 822824
enquiries@roderickprice.co.uk
www.roderickprice.co.uk
Open Mon–Fri 9am–5pm Sat 9am–noon
Sales General antiques
Frequency Occasional
Catalogues Yes

The Works Antiques Centre
Contact Steve Watts or Jon Storey
Station Road, Llandeilo, Carmarthenshire, SA19 6NH
01558 823964
Est. 2001 *Stock size* Large
No. of dealers 44
Stock General antiques and collectables
Open Tues–Sat 10am–6pm Sun 10am–4pm
Services Restorations

LLANDOVERY

Clee Tompkinson & Francis
Contact Nick Jones
Ty Ocsiwn Tywi Auction House, Llandovery, Carmarthenshire, SA18 2LY P
☎ 01269 591884/01550 720440
F 01269 595482
W www.members.aol.com/ctf99
Est. 1996
Open Mon–Fri 9am–5.30pm
Sat 9am–1pm
Sales General antiques
Frequency Monthly
Catalogues No

Phillips Antiques & French Polishing Service
Contact Phillip Wyvill-Bell
11 Market Square, Llandovery, Carmarthenshire, SA20 OAB P
☎ 01550 721355
Est. 1969 *Stock size* Large
Stock General antiques, porcelain, furniture
Open Mon–Sat 9am–5pm
Services French polishing, valuations, restoration, repairs

LLANELLI

Llanelli Antiques
Contact W Knapp
20 Inkerman Street, Llanelli, Carmarthenshire, SA15 2RL P
☎ 01554 759448
E werner@messages.co.uk
Est. 1962 *Stock size* Medium
Stock General antiques Victorian–Edwardian furniture
Open Mon–Sat 10am–1pm
Fairs Newark, Ardingly
Services Valuations, restorations

Manor Estate Auctions
Contact B Thomas
Popplewells, Swiss Valley, Llanelli, Carmarthenshire, SA14 8LZ P
☎ 01554 771938 F 01554 751818
Est. 1993
Open Mon–Fri 9am–5pm
Sat 9am–1pm
Sales General antiques, furniture
Frequency Every 2 months
Catalogues Yes

Radnedge Architectural Antiques
Contact Julian Cooper
Dafen Inn Row, Llanelli, Carmarthenshire, SA14 P
☎ 01554 755790 F 01554 755790
E rantiques@radnedge.fsworld.co.uk
W radnedge-arch-antiques.co.uk
Est. 1980 *Stock size* Large
Stock Architectural antiques, fireplaces, timber, stone etc
Open Mon–Sat 9am–5pm

LLANWRDA

Mark Rowan
Contact Mark Rowan
Garreg Fawr, Porthyrhyd, Llanwrda, Carmarthenshire, SA19 8NY P
☎ 01558 650478 F 01558 650712
E sales@markrowan.co.uk
W www.markrowan.co.uk
Est. 1975 *Stock size* Medium
Stock Country furniture and antiques
Open By appointment only

LLANYBYDDER

Jen Jones Antiques
Contact Jen Jones
Pontbrendu, Llanybydder, Carmarthenshire, SA40 9UJ P
☎ 01570 480610 F 01570 480112
E quilts@jen-jones.com
W www.jen-jones.com
Est. 1971 *Stock size* Large
Stock Welsh quilts and blankets, small Welsh country antiques
Open Mon–Sat 10am–6pm
Sun by appointment
Fairs BABAADA, Kensington Brocante

NEWCASTLE EMLYN

The Old Saddler's Antiques
Contact Mr & Mrs Coomber
Bridge Street, Newcastle Emlyn, Carmarthenshire, SA38 9DU P
☎ 01239 711615 (shop hours only)
M 07971 625113
E Dotcoomb@aol.com
Est. 1995 *Stock size* Large
Stock General antiques, country-style furniture, equestrian antiques
Open Mon–Sat 10am–5pm
winter closed Wed
Fairs Carmarthen

Riverside Antiques
Contact M Barton
Pine Croft, Carmarthen Road, Newcastle Emlyn, Carmarthenshire, SA38 9DA P
☎ 01239 710384
M 07971 751562
Est. 1971 *Stock size* Large
Stock General antiques
Open Mon–Sat 9am–6pm
Fairs Ardingly, Newark
Services Valuation, restoration, repairs

CEREDIGION

ABERYSTWYTH

The Furniture Cave
Contact P David
33 Cambrian Street, Aberystwyth, Ceredigion, SY23 1NZ
☎ 01970 611234 F 01970 611234
M 07974 465878
E furniturecave@hotmail.com
Est. 1979 *Stock size* Medium
Stock General antiques and pine
Open Mon–Fri 9am–5pm
Sat 10am–5pm
Fairs NPC, Birmingham Antiques Fair
Services Valuations, restoration, repairs

Lloyd Herbert & Jones
Contact J A Griffiths FRICS
10 Chalybeate Street, Aberystwyth, Ceredigion, SY23 1HS P
☎ 01970 624328/612559
F 01970 617934
E sales@lhj-property.co.uk
W www.lhj-property.co.uk
Est. 1904
Open Mon–Fri 9am–5.30pm
Sat 11am–3pm
Sales General antiques
Frequency Every 2 months
Catalogues No

Jim Raw-Rees & Co (ISVA)
Contact Charles Raw-Rees
1–3 Chalybeate Street, Aberystwyth, Ceredigion, SY23 1HJ P
☎ 01970 617179 F 01970 617179
M 07970 605040
E propertysales@raw-rees.co.uk
W www.raw-rees.co.uk
Est. 1948
Open Mon–Fri 9am–5.30pm Sat 9.30am–4pm

Sales General antiques
Frequency Periodically
Catalogues No

Julian Shelley Books
Contact Julian Shelley
16 Northgate Street, Aberystwyth, Ceredigion, SY23 2JS
01970 627926
julianshelley@hotmail.com
Est. 1996 *Stock size* Medium
Stock Rare and second-hand books, jewellery, collectables, items on Welsh topography
Open Mon–Sat 10am–5pm
Services Book search

Ystwyth Books (BA)
Contact Mrs H M Hinde
7 Princess Street, Aberystwyth, Ceredigion, SY23 1DX
01970 617511
Est. 1976 *Stock size* Medium
Stock Rare and second-hand books, specializing in Welsh-interest books
Open Mon–Sat 9.30am–5.15pm

CARDIGAN

J J Morris
Contact Mr Mal Evans
5 High Street, Ceredigion, Cardigan, SA43 1HJ
01239 612343 F 01239 615237
Est. 1969
Open Mon–Fri 9am–5.30pm Sat 9am–noon
Sales General antiques
Frequency Every 2 months
Catalogues No

LLANDYSUL

Fred Davies & Co (FNAVA)
Contact Fred Davies
The Square Synod Inn, Llandysul, Ceredigion, SA44 6JA
01545 580005 F 01545 580006
M 07831 852511
Est. 1992
Open Mon–Fri 9am–5pm Sat 10am–2pm
Sales General antiques and modern furniture
Frequency Monthly
Catalogues No

CONWY

COLWYN BAY

Colwyn Books (WBA)
Contact Jack Owen
66 Abergele Road, Colwyn Bay, Conwy, LL29 7PP
01492 530683 F 01492 534401
owenbooks@aol.com
www.ksap.demon.co.uk/cyberbookshops/colwynbooks
Est. 1989 *Stock size* Medium
Stock Antiquarian and second-hand books
Open Mon–Sat 9am–5.30pm closed Wed
Services Book search, translations French/English and English/French

Cryers Antiques
Contact Mr Chris Cryer
24 Abergele Road, Colwyn Bay, Conwy, LL29 7PA
01492 532457
Est. 1974 *Stock size* Large
Stock General antiques, collectables
Open Mon–Sat 11am–4.30pm
Fairs Newark, Ardingly, Swinderby
Services Valuations

North Wales Antiques
Contact Mr F Robinson
58 Abergele Road, Colwyn Bay, Conwy, LL29 7PP
01492 530521/01352 720253 (after 6pm)
Est. 1959 *Stock size* Large
Stock Antique and old furniture bought and sold
Open Mon–Sat 10am–4pm
Fairs Newark
Services House clearance, probate valuations, valuations

Rogers-Jones & Co
Contact Mr David Rogers-Jones
33 Abergele Road, Colwyn Bay, Conwy, LL29 7RU
01492 532176 F 01492 533308
www.rogersjones.ukauctioneers.com
Est. 1991
Open Mon–Thurs 9am–5pm Fri 9am–noon
Sales Furniture, ceramics, silver, paintings, collectables etc last Tues in month, 2-monthly general and collectables sales
Frequency Monthly
Catalogues Yes

CONWY

The Bookshop
Contact Mr D Crewe
21 High Street, Conwy, LL32 8DE
01492 592137
bookshopconsy.co.uk
Est. 1985 *Stock size* Medium
Stock Rare and second-hand books
Open Mon–Sat 9.30am–5pm

Paul Gibbs Antiques & Decorative Arts
Contact Paul Gibbs
25 Castle Street, Conwy, LL32 8AY
01492 593429 F 01492 593429
paul@teapotworld.co.uk
Est. 1959 *Stock size* Medium
Stock Ceramics, glass, decorative arts
Open Mon–Sat 10am–5pm
Fairs Newark
Services Valuations, restoration, repairs

Knights Gone By
Contact Mr B Tunstall
Castle Square, Conwy, LL32 8AY
01492 596119 F 01492 596119
knightsgoneby@netscapeonline.co.uk
www.knightsgoneby.com
Est. 1998 *Stock size* Medium
Stock Collectable weaponry
Open Mon–Sun 11am–5pm

DEGANWY

Castle Antiques
Contact John Nickson
Victoria Building, 71 Station Road, Deganwy, Conwy, LL31 9DF
01492 583021 F 01492 596664
Est. 1980 *Stock size* Large
Stock General antiques
Open Mon–Sat 10am–5pm
Services Valuations

LLANDUDNO

Bryan Davies & Associates
Contact Bryan Davies
4 Mostyn Street, Llandudno, Conwy, Ll30 2PS
01492 875125 F 01492 877292
llandudno@bdahomesales.co.uk
www.bdahomesales.co.uk
Est. 1908

Open Mon–Fri 9am–5pm Sat 8.30am–4pm Sun 1–3pm
Sales General antiques
Frequency Phone for details
Catalogues Yes

⊞ More Books
Contact Sue Morley
✉ 102 Mostyn Street, Llandudno, Conwy, LL30 2SW **P**
☎ 01492 878684/01244 310021 **F** 01244 310021
E sales@morebooks.co.uk
W www.morebooks.co.uk
Est. 1995 ***Stock size*** Medium
Stock Rare and second-hand books, stock of local Welsh history
Open Mon–Sat summer Sun 9.30am–5.30pm

⊞ Walters Antiques & Collectables
Contact Mrs Gillian Walters
✉ 6 Dunraven Street, Llandudno, CF40 1QE **P**
☎ 01443 421524 **F** 01443 421824
Est. 1999 ***Stock size*** Medium
Stock General antiques
Open Mon–Fri 10am–5pm
Services House clearance

LLANDUDNO JUNCTION

⊞ Collinge Antiques
Contact Nicky Collinge
✉ Old Fyffes Warehouse, Conwy Road, Llandudno Junction, Conwy, LL31 9LU **P**
☎ 01492 580022 **F** 01492 580022
E collinge.antiques@exl.co.uk
Est. 1980 ***Stock size*** Large
Stock General antiques, Georgian–Edwardian furniture
Open Mon–Sat 9am–5.30pm Sun 10.30am–4.30pm
Fairs G-Mex Manchester, Tatton Park
Services Restorations, valuations, shipping, upholstery

LLANRWST

⊞ Carrington House Antiques
Contact John Roberts or Richard Newstead
✉ Ancaster Square, Llanrwst, Conwy, LL26 0LD **P**
☎ 01492 642500 **F** 01492 642500
E richard@rnewstead.freeserve.co.uk
Est. 1975 ***Stock size*** Medium
Stock Antique pine and oak furniture
Open Mon–Sat 10am–5pm
Services Valuations

⊞ Prospect Books
Contact Mike Dingle
✉ Albert House, 18 Denbigh Street, Llanrwst, Conwy, LL26 0LL **P**
☎ 01492 640111 **F** 01492 640111
E prospectbooks@netscapeonline.co.uk
W www.members.netscapeonline.co.uk/prospectbooks
Est. 1977 ***Stock size*** Small
Stock Rare and second-hand books including some on weapons
Open Tues–Sat 9am–5pm
Fairs Arms fairs
Services Catalogues

PENMAENMAWR

⊞ Gwynedd Trading
Contact C Motter
✉ Stanley Buildings, Bangor Road, Penmaenmawr, Conwy, LL34 6LF **P**
☎ 01492 622189 **F** 01243 355499
M 07802 968819
Est. 1973 ***Stock size*** Large
Stock General antiques and shipping furniture, specializing in 17th–18thC furniture
Open By appointment
Fairs Newark, Stafford
Services Shipping worldwide

RHOS-ON-SEA

⊞ Rhos Point Books
Contact Gwyn Morris
✉ 85 The Promenade, Rhos-on-Sea, Conwy, LL28 4PR **P**
☎ 01492 545236 **F** 01492 540862
E rhos.point@btinternet.com
W www.rhos.point.btinternet.com
Est. 1984 ***Stock size*** Medium
Stock 20,000 antiquarian and second-hand titles, North Wales topography
Open Mon–Sun 10am–5.30pm July Aug 10am–9pm
Fairs Ludlow
Services Book search

DENBIGHSHIRE

CHIRK

⊞ Brocante Antiques
Contact Caroline Williams or Tina
✉ 3a St Marys Precinct, Church Street, Chirk, Wrexham, Denbighshire, LL14 5HX **P**
☎ 01691 778844 **F** 01691 778844
E brocanteantiques@btconnect.com
W www.brocanteantiques.com
Est. 1978 ***Stock size*** Large
Stock Furniture, Continental porcelain, textiles, linen, lace etc
Open Mon–Sat 10am–5.30pm
Services Valuations

⊞ Seventh Heaven
✉ Chirk Mill, Chirk, Wrexham, Denbighshire, LL14 5BU **P**
☎ 01691 777622 **F** 01691 777313
E requests@seventh-heaven.co.uk
W www.seventh-heaven.co.uk
Est. 1971 ***Stock size*** Large
Stock Antique beds, mattresses, bases, bed linen
Open Mon–Sat 9am–5pm Sun 10am–4pm

ERBISTOCK

⊞ Simon Wingett Ltd (LAPADA)
Contact Mr Simon Wingett
✉ The Garden House, Erbistock, Wrexham, Denbighshire, LL13 0DL **P**
☎ 01978 781144 **F** 01978 781144
M 07774 410889
Est. 1972 ***Stock size*** Medium
Stock 18th–19thC English furniture, paintings, objets d'art, garden sculpture
Open By appointment
Fairs LAPADA, Chelsea, Louise Walker Harrogate
Services Valuations

FRONCYSYLLTE

⌂ Chapel Antiques
Contact Mrs Eve Humber
✉ Methodist Chapel, Holyhead Road, Froncysyllte, Denbighshire, LL20 7RA **P**
☎ 01691 777624 **F** 01691 777624
Est. 1985 ***Stock size*** Medium
No. of dealers 8
Stock Wide range of antiques and collectables
Open Tues–Sun 10am–4pm

LLANGOLLEN

⊞ Books
Contact Mr Tibor Sever
✉ 17 Castle Street, Llangollen, Denbighshire, LL20 8NY **P**
☎ 01978 860334

Est. 1983 *Stock size* Large
Stock Varied stock including sci-fi, history, politics, fiction, war etc
Open Mon–Sun 9am–5pm closed 25 December

J & R Langford
Contact Mr P C Silverston
12 Bridge Street, Llangollen, Denbighshire, LL20 8PF P
01978 860182
Est. 1952 *Stock size* Medium
Stock 18th–19thC Welsh dressers, 18th–early 20thC furniture, china, pictures
Open Mon–Sat 9.30am–5.30pm Thurs 9.30am–12.30pm
Services Valuations

Passers Buy
Contact Marie Evans
8–10 Chapel Street, Llangollen, Denbighshire, LL20 8NN P
01978 860861
Est. 1978 *Stock size* Medium
Stock Range of furniture, china, brass, ceramics
Open Tues Fri Sat 11.30am–5pm or by appointment
Fairs Anglesey, Gwyn Davis Fair

RHYL

The Aquarius
Contact Mrs Gaynor Williams
18 Water Street, Rhyl, Denbighshire, LL18 1SW P
01745 332436
Est. 1980 *Stock size* Medium
Stock Period clothing, accessories, costume jewellery, lace, collectables
Open Mon–Sat 10.30am–5pm winter closed Tues am

RUTHIN

Grandpa's Collectables
Contact Yvonne Jones
2 Market Street, Ruthin, Denbighshire, LL15 1BE P
01824 705601
Est. 1998 *Stock size* Large
Stock Antiques, collectables, some French furniture
Open Tues–Sat 10am–5pm

TREVOR

Romantiques Antique Centre
Contact Mr Knight
Bryn Seion Chapel, Station Road, Trevor, Llangollen, Denbighshire, LL20 7TP P
01978 822879
M 07778 279614 (day)
E satkin1057@aol.com
W www.romantiques.co.uk
Est. 1993 *Stock size* Large
Stock Antiques, collectables
Open Mon–Fri 10am–5pm Sat Sun 11–4pm
Services Restoration of upholstery, clocks, furniture, barometers

WREXHAM

Wingett's
Contact Mr J Lloyd
29 Holt Street, Wrexham, Denbighshire, LL13 8DH P
01978 353553 F 01978 353264
E auctions@wingetts.co.uk
W www.wingetts.co.uk
Est. 1942
Open Mon–Fri 9am–5pm
Sales Weekly general sale, monthly antiques and fine art sale
Catalogues Yes

FLINTSHIRE

CONNAH'S QUAY

Whitehead & Sons
Contact Mr T Whitehead
264 High Street, Connah's Quay, Deeside, Flintshire, CH5 4DJ P
01244 818414 F 01244 82290
Est. 1995
Open Mon–Sat 9am–6pm
Sales General sales including antique china, furniture, household goods, pawnbrokers' jewellery and regular bailiff sales
Frequency Every Tuesday

EWLOE

On The Air Ltd (British Vintage Wireless Society)
Contact Steve Harris
The Vintage Technology Centre, The Highway, Ewloe, Deeside, Flintshire, CH5 3DN P
01244 530300 F 01244 530300
M 07778 767734
E info@vintageradio.co.uk
W www.vintageradio.co.uk
Est. 1990 *Stock size* Large
Stock Vintage radios, gramophones
Open Variable
Fairs NVCF (NEC)
Services Valuations, restorations, shipping

HAWARDEN

Capricorn Antiques
Contact Mr K Roberts
Ashfield Farm, Gladstone Way, Hawarden, Deeside, Flintshire, CH5 3HE P
01244 535344
Est. 1987 *Stock size* Large
Stock Early pine and Edwardian furniture, 1920s stripped oak
Open Mon–Sat 9am–5pm Sun 11am–4pm
Services Restorations, wood stripping

MOLD

J Bradburne-Price & Co
Contact Mr Roger Griffiths
16 Chester Street, Mold, Flintshire, CH7 1EG P
01352 753873 F 01352 700071
Est. 1904
Open Mon–Fri 9am–5pm Sat 9am–noon
Sales Periodic sales of antiques and modern furniture in Mold Market
Catalogues No

GWYNEDD

BANGOR

David Windsor Gallery (IPC, FATG)
Contact Mrs E Kendrick
173 High Street, Bangor, Gwynedd, LL57 1NU P
01248 364639 F 01248 364639
Est. 1970 *Stock size* Medium
Stock 1580–1850 old maps, prints, lithographs, oil paintings, watercolours
Open Mon–Sat 10am–5pm closed Wed
Services Valuations, restoration, framing

BARMOUTH

Chapel Antiques Centre
Contact Danny Jones
High Street, Barmouth, Gwynedd, LL42 IDS P
01341 281377 F 01341 281377
Est. 1993 *Stock size* Medium
No. of dealers 24

Stock General antiques, Gaudy Welsh china, country furniture
Open All week 10.30am–5pm closed Wed during off-season
Services Delivery within UK, shipping can be arranged

⊞ Fron House Antiques Decorative Items
Contact Mrs B Howard
✉ Fron House, Jubilee Road, Barmouth, Gwynedd, LL42 1EE 🅿
☎ 01341 280649 🅕 01341 280649
Ⓜ 07881 471875
Est. 1969 *Stock size* Medium
Stock General antiques, collectables
Open Mon–Sun 10am–5pm closed Wed Oct–April
Fairs Swinderby, Newark
Services Credit and debit cards accepted

BETHESDA

⊞ A E Morris Books (WBA)
Contact A E Morris
✉ 40 High Street, Bethesda, Bangor, Gwynedd, LL57 3AN 🅿
☎ 01248 602533
Est. 1986 *Stock size* Medium
Stock Rare and second-hand books, antiquarian prints
Open Mon–Sat 10am–5pm

⊞ O Law I Law
Contact Carys Dafydd
✉ 38 High Street, Bethesda, Bangor, Gwynedd, LL57 3AN 🅿
☎ 01248 600350 🅕 01248 605542
🅔 gwynfor@olawilaw.co.uk
Ⓦ www.olawilaw.co.uk
Est. 1995 *Stock size* Small
Stock General antiques
Open Mon–Sat 10am–5pm closed Wed
Fairs Anglesey

CAERNARFON

⊞ Days Gone By
Contact Sue
✉ 6 Palace Street, Caernarfon, Gwynedd, LL55 1RR
☎ 01286 678010 🅕 01286 678554
🅔 sue@daysgoneby.f9.co.uk
Ⓦ www.daysgoneby.f9.co.uk
Est. 1994 *Stock size* Medium
Stock General antiques, period furniture, collectables, jewellery
Open Mon–Sat 9.30am–5.30pm

CRICCIETH

⊞ Capel Mawr Collectors' Centre
Contact Alun Turner
✉ 21 High Street, Criccieth, Gwynedd, LL52 OBS 🅿
☎ 01766 523600
🅔 collectables@capelmawr.free-online.co.uk
Est. 1998 *Stock size* Large
Stock Rare and second-hand books, old postcards, cigarette cards, antiques etc
Trade only Yes
Open Mid-May–end Sept Mon–Sun 10am–5pm winter Tues Thurs–Sat 10am–5pm
Services Mail order

⊞ Criccieth Gallery Antiques
Contact Anita Evens
✉ London House, High Street, Criccieth, Gwynedd, LL52 ORN 🅿
☎ 01766 522836
Est. 1971 *Stock size* Medium
Stock General antiques
Open Mon–Sun 9am–5.30pm
Fairs Newark, Mona, Towy
Services Restoration of pottery and porcelain

DOLGELLAU

⊞ Cader Idris Bookshop (PBFA, WBA)
Contact Barbara or Neil Beeby
✉ 2 Maldwyn House, Finsbury Square, Dolgellau, Gwynedd, LL40 1RF
☎ 01341 421288 and 01341 423779
Est. 1987 *Stock size* Medium
Stock Antiquarian and second-hand books including Welsh topography
Open Mon–Sat 9.30am–5pm Wed 9.30am–1pm
Services Book search

PENYGROES

⊞ Maen Dylan
Contact Ken Owen
✉ Victoria Road, Penygroes, Caernarfon, Gwynedd, LL54 6HD 🅿
☎ 01286 880770
Est. 1979 *Stock size* Medium
Stock General antiques, good-quality second-hand items and household effects
Open Mon–Sat 9am–6pm
Fairs Anglesey

PONTLYFNI

⊞ Sea View Antiques
Contact Mr D Ramsell
✉ Sea View, Pontlyfni, Caernarfon, Gwynedd, LL54 5EF 🅿
☎ 01286 660436
Ⓜ 07990 976562
Est. 1997 *Stock size* Medium
Stock General antiques, collectables
Open Mon–Sun noon–6pm

PWLLDEFAID

⊞ T Evans Antiques
Contact T Evans
✉ Pwlldefaid, Aberdafon, Pwllheli, Gwynedd, LL53 8BT 🅿
☎ 01758 760215
Est. 1984 *Stock size* Medium
Stock General antiques especially Welsh country furniture
Open Mon–Sun 9am–5pm
Fairs Carmarthen, Cardiff
Services House clearance

PWLLHELI

⊞ Rodney Adams Antiques
Contact Rodney Adams
✉ Hall Place, 10 Penlan Street, Pwllheli, Gwynedd, LL53 5DU 🅿
☎ 01758 613173 🅕 01758 613173
Stock size Large
Stock General antiques, grandfather clocks and early oak furniture
Open Mon–Sat 9am–5pm Thurs 9am–1pm
Services Valuations, repairs, restorations

⊞ Penlan Pine
Contact Michael Adams
✉ Hall Place, 7 Penlan Street, Pwllheli, Gwynedd, LL53 7DH 🅿
☎ 01758 613173 🅕 01758 613173
Ⓜ 07785 313553 *Stock size* Small
Stock Reproduction and antique pine furniture
Open Mon–Sat 9am–5pm Thurs 9am–1pm
Services Valuations, restorations, repair

⊞ Period Pine
Contact Allan Stanley
✉ Units 1–3, Bron-y-Berth, Penrhos, Pwllheli, Gwynedd, LL53 7UL 🅿
☎ 01758 614343 🅕 01758 614100

Ⓜ 07768 875875
Ⓔ allan@periodpine.fsnet.co.uk
Est. 1987 *Stock size* Large
Stock General antiques. Reproduction handmade kitchens
Open Mon–Sun 9am–5pm
Services Restorations

ISLE OF ANGLESEY

BEAUMARIS

⊞ The Museum of Childhood Memories
Contact Robert Brown
✉ **1 Castle Street, Beaumaris, Isle of Anglesey, LL58 8AP** Ⓟ
☎ 01248 712498
Ⓦ www.nwi.co.uk/museumofchildhood
Est. 1973 *Stock size* Medium
Stock Childhood memorabilia, tinplate, childhood money boxes, pottery and glass, gift items based on museum exhibits
Open Mon–Sat 10.30am–5pm March–Oct Sun noon–5pm
Services Valuations

HOLYHEAD

⊞ Ann Evans (LAPADA)
Contact Mrs Ann Evans
✉ **Carna House, Station Road, Valley, Isle of Anglesey, LL65 3EB** Ⓟ
☎ 01407 741733 Ⓕ 01407 740109
Ⓜ 07850 523118
Est. 1989 *Stock size* Medium
Stock Welsh dressers, Staffordshire figures, cranberry glass, silver, country items
Open Thurs Fri Sat 10am–4.30pm
Fairs Bailey Fairs, Penmans

⊞ Gwynfair Antiques
Contact Mrs A McCann
✉ **74 Market Street, Holyhead, Isle of Anglesey, LL65 1UW** Ⓟ
☎ 01407 763740
Ⓜ 079709 68484
Est. 1986 *Stock size* Medium
Stock General Antiques
Open 10.30am–4.30pm closed Tues Thurs Sun
Services Valuations

LLANERCHYMEDD

⊞ Two Dragons Oriental Antiques
Contact Tony Andrew
✉ **8 High Streeet, Llanerchymedd, Isle of Anglesey, LL71 8EA** Ⓟ
☎ 01248 470204 or 470100 Ⓕ 01248 470040
Est. 1979 *Stock size* Large
Stock Antique Chinese country furniture, signed limited-edition prints by Charles Tunnicliffe
Open By appointment
Fairs Newark, Swinderby

MENAI BRIDGE

⊞ Better Days
Contact Mr & Mrs Rutter
✉ **33 High Street, Menai Bridge, Gwynedd, LL59 5EF** Ⓟ
☎ 01248 716657
Ⓔ rosy@betterdaysantiques.co.uk
Ⓦ www.betterdaysantiques.co.uk
Est. 1988 *Stock size* Medium
Stock General antiques
Open Mon–Sat 10.30am–4.30pm Wed 11am–1pm
Fairs Anglesey
Services House clearance

MID GLAMORGAN

ABERDARE

⊞ Market Antiques
Contact Mr Toms Glanville
✉ **15 Duke Street, Aberdare, Mid Glamorgan, CF44 7ED** Ⓟ
☎ 01685 870242 Ⓕ 01685 872453
Ⓔ toms@toms.worldonline.co.uk
Est. 1979 *Stock size* Large
Stock Second-hand and antique furniture, collectables, china, glass, pictures etc
Open Mon–Sat 9.30am–5pm
Fairs Abergavenny
Services House clearance

BRIDGEND

⊞ Hart Antiques (Textile Society)
Contact Mrs C Hart
✉ **1a Dunraven Place, Bridgend, Mid Glamorgan, CF31 1JF** Ⓟ
☎ 01656 665400 Ⓕ 01656 665400
Est. 1993 *Stock size* Large
Stock Late 18th–early 20thC decorative antiques and period textiles
Open Mon–Fri 9am–2.30pm Sat 9am–4pm phone before travelling
Fairs Specialist textile fairs, Shepton Mallet
Services Interior design

⊞ Nolton Antiques & Fine Art
Contact Mr J Gittings
✉ **66 Nolton Street, Bridgend, Mid Glamorgan, CF31 3BP** Ⓟ
☎ 01656 667774
Ⓔ julian.gittins@connectfree.co.uk
Est. 1999 *Stock size* Large
Stock Antique furniture, ceramics, paintings, clocks, ephemera, books, stamps, decorative reproductions
Open Mon–Sat 9.30am–5.30pm
Services Valuations, house clearance

⊞ Utility
Contact Mr N Sutton
✉ **20b Queen Street, Bridgend, Mid Glamorgan, CF31 1HX** Ⓟ
☎ 01656 766995
Est. 1987 *Stock size* Medium
Stock Late Victorian–Edwardian furniture and decorative items, Victorian cast-iron fireplaces and surrounds
Open Mon–Sat 10am–5pm
Services Maker of pine furniture

CAERPHILLY

⊞ G J Gittins & Sons
Contact Mr John Gittins
✉ **10 Clive Street, Caerphilly, Mid Glamorgan, CF83 1GE** Ⓟ
☎ 029 2086 8835
Ⓜ 07941 213771
Est. 1928 *Stock size* Medium
Stock General antiques
Open Mon–Sat 10am–4pm closed Wed
Services House clearance

EWENNY

⊞ Harvard Antiques
Contact Mrs E Budd
✉ **4 Wick Road, Ewenny, Bridgend, Mid Glamorgan, CF35 5BL** Ⓟ
☎ 01656 766113
Est. 1989 *Stock size* Large
Stock Good-quality furniture, porcelain, clocks, longcase clocks
Open Sat 10am–5.30pm Sun noon–5.30pm or by appointment
Services Valuations

KENFIG HILL

⊞ J & A Antiques
Contact Mrs J Lawson

✉ **1 Prince Road, Kenfig Hill, Bridgend, Mid Glamorgan, CF33 6ED** 🅿
☎ 01656 746681
Est. 1991 *Stock size* Medium
Stock Victorian–Edwardian china, glass, furniture
Open Mon–Fri 10am–4.30pm Wed 10am–12.30pm Sat 10am–1pm

MERTHYR TYDFIL

⊞ Halfway Trading
Contact Mr J McCarthy
✉ **38 Portmorlais, Merthyr Tydfil, Mid Glamorgan, CF47 8UN** 🅿
☎ 01685 350967
Est. 1995 *Stock size* Medium
Stock General range of antiques and new stock
Open Mon–Sat 9am–5pm
Services House clearance

⊞ Paul Williams Antiques
Contact Mr P Williams
✉ **The Warehouse, Warlow Street, Merthyr Tydfil, Mid Glamorgan, CF47 0YW** 🅿
☎ 01685 721481
Ⓜ 07775 828151
Est. 1985 *Stock size* Large
Stock Wide range of antique Victorian, Edwardian and Art Deco furniture, china, glass, pictures, mirrors
Open Mon–Fri 10am–5pm Sat 10am–2pm
Services House clearance

MOUNTAIN ASH

⊞ Old Oak Antiques Abercynon
Contact Mr M James
✉ **28 Margaret Street, Mountain Ash, Mid Glamorgan, CF45 4RE** 🅿
☎ 01443 742553
Ⓔ oldoak_uk@yahoo.co.uk
Est. 1997 *Stock size* Medium
Stock Victorian–Art Deco furniture, decorative items, toys, collectors' items etc
Open Mon–Sat 9am–4.30pm
Services Valuations

⊞ Trading Post
Contact Mr J Woodrow or Mrs Cath Davies
✉ **3–4 Oxford Buildings, Oxford Street, Mountain Ash, Mid Glamorgan, CF45 3HE** 🅿
☎ 01443 478855
Ⓜ 07989 332514
Est. 1997 *Stock size* Large
Stock Wide range of stock including furniture, china, glass, silver, jewellery, textiles, books, Continental furniture
Open Mon–Sat 10am–5pm closed Thurs

PONTYPRIDD

Pontypridd Sale Rooms & Auctions (ISVA)
Contact Mr K Hobbs
✉ **Old Co-op Bakery, Cefn Lane, Glyncoch, Pontypridd, Mid Glamorgan, CF37 3BP** 🅿
☎ 01443 403764 Ⓕ 01443 403764
Est. 1919
Open Wed 10am fortnightly
Sales Auction Wed 10am, viewing Tues 2–7pm
Frequency Fortnightly

PORTHCAWL

⊞ Harlequin Antiques
Contact John Ball
✉ **Dock Street, Porthcawl, Mid Glamorgan, CF36 3BL** 🅿
☎ 01656 785910
Ⓜ 07980 837844
Est. 1974 *Stock size* Medium
Stock General antiques, antiquarian books, textiles
Open Mon–Sat 10am–4pm
Services Valuations

⊞ Nostalgia
Contact Mr Paul Rossini
✉ **5 South Road, Porthcawl, Mid Glamorgan, CF36 3DH** 🅿
☎ 01656 782933 Ⓕ 01656 786913
Ⓜ 07967 006820
Est. 1999 *Stock size* Medium
Stock General antiques
Open Mon–Fri Sat 9.30am–5pm
Services Valuations, restorations, house clearance

TONYPANDY

⊞ Jeff's Antiques
Contact Mrs J Howells
✉ **88 Dunraven Street, Tonypandy, Mid Glamorgan, CF40 1AP** 🅿
☎ 01443 434963
Est. 1976 *Stock size* Large
Stock Shipping furniture, glass, porcelain, collectables
Open Mon–Sat 9.30am–5pm closed Thurs

TREHARRIS

⊞ Treharris Antiques
Contact Mr C Barker or Mrs Janet Barker
✉ **18 Perrott Street, Treharris, Mid Glamorgan, CF46 5ER** 🅿
☎ 01443 413081
Est. 1971 *Stock size* Large
Stock Militaria, china, mining memorabilia, collectable records, Welsh collectables etc
Open Always open, ring first on weekends
Services Valuations

TREORCHY

⊞ Old Exports Ltd
Contact Mrs P Evans
✉ **Unit 35, Ynyswen Industrial Estate, Treorchy, Mid Glamorgan, CF42 6EP** 🅿
☎ 01443 776410 Ⓕ 01443 776982
Ⓜ 07785 308567 or 746748
Ⓔ old.exports@virgin.net. business.virgin.net/old.exports
Est. 1980 *Stock size* Large
Stock Victorian–1920s, furniture, decorative items etc
Open Mon–Fri 9am–5pm Sat 10am–5pm
Services Packing, shipping, Far East and USA specialists

MONMOUTHSHIRE

ABERGAVENNY

J Straker Chadwick & Sons
Contact Mr L H Trumper
✉ **Market Street Chambers, Market Street, Abergavenny, Monmouthshire, NP7 5SD** 🅿
☎ 01873 852624 Ⓕ 01873 857311
Ⓔ enquiries@strakerchadwick.co.uk
Ⓦ www.strakerchadwick.co.uk
Est. 1872
Open Mon–Fri 9am–5pm Sat 9.30am–12.30pm
Sales General antiques
Frequency Monthly
Catalogues Yes

ABERSYCHAN

⊞ Emlyn Antiques
Contact Emlyn Edmonds
✉ **Ffrwd Road, Abersychan, Pontypool, Monmouthshire, NP4 8PP** 🅿
☎ 01495 774982
Est. 1985 *Stock size* Medium

Stock General antiques
Open Mon–Sat 9.30am–6pm
Services Valuations

CHEPSTOW

⊞ Foxglove Antiques
Contact Lesley Brain
⊠ **20 St Mary Street, Chepstow, Monmouthshire, NP16 5EW** Ⓟ
☎ 01291 622386
Ⓜ 07949 244611
Ⓔ foxglovesants@foxglovesants.free-online.co.uk
Est. 1995 *Stock size* Medium
Stock Antiques and collectables
Open Mon–Sat 10am–5.30pm closed Wed
Services Valuations, restorations

⊞ Plough House Interiors
Contact Peter Jones
⊠ **Plough House, Upper Church Street, Chepstow, Monmouthshire, NP16 5HU**
☎ 01291 625200
Ⓔ ploughhouse@amserve.net
Est. 1979 *Stock size* Medium
Stock General antiques, furniture including tables and chairs
Open Mon–Sat 10am–5pm
Services Valuations, upholstery and polishing

LLANBADOC

⊞ Brindley John Ayers Antique Fishing Tackle
Contact Mr B J Ayres
⊠ **Rivermill House, 1 Woodside Court, Llanbadoc, Usk, Monmouthshire, NP15 1SY** Ⓟ
☎ 01291 672710 Ⓕ 01291 673464
Ⓔ bjayers@vintagefishingtackle.com
Ⓦ vintagefishingtackle.com
Est. 1988 *Stock size* Large
Stock Antique fishing tackle
Open By appointment
Fairs Newark, Canterbury
Services Catalogues, B & B (for customers)

LLANVIHANGEL CRUCORNEY

⊞ Abergavenny Reclamation
Contact Mr Simon Thomas
⊠ **Rosenannon, Llanvihangel Crucorney, Abergavenny, Monmouthshire, NP7 7NB** Ⓟ
☎ 01873 890842
Ⓜ 0797 0318399
Est. 1993 *Stock size* Varies
Stock Architectural salvage, reclaimed building materials, flagstones and floorboards a speciality
Open By appointment

MONMOUTH

⊞ Blestium Antique Centre
Contact Brent Watkins
⊠ **The Malthouse, 10–14 St Mary Street, Monmouth, Monmouthshire, NP25 3DB**
☎ 01600 713999 Ⓕ 01600 713999
Ⓔ brent@blestium.co.uk
Ⓦ blestium.co.uk
Est. 1999 *Stock size* Large
Stock Furniture, china, collectables, clocks, silver and architectural
Open Mon–Sat 10am–6pm Sun 1–5pm

⊞ Frost Antiques & Pine
Contact Nick Frost
⊠ **8 Priory Street, Monmouth, Monmouthshire, NP25 3BR** Ⓟ
☎ 01600 716687
Ⓔ nickfrost@frostantiques.com
Ⓦ www.frostantiques.com
Est. 1956 *Stock size* Medium
Stock Pine furniture, Staffordshire figures, kitchenware, prints, china
Open Mon–Sat 9am–5pm or by appointment
Services Valuations, restorations

NEWPORT

⊞ Beechwood Antiques
Contact William Samuel
⊠ **418 Chepstow Road, Newport, Monmouthshire, NP19 8JU** Ⓟ
☎ 01633 279192 Ⓕ 01633 279192
Ⓜ 07712 1447913
Est. 1979 *Stock size* Medium
Stock General antiques
Open Mon–Sat 10.30am–5.30pm
Fairs Newark, Chepstow
Services Restoration and china repairs

⊞ Callie's Curiosity Shop
Contact Mrs K A Strangward
⊠ **2 Speke Street, Maindee, Newport, Monmouthshire, NP19 8EX** Ⓟ
☎ 01633 222005
Ⓜ 07801 149805
Est. 1996 *Stock size* Medium
Stock General antiques and collectables
Open Mon–Thurs 9.30am–4.30pm Fri Sat 10am–2pm
Fairs Berkeley Castle, Thame
Services Valuations, repairs, furniture restorations

⊞ Welsh Salvage Co (SALVO)
Contact Mr S. Lewis
⊠ **Isca Yard, Milman Street, Newport, Monmouthshire, NP20 2JL** Ⓟ
☎ 01633 212945 Ⓕ 01633 213458
Ⓦ www.welshsalvage.co.uk
Est. 1986 *Stock size* Large
Stock Fireplaces, flooring
Open Mon–Fri 8.30am–5.30pm Sat 8.30am–4pm Sun 11am–2pm
Services Restoration, repairs

TINTERN

⊞ Stella Books (PBFA)
Contact Mrs Chris Tomaszewski
⊠ **Monmouth Road, Tintern, Chepstow, Monmouthshire, NP16 6SE** Ⓟ
☎ 01291 689755 Ⓕ 01291 689998
Ⓔ enquiry@stellabooks.com
Ⓦ www.stellabooks.com
Est. 1990 *Stock size* Large
Stock Rare and out-of-print books, specializing in children's books and UK topography
Open Mon–Sun 9.30am–5.30pm
Services Book search

⊞ Tintern Antiques
Contact Dawn Floyd
⊠ **The Old Bakehouse, Tintern, Chepstow, Monmouthshire, NP16 6SE** Ⓟ
☎ 01291 689705 Ⓕ 01291 689705
Est. 1979 *Stock size* Medium
Stock General antiques including china, furniture, jewellery
Open Mon–Sun 10am–5pm

TREGARE

⊞ The Georgian Barn
Contact Sylvia Knee
⊠ **Pen-y-Walk, Tregare, Usk, Monmouthshire, NP15 2LH** Ⓟ
☎ 01291 690802
Est. 1986 *Stock size* Medium
Stock General antiques
Open Mon–Sun 10am–4pm
Services House clearance

PEMBROKESHIRE

FISHGUARD

J J Morris
Contact Mr D A Thomas
21 West Street,
Fishguard,
Pembrokeshire, SA65 9AL
☎ 01348 873836 Ⓕ 01348 874166
Ⓔ mail@jjmestateagents.co.uk
Ⓦ www.jjmestateagents.co.uk
Est. 1949
Open Mon–Fri 9am–5.30pm
Sat 9am–noon
Sales General antiques
Frequency 6–8 weeks
Catalogues No

HAVERFORDWEST

Dyfed Antiques
Contact Giles Chaplin
The Wesleyan Chapel,
Perrotts Road,
Haverfordwest,
Pembrokeshire, SA61 2JD
☎ 01437 760496 Ⓕ 01437 760496
Est. 1969 *Stock size* Large
Stock General antiques, architectural salvage, bespoke furniture
Open Mon–Sat 10am–5pm
Services Advisory and refurbishment service

Gerald Oliver Antiques
Contact Gerald Oliver
14 Albany Terrace,
Haverfordwest,
Pembrokeshire, SA61 1RH
☎ 01437 762794
Ⓔ gerald.oliver@zoom.uk
Est. 1955 *Stock size* Medium
Stock General antiques, specializing in locally sourced items, furniture and bygones
Open Mon–Sat 9am–4.30pm
Thurs 9am–1pm
Services Valuations

Kent House Antiques
Contact Mr Graham Fanstone
Kent House,
15 Market Street,
Haverfordwest,
Pembrokeshire, SA61 1NF
☎ 01437 768175
Est. 1988 *Stock size* Medium
Stock General antiques
Open Tues–Sat 10am–5pm
Services Restorations

NARBERTH

Ichthus Antiques
Contact Cheryl Evans
2 Market Square, Narberth,
Pembrokeshire, SA67 7AU
☎ 01834 860416
Est. 1998 *Stock size* Medium
Stock General antiques, linen, Welsh blankets
Open Mon–Sat 10.30am–5.30pm

The Malthouse
Contact P Griffiths or J Williams
Back Lane,
High Street, Narberth,
Pembrokeshire, SA67 7AR
☎ 01834 860303
Est. 1998 *Stock size* Medium
Stock General antiques, furniture, bric-a-brac
Open Mon–Sat 10am–5.30pm
Sun 11am–4pm
Services Pine stripping

NEWPORT

Carningli Centre
Contact Mrs Ann Gent
East Street, Newport,
Pembrokeshire, SA42 0SY
☎ 01239 820724
Est. 1997 *Stock size* Medium
Stock General antiques, second-hand books, art gallery
Open Mon–Sat 10am–5.30pm
Services Furniture restoration and polishing

PEMBROKE

Pembroke Antiques Centre
Contact Michael Blake
Wesley Chapel,
Main Street, Pembroke,
Pembrokeshire, SA71 4DE
☎ 01646 687017
Est. 1979 *Stock size* Large
Stock General antiques especially Victorian–Edwardian furniture, china, paintings, ephemera, postcards etc
Open Mon–Sat 10am–5pm
Services Repairs, restoration and valuations

Picton Collectables
Contact Mr A L Cuft
59 Main Street, Pembroke,
Pembrokeshire, SA71 4DA
☎ 01646 621734
Est. 1992 *Stock size* Medium
Stock Collectables
Open Mon–Sat 10am–4pm
Fairs Towy
Services Valuations

PEMBROKE DOCK

Treen Box Antiques
Contact Mr M D Morris
61 Bush Street,
Pembroke Dock,
Pembrokeshire, SA72 6AN
☎ 01646 621800 Ⓕ 01646 621800
Ⓜ 07971 636148
Est. 1990 *Stock size* Medium
Stock General antiques, small upholstered chairs
Open Mon–Sat 9am–5pm
or by appointment
Fairs Ardingly, Stoneleigh
Services Restorations, repairs, upholstery

Victoria Antiques
Contact Mr D Peter
49 Bush Street,
Pembroke Dock,
Pembrokeshire, SA72 6AN
☎ 01646 682652
Est. 1990 *Stock size* Medium
Stock General antiques, maritime artefacts
Open Tues Fri 10am–5pm Wed 10am–1pm Sat 10am–3pm

TEMPLETON

Barn Court Antiques
Contact David Evans
Barn Court,
Templeton, Narberth,
Pembrokeshire, SA67 8SL
☎ 01834 861224
Ⓔ barntemp@aol.com
Ⓦ www.barncourtantiques.com
Est. 1976 *Stock size* Medium
Stock 18th–19thC fine quality furniture, china and glass
Open All week 10am–5pm closed Mon during winter
Services Valuations, restorations

TENBY

Cofion Books & Postcards (PTA)
Contact A Smosarski
1 Bridge Street,
Tenby,
Pembrokeshire, SA70 7BU
☎ 01834 845741 Ⓕ 01834 843864
Est. 1987 *Stock size* Large
Stock Second-hand books, Edwardian postcards, varied collectables, specializing in

Augustus and Gwen John publications
Open All week 10.30am–5.30pm
Fairs Nottingham and London postcard fairs
Services Valuations, book search, postal approval on postcards

POWYS

BRECON

Antiques Etc
Contact Mrs S Thomas
Lion Street, Brecon, Powys, LD3 7AU
01874 622366
07971 016356
Est. 1995 *Stock size* Large
Stock General antiques
Open Mon–Sat 10am–5pm

Books, Maps & Prints
Contact Andrew Wakley
7 The Struet, Brecon, Powys, LD3 7LL
01874 622714 F 01874 622714
Est. 1973 *Stock size* Medium
Stock Books, maps and prints
Open Mon–Sat 9am–5pm
Wed 9am–1pm
Services Framing

Montague Harris & Co
Contact John Lewis
16 Ship Street, Brecon, Powys, LD3 9AD
01874 623200 F 01874 623131
E jal@montague-harris.co.uk
W www.montague-harris.co.uk
Est. 1900
Open Mon–Fri 9am–5pm
Sat 9am–1pm
Sales General antiques
Frequency Periodically
Catalogues Yes

F H Sunderland & Co (RICS , ISVA)
Contact David Pritchard
Coliseum House, 7 Wheat Street, Brecon, Powys, LD3 7DG
01874 622261 F 01874 624705
Est. 1959
Open Mon–Sat 9am–5pm
Sales Antiques and general effects
Frequency Monthly
Catalogues Yes

BUILTH WELLS

McCartneys
Contact Mrs Diana Samuel
46 High Street, Builth Wells, Powys, LD2 3AB
01982 552259 F 01982 552193
E builth@mccartneys.co.uk
W www.mccartneys.co.uk
Est. 1949
Open Mon–Fri 9am–5pm
Sat 9.30am–12.30pm
Sales General antiques, furniture and effects
Frequency Periodically
Catalogues No

Smithfield Antiques
Contact Suzanne Price
Smithfield Road, Builth Wells, Powys, LD2 3AN
01982 553022 F 01982 553022
07879 025577
E suzanne@smithfieldjoinery.fsnet.co.uk
W www.smithfield-joinery.com
Est. 2000 *Stock size* Medium
Stock General antiques, fireplaces, oak Welsh dressers
Open Mon–Sat 10am–5pm closed Wed

CILMERY

V Nejus
Contact Mr V Nejus
Comyn Cottage, Cilmery, Builth Wells, Powys, LD2 3LH
01982 553792
Est. 1972 *Stock size* Medium
Stock General antiques
Open By appointment

FOUR CROSSES

Malthouse Antiques
Contact Neville Foulkes
The Old Malthouse, Pool Road, Four Crosses, Llanymynech, Powys, SY22 6PS
01691 830015 F 01691 839099
Est. 1983 *Stock size* Medium
Stock Pine and country furniture
Open Mon–Sat 9am–6pm or by appointment
Services Valuations, restoration and repairs

KNIGHTON

Offa's Dyke Antique Centre
Contact Mr I Watkins or Mrs H Hood
4 High Street, Knighton, Powys, LD7 2AT
01547 520145
Est. 1987 *Stock size* Medium
No. of dealers 12
Stock General antiques, ceramics
Open Mon–Sat 10am–1pm and 2–5pm
Services House clearance

Islwyn Watkins Antiques
Contact Mr I Watkins
4 High Street, Knighton, Powys, LD7 1AT
01547 520145
Est. 1977 *Stock size* Large
Stock Ceramics and small country antiques
Open Mon–Sat 10am–1pm 2–5pm
Services Valuations

LLANDRINDOD WELLS

Brightwells
Contact T I Parry (FRICS, FAAV)
Lansdown Buildings, South Crescent, Llandrindod Wells, Powys, LD1 5DT
01597 824915 F 01597 825202
07778 276699
E llandrindod@brightwells.com
W www.brightwells.com
Est. 1842
Open Mon–Fri 9am–1pm 2–5pm
Sales General antiques
Frequency Periodically
Catalogues Yes

LLANFAIR CAEREINION

Heritage Restorations
Contact Jonathan Gluck
Llanfair Caereinion, Welshpool, Powys, SY21 0HD
01938 810384 F 01938 810900
E info@heritagerestorations.co.uk
W www.heritagerestorations.co.uk
Est. 1970 *Stock size* Large
Stock 18th–19thC pine furniture
Open Mon–Sat 9am–5pm
Services Restorations

LLANFYLLIN

Galata Coins
Contact Paul Withers
Old White Lion, Market Street, Llanfyllin, Powys, SY22 5BX
01691 648765 F 01691 648765
E Paul@galatacoins.demon.co.uk
W www.galatacoins.demon.co.uk/Netlist/Main.html

Est. 1974 ***Stock size*** Small
Stock Coin and medal dealers
Open By appointment
Services Valuations

Galata Print Ltd
Contact Paul Withers
Old White Lion, Market Street, Llanfyllin, Powys, SY22 5BX
01691 648765 F 01691 648765
Paul@galatacoins.demon.co.uk
www/Netlist/Main.html
Est. 1974 ***Stock size*** Large
Stock Numismatic books
Open By appointment
Services Valuations

LLANIDLOES

The Great Oak Bookshop
Contact Ross Boswell or Karin Reiter
35 Great Oak Street, Llanidloes, Powys, SY18 6BW
01686 412959 F 01686 412959
greatoak@europe.com
www.midwales.com/gob
Est. 1992 ***Stock size*** Large
Stock Books, new and second-hand
Open Mon–Fri 9.30am–5.30pm Sat 9.30am–4.30pm
Services Book search

LLANRHAEADR-YM-MOCHNANT

Browsers
Contact Mrs N Williams
Market Square, Llanrhaeadr-ym-Mochnant, Powys, SY10 0JG
01691 780220
nerys@moc.ruralwales.org
Est. 1998 ***Stock size*** Medium
Stock Antiques, curios
Open Mon–Sat 11am–5pm Sun 2–5pm closed Thurs

LLANSANTFFRAID

Tudor Antiques
Contact Menna Corbett
Central House, Llansantffraid, Powys, SY22 6AR
01691 829104
Est. 1996 ***Stock size*** Medium
Stock General antiques, Victorian china and small furniture
Open Wed–Sat 11am–5pm
Fairs Carmarthen, Anglesey

MACHYNLLETH

Dyfi Valley Bookshop (PBFA, WBA)
Contact Mr N. Beeby
6 Heol y Doll, Machynlleth, Powys, SY20 8BQ
01654 703849
beeb@dvbookshop.fsnet.co.uk
www.abebooks.com/home/dvbookshop
Est. 1988 ***Stock size*** Medium
Stock Books, rare and second-hand, specializing in archery, the Old West, firearms
Open Mon–Sat 9.30am–5pm
Services Book search, catalogues

NEWBRIDGE ON WYE

Newbridge Antiques
Contact P Allan
The Old Village Hall, Newbridge on Wye, Llandrindod Wells, Powys, LD1 6LA
01597 860654 F 01597 860655
Est. 1986 ***Stock size*** Large
Stock General antiques, furniture and architectural
Open Mon–Sat 10am–5pm Sun noon–5pm
Services Valuations, stripping and restoration

NEWTOWN

Morris Marshall & Poole
Contact Alun Davies
10 Broad Street, Newtown, Powys, SY16 2LZ
01686 625900 F 01686 623783
mmp@newtown.ereal.net
Est. 1900
Open Mon–Fri 9am–5pm Sat 9.30am–noon
Sales General antiques
Frequency Quarterly
Catalogues Yes

RHAYADER

Etcetera
Contact Mrs R A Hawthorn
Highbury Shop, North Street, Rhayader, Powys, LD6 5BT
01597 810676 or 811423
Est. 1992 ***Stock size*** Medium
Stock Good-quality period furniture
Open Mon–Sun 10am–5.30pm, Jan–Mar limited – phone first

TRECASTLE

The Fire & Stove Shop
Contact Andy Annear or Jim Portsmouth
Vicarage Row (on A40), Trecastle, Brecon, Powys, LD3 8UW
01874 636888 F 02920 614615
M 07973 916774
jim@solidfuelstoves.com
www.solidfuelstoves.com
Est. 1998
Stock Multi-fuel stoves, fires, fireplaces, tiles, inserts, surrounds, hearths, dog grates, radiators
Open Mon–Sun 10am–6pm

Trecastle Antique Centre
Contact David Skeet
Trecastle, Brecon, Powys, LD3 8UN
01874 638007
M 07971 571649
david@skeet.zx3.net
Est. 1996 ***Stock size*** Large
No. of dealers 10
Stock General antiques
Open All week 10am–5pm
Services Alterations, restorations, repairs

WELSHPOOL

A & H Antiques
Contact Mrs A. Shaw
19 High Street, Welshpool, Powys, SY21 7JP
01938 552421
M 07778 495379
anh.antiques.@amserve.net
Est. 1978 ***Stock size*** Small
Stock 18th–19thC furniture
Open Mon–Sat 9.30am–5pm closed Tues or by appointment
Fairs Stafford Bingley Hall, DMG, Shepton Mallet
Services Restoration and delivery

F E Anderson & Son (LAPADA)
Contact Ian Anderson
5 High Street, Welshpool, Powys, SY21 7JF
01938 553340 F 01938 590545
M 07889 896832
Est. 1842 ***Stock size*** Large
Stock General antiques, 17th–19thC furniture

Open Mon–Fri 9am–5pm
Sat 9am–2pm
Fairs Olympia
Services Valuations

Norman Lloyd & Co (RICS)
Contact John Harding
5 Broad Street, Welshpool, Powys, SY21 7RZ
☎ 01938 552371 Ⓕ 01938 556314
Ⓔ normanlloy@aol.com
Ⓦ www.normanlloyd.com
Est. 1900
Open Mon–Fri 9am–5.30pm
Sales General antiques
Frequency Periodically
Catalogues Yes

SOUTH GLAMORGAN

BARRY

Ray Hawkins Antiques
Contact Ray Hawkins
1A Arcade Workships, Atlantic Trading Estate, Barry, South Glamorgan, CF63 3RF Ⓟ
☎ 01446 744750 Ⓕ 01222 711778
Ⓜ 07971 575044
Ⓔ ray@hawkins.wholesalers.co.uk
Ⓦ www.hawkins-wholesales.co.uk
Est. 1975 **Stock size** Medium
Stock Furniture, statuary, reproductions
Open Mon–Fri 9am–5pm
Sat 9am–1pm
Fairs Ardingly, Newark
Services Exports furniture to USA, packing facilities

Hawkins Brothers Antiques
Contact Mrs C Robertson
21–23 Romilly Buildings, Woodham Road, Barry Docks, Barry, South Glamorgan, CF63 4JE Ⓟ
☎ 01446 746561 Ⓕ 01446 744750
Ⓔ hawkinsbrosantiques@compuserve.com
Stock size Large
Stock General antiques
Open Mon–Sat 9am–5pm

CARDIFF

Anchor Antiques (Wales) Ltd
Contact B A Brownhill
The Pumping Station, Penarth Road, Cardiff, South Glamorgan, CF11 8TT Ⓟ
☎ 029 2023 1308 Ⓕ 029 2023 2588
Est. 1989 **Stock size** Large
Stock General antiques, clocks and ceramics
Open Mon–Sun 9.30am–5.30pm closed Tues Wed
Fairs Carmarthen, Malvern and Newark

Capital Bookshop
Contact Andrew Mitchell
27 Morgan Arcade, Cardiff, South Glamorgan, CF10 lAF
☎ 029 2038 8423
Stock size Medium
Stock Rare and second-hand books including Welsh interest
Open Mon–Sat 10am–5.30pm
Fairs Book fairs, Oxford

Cardiff Antique Centre
Contact Susan Wilding
10–12 Royal Arcade, Cardiff, South Glamorgan, CF10 1AE
☎ 029 2039 8891
Est. 1975 **Stock size** Large
Stock General antiques and collectables including Welsh china, jewellery
Open Mon–Sat 10am–5.30pm
Services Valuations

Cardiff Reclamation
Contact Jeff Evans
Unit 7, Tremorfa Industrial Estate, Martin Road, Tremorfa, Cardiff, South Glamorgan, CF24 5SD Ⓟ
☎ 029 2045 8995
Est. 1987 **Stock size** Medium
Stock Architectural antiques, specializing in fireplaces and bathrooms
Open Mon–Fri 9am–5pm Sat 9am–1pm Sun 10am–1pm
Services Bath refinishing, pine stripping, sandblasting

Charlotte's Antiques
Contact Peter Cason
129 Woodville Road, Cathays, Cardiff, South Glamorgan, CF24 4DZ Ⓟ
☎ 029 2075 9809
Ⓜ 07831 619071
Est. 1975 **Stock size** Large
Stock General and period antiques
Open Mon–Fri 10am–5pm
Sat 10am–1pm

Crwys Antiques
Contact Mr Elfed Caradog
51 Crwys Road, Cardiff, South Glamorgan, CF24 4ND Ⓟ
☎ 029 2022 5318
Est. 1985 **Stock size** Small
Stock General antiques
Open Mon–Sat 10am–6pm

Decorative Heating
Contact Jim Portsmouth
Unit 2, Victoria Arcade, The Pumping Station, Cardiff, South Glamorgan, CF11 8TT Ⓟ
☎ 029 2052 2000
Ⓜ 07973 916774
Ⓔ jim@solidfuelstoves.com
Ⓦ www.solidfuelstoves.com
Est. 1998 **Stock size** Medium
Stock Multi-fuel stoves, fires, fireplaces, tiles, inserts, surrounds, hearths, dog grates, radiators
Open Mon–Sun 9am–5.30pm

W H Douglas
Contact Mr W H Douglas
161 Cowbridge Road East, Cardiff, South Glamorgan, CF11 9AH
☎ 029 2022 4861
Est. 1952 **Stock size** Medium
Stock General antiques
Open Mon–Fri 9am–5pm

Hera Antiques
Contact Neil Richards
140 Whitchurch Road, Cardiff, South Glamorgan, CF14 3LZ Ⓟ
☎ 029 2061 9472
Est. 1987 **Stock size** Large
Stock High-quality furniture, porcelain and pictures
Open Mon–Sat 10am–5pm closed Wed
Fairs The Orangery, Margam Abbey, Port Talbot
Services Restorations, valuations

Holland & Welsh
Contact Michael Nap
8 Glay-y-Llyn Industrial Estate, Taffs Well, Cardiff, South Glamorgan, CF4 7QH Ⓟ
☎ 029 2056 1795 Ⓕ 029 2021 3370
Ⓔ hollandwelsh@msn.com
Est. 1997 **Stock size** Medium
Stock Antique flooring
Open Sat–Sun 11am–4pm and by appointment
Services Restoration

Jacobs Antique Centre
Contact Mr Cooling
West Canal Wharf, Cardiff, South Glamorgan, CF10 5DB
029 2039 0939 F 029 2037 3587
Est. 1982 *Stock size* Medium
No. of dealers 40
Stock General antiques
Open Thurs–Sat 9.30am–5pm

Keepence Antiques
Contact Mr Clive Keepence
34 Clare Road, Cardiff, South Glamorgan, CF11 6RS
029 2025 5348
Est. 1969 *Stock size* Medium
Stock Victorian, Edwardian furniture, shipping goods
Open Mon–Fri 10am–4pm Sat 11am–2pm

Llanishen Antiques
Contact Mrs J Boalch
26 Crwys Road, Cardiff, South Glamorgan, CF24 4NL
029 2039 7244
Est. 1974 *Stock size* Medium
Stock General antiques including 19th–20thC furniture
Open Mon–Sat 10am–4pm
Fairs Carmarthen, Shepton Mallett
Services Restoration

Now & Then
Contact Mr A Williams
54 Crwys Road, Cardiff, South Glamorgan, CF24 4NN
029 2038 3268 F 029 2038 4945
E frongaled50@hotmail.com
Est. 1989 *Stock size* Medium
Stock General antiques
Open Mon–Sat 9am–5pm

Phillips International Auctioneers and Valuers
7–8 Park Place, Cardiff, South Glamorgan, CF10 3DP
029 2072 7980 F 029 2072 7989
W www.phillips-auction.com
Sales Regional Office. Ring for details

Pontcanna Old Books, Maps & Prints (WBA)
Contact W. A. Beynon
1 Pontcanna Street, Cardiff, South Glamorgan, CF11 9HQ
029 2046 1047 F 029 2046 1047
E wabeynon@freenetname.co.uk
Est. 1979 *Stock size* Medium
Stock Books, rare and second-hand, maps and prints, Welsh topography
Open Mon–Sat 10am–5pm
Fairs London Royal National, Bonnington
Services Restoration

The Pumping Station
Contact Mr A J Boyce
Penarth Road, Cardiff, South Glamorgan, CF11 8TT
029 2022 1085 F 029 2023 2588
M 07774 449443
Est. 1989 *Stock size* Large
No. of dealers 35
Stock General antiques
Open All week 9.30am–5.30pm

Roberts Emporium
Contact Ian Roberts
58–60 Salisbury Road, Cardiff, South Glamorgan, CF24 4AD
029 2023 5630 F 029 2064 1430
Est. 1997 *Stock size* Large
Stock General antiques, collectables
Open Mon–Sat 11am–5.30pm
Fairs Newark, Cardiff
Services Valuations, prop hire for TV and theatre

Ty-Llwyd Antiques
Contact Mr Graham Rousell
Ty-Llwyd, Lisvane Road, Lisvane, Cardiff, South Glamorgan, CF14 0SF
029 2075 4109
Est. 1988 *Stock size* Large
Stock General antiques, clocks
Open By appointment
Services House clearance

Whitchurch Books Ltd (WBA)
Contact Gale Canvin
67 Merthyr Road, Whitchurch, Cardiff, South Glamorgan, CF14 1DD
029 2052 1956 F 029 2062 3599
W www.whitchurchbooks@barclays.net
Est. 1994 *Stock size* Medium
Stock Rare and second-hand books, specializing in archaeology and history
Open Tues–Sat 10am–5.30pm
Fairs Cardiff
Services Mail order catalogues on archaeology and history

COWBRIDGE

The Antique Centre
Contact Mike Haxley
Ebenezer Chapel, 48 Eastgate, Cowbridge, South Glamorgan, CF71 7AB
01446 771190
Est. 1966 *Stock size* Large
No. of dealers 30
Stock General antiques
Open Mon–Sat 10am–5pm
Services Valuations, picture restorations, repairs

Castle Antique Clocks
Contact Mr William Webber
The Antique Centre, Ebenezer Chapel, 48 Eastgate, Cowbridge, South Glamorgan, CF71 7AB
029 2070 2313 F 029 2071 2141
E whwebber@talk21.com
Est. 1995 *Stock size* Medium
Stock Longcase clocks
Open Mon–Sat 10am–5pm
Services Valuations, restorations

Collectors Corner
Contact M Haxley
The Antique Centre, Ebenezer Chapel, 48 Eastgate, Cowbridge, South Glamorgan, CF71 7AB
01446 771190
M 07977 091665
E collectorscorner1@hotmail.com
Est. 1996 *Stock size* Medium
Stock Furniture, china, porcelain, collectables, jewellery, autographs
Open Mon–Sat 10am–5pm

Cowbridge Antiques Centre
Contact Mr T. C. Monaghan
75 Eastgate, Cowbridge, South Glamorgan, CF71 7AA
01446 775841
M 07773 486390
Est. 1995 *Stock size* Medium
No. of dealers 9
Stock Georgian–Edwardian furniture, smalls
Open Mon–Sat 10am–5pm
Services Valuations, restorations

Eastgate Antiques
Contact Liz Herbert
6 High Street, Cowbridge, South Glamorgan, CF71 7AG
01446 775111
Est. 1984 *Stock size* Medium
Stock General antiques
Open Mon–Sat 10am–1pm 2–5.30pm

⊞ The Fingerplate Co
Contact Simon Priestley
✉ **1 Golygfa Dwyrain, Llandw, Cowbridge, South Glamorgan, CF71 7NZ**
☎ 01656 890691
ⓔ fcsp@dialstart.net
ⓦ www.fresh-net.com/fingerplateco/
Est. 1995 *Stock size* Small
Stock Brassware, door plates and fingerplates
Open Mail order and Internet
Fairs Newark
Services Repair of old fingerplates, mail order, EBAY Internet auction (code name Iznibz)

WEST GLAMORGAN

CLYDACH

⊞ Antique Fireplaces
Contact Mr R Walker
✉ **Unit 13, John Player Industrial Estate, Clydach, Swansea, West Glamorgan, SA6 5BQ** Ⓟ
☎ 01792 476047 ⓕ 01792 476047
ⓜ 07973 253655
ⓦ www.celticfireplaces.co.uk
Est. 1992 *Stock size* Large
Stock Antique fireplaces
Open Wed Sat 10am–2pm or by appointment
Services Renovation

⊞ Clydach Antiques
Contact Mr R T Pulman
✉ **83 High Street, Clydach, Swansea, West Glamorgan, SA6 5LJ** Ⓟ
☎ 01792 843209
Est. 1981 *Stock size* Small
Stock General antiques
Open Mon–Fri 10am–5pm
Fairs Swansea
Services Clock repair

GURNOS

⊞ Gurnos Sales
Contact Mr Nigel Faulkner
✉ **10 Bethel Road, Gurnos, Lower Cwmtwrch, Swansea, West Glamorgan, SA9 2PS** Ⓟ
☎ 01639 849801 ⓕ 01639 849801
ⓔ nigel@gurnosales.fsnet.co.uk
Est. 1988 *Stock size* Medium
Stock General antiques and collectables
Open Mon–Fri 10am–5pm
Sat 9am–1pm
Services House clearances

MUMBLES

⊞ Gower House Antiques
Contact Mrs E S Dodds
✉ **28–30 Dunns Lane, Mumbles, Swansea, West Glamorgan, SA3 4AA** Ⓟ
☎ 01792 369844
Est. 1999 *Stock size* Medium
Stock General antiques, mirrors, lighting, chandeliers
Open Tues–Sat 10am–5.30pm
Services Valuations

NEATH

⊞ Neath Antiques
Contact Mrs S Thomas
✉ **6 Alfred Street, Neath, West Glamorgan, SA11 1EF** Ⓟ
☎ 01639 645740
ⓦ neathantiques.co.uk
Est. 1979 *Stock size* Medium
Stock General antiques, barometers and clocks
Open Mon–Sat 10am–4.30pm closed Thurs

⊞ Neath Market Curios (OMRS)
Contact Mr P D Owen
✉ **General Market, Green Street, Neath, West Glamorgan, SA11 1DP** Ⓟ
☎ 01639 641775
Est. 1989 *Stock size* Medium
Stock General collectables
Open Mon–Sat 9am–5pm
Fairs Carmarthen, Cardiff

PONTARDULAIS

⊞ Collectors
Contact Mr J D Hyorns
✉ **48 Bryngwili Road, Hendy, Pontardulais, Swansea, West Glamorgan, SA4 1XA**
☎ 01792 885141 ⓕ 01792 885141
ⓔ pjexports@pj-collectors.fsnet.co.uk
Est. 1996 *Stock size* Medium
Stock General antiques
Open Mon–Sat 10am–5.30pm
Fairs Ardingly
Services Refurbishment

⊞ The Emporium
Contact Ms Laura Jeremy
✉ **112 St Teilo Street, Pontardulais, Swansea, West Glamorgan, SA4 1SR** Ⓟ
☎ 01792 885185
ⓜ 07811 758896
ⓔ laura@the-emporium.freeserve.co.uk
Est. 1990 *Stock size* Medium
Stock Small furniture, collectables, metalware
Open Mon–Fri 10am–5.30pm
Sat 10am–1pm

SKETTY

⊞ Forget-Me-Nots
Contact Mr Anthony Thomas
✉ **43 Eversley Road, Sketty, Swansea, West Glamorgan, SA2 9DE** Ⓟ
☎ 01792 201944 ⓕ 01792 201944
Est. 1999 *Stock size* Medium
Stock Small furniture, china, Poole, Mason's, Doulton, books
Open Mon–Fri 9.30am–5pm
Sat 9.30am–4pm

⊞ Sketty Antiques
Contact Mrs P M Richards
✉ **87 Eversley Road, Sketty, Swansea, West Glamorgan, SA2 9DE** Ⓟ
☎ 01792 201616
Est. 1995 *Stock size* Medium
Stock General antiques
Open Mon–Fri 11am–5pm Sat 10am–1pm
Fairs Towy Fairs

SWANSEA

⊞ Aladdins Cave
Contact Pat Callen
✉ **2 Plymouth Street, Swansea, West Glamorgan, SA1 3QQ** Ⓟ
☎ 01792 459576
Est. 1974 *Stock size* Large
Stock General antiques and collectables, Doulton Toby jugs, brass, copper, Winstanley cats
Open Mon–Fri 9.30am–5pm
Fairs Cowbridge, Chepstow

⊞ Bygone Antiques
Contact Mr C A Oliver
✉ **122 St Helens Road, Swansea, West Glamorgan, SA1 4AW** Ⓟ
☎ 01792 468248
Est. 1970 *Stock size* Medium
Stock General antiques
Open Mon–Sat 10am–4.30pm

Collectors' Corner
Contact Mr J Tithecott
10–11 High Street, Swansea, West Glamorgan, SA1 1LE
01792 655506
Est. 1998 *Stock size* Medium
Stock Enamel badges, postcards, stamps, cigarette cards, old and new die-cast models
Open Mon–Fri 10am–4pm Sat 10am–1pm

Stripped Pine Workshop
Contact Mr John Wood
Rear of 28 Catherine Street, Swansea, West Glamorgan, SA1 4JS
01792 461236
Est. 1970 *Stock size* Medium
Stock Furniture, doors, stripped pine
Open Mon–Sat 11.30am–6pm
Services Pine stripping

Swansea Antique Centre
Contact Mr W Wright
1 King Edward Road, Swansea, West Glamorgan, SA1 4LH
01792 475194
Est. 1999 *Stock size* Large
No. of dealers 2
Stock General antiques, good furniture
Open Mon–Sat 10am–5.30pm
Services Valuations, restorations, house clearance

Upstairs Antiques
Contact Mrs M Stanley
48 St Helens Road, Swansea, West Glamorgan, SA1 4AY
01792 466522
Est. 1994 *Stock size* Medium
Stock General antiques and restoration
Open Mon–Sat 10am–5pm
Fairs Swansea
Services Re-caning and rush work

YSTRADGYNLAIS

Penybont Farm Antiques
Contact Mrs S Yankovic
Penybont Farm, Penycae, Ystradgynlais, Swansea, West Glamorgan, SA9 1SH
01639 730620
Est. 1990 *Stock size* Large
Stock General antiques, pine, china
Open Sat Sun 10am–5pm or by appointment
Services Restoration and hand stripping

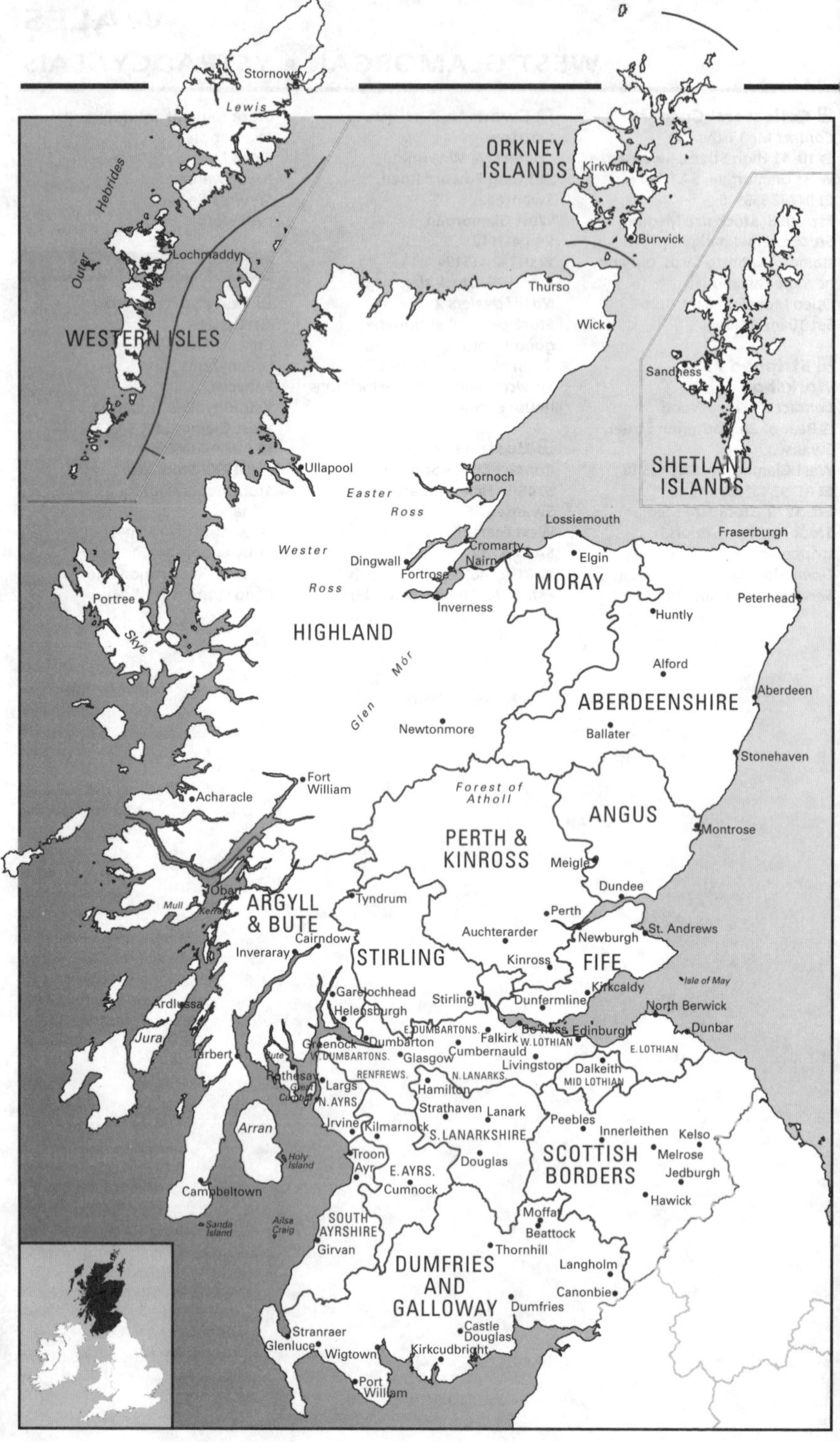

ORKNEY ISLANDS
Kirkwall
Burwick
Stornoway
Lewis
Outer Hebrides
Lochmaddy
WESTERN ISLES
Thurso
Wick
Sandness
SHETLAND ISLANDS
Ullapool
Dornoch
Easter Ross
Wester Ross
Lossiemouth
Fraserburgh
Cromarty
Nairn
Elgin
Dingwall
Fortrose
MORAY
Peterhead
Portree
Inverness
Huntly
Skye
HIGHLAND
Glen Mór
Alford
Aberdeen
ABERDEENSHIRE
Newtonmore
Ballater
Stonehaven
Fort William
Forest of Atholl
Acharacle
ANGUS
PERTH & KINROSS
Montrose
Meigle
Dundee
Oban
Mull
Kerrera
ARGYLL & BUTE
Tyndrum
Perth
St. Andrews
Auchterarder
Newburgh
Cairndow
Inveraray
STIRLING
Kinross
FIFE
Isle of May
Garelochhead
Kirkcaldy
Stirling
Dunfermline
Ardlussa
Helensburgh
North Berwick
E. DUMBARTONS.
Bo'ness
Edinburgh
Dunbar
Falkirk
W. LOTHIAN
Jura
Greenock
Dumbarton
Cumbernauld
E. LOTHIAN
Tarbert
Bute
W. DUMBARTONS.
Glasgow
Livingston
Dalkeith
RENFREWS.
N. LANARKS.
MID LOTHIAN
Rothesay
Largs
Great Cumbrae
N. AYRS
Hamilton
Strathaven
Lanark
Peebles
Arran
Irvine
Kilmarnock
S. LANARKSHIRE
Innerleithen
Kelso
Melrose
Holy Island
Troon
Ayr
Douglas
SCOTTISH BORDERS
Jedburgh
E. AYRS.
Cumnock
Hawick
Campbeltown
Moffat
Sanda Island
Ailsa Craig
SOUTH AYRSHIRE
Beattock
Girvan
Thornhill
DUMFRIES AND GALLOWAY
Langholm
Canonbie
Dumfries
Castle Douglas
Stranraer
Glenluce
Wigtown
Kirkcudbright
Port William

SCOTLAND

SCOTLAND

EDINBURGH

EDINBURGH

⊞ Armchair Books
Contact Mr D Govan
✉ **72–74 West Port, Edinburgh, EH1 2LE**
☎ 0131 229 5927
ⓔ armchairbooks@hotmail.com
Stock size Medium
Stock Books, especially Victorian illustrated books
Open Mon–Sun noon–5pm

⊞ Auckinleck
Contact William Stewart
✉ **86 Grassmarket, Edinburgh, EH1 9JR**
☎ 0131 220 0505
Est. 1979 *Stock size* Medium
Stock General antiques, Georgian–Victorian
Open Tues–Sat 10.15am–5.15pm

⊞ Bébés et Jouets
Contact Dee Urquhart
✉ **c/o Post Office, Edinburgh, EH7 6HW** Ⓟ
☎ 0131 332 5650
Ⓜ 07714 374995
ⓔ bebesetjouets@u.genie.co.uk
ⓦ http://you.genie.co.uk/bebesetjouets
Est. 1987 *Stock size* Medium
Stock Antique French bébés and German dolls, teddy bears, juvenilia and related items. Lay-away of items possible
Open By appointment only
Services Repair and restoration of antique dolls, teddies, antique costumes for dolls. Digital photographs and video of stock items. Postal service available

⊞ Belford Antiques
Contact John Belford
✉ **124 Buccleuch Street, Edinburgh, EH8 9NQ**
☎ 0131 445 4368
Ⓜ 07947 671963
Est. 1993 *Stock size* Small
Stock Furniture, collectables
Open Tues–Sat 2–6pm

⊞ Laurance Black Ltd (BADA)
Contact Laurance Black or Mrs S Campbell
✉ **60 Thistle Street, Edinburgh, EH2 1EN** Ⓟ
☎ 0131 220 3387
Est. 1989 *Stock size* Medium
Stock Scottish furniture, glass, pottery, clocks, treen
Open Mon–Fri 10.30am–4.30pm Sat 10.30am–1pm

Bonhams & Brooks Scotland
Contact Mr Mark Richards
✉ **24 Melville Street, Edinburgh, EH3 7NS** Ⓟ
☎ 0131 226 3204 Ⓕ 0131 226 3444
Ⓜ 07711 093439
ⓔ scotland@bonhams.com
ⓦ www.bonhams.com
Open Mon–Fri 9am–5pm
Sales Regional Representative for Scotland. See Head Office (London) for details

⊞ The Bookworm
Contact Peter Ritchie
✉ **210 Dalkeith Road, Edinburgh, EH16 5DT** Ⓟ
☎ 0131 662 4357
ⓔ peter.book@talk21.com
Est. 1987 *Stock size* Medium
Stock Second-hand and antique books
Open Mon–Sat 9.30am–5.30pm
Services Valuations, book search

⊞ Bow-Well Antiques
Contact Murdo McLeod
✉ **103 West Row, Edinburgh, EH1 2JP** Ⓟ
☎ 0131 225 3335 Ⓕ 0131 226 1259
Est. 1979 *Stock size* Large
Stock General and Scottish antiquities
Open Mon–Sat 10am–5pm
Fairs Ingliston
Services Shipping

⊞ Broughton Books
Contact Peter Galinsky
✉ **2a Broughton Place, Edinburgh, EH1 3RX** Ⓟ
☎ 0131 557 8010
Est. 1971 *Stock size* Medium
Stock Rare and second-hand books
Open Tues–Fri noon–6pm Sat 10.30am–5.30pm
Services Book search

⊞ Cabaret Antiques
Contact Terry Cavers
✉ **37 Grassmarket, Edinburgh, EH1 2HS** Ⓟ
☎ 0131 225 8618
Est. 1990 *Stock size* Large
Stock Art Deco, Scottish paperweights, compacts, glass, costume jewellery, ceramics
Open Mon–Sun 10.30am–5.30pm
Fairs Mammoth Fairs

⊞ Calton Gallery (BADA)
Contact Andrew Whitfield
✉ **10 Royal Terrace, Edinburgh, EH7 5AB** Ⓟ
☎ 0131 556 1010 Ⓕ 0131 558 1150
Ⓜ 07887 793781
ⓔ calton.gall@virgin.net
Est. 1980 *Stock size* Large
Stock Fine art, Scottish, marine 19th–early 20thC paintings and watercolours
Open Mon–Fri 10am–6pm Sat 10am–1pm (during exhibitions)
Services Valuations, restorations

⊞ Castle Books
Contact Mrs K Choucha
✉ **20 Rankeillor Street, Edinburgh, EH8 9HY** Ⓟ
☎ 0131 667 5174
ⓔ cathy@booksnet.freeserve.co.uk
Est. 1983 *Stock size* Small
Stock Rare and second-hand books
Open Mon–Fri 9am–5pm

⊞ D L Cavanagh Antiques
Contact Simon Cavanagh
✉ **49 Cockburn Street, Edinburgh, EH1 1BS** Ⓟ
☎ 0131 226 3391
Est. 1972 *Stock size* Large
Stock Coins, medals, silver, jewellery, collectors' items
Open Mon–Sat 11am–5.30pm
Services Valuations

⊞ Chit Chat Antiques
Contact Victoria Reid
✉ **134 St Stephen Street, Edinburgh, EH3 5AA** Ⓟ
☎ 0131 225 9660
Est. 1984 *Stock size* Small
Stock Flatware, silver plate, silver, ceramics
Open Tues–Sat 11am–5.30pm

⊞ Bobby Clyde Antiques
Contact Bobby Clyde
✉ **5a Grange Road, Edinburgh, EH9 1UH** Ⓟ
☎ 0131 667 6718
Ⓜ 07808 319496
Est. 1976 *Stock size* Medium
Stock General antiques
Open Mon Thurs Fri Sat 10.30am–5.30pm Sun noon–4pm
Services Stripping, delivery

⊞ Collector Centre
Contact Mrs K M or Mr J W Chalmers
✉ **127 Gilmore Place, Edinburgh, EH3 9PP** 🅿
☎ 0131 229 1059
Est. 1966 *Stock size* Large
Stock General antiques, mostly collectables and books, silver, militaria
Open Mon–Sat 10am–6pm closed Wed or by appointment Jul–early Sept Mon–Sat 10am–9pm Sun 1–6pm
Services Valuations, research

⊞ Da Capo Antiques
Contact Nick Carter
✉ **68 Henderson Row, Edinburgh, EH3 5BJ** 🅿
☎ 0131 557 1918
Est. 1977 *Stock size* Medium
Stock 18th–early 20thC furniture, brass bedsteads, light fittings
Open Tues–Sat 10.30am–5.30pm
Services Valuations, restorations

⊞ Alan Day Antiques (LAPADA)
Contact Mr A Day
✉ **25A Moray Place, Edinburgh, EH3 6DA** 🅿
☎ 0131 225 2590
Ⓜ 07860 533922
Ⓔ doodah.day@virgin.net
Est. 1973 *Stock size* Medium
Stock General antiques
Trade only Yes
Open By appointment

⊞ Duncan & Reid
Contact Mrs Reid
✉ **5 Tanfield, Canon Mills, Edinburgh, EH3 5DA** 🅿
☎ 0131 556 4591 Ⓕ 0131 552 8360
Ⓔ chris@cjsg.demon.co.uk
Est. 1979 *Stock size* Medium
Stock 18th–early 19thC pottery, porcelain, glass, second-hand and antiquarian books
Open Tues–Sat noon–5.30pm
Fairs Ingliston

⊞ EASY Edinburgh & Glasgow Architectural Salvage Yard (SALVO)
Contact E Barrass
✉ **Unit 6, Couper Street, Edinburgh, EH6 6HH** 🅿
☎ 0131 554 7077 Ⓕ 0131 554 3070
Ⓔ enquiries@easy-arch-salv.co.uk
Ⓦ www.easy-arch-salv.co.uk
Est. 1987 *Stock size* Medium
Stock Architectural antiques, fireplaces, doors, ranges, pews, etc
Open Mon–Sat 9am–5pm

⊞ ECS (LANA)
Contact Mr T D Brown
✉ **11 West Cross Causeway, Edinburgh, EH8 9JW** 🅿
☎ 0131 667 9095/668 2928
Ⓕ 0131 668 2926
Est. 1977 *Stock size* Large
Stock Antique coins and medals, stamps, ephemera, cigarette cards, medals
Open Mon–Sat 9am–5pm
Fairs Edinburgh, Castle Donnington
Services Valuations, auctions of coins and banknotes

⊞ Donald Ellis Antiques
Contact Donald Ellis
✉ **7 Bruntsfield Place, Edinburgh, EH10 4HN** 🅿
☎ 0131 229 4720
Est. 1969 *Stock size* Medium
Stock General antiques
Open Mon–Fri 10am–5pm closed Wed pm
Fairs Buxton
Services Restorations, clocks

⊞ Georgian Antiques (LAPADA)
Contact P or J Dixon
✉ **10 Pattison Street, Leith, Edinburgh, EH6 7HF** 🅿
☎ 0131 553 7286 Ⓕ 0131 553 6299
Ⓔ georgianantiques@btconnect.com
Ⓦ www.georgianantiques.net
Est. 1979 *Stock size* Large
Stock Very large collection of general antiques
Open Mon–Fri 8.30am–5.30pm Sat 10am–2pm
Services Valuations, shipping

⊞ Gladrags
Contact Kate Cameron
✉ **17 Henderson Row, Edinburgh, EH3 5DH** 🅿
☎ 0131 557 1916
Est. 1974 *Stock size* Large
Stock Unique selection of exquisite vintage clothes, accessories, costume jewellery, linen
Open Tues–Sat 10.30am–6pm

⊞ Goodwin's Antiques Ltd
Contact Mr B Goodwin
✉ **15–16 Queensferry Street, Edinburgh, EH2 4QW**
☎ 0131 225 4717 Ⓕ 0131 220 1412
Ⓔ bengoodwin@compuserve.com
Est. 1959 *Stock size* Large
Stock General antiques
Open Mon–Fri 9am–5.30pm Sat 9am–5pm
Services Valuations, repairs

⊞ Grant & Shaw Ltd (ABA)
Contact Alan Grant
✉ **62 West Port, Edinburgh, EH1 2LD** 🅿
☎ 0131 229 8399 Ⓕ 0131 229 8393
Ⓜ 07967 001776
Ⓔ AGrant4227@aol.com
Est. 1989 *Stock size* Medium
Stock Antiquarian literature and travel
Open By appointment
Fairs Chelsea
Services Valuations

⊞ Harlequin Antiques
Contact Charles Harkness
✉ **30 Bruntsfield Place, Edinburgh, EH10 4HJ** 🅿
☎ 0131 228 9446
Est. 1996 *Stock size* Medium
Stock General antiques
Open Mon–Sat 10am–5pm
Fairs Scone Place, Fife
Services Clock restoration

⊞ Holyrood Architectural Salvage
Contact Mr K Fowler
✉ **Holyrood Business Park, 146 Duddingston Road West, Edinburgh, EH16 4AP** 🅿
☎ 0131 661 9305 Ⓕ 0131 656 9404
Ⓔ Ken@has.abel.co.uk
Est. 1993 *Stock size* Large
Stock Period fireplaces, baths, radiators, panelled doors, brassware, stained glass
Open Mon–Sat 9am–5pm
Services Restoration of baths

⊞ Gordon Inglis Antiques
Contact Gordon Inglis
✉ **8 Barclay Terrace, Edinburgh, EH10 4HP** 🅿
☎ 0131 221 1192 Ⓕ 0131 221 1192
Ⓜ 07966 505219
Ⓔ gordon@inglisantiques.com
Ⓦ www.inglisantiques.com
Est. 1990 *Stock size* Medium
Stock Quality UK art, studio pottery, ceramics c1900, linen, books, ephemera, collectables, Scottish hand-painted pottery, Scottish Art glass

Open Mon Wed Fri Sat 1–5pm or by appointment
Services Free delivery worldwide via DHL

Allan K L Jackson
67 Causewayside, Edinburgh, EH9 1QF P
☎ 0131 668 4532
Ⓜ 07989 236443
Est. 1974 *Stock size* Medium
Stock General antiques
Open Tues–Sat 10am–5pm
Services House clearance

Kaimes Smithy Antiques
Contact Mr J Lynch
79 Howdenhall Road, Edinburgh, EH16 6PW P
☎ 0131 441 2076
Ⓜ 07973 377198
Ⓔ john@jlynch.freeserve.co.uk
Est. 1970 *Stock size* Medium
Stock 18th–19thC furniture, clocks, paintings (oils and watercolours), Chinese ceramics
Open Tues Wed Fri Sat 1.30–5pm

Alan Lawson & Son
Contact Mr A Lawson
181 Causewayside, Edinburgh, EH9 1PH P
☎ 0131 662 1991
Est. 1974 *Stock size* Medium
Stock General antiques and reproduction items
Open Mon–Sat 11.30am–5.30pm
Services Valuations, house clearance

London Road Antiques
Contact Mr R S Forrest
15 Earlston Place, Edinburgh, EH7 5SU P
☎ 0131 652 2790
Ⓔ info@19thC.com
Ⓦ www.19thC.com
Est. 1979 *Stock size* Large
Stock 19thC furniture, Victorian and Georgian wares, stripped pine
Open Mon–Sat 10am–5pm Sun 1–5pm

J D Loue
Contact Mr J D Loue
15–17 Jane Street, Edinburgh, EH6 5HE P
☎ 0131 554 7609 Ⓕ 0131 554 7609
Ⓜ 07774 678423
Est. 1967 *Stock size* Medium
Stock General antiques
Open Mon–Sat 8.30am–4.30pm
Services Valuations, reproduction furniture

J Martinez Antiques
Contact Mr J Martinez
17 Brandon Terrace, Edinburgh, EH3 5DZ P
☎ 0131 558 8720 Ⓕ 0131 558 8720
Ⓜ 07836 608090
Est. 1979 *Stock size* Medium
Stock General antiques, jewellery, clocks
Open Mon–Sat 11am–5pm
Fairs NEC, Ingliston
Services Valuations

McNaughtan's Bookshop (ABA)
Contact Elizabeth Strong
3a & 4a Haddington Place, Edinburgh, EH7 4AE P
☎ 0131 556 5897 Ⓕ 0131 556 8220
Ⓔ mcnbooks@globalnet.co.uk
Est. 1957
Stock General antiquarian and second-hand books including architecture, children's and Scottish topics
Open Tues–Sat 9.30am–5.30pm
Fairs ABA
Services Valuations

Meadow Lamps Gallery
Contact Mr Robertson
48 Warrender Park Road, Edinburgh, EH9 1HH P
☎ 0131 221 1212
Est. 1900 *Stock size* Medium
Stock Antique lighting
Open Tues Thurs Sat 10am–6pm
Fairs NEC Birmingham, Glasgow
Services Restorations

Millers Antiques
Contact Miss S Knott
187–189 Causwayside, Edinburgh, EH9 1PH P
☎ 0131 662 1429 Ⓕ 0131 662 4187
Est. 1995 *Stock size* Medium
Stock General antiques, original pine, handstripped oak, advertising and unusual collectables
Open Mon–Sat 10am–5.30pm
Fairs Newark, Swinderby
Services Pine – stripped, sanded and waxed, oak – handstripped, French polishing

T & J W Neilson Ltd (National Fireplace Association)
Contact Mr A Neilson
76 Coburg Street, Edinburgh, EH6 6HJ P
☎ 0131 554 4704 Ⓕ 0131 555 2071
Ⓔ info@chimneypiece.co.uk
Ⓦ www.chimneypiece.co.uk
Est. 1932 *Stock size* Large
Stock Antique chimney pieces, dog grates, register grates, fenders and fireplace accessories
Open Mon–Fri 9.30am–5pm Sat 9.30am–4pm
Services Shipping

Now & Then
Contact Mr D Gordon
7 & 9 West Cross Causeway, Edinburgh, EH8 9JW P
☎ 0131 668 2927 Ⓕ 0131 668 2926
Ⓜ 07976 360283
Ⓔ nowandthenuk@aol.com
Ⓦ oldtoysandantiques.co.uk
Est. 1976 *Stock size* Medium
Stock Old toys, antiques, telephones, old clocks, cameras, bicycles, automobilia, railwayana, pre-WW1 office and domestic equipment, small items of furniture
Open Tues–Sat 1–5.30pm
Fairs Edinburgh, London
Services Valuations

The Old Children's Bookshelf (PBFA)
Contact Shirley Neilson
175 Canongate Royal Mile, Edinburgh, EH8 8BN P
☎ 0131 558 3411
Est. 1998 *Stock size* Medium
Stock Children's novels, annuals, prints, comics
Open Mon–Fri 10.30am–5pm Sat 10am–5pm
Fairs PBFA

The Old Town Bookshop (PBFA)
Contact Ron Wilson
8 Victoria Street, Edinburgh, EH1 2HG P
☎ 0131 225 9237 Ⓕ 0131 229 1503
Ⓦ www.oldtownbookshop.co.uk
Est. 1978 *Stock size* Medium
Stock Antiquarian and second-hand books, maps, prints, specializing in antiquarian art books
Open Mon–Sat 10.30am–6pm
Fairs Dublin, London, Edinburgh
Services Valuations, catalogues

Past & Present (PBFA)
Contact Gary Watt

✉ **54a Clerk Street, Edinburgh, EH8 9JR**
☎ 0131 667 2004 Ⓕ 0131 667 2004
Est. 1994 *Stock size* Medium
Stock General antiques, antiquarian children's books, Art Deco
Open Mon–Fri 10am–5pm Sat 10am–6pm Sun 2–6pm
Fairs Ingliston
Services Valuations, china repair

Phillips Fine Art Auctioneers (SOFAA)
Contact Joanne Campbell
✉ **65 George Street, Edinburgh, EH2 2JL** Ⓟ
☎ 0131 225 2266 Ⓕ 0131 220 2547
Ⓦ www.phillips-auctions.com
Est. 1796
Open Mon–Fri 8.30am–5.30pm Sat 8.30am–noon
Sales Antiques and collectables
Frequency Weekly
Catalogues Yes

Reid & Reid
Contact Willie Reid
✉ **134 St Stephen Street, Edinburgh, EH3 5AA** Ⓟ
☎ 0131 225 9660
Est. 1981 *Stock size* Small
Stock Antique books and prints
Open Tues–Sat 11am–5.30pm

Royal Mile Curios
Contact Mr Martin
✉ **363 High Street, Edinburgh, EH1 1PW** Ⓟ
☎ 0131 226 4050
Est. 1875 *Stock size* Large
Stock Antique and Scottish jewellery
Open Mon–Sun 10.30am–5.30pm

Royal Mile Gallery
Contact J A Smith
✉ **272 Canongate, Edinburgh, EH8 8AA** Ⓟ
☎ 0131 558 1702
Ⓔ james@royalmilegallery.co.uk
Ⓦ www.royalmilegallery.co.uk
Est. 1994 *Stock size* Large
Stock Antiquarian maps, prints
Open Mon–Sat 11.30am–5pm
Services Valuations, framing service

James Scott
Contact James Scott
✉ **43 Dundas Street, Edinburgh, EH3 6JN**
☎ 0131 556 8260
Est. 1964 *Stock size* Medium
Stock General antiques
Open Mon–Sat 11.30am–5.30pm closed 1–2pm closed Thurs
Services Valuations

Second Edition
Contact W A Smith
✉ **9 Howard Street, Edinburgh, EH3 5JP** Ⓟ
☎ 0131 556 9403
Est. 1979 *Stock size* Large
Stock Quality books, militaria, arts, Scottish books
Open Mon–Fri noon–5.30pm Sat 9.30am–5.30pm
Services Valuations, binding

Still Life
Contact Ewan Lamont
✉ **54 Candlemaker Row, Edinburgh, EH1 2QE**
☎ 0131 225 8524
Ⓔ ewanlamont@mac.com
Ⓦ http://homepage.mac.com/ewanlamont/PhotoAlbum.html
Est. 1984 *Stock size* Large
Stock General antiques, china, glass, pictures
Open Mon–Sat noon–5pm

The Talish Gallery
Contact John Martin
✉ **168 Canongate, Edinburgh, EH8 8DF** Ⓟ
☎ 0131 557 8435
Est. 1969 *Stock size* Large
Stock Small general antiques, Oriental wares, silver
Open Mon–Sat 10am–4pm
Fairs Newark

Thomson, Roddick & Medcalf
Contact Sybelle Medcalf
✉ **The Edinburgh and Lothian Sale Room, 44/3 Harden Green Business Park, Eskbank, Edinburgh, EH22 3NX** Ⓟ
☎ 0131 454 9090 Ⓕ 0131 454 9191
Est. 1999
Open Mon–Fri 9am–5pm
Sales Antiques, fine art, general furnishings
Frequency Weekly
Catalogues Yes

Till's Bookshop
Contact Mr R Till
✉ **1 Hope Park Crescent, Edinburgh, EH8 9NA** Ⓟ
☎ 0131 667 0895
Ⓔ tillsbookshop@hotmail.com
Est. 1985 *Stock size* Medium
Stock Literature, fantasy, mystery, humanities, poetry, drama, cinema, general, first editions
Open Mon–Fri noon–7.30pm Sat 11am–6pm Sun noon–5.30pm
Services Valuations

Trinity Curios
Contact Alan Ferguson
✉ **4–6 Stanley Road, Edinburgh, EH6 4SG** Ⓟ
☎ 0131 552 8481
Ⓜ 07715 500719
Ⓔ adfer@btinternet.com
Est. 1987 *Stock size* Large
Stock Quality furniture, porcelain, silver, linen, collectables
Open Tues–Fri 10am–5pm Wed Sat noon–6pm Sun 2–5pm

Unicorn Antiques
Contact N Duncan
✉ **65 Dundas Street, Edinburgh, EH3 6RS**
☎ 0131 556 7176
Ⓔ stockbridge@ecosse.net
Ⓦ www.transcotland.com/unicorn
Est. 1969 *Stock size* Small
Stock General antiques, bric-a-brac
Open Mon–Sat 10.30am–6.30pm

West Port Books
Contact Mr H N Barrott
✉ **147 West Port, Edinburgh, EH3 9DD** Ⓟ
☎ 0131 229 4431
Ⓔ west@portbooks.freeserve.co.uk
Ⓦ www.westport.freeserve.co.uk
Est. 1979 *Stock size* Large
Stock Second-hand and antiquarian books, especially fine art books and Indian imports
Open Mon–Sat 10.30am–5.30pm

Wild Rose Antiques
Contact E or Kate Cameron
✉ **15 Henderson Row, Edinburgh, EH3 5DH** Ⓟ
☎ 0131 557 1916
Est. 1974 *Stock size* Large
Stock Select decorative table silver, ladies' and gentlemen's jewellery, porcelain, pottery, glass, metalware
Open Tues–Sat 10.30am–6pm

Richard Wood Antiques
Contact Richard Wood
✉ **66 West Port, Edinburgh, EH1 2LD** Ⓟ

☎ 0131 229 6344
Est. 1971 *Stock size* Large
Stock Small silver and Oriental items, collectables
Open Mon–Sat 10am–5pm
Fairs Ingliston Mammoth Fair

GLASGOW

GLASGOW

All Our Yesterdays
Contact Susie Robinson
✉ **6 Park Road, Kelvin Bridge, Glasgow, G4 9JG** P
☎ 0141 334 7788 ℻ 0141 339 8994
✉ antiques@allouryesterdays.fsnet.co.uk
Est. 1989 *Stock size* Large
Stock General antiques
Open Flexible Mon–Fri 11am–6pm Sat noon–5.30pm or by appointment
Services Valuations

E A Alvarino
Contact E A Alvarino
✉ **13 Radnor Street, Kelvingrove, Glasgow, G3 7UA** P
☎ 0141 334 1213
✉ EAAlvarino@aol.com
Est. 1976 *Stock size* Large
Stock General antiques
Open Mon–Fri 1–5pm
Services Valuations

Antichita
Contact Catherine Luporini
✉ **5 Abbot Street, Glasgow, G41 3XE** P
☎ 0141 632 5665
✉ antichitauk@aol.co.uk
Est. 1989 *Stock size* Large
Stock General antiques
Open Mon–Sat 10am–5pm Sun noon–4pm
Services Valuations, restorations

The Antiques Warehouse
Contact Philip Mangan
✉ **Unit 3b, Yorkhill Quay Estate, Glasgow, G3 8QE** P
☎ 0141 334 4924 ℻ 0141 400 4925
Est. 1979 *Stock size* Large
Stock General antiques
Open Mon–Fri 9am–5pm Sat 10am–5pm Sun noon–5pm
Services Valuations, restorations and repairs

Browns Clocks
Contact Jim Cairns
✉ **13 Radnor Street, Glasgow, G3 7UA** P
☎ 0141 334 6308 ℻ 0141 334 6308
✉ james@jcairns.greatxscape.net
Est. 1933 *Stock size* Medium
Stock Longcase clocks
Open Mon–Fri 10am–5pm Sat 10am–1pm
Services Restorations of all antique clocks

Butler's Furniture Galleries
Contact Laurence Butler
✉ **39 Camelon Street, Carntyne Industrial Estate, Glasgow, G32 6JS** P
☎ 0141 7785720
Ⓜ 07950 312355
✉ butlersantiques@lineone.net
Ⓦ www.butlersfurnituregalleries.co.uk
Est. 1981 *Stock size* Large
Stock Georgian–Edwardian furniture
Open Mon–Fri 10am–5pm Sun by appointment
Services Valuations, restorations

Canning Antiques
Contact Kate
✉ **24–26 Millbrae Road, Langside, Glasgow, G42 9UT**
☎ 0141 632 9853 ℻ 0141 632 9853
Est. 1997
Stock Georgian–Edwardian furniture, small mirrors
Open Mon–Fri 9am–5pm Sat 10am–5pm Sun noon–5pm
Fairs Antiques for Everyone
Services Restorations

Carpet Auctioneers Ltd (SAA)
Contact Mr T Severn
✉ **32 Washington Street, Glasgow, G3 8ZA** P
☎ 0141 2219329
Est. 1959
Open Mon–Fri 10am–4.30pm Sat 9.30am–1.30pm
Sales Phone for details

Circa
Contact Sheila Murdoch
✉ **37 Ruthven Lane, Glasgow, G12 9BG**
☎ 0141 581 3307
Est. 2000 *Stock size* Large
Stock Vintage clothing, handbags, accessories, jewellery
Open Mon–Sat 11.30am–5.30pm Sun 1–5.30pm

Arthur E Collins & Son (SAA)
Contact Leonard Kerr
✉ **141 West Regent Street, Glasgow, G2 2ST**
☎ 0141 229 1326 ℻ 0141 248 1591
Est. 1899
Open Mon–Fri 9am–5pm
Sales Pawnbroker sales
Frequency 2 per week
Catalogues Yes

Cooper Hay Rare Books (ABA)
Contact Mr C Hay
✉ **182 Bath Street, Glasgow, G2 4HG** P
☎ 0141 333 1992 ℻ 0141 333 1992
✉ chayrbooks@aol.com
Ⓦ www.abebooks.com/home/haybooks
Est. 1984 *Stock size* Medium
Stock Books, prints, specializing in Scottish art and juvenile books
Open Mon–Fri 10am–5.30pm Sat 10am–1pm
Fairs Chelsea, Bath, Edinburgh
Services Valuations, book search

Den of Antiquity
Contact Mr E Sherman
✉ **Langside Lane, 539 Victoria Road, Queens Park, Glasgow, G42 8BH** P
☎ 0141 423 7122 ℻ 0141 423 7122
✉ AntiquityGlasgow@aol.com
Ⓦ www.denofantiquity.co.uk
Est. 1969 *Stock size* Medium
Stock Antique and shipping furniture
Open Mon–Sat 9.30am–5.30pm Sun noon–5pm
Services Shipping

Finnie Antiques
Contact Bruce Finnie
✉ **103 Niddrie Road, Glasgow, G42 8PR** P
☎ 0141 423 8515 ℻ 0141 423 8515
Ⓜ 07973 315460
✉ finnie.antiques@net.ntl.com
Ⓦ www.finnieantiques.com
Est. 1971 *Stock size* Large
Stock General antiques, furniture, Arts and Crafts, lighting
Open Mon–Fri 10.30am–4.30pm Sat Sun noon–4.30pm
Fairs Antiques for Everyone, Glasgow

Flying Dutchman Antiques
Contact Hannie Van Riel

✉ Unit 3b, The Centre, Yorkhill Quay, Glasgow, G3 8QE P
☎ 0141 338 6834 F 0141 338 6834
E sales@flyingdutchman.freeserve.co.uk
Est. 1994 *Stock size* Large
Stock General antiques including European furniture
Open Mon–Fri 9am–5pm Sat 10am–5pm Sun noon–5pm

Gillmorehill Books
Contact Gerard McGonigle
✉ **43 Bank Street, Glasgow, G12 8NE**
☎ 0141 339 7504
Stock Rare and second-hand books
Open Mon–Sat 10am–6pm

Great Western Auctions
Contact Mr J H Duncan
✉ **29–37 Otago Street, Glasgow, G12 8JJ** P
☎ 0141 339 3290
E info@greatwesternauctions.com
W www.greatwesternauctions.com
Est. 1988
Open Mon–Fri 9am–5pm
Sales General antiques
Frequency fortnightly
Catalogues Yes

Kerr & McAllister (SAA)
Contact Mr Thomas McAllister
✉ **140 Niddrie Road, Glasgow, G20 7XL** P
☎ 0141 423 4271 F 0141 423 7265
Est. 1969
Open Mon–Fri 9am–5pm
Sales Household goods
Frequency Every Thurs evening
Catalogues Yes

Kittoch Antiques
Contact Una Lambie or Laura McAlonan
✉ **336 Crow Road, Broomhill, Glasgow, GL11 7HT** P
☎ 0141 339 7318
Est. 1995 *Stock size* Medium
Stock Small furniture, collectables, textiles, silver plate
Open Tues–Sat noon–5pm
Fairs Antiques for Everyone, Glasgow

Lovejoy Antiques
Contact Julie Gallagher
✉ **Unit 3b, Yorkhill Quay, Glasgow, G3 8QE** P
☎ 0141 400 2991 F 0141 400 2990
M 07710 461484
Est. 1995 *Stock size* Medium
Stock General antiques
Open Mon–Fri 9am–5pm Sat 10am–5pm Sun noon–5pm
Services Polishing

Robert McTear & Co (IAA)
Contact Miss Janet Stewart
✉ **Sky Park, 8 Elliot Place, Glasgow, G3 8EP** P
☎ 0141 221 4456 F 0141 204 5035
E enquiries@mctears.co.uk
W www.mctears.co.uk
Est. 1842
Open Mon–Fri 9am–5pm
Sales General antiques
Frequency Weekly
Catalogues Yes

Stuart Mylers
Contact Stuart Myler
✉ **93 West Regent Street, Glasgow, G2 2BA** P
☎ 01236 843736
E stuart@mylerantiques.demon.co.uk
Est. 1987 *Stock size* Medium
Stock General antiques
Open Mon–Sat 10am–5pm

Patersons Auctioneers & Valuers
Contact Robert Paterson
✉ **8 Orchard Street, Paisley, Glasgow, PA1 1UZ** P
☎ 0141 889 2435 F 0141 887 5535
Est. 1848
Open Mon–Fri 9am–5pm
Sales General antiques
Frequency Fortnightly
Catalogues Yes

Phillips Fine Art Auctioneers
Contact Judith Walters
✉ **The Beacon, 176 St Vincent Street, Glasgow, G2 5SG** P
☎ 0141 223886 F 0141 2238868
W www.phillips-auction.com
Est. 1796
Open Mon–Fri 8.30am–5.30pm
Sales General antiques
Frequency Weekly at Edinburgh
Catalogues Yes

Relics
Contact Steven Currie
✉ **Dowanside Lane, Glasgow, G12 9BZ** P
☎ 0141 341 0007
Est. 1989 *Stock size* Medium
Stock General antiques, collectables including 1960s wares
Open Mon–Sat 10.30am–6pm Sun 12.30–6pm
Services Valuations

The Renaissance Furniture Store
Contact Bruce Finnie
✉ **103 Niddrie Road, Glasgow, G42 8PR** P
☎ 0141 423 0022 F 0141 423 8515
M 07973 315460
E finnie.antiques@net.nh.com
Est. 1992 *Stock size* Medium
Stock Furniture, silver, Arts and Crafts, fireplaces
Open Mon–Fri 10.30am–5pm Sat Sun noon–5pm
Services Valuations

Restore-It
Contact Jean Eddy Devion
✉ **22 Otago Lane, Glasgow, G12 8PB** P
☎ 0141 339 7776 F 0141 647 3182
M 07770 825555
W www.restore-it.co.uk or www.maisonrouge.co.uk
Est. 1992 *Stock size* Medium
Stock General antiques and architectural salvage
Open Every day 10am–5pm
Services Restoration

Rusty Grates
Contact Tom Pearson
✉ **103 Niddrie Road, Queens Park, Glasgow, G42 8PR** P
☎ 0141 423 0022
Est. 1994 *Stock size* Medium
Stock Georgian, Victorian and Art Nouveau fireplaces
Open Mon–Fri 10am–5pm Sat Sun noon–5pm

R Rutherford
Contact Mrs R Rutherford
✉ **The Victorian Village, 93 West Regent Street, Glasgow, G2 2BA** P
☎ 0141 332 9808 F 0141 332 9808
Est. 1979 *Stock size* Medium
Stock General antiques, Scottish agates
Open Mon–Sat 10am–5pm
Services Valuations

Saratoga Trunk Yesteryear Costume & Textiles
✉ **Third Floor, 61 Hyde Park Street, Glasgow, G3 8BW** P

☎ 0141 221 4433 Ⓕ 0141 221 4433
Est. 1976 ***Stock size*** Large
Stock Vintage clothing, Victorian–1990s, linens, lace etc
Open Mon–Fri 10.30am–5pm
Services Valuations

⊞ Jeremy Sniders Antiques
Contact Jeremy Sniders
✉ **158 Bath Street, Glasgow, G2 4TB** Ⓟ
☎ 0141 332 0043 Ⓕ 0141 332 5505
Est. 1981 ***Stock size*** Medium
Stock General antiques, Scandinavian antiques, silverware, jewellery, Georg Jensen specialist
Open Mon–Sat 9am–5pm
Services Valuations

⊞ Strachan Antiques
Contact Alex Strachan
✉ **40 Darnley Street, Pollokshields, Glasgow, G41 2SE** Ⓟ
☎ 0141 429 4411
Ⓜ 07950 262346
Est. 1999 ***Stock size*** Large
Stock Arts and Crafts, Art Nouveau furniture, small collectable items
Open 10am–5pm Sun noon–5pm

⊞ The Studio
Contact Liz McKelvie
✉ **DeCourcy's Arcade, 5–21 Cresswell Lane, Glasgow, G12 8AA** Ⓟ
☎ 0141 334 8211
Ⓜ 07909 742862
Ⓦ www.decourcys.co.uk
Est. 1998 ***Stock size*** Small
Stock Books, small furniture, ceramics, pictures, glass, textiles, Glasgow-style Arts and Crafts and Art Nouveau, Talwin Morris book bindings
Open Tues–Sat 10am–5.30pm Sun noon–5pm
Services Shipping, booksearch

⊞ The Treasure Bunker Militaria Shop
Contact Mr K J Andrew
✉ **21 King Street, Glasgow, G1 5Q2**
☎ 0141 552 8164 Ⓕ 0141 552 4651
Ⓔ info@treasurebunker.com
Ⓦ www.treasurebunker.com
Est. 1985 ***Stock size*** Large
Stock Military antiques, Battle of Waterloo–WWII
Open Tues–Sat 11am–5pm
Services Worldwide mail order catalogue

⊞ Victoria Antiques Ltd
Contact Geoff Lovatt
✉ **338–350 Pollockshaws Road, Glasgow, G41 1QS** Ⓟ
☎ 0141 423 7216 Ⓕ 0141 423 6497
Ⓔ geoff6567@aol.com
Est. 1964 ***Stock size*** Large
Stock General antiques
Open Mon–Fri 9.30am–5pm Sat 10.30am–5pm
Services Valuations

⊞ Voltaire & Rousseau
Contact Mr J McGonagle
✉ **18 Otago Lane, Glasgow, G12 8PD** Ⓟ
☎ 0141 339 1811
Est. 1972 ***Stock size*** Large
Stock Rare and second-hand books, specializing in Scotland and foreign languages
Open Mon–Sat 10am–6pm
Services Valuations

⊞ Tim Wright Antiques (LAPADA)
Contact Judy or Tim Wright
✉ **147 Bath Street, Glasgow, G2 4SQ** Ⓟ
☎ 0141 221 0364 Ⓕ 0141 221 0364
Ⓦ www.timwright-antiques.com
Est. 1972 ***Stock size*** Large
Stock General antiques
Open Mon–Fri 10am–5pm Sat 10.30am–2.30pm
Services Valuations

⊞ Yesteryear
Contact Ian Taylor
✉ **14 Kildrostan Street, Glasgow, G41 4LU** Ⓟ
☎ 0141 423 0099
Est. 1973 ***Stock size*** Medium
Stock General antiques
Open Mon–Fri 9am–5pm Sat 9am–1pm
Services Valuations

ABERDEENSHIRE

ABERDEEN

⊞ The Antiquary
Contact Mr Andy Murphy
✉ **13 Marischal Street, Aberdeen, Aberdeenshire, AB11 5AD** Ⓟ
☎ 01224 464959
Ⓜ 07759 617530
Est. 2000 ***Stock size*** Large
Stock General antiques 1795–1975
Open Mon–Sat 10am–4pm closed Wed
Services Valuations

⊞ Bon-Accord Books
Contact Andrew Milne
✉ **69–75 Spital, Aberdeen, Aberdeenshire, AB24 3HX** Ⓟ
☎ 01224 643209
Ⓦ www.bon-accordbooks.co.uk
Est. 1998 ***Stock size*** Medium
Stock General and antiquarian books, Scottish, children's and modern topics, first editions
Open Mon–Fri 10.30am–5.30pm Sat 11am–4.30pm closed Wed
Fairs Aberdeen
Services Postcards, prints, pictures

⊞ Candle Close Gallery
Contact Mrs B Brown
✉ **123 Gallowgate, Aberdeen, Aberdeenshire, AB25 1BU** Ⓟ
☎ 01224 624940 Ⓕ 01224 620548
Est. 1994 ***Stock size*** Medium
Stock Collectors' items, curios, antique pine
Open Mon–Fri 10am–5.30pm Thurs 10am–7pm Sat 9am–5pm Sun noon–4pm
Fairs Newark

⊞ Grandad's Attic
Contact Carol Smith
✉ **20 Marischal Street, Aberdeen, Aberdeenshire, AB11 5AJ** Ⓟ
☎ 01224 213699
Ⓜ 07715 081751
Ⓔ decogattic@hotmail.com
Est. 1996 ***Stock size*** Medium
Stock Art Deco, ceramics, furniture
Open Tues–Fri 11am–5pm Sat 10am–5pm
Fairs Treetops – Aberdeen, Ingliston, Leeds
Services Valuations, search service

⊞ Kings Quair
Contact M or R Murdoch
✉ **197 King Street, Aberdeen, Aberdeenshire, AB24 5AH**
☎ 01224 637495
Est. 1994 ***Stock size*** Medium
Stock Rare and second-hand books
Open Mon–Sat 10am–5pm
Fairs Treetops – Aberdeen

John Milne Auctioneers (SAA)
Contact Robert Milne
9 North Silver Street, Aberdeen, Aberdeenshire, AB10 1RJ P
☎ 01224 639336 F 01224 645857
E info@john-milne.demon.co.uk
Est. 1867
Open Mon–Thur 8.30am–5pm Fri 8.30am–4pm
Sales Weekly general sales
Frequency Weekly
Catalogues Yes

The Odd Lot
Contact Mr G Mudie
24 Adelphi, Union Street, Aberdeen, Aberdeenshire, AB11 5BL P
☎ 01224 592551 F 01224 574404
M 07771 926736
E George@theoddlot.com
W www.theoddlot.com
Est. 1997 *Stock size* Medium
Stock General antiques, furniture, jewellery, Scottish antiques, books
Open Tues–Sat 11am–5pm
Fairs The Academy – Aberdeen
Services House clearance

The Old Aberdeen Bookshop
Contact Mr C Scott-Paul
140 Spital, Aberdeen, Aberdeenshire, AB24 3JU
☎ 01224 658355
Est. 1998 *Stock size* Small
Stock Rare and second-hand books
Open Mon–Sat 11am–5.30pm
Services Valuations

Rendezvous Gallery Ltd
Contact Mr C D Mead or Mr Andrew Allan
100 Forest Avenue, Aberdeen, Aberdeenshire, AB15 4TL P
☎ 01224 323247 F 01224 323247
E info@rendezvousgallery.freeserve.uk
W www.rendezvouz-gallery.co.uk
Est. 1975 *Stock size* Medium
Stock Art Nouveau, Art Deco, Scottish paintings
Open Mon–Sat 10am–6pm

Thistle Antiques (LAPADA)
Contact Mr P Bursill
28 Esslemont Avenue, Aberdeen, Aberdeenshire, AB25 1SN P
☎ 01224 634692
M 07759 429685
Est. 1969 *Stock size* Medium
Stock General antiques, Georgian–Victorian furniture, lighting
Open Mon–Fri 10am–5pm Sat 10am–1pm closed Wed

J R Webb Antiques
Contact J R Webb
23 Bon-Accord Terrace, Aberdeen, Aberdeenshire, AB11 6DP P
☎ 01224 586709 F 01224 586709
M 07801 192119
Est. 1908 *Stock size* Large
Stock General antiques, jewellery, arms and armour, especially Scottish artefacts and art
Open Mon–Fri 10am–6pm Sat 10am–1pm closed Wed
Services Valuations and probate service, restorations

Winram's Bookshop
Contact Mrs Margaret Davidson
32–36 Rosemount Place, Aberdeen, Aberdeenshire, AB25 2XB P
☎ 01224 630673 F 01224 631532
Est. 1975 *Stock size* Medium
Stock Rare and second-hand books, especially Scottish topics
Open Mon–Sat 10am–5.30pm Wed 10am–1pm
Fairs Aberdeen
Services Valuations

Colin Wood Antiques Ltd
Contact Mr C Wood
25 Rose Street, Aberdeen, Aberdeenshire, AB10 1TX P
☎ 01224 643019/644786
F 01224 644786
Est. 1969 *Stock size* Medium
Stock General and antique Scottish maps, prints
Open Mon–Sat 10am–5pm

ALFORD

David C Rogers Antiques & Interiors
Contact David Rogers
29 Main Street, Alford, Aberdeenshire, AB33 8PX P
☎ 01975 562799 F 01464 831500
M 07836 558797
Est. 1987 *Stock size* Medium
Stock General antiques, specializing in fishing items
Open Fri Sat 10am–4pm or by appointment
Fairs Newark
Services Valuations, restorations, repairs

BALLATER

Deeside Books
Contact Mr B Wayte
10 Braemar Road, Ballater, Aberdeenshire, AB35 5RL P
☎ 013397 54080 F 013397 54080
E deebook@btclick.com
Est. 1998 *Stock size* Medium
Stock Out-of-print and antiquarian books, specializing in Scottish, military, topography and fishing topics
Open Tues–Sat 10am–5pm Sun noon–5pm
Services Valuations, book search

Rowan Antiques
Contact Nikki Henderson
Tulchan House, 5–7 Victoria Road, Ballater, Aberdeenshire, AB35 5QQ P
☎ 013397 56035
Est. 1986 *Stock size* Large
Stock Georgian–Edwardian furniture, jewellery,
Open Mon–Sat 10am–5.30pm

CLOLA

Clola Antiques Centre
Contact David Blackburn
Shannas School, Clola, Aberdeenshire, Peterhead, AB42 5AB P
☎ 01771 624584
M 07836 537188
Est. 1989 *Stock size* Large
No. of dealers 6
Stock Furniture, jewellery, china, glass
Open Mon–Sat 10am–5pm Sun 11am–5pm
Services Restorations, upholstery

DUNECHT

Magic Lantern
Contact Mrs J White
Nether Corskie, Dunecht, Aberdeenshire, AB32 7EL P
☎ 01330 860678
Est. 1978 *Stock size* Medium
Stock General antiques
Services Restorations to china

FYVIE

Grampian Books (PBFA)
South Monkshill, Fyvie, Turriff, Aberdeenshire, AB53 8RQ
01651 891524 F 01651 891124
Est. 1990 *Stock size* Large
Stock Out-of-print, antiquarian and second-hand books, specializing in Scottish topics
Open By appointment
Fairs London, York, Glasgow, Edinburgh, Aberdeen
Services Valuations, purchasing library and book collections

HUNTLY

Huntly Antiques
Contact Jean Barker
43 Duke Street, Huntly, Aberdeenshire, AB54 8DT
01466 793307
Est. 1984 *Stock size* Medium
Stock General antiques
Open Mon–Sat 10am–4pm or by appointment

G G & H R Lumsden
Contact G G Lumsden
Affleck, Huntly, Aberdeenshire, AB54 6XW
01466 792686
Est. 1948
Open By appointment
Sales General antiques
Frequency Monthly
Catalogues No

INVERURIE

Thainstone Specialist Auctions
Contact Mark Barrack or L Howie
Thainstone Centre, Inverurie, Aberdeen, Aberdeenshire, AB51 5XZ
01467 623770 F 01467 623771
E tsa@goanm.co.uk
W www.tgoanm.co.uk
Est. 1942
Open Mon–Fri 9am–5pm
Sales General antiques Tues 6pm
Frequency Weekly
Catalogues Yes

KINCARDINE O'NEIL

Dunmore Antiques
Contact Pauline Baird
27 North Deeside Road, Kincardine O'Neil, Aboyne, Aberdeenshire, AB34 5AA
013398 84449 F 013398 82640
M 07711 886945
Est. 1988 *Stock size* Large
Stock General antiques, china, glass, amber jewellery
Open Thurs–Sat 10am–5pm
Fairs Newark, Treetops
Services Valuations

LAURENCEKIRK

James S T Liddle
Contact Mr B Liddle
Malvern, 65 Johnstone Street, Laurencekirk, Aberdeenshire, AB30 1AN
01561 377420 F 01561 377420
Est. 1989
Open Mon–Sat 8am–5pm
Sales General furniture
Frequency Monthly
Catalogues No

LONGHAVEN

Grannie Used To Have One
Contact Jacqui Harvey
Sanderling, Longhaven, Nr Peterhead, Aberdeenshire, AB42 0NX
01779 813223 F 01779 813223
M 07850 912364
E jacqui@grannieusedto.co.uk
W www.grannieusedto.co.uk
Est. 1991 *Stock size* Large
Stock Pottery, porcelain, furniture, glass, metalware
Open Thurs Fri 1–5pm Sat Sun 11am–5pm or by appointment
Fairs Treetops – Aberdeen, Waterside Inn – Peterhead

PORTSOY

The Curiosity Shoppe
Contact Mr A S Reynolds or Mrs P E Smith
17 Seafield Street, Portsoy, Banff, Aberdeenshire, AB45 2QT
01261 843806
M 07720 532677
E curiosityportsoy@yahoo.co.uk
Est. 1994 *Stock size* Medium
Stock General curios, clocks, musical instruments, light fittings
Open Mon–Sat 10am–5pm Sun noon–6pm
Services Instrument repair, French polishing

TARLAND

The Tower Workshops
Contact George Pirie
Aberdeen Road, Tarland, Aboyne, Aberdeenshire, AB34 4TB
013398 811544
Est. 1989 *Stock size* Large
Stock Edwardian mahogany and Georgian furniture, soft furnishings, small items, decorative objects
Open Mon–Fri 9am–5pm Sat 11am–5pm
Services Valuations, restorations, complete house commissions

ANGUS

DUNDEE

Angus Antiques
Contact John Czerek or Stanley Paget
4 St Andrew Street, Dundee, Angus, DD1 2EX
01382 322128
Est. 1972 *Stock size* Medium
Stock General antiques, militaria, jewellery
Open Mon–Fri 10am–4pm
Services Valuations

The Dundee Auction Rooms (Robert Curr & Dewar)
Contact D Dewar
Ward Road, Dundee, Angus, DD1 1LX
01382 224185 F 01382 533350
M 07889 734245
E derek@curranddewar-auction.totalserve.co.uk
Est. 1862
Open Mon–Fri 8.30am–5pm Sat 8.30am–noon
Sales General furniture, antiques, jewellery, police lost property
Frequency Weekly
Catalogues No

Dundee Philatelic Auctions (SPTA, PTS, PTA)
Contact Frank Tonelli
15 King Street, Dundee, Angus, DD1 2JD
01382 224946 F 01382 224946
Est. 1975
Open Mon–Fri 10am–1pm and 2–5pm Sat by appointment closed Wed

Sales Stamps, cigarette cards, postcards, banknotes. Public auctions held at Renfield Centre, 260 Bath St, Glasgow
Frequency 4 per annum
Catalogues Yes

B L Fenton & Son (SAA)
Contact Ben Fenton
84 Victoria Road, Dundee, Angus, DD1 2NY
01382 226227
Est. 1919
Open Mon–Fri 9am–4.45pm
Sales Antique furniture, shop stock
Frequency Every Thurs
Catalogues No

Alastair Jamieson Antiques
Contact Alastair Jamieson
212 Perth Road, Dundee, Angus, DD1 4JY
01382 322017
Est. 1997 *Stock size* Medium
Stock Wide range of antiques late Victorian–1970s
Open Mon–Sat 10am–5.30pm

Neil Livingstone (LAPADA)
Contact Neil Livingstone
3 Old Hawkhill, Dundee, Angus, DD1 5EU
01382 907788 01382 566332
07775 877715
npl@hemscott.net
Est. 1971 *Stock size* Small
Stock Continental works of art and antiques
Open By appointment only

Taymouth Architectural Antiques
Contact Graham Ellis
49–51 Magdalen Yard Road, Dundee, Angus, DD1 4NF
01382 666833 01382 666833
Est. 1991 *Stock size* Medium
Stock Antique fireplaces, Victorian fixtures and fittings, garden ornaments, antique bathrooms, doors, leaded glass
Open Tues–Sat 9.30am–5.30pm
Fairs Newark, Ardingly
Services Restorations of pine furniture, fireplaces etc

FORFAR

Forfar Auction Co Ltd
Contact Mr Rizza
Carseview Road, Forfar, Angus, DD8 3BT
01307 462197 01307 464960
Est. 1990
Open Mon–Thurs 9.30am–5pm Fri 9.30am to end of sale
Sales All household effects
Frequency Weekly
Catalogues Yes

Gow Antiques and Restoration (BAFRA)
Contact Jeremy Gow
Pitscandly Farm, Forfar, Angus, DD8 3NZ
01307 465347
07711 416786
jeremy@gowantiques.co.uk
www.gowantiques.co.uk
Est. 1991 *Stock size* Medium
Stock Furniture
Open Mon–Fri 9am–5pm or by appointment
Services Restorations

FRIOCKHEIM BY ARBROATH

M J & D Barclay
Contact M J & D Barclay
29 Gardyne Street, Friockheim by Arbroath, Angus, DD11 4SQ
01241 828265
Est. 1968 *Stock size* Medium
Stock General antiques, clocks, jewellery, porcelain
Open Mon–Sat 2pm–5pm closed Thurs
Fairs Treetops – Aberdeen

LETHAM

Idvies Antiques
Contact Mr T Slingsby
Idvies House, Letham, Forfar, Angus, DD8 2QJ
01307 818402 01307 818933
07831 709164
slingsby@compuserve.com
www.scotlandstreasures.co.uk
Est. 1989 *Stock size* Medium
Stock Furniture
Open By appointment
Services Valuations, restorations, cabinet-making

MONTROSE

Angus Architectural Antiques
Contact Les Morden
Balmain House, Lower Balmain Street, Montrose, Angus, DD10 8BQ
01674 674291 01241 830271
07831 386998
courthill@lunan46.freeserve'
Est. 1974 *Stock size* Medium
Stock Pine furniture, architectural and sanitary antiques, fireplaces
Open Mon–Sat 9am–5pm
Services Pine stripping

Harper-James (LAPADA)
Contact D James
25–27 Baltic Street, Montrose, Angus, DD10 8EX
01674 671307 01674 671307
07970 173051
harperjamesantiques@compuserve.com
www.antiquesltd.ltd.uk
Est. 1989 *Stock size* Large
Stock 18th–19thC quality furniture, porcelain, silver
Open Mon–Fri 10am–5pm Sat 10am–4pm
Fairs NEC, Aberdeen
Services Restorations, French polishing, modern polishing, upholstery

Pretty Olde Things
Contact Alison James
At James Bros Antiques, 1 Museum Street, Montrose, Angus, DD10 8HE
01674 672996 01241 830466
07778 4629303
Est. 1992 *Stock size* Medium
Stock General antiques, collectables
Open Mon–Sat 10am–5pm closed Wed
Fairs Treetops – Aberdeen

Sticks & Stones
Contact Mrs H Robertson
36–40 Baltic Street, Montrose, Angus, DD10 8EX
01674 676764
07714 601740
Est. 1995 *Stock size* Medium
Stock Victorian–Edwardian oak country furniture, Art Deco, Art Nouveau
Open Mon–Sat 10am–5pm
Fairs Treetops

ARGYLL & BUTE

COVE

Cove Curios
Contact Mrs Katherine Young

✉ **Shore Road, Clifton Place, Cove, Argyll & Bute, G84 8LR** P
☎ 01436 842222 F 01436 850261
Est. 1971 *Stock size* Medium
Stock General antiques including second-hand jewellery
Open Seasonal
Services Valuations, repairs

HELENSBURGH

Helensburgh Antique Centre
Contact Mrs P Robertson
✉ **83–85 East Clyde Street, Helensburgh, Argyll & Bute**
☎ 01436 676351 F 01436 679474
M 07712 866828
E trishrobertson@btinternet.com
W www.antiquecentre.com
Est. 1998 *Stock size* Medium
Stock General antiques
Open Tues–Sat 10am–5pm Sun 1–5pm
Services Valuations, transport

McLaren Books (ABA, PBFA)
Contact George Newlands
✉ **91 West Clyde Street, Helensburgh, Argyll & Bute, G84 8BB** P
☎ 01436 676453 F 01436 673747
E mclarenbooks@breathe.co.uk
W www.mclarenbooks.co.uk
Est. 1976 *Stock size* Medium
Stock Rare and second-hand books, especially maritime topics
Open Mon–Sat 9.30am–5pm closed 1–2pm closed Wed
Services Valuations, books purchased, book search for maritime titles

Willow Antiques
Contact D J or Mrs C Weatherstone
✉ **93 West Clyde Street, Helensburgh, Argyll & Bute, G84 8BB** P
☎ 01436 671174
Est. 1974 *Stock size* Medium
Stock General antiques
Open Tues Thurs Fri Sat 10.30am–5.30pm

OBAN

Oban Antiques
Contact Mr P R Baker
✉ **35 Stevenson Street, Oban, Argyll & Bute, PA34 5NA** P
☎ 01631 566203
E oban.antiques@lonan.screaming.net
W www.obantiques.rubylane.com
Est. 1969 *Stock size* Medium
Stock General antiques, second-hand books, prints
Open Mon–Sat 10am–5pm some seasonal variation

DUMFRIES & GALLOWAY

BEATTOCK

T W Beaty Antiques
Contact Mr T W Beaty
✉ **Lochhouse Farm, Beattock, Moffat, Dumfries & Galloway, DG10 9SG** P
☎ 01683 300451
M 07803 242408
Est. 1969 *Stock size* Medium
Stock General antiques
Open By appointment
Fairs Newark

BURNHEAD BY THORNHILL

Addendum Books (PBFA)
Contact Dr Frankie Ashton
✉ **The Lamp, Burnhead by Thornhill, Dumfries & Galloway, DG3 4AD** P
☎ 01848 331523
M 07808 050456
E addendum.books@btinternet.com
W www.addendum.books.uk
Est. 1996 *Stock size* Medium
Stock Antiquarian, rare and unusual books, specializing in Scottish literature, history and children's books
Open Tues–Sat 10am–5pm closed Thurs telephone first
Fairs Glasgow, Hexham

CASTLE DOUGLAS

Hazel's
Contact Mrs H Hall
✉ **St Andrew Street, Castle Douglas, Dumfries & Galloway, DG7 1EN** P
☎ 01556 504573 F 01556 504573
W www.castledouglas.net
Est. 1989 *Stock size* Large
Stock General antiques
Open Mon–Sat 10am–5pm
Services Valuations

DUMFRIES

Cargenbank Antiques & Tearooms
Contact Laurence Hird
✉ **Cargen Bank, Dumfries, Dumfries & Galloway, DG2 8PZ** P
☎ 01387 730303
Est. 1999 *Stock size* Medium
Stock 19thC furniture
Open Mon–Sun 11am–5pm closed Wed winter Thurs–Sun

Quarrelwood Art & Antiques
Contact Miranda van Nieuwenhuizen (Fellow of Gemmological Association)
✉ **Quarrelwood, Kirkmahoe, (Kirton), Dumfries, Dumfries & Galloway, DG1 1TE** P
☎ 01387 740654 F 01387 740000
M 07713 643434
E miranda@quarrelwoodantiques.com
W www.quarrelwoodantiques.com
Est. 1999 *Stock size* Medium
Stock Georgian–Victorian furniture, period jewellery, ceramics, glass, objets d'art
Open Wed–Sat 10am–5pm Sun 1–5pm
Services Valuations, restorations, shipping, advisory service, wedding lists

Thomson, Roddick & Medcalf
Contact Sybelle Medcalf
✉ **60 White Sands, Dumfries, Dumfries & Galloway, DG1 2RS** P
☎ 01387 255366 F 01387 266236
E office.trm@virgin.net
Est. 1899
Open Mon–Fri 9am–5pm
Sales Antiques, fine art, general furnishings
Frequency Weekly
Catalogues Yes

LOCHFOOT

Classic Pen Engineering (Writing Equipment Society)
Contact Mr D Purser
✉ **Auchenfranco Farm, Lochfoot, Dumfries, Dumfries & Galloway, DG2 8NZ** P
☎ 01387 730208 F 01387 730208
M 07403 690843
E cpe@auchenfranco.freeserve.co.uk
W www.auchenfranco.freeserve.co.uk
Est. 1994

Stock Fountain pens, dip pens, pencils
Open By appointment
Fairs Hinchingbrooke House, Huntingdon, Cambridgeshire
Services Valuations, restorations

LOCKERBIE

Cobwebs of Lockerbie Ltd
Contact Irene Beck
30 Townhead Street, Lockerbie, Dumfries & Galloway, DG11 2AE
☎ 01576 202554 Ⓕ 01576 203737
Ⓦ www.cobwebs-antiques.co.uk
Est. 1993 ***Stock size*** Large
Stock General antiques and collectables, porcelain, china, mostly Victorian–Edwardian
Open Mon–Sat 9am–5pm

MOFFAT

Ram Antiques
Contact Jean Gale
19 High Street, Moffat, Dumfries & Galloway, DG10 9SG
☎ 01683 300451
Ⓜ 07887 641631
Ⓔ jeangale@ic24.net
Est. 1969 ***Stock size*** Small
Stock General antiques
Open By appointment
Services Valuations, house clearance

STRANRAER

Lochyran Furniture Stores
Contact A Patterson
1 Cairnryan Road, Stranraer, Dumfries & Galloway, DG9 8QJ
☎ 01776 704442
Ⓦ www.lochyran.co.uk
Est. 1994 ***Stock size*** Large
No. of dealers 2
Stock Antiques, second-hand furniture
Open Mon Tues Thurs Sat 10am–4pm
Services Valuations, restorations

THORNHILL

The Hen Hoose
Contact Jo McGregor
Tynron, Thornhill, Dumfries & Galloway, DG3 4LA
☎ 01848 200418
Ⓔ info@henhoose.co.uk
Ⓦ www.henhoose.co.uk
Est. 1994 ***Stock size*** Large
Stock Collectable items from 50p to £5,000, furniture, books, bric-a-brac
Open Tues–Sun 11am–5pm
Services Valuations, restorations, tea room

WIGTOWN

The Bookcellar
Contact Robin or Marion Richmond
Beechwood, Acre Place, Wigtown, Dumfries & Galloway, DG8 9DU
☎ 01988 402653 Ⓕ 01988 403472
Ⓔ bookcellar@aol.com
Est. 1999 ***Stock size*** Medium
Stock Collectables, antiquarian books, specializing in natural history and Scottish topics
Open Mon–Sun 11am–5pm
Services Book search and shipping worldwide

The Bookshop (PBFA)
Contact John Carter
17 North Main Street, Wigtown, Dumfries & Galloway, DG8 9HL
☎ 01988 402499 Ⓕ 01988 402499
Ⓔ sales@gcbooks.demon.co.uk
Ⓦ www.gcbooks.demon.co.uk
Est. 1987 ***Stock size*** Large
Stock Antiquarian to modern books, specializing in Scottish topics and history
Open Mon–Sat 9am–5pm
Services Publishing

Ming Books
Contact Robin Richmond
Beechwood, Acre Place, Wigtown, Dumfries & Galloway, DG8 9DU
☎ 01988 402653
Ⓦ www.mingbooks.com
Est. 1982 ***Stock size*** Large
Stock Antiquarian and rare books, modern firsts, crime fiction
Open Mon–Sun 10am–6pm
Services Book search

The Old Bank Bookshop (PBFA)
Contact John Carter
8 South Main Street, Wigtown, Newton Stewart, Dumfries & Galloway, DG8 9DU
☎ 01988 402688
Est. 1987 ***Stock size*** Large
Stock Rare and second-hand books, specializing in archaeology and art topics
Open Mon–Sat 9am–5pm Sun 1–5pm
Services Framing

Priory Antiques
Contact Mary Arnott
29 George Street, Wigtown, Newton Stewart, Dumfries & Galloway, DG8 8NS
☎ 01988 500517
Ⓜ 07887 554537
Est. 1988 ***Stock size*** Medium
Stock General antiques
Open Usually Mon–Sun 10.30am–5pm
Services Valuations

EAST AYRSHIRE

KILMARNOCK

D & D Programmes
Contact Mr D Stevenson
49 Titchfield Street, Kilmarnock, Ayrshire, KA1 1QS
☎ 01563 573316
Ⓔ d-d-programmes@ukf.net
Ⓦ www.d-d-programmes.ukf.net
Est. 1998 ***Stock size*** Medium
Stock Football memorabilia
Open Tues–Sat 10am–5pm Fri 10am–8pm
Fairs Glasgow, Alloway
Services Mail order catalogue available

EAST LOTHIAN

GULLANE

Gullane Antiques
Contact Elizabeth Lindsey
5 Rosebery Place, Gullane, East Lothian, EH31 2AN
☎ 01620 842994
Est. 1980 ***Stock size*** Large
Stock General antiques, mixed porcelain, glass
Open Mon Tues Fri Sat 10.30am–1pm 2.30–5pm

HADDINGTON

The Thomas Chippendale School of Furniture (SSCR)
Contact Mr Anselm Fraser

✉ Myreside, Gifford, Haddington, East Lothian, EH41 4JA 🅿
☎ 01620 810680 Ⓕ 01620 810701
Ⓔ info@chippendale.co.uk
Ⓦ www.chippendale.co.uk
Est. 1982 *Stock size* Medium
Stock Antique and contemporary furniture
Open Mon–Fri 7.30am–5pm
Services Restorations, repairs, custom-built commissions

⊞ Yester-Days
Contact Betty Logan
✉ **79 High Street, Haddington, East Lothian, EH41 3ET** 🅿
☎ 01620 824543
Est. 1992 *Stock size* Small
Stock Antiques, collectables
Open Tues Wed Fri Sat 11am–4.30pm

NORTH BERWICK

⊞ Lindsey Antiques
Contact Stephen Lindsey
✉ **49a Kirk Ports, North Berwick, East Lothian, EH39 4HL** 🅿
☎ 01620 894114
Est. 1995 *Stock size* Medium
Stock Furniture, ceramics, glass, pictures, etc
Open Mon–Sat 10.30am–5pm closed Thurs

⊞ The Penny Farthing
Contact Stuart Tait
✉ **23 Quality Street, North Berwick, East Lothian, EH39 4HR** 🅿
☎ 01620 894400 Ⓕ 01620 894400
Est. 1989 *Stock size* Medium
Stock Rare, antiquarian and second-hand books, specializing in travel and children's books
Open Mon–Sat 9am–5.30pm Sun 2–5.30pm
Fairs Meadowbank, Edinburgh

⊞ Soltire Antiques Ltd
Contact Andrew Young
✉ **Fenton Barns, Drem, North Berwick, East Lothian, EH39 5BW** 🅿
☎ 01620 850677
Ⓜ 07951 371861
Est. 2001 *Stock size* Large
Stock Antiques, collectables, pine, Victorian, Edwardian furniture, fireplaces, clocks, pews
Open Mon–Sun 10.30am–5pm

FIFE

ABERDOUR

⊞ Antiques & Gifts
✉ **26 High Street, Aberdour, Fife, KY3 0SW** 🅿
☎ 01383 860523
Est. 1969 *Stock size* Small
Stock General antiques
Open Tues 2–5pm Wed 10am–12.30pm Thurs–Sat 10am–5pm closed 12.30–2pm

CERES

⊞ Ceres Antiques
Contact Evelyn Norrie
✉ **1 The Butts, Ceres, Cupar, Fife, KY15 5NF** 🅿
☎ 01334 828384
Est. 1969 *Stock size* Medium
Stock General antiques, specializing in linen and lace
Open Mon–Sun 10am–6pm or by appointment
Fairs Newark, Birmingham and Harrogate

CUPAR

Oliver & Son
Contact Dorothy Wang
✉ **11 East Road, Cupar, Fife, KY15 4HQ** 🅿
☎ 01334 657002 Ⓕ 01334 653807
Ⓜ 07850 013191
Est. 1998
Open Mon–Fri 9am–5pm Sat Sun 10am–4pm
Sales Quarterly antiques and collectors' sales, fortnightly general antiques and household furniture sales
Frequency Fortnightly
Catalogues Yes

DUNFERMLINE

Dunfermline Auction Company Ltd
Contact Mr G Mitchell
✉ **Castleblair Lane, Dunfermline, Fife, KY12 7DP** 🅿
☎ 01383 727434 Ⓕ 01383 729899
Ⓦ www.dunfermlineauction.co.uk
Open Mon–Fri 9am–5.15pm Sat 9am–12.30pm
Sales Antiques, collectables
Frequency 3 per month
Catalogues Yes

DYSART

⊞ Second Notions Antiques
Contact Jim Sinclair
✉ **4b Normand Road, Dysart, Kirkcaldy, Fife, KY1 2XJ** 🅿
☎ 01592 650505 Ⓕ 01592 652792
Ⓜ 07977 119787
Ⓔ james@sinclair1155.freeserve.co.uk
Est. 1994 *Stock size* Medium
Stock General antiques
Open Mon–Fri noon–5pm Sat 10am–5pm
Fairs Swinderby
Services Exporting of containers

FALKLAND

⊞ Falkland Antiques
Contact Mrs Aileen Davies
✉ **High Street, Falkland, Fife, KY15 7BZ** 🅿
☎ 01337 857966 Ⓕ 01337 857966
Est. 1989 *Stock size* Medium
Stock General antiques, Scottish and English ceramics, antique and second-hand jewellery
Open Mon–Sun 10am–5.30pm
Services Professional china and ceramics restoration

INVERKEITHING

⊞ Bargain Centre
Contact Hilda Fleming
✉ **3 Boreland Road, Inverkeithing, Fife, KY11 1NK** 🅿
☎ 01383 416727 Ⓕ 01383 418054
Ⓦ www.bargaincentre.com
Est. 1982 *Stock size* Large
Stock General antiques, bric-a-brac, office furniture
Open Mon–Sat 9am–5pm

KIRKCALDY

⊞ Book-ends
Contact M Potter
✉ **Sailors Walk, 449 High Street, Kirkcaldy, Fife, KY1 2SN** 🅿
☎ 01592 205294
Ⓔ maureen@bookends.freeserve.co.uk
Est. 1990 *Stock size* Medium
Stock Rare and second-hand books, specializing in Scottish topics
Open Tues–Sat 10am–5pm
Services Book search

⊞ A K Campbell & Son
Contact Mr A K Campbell
✉ **262 High Street, Kirkcaldy, Fife, KY1 1LA** 🅿

☎ 01592 597022
Est. 1977 *Stock size* Medium
Stock General antiques, militaria, furniture, bric-a-brac, postcards, banknotes
Open Mon–Sat 10am–5pm
Services Valuations, house and estate clearance

A K Campbell & Son
Contact Mr A K Campbell
277 High Street, Kirkcaldy, Fife, KY1 1JH 🅿
☎ 01592 264305/597161
Est. 1977 *Stock size* Medium
Stock Family jewellery including antique jewellery, silver
Open Mon–Sat 10am–5pm
Services Valuations, repairs, goods purchased

The Golden Past
Contact Fiona Campbell
90 Rosslyn Street, Kirkcaldy, Fife, KY1 3AD 🅿
☎ 01592 653185
Est. 1983 *Stock size* Small
Stock General antiques, pine furniture
Open Tues–Sun 10am–5pm
Services Pine stripping

M D's Auction Co
Contact Mark Harnden
Unit 15–17, Smeaton Industrial Estate, Hayfield Road, Kirkcaldy, Fife, KY1 2HE 🅿
☎ 01592 599969 Ⓕ 01592 640969
Ⓜ 07970 737401
Ⓔ navatmds@aol.com
Ⓦ www.mdsauction.co.uk
Est. 1989
Open Mon–Fri 9am–5pm Sat 10am–1pm
Sales 500 lots, Thurs 6.30pm
Frequency Weekly
Catalogues Yes

LEVEN

Johnson's Auctions
Contact Maureen Johnson
Station Road, Leven, Fife, KY8 4QU
☎ 01333 423438
Est. 1910
Open Mon–Fri 10am–5pm
Sales General antiques
Frequency Fortnightly
Catalogues No

MARKINCH

Squirrel Antiques
Contact Sheila Green
13 Commercial Street, Markinch, Fife, KY7 6DE 🅿
☎ 01592 754386 Ⓕ 01592 754386
Ⓜ 07850 912801
Est. 1984 *Stock size* Medium
Stock General antiques, restored pine, Scottish pottery
Open Mon–Sat 9am–5pm closed Wed or by appointment
Fairs Ingliston
Services Valuations

NEWBURGH

Henderson-Dark Antiques Ltd
Contact Dawn Dark
237–241 High Street, Newburgh, Fife, KY14 6DY 🅿
☎ 01337 842000
Ⓜ 07714 048510
Est. 1990 *Stock size* Medium
Stock Good quality 18th–19thC small items, furniture
Open Every day 10am–5.30pm
Fairs NEC
Services Valuations, restorations and shipping

Newburgh Antiques
Contact Miss D J Fraser
222 High Street, Newburgh, Cupar, Fife, KY14 9HH 🅿
☎ 01337 841026
Est. 1989 *Stock size* Small
Stock General antiques
Open Tues–Sat 10am–5pm

NEWPORT-ON-TAY

Mair Wilkes Books (PBFA)
Contact James Mair
3 St Marys Lane, Newport-on-Tay, Fife, DD6 8AH 🅿
☎ 01382 542260 Ⓕ 01382 542260
Est. 1969 *Stock size* Large
Stock Large selection of rare, second-hand, antiquarian and out-of-print books, specializing in Scottish topics and psychology
Open Tues–Fri 10am–5pm closed 12.30–2pm Sat 10am–5.30pm
Services Valuations, book search

PITTENWEEM

Harbour Antiques
Contact R Clark
27 High Street, Pittenweem, Fife, KY10 2LA 🅿
☎ 01333 312870
Ⓜ 07711 300136
Est. 1984 *Stock size* Medium
Stock General antiques, Wemyss ware
Open Mon–Sun 10.30am–5pm
Services Valuations, goods purchased

ST ANDREWS

Bouquiniste
Contact Mrs E A Anderson
31 Market Street, St Andrews, Fife, KY16 9NS
☎ 01334 476724
Est. 1981 *Stock size* Medium
Stock Rare and second-hand books
Open Mon–Sat 10am–5pm

A K Campbell & Son
Contact Mr A K Campbell
84c Market Street, St Andrews, Fife, KY16 9PA 🅿
☎ 01334 474214
Est. 1977 *Stock size* Medium
Stock Jewellery
Open Mon–Sat 10am–5pm
Services Valuations, repairs

Macgregor Auctions
Contact Mrs Graham
56 Largo Road, St Andrews, Fife, KY16 8RP 🅿
☎ 01334 472431 Ⓕ 01334 479606
Est. 1857
Open Viewing and sale days only
Sales Sale Thurs Fri 10.30am, viewing day prior 9am–7pm
Frequency Fortnightly
Catalogues Yes

Old St Andrews Gallery
Contact David Brown
9 Albany Place, St Andrews, Fife, KY16 9HH 🅿
☎ 01334 477840
Est. 1969 *Stock size* Medium
Stock General antiques, Scottish jewellery, silver, golf memorabilia
Open Mon–Sat 10am–5pm
Services Valuations, restorations

HIGHLAND

AULDEARN

Auldearn Antiques
Contact Roger Milton

✉ Dalmore Manse,
Cethen Road, Auldearn, Nairn,
Inverness-shire, IV12 5HZ P
☎ 01667 453087
Ⓜ 07803 318801
Est. 1984 *Stock size* Large
Stock General antiques
Open Mon–Sun 9.30am–5.30pm
Services Valuations, restorations and repairs

BEAULY

⊞ Iain Marr (HADA)
Contact Iain Marr
✉ 3 Mid Street, Beauly,
Inverness-shire, IV4 7DP P
☎ 01463 782372 Ⓕ 01463 783263
Ⓜ 07860 914191
Ⓔ iainmarr@supanet.com
Ⓦ www.iain-marr-antiques.com
Est. 1974 *Stock size* Medium
Stock General antiques, authorized seller on Sothebys.com
Open Mon–Sat 10.30am–5.30pm closed 1–2pm closed Thurs
Services Valuations

CROMARTY

⊞ The Emporium (HOST)
Contact Sara Baker or Vivienne Griffiths
✉ 11–13 High Street, Cromarty,
Ross-shire, IV11 8UZ P
☎ 01381 600551
Ⓔ emporium@cali.co.uk
Est. 1990 *Stock size* Large
Stock General antiques, small items, second-hand books, collectables
Open Mon–Sun 9.30am–6pm
Services Valuations, tea and coffee shop

DINGWALL

Dingwall R U A Partnership (IAA)
Contact Kenneth MacKay
✉ 15 Tulloch Street, Dingwall,
Ross-shire, IV15 9TT P
☎ 01349 863252 Ⓕ 01349 865062
Ⓔ dingwallmart@cqm.co.uk
Open Mon–Fri 8am–5pm
Sales General antiques
Frequency weekly
Catalogues No

DORNOCH

⊞ Castle Close Antiques
Contact George or Joyce McLean
✉ Castle Street, Dornoch,
Highland, IV25 3SN P
☎ 01862 810405 Ⓕ 01862 810405
Ⓔ enquiries@castle-close-antiques.com
Ⓦ www.castle-close-antiques.com
Est. 1983 *Stock size* Medium
Stock General antiques including jewellery, china
Open Mon–Sat 10am–5pm closed 1–2pm Thurs half day
Fairs Inverness, Aberdeen

⊞ Little Treasures
Contact Mrs A Taylor
✉ Shore Road, Dornoch,
Highland, IV25 3LS P
☎ 01862 811175
Est. 1993 *Stock size* Medium
Stock General antiques, small items, curios, costume jewellery
Open Mon–Sat 10am–5pm
Services Valuations

FORTROSE

⊞ Cathedral Antiques
Contact Mrs Patricia MacColl
✉ 45 High Street, Fortrose,
Ross-shire, IV10 8SU P
☎ 01381 620161
Ⓔ cathant@btinternet.com
Est. 1996 *Stock size* Medium
Stock General antiques, 19thC furniture, ceramics
Open Fri Sat 10am–5pm or by appointment
Fairs Highlands, Inverness
Services Valuations

INVERNESS

⊞ County Furniture Antiques
Contact Mr F Rizza
✉ 8a Harbour Road, Inverness,
Inverness-shire, IV1 1SY P
☎ 01463 715688
Ⓜ 07769 906966
Est. 1984 *Stock size* Medium
Stock General antiques
Trade only Mainly trade
Open Mon–Wed 10am–5pm or by appointment
Services Valuations

Frasers Auctioneers
Contact Mrs A Henderson
✉ 8a Harbour Road,
Inverness,
Inverness-shire, IV1 1SY P
☎ 01463 232395 Ⓕ 01463 233634
Est. 1900
Open Tues 9am–5pm
Wed 9am–6pm
Sales General antiques
Frequency Weekly
Catalogues Yes

NAIRN

⊞ Moray Antiques
Contact Melanie Muir
✉ 78 High Street, Nairn,
Inverness-shire, IV12 4AU P
☎ 01667 455570 Ⓕ 01667 455570
Est. 1997 *Stock size* Medium
Stock General antiques, silver, porcelain
Open Mon–Sat 10.30am–5pm
Services Valuations, restorations

⊞ Sun-City Indoor Market
Contact S Morris
✉ 126 Harbour Street, Nairn,
Inverness-shire, IV12 4AI P
☎ 01667 456300
Est. 1989 *Stock size* Large
Stock General antiques
Open Mon 9am–5pm
Sun noon–5pm
Services Valuations and house clearance

NEWTONMORE

⊞ The Antique Shop
Contact John Harrison
✉ Main Street, Newtonmore,
Inverness-shire, PH20 1DD P
☎ 01540 673272
Ⓜ 07713 093801
Est. 1990 *Stock size* Medium
Stock General antiques, scientific instruments, second-hand books
Open Mon–Sat 10am–5pm

MIDLOTHIAN

MUSSELBURGH

⊞ Early Technology
Contact Michael Bennett-Levy
✉ Monkton House,
Old Craighall,
Musselburgh,
Midlothian, EH21 8SF P
☎ 0131 665 5753
Ⓔ levy@virgin.net
Ⓦ www.earlytech.com
Est. 1971 *Stock size* Large
Stock Early electrical and mechanical antiques
Open Mon–Sun 7am–7pm
Fairs Ingliston
Services Valuations, restorations

MORAY

ELGIN

West End Antiques (HADA)
Contact Mr F Stewart
35 High Street, Elgin, Moray, IV30 1EE
01343 547531
07977 821440
Est. 1971 *Stock size* Large
Stock General antiques, silver, furniture
Open Mon–Sat 9.30am–5pm closed 12.30–1.30pm closed Wed pm
Services Valuations

FORRES

Forres Saleroom
Contact Alexander Morris
Tytler Street, Forres, Moray, IV36 1EL
01309 672422 F 01309 673339
Est. 1895
Open Mon–Fri 9am–5pm Sat 9am–noon
Sales General antiques
Frequency Weekly
Catalogues Yes

GRANTOWN ON SPEY

Strathspey Gallery (LAPADA, HADA)
Contact James or Stephanie Franses
40 High Street, Grantown on Spey, Moray, PH26 3EH
01479 873290/873434
07831 287762
antiques@strathspey.prestel.co.uk
Est. 1969 *Stock size* Medium
Stock General antiques
Open Tues Wed Fri Sat 10am–5pm
Services Valuations

LOSSIEMOUTH

Harbour Treasures
Contact Janice Raynes
1 Pitgaveny Quay, Lossiemouth, Moray, IV31 6TW
01343 815880
Est. 1997 *Stock size* Large
Stock General antiques and collectables
Open Mon–Sun 10am–5pm
Fairs Newark, Swinderby and Ardingly
Services Tea rooms, free delivery within 200 miles

PORTGORDON

Hannah's Heirlooms
Contact Linda Sherman
9 Gordon Street, Portgordon, Moray, AB56 5QR
01542 832153
Est. 1997 *Stock size* Large
Stock General antiques including Victorian furniture and china
Open Mon–Sun 9.30am–5.30pm
Services Valuations, restorations and repairs

NORTH AYRSHIRE

FAIRLIE

E A Alvarino Fairlie Antiques
Contact E A Alvarino
86 Main Road, Fairlie, Largs, North Ayrshire, KA29 0AD
01475 568613
oldfairlie@aol.com
Est. 1976 *Stock size* Small
Stock General antiques
Services Valuations

ISLE OF ARRAN

The Stable Antiques
Contact Alistair Linton
Balmichael Visitors Centre, Shiskine Brodick, Isle of Arran, North Ayrshire, KA27 8DT
01770 860468
07747 723791
Est. 1984 *Stock size* Medium
Stock General antiques
Open Summer Mon–Sun 10am–5pm winter Wed–Sun 10am–5pm
Services Furniture restoration

LARGS

Narducci Antiques
Contact Mr G Narducci
11 Waterside Street, Largs, North Ayrshire, KA30 9LW
01475 672612/01294 461687 F 01294 470002
07771 577777/07831 100152
Est. 1969 *Stock size* Large
Stock General antiques, shipping goods
Open By appointment
Services Packing, shipping, European haulage

Nicolson Maps
Contact Malcolm Nicolson
3 Frazer Street, Largs, North Ayrshire, KA30 9HP
01475 689242 F 01475 689242
enquiries@nicolsonmaps.com
www.nicolsonmaps.com
Est. 1979 *Stock size* Medium
Stock General maps and charts
Open Mon–Fri 9am–5pm
Fairs International Map Association
Services Free postal service

PERTH & KINROSS

ABERNYTE

A D Antiques
Contact Alison Davey
Abernyte Antiques, Scottish Antique and Art Centre, Abernyte, Perth & Kinross, PH14 9SJ
0131 553 6462 F 0131 553 6462
07939 508171
alison@adantiques.freeserve.co.uk
www.thesaurus.co.uk/adantiques
Est. 1997 *Stock size* Medium
Stock Decorative arts
Open By appointment
Fairs NEC, Bingley Hall

The Old Church Antiques
Contact George Whitla
The Old Church, Scottish Antique and Art Centre, Abernyte, Perth, Perth & Kinross, PH14 9SJ
01828 686642/01250 886276
Est. 1999 *Stock size* Medium
Stock General antiques, clocks, books
Open Mon–Sun 11am–5pm
Services Valuations, clock repairs

Scottish Antique and Art Centre
Contact Tracy Walsh
Abernyte, Perthshire, PH14 9SJ
01828 686401 F 01828 686199
tracy@saac.demon.co.uk
www.scottish-antiques.com
Est. 1999 *Stock size* Large
No. of dealers 90
Stock Georgian, Victorian, general antiques and collectables
Open Mon–Sun 10am–5pm

Services Valuations, restorations and repairs, shipping, parking for 400 cars, coffee shop, new food hall

AUCHTERARDER

Ian Burton Antique Clocks (NAWCC, AHS)
Contact Ian Burton
125 High Street, Auchterarder, Perth & Kinross, PH3 1AA
01334 479979 Ⓜ 07785 114800
iansclocks@aol.com
www.ianburton.com
Est. 1974 *Stock size* Large
Stock Antique clocks, especially longcase and mystery
Open Mon–Sat 9am–5pm

K Stanley & Son
Contact Chris Stanley
20b Townhead, Auchterarder, Perth & Kinross, PH3 1AH
01764 662252 Ⓕ 01764 662252
Ⓜ 07778 311653
ksantique@aol.com
Est. 1956 *Stock size* Medium
Stock General antiques
Open Mon–Sat 10am–5pm Sun noon–5pm

Times Past Antiques
Contact Andrew or Neil Brown
Broadfold Farm, Auchterarder, Perth & Kinross, PH3 1DR
01764 663166 Ⓕ 01764 663166
Est. 1974 *Stock size* Large
Stock Stripped antique pine
Open Mon–Fri 8am–4.30pm Sat Sun 10am–3.30pm
Services Restorations, stripping, exporting

John Whitelaw & Sons (LAPADA)
Contact Alan or Ian Whitelaw
125 High Street, Auchterarder, Perth & Kinross, PH3 1AA
01764 662482 Ⓕ 01764 663577
Ⓜ 07836 725558
jwsantique@aol.com
www.whitelawantiques.com
Est. 1959 *Stock size* Large
Stock General antiques, Georgian furniture
Open Mon–Sat 9am–5pm
Fairs NEC, LAPADA
Services Repairs, restorations

BLAIRGOWRIE

Roy Sim Antiques
Contact Roy Sim
The Granary Warehouse, Lower Mill Street, Blairgowrie, Perthshire, PH10 6AQ
01250 873860 Ⓕ 01250 873860
roy.sim@lineone.net
Est. 1977 *Stock size* Large
Stock Antique furniture, decorative and collectable items, longcase clocks, wall and mantel clocks, copper, brassware
Open Mon–Sat 9am–5.30pm Sun 12.30–5pm

BRIDGE OF EARN

Imrie Antiques & Interiors (LAPADA)
Contact Ian Imrie
Imrie House, Back Street, Bridge of Earn, Perth, Perth & Kinross, PH2 9AE
01738 812784
Est. 1966 *Stock size* Large
Stock General antiques
Open Mon–Sat 9am–5pm
Services Valuations, restorations and repairs

CRIEFF

Antiques & Fine Arts
Contact Mrs S Drysdale
11 Comrie Street, Crieff, Perth & Kinross, PH7 4AX
01764 654496
Est. 1984 *Stock size* Medium
Stock General antiques
Open Mon–Sat 10am–6pm closed 1–2.20pm

DOUNE

Scottish Antique and Arts Centre
Contact Tracy Walsh
Muir of Cambus, Doune, Perth & Kinross, FH16 6HD
01786 841203 Ⓕ 01786 842070
victoria@saac.demon.co.uk
www.scottish-antiques.com
Est. 1974 *Stock size* Large
No. of dealers 80
Stock Georgian–Victorian, general antiques and collectables
Open Mon–Sun 10am–5pm
Services Valuations, shipping, coffee shop

DUNKELD

Dunkeld Antiques (LAPADA)
Contact David Dytch
Tay Terrace, Dunkeld, Perth & Kinross, PH8 0AQ
01350 728832 Ⓕ 01350 727008
Ⓜ 07713 074932
sales@dunkeldantiques.com
www.dunkeldantiques.com
Est. 1986 *Stock size* Large
Stock General antiques, specializing in 18thC and 19thC furniture
Open Mon–Sat 10am–5pm Sun noon–5pm

GLENDOICK

Glendoick Antiques
Contact Malcolm Wood
The School House, Glendoick, Perth & Kinross, PH2 7NR
01738 860870
Est. 1995 *Stock size* Large
Stock Quality antiques, Georgian–Edwardian dining furniture
Open Mon–Sun 10.30am–5pm

INCHTURE

Inchmartine Fine Art
Contact Paul Stephens
Inchmartine house, Inchture, Perth & Kinross, PH14 9QQ
01828 686412 Ⓕ 01828 686748
Ⓜ 07702 190128
paul@toolbazaar.freeserve.co.uk
Est. 1997 *Stock size* Medium
Stock 19th–early 20thC Scottish paintings
Open Mon–Sat 9am–5.30pm
Fairs Buxton, Chester, Glasgow
Services Valuations, cleaning and framing

Inchmartine Restorations
Contact Andrew Stephens
Inchmartine house, Inchture, Perth & Kinross, PH14 9QQ
01828 686412 Ⓕ 01828 686748
ir@toolbazaar.freeserve.co.uk
www.toolbazaar.co.uk
Est. 1989 *Stock size* Medium
Stock 18th–19thC furniture
Open Mon–Sat 9am–5.30pm
Fairs Buxton, Gleneagles
Services Valuations and cabinet-making

Inchmartine Tool Bazaar
Contact Andrew Stephens
Inchmartine house, Inchture, Perth & Kinross, PH14 9QQ
01828 686096 Ⓕ 01828 686748

ⓔ andrew@toolbazaar.freeserve.co.uk
ⓦ www.toolbazaar.co.uk
Est. 1991 ***Stock size*** Large
Stock Old cabinet-making and woodworking tools
Open Mon–Sat 9am–5.30pm
Fairs Buxton, Gleneagles, Tatton

⊞ C S Moreton Antiques
Contact Paul Stephens
✉ Inchmartine House, Inchture, Perth & Kinross, PH14 9QQ Ⓟ
☎ 01828 686412 ⓕ 01828 686748
ⓜ 07702 190128
ⓔ paul@toolbazaar.freeserve.co.uk
Est. 1854 ***Stock size*** Medium
Stock Period furniture, Oriental rugs, paintings, objets d'art, old hand tools
Open Mon–Sat 9am–5.30pm
Fairs Buxton, Chester, Glasgow
Services Valuations, restorations and shipping

KILLIN

⊞ Maureen H Gauld
Contact Maureen Gauld
✉ Craiglee Main Street, Killin, Perth & Kinross, FK21 8UN Ⓟ
☎ 01567 820475 ⓕ 01567 820605
ⓔ KillinGallery@FSBDial.co.uk
ⓦ www.killingallery,com
Est. 1973 ***Stock size*** Medium
Stock Silver, china, glass antiques
Open Mon–Sat 10am–5pm or by appointment

⊞ Killin Gallery
Contact J Gauld
✉ Craiglea Main Street, Killin, Perth & Kinross, FK21 8UN Ⓟ
☎ 01567 820475 ⓕ 01567 820605
ⓔ killingallery@FSBDial.co.uk
ⓦ www.killingallery.com
Est. 1994 ***Stock size*** Medium
Stock Furniture, paintings, etchings
Open Mon–Sat 10am–5pm or by appointment

KINROSS

⊞ Miles Antiques (LAPADA)
Contact Ken and Sue Miles
✉ Mill Street, Kinross, Perth & Kinross, KY13 8DR Ⓟ
☎ 01577 864858 ⓕ 01577 863881
ⓜ 07836 315589
Est. 1978 ***Stock size*** Large
Stock Principally Victorian furniture, Georgian furniture, clocks, porcelain, decorative objects
Open Mon–Fri noon–5pm or by appointment

⊞ Tudor House Antiques
Contact John Neville
✉ 11 South Street, Milnathort, Kinross, Perth & Kinross, KY13 9XA Ⓟ
☎ 01577 863185 ⓕ 01577 863185
Est. 1978 ***Stock size*** Small
Stock General antiques
Open Tues Wed 1–5pm Fri Sat 10am–5pm
Services Valuations, restorations and repairs

MEIGLE

⊞ Airlie Antiques
Contact J W McGill
✉ Alyth Road, Meigle, Blairgowrie, Perth & Kinross, PH12 8RS Ⓟ
☎ 01828 640617 ⓕ 01828 640617
ⓜ 07713 889205
ⓔ shop@airlieantiques.co.uk
ⓦ www.airlieantiques.co.uk
Est. 1981 ***Stock size*** Medium
Stock Antique glassware, Perthshire glass, Georgian and Victorian furniture
Open Mon–Sun noon–5pm or by appointment
Fairs Newark, Edinburgh
Services Valuations

⊞ Airlie Antiques (Textiles)
Contact Mrs J McGill
✉ Alyth Road, Meigle, Blairgowrie, Perth & Kinross, PH12 8RS Ⓟ
☎ 01828 640617 ⓕ 01828 640617
ⓔ jmcgill@tesco.net
Est. 1982 ***Stock size*** Medium
Stock Antique textiles, country antiques
Open Mon–Fri 2–5pm Sat 10am–5pm closed Wed

⊞ Herrald of Edinburgh
Contact Bruce Herrald
✉ Kings of Kinloch, Meigle, Blairgowrie, Perth & Kinross, PH12 8QX Ⓟ
☎ 01828 640273 ⓕ 01828 640273
ⓜ 07711 285132
ⓔ herrald@sol.co.uk
ⓦ www.sol.co.uk/a/antiquesherrald
Est. 1882 ***Stock size*** Large
Stock General antiques
Open Mon–Sat 9.30am–5pm Sun 2–5pm
Services Valuations, restorations and repairs

MUTHILL

⊞ Upstairs-Downstairs
Contact Elizabeth Richardson
✉ 18 Drummond Street, Muthill, Crieff, Perth & Kinross, PH5 2AN Ⓟ
☎ 01764 681737
ⓜ 07803 461465
Est. 1996 ***Stock size*** Small
Stock General antiques, Victorian, Edwardian, Arts and Crafts, Art Nouveau, small furniture items, Continental glass, golf paraphernalia
Open Mon–Sun 2–5.30pm or by appointment

PERTH

⊞ Ainslie's Antiques
Contact Robert Ainslie
✉ Unit 3, Gray Street, Perth, Perth & Kinross, PH2 0JH Ⓟ
☎ 01738 636825
Est. 1959 ***Stock size*** Large
Stock General antiques including Victorian and Edwardian furniture
Open Mon–Fri 9am–5pm or by appointment
Fairs Newark

Lindsay Burns & Co (SAA)
Contact Mr L Burns
✉ 6 King Street, Perth, Perth & Kinross, RH2 8JA Ⓟ
☎ 01738 633888 ⓕ 01738 441322
ⓔ lindsayburns@btconnect.com
ⓦ www.lburnscoauctions.co.uk
Est. 1982
Open Mon–Fri 9am–5pm Sat 9am–noon
Sales General antiques, household effects bi-weekly Thurs 10.30am, viewing day prior to sale
Frequency Bi-weekly
Catalogues Yes

⊞ Design Interiors
Contact Margaret Blane
✉ 55 South Street, Perth, Perth & Kinross, PH2 8PD Ⓟ
☎ 01738 635360
ⓔ robert.blane@btinternet.com
Est. 1989 ***Stock size*** Medium

Stock General antiques and collectables
Open Mon–Sat 10am–5.30pm
Services China restoration, picture cleaning, framing

⊞ Alexander S Deuchar & Son
Contact A S Deuchar
✉ 12 South Street, Perth, Perth & Kinross, PH2 8PG 🅿
☎ 01738 626297
Est. 1911 ***Stock size*** Medium
Stock General antiques
Open Mon–Fri 10am–5pm

Loves Auction Rooms (SAA)
Contact Mrs E Reid
✉ 52–54 Canal Street, Perth, Perth & Kinross, PH2 8LF 🅿
☎ 01738 633337 Ⓕ 01738 629830
Est. 1869
Open Mon–Fri 9am–5.30pm Sat 9am–noon
Sales Antiques quarterly, household effects weekly
Frequency Weekly & quarterly
Catalogues Yes (quarterly sales only)

⊞ Perth Antiques
Contact Robert Blane
✉ 50 South Street, Perth, Perth & Kinross, PH2 8PD 🅿
☎ 01738 440888
Ⓜ 07939 196750
Ⓔ robert.blane@btinternet.com
Est. 1998 ***Stock size*** Large
Stock General antiques, porcelain, Clarice Cliff, Belleek, Moorcroft, Art Deco pottery, Monart glass, chintz
Open Mon–Sat 10am–5pm

⊞ Whisper of the Past
Contact Laura Wilson
✉ 15 George Street, Perth, Perth & Kinross, PH1 5JY 🅿
☎ 01738 635472
Est. 1981 ***Stock size*** Medium
Stock Country antiques
Open Mon–Sat 9.30am–5pm Jan–Mar closed Wed

⊞ Yesterdays Today
Contact W MacGregor
✉ 267 Old High Street, Perth, Perth & Kinross, PH1 5QN 🅿
☎ 01738 443534
Ⓜ 07713 897793
Ⓔ yesterdaystoday@talk21.com
Est. 1995 ***Stock size*** Medium
Stock Scottish pottery and glass, jewellery, silver, Royal Doulton, Beswick
Open Mon–Sat 9am–5pm
Services Valuations

PITLOCHRY

⊞ Blair Antiques
Contact Duncan Huie
✉ 14 Bonnethill Road, Pitlochry, Perth & Kinross, PH16 5BS 🅿
☎ 01796 472624 Ⓕ 01796 474202
Ⓔ adhuie@aol.com
Est. 1976 ***Stock size*** Medium
Stock General antiques, art
Open Mon–Fri 9am–5pm closed 12.30–2pm
Services Valuations

RAIT

⊞ Edward Bowry
Contact Edward Bowry
✉ Rait Village Antique Centre, Rait, Perth, Perth & Kinross, PH2 7RT 🅿
☎ 01821 670318
Est. 1990 ***Stock size*** Medium
Stock Furniture, old woodworking tools, sporting items
Open Mon–Sat 10.30am–5pm
Services Valuations, restorations and repairs

⊞ Fair Finds Antiques
Contact Lynda Templeman
✉ Rait Village Antiques Centre, Rait, Perth, Perth & Kinross, PH2 7RT 🅿
☎ 01821 670379 Ⓕ 01821 670379
Ⓜ 07720 394750
Est. 1969 ***Stock size*** Large
Stock Furniture, Wemyss ware, general antiques
Open Mon–Sat 10am–5pm Sun 12.30–4.30pm

⊞ Gordon Loraine Antiques
Contact Liane or Gordon Loraine
✉ The Cartshed, Rait Village Antiques Centre, Rait, Perth, Perth & Kinross, PH2 7RT 🅿
☎ 01821 670760 Ⓕ 01821 670760
Ⓜ 07798 550017
Est. 1991 ***Stock size*** Medium
Stock Good-quality Georgian–Edwardian furniture, decorative items and collectables
Open Mon–Sat 10am–5pm

⊞ Newton Antiques
Contact Lindsay Newton
✉ Rait Village Antiques Centre, Rait Farm, Rait, Perth, Perth & Kinross, PH2 7RT 🅿
☎ 01821 670205
Est. 1981 ***Stock size*** Medium
Stock General antiques, textiles, cushions, decorative items
Open Mon–Sat 10.30am–5pm

Rait Village Antiques Centre
Contact Lynda Templeman
✉ Rait, Perth, Perth & Kinross, PH2 7RT 🅿
☎ 01821 670379 Ⓕ 01821 670379
Ⓜ 07720 394750
Est. 1985 ***Stock size*** Large
No. of dealers 8
Stock Furniture, silver, pottery, porcelain, woodworking tools, Wemyss ware, rugs
Open Mon–Sat 10am–5pm some dealers Sun 12.30–4.30pm
Services Valuations, restorations

RUMBLING BRIDGE

⊞ Bridge Bygones Antiques
Contact David or Angela de Boer
✉ The Bungalow, Rumbling Bridge, Kinross, Perth & Kinross, KY13 0PT 🅿
☎ 01577 840280/840251
Ⓔ jamesrussell@bridgebygones.freeserve.co.uk
Ⓦ www.bridgebygones.freeserve.co.uk
Est. 1984 ***Stock size*** Medium
Stock General antiques, Victorian and later furniture and effects
Open Sat Sun noon–5pm or by appointment
Services Restorations and re-upholstery

SCONE

Ian M Smith Auctioneers & Valuers
Contact Iain Smith
✉ Unit 18, Perth Airport Business Park, Scone, Perth, Perth & Kinross, PH2 6NP 🅿
☎ 01738 551110 Ⓕ 01738 551110
Ⓜ 07836 770664
Ⓔ imsauctions@beeb.net
Est. 1994
Open Mon–Fri 9am–5pm Sat 10am–1pm
Sales General antiques
Frequency Fortnightly
Catalogues No

STANLEY

Coach House Antiques Ltd (PADA)
Contact John Walker
Charleston, Stanley, Perth & Kinross, PN1 4PN
01738 828627
07710 122244
www.goodtradecall.com
Est. 1970 *Stock size* Medium
Stock Period furniture, decorative items, garden items
Open By appointment
Services Valuations, restorations, shipping

RENFREWSHIRE

GREENOCK

McTear's (SAA, IAA)
Contact Brian Clements
22 Forsyth Street, Greenock, Renfrewshire, PA16 8DX
01475 730343 01475 726436
07767 376642
enquiries@mctears.co.uk
www.mctears.co.uk
Est. 1842
Open Mon–Fri 8.30am–5pm
Sales General antiques
Frequency Weekly
Catalogues Yes

D B Warne Ltd (SAA)
Contact L Haynes
2 Houston Street, Greenock, Renfrewshire, PA16 8ND
01475 723150 01475 723150
corains@easynet.co.uk
Est. 1921
Open Mon–Fri 9.30am–4pm
Sales General antiques
Frequency Weekly
Catalogues Yes

KILBARCHAN

Gardners 'The Antique Shop' (LAPADA)
Contact George or Robert Gardner
Ward End House, Kibbleston Road, Kilbarchan, Johnstone, Renfrewshire, PA10 2PN
01505 702292 01505 702292
gardantiques@colloquium.co.uk
Est. 1950 *Stock size* Large
Stock General antiques, Georgian–1930s
Open Mon–Fri 9am–6pm Sat 10am–5pm

McQuade Antiques
7 Shuttle Street, Kilbarchan, Johnstone, Renfrewshire, PA10 2JN
01505 704249
07860 729598
Est. 1967 *Stock size* Medium
Stock General antiques
Open Mon–Fri 10am–5.30pm Sun 2–5.30pm
Fairs Newark

KILMALCOLM

Kilmalcolm Antiques
Contact Hilary McLean
Stewart Place, Bridge of Weir Road, Kilmalcolm, Renfrewshire, PA13 4AF
01505 873149 01505 873149
07850 126150
Est. 1974 *Stock size* Large
Stock General antiques, Scottish paintings, pottery, Georgian–Victorian furniture
Open Mon–Sat 10am–1pm 2.30–5.30pm
Fairs Hopeton House, Margam

PAISLEY

Corrigan Antiques
Contact Mr John Corrigan
23 High Calside, Paisley, Renfrewshire, PA2 6BY
0141 889 6653 0141 848 9700
07802 631110
john.@corriganantiques3.freeserve.co.uk
Est. 1939 *Stock size* Small
Stock Decorative antiques
Open By appointment only

SCOTTISH BORDERS

COLDSTREAM

Fraser Antiques
Contact R Fleming
65 High Street, Coldstream, Scottish Borders, TD12 4DL
01890 882450 01890 882451
Est. 1968 *Stock size* Medium
Stock General antiques
Open Tues–Fri 10am–5pm closed 1–2pm Sat 9.30am–1pm or by appointment
Services Valuations, restorations

GALASHIELS

Hall's Auctioneers
Contact Michael Hall
Ladhope Vale House, Ladhope Vale, Galashiels, Scottish Borders, TD1 1BT
01896 754477 01896 754477
Est. 1995
Open Mon–Fri 9am–5pm Sat 9am–noon or by appointment
Sales General antiques and collectables
Frequency Every 3-4 weeks
Catalogues Yes

INNERLEITHEN

The Glory Hole
Contact Paul MacNaughton
29 High Street, Innerleithen, Scottish Borders, EH44 6HA
01896 831306
07710 771055
Est. 1996 *Stock size* Medium
Stock General antiques, specializing in old printing items
Open Mon–Fri 11am–5pm closed Tues
Fairs Border fairs

Keepsakes
Contact Mrs M Maxwell
96 High Street, Innerleithen, Scottish Borders, EH44 6HF
01896 831369
07773 477291
rmaxwell@lineone.net
www.website.lineone.net/~rmaxwell
Est. 1979 *Stock size* Medium
Stock General antiques, dolls, toys, Art Deco
Open Mon Thurs–Sat 11am–4.30pm
Fairs Ingliston

The Last Century Antiques
Contact Keith or Gill Miller
34 High Street, Innerleithen, Scottish Borders, EH44 6HF
01896 831759
last.century@biinternet.com
Est. 1989 *Stock size* Medium
Stock General antiques including glass, cutlery, curtains
Open Mon–Sat 11am–4.30pm
Fairs Ingliston
Services Valuations

JEDBURGH

R & M Turner (Antiques & Fine Art) Ltd (LAPADA)
Contact Mr R J Turner
34–36 High Street, Jedburgh, Roxburghshire, TD8 6AG

☎ 01835 863445 Ⓕ 01835 863349
Est. 1966 *Stock size* Large
Stock Fine art, clocks, furniture, jewellery, bric-a-brac, porcelain, reproductions
Open Mon–Fri 9.30am–5.30pm Sat 10am–5pm
Services Valuations, restorations, shipping

MELROSE

Border Country Furniture
Contact Denni or Christine Reid
✉ **2 Palma Place, Melrose, Scottish Borders, TD6 9PR** Ⓟ
☎ 01896 823700 Ⓕ 01896 823700
Est. 1974 *Stock size* Large
Stock General antiques, hand-made furniture
Open Mon–Sat 10am–5pm Thurs 10am–1pm Sun 2–4pm
Services Made-to-measure tables and fireplaces

John Swan & Sons Plc
Contact Frank Forrest
✉ **Newtown St Boswells, Melrose, Scottish Borders, TD6 0PD** Ⓟ
☎ 01835 822214 Ⓕ 01835 823860
Ⓔ stboswells@johnswan.demon.co.uk
Est. 1899
Open Mon–Fri 9am–5pm
Sales General antiques and house clearance
Catalogues Yes

PEEBLES

Veteran Antiques and Collectables
Contact Paul Kelly
✉ **61 High Street, Peebles, Scottish Borders, EH45 8AN** Ⓟ
☎ 01721 724228
Est. 1996 *Stock size* Medium
Stock General antiques
Open Mon–Sat 10.30am–5pm or by appointment
Fairs NEC, Newark
Services Valuations

SOUTH AYRSHIRE

AYR

Lochyran Furniture Stores
Contact A Patterson
✉ **12 Kirkport, Ayr, South Ayrshire, KA7 1QB** Ⓟ
☎ 01292 282821
Ⓦ www.lochyran.co.uk
Est. 1994 *Stock size* Large
No. of dealers 2
Stock General antiques
Open Mon–Sat 10am–5pm

GIRVAN

Ainslie Books
Contact Mr G Clark
✉ **28 Hamilton Street, Girvan, South Ayrshire, KA26 9EY** Ⓟ
☎ 01465 715453 Ⓕ 01465 715453
Est. 1996 *Stock size* Medium
Stock Rare and second-hand books, specializing in Scottish and Ayrshire topics
Open Mon–Sat 10am–5pm
Services Book search

Clamjamfrey
Contact Ingrid Powell
✉ **26 Hamilton Street, Girvan, South Ayrshire, KA26 9EY** Ⓟ
☎ 01465 715621
Ⓜ 07867 910492
Ⓔ clamjam@ukonline.co.uk
Est. 1997 *Stock size* Medium
Stock General antiques, Denby and Poole pottery
Open Mon–Sat 10am–5pm
Fairs Ingliston, Edinburgh, Swinderby
Services Valuations

PRESTWICK

Crossroads Antiques
Contact Mr T O'Keeffe
✉ **7 The Cross, Prestwick, South Ayrshire, KA9 1AJ** Ⓟ
☎ 01292 474004
Est. 1989 *Stock size* Medium
Stock General antiques, furniture, china
Open Mon–Sat 10.30am–5pm

TROON

IDS Valuation Consultants (BWCG)
Contact Iain Sutherland
✉ **79 Templehill, Troon, South Ayrshire, KA10 6BQ** Ⓟ
☎ 01292 315999 Ⓕ 01292 316611
Est. 1995 *Stock size* Medium
Stock General antiques
Open Mon–Sat 9.30am–5.30pm or by appointment
Fairs Ayr
Services Valuations, full consultation service

Tantalus Antiques (BWCG)
Contact Iain Sutherland
✉ **79 Templehill, Troon, South Ayrshire, KA10 6BQ** Ⓟ
☎ 01292 315999 Ⓕ 01292 316611
Ⓔ idsantique@aol.com
Est. 1997 *Stock size* Medium
Stock General antiques, furniture, jewellery, clocks, watches
Open Mon–Sat 10am–5pm or by appointment
Fairs Ayr
Services Full consultation and restoration service

SOUTH LANARKSHIRE

HAMILTON

L S Smellie & Sons Ltd (SAA)
Contact Mr R Smellie
✉ **Lower Auchingramont Road, Hamilton, South Lanarkshire, ML3 6HW** Ⓟ
☎ 01698 282007 Ⓕ 01698 207473
Ⓔ andrew@LSSmellie.co.uk
Ⓦ www.LSSmellie.co.uk
Est. 1874
Open Mon–Fri 8am–5pm
Sales General antiques
Frequency Weekly & quarterly
Catalogues Yes

LANARK

Recollections
Contact Mr A Roebock
✉ **9 Westport, Lanark, South Lanarkshire, ML11 9HD** Ⓟ
☎ 01555 663668
Est. 1996 *Stock size* Medium
Stock General antiques
Open Mon–Sat 9am–5pm
Fairs Scot fairs, Glasgow, Edinburgh
Services Valuations

STRATHAVEN

Suedan Antiques
Contact Mrs M Hardie
✉ **5 Main Street, Strathaven, South Lanarkshire, ML10 6AJ** Ⓟ
☎ 01357 529854
Ⓜ 07801 367768
Est. 1997 *Stock size* Large
Stock General antiques
Open Mon–Sat 10.30am–4.30pm closed Wed
Services Valuations, repairs

STIRLING

BRIDGE OF ALLAN

⊞ Bridge of Allan Books (PBFA)
✉ **2 Henderson Street, Bridge of Allan, Stirling, FK9 4HT** P
☎ 01786 834483
E books@bridgeofallen.fsnet.co.uk
Est. 1985 *Stock size* Medium
Stock Antiquarian, rare and second-hand books, prints, specializing in Scottish and field sports
Open Mon–Sat 10am–5pm
Services Free book search

Key to Symbols

- ⊞ = Dealer
- 🏛 = Antiques Centre
- 🔨 = Auction House
- ✉ = Address
- P = Parking
- ☎ = Telephone No.
- M = Mobile tel No.
- F = Fax No.
- E = E-mail address
- W = Website address

DOUNE

⊞ Bluebell Collectables
Contact Charlie Claydon
✉ **4 Main Street, Doune, Stirling, FK16 6BJ** P
☎ 01786 842828 F 0141 571 5694
E militaria@stirling.co.uk
W www.militaria.stirling.co.uk
Est. 1994 *Stock size* Medium
Stock Collectables, regimental badges
Open Tues–Sat 10.30am–4.30pm closed Wed
Fairs Ingliston, Lancaster, Liverpool
Services Medal research

FALKIRK

🔨 Auction Rooms (NAVA)
Contact Robert Penman
✉ **Central Auction Hall, Bankside, Falkirk, Stirling, FK2 7XR** P
☎ 01324 623000 F 01324 630343
E robert@auctionroomsfalkirk.co.uk
W www.auctionroomsfalkirk.co.uk
Est. 1999
Open Mon Thurs Fri 9am–5pm Tues 8am–8pm Wed 8am–6pm Sat 9am–noon
Sales General antiques sales every Wed evening
Frequency Weekly
Catalogues Yes

⊞ Fairweathers
Contact Jane Wheeler
✉ **54 Vicars Street, Falkirk, Stirling, FK1 1JB**
☎ 01324 633569
Est. 1984 *Stock size* Small
Stock Collectors items, curios
Open Mon–Sat 9.30am–5.30pm

GARGUNNOCK

⊞ Country Home Antiques
Contact P Christie
✉ **Mains Farm, Gargunnock, Stirling, FK8 3AY** P
☎ 01786 860509 F 01786 860509
E gargunnock@aol.com or antiquestrader@aol.com
W www.scotlandroom.com
Est. 1979 *Stock size* Large
Stock General antiques
Open Mon–Fri 9am–5pm Sat 10am–5pm Sun 12.30–5pm
Services Stripping, waxing, upholstery, French polishing, full restoration, shipping

STIRLING

⊞ Abbey Antiques
Contact Stuart Campbell
✉ **35 Friars Street, Stirling, FK8 1HA** P
☎ 01786 447840
M 07801 692126
Est. 1984 *Stock size* Medium
Stock General antiques
Open Mon–Sat 9.30am–5pm
Services Valuations

⊞ Stewart Sales Rooms
Contact Mrs Watson-Fargie
✉ **14 Dumbarton Road, Stirling, FK8 2LG** P
☎ 01786 473414
Est. 1969 *Stock size* Large
Stock General antiques
Open Mon–Sat 10am–4pm closed Wed
Services Valuations

STRATHBLANE

⊞ What Nots Antiques
Contact Frank Bruce
✉ **16 Milngavie Road, Strathblane, Stirling, G63 9EH** P
☎ 01360 770310
Est. 1969 *Stock size* Medium
Stock General antiques, clocks, selection of horse-drawn vehicles
Open Mon–Sun 9.30am–5pm

WEST LOTHIAN

BO'NESS

🔨 Grosvenor's Auctions
Contact Charles
✉ **Bomains Industrial Estate, Linlithgow Road, Bo'Ness, West Lothian, EH51 0QG** P
☎ 01506 829900 F 01506 829900
W www.grosvenors-auction.com
Open Sun 10am–4pm Mon 3–6.30pm Tues–Sat 10am–5pm
Sales General antiques
Frequency Weekly
Catalogues Yes

🔨 D J Manning Auctioneers, Valuers & Appraisers (IAA)
Contact D J Manning
✉ **Bridgeness, Carriden, Bo'Ness, West Lothian, EH51 9SF** P
☎ 01506 827693 F 01506 826495
E info@djmanning.co.uk
W www.djmanning.co.uk
Est. 1969
Open Mon–Fri 9am–5pm
Sales Books, general antiques, collectables
Frequency Quarterly
Catalogues Yes

FAULDHOUSE

⊞ Sunnyside Antiques
Contact Mark Attwood
✉ **Units 1–2, Bridge Street, Fauldhouse, West Lothian, EH47 9AU** P
☎ 0800 298 5877 F 01501 763778
M 07798 640629
E info@periodantiques.net
W www.periodantiques.net
Est. 1995 *Stock size* Medium
Stock 17th–19thC period furniture, longcase clocks
Open By appointment only
Fairs NEC, Newark
Services Restorations, shipping

LINLITHGOW

⊞ County Antiques
Contact Mrs Flynn
✉ **30 High Street, Linlithgow, West Lothian, EH49 7AE** P
☎ 01506 671201
Est. 1992 *Stock size* Medium
Stock General antiques, jewellery
Open Mon–Sat 10am–5pm
Fairs Edinburgh
Services Valuations and jewellery repairs

⊞ Heritage Antiques
Contact Ann Davidson
✉ **222 High Street, Linlithgow, West Lothian, EH49 7ES** P
☎ 01506 847460
E anantiques@aol.com
W www.members.aol.com/antiques
Est. 1992 *Stock size* Medium
Stock General antiques
Open Mon–Sat 10.30am–5pm closed Wed
Fairs Ingliston
Services Valuations

CHANNEL ISLANDS

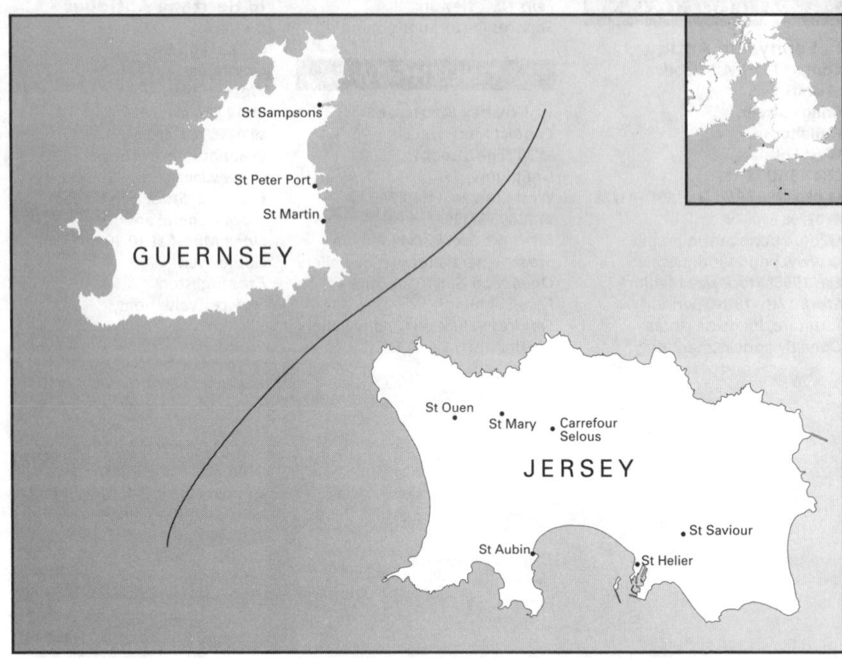

GUERNSEY

ST PETER PORT

Stephen Andrews Gallery
Contact Stephen Andrews
5 College Terrace, The Grange, St Peter Port, Guernsey, GY1 2PX
01481 710380
Est. 1984 *Stock size* Large
Stock Pottery, porcelain, furniture, silver
Open Mon–Sat 9.30am–5pm
Fairs Guernsey Antiques Fair

Antique Newspapers (ESoc)
Contact David Godfrey
PO Box 396, St Peter Port, Guernsey, GY1 3FW
01481 712990 01481 725168
antiquenews@guernsey.net
www.antiquenewspapers.co.uk
Est. 1971 *Stock size* Large
Stock Antiquarian newspapers 1641–1865, naval and military lists
Open Mail order
Services Lists on any subject from 1641–1865

Bonhams & Brooks
Contact Keith Baker or Norman Wilkinson
Allez Street Auction Rooms, St Peter Port, Guernsey, GY1 1NG
01481 722700 01481 723306
guernsey@bonhams.com
Est. 1977
Open Mon–Fri 9am–5pm
Sales General sales every 2 weeks Thurs 2.15pm, viewing previous Tues and Wed 9am–5pm. Sales of selected antiques (Jun Nov)
Frequency Every 2 weeks
Catalogues Yes

Channel Islands Galleries Ltd
Contact Geoffrey Gavey
Trinity Square, St Peter Port, Guernsey, GY1 ILX
01481 723247 01481 714669
geoff.gavey@cigalleries.f9.co.uk
www.cigalleries.f9.co.uk
Est. 1970 *Stock size* Medium
Stock Channel Island antique maps, prints, watercolours, oil paintings, out-of-print books, bank notes, coins
Open Mon–Fri 10am–5pm Sat 10am–1pm
Services Valuations, restorations, conservation

The Collectors Centre
Contact Andrew Rundle
1 Sausmarez Street, St Peter Port, Guernsey, GY1 2PT
01481 725209
Est. 1985 *Stock size* Medium
Stock Antique prints, engravings, old postcards, coins, bank notes, memorabilia, stamps
Open Mon–Sat 10.30am–6pm
Services Valuations for collectables, mail order, postal auctions, free catalogue

W De La Rue Antiques
Contact William de La Rue
29 Mill Street, St Peter Port, Guernsey, GY1 1HG
01481 723177
Est. 1975 *Stock size* Medium
Stock General antiques, collectors' items

Open Mon–Sat 10am–12.30pm 2–4pm closed Thurs pm
Services Valuations, buying

Ann Drury Antiques
Contact Ann Drury
1 Mansell Street, St Peter Port, Guernsey, GY1 1HP
01481 716193
07781 104304
Est. 1969 *Stock size* Large
Stock 18th–20thC furniture, decorative antiques
Open Mon–Sat 10am–noon 2–4pm closed Thurs
Fairs Guernsey Antiques Fair
Services Valuations

Mahogany
Contact Angela Edwards
7 Mansell Street, St Peter Port, Guernsey, GY1 1HP
01481 727574 01481 727574
Est. 1980 *Stock size* Large
Stock General antiques, collectables
Open Mon–Sat 10am–12.30pm 2–5pm half day Thurs
Fairs Guernsey Antiques Fair, Beau Sejours Fair

N St J Paint and Sons Ltd (NAG)
Contact Michael or Paul Paint
26 Le Pollet, St Peter Port, Guernsey, GY1 1WQ
01481 722229 01481 710241
paint@guernsey.net
Est. 1947 *Stock size* Large
Stock General antiques, jewellery, silver, objets d'art
Open Mon–Sat 9am–5.30pm
Services Valuations, restorations and repairs (goldsmiths and silversmiths)

Parasol Antiques
Contact Marianne Barwick
23 Mansell Street, St Peter Port, Guernsey, GY1 1HP P
01481 710780 01481 710780
07781 118715
Est. 1993 *Stock size* Medium
Stock Jewellery, silver, furniture, copper, brass, pictures
Open Mon–Sat 10am–5pm Thurs 10am–1pm
Fairs Guernsey Antiques Fair
Services Valuations, restorations

St James's Gallery Ltd
Contact Mrs C Whittam
Smith Street, St Peter Port, Guernsey, GY1 2JQ P
01481 720070 01481 721132
stjamesantiques@gtonline.net
Est. 1979 *Stock size* Large
Stock Post-1830s furniture, paintings, silver, porcelain
Open Mon–Fri 9.30am–1pm 2–5pm Sat 9.30am–1pm
Fairs Olympia (under the name of Havilland Antiques Ltd)
Services Valuations

ST SAMPSONS

The Old Curiosity Shop
Contact Mrs Stevens-Cox
Commercial Road, St Sampsons, Guernsey, GY2 4QP P
01481 245324
Est. 1978 *Stock size* Medium
Stock General small antiques, collectables, second-hand books
Open Tues Wed Fri Sat 10.30am–4.30pm
Fairs Guernsey Antiques Fair
Services Framing

Pretty Things
Contact Myrtle Domiall
Petites Capelles, St Sampsons, Guernsey, GY2 4GX P
01481 47391 01481 42215
Est. 1984 *Stock size* Large
Stock General antiques and collectables (no furniture)
Open Mon–Sat 9.30am–12.30pm 2.30–5pm closed Thurs

Ray & Scott Ltd (NAG)
Contact M Search
The Bridge, St Sampsons, Guernsey, GY2 4QN P
01481 244610 01481 244610
Est. 1962 *Stock size* Large
Stock Fine jewellery, clocks, silver, second-hand watches
Open Mon–Sat 9am–5pm
Fairs Guernsey Antiques Fair, Beau Sejours Fair
Services Valuations, restoration of jewellery, antique clocks, gold and silversmiths

VALE

Havilland Antiques Ltd (LAPADA)
Contact Mrs C Whittam
Crossways Centre, Braye Road, Vale, Guernsey, GY3 5PH
01481 723999 01481 721132
stjamesantiques@gtonline.net
Est. 1989 *Stock size* Large
Stock Post-1830s furniture, paintings, silver, porcelain
Open By appointment
Fairs Olympia

CARREFOUR SELOUS

David Hick Antiques
Contact David Hick
Alexandra House, Carrefour Selous, St Lawrence, Jersey, JE3 1GL P
01534 865965 01534 865448
hickantiques@cinergy.co.uk
Est. 1974 *Stock size* Large
Stock Furniture, silver, porcelain
Open Wed Fri Sat 9.30am–5pm

JERSEY

ST HELIER

Antiques Warehouse
Contact Tim Morley
Robin Place, St Helier, Jersey, JE2 4LT P
01534 873932 01534 506833
07797 720234
Est. 1988 *Stock size* Large
Stock General antiques
Open Mon–Sat 8am–5.30pm
Fairs Mainly French fairs
Services Restorations, shipping

Bonhams & Brooks
Contact Su Gay
Don Street, St Helier, Jersey, JE2 4TR
01534 722441 01534 759354
jersey@bonhams.com
www.bonhams.com
Est. 1940
Open Mon–Fri 9am–5pm
Sales Antiques and modern sales alternate Wed at 10.30am, viewing previous Mon Tues 9am–5pm. Fine sales May and Nov. Channel Islands interest auction March
Frequency Every 2 weeks
Catalogues Yes

Brown's Times Past Antiques
Contact Mick Brown
28 Burrard Street, St Helier, Jersey, JE2 4WS P
01534 737090 /735264
Est. 1984 *Stock size* Medium
Stock Georgian–Edwardian furniture, ceramics, 19thC pottery and glass

CHANNEL ISLANDS

JERSEY • ST MARY

Open Mon–Sat 9am–5pm or by appointment
Services Valuations

⊞ John Cooper Antiques
Contact John Cooper
✉ **16 Central Market, St Helier, Jersey, JE2 4WL**
☎ 01534 723600
Est. 1982 *Stock size* Medium
Stock General, mostly small items including jewellery
Open Mon–Sat 9am–5.30pm Thurs half day

⊞ David Hick Antiques
Contact David Hick
✉ **45 Halkett Place, St Helier, Jersey, JE2 4WQ** P
☎ 01534 721162 F 01534 721162
E hickantiques@cinergy.co.uk
Est. 1974 *Stock size* Large
Stock Furniture, silver, porcelain
Open Mon–Sat 10am–5pm Thurs 10am–1pm

⊞ Jeremiah's Fine Time Pieces and Antiques (AHA)
Contact Kevin O'Keeffe
✉ **14½ Queen Street, St Helier, Jersey, JE2 4WD**
☎ 01534 723153 F 01534 723153
E jeremiahsjersey@hotmail.com
Est. 1989 *Stock size* Small
Stock Clocks, watches, paintings, objets d'art
Open Mon–Fri 10am–4pm
Fairs USA, Germany
Services Valuations, restorations

⊞ Jersey Coin Company
Contact V or S Dougan
✉ **26 Halkett Street, St Helier, Jersey, JE2 4WJ**
☎ 01534 725743 F 01534 509094
Est. 1965 *Stock size* Medium
Stock Antique coins, bank notes, medals, WWII weapons
Open Mon–Sat 9am–5pm
Services Valuations, jewellery repairs

⊞ Peter Le Vesconte Collectables
Contact Peter Le Vesconte
✉ **62 Stopford Road, St Helier, Jersey, JE2 4LZ** P
☎ 01534 732481 F 01534 732481
E p-l-v-collectables@psilink.co.je
Est. 1981 *Stock size* Large
Stock Dinky and Corgi toys, mint and boxed toys, militaria (especially WWII) new collectors' toys
Open Mon–Sat 10am–3pm closed Thurs
Fairs Jersey Toy and Phone Card Collectors Fair
Services Toy valuations

⊞ Park Antiques
Contact P Cowan
✉ **16 Burrard Street, St Helier, Jersey, JE2 4WF**
☎ 01534 280784 F 01534 618129
E park@igl.net
Est. 1969 *Stock size* Large
Stock English and continental European furniture
Open By appointment only

⊞ A & R Ritchie
Contact A and R Ritchie
✉ **7 Duhamel Place, St Helier, Jersey, JE2 4TP** P
☎ 01534 873805
Est. 1973 *Stock size* Medium
Stock Collectables, brass, china, glass, toys, silver, jewellery, scent bottles, militaria
Open Mon–Sat 10am–5pm
Services Restorations – militaria and ivory

⊞ Robert's Antiques
Contact Robert Michieli
✉ **14 York Street, St Helier, Jersey, JE2 3RQ**
☎ 01534 509071
M 07798 876553
Est. 1979 *Stock size* Medium
Stock English silver, porcelain, jewellery, glass
Open Mon–Sat 9am–5.30pm or by appointment
Services Valuations

⊞ Thomson's Antiques
Contact Ray or Chris Thomson
✉ **44 Don Street, St Helier, Jersey, JE2 4TR** P
☎ 01534 618673
M 07797 735981
Est. 1967 *Stock size* Large
Stock Collectors' items, furniture, clocks, silver
Open Mon–Sat 10am–4pm

⊞ Thomson's Antiques
Contact Ray or Chris Thomson
✉ **60 Kensington Place, St Helier, Jersey, JE2 3PA**
☎ 01534 723673
M 07797 735981
Est. 1967 *Stock size* Large
Stock General antiques, furniture
Open Mon–Sat 10am–6pm

ST MARY

⊞ Country House and Cottage Antiques
Contact Sarah Johnson
✉ **Rue Esboeufs, St Mary, Jersey, JE3 3EQ** P
☎ 01534 862547
Est. 1984 *Stock size* Large
Stock Georgian–Edwardian, oak, pine and mahogany furniture, china, glass, ceramics, silver
Open Mon–Fri 10am–4pm Sat 9am–1pm
Fairs St Mary's Fair
Services Valuations

ST OUEN

⊞ Stephen Cohu Antiques
Contact Stephen Cohu
✉ **The Village Gallery, La Ville de L'Eglise, St Ouen, Jersey, JE3 2LR** P
☎ 01534 485177
M 07797 723895
Est. 1993 *Stock size* Large
Stock General antiques
Open In season Tues Thurs–Sat 10am–5pm Aug Sat Jan–Mar by appointment only
Fairs Newark, NEC
Services Valuations, restorations

ST SAVIOUR

⊞ Pine for Pine Antiques
Contact Mrs Brenda Clyde Smith
✉ **Chateau Clairval, St Saviour, Jersey, JE2 7HN** P
☎ 01534 737173/724748 F 01534 618384
Est. 1974 *Stock size* Medium
Stock Georgian–Edwardian pine furniture
Open Mon–Fri 10am–4pm Sat 10am–2pm

NORTHERN IRELAND

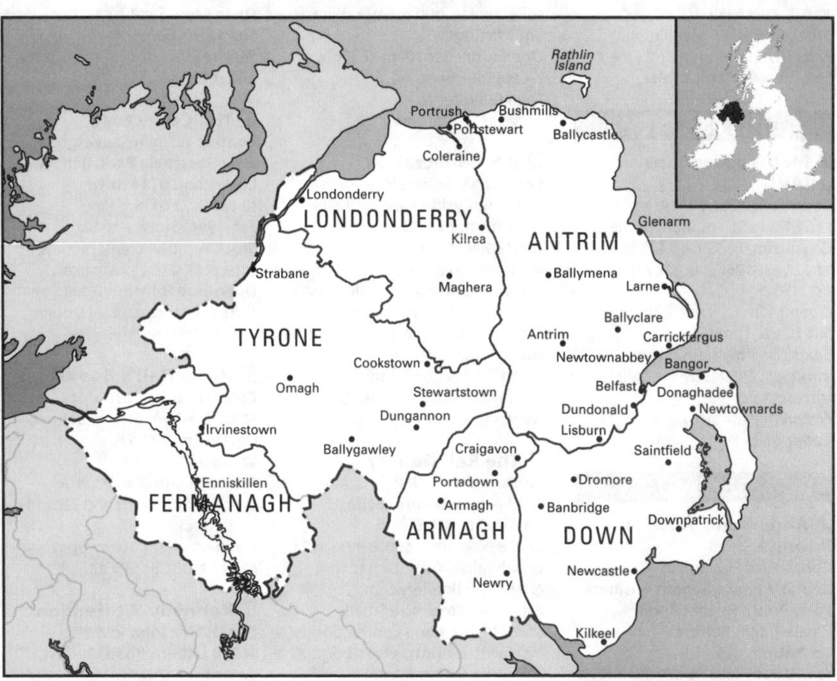

CO ANTRIM

AHOGHILL

⊞ Once Upon a Time Antiques
Contact Sean or Ronan McLaughlin
✉ **13 Church Street, Ahoghill, Co Antrim, BT42 2PA** 🅿
☎ 028 2587 1244 🅕 028 2565 6666
Est. 1973 *Stock size* Large
Stock Jewellery, furniture, general antiques
Open Mon–Sat 10am–6pm
Services Valuations, restorations

ANTRIM

⊞ Country Antiques (LAPADA)
Contact David Wolfenden
✉ **219 Lisnevenagh Road, Antrim, Co Antrim, BT41 2JT** 🅿
☎ 028 9442 9498 🅕 028 9442 9498
Ⓜ 07768 128800
🅔 antiquewolfirl@aol.com
Ⓦ www.country-antiques-wolfenden.co.uk
Est. 1984 *Stock size* Large
Stock Furniture, jewellery, general antiques
Open Mon–Sat 10am–6pm
Services Valuations, restorations

⊞ Village Antiques
Contact Mr W J Baird
✉ **99 Main Street, Randalstown, Antrim, Co Antrim, BT41 3BB** 🅿
☎ 028 9447 8686
Ⓜ 07703 594522
Est. 1998 *Stock size* Medium
Stock General antiques, furniture
Open Mon–Sat 10am–6pm
Services Restorations and clock repairs

BALLINDERRY

⊞ Ballinderry Antiques
Contact Mr W Mills
✉ **2 Ballinderry Road, Ballinderry, Upper Lisburn, Co Antrim, BT28 2EP** 🅿
☎ 028 9265 1046 🅕 028 9265 1580
Est. 1959 *Stock size* Large
Stock Antique furniture, silver
Open Mon–Sat 10am–5.30pm
Thurs 10am–9pm
Fairs Newark
Services Valuations

BALLYCASTLE

P J McIlroy & Son
Contact Mr Sean McIlroy FNAEA
✉ **11 Ann Street, Ballycastle, Co Antrim, BT54 6AA** 🅿
☎ 028 2076 2353 🅕 028 2076 2126
🅔 leo@pjmcilroy.freeserve.co.uk
Est. 1967
Open Mon–Fri 9am–5.30pm
Sat 9am–12.30pm
Sales General antiques, paintings
Frequency Monthly
Catalogues Yes

BALLYMENA

⊞ Angela's Antiques
Contact Angela McClelland
✉ **75 Wellington Street, Ballymena, Co Antrim, BT43 6AD**
☎ 028 2564 1999
Est. 1993 *Stock size* Large
Stock Porcelain, jewellery, furniture, general antiques
Open Mon–Sat 9.30am–5pm

⊞ Lorraine's Antiques
Contact Ms Lorraine Wylie
✉ **84 Galgorm Road, Ballymena, Co Antrim, BT42 1AA** 🅿

☎ 028 2564 5359
Stock Porcelain, jewellery
Fairs Ulster Antique and Fine Art Fair, Temple Patrick (Mar)

BALLYMONEY

McAfee Auctions (NIAVI)
Contact Mr Gerry McAfee
✉ **51 Main Street, Ballymoney, Co Antrim, BT53 6AN** P
☎ 028 2766 7676 F 028 2766 7666
Est. 1992
Open Mon–Fri 9am–5.30pm Sat 10am–1pm
Sales Monthly sales of general antiques. Quarterly specialist Irish art sales
Frequency Monthly
Catalogues Yes

BELFAST

Anderson's Auction Rooms
Contact Mr Flanaghan
✉ **Unit 7 Prince Regent Business Park, Prince Regent Road, Castlereagh, Belfast, Co Antrim, BT5 6QR**
☎ 028 9040 1888 F 028 9040 1177
Est. 1979
Open Mon–Thur 9am–5pm Fri 9am–4pm late viewing Tues until 8pm
Sales Antiques and general every Wednesday, specialized fine art and antiques sales 3 times per annum
Frequency Every Wed
Catalogues No

Antiquarian
Contact Mr Eric Lauro
✉ **67 Royal Avenue, Belfast, Co Antrim, BT1 1FE** P
☎ 028 9032 7301
Stock Guns, swords, wartime memorabilia, watches, clocks, stamps, coins
Open Mon–Sat 9am–5.30pm Thurs 10am–9pm
Services Valuations, repairs

Archives Antique Centre
Contact Mr Laurence Johnston
✉ **88 Donegal Pass, Belfast, Co Antrim, BT7 1BX** P
☎ 028 9023 2383
M 07889 104719
Est. 1989 *Stock size* Large
Stock General antiques and collectables, pub memorabilia, light fittings
Open Mon–Sat 10am–5.30pm or by appointment
Fairs Culloden
Services Valuations

B B Collectables
Contact Mr Robert Holden
✉ **17 Sunnyside Park, Belfast, Co Antrim, BT7 3DT**
☎ 028 9087 8133
E bbcollectables@yahoo.com
W www.holden.free-online.co.uk
Est. 1993 *Stock size* Medium
Stock General antique furniture, collectables, curios
Open Trades only at fairs
Fairs Mary Magdalen Hall, Newman House

The Bell Gallery
Contact Nelson Bell
✉ **13 Adelaide Park, Belfast, Co Antrim, BT9 6FX** P
☎ 028 9066 2998 F 028 9038 1524
E bellgallery@btinternet.com
W www.bellgallery.com
Est. 1964 *Stock size* Small
Stock Irish art and contemporary Irish artists, prints, silver, bog oak jewellery, Irish books
Services Valuations

Bloomfield Auctions
Contact Mr George Gribben
✉ **288 Deersbridge Road, Belfast, Co Antrim, BT5 1DX** P
☎ 028 9045 6404 F 028 9045 6404
Est. 1991
Open Mon–Fri 10am–5pm
Sales Antiques, fine art
Frequency Every Tues at 6.30pm
Catalogues No

Bookfinders
Contact Miss Mary Denver
✉ **47 University Road, Belfast, Co Antrim, BT7 1ND**
☎ 028 9032 8269
Est. 1985 *Stock size* Large
Stock Antiquarian, rare and second-hand books
Open Mon–Sat 10am–5.30pm
Services Book search

Cellar Antiques
Contact Jonathan Megaw
✉ **Belfast Castle, Antrim Road, Belfast, Co Antrim, BT15 5GR** P
☎ 028 9077 6925 ext 31
Est. 1984 *Stock size* Medium
Stock Jewellery, general antiques, collectables
Open Mon–Sat 12.30–10pm Sun 12.30–5pm
Services Valuations, restorations and repairs

The Collector
Contact William Seawright
✉ **42 Rosscoole Park, Belfast, Co Antrim, BT14 8JX**
☎ 028 9071 0115
Est. 1964 *Stock size* Large
Stock Antique coins, medals, cigarette cards, postcards
Open Trades through fairs only
Fairs All major fairs in Dublin and Belfast

Harry Hall's Bookshop
Contact Mr Bernard Hope
✉ **39 Gresham Street, Belfast, Co Antrim, BT1 1JL**
☎ 028 9024 1923
Est. 1970 *Stock size* Large
Stock Antiquarian and second-hand books
Open Mon–Sat 10am–5pm
Fairs Belfast Book Fair

Kennedy Wolfenden
Contact Mr John Irwin
✉ **218 Lisburn Road, Belfast, Co Antrim, BT9 6GD** P
☎ 028 9038 1775 F 028 9038 1147
M 07831 453038
E eleanorwolfenden@hotmail.com
W www.antiquesni.co.uk or www.kwauctionsni.co.uk
Est. 1974 *Stock size* Large
Stock Antique furniture, porcelain, jewellery, silver, paintings
Open Mon–Sat 9am–5.30pm
Services Valuations

Morgan's Auctions
Contact Mr Haliday or Mr Morgan
✉ **6 Duncrue Crescent, Duncrue Road, Belfast, Co Antrim, BT3 9BW** P
☎ 028 9077 1552 F 028 9077 4503
Est. 1985
Open Mon 9am–6pm Tues–Fri 9am–5pm
Sales General and antiques
Frequency Every Tues 11am
Catalogues No

Oakland Antiques
Contact Donald McCluskey
✉ **135–137 Donegal Pass, Belfast, Co Antrim, BT7 1DS** P
☎ 028 9023 0176 F 028 9024 8144
M 07831 176438

e sales@oaklandnl.com
w www.oaklandnl.com
Est. 1975 *Stock size* Large
Stock Georgian–Edwardian furniture, silver, clocks, glass, bronze, spelter, marble, English and Oriental porcelain, oil paintings, watercolours, longcase clocks
Open Mon–Sat 10am–5.30pm
Fairs Ulster Antique and Fine Art Fair
Services Deliveries to anywhere in Northern Ireland

Past & Present
Contact Trevor or Frances McNally
58–60 Donegal Pass, Belfast, Co Antrim, BT7 1BU P
☎ 028 9033 3137 f 028 9033 3137
Est. 1985 *Stock size* Medium
Stock Victorian–Edwardian furniture, collectables
Open Mon–Sat 10.30am–5pm

Phoenix Gallery
Contact Vivienne Jackson
82 Donegal Pass, Belfast, Co Antrim, BT7 1BX P
☎ 028 9023 8246
Est. 2000 *Stock size* Large
Stock General antiques, art
Open Mon–Sat 10am–5pm

John Ross & Company (NIAVI)
Contact Mr Daniel Clarke
37 Montgomery Street, Belfast, Co Antrim, BT1 4NX P
☎ 028 9032 5448 f 028 9033 3642
Est. 1919
Open Mon–Fri 9am–5pm late viewing Wed
Sales Quarterly sales of Irish paintings, monthly sales of antiques, weekly general sales
Frequency Weekly
Catalogues Yes

P & B Rowan (IADA)
Contact Peter or Briad Rowan
Carleton House, 92 Malone Road, Belfast, Co Antrim, BT9 5HP P
☎ 028 9066 6448 f 028 9066 3725
e peter@pbrowan.thegap.com
Est. 1973 *Stock size* Large
Stock Antiquarian books
Open By appointment
Fairs Irish Antiques Dealers Fair, PBFA (May/Jun)
Services Valuations

Stormont Antiques
Contact Mrs Ann McMurray
2a Sandown Road, Upper Newtownards Road, Belfast, Co Antrim, BT5 6GY P
☎ 028 9047 2586
Est. 1979 *Stock size* Large
Stock Jewellery, silver
Open Mon–Fri 11.30am–5pm Sat 11.30am–4pm
Services Valuations, restorations

Terrace Antiques
Contact Peter or Anne Houston
441a Lisburn Road, Belfast, Co Antrim, BT9 7EY P
☎ 028 9066 3943
Est. 1985 *Stock size* Medium
Stock Jewellery, small furniture, linens, general antiques
Open Tues–Sat 10.30am–5pm
Fairs Ulster Antique and Fine Art Fair
Services Jewellery repairs, valuations, house clearance

The Wake Table
Contact Mr P Rosenberg
40 Donegal Pass, Belfast, Co Antrim, BT7 1BS
028 9032 2147
Est. 1996 *Stock size* Medium
Stock General antiques
Open Mon–Sat 9am–5pm
Fairs Ulster Antique and Fine Art Fair

BUSHMILLS

Brian R Bolt Antiques (IADA)
Contact Brian or Helen Bolt
88 Ballaghmore Road, Portballintrae, Bushmills, Co Antrim, BT57 8RL
028 2073 1129 028 2073 1129
07712 579802
brianbolt@antiques88.freeserve.co.uk
Est. 1979 *Stock size* Medium
Stock Antique and 20thC silver and objects of virtue, decorative arts, antique and 20thC glass, treen, general small items
Open Tues–Sat 11am–5.30pm or by appointment
Services Valuations, search, worldwide postal service

Causeway Books
Contact Mr D Speers
110 Main Street, Bushmills, Co Antrim, BT57 8QD
028 2073 2596
Est. 1989 *Stock size* Medium
Stock General antiquarian books
Open Mon–Sat 10am–5.30pm

Dunluce Antiques and Crafts
Contact Ms Clare Ross
33 Ballytober Road, Bushmills, Co Antrim, BT57 8UU
028 207 31140
Est. 1978 *Stock size* Small
Stock General antiques
Open Mon–Thurs 10am–6pm Sat 2–6pm
Services Valuations and porcelain restoration

CARRICKFERGUS

Robert Christie Antiques (IADA)
Contact Robert Christie
The Courtyard, 38 Scotch Quarter, Carrickfergus, Co Antrim, BT38 7DP
028 9336 1333 028 9334 1149
07802 968846
Est. 1976 *Stock size* Medium
Stock 18th–19thC furniture, clocks, silver and plate, pottery, porcelain
Open Tue–Sat 11am–5pm or by appointment
Fairs Northern Ireland Antiques Fair, Ulster Antique and Fine Art Fair
Services Valuations

Lennox Auctions and Valuers
Contact Mr A Lennox
The Basement, 41b Ellis Street, Carrickfergus, Co Antrim, BT38 8AY
028 9335 1522/028 9337 8527 (pm)
028 9335 1522
Est. 1987
Open Mon–Fri 9.30am–5pm Sat 9.30am–1pm
Sales Weekly sales Thurs 7pm, viewing all day Thurs. Telephone for details. Also total house clearance sales
Frequency Weekly
Catalogues No

CARRYDUFF

Carryduff Group Ltd
Contact Mr Robert Jenkins
10 Comber Road, Carryduff, Co Antrim, BT8 8AM
028 9081 3775 028 9081 4518
Est. 1996
Open Mon–Fri 9am–6pm
Sales General antiques
Frequency Monthly
Catalogues Yes

GLARRYFORD

Antique Builders Suppliers
Contact Mr Hastings White
94 Duneoin Road, Drumminning, Glarryford, Co Antrim, BT44 9HH
028 2568 5444
07860 675908
sales@whites-architecturalsalvage.com
www.whites-architecturalsalvage.com
Est. 1983 *Stock size* Large
Stock Architectural salvage, Bangor blue slates, beams, tiles, stained glass windows, chimney pots, weathervanes, hardwood flooring, baths, etc
Open Mon–Sat 7am–11pm
Services Delivery

GLENGORMLEY

Acorns
Contact Mr P McComb
4 Portland Avenue, Glengormley, Co Antrim, BT36 5EY
028 9080 4100
Est. 1999 *Stock size* Medium
Stock Furniture, general antiques
Open Mon–Sat 9.30am–5.30pm
Services Local delivery

KELLS

Cottage Antiques
Contact Rachael Hiles
25 Greenfield Road, Kells, Co Antrim, BT42 3JL
028 2589 2169
07808 161052
Est. 1969 *Stock size* Large
Stock General antiques
Open Fri–Sat 1–5.30pm

LARNE

Bric-A-Brac
Contact Mr J McIlwaine
4 Riverdale, Larne, Co Antrim, BT40 1LB
028 2827 5657
Est. 1974 *Stock size* Large
Stock General antiques including clocks, furniture, oil lamps, jewellery, paintings
Open Mon–Sat 9am–5.30pm Tues 9am–2pm

Cobwebs
Contact Mrs D Knox
94c Agnew Street, Larne, Co Antrim, BT40 1RE
028 2826 7127
Stock General antiques, clocks, antique fireplaces, antique pine
Open Wed–Sat 11.00am–4.30pm

Colin Wilkinson and Co (IRRV)
Contact Mr Colin Wilkinson
The Auction Mart, 7 Point Street, Larne, Co Antrim, BT40 1HY
028 2826 0037 028 2826 0497
Est. 1900
Open Mon–Fri 9.30am–5pm

Sales General antiques, paintings, silver, porcelain
Frequency Monthly
Catalogues Yes

LISBURN

⊞ Trevor Falconer Antiques
Contact Trevor Falconer
✉ **51 Bridge Street, Lisburn, Co Antrim, BT28 1BZ** 🅿
☎ 028 9260 5879
Est. 1984 *Stock size* Medium
Stock Antique country furniture, militaria, clocks, Irish pine
Open Mon–Sat 10am–5pm
Services Restorations and pine stripping

⊞ Jiri Books
Contact Jim and Rita Swindall
✉ **11 Mill Road, Lisburn, Co Antrim, BT27 5TT** 🅿
☎ 028 9082 6443 Ⓕ 028 9082 6443
Ⓔ jiri.books@dnet.co.uk
Est. 1978 *Stock size* Medium
Stock Largely Irish interest, second-hand and antiquarian books
Open By appointment only
Fairs Organizes Annual Belfast Second-hand and Antiquarian Bookfair (part of the Belfast Festival)
Services Book searches

⊞ Parvis (IADA)
Contact Parvis or Meriel Sigaroudinia
✉ **Mountain View House, 40 Sandy Lane, Ballyskeagh, Lisburn, Co Antrim, BT27 5TL** 🅿
☎ 028 9062 1824 Ⓕ 028 9062 3311
Ⓜ 07801 347358
Ⓔ parvissig@aol.com
Ⓔ info@parvis.co.uk
Ⓦ www.parvis.co.uk
Est. 1973 *Stock size* Large
Stock Oriental and European carpets, rugs, tapestries, bronze sculptures, upholstered furniture, lamps
Open By appointment at any time
Fairs IADA Exhibition, Northern Ireland Antiques Fair
Services Valuations, restorations, consultancy, own exhibitions

Temple Auctions Ltd
Contact Mr Robin Graham
✉ **133 Carryduff Road, Temple, Lisburn, Co Antrim, BT27 6YL** 🅿
☎ 028 9263 8777 Ⓕ 028 9263 8640
Est. 1981
Open Mon–Fri 9am–5.30 pm or by appointment
Sales General antiques, jewellery, paintings
Frequency Every 3 weeks
Catalogues No

⊞ Van-Lyn Antiques
Contact V or W Hastings
✉ **300 Comber Road, Lisburn, Co Antrim, BT27 6TA** 🅿
☎ 028 9263 8358
Ⓜ 07899 935990
Est. 1979 *Stock size* Medium
Stock General, antique furniture, porcelain, brass, glass, books
Open Mon–Sat 9am–9pm

NEWTOWNABBEY

⊞ MacHenry Antiques (IADA)
Contact Rupert or Anne MacHenry
✉ **1–7 Glen Road, Jordanstown, Newtownabbey, Co Antrim, BT37 0RY** 🅿
☎ 028 9086 2036 Ⓕ 028 9085 3281
Ⓜ 07831 135226
Ⓔ rupertmachenry@ukgateway.net
Est. 1964 *Stock size* Medium
Stock 18th–19thC furniture, paintings
Open Mon–Sat 2–7pm or by appointment
Fairs Ulster Antique and Fine Art Fair
Services Valuation for insurance, probate and family division, restoration

Wilson's Auctions (NAVA, IAVI)
Contact Mr Richard Bell
✉ **22 Mallusk Road, Newtownabbey, Co Antrim, BT36 8PP** 🅿
☎ 028 9034 2626 Ⓕ 028 9034 2528
Ⓔ richardbell@wilsonsauctions.com
Ⓦ www.wilsonsauctions.com
Est. 1964
Open Mon–Fri 9am–6pm, viewing Sun noon–5pm
Sales Monthly sales on the last Mon of month at 7pm, also quarterly sales of Irish art. Other specialist sales throughout the year
Frequency Monthly
Catalogues Yes

PORTRUSH

⊞ Alexander Antiques
Contact Mr David Alexander
✉ **108 Dunluce Road, Portrush, Co Antrim, BT56 8NB** 🅿
☎ 028 7082 2783 Ⓕ 028 7082 2364
Ⓔ alexanderantique@aol.com
Est. 1973 *Stock size* Large
Stock Georgian–Edwardian furniture
Open Mon–Sat 10am–6pm
Services Valuations, restorations

⊞ Atlantic Antiques
Contact Mr Samuel Dickie
✉ **22 Portstewart Road, Portrush, Co, Antrim, BT56 8EQ**
☎ 028 7082 5988
Est. 1997 *Stock size* Medium
Stock General antiques
Open Mon–Sat 11am–6pm Sun 2–6pm

⊞ Kennedy Wolfenden
Contact Miss Eleanor Wolfenden
✉ **86 Main Street, Portrush, Co Antrim, BT56 8BN**
☎ 028 7082 2995 Ⓕ 028 7082 5587
Ⓜ 07831 453038
Ⓔ eleanorwolfenden@hotmail.com
Ⓦ www.kwauctionsni.co.uk
Est. 1974 *Stock size* Large
Stock Antique furniture, porcelain, jewellery, silver and paintings
Open Mon–Sat 11am–5.30pm Jul–Aug later
Services Valuations

CO ARMAGH

ARMAGH

⊞ Craobh Rua Rare Book (PBFA)
Contact Mr James Vallely
✉ **12 Woodford Gardens, Armagh, Co Armagh, BT60 2AZ**
☎ 028 3752 6938
Ⓔ Craobh@btinternet.com
Est. 1990 *Stock size* Medium
Stock Books, prints, selection of newspaper prints relating to 19thC Ireland
Open By appointment only
Fairs National Book Fair, Dublin
Services Catalogue, mail order

LOUGHALL

⊞ Heritage Antiques
Contact Ms Heather Teggart

✉ **Dispensary House, 88 Main Street, Loughall, Co Armagh, BT61 8HZ** 🅿
☎ 028 3889 1314
Ⓜ 07710 38557
Est. 1981 *Stock size* Small
Stock Clocks, small furniture
Open Tues–Fri 2–5pm Sat 11am–5.30pm
Services Clock and barometer repairs

MOIRA

⊞ Four Winds Antiques
Contact Mr John Cairns
✉ **66a Main Street, Moira, Co Armagh, BT67 0LQ** 🅿
☎ 028 9261 2226
Ⓜ 07768 292369 (John)/07713 081748 (Tina)
Est. 1994 *Stock size* Large
Stock Georgian–Edwardian furniture, porcelain, longcase and bracket clocks
Open Mon–Sat 10am–5.30pm or by appointment

⊞ Moyrah Antiques
Contact Mrs Dorothy Smith
✉ **98 Main Street, Moira, Craigavon, Co Armagh, BT67 0LH**
☎ 028 9261 1272
Ⓜ 07710 611037
Est. 1987 *Stock size* Medium
Stock General antiques, porcelain, jewellery
Open Mon–Sat 10.30am–5.30pm

PORTADOWN

Wilson's Auctions Ltd (Portadown) (NAVA, IAVI)
Contact Michael Tomalin
✉ **65 Seagoe Industrial Estate, Portadown, Craigavon, Co Armagh, T63 5QE** 🅿
☎ 028 3833 6433 Ⓕ 028 3833 6618
Ⓔ mtomalin@virgin.net
Ⓦ www.wilsons-auctions.com
Est. 1964
Open Mon–Fri 9am–6pm and on auction nights
Sales Antiques, fine art and disposal auctions Wed 7pm. Advisable to phone ahead for sale details
Frequency Telephone for details
Catalogues Yes

CO DOWN

BALLYNAHINCH

⊞ Davidson Books
Contact Mr Arthur Davidson
✉ **34 Broomhill Road, Spa, Ballynahinch, Co Down, BT24 8QD** 🅿
☎ 028 9756 2502 Ⓕ 028 9756 2502
Est. 1959 *Stock size* Large
Stock Antiquarian books, especially Irish
Open By appointment only
Fairs Annual Belfast Second-hand and Antiquarian Bookfair, De Burca fair
Services Valuations

⊞ The French Warehouse
Contact Heather Cowdy
✉ **72 Dunmore Road, Spa, Ballynahinch, Co Down, BT24 8PR** 🅿
☎ 02897 561774
Ⓔ frenchwarehouse@nireland.com
Ⓦ www.french-warehouse.com
Est. 1988 *Stock size* Large
Stock Antique French beds, 19thC French furniture
Open By appointment
Services Shipping

BANGOR

⊞ Pages Bookshop
Contact Mr Harry Hichens
✉ **12 High Street, Bangor, Co Down, BT20 5AY** 🅿
☎ 028 9145 3061
Est. 1979 *Stock size* Large
Stock Rare antiquarian books
Open Mon–Sat 10am–5.30pm
Services Book search

⊞ Todd Antiques
Contact Mrs E Heyes
✉ **30 Gray's Hill, Bangor, Co Down, BB3 0HB** 🅿
☎ 028 9145 5850
Est. 1988 *Stock size* Medium
Stock Silver jewellery, clocks, small furniture items
Open Tues–Sat 9.30am–4.30pm closed Thurs
Services Clock and jewellery repairs

COMBER

⊞ Bobby Douglas
Contact Mr Bobby Douglas
✉ **31 Ballykeigle Road, Comber, Co Down, BT23 5SD** 🅿
☎ 028 9752 8351
Est. 1964 *Stock size* Medium
Stock Irish Georgian furniture (pre-1837)
Open Any time by appointment
Services Valuations

⊞ Reflections
Contact Mr Nick Williams
✉ **9 Killinchy Street, Comber, Co Down, BT23 5AP** 🅿
☎ 028 9187 0809
Ⓜ 07748 948325
Est. 1994 *Stock size* Small
Stock 19thC country furniture, decorative items, clocks
Open Mon–Sat 10am–5pm
Services Restoration and French polishing

DONAGHADEE

⊞ Antiquarian Booksellers
Contact M C McAlister
✉ **Prospect House, 4 Millisle Road, Donaghadee, Co Down, BT21 0HY** 🅿
☎ 028 9188 2990 Ⓕ 028 9188 2990
Ⓔ rarebooks@phb.dnet.co.uk
Ⓦ www.booksulster.com
Est. 1981 *Stock size* Medium
Stock Antiquarian and out-of-print books, Ireland, travel, fine buildings and natural history specialities
Open Strictly by appointment only
Fairs Wellington Park (Nov)

⊞ Ferran's Antiques
Contact Justin or Vivien Ferran
✉ **2 Meetinghouse Street, Donaghadee, Co Down, BT21 0HJ** 🅿
☎ 028 9188 2642
Ⓜ 07711 085563
Est. 1988 *Stock size* Medium
Stock 18th–19thC furniture
Open By appointment only
Fairs Culloden Antique Fair, Northern Ireland
Services Restorations

DUNDONALD

⊞ Stacks Bookshop
Contact Mr Jim Tollerton
✉ **67 Comber Road, Dundonald, Co Down, BT16 0AE** 🅿
☎ 028 9048 6880
Est. 1992 *Stock size* Medium
Stock Antiquarian Irish, religious, military and poetry books

Open Mon–Sat 10am–6pm
Fairs Annual Belfast Second-hand and Antiquarian Bookfair

GREY ABBEY

Archway Antiques
Contact Mrs Boo Hughes
Hoops Courtyard, Main Street, Grey Abbey, Newtownards, Co Down, BT22 2NE
☎ 028 4278 8889
Ⓜ 07703 330900
Est. 1989 *Stock size* Large
Stock 18th–19thC porcelain, 19thC glass, jewellery, furniture, silver, kitchenware, linen, pictures
Open Wed Fri Sat 11am–5pm or by appointment
Fairs Ulster Antique and Fine Art Fair, Culloden
Services Valuations, house clearance

Phyllis Arnold Antiques
Contact Ms Phyllis Arnold
Hoops Courtyard, Grey Abbey, Newtownards, Co Down, BT22 2NE
☎ 028 4278 8199 Ⓕ 028 9185 3322
Est. 1973 *Stock size* Medium
Stock Maps, prints, furniture, silver, general
Open Wed Fri Sat 11am–5pm
Services Framing, conservation

Old Forge Collectables
Contact David or Christine Eynon
5 Main Street, Grey Abbey, Co Down, BT22 2NE
☎ 028 9181 0422 Ⓕ 028 9181 0422
Ⓜ 0780 860 5644
Ⓔ info@oldforge.downtownfm.com
Ⓦ www.oldforgecollectables.co.uk
Est. 1989 *Stock size* Medium
Stock Very comprehensive selection of discontinued porcelain and china
Open Tues–Fri 1–5pm
Sat 11am–5pm
Mon by appointment

Ann Shaw Antiques
Contact Ann Shaw
Hoops Courtyard, 79 Main Street, Grey Abbey, Newtownards, Co Down, BT22 2NE
☎ 028 9066 0975
Est. 1972 *Stock size* Medium
Stock Jewellery, silver, furniture, general
Open Wed Fri Sat 11am–5pm
Fairs Olympia, Grosvenor House
Services Upholstery

HILLSBOROUGH

Bowers' Auctioneers
Contact Mr Bowers
1 Dromore Road, Hillsborough, Co Down, BT26 6HS
☎ 028 9268 3840 Ⓕ 028 9268 9528
Ⓔ billy@bowersantiques.co.uk
Est. 1987
Open Mon–Fri 9am–5pm
Sales Antique furniture, fine art, house sales
Frequency Quarterly
Catalogues Yes

HOLYWOOD

Jacquart Antiques
Contact Mr Dan Uprichard
10–12 Hibernia Street, Holywood, Co Down, BT18 9JE
☎ 028 9042 6642 Ⓕ 028 9752 1109
Ⓜ 07831 548803
Ⓔ jacquart@nireland.com
Ⓦ www.jacquart.co.uk
Est. 1992 *Stock size* Large
Stock Imported French antiques, mainly 19th century furniture (walnut, oak), mirrors, rare items
Open Mon–Sat 10am–5.30pm or by appointment
Fairs Ulster Antique and Fine Art Fair
Services Interior-design item search

KILLYLEAGH

Tout Le Monde
Contact Mr Tony Forsyth
12–14 Shore Street, Killyleagh, Co Down, BT30 9QJ
☎ 028 4482 8509 Ⓕ 028 4482 8509
Ⓔ aforsyth@mac.com
Ⓦ wwwtoutlemonde.co.uk
Est. 1998 *Stock size* Medium
Stock Old country furniture, French, Chinese, Irish antiques
Open Mon–Sat 9am–5pm or by appointment

NEWRY

Cornmarket Curios
Contact Rory and Patricia Byrne
21 Cornmarket, Newry, Co Down, BT35 8BG
☎ 028 3026 5958
Est. 1978 *Stock size* Large
Stock General antiques, antiquarian and second-hand books
Open Thurs 11am–8pm
Fri–Sat 11am–5pm

NEWTOWNARDS

Ballyalton House Architectural Antiques (SALVO)
Contact Leonard Cave
Ballyalton House, 39 Ballyrainey Road, Newtownards, Co Down, BT23 5AD
☎ 028 9181 3235 Ⓕ 028 9181 3235
Ⓔ andrew@ballyalton.freeserve.co.uk
Ⓦ www.ballyalton.freeserve.co.uk
Est. 1993 *Stock size* Large
Stock General architectural antiques, largest stock of bathrooms in Ireland. Newly quarried stone, granite
Open Mon–Sat 8am–6pm

Bangor Public Auctions
Contact Mr G Holden-Downes
11 Greenway Industrial Estate, Conlig, Newtownards, Co Down, BT23 7SU
☎ 028 9145 0494 Ⓕ 028 9127 5993
Ⓦ www.irishantiquesonline.com
Est. 1991
Open Mon Tues Fri 9am–5pm
Sales General antiques sales every Thurs 6pm
Frequency Weekly
Catalogues No

Castle Antiques
Contact Peter Moore
6 Regency Manor, Newtownards, Co Down, BT23 8ZD
☎ 028 9181 5710
Ⓜ 07113 451440
Ⓔ info@castleantiques.co.uk
Ⓦ www.castleantiques.co.uk
Est. 1989 *Stock size* Medium
Stock Collectables, clocks
Open By appointment

PORTAFERRY

Time & Tide Antiques (IADA, MAPH)
Contact Mr David Dunlop
Rock Angus House, 2 Ferry Street, Portaferry, Co Down, BT22 1PB
☎ 028 4272 8935 Ⓕ 028 4272 9825
Est. 1990 *Stock size* Large
Stock Clocks, barometers,

nautical items, marine instruments, fine small furniture
Open Wed Fri Sat noon–5.30pm or by appointment
Fairs Ulster Antique and Fine Art Fair
Services Restorations

SAINTFIELD

Agar Antiques
Contact Ms Rosie Agar
92 Main Street, Saintfield, Co Down, BT24 7AD
028 9751 1214
Est. 1991 *Stock size* Medium
Stock Victorian furniture, ceramics, jewellery, Oriental antiques, Delftware, lighting
Open Mon–Sat 11am–5pm
Services Valuations

Antiques at the Stile
Contact Mr Graham Hancock
52 Main Street, Saintfield, Co Down, BT24 7AB
028 9751 0844
07831 587078
Est. 1989 *Stock size* Large
Stock Georgian–Edwardian furniture, clocks, porcelain
Open Tues–Sat 10am–5.30pm or by appointment
Services Valuations

Ashley Pine
Contact Ms Trudy Martin
88 Main Street, Saintfield, Co Down, BT24 7AB
028 9751 1855 Fax 028 9751 1855
trudy@ashleypine.totalserve.co.uk
www.ceenet.co.uk/ashleypine
Est. 1995 *Stock size* Medium
Stock General antiques, furniture, kitchens built using salvaged materials
Open Mon 12.30–5pm Tues–Fri 10.30am–5pm Sat 10am–5.30pm
Fairs International Antique and Collectables Fair at RAF Swinderby

Attic Antiques
Contact Mr Reuben Doyle
90 Main Street, Saintfield, Co Down, BT24 7AB
028 9751 1057
07803 169799
Est. 1980 *Stock size* Large
Stock General antiques, jewellery, bric-a-brac, large selection of stripped pine
Open Mon–Fri 10am–5pm Sat 10am–5.30pm
Fairs International Antique and Collectables Fair at RAF Swinderby Stafford
Services Export worldwide, house clearance

Attic Pine
Contact Mr Reuben Doyle
90a Main Street, Saintfield, Co Down, BT24 7AB
028 9751 1057
Est. 1996
Stock Irish and Continental pine, reclaimed furniture
Open Mon–Sat 10am–5pm
Services Stripping

Peter Francis Antiques
Contact Mr Peter Francis
92 Main Street, Saintfield, Co Down, BT24 7AD
028 9751 1214
Est. 1997 *Stock size* Small
Stock Irish and English ceramics and glass, Oriental, miscellaneous
Open Mon–Sat 11am–5pm
Services Valuations

Saintfield Antiques & Fine Books
Contact Mr Joseph Leckey
68 Main Street, Saintfield, Co Down, BT24 7AB
028 9752 8428 Fax 028 9752 8428
home@antiquesireland.com
www.antiquesireland.com
Est. 1982 *Stock size* Large
Stock Porcelain 1750–1850, silver (especially Georgian), British and European glass, antiquarian books
Open Thurs–Sat 11.30am–5pm or by appointment
Fairs All fairs organized by L&M Fairs Ltd
Services Book search

SEAPATRICK

Mill Court Antiques
Contact Ms Gillian Close
99 Lurgan Road, Seapatrick, Banbridge, Co Down, BT32 4NE
028 4066 2909
gillian@drumbanagher.freeserve.co.uk
Est. 1979 *Stock size* Medium
Stock Furniture, ceramics, collectables, jewellery
Open By appointment only 11.30am–5.30pm closed Thurs
Services Valuations, restorations

CO FERMANAGH

BALLINAMALLARD

Ballindullagh Barn
Contact Mr Roy Armstrong
Ballindullagh, Ballinamallard, Co Fermanagh, BT94 2NY
028 6862 1802
Est. 1988 *Stock size* Large
Stock Pine country furniture
Open Mon–Sat 8am–6pm
Services Valuations, restorations

ENNISKILLEN

Cloughcor House Antiques
Contact Mr Ian Black
22 Shore Road, Enniskillen, Co Fermanagh, BT74 7EF
028 6632 4805 Fax 028 6632 8828
07774 758827
Est. 1964 *Stock size* Large
Stock Victorian–Edwardian furniture, continental European pine, small silver wares
Open Mon–Sat 9.30am–5.30pm
Services Valuations, restorations and delivery

TEMPO

Marion Langham (IADA, CINOA)
Contact Marion Langham
Clanranagh, Tempo, Co Fermanagh, BT94 3FJ
028 6654 1247 Fax 028 6654 1690
LL@ladymarion.co.uk
www.ladymarion.co.uk
Est. 1982 *Stock size* Large
Stock Belleek, paperweights
Open By appointment
Fairs NEC, Newark
Services Valuations, advice

CO LONDONDERRY

AGHADOWEY

Sarah Rose Antiques
Contact Mr Jim McCaughey
51 Ardreagh Road, Aghadowey, Coleraine, Co Londonderry, BT51 4DN
028 7086 8722
www.srantiques.co.uk

Est. 1989 *Stock size* Medium
Stock General antiques, pine
Open Mon–Sat 10am–5.30pm

COLERAINE

The Forge Antiques
Contact Margaret or Graham Walker
24–26 Long Commons, Coleraine, Co Londonderry, BT52 1LH
028 7035 1339
Est. 1966 *Stock size* Large
Stock Jewellery, silver, porcelain, furniture, clocks
Open Mon–Sat 10am–5.30pm closed Thurs

Fountain Antique Studios & Workshop
Contact Ms Anne Morton
Fountain Villas, 31 Millburn Road, Coleraine, Co Londonderry, BT52 1QT
028 703 52260 F 028 703 54268
M 07771 525650
Est. 1989 *Stock size* Medium
Stock Kitchenware, furniture, stripped pine, porcelain
Open Mon–Sat 2–5.30pm or by appointment

KILREA

Beeswax Antiques
Contact Pat McNeill
6 Church Street, Kilrea, Co Londonderry, BT51 5QU
028 2564 1104
Est. 1987 *Stock size* Large
Stock Mahogany and pine furniture, general smalls
Open Mon–Sat 10.30am–5.30pm
Fairs Newark fair every other month
Services Valuations, restorations

LONDONDERRY

Foyle Antiques
Contact Mr John Helfery
The Old Farmhouse, 16 Whitehouse Road, Londonderry, Co Londonderry, BT48 0NE
028 7126 7626 F 028 7126 7626
E john@foyleantiques.com
W foyleantiques.com
Est. 1984 *Stock size* Large
Stock Antiques and reproduction furniture. Showhouse with 16 furnished period rooms
Open Mon–Sat 10am–6pm Sun 2–6pm
Services Restorations, upholstery

Foyle Books
Contact Ken Thatcher or A Byrne
12 Magazine Street, Londonderry, Co Derry, BT48 6HH
028 7137 2530
Est. 1989 *Stock size* Medium
Stock Antiquarian books, general, books on Derry and Donegal a speciality
Open Mon–Fri 11am–5pm Sat 10am–5pm
Services Valuations

Marcus Griffin Speciallists in Silver Jewellery
Contact Ms Marcus Griffin
2 London Street, Londonderry, Co Londonderry, BT48 6RQ
028 7130 9495
Est. 1974 *Stock size* Large
Stock General antiques, furniture, silver, fossils, objets d'art
Open Mon–Sat 10am–5pm
Fairs International Antique and Collectables Fair at RAF Swinderby

The Whatnot
Contact Ms Margot O'Dowd
22 Bishop Street, Londonderry, Co Londonderry, BT48 6TP
028 7128 8333
Est. 1984 *Stock size* Medium
Stock General antiques
Open Mon–Sat 11am–5pm

PORTSTEWART

Irish Art Group (PTA)
Contact Michael Hughes
49 The Promenade, Portstewart, Co Londonderry, BT55 7AE
028 7083 4600 F 028 7083 4600
E michael@irishartgroup.com
W www.irishartgroup.com
Est. 1982 *Stock size* Large
Stock Irish art, prints, collectables, maps, postcards, cigarette cards, fountain pens
Open Mon–Sat 11am–1pm 2–5pm
Fairs NEC Spring & Autumn
Services Catalogue (6 times a year)

CO TYRONE

AUGHNACLOY

Lucy Forsythe Antiques
Contact Albert or Lucy Forsythe
The Old Rectory, 24 Carnteel Road, Aughnacloy, Co Tyrone, BT69 6DU
028 855 57522 F 028 855 57522
Est. 1962 *Stock size* Large
Stock French provincial farmhouse tables, Irish pine country furniture, Chinese rural antiques
Open Mon–Sat 9am–5pm or by appointment

BALLYCOLMAN

Melmount Auctions
Contact Mr Michael McNamee
Unit C, Ballycolman Industrial Estate, Ballycolman, Co Tyrone, BT82 9PH
028 7138 2223
Est. 1992
Open Mon–Fri 9.30am–5.30pm Thurs 9.30am–1pm
Sales General antiques
Frequency Weekly
Catalogues Yes

BALLYGAWLEY

Old Mill Antiques
Contact Michael and Rose Lippett
The Old Mill, Tulnavern Road, Ballygawley, Co Tyrone, BT70 2HH
028 855 67470 F 028 855 67466
M 07831 866235
Est. 1970 *Stock size* Large
Stock General antiques
Open Mon–Sat 10am–5.30pm Thurs 10am–9pm

COOKSTOWN

Cookstown Antiques (RICS)
Contact Mrs Glymis Jebb
16 Oldtown Street, Cookstown, Co Tyrone, BT80 8EF
028 8676 5279 F 028 8676 2946
M 07808 0788417
Est. 1980 *Stock size* Small
Stock Jewellery, china, small antiques, militaria including WWI medals

Open Thurs Fri 2–5.30pm
Sat 10.30am–5.30pm
Services Valuations

MOY

⊞ Moy Antique Pine
Contact Mr Barry MacNeice
✉ 15 Charlemont Street, Moy, Dungannon, Co Tyrone, BT71 7SG 🅿
☎ 028 8778 9909 Ⓕ 028 8778 4895
Ⓜ 07909 538784
Ⓔ macneice@fsnet.co.uk
Est. 1974 *Stock size* Large
Stock General antiques
Open Mon–Sat 9am–6pm
Services Freestanding kitchens made with antique wood

⊞ Moy Antiques
Contact Mr Lawrence MacNeice
✉ 12 The Square, Moy, Dungannon, Co Tyrone, BT71 7SG 🅿
☎ 028 8778 4895/4755
Ⓕ 028 8778 4895
Ⓔ sales@moyantiques.freeserve.co.uk
Est. 1979 *Stock size* Large
Stock General antique furniture, garden statues, original marble fireplaces
Open Mon–Sat 9.30am–6pm
Fairs Newark, Ardingly
Services Valuations

OMAGH

Dromore Road Auction Rooms
Contact Mr Oliver Gormley
✉ Unit 3, Dromore Road Industrial Estate, Omagh, Co Tyrone, BT78 1QZ 🅿
☎ 028 8224 7738 Ⓕ 028 8225 2797
Ⓔ info@gormleys.ie
Ⓦ www.gormleys.ie
Est. 1989
Open Mon–Sat 9am–6pm
Sales General sales every Thurs, regular sales of antiques and paintings
Frequency Weekly
Catalogues Yes

⊞ Gormley Antique Gallery
Contact Mr Oliver Gormley
✉ Unit 4, Dromore Road, Omagh, Co Tyrone, BT79 IQ2 🅿
☎ 028 8225 2797 Ⓕ 028 8225 2797
Est. 1989 *Stock size* Large
Stock General antiques and paintings
Open Mon–Sat 9am–6pm Tues Fri 9am–8.30pm
Fairs Newark
Services Valuations, restorations

⊞ Kelly Antiques
Contact Mr Louis Kelly
✉ Mullaghmore House, Old Mountfield Road, Omagh, Co Tyrone, BT79 7EX 🅿
☎ 028 8224 2314 Ⓕ 028 8225 0262
Ⓔ info@kellyantiques.com
Ⓦ www.kellyantiques.com
Est. 1936 *Stock size* Large
Stock Period fireplaces, hardwood furniture, bedroom suites, tables, chairs, lighting
Open Mon–Fri 10am–7pm Sat 10am–5pm
Services Restorations, private auctions, due to open an international college teaching restoration techniques

⊞ Viewback Auctions
Contact Mr G Simpson
✉ 8–10 Castle Place, Omagh, Co Tyrone, BT78 5ER 🅿
☎ 028 8224 6271 Ⓕ 028 8224 6271
Ⓜ 0776 0275247
Ⓔ viewback@talk21.com
Est. 1979 *Stock size* Large
Stock General antiques
Open Mon–Sat 10am–6pm
Fairs Newark
Services Auctioneering

STEWARTSTOWN

⊞ Silversaddle Antiques
Contact Vivian Smith
✉ West Street, Stewartstown, Co Tyrone, BT71 5HT 🅿
☎ 028 8773 8088
Est. 1900 *Stock size* Large
Stock Georgian–Edwardian furniture, clocks, Victorian chandeliers
Open Mon–Sat 10.30am–6pm Thurs until 9pm
Services Valuations, restorations

⊞ P J Smith (Fair Trades)
Contact Patrick Smith
✉ 1 North Street, Stewartstown, Co Tyrone, BT71 5JE 🅿
☎ 028 8773 8071
Ⓦ ww.pjsmith-antique-fireplace.co.uk
Est. 1979 *Stock size* Large
Stock Antique fireplaces (largest stock in Ireland), stained glass, beds
Open Mon–Fri 10.30am–1pm 1.40–6pm Thurs until 9pm Sat 10.30am–6pm
Services Restorations

REPUBLIC OF IRELAND

REPUBLIC OF IRELAND

CO CARLOW

BORRIS

Joe Dunne Auctioneers & Valuers (IAVI)
Contact Joe Dunne
Borris, Co Carlow, Ireland P
☎ 050 373191 F 050 373536
E movehome@dunnesofborris.com
W www.dunnesofborris.com
Est. 1984
Open Tues–Sat 9.30am–5pm
Sales Antiques and general household, antiques sales twice yearly
Frequency Every 6 weeks
Catalogues Yes

CO CAVAN

BALLINEA

F J McAvenues & Son
Contact Dennis McAvenues
7 Lower Bridge Street, Ballinea, Co Cavan, Ireland P
☎ 04995 22204
Est. 1964 *Stock size* Large
Stock General antiques, furniture, jewellery, silver, clocks
Open Mon–Fri 2–6pm Sat Sun 11am–5pm
Services Valuations

CO CLARE

CLARECASTLE

The Antique Loft
Contact Paul Walsh or Paul Deloughrey
Barrack Street, Clarecastle, Co Clare, Ireland P
☎ 065 6841969 F 065 6841969
Est. 1991 *Stock size* Large
Stock Victorian furniture, collectables, Persian rugs
Open Mon–Sat 9am–6.30pm Sun by appointment

ENNIS

Tony Honan
Contact Mr Tony Honan
14 Abbey Street, Ennis, Co Clare, Ireland
☎ 065 682 8137
Est. 1974 *Stock size* Large
Stock Clocks, oil lamps
Open Mon–Sat 10am–6pm

CO CORK

BALLYDEHOB

Schull Books
Contact Barbara or Jack O'Connell
Ballydehob, Co Cork, Ireland P
☎ 028 37317 F 028 37317
E schullbooks@eircom.net
W www.schullbooks.com
Est. 1981 *Stock size* Medium
Stock Antiquarian books, second-hand books, military history a speciality
Open June–Sept Mon–Sat 11am–6pm other times by appointment
Fairs All major Irish book fairs
Services Valuations

BANDON

Galvins Antiques
Contact Maisie Galvin
Clonakilty Road, Bandon, Co Cork, Ireland P
☎ 023 20983 F 023 20555
Est. 1991 *Stock size* Medium
Stock Antiques and collectables
Open Mon–Sat 10am–5pm closed 1–2pm

BANTRY

The Bantry Bookstore (IAB)
Contact Michael Carroll
New Street, Bantry, Co Cork, Ireland P
☎ 027 50064 F 027 52042
E bantrybk@iol.ie
W www.irelandbooks.com www.bantrybk.com
Est. 1992 *Stock size* Large
Stock Antiquarian books, including rare Irish books, Irish history books, collectors' items, second-hand books
Open Mon–Sun 9.30am–5.30pm closed Sun 15 Oct–15 Jun
Services Restorations

CHARLEVILLE

Fortlands Antiques (IADA)
Contact Mary or Carol O'Connor
Fortlands, Charleville, Co Cork, Ireland P
☎ 063 81295 F 063 81295
Est. 1974 *Stock size* Large
Stock Georgian–Victorian furniture, silver, brass, china, objets d'art
Open Mon–Sat 11am–5pm Sun 2–5pm
Fairs Irish Antique Dealers' Fair
Services Valuations, restorations

CLONAKILTY

Boyle's Antiques
Contact Joyce Boyle
35 Ashe Street, Clonakilty, Co Cork, Ireland P
☎ 02334 222
Est. 1993 *Stock size* Small
Stock Gilt mirrors, overmantels, jewellery
Open Mon–Sat 10am–6pm closed Wed pm Jan–Mar Thurs–Sat only
Services Valuations

CORK

Antiques & Curios Centre
Contact Liam Hurley
No 3 Adelaide Street, Cork, Co Cork, Ireland P
☎ 021 4395320
Est. 1987 *Stock size* Large
Stock Country furniture, general antiques
Open Mon–Sat 9.30am–5.30pm

Devonshire Antiques
Contact John O'Brien
9 Carroll's Quay, Cork, Co Cork, Ireland P
☎ 021 4509300
M 0863 081943
Est. 1995 *Stock size* Large
Stock Furniture, fireplaces
Open Mon–Sat 10am–5.30pm

Georgian Antiques (LAPADA, CINOA, IADA)
Contact Patrick Jones
21 Lavitts Quay, Cork, Co Cork, Ireland
☎ 021 4278153 F 021 4279365
M 0872 563721
E info@georgianantiquesltd.com
W www.georgianantiquesltd.com
Est. 1998 *Stock size* Large
Stock 18th–19thC Irish, English and continental European furniture, decorations
Open Mon–Fri 2–5pm Sat 10am–5pm
Fairs Irish Antique Dealers' Fair, The Annual Cork Antiques Fair

Goodwood Pine Furniture
Contact Tedge or Cathy Mullane
Rosebank, Old Blackrock Road, Cork, Co Cork, Ireland
021 4318418 021 4318418
Est. 1990 *Stock size* Large
Stock General antiques, architectural salvage
Open Mon–Fri 9am–6pm Sat 10am–2pm

Goodwoods
Contact Mr T O'Mullane
Rosebank, Old Blackrock Road, Cork, Co Cork, Ireland
021 431 8418 021 431 8418
Est. 1992 *Stock size* Medium
Stock Architectural salvage, doors, baths, fireplaces, sinks, etc
Open Mon–Fri 9am–6pm Sat 10am–2pm

Helga's Antiques
Contact Helga McCarthy Cleary or John McCarthy
7 Cross Street, Cork, Co Cork, Ireland
021 4270034 021 4274222
0868 727075
Est. 1994 *Stock size* Large
Stock General
Open Mon–Sat 9.30am–5pm or by appointment
Services Valuations, restorations, French polishing

Ann McCarthy
Contact Ann McCarthy
2 Paul's Lane, Huguenot Quarter, Cork, Co Cork, Ireland
021 4273755
Est. 1985 *Stock size* Large
Stock Silver, linen, china, glass, lace
Open Mon–Sat 10am–6pm
Services Valuations

Mills Antiques
Contact David Coon or Orla Clarke
3 Paul's Lane, Huguenot Centre, Cork, Co Cork, Ireland
021 4273528
Est. 1981 *Stock size* Large
Stock General small items, small furniture, paintings, prints, objets d'art
Open Mon–Sat 10am–6pm
Services Painting and frame restoration

Diana O'Mahony Antiques & Jewellery (IADA, BGA)
Contact Diana or Niamh O'Mahony
8 Winthrop Street, Cork, Co Cork, Ireland
021 4276599
Est. 1970 *Stock size* Large
Stock Victorian jewellery, diamond pieces, Georgian and Victorian silver, Cork and Dublin silver, small furniture
Open Mon–Sat 9.30am–5.30pm
Services Valuations, pearl restringing, remounting

Royal Carberry Books
Contact Gerald Feehan
36 Beechwood Park, Ballinlough, Cork, Co Cork, Ireland
021 4294191 021 4294191
mgfeehan@teircom.net
Est. 1976 *Stock size* Medium
Stock Antiquarian and out-of-print books, books of Irish interest, postcards
Open By appointment only
Fairs All major Irish book fairs
Services Valuations and book search facility

Stokes Clocks
Contact Philip Stokes
48 MacCurtain Street, Cork, Co Cork, Ireland
021 4551195 021 4509125
stokesclocks@eircom.net
Est. 1969 *Stock size* Large
Stock Clocks, watches, barometers
Open Mon–Fri 9.15am–6pm Sat 10am–5pm
Services Valuations, restorations

Victoria's Antiques
Contact Ms Frances Lynch
2 Oliver Plunkett Street, Cork, Co Cork, Ireland
021 4272752 021 4278814
Est. 1987 *Stock size* Large
Stock Jewellery, silver gifts, small items of furniture
Open Mon–Sat 10.30am–6pm
Services Valuations, restorations

Joseph Woodward & Sons Ltd (IAVI)
Contact Tom Woodward
26 Cook Street, Cork, Co Cork, Ireland
021 4273327 021 4272891
auctions@woodward.ie
www.woodward.ie
Est. 1883
Open Mon–Fri 9.15am–5.30pm
Sales Antiques, paintings, silver, porcelain. Twice-yearly specialist Irish silver auctions. Internet catalogues available
Frequency Monthly
Catalogues Yes

FERMOY

Country Furniture
Contact Seamus Kirby
Johnstown, Fermoy, Co Cork, Ireland
025 38244 025 38244
0868 126883
Est. 1990 *Stock size* Large
Stock Antique fireplaces, pine, salvage
Open Mon–Sat 9am–6pm Sun 2–6pm other times by appointment only
Services Pine stripping

KINSALE

Linda's Antiques
Contact Linda or Laura Walsh
Main Street, Kinsale, Co Cork, Ireland
021 4774754 021 4774441
lindasjewellery@eircom.net
www.dragnet-systems.ie/dira/antique
Est. 1992
Stock Jewellery, prints, silver, porcelain
Open Mon–Sat 10.30am–6pm Sun 2–6pm
Fairs Cork Antiques Fair

LEAP

Ovne Antique Stoves
Contact Tom Keane or Claire Graham
Main Street, Leap, Co Cork, Ireland
028 34917
0868 555635
info@ovnestoves.com
www.ovnestoves.com
Est. 1990 *Stock size* Medium
Stock Antique stoves from all around the world 1840–1950
Open Mon–Sat 10am–6pm

MALLOW

Linda's Antiques (IADA)
Contact Linda or Laura Walsh

✉ 1st Floor, 151 West End, Mallow, Co Cork, Ireland P
☎ 022 43048 ⓕ 021 4774441
ⓜ 0872 502467
ⓔ lindasjewellery@eircom.net
ⓦ www.dragnet-systems.ie/dira/antique
Est. 1974 *Stock size* Large
Stock Antique jewellery, silver, porcelain, paintings, prints, books
Open Fri–Sat 11.30am–5.30pm
Fairs Annual Cork Antiques Fair
Services Valuations, proprietor is a gemologist

⊞ McMahon's Antiques
Contact Mr McMahon
✉ Dromagh, Mallow, Co Cork, Ireland P
☎ 029 78119
Est. 1977 *Stock size* Large
Stock Pre-War, general antiques
Open Mon–Sat 10am–9pm Sun noon–9pm

SCHULL

⊞ Fuschia Books
Contact Ms Mary Mackey
✉ Main Street, Schull, Co Cork, Ireland P
☎ 028 28016 ⓕ 028 28016
ⓔ fuschiabooks@eircom.net
ⓦ www.fuschiabooks.com
Est. 1984 *Stock size* Small
Stock Antiquarian stock, especially Irish books, prints
Open Mon–Sat Summer 10am–6pm winter 11am–4pm
Services Valuations and book searches

SKIBEREEN

⊞ Moylurg Antiques
Contact Timothy MacDermot-Roe
✉ The Mall, Skibereen, Skibbereen, Co Cork, Ireland P
☎ 028 36396 ⓕ 028 36396
Est. 1993 *Stock size* Small
Stock General, furniture, pictures, porcelain, Indian furniture and artefacts
Open May–Sept Tues–Sun 11am–8pm Mon by appointment only
Services Valuations

CO DONEGAL

BUNDORAN

⊞ Vincent McGowan Antiques
Contact Mr Vincent McGowan
✉ 2–3 Main Street, Bundoran, Co Donegal, Ireland P
☎ 072 41536
Est. 1981 *Stock size* Medium
Stock Georgian–Edwardian furniture, small items, clocks, jewellery, Belleek
Open By appointment
Services Valuations, restorations

CARNDONAGH

⊞ The Bookshop
Contact Mr Michael Herron
✉ Carnfair Shopping Arcade, Carndonagh, Co Donegal, Ireland P
☎ 077 74389 ⓕ 077 74313
Est. 1987 *Stock size* Large
Stock Irish interest, science, 19thC antiquarian section, general stock
Open Mon–Sat 11am–7pm Sun 2–7pm
Fairs De Burca, Annual Belfast Second-hand and Antiquarian Bookfair
Services Catalogues 4 or 5 a year

DONEGAL

⊞ Millcourt Antiques
Contact Tom Dooley
✉ Millcourt Mews, Donegal, Co Donegal, Ireland P
☎ 073 23222 ⓕ 073 23274
Est. 1995 *Stock size* Medium
Stock Georgian–Victorian furniture
Open Mon–Sat 9.30am–5.30pm
Services Valuations

⊞ Sean Thomas Antiques (IADA)
Contact Sean or Noreen Thomas
✉ Killymard House, Donegal, Co Donegal, Ireland P
☎ 073 35024
Est. 1961 *Stock size* Small
Stock General
Open Mon–Sat 10am–6pm
Services Valuations

DUNFANAGHY

⊞ The Gallery
Contact Alan and Moira Harley
✉ Dunfanaghy, Co Donegal, Ireland P
☎ 074 36224
Est. 1968 *Stock size* Medium
Stock Silver, brass, Asian antiques, pottery, porcelain, jewellery, clocks
Open Mon–Sat 10am–7pm
Services Picture framing

CO DUBLIN

BLACKROCK

Adams Blackrock (IAVI)
Contact Ms Martina Noonan
✉ 38 Main Street, Blackrock, Co Dublin, Ireland
☎ 01 288 5146 ⓕ 01 288 7820
ⓔ info@irishart&antiques.com
Est. 1947
Open Mon–Fri 9.30am–5.30pm Every fortnight Sat 10am–1pm Sun 2–5pm alternate Mon 9.30am–7pm
Sales 20 furniture fine art auctions per annum, 4 Irish and continental European paintings auctions per annum, 4 jewellery and silver sales per annum, regular house contents sales
Catalogues Yes

⊞ De Burca Rare Books (IADA, ABA, PBFA, ASBI)
Contact Mr Eamon de Burca
✉ Cloongashel, 27 Priory Drive, Blackrock, Co Dublin, Ireland P
☎ 01 288 2159 ⓕ 01 283 4080
ⓔ deburca@indigo.ie
Stock Irish antiquarian fine books, maps, prints, manuscripts
Open Mon–Fri 9am–6pm Sat 10am–1pm
Fairs London and New York book fairs
Services Mail-order service, book search, valuations, book binding

HOK Fine Art (IAVI)
Contact Ms Sarah Kenny
✉ 4 Main Street, Blackrock, Co Dublin, Ireland P
☎ 01 288 1000 ⓕ 01 288 0838
ⓔ fineart@hok.ie
ⓦ www.hok.ie
Est. 1944
Open 8.45am–5.45pm
Sales Biannual fine art and furniture sales held at Royal Dublin Society. Blackrock fine art and furniture sales Wed every 6

weeks. House contents sales countrywide. Phone for details
Frequency 6 weeks
Catalogues Yes

⊞ Peter Linden Oriental Rugs and Carpets (IADA, IRC)
Contact Mr Peter Linden
✉ **15 George's Avenue, Blackrock, Co Dublin, Ireland** 🅿
☎ 01 288 5875 Ⓕ 01 283 5616
Ⓔ lind@indigo.ie
Ⓦ www.peterlinden.com
Est. 1980 ***Stock size*** Large
Stock Oriental rugs, carpets, kilims, tapestries
Open Mon–Sat 10am–5.30pm
Fairs Irish Antique Dealers' Fair
Services Valuations, restorations

⊞ Treasure Chest Antiques
Contact Mr Norman Ludgate
✉ **49 Main Street, Blackrock, Co Dublin, Ireland** 🅿
☎ 01 288 9961
Ⓜ 0872 831027
Ⓔ treasurechest@iol.ie
Est. 1992
Stock Lighting, small furniture, silver, jewellery, general antiques
Open Mon–Fri 11am–6pm Sat 11.30am–6pm closed Thurs

CLONTARF

⊞ Glenbower Books
Contact Mr Martin Walsh
✉ **46 Howth Road, Clontarf, Dublin 3, Ireland**
☎ 01 833 5305 Ⓕ 01 833 5305
Ⓔ oldbook@eircom.net
Ⓦ www.abebooks.com/home/glenbowerbooks
Est. 1992 ***Stock size*** Large
Stock Antiquarian books
Open Book fair and Internet trading only
Fairs National Book Fair, Dublin Book Fair

DUBLIN

James Adam
✉ **26 St Stephen's Green, Dublin 2, Co Dublin, Ireland** 🅿
☎ 01 676 0261 Ⓕ 01 662 4725
Ⓔ info@jamesadam.ie
Ⓦ www.jamesadam.ie
Est. 1887
Sales Specialist sales throughout the year of Irish art, vintage wine, militaria, toys and ceramics, phone for details
Catalogues Yes

⊞ Anthony Antiques Ltd (IADA)
Contact Jeffrey or Roger Dell
✉ **7–9 Molesworth Street, Dublin 2, Co Dublin, Ireland** 🅿
☎ 01 677 7222 Ⓕ 01 677 7222
Ⓔ anthonyantiques@oceanfree.net
Ⓦ www.irelandantiques.com/anthony
Est. 1963 ***Stock size*** Large
Stock Decorative antique furniture, mirrors, brass, chandeliers
Open Mon–Sat 9am–6pm
Fairs Irish Antique Dealers' Fair

⊞ Antique Prints (IADA)
Contact Hugh or Anne Iremonger
✉ **16 South Anne Street, Dublin 2, Co Dublin, Ireland** 🅿
☎ 01 671 9523 or 01 269 8373
Ⓔ antiqueprints_irl@yahoo.ie
Est. 1969

Stock 17th–20thC prints, maps, books, *incunabulae*
Open Mon–Sat 11am–5.30pm

⊞ Architectural Antiques and Salvage
Contact Mr S Bird or Mr S Flanagan
✉ **31 South Richmond Street, Dublin, Co Dublin, Ireland** P
☎ 01 478 4245 F 01 478 4245
W www.arcantiques.ie
Est. 1996 *Stock size* Medium
Stock Architectural salvage, fonts, statues, fireplaces, ecclesiastical robes
Open Mon–Sat 10am–6pm

⊞ Architectural Classics
Contact Mr Niall McDonagh
✉ **South Gloucester Street, Dublin 2, Co Dublin, Ireland** P
☎ 086 8207700 F 01 6773318
E info@architecturalclassics.com
W www.architecturalclassics.com
Est. 1986 *Stock size* Large
Stock Antique lighting, door furniture, period fireplaces, garden statuary
Open Mon–Fri 9am–5.30pm Sat 9am–2pm
Fairs IADA fairs, Dublin
Services Valuations, restorations

⊞ Benezet Antiques
Contact Ms Sarah Halpin
✉ **101a Rathgar Road, Dublin 6, Co Dublin, Ireland** P
☎ 01 490 8361 F 01 490 8361
Est. 1979 *Stock size* Medium
Stock Gilt furnishings, furniture, paintings
Open Mon–Sat 10am–5pm or by appointment
Services Valuations

⊞ Christy Bird
Contact Christy Bird
✉ **32 South Richmond Street, Dublin, Co Dublin, Ireland** P
☎ 01 475 4049 F 01 475 8708
E christybird@ireland.com
W www.christybird.com
Est. 1945 *Stock size* Large
Stock Antique furniture
Open Mon–Sat 10am–6pm
Services Restorations

⊞ Lorcan Brereton (IADA)
Contact Mr Diarmuid Brereton
✉ **29 South Anne Street, Dublin 2, Co Dublin, Ireland**
☎ 01 677 1462 F 01 677 1125
Est. 1912
Stock Antique and modern jewellery, silver
Open Mon–Sat 9.15am–5.30pm
Fairs IADA annual fair
Services Valuations, restorations

⊞ Edward Butler (IADA)
Contact Peter or Elizabeth Bateman
✉ **14 Bachelor's Walk, Dublin 1, Co Dublin, Ireland**
☎ 01 873 0296 F 01 873 0296
M 0872 486916
E bateman@iol.ie
W www.edwardbutlerantiques.com
Est. 1850 *Stock size* Large
Stock Nautical and scientific instruments, 18th–19thC furniture, paintings, clocks
Open Mon–Fri 10.30am–4.45pm
Fairs Irish Antique Dealers' Fair

⊞ Cathach Books
Contact Ms Enda Cunningham
✉ **10 Duke Street, Dublin 2, Co Dublin, Ireland** P
☎ 01 671 8676 F 01 671 5120
E cathach@rarebooks.ie
W www.rarebooks.ie
Est. 1964 *Stock size* Medium
Stock Irish 20thC literature, rare signed editions, Irish history, antiquarian prints, maps
Open Mon–Sat 9.30am–5.45pm
Services Valuations

⊞ Caxton Prints (IADA CINOA)
Contact Ronan Teevan or Liam Fitzpatrick
✉ **63 Patrick Street, Dublin 8, Co Dublin, Ireland** P
☎ 01 453 0060 F 01 453 0060
M 0872 429799
E caxton@e-merge.ie
Est. 1989 *Stock size* Small
Stock Old Masters, 17th–18thC decorative prints
Open Mon–Sat 10.30am–5.30pm
Fairs Irish Antique Dealers' Fair
Services Valuations

⊞ Chapters Book and Music Store (BA)
Contact Mr William Kinsella
✉ **108–109 Middle Abbey Street, Dublin 1, Co Dublin, Ireland** P
☎ 01 872 3297 (books) 01 873 0484 (music) F 01 872 3044/7404
Est. 1983 *Stock size* Large
Stock Antiquarian books, collectable vinyls, CDs, Irish music
Open Mon–Sat 9.30am–6.30pm Thurs 9.30am–8pm Sun 1–6.30pm

⊞ Conlan Antiques
Contact Mr Michael Conlan
✉ **22 Lower Clanbrassil Street, Dublin 8, Co Dublin, Ireland** P
☎ 01 453 7323
Est. 1970 *Stock size* Large
Stock General antiques, prints, watercolours, paintings, clocks, fireplaces
Open Mon–Sat 10am–6pm

⊞ Courtville Antiques (IADA, CINOA)
Contact Ms Grainne Pierse
✉ **Powerscourt Townhouse Centre, South William Street, Dublin 2, Co Dublin, Ireland** P
☎ 01 679 4042 F 01 679 4042
Est. 1964 *Stock size* Large
Stock Victorian and Art Deco jewellery, silver, paintings, decorative items
Open Mon–Sat 10am–6pm
Fairs Irish Antique Dealers' Fair
Services Commission purchasing

⊞ Delphi Antiques
Contact Mr Declan Corrigan
✉ **Powerscourt Townhouse Centre, South William Street, Dublin 2, Co Dublin, Ireland** P
☎ 01 679 0331
E declancorrigan@netscape.net declancorrigan@sothebys.com
Est. 1987 *Stock size* Large
Stock Georgian–Edwardian jewellery, Continental and European ceramics, Irish Belleek
Open Mon–Sat 10.30am–5.30pm
Services Restorations

⊞ Michael Duffy Antiques
Contact Mr Michael Duffy
✉ **9–10 Parnell Street, Dublin 1, Co Dublin, Ireland** P
☎ 01 872 6928 F 01 872 6928
M 0872 562326
Est. 1949 *Stock size* Medium
Stock General Victorian antiques
Open Mon–Sat 10am–5pm

⊞ Samuel Elliot
Contact Mr Samuel Elliot
✉ **12 Fade Street, Dublin 2, Co Dublin, Ireland** P
☎ 01 671 1174
Est. 1961 *Stock size* Small
Stock Pocket watches, wrist watches, Rolex
Open Mon–Fri 9.30am–6pm Sat by appointment
Services Valuations, restorations

⊞ John Farrington Antiques (IADA)
Contact Mr John Farrington
✉ **32 Drury Street, Dublin 2, Co Dublin, Ireland** 🅿
☎ 01 679 1899
Ⓔ johnfarringtonantiques@dircon.net
Est. 1979 *Stock size* Large
Stock Fine-quality jewellery, silver, gilt mirrors
Open Tues–Sat 10.30am–5pm
Fairs Dublin Horse Show, Irish Antique Dealers' Fair

⊞ Flanagans Ltd
Contact Brian or Peter Flanagan
✉ **Deerpark Road, Mount Merrion, Dublin, Co Dublin, Ireland** 🅿
☎ 01 288 0218 Ⓕ 01 288 1336
Ⓔ flan@iol.ie
Ⓦ www.theflanagan.com
Est. 1974 *Stock size* Large
Stock Antique pianos, 19thC furniture
Open Mon–Sat 10am–6pm Thurs 10am–9pm
Services Restorations

⊞ Fleury Antiques (IADA)
Contact C or D Fleury
✉ **57 Francis Street, Dublin 8, Co Dublin, Ireland**
☎ 01 473 0878 Ⓕ 01 473 0371
Ⓔ fleuryantiques@eircom.ie
Ⓦ www.fleuryantiques.com
Est. 1979 *Stock size* Large
Stock 18th–19thC furniture, sculptures, paintings, decorative objects, porcelain, silver
Open Mon–Sat 9am–6pm

🔨 Herman & Wilkinson (IAVI)
Contact Mr David Herman or Mr Ray Wilkinson
✉ **161 Lower Rathmines Road, Dublin 6, Co Dublin, Ireland** 🅿
☎ 01 497 2245 Ⓕ 01 496 2245
Ⓔ hwauct@indigo.ie
Est. 1970
Open Mon–Fri 9.30am–5.30pm
Sales Monthly antiques and fine art sales, Thurs 10am, viewing Wed 10am–9pm
Frequency Monthly
Catalogues Yes

⊞ Patrick Howard Antiques (IADA)
Contact Patrick Howard
✉ **60 Francis Street, Dublin 8, Co Dublin, Ireland** 🅿
☎ 01 473 1126 Ⓕ 01 473 1126
Ⓜ 0872 331870
Ⓔ phowardantiques@hotmail.com
Stock size Large
Stock Decorative arts, furniture, paintings, prints and lighting
Open Mon–Sat 9.30am–6pm
Fairs Irish Antique Dealers' Fair

⊞ The Jewel Casket (IADA)
Contact Mr Keith Cusack
✉ **17 South Anne Street, Dublin 2, Co Dublin, Ireland**
☎ 01 671 1262
Est. 1989 *Stock size* Large
Stock Antique jewellery, silver, curios
Open Tues–Sat 9.30am–6pm
Services Jewellery repairs

⊞ Kevin Jones Antiques (IADA)
Contact Mr Kevin Jones
✉ **65–66 Francis Street, Dublin 8, Co Dublin, Ireland** 🅿
☎ 01 454 6626
Ⓜ 0876 29790
Ⓔ jonesantiques@aircom.net
Est. 1989 *Stock size* Large
Stock 18th–19thC furniture, paintings, objets d'art
Open Mon–Sat 10am–5.30pm

⊞ Gerald Kenyon Antiques (IADA, CINOA)
Contact Mr Gerald A Kenyon
✉ **6 Great Strand Street, Dublin 1, Co Dublin, Ireland** 🅿
☎ 01 873 0625 Ⓕ 01 873 0882
Ⓔ mark@kenyon-antiques.com
Ⓦ www.kenyon-antiques.com
Est. 1740 *Stock size* Large
Stock Fine Georgian furniture, works of art, collectors' items
Open Mon–Fri 9am–6pm
Fairs Irish Antique Dealers' Fair, Dublin Antiques Fair
Services Interior decoration

⊞ McGovern's Corner
Contact Pat McGovern
✉ **87–88 Cork Street, Dublin 8, Co Dublin, Ireland** 🅿
☎ 01 453 5979
Est. 1960 *Stock size* Large
Stock Architectural salvage
Open Mon–Fri 9am–5pm Sat 9am–1pm

⊞ Mitofsky Antiques (IADA)
Contact Anne Citron
✉ **8 Rathfarnham Road, Terenure, Dublin 6, Co Dublin, Ireland** 🅿
☎ 01 492 0033 Ⓕ 01 492 0188
Ⓔ info@mintofskyartdeco.com
Ⓦ www.mintofskyartdeco.com
Est. 1994 *Stock size* Large
Stock Art Deco, Art Nouveau, Arts and Crafts
Open Mon–Sat 10am–5.30pm
Fairs The Kings Hall (Belfast), IADA

⊞ Roxane Moorhead Antiques (IADA)
Contact Ms Roxane Moorhead
✉ **65–66 Francis Street, Dublin 8, Co Dublin, Ireland**
☎ 01 453 3962
Ⓜ 0868 147451
Est. 1979 *Stock size* Medium
Stock 18th–19thC furniture, porcelain, mirrors, chandeliers
Open Mon–Sat 10am–5.30pm
Fairs Irish Antique Dealers' Fair
Services Valuations

⊞ Neptune Gallery (IADA, FATG)
Contact Mr Andrew Bonar Law
✉ **41 South William Street, Dublin 2, Co Dublin, Ireland** 🅿
☎ 01 671 5021 Ⓕ 01 671 5021
Ⓔ abl@neptune-gallery.ie
Est. 1963 *Stock size* Medium
Stock Irish maps, prints, watercolours, books
Open Mon–Fri 10am–6pm Sat 10am–1pm
Fairs Irish Antique Dealers' Fair
Services Valuations, framing, restoration

⊞ Gordon Nichol Antiques (IADA CINOA)
Contact Mr Gordon Nichol
✉ **67–68 Francis Street, Dublin 8, Co Dublin, Ireland** 🅿
☎ 01 454 3322 Ⓕ 01 473 5020
Est. 1985 *Stock size* Large
Stock 18th–19thC Irish, English and Continental furniture, chimney pieces, decorative objects
Open Mon–Sat 10.30am–4pm

🔨 O'Reillys (IAVI)
Contact Mr Michael Jordan
✉ **126 Francis Street, Dublin 8, Co Dublin, Ireland** 🅿
☎ 01 453 0311 Ⓕ 01 453 0226
Est. 1952
Open Mon–Fri 9.30am–5pm

Sales Fine jewellery and silverware monthly sale Wed 1pm, viewing Sun noon–4pm Mon Tues 11am–6pm Wed 10am–12.30pm prior to sale
Frequency Monthly
Catalogues Yes

O'Sullivan Antiques (IADA AADL)
Contact Ms Chantal O'Sullivan
43–44 Francis Street, Dublin 8, Co Dublin, Ireland
01 454 1143 F 01 454 1156
M 0862 543399
E info@osullivanantiques.com
W www.osullivanantiques.com
Est. 1991 *Stock size* Large
Stock 18th–19thC furniture, paintings, mirrors, chandeliers, mantelpieces, garden furniture
Open Mon–Fri 9am–6pm Sat 10am–6pm
Fairs Irish Antique Dealers' Fair
Services Valuations, restoration and upholstery

Oman Antique Galleries (IADA)
Contact Rosemary Whelan
114–116 Capel Street, Dublin 1, Co Dublin, Ireland
01 872 4477 F 01 872 4520
E oman@indigo.ie
W www.irelandantiques.com
Est. 1974 *Stock size* Large
Stock Georgian–Edwardian furniture, works of art
Open Mon–Sat 9am–5.30pm
Fairs Irish Antique Dealers' Fair, Kerrygold Horseshow Fair
Services Packing and shipping

Rathmines Bookshop (BABI)
Contact Mr James Kinsella
201 Lower Rathmines Road, Dublin 6, Co Dublin, Ireland
01 496 1064 F 01 496 1064
Est. 1986 *Stock size* Large
Stock Irish books, first editions
Open Mon–Sat 10am–7pm

Rufus the Cat
Contact Aidan & Gail Kinsella
20–22 Market Arcade, George Street, Dublin 2, Co Dublin, Ireland
01 677 0406
Est. 1964 *Stock size* Large
Stock Gentlemen's clothing and collectable accessories – smoking jackets, cuff links, ash trays etc
Open Mon–Sat 10.30am–6pm

Esther Sexton Antiques (IADA)
Contact Ms Esther Sexton
51 Francis Street, Dublin 8, Co Dublin, Ireland
01 473 0909 *Stock size* Large
Stock Victorian and Edwardian furniture, decorative items
Open Mon–Fri 10.30am–5.50pm
Fairs Irish Antique Dealers' Fair

The Silver Shop (IADA)
Contact Mr Ian Haslam
Powerscourt Townhouse Centre, South William Street, Dublin 2, Co Dublin, Ireland
01 679 4147 F 01 679 4147
E ianhaslam@eircom.net
Est. 1979 *Stock size* Large
Stock 18th–19thC silver, porcelain, portrait miniatures
Open Mon–Sat 11am–6pm Thurs 11am–8pm
Fairs Irish Antique Dealers' Fair
Services Valuations

Stokes Books
Contact Mr Stephen Stokes
19 Market Arcade, South Great George's Street, Dublin 2, Co Dublin, Ireland
01 671 3584 F 01 671 3181
E stokesbooks@oceanfree.net
Est. 1982 *Stock size* Small
Stock General antiquarian. Catalogues available. Books on Irish history and literature a speciality
Open Mon–Sat 11am–5.30pm
Fairs De Burca fair and Annual Belfast Second-hand and Antiquarian Bookfair
Services Valuations for probate and insurance

Timepiece Antique Clocks (IADA)
Contact Kevin Chellar
57–58 Patrick Street, Dublin 8, Co Dublin, Ireland
01 454 0774 F 01 454 0744
M 0872 260212
E timepieceireland@eircom.net
Est. 1983 *Stock size* Large
Stock 18th–19thC clocks
Open Tues–Sat 10am–5pm
Fairs Irish Antique Dealers' Fair, Burlington Antiques Fair
Services Valuations, restorations

Town & Country Auctioneers (IAVI)
Contact Ms Helen Thornton
4 Lower Ormond Quay, Dublin 1, Co Dublin, Ireland
01 872 8300/7401 F 01 872 8002
Est. 1992
Open Mon–Fri 9am–5pm
Sales Large house contents sales, Victorian and Georgian furniture
Frequency Every Wed and Sun – 122 per annum

Upper Court Manor Antiques (IADA)
Contact Mr Patrick Fitzgerald
54 Francis Street, Dublin 8, Co Dublin, Ireland
01 473 0037 F 01 473 0037
E uppercourtmanorantiques@iol.ie
Est. 1994 *Stock size* Large
Stock English and Irish 18th–19thC furniture
Open Mon–Sat 10am–6pm
Fairs IADA Exhibition

Jenny Vander
Contact Aidan or Gail Kinsella
4 Exchequer Street, Dublin 2, Co Dublin, Ireland
01 677 0406
Est. 1964 *Stock size* Large
Stock Clothing (including evening dress), lace, 1930s–1950s jewellery
Open Mon–Sat 10.30am–6pm

The Victorian Salvage and Joinery Co Ltd (SALVO)
Contact Mark McDonagh
46–47 Townsend Street, Dublin 2, Co Dublin, Ireland
01 672 7000 F 01 672 7435
M 0872 551299
E vicsalv@indigo.ie
W www.victorian-salvage.com
Est. 1999 *Stock size* Large
Stock Reclaimed building materials
Open Mon–Fri 8.30am–5.30 Sat 9am–2pm
Services Valuations, restorations, shipping

Weir and Sons
Contact Allan Kilpatrick
96–99 Grafton Street, Dublin 2, Co Dublin, Ireland
01 677 9678 F 01 677 7739
E weirs@indigo.ie
Est. 1869 *Stock size* Large
Stock Silverware (especially Irish), jewellery, pocket and wrist watches
Open Mon–Sat 9am–5.30pm
Services Valuations, restorations

J W Weldon (IADA)
Contact James or Martin Weldon
55 Clarendon Street, Dublin 2, Co Dublin, Ireland
01 677 1638 F 01 670 7958
E antiques@weldonsofdublin.com
W www.weldonsofdublin.com
Est. 1900 *Stock size* Large
Stock Irish and diamond jewellery, antique and provincial Irish silver
Open Mon–Sat 10am–5.30pm
Fairs IADA

Whyte's
Contact Ian Whyte
30 Marlborough Street, Dublin 1, Co Dublin
01 874 6161 F 01 874 6020
E info@whytes.ie
W www.whytes.ie
Est. 1783
Open Mon–Fri 10am–1pm 2–6pm
Sales 8 to 10 sales annually of Irish art and collectables
Catalogues Yes

The Winding Stair Bookshop
Contact Mr Kevin Connolly
40 Lower Ormond Quay, Dublin 1, Co Dublin, Ireland
01 873 3292 F 01 873 3292
E windingstairbooks@tinet.ie
W www.windingstair.ie
Est. 1982 *Stock size* Large
Stock New, second-hand and antiquarian books, Irish-interest books a speciality
Open Mon–Sat 9.30am–6pm Sun 1–6pm

Yesteryear Antiques
Contact Cyril Wall
12 North Frederick Street, Dublin 1, Co Dublin, Ireland
01878 3567
Est. 1981 *Stock size* Small
Stock Collectables
Open Tues–Fri 10am–5.30pm Sat 10am–4pm

DUN LAOGHAIRE

James Fenning, Old and Rare Books (ABA)
Contact Mr James Fenning
12 Glenview, Rochestown Avenue, Dun Laoghaire, Co Dublin, Ireland
01 285 7855 F 01 285 7919
E fenning@indigo.ie
Est. 1969 *Stock size* Small
Stock Antiquarian books
Open By appointment
Services Valuations

Naughton's Booksellers
Contact Ms Susan Naughton
8 Marine Terrace, Dun Laoghaire, Co Dublin, Ireland
01 280 4392
E sales@naughtonsbooks.com
W www.naughtonsbooks.com
Est. 1978 *Stock size* Medium
Stock Second-hand and antiquarian books
Open By appointment

The Old Shop
Contact Ms Siobhan Nugent
St Michael's Mall, Dun Laoghaire Shopping Centre, Co Dublin, Ireland
01 280 9915
Est. 1976 *Stock size* Large
Stock Jewellery, silver, porcelain
Open Mon–Sat 9.30am–6pm

Through the Looking Glass
Contact Ms Anna Connolly
2 Salthill Place, Dun Laoghaire, Co Dublin, Ireland
01 280 6577
Est. 1989 *Stock size* Large
Stock Mirrors, general
Open Tues–Sat 10.30am–5.30pm
Services Restoration of mirrors

MALAHIDE

Drums Malahide
Contact Dennis Drum
Malahide, Co Dublin, Ireland
01 845 2819 F 01 845 3356
Est. 1974
Open Mon–Fri 9am–5pm closed 1–2pm
Sales Fine art sales monthly on Thurs at 7pm, regular fortnightly mixed household sales Thurs
Catalogues Yes

Malahide Antique Shop
Contact Mr Frank Donellan
14 New Street, Malahide, Co Dublin, Ireland
01 845 2900
Est. 1974 *Stock size* Large
Stock Jewellery, silver, Georgian furniture, pictures, porcelain
Open Mon–Sat 10am–5.30pm closed 1–2pm
Services Valuations, restorations

MONKSTOWN

Bonhams & Brooks
Contact David Dunn
Belgrave House, Belgrave Square, Monkstown, Co Dublin, Ireland
01 280 8126 F 01 280 9274
W www.bonhams.com
Open Mon–Fri 9am–5pm
Sales Regional Representative for Ireland

SANDYCOVE

Sandycove Fine Arts (IADA)
Contact Ms Fiona O'Reilly
55 Glasthule Road, Sandycove, Co Dublin, Ireland
01 280 5956
Est. 1993 *Stock size* Medium
Stock Antique furniture, paintings, china, glass, silver, silver plate
Open Mon–Sat 10.30am–1pm 2–6pm

STILLORGAN

Beaufield Mews Antiques (IADA)
Contact Ms Jill Cox
Woodlands Avenue, Stillorgan, Co Dublin, Ireland
01 288 0375 F 01 288 6945
M 0872 427360
E beaumews@iol.ie
W www.antiquesireland.ie
Est. 1948 *Stock size* Large
Stock Early Irish glass and porcelain, 18th–19thC small items of furniture, pictures
Open Tues–Sat 3–9pm Sun 1–5pm
Fairs Irish Antique Dealers' Fair
Services Valuations, award-winning restaurant on site

CO GALWAY

ATHLONE

Arcadia Antiques & Fine Art (IADA)
Contact Ms Imelda O'Flynn
Church Street, Athlone, Co Galway, Ireland
0902 74671
Est. 1971 *Stock size* Large

Stock Fine Victorian jewellery, silver, objets d'art, prints, dolls
Open Mon–Sat 9.30am–6pm
Services Jewellery restoration

CLARENBRIDGE

Clarenbridge Antiques
Contact Mr Martin Griffin
Limerick Road (N18), Clarenbridge, Co Galway, Ireland
091 796522 091 796522
clarenbridgeantiques@tinet.ie
www.homepage.tinet.ie/~clarenbridgeantiques
Est. 1981 *Stock size* Large
Stock Irish pine furniture, country antiques, mahogany and collectables
Open Summer Mon–Sun winter Mon–Sat 9am–6pm
Services Pine stripping

GALWAY

Cobwebs (IADA)
Contact Mrs Phyllis MacNamara
7 Quay Lane, Galway, Co Galway, Ireland
091 564388 091 564235
0872 375745
cobwebs@tinet.ie
www.cobwebsgalway.com
Est. 1972 *Stock size* Large
Stock Sporting antiques, jewellery, collectables
Open Mon–Sat 9.30am–5.30pm
Fairs Irish Antique Dealers Fair

Corrib Antiques
Contact Ms Gretta Boland
The Bridge Mills, Galway, Co Galway, Ireland
091 564938
Est. 1987 *Stock size* Medium
Stock Mahogany and pine furniture, general, jewellery
Open Mon–Sat 10am–5.30pm
Fairs Galway Antique Fair – Galway Bay Hotel

Maguire Antiques of Galway Ltd
Contact Phillip or Martin Maguire
Tuam Rd Centre, Tuam Rd, Galway, Co Galway, Ireland
091 770799 091 771433
Est. 1949 *Stock size* Large
Stock General antiques, fine art, paintings, porcelain
Open Mon–Sat 9.30am–6pm
Services Valuations

Tempo Antiques
Contact Frank or Phil Greeley
9 Cross Street, Galway, Co Galway, Ireland
091 562282
info@tempoantiques.com
www.tempoantiques.com
Est. 1995 *Stock size* Large
Stock Victorian–Edwardian, Art Deco antique jewellery, silver, porcelain, collectables
Open Mon–Sat 9.30am–6.30pm open later in summer
Fairs Galway Bay Hotel

Twice As Nice
Contact Ms Deirdre Grandee
5 Quay Street, Galway, Co Galway, Ireland
091 566332
grandideirdre@hotmail.com
Est. 1987 *Stock size* Medium
Stock Period clothes, lace, linen, jewellery
Open Mon–Sat 10am–6pm

The Winding Stair
Contact Mr Val Tyrell
4 Mainguard Street, Galway, Co Galway, Ireland
091 561682
tyrell@eircom.net
Est. 1991 *Stock size* Medium
Stock Prints, lighting, furniture, bathroom fittings, jewellery, collectables, general antiques
Open Mon–Sat 10am–6pm
Services Shipping – small items only

GORT

Honan's Antiques
Contact Brian or Margaret Honan
Crowe Street, Gort, Co Galway, Ireland
091 631407 091 631816
honanantiques@eircom.net
www.honanantiques.com
Est. 1976 *Stock size* Large
Stock Antique pine, clocks, lamps, Victorian fireplaces, advertising signs, mirrors, pub fittings etc
Open Mon–Sat 10am–6pm
Services Pine stripping

KINVARA

Penny Farthing Antiques
Contact Olive or Neil Bradley
Main Street, Kinvara, Co Galway, Ireland
09163 7720
www.pennyfarthing.ie
Est. 1997 *Stock size* Medium
Stock Furniture, china, pictures, collectables
Open Mon–Sun noon–5pm closed Tues

MOYCULLEN

Moycullen Village Antiques (IADA)
Contact Ms Maura Duffy
Main Street, Moycullen, Co Galway, Ireland
091 555303 091 555303
0868 235976
Est. 1989 *Stock size* Large
Stock Fine Regency–Edwardian furniture, paintings, prints, fine china, silver
Open Mon–Sat 9.45am–5.30pm Sun 2–5.30pm
Fairs Dublin Horse Show and IADA (Mar, Dec)
Services Valuations, restorations

CO KERRY

ABBEYDORNEY

Abbey Antiques
Contact Jerry O'Donovan
Main Street, Abbeydorney, Co Kerry, Ireland
066 7135460
Est. 1989 *Stock size* Large
Stock Victorian fireplaces, Georgian–Edwardian furniture
Open Sun or by appointment

CAHIRSIVEEN

Biggs Antique Shop (MADA)
Contact Denyce Biggs
Old Road, Cahirsiveen, Co Kerry, Ireland
066 947 2580
Est. 1975 *Stock size* Large
Stock 1830–1950s small portable antiques including cutlery
Open Tues–Sat 10.30am–6pm Sun call first
Services Valuations

DINGLE

Fado Antiques (FATG)
Contact Pat or Eve Hennessy
Main Street, Dingle, Co Kerry, Ireland

☎ 091 51452 Ⓕ 091 51452
Ⓜ 0872 038123
Est. 1980 *Stock size* Large
Stock General, paintings, original Irish art, clocks
Open May–Nov 10am–10pm winter by appointment
Services Valuations, cleaning and framing

TRALEE

⊞ O'Keeffe's Antiques and Interiors
Contact Maurice or Jane O'Keeffe
✉ **15 Princes Street, Tralee, Co Kerry, Ireland** Ⓟ
☎ 066 718 0613/066 712 5635
Ⓕ 066 712 5635
Ⓔ okeeffeantiques2@eircom.net
Est. 1860 *Stock size* Large
Stock 8 rooms in a Georgian town house, fully decorated in period furnishings, all items for sale
Open Tues–Sat 9.30am–6pm
Services Valuations, restorations

CO KILDARE

MAYMOOTH

⊞ Hugh Cash Antiques
Contact Hugh Cash
✉ **Main Street, Maynooth, Co Kildare, Ireland** Ⓟ
☎ 01 628 5946
Ⓜ 0872 434510
Est. 1969 *Stock size* Large
Stock Georgian–Edwardian furniture
Open By appointment
Services Valuations

CO KILKENNY

CASTLECOMER

Mealy's Ltd (IAVI)
Contact Fonsie or George Mealy
✉ **Chatsworth Street, Castlecomer, Co Kilkenny, Ireland** Ⓟ
☎ 056 41229/41413 Ⓕ 056 41627
Ⓔ secinfo@mealys.iol.ie
Ⓦ www.mealys.com
Est. 1934
Open Mon–Fri 9am–1pm 2–6pm
Sales 2 antiquarian book auctions per year, viewing days prior to auction. Also fine art sales
Frequency 8 per year
Catalogues Yes

FRESHFORD

⊞ Cass Freshford Antiques
Contact Michael Cass
✉ **Bohercrussia Street, Freshford, Co Kilkenny, Ireland** Ⓟ
☎ 056 32240
Ⓔ cassantiques@dol.ie
Est. 1966 *Stock size* Medium
Stock Antique furniture
Open Mon–Sat 9am–5pm
Services Restorations

⊞ Upper Court Manor Antiques (IADA)
Contact Patrick Fitzgerald
✉ **Upper Court Manor, Freshford, Co Kilkenny, Ireland** Ⓟ
☎ 056 32174 Ⓕ 056 32325
Ⓔ antiques@indigo.ie
Est. 1989 *Stock size* Large
Stock English and Irish 19thC furniture
Open Mon–Fri 10am–5.30pm
Fairs Irish Antique Dealers' Fair, Burlington Antiques Fair
Services Restorations, shipping, packing

CO LAOIS

DURROW

C Sheppard and Sons (IAVI)
Contact Michael Sheppard
✉ **The Square, Durrow, Co Laois, Ireland** Ⓟ
☎ 050 236123 Ⓕ 050 236546
Ⓔ info@sheppards.ie
Est. 1949
Open Mon–Sat 10am–1pm 2–6pm
Sales General antiques, porcelain, furniture, fine arts
Frequency Every 2–3 months
Catalogues Yes

PORTARLINGTON

⊞ McDonnell's Antique Furniture
Contact Ray McDonnell
✉ **Cloneyhurke, Portarlington, Co Laois, Ireland** Ⓟ
☎ 05024 3304
Est. 1981 *Stock size* Large
Stock Religious furniture, pulpits, pews, statuary, pine and farmhouse furniture
Open Mon–Sat 8am–8pm

CO LEITRIM

CARRICK ON SHANNON

⊞ Trinity Rare Books
Contact Nick or Joanna Kaszuk
✉ **Bridge Street, Carrick on Shannon, Co Leitrim, Ireland** Ⓟ
☎ 078 22144
Ⓔ nickk@indigo.ie
Ⓦ www.indigo.ie/~nickk
Est. 1999 *Stock size* Medium
Stock Antiquarian fine bindings, books, modern first editions
Open Mon–Sat 9.30am–6pm
Services Book search

CO LIMERICK

ADARE

⊞ Carol's Antiques (IADA, CINOA)
Contact Ms Carol O'Connor
✉ **Main Street, Adare, Co Limerick, Ireland** Ⓟ
☎ 061 396977 Ⓕ 061 396991
Ⓜ 0862 478827
Ⓔ coconnor@indigo.ie
Ⓦ www.carolsantiquesadare.com
Est. 1979 *Stock size* Large
Stock Georgian–Victorian furniture, silver, brass, porcelain, objets d'art, jewellery
Open Mon–Sat 9.30am–5.30pm Sun 12.30–5pm
Fairs Irish Antique Dealers' Fair, Annual Cork Antiques Fair
Services Interior decoration

⊞ Manor Antiques
Contact Mr Simon Quilligan
✉ **Main Street, Adare, Co Limerick, Ireland** Ⓟ
☎ 061 396515 or 069 64869
Ⓜ 0868 365196
Est. 1914 *Stock size* Large
Stock Georgian–Victorian furniture, general antiques
Open Sat 10am–5.30pm or by appointment
Services Shipping

⊞ George Stacpoole (IADA)
Contact Mr George Stacpoole
✉ **Main Street, Adare, Co Limerick, Ireland** Ⓟ
☎ 061 396409 Ⓕ 061 396733

ⓔ stacpool@iol.ie
ⓦ www.georgestacpooleantiques.com
Est. 1962 ***Stock size*** Medium
Stock Furniture, silver, books, pictures, china, prints
Open Mon–Sat 10am–5.30pm
Fairs IADA exhibitions – Dublin, Cork, Limerick
Services Valuations and interior decoration

LIMERICK

⊞ Ann's Antiques
Contact Ann O'Doherty
✉ **32 Mallow Street, Limerick, Co Limerick, Ireland** 🅿
☎ 061 302492 ⓕ 061 413035
Est. 1984 ***Stock size*** Medium
Stock Mid–late Victorian furniture
Open Tues–Fri 11am–5pm or by appointment
Services Valuations, search

⊞ Bygones Antiques
Contact Mr John Costello
✉ **16 Nicholas Street, Limerick, Co Limerick, Ireland** 🅿
☎ 061 417339
Est. 1979 ***Stock size*** Medium
Stock Antique pine furniture and beds
Open Mon–Fri 9am–5.30pm half day Sat
Services Pine stripping

⊞ John Gunning Antiques
Contact Mr John Gunning
✉ **2 Castle Street, Limerick, Co Limerick, Ireland** 🅿
☎ 061 410535
Est. 1970 ***Stock size*** Large
Stock General antiques
Open Mon–Sat 10am–5pm

⊞ Noonan Antiques
Contact Jim Noonan
✉ **16–17 Ellen Street, Limerick, Co Limerick, Ireland** 🅿
☎ 061 413861 ⓕ 061 413861
ⓜ 0872 539165
ⓔ jandanoonan@eircom.net
Est. 1985 ***Stock size*** Medium
Stock Antique jewellery, furniture
Open Mon–Sat 10am–5pm

⊞ O'Toole Antiques & Decorative Galleries (IADA)
Contact Noel O'Toole
✉ **Upper William Street, Limerick, Co Limerick, Ireland** 🅿
☎ 061 414490 ⓕ 061 411378
ⓜ 0862 550985
ⓔ noel.o.toole.antiques@oceanfree.net
Est. 1979 ***Stock size*** Large
Stock 18th–19thC furniture, pictures, fireplaces, mirrors and porcelain
Open Mon–Sat 9.30am–6pm
Fairs IADA
Services Valuations, restorations

Sextons Auctioneers
Contact Lionel, Melissa or Anmarie Sexton
✉ **78 O'Connell Street, Limerick, Co Limerick, Ireland**
☎ 061 310430
ⓜ 0872 506824
ⓔ sextonma@indigo.ie
Est. 1894
Sales Antique furniture and fine art
Catalogues No

⊞ Tess Antiques
Contact Ms Tess Costello
✉ **5 Roches Street, Limerick, Ireland** 🅿
☎ 061 416643
ⓜ 0872 960624
ⓔ tessantiques@eircom.net
Est. 1980 ***Stock size*** Medium
Stock Jewellery, silver, porcelain
Open Tues–Sat 10am–5pm

CO LOUTH

DROGHEDA

⊞ Greene's Antiques Galleries (IADA)
Contact Austin Greene
✉ **The Mall, Drogheda, Co Louth, Ireland** 🅿
☎ 04198 38286/36212
ⓕ 04198 38286
Est. 1886 ***Stock size*** Large
Stock Furniture, Irish silver, paintings
Open Mon–Sat 10am–12.30pm 2–5pm

DUNDALK

⊞ Hall's Curio Shop
Contact Margaret or Rory Hall
✉ **9–10 Jocelyn Street, Dundalk, Co Louth, Ireland**
☎ 042 933 4902
Est. 1971 ***Stock size*** Large
Stock Jewellery, paintings, silver, general
Open Mon–Sat 10am–1pm 2–6pm closed Thurs or by appointment
Services Valuations

CO MAYO

ACHILL SOUND

⊞ Roger Grimes (IADA)
Contact Roger Grimes
✉ **Old Rectory, Achill Sound, Co Mayo, Ireland** 🅿
☎ 098 27823 ⓕ 098 27823
ⓜ 0872 339221
ⓦ www.vparker.com
Est. 1977
Stock 17th–19thC provincial furniture, metalware, china, pictures, prints, eccentricities
Open Daily in the summer or by appointment
Fairs IADA
Services Valuations

⊞ Vanessa Parker Rare Books (IADA)
Contact Vanessa Parker
✉ **Old Rectory, Achill Sound, Co Mayo, Ireland** 🅿
☎ 098 27823 ⓕ 098 27823
ⓜ 0872 339221
ⓦ www.vparker.com
Est. 1977
Stock Antiquarian books, folklore, literature, Irish, 19th–20thC children's books.
Open Daily in the summer or by appointment
Fairs IADA
Services Valuations

WESTPORT

⊞ Jonathan Beech Antique Clocks (IADA, CINOA)
Contact Mr Jonathan Beech
✉ **Killeenacoff House, Cloona, Westport, Co Mayo, Ireland** 🅿
☎ 098 28688 ⓕ 098 28688
ⓜ 0872 226247
ⓔ jbeech@anu.ie
ⓦ www.antiques-ireland.com
Est. 1984 ***Stock size*** Medium
Stock Clocks
Open Mon–Sat 9.30am–5.30pm or by appointment
Fairs Irish Antique Dealers' Fair, Dublin, Galway, Limerick
Services Valuations, restorations

Bygones of Ireland Ltd
Contact John or Lia Van Wensveen
Lodge Road, Westport, Co Mayo, Ireland P
☎ 098 26132/25701 F 098 26132
E bygones@anu.ie
W www.anu.ie/bygones
Est. 1983 *Stock size* Large
Stock Irish and European antique pine and country furniture
Open Mon–Sat 9am–5.30pm

Satch Kiely (IADA, LAPADA)
Contact Mrs Satch Kiely
Westport Quay, Westport, Co Mayo, Ireland P
☎ 098 25775 F 098 25957
Est. 1985 *Stock size* Large
Stock 18th–19thC furniture, Irish and English silver, colonial lamps, fossil bog oak and Biedermeier
Open Mon–Sat 2–6pm or by appointment
Fairs Irish Antique Dealers' Fair, Annual Cork Antiques Fair, Galway and Hunt Museum, Limerick
Services Valuations

Westport House Antique Shop (IADA)
Contact Earl of Altamont
Westport, Co Mayo, Ireland P
☎ 098 25430/25404 F 098 25206
E info@westporthouse.ie
W www.westporthouse.ie
Est. 1969 *Stock size* Medium
Stock General antiques, prints, postcards, silver, silver plate, jewellery
Open Daily April–June 2–5pm Jul Aug 11.30am–5.30pm or by appointment

CO MEATH

GORMANSTOWN

Delvin Farm Antiques
Contact J or B McCrane
Gormanstown, Co Meath, Ireland P
☎ 01 841 2285 F 01 841 3730
E info@delvinfarmpine.com
W www.delvinfarmpine.com
Est. 1974 *Stock size* Large
Stock Antique country furniture
Open Mon–Sat 9am–5pm

KELLS

Oliver Usher (IAVI)
Contact Mr Oliver Usher
John Street, Kells, Co Meath, Ireland P
☎ 046 41097 F 046 41097
E oliverusher@ireland.com
Est. 1978
Open Mon–Fri 9.30am–5.30pm
Sales Antique and high-class furniture sale Tues 5pm mid month at Kells, viewing Sun 2–6pm Mon 11am–7pm Tues 11am–5pm. Monthly general household sale in CYWS Hall, Navan first Fri of month 6.30pm (no catalogue), viewing Fri 11am–6.30pm. Spring and Autumn sale at The Conyngham Arms Hotel, Slane
Frequency Monthly
Catalogues Yes

George Williams Antiques (IADA)
Contact George Williams
The Annexe, Newcastle House, Kilmainhamwood, Kells, Co Meath, Ireland P
☎ 046 52740
M 0872 529959
E gwilliams@eircom.net
W www.georgian-antiques.com
Est. 1987 *Stock size* Medium
Stock 18th–19thC furniture, paintings
Open By appointment
Fairs IADA Exhibition, Dublin (Sept)
Services Purchasing on commission, valuations

OLDCASTLE

Mullen Bros Auctions
Contact Michael Mullen,
Oldcastle, Co Meath, Ireland P
☎ 04 985 41107 F 04 985 41107
Est. 1962
Open Tues–Fri 10am–6pm closed Sun Mon
Sales General antiques and household goods 1st Tues of every month 6.30pm, viewing 3 days prior
Catalogues No

CO OFFALY

BIRR

Ivy Hall Antiques (IADA, CINOA)
Contact Mrs Ena Hoctor
Carrig, Birr, Co Offaly, Ireland P
☎ 0509 20148
Est. 1967 *Stock size* Large
Stock 18th–19thC silver, porcelain, furniture, pictures
Open By appointment

EDENDERRY

Edenderry Architectural Salvage Ltd
Contact Brian Murphy
Monasteroris Industrial Estate, Edenderry, Co Offaly, Ireland P
☎ 040 533156 F 040 533156
M 0862 595367
E bpmurphy@iol.ie
Est. 1995 *Stock size* Large
Stock Reclaimed flooring, bricks, radiators, doors, baths, sinks, beams, woodblock, railway sleepers, cobblestones, fireplaces
Open Mon–Fri 9am–5pm
Services Cutting and planing of reclaimed timber beams and flooring

CO SLIGO

SLIGO

Louis J Doherty and Sons
Contact Mr John McSharry
Tealing Street, Sligo, Co Sligo, Ireland P
☎ 071 69494 F 071 69494
E ljdoherty@tinet.ie
Est. 1976 *Stock size* Large
Stock Large furniture, bedroom suites, settees, display cabinets, overmantels, pianos, general antiques
Open Mon–Sat 9.30am–1pm 2–6pm
Services Valuations

Georgian Village Antiques
Contact Louis and John Doherty
Johnstons Court, Sligo, Co Sligo, Ireland P
☎ 071 62421 F 071 69494
E ljdoherty@tinet.ie
Est. 1976 *Stock size* Medium

Stock Small furniture items, jewellery, porcelain, glass
Open Mon–Sat 10am–6pm
Services Valuations

CO TIPPERARY

BALLINDERRY

Kilgarvan Antique Centre
Contact Denise Shaw
Kilgarvan Quay, Ballinderry, Nenagh, Co Tipperary, Ireland
☎ 067 22047
deniseshaw27@hotmail.com
Est. 1947 *Stock size* Medium
Stock Georgian antiques, mirrors, general china
Open Mon–Sat 10am–7pm Sun after 3pm Apr–Oct by appointment
Services Restoration of giltwood mirrors and antique furniture, restoration and polishing of wooden and carved furniture

BIRDHILL

Delany Antiques
Contact Mr P Delany
Cragg House, Birdhill, Birdhill, Co Tipperary, Ireland
☎ 06 137 8180
Est. 1980 *Stock size* Medium
Stock Architectural salvage, mirrors, bar interiors
Open By appointment only
Services Upholstery

CAHIR

Abbey Antiques (IADA)
Contact Mr Michael Kennedy
Abbey Street, Cahir, Co Tipperary, Ireland
☎ 052 41187 Fax 052 41187
Mobile 0872 728844
celine@antiquesireland.ie
www.antiquesireland.ie
Est. 1992 *Stock size* Large
Stock Georgian–Edwardian furniture, lighting, objets d'art
Open Mon–Sat 10.30am–5.30pm
Services Shipping

Fleury Antiques (IADA)
Contact C or D Fleury or P Reidy
The Square, Cahir, Co Tipperary, Ireland
☎ 052 41226 Fax 052 41819
fleuryantiques@eircom.ie
www.fleuryantiques.com
Est. 1978 *Stock size* Medium
Stock 18th–19thC furniture, sculptures, paintings, decorative objects, jewellery, porcelain, silver
Open Mon–Sat 9am–6pm
Fairs No

CLONMEL

Glenconnor Antiques
Contact Richard Hanna
Glenconnor House, Clonmel, Co Tipperary, Ireland
☎ 052 27606 Fax 052 29196
Mobile 0872 870214
Est. 1991 *Stock size* Medium
Stock Victorian mahogany, walnut furniture
Open Tues–Sat 10am–6pm or by appointment
Services Valuations, restorations

NEWPORT

Delaney Antiques
Contact Patrick Delaney
Cragg House, Cragg, Birdhill, Co Tipperary, Ireland
☎ 061 378180 Fax 061 378180
Est. 1979 *Stock size* Large
Stock Architectural salvage, bath fittings, accessories
Open By appointment
Services Valuations, upholstery

CO WATERFORD

WATERFORD

R J Keighery (IPAV)
Contact Rody or Ann Keighery
Georges Quay, Waterford, Co Waterford, Ireland
☎ 05 187 3692 Fax 05 187 3692
Est. 1948
Open Mon–Sun 9am–5.30pm
Sales Six weekly antiques and general furniture sale Mon 2pm, view Fri Sat Sun noon–6pm
Frequency Six weekly
Catalogues Yes

R J Keighery
Contact Rody or Ann Keighery
27 William Street, Waterford, Co Waterford, Ireland
☎ 051 873692
Est. 1948 *Stock size* Large
Stock Antiques, furniture, china, silver, collectables
Open Mon–Sat 9am–5.30pm
Services Valuations

The Salvage Shop
Contact Sean Corcoran
Airport Road, Waterford, Co Waterford, Ireland
☎ 051 873260 Fax 051 858323
Mobile 0872 524657
salvage@iol.ie
www.bang2000.com
Est. 1991 *Stock size* Large
Stock Architectural salvage and reclaimed wood furniture
Open Mon–Fri 8am–5.30pm Sat 10am–3pm
Fairs Beyond the Hall Door
Services Restorations, interior design, catalogues

Times Past
Contact James O'Hanlon
16 The Quay, Waterford, Ireland
☎ 051 853036 Fax 051 853036
Mobile 0872 503557
Est. 1989 *Stock size* Large
Stock General antiques, fireplaces and furniture, smalls
Open Mon–Sat 10am–5pm
Services Pine stripping

CO WEXFORD

WEXFORD

Forum Antiques
Contact Nora Liddy
Selskar, Wexford, Co Wexford, Ireland
☎ 053 21055 Fax 053 23630
info@selskarantiques.com
www.selskarantiques.com
Est. 1996 *Stock size* Medium
Stock Antiquarian books, maps, prints, china, collectables
Open Tues–Sat 11am–5.30pm
Fairs National Book Fairs
Services Book valuations

Selskar Abbey Antiques
Contact Irene Walker
Selskar Court, Wexford, Co Wexford, Ireland
☎ 053 23630 Fax 053 23630
Mobile 0876 791095
info@selskarantiques.com
www.selskarantiques.com
Est. 1984 *Stock size* Medium
Stock Antique jewellery, fine

china, small furniture items, pictures, glass, collectables
Open Mon–Sat 10am–6pm
Fairs National fairs, O'Donnell Fairs
Services Valuations

CO WICKLOW

BRAY

⊞ Clancy Chandeliers (IADA)
Contact Ger, Derek or Tommy Clancy
✉ **Villanova, Ballywaltrim, Bray, Co Wicklow, Ireland** 🅿
☎ 0128 63460 Ⓕ 0128 63460
Ⓔ info@clancychandeliers.com
Ⓦ www.clancychandeliers.com
Est. 1989 ***Stock size*** Large
Stock Period and reproduction chandeliers, wall lights, hall lanterns
Open Strictly by appointment
Fairs IADA Exhibition, Dublin (Sept) and Dublin Antiques Fair (Mar Nov)
Services Professional cleaning, restoration, hanging service

GREYSTONES

Il Antiques
Contact Beth O'Riordan
✉ **Church Road, Greystones, Co Wicklow, Ireland** 🅿
☎ 01 287 5651
Est. 1990 ***Stock size*** Medium
Stock Furniture, porcelain, pottery, ceramics, silver, jewellery, linens, glass
Open Mon–Sat 10.30am–5.30pm

⊞ Ormonde Antiques
Contact Mr John Gammell
✉ **Victoria Road, Greystones, Co Wicklow, Ireland** 🅿
☎ 01 287 3355
Est. 1967 ***Stock size*** Large
Stock Furniture, mirrors
Open Mon–Sat 9.30am–5.30pm closed Wed
Services Valuations, restorations, French polishing

RADHDRUM

⊞ Cathair Books
Contact Mr Eugene Mallon
✉ **Pound Brook Lane, Radhdrum, Co Wicklow, Ireland** 🅿
☎ 040 446939 Ⓕ 040 446939
Ⓔ cathairbks@eircom.net
Ⓦ www.abebooks.com/home/cathair_books
Est. 1974 ***Stock size*** Medium
Stock Irish-interest books, prints, maps, postcards
Open Mail order or by appointment
Fairs Dublin book fair and provincial fairs in Limerick and Belfast
Services Valuations

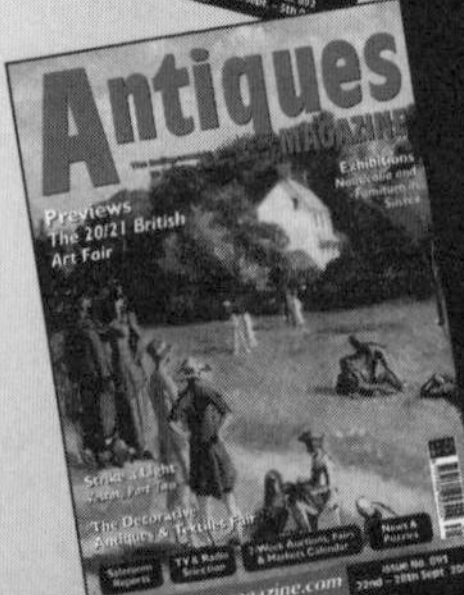

Associated Services

ARCHITECTURAL

Jacob Butler – Period Joinery Specialist
Contact Jacob Butler
✉ **301–302 Via Gellia Mills, Via Gellia Road, Bonsall, Matlock, Derbyshire, DE4 2AJ** P
☎ 01629 822170/825640
ⓔ jacob.butler@virgin.net
ⓦ www.phopkins.demon.co.uk/jacob.html
Est. 1987
Services Repair and restoration of period joinery and furniture
Open By appointment

Zygmunt Chelminski (UKIC)
Contact Mr Z Chelminski
✉ **Studio GE1, 2 Michael Road, London, SW6 2AD** P
☎ 020 7610 9731 ⓕ 020 7610 9731
ⓜ 07770 585130
Est. 1995
Services Marble, stone, terracotta, alabaster and coldstone repair and restoration. English Heritage approved contractor
Open Mon–Fri 10am–5pm appointment advisable

Heritage Architectural Restoration
Contact Richard Powell
✉ **Tyne Court, Haddington, East Lothian, EH41 4BL** P
☎ 01620 825499
Est. 1995
Services Refurbishing and restoration of all architectural woodwork, internal woodwork and furniture
Open By appointment

Iron Wright
Contact Mr F Sporik
✉ **Arch 13b, Parkfield Industrial Estate, Culvert Place, London, SW11 5BA** P
☎ 020 7622 7495 ⓕ 020 7652 4089
Est. 1994
Services Repair and restoration of cast-iron fireplaces
Open Mon–Fri 8am–6pm Sat by appointment

Kelly Antiques
Contact Mr Louis Kelly
✉ **Mullaghmore House, Old Mountfield Road, Omagh, Co Tyrone, BT79 7EX** P
☎ 028 8224 2314 ⓕ 028 8225 0262
ⓔ info@kellyantiques.com
ⓦ www.kellyantiques.com
Est. 1936
Services Fireplace restorations including wood, slate, sandstone, granite and cast-iron, also comprehensive furniture restorations
Open Mon–Fri 10am–7pm Sat 10am–5pm

Melluish & Davis
Contact Mr J Davis
✉ **11 Hampton Lane, Hanworth, Middlesex, TW13 6NN** P
☎ 020 7622 5731 ⓕ 020 8893 4178
Est. 1972
Services Restoration of marble chimney pieces, sculpture and garden ornaments
Open By appointment

Saltney Restoration Services
Contact Mr J Moore
✉ **50 St Mark's Road, Chester, Cheshire, CH4 8DQ** P
☎ 01244 312529 ⓕ 01244 312529
ⓜ 07713 823383
Est. 1967
Services Brick, metal, steel, glass, furniture, stone, lighting and sanitary ware restoration
Open By appointment

Salvo
Contact Hazel Maltravers
✉ **Ford Village, Berwick upon Tweed, Northumberland, TD15 2QG**
☎ 01890 820333 ⓕ 01890 820499
ⓔ salvo@salvo.co.uk
ⓦ www.salvo.co.uk
Est. 1992
Services Provider of information about architectural antiques and reclaimed materials. Salvo publish *Salvo News* every two weeks, Salvo magazines and an auction price guide

BOOKS

C & A J Barmby
Contact C Barmby
✉ **140 Lavender Hill, Tonbridge, Kent, TN9 2AY**
☎ 01732 771590 ⓕ 01732 771590
ⓔ bookpilot@aol.com
Est. 1970
Services Reference books on antiques, display stands, accessories, packaging material
Trade only Yes
Open By appointment

The Book Depot
Contact Conrad Wiberg
✉ **111 Woodcote Avenue, London, NW7 2PD**
☎ 020 8906 3708 ⓕ 020 8906 3708
Est. 1980
Services Free book search for any book
Open Mon–Sun 9am–5pm postal business

H P Book Finders
Contact Mr Martin Earl
✉ **Mosslaird, Brig O'Turk, Callander, Scotland, FK17 8HT** P
☎ 01877 376377 ⓕ 01877 376377
ⓔ martin@hp-bookfinders.co.uk
ⓦ www.hp-bookfinders.co.uk
Est. 1984
Services Booksearch
Open 8am–6pm

F Hutton (Bookbinder) (SOBB)
Contact Felicity Hutton
✉ **Langore House, Langore, Launceston, Cornwall, PL15 8LD** P
☎ 01566 773831
Est. 1985
Services Bookbinding and restoration
Open Telephone first

Meadowcroft Books
Contact Mr A Parry
✉ **21 Upper Bognor Road, Bognor Regis, West Sussex, PO21 1JA** P
☎ 01243 868614 ⓕ 01243 868714
ⓔ enquiries@meadowcroftbooks.demon.co.uk
ⓦ www.meadowcroftbooks.demon.co.uk
Est. 1996
Services Booksearch
Open By appointment

BOXES

William Heffer Antiques
Contact Mr W Heffer
✉ **37 Victoria Park, Cambridge, Cambridgeshire, CB4 3EJ** P
☎ 01223 362825
ⓔ hefferw.vicpark@dial.pipex.com
Est. 1972
Services Small restoration work, caddies, jewellery boxes
Open By appointment

Alan and Kathy Stacy (BAFRA)
Contact Alan Stacey
✉ **PO Box 2771, Wincanton, Somerset, BA9 9YY** Ⓟ
☎ 01963 33988 Ⓕ 01963 32555
Ⓔ akstacey@cwcom.net
Est. 1990
Services Restoration of tortoiseshell, ivory, shagreen, mother-of-pearl and bone
Open By appointment

CANING

Cane and Rush Works
Contact Miss J Swan
✉ **6c Sylvan Road, London, E11 1QH** Ⓟ
☎ 020 8530 7052
Est. 1981
Services Caning and rushing, country chairs, chair seats, bergère suites and sofas
Open By appointment

Cane Corner
Contact Bridgette Stone
✉ **Behind East Budleigh Garage, Lower Budleigh, East Budleigh, Devon, EX9 7DL** Ⓟ
☎ 01395 446166
Est. 1985
Services Antique and modern chairs professionally reseated with split cane and rush
Open Mon–Fri 9am–5.30pm

The Cane Workshop
Contact Mr K Mason
✉ **Squires Garden Centre, Sixth Cross Road, Twickenham, Middlesex, TW2 5PA** Ⓟ
☎ 020 8943 4869 Ⓕ 020 8943 4869
Est. 1976
Services Caning, rushing, cords and willows
Open Tues–Sat 9am–5pm

Caners & Upholders
Contact Steve Warrington
✉ **12 Soberton Road, Bournemouth, Dorset, BH8 9BG** Ⓟ
☎ 01202 399339
Ⓔ steven.warrington@virgin.net.
Est. 1989
Services Cane and rush repair and restoration
Open Mon–Fri 9am–5pm or by appointment

Chair Repair
Contact Denise Viles
✉ **7 Palace Cottages, Exmouth, Devon, EX8 1RP**
☎ 01395 269438
Est. 1999
Services Repairs to rush cane and upholstered furniture, specializing in antique rush and cane seats (bergère suites)
Open Workshop by appointment

Peter Maitland
Contact Mr P J Maitland
✉ **27 Berkeley Road, Bishopstone, Bristol, BS7 8HF** Ⓟ
☎ 0117 942 6870
Est. 1990
Services Chair restoration, rush seating and caning
Open Mon–Fri 9am–5pm or by appointment

CARPETS & RUGS

Lannowe Oriental Textiles
Contact Joanna Titchell
✉ **Near Bath, Wiltshire**
☎ 01225 891487 Ⓕ 01225 891182
Ⓜ 07714 70 3535
Ⓔ joanna@lannowe.co.uk
Est. 1976
Services Washing, restoration and conservation of Oriental carpets, rugs and tapestries
Open By appointment

M & M Restoration
Contact Mrs M Druet
✉ **Mantel House, Broomhill Road, London, SW18 4JQ** Ⓟ
☎ 020 8871 5098 Ⓕ 020 8877 1940
Ⓜ 07850 310104
Est. 1985
Services Restoration and cleaning of antique tapestries, carpets, textiles
Open Mon–Fri 9am–6pm

CERAMICS

SOUTH EAST

Carol Basing
Contact Carol Basing
✉ **41 Prospect Road, Sevenoaks, Kent, TN13 3UA**
☎ 01732 456695
Est. 1984
Services Ceramic repair and restoration
Open Mon–Sun 9am–5pm

Grenville Godfrey
Contact Mr G Godfrey
✉ **60 Watts Lane, Eastbourne, East Sussex, BN21 2LL** Ⓟ
☎ 01323 735595
Est. 1997
Services Repair and restoration of ceramics
Open By appointment

Helen Warren China Restoration
Contact Helen Warren
✉ **5 Clerksfield, Headcorn, Kent, TN27 9QJ** Ⓟ
☎ 01622 891700
Ⓔ conservation@ifwarren.demon.co.uk
Ⓦ www.ifwarren.demon.co.uk
Est. 1990
Services Ceramic repair and restoration
Open By appointment

Laurie Wheeler Restorations
Contact Laurie Wheeler
✉ **Great Knell Farm Cottage, Molland Lane, Ash, Canterbury, Kent, CT3 2ED** Ⓟ
☎ 01304 813550 Ⓕ 01304 813550
Ⓔ laurieandnikki@eurobell.com
Est. 1979
Services Restoration of antique porcelain, pottery, Parian, gilding and enamelling. Tuition also available
Open By appointment

LONDON

The Conservation Studio (ICOM, ILC, UKIC)
Contact Mrs F Hayward
✉ **77 Troutbeck, Albany Street, London, NW1 4EJ** Ⓟ
☎ 020 7387 4994 Ⓕ 020 7387 4994
Est. 1993
Services Restoration and conservation of ceramics, glass, metalwork, ivory and soapstone, specializing in gilding, painting on glass and ceramics
Open Mon–Fri 8.30am–4.30pm Sat by appointment

G W Conservation (OCS)
Contact Ms Gillian Quartly-Watson
✉ **5S Hewlett House, Havelock Avenue, London, SW8 4AS** Ⓟ
☎ 020 7498 5938 Ⓕ 020 7498 5938
Ⓜ 07710 355743
Ⓔ stylish.moves@virgin.net
Est. 1991

Services Conservation of ceramics and related objects
Open Mon–Fri 10am–6pm or by appointment

Rosemary Hamilton China Repairs (IDDA)
Contact Mrs R Hamilton
✉ **44 Moreton Street, London, SW1V 2PB** P
☎ 020 7828 5018 F 020 7828 1325
Est. 1993
Services China repairs and restorations
Open Mon–Fri 9.30am–5.30pm

SOUTH

Brook Studio
Contact Mrs Joanna Holland
✉ **The Granary, 2 Church Road, Pangbourne, Berkshire, RG8 7AA** P
☎ 0118 9842014/9713249
E joanna@holland.demon.co.uk
Est. 1978
Services Good-quality china and porcelain restoration
Open By appointment

Norman Flynn Restorations
Contact Mr N Flynn
✉ **2 Lind Road, Sutton, Surrey, SM1 4QY** P
☎ 020 8661 9505
Est. 1972
Services Porcelain, pottery, enamel restoration
Open Tues–Fri 8.30am–3.30pm

Sarah Peek
Contact Miss S Peek
✉ **The Battery House, Petworth House, Petworth, West Sussex, GU28 ODP** P
☎ 01798 342763 F 01798 342763
E conservation@sarahpeek.co.uk
W www.sarahpeek.co.uk
Est. 1995
Services Restoration of ceramics, glass, enamels
Open By appointment

Regency Antiques
Contact R De Santini
✉ **Bognor Regis, West Sussex**
☎ 01243 861643 F 01243 861643
M 07947 597311
Est. 1978
Services Porcelain and furniture restoration
Open Mon–Fri 9.30am–5.30pm by appointment

Sheila Southwell Studio (BCPAA, IPAA)
Contact Mrs S Southwell
✉ **7 West Street, Burgess Hill, West Sussex, RH15 8NN** P
☎ 01444 244307
Est. 1969
Services Restoration of ceramics, china, porcelain, earthenware. Commissions accepted for hand-painted, commemorative porcelain for any occasion
Open By appointment

WEST COUNTRY

Addington Studio Ceramic Repairs
Contact Pam Warner
✉ **1 Addington Cottages, Upottery, Honiton, Devon, EX14 9PN** P
☎ 01404 861519 F 01404 861308
E addington.studio@virgin.net
Est. 1991
Services Restoration and conservation of ceramics and glass. Tuition given. Collection and delivery service to London
Open By appointment

Antique China and Porcelain Restoration
Contact Mr Carl Garratt
✉ **6 Enfield Drive, Evercreech, Shepton Mallet, Somerset, BA4 6LL** P
☎ 01749 831116
Est. 1978
Services Restoration of antique china, oil paintings and objets d'art
Open By appointment

Ceramic Restoration
Contact Martina Gray or Emma Organ
✉ **Unit 1, 24 Cheap Street, Sherborne, Dorset, DT9 3PX** P
☎ 01935 813128
Est. 1989
Services Restoration and conservation of ceramics
Open Mon–Fri 10am–12.30pm Sat 1.30pm–4pm by appointment

China and Glass Restoration
Contact Mrs Susan Birch
✉ **The Shoe, Old Hollow, Mere, Warminster, Wiltshire, BA12 6EG** P
☎ 01747 861703
Est. 1993
Services China and glass restoration
Open By appointment

Peter Martin Ceramic Restoration
Contact Mr P Martin
✉ **11 Eastbourne Terrace, Westward Ho, Bideford, Devon, EX39 1HG** P
☎ 01237 421446
E pmcr@madasafish.com
Est. 1996
Services Modern and antique ceramic restoration, specializing in decorative china and porcelain antiques
Open Strictly by appointment

Reference Works
Contact Joy or Barry Lamb
✉ **The Last Resort, 9 Commercial Road, Swanage, Dorset, BH19 1DF** P
☎ 01929 424423 F 01929 422597
E sales@referenceworks.co.uk
W www.referenceworks.co.uk
Est. 1984
Services Mail order reference books on pottery and porcelain (mail order address is 12 Commercial Road, Swanage). Consultants and advisers on British ceramics. Monthly illustrated newsletters and book lists
Open Phone for catalogue

EAST

Emma Bradshaw Ceramic Restorations (UKIC)
Contact Emma Bradshaw
✉ **Blake House Craft Centre, 7 Blake End, Rayne, Nr Braintree, Essex, CM7 8SH** P
☎ 01376 529180
Est. 1991
Services Conservation and restoration of bone china, earthenware, porcelain, stoneware, terracotta, early English pottery
Open By appointment

Ceramic Restorations
Contact Miss Syms
✉ **10 Valley Lane, Holt, Norfolk, NR25 6SF** P
M 07748 901093
E victoriasyms@hotmail.com
Est. 1989
Services Ceramics, pottery and porcelain restorations,

specializing in English blue-and-white transfer ware
Open By appointment

HEART OF ENGLAND

The China Repairers
Contact Mrs A Chalmers
✉ **1 Street Farm Workshops, Doughton, Tetbury, Gloucestershire, G18 8TH** 🅿
☎ 01666 503551
Est. 1989
Services China, mirror and picture frame restoration (By Appointment to HRH The Prince of Wales)
Open Mon–Fri 9am–5pm

Gray Arts
Contact Mr A Gray
✉ **Unit 21b, The Maltings, School Lane, Amersham, Buckinghamshire, HP7 0ET** 🅿
☎ 01494 726502 Ⓕ 01494 726502
Ⓜ 07714 274410
Est. 1979
Services Porcelain restoration, clock and watch dial restoration
Trade only Yes
Open By appointment

George Perkins
Contact Mr George Perkins
✉ **2 Dell Spring, Buntingford, Hertfordshire, SG9 9BF** 🅿
☎ 01763 273139 Ⓕ 01763 273139
Est. 1997
Services Porcelain restoration
Open By appointment

The Traditional Studio
Contact Miss V Green
✉ **Welwyn Equestrian Centre, Potters Heath Road, Welwyn, Hertfordshire, AL6 9SZ** 🅿
☎ 01438 814808 Ⓕ 01438 814808
Ⓜ 07899 745316
Est. 1997
Services Ceramics, porcelain, pottery, furniture, plaster, stonework repair, restoration, gilding, frame restoration. Free estimates and advice
Open Mon–Fri 9am–5pm

MIDLANDS

Ashdale China Restoration
Contact Mr R Gregory
✉ **19 Boothby Avenue, Ashbourne, Derbyshire, DE6 1EL** 🅿
☎ 01335 345965
Ⓜ 07961 957530
Ⓦ www.ashdalechina.co.uk
Est. 1984
Services Repairs and restorations
Open By appointment

Roger Hawkins Restoration
Contact R Hawkins
✉ **Unit 4, The Old Dairy, Winkburn, Newark, Nottinghamshire, NG22 8PQ**
☎ 01636 636666
Est. 1980
Services Restorations of all types of pottery, porcelain. Tuition given
Open By appointment

Ravensdale Studios
Contact Mr S Nicholls
✉ **77a Roundwell Street, Tunstall, Stoke-on-Trent, Staffordshire, ST6 5AW** 🅿
☎ 01782 836810 Ⓕ 01782 836810
Ⓔ restore@ravensdale69.fsnet.co.uk
Ⓦ www.ravensdalestudios.co.uk
Est. 1988
Services Ceramic restoration
Open Mon–Fri 9am–5pm

Warwick-Wright Restoration
Contact Mr S MacGarvey
✉ **19b Wem Business Park, New Street, Wem, Shrewsbury, Shropshire, SY4 5JX** 🅿
☎ 01939 234879
Ⓦ www.porcelain-restoring.co.uk
Est. 1992
Services Porcelain restoration
Open Mon–Fri 8.30am–4.30pm

YORKSHIRE & LINCOLNSHIRE

A M Hurrell
Contact Miss A M Hurrell
✉ **49 Bolton Road, Silsden, Keighley, West Yorkshire, BD20 0JY** 🅿
☎ 01535 652969
Est. 1989
Services China restoration
Open By appointment

Kaleidescope Porcelain and Pottery Restorers
Contact Mr F Roberts
✉ **Rose Marie, Main Road, Potterhanworth, Lincoln, Lincolnshire, LN4 2DT** 🅿
☎ 01522 793869 Ⓕ 01522 793869
Est. 1985
Services Antique repairs and restorations, also restores modern pieces on request
Open Mon–Fri 9am–6pm Sat 9am–noon

The Pottery & Porcelain Restoration Co
Contact Mr Tom Cosens
✉ **30 Wharf Street, Sowerby Bridge, West Yorkshire, HX6 2AEW** 🅿
☎ 01422 834828
Ⓔ potrestore@aol.com
Est. 1990
Services Repairs, restoration to all ceramics and spelter
Open Mon–Fri 9am–5pm by appointment

Barbara Skillen Porcelain and Pottery Restoration
Contact Barbara Skillen
☎ 0114 255 4088
Est. 1994
Services Porcelain and pottery restoration
Open By appointment

NORTH EAST

Artisans
Contact Mr C Hobs
✉ **Unit 68, Enterprise Centre, 70 Brunswick Street, Stockton-on-Tees, Cleveland, TS18 1DW** 🅿
☎ 01642 801020 Ⓕ 01642 391351
Ⓜ 07971 831356
Est. 1991
Services Restoration, repairs to antique china and glassware
Open Mon–Fri 9am–5pm Sat 9am–2pm

NORTH WEST

Domino Restorations
Contact Mrs J Hargreaves
✉ **c/o G B Antiques Centre, Lancaster Leisure Park, Wyresdale Road, Lancaster, Lancashire, LA1 3LA** 🅿
Ⓜ 07710 223170
Est. 1979
Services Porcelain and china restoration, jewellery repairs. Repair and restoration of glassware, metalware, tortoiseshell and ivory, spelter, bronze
Open By appointment

ASSOCIATED SERVICES

CLOCKS

Monogram Studios
Contact Mr David R Adams
✉ **25 Kinsey Street, Congleton, Cheshire, CW12 1ES** 🅿
☎ 01260 273957
Est. 1962
Services Pottery and porcelain repair and restoration
Open Mon–Fri 8.30am–5pm

Porcelain Repairs
Contact Mr I Norman
✉ **240 Stockport Road, Cheadle Heath, Stockport, Cheshire, SK3 0LX** 🅿
☎ 0161 428 9599 Ⓕ 0161 286 6702
Ⓔ porrep@cs.com
Est. 1976
Services Repair and restoration of all ceramics. Collection and delivery service to central London
Open By appointment during office hours

WALES

Ceramic Restoration (GADR)
Contact Lynette Pierce
✉ **Glan-Hafren Studio, Abermule, Montgomery, Powys, SY15 6NA** 🅿
☎ 01686 630219
Ⓜ 07950 025742
Est. 1995
Services China and pottery repairs and restoration, figurines a speciality
Trade only Yes
Open By appointment

SCOTLAND

Ellen L Breheny
Contact Ellen L Breheny
✉ **10 Glenisla Gardens, Edinburgh, EH9 2HR** 🅿
☎ 0131 667 2620
Ⓔ ellen@breheny.com
Est. 1988
Services Conservation and restoration of ceramics, glass and related materials
Open Mon–Fri 10am–6pm

Renaissance China Restoration
Contact Miss S Harvey
✉ **30 West Annadale Street, Edinburgh, EH7 4JY** 🅿
☎ 0131 557 2762
Est. 1984
Services Invisible ceramic restoration
Open Mon–Fri 10am–5pm

REPUBLIC OF IRELAND

Lorna Barnes Conservation (IPCRA, ICCOM)
Contact Lorna Barnes
✉ **158 Rialto Cottages, Rialto, Dublin 8, Co Dublin, Ireland** 🅿
☎ 01 473 6205
Ⓔ barneslorna@hotmail.com
Est. 2000
Services Conservation of glass, ceramic and stone objects, condition surveys, advice on packaging and storage
Open Mon–Fri 9am–6pm

CLOCKS

Anthony Allen Conservation, Restoration, Furniture and Artefacts (BAFRA, UKIC)
Contact Anthony Allen
✉ **The Old Wharf Workshop, Redmoor Lane, Newtown, High Peak, Derbyshire, SK22 3JL** 🅿
☎ 01663 745274 Ⓕ 01663 745274
Est. 1970
Services Restoration of clock cases and movements, gilding, marquetry, Boulle, upholstery, metalwork, 17th–19thC furniture
Open Mon–Fri 8am–5pm

David Ansell (BAFRA, BHI)
Contact David Ansell
✉ **48 Dellside, Harefield, Middlesex, UB9 6AX** 🅿
☎ 01895 824648
Ⓜ 07976 222610
Ⓔ dansell@globalnet.co.uk
Est. 1990
Services Repairs and restoration of clocks
Open Mon–Sun 8.30am–5.30pm or by appointment

Antique Renovations
Contact Stephen or Alan Gartland
✉ **Unit 1, Lavenham Craft Units, Brent Eleigh Road, Lavenham, Sudbury, Suffolk, CO10 9PE** 🅿
☎ 01787 248511
Est. 1960
Services Repair, cabinet work and French polishing
Recommended by ERCOL. Specializing in clock case repair
Open Mon–Fri 8.30am–5pm Sat 9am–1pm

The Barometer Shop (BHI)
Contact Mr R Cookson
✉ **New Street, Leominster, Herefordshire, HR6 8DP** 🅿
☎ 01568 610200 Ⓕ 01568 610200
Ⓜ 07771 548037
Est. 1969
Services Supply and restoration of antique clocks and barometers
Open Mon–Fri 9am–5pm Sat 10am–4pm

David Bates
Contact Mr David Bates
✉ **Church Cottage, Church Lane, Cawston, Norwich, Norfolk, NR10 4AJ** 🅿
☎ 01603 871687
Est. 1995
Services Restoration of painted and brass clock dials
Open Mon–Fri 9am–5pm

Symon E Boyd Clock Restorer (BHI)
Contact Mr S Boyd
✉ **54 Buxton Road, Disley, Stockport, Cheshire, SK12 2EY** 🅿
☎ 01663 763999
Est. 1984
Services Repair and restoration of clocks, barometers, musical boxes and automata
Open By appointment

J W Carpenter Antique Clock Restorer (BHI)
Contact John Carpenter
✉ **Gable Cottage, Beacon Lane, Woodnesborough, Sandwich, Kent, CT13 0PD** 🅿
☎ 01304 813909 Ⓕ 01304 813909
Ⓔ john@ticking.freeserve.co.uk
Est. 1970
Services Antique clock repair and restoration
Open By appointment

Clockcraft
Contact Mr D Peveley
✉ **13 High Street, Bridlington, East Yorkshire, YO16 4PR** 🅿
☎ 01262 602802
Est. 1984
Services Clock repairs and restoration, all periods and all types
Open Mon–Sat 9am–5pm

Gray Arts
Contact Mr A Gray
✉ **Unit 21b, The Maltings, School Lane, Amersham, Buckinghamshire, HP7 0ET** Ⓟ
☎ 01494 726502 Ⓕ 01494 726502
Ⓜ 07714 274410
Est. 1979
Services Porcelain restoration, clock and watch dial restoration
Trade only Yes
Open By appointment

Richard Higgins Conservation (BAFRA, UKIC)
Contact Richard Higgins
✉ **The Old School, Longnor, Nr Shrewsbury, Shropshire, SY5 7PP** Ⓟ
☎ 01743 718162 Ⓕ 01743 718022
Ⓔ richardhigginsco@aol.com
Est. 1988
Services Restoration of all fine furniture, clocks, movements, dials and cases, casting, plating, Boulle, gilding, lacquerwork, carving, period upholstery
Open Mon–Fri 8am–6pm

E Hollander (BWCG, BHI)
Contact Mr D J Pay
✉ **1 Bennets Castle, 89 The Street, Capel, Dorking, Surrey, RH5 5JX** Ⓟ
☎ 01306 713377 Ⓕ 01306 712013
Est. 1860
Services Repair and restoration of clocks, barometers, watches
Open Mon–Fri 8am–4.30pm or by appointment

Horological Workshops (BHI, BADA)
Contact Mr M D Tooke
✉ **204 Worplesdon Road, Guildford, Surrey, GU2 9UY** Ⓟ
☎ 01483 576496 Ⓕ 01483 452212
Ⓔ enquiries@horologicalworkshops.com
Est. 1968
Services Full restoration of antique clocks
Open Tues–Fri 8.30am–5.30pm Sat 9am–12.30pm

Gavin Hussey Antique Restoration (BAFRA)
Contact G Hussey
✉ **4 Brook Farm, Clayhill Road, Leigh, Reigate, Surrey, RH2 8PA** Ⓟ
☎ 01306 611634 Ⓕ 01293 782595
Ⓦ www.restoreantiques.com
Est. 1994
Services Full restoration of furniture and clocks
Open Mon–Fri 8.30am–5.30pm or by appointment

Llewellyn Clocks
Contact Mr C Llewellyn
✉ **12 Gibson Crescent, Sandbach, Cheshire, CW11 3HW** Ⓟ
☎ 01270 768525
Est. 1976
Services Complete antique clock repair and restoration
Open By appointment

Robert Loomes Clock Restoration (BWCG, MBHI)
Contact Mr R Loomes
✉ **3 St Leonards Street, Stamford, Lincolnshire, PE9 2HU** Ⓟ
☎ 01780 481319
Ⓦ www.dialrestorer.co.uk
Est. 1987
Services Antique repair and restoration
Open Mon–Fri 9am–5pm or by appointment

C Moss
Contact Mr C Moss
✉ **59 Walcot Street, Bath, Somerset, BA1 5BN** Ⓟ
☎ 01225 445892 Ⓕ 01225 445892
Ⓜ 07779 161731
Est. 1985
Services Clock case restoration, marquetry, parquetry, walnut furniture
Open By appointment

Oxford Longcase Clocks
Contact Mr Paul Carroll
✉ **76 Courtland Road, Rose Hill, Oxford, Oxfordshire, OX4 4JB** Ⓟ
☎ 01865 779660
Est. 1978
Services Clock and barometer repair
Open Mon–Fri 8am–5pm Sat 8am–noon

Reeves Restoration at the Coach House Antiques
Contact Mrs L Reeves
✉ **The Coach House, 60 Station Approach, Gomershall, Surrey, GU5 9NP** Ⓟ
☎ 01483 203838 Ⓕ 01483 202999
Ⓔ coach_house.antiques@virgin.net
Ⓦ www.coachhouseantiques.com
Est. 1984
Services Antique clock, furniture and upholstery restoration, calligraphy, painting
Open Mon–Sun 10am–5pm closed Thurs

J K Speed Antique Furniture Restoration
Contact Mr J Speed
✉ **The Workshop, Thornton Road, New York, Lincoln, Lincolnshire, LN4 4YL** Ⓟ
☎ 01205 280313
Ⓜ 07761 242219
Est. 1964
Services Antique repair and restoration, light upholstery, specializing in case repair of longcase clocks
Open Mon–Fri 9am–5.30pm

Sundial Antique Clock Service
Contact Mr Peter Mole
✉ **64 The Parade, Brighton Road, Hooley, Coulsdon, Surrey, CR5 3EE** Ⓟ
☎ 01737 551991 Ⓕ 01737 551991
Ⓜ 07733 408535
Ⓔ sundialclocks@hooley68.fsnet.co.uk
Est. 1965
Services Barometer and clock restoration, specializing in longcase clock repair
Open By appointment

Robert P Tandy (BAFRA)
Contact Robert P Tandy
✉ **Unit 5, Manor Workshops, West End, Nailsea, Bristol, North Somerset, BS48 4DD** Ⓟ
☎ 01275 856378
Est. 1987
Services Antique furniture and longcase clock casework restoration
Open Mon–Fri 10am–6pm

Time Restored
Contact J H Bowler-Reed
✉ **20 High Street, Pewsey, Wiltshire, SN9 5AQ** Ⓟ
☎ 01672 563544
Est. 1978
Services Restoration of antique clocks, musical boxes and barometers
Open Mon–Fri 10am–6pm

Timecraft Clocks (BHI)
Contact Mr G Smith
✉ **Unit 2, 24 Cheap Street, Sherborne, Dorset, DT9 3PX** Ⓟ
☎ 01935 817771

ASSOCIATED SERVICES

CONSERVATION

Est. 1994
Services Clock restoration and repair
Open Tue–Fri 10.30am–5.30pm Sat 10.30am–5pm

Warwick Antique Restorations (UKIC)

Contact Mr R Lawman
✉ **32 Beddington Lane, Croydon, Surrey, CR0 4TB** 🅿
☎ 020 8688 4511
ⓔ boris@sutton74.freeserve.co.uk
Est. 1976
Services Antique clock restoration, leathering, rushing, upholstery, caning, brass work
Open Tues–Sat 9.30am–5pm

Wheelers (BHI, BWCG)

Contact Mr T P Wheeler
✉ **14–16 Bath Place, Worthing, West Sussex, BN11 3AA**
☎ 01903 207656
Est. 1991
Services Antique clock repair, restoration, sales
Open Mon–Sat 9am–5pm

CONSERVATION

Archaeological Conservator (ICHAWI, ILC, IPCRA)

Contact Susannah Kelly
✉ **14 Greenmount Lawns, Terenure, Dublin 6, Republic of Ireland** 🅿
☎ 01 492 7695/01 716 8503
Ⓜ 08728 48752
ⓔ csmchale@gofree.indigo.ie
Est. 1993
Services Conservation of archaeological and historical objects
Open Mon–Fri 9am–6pm

Heritage Care (ICHAWI, IPCRA, IMA)

Contact Adrian Kennedy
✉ **Dublin, Ireland**
☎ 01 459 9745
ⓔ adrian@iegateway.net
Est. 1998
Services Conservation and restoration of museum, folk-life and religious type objects dating from archaeological finds to 20thC items
Open Mon–Fri 7.30am–5.30pm

Plowden and Smith Ltd (MGA)

Contact James Fielden
✉ **190 St Ann's Hill, London, SW18 2RT** 🅿
☎ 020 8874 4005 Ⓕ 020 8874 7248
ⓔ info@plowden-smith.co.uk
Ⓦ www.plowden-smith.co.uk
Est. 1966
Services Repair and restoration of paintings, furniture, stone, metalwork, decorative arts, object mounting, exhibitions
Open Mon–Fri 9am–5pm

Gordon Richardson

Contact Gordon Richardson
✉ **36 Silverknowes Road, Edinburgh, EH4 5LG** 🅿
☎ 0131 312 7959
ⓔ grconserve@supanet.com
Ⓦ www.homestead.com/grconserve/index~nsg.html
Services Conservation and restoration of paintings, pictures, prints, drawings, globes, scientific instruments, silverware, metalware, military artefacts, ships' models, decorative objects
Open By appointment

Textile Conservation (UKIC)

Contact Frances Lennard
✉ **Ivy House Farm, Wolvershill Road, Banwell, Somerset, BS29 6LB** 🅿
☎ 01934 822449 Ⓕ 01934 822449
ⓔ huttonlennard@compuserve.com
Est. 1989
Services Textile conservation
Open Mon–Fri 9am–5pm

Textile Conservation Services

Contact Miss L Bond
✉ **3–4 West Workshops, Welbeck, Worksop, Nottinghamshire, S80 3LW** 🅿
☎ 01909 481655 Ⓕ 01909 481655
ⓔ textile.conservation@tesco.net
Est. 1984
Services The conservation of costume, lace and small textiles. Talks and courses on costume and textiles
Open By appointment

Voitek Conservation of Works of Art (IPC)

Contact Mrs E Sobczynski
✉ **9 Whitehorse Mews, Westminster Bridge Road, London, SE1 7QD** 🅿
☎ 020 7928 6094 Ⓕ 020 7928 6094
ⓔ voitekcwa@btinternet.com
Est. 1972
Services Conservation of prints, drawings, watercolours, maps, conservation mounting and project planning
Open By appointment

CONSULTANCY

Tim Corfield Professional Antiques Consultant

Contact Tim Corfield
✉ **Beechcroft, Buckholt Road, Broughton, Stockbridge, Hampshire, SO20 8DA** 🅿
☎ 01794 301141 Ⓕ 01794 301141
Ⓜ 07798 881383
ⓔ antique@tcp.co.uk
Ⓦ www.antiques-hunter.com
Est. 1992
Services Advising clients on purchases at auction or in the trade
Open By appointment

Robert Kleiner and Co Ltd (BADA, CINOA)

Contact Robert Kleiner or Jane de Hurtig
✉ **30 Old Bond Street, London, W1S 4AE** 🅿
☎ 020 7629 1814 Ⓕ 020 7629 1239
ⓔ robert.kleiner@virgin.net
Ⓦ www.cloudband.com/gallery/kleiner/playthings
Est. 1989
Services Advice on purchase and sale of Chinese works of art, jades, porcelain, snuff bottles, valuations of collections. Specialist in Chinese Snuff Bottles.
Open Mon–Fri 9.30am–5.30pm

DISPLAY EQUIPMENT

Arcade Arts Ltd

Contact Mr K Hewitt or Monika Wengraf-Hewitt
✉ **25 West Hill Road, London, SW18 1LL** 🅿
☎ 020 8265 2564 Ⓕ 020 8874 2982
Est. 1997
Services Repair and renovation of art objects and makers of display stands
Open By appointment

Timbercraft

Contact Mr A J Fishwick
✉ **Bottomley Yard, Bottomley Street, Nelson, Lancashire, BB9 9SW** 🅿

☎ 01282 611277 Ⓕ 01282 615651
Est. 1997
Services Makers of display units for antique thimbles, spoons, cabinets for medals etc
Open By appointment

DOCUMENTATION AND PROVENANCE

DIVA (Digital Inventory and Visual Archive)
Contact Mr R Haycraft
✉ **The Lamb Arcade, High Street, Wallingford, Oxfordshire, OX10 0BS** Ⓟ
☎ 01491 839622
Ⓔ rohaycraft@fsbdial.co.uk
Ⓦ www.juststolen.com
Est. 1980
Services Archive documentation, provision of logbook and provenance history, stolen property displayed on website
Open Mon–Fri 9am–5.30pm

ENAMEL

Mark Newland Enamel Restorer
Contact Mr M Newland
✉ **1 Whitehouse Way, Southgate, London, N14 7LX** Ⓟ
☎ 020 8361 0429
Est. 1982
Services Restoration of enamelled jewellery and objets d'art
Open By appointment

ETHNOGRAPHICS

George Monger
Contact Mr G Monger
✉ **Unit 6, The Barn, Glebe Farm Industrial Units, Onehouse, Stowmarket, Suffolk, IP14 3HL** Ⓟ
☎ 01449 677900 Ⓕ 01449 674803
Ⓜ 07703 441265
Ⓔ geoMcons@tinyworld.co.uk
Est. 1995
Services Conservation and restoration, including social and industrial history and ethnography of pieces
Open By appointment

FLOORS

Holland & Welsh
Contact Michael Nap
✉ **8 Glay-y-Llyn, Industrial Estate, Taffs Well, Cardiff, South Glamorgan, CF4 7QH** Ⓟ
☎ 029 2056 1795 Ⓕ 029 2021 3370
Ⓔ hollandwelsh@msn.com
Est. 1997
Services Supply and installation of antique flooring
Open Sat–Sun 11am–4pm and by appointment

FRAMING

Baron Art
Contact Mr A Baron
✉ **9 Chapel Yard, Albert Street, Holt, Norfolk, NR25 6HJ** Ⓟ
☎ 01263 713430 Ⓕ 01263 711670
Ⓔ baronart@aol.com
Est. 2001
Services Framing
Open Mon–Sat 9am–5pm

Douglas McLeod Period Frames
Contact Suzie McLeod
✉ **22–24 Trinity Street, Salisbury, Wiltshire, SP1 2BD** Ⓟ
☎ 01722 337565 Ⓕ 01722 337565
Est. 1982
Services Restoration of old frames, picture restoration, carving, gilding, lacewing framing
Open Mon–Fri 9am–5pm Sat 10am–4pm

FURNITURE

SOUTH EAST

T M Akers Antique Restoration (BAFRA)
Contact Mr T M Akers
✉ **39 Chancery Lane, Beckenham, Kent, BR3 2NR** Ⓟ
☎ 020 8650 9179
Ⓜ 07768 948421
Ⓦ www.akersofantiques.com
Est. 1979
Services Period antique furniture restoration
Open Mon–Fri 9am–5pm

Antique Restoration
Contact Mr S Bigwood
✉ **Unit 5, Nuralite Industrial Estate, Canal Road, Higham, Rochester, Kent, ME3 7HX** Ⓟ
☎ 01474 823866
Ⓔ sales@bigwoodantiques.com
Ⓦ www.antiquesrestoration.co.uk
Est. 1984
Services Complete restoration of all antique furniture
Open Mon–Fri 8.30am–5pm

Antique Restorations (BAFRA)
Contact Raymond Konyn
✉ **The Old Wheelwrights', Brasted Forge, Brasted, Kent, TN16 1JL** Ⓟ
☎ 01959 563863 Ⓕ 01959 561262
Ⓔ antique@antique-restorations.org.uk
Ⓦ www.antique-restorations.org.uk
Est. 1979
Services Full antique furniture restoration, pre-1900 furniture sourcing and acquisition, replica brass foundry castings
Open Mon–Fri 9am–5pm

Ashdown Antiques Restoration
Contact Robert Hale
✉ **Old Forge Farm, Old Forge Lane, Horney Common, Uckfield, East Sussex, TB22 3EL** Ⓟ
☎ 01825 713003
Est. 1975
Services Furniture restorer
Open By appointment

Bespoke Furniture
Contact Mr M McEwan
✉ **Ladwood Farm, Acrise, Folkestone, Kent, CT18 8LL** Ⓟ
☎ 01303 893635
Est. 1994
Services Restoration of antique furniture. Traditional or contemporary individual pieces of furniture made to order
Open Mon–Fri 8.30am–5pm Sat 9am–2pm Sun by appointment

Maxwell Black
Contact Mr M Black
✉ **Brook House Studio, Novington Lane, East Chiltington, Lewes, East Sussex, BN7 3AX** Ⓟ
☎ 01273 890175
Est. 1979
Services All types of antique furniture restoration
Open Mon–Fri 8am–6pm

Brightling Restoration
Contact N M J Haken
✉ **Little Worge Farm, Brightling, Robertsbridge, East Sussex, TN32 5HN** Ⓟ
☎ 01424 838424 Ⓕ 01424 838681
Ⓔ brightlingrest@cs.com
Est. 2000
Services Restoration of English and Continental furniture
Open Mon–Fri 8am–4.30pm

FURNITURE

Benedict Clegg (BAFRA)
Contact Mr Benedict Clegg
✉ **Rear of 20 Camden Road, Tunbridge Wells, Kent, TN1 2PY**
☎ 01892 548095
Est. 1987
Services Antique furniture repair and restoration
Open Mon–Fri 9am–5pm

D & C Antique Restorations
Contact Mr C Voles
✉ **1–4 Upper Gardner Street, Brighton, East Sussex, BN1 4AN** P
☎ 01273 670344
Est. 1993
Services Complete antique furniture restoration
Open Mon–Fri 8am–5.30pm

W H Earles
Contact Mr W H Earles
✉ **60 Castle Road, Tankerton, Whitstable, Kent, CT5 2EA** P
☎ 01227 264346
Est. 1978
Services English, Continental and most period furniture restoration and papier mâché
Open Mon–Fri 8.30am–6pm

Luke Evans Antiques
Contact Mr Luke Evans
✉ **19 Pycombe Street, Pycombe, East Sussex, BN45 7EE** P
☎ 01273 504359
Est. 1998
Services Furniture restoration, upholstery, re-caning, re-leathering, pine stripping, furniture finding service
Open Mon–Sat 9am–6pm

Farm Cottage Antiques
Contact Mrs Lynn Winder
✉ **Basement, 6a Claremont Road, Seaford, East Sussex, BN25 2AY** P
☎ 01323 896766 ℻ 01323 894982
Est. 1995
Services Furniture restoration
Open By appointment

Glassenbury Antique Pine
Contact Clive Cowell
✉ **Iden Green, Goudhurst, Cranbrook, Kent, TN17 2PA** P
☎ 01580 212022 ℻ 01580 212944
Est. 1985
Services Repair and restoration, makes on commission
Open Mon–Fri 8.30am–5.30pm
Sat 10am–1pm

Heritage Restoration
Contact Mr D R Johnson
✉ **782 Lower Rainham Road, Rainham, Gillingham, Kent, ME8 7UD** P
☎ 01634 374609
Est. 1989
Services Antique furniture restoration
Open Mon–Fri 9am–5pm

T C Hinton
Contact T C Hinton
✉ **The Board Stores, Spencer Mews, Rear of 20 Camden Rd, Tunbridge Wells, Kent, TN1 2PY** P
☎ 01892 547515 ℻ 01892 547515
ⓔ hintonbusiness@talk21.com
Est. 1979
Services Restoration and conservation of antique furniture, French polishing, gilding, painted furniture, antique paint effects
Open Mon–Fri 9am–1pm
2–5.30pm

R G Jones
Contact R G Jones
✉ **1 Brickfield Cottage, Bilting, Ashford, Kent, TN25 4ER** P
☎ 01233 812849
Est. 1985
Services Antique restoration, gilding
Open Mon–Fri 9am–4pm

R Lindsell
Contact R Lindsell
✉ **2b Southwood Road, Ramsgate, Kent, G11 0AA** P
☎ 01843 588845
Est. 1973
Services Furniture repair and restoration, French polishing
Open Mon–Fri 9am–6pm

Timothy Long Restoration (BAFRA)
Contact Timothy Long
✉ **St John's Church, London Road, Dunton Green, Sevenoaks, Kent, TN13 2TE** P
☎ 01732 743368
Est. 1978
Services Antique furniture restoration, marquetry, Boulle, clock cases, upholstery, cabinet work and polishing
Open Mon–Fri 8am–5pm

The Old Forge
Contact Mr Burgess
✉ **South Street, Rotherfield, Crowborough, East Sussex, TN6 3LR** P
☎ 01892 852060
Est. 1979
Services Furniture restoration
Open Mon–Fri 8am–6pm
Sat 8am–2pm

Park View Antiques
Contact Patrick Leith-Ross
✉ **High Street, Durgates, Wadhurst, East Sussex, TN5 6DE** P
☎ 01892 740264 ℻ 01892 740264
Ⓜ 07970 202036
ⓔ leithross@btconnect.com
Est. 1985
Services Furniture restoration
Open By appointment

Phillburys
Contact Mr G C Rattenbury
✉ **Unit 2, Udimore Workshop, School Lane, Udimore, Rye, East Sussex, TN31 6AS** P
☎ 01797 222361
Est. 1982
Services Restoration of antique furniture
Open Mon–Sat 8am–6pm

Marco Pitt (BADA)
Contact Mr Marco Pitt
✉ **New England House, New England Street, Brighton, East Sussex, BN1 4GH** P
☎ 01273 685009
Ⓜ 07721 022480
Est. 1978
Services Complete furniture restoration, specializing in Russian and European pieces
Open Mon–Fri 9am–6pm
Sat 9am–1pm

Paul M Read Antique Furniture Restoration
Contact Paul Read
✉ **Brasted Forge, The Green, High Street, Brasted, Westerham, Kent, TN16 1JL** P
☎ 01959 565733 ℻ 01959 565733
Est. 1986
Services Full furniture restoration, cabinet-making, marquetry, inlaying, carving, turning, gilding,

leather work, full clock restoration service, upholstery, cane and rush seating, traditional French polishing, on-site polishing and specialist wood finishes
Open By appointment

T Straw Restoration
Contact Mr T Straw
✉ **Unit 4, The Oast Hurst Farm, Mountain Street, Chilham, Canterbury, Kent, CT4 8DH** 🅿
☎ 01227 732485
Ⓜ 07961 944014
Est. 1989
Services Antique furniture restoration
Open Mon–Fri 8am–6pm or by appointment

V Stringer
Contact Mr V Stringer
✉ **Unit 5, Acorn House, The Broyle, Ringmer, Lewes, East Sussex, BN8 5NN** 🅿
☎ 01273 814434 Ⓕ 01273 814434
Est. 1989
Services Antique restoration, reproduction polishers, furniture makers
Open Mon–Fri 8am–6pm Sat 8am–noon

Temple Jones Restoration
Contact E or Miss B Temple Jones
✉ **The Workshop, Burwash Common Post Office, Heathfield Road, Burwash Common, East Sussex, TN19 7LT** 🅿
☎ 01435 883130 Ⓕ 01435 883130
Ⓜ 07802 415138
Ⓔ temple-jones@talk21.com
Est. 1996
Services Restoration and conservation work to period antique furniture
Open Mon–Sat 8am–6pm

LONDON

J Abrahart
Contact Mr J Abrahart
✉ **62a Valetta Road, London, W3 7TN** 🅿
☎ 020 8746 7260
Est. 1955
Services Antique furniture repair and restoration, French polishing
Open By appointment

Adams Restorations
Contact Mr A Klappholz
✉ **273 Green Lanes, Brownswood Road, London, N4 2EX** 🅿
☎ 020 7281 9604 Ⓕ 020 7281 9604
Ⓜ 07778 802877
Ⓔ aklappholz@ukgateway.net
Est. 1987
Services Furniture repair and restoration
Open Mon–Sat 8am–5pm

G Albanese
Contact Mr G Albanese
✉ **Unit 3a, 100 Rosebery Avenue, London, E12 6PS** 🅿
☎ 020 8471 5417
Est. 1978
Services Antiques restoration and cabinet-making
Trade only Yes
Open Mon–Fri 7am–5pm

Antique Restorations (BAFRA)
Contact Mr A Smith
✉ **45 Windmill Road, Brentford, Middlesex, TW8 0QQ** 🅿
☎ 020 8568 5249 Ⓕ 020 8568 5249
Est. 1987
Services Restorers of painted and decorated furniture. Specialists in Oriental laquering, Japanning, gilding
Open Mon–Fri 9am–5.30pm or by appointment

B S H Antique Restorers Ltd
Contact Mr B S Howells
✉ **7a Tynemouth Terrace, Tynemouth Road, London, N15 4AP** 🅿
☎ 020 8808 7965 Ⓕ 020 8801 5313
Est. 1978
Services 18th–19thC antique furniture restoration, leatherwork, gilding, marquetry and copy brasswork
Open Mon–Fri 6.30am–3.30pm

Mark Baker
Contact Mr M Baker
✉ **74 The Green, Twickenham, Middlesex, TW2 5AG** 🅿
☎ 020 8891 5309
Est. 1992
Services Complete furniture repair and restoration, turning, marquetry, inlay work, cabinet-making
Open Mon–Fri 9am–6pm

Ballantyne Booth Ltd
Contact Mr Scott Bowram
✉ **Wendover House, 2a Wendover Road, London, NW10 4R7** 🅿
☎ 020 965 2777 Ⓕ 020 965 2777
Est. 1983
Services Cabinet work, veneering, glazing, carving, polishing, upholstery, conservation and restoration
Open Mon–Fri 9am–5.30pm

Bell House Restoration
Contact Mr R Humphrey
✉ **20–22 Beardell Street, London, SE19 1TP** 🅿
☎ 020 8761 9002 Ⓕ 020 8761 9012
Ⓜ 07771 801269
Ⓔ bellhouserestore@aol.com
Est. 1984
Services Antique furniture restoration, gilding, polishing, colouring, turning, veneering, restorations abroad, simulation
Open Mon–Fri 8am–5pm

Church Lane Restorations (LAPADA)
Contact Mr Evans or Mr Vincent
✉ **1 Church Lane, Teddington, Middlesex, TW11 8PA** 🅿
☎ 020 8977 2526 Ⓕ 020 8977 2526
Est. 1969
Services Complete repair and restoration service, cabinet-making, polishing, carving
Open Mon–Thurs 7.30am–5pm Fri 7.30am–4pm

The Collector's Workshop
Contact Mr B Brannan
✉ **Heathrow House, Factory Lane, London, N17 9BY** 🅿
☎ 020 8808 1920 Ⓕ 020 8808 1920
Ⓜ 07778 754754
Est. 1968
Services Antique furniture repair and restoration, upholstery, carving, gilding
Open By appointment

W J Cook (BAFRA)
Contact Mr B Cook
✉ **167 Battersea High Street, London, SW11 3JS** 🅿
☎ 020 7736 5329
Est. 1963
Services Furniture polishing, restoration, upholstery, gilding
Open By appointment

George Cooke
Contact Mr G Cooke

✉ Unit GE 3,
Cooper House,
2 Michael Road,
London,
SW6 2AD 🅿
☎ 020 7610 9066
Ⓜ 07932 007412
Ⓔ george@gcrestoration.fsnet.co.uk
Est. 1993
Services Antique restoration and conservation, including French polishing, veneering, turning, cabinet-making
Open Mon–Fri 8am–6pm
Sat by appointment

The Craftsman's Joint
Contact Mrs Jo Hollis
✉ **175 Kingston Road, London, SW19 1LH** 🅿
☎ 020 8545 0655 Ⓕ 020 8395 4566
Ⓔ craftsmans_joint@yahoo.co.uk
Ⓦ www.craftsmansjoint.co.uk
Est. 1991
Services Furniture restoration, cabinet-making, French polishing, upholstery, caning, leatherwork
Open Mon–Fri 9.30am–5.30pm
Sat 10am–2pm closed Wed or by appointment

Crawford Antiques
✉ **87 Cricklewood Lane, London, NW2 1HR** 🅿
☎ 020 8450 3660
Est. 1969
Services Antiques repairs and French polishing
Open Mon–Sat 9am–6pm

Robert H Crawley (BAFRA)
Contact Mr R Crawley
✉ **75 St Mary's Road, London, W5 5RH** 🅿
☎ 020 8566 5074 Ⓕ 020 8810 0878
Ⓔ antique.restorer@virgin.net
Est. 1979
Services Antique furniture restoration
Open Mon–Fri 8.30am–4.30pm

G and D Davis Antique Restorers
Contact Mr G Davis
✉ **135 Bowes Road, London, N13 4SE** 🅿
☎ 020 8889 4951
Est. 1982
Services Antique furniture restoration, caning, upholstery
Open Mon–Sat 9am–6pm

Elizabeth Street Antiques and Restoration Services
Contact Mr Naik
✉ **35 Elizabeth Street, London, SW1 9RP** 🅿
☎ 020 7730 6777
Est. 1993
Services Antique restoration, marquetry, French polishing, upholstery. Sells antiques
Open Mon–Sat 8am–7pm

Fens Restoration and Sales
Contact Mrs M Saville
✉ **46 Lots Road, London, SW10 0QF** 🅿
☎ 020 7352 9883
Est. 1979
Services Repair and restoration of furniture, stripping
Open Mon–Fri 9am–5pm
Sat by appointment

Ivo Geikie-Cobb
Contact Mr I Geikie-Cobb
✉ **Unit 32, Charterhouse Works, Eltringham Street, London, SW18 1TD** 🅿
☎ 020 8874 3767 Ⓕ 020 8874 3767
Ⓜ 07761 561569
Ⓔ restore@ivogc.com
Ⓦ www.ivogc.com
Est. 1991
Services Antique furniture conservation and restoration, gilding, upholstery, re-leathering, French polishing, veneering, architectural restoration
Open Mon–Fri 9.30am–5.30pm

H J Hatfield and Son
✉ **42 St Michael's Street, London, W2 1QP** 🅿
☎ 020 7723 8265 Ⓕ 020 7706 4562
Ⓔ hjhatfield@msn.com
Est. 1834
Services Restoration of furniture, porcelain, paintings, Boulle, upholstery, lacquerwork, metalwork, chandeliers, marble
Open Mon–Fri 9am–1pm 2–5pm

Hatter Antiques & Restoration
Contact Mr P Harris
✉ **291 Sydenham Road, London, SE26 5EW** 🅿
☎ 020 8659 0333
Est. 1987
Services Antique furniture repair and restoration, upholstery, French polishing, woodwork repair
Open Mon–Sat 8.30am–7.30pm

Hens Teeth Antiques
Contact Mr M Murray
✉ **20 Park Hall Road, London, N2 9PU** 🅿
☎ 020 8883 0755
Ⓜ 07970 625359
Ⓔ hens.teeth@virgin.net
Est. 1997
Services Furniture repair and restoration, polishing, gilding, upholstery
Open By appointment

Hope and Piaget (BAFRA)
Contact Mr B Duffy or Mrs K Keate
✉ **Unit 12–13, Burmarsh Workshops, Marsden Street, London, NW5 3JA** 🅿
☎ 020 7267 6040 Ⓕ 020 7267 6040
Ⓔ mail@hope-piaget.co.uk
Est. 1982
Services Conservation and restoration of 18th–19thC furniture, Japanning, laquerwork, gilding, carving, tortoiseshelling
Open Mon–Fri 9.30am–6pm

Hornsby Furniture Restoration Ltd
Contact Mr M Gough
✉ **35 Thurloe Place, London, SW7 2HJ** 🅿
☎ 020 7225 2888 Ⓕ 020 7838 0235
Ⓔ hornsby@antiquefurniturefood.com
Ⓦ www.antiquefurniturefood.com
Est. 1890
Services Antique furniture restoration including gilding, cabinet-making, upholstery, bespoke furniture, French polishing, caning
Open Mon–Fri 8am–5.30pm
Sat 9am–12.30pm

Magical Restorations
Contact Mr F Hussain
✉ **3 Wilson Walk, Chiswick, London, W4 1TP** 🅿
☎ 020 8741 3799
Est. 1997
Services Furniture repair and restoration, carving, gilding, French polishing
Open Mon–Fri 9am–5pm

M Merritt
Contact Mr M Merritt

✉ **8 Brightfield Road, London, SE12 8QF** 🅿
☎ 020 8852 7577 Ⓕ 020 8852 7577
Est. 1983
Services Antique furniture restoration, cabinet-making, veneering
Open Mon–Fri 9am–5pm

Richard G Phillips Ltd
Contact Mr R G Phillips
✉ **95–99 Shernhall Street, London, E17 9HS** 🅿
☎ 020 8509 9075 Ⓕ 020 8509 9077
Est. 1984
Services Antique furniture restoration. Also manufactures classical English furniture and decorative four-poster beds
Open By appointment

Piers Furniture Repair Workshop
Contact Mr P Tarrant-Willis
✉ **The Old Air Raid Shelter, Athlone Street, London, NW5 4LN** 🅿
☎ 020 7209 5824
Est. 1998
Services Antique furniture repair and restoration including French polishing
Open By appointment

Quality Restorations Limited
Contact Mr A Dwyer
✉ **Ionna House, Humber Road, London, NW2 6EN** 🅿
☎ 020 8830 5888 Ⓕ 020 8450 9296
Ⓔ info@qfw.co.uk
Ⓦ www.qfw.co.uk
Est. 1994
Services Full repair and restoration of all types of furniture, French polishing, waxing, high-density gloss and satin finish, oiling
Open By appointment

R M W Restorations
Contact Mr R Mark-Wardlaw
✉ **Unit B08, Acton Business Centre, School Road, London, NW10 6TD** 🅿
☎ 020 8965 2938 Ⓕ 020 8965 2938
Est. 1986
Services Antique furniture repair and restoration, traditional and modern finishes, insurance work, cabinet work, polishing
Open Mon–Fri 10am–6pm

Regency Restoration
Contact Mrs E Ball
✉ **Studio 21, Thames House, 140 Battersea Park Road, London, SW11 4NB** 🅿
☎ 020 7622 5275 Ⓕ 020 7498 1803
Est. 1987
Services Restoration of 18th–19thC mirrors, picture frames, English and Continental painted and gilded furniture, architectural gilding, church interiors, polychrome sculpture, laquerwork, oil paintings, carving
Open Mon–Fri 9.30am–5.30pm

Remstone Contracts
Contact Mr D Louden
✉ **69a Southgate Road, London, N1 3JS** 🅿
☎ 020 7359 3536 Ⓕ 020 7359 3536
Est. 1968
Services Furniture restoration and repair, polishing, leather colouring
Open Mon–Fri 8am–5.30pm

David N Salmon
Contact Mr D Salmon
✉ **16a Southam Street, London, W10 5PH** 🅿
☎ 020 8968 3700 Ⓕ 020 8968 3700
Est. 1994
Services Repair and restoration of country and Georgian furniture, carving, veneering and gilding, hand-made furniture made from recycled timber when possible
Open By appointment

Michael Slade
Contact M Slade
✉ **42 Quernmore Road, London, N4 4QP** 🅿
☎ 020 8341 3194
Ⓔ mikeslade@ntl.com
Est. 1984
Services Antique repairs and restoration, furniture maker, upholstery, French polishing. Furniture sales
Open By appointment

H A Smith & Son
Contact Mr A Smith
✉ **36a Nelson Road, Harrow on the Hill, Harrow, Middlesex, HA1 3ET** 🅿
☎ 020 8864 2335
Est. 1920
Services Antique and modern furniture restoration, repair and upholstery
Open Mon–Fri 9am–6pm
Sat 10am–2pm

Tony's Antique Restoration
Contact Tony Brown
✉ **Unit 13, Downham Enterprise Centre, London, SE6 1TE** 🅿
☎ 020 8461 5757 Ⓕ 020 8461 5757
Est. 1997
Services Antiques restoration including stripping, polishing, marquetry and inlaying
Open Mon–Fri 9.30am–4.30pm

Angela Vernon Bates
Contact Mrs A Vernon Bates
✉ **Candid Studio, 3 Torrens Street, London, EC1V 1NQ** 🅿
☎ 020 7833 2133 Ⓕ 020 7833 2133
Est. 1991
Services Antiques repair and restoration of small items, painted surfaces, re-lining of boxes, frames, töle gilding, papier mâché, painted textiles and furniture
Open By apppointment

P Walters Ltd
Contact David Walters
✉ **3 Harold Road, Harringey, London, N15 4PL**
☎ 020 8808 5889 Ⓕ 020 8808 0227
Est. 1937
Services Repair and restoration of antiques, cabinet-maker
Trade only Yes
Open Mon–Fri 8am–5.30pm

Woodbourne Antiques and Furniture Makers
Contact Mr G Evans
✉ **Unit 35, Cromwell Industrial Estate, Staffa Road, London, E10 7QZ** 🅿
☎ 020 8539 5575 Ⓕ 020 8539 5575
Est. 1984
Services Furniture makers, chair copying, repair and restoration of antique furniture
Open Mon–Fri 8am–6pm
Sat 8am–1pm

SOUTH

Antique Restorers
Contact Mr W Barker
✉ **2 Station Approach, Stoneleigh, Epsom, Surrey, KT19 0QZ** 🅿
☎ 020 8393 9111

Est. 1980
Services Upholstery, French polishing, furniture repairs, cane and rush seating. Also sell antique and second-hand tools
Open Mon–Fri 9.30am–4.30pm

B H Woodfinishes
Contact Mr C Hopkins
✉ **Unit 22, Church Lane Industrial Estate, Church Lane, Horsham, West Sussex, RH13 6LU** Ⓟ
☎ 01403 891551 Ⓕ 01403 891551
Ⓜ 07850 051607
Ⓔ sales@bhwoodfinishes.co.uk
Ⓦ www.bhwoodfinishes.co.uk
Est. 1988
Services Strip and repolish, wood repairs, French polishing, leathering, gilding. On-site work (bannisters, staircases etc)
Open Mon–Fri 9am–5pm

Colin Bell, Ben Norris and Co (BAFRA)
Contact Colin Bell
✉ **Knowl Hill Farm, Knowl Hill, Kingsclere, Newbury, Berkshire, RG15 8NJ** Ⓟ
☎ 01635 297950 Ⓕ 01635 299851
Est. 1980
Services Restoration of antique furniture and gilding, reproduction cabinet-making, furniture made to order
Open Mon–Fri 8.30am–5pm

A E Booth and Son (BAFRA)
Contact David or Ann Booth
✉ **9 High Street, Ewell, Surrey, KT17 1SG** Ⓟ
☎ 020 8393 5245 Ⓕ 020 8393 5245
Est. 1934
Services Restoration of antique and reproduction furniture including polishing and upholstery
Open Mon–Sat 9am–4.45pm

C T Bristow
Contact Mr Bristow
✉ **Lydgate, Seale Lane, Seale, Farnham, Surrey, GU10 1LF** Ⓟ
☎ 01252 782775
Est. 1971
Services French polishing, fine antique furniture restoration
Open By appointment

The Cabinet Repair Shop
Contact Mrs H Embling
✉ **Woodlands Farm, Blacknest Road, Blacknest, Alton, Hampshire, GU34 4BQ** Ⓟ
☎ 01252 794260 Ⓕ 01252 794260
Est. 1984
Services Restoration of antique and modern furniture, insurance claim work
Open Mon–Fri 8am–5pm
Sat by appointment

Peter Casebow (BAFRA)
Contact Mr P Casebow
✉ **Pilgrims Mill Lane, Worthing, West Sussex, BN13 3DE** Ⓟ
☎ 01903 264045
Ⓜ 07790 339602
Ⓔ pcasebow@hotmail.com
Est. 1987
Services Restoration of period furniture including square-piano restoration
Open By appointment

B Castle
Contact Mr B Castle
✉ **2 Charmandean Road, Worthing, West Sussex, BN14 9LB** Ⓟ
☎ 01903 239702
Est. 1982
Services Antique repair and restoration of small furniture, decorative items, woodcarver
Open Mon–Sat by appointment

Ralph Clee
Contact Mr R Clee
✉ **Quell Farm, Greatham, Pulborough, West Sussex, RH20 2ES** Ⓟ
☎ 01798 874228
Est. 1995
Services Furniture restoration, polishing
Open Mon–Fri 8.30am–6pm
Sat by appointment

Alan Cooper Antique Restorations
Contact Alan Cooper
✉ **Unit 7, Park Farm, Hundred Acre Lane, Wivelsfield Green, Haywards Heath, West Sussex, RH17 7RU** Ⓟ
☎ 01273 890017
Est. 1973
Services Antiques repair, French polishing, restoration
Open Mon–Fri 8am–3pm

Copperwheat Restoration
Contact Carole Copperwheat
✉ **Rear of Pascall Atkey, 29–30 High Street, Cowes, Isle of Wight, PO31 7RX** Ⓟ
☎ 01983 281011
Ⓜ 07720 399670
Est. 1985
Services Antique furniture repair, restoration, commissions
Open Any time by prior phone call

Corwell
Contact Mr S Corbin
✉ **Unit 6, Amners Farm, Burghfield, Reading, Berkshire, RG30 3UE** Ⓟ
☎ 0118 983 3404 Ⓕ 0118 983 3404
Ⓔ info@corwell.co.uk
Ⓦ www.corwell.co.uk
Est. 1989
Services Antique restoration, cabinet-making
Open Mon–Fri 9am–5pm Sat 9am–2pm

Davenports Antiques
Contact Mr C Height
✉ **Unit 5, Woodgate Centre, Oak Tree Lane, Woodgate, Chichester, West Sussex, PO20 6GU** Ⓟ
☎ 01243 544242
Ⓜ 07932 690210
Est. 1980
Services Antique furniture restoration
Open Mon–Fri 8.30am–6pm

Sonia Demetriou
Contact Sonia Demetriou
✉ **2 Elbridge Farm Buildings, Chichester Road, Bognor Regis, West Sussex, PO21 5EG** Ⓟ
☎ 01243 842235 Ⓕ 01243 842235
Est. 1977
Services Restoration of antique painted furniture and objets d'art
Open Mon–Fri 9.30am–6pm
Sat by appointment

R G Dewdney
Contact Mr R G Dewdney
✉ **Norfolk Road, South Holmwood, Dorking, Surrey, RH5 4LA** Ⓟ
☎ 01306 888174 Ⓕ 01306 742636
Est. 1968
Services General antiques repairs and restoration, leatherwork
Open Mon–Fri 9am–6pm

Downland Furniture Restoration
Contact Mr S Macintyre
✉ **Wepham Farmyard, Wepham, Arundel, West Sussex, BN18 9RQ** P
☎ 01903 883387
Est. 1984
Services Furniture restoration and conservation
Open Mon–Fri 9am–5pm

Dunn and Wright
Contact Mr A Dunn
✉ **Rear of 128 Sheen Road, Richmond, Surrey, TW9 1UR** P
☎ 020 8948 7032
Est. 1974
Services Furniture repair and restoration
Open Mon–Fri 8am–5.30pm

R C Elderton
Contact R C Elderton
✉ **Home Farm, Mill Lane, Hawkley, Liss, Hampshire, GU33 6NU** P
☎ 01420 538374
E woodman@cix.co.uk
W www.cix.co.uk/~woodman/
Est. 1976
Services Antique furniture restorations, new bespoke solid wood furniture, metalworking repairs, woodturning
Open Mon–Fri 9am–5pm or by appointment

F and R Restorations
Contact Mr G R Fisher
✉ **39b Walton Street, Tadworth, Surrey, KT20 7RR** P
☎ 01737 819918 F 01737 819518
E fandr.restoration@virgin.net
W www.fandrrestorations.co.uk
Est. 1999
Services Antique furniture restorations, sales of antique and contemporary design furniture
Open Mon–Sat 8.30am–6pm

G and R Fraser-Sinclair (BAFRA)
Contact Mr G Fraser-Sinclair
✉ **Haysbridge Farm, Brickhouse Lane, South Godstone, Godstone, Surrey, RH9 8JW** P
☎ 01342 844112 F 01342 844112
Est. 1978
Services General restoration of 18thC furniture
Open Mon–Fri 8am–5.30pm

A D Gardner
Contact Mr Gardner
✉ **2a East Road, Reigate, Surrey, RH2 9EX** P
☎ 01737 222430
Est. 1969
Services Antique repair and restoration, fine French polishing, caning, leathering, upholstery
Open Mon–Fri 8.30am–5.30pm

Tony Gardner
Contact Mr T Gardner
✉ **The Boiler House, Morden Hall Park, Morden, Surrey, SM4 5JD** P
☎ 020 8687 1991
M 07979 642895
Est. 1980
Services Furniture restoration, French polishing, caning and rushing. Situated in a National Trust property
Open Thurs–Mon 10am–4pm

Goodwood Furniture Restoration (BAFRA)
Contact Bruce Neville
✉ **21 Richmond Road, Westerton, Chichester, West Sussex, PO18 0PQ** P
☎ 01243 778614
M 07719 778079
E bruce@goodwoodrestoration.co.uk
W www.goodwoodrestoration.co.uk
Est. 1991
Services Antique furniture restoration, cabinet-making
Open Mon–Sat 8.30am–5.30pm

G E Griffith
Contact Mr G E Griffin
✉ **43a Brighton Road, South Croydon, Surrey, CR2 6EB** P
☎ 020 8688 3130
M 07970 412679
E ted@gegriffin.freeserve.co.uk
Est. 1896
Services Antiques restoration, re-upholstery, china restoration
Open Mon–Fri 8am–6pm Sat 10am–4pm

G J Hall, Antique Furniture Restoration
Contact Mr G J Hall
✉ **1st Floor, Eagle Works, High Street, Hartley Wintney, Hampshire, RG27 8NU** P
☎ 01252 845052
M 07711 846712
Est. 1984
Services Restoration and conservation of fine antique furniture, copy chair making, French polishing, insurance work, design commissions
Open Mon–Fri 9.30am–5.30pm

Hedgecoe and Freeland (BAFRA, LAPADA)
Contact Justin Freeland
✉ **Rowan House, 21 Burrow Hill Green, Chobham, Woking, Surrey, GU24 8QP** P
☎ 01276 858206 F 01276 857352
M 07771 953870
Est. 1969
Services Cabinet-making, polishing, upholstery, metalwork, gilding, lacquerwork and paintwork
Open Mon–Fri 8am–5.30pm

Stuart Hobbs Antique Furniture Restoration (BAFRA)
Contact Mr S Hobbs
✉ **Meath Paddock, Meath Green Lane, Horley, Surrey, RH6 8HZ** P
☎ 01293 782349 F 01293 773467
Est. 1981
Services Furniture, longcase, bracket clock and barometer restoration
Open By appointment

Jeff Howlett Restoration @ Great Grooms Antique Centres (BAFRA)
Contact Jeff Howlett
✉ **Unit 4, Charnham Lane, Hungerford, Berkshire, RG17 0EY** P
☎ 01488 684674 F 01488 686178
E jeffhowlett@antiquefurniturerestorers.com
W www.antiquefurniturerestorers.com
Est. 1989
Services Full restoration and conservation of all antiques
Open Mon–Fri 8am–6pm Sat by appointment

Howard Hunt Antiques
Contact Mr H Hunt
✉ **The White Hut, Thackhams Farm, Bottle Lane, Mattingley, Hook, Hampshire, RG27 8LJ** P
☎ 01256 881111 F 01256 881111
Est. 1989
Services Repair and restoration of furniture, mirrors, porcelain, upholstery, leathering, gilding
Open Mon–Fri 9am–6pm Sat 9am–4pm

FURNITURE

David C E Lewry (BAFRA)
Contact Mr D Lewry
✉ **Wychelms, 66 Gorran Avenue, Rowner, Gosport, Hampshire, PO13 0NF** Ⓟ
☎ 01329 286901 Ⓕ 01329 289964
Ⓜ 07785 766844
Ⓔ davidjoanlewry@talk21.com
Est. 1979
Services Complete repair and restoration service
Open By appointment

John Lloyd (BAFRA)
✉ **The Old Bakehouse, The Street, Bolney, West Sussex, RH17 5PG** Ⓟ
☎ 01444 881988 Ⓕ 01444 881988
Ⓜ 07941 124772
Ⓔ lloydjohn@aol.com
Est. 1989
Services Complete repair and restoration of period, reproduction and modern furniture
Open By appointment

C Lopez
Contact Mr C Lopez
✉ **151 London Road, Burgess Hill, West Sussex, RH15 8LH** Ⓟ
☎ 01444 243176 Ⓕ 01444 254208
Est. 1977
Services Antique furniture restoration and handmade chair copying
Open Mon–Fri 9am–1pm 2–6pm Sat 9am–1pm

Lush Restoration
Contact Mr M Lush
✉ **64d Old Milton Road, New Milton, Hampshire, BN25 6DX** Ⓟ
☎ 01425 629680
Est. 1992
Services Repair and restoration
Open Mon–Fri 8am–1pm 2–5pm

Lymington Restoration
Contact Mr M Cooper
✉ **Fairlea House, 110–112 Marsh Lane, Lymington, Hampshire, SO41 9EE** Ⓟ
☎ 01590 677558 Ⓕ 01590 677558
Est. 1996
Services Restoration of antique furniture, gilding, upholstery
Open Mon–Sat 9am–5pm

Maybury Antique Restoration
Contact Mr B Everitt
✉ **Maybury Rough Cottage, Lytton Road, Woking, Surrey, GU22 7EH** Ⓟ
☎ 01483 762812
Est. 1989
Services All furniture repairs, gilding, leathering, upholstering, French polishing
Open Mon–Fri 8am–6pm Sat 8am–1pm

A F Mrozinski
Contact Mr Mrozinski
✉ **44 Elizabeth Road, Farncombe, Godalming, Surrey, GU7 3PZ** Ⓟ
☎ 01483 415028
Est. 1979
Services Antique furniture repair, French polishing
Open Mon–Fri 7.30am–5pm

Timothy Naylor Associates (BAFRA)
Contact T Naylor
✉ **24 Bridge Road, Chertsey, Surrey, KT16 8JN** Ⓟ
☎ 01932 567129 Ⓕ 01932 564948
Ⓔ timothy.naylor@talk21.com
Est. 1988
Services Georgian and Regency furniture restoration
Open Mon–Fri 8.30am–5pm

K S Pawlowski
Contact K S Pawlowski
✉ **Unit 3, Turner Dumbrell Workshops, North End, Ditchling, Hassocks, West Sussex, BN6 8TG** Ⓟ
☎ 01273 846003
Est. 1983
Services Conservation and restoration of antique furniture
Open Mon–Fri 9am–5.30pm Sat 9am–1pm

Eva-Louise Pepperall (BAFRA)
Contact E Pepperall
✉ **Dairy Lane Cottage, Walberton, Arundel, West Sussex, BN18 0PT** Ⓟ
☎ 01243 551282
Est. 1977
Services Restoration of antique furniture, gilding, lacquer work
Open By appointment

Simon Peterson (BAFRA)
✉ **Whitelands, West Dean, Chichester, West Sussex, PO18 0RL** Ⓟ
☎ 01243 811900
Ⓔ sp@hotglue.fsnet.co.uk
Est. 1992
Services Repair and restoration of antique furniture and clocks, Boulle work, marquetry
Open By appointment

Mr Pickett's
Contact Mr M Pickett
✉ **Top Barn, Old Park Lane, Bosham, Nr Chichester, West Sussex, PO18 8EX** Ⓟ
☎ 01243 574573 Ⓕ 01243 572255
Ⓜ 07779 997012
Ⓔ info@mrpicketts.com
Ⓦ www.mrpicketts.com
Est. 1991
Services Paint stripping, sanding, waxing, full restoration, bespoke items made to order from reclaimed pine
Open Mon–Fri 8am–5pm Sat 8am–4pm Sun by appointment

Albert Plumb Furniture Co (BAFRA)
Contact Mrs S Plumb
✉ **Itchenor Green, Chichester, West Sussex, PO20 7DA** Ⓟ
☎ 01243 513701 Ⓕ 01243 513700
Est. 1977
Services Antique furniture restorers and upholsterers. Bespoke cabinet-makers
Open Mon–Fri 8.30am–6.30pm or by appointment

D Potashnick
Contact Mr D Potashnick
✉ **7 The Parade, 73 Stoats Nest Road, Coulsdon, Surrey, CR5 2JJ** Ⓟ
☎ 020 8660 8403
Est. 1969
Services Restoration of furniture
Open Mon–Fri 9am–5pm or by appointment

Renaissance
Contact Mr Peter Cross
✉ **11 Enterprise Close, Croydon, Surrey, CR0 3RZ** Ⓟ
☎ 020 8664 9686 Ⓕ 020 8664 9737
Est. 1996
Services Furniture and frame repair and restoration
Open Mon–Fri 10am–6.30pm

The Restoration Co
Contact Mr J Howard
✉ **The Coach House, Dorney Court, Dorney, Windsor, Berkshire, SL4 6QL** Ⓟ
☎ 01628 660708

Est. 1991
Services Restoration of 18th–19thC furniture, carving, gilding, upholstery, metalwork
Open Mon–Fri 8am–5.30pm

David A Sayer Antique Furniture Restorer (BAFRA)
Contact David Sayer
✉ **Courtlands, Park Road, Banstead, Surrey, SM7 3EF** Ⓟ
☎ 01737 352429 Ⓕ 01737 373255
Ⓜ 07775 636009
Ⓔ dsayer@courtlands98.freeserve.co.uk
Ⓦ www.bafra.org.uk/members/dsayer.html
Est. 1985
Services Comprehensive repair, restoration and conservation service of English and Continental furniture
Open Mon–Fri 8am–6pm

Michael Schryver Antiques
Contact Mr M Schryver
✉ **The Granary, 10 North Street, Dorking, Surrey, RH4 1DN** Ⓟ
☎ 01306 881110 Ⓕ 01306 876168
Est. 1971
Services 18thC furniture restoration
Open Mon–Fri 8.30am–5.30pm Sat 8am–noon or by appointment

Seagers Restorations
Contact Mr M L Cheater
✉ **Seagers Farm, Stuckton, Fordingbridge, Hampshire, SP6 2HG** Ⓟ
☎ 01425 652245
Est. 1962
Services Restoration of furniture of all ages
Open Mon–Fri 9am–5.30pm or by appointment

Andrew Sharp Antique Restoration Ltd
Contact Mr A Sharp
✉ **Unit 1, Forest Villa Courtyard, Lyndhurst Road, Brockenhurst, Hampshire, SO42 7RL** Ⓟ
☎ 01590 622577
Est. 1996
Services Sale and restoration of Georgian–Victorian furniture
Open Mon–Sat 9am–5.30pm

Surrey Restoration Ltd
Contact Emily McGhee
✉ **Highway Farm, Horsley Road, Downside, Cobham, Surrey, KT11 3JZ** Ⓟ
☎ 01932 868883 Ⓕ 01483 268285
Ⓔ emcghee@surreyrestoration.freeserve.co.uk
Est. 1994
Services Antique furniture restoration, interior wooden panelling of period houses
Open Mon–Sat 8.30am–6.30pm

Sussex Woodcraft
Contact Mr Waters
✉ **15 Drayton Cottages, Drayton Lane, Drayton, Chichester, West Sussex, PO20 6BN** Ⓟ
☎ 01243 788830
Est. 1937
Services Cabinet-making and restoration
Open Mon–Fri 8am–5pm

T S Restorations
Contact T Street
✉ **13 Blatchford Close, Horsham, West Sussex, RH13 5RG** Ⓟ
☎ 01403 273766
Est. 1989
Services Antiques repair and restoration
Open Mon–Fri 8am–5pm

Roy Temple Polishing
Contact Mr R Temple
✉ **Unit 14, Seeplands Farm, Twyford Road, Wargrave, Reading, Berkshire, RG10 8DL** Ⓟ
☎ 01189 402211/01628 660106
Ⓕ 01189 402211
Est. 1996
Services Furniture repair and restoration, polishing, leathering
Open Mon–Sat 9am–5pm

Thread Bare Upholstery (AMU)
Contact Mr Martin Colwill
✉ **186a Bitterne Road, Bitterne, Southampton, Hampshire, SO18 1BE** Ⓟ
☎ 023 8077 3933/8021 1721
Ⓕ 023 8077 3933/8021 1721
Ⓜ 0789 9695479
Ⓦ www.threadbareupholstery.co.uk
Est. 1985
Services Furniture restoration, French polishing, reupholstery
Open Tue–Fri 10am–5pm Sat 10am–4pm

T R J Troke
Contact T Troke
✉ **22 Fairview Road, Hungerford, Berkshire, RG17 0BT** Ⓟ
☎ 01488 683310
Est. 1975
Services Antique furniture repair and restoration
Open By appointment

Martin Tucker Antique Restoration
Contact M Tucker
✉ **Springbok Estate, Alfold, Cranleigh, Surrey, GU6 8HR** Ⓟ
☎ 01403 753090
Est. 1984
Services Furniture restoration, French polishing
Open Mon–Fri 9am–5pm

D G Weston
Contact Mr I L Weston
✉ **33 Rowan Drive, Newbury, Berkshire, RG14 1LY** Ⓟ
☎ 01635 43022
Ⓜ 07803 752420
Est. 1958
Services Antiques repair and restoration, French polishing, leather lining, upholstery
Open Mon–Fri 9am–5.30pm

G Williams
Contact Graham Williams
✉ **The Builders Yard, Church Street, Betchworth, Surrey, RH3 7DN** Ⓟ
☎ 01737 843266
Est. 1975
Services General restoration, desk-top leathering, gold tooling, French polishing
Open Mon–Fri 9am–6pm Sat 10am–2pm

Wotruba and Son
Contact F F Wotruba
✉ **Manor Farm, Chilworth Old Village, Southampton, Hampshire, SO16 7JP** Ⓟ
☎ 023 8076 6411
Ⓜ 07887 712401
Est. 1995
Services Antiques restoration, upholstery
Open Mon–Fri 1–5pm or by appointment

WEST COUNTRY

4b Antiques and Interiors
Contact Jonathan Plant

✉ **4b Northgate Street, Devizes, Wiltshire, SN10 1JL** 🅿
☎ 01380 729275
Est. 1972
Services Furniture restoration
Open Mon–Fri 8am–5pm or by appointment

Antique Restoration
Contact George Judd
✉ **East Farm, Winterbourne Gunner, Salisbury, Wiltshire, SP4 6EW** 🅿
☎ 01980 610576/611828
Est. 1975
Services Furniture, porcelain and painting restoration, cabinet-making, upholstery
Open Mon–Fri 9am–7pm

David Battle Antique Furniture Restoration and Conservation (BAFRA)
Contact David Battle
✉ **Brightley Pound, Umberleigh, Devon, EX37 9AL** 🅿
☎ 01769 540483
Ⓔ david@brightley.clara.net
Ⓦ brightley.clara.net
Est. 1984
Services Comprehensive service for English and Continental period furniture
Open By appointment

Peter Binnington (BAFRA)
Contact Mr Peter Binnington
✉ **Barn Studio, Botany Farm, East Lulworth, Wareham, Dorset, BH20 5QH** 🅿
☎ 01929 400224 Ⓕ 01929 400744
Est. 1979
Services General furniture restoration and gilding, specialist in *verre églomisé*
Open By appointment

Boughey Antique Restoration
Contact Dave Boughey
✉ **Manor Farm Workshop, Millbrook, Torpoint, Cornwall, PL10 1AN** 🅿
☎ 01752 829008 Ⓕ 01752 829008
Ⓜ 07970 540644
Est. 1960
Services Furniture restoration, cabinet-making, porcelain and pottery restoration
Open Mon–Fri 8am–5.30pm or by appointment

Jason Bowen
Contact Mr J Bowen
✉ **Unit 2, Alexandra Court, Yeovil, Somerset, BA21 5AL** 🅿
☎ 01935 474446
Est. 1984
Services Furniture restoration, French polishing, gilding, carving, cabinet-making
Open Mon–Sat 8.30am–5pm

M and S Bradbury (BAFRA)
Contact Mr S Bradbury
✉ **The Barn, Hanham Lane, Paulton, Bristol, BS39 7PF** 🅿
☎ 01761 418910
Est. 1988
Services Furniture restoration including clock cases
Open Mon–Fri 8am–5pm

Sarah & Gary Brumfitt
Contact Sarah or Gary Brumfitt
✉ **Watershed Studio, East Street, Salisbury, Wiltshire, SP2 7SF**
☎ 01722 335532/334877
Est. 1992
Services Antiques repair and restoration, gilding, painted effects
Open By appointment

J E Cadman
Contact Mr Cadman
✉ **15 Norwich Road, Bournemouth, Dorset, BH2 5QZ** 🅿
☎ 01202 290973
Est. 1901
Services Antiques restoration, mostly furniture
Open Mon–Fri 9am–5pm

Castle House (BAFRA)
Contact Mr Michael Durkee
✉ **Castle House, Units 1 and 3, Bennetts Field Estate, Wincanton, Somerset, BA9 9DT** 🅿
☎ 01963 33885 Ⓕ 01963 31278
Est. 1975
Services Antique furniture restoration and conservation
Open Mon–Fri 8.30am–5pm

Christopher Cole
Contact Mr C Cole
✉ **The Workshop, 36 Claude Avenue, Oldfield Park, Bath, Somerset, BA2 1AG** 🅿
☎ 01225 310298 Ⓕ 01225 310298
Est. 1994
Services Antique furniture restoration, carving, turning, French polishing
Open Mon–Fri 8.30am–7pm

David Collyer Antique Restorations
Contact David Collyer
✉ **Tunley Farm, Tunley, Bath, Somerset, BA2 0DL** 🅿
☎ 01761 472727 Ⓕ 01761 472727
Ⓜ 07889 725508
Ⓔ davidcollyer@fsbdial.co.uk
Est. 1985
Services Furniture restoration and repair
Open Mon–Fri 9am–5.30pm or by appointment

W J Cook (BAFRA)
Contact Mr B Cook
✉ **High Trees, Savernake Forest, Nr Marlborough, Wiltshire, SN8 4NE** 🅿
☎ 01672 513017 Ⓕ 01672 514455
Est. 1963
Services Furniture polishing, restoration, upholstery, gilding
Open By appointment

Mark Coray Fine Antique Furniture Restoration (BAFRA)
Contact Mark Coray
✉ **The Coach House Workshops, Ford Street, Wellington, Somerset, TA21 9PG** 🅿
☎ 01823 663766/667284
Ⓜ 07979 245524
Est. 1999
Services All antique furniture restoration, gilding, furniture made to order
Open Mon–Fri 9am–5pm

N G and C Coryndon (BAFRA)
Contact N G Coryndon or Simon Butler
✉ **Rainscombe Farm, Oare, Marlborough, Wiltshire, SN8 4HZ** 🅿
☎ 01672 562581 Ⓕ 01672 563 995
Ⓔ simonbutler@coryndon.fsbusiness.co.uk
Est. 1964
Services General restoration of furniture, gilding, paint finishes. Collection and delivery if required
Open Mon–Fri 8.30am–4.30pm

D M Antique Restoration
Contact Mr D Pike
✉ **Purn Farm, Bridgewater, Bleadon, Weston-super-Mare, Somerset, BS24 0AN** 🅿
☎ 01934 811120

Est. 1983
Services Restoration of furniture and chests-of-drawers
Open Mon–Fri 8am–5pm

M L Davis
Contact Mr M L Davis
✉ **Rear of 1079 Christchurch Road, Bournemouth, Dorset, BH7 6BQ** Ⓟ
☎ 01202 434684
Est. 1987
Services Full restoration of furniture, brass cleaning
Open Mon–Fri 8.30am–5.30pm or by appointment

Simon Dodson
Contact Mr Dodson
✉ **The Workshop, Odd Penny Farm, Crudwell, Malmesbury, Wiltshire, SN16 9SJ** Ⓟ
☎ 01285 770810
Est. 1992
Services Antique furniture restoration
Open Mon–Sat 9am–6pm

Christopher John Douglas
Contact Mr C J Douglas
✉ **Befferlands Farm Workshop, Berne Lane, Charmouth, Bridport, Dorset, DT6 6RD** Ⓟ
☎ 01297 561120
Ⓜ 07989 161019
Est. 1975
Services Restoration of antique furniture, old pine, Art Deco
Open Mon–Fri 9am–6pm

Dudley and Spencer
Contact John Spencer or Ray Dudley
✉ **Unit 21, Signal Way, Central Trading Estate, Swindon, Wiltshire, SN3 1PD** Ⓟ
☎ 01793 535394
Est. 1969
Services Furniture restoration, upholstery
Open Mon–Fri 7am–6pm

A A Eddy and Son
Contact Mr K Eddy or Mr M Eddy
✉ **1a Elphinstone Road, Peverell, Plymouth, Devon, PL2 3QQ** Ⓟ
☎ 01752 787138 Ⓕ 01752 789013
Est. 1889
Services Full repairs and restoration, French polishing. Free estimates in the Plymouth area
Open Mon–Fri 7.30am–5pm

Esox Antique Restoration
Contact Mr B Elston
✉ **Unit 8, Dobles Lane Industrial Estate, Holsworthy, Devon, EX22 6HL** Ⓟ
☎ 01409 259090
Ⓜ 07967 283602
Est. 1987
Services Full furniture restoration, French polishing
Open Mon–Fri 9am–5pm or by appointment

Gilboy's
Contact Mr S Gilboys
✉ **Hall Farm, Riverford, Staverton, Totnes, Devon, TQ9 6AH** Ⓟ
☎ 01803 762763
Est. 1992
Services Restoration, French polishing, modern furniture finishes (dining room table heatproofing). Maker of replacement doors
Open Mon–Fri 9am–5pm

Philip Hawkins Furniture (BAFRA)
Contact Mr P Hawkins
✉ **Glebe Workshop, Semley, Shaftesbury, Dorset, SP7 9AP** Ⓟ
☎ 01747 830830 Ⓕ 01747 830830
Ⓔ hawkinssemley@hotmail.com
Est. 1987
Services Restoration and replication of antique furniture
Open Mon–Fri 9am–5pm or by appointment

Bruce Isaac
Contact Mr Bruce Isaac
✉ **Crown Works, 114a Rodden Road, Frome, Somerset, BA11 2AW** Ⓟ
☎ 01373 453277 Ⓕ 01373 830849
Ⓜ 07711 399165
Est. 1990
Services Furniture restoration
Open Mon–Fri 8am–5pm

Mike Keeley
Contact Mike Keeley
✉ **205 Old Church Road, Clevedon, Somerset, BS21 7UD** Ⓟ
☎ 01275 873418
Ⓔ mike.keeley@tesco.net
Est. 1980
Services General repairs to antique furniture, specializing in dining furniture
Open By appointment Mon–Fri 9am–5pm

M & J Lazenby Antique Restoration
Contact Mark Lazenby
✉ **The Old Bakery, Terrace View, Horsecastles, Sherborne, Dorset, DT9 3HE**
☎ 01935 816716
Est. 1987
Services Full furniture restoration service
Open Mon–Fri 8am–5pm

Market Place Antiques Restorations
Contact Martin Bryan Turner
✉ **Nuttaberry Works, Nuttaberry Industrial Estate, Bideford East, Bideford, Devon, EX39 4DU** Ⓟ
☎ 01237 476628
Est. 1984
Services Antique furniture restoration
Open By appointment

Alf McKay
Contact Mr A McKay
✉ **Manor Barn, Hewish, Crewkerne, Somerset, TA18 8PT** Ⓟ
☎ 01460 78916 Ⓕ 01460 78916
Ⓜ 07720 810750
Est. 1972
Services Restorations, cabinet-maker, traditional furniture, architectural salvage
Open By appointment

Rod Naylor
Contact Angela Naylor
✉ **208 Devizes Road, Hilperton, Trowbridge, Wiltshire, BA14 7QP** Ⓟ
☎ 01225 754497 Ⓕ 01225 754497
Ⓔ rod.naylor@virgin.net
Ⓦ www.freespace.virgin.net/laura.naylor/index.htm
Est. 1970
Services Restoration of antique wood carvings, supplies replicas of hard-to-find items and materials for caddies, boxes, desks etc, cabinet-making, supplier of power carving machinery and tools
Open By appointment

Newmans (BAFRA)
Contact Tony Newman
✉ **Tithe Barn, Crowbombe, Somerset, TA4 4AQ** Ⓟ
Ⓜ 07778 615945
Ⓔ tony@cheddon.fsnet.co.uk
Est. 1991

Services All types of restoration
Open Sun–Mon 9am–5pm
or by appointment

Oakfield Cabinet Makers
Contact Mr X Haines
✉ **Unit 8, Mount Pleasant, Offwell, Honiton, Devon, EX14 9RN** 🅿
☎ 01404 46858
Est. 1989
Services Cabinet-making and restoration
Open Mon–Fri 7.30am–6pm

Ottery Antique Restorers (BAFRA)
Contact Mr C James
✉ **Wincanton Business Park, Wessex Way, Wincanton, Somerset, BA9 9RR** 🅿
☎ 01963 34572 Ⓕ 01963 34572
Ⓜ 07770 923955
Ⓔ charles@otteryantiques.co.uk
Ⓦ www.otteryantiques.co.uk
Est. 1986
Services Furniture restoration
Open Mon–Fri 7.30am–5.30pm

Park Lane Restoration
Contact Matthew Channell
✉ **Unit 2, Marston Park Lane, St Clement, Truro, Cornwall, TR1 1SX** 🅿
☎ 01872 223944
Ⓜ 07774 798198
Est. 1984
Services 18th–19thC furniture restoration, cabinet veneering, stripping and French polishing. Fire, flood, shipping damage insurance work
Open Mon–Fri 8am–6pm

Alexander Paul Restorations
Contact Dave Steele
✉ **Fenny Bridges, Honiton, Devon, EX14 1PJ** 🅿
☎ 01404 850881 Ⓕ 01404 850881
Ⓔ alexanderpaulre@aol.com
Est. 2000
Services Full restoration including French polishing, turning, veneering
Open Mon–Fri 9am–5.30pm
Sat 10am–4pm

R L Peploe
Contact Mr Peploe
✉ **18 Hughenden Road, Clifton, Bristol, BS8 2TT** 🅿
☎ 0117 923 9349
Est. 1986
Services Cabinet work, gilding, carving, general finishing
Open Mon–Fri 9am–5pm

J Perrin
Contact Mr Perrin
✉ **Hope Chapel, Pitney, Langport, Somerset, TA10 9AE** 🅿
☎ 01458 251150 Ⓕ 01458 251150
Est. 1971
Services Furniture restoration
Open Mon–Sat 8am–6pm

Piers Pisani Antiques
Contact Mr Piers Pisani
✉ **The Old Chapel, Marston Road, Sherborne, Dorset, DT9 4BL** 🅿
☎ 01935 814789 Ⓕ 01935 815209
Ⓜ 07973 373753
Ⓔ antiques@pierspisani.sagehost.co.uk
Ⓦ www.pierspisani.com
Est. 1987
Services Full furniture restoration, cabinet-making
Open Mon–Sat 8.30am–6pm

Revival
Contact Mr B Gould
✉ **South Road, Timsbury, Bath, Somerset, BA3 1LD** 🅿
☎ 01761 472255
Est. 1979
Services Antiques restoration, upholstery, French polishing
Open Mon–Fri 7am–4.30pm

Rosewood Restoration
Contact Liz Cain
✉ **The Courtyard Home Farm, St Audries, Williton, Taunton, Somerset, TA4 4DP** 🅿
☎ 01984 633701 Ⓕ 01984 633701
Est. 1995
Services Restoration, cabinet-making, gilding, upholstery
Open Thurs–Tues 10am–4pm

F B Sadowski
Contact Mr Sadowski
✉ **Unit 2, Plot 1a, Rospeath Estate, Crowlas, Penzance, Cornwall, TR20 8DU** 🅿
☎ 01736 741083
Est. 1910
Services Furniture restoration. Repairs including Boulle work, marquetry
Open Mon–Fri 9.30am–5pm

Graham Sparks Restoration
Contact Mr Graham Sparks
✉ **Unit 63, Tone Mill, Tonedale, Wellington, Somerset, TA21 0AB** 🅿
☎ 01823 663636 Ⓕ 01823 667393
Est. 1979
Services Furniture restoration, upholstery, cabinet-making. Selection of desks, cabinets etc always in stock
Open Mon–Fri 8am–6pm
Sat 8am–1pm

St Thomas Antiques
Contact Ken Holdsworth
✉ **74 St Thomas Street, Wells, Somerset, BA5 2UZ** 🅿
☎ 01749 672520
Est. 1969
Services Repairs, repolishing
Open Mon–Fri 10am–4pm
closed Wed

Robert P Tandy (BAFRA)
Contact Robert P Tandy
✉ **Unit 5, Manor Workshops, West End, Nailsea, Bristol, North Somerset, BS48 4DD** 🅿
☎ 01275 856378
Est. 1987
Services Antique furniture and longcase clock casework restoration
Open Mon–Fri 10am–6pm

John Thorpe Fine Furniture
Contact Mr John Thorpe-Dixon
✉ **Units 1–2, Old Station Yard, Egloskerry, Launceston, Cornwall, PL15 8ST** 🅿
☎ 01566 785544 Ⓕ 01566 785544
Est. 1990
Services Antique furniture restoration, cabinetry, refinishing. Covers London and all areas west of London
Open Mon–Fri 9am–5pm

N S L Tomson
Contact Nick Tompson
✉ **Unit 1, Centurion Works, Union Road, Kingsbridge, Devon, TQ7 1EF** 🅿
☎ 01548 854380
Est. 1981
Services French polishing and furniture restoration
Open Mon–Sat 8am–6pm
and by appointment

Turnpike Cottage Antiques & Tearoom
Contact Mrs S Green or Mr T A Green
✉ **6 The Square Gerrans, Portscathe, Truro, Cornwall, TR2 5EB** Ⓟ
☎ 01872 580853
Est. 1988
Services French polishing, furniture repairs, carving, over 40 years experience. Also antiques shop and tea room
Open Mon–Sun 11am–1.30pm 3–6pm winter 3–6pm closed Thurs

Brian Walker (FOMC)
Contact Mr Walker
✉ **Westwood, Dinton Road, Forant, Salisbury, Wiltshire, SP3 5JW** Ⓟ
☎ 01722 714370 Ⓕ 01722 714853
Est. 1972
Services Furniture restoration and maker
Open Mon–Fri 8am–6pm or by appointment

Westmoor Furniture
Contact Gary Male
✉ **Unit 3, Alfords Yard, Westmoor Lane, Hambridge, Langport, Somerset, TA10 0AS** Ⓟ
☎ 01460 281535
Est. 1994
Services Antiques restoration and repairs, custom-made furniture
Open Mon–Fri 9am–6pm

N D Whibley Restorations
Contact Mr Whibley
✉ **1166 Ringwood Road, Bear Cross, Bournemouth, Dorset, BH11 9LG** Ⓟ
☎ 01202 575167
Est. 1975
Services Polishing and restoration of furniture, clock cases, medical cases, scientific instrument cases
Open By appointment

Wood 'n' Things
Contact Mr William Page
✉ **Cross Lanes Farm, Cross Lanes, Pill, Bristol, BS20 0JJ** Ⓟ
☎ 01275 371660
Est. 1983
Services Furniture restoration, cabinet-making
Open Mon–Fri 9am–6pm advisable to call first

EAST

Abbey Antique Restorers
Contact Mr David Carter
✉ **Coxford Abbey Farmhouse, Coxford, King's Lynn, Norfolk, PE31 6TB** Ⓟ
☎ 01485 528043
Ⓦ www.abbey-restorations.co.uk
Est. 1969
Services Conservation and restoration of antique furniture
Open Mon–Sun 9am–6pm

Acorn Antique Restoration Services
Contact Mr V Lawson
✉ **9 Taverham Chase, Taverham, Norwich, Norfolk, NR8 6NZ** Ⓟ
☎ 01603 260446
Ⓜ 0771 322 5674
Est. 1998
Services French polishing, furniture restoration, general small repairs, wood turning service
Open Mon–Sat 9am–6pm

Antiques and Restoration
Contact Mr R Rush
✉ **Unit 5, Penny Corner, Farthing Road, Ipswich, Suffolk, IP1 5AP** Ⓟ
☎ 01473 464609 Ⓕ 01473 464609
Ⓜ 07939 220041
Ⓔ info@antiquesandrestoration.co.uk
Ⓦ www.antiquesandrestoration.co.uk
Est. 1997
Services Restorations
Open Mon–Fri 8am–6pm Sat 8am–1.30pm

M Barrett Restoration
Contact Mr M Barrett
✉ **Unit 7, Warbraham Farm, Heath Road, Burwell, Cambridge, Cambridgeshire, CB5 0AP** Ⓟ
☎ 01638 741700 Ⓕ 01638 741700
Est. 1987
Services Pre-1940s furniture restoration
Open Mon–Fri 8.30am–5pm

Clive Beardall (BAFRA)
Contact Mr Clive Beardall
✉ **104b High Street, Maldon, Essex, CM9 7ET** Ⓟ
☎ 01621 857890 Ⓕ 01621 850753
Ⓔ info@clivebeardall.co.uk
Ⓦ www.clivebeardall.co.uk
Est. 1982
Services Specializing in period furniture restoration, traditional hand French polishing, wax polishing, reupholstery, marquetry, carving, gilding, leather desk-lining, rush and cane seating, decorative finishes, bespoke cabinet-making, valuations
Open Mon–Fri 8am–5.30pm Sat 9am–4pm

Beechams Furniture (EADA)
Contact Mr George or Stan Beecham
✉ **2 Romside Commercial Centre, 149 North Street, Romford, Essex, RM1 1ED** Ⓟ
☎ 01708 745778 Ⓕ 01708 764328
Ⓜ 07950 023332
Ⓔ stan@beechams.altodigital.co.uk
Ⓦ www.beechamsfurniture.co.uk
Est. 1969
Services Chair, table, cabinet manufacture, restoration, polishing, upholstery, gilding, chair caning
Open Mon–Fri 8.30am–5pm

K W Box
Contact Mr K W Box
✉ **The Workshop, Upper Street, Stratford St Mary, Colchester, Essex, CO7 6JN** Ⓟ
☎ 01206 322673
Est. 1985
Services 17th–18th and early 19thC furniture restoration and one-off cabinet-making to order. 21 years experience
Open Mon–Fri 8am–6pm Sat 8am–1pm

Bradshaw Fine Wood Furniture Ltd
Contact Mr Chris Shaw-Williams
✉ **Unit 12, Clovelly Works, Chelmsford Road, Rawreth, Wickford, Essex, SS11 8SY** Ⓟ
☎ 01268 571414 Ⓕ 01268 571314
Est. 1988
Services French polishing, furniture restoration and repair work
Open Mon–Fri 8am–6pm

Clare Hall Co
Contact Mr M Moore
✉ **The Barns, Clare Hall, Clare, Sudbury, Suffolk, CO10 8PJ** Ⓟ

☎ 01787 278445 ⓕ 01787 278803
Est. 1960
Services Restoration of all antiques including polishing and upholstery. Replicas of antique globes and four-poster beds
Open By appointment

P Dawson Furniture Restorers
Contact Mr Paul Dawson
✉ **Unit 0, Dodnash Priory Farm, Hazel Shrub, Bentley, Ipswich, Suffolk, IP9 2DF** 🅿
☎ 01473 311947 ⓕ 01473 462397
ⓜ 07718 958415
ⓔ paul@dawson21.freeserve.co.uk
Est. 1996
Services Restoration and sales of 17th–20thC furniture £50–£3,000 and reproductions
Open Mon–Sat 8am–6pm

Michael Dolling (BAFRA)
Contact Mr Michael Dolling
✉ **Church Farm, Barns, Glandford, Holt, Norfolk, NR25 7JR** 🅿
☎ 01263 741115
Est. 1986
Services General furniture restoration and repair
Open Mon–Fri 9am–5pm

Essex Reupholstery Services
Contact Mr S T Richardson
✉ **49 Chestnut Grove, Southend on Sea, Essex, SS2 5HG**
☎ 01702 464775 ⓕ 01702 305684
Est. 1987
Services Restoration of antique furniture, paddings, reupholstery
Open Mon–Fri 8am–5pm

Forge Studio Workshops
Contact Mr D Darton
✉ **Stour Street, Manningtree, Essex, CO11 1BE** 🅿
☎ 01206 396222 ⓕ 01206 396222
Est. 1979
Services Antique furniture restoration
Open Mon–Fri 8.30am–5.30pm Sat 8.30am–1pm

Furse Restoration
Contact Mr Fred Furse
✉ **Beechcroft, Damases Lane, Boreham, Chelmsford, Essex, CM3 3AL** 🅿
☎ 01245 466744 ⓕ 01245 466744
ⓔ andrew@furserestoration.co.uk
ⓦ www.furserestoration.co.uk
Est. 1993
Services Antique restoration, bespoke cabinet-making, French polishing, veneer design and pressing
Open Mon–Fri 8am–6pm Sat 9am–4pm

P Godden
Contact Mr P Godden
✉ **32 Darcy Road, Old Heath, Colchester, Essex, CO2 8BB** 🅿
☎ 01206 790349
Est. 1942
Services Antique furniture restoration
Open Mon–Sat 9am–5pm

Haig and Hosford
Contact Mr J Hosford
✉ **The Workshop, Trews Chase, High Street, Kelvedon, Colchester, Essex, CO5 9AQ** 🅿
☎ 01376 571502
Est. 1981
Services French polishing, antique restoration
Open Mon–Fri 8.30am–5pm Sat 8.30am–1pm

Brian Harris Furniture Restorations (BAFRA, EADA)
Contact Brian Harris
✉ **40 Lower Street, Stansted Mountfitchet, Essex, CM24 8LR** 🅿
☎ 01279 812233
Est. 1956
Services Antique furniture restoration including carving, gilding, French polishing, inlay work. Also restoration of clocks, barometers and ceramics
Open Mon–Sat 9am–5pm

Jeff Ingall
Contact Mr J Ingall
✉ **33 Hillside Road, Southminster, Essex, CM0 7AL** 🅿
☎ 01621 772686
Est. 1989
Services Antique furniture restorer, furniture maker
Open Mon–Sun 9am–6pm

S Layt
Contact Mr S Layt
✉ **Units 27–28, Barns Stables, Timworth Green, Bury St Edmunds, Suffolk, IP31 1HS** 🅿
☎ 01284 729072
Est. 1999
Services Antique furniture restoration, French polishing
Open Mon–Fri 8am–5.30pm

Maisey Restoration
Contact Mr Steve Maisey
✉ **Clark's Yard, High Street, Cavendish, Sudbury, Suffolk, CO10 8AT** 🅿
☎ 01787 281331
Est. 1991
Services Repair, restoration and French polishing
Open Mon–Fri 8am–5pm

Andrew A Matthews Restoration (BAFRA)
Contact Mr A A Matthews
✉ **25 Mawson Road, Cambridge, Cambridgeshire, CB1 2DZ** 🅿
☎ 01223 524728
ⓜ 07808 590370
Est. 1998
Services Antiques restoration and conservation, cabinet work, veneering, turning, key-making, lock repair, polishing, upholstery, rushing and caning
Open By appointment

R J McPhee
Contact Mr R J McPhee
✉ **20 Muspole Street, Norwich, Norfolk, NR3 1DJ** 🅿
☎ 01603 667701 ⓕ 01603 667701
ⓔ richardj.mcphee@tesco.net
ⓦ www.yell.co.uk/sites/rjmcphee
Est. 1980
Services 17th–18thC fine antique furniture restoration
Open Mon–Fri 8am–1pm 2–5pm or Sat by appointment

Norfolk Galleries
Contact Mr G Cumbley or Mr B Houchen
✉ **1 Stanley Street, King's Lynn, Norfolk, PE30 1PF**
☎ 01553 765060
Est. 1971
Services Full restoration service
Open Mon–Fri 8.30am–5.30pm

Peter Norman Antiques
Contact Mr Tony Marpole
✉ **55 North Street, Burwell, Cambridge, Cambridgeshire, CB5 0BA** 🅿
☎ 01638 616914
Est. 1977
Services General antiques

restoration, woodwork, caning, reupholstery, relining and restoring oils
Open Mon–Sat 9am–5.30pm prior warning best

Mark Peters Antiques
Contact Mr M Peters
✉ **Green Farm Cottage, Oak Road, Thurston, Bury St Edmunds, Suffolk, IP31 3SN** P
☎ 01359 230888 F 01359 233384
Est. 1977
Services Antique furniture restoration
Open Mon–Fri 8am–5pm Sat 9am–noon

Phoenix Restoration (BAFRA)
Contact Mr D Comben
✉ **Highlands Farm, Southend Road, Rettenden Common, Chelmsford, Essex, CM3 8EB** P
☎ 01245 327111 F 01245 327111
Est. 1998
Services General antique furniture restoration
Open By appointment

Ludovic Potts Restorations (BAFRA)
Contact Mr Ludovic Potts
✉ **Unit 1–1a, Station Road, Haddenham, Ely, Cambridgeshire, CB6 3XD** P
☎ 01353 741537 F 01353 741822
M 07889 341671
E mail@restorers.co.uk
W www.restorers.co.uk
Est. 2001
Services Modern and antique furniture restoration
Open By appointment

Repair Convert Furniture
Contact Mr John McKenna
✉ **The Barn, 86 Norsey Road, Billericay, Essex, CM11 1AT** P
☎ 01277 653088
Est. 1969
Services Antique furniture restoration and cabinet-maker
Open Mon–Fri 8.30am–4.30pm

Richard's Polishing
Contact Mr R Bufton
✉ **Bentley Road, Weeley Heath, Clacton on Sea, Essex, CO16 9DP** P
☎ 01255 831539
M 07712 873864
E sos@sos.uk.com
W www.sos.uk.com
Est. 1979
Services Antique restoration, all polish finishes
Open Mon–Fri 7.30am–5pm

Robert's Antiques
Contact Mr Robert King
✉ **The Barn, South Street, Risby, Bury St Edmunds, Suffolk, IP28 6QU** P
☎ 01284 811440 F 01284 811440
E roberts-antiques@ic24.com
Est. 1978
Services Upholstery, French polishing
Open Mon–Fri 8.30am–5pm

D J Short
Contact Mr D Short
✉ **The Stables, High Street, Horseheath, Cambridge, Cambridgeshire, CB1 6QN** P
☎ 01223 891983
Est. 1969
Services Antique furniture restoration, upholstery
Open Mon–Fri 9am–5pm Sat 9am–1pm

R J Smith Restoration
Contact Mr R J Smith
✉ **Unit 6A, Rear of Keimar House, Tut Hill, Fornham All Saints, Bury St Edmonds, Suffolk, IP28 6LE** P
☎ 01284 704894
M 07771 535863
Est. 1991
Services Repair and restoration of Georgian–Edwardian furniture, French polishing
Open Mon–Sat 8.30am–5.30pm

R A Surridge
Contact Mr R Surridge
✉ **The Barn, Thistledown, Latchingdon Road, Cold Norton, Chelmsford, Essex, CM3 6HR** P
☎ 01621 828036 F 01621 828036
Est. 1978
Services Antique restoration and cabinet-maker
Open Mon–Fri 8am–5pm

Teywood Ltd
Contact Mr K Cottee
✉ **East Gores Farm, Salmons Lane, Coggeshall, Essex, CO6 1RZ** P
☎ 01376 563025 F 01376 563025
Est. 1984
Services Antique furniture restoration and cabinet-maker
Open Mon–Fri 9am–5pm

Whitfield Restoration
Contact Mr J Palmor
✉ **London Road, Cockford, Colchester, Essex, CO6 1LG** P
☎ 01206 213212
Est. 1990
Services Antique restoration of furniture, cabinet-making, French polishing
Open Mon–Sat 8.30am–5pm

Justin Wood Restoration
Contact Justin Wood
✉ **Manor Farm Dairy, Manor Road, Hasketon, Woodbridge, Suffolk, IP13 6HZ** P
☎ 01394 387791
M 07712 131820
E justin.wood@antique-restoration.net
W www.antique-restoration.net
Est. 1997
Services Quality restoration, French polishing, woodcarving, cabinet-making
Open Mon–Fri 9am–5pm Sat 9am–noon

Woodside Restoration Services (GADR)
Contact Mr Tony Payne
✉ **Mulberry Farm, Ashfield Road, Elmswell, Bury St Edmunds, Suffolk, IP30 9HG** P
☎ 01359 244244 F 01359 244244
E mulberry@hotmail.com
Est. 1969
Services Full restoration service of furniture, brass, steel and upholstery
Open By appointment

HEART OF ENGLAND

A C Restorations
Contact Mr Adrian Clark
✉ **Unit 9d, Quickbury Farm, Hatfield Heath Road, Sawbridgeworth, Hertfordshire, CM21 9HY** P
☎ 01279 721583
M 07905 156976
E adrian.clark1@virgin.net
Est. 1993
Services Furniture restoration, polishing, leather lining, carving, general services
Open Mon–Fri 9am–5.30pm

ASSOCIATED SERVICES

FURNITURE

Antique and Modern Restoration by Richard Parsons
Contact Mr R Parsons
✉ **85 Pondcroft Road, Knebworth, Hertfordshire, SG3 6DE** 🅿
☎ 01438 812200
Est. 1980
Services Antique and modern furniture restoration, French polishing
Open Mon–Fri 8.30am–6pm or by appointment

Antique Restoration & Polishing
Contact Mr M P Wallis
✉ **1 The Row, Hawridge, Chesham, Buckinghamshire, HP5 2UH** 🅿
☎ 01494 758172 Ⓕ 01494 758701
Ⓔ mikewallis@hawridge.freeserve.co.uk
Est. 1968
Services General antique furniture restoration and polishing
Open By appointment

Keith Bawden (BAFRA)
Contact Keith Bawden
✉ **Mews Workshops, Montpelier Retreat, Cheltenham, Gloucestershire, GL50 2XG** 🅿
☎ 01242 230320
Est. 1975
Services Full antique restoration service of furniture, clocks, watercolours, jewellery, ceramics and Oriental carpets
Open Mon–Fri 7am–4.30pm

R Beesly
Contact Mr R Beesly
✉ **41 High Street, Broom, Biggleswade, Bedfordshire, SG18 9NA** 🅿
☎ 01767 314918
Est. 1974
Services Cabinet-maker, French polishing clock repairs
Open Mon–Sat 8am–6pm or by appointment

Richard Bolton Furniture Restorer (BAFRA)
Contact Richard Bolton
✉ **Painswick House, Old Dairy Workshop, Gloucester Road, Painswick, Gloucestershire, GL6 6TH** 🅿
☎ 01452 814881
Est. 1981
Services Restoration of fine antique furniture
Open Mon–Fri 9am–5pm

Andy Briggs
Contact Andy Briggs
✉ **2 Folly View, Bampton Road, Black Bourton, Oxfordshire, OX18 2PD** 🅿
☎ 01993 842623
Ⓜ 07977 936882
Est. 1991
Services Restoration and conservation of town and country furniture, cabinet-making, items bought and sold, copies of stolen items made
Open By appointment

Peter Campion Restorations (BAFRA)
Contact Peter Campion
✉ **The Old Dairy, Rushley Lane, Winchcombe, Nr Cheltenham, Gloucestershire, GL54 5JE** 🅿
☎ 01242 604403 Ⓕ 01242 604403
Ⓔ petercampion@ukonline.co.uk
Ⓦ www.petercampion.co.uk
Est. 1959
Services Restoration and conservation of furniture, barometers, clock cases. Also cabinet work, inlays, brass, veneering, polishing, furniture designed and made to order
Open Mon–Fri 9am–5.30pm

Charnwood Antiques (EADA)
Contact Mr Nigel Hoy
✉ **Unit 2e, The Maltings, Station Road, Sawbridgeworth, Hertfordshire, CM21 9JX** 🅿
☎ 01279 600562 Ⓕ 01279 600562
Ⓜ 07957 551899
Est. 1988
Services Cabinet-maker, antique furniture restoration, upholstery, cabinet lining, French polishing
Open Tues–Fri 10am–5pm Sat Sun 11am–5pm

Chess Antique Restorations
Contact Mr T Chapman
✉ **85 Broad Street, Chesham, Buckinghamshire, HP5 3EF** 🅿
☎ 01494 783043 Ⓕ 01494 791302
Ⓔ chessres@aol.com
Est. 1969
Services All cabinet work, hand finishing, upholstery, ceramics, metalwork, picture restoration, traditional polishing
Open Mon–Fri 9am–5pm

N A Copp
Contact Nigel Copp
✉ **Red Lane, Tewkesbury, Gloucestershire, GL20 5BQ** 🅿
☎ 01684 293935
Est. 1984
Services Restoration of antique furniture, maker of kitchens
Open Mon–Fri 8.30am–5.30pm

Martin Coulborn Restorations
Contact Mr M Coulborn
✉ **Canterbury House, Bridge Road, Frampton on Severn, Gloucestershire, GL2 7HE** 🅿
☎ 01452 740334
Est. 1978
Services Antique furniture restoration, maker of replica 18thC-style furniture
Open Mon–Fri 9am–1pm 2–5pm

Country Chairmen and Dovetail Restoration
Contact Mr Tony Handley
✉ **Home Farm, Ardington, Wantage, Oxfordshire, OX12 8PD** 🅿
☎ 01235 833614 Ⓕ 01235 833110
Ⓔ countrychairmen@compuserve.com
Est. 1973
Services Antique and modern furniture restoration
Open Mon–Fri 8.30am–5.30pm or Sat by appointment

D H R Ltd (BAFRA, UKIC)
Contact Mr David Hordern
✉ **8–10 Lea Lane, Thame Road, Long Crendon, Aylesbury, Buckinghamshire, HP18 9RN** 🅿
☎ 01844 202213 Ⓕ 01844 202214
Est. 1985
Services All antique furniture restoration services
Open Mon–Fri 9am–5.30pm

D M E Restorations Ltd (BAFRA)
Contact Duncan Everitt
✉ **11 Church Street, Ampthill, Bedfordshire, MK45 2PL** 🅿
☎ 01525 405819 Ⓕ 01525 756177
Ⓜ 07778 015121
Ⓔ duncan@dmerestorations.com
Ⓦ www.dmerestorations.com
Est. 1986
Services Restoration and conservation of antique furniture
Open Mon–Fri 8am–5pm or by appointment

P M Dupuy
Contact Mr P Dupuy
✉ **132 Bletchley Road, Newton Longville, Milton Keynes, Buckinghamshire, MK17 0AA** Ⓟ
☎ 01908 367168
Est. 1978
Services Restoration of antique furniture, all woodwork repairs, French and wax polishing, hand-stripping
Open Mon–Sat 9am–6pm

J W Eaton
Contact Mr J Eaton
✉ **The Barn, Tupsley Court Farm, Hampton Dene Road, Hereford, Herefordshire, HR1 1UX** Ⓟ
☎ 01432 354344
Est. 1990
Services General antique restoration
Open Mon–Fri 9am–5pm

C G Elmer-Menage
Contact Mr C Elmer
✉ **Unit 12, Elmsfield Industrial Estate, Worcester Road, Chipping Norton, Oxfordshire, OX7 5XL** Ⓟ
☎ 01608 644024
Est. 1978
Services Restoration of 18th–19thC furniture, marquetry, bespoke furniture maker
Open By appointment

Gloucestershire Furniture Hospital
Contact Mr M Deane
✉ **Commonfields Farm, Lower Boulsdon, Newent, Gloucestershire, GL18 1JH** Ⓟ
☎ 01531 822881
Est. 1999
Services Antique and modern furniture repair including upholstery, caning and French polishing. Collection service
Open Mon–Sat 8am–6pm

Robert Gripper Restoration
Contact Mr R Gripper
✉ **Manor Barn, Manor Farm, Ascott-under-Wychwood, Chipping Norton, Oxfordshire, OX7 6AL** Ⓟ
☎ 01993 831960 Ⓕ 01993 830395
Ⓔ robgripper@aol.com
Est. 1982
Services Antique furniture restoration, modern insurance work
Open Mon–Fri 9am–5pm

Hart Antiques
Contact Mr M Hart
✉ **Widmere Cottage, Parmoor, Frieth, Henley on Thames, Oxfordshire, RG9 6NH** Ⓟ
☎ 01491 571669 Ⓕ 01491 571917
Ⓜ 07816 122730
Est. 1985
Services Antique furniture restoration including upholstery, gilding and lacquerwork
Open Mon–Sat 9am–6pm

Roland Haycraft (GADR)
Contact Mr R Haycraft
✉ **The Lamb Arcade, High Street, Wallingford, Oxfordshire, OX10 0BS** Ⓟ
☎ 01491 839622
Ⓔ rohaycraft@fsbdial.co.uk
Ⓦ www.juststolen.com
Est. 1980
Services Antique furniture restorations and cabinet-making
Open Mon–Fri 9am–5.30pm

Alan Hessel (BAFRA)
Contact Mr A Hessel
✉ **The Old Town Workshop, St George's Close, Moreton-in-Marsh, Gloucestershire, GL56 0LP** Ⓟ
☎ 01608 650026 Ⓕ 01608 650026
Ⓜ 07860 225608
Est. 1975
Services Restoration of fine 17th–19thC furniture
Open Mon–Fri 8.30am–5pm or by appointment

Stephen Hill (BAFRA)
Contact Stephen Hill
✉ **11 Cirencester Workshops, Brewery Court, Cirencester, Gloucestershire, GL7 1JH** Ⓟ
☎ 01285 658817
Ⓜ 07976 722028
Est. 1979
Services Restoration of 17th–19thC furniture
Open Mon–Fri 9am–5pm

John Hulme
Contact Mr J Hulme
✉ **11a High Street, Chipping Norton, Oxfordshire, OX7 5AD** Ⓟ
☎ 01608 641692 Ⓕ 01608 641692
Est. 1980
Services Antique furniture restoration and conservation
Open Mon–Fri 7.30am–6pm

Icknield Restorations
Contact Simon Pallister
✉ **Icknield Farm, Tring Road, Dunstable, Bedfordshire, LU6 2JX** Ⓟ
☎ 01525 222883
Est. 1994
Services Antique furniture restoration
Open Mon–Fri 9.30am–6pm

Ipsden Woodcraft
Contact Mr M Small
✉ **The Post Office, The Street, Ipsden, Wallingford, Oxfordshire, OX10 6AG** Ⓟ
☎ 01494 680262
Est. 1981
Services Antique furniture restoration
Open Mon–Fri 8am–6pm

J R Jury & Son
Contact Mr Ken Jury
✉ **Springfields, Cobhall Common, Allensmore, Hereford, Herefordshire, HR2 9BJ** Ⓟ
☎ 01432 279108
Est. 1974
Services Antique furniture restorers, French polishing
Open Mon–Fri 8am–5pm

Robert Lawrence-Jones
Contact Robert Lawrence-Jones
✉ **Frogmarsh Mill, Stroud, Gloucestershire, GL5 5ET** Ⓟ
☎ 01453 872817
Est. 1980
Services Cabinet-maker, furniture restorer
Open Mon–Fri 9am–5pm

E C Legg and Son
Contact Mr C Legg
✉ **3 College Farm Buildings, Tetbury Road, Cirencester, Gloucestershire, GL7 6PY** Ⓟ
☎ 01285 650695
Est. 1903
Services Furniture restoration, carving, rushing, leather laying
Open Mon–Fri 9am–5pm
Sat 9am–noon

Andrew Lelliott
Contact Mr A Lelliott
✉ **Avening Park Workshop, West End, Avening, Tetbury, Gloucestershire, GL8 8NE** Ⓟ

☎ 01453 835783 Ⓕ 01453 832652
Ⓔ family@lelliotglos.freeserve.co.uk
Ⓦ www.andrewlelliot.sagenet.co.uk
Est. 1985
Services Furniture and clock case restoration, matching mouldings
Open By appointment

Clive Loader Restorations
Contact Mr C Loader
✉ **Stables Workshop, Lodge Cottage, High Street, Shipton under Wychwood, Oxfordshire, OX7 6DG** Ⓟ
☎ 01993 832727
Est. 1984
Services Antique furniture restoration
Open Mon–Fri 8am–5pm

M K Restorations
Contact Mr M Knight
✉ **Unit 8e4, Quickbury Farm, Hatfield Heath Road, Sawbridgeworth, Hertfordshire, CM21 9HY** Ⓟ
☎ 01279 726664
Ⓜ 07939 438587
Est. 1992
Services Antique furniture restoration
Open Mon–Sat 9am–6.30pm

Peter Makin (BAFRA)
Contact Mr P Makin
✉ **Dray House, The Maltings, School Lane, Amersham, Buckinghamshire, HP7 0ES** Ⓟ
☎ 01494 434688
Ⓔ hotleybott@aol.com
Est. 1992
Services Repair and restoration of 18th–19thC furniture, clock cases etc, including gilding, marquetry
Open Mon–Fri 9am–5.30pm Sat 9am–noon

Miracle Finishing
Contact Mr C Howes or Mr A Howes
✉ **The Cottage, Woodhall Farm, Hatfield, Hertfordshire, AL9 5NU** Ⓟ
☎ 01707 270587 Ⓕ 01707 270587
Ⓜ 07790 696631
Est. 1992
Services Furniture restoration, French polishing, reupholstery, pine stripping
Open Mon–Fri 8.30am–5pm

J Moore Restorations
Contact Mr J Moore
✉ **College Farm House Workshops, Chawston Lane, Chawston, Bedford, Bedfordshire, MK44 3BH** Ⓟ
☎ 01480 214165
Est. 1975
Services All aspects of furniture restoration, particularly period furniture
Open Mon–Fri 9am–5pm

Clive Payne (BAFRA, LAPADA)
Contact Clive Payne
✉ **Unit 4, Mount Farm, Junction Road, Churchill, Chipping Norton, Oxfordshire, OX7 6NP** Ⓟ
☎ 01608 658856 Ⓕ 01608 658856
Ⓜ 07801 088363
Ⓔ clive.payne@virgin.net
Ⓦ www.clivepayne.com
Est. 1986
Services Antique furniture restoration, specializing in country furniture and Georgian mahogany
Open Mon–Fri 9am–5pm

Charles Perry Restorations Ltd (BAFRA)
Contact John Carr
✉ **Praewood Farm, Hemel Hempstead Road, St Albans, Hertfordshire, AL3 6AA** Ⓟ
☎ 01727 853487 Ⓕ 01727 846668
Ⓔ cperry@praewood.freeserve.co.uk
Est. 1986
Services Anything associated with antique furniture restoration including carving, gilding, caning and upholstery
Open Mon–Fri 8.30am–5.30pm

Nathan Polley Antique Restoration
Contact Mr N Polley
✉ **The Barn, Upton Grove, Tetbury Upton, Tetbury, Gloucestershire, GL8 8LR** Ⓟ
☎ 01666 504997
Ⓜ 07977 263236
Ⓔ npolleyrestorations@yahoo.co.uk
Est. 1995
Services Repair and restoration
Open Mon–Fri 8am–6.30pm Sat 8am–4pm

R J Poynter
Contact Mr R Poynter
✉ **Lyndhurst, Westland Green, Little Hadham, Ware, Hertfordshire, SG11 2AF** Ⓟ
☎ 01279 842395
Est. 1984
Services Antique furniture restoration
Open Mon–Fri 10am–5pm Sat by appointment

Saracen Restoration
Contact Mr C Mills
✉ **Upton Downs Farm, Burford, Oxfordshire, OX18 4LY** Ⓟ
☎ 01993 822987 Ⓕ 01993 823701
Ⓜ 07958 907255
Ⓔ cmills6702@aol.com
Est. 1992
Services Full restoration service including marquetry, French polishing, gilding
Open Mon–Sat 9am–5.30pm

J Smith
Contact Mr J Smith
✉ **Calleva House, 6 High Street, Wallingford, Oxfordshire, OX10 0BP** Ⓟ
☎ 01491 835185
Est. 1994
Services Antique furniture restoration, conservation of original finishes
Open Mon–Fri 9am–5.30pm

Starkadder
Contact Mr C Rosser
✉ **Unit 4–13, Ditchford Farm, Stretton on Fosse, Moreton-in-Marsh, Gloucestershire, GL56 9RD** Ⓟ
☎ 01608 664885
Est. 1998
Services Antique furniture restoration
Open By appointment

Sunningend Joiners and Cabinet Makers Ltd
Contact Mr R J Duester
✉ **Industrial Estate, Station Road, Bourton-on-the-Water, Cheltenham, Gloucestershire, GL54 2EP** Ⓟ
☎ 01451 820761 Ⓕ 01451 820761
Est. 1972
Services Joinery, cabinet-making, antique furniture restoration
Open By appointment

Timber Restorations
Contact Mr S Shannon
✉ **Hyde Hall Barn, Sandon, Buntingford, Hertfordshire, SG9 0RU** Ⓟ
☎ 01763 274849 Ⓕ 01763 274849
Ⓜ 07973 748644
Est. 1997
Services Spray lacquering, French polishing, furniture repairs, caustic and non-caustic stripping, wax polishing, furniture sales, leather top inlay
Open Mon–Sat 9am–5pm

Christopher Tombs
Contact Mr C G Tombs
✉ **Unit 45, Northwick Business Centre, Blockley, Moreton-in-Marsh, Gloucestershire, GL56 9RF** Ⓟ
☎ 01386 700085
Est. 1994
Services English furniture restoration
Open Mon–Fri 8am–5pm

Clifford J Tracy (BAFRA)
Contact Clifford Tracy
✉ **3 Shaftesbury Industrial Centre, Icknield Way, Letchworth, Hertfordshire, SG6 1HE** Ⓟ
☎ 01462 684855 Ⓕ 01462 684833
Ⓜ 07831 326488
Est. 1961
Services Antique furniture restoration, marquetry, brasswork, tortoiseshell, ivory work, wax polishing, re-upholstery, leather top lining, period panelling restoration, deinfestation. Also specialist cabinet-makers
Open Mon–Thurs 7am–4pm
Fri 7am–3pm

Truman and Bates
Contact Mr P Truman
✉ **Classic Works, Station Road, Banbury, Oxfordshire, OX15 5LS** Ⓟ
☎ 01608 730433
Est. 1961
Services Restoration of antique furniture, French polishing
Open Mon–Fri 8am–5pm

P M Welch
Contact Mr P Welch
✉ **The Sitch, Longborough, Moreton-in-Marsh, Gloucestershire, GL56 0QJ** Ⓟ
☎ 01451 832046 Ⓕ 01451 870552
Ⓔ restoration.antiques@virgin.net
Ⓦ www.antiques-restorers.com
Est. 1969
Services Restoration of English and Continental furniture
Open Mon–Fri 7.45am–5.30pm
Sat 7.45am–noon

Robert Williams (BAFRA)
Contact Mr Robert Williams
✉ **32 Church Street, Willingham, Cambridge, Cambridgeshire, CB4 5HT** Ⓟ
☎ 01954 260972
Est. 1980
Services Restoration of carving, ivory, mother-of-pearl, bonework, papier mâché, tortoiseshell, weapons. Also cabinet-making and locksmith
Open Mon–Fri 9am–5pm

MIDLANDS

Anthony Allen Conservation, Restoration, Furniture and Artefacts (BAFRA, UKIC)
Contact Anthony Allen
✉ **The Old Wharf Workshop, Redmoor Lane, Newtown, High Peak, Derbyshire, SK22 3JL** Ⓟ
☎ 01663 745274 Ⓕ 01663 745274
Est. 1970
Services Restoration of 17th–19thC furniture, gilding, marquetry, Boulle, upholstery, metalwork, clock cases and movements
Open Mon–Fri 8am–5pm

The Antiques Workshop
Contact Mr Paul Burrows
✉ **68 Yoxall Road, Solihull, West Midlands, B90 3RP** Ⓟ
☎ 0121 744 1744
Ⓜ 07860 16878
Est. 1988
Services Furniture restoration
Open Mon–Sat 9am–5pm
closed Wed

M G Bassett
Contact Mrs G Bassett or Mr M Bassett
✉ **38 Church Street, Ashbourne, Derbyshire, DE6 1AJ** Ⓟ
☎ 01335 347750 (workshop)
01335 300061 (shop)
Ⓕ 01335 300061
Ⓔ mgbassett@aol.com
Est. 1979
Services Restoration of English and French country furniture and decorative items
Trade only Yes
Open Mon–Fri 9am–5pm
closed Wed

Belle Vue Restoration
Contact Mr Peter Grady
✉ **19 Belle Vue Road, Shrewsbury, Shropshire, SY3 7LN** Ⓟ
☎ 01743 272210
Est. 1984
Services Antique furniture restoration
Open Mon–Fri 8am–5.30pm

S C Brown
Contact Mr S C Brown
✉ **53 Melton Road, Birmingham, West Midlands, B14 7ET** Ⓟ
☎ 0121 441 1479
Est. 1981
Services Antique furniture restoration, furniture designed and made
Open Mon–Sat 8am–5.30pm

Byethorpe Furniture
Contact Mr B Yates
✉ **Shippen Rural Business Centre, Church Farm, Barlow, Derbyshire, S18 7TR** Ⓟ
☎ 0114 289 9111 Ⓕ 0114 289 9111
Ⓦ www.byethorpe.com
Est. 1995
Services Antique restoration, maker of bespoke furniture
Open Mon–Sat 9.30am–5.30pm

Century Tables
Contact Mr R Matthews
✉ **80 Hemming Street, Kidderminster, Worcestershire, DY11 6NB** Ⓟ
☎ 01562 747172
Est. 1974
Services Complete furniture restoration and repair, French polishing, marquetry, marble work etc
Open By appointment

Ian Dewar
Contact Mr Ian Dewar
✉ **55 Whateleys Drive, Kenilworth, Warwickshire, CV8 2GY** Ⓟ
☎ 01926 856767
Ⓔ DewarRestoration@aol.com
Est. 1989

Services Antique furniture restoration, French polishing
Open Mon–Fri 8.30am–5.30pm

G M H Restoration
Contact Mr G Hale
✉ **56c Market Street, Kingswinford, West Midlands, DY6 9LE** 🅿
☎ 01384 279670
Est. 1993
Services Furniture restoration
Open Mon–Fri 8.30am–6pm

T J Gittins
Contact Mr T J Gittins
✉ **The Old Barn, Nagington Grange, Childs Ercall, Market Drayton, Shropshire, TF9 2TW**
☎ 01952 840409
Services Antique furniture restoration

Guy Goodwin Restoration
Contact Mr Guy Goodwin
✉ **1a St John's, Warwick, Warwickshire, CV34 4NE** 🅿
☎ 01926 407409 ⓕ 01926 407409
Est. 1979
Services Antique furniture restoration
Open Mon–Fri 9am–5.30pm

Grantham Workshops Cabinet Makers
Contact Peter Grantham
✉ **51a–57 Union Street, Kettering, Northamptonshire, NN16 9DA**
☎ 01536 411461 ⓕ 01536 392239
ⓔ info@antiquerestore.co.uk
ⓦ www.antiquerestore.co.uk
Est. 1979
Services Conservation and restoration of antique furniture. Veneer and inlay replacement, French polishing and colouring

Gullheath Ltd
Contact Mr Mike Hammond
✉ **Beeches Road, Rowley Regis, West Midlands, B65 0AT** 🅿
☎ 0121 559 2555 ⓕ 0121 559 2555
ⓔ mikehammond@supanet.com
Est. 1977
Services Complete antique furniture restoration
Open Mon–Fri 8am–4.30pm

S Herberholz (BAFRA)
Contact Mr S Herberholz
✉ **Middleton Hall, Middleton, Tamworth, Staffordshire, B78 2AE** 🅿
☎ 01827 282858
ⓜ 07973 151681
Est. 1997
Services Complete repair and restoration of antique furniture, including metalwork, turning, upholstery, carving, caning, gilding, porcelain restoration
Open Wed–Sun 11am–5pm

Richard Higgins Conservation (BAFRA, UKIC)
Contact Richard Higgins
✉ **The Old School, Longnor, Nr Shrewsbury, Shropshire, SY5 7PP** 🅿
☎ 01743 718162 ⓕ 01743 718022
ⓔ richardhigginsco@aol.com
Est. 1988
Services Restoration of all fine furniture, clocks, movements, dials and cases, casting, plating, Boulle, gilding, lacquerwork, carving, period upholstery
Open Mon–Fri 8am–6pm

Hope Antiques
Contact Mr D White
✉ **The Coach House, Spring Croft, Hartwell Lane, Rough Close, Stoke-on-Trent, Staffordshire, ST3 7NG** 🅿
☎ 01782 399022 ⓕ 01782 399022
ⓜ 07720 160078
ⓔ hopeantiques@btintenet.com
Est. 1986
Services Repair and restoration of furniture, French polishing, pine stripping, inlay work. Country oak furniture made to order (from wood no less than 150 years old)
Open Mon–Sat 8am–6pm

John Hubbard Antiques Restoration & Conservation (LAPADA, CINOA)
Contact John Hubbard
✉ **Castle Ash, Birmingham Road, Blakedown, Worcestershire, DY10 3JE** 🅿
☎ 01562 701020 ⓕ 01562 700001
ⓜ 07775 872221
ⓔ jphubbard@aol.com
Est. 1968
Services Furniture restoration, French polishing, desktop leathers, upholstery
Open By appointment Mon–Fri 9am–5.30pm

Kings of Loughborough
Contact Mr A King
✉ **9b Hanford Way, Loughborough, Leicestershire, LE11 1SL** 🅿
☎ 01509 236335
Est. 1971
Services Repairs, restorations and cabinet-making
Open Mon–Fri 8am–5pm

Lincoln Restorations
Contact Andrew Lincoln
✉ **54 Mill Road, High Heath, Pelsall, Walsall, West Midlands, WS4 1BS** 🅿
☎ 01922 693999
Est. 1986
Services Full antique furniture restoration
Open Mon–Fri 8.30am–6pm

Mackenzie & Smith (BAFRA, UKIC)
Contact Mr Tim Smith
✉ **The Old Sorting Office, 7 Corve Street, Ludlow, Shropshire, SY8 1DB** 🅿
☎ 01584 877133
Est. 1998
Services 17th–19thC furniture restoration, clock case restoration
Open Mon–Fri 9am–5pm

Malvern Studios (BAFRA, UKIC, LGCI, NCCR)
Contact Jeff Hall
✉ **56 Cowleigh Road, Malvern, Worcestershire, WR14 1QD** 🅿
☎ 01684 574913 ⓕ 01684 569475
Est. 1961
Services Restoration of any form of furniture and panelling, including Boulle, gilding, tortoiseshell, black lacquer, chinoiserie, satinwood, hand-painted cameos
Open Mon Tues Thurs 9am–5.15pm Fri Sat 9am–4.45pm

Nigel Mayall
Contact Mr N Mayall
✉ **44 Load Street, Bewdley, Worcestershire, DY12 2AP** 🅿
☎ 01299 401431
Est. 1989
Services High-class French polishing, repairs, minor restorations, re-leathering, veneer repairs
Open Mon–Fri 10am–6pm

Melbourne Hall Furniture
Contact Mr N Collumbell
✉ **Old Saw Mill Craft Centre, Melbourne Hall, Melbourne, Derby, Derbyshire, DE73 1EA** P
☎ 01332 864131
Est. 1982
Services Repairs and restorations, French polishing
Open By appointment

Paul Mitchell
Contact Mr P J Mitchell
✉ **The Restoration Workshop, Grove Place, Raunds, Wellingborough, Northamptonshire, NN9 6DU** P
☎ 01933 622336
ⓔ mtchllmtch@aol.com
Est. 1974
Services Repairs, restorations, decorative paint finishes, gilding
Open By appointment

K Needham Restoration
Contact Kevin Needham
✉ **Unit 2, Old Hall Workshops, School Road, Beely, Derbyshire, DE4 2NU** P
☎ 01629 735455
Est. 1993
Services Repair and restoration
Open Mon–Sat 9am–5pm

Painswick Antiques
✉ **6 Churchgate, Retford, Nottinghamshire, DN22 6PQ** P
☎ 01777 706278
Est. 1977
Services Repair and restoration
Open Mon–Sat 9am–6pm

Perkins Stockwell and Co Ltd
Contact Mr J Stockwell
✉ **Abbey House, Abbey Gate, Leicester, Leicestershire, LE4 0AB** P
☎ 01162 516501 ⓕ 01162 510697
Est. 1760
Services Repair and restoration of furniture
Open Mon–Fri 7am–4pm

Regency Furniture Restoration
Contact Mr M Houghton
✉ **29 St Kenelm's Avenue, Halesowen, West Midlands, B63 1DW** P
☎ 0121 550 8356 ⓕ 0121 550 8356
Ⓜ 07966 434947
Est. 1997
Services Antique furniture restoration and cabinet-making
Open Mon–Fri 8am–5pm or by appointment

Reindeer Restorations
Contact Mr K Stimpson
✉ **43 Watling Street, Pottersbury, Towcester, Northamptonshire, NN12 7QD** P
☎ 01908 542633
Est. 1984
Services Reproductions, restoration
Open Mon–Fri 8am–4.30pm or by appointment

Renaissance Antiques
Contact Mr S Macrow
✉ **18 Marshall Lake Road, Shirley, Solihull, West Midlands, B90 4PL** P
☎ 0121 745 5140
Est. 1979
Services Antique furniture restoration
Open Mon–Sat 9am–5pm

Restoration Rooms (AMU)
Contact Miss Jo MacDonald or Miss Susan Robinson
✉ **Machins Business Centre, Wood Street, Ashby de la Zouch, Leicestershire, LE65 1EL** P
☎ 01530 417510 ⓕ 01530 417510
Est. 1997
Services Repairs, restorations and reupholstery
Open Mon–Fri 9am–5pm

Tim Ross-Bain
Contact Mr T Ross-Bain
✉ **Halford Bridge, Fosse Way, Halford, Shipston-on-Stour, Warwickshire, CV36 5BN** P
☎ 01789 740778 ⓕ 01789 740778
Est. 1979
Services Antique furniture restoration, interior decoration and repair, cabinet-making
Open 24 hours by appointment

Sealcraft
Contact Mr P M Sealey
✉ **107 New Road, Bromsgrove, Worcestershire, B60 2LJ** P
☎ 01527 872677
Est. 1995
Services Antiques restoration and repair, French polishing
Open By appointment

Simmons & Miles
Contact Mr S Simmons
✉ **The Workshop, Main Road, Wensley, Matlock, Derbyshire, DE4 2LH** P
☎ 01629 734826 ⓕ 01629 734826
Ⓦ www.simmonsandmiles.co.uk
Est. 1988
Services Antique furniture restoration. Specialist courses available
Open By appointment

Phillip Slater (BAFRA)
Contact Phillip Slater
✉ **93 Hewell Road, Barnt Green, Birmingham, West Midlands, B45 8NL** P
☎ 0121 445 4942 ⓕ 0121 445 4942
Est. 1977
Services Furniture and longcase clock restoration. All aspects of polishings and finishings including wax and French polishing, marquetry, inlay
Open Mon–Fri 9am–5.30pm Sat 9am–1pm

Anthony Smith
Contact Mr A Smith
✉ **Perton Court Farm, Jenny Walkers Lane, Wolverhampton, West Midlands, WV6 7HB** P
☎ 01902 380303 ⓕ 01902 380303
Est. 1969
Services Antique and quality furniture restoration
Open Mon–Fri 8.30am–5pm

Mark Smitten Cabinet Makers
Contact Mr M Smitten
✉ **Weston Trading Estate, Weston sub Edge, Evesham, Worcestershire, WR11 5QQ** P
☎ 01386 841205
Est. 1986
Services Complete antiques repair and restoration service, French polishing, veneering
Open Mon–Fri 8am–6pm

J A Snelson
Contact Mr J A Snelson
✉ **Jennett Tree Farm, Jennett Tree Lane, Callow End, Worcestershire, WR2 4UA** P
☎ 01905 831887
Ⓜ 07803 469122
Est. 1984
Services Fine antique restoration, French polishing, cabinet work

Open Mon–Fri 9am–5pm Sat 9am–noon

J W Stevens and Son
Contact Mr M J Stevens
✉ **61 Main Street, Lubenham, Market Harborough, Leicestershire, LE16 9TF** 🅿
☎ 01858 463521
Est. 1947
Services Antique furniture restorations
Open By appointment

Sympathetic Restorations
Contact Mr N Welsh
✉ **21–22 Monkmoor Farm, Monkmoor Road, Shrewsbury, Shropshire, SY2 5TL** 🅿
☎ 01743 340542 Ⓕ 01743 340542
Ⓜ 07971 208429
Ⓔ nicholas_welsh@hotmail.com
Est. 1994
Services Restoration of antique furniture, architectural features, insurance work, modern and traditional polishing, furniture made to order
Open Mon–Fri 8am–5pm weekends by appointment

Treedale Antiques
Contact Mr G Warren
✉ **Pickwell Lane, Little Dalby, Melton Mowbray, Leicestershire, LE14 2XB** 🅿
☎ 01664 454535 Ⓕ 01572 757521
Est. 1968
Services 16th–18thC furniture restoration
Open Mon–Sun 8am–6pm

Richard Walker – Antique Restoration
Contact Mr R Walker
✉ **302 Via Gellia Mills, Via Gellia Road, Bonsall, Matlock, Derbyshire, DE4 2AJ** 🅿
☎ 01629 636012/825640
Est. 1992
Services Furniture repair and restoration
Open By appointment

Simon Waterhouse Designs
Contact Mr S Capewell
✉ **The Jinney Ring Craft Centre, Hanbury, Bromsgrove, Worcestershire, B60 4BU** 🅿
☎ 01527 874787821182
Services Complete restoration and repair service, French polishing, veneering, leathering, inlay work, upholstery, Japanning. Furniture copying service
Open Tues–Sun 10.30am–5.30pm

Weedon Bec Antiques
Contact Mr N N Astbury
✉ **Rear of the Plough, Everdon, Daventry, Northamptonshire, NN11 3BL** 🅿
☎ 01327 361614 Ⓕ 01327 361614
Est. 1989
Services Antique repair and restoration
Open By appointment

E White Antique Restoration
Contact Mr E White
✉ **Abbey House, 115 Woods Lane, Derby, Derbyshire, DE22 3UE** 🅿
☎ 01332 331426
Ⓔ shirley.white1@btinternet.com
Est. 1969
Services Antique furniture repair and restoration
Open By appointment

Wizzards Furniture Transformers
Contact D Hayes
✉ **The Old Stables, Meadow Lane, Nottingham, Nottinghamshire, NG2 3HQ** 🅿
☎ 0115 986 7484 Ⓕ 0115 986 7484
Est. 1994
Services Furniture repairs and restorations
Open Mon–Fri 8.30am–5pm

Wood Restorations
Contact Mr Peter Wood
✉ **Eastfields Farm, Crick Road, Rugby, Warwickshire, CV23 0AB** 🅿
☎ 01788 822253 Ⓕ 01788 822253
Est. 1969
Services Furniture restoration
Open By appointment

YORKSHIRE & LINCOLNSHIRE

David Bailes of Knaresborough
Contact Mr P Oliver
✉ **Finkle Street, Knaresborough, North Yorkshire, HG5 8AA** 🅿
☎ 01423 868438
Est. 1961
Services Antiques repair, restoration
Open Mon–Sat 8am–5.30pm

Anthony James Beech (BAFRA, UKIC)
Contact Mr Anthony Beech
✉ **The Stable Courtyard, Burghley House, Stamford, Lincolnshire, PE9 3JY** 🅿
☎ 01780 481199
Est. 1998
Services Period furniture conservation and restoration
Open By appointment

Adrian J Black
Contact Mr A J Black
✉ **36a Freeman Street, Grimsby, Lincolnshire, DN32 7AG**
☎ 01472 355668
Est. 1968
Services Antique furniture repair and restoration
Open By apppointment

Kenneth F Clifford
Contact Mr K Clifford
✉ **29 St Aubyn's Place, York, North Yorkshire, YO24 1EQ** 🅿
☎ 01904 635780
Est. 1982
Services Antiques repair and restoration
Open By appointment

D A Copley
Contact Mr D A Copley
✉ **54a New Lane, Siddal, Halifax, West Yorkshire, HX3 9AL** 🅿
☎ 01422 351854
Est. 1949
Services Antiques repairs and restorations, French polishing
Open Mon–Fri 8am–5pm Sat 8am–noon

Edmund Czajkowski & Son (BAFRA)
Contact Michael Czajkowski
✉ **96 Tor O Moor Road, Woodhall Spa, Lincolnshire, LN10 6SB** 🅿
☎ 01526 352895 Ⓕ 01526 352895
Ⓔ michael.czajkowski@ntlworld.com
Est. 1951
Services Restoration of antique furniture, clocks, barometers
Open Mon–Sat 8.30am–5pm

R D Dunning
Contact Mr R Dunning
✉ **Scaife Cottage, Gate Helmsley, York, North Yorkshire**
☎ 01759 371961
Est. 1972
Services Antique furniture repair and restoration
Open Mon–Fri 9am–6pm

French House Antiques
Contact Steve
✉ **74 Micklegate, York, North Yorkshire, YO1 6LF** P
☎ 01904 624465 F 01904 629965
E info@thefrenchhouse.co.uk
W www.thefrenchhouse.co.uk
Est. 1995
Services Restoration of antique French furniture
Open Mon–Sat 9.30am–5.30pm

Rodney S Kemble Fine Furniture (BAFRA)
Contact Rodney Kemble
✉ **16 Cragvale Terrace, Glusburn, Nr Keighley, West Yorkshire, BD20 8QU** P
☎ 01535 636954
Est. 1984
Services Restoration of 18th–19thC English furniture, especially mahogany and walnut including veneer work and gilding. Also restoration of clock cases, writing slopes, decorative boxes, barometers

Ogee Restorations
Contact Mr L Jackson
✉ **32a Cambridge Street, Cleethorpes, Lincolnshire, DN35 8HD** P
☎ 01472 601701 F 01472 601701
M 07977 860823
Est. 1973
Services Repair, restoration, veneering, inlaying
Open Mon–Sat 8am–5pm

Paraphernalia
Contact Mrs R Thomas
✉ **12 Harland Place, High Street, Norton, Stockton-on-Tees, North Yorkshire, TS20 1AL** P
☎ 01642 535940
Est. 1984
Services Repairs and restorations, tea room
Open Mon–Sat 9.30am–5pm

Period Furniture Ltd (LAPADA)
Contact Mr S Bowyer
✉ **Moorside, Tockwith, York, North Yorkshire, YO26 7QG** P
☎ 01423 358399 F 01423 359050
E pf@period-furniture.co.uk
W www.antique-furniture.co.uk
Est. 1985
Services Antiques repair and restoration, sales of Georgian–Edwardian furniture
Trade only Sat
Open Mon–Fri 8am–4.30pm Sat 9am–4.30pm

T L Phelps Fine Furniture Restoration (BAFRA)
Contact Mr T Phelps
✉ **8 Mornington Terrace, Harrogate, North Yorkshire, HG1 5DH** P
☎ 01423 524604
Est. 1984
Services Repair, restoration and conservation of high-quality period furniture with old waxed and polished surfaces
Open By appointment

A G Podmore & Son
Contact Andrew Podmore
✉ **Unit 1D, North Minster Business Park, Northfield Lane, Poppleton, York, North Yorkshire, YO26 6QU** P
☎ 01904 799800
Est. 1968
Services Antique furniture restoration
Open Mon–Fri 9am–5pm

Rainbow Bridge
Contact Mr N Lambert
✉ **57A Oxbridge Lane, Stockton-on-Tees, Cleveland, TS18 4AP** P
☎ 01642 643033
Est. 1989
Services Antique repairs and restorations
Open Mon–Sat 10am–5pm

John W Saggers
Contact Mr J Saggers
✉ **Chapel Hill, Woolsthorpe by Belvoir, Grantham, Lincolnshire, NG32 1NG** P
☎ 01476 870756 F 01476 870756
Est. 1966
Services Antiques repair and restoration
Open By appointment

K J Sarginson Fine Furniture (AIOC)
Contact Mr K Sarginson
✉ **The Joinery, Escrick Grange, Stillingfleet Road, Escrick, York, North Yorkshire, YO19 6EB** P
☎ 01904 728202 F 01904 728202
Est. 1991
Services Antique restorations and repairs of fine furniture. Dining tables a speciality
Open Mon–Fri 8.15am–5.30pm or by appointment

Gerald Shaw
Contact Mr M G Shaw
✉ **Jansville, Quarry Lane, Harrogate, North Yorkshire, HG1 3HR** P
☎ 01423 503590 F 01423 503590
Est. 1956
Services Repair, restoration of antique furniture
Open By appointment

Tony Smart Restorations
Contact Tony Smart
✉ **Fold House, Glebe Farm, Lund, Beverley, East Yorkshire, YO25 9TT** P
☎ 01377 217438
Est. 1971
Services General fine furniture restoration
Open Mon–Fri 9am–5pm

J K Speed Antique Furniture Restoration
Contact Mr J Speed
✉ **The Workshop, Thornton Road, New York, Lincoln, Lincolnshire, LN4 4YL** P
☎ 01205 280313
M 07761 242219
Est. 1964
Services Antique repair and restoration, light upholstery, specializing in case repair of longcase clocks
Open Mon–Fri 9am–5.30pm

Spires Restoration
Contact Mr G Bexon
✉ **32 Upgate, Louth, Lincolnshire, LN11 9ET** P
☎ 01507 600707
F 01507 602588
M 07866 230725
Est. 1994
Services Repair and restoration of furniture
Open Mon–Fri 8am–5pm or by appointment

Tomlinson Antiques (LAPADA)
Contact Mike Grant
✉ **Moorside, Tockwith, North Yorkshire, YO26 7QG** P
☎ 01423 358833 F 01423 358188
E info@tomlinsonfurniture.com
W antique-furniture.co.uk
Est. 1977
Services Repair and restoration of furniture
Open Mon–Sat 9am–4.30pm Sun 10am–4pm

Neil Trinder (BAFRA)
Contact Mr N Trinder
✉ **Burrowlee House, Broughton Road, Sheffield, South Yorkshire, S6 2AS** 🅿
☎ 0114 285 2428
Est. 1985
Services Furniture restoration including gilding, upholstery, marquetry etc
Open By appointment

Clive Underwood Antiques
Contact Mr Clive Underwood
✉ **Rose Cottage, 46 High Street, Colsterworth, Grantham, Lincolnshire, NG33 5NF** 🅿
☎ 01476 860689
Est. 1964
Services Restoration of 17th–18thC furniture, also rushing and caning. Dining chairs made to match existing
Open Mon–Fri 8am–5.30pm

Westway Pine
Contact Mr J Dzierzek
✉ **Carlton Lane, Helmsley, York, North Yorkshire, YO62 5HB** 🅿
☎ 01439 771399 Ⓕ 01439 770172
Ⓜ 07798 651155
Ⓔ derzie@supanet.co.uk
Est. 1986
Services Antique reproductions and restoration
Open Mon–Fri 9am–5pm Sat 10am–5pm Sun by appointment

B D Whitham
Contact Mr B D Whitham
✉ **1 South View Cottage, Draughton, Skipton, North Yorkshire, BD23 6EF** 🅿
☎ 01756 710422
Est. 1984
Services Repair and restoration, upholstery
Open Mon–Fri 9am–6pm and by appointment

Nigel Wright
Contact Mr N Wright
✉ **Burrowlee House, Broughton Road, Sheffield, South Yorkshire, S6 2AS** 🅿
☎ 0114 234 1403
Est. 1983
Services Complete repair and restoration of antique furniture, veneering, inlays, French polishing, colouring, etc
Open By appointment

NORTH EAST

G M Athey
Contact Mr Athey
✉ **Corner Shop, Narrowgate, Alnwick, Northumberland, NE66 1JQ** 🅿
☎ 01665 604229
Ⓜ 07836 718350
Ⓦ www.atheysantiques.com
Est. 1982
Services Full restoration, French polishing, upholstery. Deals in Georgian and Victorian furniture and china
Open Mon–Sat 8am–4.30pm

Richard Pattison
Contact Richard Pattison
✉ **Unit 4, New Kennels, Blagdon Estate, Seaton Burn, Newcastle-upon-Tyne, Tyne and Wear, NE13 6DB** 🅿
☎ 01670 789888
Est. 1977
Services Traditional antique furniture restoration
Open Mon–Sat 9am–5pm

Richard Zabrocki & Son
Contact Mr I Zabrocki
✉ **Hoults Estate, Walker Road, Newcastle-upon-Tyne, Tyne & Wear, NE6 1AB** 🅿
☎ 0191 265 5989
Est. 1949
Services Repair and restoration of antique furniture
Open By appointment

NORTH WEST

Antique Furniture Restoration & Conservation (BAFRA)
Contact Eric Smith
✉ **The Old Church, Park Road, Darwen, Lancashire, BB3 2LD** 🅿
☎ 01254 776222
Ⓜ 07977 811067
Ⓔ ericsmith@restorations.ndo.co.uk
Est. 1965
Services Furniture restoration
Open Mon–Sun 9am–7pm

Arrowsmith Antiques & Restoration
Contact Mr P Arrowsmith
✉ **Unit 7–8, Waterside Mill, Waterside, Macclesfield, Cheshire, SK11 7HG** 🅿
☎ 01625 611880
Est. 1977
Services Complete repair and restoration service of high-quality antique furniture
Open Mon–Fri 8.30am–5.30pm Sat 10am–2pm

K Bennett
Contact Mr Keith Bennett
✉ **Oak House Farm, Wycollar, Colne, Lancashire, BB8 8SY** 🅿
☎ 01282 866853
Est. 1973
Services Antique furniture restoration
Open By appointment

Steve Blackwell French Polishers
Contact Mr S Blackwell
✉ **Bute Mill, Essex Street, Preston, Lancashire, PR1 1QE** 🅿
☎ 01772 821004 Ⓕ 01772 432270
Ⓜ 07929 170114
Est. 1989
Services Full antique furniture restoration service and modern finishes
Open Mon–Thurs 8am–5pm Fri 8am–4.30pm

M Bradley
Contact Mr M Bradley
✉ **588 Hawthorne Road, Bootle, Merseyside, L20 6JZ** 🅿
☎ 0151 922 5901
Est. 1969
Services Antique furniture restoration, French polishing, repairs, upholstery repairs
Open Mon–Fri 9am–5pm Sat 9am–noon

Michael Clayton French Polisher
Contact Mr M Clayton
✉ **The Workshop, Lestrange Street, Cleethorpes, Lancashire, BU35 7HS** 🅿
☎ 01472 602795
Est. 1979
Services French polishing
Open By appointment

Rory Fraser
Contact Mr R Fraser
✉ **Goyt Mill, Upper Hibbert Lane, Marple, Stockport, Cheshire, SK6 7HX** 🅿
☎ 0161 427 2122
Est. 1993
Services Good-quality antique furniture restoration, French polishing, leathers fitted, woodturning, carving
Open Mon–Fri 9am–5pm

Hamilton Antique Restoration
Contact Mr C Sayle
✉ **1a Orry Place, Douglas, Isle of Man**
☎ 01624 662483
Est. 1989
Services Complete furniture repair and restoration service, upholstery
Open By appointment

Michael Holroyd Restorations
Contact Mr M Holroyd
✉ **Pendle Antique Centre, Union Mill, Watt Street, Sabden, Clitheroe, Lancashire, BB7 9ED** P
☎ 01282 771112
Ⓜ 07711 011465
Est. 1996
Services Complete repair and restoration service including spray finish, wax finish, French polishing, cabinet-making and veneering
Open Mon–Sat 8am–5pm

Hopkins Antique Restoration
Contact Mr Mark Hopkins
✉ **Unit 1, Excelsior Works, Charles Street, Heywood, Lancashire, OL10 2HW** P
☎ 01706 620549
Est. 1987
Services Antique furniture restoration, French polishing
Open Mon–Sat 9am–5pm

J Kershaw Fine Furniture Restoration
Contact Mr J Kershaw
✉ **Normans Hall Farm, Shrigley Road, Pott Shrigley, Macclesfield, Cheshire, SK10 5SE** P
☎ 01625 560808 Ⓕ 01625 573222
Est. 1985
Services Full repair and restoration service including French polishing, inlay work, marquetry, lacquerwork
Open By appointment

Peter Lawrenson
Contact Margaret Lawrenson
✉ **Brook Cottage, Scronkey Pilling, Preston, Lancashire, PR3 6SQ** P
☎ 01253 790671
Est. 1984
Services Furniture restoration
Open By appointment

M & M Restoration Work Ltd
Contact Mrs M Bean
✉ **Rock Cottage, Castletown, Isle of Man, IM9 4PJ** P
☎ 01624 823620 Ⓕ 01624 822463
Est. 1993
Services Repair and restoration of furniture, upholstery, caning, rushing etc
Open By appointment

Macdonalds Restoration
Contact Mr A Macdonald
✉ **Unit 4, Gladstone Park, Ramsey, Isle of Man, IM8 2LE** P
☎ 01624 812791
Est. 1980
Services Traditional antique and modern furniture repair and restoration, upholstery, cabinet-making etc
Open Mon–Sun 8am–6pm

Mansion House Antiques
Contact Mr Andrew Smith
✉ **11 Hand Lane, Leigh, Lancashire, WN7 3LP** P
☎ 01942 605634
Est. 1995
Services Antique furniture restoration
Open By appointment

Pilgrims Progress Antiques
Contact Mr S Hyams
✉ **1a–3a Bridgewater Street, Bridgewater, Liverpool, Merseyside, L10 0AR** P
☎ 0151 7087815 Ⓕ 0151 7087815
Ⓔ pilgrimsprog@fsb.dial.co.uk
Ⓦ www.pilgrimsprogress.co.uk
Est. 1987
Services Complete repair and restoration service, traditional upholstery, caning, veneering, French polishing, sales of 19th–20thC furniture
Open Mon–Fri 9am–5pm
Sat 1–4pm

R S M Antique Restoration
Contact Mr Robin Stone
✉ **The Stables, Black Eaves Street, Blackpool, Lancashire, FY1 2HW** P
☎ 01253 623839 Ⓕ 01253 623839
Est. 1972
Services Antique furniture, clocks, barometer, restoration, marquetry cutting
Open Mon–Fri 9am–6pm

T N Richards
Contact Mr D Richards
✉ **Hamilton Place, Chester, Cheshire, CH1 2BH** P
☎ 01244 320241
Est. 1975
Services Complete repair and restoration service
Open By appointment

R J H Rimmel
Contact Mr R J H Rimmel
✉ **3 Newton Bank Cottages, Newton Hall Road, Mobberley, Cheshire, WA16 7LB** P
☎ 01565 873847
Est. 1974
Services Full furniture restoration service, special commissions and church work undertaken
Open By appointment

J D Worrall
Contact Mr J Worrall
✉ **Goyt Mill, The Old Brickworks, Pott, Shingley, Stockport, Cheshire, SK6 7HX** P
☎ 01663 733817
Est. 1997
Services Complete antiques repair and restoration including upholstery, carving, gilding, veneer, inlay, cabinet work and French polishing
Open By appointment

WALES

Iain Ashcroft Furniture
Contact Mr Ian Ashcroft
✉ **Ty Canol Farm, Sunbank, Llangollen, Denbighshire, LL20 7UL** P
☎ 01978 860392 Ⓕ 01978 860392
Est. 1987
Services Antique furniture, restoration, carving, inlaying
Open Mon–Fri 9am–5pm

D J Gravell
Contact D J Gravell
✉ **Unit 5, Aber Court, Ferryboat Close Enterprise Park, Morrison, Swansea, West Glamorgan, SA6 8QN** P
☎ 01792 310202 Ⓕ 01792 795471
Ⓔ jgravell@universalwoodfinishers.co.uk
Ⓦ www.universalwoodfinishers.co.uk
Est. 1989
Services Antique furniture repair and restoration
Open Mon–Fri 8.30am–5.30pm
Sat 9–11am

ASSOCIATED SERVICES

FURNITURE

Hera Restorations
Contact Neil Richards
✉ **Cardiff, South Glamorgan**
☎ 029 2075 5379 Ⓕ 01222 761660
Est. 1995
Services Full French polishing, veneering, carving
Open By appointment

Heritage Workshop
Contact Mr G Lloyd
✉ **14B, rear of 1 Iestyn Street, Cardiff, South Glamorgan, CF11 9HT** Ⓟ
☎ 029 2039 0097
Ⓜ 07931 681743
Est. 1981
Services Restoration of furniture. Makes oak and pine furniture to order. Period architectural restoration, specializing in fireplaces
Open Mon–Sat 9am–5pm

B G Jones
Contact B G Jones
✉ **Cwmbury Honey Farm, Ferryside, Carmarthenshire, SA17 5TW** Ⓟ
☎ 01267 267318
Ⓔ brian_jones@cwmburryfarm.freeserve.co.uk
Est. 1986
Services Antiques repair and restoration of furniture
Open Mon–Fri 9am–5pm

G A Parkinson
Contact Mr G A Parkinson
✉ **Glanrapon, Secontmill Road, Caernarfon, Gwynedd, LL55 2YL** Ⓟ
☎ 01286 672865
Est. 1949
Services French polishing, repairs, restoration
Open Mon–Sat 9am–5pm

Pastiche
Contact Mr S Pesticcio
✉ **15 Duxford Close, Llandaff, Cardiff, South Glamorgan, CF5 2DZ** Ⓟ
☎ 02920 309559
Ⓜ 07811 594257
Est. 1975
Services Period and traditional restoration and redecoration of Victorian furniture and property
Open By appointment

Phoenix Conservation.com (BAFRA, UKIC)
Contact Hugh Haley
✉ **Selwyn Forge, Tenby Road, St Clears, Carmarthenshire, SA33 4JP** Ⓟ
☎ 01994 232109
Ⓔ phoenixconservation@hotmail.com
Ⓦ www.phoenixconservation.com
Est. 1992
Services Welsh oak and antique furniture restoration and repair
Open By appointment

T N Richards
Contact Mr D Richards
✉ **Caergynog, Llanbedr, Gwynedd, LL45 2PL** Ⓟ
☎ 01341 241485
Est. 1974
Services Complete repair and restoration service
Open By appointment

Snowdonia Antiques
Contact Jeffery Collins
✉ **Bank Building, Station Road, Llanrwst, Gwynedd, LL26 0EP** Ⓟ
☎ 01492 640789 Ⓕ 01492 641800
Ⓜ 07802 503552
Est. 1965
Services Antiques repair and restoration
Open Mon–Sat 9am–5pm
Sun by appointment

St Helen's Restoration
Contact Jane McCarthy
✉ **87–88 St Helen's Avenue, Swansea, West Glamorgan, SA1 4NN** Ⓟ
☎ 01792 465240 Ⓕ 01792 467788
Ⓔ jo@artsnetwork.co.uk
Est. 1979
Services Antiques repair and restoration, upholstery, French polishing
Open Mon–Fri 9am–5pm
Sat 9.30am–1pm

SCOTLAND

Adam Antiques & Restoration
Contact Charles Bergius
✉ **23c Dundas Street, Edinburgh, EH3 6QQ** Ⓟ
☎ 0131 556 7555 Ⓕ 0131 556 7555
Est. 1983
Services Quality repairs to 18th–19thC furniture. Sales of 18th–19thC mainly mahogany furniture and associated furnishings
Open Mon–Sat 10.30am–6pm

Antique Furniture Restoration
Contact David Carson
✉ **108b Causewayside, Edinburgh, EH9 1PU** Ⓟ
☎ 0131 667 1067
Ⓜ 07779 824543
Ⓔ carsonantrest@btinternet
Est. 1994
Services Repair and restoration of all old and antique furniture
Open Mon–Fri 10am–6pm
Sat 10am–2pm

Castle Restoration
Contact Peter Nicholson
✉ **Auchtertool House, Auchtertool, Kirkcaldy, Fife, KY2 5XW** Ⓟ
☎ 01592 780371 Ⓕ 01592 780371
Est. 1964
Services Repair and restoration of all antiques, French polishing
Open By appointment

The Chairman of Bearsden
Contact David Snutterton
✉ **At 16 Highborough Road, The Mews, Caledon Lane, Hillhead, Glasgow, G12 9YE** Ⓟ
☎ 0141 334 2727 Ⓕ 0141 334 4747
Ⓔ sales@thechairmanofbearsden.co.uk
Ⓦ www.thechairmanofbearsden.co.uk
Est. 1990
Services Furniture restoration and upholstery, French polishing, cabinet-making, bergère suites, cane and rush seating
Open Mon–Sat 9am–5pm

Chisholme Antiques
Contact Kim Roberts
✉ **5 Orrock Place, Hawick, Scottish Borders, TD9 0HQ** Ⓟ
☎ 01450 376928
Est. 1979
Services Antiques repair and restoration of furniture, cabinet-making
Open Mon–Fri 9am–5pm

Chylds Hall Fine Furniture Restoration
Contact Stephen Pickering
✉ **Old Dairy Cottage, Upper Stepford, Dunscore, Dumfries & Galloway, DG2 0JP** Ⓟ
☎ 01387 820558
Est. 1991

Services Fine furniture restoration, period paint finish restoration, French polishing
Open By appointment

Douglas & Kay
Contact Mr P Kay
✉ **Next to 200 Eglington Street, Glasgow, G5 9QJ** P
☎ 0141 429 6908
Ⓜ 0797 4494618
Est. 1948
Services Repair and restoration of furniture, French polishing
Open By appointment

Roland Gomm
Contact Roland Gomm
✉ **65 Constitution Street, Edinburgh, EH6 7AF** P
☎ 0131 467 5525
Ⓜ 07947 179774
Est. 1986
Services French polishing, restoration of fine antique furniture, upholstery
Open Mon–Sat 10am–6pm

Alastair Gunn
✉ **46e Bavelaw Road, Balerno, Midlothian, EH14 7AE** P
☎ 0131 449 4032
Est. 1989
Services Antique reproduction and restoration
Open Mon–Sat 9am–6pm

The Hen Hoose
Contact Jo McGregor
✉ **Tynron, Thornhill, Dumfriesshire, DG3 4LA** P
☎ 01848 200418
Ⓦ www.henhoose.co.uk
Est. 1994
Services French polishing, caning, rushing, upholstery, general antique repair
Open Tues–Sun 11am–5pm

Inchmartine Restorations (BAFRA)
Contact Andrew Stephens
✉ **Inchmartine House, Inchture, Perth, Perthshire, PH14 9QQ** P
☎ 01828 686412 Ⓕ 01828 686748
Ⓔ ir@toolbazaar.freeserve.co.uk
Ⓦ www.toolbazaar.co.uk
Est. 1990
Services Restores antique furniture pre-1840
Open Mon–Sat 9am–5.30pm

The Tower Workshops
Contact George Pirie
✉ **Aberdeen Road, Tarland, Aboyne, Aberdeenshire, AB34 4TB** P
☎ 013398 811544
Est. 1989
Services Antiques restorers and dealers
Open Mon–Fri 9am–5pm
Sat 11am–5pm

William Trist (BAFRA)
Contact Willliam Trist
✉ **135 St Leonard's Street, Edinburgh, EH8 9RB** P
☎ 0131 667 7775 Ⓕ 0131 667 4333
Services Restoration and conservation of antique furniture and panelling, Cabinet and chair-makers, cane and rush chair seating, upholstery
Open Mon–Fri 8am–6pm but appointment advisable

Graham Watson
✉ **The Workshop, Mill Lynd, Greenlaw, Scottish Borders, TD10 6UA** P
☎ 01361 810770/810593
Est. 1996
Services Furniture restoration, French polishing
Open Mon–Sat 8am–5pm

NORTHERN IRELAND

Antique Services
Contact David Hosgood
✉ **288 Beersbridge Road, Belfast, Co Antrim, BT5 5DY** P
☎ 028 9020 3933
Est. 1984
Services Restoration, re-polishing
Open Mon–Fri 8am–5pm
Sat 8am–1pm

Courtyard Restoration
Contact Mr Shaun Butler
✉ **The Old Mill, 2 Parkfield Road, Ballymena, Co Antrim, BT42 2QS** P
☎ 028 2587 8875
Ⓜ 07967 144784
Est. 1995
Services Furniture restoration
Open Mon–Sat 10am–6pm

Crozier Antique Furniture Restoration
Contact Mr Peter Crozier
✉ **39 Tassagh Road, Keady, Co Armagh, BT60 3TU** P
☎ 028 3753 8242
Est. 1986
Services Restoration
Open Mon–Fri 9am–6pm or by appointment

REPUBLIC OF IRELAND

Conservation Restoration Centre for Furniture and Wooden Artefacts (UKIC, ICHAWI)
Contact Colin Piper ACR IICHAWI
✉ **Letterfrack, Co Galway, Ireland** P
☎ 095 41036 Ⓕ 095 41112
Services Conservation and restoration of all historic furniture and related objects. Museum conservation, cabinet-making, French polishing, veneer work, turning and woodcarving, marquetry, Boulle work, metal work repairs, *pietre dure* and marble repair
Open Mon–Fri 9am–5.30pm or by appointment

E Fitzpatrick
Contact E Fitzpatrick
✉ **17 Sidney Park, Wellington Road, Cork, Co Cork, Ireland** P
☎ 021 450 3084
Est. 1989
Services Repair and restoration of antique furniture
Open By appointment

Val Hughes (IPCRA)
Contact Mr Val Hughes
✉ **132 Arden Vale, Tullamore, Co Offaly, Ireland** P
☎ 0506 22600
Ⓔ valhughestull@eircom.net
Est. 1990
Services Conservation and restoration of antique and fine furniture
Open Mon–Sat 8.30am–6pm

Stephen McDonnell (BAFRA)
Contact Mr McDonnell
✉ **2 Anglesea Lane, Dun Laoghaire, Co Dublin, Ireland** P
☎ 01 280 7077 Ⓕ 01 284 2268
Ⓜ 07863 363537

Est. 1994
Services Furniture restoration, traditional finishing, French polishing, cabinet repairs
Open Tues–Sat 9am–5.30pm

GILDING

Alison Cosserat
Contact Miss Alison Cosserat
✉ **13f Tonedale Mills, Tonedale, Wellington, Somerset, TA21 0AW** P
☎ 01823 665279
Ⓜ 07989 465427
Est. 1997
Services Gold leaf specialist
Open Mon–Fri 10am–6pm

Michael Ferris
Contact Mr M Ferris
✉ **Rose Cottage, Chapel Lane, South Cockerington, Louth, Lincolnshire, LN11 7EB** P
☎ 01507 327463 Ⓕ 01507 327463
Est. 1979
Services Antiques repairs and restorations
Open By appointment

Mark Finamore
Contact Mark Finamore
✉ **63 Orford Road, Walthamstow, London, E17 9NJ** P
☎ 020 8521 9407
Est. 1981
Services General antiques service, furniture restoration and conservation
Open Mon–Fri 10.30am–6pm or Sat by appointment

R G Jones
Contact R G Jones
✉ **1 Brickfield Cottage, Bilting, Ashford, Kent, TN25 4ER** P
☎ 01233 812849
Est. 1985
Services Antique restoration, gilding
Open Mon–Fri 9am–4pm

Vigi Sawdon
Contact Vigi Sawdon
✉ **79–81 Ledbury Road, London, W11 2AG** P
☎ 020 7229 9321/2033
Ⓕ 020 7229 2033
Ⓔ vigisawdon@virgin.net
Est. 1994
Services Gilding and restoration of old wooden, gesso and composite mirrors, architectural pieces, frames. Also provides special paint effects
Open By appointment

GLASS

F W Aldridge Ltd
Contact Miss Angela Garwood
✉ **28 Mead Industrial Park Riverway, Harlow, Essex, CM20 2SE** P
☎ 01279 442876 Ⓕ 01279 445764
Ⓔ angela@fwaldridge.abk.co.uk
Ⓦ www.fwaldridgeglass.com
Est. 1926
Services Repair and restoration of glass, provides Bristol glass for antique and modern table silverware, all glass and silver restoration
Open Mon–Fri 9am–5.30pm

Lorna Barnes Conservation (IPCRA, ICCOM)
Contact Lorna Barnes
✉ **158 Rialto Cottages, Rialto, Dublin 8, Co Dublin, Ireland** P
☎ 01 473 6205
Ⓔ barneslorna@hotmail.com
Est. 2000
Services Conservation of glass, ceramic and stone objects, condition surveys, advice on packaging and storage
Open Mon–Fri 9am–6pm

Facets Glass Restoration
Contact Mrs K Moore
✉ **107 Boundary Road, London, E17 8NQ** P
☎ 020 8520 3392 Ⓕ 020 8520 3392
Ⓜ 07778 758304
Ⓔ repairs@facetsglass.co.uk
Ⓦ www.facetsglass.co.uk
Est. 1996
Services Antique glass restoration including supply of blue glass liners for table silverware, re-bristling hair brushes, cutlery restoration, flute and trumpet stopper suppliers
Open Mon Tues 1–5pm or by appointment

Fran Hall Glass Restoration
Contact Mrs Fran Hall
✉ **49 Grove Road, Beccles, Suffolk, NR34 9RE** P
☎ 01502 717246
Services Glass restoration including decanter cleaning
Open By appointment

Martyn Pearson Glass
Contact Martyn Pearson
✉ **The Stables Craft Centre, Halfpenny Green Vineyard, Tom Lane, Bobbington, Staffordshire, DY7 5EP** P
☎ 01384 221399
Ⓜ 07951 305617
Est. 1995
Services Glass cutting, engraving and repairs
Open Mon–Sun 11am–5pm

Red House Glasscrafts
Contact Mrs J Oakley or B Taylor
✉ **Stuart Crystal Museum, Red House Glassworks, Vine Lane, Wordsley, Stourbridge, West Midlands, DY8 4AA** P
☎ 01384 76018 Ⓕ 01384 76018
Ⓦ www-antiques-ukdealers.com/redhouse
Est. 1987
Services Repair and restoration of antique crystal
Open Mon–Fri 9am–5pm Sat 10am–4pm

Romanov Restoration
Contact Ludmila Romanova
✉ **51 Sutherland Avenue, London, SW9 2HF** P
☎ 020 7286 1430
Est. 1982
Services Painting and icon restoration using traditional Russian methods, glass and bronze restoration
Open By appointment

GRAMOPHONES & RADIOS

Philip Knighton the Gramophone Man (RETRA)
Contact Philip Knighton
✉ **11 North Street, Wellington, Somerset, TA21 8LX** P
☎ 01823 661618 Ⓕ 01823 661618
Ⓔ gramman@msn.com
Est. 1981
Services Supplies and restores gramophones, early wirelesses and sells 78rpm records
Open Mon–Sat 10am–5.30pm

Talking Points Antiques
Contact Mr Paul Austwick

✉ 66 West Street,
Sowerby Bridge,
West Yorkshire, HX6 3AP P
☎ 01422 834126
e tpagrams@aol.com
Est. 1985
Services Repair, refurbishment and restoration of wind-up gramophones. Sales of general antiques
Open Thurs Fri Sat 10.30am–5.30pm and by appointment

The Wireless Works
Contact Rob Rusbridge
✉ **40 Fore Street, Bugle, St Austell, Cornwall, PL26 8PE** P
☎ 01726 852284 f 01726 852284
e rob@wirelessworks.co.uk
w www.wirelessworks.co.uk
Est. 1995
Services Radio, gramophone and antique electronics repairs, restorations, rebuilding and trading
Open Mon–Sat 9am–5pm

INLAY WORK

Paul Waldmann Woodwork (Conservation Unit)
Contact Mr P Waldmann
✉ **41 Norfolk Street, Cambridge, Cambridgeshire, CB1 2LD** P
☎ 01223 314001
m 07740 167055
e paul.mann@cwcom.net
Est. 1982
Services Antique furniture restoration, cabinet-making
Open By appointment

KITCHENWARE

Craftsman Antiques
Contact Mark Haines
✉ **Unit 1, Maindy Lane, Maindy Road, Cathay, Cardiff, West Glamorgan, CF24 4XN** P
☎ 01291 625145 f 01291 625145
m 07836 634712
e mark@oakden.com
w www.oakden.com
Est. 1968
Services Furniture, antiques repair and restoration, kitchenware
Open All week 9am–5pm

LEATHER

Antique Leathers (LAPADA, AMU)
Contact Jackie Crisp
✉ **Unit 2, Bennetts Field Trading Estate, Wincanton, Somerset, BA9 9DT** P
☎ 01963 33163 f 01963 33164
e info@antique-leathers.co.uk
w www.antique-leathers.co.uk
Est. 1965
Services Hand-dyed leatherwork on desk tops, gold tooling, traditional upholstery, leather chair repairs and restorations, bookshelf edging
Open Mon–Fri 9.30am–5pm

J Crisp (AMU)
Contact Mr J Crisp
✉ **48 Roderick Road, London, NW3 2NL** P
☎ 020 7485 8566 f 020 7485 8566
Est. 1979
Services Loose leather services, traditional upholstery, French and leather polishing, table liners, leather gilding
Open Mon–Fri 10am–6pm visitors by appointment

Director Furniture Leathergilders
Contact Mrs M Taylor
✉ **39 Severn Stoke, Worcester, Worcestershire, WR8 9JA** P
☎ 01905 371339
Est. 1984
Services Replacement leather tops for the antiques trade, gilded or ungilded. Full grain hide or skiver
Open By appointment

Leather Conservation Centre (UKIC, SSCR)
Contact Roy Thomson
✉ **University College Campus, Boughton Green Road, Moulton Park, Northampton, Northamptonshire, NN2 7AN** P
☎ 01604 719766 f 01604 719649
e lcc@northampton.ac.uk
Est. 1978
Services Conservation and restoration of leather objects, research, training and information for leather and leather conservation
Open Mon–Fri 9am–5pm

Stanstead Abbotts Leathers
Contact Mrs L Ray
✉ **Hedges, Commonside Road, Harlow, Essex, CM18 7EY** P
☎ 01279 453914 f 01279 432295
Est. 1981
Services Table liners
Open Mon–Fri 9am–5.30pm

Stocks and Chairs Antique Restoration
Contact Kevin Beale
✉ **The Old Church Hall, Hardy Road, Parkstone, Poole, Dorset, BH14 9HN** P
☎ 01202 718418 f 01202 718918
e email@stocksandchairsantiques.com
w www.stocksandchairsantiques.com
Est. 1979
Services Full restoration service, specializing in hand-dyed leather
Open Mon–Fri 9am–5pm weekends by appointment

Woolnough (AC) Ltd
Contact Mr A Cullen
✉ **Units W107–110, First Floor, Holywell Centre, 1 Phipp Street, London, EC2A 4PS** P
☎ 020 7739 6603 f 020 7739 8975
Est. 1885
Services Desk top leathering, leather upholstery, bookshelf edging, chairback embossing and distressed hand-stained leather upholstery
Open Mon–Fri 7am–3.30pm

LIGHTING

Dernier and Hamlyn Ltd
✉ **Unit 5, Croydon Business Centre, 214 Purley Way, Croydon, Surrey, CR0 4XG** P
☎ 020 8760 0900 f 020 8760 0955
w www.dernier-hamlyn.com
Est. 1888
Services Traditional and contemporary bespoke lighting specialists, manufacturing and restoration. Holders of royal warrant for manufacture and restoration to HM Queen
Open Mon–Fri 9am–6pm

Karim Restorations
Contact Mr A Karim
✉ **Studio 6, The Bull Theatre Gallery, Barnet, Hertfordshire, EN5 5SJ** P
☎ 020 8449 928647
e aminsemail@e.mail.com
Est. 1984

Services Restoration of Art Nouveau, Arts and Crafts, pewter, castings and lighting
Open Mon–Fri 10am–5pm

Sargeant Restorations
Contact David and Ann Sargeant
✉ **21 The Green, Westerham, Kent, TN16 1AX** Ⓟ
☎ 01959 562130 Ⓕ 01959 561989
Ⓜ 07771 553624
Est. 1989
Services Restoration of all light fittings, lustres, candelabra
Open Mon–Sat 9am–5.30pm

David Turner
Contact Mr D Turner
✉ **24 Tottenham Road, London, N1 4BZ** Ⓟ
☎ 020 7241 5400 Ⓕ 020 7241 5416
Ⓔ david.turner@teleregion.co.uk
Est. 1987
Services Repair and restoration of metalwork, lighting, decorative antiques
Open Mon–Fri 9.30am–6pm

MARBLE

Rimmer Restoration
Contact Mr J S Rimmer
✉ **14 Hastings Place, Lytham, Lancashire, FY8 5LZ** Ⓟ
☎ 01253 794521 Ⓕ 01253 794521
Est. 1987
Services Marble restorer
Open By appointment

MARQUETRY

A Dunn and Son
Contact Mr R Dunn
✉ **8 Wharf Road, Chelmsford, Essex, CM2 6LU** Ⓟ
☎ 01245 354452 Ⓕ 01245 494991
Est. 1896
Services Makers of marquetry and Boulle
Open Mon–Fri 8am–6pm
Sat by appointment

Gow Antiques and Restoration (BAFRA)
Contact Jeremy Gow
✉ **Pitscandly Farm, Forfar, Angus, DD8 3NZ** Ⓟ
☎ 01307 465342
Ⓜ 07711 416786
Ⓔ jeremy@gowantiques.co.uk
Ⓦ www.gowantiques.co.uk
Est. 1991
Services Specialists in restoration of European furniture, 17th–18thC marquetry
Open Mon–Fri 9am–5pm or by appointment

METAL

Antique Restorations
Contact Mr C Christofi
✉ **Unit 23a, Rosebery Industrial Park, Rosebery Avenue, London, N17 9SR** Ⓟ
☎ 020 8880 9697 Ⓕ 020 8880 9697
Est. 1968
Services Repair, restoration and refinishing to all metalwork, re-gilding, repairing and casting
Open Mon–Fri 8am–6pm

John Armistead
Contact Mr John Armistead
✉ **Malham Cottage, Bellingdon, Chesham, Buckinghamshire, HP5 2UR** Ⓟ
☎ 01494 758209 Ⓕ 01494 758209
Est. 1979
Services Repair and restoration of all antique metalwork including casting, replacement of missing parts, lighting
Open Mon–Fri 9am–5pm

B W Restorations
Contact Mr B W Harris
✉ **44 Hayling Rise, Worthing, West Sussex, BN13 3AG** Ⓟ
☎ 01903 871562 Ⓕ 01903 603846
Ⓜ 07966 539854
Est. 1984
Services Restoration of bronze sculptures
Open Mon–Sun 8am–6pm

Bold as Brass Polishers
Contact Mark Mapley
✉ **Unit 13, Visicks Works, Perranarworthal, Truro, Cornwall, TR3 7NR** Ⓟ
☎ 01872 864207
Est. 1994
Services Brass and copper polishing
Open Mon–Fri 9.15am–4.30pm

Bristol Restoration Workshop
Contact Mr Hall
✉ **8 Devon Road, Bristol, BS5 9AD** Ⓟ
☎ 0117 954 2114 Ⓕ 0117 954 2114
Est. 1979
Services Metalware restoration and repair
Open Mon–Fri 8am–5pm

Michael Brook Antique Metal Restoration (BAFRA)
Contact Mr M Brook
✉ **192 Camberwell Grove, London, SE5 8RJ** Ⓟ
☎ 020 7708 0467 Ⓕ 020 7708 0467
Ⓦ www.antiquemetalrestoration.co.uk
Est. 1988
Services Antique metal restoration, repair and patination of bronzes, specializing in ormolu cleaning and repair
Open By appointment

E Hansen
Contact Mr E Hansen
✉ **6 Shalbourne Close, Hungerford, Berkshire, RG17 0QH** Ⓟ
☎ 01488 684772
Ⓜ 07885 511986
Ⓔ epgerdes-hans@amserve.net
Est. 1985
Services Metal restoration
Open Mon–Fri 9am–6pm

Rupert Harris Conservation (ILC, UKIC, NACE, SPAB, ICOM)
Contact Ms Roberts
✉ **Unit 5C, 1 Fawe Street, London, E14 6PD** Ⓟ
☎ 020 7987 6231/7515 2020
Ⓕ 020 7987 7994
Ⓔ enquiries@rupertharris.com
Ⓦ www.rupertharris.com
Est. 1982
Services Conservation and restoration of fine metalwork and sculpture
Trade only Yes
Open By appointment

Karim Restorations
Contact Mr A Karim
✉ **Studio 6, The Bull Theatre Gallery, Barnet, Hertfordshire, EN5 5SJ** Ⓟ
☎ 020 8449 928647
Ⓔ aminsemail@e.mail.com
Est. 1984
Services Restoration of Art Nouveau, Arts and Crafts, pewter, castings and lighting
Open Mon–Fri 10am–5pm

Metalwork Restoration Services
Contact Ms G Salmon
✉ **59 Trafalgar Street, Sheffield, South Yorkshire, S1 4GN** P
☎ 0114 249 3308
Est. 1993
Services Metalwork restoration, bronze, silver, brass etc
Open By appointment

Renaissance Ironwork
Contact Robert Helyer
✉ **Woodsend House, Old London Road, Copdock, Ipswich, Suffolk, IP8 3JP** P
☎ 01473 730017 Ⓕ 01473 730017
Est. 1969
Services Makers of antique metal furniture fittings and decorative ironwork. Antique metal restorations
Trade only Yes
Open By appointment

Shawlan Antiques (LAPADA)
Contact Mr Shawn Parmakis
✉ **415 Whitehorse Road, Thornton Heath, Surrey, CR7 8SD** P
☎ 020 8684 5082 Ⓕ 020 8684 5082
Ⓜ 07889 510253
Est. 1974
Services Metal restorations, foundry work, patination, gilding, chasing
Open Mon–Fri 8am–6pm Sat 8am–5pm

David Turner
Contact Mr D Turner
✉ **24 Tottenham Road, London, N1 4BZ** P
☎ 020 7241 5400 Ⓕ 020 7241 5416
Ⓔ david.turner@teleregion.co.uk
Est. 1987
Services Repair and restoration of metalwork, lighting, decorative antiques
Open Mon–Fri 9.30am–6pm

MILITARIA

Bailiff Forge Manufacturing
Contact Mr John Denbigh or Mr Tom Kay
✉ **Unit 53, Colne Valley Workshops, Linthwaite, Huddersfield, West Yorkshire, HD7 5QG** P
☎ 01484 846973 Ⓕ 01484 846973
Ⓔ bailifforge@jedenbigh.freeserve.uk
Ⓦ www.baliff-forge.co.uk
Est. 1984
Services Restorations to swords and armour
Open Mon–Fri 10am–6pm Sat 2–6pm

The Queen's Shilling
Contact Mrs A Wolf
✉ **87 Commercial Road, Parkstone, Poole, Dorset, BH14 0JD** P
☎ 01202 723335
Est. 1986
Services Medal mounting, blazer badges for uniforms, sells memorabilia
Open Mon–Sat 9am–5pm half day Wed

Chris Rollason Home Counties Medal Services
Contact Mr C Rollason
✉ **53 Bodiam Crescent, Hampden Park, Eastbourne, East Sussex, BN22 9HQ** P
☎ 01323 506012
Est. 1979
Services Full-size medals restored and mounted to wear or in frame or case. Miniature dress medals supplied and mounted. Regimental ties, blazer badges, buttons, medal accessories also supplied
Open Mon–Fri 9am–5pm

MUSICAL INSTRUMENTS

A Frayling-Cork (BAFRA)
Contact Mr A Frayling-Cork
✉ **2 Mill Lane, Wallingford, Oxfordshire, OX10 0DH** P
☎ 01491 826221
Est. 1979
Services Antique furniture repair, restoration, French polishing, metal fittings, specializing in musical instruments
Open By appointment 24hr answerphone

Michael Parfett
Contact Mr M Parfett
✉ **Unit 058, 31 Clerkenwell Close, London, EC1R** P
☎ 020 7490 8768 Ⓕ 020 7253 5535
Ⓜ 07939 334645
Ⓦ www.michaelparfett.co.uk
Est. 1990
Services Keyboard musical instrument restoration, also harps and stringed instruments, lacquerwork, gilding
Open By appointment

ORIENTAL

E & C Royall
Contact Mr C Royall
✉ **10 Waterfall Way, Medbourne, Market Harborough, Leicestershire, LE16 8EE** P
☎ 01858 565744
Est. 1981
Services Repairs, restorations
Open Mon–Sat 9am–5pm or by appointment

PACKERS

Michael Allcroft Antiques
Contact Michael Allcroft
✉ **203 Buxton Road, Newtown, Disley, Nr Stockport, Cheshire, SK12 2RA** P
☎ 01663 744014 Ⓕ 01663 744014
Ⓜ 07798 781642
Est. 1986
Services Packing and export abroad, English oak ideal for the Japanese market
Open Mon–Fri noon–6pm Sat 10am–1pm or by appointment

Anglo Pacific (Fine Art) Ltd (LAPADA)
Contact Malcolm Disson
✉ **Unit 2, Bush Industrial Estate, Standard Road, London, NW10 6DF** P
☎ 020 8838 8008 Ⓕ 020 8453 0225
Ⓔ antiques@anglopacific.co.uk
Ⓦ www.anglopacific.co.uk
Est. 1977
Services Packing, shipping and international removals. Also valuations and restorations
Open Mon–Fri 8.30am–5.30pm

Derbyshire Removals
Contact Michael Powell
✉ **Butterley Cottage, Butterley Lane, Ashover, Derbyshire, S45 0JU** P
☎ 01629 582762/01246 202289
Ⓜ 07774 422561
Est. 1987
Services Removal service of antique and fine furniture and packing
Open Ring anytime

Alan Franklin Transport
Contact Miss S Cowan

✉ **26 Blackmoor Road, Verwood, Dorset, BH31 6BB**
☎ 01202 826539 Ⓕ 01202 827337
Ⓔ alanfranklin@lineone.net
Ⓦ www.alanfranklintransport.co.uk
Est. 1975
Services Specialist carriers of antiques and fine art world wide
Open Mon–Fri 8.30am–5.30pm

Gander and White Shipping Ltd (BADA, LAPADA)
Contact O Howell
✉ **21 Lillie Road, London, SW6 1UE** Ⓟ
☎ 020 7381 0571 Ⓕ 020 7381 5428
Ⓔ info@ganderandwhite.com
Ⓦ www.ganderandwhite.com
Est. 1933
Services Packing and shipping
Open Mon–Fri 9am–5.30pm

Hedleys Humpers (LAPADA, BADA, BIFA, BAR, IATA)
✉ **3 St Leonards Road, London, NW10 6SX** Ⓟ
☎ 020 8965 8733 Ⓕ 020 8965 0249
Ⓔ mg@hedleyshumpers.com
Ⓦ www.hedleyshumpers.com
Est. 1973
Services Door-to-door delivery by road, sea and air of single items to full container loads. Arrange collection, export, packing, insurance and all export and customs paperwork on customer's behalf
Open Mon–Fri 8am–6pm

International Furniture Exporters Ltd
Contact Iris Mitchell
✉ **Old Cement Works, South Heighton, Newhaven, East Sussex, BN9 0HS** Ⓟ
☎ 01273 611251 Ⓕ 01273 611574
Ⓦ www.asweb.co.uk/ife
Est. 1990
Services Make furniture and export
Open By appointment

Kuwahara Ltd (LAPADA, HHGFAA)
Contact Yukio Kuwahara
✉ **6 McNicol Drive, London, NW10 7AW** Ⓟ
☎ 020 8963 1100 Ⓕ 020 8963 0100
Ⓔ yukio@kuwahara.co.uk
Ⓦ www.kuwahara.co.uk
Est. 1983
Services Fine art packing and shipping, door-to-door transport around the world by land, air or sea
Trade only Yes
Open Mon–Fri 9am–5.30pm

C and N Lawrence
Contact Mr N Lawrence
✉ **7 Church Walk, Brighton Road, Horley, Surrey, RH6 7EE**
☎ 01293 783243
Est. 1983
Services Removals, shipping, packing for antiques trade
Trade only Yes
Open Mon–Fri 9am–5pm

John Morgan and Sons (FIDI, OMI, BAR, HHGFAA, ERC)
Contact Mr William Morgan
✉ **Removal House, 30 Island Street, Belfast, Co Antrim, BT4 1DH** Ⓟ
☎ 028 9073 2333 Ⓕ 028 9045 7402
Ⓔ info@morganremovals.com
Ⓦ www.morganremovals.com
Est. 1915
Services Specialist antique removals and local, worldwide household removals
Open Mon–Fri 9am–5.30pm

PDQ Air Freight/Art Move (LAPADA, CINOA, GTA, BASC, BIFA)
✉ **Unit 4, Court 1, Challenge Road, Ashford, Middlesex, TW15 1AX**
☎ 01784 243695 Ⓕ 01784 242237
Ⓔ artmove@pdq.uk.com
Ⓦ www.pdq.uk.com
Est. 1983
Services Packing and shipping, fair logistics, hand-carry couriers, bonded warehouse
Open Mon–Fri 9am–5.30pm

Seabourne Mailpack Worldwide (LAPADA)
Contact Jonathan Cohen
✉ **Unit 13, Saxon Way, Moor Lane, Harmondsworth, Middlesex, UB7 0LW** Ⓟ
☎ 020 8897 3888
Ⓜ 07770 612134
Ⓦ www.seabourne-mailpack.co.uk
Est. 1962
Services Export packing and world wide delivery of fine art, antiques, furniture, etc
Open Mon–Fri 9am–5pm

The Shipping Company
Contact Matt Walton
✉ **Bourton Industrial Park, Bourton-on-the-Water, Cheltenham, Gloucestershire, GL54 2HQ** Ⓟ
☎ 01451 822451 Ⓕ 01451 810985
Ⓜ 07971 425978
Ⓔ enquiries@theshippingcompanyltd.com
Est. 1998
Services Packing and shipping of antiques worldwide
Open Mon–Fri 9am–6pm phone mobile at other times

A J Williams Shipping (LAPADA)
Contact Jennifer Williams
✉ **607 Sixth Avenue, Central Business Park, Petherton Road, Hengrove, Bristol, BS14 9BZ** Ⓟ
☎ 01275 892166 Ⓕ 01275 891333
Ⓔ aj.williams@btclick.com
Est. 1977
Services Packing and shipping of antiques and fine art worldwide
Open Mon–Fri 9am–5.30pm or by appointment

PAINTED FURNITURE

Joyce Ellis
Contact Joyce Ellis
✉ **Yew Tree Farm, Stratford Road, Wootton Wawen, Solihull, West Midlands, B95 6BY** Ⓟ
☎ 01564 795401 Ⓕ 01564 795401
Ⓜ 07712 126048
Est. 1989
Services Restoration of painted furniture and pen work, general restoration
Open Tues–Sun 9am–5.30pm

M Tocci
Contact Mr M Tocci
✉ **81 Southern Row, London, W10 5AL** Ⓟ
☎ 020 8960 4826
Est. 1978
Services Gilding, painted furniture restoration, lacquer on furniture and decorations
Open Mon–Fri 8am–4.30pm

PAPER

Cameron Preservation (IPCRA, IPC, SAPCON)
Contact Mr Elgin Cameron

✉ **Flush Business Centre, Flush Place, Lurgan, Co Armagh, BT66 7DT** Ⓟ
☎ 028 3834 3099 Ⓕ 028 3834 3099
Est. 1993
Services Restoration of art on paper, archives, manuscripts, books etc, also vellum, parchment, globes
Open Mon–Fri 8.30am–5.15 Sat 8.30am–noon

PICTURE RESTORATION

Roger Allan
Contact Mr R Allan
✉ **The Old Red Lion, Bedlingfield, Eye, Suffolk, IP23 7LQ** Ⓟ
☎ 01728 628491
Est. 1973
Services Picture restorer, furniture restorer
Trade only Yes
Open By appointment

Framing & Restoration Workshop
Contact Alex Wildman
✉ **First Floor, Higherford Mill, Barrowford, Lancashire, BB9 6JH** Ⓟ
Est. 1970
Services Picture and frame restoration
Open Please ring

Alyson Lawrence
Contact Alyson Lawrence
✉ **Lev Antiques Ltd, 97a Kensington Church Street, London, W8 7LN** Ⓟ
☎ 020 7727 9248 Ⓕ 020 7727 9248
Ⓜ 07768 470473
Ⓔ alyson@richardlawrence.co.uk
Est. 1984
Services Restoration of 17th–20thC oil paintings
Open Tues–Sat 10.30am–5.45pm or by appointment

Romanov Restoration
Contact Ludmila Romanova
✉ **51 Sutherland Avenue, London, SW9 2HF** Ⓟ
☎ 020 7286 1430
Est. 1982
Services Painting and icon restoration using traditional Russian methods, glass and bronze restoration
Open By appointment

PINE

Heritage Restorations
Contact Jonathan Gluck
✉ **Llanfair Caereinion, Welshpool, Powys, SY21 0HD** Ⓟ
☎ 01938 810384 Ⓕ 01938 810900
Ⓔ info@heritagerestorations.co.uk
Ⓦ www.heritagerestorations.co.uk
Est. 1970
Services Antique furniture, repair and restoration, specializing in 18th–19thC pine
Open Mon–Sat 9am–5pm

Oldwoods Pine Furniture
Contact Sid Duck
✉ **Unit 4, Colston Yard, Colston Street, Bristol, BS1 5BD** Ⓟ
☎ 0117 9299023
Est. 1980
Services Furniture repairs, restorations, buying and selling
Open By appointment

The Pine Mine
Contact Mr David Crewe-Read
✉ **100 Wandsworth Bridge Road, London, SW6 2TF** Ⓟ
☎ 020 7736 1092 Ⓕ 020 7736 5283
Ⓔ pinemine@hotmail.com
Est. 1972
Services Country furniture and antique pine repair and restoration, bespoke furniture maker
Open Mon–Sat 9.30am–5.30pm Sun 11am–4pm

Ed Thomas Old Country Pine
Contact Mr E Thomas
✉ **Unit 9, Yates Brothers Estate, Lime Lane, Pelsall, Walsall, West Midlands, WS3 5AS** Ⓟ
☎ 01543 360097 Ⓕ 01543 360097
Ⓜ 07966 243477
Ⓔ edthomasoldcountrypine@altavista.com
Est. 1981
Services Made-to-measure pine furniture using only old original pine.
Open Mon–Sat 9am–5.30pm

Wood Be Good
Contact Mr Dennis Langford
✉ **1 Jarrow Road, London, SE16 3JR** Ⓟ
☎ 020 7232 2639 Ⓕ 020 8657 6610
Est. 1984
Services Pine furniture repair and restoration, pine stripping
Open Mon–Sat 7am–5pm

PLASTERWORK

Seamas O'Heocha Teoranta (IPCRA)
Contact Seamas O'Heocha
✉ **Corbally, Barna, Galway, Co Galway, Ireland** Ⓟ
☎ 091 590256 Ⓕ 091 590256
Ⓜ 087 2581150
Ⓔ soheocha@indigo.ie
Est. 1987
Services Ornate plasterwork restoration and conservation
Open Mon–Fri 9am–6pm

SCIENTIFIC

Osborne Antiques
Contact Mrs L Osborne
✉ **91 Chester Road, New Oscot, Sutton Coldfield, West Midlands, B73 5BA** Ⓟ
☎ 0121 355 6667 Ⓕ 0121 354 7166
Ⓔ chris@barometerparts.co.uk
Ⓦ www.barometerparts.co.uk
Est. 1975
Services Barometer parts suppliers, scientific glass blowers
Open Tues–Thurs 9am–5pm Fri 9am–5.30pm Sat 9.15am–1pm closed 1–2pm

SCULPTURE

Graciela Ainsworth
Contact Graciela
✉ **Unit 10 Bonnington Mill, 72 Newhaven Road, Edinburgh, EH6 5QG** Ⓟ
☎ 0131 555 1294 Ⓕ 0131 467 7080
Ⓔ graciela@graciela-ainsworth.com
Est. 1990
Services Conservation of statues, monuments, stone sculptures. Carving commissions
Open Mon–Fri 9am–6pm

Taylor Pearce Restoration Services Ltd
Contact Mr K Taylor
✉ **Fishers Court, Besson Street, London, SE14 5AF** Ⓟ
☎ 020 7252 9800 Ⓕ 020 7277 8169
Ⓔ admin@taylorpearce.com
Est. 1985
Services Sculpture, conservation and restoration of stone, bronze, plaster and terracotta. By appointment to HM Queen
Open By appointment

SILVER

Wellington Gallery (LAPADA)
Contact Mrs M Barclay
✉ **1 St John's Wood High Street, London, NW8 7NG** Ⓟ
☎ 020 7586 2620 Ⓕ 020 7483 0716
Est. 1979
Services Restoration of silver and silver plate, gilding, engraving, jewellery, glass, upholstery, paintings, porcelain, furniture, framing, valuations
Open Mon–Fri 10.30am–6pm
Sat 10am–6pm

STONEWORK

Voitek Conservation of Works of Art
Contact Mr W Sobczynski
✉ **9 Whitehorse Mews, Westminster Bridge Road, London, SE1 7QD** Ⓟ
☎ 020 7928 6094 Ⓕ 020 7928 6094
Ⓔ voitekcwa@btinternet.com
Est. 1972
Services Conservation and restoration of marble, stone, terracotta, wood
Open By appointment

STRIPPING

Back to the Wood
Contact Mr J Davis
✉ **Riverside Works, Riverside Road, Watford, Hertfordshire, WD1 4HY** Ⓟ
☎ 01923 222943
Ⓜ 07976 297008
Est. 1981
Services Pine stripping, Victorian–Edwardian fireplaces a speciality
Open Mon–Sat 9am–5pm

Cameo Antiques
Contact Mrs S Hinton
✉ **3 Liverpool Road East, Church Lawton, Stoke-on-Trent, Staffordshire, ST7 3AQ** Ⓟ
☎ 01782 772555
Est. 1985
Services Complete repair and restoration of furniture, stripping
Open Mon–Fri 9am–6pm
Sat 9am–4pm

E Carty
Contact Mr E Carty
✉ **51 Trinity Street, Gainsborough, Lincolnshire, DN21 1JF** Ⓟ
☎ 01427 614452
Ⓜ 07733 474895
Est. 1976
Services Stripping and restoration
Open By appointment

Chiltern Strip & Polish
Contact Mr B Black
✉ **Kitchener Works, Kitchener Road, High Wycombe, Buckinghamshire, HP11 2SJ** Ⓟ
☎ 01494 438052
Est. 1986
Services Repairs and repolishing. Sale of antique furniture
Open Mon–Fri 9am–5pm Sat 9am–12.30pm

Dip 'n' Strip
Contact P Coates
✉ **88 Barkly Road, Beeston, Leeds, West Yorkshire, LS11 7ES** Ⓟ
☎ 0113 272 0064
Est. 1982
Services Antiques repairs and restorations
Open Mon–Fri 9am–6pm

Dip 'n' Strip
Contact Brendan Peoples
✉ **Singer Station, Singers Building, Kilbourne Road, Clydebank, Dunbartonshire, G81 2JQ** Ⓟ
☎ 0141 9529111460
Est. 1980
Services Furniture restoration
Open Mon–Fri 9am–5pm

The Door Stripping Company Ltd
Contact Mr B Findley
✉ **32 Main Road, Renishaw, Sheffield, South Yorkshire, S21 3UT** Ⓟ
☎ 01246 435521
Est. 1984
Services Pine stripping, non-caustic restoration of furniture
Open Mon–Fri 9am–5pm
Sat–Sun 11am–2pm

Hunts Pine Stripping Services
Contact Mr W Dougherty
✉ **Unit 6a, Victoria Farm, Water Lane, York, North Yorkshire, YO30 6PQ** Ⓟ
☎ 01904 690561
Est. 1984
Services Antiques repair and restoration
Open Mon–Fri 9am–5.30pm
Sat 9am–2.30pm

Miracle Stripping
Contact Mr C Howes or Mr A Howes
✉ **The Cottage, Woodhall Farm, Hatfield, Hertfordshire, AL9 5NU** Ⓟ
☎ 01707 270587 Ⓕ 01707 270587
Ⓜ 07790 696631
Est. 1992
Services Stripping of doors, cast-iron fireplaces etc
Open Mon–Fri 8.30am–5pm

Mr Dip
Contact Mr G Broadbridge
✉ **3 Knutsford Road, Alderley Edge, Cheshire, SK9 7SD** Ⓟ
☎ 01625 584896
Est. 1983
Services Wood stripping, hardwood, softwood and antique items, furniture and fireplaces
Open Mon–Fri 10am–4pm
Sat 10am–2pm closed Wed

Salisbury Stripping Co
Contact Karen Montlake
✉ **48–54 Milford Street, Salisbury, Wiltshire, SP1 2BP**
☎ 01722 413595/718203
Ⓕ 01722 416395
Ⓔ enquiries@myriad-antiques.co.uk
Ⓦ www.myriad-antiques.co.uk
Est. 1994
Services Paint and varnish stripping of furniture and doors, caustic and non-caustic processes, full restoration
Open Mon–Sat 9.30am–5pm
Sun by appointment

Strip It Ltd
Contact Mr Panton
✉ **109–111 Pope Street, Birmingham, West Midlands, B1 3AG** Ⓟ
☎ 0121 243 4001
Est. 1983
Services Stripping furniture
Open Mon–Sat 8am–5.30pm

Strippadoor Ltd
Contact Danny Russell

✉ Victoria House,
Higher Bury Street, Stockport,
Cheshire, SK4 1BJ **P**
☎ 0161 477 8980 **F** 0161 477 6302
Est. 1979
Services Stripping of doors, fireplaces, fire surrounds and furniture
Open Mon–Fri 8.30am–5.30pm
Sat 10.30am–2.30pm

Stripped Pine Workshop
Contact Mr John Wood
✉ **Rear of 28 Catherine Street, Swansea, West Glamorgan, SA1 4JS P**
☎ 01792 461236
Est. 1970
Services Pine stripping
Open Mon–Sat 11.30am–6pm

The Stripper
Contact Mr K Pinder
✉ **Sneaton Lane, Ruswarp, Whitby, North Yorkshire, YO22 5HL P**
☎ 01947 820035/880966
Est. 1995
Services Antiques repair and restoration
Open Mon–Fri 8am–6pm
Sat 8am–noon

The Stripping Store
Contact Jeff Low
✉ **57 Newhall Street, Glasgow, G40 1LA P**
☎ 0141 550 8195
M 07796 501633
Est. 1997
Services Hand stripping of period and traditional furniture
Open Mon–Sat 10am–6pm

Windsor Antiques
Contact Mr G Henderson
✉ **Rosemary Farm, Rosemary Lane, Castle Hedingham, Halstead, Essex, CO9 3AJ P**
☎ 01787 461653
Est. 1981
Services Furniture and paint stripping
Open By appointment

SUPPLIERS

Richard Barry Southern Marketing Ltd
Contact Mr Richard Fill
✉ **Unit 1–2, Chapel Place, North Street, Portslade, Brighton, East Sussex, BN41 1DR P**
☎ 01273 419471 **F** 01273 421925
Est. 1978
Services Suppliers to the antiques trade of all wood-finishing materials
Open Mon–Fri 8am–5pm

Chemicals Ltd
Contact Sales department
✉ **Unit 2, Ringtail Place, Burscough Industrial Estate, Burscough, Lancashire, L40 7SD P**
☎ 01704 897700 **F** 01704 897237
E sales@paramose.com
Est. 1982
Services Original and water washable strippers, Paramose stripping machines, restoration materials
Open Mon–Fri 9am–5pm

Classic Finishes
Contact Mark Baker
✉ **St Julien's Wharf, 131–133 King Street, Norwich, Norfolk, NR1 1QE P**
☎ 01603 760374 **F** 01603 660477
E enq@classicfinishes.co.uk
W www.classicfinishes.co.uk
Est. 1985
Services Restoration materials, advice, specialist paints, French and wax polishes
Open Mon–Fri 8.30am–5.30pm
Sat 9am–1pm

Pendelfin Studio Ltd
Contact Mrs Morley
✉ **Cameron Mill, Housin Street, Burnley, Lancashire, BB10 1PP P**
☎ 01282 432301 **F** 01282 459464
E boswell@pendelfin.co.uk
W www.pendelfin.co.uk
Est. 1953
Services Suppliers to retail outlets of collectable stonecraft rabbits and village pieces
Open Mon–Fri 9am–5pm

John Penny Antique Services
Contact Mr J Penny
✉ **Unit 10, City Industrial Park, Southern Road, Southampton, Hampshire, SO15 0HA P**
☎ 023 8023 2066 **F** 023 8021 2129
Est. 1981
Services Suppliers of furniture restoration materials
Open Mon–Fri 9am–5pm
Sat 9am–12.30pm

Restoration Supplies
Contact Mrs M O'Connell
✉ **The Corn Mill, Claremont, Wyke, Bradford, West Yorkshire, BD12 9JJ**
☎ 01274 691461
Est. 1989
Services Restoration supplies
Open Mon–Sat 10.30am–6pm
closed Wed

Suffolk Brass Ltd
Contact Mr M Peters
✉ **Thurston, Bury St Edmunds, Suffolk, IP31 3SN**
☎ 01359 233383 **F** 01359 233384
E suffolkbrass@aol.com
Est. 1987
Services Supplies replica cast brass handles from catalogue
Trade only Yes
Open Mail order only

TEXTILES

Lannowe Oriental Textiles
Contact Joanna Titchell
✉ **Near Bath, Wiltshire**
☎ 01225 891487 **F** 01225 891182
M 0771 470 3535
E joanna@lannowe.co.uk
Est. 1976
Services Washing, restoration and conservation of Oriental carpets, rugs and tapestries
Open By appointment

M & M Restoration
Contact Mrs M Druet
✉ **Mantel House, Broomhill Road, London, SW18 4JQ P**
☎ 020 8871 5098 **F** 020 8877 1940
M 07850 310104
Est. 1985
Services Restoration and cleaning of antique tapestries, carpets and textiles
Open Mon–Fri 9am–6pm

Textile Conservation
Contact Frances Lennard
✉ **Ivy House Farm, Wolvershill Road, Banwell, Somerset, BS29 6LB P**
☎ 01934 822449 **F** 01934 822449

ⓔ huttonlennard@compuserve.com
Est. 1989
Services Textile conservation
Open Mon–Fri 9am–5pm

Textile Conservation Services
Contact Miss Lyndall Bond
✉ **3–4 West Workshop, Welbeck, Worksop, Nottinghamshire, S80 3LW** Ⓟ
☎ 01909 481655 ⓕ 01909 481655
ⓔ textile.conservation@tesco.net
Est. 1984
Services The conservation of costume, lace and small textiles. Talks and courses on costume and textiles
Open By appointment

TOYS

Haddon Rocking Horses
Contact Paul Stollery
✉ **5 Telford Road, Clacton-on-Sea, Essex, CO15 4LP** Ⓟ
☎ 01255 424745 ⓕ 01255 475505
ⓔ millers@rockinghorses.uk.com
ⓦ www.rockinghorses.uk.com
Est. 1971
Services Restorers and manufacturers of rocking horses
Open Mon–Thurs 8am–5pm Fri 8am–1pm

Stevenson Brothers (British Toymakers Guild)
Contact Mark Stevenson or Sue Russell
✉ **The Workshop, Ashford Road, Bethersden, Ashford, Kent, TN26 3AP** Ⓟ
☎ 01233 820363 ⓕ 01233 820580
ⓔ sale@stevensonbros.com
ⓦ www.stevensonbros.com
Est. 1982
Services Restoration of rocking horses and children's pedal cars
Open Mon–Fri 9am–6pm Sat 10am–1pm

TUITION

Richard Bolton Furniture Restorer (BAFRA)
Contact Richard Bolton
✉ **Painswick House, Old Dairy Workshop, Gloucester Road, Painswick, Gloucestershire, GL6 6TH** Ⓟ
☎ 01452 814881
Est. 1981
Services Tuition on the restoration of fine antique furniture
Open Mon–Fri 9am–5pm

Leather Conservation Centre (UKIC, SSCR)
Contact Roy Thomson
✉ **University College Campus, Boughton Green Road, Moulton Park, Northampton, Northamptonshire, NN2 7AN** Ⓟ
☎ 01604 719766 ⓕ 01604 719649
ⓔ lcc@northampton.ac.uk
Est. 1978
Services Conservation and restoration of leather objects, research, training and information for leather and leather conservation
Open Mon–Fri 9am–5pm

The Thomas Chippendale School of Furniture (SSCR)
Contact Mr Anselm Fraser
✉ **The Thomas Chippendale School of Furniture, Myreside, Gifford, Haddington, East Lothian, EH41 4JA** Ⓟ
☎ 01620 810680 ⓕ 01620 810701
ⓔ info@chippendale.co.uk
ⓦ www.chippendale.co.uk
Est. 1982
Services International school of furniture, professional training of people to design, make and restore furniture
Open Mon–Fri 7.30am–5pm

The Wiston Project School
Contact Mr N Wears
✉ **The Old School, Wiston, Haverfordwest, Pembrokeshire, SA62 4PS** Ⓟ
☎ 01437 731579
Est. 1988
Services School of furniture making
Open By appointment

Peter Young Auctioneers
Contact Mr P Young
✉ **Doncaster Road, Bawtry, Doncaster, South Yorkshire, DN10 6NQ** Ⓟ
☎ 01302 711770 ⓕ 01302 711770
ⓜ 070801 079818
ⓔ auction@auction.demon.co.uk
ⓦ www.auction.demon.co.uk
Est. 1961
Services Regular timetable of antiques lectures for local further education groups, plus antiques visits, excursions and holidays
Open Mon–Fri 9.30am–5.30pm

UPHOLSTERY

SOUTH EAST

Deal Upholstery Services
Contact Mr P E Cavanagh
✉ **116 Downs Road, Walmer, Deal, Kent, G14 7TF** Ⓟ
☎ 01304 372297
Est. 1988
Services Antique and modern upholstery, loose covers
Open Mon–Fri 9am–5pm

Norris of Blackheath
Contact Paul Norris
✉ **Dimpleshaven, Pett Road, Pett, East Sussex, TN35 4HE** Ⓟ
☎ 01424 812129
Services Upholstery, free estimates, pick-up and delivery
Open Mon–Fri 8am–6pm

T J Upholstery
Contact Mr Tim Jenner
✉ **Unit One, Hill House Farm, High Street, Wadhurst, East Sussex, TN5 6AA** Ⓟ
☎ 01892 784417
ⓜ 07867 672707
Est. 1979
Services Traditional upholstery
Open By appointment

The Upholsterers Workshop (AMU)
Contact Mr Rodney Henham
✉ **Church Farm Studio, Penhurst, Battle, East Sussex, TN33 9QP** Ⓟ
☎ 01424 893277 ⓕ 01424 893277
Est. 1996
Services Traditional upholsterers
Open Mon–Fri 8am–4.30pm Sat 8am–1pm or by appointment

LONDON

Kantuta
Contact Mrs N Wright
✉ **1d Gleneagle Road, London, SW16 6AX** Ⓟ
☎ 020 8677 6701
Est. 1986
Services Upholstery and furniture and restoration
Open Mon–Sat 10am–6pm

SOUTH

Dee Cee Upholstery
Contact Mr D A Caplen

✉ **502 Portswood Road, Portswood, Southampton, Hampshire, SO17 3SP** Ⓟ
☎ 023 8055 5888 Ⓕ 023 8067 6761
Ⓔ enquiries@deeceeupholstery.co.uk
Ⓦ www.deeceeupholstery.co.uk
Est. 1978
Services Traditional upholstery specialist, all upholstery and DIY supplies
Open Mon–Thurs 8am–5.30pm Fri 8am–5pm Sat 9am–1pm or by appointment

Hartley Upholstery and Antique Restorations
✉ **Unit 2, Priors Farm, Reading Road, Mattingley, Hook, Hampshire, RG27 8JU** Ⓟ
☎ 0118 932 6567 Ⓕ 0118 932 6567
Est. 1984
Services Upholstery, French polishing and cabinet work. Commissions undertaken
Open Mon–Sat 9am–5pm or by appointment

Hythe Furnishings
Contact Mr G Batchelor
✉ **16 Marsh Parade, Hythe, Southampton, Hampshire, SO45 6AN** Ⓟ
☎ 023 8084 5727
Est. 1997
Services Reupholstery and reconditioning of furniture
Open Mon–Fri 9am–5.30pm Sat 9am–4pm closed Wed

A H Smith & Son
Contact Mr M Smith
✉ **3, 6–7 The Parade, Old Lodge Lane, Purley, Surrey, CR8 4DG** Ⓟ
☎ 020 8660 1211 Ⓕ 020 8660 1211
Est. 1949
Services Upholstery, French polishing, antiques repairs
Open Mon–Fri 9am–5pm Sat 9am–1pm

Suite Dreams Upholstery
Contact Len Double
✉ **Larkwhistle Cottage, Christmas Hill, Sutton Scotney, Winchester, Hampshire, SO21 3ET** Ⓟ
☎ 01962 885630 Ⓕ 01962 885630
Ⓜ 07860 843691
Est. 1991
Services Traditional, modern upholstery, loose covers a speciality
Open Mon–Sat 9am–6pm

WEST COUNTRY

Daniel Fox Upholstery
Contact Mr D Fox
✉ **Goulds Farm, Nethercott, Braunton, Devon, EX33 1HT** Ⓟ
☎ 01271 815998
Est. 1994
Services Re-upholstery
Open Mon–Fri 9am–5pm

Russell Hudson Upholsterer
Contact Mr R Hudson
✉ **Unit 2e, Riverside Business Park, Riverside Road, Bath, Somerset, BA2 3DW** Ⓟ
☎ 01225 400003
Ⓔ rhudson@fdn.co.uk
Est. 1985
Services Antique re-upholstery
Open Mon–Fri 8.30am–5.30pm

M J R Upholstery
Contact Mr M J Rowbrey
✉ **Unit 7, Cornishway South, Galmington Trading Estate, Taunton, Somerset, TA1 5NQ** Ⓟ
☎ 01823 338793
Est. 1988
Services Re-upholstery
Open Mon–Fri 9am–5pm

Rocco d'Ambrosio
Contact Mrs R Crees
✉ **94 Benedict Street, Glastonbury, Somerset, BA6 9EZ** Ⓟ
☎ 01458 831541
Est. 1969
Services Upholstery restoration, French polishing, dealer, furniture restoration
Open Mon–Fri 9am–6pm or by appointment

Cyril C Wills
Contact Mr Wills
✉ **Oak Tree Yard, Upper Manor Road, Paignton, Devon, TQ3 2TP** Ⓟ
☎ 01803 558039 Ⓕ 01803 558039
Est. 1929
Services Upholstery, chair frame and furniture repair
Open Mon–Fri 9am–5pm

EAST

Decorcraft Upholsterers
Contact Mr A Wise
✉ **Sand Acre, Elmham Drive, Nacton, Ipswich, Suffolk, IP10 0DG** Ⓟ
☎ 01473 659396 Ⓕ 01473 659396
Est. 1975
Services Upholstery
Open Mon–Sat 9am–6pm

Lomas Pigeon & Co Ltd (AMU, BAFRA)
Contact Mr W A J Pigeon
✉ **37 Beehive Lane, Chelmsford, Essex, CM2 9TQ** Ⓟ
☎ 01245 353708 Ⓕ 01245 355211
Ⓔ wpigeon@compuserve.com
Ⓦ www.lomas-pigeon.co.uk
Est. 1938
Services Upholstery, antique restoration, French polishing, cabinet-making
Open Mon–Fri 10am–4pm Sat 9am–noon closed Wed

HEART OF ENGLAND

Churchill Upholstery
Contact David Matthews
✉ **Unit 1, Mount Farm, Junction Road, Churchill, Chipping Norton, Oxfordshire, OX7 6NP** Ⓟ
☎ 01608 658139 Ⓕ 01608 658139
Ⓜ 07957 355114
Est. 1986
Services Antique re-upholstery and soft furnishings
Open Mon–Fri 8am–5.30pm Sat 8am–noon

MIDLANDS

K Davenport
Contact Mr M Davenport
✉ **The Queens Yard, Madac Place, Beatrice Street, Oswestry, Shropshire, SY11 1QJ** Ⓟ
☎ 01691 652293 Ⓕ 01691 652293
Ⓜ 07885 817026
Ⓔ kdavenportinteriors@theinternetpages.co.uk
Ⓦ www.kdavenportinteriors.co.uk
Est. 1965
Services Re-upholstery and restoration of antique furniture
Open Mon–Fri 8.30am–5pm

Heath Upholstery
Contact Mr A Heath
✉ **Marychurch Road, Bucknall, Stoke-on-Trent, Staffordshire, ST2 9BJ** Ⓟ

☎ 01782 268802 Ⓕ 01782 268802
Ⓜ 07974 929221
Ⓔ a.heath@fsbdial.co.uk
Est. 1973
Services Antique upholstery and contract work
Open Mon–Fri 8.30am–6pm or by appointment

Imperial Upholstery
Contact Mr N Scattergood
✉ **Ferry Street, Stapenhill, Burton-on-Trent, Staffordshire, DE15 9EU** Ⓟ
☎ 01283 512327 Ⓕ 01283 512327
Est. 1993
Services Upholstery, antique restoration, French polishing
Open Mon–Sat 9am–6pm

John Reed and Son Upholsterers (AMU)
Contact Mr J Reed
✉ **141 Regent Street, Kettering, Northamptonshire, NN16 8QH** Ⓟ
☎ 01536 510584 Ⓕ 01536 510584
Ⓔ johnreed.andson@lineone.net
Ⓦ www.johnreedandsons.com
Est. 1973
Services Repairs, restorations, French and spray polishing
Open Mon–Fri 8am–5.30pm

Sitting Pretty
Contact Mrs J Deaville
✉ **2 Groundslow Cottages, Tittensor, Stoke-on-Trent, Staffordshire, ST12 9HJ** Ⓟ
☎ 01782 373766 Ⓕ 01782 373766
Est. 1989
Services Upholstery, repair and restoration of furniture
Open By appointment

P Woodcock & Co
Contact Mr Paul Day
✉ **56a Salop Road, Oswestry, Shropshire, SY11 2RQ** Ⓟ
☎ 01691 653317/0800 524 0008
Ⓕ 01691 679724
Est. 1954
Services Upholstery and restoration of antique furniture
Open Mon–Fri 7.15am–5pm Sat 9am–4pm

YORKSHIRE & LINCOLNSHIRE

Paul Rawciffe Upholstery Services
Contact Mr P Rawciffe
✉ **Unit 10, New Enterprise Centre, Humber Bank South, South Quay, Grimsby, Lincolnshire, DN31 3SD** Ⓟ
☎ 01472 251732
Ⓜ 07714 436710
Est. 1989
Services Repair, restoration
Open Mon–Fri 8am–5pm

NORTH WEST

E Callister
Contact Mr E Callister
✉ **127 Lark Lane, Liverpool, Merseyside, L17 8UR** Ⓟ
☎ 0151 727 5679
Est. 1964
Services Re-upholstery, French polishing
Open Mon–Fri 9am–5pm Sat 9am–noon

J E Hatcher & Son
Contact Mr C Hatcher
✉ **121a Victoria Road West, Cleveleys, Thornton Cleveleys, Lancashire, FY5 3LA** Ⓟ
☎ 01253 853162
Est. 1946
Services Traditional upholstery
Open Mon–Fri 8.30am–5.30pm Sat 8.30am–11am

WALES

Cliff Amey & Son (AMU)
Contact Cliff Amey
✉ **12 Clive Road, Canton, Cardiff, South Glamorgan, CF5 1HJ** Ⓟ
☎ 02920 233462 Ⓕ 02920 233462
Ⓔ dennis.amey@talk21.com
Est. 1951
Services Upholstery
Open Mon–Fri 8am–5pm

S M Upholstery Ltd
Contact P Morgan
✉ **212a Whitchurch Road, Cardiff, South Glamorgan, CF14 3NB** Ⓟ
☎ 029 2061 7579 Ⓕ 029 2061 7579
Est. 1974
Services Traditional upholstery
Open Mon–Fri 9.30am–1pm 2–5pm Sat 9.30am–1pm

SCOTLAND

Just Chairs
Contact Mr R Kerr
✉ **Sunnyside, Baster Road, Edinburgh, EH7 5RA** Ⓟ
☎ 0131 652 0320
Est. 1984
Services Traditional upholstery, antique chairs (restored) bought and sold
Open Mon–Fri 8am–5pm

Sherman Upholstery
Contact Jim Sherman
✉ **Blairdaff Street, Buckie, Morayshire, AB56 1PT** Ⓟ
☎ 01542 834680 Ⓕ 01542 834680
Ⓜ 07703 881903
Ⓔ linda@sherman73.freeserve.co.uk
Est. 1956
Services Antiques repair and restoration
Open Mon–Fri 8.30am–4.30pm Sat 8.30am–noon

W M Stark
Contact William Stark
✉ **88 Peddie Street, Dundee, Tayside, DD1 5LT** Ⓟ
☎ 01382 660040
Est. 1977
Services Upholstery, re-covering
Open Mon–Fri 8am–4.30pm

VALUERS

Lennox Auctions and Valuers
Contact Mr A Lennox
✉ **The Basement, 41b Ellis Street, Carrickfergus, Co Antrim, BT38 8AY** Ⓟ
☎ 028 9335 1522/028 9337 8527
Ⓕ 028 9335 1522
Est. 1987
Services Valuations on porcelain and glass
Open Mon–Fri 9.30am–5pm Sat 9.30am–1pm

Nicholas Somers Chartered Arts and Antiques Surveyor
Contact Nicholas Somers, FRICS, FRSA, FIAVI
✉ **45B Lurline Gardens, Battersea, London, SW11 4DD** Ⓟ
☎ 020 7627 1248 Ⓕ 020 7622 9587
Ⓜ 07836 698889
Est. 1990
Services Insurance valuations and sales advice for antiques, fine art and chattels. Expert witness work. Offices in Bath
Open By appointment

Sotheby's (International Auctioneers)
Contact William Montgomery
✉ **The Estate Office, Grey Abbey, Newtownards, Co Down, BT22 2QA** Ⓟ
☎ 028 4278 8668 Ⓕ 028 4278 8652
Ⓔ william.montgomery@sothebys.com
Ⓦ www.sothebys.com
Est. 1979
Services Sotheby's Northern Ireland office provides free valuations of antiques for sale by auction. Insurance valuations can be arranged, and advice given on buying, selling and restoration. Free transport of goods for auction is provided to Sotheby's in England
Open By appointment

Weller King
Contact Alastair Dixon
✉ **36 High Street, Steyning, West Sussex, BN44 3YE** Ⓟ
☎ 01903 816633 Ⓕ 01903 816644
Ⓜ 07796 174381
Ⓔ enquiries@wellerking.com
Ⓦ www.wellerking.com
Est. 1993
Services Insurance, probate and market valuations, expert witness work
Open Mon–Fri 9am–5.30pm

Weller King
Contact Alastair Dixon
✉ **62 Pall Mall, London, SW1Y 5HZ** Ⓟ
☎ 020 7839 4702 Ⓕ 020 7839 0444
Ⓜ 07796 174381
Ⓔ enquiries@wellerking.com
Ⓦ www.wellerking.com
Est. 1993
Services Insurance, probate and market valuations, expert witness work
Open Mon–Fri 9am–5.30pm

WRITING

Classic Pen Engineering (Writing Equipment Society)
Contact Mr D Purser
✉ **Auchenfranco Farm, Lochfoot, Dumfries, Dumfries & Galloway, G2 8NZ** Ⓟ
☎ 01387 730208 Ⓕ 01387 730208
Ⓜ 07703 690843
Ⓔ cpe@auchenfranco.freeserve.co.uk
Ⓦ www.auchenfranco.freeserve.co.uk
Est. 1994
Services Complete refurbishment of writing instruments. Sales and valuations of fountain pens, dip pens and pencils
Open By appointment

Fairs

Every effort has been made to ensure that this information is correct at the time of going to press. However it is highly recommended that you telephone to confirm the details are still as stated You may also discover that the event organizer has several additional events, which could not be included at the time of going to press. If you would like your fair(s) to be included in next year's directory, please inform us by October 1st 2002. (FWC = Free with Card).

JANUARY

16–21

LAPADA Fine Art & Antiques Fair
☎ 0121 7674789
Ⓔ antiques@necgroup.co.uk
Ⓦ www.lapadafair.co.uk
Location NEC, Birmingham Ⓟ
Est. 1993
Open Weekdays 11am–8pm Fri 11am–7pm Sat Sun 11am–6pm
Entrance fee 16th £7 17th–21st £6
Details 100 dealers

17–20

Penmans West London Antiques & Fine Art Fair
Contact Caroline Penman
☎ 01444 482514 Ⓕ 01444 482412
Ⓜ 07774 850044
Ⓔ info@penman-fairs.co.uk
Ⓦ www.penman-fairs.co.uk
Location Kensington Town Hall, Hornton Street, London W8 Ⓟ
Est. 1975
Open Thurs noon–8pm Fri Sat 11am–6pm Sun 11am–5pm
Entrance fee £4
Details 60 stands, vetted quality, traditional and decorative

18–20

Shepton Mallet Antiques & Collectors Fair
Contact Caroline Cleary
☎ 01636 702326 Ⓕ 01636 707923
Ⓦ www.dmgantiquefairs.com
Location Royal Bath and West Showground, Shepton Mallett, Somerset Ⓟ
Est. 1997
Open Fri 1–5pm Sat 8.30am–5pm Sun 10am–4pm
Entrance fee Fri £10 Sat 8.30am £7.50 9.30am £5 Sun £5
Details Up to 600 exhibitors

19

Antiques Fair
Contact Barry Phillips
☎ 01945 870160 Ⓕ 01945 870660
Ⓜ 07860 517048
Location Castle Hall, Hertford, Hertfordshire Ⓟ
Est. 1976
Open 10am–4.30pm
Entrance fee £1 Senior citizens 75p Trade FWC from 9am
Details Refreshments, ground floor, level access

Chelsea Town Hall
Contact Matthew Adams
☎ 020 7254 4054
Ⓦ www.adams-antiques-fairs.co.uk
Location Chelsea Town Hall, King's Road, Chelsea, London SW3 Ⓟ
Est. 1994
Open 10am–5.30pm
Entrance fee 50p
Details 70+ exhibitors

Commonwealth Institute Coin Fair
Contact Mrs Monk
☎ 020 8656 4583 Ⓕ 020 8656 4583
Location The Commonwealth Institute, Kensington High Street, London, W8 Ⓟ
Est. 1988
Open 9.30am–2.30pm
Entrance fee £1
Details English, foreign and ancient coins, antiquities, medallions, tokens and some bank notes

20

Antiques and Collectables Fair
Contact Joan Murray
☎ 00 353 1 6708260
Ⓕ 00 353 1 6708295
Ⓜ 00 353 87 2670607
Ⓔ AntiquesFairsIreland@esatclear.ie
Ⓦ www.antiquesfairsireland.com
Location Newman House, 85 St Stephen's Green, Dublin 2
Open 11am–6pm
Entrance fee 2 Euros
Details 40 dealers, wide range of antiques and collectors items

Antiques & Collectors Fair
Contact Barry Phillips
☎ 01945 870160 Ⓕ 01945 870660
Ⓜ 07860 517048
Ⓔ janba@supanet.com
Location Knights Hill Hotel, South Wooton, King's Lynn Ⓟ
Open 10am–4.30pm
Entrance fee £1 Senior citizens 75p Trade FWC from 9am
Details Refreshments, ground floor, level access

Aquarius Fairs
Contact Elaine
☎ 01256 465559/363311
Location Heckfield Memorial Hall, Church Lane, Heckfield, Hook, Hampshire Ⓟ
Open 9.15am–4.30pm
Entrance fee 40p
Details 30 dealers

Athena Fayres
Contact Mr A Tonks
☎ 01489 578093 (day) 01489 584633 (eve)
Location The Village Hall, Minstead, Nr Lyndhurst, about a mile from the end of the M27 Ⓟ
Est. 1990
Open Trade 10am Public 10.30am–4pm
Entrance fee 50p Trade 80p
Details Around 25 stalls

Biggleswade Antiques Fairs
☎ 01234 871449 Ⓕ 01234 871449
Ⓜ 07778 789917
Location The Weatherley Centre, Eagle Farm Road, Biggleswade, Bedfordshire
Open 9.30am–4.30pm

Bob Evans Fairs
☎ 01664 812627 Ⓕ 01664 813727
Location Hereford Leisure Centre, Holmer Road, Hertfordshire Ⓟ
Open Trade 8am Public 9.30am–4.30pm
Details 200 stalls

Chenevare Fairs
Contact Peter or John
☎ 01384 441628/872697
Ⓔ johnbills@skybiz.com
Ⓦ http://skybusiness.com/chenevare
Location Bridgnorth Sports and Leisure Centre, Northgate, Bridgnorth, Shropshire Ⓟ
Est. 1996
Open 9.30am–4pm
Entrance fee Adults 90p Concessions 60p
Details Capacity 60 stalls
Trade only Trade admission free before 10am

Hatfield Antiques & Collectors Fair
Contact Richard Millar
☎ 01279 871110 Ⓕ 01279 871917
Location Red Lion, Great North Road, Hatfield, Hertfordshire Ⓟ
Open Trade with card 9.30am Public 10.30am–4.30pm

Entrance fee Adults 90p Concessions 70p Children 16 and under free Trade FWC
Details Up to 56 stalls

J and K Fairs
☎ 01472 813281
Location Lincolnshire Showground, Lincoln P
Est. 1981
Open Trade 7am Public 10am–5pm
Entrance fee 90p
Details 200 dealers

Mark Carter Militaria & Medal Fairs
☎ 01753 534777
Location The Princes Hall, Princes Way, Aldershot, Hampshire P
Open Preview 9.30am Public 10.30am–3.30pm
Entrance fee £1.50 Preview £3 Accompanied children free
Details Between 110 and 125 tables of quality militaria, books and medals

Monmouthshire County Antiques & Collectors Fair
Contact Mr G B Harris
☎ 01873 735811 F 01873 735829
E markets@monmouthshire.gov.uk
Location The Market Hall (next to the Town Hall), Abergavenny, Monmouthshire P
Est. 1996
Open 6am–5pm
Entrance fee Free
Details 60 dealers, refreshments

Scotfairs Antique and Collectors Fair
Contact Mr R M Torrens
☎ 01764 654555 F 01764 654340
Location Moir Hall, Mitchell Library, Granville Street, Glasgow P
Open Trade 8am Public 10am–4pm
Entrance fee Trade free Public £1 Accompanied children free
Details 65 stands

The London Textiles, Vintage Fashion and Accessories Fair
Contact Paola Francia-Gardiner
☎ 020 8543 5075 F 020 8404 6262
Location Hammersmith Town Hall, King Street, London, W6 P
Open 10am–5pm
Entrance fee £4
Details 85 stands

25–27

Galloway Antiques Fairs
☎ 01423 522122 F 01423 522122
M 07966 528725
E susan@gallowayfairs.co.uk
W www.gallowayfairs.co.uk
Location The Old Swan Hotel, Harrogate, North Yorkshire P
Open 10.30am–5pm
Entrance fee £3.50–£4.50

26

Blackpool Winter Gardens Antiques and Collectors Fair
☎ 01253 782828 F 01253 714715
Location Blackpool Winter Gardens, Blackpool, Lancashire P
Open Trade 7.30am Public 9am–4pm
Entrance fee Trade FWC
Details 250 stalls

Browser's Antique & Collectors Fair
☎ 01189 863934
Location Village Hall, Station Road, Pangbourne, Berkshire (on A329 off A4, M4 Jct 12/13) P
Open Trade 9.30am Public 10am–4pm
Entrance fee 25p Accompanied children free
Details 24 stalls max, refreshments

Chingford Antiques & Collectors Fair
Contact Richard Millar
☎ 01279 871110 F 01279 871917
Location Assembly Hall, The Green, Station Road, Chingford P
Open Trade with card 9.30am Public 10.30am–4pm
Entrance fee Adults £1 Concessions 70p Children 16 and under free Trade FWC
Details Over 70 stalls

Pamela Robertson Antique and Collectors Fair
Contact Pamela Robertson
☎ 01244 678106
E gprobertson@robertson58.fsnet.co.uk
Location Northgate Arena, Victoria Road, Cheshire P
Open 10am–4.30pm
Entrance fee £1.50 Seniors £1
Details Capacity 150 stalls selling all small antiques and collectables

Scotfairs Antique and Collectors Fair
Contact Mr R M Torrens
☎ 01764 654555 F 01764 654340
Location The Citadel Leisure Centre, Ayr Baths, South Beach Road, Ayr P
Open Trade 8am Public 10am–4pm
Entrance fee Trade free Public £1 Accompanied children free
Details 100 stands

26–27

Bob Evans Fairs
☎ 01664 812627 F 01664 813727
Location Sport Village, Drayton High Road, Hellesdon, Norwich P
Open Trade 8am Public 9.30am–4.30pm
Details 300 stalls

Buxton Antique and Collectors Fair
Contact Mr David Fletcher
☎ 0161 773 7001
Location Pavilion Gardens, Buxton, Derbyshire P
Est. 1976
Open 9am–5pm
Details 100 stalls

Detling International Antiques & Collectors Fair
Contact Caroline Cleary
☎ 01636 702326 F 01636 707923
W www.dmgantiquefairs.com
Location Kent County Showground, Detling, Nr Maidstone, Kent P
Est. 1998
Open Sat 8.30am–5pm Sun 10am–4pm
Entrance fee Sat 8.30am £5 Sat 10am £3.50 Sun £3.50
Details Up to 500 exhibitors

The Long Melford
Contact Graham Turner
☎ 01473 658224
E ggt@btinternet.com
Location Village Memorial Hall, Long Melford, Suffolk P
Est. 1990

Open Trade 9.30am Public 10am–4.30pm
Details Strict 1930 date-line, 40 dealers, quality stock

The Original Long Melford Fair
Contact Tom Burt
☎ 01787 280306
Location The Old School, Long Melford, Suffolk
Est. 1976
Open Trade 8.30am Public 9.30am–5pm
Entrance fee Trade FWC
Details 50 stalls each day

27

Antique and Collectors Fair
Contact John Slade
☎ 020 8894 0218
Ⓦ www.antiquefairs.co.uk
Location Canons Leisure Centre, Madeira Road, Mitcham, Surrey 🅿
Open 8.30am–4.30pm
Entrance fee £1.50
Details 145 stalls

Antiques and Collectables Fair
Contact Joan Murray
☎ 00 353 1 6708295
Ⓕ 00 353 1 6708295
Ⓜ 00 353 87 2670607
Ⓔ antiquesfairsireland@esatclear.ie
Ⓦ www.antiquesfairsireland.com
Location Royal Marine Hotel, Dun Laoghaire, Co Dublin
Open 11am–6pm
Entrance fee 4 Euros
Details 50 dealers, wide range of antiques and collectors' items

Art Deco Fair with 20thC Decorative Arts
Contact Ann Zierold
☎ 01824 750500 Ⓕ 01824 750490
Location Chester Racecourse 🅿
Est. 1996
Open 9.30am–4pm
Details 80 stands, no copies or reproductions

Athena Fayres
Contact Mr A Tonks
☎ 01489 578093 (day)/584633 (eve)
Location Community Centre, Mill Lane, Wickham, Hampshire 🅿
Est. 1988
Open Trade 10am Public 11am–4.30pm
Entrance fee 80p Trade £1.50
Details Around 78 stalls

Biggleswade Antiques Fairs
☎ 01234 871449 Ⓕ 01234 871449
Ⓜ 07778 789917
Location The Addison Centre, Kempston, Bedford
Open 10am–4.30pm

Bloomsbury Postcard & Collectors Fair
Contact Clive Smith
☎ 020 8202 9080/8203 1500
Ⓕ 020 8203 7031
Ⓔ bloomsbury@memoriespostcards.co.uk
Ⓦ www.memoriespostcards.co.uk
Location Galleon Suite, Royal National Hotel, Bedford Way, London, WC1 🅿
Est. 1976
Open Early entry 8am Public 10am–5pm
Entrance fee £1 early entry £5
Details 120 stands of postcards, printed ephemera, autographs, programmes, photos, cigarette cards, postal history etc

Burford Antiques Fair
Contact Andy Briggs
☎ 01993 842623
Ⓜ 07977 936882
Ⓔ andy@fatcatfairs.co.uk
Ⓦ www.fatcatfairs.co.uk
Location Burford School, Burford, Oxfordshire 🅿
Est. 1990
Open 9am–4pm
Details 40 stands, refreshments available

Chenevare Fairs
Contact Peter or John
☎ 01384 441628/872697
Ⓔ johnbills@skybiz.com
Ⓦ http://skybusiness.com/chenevare
Location Hagley Community Centre, Worcester Road, West Hagley, Hereford & Worcester 🅿
Est. 1985
Open Trade 10am Public 9.30am–4pm
Entrance fee 75p Concessions 50p Trade FWC before 10am
Details Capacity 35 stalls

Elstree Moat House Hotel
Contact Colin Edwards
☎ 01462 671688
Location Elstree Moathouse Hotel, adjacent to Borehamwood exit, 2 miles south of M25, Hertfordshire
Open Trade 9.30am Public 10.30am–5pm
Details 80+ stalls, 1930 date-line

Midland Clock & Watch Fair
☎ 01895 834694/834357
Ⓕ 01895 832329/832904
Location National Motorcycle Museum, M42 Exit 6, West Midlands 🅿
Open 9am–2.30pm
Entrance fee 9am £5 11am–2.30pm £2.50 Accompanied children free
Details 153 stands, each fair displaying about £3 million worth of antique clocks, watches, parts and books, refreshments available, free valuations

R and S Western Fairs
Contact Bob or Shenda
☎ 01726 812558
Ⓜ 07710 561306
Ⓔ robert.allgrove@virgin.net
Location Trenython Manor, Tywardreath, Nr Par, Cornwall 🅿
Est. 2001
Open Trade and setup 9.30am Public 10.30am–4.30pm
Details 38 dealers, bar, restaurant, wheelchair access

30

The Big Brum
Contact Carol Baskin
☎ 01782 595805 Ⓕ 01782 596133
Ⓔ info@antiqueforumgroup.com
Ⓦ www.antiqueforumgroup.com
Location St Martins Market (The Rag), Edgbaston Street, Birmingham 🅿
Open From 7.30am
Entrance fee Free
Details 700 stands plus 500 unreserved stalls

31

Antique & Collectors Fair
Contact Stancie Kutler
☎ 01270 624288
Location Nantwich Civic Hall, Market Street, Nantwich, Cheshire, M6 Jct 16 🅿
Est. 1974
Open Trade 8am Public 10am–5pm

Details Refreshments, up to 75 stalls

31–3 Feb

The 32nd Harrogate Winter Antiques and Fine Art Fair
☎ 01277 214677 Ⓕ 01277 214550
Ⓔ admin@baileyfairs.co.uk
Ⓦ www.baileyfairs.co.uk
Location Pavilions of Harrogate, Great Yorkshire Showground Ⓟ
Open Thurs 2–6pm Fri Sat 11am–6pm Sun 11am–5pm
Entrance fee £5
Details 80 dealers, vetted and date-lined

FEBRUARY

1–3

Galloway Antiques Fairs
☎ 01423 522122 Ⓕ 01423 522122
Ⓜ 07966 528725
Ⓔ susan@gallowayfairs.co.uk
Ⓦ www.gallowayfairs.co.uk
Location Shrigley Hall, Nr Macclesfield, Cheshire Ⓟ
Open 10.30am–5pm
Entrance fee £3.50–£4.50

The International Antiques and Collectors Fair at RAF Swinderby
Contact Mr J Ball
☎ 01298 27493/73188
Ⓜ 07860 797200
Location RAF Swinderby, A46 between Newark and Lincoln Ⓟ
Open Fri 7am–5pm Sat Sun 8am–5pm
Entrance fee Fri trade day £7.50 Sat Sun £3
Details Over 2000 stands

2

Antiques & Collectors Fair
Contact Ann Zierold
☎ 01824 750500 Ⓕ 01824 750490
Location Mountford Hall, Students Union Building, Liverpool University
Est. 1970
Open 9.30am–4pm
Entrance fee £1.50 Concessions £1.20
Details Up to 130 dealers

E W Services Antiques Fair
Contact David Smith
☎ 01933 224674
Location Buckingham Community Centre, Cornwalls Meadow Shopping Precinct, Buckingham Ⓟ
Est. 1993
Details 25 dealers

Jade Fairs
Contact Mr C B Thornber
☎ 01253 733420
Ⓜ 07887 952864
Location Lowther Pavilion, The Promenade, Lytham St Anne's, Lancashire Ⓟ
Est. 1978
Open 9.30am–4.30pm
Entrance fee £1 Concessions 70p
Details 56 dealers of antiques and collectables

Marcel Fairs
Contact Marcel Epstein
☎ 020 8950 1844 Ⓕ 020 8950 1844
Ⓜ 07887 648255
Location St Paul's Church Hall, Mill Hill, Ridgeway, London, NW7 Ⓟ
Open Trade 8am Public 9am–4pm
Entrance fee 50p
Details 1950s date-line, 30–35 dealers, small furniture

Scotfairs Antique and Collectors Fair
Contact Mr R M Torrens
☎ 01764 654555 Ⓕ 01764 654340
Location Albert Halls, Dumbarton Road, Stirling Ⓟ
Open Trade 8am Public 10am–4pm
Entrance fee Trade free Public £1 Accompanied children free
Details 65 stands

Victoriana's Fairs
Contact Mrs Kyzor
☎ 01543 425380
Location Walsall Town Hall, Walsall, West Midlands
Est. 1979
Open 10am–4pm
Details 35–40 stalls of antiques and collectables

2–3

Saffron Walden Antiques and Fine Art Fair
Contact Colin Edwards
☎ 01462 671688
Location Saffron Walden County High School, Audley End Road, Saffron Walden, Essex
Open 10am–5pm

Swansea Antiques Fair
Contact Carol Pugh
☎ 01267 236569
Ⓕ 01267 220444
Ⓜ 07885 333845
Ⓔ antiques@towy-fairs.co.uk
Ⓦ www.towy-fairs.co.uk
Location Brangwyn Hall, Swansea Ⓟ
Open 10am–5pm
Entrance fee £3 Accompanied children free
Details 100 stands

3

Antiques and Collectables Fair
Location Newman House, 85 St Stephen's Green, Dublin 2
Details See Antiques and Collectables Fair 20 January

Antiques & Collectors Fair
Contact Yvonne Stimson
☎ 020 83101388
Ⓕ 020 83101388
Ⓜ 07976 814588
Location Crook Log Sports Centre, Brampton Road, Bexleyheath, Kent Ⓟ
Open Trade/Early Bird 9am Public 10am–4.30pm
Entrance fee 9am £2.00 10am £1.50
Details Up to 170 stands, refreshments available, licensed bar

Best of Fairs
Contact Tom Burt
☎ 01787 280306
Location The Village Hall, Copdock, 3 miles west of Ipswich
Open Trade 7.30am Public 9.30am–5pm
Entrance fee Trade FWC
Details 50 stalls

Brocante
Contact Matthew Adams
☎ 020 7254 4054
Ⓦ www.adams-antiques-fairs.co.uk
Location Kensington Town Hall, Hornton Street, London, W8 Ⓟ
Est. 1997
Open Preview 9–11am General opening 11am–5pm
Entrance fee Preview £15 11am £3 Accompanied children free
Details 100 exhibitors selling decorative antiques and textiles

FEBRUARY

Chatsworth Fairs
Contact Marie
☎ 0114 2351502
Ⓜ 07801 283115
Location Cedar Court Hotel, M1 Jct 39 , Wakefield, West Yorkshire 🅿
Open 9.30am–4.30pm
Entrance fee £1
Details Capacity for 70 dealers

Clock & Watch Dealers Fair
Contact Mr Lionel Parker
☎ 01691 831162
Ⓔ fairs@oswatch.fsnet.co.uk
Location The Grove Leisure Centre, London Road, Balderton, Nr Newark, Nottinghamshire 🅿
Open 8.30am–3pm
Entrance fee £5 before 10am £2 after
Details 65 stalls offering clocks, watches and jewellery

Cross Country Fairs Ltd
Contact Mr Harding
☎ 07860 863300
Location Copthorne Hotel, Effingham Park, West Sussex 🅿
Open 9am–4.30pm
Entrance fee £2 Children free Trade FWC until 10am
Details 145 stands

Hampstead Antique Collectors Fair
Contact Julie Garner
☎ 020 8203 7223
Location Hampstead Community Centre, High Street, Hampstead, London
Est. 1984
Open 10.30am–5pm
Entrance fee 20p
Details 20 dealers

Harlequin Fairs
Contact Colin Edwards
☎ 01462 671688
Location Centre for Epilepsy, Chalfont Common, Chalfont St Peter, Buckinghamshire
Open Trade 9.30am Public 10am–4.30pm
Details 50+ stalls, 1940 date-line

Ipswich Antiques and Collectables Fair
Contact Vicky Roberts-Barber
☎ 01473 688201/780720
Location Ipswich County Hotel (formerly Ipswich Moat House) Copdock, Ipswich, Suffolk 🅿
Open Trade 8.30am Public 9am–5pm
Details 100 stalls, refreshments, bar

Lechlade Antiques Fair
Contact Andy Briggs
☎ 01993 842623 Ⓜ 07977 936882
Ⓔ andy@fatcatfairs.co.uk
Ⓦ www.fatcatfairs.co.uk
Location The New Memorial Hall, Burford Road, Lechlade, Gloucestershire 🅿
Est. 1993
Open 9am–4.30pm
Entrance fee 50p Trade FWC
Details 35 stands, refreshments available

Magnum Antiques Fairs
Contact Stewart Watt
☎ 01491 681009
Location Midhurst, The Grange Centre, Bepton Road, West Sussex 🅿
Open 10am–4.30pm
Entrance fee £1
Details 130 stands

Malvern Antiques & Collectors Fair
Contact Caroline Cleary
☎ 01636 702326 Ⓕ 01636 707923
Ⓦ www.dmgantiquefairs.com
Location Three Counties Showground, Malvern, Worcestershire 🅿
Est. 1997
Open 8.30am–5pm
Entrance fee 8.30am £3.50 10am £2.50
Details Up to 200 exhibitors

Mark Carter Militaria & Medal Fairs
☎ 01753 534777
Location Yate Leisure Centre, Kennedy Way, Yate, Bristol 🅿
Open Preview 9.30am Public 10.30am–3.30pm
Entrance fee £1.50 Preview £3 Accompanied children free
Details Between 90 and 100 tables of quality militaria, books and medals

Scotfairs Antique and Collectors Fair
Contact Mr R M Torrens
☎ 01764 654555 Ⓕ 01764 654340
Location Meadowbank Stadium, London Road, Edinburgh 🅿
Open Trade 8am Public 10am–4pm
Entrance fee Trade free Public £1 Accompanied children free
Details 135 stands

Twickenham Rugby Ground Art Deco Fair
Contact Jean May
☎ 0121 430 3767 Ⓕ 0121 436 7912
Location Twickenham Rugby Ground 🅿
Est. 2000
Open Trade 8.30am Public 9.30am–4.30pm
Entrance fee £2
Details 85 stalls, furniture

Wessex Fairs
Contact Mrs Jo Wanford
☎ 01278 789568
Location Holiday Inn, Taunton, Somerset, M5 Jct 25 🅿
Est. 1986
Open 10am–4.30pm
Entrance fee £1 Trade FWC
Details Stall capacity 20, refreshments available

4–5

Newark International Antiques & Collectors Fair
Contact Caroline Cleary
☎ 01636 702326 Ⓕ 01636 707923
Ⓦ www.dmgantiquefairs.com
Location Newark & Notts Showground, Newark 🅿
Est. 1997
Open Mon 5.30am–6pm Tues 8am–4pm
Entrance fee Mon £20 (includes Tuesday entry) Tues £5
Details Up to 4000 exhibitors

6

The Long Melford
Contact Graham Turner
☎ 01473 658224
Ⓔ ggt@btinternet.com
Location Village Memorial Hall, Long Melford, Suffolk 🅿
Est. 1990
Open Trade 9am Public 9.30am–4pm
Details Strict 1930 date-line, 40 dealers, quality stock

8–10

Galloway Antiques Fairs
☎ 01423 522122 Ⓕ 01423 522122
Ⓜ 07966 528725
Ⓔ susan@gallowayfairs.co.uk

Ⓦ www.gallowayfairs.co.uk
Location The Bowes Museum, Barnard Castle, Co Durham Ⓟ
Open 10.30am–5pm
Entrance fee £3.50–£4.50

Penmans Petersfield Antiques Fair
Contact Caroline Penman
☎ 01444 482514 Ⓕ 01444 482412
Ⓜ 07774 850044
Ⓔ info@penman-fairs.co.uk
Ⓦ www.penman-fairs.co.uk
Location Festival Hall, Heath Road, Petersfield, Hampshire Ⓟ
Open Fri Sat 11am–6pm Sun 11am–5pm
Entrance fee £3
Details 43 stands of vetted traditional and decorative antiques

Stafford Bingley Hall
Contact Helen Bowman or Ben Wray
☎ 07071 284333 Ⓕ 07071 284334
Ⓔ info@antiquesfairs.com
Ⓦ www.antiquesfairs.com
Location The Bingley Hall, County Showground Ⓟ
Est. 1974
Open Fri Trade 8.30am Public 10am–5pm Sat 9.30am–5pm
Details Over 400 exhibitors including furniture

9

Aquarius Fairs
Contact Elaine
☎ 01256 465559/363311
Location The Harlington Centre, High Street, Fleet, Hampshire Ⓟ
Open 9.15am–4.30pm
Entrance fee Free

Athena Fayres
Contact Mr A Tonks
☎ 01489 578093 (day) 01489 584633 (eve)
Location Lockswood Community Centre, Locks Heath Shopping Centre, Locks Heath, Nr Fareham, Hants Ⓟ
Est. 1984
Open Trade 9.30am Public 10am–4pm
Entrance fee 30p Trade 60p
Details Around 32 stalls

Chelsea Town Hall
Location Chelsea Town Hall, King's Road, Chelsea, London
Details See Chelsea Town Hall 19 January

Devon County Antiques Fairs
☎ 01363 82571 Ⓕ 01363 82312
Ⓔ dcaf@antiques-fairs.com
Ⓦ www.antiques-fairs.com
Location Matford Centre in the Exeter Livestock Centre, Marsh Barton, Exeter Ⓟ
Open 9am–4.30pm
Entrance fee 9–10am £3.50 10am–4.30pm £2.50 Children free
Details 230 stands inside, 350 outside, restaurant, bar, good disabled and wheelchair access

London Coin Fair
Contact Mr H Simmons
☎ 020 7831 2080 Ⓕ 020 7831 2090
Ⓔ lcf@simmonsgallery.co.uk
Ⓦ www.simmonsgallery.co.uk
Location Holiday Inn, Bloomsbury, Coram Street, London WC1 Ⓟ
Est. 1970
Open 9.30am–5pm
Entrance fee £3 Concessions for families and OAPs
Details 70–85 dealers

9–10

Harpenden Antiques and Fine Art Fair
Contact Colin Edwards
☎ 01462 671688
Location Rothamsted Conference Centre, on A1081 Harpenden–St Albans road, Hertfordshire
Open 10am–5pm
Details 1930 date-line

10

Antique and Collectors Fair
Contact John Slade
☎ 020 8894 0218
Ⓦ www.antiquefairs.co.uk
Location Woking Leisure Centre, Kingfield Road, Woking, Surrey Ⓟ
Open 8.30am–4.30pm
Entrance fee £1.50
Details 175 stalls

Antiques & Collectors Fairs
☎ 01753 685098
Location Runnymeade Hotel & Spa, Windsor Road, Egham, Surrey Ⓟ
Est. 1974
Open 11am–5pm
Details Approximately 70 stalls, refreshments available

Biggleswade Antiques Fairs
☎ 01234 871449 Ⓕ 01234 871449
Ⓜ 07778 789917
Location The Marriott Hotel, Huntingdon, Cambridgeshire, off A14
Open 10am–4.30pm

Bob Evans Fairs
☎ 01664 812627 Ⓕ 01664 813727
Location Sports Connexion, Ryton on Dunsmore, Coventry Ⓟ
Open Trade 8am Public 9.30am–4.30pm
Details 300 stalls

Chenevare Fairs
Contact Peter or John
☎ 01384 441628/872697
Ⓔ johnbills@skybiz.com
Ⓦ http://skybusiness.com/chenevare
Location Kinver Leisure Centre, Enville Road, Kinver, Stourbridge, West Midlands Ⓟ
Est. 1990
Open 9.30am–4pm
Entrance fee 90p Concessions 60p Trade free before 10am
Details Capacity 80 stalls

Crispin Fairs
Contact Mrs P Wyatt
☎ 0118 983 3020
Location Victoria Hall, Hartley Wintney, Hampshire Ⓟ
Est. 1993
Open Trade 8.30am Public 10am–4.30pm
Entrance fee 50p
Details 40 stalls

Devon County Antiques Fairs
☎ 01363 82571 Ⓕ 01363 82312
Ⓔ dcaf@antiques-fairs.com
Ⓦ www.antiques-fairs.com
Location Westland Sports and Social Club, Westbourne Close, Yeovil, Somerset Ⓟ
Open 9am–4.30pm
Entrance fee 9am–10am £2 10am–4.30pm
Details 200 stands, restaurant, bar

FAIRS
FEBRUARY

Furze Hill
Contact Graham Turner
☎ 01473 658224
Ⓔ ggt@btinternet.com
Location Furze Hill, Banqueting Centre, Margaretting, Nr Chelmsford Ⓟ
Est. 1980
Open Trade 9.30am Public 10am–4.30pm
Details 60 dealers on 2 floors, quality exhibits

Lostwithiel Antiques Fair
Contact Richard Bonehill
☎ 01872 225200 or 01736 793213
Ⓔ richard@bonehill3.freeserve.co.uk
Ⓦ www.bonehill3.freeserve.co.uk
Location Community Centre, Lostwithiel, Cornwall Ⓟ
Est. 1989
Open Trade 9.30am Public 10am–4.30pm
Entrance fee 25p

Midas Antique Fair
Contact Joy Alder
☎ 01494 674170
Location The Bellhouse Hotel, Oxford Road (A40), Beaconsfield, Bucks Ⓟ
Open 10.30am–5pm
Details 60 date-lined stands of general antiques and collectables, refreshments, licenced bar

Pennyfarthing Fayres
Contact Maureen Carson
☎ 0208 4413425
Location Potters Bar, Hertfordshire Ⓟ
Est. 1991
Open Trade 9am Public 10am–4.30pm
Entrance fee Trade FWC Public £1 OAPs 50p
Details 70 stands of antiques and collectables

Royal Horticultural Hall
Contact Matthew Adams
☎ 020 72544054
Ⓦ www.adams-antiques-fairs.co.uk
Location Royal Horticultural Hall, Lawrence Hall, Greycoat Street, London SW1 Ⓟ
Est. 1972
Open 9.30am–4.30pm
Entrance fee £2.50
Details 240+ antiques dealers

13

Marks Tey
Contact Graham Turner
☎ 01473 658224
Ⓔ ggt@btinternet.com
Location Parish Hall, Marks Tey, Essex Ⓟ
Est. 2002
Open Trade 9.30am Public 10am–4pm
Details 1940 date-line

Newbury Racecourse
Contact Matthew Adams
☎ 020 7254 4054
Ⓦ www.adams-antiques-fairs.co.uk
Location Newbury Racecourse, Newbury, Berkshire Ⓟ
Open 10am–5pm
Entrance fee £2 Trade FWC
Details 300 stands, 200 outdoor pitches

14

Paraphernalia Fairs
Contact Jill Robinson
☎ 01305 860012
Location Lyndhurst Community Centre, Lyndhurst, New Forest, Hampshire Ⓟ
Est. 1995
Open Trade 9am Public 9.30am–4pm
Entrance fee 50p Trade FWC
Details 40 stands, antique and collectors flea market

14–17

Penmans Chester Antiques & Fine Art Show
Contact Caroline Penman
☎ 01444 482514 Ⓕ 01444 482412
Ⓜ 07774 850044
Ⓔ info@penman-fairs.co.uk
Ⓦ www.penman-fairs.co.uk
Location County Grandstand, Chester Racecourse, Cheshire Ⓟ
Est. 1990
Open Thurs noon–8pm Fri Sat 11am–6pm Sun 11am–5pm
Entrance fee £4
Details 60 stands on 3 floors, fine antiques and art

15–17

Galloway Antiques Fairs
☎ 01423 522122 Ⓕ 01423 522122
Ⓜ 07966 528725
Ⓔ susan@gallowayfairs.co.uk
Ⓦ www.gallowayfairs.co.uk
Location Stonyhurst College, Nr Clitheroe, Lancashire Ⓟ
Open 10.30am–5pm
Entrance fee £3.50–£4.50

16

Commonwealth Institute Coin Fair
Location The Commonwealth Institute, Kensington High Street, London W8
Details See Commonwealth Institute Coin Fair 19 January

Southport Antiques and Collectors Fair
☎ 01253 782828 Ⓕ 01253 714715
Location Southport Floral Hall, the Promenade, Southport, Merseyside Ⓟ
Open Trade 8.30am Public 9.30am–4pm
Entrance fee Trade FWC
Details 200 stalls

16–17

53rd Luton Antiques Fair
Contact Rodney Week
☎ 01234 381701 Ⓕ 01234 381701
Location Putteridge Bury House, A505 Luton to Hitchin Road, Luton, Bedfordshire Ⓟ
Est. 1973
Open Sat 11am–5pm Sun 10am–5pm
Entrance fee £2.50
Details 40+ stands, 1910 date-line, restaurant

Antiques & Collectors Fair
Contact Barry Phillips
☎ 01945 870160 Ⓕ 01945 870660
Ⓜ 07860 517048
Ⓔ janba@supanet.com
Location Burgess Hall, St Ives Recreation Centre, St Ives, Cambridgeshire Ⓟ
Open 10am–4.30pm
Entrance fee £1 Senior citizens 75p Trade FWC from 9am
Details Refreshments, ground floor, level access

Beckett Antique Fairs
Contact Alan
☎ 0114 2890656
Location Doncaster Race Exhibition Centre, Doncaster Ⓟ

Open Trade 8.30am Public 10am–4.30pm
Entrance fee £1.50 OAPs Children 50p
Details 240 stands, refreshments available

Bob Evans Fairs
☎ 01664 812627 Ⓕ 01664 813727
Location International Centre, St Quentin Gate, Telford Ⓟ
Open Trade 8am Public 9.30am–4.30pm
Details 300 stalls

Classic Antiques Fairs
Contact Bob Foundling
☎ 0121 476 5798 Ⓕ 0121 476 5798
Ⓦ www.classic-antiques-fairs.co.uk
Location The Heritage Motor Centre, Gaydon, Warwickshire, Jct 12, M40, midway between Warwick and Banbury Ⓟ
Est. 1994
Open Sat Trade 9.30am Public 10am–5pm Sun 10.30am–5pm
Details Approximately 50 dealers selling high quality antiques, date-lined, stand fitted

17

Antiques and Collectables Fair
Location Newman House, 85 St Stephen's Green, Dublin 2
Details See Antiques and Collectables Fair 20 January

Aquarius Fairs
Location Heckfield Memorial Hall, Church Lane, Heckfield, Hook, Hampshire
Details See Aquarius Fairs 20 January

Athena Fayres
Location The Village Hall, Minstead, Nr Lyndhurst, about a mile from the end of the M27
Details See Athena Fayres 20 January

Battersea Town Hall Art Deco Fair
Contact Jean May
☎ 0121 430 3767 Ⓕ 0121 436 7912
Location Battersea Town Hall Ⓟ
Est. 1991
Open Trade 8.30am Public 9.30am–4.30pm
Entrance fee £2
Details 120 stalls, furniture

Biggleswade Antiques Fairs
Location The Weatherley Centre, Eagle Farm Road, Biggleswade, Bedfordshire
Details See Biggleswade Antiques Fairs 20 January

Brunel Clock & Watch Fair
☎ 01895 834694/834357 Ⓕ 01895 832329/832904
Location Brunel University, Kingston Lane, Uxbridge, Middlesex Ⓟ
Open 9am–2.30pm
Entrance fee 9am £5 11am–2.30pm £2.50 Accompanied children free
Details 153 stands, each fair displaying about £3 million worth of antique clocks, watches, parts and books, refreshments available, free valuations

Hatfield Antiques & Collectors Fair
Location Red Lion, Great North Road, Hatfield, Hertfordshire
Details See Hatfield Antiques & Collectors Fair 20 January

Monmouthshire County Antiques & Collectors Fair
Location The Market Hall next to the Town Hall), Abergavenny, Monmouthshire
Details See Monmouthshire County Antiques & Collectors Fair 20 January

Newmarket Antiques & Collectors Fair
Contact Caroline Cleary
☎ 01636 702326
Ⓕ 01636 707923
Ⓦ www.dmgantiquefairs.com
Location Millennium Grandstand, Rowley Mile Racecourse, Newmarket, Suffolk Ⓟ
Est. 1993
Open 8am–4pm
Entrance fee 8am £10 10am £3
Details Up to 250 exhibitors

Scotfairs Antique and Collectors Fair
Location Moir Hall, Mitchell Library, Granville Street, Glasgow
Details See Scotfairs Antique and Collectors Fair 20 January

19

The Sandown Park Antique Fair
Contact Alan or Ludi Kipping
☎ 0207 249 4050 Ⓕ 0207 249 5060
Ⓔ alan&ludi@ww-antique-fairs.demon.co.uk
Ⓦ www.ww-antique-fairs.demon.co.uk
Location The Exhibition Centre, Sandown Park Racecourse, Esher, Surrey Ⓟ
Open Preview noon–2pm General admission 2–6pm
Entrance fee Preview £10 General £3
Details 550 stands under cover in 2 large exhibition halls

20

Evening Antiques/Collectors Fairs
Contact Carol Baskin
☎ 01782 595805 Ⓕ 01782 596133
Ⓔ info@antiqueforumgroup.com
Ⓦ www.antiqueforumgroup.com
Location St Martins Market (The Rag), Edgbaston Street, Birmingham Ⓟ
Open 4–8pm
Entrance fee Free
Details 300 stalls only inside

23

Antiques Fair
Location Castle Hall, Hertford, Hertfordshire
Details See Antiques Fair 19 January

Blackpool Winter Gardens Antiques and Collectors Fair
Location Blackpool Winter Gardens, Blackpool, Lancashire
Details See Blackpool Winter Gardens Antiques and Collectors Fair 26 January

Browser's Antique & Collectors Fair
Location Village Hall, Station Road, Pangbourne, Berkshire (on A329 off A4, M4 Jct 12/13)
Details See Browser's Antique & Collectors Fair 26 January

Chingford Antiques & Collectors Fair
Location Assembly Hall, The Green, Station Road, Chingford,

Details See Chingford Antiques & Collectors Fair 26 January

Pamela Robertson Antique and Collectors Fair
Location Northgate Arena, Victoria Road, Cheshire
Details See Pamela Robertson Antique and Collectors Fair 26 January

Scotfairs Antique and Collectors Fair
Location The Citadel Leisure Centre, Ayr Baths, South Beach Road, Ayr
Details See Scotfairs Antique and Collectors Fair 26 January

23–24

Detling International Antiques & Collectors Fair
Location Kent County Showground, Detling, Nr Maidstone, Kent
Details See Detling International Antiques & Collectors Fair 26–27 January

The Original Long Melford Fair
Location The Old School, Long Melford, Suffolk
Details See The Original Long Melford Fair 26–27 January

West Midlands Antique Fairs
Contact Jenny Wakeham
☎ 01743 271444 Ⓕ 01743 352353
Location Prestwood Complex, Stafford County Showground Ⓟ
Est. 1973
Open Trade 8.30am Public 10am–5pm
Entrance fee 8.30am £3 10am £2 Trade FWC
Details More than 280 stalls in 3 halls offering furniture, porcelain, paintings, clocks, Arts and Crafts, jewellery and collectables

24

Antique and Collectors Fair
Location Canons Leisure Centre, Madeira Road, Mitcham, Surrey
Details See Antique and Collectors Fair 27 January

Antiques and Collectables Fair
Contact Joan Murray
☎ 00 353 1 6708295 Ⓕ 00 353 1 6708295
Ⓜ 00 353 87 2670607
Ⓔ antiquesfairsireland@esatclear.ie
Ⓦ www.antiquesfairsireland.com
Location Clontarf Castle, Castle Avenue, Dublin Ⓟ
Open 11am–6pm
Entrance fee Adults £2 Accompanied children free
Details 60 dealers, wide range of antiques and collectors items, bar and restaurant

Antiques & Collectors Fair
Location Knights Hill Hotel, South Wooton, King's Lynn
Details See Antiques & Collectors Fair 20 January

Athena Fayres
Location Community Centre, Mill Lane, Wickham, Hampshire
Details See Athena Fayres 27 January

Biggleswade Antiques Fairs
Location The Addison Centre, Kempston, Bedford
Details See Biggleswade Antiques Fairs 27 January

Bloomsbury Postcard & Collectors Fair
Location Galleon Suite, Royal National Hotel, Bedford Way, London, WC1
Details See Bloomsbury Postcard and Collectors Fair 27 January

Bob Evans Fairs
☎ 01664 812627 Ⓕ 01664 813727
Location Leisure Village, Thurston Drive, Kettering Ⓟ
Open Trade 8am Public 9.30am–4.30pm
Details 300 stalls

Burford Antiques Fair
Location Burford School, Burford, Oxfordshire
Details See Burford Antiques Fair 27 January

Chenevare Fairs
Location Hagley Community Centre, Worcester Road, West Hagley, Hereford & Worcester
Details See Chenevare Fairs 27 January

Elstree Moat House Hotel
Location Elstree Moathouse Hotel, adjacent to Borehamwood exit, 2 miles south of M25
Details See Elstree Moat House Hotel 27 January

R and S Western Fairs
Location Trenython Manor, Tywardreath, Nr Par, Cornwall
Details See R and S Western Fairs 27 January

Waterfront Place
Contact Graham Turner
☎ 01473 658224 Ⓕ 01473 658224
Location Waterfront Place, Chelmsford, Essex Ⓟ
Open Trade 9.30am Public 10am–4.30pm
Details 1935 date-line

Wessex Fairs
Contact Mrs Jo Wanford
☎ 01278 789568
Location Winter Gardens, Weston-Super-Mare, Somerset Ⓟ
Est. 1986
Open 10am–4.30pm
Entrance fee Trade FWC
Details Stall capacity 60+, refreshments available

6–27

Ardingly International Antiques & Collectors Fair
Contact Caroline Cleary
☎ 01636 702326 Ⓕ 01636 707923
Ⓦ www.dmgantiquefairs.com
Location South of England Centre, Ardingly, West Sussex Ⓟ
Est. 1997
Open Tues 10am–6pm Wed 8am–4pm
Entrance fee Tues £20 (includes Wed entry) Wed £5
Details Up to 1700 exhibitors

26–3 Mar

The Olympia Fine Art and Antiques Fair
☎ 020 7370 8186/8212
Ⓕ 020 7370 8221
Ⓔ olympia-antiques@eco.co.uk
Ⓦ www.olympia-antiques.com
Location Olympia, London Ⓟ
Est. 1994
Open 26th 5pm–10pm 27th 11am–9pm 28th–1st 11am–8pm 2nd 11am–7pm 3rd 11am–5pm

Entrance fee £5
Details 180 exhibitors, offering wide range of antiques and works of art, all items examined by experts

28

Antique & Collectors Fair
Location Nantwich Civic Hall, Market Street, Nantwich, Cheshire, M6 Jct 16
Details See Antique & Collectors Fair 31 January

28–3 Mar

The Milton Keynes Antiques Fair
Contact David Smith
☎ 01933 224674
Location Middleton Hall, at thecentre:mk, Milton Keynes Shopping Centre Ⓟ
Est. 1993
Entrance fee Free
Details Stand-fitted and tabletop sections, 1939 date-line, 86 dealers

MARCH

2

Antiques & Collectors Fair
Location Mountford Hall, Students Union Building, Liverpool University
Details See Antiques & Collectors Fair 2 February

Marcel Fairs
Location St Paul's Church Hall, Mill Hill, Ridgeway, London, NW7
Details See Marcel Fairs 2 February

Victoriana's Fairs
Location Walsall Town Hall, Walsall, West Midlands
Details See Victoriana's Fairs 2 February

2–3

Buxton Antique and Collectors Fair
Location Pavilion Gardens, Buxton, Derbyshire
Details See Buxton Antique and Collectors Fair 26–27 January

Devon County Antiques Fairs
☎ 01363 82571 Ⓕ 01363 82312
Ⓔ dcaf@antiques-fairs.com
Ⓦ www.antiques-fairs.com
Location Westpoint Exhibition Centre, Clyst St Mary, Exeter Ⓟ
Open Sat 8–10am Sat–Sun 10am–5pm
Entrance fee Sat 8–10am £6.50 Sat–Sun 10am–5pm £4.50 Children free
Details 500 stands in one hall, restaurant and bar, good disabled and wheelchair access

3

Best of Fairs
Location The Village Hall, Copdock, 3 miles west of Ipswich
Details See Best of Fairs 3 February

Bob Evans Fairs
☎ 01664 812627 Ⓕ 01664 813727
Location The Cresset, Bretton Centre, Peterborough Ⓟ
Open Trade 8am Public 9.30am–4.30pm
Details 200 stalls

Chatsworth Fairs
Location Cedar Court Hotel, Jct 39 M1, Wakefield
Details See Chatsworth Fairs 3 February

Chiswick Town Hall Art Deco Fair
Contact Jean May
☎ 0121 430 3767 Ⓕ 0121 436 7912
Location Chiswick Town Hall Ⓟ
Est. 1988
Open 9.30am–4pm
Entrance fee £1.50
Details 65 stalls, furniture

Clock & Watch Dealers Fair
Contact Mr Lionel Parker
☎ 01691 831162
Ⓔ fairs@oswatch.fsnet.co.uk
Location Haydock Park racecourse, M6 Jct 23 Ⓟ
Open 8.30am–3pm
Entrance fee £5 before 10am £2 after
Details 85 stalls offering clocks, watches and jewellery

Cross Country Fairs Ltd
Location Copthorne Hotel, Effingham Park, West Sussex
Details See Cross Country Fairs Ltd 3 February

Hampstead Antique Collectors Fair
Location Hampstead Community Centre, High Street, Hampstead, London
Details See Hampstead Antique Collectors Fair 3 February

Harlequin Fairs
Location Centre for Epilepsy, Chalfont Common, Chalfont St Peter, Buckinghamshire
Details See Harlequin Fairs 3 February

International Antique Textile Fair Manchester
Contact Walter Bowyer
☎ 020 85232399
Location Armitage Centre, Moseley Road, Fallowfield, Manchester Ⓟ
Open Trade 8am Public 10am–5pm
Entrance fee Public £5 Trade £10
Details 70 stands

Ipswich Antiques and Collectables Fair
Location Ipswich County Hotel (formerly Ipswich Moat House) Copdock, Ipswich, Suffolk
Details See Ipswich Antiques and Collectables Fair

J and K Fairs
Location Lincolnshire Showground, Lincoln
Details See J and K Fairs 20 January

Lechlade Antiques Fair
Location The New Memorial Hall, Burford Road, Lechlade, Gloucestershire
Details See Lechlade Antiques Fair 3 February

Malvern Antiques & Collectors Fair
Location Three Counties Showground, Malvern, Worcestershire
Details See Malvern Antiques & Collectors Fair 3 February

Royal Horticultural Hall
Location Royal Horticultural Hall, Lawrence Hall, Greycoat Street, London SW1

Details See Royal Horticultural Hall 10 February

Scotfairs Antique and Collectors Fair
Location Meadowbank Stadium, London Road, Edinburgh
Details See Scotfairs Antique and Collectors Fair
3 February
3 February

Wessex Fairs
Location Holiday Inn, Taunton, Somerset, M5 Jct 25
Details See Wessex Fairs
3 February

6

The Long Melford
Location Village Memorial Hall, Long Melford, Suffolk
Details See The Long Melford
6 February

7

Paraphernalia Fairs
Location Lyndhurst Community Centre, Lyndhurst, New Forest, Hampshire
Details See Paraphernalia Fairs
14 February

7–10

Bath Annual Decorative & Antiques Fair
Contact Robin Coleman
☎ 01225 851466 Ⓕ 01225 851120
Location The Pavilion, North Parade Road, Bath Ⓟ
Est. 1983
Open Wed Trade only 1pm–8pm Thurs 1pm–7pm Fri 11am–7pm Sat 11am–5pm
Entrance fee £2.50 Trade free with card
Details 45 dealers, BABAADA members and invited guests

The 33rd Cheshire Spring Antiques Fair
☎ 01277 214677 Ⓕ 01277 214550
Ⓔ admin@baileyfairs.co.uk
Ⓦ www.baileyfairs.co.uk
Location Tatton Park, Knutsford, Cheshire Ⓟ
Open Thurs 2–6pm Fri Sat 11am–6pm Sun 11am–5pm
Entrance fee £5
Details 50 dealers, vetted and date-lined

8–10

Galloway Antiques Fairs
☎ 01423 522122 Ⓕ 01423 522122
Ⓜ 07966 528725
Ⓔ susan@gallowayfairs.co.uk
Ⓦ www.gallowayfairs.co.uk
Location Stansted House, Rowlands Castle, Hants Ⓟ
Open 10.30am–5pm
Entrance fee £3.50–£4.50

9

Aquarius Fairs
Location The Harlington Centre, High Street, Fleet, Hampshire
Details See London Coin Fair
9 February

Athena Fayres
Location Lockswood Community Centre, Locks Heath Shopping Centre, Locks Heath, Nr Fareham, Hants
Details See Athena Fayres
9 February

Chelsea Town Hall
Location Chelsea Town Hall, King's Road, Chelsea, London
Details See Chelsea Town Hall
19 January

Scotfairs Antique and Collectors Fair
Location Albert Halls, Dumbarton Road, Stirling
Details See Scotfairs Antique and Collectors Fair 2 February

9–10

Carmarthen Antiques & Collectors Fair
Contact Carol Pugh
☎ 01267 236569 Ⓕ 01267 220444
Ⓜ 07885 333845
Ⓔ antiques@towy-fairs.co.uk
Ⓦ www.towy-fairs.co.uk
Location United Counties Showground, Carmarthen Ⓟ
Est. 1993
Open 10am–5pm
Entrance fee £3 Accompanied children free
Details 180 dealers

10

Antique and Collectors Fair
Location Woking Leisure Centre, Kingfield Road, Woking, Surrey
Details See Antique and Collectors Fair 10 February

Antique Map Fair
☎ 01242 514287 Ⓕ 01242 513890
Ⓦ www.antiquemaps.co.uk
Location The Bonnington Hotel, Southampton Row, midway between Holborn and Russell Square tube stations, London
Est. 1982
Open 11am–6pm
Entrance fee Free
Details 18 dealers

Antiques and Collectables Fair
Location Newman House, 85 St Stephen's Green, Dublin 2
Details See Antiques and Collectables Fair 20 January

Biggleswade Antiques Fairs
☎ 01234 871449 Ⓕ 01234 871449
Ⓜ 07778 789917
Location Thistle Hotel (formerly Blakemore Hotel), Little Wymondley, Nr Hitchin, Herts
Open 9.30am–4.30pm

Crispin Fairs
Location Victoria Hall, Hartley Wintney, Hampshire
Details See Crispin Fairs
10 February

Furze Hill
Location Furze Hill, Banqueting Centre, Margaretting, Nr Chelmsford
Details See Furze Hill 10 February

Lostwithiel Antiques Fair
Location Community Centre, Lostwithiel, Cornwall
Details See Lostwithiel Antiques Fair 10 February

Mark Carter Militaria & Medal Fairs
☎ 01753 534777
Location Stratford Leisure Centre & Visitor Centre, Bridgfoot, Stratford upon Avon, Warwickshire Ⓟ
Open Preview 9.30am Public 10.30am–3.30pm
Entrance fee £1.50 Preview £3 Accompanied children free
Details 90 tables of quality militaria, books and medals

Midas Antique Fair
Location The Bellhouse Hotel, Oxford Road (A40), Beaconsfield, Bucks
Details See Midas Antique Fair 10 February

Pennyfarthing Fayres
Location Potters Bar
Details See Pennyfarthing Fayres 10 February

The London Textiles, Vintage Fashion and Accessories Fair
Location Hammersmith Town Hall, King Street, London, W6
Details See The London Textiles, Vintage Fashion and Accessories Fair 20 January

13

Marks Tey
Location Parish Hall, Marks Tey, Essex
Details See Marks Tey 13 February

13–19

The BADA Antiques and Fine Art Fair
☎ 020 7589 6108
Ⓦ www.bada-antiques-fair.co.uk
Location The Duke of York's Headquarters, King's Road, London, SW3
Est. 1993
Open 13th 11am–9pm 14th 11am–5.30pm 15th 11am–8pm 16th–17th 11am–6pm 18th 11am–8pm 19th 11am-6pm
Entrance fee Single entry £10 Double entry £15 Yearbook £9 inc p&p Events (including fair entry) Single £13 Double £19 Further per person is £8
Details Approximately 95 deakers, members of the British Antique Dealers Association, selling art and antiques

15–17

Cheshire County Antiques Fair
Contact Anne Harwood
☎ 01249 661111 Ⓕ 01249 661111
Ⓔ enquiries@cooperantiquesfairs.co.uk
Ⓦ www.cooperantiquesfairs.co.uk
Location Arley Hall, Nr Knutsford, Cheshire
Open Fri noon–5pm Sat Sun 11am–5pm
Entrance fee £4 Children under 16 and OAPs free

Galloway Antiques Fairs
☎ 01423 522122 Ⓕ 01423 522122
Ⓜ 07966 528725
Ⓔ susan@gallowayfairs.co.uk
Ⓦ www.gallowayfairs.co.uk
Location Ripley Castle, Ripley, Nr Harrogate, North Yorkshire Ⓟ
Open 10.30am–5pm
Entrance fee £3.50–£4.50

Stafford Bingley Hall
Location The Bingley Hall, County Showground
Details See Stafford Bingley Hall 8–10 February

The 19th Hertfordshire Antiques and Fine Art Fair
☎ 01277 214677 Ⓕ 01277 214550
Ⓔ admin@baileyfairs.co.uk
Ⓦ www.baileyfairs.co.uk
Location Hatfield House, Hatfield, Hertfordshire Ⓟ
Open 11am–5pm
Entrance fee £4
Details 40 dealers, vetted and date-lined

15–24

Penmans Chelsea Antiques Fair
Contact Caroline Penman
☎ 01444 482514 Ⓕ 01444 482412
Ⓜ 07774 850044
Ⓔ info@penman-fairs.co.uk
Ⓦ www.penman-fairs.co.uk
Location Chelsea Old Town Hall, King's Road, London, SW3 Ⓟ
Est. 1950
Open Weekdays 11am–8pm Sat 11am–7pm Sun 11am–5pm
Entrance fee £5
Details Fine traditional antiques from 40 top British exhibitors

16

Commonwealth Institute Coin Fair
Location The Commonwealth Institute, Kensington High Street, London, W8
Details See Commonwealth Institute Coin Fair 19 January

Devon County Antiques Fairs
Location Matford Centre in the Exeter Livestock Centre, Marsh Barton, Exeter
Details See Devon County Antiques Fairs 9 February

16–18

4th International Irish Antiques and Fine Art Fair
Contact Louis O'Sullivan
☎ 00 353 1 285 9294
Location Royal Dublin Society, Ballsbridge, Dublin 4, Ireland Ⓟ
Open 11am–7pm
Entrance fee 7 Euros
Details Fair Date-lines: pre-1900: prints, photos; pre-1925: furniture, metalwork, architectural fittings; pre-1930: glass, china, clocks; pre-1940: works of art, silver, etchings, lighting, clocks; pre-1950: jewellery, paintings, drawings

17

Alexandra Palace
Contact Lindy Berkman
☎ 020 88837061 Ⓕ 020 82458361
Ⓦ www.pigandwhistlepromotions.com
Location Wood Green, London Ⓟ
Open Trade 10am Public 11.30am–5pm
Entrance fee Trade £6 Public £4 Children free
Details London's largest antiques fair, over 700 stands, furniture from 18th–20thC

Antiques & Collectors Fair
Location Crook Log Sports Centre, Brampton Road, Bexleyheath, Kent
Details See Antiques & Collectors Fair 3 February

Aquarius Fairs
Location Heckfield Memorial Hall, Church Lane, Heckfield, Hook, Hampshire
Details See Aquarius Fairs 20 January

Biggleswade Antiques Fairs
Location The Weatherley Centre, Eagle Farm Road, Biggleswade, Bedfordshire
Details See Biggleswade Antiques Fairs 20 January

Bob Evans Fairs
Location Hereford Leisure Centre, Holmer Road
Details See Bob Evans Fairs 20 January

Grand Glass Fair
Contact John Slade
☎ 020 8894 0218
Ⓦ www.antiquefairs.co.uk
Location Woking Leisure Centre, Kingfield Road, Woking, Surrey 🅿
Open 9.30am–4pm
Entrance fee £2.50
Details 145 stalls

Hatfield Antiques & Collectors Fair
Location Red Lion, Great North Road, Hatfield, Hertfordshire
Details See Hatfield Antiques & Collectors Fair 20 January

Monmouthshire County Antiques & Collectors Fair
Location The Market Hall (next to the Town Hall), Abergavenny, Monmouthshire
Details See Monmouthshire County Antiques & Collectors Fair 20 January

19–21

12th Annual Antique and Fine Art Fair
☎ 028 9181 5710 Ⓕ 028 9182 0637
Ⓔ info@castleantiques.co.uk
Ⓦ www.castleantiques.co.uk
Location Templeton Hotel, Templepatrick 🅿
Open Tues Wed 2–9pm Thurs noon–9pm

22–23

Peterborough Festival of Antiques
☎ 01664 812627 Ⓕ 01664 813727
Location East of England Showground 🅿
Open Trade 6am Public 9am–4.30pm
Details Over 1000 stalls

22–24

Galloway Antiques Fairs
☎ 01423 522122 Ⓕ 01423 522122
Ⓜ 07966 528725
Ⓔ susan@gallowayfairs.co.uk
Ⓦ www.gallowayfairs.co.uk
Location Naworth Castle, Brampton, Cumbria 🅿
Open 10.30am–5pm
Entrance fee £3.50–£4.50

Shepton Mallet Antiques & Collectors Fair
Location Royal Bath and West Showground, Shepton Mallett, Somerset
Details See Shepton Mallet Antiques & Collectors Fair 18–20 January

23

Browser's Antique & Collectors Fair
Location Village Hall, Station Road, Pangbourne, Berkshire (on A329 off A4, M4 Jct 12/13)
Details See Browser's Antique & Collectors Fair 26 January

Southport Antiques and Collectors Fair
Location Southport Floral Hall, the Promenade, Southport, Merseyside
Details See Southport Antiques and Collectors Fair 16 February

24

Antique and Collectors Fair
Location Canons Leisure Centre, Madeira Road, Mitcham, Surrey
Details See Antique and Collectors Fair 27 January

Antiques and Collectables Fair
Location Newman House, 85 St Stephen's Green, Dublin 2
Details See Antiques and Collectables Fair 20 January

Antiques & Collectors Fair
Location Knights Hill Hotel, South Wooton, King's Lynn
Details See Antiques & Collectors Fair 20 January

Art Deco Fair with 20thC Decorative Arts
Contact Ann Zierold
☎ 01824 750500 Ⓕ 01824 750490
Location Leeds Royal Armouries 🅿
Est. 1997
Open 9.30am–4pm
Details 80 stands, no copies or reproductions

Athena Fayres
Location The Village Hall, Minstead, Nr Lyndhurst, about a mile from the end of the M27
Details See Athena Fayres 20 January

Biggleswade Antiques Fairs
Location The Addison Centre, Kempston, Bedford
Details See Biggleswade Antiques Fairs 27 January

Bloomsbury Postcard & Collectors Fair
Location Galleon Suite, Royal National Hotel, Bedford Way, London, WC1
Details See Bloomsbury Postcard and Collectors Fair 27 January

Brocante
Location Kensington Town Hall, Hornton Street, London, W8
Details See Brocante 3 February

Burford Antiques Fair
Location Burford School, Burford, Oxfordshire
Details See Burford Antiques Fair 27 January

Elstree Moat House Hotel
Location Elstree Moathouse Hotel, adjacent to Borehamwood exit, 2 miles south of M25
Details See Elstree Moat House Hotel 27 January

J and K Fairs
Location Lincolnshire Showground, Lincoln
Details See J and K Fairs 20 January

Scotfairs Antique and Collectors Fair
Location Moir Hall, Mitchell Library, Granville Street, Glasgow
Details See Scotfairs Antique and Collectors Fair 20 January

Wessex Fairs
Contact Mrs Jo Wanford
☎ 01278 789568
Location Combe Lodge, A368, Blagdon, Nr Church Hill, North Somerset 🅿

Est. 2001
Open 10am–4.30pm
Entrance fee £1 Trade FWC
Details Stall capacity 40, refreshments available

27

The Big Brum
Location St Martins Market (The Rag), Edgbaston Street, Birmingham
Details See The Big Brum 30 January

28

Antique & Collectors Fair
Location Nantwich Civic Hall, Market Street, Nantwich, Cheshire, M6 Jct 16
Details See Antique & Collectors Fair 31 January

29

Antique and Collectors Fair
Location Woking Leisure Centre, Kingfield Road, Woking, Surrey
Details See Antique and Collectors Fair 10 February

Magnum Antiques Fairs
Contact Stewart Watt
☎ 01491 681009
Location Guildford, Surrey University Sports Hall, Just off the A3 🅿
Open 10am–4.30pm
Entrance fee £1.25
Details 110 stands

29–1 Apr

Galloway Antiques Fairs
☎ 01423 522122 Ⓕ 01423 522122
Ⓜ 07966 528725
Ⓔ susan@gallowayfairs.co.uk
Ⓦ www.gallowayfairs.co.uk
Location Cranleigh School, Cranleigh, Surrey 🅿
Open 10.30am–5pm
Entrance fee £3.50–£4.50

30

Antiques Fair
Location Castle Hall, Hertford, Hertfordshire
Details See Antiques Fair 19 January

Blackpool Winter Gardens Antiques and Collectors Fair
Location Blackpool Winter Gardens, Blackpool, Lancashire
Details See Blackpool Winter Gardens Antiques and Collectors Fair 26 January

Scotfairs Antique and Collectors Fair
Location The Citadel Leisure Centre, Ayr Baths, South Beach Road, Ayr
Details See Scotfairs Antique and Collectors Fair 26 January

30–1 Apr

Beckett Antique Fairs
Location Doncaster Race Exhibition Centre, Doncaster
Details See Beckett Antique Fairs 16–17 February

The 2nd North Norfolk Fine Art and Antiques Fair
Contact Liz Allport
☎ 01603 737631 Ⓕ 01603 737631
Ⓜ 07747 843074
Ⓔ liz.allport@lineone.net
Ⓦ www.lomaxantiquesfairs.co.uk
Location Sussex Barn, Nr Burnham Market, Norfolk 🅿
Open 30th 11am–6pm 31st 10.30am–6pm 1st 10.30am–5pm

The Original Long Melford Fair
Location The Old School, Long Melford, Suffolk
Details See The Original Long Melford Fair 26–27 January

30–31

Little Easton Manor
Contact Graham Turner
☎ 01473 658224
Ⓔ ggt@btinternet.com
Location Little Easton Manor, Nr Great Dunmow, Essex 🅿
Open Trade 9.30am Public 10am–4.30pm
Details Beautiful venue in historic barn theatre, quality dealers

31

Antique and Collectors Fair
Contact Jocelyn Gibbons
☎ 01442 890339
Location Berkhampstead Sports Centre, Lagley Meadow, Douglas Gardens, Berkhampstead, Hertfordshire
Open 10am–4.30pm
Details 130 stalls

Art Nouveau and Art Deco Fair
Contact John Slade
☎ 020 8894 0218
Ⓦ www.antiquefairs.co.uk
Location Woking Leisure Centre, Kingfield Road, Woking, Surrey 🅿
Open Trade 8am Public 9am–4.30pm
Entrance fee £2
Details 200 stalls

Athena Fayres
Location Community Centre, Mill Lane, Wickham, Hampshire
Details See Athena Fayres 27 January

Bob Evans Fairs
Location Sports Connexion, Ryton-on-Dunsmore, Coventry, Warwickshire
Details See Bob Evans Fairs 10 February

Chenevare Fairs
Location Hagley Community Centre, Worcester Road, West Hagley, Hereford & Worcester
Details See Chenevare Fairs 27 January

Midland Clock & Watch Fair
Location National Motorcycle Museum, M42 Exit 6, West Midlands
Details See Midland Clock & Watch Fair 27 January

R and S Western Fairs
Location Trenython Manor, Tywardreath, Nr Par, Cornwall
Details See R and S Western Fairs 27 January

Royal Horticultural Hall
Location Royal Horticultural Hall, Lawrence Hall, Greycoat Street, London SW1
Details See Royal Horticultural Hall 10 February

APRIL

31–1 Apr

Antiques & Collectors Fair
Location Burgess Hall, St Ives Recreation Centre, St Ives, Cambridgeshire
Details See Antiques & Collectors Fair 16–17 February

The Beaconsfield Fine Art and Antiques Fair
Contact Joy Alder
☎ 01494 674170
Location The Bellhouse Hotel, Oxford Road (A40), Beaconsfield, Bucks 🅿
Open 11am–5pm
Details Vetted, partial stand-fitted, quality fair

Wessex Fairs
Location Winter Gardens, Weston-Super-Mare
Details See Wessex Fairs 24 February

APRIL

1

13th Annual Easter Antique and Fine Art Fair
☎ 028 9181 5710 Ⓕ 028 9182 0637
Ⓔ info@castleantiques.co.uk
Ⓦ www.castleantiques.co.uk
Location The Causeway Coast Hotel, Portrush 🅿
Open 11am–7pm

Antique Collectors Jamboree
Contact Stancie Kutler
☎ 01270 624288
Location Nantwich Civic Hall, Market Street, Nantwich, Cheshire, M6 Jct 16 🅿
Est. 1974
Open Trade 8am Public 10am–5pm
Details Refreshments, up to 75 stalls

Antiques and Collectables Fair
Location Royal Marine Hotel, Dun Laoghaire, Co Dublin
Details See Antiques and Collectables Fair 27 January

Antiques and Collectors Fair
Contact Sandra Mather
☎ 01744 750606 Ⓕ 01744 750606
Ⓔ sandracca@aol.com
Ⓦ www.crafts@supanet.com
Location Wilmslow Leisure Centre, Wilmslow, Cheshire 🅿
Open 10am–5pm
Entrance fee £1
Details 75 stalls, refreshments

Bob Evans Fairs
Location Leisure Village, Thurston Drive, Kettering
Details See Bob Evans Fairs 24 February

Magnum Antiques Fairs
Contact Stewart Watt
☎ 01491 681009
Location Winchester, River Park Leisure Centre, Gordon Road 🅿
Open 10am–4.30pm
Entrance fee £1.25
Details 170 stands

Pamela Robertson Antique and Collectors Fair
Location Northgate Arena, Victoria Road, Cheshire
Details See Pamela Robertson Antique and Collectors Fair 26 January

Wembley Antiques & Collectors Fair
Contact Caroline Cleary
☎ 01636 702326 Ⓕ 01636 707923
Ⓦ www.dmgantiquefairs.com
Location Hall 3, Wembley Exhibition Centre, Wembley, London 🅿
Est. 1999
Open 7.30am–4pm
Entrance fee 7.30am £10 10am £3.50
Details Held on a bank holiday, 400 stalls, café

2

The Sandown Park Antique Fair
Location The Exhibition Centre, Sandown Park Racecourse, Esher, Surrey
Details See Sandown Park Antique Fair 19 February

Newbury Racecourse
Location Newbury Racecourse, Newbury, Berkshire
Details See Newbury Racecourse February 13

The Long Melford
Location Village Memorial Hall, Long Melford, Suffolk
Details See The Long Melford 6 February

4

Paraphernalia Fairs
Location Lyndhurst Community Centre, Lyndhurst, New Forest, Hampshire
Details See Paraphernalia Fairs 14 February

5–7

Antiques for Everyone
Ⓔ antiques@necgroup.co.uk
Ⓦ www.antiquesforeveryone.co.uk
Location G-Mex, Manchester 🅿
Est. 1985
Open Weekdays 11am–8pm weekends 11am–6pm
Entrance fee £5
Details Approximately 200 dealers

South Cotswolds Antiques Fair
Contact Anne Harwood
☎ 01249 661111 Ⓕ 01249 661111
Ⓔ enquiries@cooperantiquesfairs.co.uk
Ⓦ www.cooperantiquesfairs.co.uk
Location Westonbirt School, Nr Tetbury, Gloucestershire
Open Fri noon–5pm Sat Sun 11am–5pm
Entrance fee £4 Children under 16 and OAPs free

The International Antiques and Collectors Fair at RAF Swinderby
Location RAF Swinderby, A46 between Newark and Lincoln
Details See The International Antiques and Collectors Fair at RAF Swinderby 1–3 February

6

Antiques & Collectors Fair
Location Mountford Hall, Students Union Building, Liverpool University
Details See Antiques & Collectors Fair 2 February

Chingford Antiques & Collectors Fair
Location Assembly Hall, The Green, Station Road, Chingford,
Details See Chingford Antiques & Collectors Fair 26 January

E W Services Antiques Fair
Location Buckingham Community Centre, Cornwalls Meadow Shopping Precinct, Buckingham
Details See E W Services Antiques Fair 2 February

Marcel Fairs
Location St Paul's Church Hall, Mill Hill, Ridgeway, London, NW7
Details See Marcel Fairs 2 February

Victoriana's Fairs
Location Walsall Town Hall, Walsall, West Midlands
Details See Victoriana's Fairs 2 February

6–7

3rd Mid Beds Antiques Fair
Contact Rodney Week
☎ 01234 381701 Ⓕ 01234 381701
Location Silsoe Conference Centre, Bedfordshire Ⓟ
Est. 2001
Open Sat 11am–5pm Sun 10am–5pm
Entrance fee £2.50
Details 40+ stands, 1930 date-line, restaurant

Bob Evans Fairs
Location Sport Village, Drayton High Road, Hellesdon, Norwich
Details See Bob Evans Fairs 26–27 January

Buxton Antique and Collectors Fair
Location Pavilion Gardens, Buxton, Derbyshire
Details See Buxton Antique and Collectors Fair 26–27 January

7

Antiques and Collectables Fair
Location Newman House, 85 St Stephen's Green, Dublin 2
Details See Antiques and Collectables Fair 20 January

Battersea Town Hall Art Deco Fair
Location Battersea Town Hall
Details See Battersea Town Hall Art Deco Fair February 17

Best of Fairs
Location The Village Hall, Copdock, 3 miles west of Ipswich
Details See Best of Fairs 3 February

Biggleswade Antiques Fairs
☎ 01234 871449 Ⓕ 01234 871449
Ⓜ 07778 789917
Location Kimbolton Castle, Huntingdon, Cambridgeshire
Open 10am–4.30pm
Details Date-line 1940s

Chatsworth Fairs
Location Cedar Court Hotel, Jct 39 M1, Wakefield
Details See Chatsworth Fairs 3 February

Cross Country Fairs Ltd
Location Copthorne Hotel, Effingham Park, West Sussex
Details See Cross Country Fairs Ltd 3 February

Hampstead Antique Collectors Fair
Location Hampstead Community Centre, High Street, Hampstead
Details See Hampstead Antique Collectors Fair 3 February

Harlequin Fairs
Location Centre for Epilepsy, Chalfont Common, Chalfont St Peter, Buckinghamshire
Details See Harlequin Fairs 3 February

Ipswich Antiques and Collectables Fair
Location Ipswich County Hotel (formerly Ipswich Moat House) Copdock, Ipswich, Suffolk
Details See Ipswich Antiques and Collectables Fair

Lechlade Antiques Fair
Location The New Memorial Hall, Burford Road, Lechlade, Gloucestershire
Details See Lechlade Antiques Fair 3 February

Magnum Antiques Fairs
Location Midhurst, The Grange Centre, Bepton Road
Details See Magnum Antiques Fairs 3 February

Malvern Antiques & Collectors Fair
Location Three Counties Showground, Malvern, Worcestershire
Details See Malvern Antiques & Collectors Fair 3 February

Mark Carter Militaria & Medal Fairs
Location The Princes Hall, Princes Way, Aldershot, Hampshire
Details See Mark Carter Militaria & Medal Fairs 20 January

Scotfairs Antique and Collectors Fair
Location Meadowbank Stadium, London Road, Edinburgh
Details See Scotfairs Antique and Collectors Fair 3 February

Wessex Fairs
Location Holiday Inn, Taunton, Somerset, M5 Jct 25
Details See Wessex Fairs 3 February

8–9

Little Chelsea Antiques Fair
Contact Carol Pugh
☎ 01267 236569 Ⓕ 01267 220444
Ⓜ 07885 333845
Ⓔ antiques@towy-fairs.co.uk
Ⓦ www.towy-fairs.co.uk
Location Chelsea Old Town Hall, King's Road, London, SW3 Ⓟ
Open 10am–5pm
Entrance fee £3 Accompanied children free Trade FWC
Details Vetted and date-lined quality fair

Newark International Antiques & Collectors Fair
Location Newark & Notts Showground, Newark
Details See Newark International Antiques & Collectors Fair 4–5 February

10

Marks Tey
Location Parish Hall, Marks Tey, Essex
Details See Marks Tey 13 February

APRIL

12–14

TVADA Spring Fair
Contact Jill Mair
☎ 01865 341639
Location The Blue Coat School, Sonning-on-the-Thames, Berkshire Ⓟ
Est. 1989
Open Fri Sat 11am–6pm Sun 11am–5pm
Entrance fee £5
Details 40+ stands, fully licensed restaurant

13

Aquarius Fairs
Location The Harlington Centre, High Street, Fleet, Hampshire
Details See Aquarius Fairs 9 February

Athena Fayres
Location Lockswood Community Centre, Locks Heath Shopping Centre, Locks Heath, Nr Fareham, Hants
Details See Athena Fayres 9 February

Chelsea Town Hall
Location Chelsea Town Hall, King's Road, Chelsea, London SW3
Details See Chelsea Town Hall 19 January

Commonwealth Institute Coin Fair
Location The Commonwealth Institute, Kensington High Street, London, W8
Details See Commonwealth Institute Coin Fair 19 January

Devon County Antiques Fairs
Location Matford Centre in the Exeter Livestock Centre, Marsh Barton, Exeter

Details See Devon County Antiques Fairs 9 February

13–14

Harpenden Antiques and Fine Art Fair
Location Rothamsted Conference Centre, on A1081 Harpenden–St Albans road
Details See Harpenden Antiques and Fine Art Fair 9–10 February

The Original Long Melford Fair
Location The Old School, Long Melford, Suffolk
Details See The Original Long Melford Fair 26–27 January

West Midlands Antique Fairs
Location Prestwood Complex, Stafford County Showground
Details See West Midlands Antique Fairs 23–24 February

14

Antique and Collectors Fair
Location Woking Leisure Centre, Kingfield Road, Woking, Surrey
Details See Antique and Collectors Fair 10 February

Antique Map Fair
Location The Bonnington Hotel, Southampton Row, midway between Holborn and Russell Square tube stations, London
Details See Antique Map Fair 10 March

Antiques & Collectors Fairs
Location Runnymeade Hotel & Spa, Windsor Road, Egham, Surrey
Details See Antiques & Collectors Fair 10 February

Art Deco Fair with 20thC Decorative Arts
Location Chester Racecourse
Details See Art Deco Fair with 20thC Decorative Arts 27 January

Chenevare Fairs
Location Kinver Leisure Centre, Enville Road, Kinver, Stourbridge, West Midlands
Details See Chenevare Fairs 10 February

Crispin Fairs
Location Victoria Hall, Hartley Wintney, Hampshire
Details See Crispin Fairs 10 February

Devon County Antiques Fairs
Location Westland Sports and Social Club, Westbourne Close, Yeovil, Somerset
Details See Devon County Antiques Fairs 10 February

Furze Hill
Location Furze Hill, Banqueting Centre, Margaretting, Nr Chelmsford, Essex
Details See Furze Hill 10 February

Lostwithiel Antiques Fair
Location Community Centre, Lostwithiel, Cornwall
Details See Lostwithiel Antiques Fair 10 February

Midas Antique Fair
Location The Bellhouse Hotel, Oxford Road (A40), Beaconsfield, Bucks
Details See Midas Antique Fair 10 February

Pennyfarthing Fayres
Location Potters Bar, Hertfordshire
Details See Pennyfarthing Fayres 10 February

16–21

The Decorative Antiques and Textiles Fair
Contact Patricia Harvey
☎ 020 76245173 Ⓕ 020 76258326
Ⓔ fairs@decorativefair.com
Ⓦ www.decorativefair.com
Location The Marquee, Battersea Park, London Ⓟ
Est. 1985
Open 16th noon–8pm 17th–19th 11am–8pm 20th 11am–7pm 21st 10am–6pm
Entrance fee £6 including catalogue
Details 100 dealers

17

Evening Antiques/Collectors Fairs
Location St Martins Market (The Rag), Edgbaston Street, Birmingham
Details See Evening Antiques/Collectors Fairs 20 February

17–21

The 8th Claridge's Antiques and Fine Art Fair
☎ 01277 214677 Ⓕ 01277 214550
Ⓔ admin@baileyfairs.co.uk
Ⓦ www.baileyfairs.co.uk

Location Claridge's Hotel, London, W1 P
Entrance fee £5
Details 50 dealers, vetted and date-lined

19–21

Galloway Antiques Fairs
☎ 01423 522122 F 01423 522122
M 07966 528725
E susan@gallowayfairs.co.uk
W www.gallowayfairs.co.uk
Location Brandling House, High Gosforth Park, Newcastle Upon Tyne P
Open 10.30am–5pm
Entrance fee £3.50–£4.50

20

Antiques Fair
Location Castle Hall, Hertford, Hertfordshire
Details See Antiques Fair 19 January

Chingford Antiques & Collectors Fair
Location Assembly Hall, The Green, Station Road, Chingford,
Details See Chingford Antiques & Collectors Fair 26 January

Scotfairs Antique and Collectors Fair
Location Albert Halls, Dumbarton Road, Stirling
Details See Scotfairs Antique and Collectors Fair 2 February

20–21

Beckett Antique Fairs
Location Doncaster Race Exhibition Centre, Doncaster
Details See Beckett Antique Fairs 16–17 February

Bob Evans Fairs
Location International Centre, St Quentin Gate, Telford, Shropshire
Details See Bob Evans Fairs 16–17 February

Saffron Walden Antiques and Fine Art Fair
Location Saffron Walden County High School, Audley End Road, Saffron Walden, Essex
Details See Saffron Walden Antiques and Fine Art Fair 2–3 February

The Long Melford
Location Village Memorial Hall, Long Melford, Suffolk
Details See The Long Melford 26–27 January

21

Antiques and Collectables Fair
Location Newman House, 85 St Stephen's Green, Dublin 2
Details See Antiques and Collectables Fair 20 January

Antiques & Collectors Fair
Location Knights Hill Hotel, South Wooton, King's Lynn
Details See Antiques & Collectors Fair 20 January

Aquarius Fairs
Location Heckfield Memorial Hall, Church Lane, Heckfield, Hook, Hampshire
Details See Aquarius Fairs 20 January

Athena Fayres
Location The Village Hall, Minstead, Nr Lyndhurst, Hampshire, about a mile from the end of the M27
Details See Athena Fayres 20 January

Biggleswade Antiques Fairs
Location The Weatherley Centre, Eagle Farm Road, Biggleswade, Bedfordshire
Details See Biggleswade Antiques Fairs 20 January

Brunel Clock & Watch Fair
Location Brunel University, Kingston Lane, Uxbridge, Middlesex
Details See Brunel Clock & Watch Fair 17 February

Chenevare Fairs
Location Bridgnorth Sports and Leisure Centre, Northgate, Bridgnorth, Shropshire
Details See Chenevare Fairs 20 January

Hatfield Antiques & Collectors Fair
Location Red Lion, Great North Road, Hatfield, Hertfordshire
Details See Hatfield Antiques & Collectors Fair 20 January

J and K Fairs
Location Lincolnshire Showground, Lincoln
Details See J and K Fairs 20 January

Monmouthshire County Antiques & Collectors Fair
Location The Market Hall (next to the Town Hall), Abergavenny, Monmouthshire
Details See Monmouthshire County Antiques & Collectors Fair 20 January

Newmarket Antiques & Collectors Fair
Location Millennium Grandstand, Rowley Mile Racecourse, Newmarket, Suffolk
Details See Newmarket Antiques & Collectors Fair 17 February

Scotfairs Antique and Collectors Fair
Location Moir Hall, Mitchell Library, Granville Street, Glasgow
Details See Scotfairs Antique and Collectors Fair 20 January

23–24

Ardingly International Antiques & Collectors Fair
Location South of England Centre, Ardingly, West Sussex
Details See Ardingly International Antiques & Collectors Fair 26–27 February

25

Antique & Collectors Fair
Location Nantwich Civic Hall, Market Street, Nantwich, Cheshire, M6 Jct 16
Details See Antique & Collectors Fair 31 January

25–28

Penmans 7th Annual Chelsea Art Fair
Contact Caroline Penman
☎ 01444 482514 F 01444 482412
M 07774 850044
E info@penman-fairs.co.uk
W www.penman-fairs.co.uk
Location Chelsea Old Town Hall, King's Road, London SW3 P
Est. 1995
Open Thurs Fri 11am–9pm Sat 11am–7pm Sun 11am–5pm

Entrance fee £6
Details 40 leading galleries offer contemporary and 20thC art

The 6th Harrogate Spring antiques and Fine Art Fair
☎ 01277 214677 Ⓕ 01277 214550
Ⓔ admin@baileyfairs.co.uk
Ⓦ www.baileyfairs.co.uk
Location Pavilions of Harrogate, Great Yorkshire Showground Ⓟ
Open Thurs 2–6pm Fri Sat 11am–6pm Sun 11am–5pm
Entrance fee £5
Details 80 dealers, vetted and date-lined

26–27

The 68th London Arms Fair
Contact Mrs Durrant
☎ 020 8539 5278
Location Royal National Hotel, Woburn Place, Holborn, London WC1 Ⓟ
Est. 1968
Details Antique arms, armour and militaria, 120 tables

27

Blackpool Winter Gardens Antiques and Collectors Fair
Location Blackpool Winter Gardens, Blackpool, Lancashire
Details See Blackpool Winter Gardens Antiques and Collectors Fair 26 January

Browser's Antique & Collectors Fair
Location Village Hall, Station Road, Pangbourne, Berkshire (on A329 off A4, M4 Jct 12/13)
Details See Browser's Antique & Collectors Fair 26 January

Scotfairs Antique and Collectors Fair
Location The Citadel Leisure Centre, Ayr Baths, South Beach Road, Ayr
Details See Scotfairs Antique and Collectors Fair 26 January

27–28

Cardiff Antiques & Collectors Fair
Contact Carol Pugh
☎ 01267 236569 Ⓕ 01267 220444
Ⓜ 07885 333845
Ⓔ antiques@towy-fairs.co.uk
Ⓦ www.towy-fairs.co.uk
Location Cardiff Bowls Club, Sophia Gardens, Cardiff Ⓟ
Est. 2001
Open 10am–5pm
Entrance fee £3 Accompanied children free
Details 120 stands

Detling International Antiques & Collectors Fair
Location Kent County Showground, Detling, Nr Maidstone, Kent
Details See Detling International Antiques & Collectors Fair 26–27 January

28

Antique and Collectors Fair
Location Canons Leisure Centre, Madeira Road, Mitcham, Surrey
Details See Antique and Collectors Fair 27 January

Athena Fayres
Location Community Centre, Mill Lane, Wickham, Hampshire
Details See Athena Fayres 27 January

Bloomsbury Postcard & Collectors Fair
Location Galleon Suite, Royal National Hotel, Bedford Way, London, WC1
Details See Bloomsbury Postcard and Collectors Fair 27 January

Burford Antiques Fair
Location Burford School, Burford, Oxfordshire
Details See Burford Antiques Fair 27 January

Chenevare Fairs
Location Hagley Community Centre, Worcester Road, West Hagley, Hereford & Worcester
Details See Chenevare Fairs 27 January

Mark Carter Militaria & Medal Fairs
Location Yate Leisure Centre, Kennedy Way, Yate, Bristol
Details See Mark Carter Militaria & Medal Fairs 3 February

R and S Western Fairs
Location Trenython Manor, Tywardreath, Nr Par, Cornwall
Details See R and S Western Fairs 27 January

The London Textiles, Vintage Fashion and Accessories Fair
Location Hammersmith Town Hall, King Street, London, W6
Details See The London Textiles, Vintage Fashion and Accessories Fair 20 January

MAY

1

The Long Melford
Location Village Memorial Hall, Long Melford, Suffolk
Details See The Long Melford 6 February

2

Paraphernalia Fairs
Location Lyndhurst Community Centre, Lyndhurst, New Forest, Hampshire
Details See Paraphernalia Fairs 14 February

2–5

The Harrogate Antique & Fine Art Fair
Contact Louise Walker
☎ 01823 323363 Ⓕ 01823 271072
Ⓦ www.harrogateantiquefair.com
Location Hall A and B, Harrogate International Centre, Ripon Road, Harrogate, North Yorkshire Ⓟ
Open Thurs Fri 11am–8pm Sat Sun 11am–6pm
Entrance fee £6 including catalogue
Details High quality antiques & fine art

3–6

Galloway Antiques Fairs
☎ 01423 522122 Ⓕ 01423 522122
Ⓜ 07966 528725
Ⓔ susan@gallowayfairs.co.uk
Ⓦ www.gallowayfairs.co.uk
Location Eridge Park, Nr Crowborough, East Sussex Ⓟ

Open 10.30am–5pm
Entrance fee £3.50–£4.50

4

Antiques & Collectors Fair
Location Mountford Hall, Students Union Building, Liverpool University
Details See Antiques & Collectors Fair 2 February

Chelsea Town Hall
Location Chelsea Town Hall, King's Road, Chelsea, London SW3
Details See Chelsea Town Hall 19 January

Commonwealth Institute Coin Fair
Location The Commonwealth Institute, Kensington High Street, London, W8
Details See Commonwealth Institute Coin Fair 19 January

E W Services Antiques Fair
Location Buckingham Community Centre, Cornwalls Meadow Shopping Precinct, Buckingham
Details See E W Services Antiques Fair 2 February

Marcel Fairs
Location St Paul's Church Hall, Mill Hill, Ridgeway, London, NW7
Details See Marcel Fairs 2 February

Victoriana's Fairs
Location Walsall Town Hall, Walsall, West Midlands
Details See Victoriana's Fairs 2 February

4–5

Devon County Antiques Fairs
Location Westpoint Exhibition Centre, Clyst St Mary, Exeter
Details See Devon County Antiques Fair 2–3 February

May,4–6

The Original Long Melford Fair
Location The Old School, Long Melford, Suffolk
Details See The Original Long Melford Fair 26–27 January

West Midlands Antique Fairs
Location Prestwood Complex, Stafford County Showground
Details See West Midlands Antique Fairs 23–24 February

5

Best of Fairs
Location The Village Hall, Copdock, 3 miles west of Ipswich
Details See Best of Fairs 3 February

Chatsworth Fairs
Location Cedar Court Hotel, Jct 39 M1, Wakefield
Details See Chatsworth Fairs 3 February

Clock & Watch Dealers Fair
Location Haydock Park racecourse, M6 Jct 23
Details See Clock & Watch Dealers Fair 3 March

Cross Country Fairs Ltd
Location Copthorne Hotel, Effingham Park, West Sussex
Details See Cross Country Fairs Ltd 3 February

Hampstead Antique Collectors Fair
Location Hampstead Community Centre, High Street, Hampstead
Details See Hampstead Antique Collectors Fair 3 February

Harlequin Fairs
Location Centre for Epilepsy, Chalfont Common, Chalfont St Peter, Buckinghamshire
Details See Harlequin Fairs 3 February

Ipswich Antiques and Collectables Fair
Location Ipswich County Hotel (formerly Ipswich Moat House) Copdock, Ipswich, Suffolk
Details See Ipswich Antiques and Collectables Fair

Lechlade Antiques Fair
Location The New Memorial Hall, Burford Road, Lechlade, Gloucestershire
Details See Lechlade Antiques Fair 3 February

Malvern Antiques & Collectors Fair
Location Three Counties Showground, Malvern, Worcestershire
Details See Malvern Antiques & Collectors Fair 3 February

5–6

Wessex Fairs
Location Winter Gardens, Weston-Super-Mare, Somerset
Details See Wessex Fairs 24 February

6

8th Annual Charity Antique and Fine Art Fair
☎ 028 9181 5710 Ⓕ 028 9182 0637
Ⓔ info@castleantiques.co.uk
Ⓦ www.castleantiques.co.uk
Location Queen's Hall, Newtownards Ⓟ
Open 11am–5pm

Antique Collectors Jamboree
Location Nantwich Civic Hall, Market Street, Nantwich, Cheshire, M6 Jct 16
Details See Antique Collectors Jamboree 1 April

Antiques and Collectables Fair
Location Clontarf Castle, Castle Avenue, Dublin
Details See Antiques Fairs Ireland 24 February

Bob Evans Fairs
Location The Cresset, Bretton Centre, Peterborough, Cambridgeshire
Details See Bob Evans Fairs 3 March

J and K Fairs
Location Lincolnshire Showground, Lincoln
Details See J and K Fairs 20 January

Magnum Antiques Fairs
Location Winchester, River Park Leisure Centre, Gordon Road

Details See Magnum Antiques Fairs 1 April

Pamela Robertson Antique and Collectors Fair
Location Northgate Arena, Victoria Road, Cheshire
Details See Pamela Robertson Antique and Collectors Fair 26 January

Wembley Antiques & Collectors Fair
Location Hall 3, Wembley Exhibition Centre, Wembley, London
Details See Wembley Antiques & Collectors Fair 1 April

8

Marks Tey
Location Parish Hall, Marks Tey, Essex
Details See Marks Tey 13 February

The Big Brum
Location St Martins Market (The Rag), Edgbaston Street, Birmingham
Details See The Big Brum 30 January

10–12

Hylands House
Contact Graham Turner
☎ 01473 658224 Ⓕ 01473 658224
Location Hylands Park, Chelmsford, Essex Ⓟ
Open Fri gala 7pm–10pm Sat Sun Trade 9.30am Public 10am–4.30pm
Details Outstanding grade II listed building, quality fair

Shepton Mallet Antiques & Collectors Fair
Location Royal Bath and West Showground, Shepton Mallett, Somerset
Details See Shepton Mallet Antiques & Collectors Fair 18–20 January

11

Athena Fayres
Location Lockswood Community Centre, Locks Heath Shopping Centre, Locks Heath, Nr Fareham, Hants
Details See Athena Fayres 9 February

Scotfairs Antique and Collectors Fair
Location Albert Halls, Dumbarton Road, Stirling
Details See Scotfairs Antique and Collectors Fair 2 February

11–12

Art Deco Fair with 20thC Decorative Arts
Contact Ann Zierold
☎ 01824 750500 Ⓕ 01824 750490
Location Royal Highland Centre, Edinburgh Ⓟ
Est. 2002
Open Sat 11am–5pm Sun 9.30am–4pm
Details Over 100 stands, no copies or reproductions, lectures

Beckett Antique Fairs
Location Doncaster Race Exhibition Centre, Doncaster
Details See Beckett Antique Fairs 16–17 February

11–18

38th Buxton Antiques Fair
Contact Roger or Mary Heath-Bullock
☎ 01483 422562 Ⓕ 01483 422562
Ⓦ www.buxtonantiquesfair.co.uk
Location Pavilion Gardens, Buxton, Derbyshire Ⓟ
Est. 1965
Open First Sat noon–8pm Sun Mon noon–6pm Tues–Thurs noon–9pm Fri–Sat noon–6pm
Details Annual vetted & date-lined fair

12

Alexandra Palace
Location Wood Green, London
Details See Alexandra Palace 17 March

Antique and Collectors Fair
Location Woking Leisure Centre, Kingfield Road, Woking, Surrey
Details See Antique and Collectors Fair 10 February

Antique Map Fair
Location The Bonnington Hotel, Southampton Row, midway between Holborn and Russell Square tube stations, London
Details See Antique Map Fair 10 March

Antiques and Collectables Fair
Location Newman House, 85 St Stephen's Green, Dublin 2
Details See Antiques and Collectables Fair 20 January

Antiques & CollectorsFairs
Location Runnymeade Hotel & Spa, Windsor Road, Egham, Surrey
Details See Antiques & Collectors Fair 10 February

Aquarius Fairs
Location The Harlington Centre, High Street, Fleet, Hampshire
Details See Aquarius Fairs 9 February

Bob Evans Fairs
Location Sports Connexion, Ryton-on-Dunsmore, Coventry
Details See Bob Evans Fairs 10 February

Chenevare Fairs
Location Kinver Leisure Centre, Enville Road, Kinver, Stourbridge, West Midlands
Details See Chenevare Fairs 10 February

Crispin Fairs
Location Victoria Hall, Hartley Wintney, Hampshire
Details See Crispin Fairs 10 February

Lostwithiel Antiques Fair
Location Community Centre, Lostwithiel, Cornwall
Details See Lostwithiel Antiques Fair 10 February

Midas Antique Fair
Location The Bellhouse Hotel, Oxford Road (A40), Beaconsfield, Bucks
Details See Midas Antique Fair 10 February

Pennyfarthing Fayres
Location Potters Bar
Details See Pennyfarthing Fayres 10 February

The Original National Glass Collectors Fair
Contact Patricia Hier

☎ 01260 271975 Ⓕ 01260 271975
Ⓔ dil.hier@talk21.com
Location National Motorcycle Museum, Jct 6 M42, Midlands Ⓟ
Open 9.30am–3.30pm
Details Over 100 dealers selling all types of glass including ancient, 18thC drinking glasses, Victorian pressed, Art Deco, Art Nouveau, paperweights and studio glass

16–19

Antiques for Everyone
Ⓔ antiques@necgroup.co.uk
Ⓦ www.antiquesforeveryone.co.uk
Location NEC Birmingham, Hall 5 Ⓟ
Est. 1985
Open Weekdays 11am–8pm weekends 11am–6pm
Entrance fee 16th £7 17th–19th £6
Details Over 600 dealers

18

Antiques Fair
Location Castle Hall, Hertford, Hertfordshire
Details See Antiques Fair 19 January

Jade Fairs
Location Lowther Pavilion, The Promenade, Lytham St Anne's, Lancashire
Details See Jade Fairs 2 February

Scotfairs Antique and Collectors Fair
Location Meadowbank Stadium, London Road, Edinburgh
Details See Scotfairs Antique and Collectors Fair 3 February

19

Antiques & Collectors Fair
Location Crook Log Sports Centre, Brampton Road, Bexleyheath, Kent
Details See Antiques & Collectors Fair 3 February

Antiques & Collectors Fair
Location Knights Hill Hotel, South Wooton, King's Lynn
Details See Antiques & Collectors Fair 20 January

Aquarius Fairs
Location Heckfield Memorial Hall, Church Lane, Heckfield, Hook, Hampshire
Details See Aquarius Fairs 20 January

Athena Fayres
Location The Village Hall, Minstead, Nr Lyndhurst, about a mile from the end of the M27
Details See Athena Fayres 20 January

Biggleswade Antiques Fairs
Location The Weatherley Centre, Eagle Farm Road, Biggleswade, Bedfordshire
Details See Biggleswade Antiques Fairs 20 January

Hatfield Antiques & Collectors Fair
Location Red Lion, Great North Road, Hatfield, Hertfordshire
Details See Hatfield Antiques & Collectors Fair 20 January

Monmouthshire County Antiques & Collectors Fair
Location The Market Hall (next to the Town Hall), Abergavenny, Monmouthshire
Details See Monmouthshire County Antiques & Collectors Fair 20 January

Royal Horticultural Hall
Location Royal Horticultural Hall, Lawrence Hall, Greycoat Street, London SW1
Details See Royal Horticultural Hall 10 February

Scotfairs Antique and Collectors Fair
Location Moir Hall, Mitchell Library, Granville Street, Glasgow
Details See Scotfairs Antique and Collectors Fair 20 January

Wessex Fairs
Location Holiday Inn, Taunton, Somerset, M5 Jct 25
Details See Wessex Fairs 3 February

22

Newbury Racecourse
Location Newbury Racecourse, Newbury, Berkshire
Details See Newbury Racecourse February 13

25

Browser's Antique & Collectors Fair
Location Village Hall, Station Road, Pangbourne, Berkshire (on A329 off A4, M4 Jct 12/13)
Details See Browser's Antique & Collectors Fair 26 January

Chelsea Town Hall
Location Chelsea Town Hall, King's Road, Chelsea, London SW3
Details See Chelsea Town Hall 19 January

Chingford Antiques & Collectors Fair
Location Assembly Hall, The Green, Station Road, Chingford,
Details See Chingford Antiques & Collectors Fair 26 January

London Coin Fair
Location Holiday Inn, London Bloomsbury, Coram Street, WC1
Details See London Coin Fair 9 February

Scotfairs Antique and Collectors Fair
Location The Citadel Leisure Centre, Ayr Baths, South Beach Road, Ayr
Details See Scotfairs Antique and Collectors Fair 26 January

25–26

Carmarthen Antiques & Collectors Fair
Location United Counties Showground, Carmarthen
Details See Carmarthen Antiques & Collectors Fair 9–10 March

Gawsworth Antiques Fair
Contact Sandra Mather
☎ 01744 750606 Ⓕ 01744 750606
Ⓔ sandracca@aol.com
Ⓦ www.crafts@supanet.com
Location Gawsworth Hall, Macclesfield, off A536, Cheshire Ⓟ
Open 10am–5pm
Entrance fee £1.50
Details 75–85 stalls, refreshments

25–27

The Original Long Melford Fair
Location The Old School, Long Melford, Suffolk
Details See The Original Long Melford Fair 26–27 January

26

Antique and Collectors Fair
Location Canons Leisure Centre, Madeira Road, Mitcham, Surrey
Details See Antique and Collectors Fair 27 January

Antiques and Collectables Fair
Location Newman House, 85 St Stephen's Green, Dublin 2
Details See Antiques and Collectables Fair 20 January

Antiques & Collectors Fair
Location Burgess Hall, St Ives Recreation Centre, St Ives, Cambridgeshire
Details See Antiques & Collectors Fair 16 February

Athena Fayres
Location Community Centre, Mill Lane, Wickham, Hampshire
Details See Athena Fayres 27 January

Bloomsbury Postcard & Collectors Fair
Location Galleon Suite, Royal National Hotel, Bedford Way, London, WC1
Details See Bloomsbury Postcard and Collectors Fair 27 January

Burford Antiques Fair
Location Burford School, Burford, Oxfordshire
Details See Burford Antiques Fair 27 January

Chenevare Fairs
Location Hagley Community Centre, Worcester Road, West Hagley, Hereford & Worcester
Details See Chenevare Fairs 27 January

Mark Carter Militaria & Medal Fairs
Location Stratford Leisure Centre & Visitor Centre, Bridgfoot, Stratford upon Avon, Warwickshire
Details See Mark Carter Militaria & Medal Fairs 10 March

Midland Clock & Watch Fair
Location National Motorcycle Museum, M42 Exit 6, West Midlands
Details See Midland Clock & Watch Fair 27 January

R and S Western Fairs
Location Trenython Manor, Tywardreath, Nr Par, Cornwall
Details See R and S Western Fairs 27 January

The National Vintage Tackle Fair
Contact Bob Turner
☎ 01934 416492
Location Abbey Sports Stadium, Birmingham Road, Redditch, Worcestershire P
Est. 1999
Open 10am–4pm
Entrance fee £1
Details 50 stalls

Wessex Fairs
Location Combe Lodge, A368, Blagdon, Nr Church Hill, North Somerset
Details See Wessex Fairs 24 March

27

Pamela Robertson Antique and Collectors Fair
Location Northgate Arena, Victoria Road, Cheshire
Details See Pamela Robertson Antique and Collectors Fair 26 January

30

Antique & Collectors Fair
Location Nantwich Civic Hall, Market Street, Nantwich, Cheshire, M6 Jct 16
Details See Antique & Collectors Fair 31 January

JUNE

1

Antiques & Collectors Fair
Contact Ann Zierold
☎ 01824 750500 F 01824 750490
Location St George's Hall, Lime Street, Liverpool
Est. 1970
Open 9.30am–4pm
Entrance fee £1.50 Concessions £1.20
Details Up to 130 dealers

Devon County Antiques Fairs
Location Matford Centre in the Exeter Livestock Centre, Marsh Barton, Exeter
Details See Devon County Antiques Fairs 9 February

E W Services Antiques Fair
Location Buckingham Community Centre, Cornwalls Meadow Shopping Precinct, Buckingham
Details See E W Services Antiques Fair 2 February

Marcel Fairs
Location St Paul's Church Hall, Mill Hill, Ridgeway, London, NW7
Details See Marcel Fairs 2 February

Victoriana's Fairs
Location Walsall Town Hall, Walsall, West Midlands
Details See Victoriana's Fairs 2 February

1–3

Jubileee Petersfield Fair
Contact Caroline Penman
☎ 01444 482514 F 01444 482412
M 07774 850044
E info@penman-fairs.co.uk
W www.penman-fairs.co.uk
Location Festival Hall, Heath Road, Petersfield, Hants P
Open Sat Sun 11am–6pm Mon 11am–5pm
Entrance fee £3
Details Phone for details

The 10th Langley Park Spring Antiques Fair
Contact Liz Allport
☎ 01603 737631 F 01603 737631

Ⓜ 07747 843074
Ⓔ liz.allport@lineone.net
Ⓦ www.lomaxantiquesfairs.co.uk
Location Langley Park School, Loddon, Norfolk Ⓟ
Open 1st 2pm–7pm 2nd 10.30am–6pm 3rd 10.30am–5pm

2

Best of Fairs
Location The Village Hall, Copdock, 3 miles west of Ipswich
Details See Best of Fairs 3 February

Brocante
Location Kensington Town Hall, Hornton Street, London, W8
Details See Brocante 3 February

Cross Country Fairs Ltd
Location Copthorne Hotel, Effingham Park, West Sussex
Details See Cross Country Fairs Ltd 3 February

Devon County Antiques Fairs
Location Westland Sports and Social Club, Westbourne Close, Yeovil, Somerset
Details See Devon County Antiques Fairs 10 February

Hampstead Antique Collectors Fair
Location Hampstead Community Centre, High Street, Hampstead
Details See Hampstead Antique Collectors Fair 3 February

Harlequin Fairs
Location Centre for Epilepsy, Chalfont Common, Chalfont St Peter, Buckinghamshire
Details See Harlequin Fairs 3 February

Ipswich Antiques and Collectables Fair
Location Ipswich County Hotel (formerly Ipswich Moat House) Copdock, Ipswich, Suffolk
Details See Ipswich Antiques and Collectables Fair

Lechlade Antiques Fair
Location The New Memorial Hall, Burford Road, Lechlade, Gloucestershire
Details See Lechlade Antiques Fair 3 February

Malvern Antiques & Collectors Fair
Location Three Counties Showground, Malvern, Worcestershire
Details See Malvern Antiques & Collectors Fair 3 February

Scotfairs Antique and Collectors Fair
Location Meadowbank Stadium, London Road, Edinburgh
Details See Scotfairs Antique and Collectors Fair 3 February

2–3

Antiques and Collectables Fair
Location Royal Marine Hotel, Dun Laoghaire, Co Dublin
Details See Antiques and Collectables Fair 27 January

Wessex Fairs
Location Winter Gardens, Weston-Super-Mare, Somerset
Details See Wessex Fairs 24 February

3

Art Nouveau and Art Deco Fair
Location Woking Leisure Centre, Kingfield Road, Woking, Surrey
Details See Art Nouveau and Art Deco Fair 31 March

J and K Fairs
Location Lincolnshire Showground, Lincoln
Details See J and K Fairs 20 January

Magnum Antiques Fairs
Location River Park Leisure Centre, Gordon Road, Winchester, Hampshire
Details See Magnum Antiques Fairs 1 April

4

Antique Collectors Jamboree
Location Nantwich Civic Hall, Market Street, Nantwich, Cheshire, M6 Jct 16
Details See Antique Collectors Jamboree 1 April

Wembley Antiques & Collectors Fair
Location Hall 3, Wembley Exhibition Centre, Wembley, London
Details See Wembley Antiques & Collectors Fair 1 April

5

The Long Melford
Location Village Memorial Hall, Long Melford, Suffolk
Details See The Long Melford 6 February

6

Paraphernalia Fairs
Location Lyndhurst Community Centre, Lyndhurst, New Forest, Hampshire
Details See Paraphernalia Fairs 14 February

6–16

The Olympia Fine Art and Antiques Fair
☎ 020 7370 8186/8212
Ⓕ 020 7370 8221
Ⓔ olympia-antiques@eco.co.uk
Ⓦ www.olympia-antiques.com
Location Olympia, London Ⓟ
Est. 1971
Open 6th 11am–6pm 7th 11am–8pm 8th–9th 11am–7pm 10th closed 11th–14th 11am–8pm 15th 11am–7pm 16th 11am–5pm
Entrance fee £7 includes admission to ABA or Harvey Fair
Details 400 exhibitors, offering wide range of antiques and works of art, all items examined by experts

7–8

Antique Map Fair
Location The Bonnington Hotel, Southampton Row, midway between Holborn and Russell Square tube stations, London
Details See Antique Map Fair 10 March

7–9

Cheshire County Antiques Fair
Location Arley Hall, Nr Knutsford, Cheshire

Details See Cheshire County Antiques Fair 15–17 March

Galloway Antiques Fairs
☎ 01423 522122 Ⓕ 01423 522122
Ⓜ 07966 528725
Ⓔ susan@gallowayfairs.co.uk
Ⓦ www.gallowayfairs.co.uk
Location Seaford College, Nr Petworth, West Sussex Ⓟ
Open 10.30am–5pm
Entrance fee £3.50–£4.50

The International Antiques and Collectors Fair at RAF Swinderby
Location RAF Swinderby, A46 between Newark and Lincoln
Details See The International Antiques and Collectors Fair at RAF Swinderby 1–3 February

8

Athena Fayres
Location Lockswood Community Centre, Locks Heath Shopping Centre, Locks Heath, Nr Fareham, Hants
Details See Athena Fayres 9 February

Blackpool Winter Gardens Antiques and Collectors Fair
Location Blackpool Winter Gardens, Blackpool, Lancashire
Details See Blackpool Winter Gardens Antiques and Collectors Fair 26 January

Scotfairs Antique and Collectors Fair
Location Albert Halls, Dumbarton Road, Stirling
Details See Scotfairs Antique and Collectors Fair 2 February

8–9

Harpenden Antiques and Fine Art Fair
Location Rothamsted Conference Centre, on A1081 Harpenden–St Albans road, Hertfordshire
Details See Harpenden Antiques and Fine Art Fair 9–10 February

9

Antique and Collectors Fair
Location Woking Leisure Centre, Kingfield Road, Woking, Surrey
Details See Antique and Collectors Fair 10 February

Aquarius Fairs
Location The Harlington Centre, High Street, Fleet, Hampshire
Details See Aquarius Fairs 9 February

Biggleswade Antiques Fairs
Location Kimbolton Castle, Huntingdon, Cambridgeshire
Details See Biggleswade Antiques Fairs 7 April

Chenevare Fairs
Location Kinver Leisure Centre, Enville Road, Kinver, Stourbridge, West Midlands
Details See Chenevare Fairs 10 February

Clock & Watch Dealers Fair
Location The Grove Leisure Centre, London Road, Balderton, Nr Newark
Details See Clock & Watch Dealers Fair 3 February

Crispin Fairs
Location Victoria Hall, Hartley Wintney, Hampshire
Details See Crispin Fairs 10 February

Lostwithiel Antiques Fair
Location Community Centre, Lostwithiel, Cornwall
Details See Lostwithiel Antiques Fair 10 February

Midas Antique Fair
Location The Bellhouse Hotel, Oxford Road (A40), Beaconsfield, Bucks
Details See Midas Antique Fair 10 February

Pennyfarthing Fayres
Location Potters Bar
Details See Pennyfarthing Fayres 10 February

Royal Horticultural Hall
Location Royal Horticultural Hall, Lawrence Hall, Greycoat Street, London SW1
Details See Royal Horticultural Hall 10 February

10–11

Newark International Antiques & Collectors Fair
Location Newark & Notts Showground, Newark, Nottinghamshire
Details See Newark International Antiques & Collectors Fair 4–5 February

12

Marks Tey
Location Parish Hall, Marks Tey, Essex
Details See Marks Tey 13 February

12–18

The Grosvenor House Art & Antiques Fair
Contact Nicola Winwood
☎ 020 7399 8100 Ⓕ 020 7495 8747
Ⓔ info@grosvenor-antiquesfair.co.uk
Ⓦ www.grosvenor-antiquesfair.co.uk
Location Le Méridien Grosvenor House, Park Lane, London, W1K 7TN Ⓟ
Est. 1934
Open 12th 14th 11am–8pm 13th 15th–18th 11am–6pm
Entrance fee Single £16 Double £27
Details 90 of the world's leading art and antique dealers

14–16

Galloway Antiques Fairs
☎ 01423 522122 Ⓕ 01423 522122
Ⓜ 07966 528725
Ⓔ susan@gallowayfairs.co.uk
Ⓦ www.gallowayfairs.co.uk
Location Duncombe Park, Helmsely, North Yorkshire Ⓟ
Open 10.30am–5pm
Entrance fee £3.50–£4.50

Stafford Bingley Hall
Location The Bingley Hall, County Showground
Details See Stafford Bingley Hall 8–10 February

14–17

International Ceramics Fair & Seminar
Contact Mr B Haughton
☎ 020 7734 5491 Ⓕ 020 7494 4604
Ⓔ info@haughton.com
Ⓦ www.haughton.com

Location Park Lane Hotel Ballroom, Piccadilliy, London, W1 🅿
Est. 1982
Open 11am–7pm
Entrance fee £10
Details 45 dealers selling ceramics and glass from antiquities to contemporary studio wares,15 lectures and loan exhibition

15

Chelsea Town Hall
Location Chelsea Town Hall, King's Road, Chelsea, London SW3
Details See Chelsea Town Hall 19 January

Commonwealth Institute Coin Fair
Location The Commonwealth Institute, Kensington High Street, London, W8
Details See Commonwealth Institute Coin Fair 19 January

Devon County Antiques Fairs
☎ 01363 82571 Ⓕ 01363 82312
Ⓔ dcaf@antiques-fairs.com
Ⓦ www.antiques-fairs.com
Location Salisbury Leisure Centre, The Butts, Hulse Road, Salisbury, Wiltshire 🅿
Open 9am–4.30pm
Entrance fee 9–10am £2 10am–4.30pm £1.50
Details 140 stands, snack bar, good disabled access

15–16

Buxton Antique and Collectors Fair
Location Pavilion Gardens, Buxton, Derbyshire
Details See Buxton Antique and Collectors Fair 26–27 January

The London Antique Textiles Fair
Contact Paola Francia-Gardiner
☎ 020 8543 5075 Ⓕ 020 8404 6262
Location Hammersmith Town Hall, King Street, London, W6 🅿
Open 10am–5pm
Entrance fee Sat £5 Sun £3.50

16

Antiques and Collectables Fair
Location Newman House, 85 St Stephen's Green, Dublin 2
Details See Antiques and Collectables Fair 20 January

Athena Fayres
Location The Village Hall, Minstead, Nr Lyndhurst, about a mile from the end of the M27
Details See Athena Fayres 20 January

Battersea Town Hall Art Deco Fair
Location Battersea Town Hall
Details See Battersea Town Hall Art Deco Fair February 17

Biggleswade Antiques Fairs
Location The Weatherley Centre, Eagle Farm Road, Biggleswade, Bedfordshire
Details See Biggleswade Antiques Fairs 20 January

Monmouthshire County Antiques & Collectors Fair
Location The Market Hall (next to the Town Hall), Abergavenny, Monmouthshire
Details See Monmouthshire County Antiques & Collectors Fair 20 January

Newmarket Antiques & Collectors Fair
Location Millennium Grandstand, Rowley Mile Racecourse, Newmarket, Suffolk
Details See Newmarket Antiques & Collectors Fair 17 February

Scotfairs Antique and Collectors Fair
Location Moir Hall, Mitchell Library, Granville Street, Glasgow
Details See Scotfairs Antique and Collectors Fair 20 January

18

The Sandown Park Antique Fair
Location The Exhibition Centre, Sandown Park Racecourse, Esher, Surrey
Details See Sandown Park Antique Fair 19 February

19

The Big Brum
Location St Martins Market (The Rag), Edgbaston Street, Birmingham
Details See The Big Brum 30 January

20–21

Buxton Antique and Collectors Fair
Location Pavilion Gardens, Buxton, Derbyshire
Details See Buxton Antique and Collectors Fair 26–27 January

21–23

Galloway Antiques Fairs
☎ 01423 522122 Ⓕ 01423 522122
Ⓜ 07966 528725
Ⓔ susan@gallowayfairs.co.uk
Ⓦ www.gallowayfairs.co.uk
Location Blair Castle, Blair Atholl, Pitlochry, Perthshire 🅿
Open 10.30am–5pm
Entrance fee £3.50–£4.50

22

Browser's Antique & Collectors Fair
Location Village Hall, Station Road, Pangbourne, Berkshire (on A329 off A4, M4 Jct 12/13)
Details See Browser's Antique & Collectors Fair 26 January

Scotfairs Antique and Collectors Fair
Location The Citadel Leisure Centre, Ayr Baths, South Beach Road, Ayr
Details See Scotfairs Antique and Collectors Fair 26 January

23

Antique and Collectors Fair
Location Canons Leisure Centre, Madeira Road, Mitcham, Surrey
Details See Antique and Collectors Fair 27 January

Biggleswade Antiques Fairs
Location The Addison Centre, Kempston, Bedford
Details See Biggleswade Antiques Fairs 27 January

Bloomsbury Postcard & Collectors Fair
Location Galleon Suite, Royal National Hotel, Bedford Way, London, WC1
Details See Bloomsbury Postcard and Collectors Fair 27 January

Brunel Clock & Watch Fair
Location Brunel University, Kingston Lane, Uxbridge, Middlesex
Details See Brunel Clock & Watch Fair 17 February

Burford Antiques Fair
Location Burford School, Burford, Oxfordshire
Details See Burford Antiques Fair 27 January

Mark Carter Militaria & Medal Fairs
Location The Princes Hall, Princes Way, Aldershot, Hampshire
Details See Mark Carter Militaria & Medal Fairs 20 January

Wessex Fairs
Location Winter Gardens, Weston-Super-Mare, Somerset
Details See Wessex Fairs 24 February

27

Antique & Collectors Fair
Location Nantwich Civic Hall, Market Street, Nantwich, Cheshire, M6 Jct 16
Details See Antique & Collectors Fair 31 January

28–30

Shepton Mallet Antiques & Collectors Fair
Location Royal Bath and West Showground, Shepton Mallett, Somerset
Details See Shepton Mallet Antiques & Collectors Fair 18–20 January

29

Antiques Fair
Location Castle Hall, Hertford, Hertfordshire
Details See Antiques Fair 19 January

Pamela Robertson Antique and Collectors Fair
Location Northgate Arena, Victoria Road, Cheshire
Details See Pamela Robertson Antique and Collectors Fair 26 January

Southport Antiques and Collectors Fair
Location Southport Floral Hall, the Promenade, Southport, Merseyside
Details See Southport Antiques and Collectors Fair 16 February

29–30

Saffron Walden Antiques and Fine Art Fair
Location Saffron Walden County High School, Audley End Road, Saffron Walden, Essex
Details See Saffron Walden Antiques and Fine Art Fair 2–3 February

The Original Long Melford Fair
Location The Old School, Long Melford, Suffolk
Details See The Original Long Melford Fair 26–27 January

West Midlands Antique Fairs
Location Prestwood Complex, Stafford County Showground
Details See West Midlands Antique Fairs 23–24 February

30

Antique & Collectors Fair
Location Berkhampstead Sports Centre, Langley Meadow, Douglas Gardens, Berkhampstead, Hertfordshire
Details See Antique and Collectors Fair 31 March

Antiques and Collectables Fair
Location Newman House, 85 St Stephen's Green, Dublin 2
Details See Antiques and Collectables Fair 20 January

Athena Fayres
Location Community Centre, Mill Lane, Wickham, Hampshire
Details See Athena Fayres 27 January

Chenevare Fairs
Location Hagley Community Centre, Worcester Road, West Hagley, Hereford & Worcester
Details See Chenevare Fairs 27 January

R and S Western Fairs
Location Trenython Manor, Tywardreath, Nr Par, Cornwall
Details See R and S Western Fairs 27 January

The London Textiles, Vintage Fashion and Accessories Fair
Location Hammersmith Town Hall, King Street, London, W6
Details See The London Textiles, Vintage Fashion and Accessories Fair 20 January

Wessex Fairs
Location Combe Lodge, A368, Blagdon, Nr Church Hill, North Somerset
Details See Wessex Fairs 24 March

JULY

3

The Long Melford
Location Village Memorial Hall, Long Melford, Suffolk
Details See The Long Melford 6 February

4

Paraphernalia Fairs
Location Lyndhurst Community Centre, Lyndhurst, New Forest, Hampshire
Details See Paraphernalia Fairs 14 February

6

Antiques & Collectors Fair
Location St George's Hall, Lime Street, Liverpool
Details See Antiques & Collectors Fair 1 June

E W Services Antiques Fair
Location Buckingham Community Centre, Cornwalls Meadow Shopping Precinct, Buckingham
Details See E W Services Antiques Fair 2 February

Marcel Fairs
Location St Paul's Church Hall, Mill Hill, Ridgeway, London, NW7
Details See Marcel Fairs 2 February

Victoriana's Fairs
Location Walsall Town Hall, Walsall, West Midlands
Details See Victoriana's Fairs 2 February

6–7

Devon County Antiques Fairs
Location Westpoint Exhibition Centre, Clyst St Mary, Exeter, Devon
Details See Devon County Antiques Fair 2–3 February

7

Best of Fairs
Location The Village Hall, Copdock, 3 miles west of Ipswich
Details See Best of Fairs 3 February

Cross Country Fairs Ltd
Location Copthorne Hotel, Effingham Park, West Sussex
Details See Cross Country Fairs Ltd 3 February

Hampstead Antique Collectors Fair
Location Hampstead Community Centre, High Street, Hampstead
Details See Hampstead Antique Collectors Fair 3 February

Harlequin Fairs
Location Centre for Epilepsy, Chalfont Common, Chalfont St Peter, Buckinghamshire
Details See Harlequin Fairs 3 February

Ipswich Antiques and Collectables Fair
Location Ipswich County Hotel (formerly Ipswich Moat House) Copdock, Ipswich, Suffolk
Details See Ipswich Antiques and Collectables Fair

J and K Fairs
Location Lincolnshire Showground, Lincoln
Details See J and K Fairs 20 January

Lechlade Antiques Fair
Location The New Memorial Hall, Burford Road, Lechlade, Gloucestershire
Details See Lechlade Antiques Fair 3 February

Scotfairs Antique and Collectors Fair
Location Meadowbank Stadium, London Road, Edinburgh
Details See Scotfairs Antique and Collectors Fair 3 February

10

Marks Tey
Location Parish Hall, Marks Tey, Essex
Details See Marks Tey 13 February

11–14

Snape
Contact Graham Turner
☎ 01473 658224
Ⓔ ggt@btinternet.com
Location The Village Hall, Snape, Suffolk Ⓟ
Open Trade 9.30am Public 10am–4.30pm
Details 1930 date-line

12–14

The 33rd Cheshire Summer Antiques and Fine Art Fair
☎ 01277 214677 Ⓕ 01277 214550
Ⓔ admin@baileyfairs.co.uk
Ⓦ www.baileyfairs.co.uk
Location Tatton Park, Knutsford Ⓟ
Open Fri 1–6pm Sat 11am–6pm Sun 11am–5pm
Entrance fee £5
Details 40 dealers, vetted and date-lined

13

Aquarius Fairs
Location The Harlington Centre, High Street, Fleet, Hampshire
Details See Aquarius Fairs 9 February

Athena Fayres
Location Lockswood Community Centre, Locks Heath Shopping Centre, Locks Heath, Nr Fareham, Hants
Details See Athena Fayres 9 February

Chelsea Town Hall
Location Chelsea Town Hall, King's Road, Chelsea, London SW3
Details See Chelsea Town Hall 19 January

14

Antique and Collectors Fair
Location Woking Leisure Centre, Kingfield Road, Woking, Surrey
Details See Antique and Collectors Fair 10 February

Antique Map Fair
Location The Bonnington Hotel, Southampton Row, midway between Holborn and Russell Square tube stations, London
Details See Antique Map Fair 10 March

Antiques and Collectables Fair
Location Newman House, 85 St Stephen's Green, Dublin 2
Details See Antiques and Collectables Fair 20 January

Athena Fayres
Location The Village Hall, Minstead, Nr Lyndhurst, about a mile from the end of the M27
Details See Athena Fayres 20 January

Chenevare Fairs
Location Kinver Leisure Centre, Enville Road, Kinver, Stourbridge, West Midlands
Details See Chenevare Fairs 10 February

Lostwithiel Antiques Fair
Location Community Centre, Lostwithiel, Cornwall
Details See Lostwithiel Antiques Fair 10 February

Malvern Antiques & Collectors Fair
Location Three Counties Showground, Malvern, Worcestershire
Details See Malvern Antiques & Collectors Fair 3 February

FAIRS

JULY

Midas Antique Fair
Location The Bellhouse Hotel, Oxford Road (A40), Beaconsfield, Bucks
Details See Midas Antique Fair 10 February

Royal Horticultural Hall
Location Royal Horticultural Hall, Lawrence Hall, Greycoat Street, London SW1
Details See Royal Horticultural Hall 10 February

Wessex Fairs
Location Combe Lodge, A368, Blagdon, Nr Church Hill, North Somerset
Details See Wessex Fairs 24 March

16–17

Ardingly International Antiques & Collectors Fair
Location South of England Centre, Ardingly, West Sussex
Details See Ardingly International Antiques & Collectors Fair 26–27 February

18–21

35th Annual Snape Antiques Fair
Contact Anne Harwood
☎ 01249 661111 Ⓕ 01249 661111
Ⓔ enquiries@cooperantiquesfairs.co.uk
Ⓦ www.cooperantiquesfairs.co.uk
Location Snape, Suffolk
Open Thurs 11am–8pm Fri Sat 11am–6pm Sun 11am–5pm
Entrance fee £4 Children under 16 and OAPs free

20

Antiques Fair
Location Castle Hall, Hertford, Hertfordshire
Details See Antiques Fair 19 January

Commonwealth Institute Coin Fair
Location The Commonwealth Institute, Kensington High Street, London, W8
Details See Commonwealth Institute Coin Fair 19 January

Scotfairs Antique and Collectors Fair
Location The Citadel Leisure Centre, Ayr Baths, South Beach Road, Ayr
Details See Scotfairs Antique and Collectors Fair 26 January

20–21

Carmarthen Antiques & Collectors Fair
Location United Counties Showground, Carmarthen
Details See Carmarthen Antiques & Collectors Fair 9–10 March

Detling International Antiques & Collectors Fair
Location Kent County Showground, Detling, Nr Maidstone, Kent
Details See Detling International Antiques & Collectors Fair 26–27 January

Little Easton Manor
Location Little Easton Manor, Nr Great Dunmow, Essex
Details See Little Easton Manor 30–31 March

21

Biggleswade Antiques Fairs
Location The Weatherley Centre, Eagle Farm Road, Biggleswade, Bedfordshire
Details See Biggleswade Antiques Fairs 20 January

Clock & Watch Dealers Fair
Location Haydock Park racecourse, M6 Jct 23
Details See Clock & Watch Dealers Fair 3 March

Monmouthshire County Antiques & Collectors Fair
Location The Market Hall (next to the Town Hall), Abergavenny, Monmouthshire
Details See Monmouthshire County Antiques & Collectors Fair 20 January

Scotfairs Antique and Collectors Fair
Location Moir Hall, Mitchell Library, Granville Street, Glasgow
Details See Scotfairs Antique and Collectors Fair 20 January

24

The Big Brum
Location St Martins Market (The Rag), Edgbaston Street, Birmingham
Details See The Big Brum 30 January

25

Antique & Collectors Fair
Location Nantwich Civic Hall, Market Street, Nantwich, Cheshire, M6 Jct 16
Details See Antique & Collectors Fair 31 January

26–28

Galloway Antiques Fairs
Location Cranleigh School, Cranleigh, Surrey
Details See Galloway Antiques Fairs 29 March

27

Browser's Antique & Collectors Fair
Location Village Hall, Station Road, Pangbourne, Berkshire (on A329 off A4, M4 Jct 12/13)
Details See Browser's Antique & Collectors Fair 26 January

Pamela Robertson Antique and Collectors Fair
Location Northgate Arena, Victoria Road, Cheshire
Details See Pamela Robertson Antique and Collectors Fair 26 January

Scotfairs Antique and Collectors Fair
Location Albert Halls, Dumbarton Road, Stirling
Details See Scotfairs Antique and Collectors Fair 2 February

27–28

The Original Long Melford Fair
Location The Old School, Long Melford, Suffolk
Details See The Original Long Melford Fair 26–27 January

28

Antique and Collectors Fair
Location Canons Leisure Centre, Madeira Road, Mitcham, Surrey
Details See Antique and Collectors Fair 27 January

Antiques and Collectables Fair
Location Newman House, 85 St Stephen's Green, Dublin 2
Details See Antiques and Collectables Fair 20 January

Athena Fayres
Location Community Centre, Mill Lane, Wickham, Hampshire
Details See Athena Fayres 27 January

Bloomsbury Postcard & Collectors Fair
Location Galleon Suite, Royal National Hotel, Bedford Way, London, WC1
Details See Bloomsbury Postcard and Collectors Fair 27 January

Burford Antiques Fair
Location Burford School, Burford, Oxfordshire
Details See Burford Antiques Fair 27 January

Chenevare Fairs
Location Hagley Community Centre, Worcester Road, West Hagley, Hereford & Worcester
Details See Chenevare Fairs 27 January

R and S Western Fairs
Location Trenython Manor, Tywardreath, Nr Par, Cornwall
Details See R and S Western Fairs 27 January

Wessex Fairs
Location Winter Gardens, Weston-Super-Mare, Somerset
Details See Wessex Fairs 24 February

AUGUST

1

Paraphernalia Fairs
Location Lyndhurst Community Centre, Lyndhurst, New Forest, Hampshire
Details See Paraphernalia Fairs 14 February

3

Devon County Antiques Fairs
Location Matford Centre in the Exeter Livestock Centre, Marsh Barton, Exeter
Details See Devon County Antiques Fairs 9 February

E W Services Antiques Fair
Location Buckingham Community Centre, Cornwalls Meadow Shopping Precinct, Buckingham
Details See E W Services Antiques Fair 2 February

Marcel Fairs
Location St Paul's Church Hall, Mill Hill, Ridgeway, London, NW7
Details See Marcel Fairs 2 February

Victoriana's Fairs
Location Walsall Town Hall, Walsall, West Midlands
Details See Victoriana's Fairs 2 February

4

Ardingly International Antiques & Collectors Fair
Contact Caroline Cleary
☎ 01636 702326 Ⓕ 01636 707923
Ⓦ www.dmgantiquefairs.com
Location South of England Centre, Ardingly, West Sussex 🅿
Est. 1997
Open 8am–4pm
Entrance fee 8am £10 10am £3
Details Up to 350 exhibitors

Best of Fairs
Location The Village Hall, Copdock, 3 miles west of Ipswich
Details See Best of Fairs 3 February

Cross Country Fairs Ltd
Location Copthorne Hotel, Effingham Park, West Sussex
Details See Cross Country Fairs Ltd 3 February

Devon County Antiques Fairs
Location Westland Sports and Social Club, Westbourne Close, Yeovil, Somerset
Details See Devon County Antiques Fairs 10 February

Hampstead Antique Collectors Fair
Location Hampstead Community Centre, High Street, Hampstead
Details See Hampstead Antique Collectors Fair 3 February

Harlequin Fairs
Location Centre for Epilepsy, Chalfont Common, Chalfont St Peter, Buckinghamshire
Details See Harlequin Fairs 3 February

J and K Fairs
Location Lincolnshire Showground, Lincoln
Details See J and K Fairs 20 January

Lechlade Antiques Fair
Location The New Memorial Hall, Burford Road, Lechlade, Gloucestershire
Details See Lechlade Antiques Fair 3 February

Magnum Antiques Fairs
Location Midhurst, The Grange Centre, Bepton Road
Details 135 stands

Malvern Antiques & Collectors Fair
Location Three Counties Showground, Malvern, Worcestershire
Details See Malvern Antiques & Collectors Fair 3 February

5

Antiques and Collectables Fair
Location Royal Marine Hotel, Dun Laoghaire, Co Dublin
Details See Antiques and Collectables Fair 27 January

7

The Long Melford
Location Village Memorial Hall, Long Melford, Suffolk
Details See The Long Melford 6 February

AUGUST

8–11

Antiques for Everyone

E antiques@necgroup.co.uk
W www.antiquesforeveryone.co.uk
Location NEC Birmingham, Hall 5 P
Est. 1985
Open Weekdays 11am–8pm weekends11am–6pm
Entrance fee 8th £7 9th–11th £6
Details Over 600 dealers

10

Aquarius Fairs

Location The Harlington Centre, High Street, Fleet, Hampshire
Details See Aquarius Fairs 9 February

11

Antique and Collectors Fair

Location Woking Leisure Centre, Kingfield Road, Woking, Surrey
Details See Antique and Collectors Fair 10 February

Antique Map Fair

Location The Bonnington Hotel, Southampton Row, midway between Holborn and Russell Square tube stations, London
Details See Antique Map Fair 10 March

Antiques and Collectables Fair

Location Newman House, 85 St Stephen's Green, Dublin 2
Details See Antiques and Collectables Fair 20 January

Chenevare Fairs

Location Kinver Leisure Centre, Enville Road, Kinver, Stourbridge, West Midlands
Details See Chenevare Fairs 10 February

Lostwithiel Antiques Fair

Location Community Centre, Lostwithiel, Cornwall
Details See Lostwithiel Antiques Fair 10 February

Mark Carter Militaria & Medal Fairs

Location Yate Leisure Centre, Kennedy Way, Yate, Bristol
Details See Mark Carter Militaria & Medal Fairs 3 February

Midas Antique Fair

Location The Bellhouse Hotel, Oxford Road (A40), Beaconsfield, Bucks
Details See Midas Antique Fair 10 February

Newmarket Antiques & Collectors Fair

Location Millennium Grandstand, Rowley Mile Racecourse, Newmarket, Suffolk
Details See Newmarket Antiques & Collectors Fair 17 February

Scotfairs Antique and Collectors Fair

Location Meadowbank Stadium, London Road, Edinburgh
Details See Scotfairs Antique and Collectors Fair 3 February

14

Evening Antiques/Collectors Fairs

Location St Martins Market (The Rag), Edgbaston Street, Birmingham
Details See Evening Antiques/Collectors Fairs 20 February

Marks Tey

Location Parish Hall, Marks Tey, Essex
Details See Marks Tey 13 February

16–18

South Cotswolds Antiques Fair

Location Westonbirt School, Nr Tetbury, Gloucestershire
Details See South Cotswolds Antiques Fair 5 April

Stafford Bingley Hall

Location The Bingley Hall, County Showground
Details See Stafford Bingley Hall 8–10 February

The International Antiques and Collectors Fair at RAF Swinderby

Location RAF Swinderby, A46 between Newark and Lincoln
Details See The International Antiques and Collectors Fair at RAF Swinderby 1–3 February

17

Commonwealth Institute Coin Fair

Location The Commonwealth Institute, Kensington High Street, London, W8
Details See Commonwealth Institute Coin Fair 19 January

18

Athena Fayres

Location The Village Hall, Minstead, Nr Lyndhurst, about a mile from the end of the M27
Details See Athena Fayres 20 January

Mark Carter Militaria & Medal Fairs

Location The Princes Hall, Princes Way, Aldershot, Hampshire
Details See Mark Carter Militaria & Medal Fairs 20 January

Midland Clock & Watch Fair

Location National Motorcycle Museum, M42 Exit 6, West Midlands
Details See Midland Clock & Watch Fair 27 January

Monmouthshire County Antiques & Collectors Fair

Location The Market Hall (next to the Town Hall), Abergavenny, Monmouthshire
Details See Monmouthshire County Antiques & Collectors Fair 20 January

Scotfairs Antique and Collectors Fair

Location Moir Hall, Mitchell Library, Granville Street, Glasgow
Details See Scotfairs Antique and Collectors Fair 20 January

19–20

Newark International Antiques & Collectors Fair

Location Newark & Notts Showground, Newark
Details See Newark International Antiques & Collectors Fair 4–5 February

23–25

Antiques for Everyone
E antiques@necgroup.co.uk
W www.antiquesforeveryone.co.uk
Location SECC, Glasgow P
Est. 1985
Open Weekdays 11am–8pm weekends 11am–6pm
Entrance fee £5
Details Approximately 200 dealers, pre-1940 date-line in section 1 excluding modern art

23–26

Galloway Antiques Fairs
☎ 01423 522122 F 01423 522122
M 07966 528725
E susan@gallowayfairs.co.uk
W www.gallowayfairs.co.uk
Location Rookesbury Park, Wickham, Nr Fareham, Hampshire P
Open 10.30am–5pm
Entrance fee £3.50–£4.50

24

Antiques Fair
Location Castle Hall, Hertford, Hertfordshire
Details See Antiques Fair 19 January

Browser's Antique & Collectors Fair
Location Village Hall, Station Road, Pangbourne, Berkshire (on A329 off A4, M4 Jct 12/13)
Details See Browser's Antique & Collectors Fair 26 January

Scotfairs Antique and Collectors Fair
Location The Citadel Leisure Centre, Ayr Baths, South Beach Road, Ayr
Details See Scotfairs Antique and Collectors Fair 26 January

24–26

Beckett Antique Fairs
Location Doncaster Race Exhibition Centre, Doncaster
Details See Beckett Antique Fairs 16–17 February

Buxton Antique and Collectors Fair
Location Pavilion Gardens, Buxton, Derbyshire
Details See Buxton Antique and Collectors Fair 26–27 January

Framlingham College
Contact Graham Turner
☎ 01473 658224
E ggt@btinternet.com
Location Framlingham College, Framlingham, Suffolk P
Open Trade 9.30am Public 10am–4.30pm
Details 1930 date-line

The Original Long Melford Fair
Location The Old School, Long Melford, Suffolk
Details See The Original Long Melford Fair 26–27 January

25

Antique and Collectors Fair
Location Canons Leisure Centre, Madeira Road, Mitcham, Surrey
Details See Antique and Collectors Fair 27 January

Antiques and Collectables Fair
Location Newman House, 85 St Stephen's Green, Dublin 2
Details See Antiques and Collectables Fair 20 January

Athena Fayres
Location Community Centre, Mill Lane, Wickham, Hampshire
Details See Athena Fayres 27 January

Bloomsbury Postcard & Collectors Fair
Location Galleon Suite, Royal National Hotel, Bedford Way, London, WC1
Details See Bloomsbury Postcard and Collectors Fair 27 January

Chenevare Fairs
Location Hagley Community Centre, Worcester Road, West Hagley, Hereford & Worcester
Details See Chenevare Fairs 27 January

R and S Western Fairs
Location Trenython Manor, Tywardreath, Nr Par, Cornwall
Details See R and S Western Fairs 27 January

25–26

Antiques & Collectors Fair
Location Burgess Hall, St Ives Recreation Centre, St Ives, Cambridgeshire
Details See Antiques & Collectors Fair 16–17 February

Jade Fairs
Location Lowther Pavilion, The Promenade, Lytham St Anne's, Lancashire
Details See Jade Fairs 2 February

The Beaconsfield Fine Art and Antiques Fair
Location The Bellhouse Hotel, Oxford Road (A40), Beaconsfield, Bucks
Details See The Beaconsfield Fine Art and Antiques Fair 31–1 March

Wessex Fairs
Location Winter Gardens, Weston-Super-Mare
Details See Wessex Fairs 24 February

26

13th Annual August Antique and Fine Art Fair
☎ 028 9181 5710 F 028 9182 0637
E info@castleantiques.co.uk
W www.castleantiques.co.uk
Location The Causeway Coast Hotel, Portrush P
Open 11am–7pm

Antique Collectors Jamboree
Location Nantwich Civic Hall, Market Street, Nantwich, Cheshire, M6 Jct 16
Details See Antique Collectors Jamboree 1 April

Art Nouveau and Art Deco Fair
Location Woking Leisure Centre, Kingfield Road, Woking, Surrey
Details See Art Nouveau and Art Deco Fair 31 March

Magnum Antiques Fairs
Location Winchester, River Park Leisure Centre, Gordon Road
Details See Magnum Antiques Fairs 1 April

Pamela Robertson Antique and Collectors Fair
Location Northgate Arena, Victoria Road, Cheshire
Details See Pamela Robertson Antique and Collectors Fair 26 January

Wembley Antiques & Collectors Fair
Location Hall 3, Wembley Exhibition Centre, Wembley, London
Details See Wembley Antiques & Collectors Fair 1 April

28

Newbury Racecourse
Location Newbury Racecourse, Newbury, Berkshire
Details See Newbury Racecourse February 13

29

Antique & Collectors Fair
Location Nantwich Civic Hall, Market Street, Nantwich, Cheshire, M6 Jct 16
Details See Antique & Collectors Fair 31 January

30–1 Sept

Galloway Antiques Fairs
Location Naworth Castle, Brampton, Cumbria
Details See Galloway Antiques Fairs 22–24 March

31

Chelsea Town Hall
Location Chelsea Town Hall, King's Road, Chelsea, London SW3
Details See Chelsea Town Hall 19 January

Scotfairs Antique and Collectors Fair
Location Albert Halls, Dumbarton Road, Stirling
Details See Scotfairs Antique and Collectors Fair 2 February

31–1 Sept

Devon County Antiques Fairs
Location Westpoint Exhibition Centre, Clyst St Mary, Exeter
Details See Devon County Antiques Fair 2–3 February

Gawsworth Antiques Fair
Location Gawsworth Hall, Macclesfield, off A536, Cheshire
Details See Gawsworth Antiques Fair 25–26 May

The Long Melford
Location Village Memorial Hall, Long Melford, Suffolk
Details See The Long Melford 26–27 January

SEPTEMBER

1

Antiques and Collectables Fair
Location Newman House, 85 St Stephen's Green, Dublin 2
Details See Antiques and Collectables Fair 20 January

Battersea Town Hall Art Deco Fair
Location Battersea Town Hall
Details See Battersea Town Hall Art Deco Fair 17 February

Best of Fairs
Location The Village Hall, Copdock, 3 miles west of Ipswich
Details See Best of Fairs 3 February

Bob Evans Fairs
Location Sports Connexion, Ryton on Dunsmore, Coventry
Details See Bob Evans Fairs 10 February

Cross Country Fairs Ltd
Location Copthorne Hotel, Effingham Park, West Sussex
Details See Cross Country Fairs Ltd 3 February

Hampstead Antique Collectors Fair
Location Hampstead Community Centre, High Street, Hampstead
Details See Hampstead Antique Collectors Fair 3 February

Harlequin Fairs
Location Centre for Epilepsy, Chalfont Common, Chalfont St Peter, Buckinghamshire
Details See Harlequin Fairs 3 February

Ipswich Antiques and Collectables Fair
Location Ipswich County Hotel (formerly Ipswich Moat House) Copdock, Ipswich, Suffolk
Details See Ipswich Antiques and Collectables Fair

J and K Fairs
Location Lincolnshire Showground, Lincoln
Details See J and K Fairs 20 January

Lechlade Antiques Fair
Location The New Memorial Hall, Burford Road, Lechlade, Gloucestershire
Details See Lechlade Antiques Fair 3 February

Malvern Antiques & Collectors Fair
Location Three Counties Showground, Malvern, Worcestershire
Details See Malvern Antiques & Collectors Fair 3 February

Scotfairs Antique and Collectors Fair
Location Meadowbank Stadium, London Road, Edinburgh
Details See Scotfairs Antique and Collectors Fair 3 February

4

The Long Melford
Location Village Memorial Hall, Long Melford, Suffolk
Details See The Long Melford 6 February

5

Paraphernalia Fairs
Location Lyndhurst Community Centre, Lyndhurst, New Forest, Hampshire
Details See Paraphernalia Fairs 14 February

5–8

The 33rd Cheshire Autumn Antiques and Fine Art Fair
☎ 01277 214677 Ⓕ 01277 214550
Ⓔ admin@baileyfairs.co.uk
Ⓦ www.baileyfairs.co.uk

Location Tatton Park, Knutsford P
Open Thurs 2–6pm Fri Sat 11am–6pm Sun 11am–5pm
Entrance fee £5
Details 50 dealers, vetted and date-lined

6–8

Oak and Country Antiques Fair
Contact Anne Harwood
☎ 01249 661111 F 01249 661111
E enquiries@cooperantiquesfairs.co.uk
W www.cooperantiquesfairs.co.uk
Location Kentwell Hall, Long Melford, Suffolk
Open Fri noon–5pm Sat Sun 11am–5pm
Entrance fee £3.50 Children under 16 and OAPs free

Penmans Petersfield Antiques Fair
Contact Caroline Penman
☎ 01444 482514 F 01444 482412
M 07774 850044
E info@penman-fairs.co.uk
W www.penman-fairs.co.uk
Location Festival Hall, Heath Road, Petersfield, Hants P
Open Thurs noon–8pm Fri Sat 11am–6pm Sun 11am–5pm
Details 43 stands of vetted traditional and decorative antiques

7

Antiques & Collectors Fair
Location St George's Hall, Lime Street, Liverpool
Details See Antiques & Collectors Fair 1 June

Chelsea Town Hall
Location Chelsea Town Hall, King's Road, Chelsea, London SW3
Details See Chelsea Town Hall 19 January

E W Services Antiques Fair
Location Buckingham Community Centre, Cornwalls Meadow Shopping Precinct, Buckingham
Details See E W Services Antiques Fair 2 February

Marcel Fairs
Location St Paul's Church Hall, Mill Hill, Ridgeway, London, NW7
Details See Marcel Fairs 2 February

Victoriana's Fairs
Location Walsall Town Hall, Walsall, West Midlands
Details See Victoriana's Fairs 2 February

7–8

Bob Evans Fairs
Location International Centre, St Quentin Gate, Telford
Details See Bob Evans Fairs 16–17 February

Cardiff Antiques & Collectors Fair
Location Cardiff Bowls Club, Sophia Gardens
Details See Cardiff Antiques & Collectors Fair 27–28 April

8

Antique and Collectors Fair
Location Woking Leisure Centre, Kingfield Road, Woking, Surrey
Details See Antique and Collectors Fair 10 February

Antique Costume & Textile Fair
Contact Margaret Bolger
☎ 0151 6394920
E artfairs@artizania.co.uk
W www.artizania.co.uk
Location Armitage Centre, Sallowfield, Manchester
Est. 1996
Open Trade 8am Public 10am–5.30pm
Entrance fee 8am–2pm £3 2–5.30pm £2
Details 130+ stalls, 1960 date-line

Antique Map Fair
Location The Bonnington Hotel, Southampton Row, midway between Holborn and Russell Square tube stations, London
Details See Antique Map Fair 10 March

Brunel Clock & Watch Fair
Location Brunel University, Kingston Lane, Uxbridge, Middlesex
Details See Brunel Clock & Watch Fair 17 February

Chenevare Fairs
Location Kinver Leisure Centre, Enville Road, Kinver, Stourbridge, West Midlands
Details See Chenevare Fairs 10 February

Crispin Fairs
Location Victoria Hall, Hartley Wintney, Hampshire
Details See Crispin Fairs 10 February

Furze Hill
Location Furze Hill, Banqueting Centre, Margaretting, Nr Chelmsford
Details See Furze Hill 10 February

Lostwithiel Antiques Fair
Location Community Centre, Lostwithiel, Cornwall
Details See Lostwithiel Antiques Fair 10 February

Midas Antique Fair
Location The Bellhouse Hotel, Oxford Road (A40), Beaconsfield, Bucks
Details See Midas Antique Fair 10 February

Pennyfarthing Fayres
Location Potters Bar
Details See Pennyfarthing Fayres 10 February

Royal Horticultural Hall
Location Royal Horticultural Hall, Lawrence Hall, Greycoat Street, London SW1
Details See Royal Horticultural Hall 10 February

10–11

Ardingly International Antiques & Collectors Fair
Location South of England Centre, Ardingly, West Sussex
Details See Ardingly International Antiques & Collectors Fair 26–27 February

11

Marks Tey
Location Parish Hall, Marks Tey, Essex
Details See Marks Tey 13 February

FAIRS

SEPTEMBER

13–15

Galloway Antiques Fairs
Location Eridge Park, Nr Crowborough, East Sussex
Details See Galloway Antiques Fairs 3–6 May

13–22

Penmans Chelsea Antiques Fair
Location Chelsea Old Town Hall, King's Road, London, SW3
Details See Penmans Chelsea Antiques Fair 15–24 March

14

9th Annual Charity Antique and Fine Art Fair
Location Queen's Hall, Newtownards
Details See 8th Annual Charity Antique and Fine Art Fair 6 May

Aquarius Fairs
Location The Harlington Centre, High Street, Fleet, Hampshire
Details See Aquarius Fairs 9 February

Athena Fayres
Location Lockswood Community Centre, Locks Heath Shopping Centre, Locks Heath, Nr Fareham, Hants
Details See Athena Fayres 9 February

Devon County Antiques Fairs
Location Matford Centre in the Exeter Livestock Centre, Marsh Barton, Exeter
Details See Devon County Antiques Fairs 9 February

Scotfairs Antique and Collectors Fair
Location Albert Halls, Dumbarton Road, Stirling
Details See Scotfairs Antique and Collectors Fair 2 February

14–15

Carmarthen Antiques & Collectors Fair
Location United Counties Showground, Carmarthen
Details See Carmarthen Antiques & Collectors Fair 9–10 March

Detling International Antiques & Collectors Fair
Location Kent County Showground, Detling, Nr Maidstone, Kent
Details See Detling International Antiques & Collectors Fair 26–27 January

Saffron Walden Antiques and Fine Art Fair
Location Saffron Walden County High School, Audley End Road, Saffron Walden
Details See Saffron Walden Antiques and Fine Art Fair 2–3 February

West Midlands Antique Fairs
Location Prestwood Complex, Stafford County Showground
Details See West Midlands Antique Fairs 23–24 February

15

Antiques and Collectables Fair
Location Newman House, 85 St Stephen's Green, Dublin 2
Details See Antiques and Collectables Fair 20 January

Aquarius Fairs
Location Heckfield Memorial Hall, Church Lane, Heckfield, Hook, Hampshire
Details See Aquarius Fairs 20 January

Art Deco Fair with 20thC Decorative Arts
Location Leeds Royal Armouries
Details See Art Deco Fair with 20thC Decorative Arts 24 March

Athena Fayres
Location The Village Hall, Minstead, Nr Lyndhurst, about a mile from the end of the M27
Details See Athena Fayres 20 January

Biggleswade Antiques Fairs
Location The Weatherley Centre, Eagle Farm Road, Biggleswade, Bedfordshire
Details See Biggleswade Antiques Fairs 20 January

Bob Evans Fairs
Location Leisure Village, Thurston Drive, Kettering
Details See Bob Evans Fairs 24 February

Chenevare Fairs
Location Bridgnorth Sports and Leisure Centre, Northgate, Bridgnorth, Shropshire
Details See Chenevare Fairs 20 January

Hatfield Antiques & Collectors Fair
Location Red Lion, Great North Road, Hatfield, Hertfordshire
Details See Hatfield Antiques & Collectors Fair 20 January

Monmouthshire County Antiques & Collectors Fair
Location The Market Hall (next to the Town Hall), Abergavenny, Monmouthshire
Details See Monmouthshire County Antiques & Collectors Fair 20 January

Scotfairs Antique and Collectors Fair
Location Moir Hall, Mitchell Library, Granville Street, Glasgow
Details See Scotfairs Antique and Collectors Fair 20 January

The London Textiles, Vintage Fashion and Accessories Fair
Location Hammersmith Town Hall, King Street, London, W6
Details See The London Textiles, Vintage Fashion and Accessories Fair 20 January

18

The Big Brum
Location St Martins Market (The Rag), Edgbaston Street, Birmingham
Details See The Big Brum 30 January

18–22

The 52nd Northern Antiques Fair
☎ 01277 214677 Ⓕ 01277 214550
Ⓔ admin@baileyfairs.co.uk
Ⓦ www.baileyfairs.co.uk

Location Pavilions of Harrogate, Great Yorkshire Showground 🅿
Entrance fee £10
Details 80 dealers, vetted and date-lined

20–22

Galloway Antiques Fairs
Location The Old Swan Hotel, Harrogate, North Yorkshire
Details See Galloway Antiques Fairs 25–27 January

Shepton Mallet Antiques & Collectors Fair
Location Royal Bath and West Showground, Shepton Mallett
Details See Shepton Mallet Antiques & Collectors Fair 18–20 January

21

Antiques Fair
Location Castle Hall, Hertford, Hertfordshire
Details See Antiques Fair 19 January

Chingford Antiques & Collectors Fair
Location Assembly Hall, The Green, Station Road, Chingford
Details See Chingford Antiques & Collectors Fair 26 January

Commonwealth Institute Coin Fair
Location The Commonwealth Institute, Kensington High Street, London W8
Details See Commonwealth Institute Coin Fair 19 January

22

Alexandra Palace
Location Wood Green, London
Details See Alexandra Palace 17 March

Antique and Collectors Fair
Location Canons Leisure Centre, Madeira Road, Mitcham, Surrey
Details See Antique and Collectors Fair 27 January

Antiques & Collectors Fair
Location Crook Log Sports Centre, Brampton Road, Bexleyheath, Kent
Details See Antiques & Collectors Fair 3 February

Antiques & Collectors Fair
Location Knights Hill Hotel, South Wooton, King's Lynn
Details See Antiques & Collectors Fair 20 January

Biggleswade Antiques Fairs
Location The Marriott Hotel, Huntingdon, Cambridgeshire, off A14
Details See Biggleswade Antiques Fairs 10 February

Bloomsbury Postcard & Collectors Fair
Location Galleon Suite, Royal National Hotel, Bedford Way, London, WC1
Details See Bloomsbury Postcard and Collectors Fair 27 January

Bob Evans Fairs
Location The Cresset, Bretton Centre, Peterborough
Details See Bob Evans Fairs 3 March

Burford Antiques Fair
Location Burford School, Burford, Oxfordshire
Details See Burford Antiques Fair 27 January

Clock & Watch Dealers Fair
Location Haydock Park racecourse, M6 Jct 23
Details See Clock & Watch Dealers Fair 3 March

Royal Horticultural Hall
Location Royal Horticultural Hall, Lawrence Hall, Greycoat Street, London SW1
Details See Royal Horticultural Hall 10 February

Wessex Fairs
Location Winter Gardens, Weston-Super-Mare
Details See Wessex Fairs 24 February

24–29

The Decorative Antiques and Textiles Fair
Contact Patricia Harvey
☎ 020 76245173 Ⓕ 020 76258326
Ⓔ fairs@decorativefair.com
Ⓦ www.decorativefair.com
Location The Marquee, Battersea Park 🅿
Est. 1985
Open 24th noon–8pm 25th–27th 11am–8pm 28th 11am–7pm 29th 10am–6pm
Entrance fee £6 including catalogue
Details 100–120 dealers

25–29

Irish Antique Dealers Fair
Contact Louis O'Sullivan
☎ 00 353 1 2859294
Location Royal Dublin Society, Ballsbridge, Dublin 4, Ireland 🅿
Open 11am–7pm
Entrance fee 700 Euros
Details Fair Date-lines: pre-1900: prints, photos; pre-1925: furniture, metalwork, architectural fittings; pre-1930: glass, china, clocks; pre-1940: works of art, silver, etchings, lighting, clocks; pre-1950: jewellery, paintings, drawings

26

Antique & Collectors Fair
Location Nantwich Civic Hall, Market Street, Nantwich, Cheshire, M6 Jct 16
Details See Antique & Collectors Fair 31 January

27–1 Oct

The Harrogate Antiques Fair
Contact Louise Walker
☎ 01823 323363 Ⓕ 01823 271072
Ⓦ www.harrogateantiquefair.com
Location Hall A, Harrogate International Centre, Ripon Road, Harrogate, North Yorkshire 🅿
Entrance fee £7.50 including catalogue
Details High quality antiques & fine art, call for further information

27–28

The 69th London Arms Fair
Location Royal National Hotel, Woburn Place, Holborn, London WC1

Details See The 68th London Arms Fair 26–27 April

28

Browser's Antique & Collectors Fair

Location Village Hall, Station Road, Pangbourne, Berkshire (on A329 off A4, M4 Jct 12/13)
Details See Browser's Antique & Collectors Fair 26 January

Devon County Antiques Fairs

Location Salisbury Leisure Centre, The Butts, Hulse Road, Salisbury
Details See Devon County Antiques Fairs 15 June

Pamela Robertson Antique and Collectors Fair

Location Northgate Arena, Victoria Road, Cheshire
Details See Pamela Robertson Antique and Collectors Fair 26 January

Scotfairs Antique and Collectors Fair

Location The Citadel Leisure Centre, Ayr Baths, South Beach Road, Ayr
Details See Scotfairs Antique and Collectors Fair 26 January

28–29

Beckett Antique Fairs

Location Doncaster Race Exhibition Centre, Doncaster
Details See Beckett Antique Fairs 16–17 February

Bob Evans Fairs

Location Sport Village, Drayton High Road, Hellesdon, Norwich
Details See Bob Evans Fairs 26–27 January

The Original Long Melford Fair

Location The Old School, Long Melford, Suffolk
Details See The Original Long Melford Fair 26–27 January

29

Antique and Collectors Fair

Location Berkhampstead Sports Centre, Lagley Meadow, Douglas Gardens, Berkhampstead, Hertfordshire
Details See Antique and Collectors Fair 31 March

Antiques and Collectables Fair

Location Clontarf Castle, Castle Avenue, Dublin
Details See Antiques Fairs Ireland 24 February

Athena Fayres

Location Community Centre, Mill Lane, Wickham, Hampshire
Details See Athena Fayres 27 January

Biggleswade Antiques Fairs

Location The Addison Centre, Kempston, Bedford
Details See Biggleswade Antiques Fairs 27 January

Chatsworth Fairs

Location Cedar Court Hotel, Jct 39 M1, Wakefield
Details See Chatsworth Fairs 3 February

Chenevare Fairs

Location Hagley Community Centre, Worcester Road, West Hagley, Hereford & Worcester
Details See Chenevare Fairs 27 January

Grand Glass Fair

Location Woking Leisure Centre, Kingfield Road, Woking, Surrey
Details See Grand Glass Fair 17 March

R and S Western Fairs

Location Trenython Manor, Tywardreath, Nr Par, Cornwall
Details See R and S Western Fairs 27 January

Wessex Fairs

Location Combe Lodge, A368, Blagdon, Nr Church Hill, North Somerset
Details See Wessex Fairs 24 March

OCTOBER

1

The Sandown Park Antique Fair

Location The Exhibition Centre, Sandown Park Racecourse, Esher, Surrey
Details See Sandown Park Antique Fair 19 February

2

The Long Melford

Location Village Memorial Hall, Long Melford, Suffolk
Details See The Long Melford 6 February

3

Paraphernalia Fairs

Location Lyndhurst Community Centre, Lyndhurst, New Forest, Hampshire
Details See Paraphernalia Fairs 14 February

3–6

35th Surrey Antiques Fair

Contact Roger or Mary Heath-Bullock
☎ 01483 422562 Ⓕ 01483 422562
Ⓦ www.surreyantiquesfair.co.uk
Location Guildford Civic, Guildford, Surrey 🅿
Est. 1968
Open Thurs–Sat 11am–7pm Sun 11am–6pm
Details Annual event with more than 40 dealers of antiques and fine art from around the country

The Milton Keynes Antiques Fair

Location Middleton Hall, at thecentre:mk, Milton Keynes Shopping Centre
Details See The Milton Keynes Antiques Fair 28–3 February

4–5

Peterborough Festival of Antiques

Location East of England Showground
Details See Peterborough Festival of Antiques 22–23 March

4–6

Cheshire County Antiques Fair
Location Arley Hall, Nr Knutsford, Cheshire
Details See Cheshire County Antiques Fair 15–17 March

Stafford Bingley Hall
Location The Bingley Hall, County Showground
Details See Stafford Bingley Hall 8–10 February

5

Antiques & Collectors Fair
Location St George's Hall, Lime Street, Liverpool
Details See Antiques & Collectors Fair 1 June

Jade Fairs
Location Lowther Pavilion, The Promenade, Lytham St Anne's, Lancashire
Details See Jade Fairs 2 February

Marcel Fairs
Location St Paul's Church Hall, Mill Hill, Ridgeway, London, NW7
Details See Marcel Fairs 2 February

Victoriana's Fairs
Location Walsall Town Hall, Walsall, West Midlands
Details See Victoriana's Fairs 2 February

5–6

Buxton Antique and Collectors Fair
Location Pavilion Gardens, Buxton, Derbyshire
Details See Buxton Antique and Collectors Fair 26–27 January

Little Easton Manor
Location Little Easton Manor, Nr Great Dunmow, Essex
Details See Little Easton Manor 30–31 March

6

Antiques and Collectables Fair
Location Newman House, 85 St Stephen's Green, Dublin 2
Details See Antiques and Collectables Fair 20 January

Chiswick Town Hall Art Deco Fair
Location Chiswick Town Hall
Details See Chiswick Town Hall Art Deco Fair March 3

Cross Country Fairs Ltd
Location Copthorne Hotel, Effingham Park, West Sussex
Details See Cross Country Fairs Ltd 3 February

Hampstead Antique Collectors Fair
Location Hampstead Community Centre, High Street, Hampstead
Details See Hampstead Antique Collectors Fair 3 February

Harlequin Fairs
Location Centre for Epilepsy, Chalfont Common, Chalfont St Peter, Buckinghamshire
Details See Harlequin Fairs 3 February

Ipswich Antiques and Collectables Fair
Location Ipswich County Hotel (formerly Ipswich Moat House) Copdock, Ipswich, Suffolk
Details See Ipswich Antiques and Collectables Fair

J and K Fairs
Location Lincolnshire Showground, Lincoln
Details See J and K Fairs 20 January

Lechlade Antiques Fair
Location The New Memorial Hall, Burford Road, Lechlade, Gloucestershire
Details See Lechlade Antiques Fair 3 February

Magnum Antiques Fairs
Location Midhurst, The Grange Centre, Bepton Road
Details 135 stands

Scotfairs Antique and Collectors Fair
Location Meadowbank Stadium, London Road, Edinburgh
Details See Scotfairs Antique and Collectors Fair 3 February

Wessex Fairs
Location Holiday Inn, Taunton, Somerset, M5 Jct 25
Details See Wessex Fairs 3 February

7–8

Little Chelsea Antiques Fair
Location Chelsea Old Town Hall, King's Road, London, SW3
Details See Little Chelsea Antiques Fair 8–9 April

9

Marks Tey
Location Parish Hall, Marks Tey, Essex
Details See Marks Tey 13 February

9–13

LAPADA Fine Art & Antiques Fair
Ⓔ antiques@necgroup.co.uk
Ⓦ www.lapadafair.co.uk
Location Commonwealth Institute, London, W8 🅿
Est. 1993
Open Weekdays 11am–8pm weekends 11am–6pm
Entrance fee £8 Double entry £14 Accompanied children free
Details 100 dealers

11–13

Galloway Antiques Fairs
Location The Bowes Museum, Barnard Castle, Co Durham
Details See Galloway Antiques Fairs 8–10 February

12

Aquarius Fairs
Location The Harlington Centre, High Street, Fleet, Hampshire
Details See Aquarius Fairs 9 February

Athena Fayres
Location Lockswood Community Centre, Locks HeathShopping Centre, Locks Heath, Nr Fareham, Hants
Details See Athena Fayres 9 February

Devon County Antiques Fairs
Location Matford Centre in the Exeter Livestock Centre, Marsh Barton, Exeter
Details See Devon County Antiques Fairs 9 February

OCTOBER

Scotfairs Antique and Collectors Fair
Location Albert Halls, Dumbarton Road, Stirling
Details See Scotfairs Antique and Collectors Fair 2 February

12–13

Harpenden Antiques and Fine Art Fair
Location Rothamsted Conference Centre, on A1081 Harpenden–St Albans road
Details See Harpenden Antiques and Fine Art Fair 9–10 February

13

Antique and Collectors Fair
Location Woking Leisure Centre, Kingfield Road, Woking, Surrey
Details See Antique and Collectors Fair 10 February

Antique Map Fair
Location The Bonnington Hotel, Southampton Row, midway between Holborn and Russell Square tube stations, London
Details See Antique Map Fair 10 March

Antiques & Collectors Fair
Location Burgess Hall, St Ives Recreation Centre, St Ives, Cambridgeshire
Details See Antiques & Collectors Fair 16 February

Art Deco Fair with 20thC Decorative Arts
Location Chester Racecourse
Details See Art Deco Fair with 20thC Decorative Arts 27 January

Athena Fayres
Location The Village Hall, Minstead, Nr Lyndhurst, about a mile from the end of the M27
Details See Athena Fayres 20 January

Best of Fairs
Location The Village Hall, Copdock, 3 miles west of Ipswich
Details See Best of Fairs 3 February

Biggleswade Antiques Fairs
Location Thistle Hotel (formerly Blakemore Hotel), Little Wymondley, Nr Hitchin, Herts
Details See Biggleswade Antiques Fairs 10 March

Bob Evans Fairs
Location Hereford Leisure Centre, Holmer Road
Details See Bob Evans Fairs 20 January

Chenevare Fairs
Location Kinver Leisure Centre, Enville Road, Kinver, Stourbridge, West Midlands
Details See Chenevare Fairs 10 February

Crispin Fairs
Location Victoria Hall, Hartley Wintney, Hampshire
Details See Crispin Fairs 10 February

Devon County Antiques Fairs
Location Westland Sports and Social Club, Westbourne Close, Yeovil, Somerset
Details See Devon County Antiques Fairs 10 February

Furze Hill
Location Furze Hill, Banqueting Centre, Margaretting, Nr Chelmsford
Details See Furze Hill 10 February

Lostwithiel Antiques Fair
Location Community Centre, Lostwithiel, Cornwall
Details See Lostwithiel Antiques Fair 10 February

13

Malvern Antiques & Collectors Fair
Location Three Counties Showground, Malvern, Worcestershire
Details See Malvern Antiques & Collectors Fair 3 February

Mark Carter Militaria & Medal Fairs
Location Stratford Leisure Centre & Visitor Centre, Bridgfoot, Stratford upon Avon, Warwickshire
Details See Mark Carter Militaria & Medal Fairs 10 March

Midas Antique Fair
Location The Bellhouse Hotel, Oxford Road (A40), Beaconsfield, Bucks
Details See Midas Antique Fair 10 February

Pennyfarthing Fayres
Location Potters Bar
Details See Pennyfarthing Fayres 10 February

Royal Horticultural Hall
Location Royal Horticultural Hall, Lawrence Hall, Greycoat Street, London SW1
Details See Royal Horticultural Hall 10 February

16

Evening Antiques/Collectors Fairs
Location St Martins Market (The Rag), Edgbaston Street, Birmingham
Details See Evening Antiques/Collectors Fairs 20 February

18–20

Galloway Antiques Fairs
Location Seaford College, Nr Petworth, West Sussex
Details See Galloway Antiques Fairs 7–9 June

The 10th Buxton Autumn Fine Art and Antiques Fair
☎ 01277 214677 Ⓕ 01277 214550
Ⓔ admin@baileyfairs.co.uk
Ⓦ www.baileyfairs.co.uk
Location Pavilion Gardens Buxton, Derbyshire Ⓟ
Open Fri 1–6pm Sat 11am–6pm Sun 11am–5pm
Entrance fee £5

The International Antiques and Collectors Fair at RAF Swinderby
Location RAF Swinderby, A46 between Newark and Lincoln
Details See The International Antiques and Collectors Fair at RAF Swinderby 1–3 February

19–20

Classic Antiques Fairs
Location The Heritage Motor Centre, Gaydon, Warwickshire, Jct 12, M40, midway between Warwick and Banbury
Details See Classic Antiques Fairs 16–17 February

20

Antiques and Collectables Fair
Location Newman House, 85 St Stephen's Green, Dublin 2
Details See Antiques and Collectables Fair 20 January

Aquarius Fairs
Location Heckfield Memorial Hall, Church Lane, Heckfield, Hook, Hampshire
Details See Aquarius Fairs 20 January

Battersea Town Hall Art Deco Fair
Location Battersea Town Hall
Details See Battersea Town Hall Art Deco Fair February 17

Biggleswade Antiques Fairs
Location The Weatherley Centre, Eagle Farm Road, Biggleswade, Bedfordshire
Details See Biggleswade Antiques Fairs 20 January

Brocante
Location Kensington Town Hall, Hornton Street, London, W8
Details See Brocante 3 February

Clock & Watch Dealers Fair
Location The Grove Leisure Centre, London Road, Balderton, Nr Newark
Details See Clock & Watch Dealers Fair 3 February

Hatfield Antiques & Collectors Fair
Location Red Lion, Great North Road, Hatfield, Hertfordshire
Details See Hatfield Antiques & Collectors Fair 20 January

Monmouthshire County Antiques & Collectors Fair
Location The Market Hall (next to the Town Hall), Abergavenny, Monmouthshire
Details See Monmouthshire County Antiques & Collectors Fair 20 January

Scotfairs Antique and Collectors Fair
Location Moir Hall, Mitchell Library, Granville Street, Glasgow
Details See Scotfairs Antique and Collectors Fair 20 January

20–21

54th Luton Antiques Fair
Location Putteridge Bury House, A505 Luton to Hitchin Road, Luton
Details See 53rd Luton Antiques Fair 16–17 February

21–22

Newark International Antiques & Collectors Fair
Location Newark & Notts Showground, Newark
Details See Newark International Antiques & Collectors Fair 4–5 February

23

Newbury Racecourse
Location Newbury Racecourse, Newbury, Berkshire
Details See Newbury Racecourse February 13

24–27

Penmans Chester Antiques & Fine Art Show
Location County Grandstand, Chester Racecourse, Cheshire
Details See Penmans Chester Antiques & Fine Art Show 14–17 February

25–27

Galloway Antiques Fairs
Location Stonyhurst College, Nr Clitheroe, Lancashire
Details See Galloway Antiques Fairs 15–17 February

The 11th East Anglian Antique Dealers Fair
Contact Liz Allport
☎ 01603 737631 Ⓕ 01603 737631
Ⓜ 07747 843074
Ⓔ liz.allport@lineone.net
Ⓦ www.lomaxantiquesfairs.co.uk
Location Langley Park School, Loddon, Norfolk Ⓟ
Open 25th 2–7pm 26th 10.30am–6pm 27th 10.30am–5pm

TVADA Autumn Fair
Contact Jill Mair
☎ 01865 341639
Location Radley College, Nr Abingdon, Oxon Ⓟ
Est. 1989
Open Fri Sat 11am–6pm Sun 11am–5pm
Entrance fee £5
Details 35+ stands, fully licensed restaurant

26

Antiques Fair
Location Castle Hall, Hertford, Hertfordshire
Details See Antiques Fair 19 January

Browser's Antique & Collectors Fair
Location Village Hall, Station Road, Pangbourne, Berkshire (on A329 off A4, M4 Jct 12/13)
Details See Browser's Antique & Collectors Fair 26 January

Commonwealth Institute Coin Fair
Location The Commonwealth Institute, Kensington High Street, London, W8
Details See Commonwealth Institute Coin Fair 19 January

Pamela Robertson Antique and Collectors Fair
Location Northgate Arena, Victoria Road, Cheshire
Details See Pamela Robertson Antique and Collectors Fair 26 January

Scotfairs Antique and Collectors Fair
Location The Citadel Leisure Centre, Ayr Baths, South Beach Road, Ayr
Details See Scotfairs Antique and Collectors Fair 26 January

NOVEMBER

26–27

Swansea Antiques Fair
Location Brangwyn Hall, Swansea
Details See Swansea Antiques Fair 2–3 February

The Original Long Melford Fair
Location The Old School, Long Melford, Suffolk
Details See The Original Long Melford Fair 26–27 January

27

Antique and Collectors Fair
Location Canons Leisure Centre, Madeira Road, Mitcham, Surrey
Details See Antique and Collectors Fair 27 January

Antiques & Collectors Fair
Location Knights Hill Hotel, South Wooton, King's Lynn
Details See Antiques & Collectors Fair 20 January

Athena Fayres
Location Community Centre, Mill Lane, Wickham, Hampshire
Details See Athena Fayres 27 January

Biggleswade Antiques Fairs
Location Kimbolton Castle, Huntingdon, Cambridgeshire
Details See Biggleswade Antiques Fairs 7 April

Bloomsbury Postcard & Collectors Fair
Location Galleon Suite, Royal National Hotel, Bedford Way, London, WC1
Details See Bloomsbury Postcard and Collectors Fair 27 January

Bob Evans Fairs
Location Sports Connexion, Ryton on Dunsmore, Coventry
Details See Bob Evans Fairs 10 February

Burford Antiques Fair
Location Burford School, Burford, Oxfordshire
Details See Burford Antiques Fair 27 January

Chatsworth Fairs
Location Cedar Court Hotel, Jct 39 M1, Wakefield
Details See Chatsworth Fairs 3 February

Chenevare Fairs
Location Hagley Community Centre, Worcester Road, West Hagley, Hereford & Worcester
Details See Chenevare Fairs 27 January

J and K Fairs
Location Lincolnshire Showground, Lincoln
Details See J and K Fairs 20 January

R and S Western Fairs
Location Trenython Manor, Tywardreath, Nr Par, Cornwall
Details See R and S Western Fairs 27 January

Wessex Fairs
Location Winter Gardens, Weston-Super-Mare
Details See Wessex Fairs 24 February

27–28

Antiques and Collectables Fair
Location Royal Marine Hotel, Dun Laoghaire, Co Dublin
Details See Antiques and Collectables Fair 27 January

29–30

Ardingly International Antiques & Collectors Fair
Location South of England Centre, Ardingly, West Sussex
Details See Ardingly International Antiques & Collectors Fair 26–27 February

31

Antique & Collectors Fair
Location Nantwich Civic Hall, Market Street, Nantwich, Cheshire, M6 Jct 16
Details See Antique & Collectors Fair 31 January

NOVEMBER

1–3

Galloway Antiques Fairs
Location Duncombe Park, Helmsley, North Yorkshire
Details See Galloway Antiques Fairs 14–16 June

The 20th Hertfordshire Antiques and Fine Art Fair
☎ 01277 214677 Ⓕ 01277 214550
Ⓔ admin@baileyfairs.co.uk
Ⓦ www.baileyfairs.co.uk
Location Hatfield House, Hatfield, Hertfordshire Ⓟ
Open 11am–5pm
Entrance fee £4
Details 40 dealers, vetted and date-lined

2

Antiques & Collectors Fair
Location St George's Hall, Lime Street, Liverpool
Details See Antiques & Collectors Fair 1 June

E W Services Antiques Fair
Location Buckingham Community Centre, Cornwalls Meadow Shopping Precinct, Buckingham
Details See E W Services Antiques Fair 2 February

Jade Fairs
Location Lowther Pavilion, The Promenade, Lytham St Anne's, Lancashire
Details See Jade Fairs 2 February

Marcel Fairs
Location St Paul's Church Hall, Mill Hill, Ridgeway, London, NW7
Details See Marcel Fairs 2 February

Scotfairs Antique and Collectors Fair
Location Albert Halls, Dumbarton Road, Stirling
Details See Scotfairs Antique and Collectors Fair 2 February

Victoriana's Fairs
Location Walsall Town Hall, Walsall, West Midlands
Details See Victoriana's Fairs 2 February

2–3

Beckett Antique Fairs
Location Doncaster Race Exhibition Centre, Doncaster
Details See Beckett Antique Fairs 16–17 February

Bob Evans Fairs
Location Sport Village, Drayton High Road, Hellesdon, Norwich
Details See Bob Evans Fairs 26–27 January

Buxton Antique and Collectors Fair
Location Pavilion Gardens, Buxton, Derbyshire
Details See Buxton Antique and Collectors Fair 26–27 January

Devon County Antiques Fairs
Location Westpoint Exhibition Centre, Clyst St Mary, Exeter
Details See Devon County Antiques Fair 2–3 February

3

Antique Map Fair
Location The Bonnington Hotel, Southampton Row, midway between Holborn and Russell Square tube stations, London
Details See Antique Map Fair 10 March

Antiques and Collectables Fair
Location Newman House, 85 St Stephen's Green, Dublin 2
Details See Antiques and Collectables Fair 20 January

Best of Fairs
Location The Village Hall, Copdock, 3 miles west of Ipswich
Details See Best of Fairs 3 February

Cross Country Fairs Ltd
Location Copthorne Hotel, Effingham Park, West Sussex
Details See Cross Country Fairs Ltd 3 February

Hampstead Antique Collectors Fair
Location Hampstead Community Centre, High Street, Hampstead
Details See Hampstead Antique Collectors Fair 3 February

Harlequin Fairs
Location Centre for Epilepsy, Chalfont Common, Chalfont St Peter, Buckinghamshire
Details See Harlequin Fairs 3 February

Ipswich Antiques and Collectables Fair
Location Ipswich County Hotel (formerly Ipswich Moat House) Copdock, Ipswich, Suffolk
Details See Ipswich Antiques and Collectables Fair

Lechlade Antiques Fair
Location The New Memorial Hall, Burford Road, Lechlade, Gloucestershire
Details See Lechlade Antiques Fair 3 February

Malvern Antiques & Collectors Fair
Location Three Counties Showground, Malvern, Worcestershire
Details See Malvern Antiques & Collectors Fair 3 February

Mark Carter Militaria & Medal Fairs
Location The Princes Hall, Princes Way, Aldershot, Hampshire
Details See Mark Carter Militaria & Medal Fairs 20 January

Midland Clock & Watch Fair
Location National Motorcycle Museum, M42 Exit 6, West Midlands
Details See Midland Clock & Watch Fair 27 January

Royal Horticultural Hall
Location Royal Horticultural Hall, Lawrence Hall, Greycoat Street, London SW1
Details See Royal Horticultural Hall 10 February

Scotfairs Antique and Collectors Fair
Location Meadowbank Stadium, London Road, Edinburgh
Details See Scotfairs Antique and Collectors Fair 3 February

Wessex Fairs
Location Holiday Inn, Taunton, Somerset, M5 Jct 25
Details See Wessex Fairs 3 February

5

The Sandown Park Antique Fair
Location The Exhibition Centre, Sandown Park Racecourse, Esher, Surrey
Details See Sandown Park Antique Fair 19 February with firework party

6

The Long Melford
Location Village Memorial Hall, Long Melford, Suffolk
Details See The Long Melford 6 February

7

Paraphernalia Fairs
Location Lyndhurst Community Centre, Lyndhurst, New Forest, Hampshire
Details See Paraphernalia Fairs 14 February

7–10

Penmans Bath Antiques & Fine Art Fair
Contact Caroline Penman
☎ 01444 482514 Ⓕ 01444 483412
Ⓜ 07774 850044
Ⓔ info@penman-fairs.co.uk
Ⓦ www.penman-fairs.co.uk
Location The Pavilion, North Parade Road, Bath Ⓟ
Open Thurs noon–8pm Fri Sat 11am–6pm Sun 11am–5pm
Entrance fee £4
Details 55 stands of decorative and traditional vetted antiques and art

8–10

Galloway Antiques Fairs
☎ 01423 522122 Ⓕ 01423 522122
Ⓜ 07966 528725
Ⓔ susan@gallowayfairs.co.uk
Ⓦ www.gallowayfairs.co.uk
Location Firle Place, Nr Lewes, East Sussex Ⓟ
Open 10.30am–5pm
Entrance fee £3.50–£4.50

FAIRS

NOVEMBER

9

Aquarius Fairs
Location The Harlington Centre, High Street, Fleet, Hampshire
Details See Aquarius Fairs 9 February

Athena Fayres
Location Lockswood Community Centre, Locks Heath Shopping Centre, Locks Heath, Nr Fareham, Hants
Details See Athena Fayres 9 February

Belfast Book Fair
Contact Jim or Rita Swindall
☎ 028 90826443 Ⓕ 028 90826443
Ⓔ jiribooks@dnet.co.uk
Location Wellington Park Hotel Ⓟ
Est. 1982
Open 10am–5pm
Entrance fee £2 Concessions £1
Details 45 dealers exhibiting, refreshments

London Coin Fair
Location Holiday Inn, London Bloomsbury, Coram Street, WC1
Details See London Coin Fair 9 February

Southport Antiques and Collectors Fair
Location Southport Floral Hall, the Promenade, Southport, Merseyside
Details See Southport Antiques and Collectors Fair 16 February

9–10

Detling International Antiques & Collectors Fair
Location Kent County Showground, Detling, Nr Maidstone, Kent
Details See Detling International Antiques & Collectors Fair 26–27 January

The Northern Ireland Antiques and Fine Art Fair
Contact Kirsty Thompson
☎ 028 9127 5050
Ⓔ kthompson@carmah.com
Ⓦ www.carmah.com
Location Culloden Hotel, Bangor Road, Belfast, Co Down Ⓟ
Open Sat 2–10pm Sun 2–9pm
Details 40 dealers. Provisional date, phone for details of fair

West Midlands Antique Fairs
Location Prestwood Complex, Stafford County Showground
Details See West Midlands Antique Fairs 23–24 February

10

Antiques & Collectors Fairs
Location Runnymeade Hotel & Spa, Windsor Road, Egham, Surrey
Details See Antiques & Collectors Fair 10 February

Art Deco Fair with 20thC Decorative Arts
Location Leeds Royal Armouries
Details See Art Deco Fair with 20thC Decorative Arts 24 March

Athena Fayres
Location The Village Hall, Minstead, Nr Lyndhurst, about a mile from the end of the M27
Details See Athena Fayres 20 January

Biggleswade Antiques Fairs
Location The Marriott Hotel, Huntingdon, Cambridgeshire, off A14
Details See Biggleswade Antiques Fairs 10 February

Bob Evans Fairs
Location Leisure Village, Thurston Drive, Kettering
Details See Bob Evans Fairs 24 February

Chenevare Fairs
Location Kinver Leisure Centre, Enville Road, Kinver, Stourbridge, West Midlands
Details See Chenevare Fairs 10 February

Crispin Fairs
Location Victoria Hall, Hartley Wintney, Hampshire
Details See Crispin Fairs 10 February

Furze Hill
Location Furze Hill, Banqueting Centre, Margaretting, Nr Chelmsford
Details See Furze Hill 10 February

J and K Fairs
Location Lincolnshire Showground, Lincoln
Details See J and K Fairs 20 January

Lostwithiel Antiques Fair
Location Community Centre, Lostwithiel, Cornwall
Details See Lostwithiel Antiques Fair 10 February

Midas Antique Fair
Location The Bellhouse Hotel, Oxford Road (A40), Beaconsfield, Bucks
Details See Midas Antique Fair 10 February

Pennyfarthing Fayres
Location Potters Bar
Details See Pennyfarthing Fayres 10 February

Scotfairs Antique and Collectors Fair
Location Moir Hall, Mitchell Library, Granville Street, Glasgow
Details See Scotfairs Antique and Collectors Fair 20 January

The London Textiles, Vintage Fashion and Accessories Fair
Location Hammersmith Town Hall, King Street, London, W6
Details See The London Textiles, Vintage Fashion and Accessories Fair 20 January

The Original National Glass Collectors Fair
Location National Motorcycle Museum, Jct 6 M42, Midlands
Details See The Original National Glass Collectors Fair 12 May

11–17

The Olympia Fine Art and Antiques Fair
☎ 020 7370 8186/8212
Ⓕ 020 7370 8221
Ⓔ olympia-antiques@eco.co.uk
Ⓦ www.olympia-antiques.com
Location Olympia, London Ⓟ
Est. 1989
Open 11th 5pm–10pm 12th 11am–9pm 13th–15th 11am–8pm 16th 11am–7pm 17th 11am–5pm
Entrance fee £5

Details 240 exhibitors, offering wide range of antiques and works of art, all items examined by experts

13

Marks Tey
Location Parish Hall, Marks Tey, Essex
Details See Marks Tey 13 February

The Big Brum
Location St Martins Market (The Rag), Edgbaston Street, Birmingham
Details See The Big Brum 30 January

15–17

Galloway Antiques Fairs
☎ 01423 522122 Ⓕ 01423 522122
Ⓜ 07966 528725
Ⓔ susan@gallowayfairs.co.uk
Ⓦ www.gallowayfairs.co.uk
Location Scone Palace, Perth Ⓟ
Open 10.30am–5pm
Entrance fee £3.50–£4.50

Shepton Mallet Antiques & Collectors Fair
Location Royal Bath and West Showground, Shepton Mallett, Somerset
Details See Shepton Mallet Antiques & Collectors Fair 18–20 January

16

Antiques Fair
Location Castle Hall, Hertford, Hertfordshire
Details See Antiques Fair 19 January

Commonwealth Institute Coin Fair
Location The Commonwealth Institute, Kensington High Street, London, W8
Details See Commonwealth Institute Coin Fair 19 January

Pamela Robertson Antique and Collectors Fair
Location Northgate Arena, Victoria Road, Cheshire
Details See Pamela Robertson Antique and Collectors Fair 26 January

16–17

Saffron Walden Antiques and Fine Art Fair
Location Saffron Walden County High School, Audley End Road, Saffron Walden
Details See Saffron Walden Antiques and Fine Art Fair 2–3 February

The London Antique Textiles Fair
Contact Paola Francia-Gardiner
☎ 020 8543 5075 Ⓕ 020 8404 6262
Location Hammersmith Town Hall, King Street, London, W6 Ⓟ
Open Sat 3pm–8pm Sun 10am–5pm
Entrance fee Sat £5 Sun £3.50

The Long Melford
Location Village Memorial Hall, Long Melford, Suffolk
Details See The Long Melford 26–27 January

17

Alexandra Palace
Location Wood Green, London
Details See Alexandra Palace 17 March

Antiques and Collectables Fair
Location Newman House, 85 St Stephen's Green, Dublin 2

Details See Antiques and Collectables Fair 20 January

Aquarius Fairs
Location Heckfield Memorial Hall, Church Lane, Heckfield, Hook, Hampshire
Details See Aquarius Fairs 20 January

Biggleswade Antiques Fairs
Location The Weatherley Centre, Eagle Farm Road, Biggleswade, Bedfordshire
Details See Biggleswade Antiques Fairs 20 January

Bob Evans Fairs
Location The Cresset, Bretton Centre, Peterborough
Details See Bob Evans Fairs 3 March

Chenevare Fairs
Location Bridgnorth Sports and Leisure Centre, Northgate, Bridgnorth, Shropshire
Details See Chenevare Fairs 20 January

Hatfield Antiques & Collectors Fair
Location Red Lion, Great North Road, Hatfield, Hertfordshire
Details See Hatfield Antiques & Collectors Fair 20 January

Monmouthshire County Antiques & Collectors Fair
Location The Market Hall (next to the Town Hall), Abergavenny, Monmouthshire
Details See Monmouthshire County Antiques & Collectors Fair 20 January

Wessex Fairs
Location Combe Lodge, A368, Blagdon, Nr Church Hill, North Somerset
Details See Wessex Fairs 24 March

23

Browser's Antique & Collectors Fair
Location Village Hall, Station Road, Pangbourne, Berkshire (on A329 off A4, M4 Jct 12/13)
Details See Browser's Antique & Collectors Fair 26 January

23–24

4th Mid Beds Antiques Fair
Location Silsoe Conference Centre
Details See 3rd Mid Beds Antiques Fair 6–7 April

Antiques & Collectors Fair
Location Burgess Hall, St Ives Recreation Centre, St Ives, Cambridgeshire
Details See Antiques & Collectors Fair 16–17 February

The Original Long Melford Fair
Location The Old School, Long Melford, Suffolk
Details See The Original Long Melford Fair 26–27 January

DECEMBER

24

Antique and Collectors Fair
Location Canons Leisure Centre, Madeira Road, Mitcham, Surrey
Details See Antique and Collectors Fair 27 January

Antiques and Collectables Fair
Location Clontarf Castle, Castle Avenue, Dublin
Details See Antiques Fairs Ireland 24 February

Athena Fayres
Location Community Centre, Mill Lane, Wickham, Hampshire
Details See Athena Fayres 27 January

Battersea Town Hall Art Deco Fair
Location Battersea Town Hall
Details See Battersea Town Hall Art Deco Fair February 17

Biggleswade Antiques Fairs
Location The Addison Centre, Kempston, Bedford
Details See Biggleswade Antiques Fairs 27 January

Bob Evans Fairs
Location Hereford Leisure Centre, Holmer Road
Details See Bob Evans Fairs 20 January

Burford Antiques Fair
Location Burford School, Burford, Oxfordshire
Details See Burford Antiques Fair 27 January

Chatsworth Fairs
Location Cedar Court Hotel, Jct 39 M1, Wakefield
Details See Chatsworth Fairs 3 February

Chenevare Fairs
Location Hagley Community Centre, Worcester Road, West Hagley, Hereford & Worcester
Details See Chenevare Fairs 27 January

Clock & Watch Dealers Fair
Location Haydock Park racecourse, M6 Jct 23
Details See Clock & Watch Dealers Fair 3 March

J and K Fairs
Location Lincolnshire Showground, Lincoln
Details See J and K Fairs 20 January

Newmarket Antiques & Collectors Fair
Location Millennium Grandstand, Rowley Mile Racecourse, Newmarket, Suffolk
Details See Newmarket Antiques & Collectors Fair 17 February

R and S Western Fairs
Location Trenython Manor, Tywardreath, Nr Par, Cornwall
Details See R and S Western Fairs 27 January

Wessex Fairs
Location Winter Gardens, Weston-Super-Mare
Details See Wessex Fairs 24 February

25

Antiques & Collectors Fair
Location Crook Log Sports Centre, Brampton Road, Bexleyheath, Kent
Details See Antiques & Collectors Fair 3 February

27

Bloomsbury Postcard & Collectors Fair
Location Galleon Suite, Royal National Hotel, Bedford Way, London, WC1
Details See Bloomsbury Postcard and Collectors Fair 27 January

28

Antique & Collectors Fair
Location Nantwich Civic Hall, Market Street, Nantwich, Cheshire, M6 Jct 16
Details See Antique & Collectors Fair 31 January

28–1 Dec

Antiques for Everyone
Ⓔ antiques@necgroup.co.uk
Ⓦ www.antiquesforeveryone.co.uk
Location NEC Birmingham, Hall 5 P
Est. 1985
Open Weekdays 11am–8pm 11am–6pm weekends
Entrance fee 28th £7 29th–1st £6
Details Over 600 dealers

29–1 Dec

The Autumn Antiques Fair
Contact Louis O'Sullivan
☎ 00 3531 2859294
Location Royal Dublin Society, Ballsbridge, Dublin 4, Ireland P
Open 11am–7pm
Entrance fee 7 Euros
Details Over 30 dealers

The International Antiques and Collectors Fair at RAF Swinderby
Location RAF Swinderby, A46 between Newark and Lincoln
Details See The International Antiques and Collectors Fair at RAF Swinderby 1–3 February

30

Devon County Antiques Fairs
Location Salisbury Leisure Centre, The Butts, Hulse Road, Salisbury
Details See Devon County Antiques Fairs 15 June

Scotfairs Antique and Collectors Fair
Location The Citadel Leisure Centre, Ayr Baths, South Beach Road, Ayr
Details See Scotfairs Antique and Collectors Fair 26 January

30–1 Dec

Buxton Antique and Collectors Fair
Location Pavilion Gardens, Buxton, Derbyshire
Details See Buxton Antique and Collectors Fair 26–27 January

DECEMBER

1

Antiques and Collectables Fair
Location Newman House, 85 St Stephen's Green, Dublin 2
Details See Antiques and Collectables Fair 20 January

Best of Fairs
Location The Village Hall, Copdock, 3 miles west of Ipswich
Details See Best of Fairs 3 February

Brocante
Location Kensington Town Hall, Hornton Street, London, W8
Details See Brocante 3 February

Cross Country Fairs Ltd
Location Copthorne Hotel, Effingham Park, West Sussex
Details See Cross Country Fairs Ltd 3 February

Hampstead Antique Collectors Fair
Location Hampstead Community Centre, High Street, Hampstead
Details See Hampstead Antique Collectors Fair 3 February

Harlequin Fairs
Location Centre for Epilepsy, Chalfont Common, Chalfont St Peter, Buckinghamshire
Details See Harlequin Fairs 3 February

Ipswich Antiques and Collectables Fair
Location Ipswich County Hotel (formerly Ipswich Moat House) Copdock, Ipswich, Suffolk
Details See Ipswich Antiques and Collectables Fair

Lechlade Antiques Fair
Location The New Memorial Hall, Burford Road, Lechlade, Gloucestershire
Details See Lechlade Antiques Fair 3 February

Magnum Antiques Fairs
Location Midhurst, The Grange Centre, Bepton Road
Details 135 stands

Malvern Antiques & Collectors Fair
Location Three Counties Showground, Malvern, Worcestershire
Details See Malvern Antiques & Collectors Fair 3 February

Pennyfarthing Fayres
Location Potters Bar
Details See Pennyfarthing Fayres 10 February

Scotfairs Antique and Collectors Fair
Location Meadowbank Stadium, London Road, Edinburgh
Details See Scotfairs Antique and Collectors Fair 3 February

Wessex Fairs
Location Holiday Inn, Taunton, Somerset, M5 Jct 25
Details See Wessex Fairs 3 February

2–3

Newark International Antiques & Collectors Fair
Location Newark & Notts Showground, Newark
Details See Newark International Antiques & Collectors Fair 4–5 February

4

Newbury Racecourse
Location Newbury Racecourse, Newbury, Berkshire
Details See Newbury Racecourse February 13

The Long Melford
Location Village Memorial Hall, Long Melford, Suffolk
Details See The Long Melford 6 February

5

Paraphernalia Fairs
Location Lyndhurst Community Centre, Lyndhurst, New Forest, Hampshire
Details See Paraphernalia Fairs 14 February

6–8

Galloway Antiques Fairs
Location Stansted House, Rowlands Castle, Hants/West Sussex
Details See Galloway Antiques Fairs 8–10 March

Stafford Bingley Hall
Location The Bingley Hall, County Showground Staffordshire
Details See Stafford Bingley Hall 8–10 February

7

Antiques & Collectors Fair
Location St George's Hall, Lime Street, Liverpool
Details See Antiques & Collectors Fair 1 June

Athena Fayres
Location Lockswood Community Centre, Locks Heath Shopping Centre, Locks Heath, Nr Fareham, Hants
Details See Athena Fayres 9 February

Chelsea Town Hall
Location Chelsea Town Hall, King's Road, Chelsea, London SW3
Details See Chelsea Town Hall 19 January

Devon County Antiques Fairs
Location Matford Centre in the Exeter Livestock Centre, Marsh Barton, Exeter
Details See Devon County Antiques Fairs 9 February

Marcel Fairs
Location St Paul's Church Hall, Mill Hill, Ridgeway, London, NW7
Details See Marcel Fairs 2 February

Victoriana's Fairs
Location Walsall Town Hall, Walsall, West Midlands
Details See Victoriana's Fairs 2 February

7–8

Harpenden Antiques and Fine Art Fair
Location Rothamsted Conference Centre, on A1081 Harpenden–St Albans road
Details See Harpenden Antiques and Fine Art Fair 9–10 February

8

Antique and Collectors Fair
Location Woking Leisure Centre, Kingfield Road, Woking, Surrey
Details See Antique and Collectors Fair 10 February

FAIRS

DECEMBER

Antiques and Collectables Fair
Location Newman House, 85 St Stephen's Green, Dublin 2
Details See Antiques and Collectables Fair 20 January

Antiques & Collectors Fairs
Location Runnymeade Hotel & Spa, Windsor Road, Egham, Surrey
Details See Antiques & Collectors Fair 10 February

Athena Fayres
Location The Village Hall, Minstead, Nr Lyndhurst, about a mile from the end of the M27
Details See Athena Fayres 20 January

Chenevare Fairs
Location Kinver Leisure Centre, Enville Road, Kinver, Stourbridge, West Midlands
Details See Chenevare Fairs 10 February

Chiswick Town Hall Art Deco Fair
Location Chiswick Town Hall
Details See Chiswick Town Hall Art Deco Fair March 3

Crispin Fairs
Location Victoria Hall, Hartley Wintney, Hampshire
Details See Crispin Fairs 10 February

Devon County Antiques Fairs
Location Westland Sports and Social Club, Westbourne Close, Yeovil, Somerset
Details See Devon County Antiques Fairs 10 February

Furze Hill
Location Furze Hill, Banqueting Centre, Margaretting, Nr Chelmsford
Details See Furze Hill 10 February

J and K Fairs
Location Lincolnshire Showground, Lincoln
Details See J and K Fairs 20 January

Lostwithiel Antiques Fair
Location Community Centre, Lostwithiel, Cornwall
Details See Lostwithiel Antiques Fair 10 February

Midas Antique Fair
Location The Bellhouse Hotel, Oxford Road (A40), Beaconsfield, Bucks
Details See Midas Antique Fair 10 February

11

Marks Tey
Location Parish Hall, Marks Tey, Essex
Details See Marks Tey 13 February

The Big Brum
Location St Martins Market (The Rag), Edgbaston Street, Birmingham
Details See The Big Brum 30 January

14

Antiques Fair
Location Castle Hall, Hertford, Hertfordshire
Details See Antiques Fair 19 January

Aquarius Fairs
Location The Harlington Centre, High Street, Fleet, Hampshire
Details See Aquarius Fairs 9 February

Browser's Antique & Collectors Fair
Location Village Hall, Station Road, Pangbourne, Berkshire (on A329 off A4, M4 Jct 12/13)
Details See Browser's Antique & Collectors Fair 26 January

Pamela Robertson Antique and Collectors Fair
Location Northgate Arena, Victoria Road, Cheshire
Details See Pamela Robertson Antique and Collectors Fair 26 January

Scotfairs Antique and Collectors Fair
Location Albert Halls, Dumbarton Road, Stirling
Details See Scotfairs Antique and Collectors Fair 2 February

14–15

Carmarthen Antiques & Collectors Fair
Location United Counties Showground, Carmarthen
Open 10am–4pm
Details See Carmarthen Antiques & Collectors Fair 9–10 March

The Original Long Melford Fair
Location The Old School, Long Melford, Suffolk
Details See The Original Long Melford Fair 26–27 January

15

Antiques & Collectors Fair
Location Knights Hill Hotel, South Wooton, King's Lynn
Details See Antiques & Collectors Fair 20 January

Aquarius Fairs
Location Heckfield Memorial Hall, Church Lane, Heckfield, Hook, Hampshire
Details See Aquarius Fairs 20 January

Biggleswade Antiques Fairs
Location The Weatherley Centre, Eagle Farm Road, Biggleswade, Bedfordshire
Details See Biggleswade Antiques Fairs 20 January

Bloomsbury Postcard & Collectors Fair
Location Galleon Suite, Royal National Hotel, Bedford Way, London, WC1
Details See Bloomsbury Postcard and Collectors Fair 27 January

Brunel Clock & Watch Fair
Location Brunel University, Kingston Lane, Uxbridge, Middlesex
Details See Brunel Clock & Watch Fair 17 February

Chenevare Fairs
Location Hagley Community Centre, Worcester Road, West Hagley, Hereford & Worcester

Details See Chenevare Fairs 27 January

Hatfield Antiques & Collectors Fair
Location Red Lion, Great North Road, Hatfield, Hertfordshire
Details See Hatfield Antiques & Collectors Fair 20 January

Mark Carter Militaria & Medal Fairs
Location Yate Leisure Centre, Kennedy Way, Yate, Bristol
Details See Mark Carter Militaria & Medal Fairs 3 February

Monmouthshire County Antiques & Collectors Fair
Location The Market Hall (next to the Town Hall), Abergavenny, Monmouthshire
Details See Monmouthshire County Antiques & Collectors Fair 20 January

Royal Horticultural Hall
Location Royal Horticultural Hall, Lawrence Hall, Greycoat Street, London SW1
Details See Royal Horticultural Hall 10 February

Scotfairs Antique and Collectors Fair
Location Moir Hall, Mitchell Library, Granville Street, Glasgow
Details See Scotfairs Antique and Collectors Fair 20 January

21

Chingford Antiques & Collectors Fair
Location Assembly Hall, The Green, Station Road, Chingford
Details See Chingford Antiques & Collectors Fair 26 January

Commonwealth Institute Coin Fair
Location The Commonwealth Institute, Kensington High Street, London, W8
Details See Commonwealth Institute Coin Fair 19 January

Scotfairs Antique and Collectors Fair
Location The Citadel Leisure Centre, Ayr Baths, South Beach Road, Ayr
Details See Scotfairs Antique and Collectors Fair 26 January

21–22

South Cotswolds Xmas Antiques Fair
Contact Anne Harwood
☎ 01249 661111 Ⓕ 01249 661111
Ⓔ enquiries@cooperantiquesfairs.co.uk
Ⓦ www.cooperantiquesfairs.co.uk
Location Westonbirt School, Nr Tetbury, Gloucestershire
Open Sat Sun 11am–5pm
Entrance fee £3.50 Children under 16 and OAPs free

26

Antique & Collectors Fair
Location Nantwich Civic Hall, Market Street, Nantwich, Cheshire, M6 Jct 16
Details See Antique & Collectors Fair 31 January

Blackpool Winter Gardens Antiques and Collectors Fair
☎ 01253 782828 Ⓕ 01253 714715
Location Empress Ballroom, Blackpool Winter Gardens, Blackpool, Lancashire Ⓟ
Open Trade 7.30am Public 9.30am–4pm
Entrance fee 7.30am–9pm £5 plus card 9.30am–5pm £2.50
Details 200 stalls

Jade Fairs
Location Lowther Pavilion, The Promenade, Lytham St Anne's, Lancashire
Details See Jade Fairs 2 February

27

Art Nouveau and Art Deco Fair
Location Woking Leisure Centre, Kingfield Road, Woking, Surrey
Details See Art Nouveau and Art Deco Fair 31 March

Wembley Antiques & Collectors Fair
Location Hall 3, Wembley Exhibition Centre, Wembley, London
Details See Wembley Antiques & Collectors Fair 1 April

27–29

West Midlands Antique Fairs
Location Prestwood Complex, Stafford County Showground
Details See West Midlands Antique Fairs 23–24 February

28

Bob Evans Fairs
Location Sports Connexion, Ryton on Dunsmore, Coventry
Details See Bob Evans Fairs 10 February

28–29

Beckett Antique Fairs
Location Doncaster Race Exhibition Centre, Doncaster
Details See Beckett Antique Fairs 16–17 February

Buxton Antique and Collectors Fair
Location Pavilion Gardens, Buxton, Derbyshire
Details See Buxton Antique and Collectors Fair 26–27 January

The Original Long Melford Fair
Location The Old School, Long Melford, Suffolk
Details See The Original Long Melford Fair 26–27 January

29

Antique and Collectors Fair
Location Berkhampstead Sports Centre, Lagley Meadow, Douglas Gardens, Berkhampstead, Hertfordshire
Details See Antique and Collectors Fair 31 March

Athena Fayres
Contact Mr A Tonks
☎ 01489 578093 (day) 01489 584633 (eve)
Location Community Centre, Mill Lane, Wickham, Hampshire Ⓟ
Est. 1988
Open Trade 10am Public 11am–4pm
Entrance fee 80p Trade £1.50
Details Around 78 stalls

The BACA *Winners...*

CATEGORY 1
General Antiques Dealer

LONDON (INSIDE M25)
sponsored by 

Windsor House Antiques
28-29 Dover Street, Mayfair, London W1X 3PA

UK (OUTSIDE M25) *sponsored by* ANTIQUE STREET www.antiquestreet.co.uk
David J. Hansord & Son
6 & 7 Castle Hill, Lincoln,
Lincolnshire LN1 3AA

CATEGORY 2
Specialist Antiques Dealers

FURNITURE
Norman Adams
8-10 Hans Road, Knightsbridge,
London SW3 1RX

CERAMICS
Roderick Jellicoe
3a Campden Street, off Kensington Church St,
London W8 7EP

CLOCKS, WATCHES & SCIENTIFIC INSTRUMENTS
Brian & Joy Loomes
Calf Haugh Farmhouse, Pateley Bridge,
Harrogate, N. Yorks HG3 5HW

SILVER & PLATE
Nicholas Shaw Antiques
Great Grooms Antiques Centre, Parbrook,
Billingshurst, West Sussex RH14 9EU

COLLECTABLES
Ropewalk Antiques
Rye, East Sussex TN31 7NA

TOYS & DOLLS
Yesterday Child
Angel Arcade, 118 Islington High Street,
London N1 8EG

JEWELLERY
N. Bloom & Son
The New Bond St Antiques Centre,
124 New Bond Street, London W1S 1DX

ARMS & ARMOUR
Trident Arms
96-98 Derby Road, Nottingham NG1 5FB

COSTUMES & TEXTILES
Linda Wrigglesworth Ltd
34 Brook Street, London W1K 5DN

ARCHITECTURAL & GARDEN
LASSCO
The London Architectural Salvage
and Supply Co, St Michael's Church,
Mark Street, London EC2 4ER

CATEGORY 3
Auction Houses

LONDON (INSIDE M25)
Phillips
101 New Bond Street, London W1S 1SR

UK (OUTSIDE M25)
Tennants Auctioneers
The Auction Centre, Leyburn,
N. Yorkshire DL8 5SG

CATEGORY 4
Associated Awards

For a significant contribution to the popular appreciation of Antiques
The BBC Antiques Roadshow

FAIR OF THE YEAR
Olympia Fine Art & Antiques Fair
June 2000, Olympia, London

BEST IN-HOUSE EXHIBITION *sponsored by* Antiques Trade GAZETTE
Pelham Galleries
"East and West:
Masterpieces of Lacquer Furniture",
24-25 Mount Street, London W1Y 5RB

AUCTIONEER OF THE YEAR
Ben Lloyd
Mallams, Bocardo House, St Michael's Street,
Oxford OX1 2DR

BEST ANTIQUES WRITER *sponsored by* freeserve www.freeserve.com
Christopher Wood
Christopher Wood Gallery, 20 Georgian House,
10 Bury Street, London SW1Y 6AA

SERVICES AWARD: BEST FREIGHT CARRIER *sponsored by* CHRISTIE'S
Lockson
29 Broomfield Street, London E14 6BX

MILLER'S CLUB **BEST ANTIQUES TOWN/VILLAGE**
Horncastle, Lincolnshire

Indexes

In the Index of Specialists and the General Index, shops and businesses beginning with a forename are listed alphabetically by surname: thus R G Archer Books is listed under A and Michael Saffell Antiques appears under S.

The county in which a city, town or village has been placed in the Directory is also given In the Index of Place Names. Note that this is not always the county given in the address that forms part of the entry.

KEY TO MEMBER ORGANISATIONS

In order to make the information in this book more concise we have used the following abbreviations where applicable.

AAFAA Alresford Antique & Fine Arts Association`
ABA Antiquarian Booksellers' Association
ACC Antique Collectors' Club
ADA Antique Dealers' Association
ADDA Art Deco Dealers' Association
ADS Antique Dealers' Society
AFAA Association of Fine Art Auctioneers
AHA American Horological Association
AHS Antiquarian Horological Society
AMU Association Master Upholsterers
AMUSF Association of Master Upholsterers & Soft Furnishers
ANA American Numismatic Association
ARVA Association of Regional Valuers & Auctioneers
ASDA American Stamp Dealers' Association
ASVA Association of Society of Valuers & Auctioneers
AU Association of Upholsterers
BA Booksellers' Association
BABA-ADA Bath & Bradford on Avon Antique Dealers' Association
BABI Booksellers' Association of Britain & Ireland
BADA British Antique Dealers' Association
BAFRA British Antique Furniture Restorers' Association
BAR British Association of Removers
BCPAA British China & Porcelain Artists' Association
BGA British Gemologists' Association
BHI British Horological Institute
BIFA British International Freight Association
BJA British Jewellers' Association
BNTA British Numismatic Trade Association
BTCM British Traditional Cabinet Makers
BWCG British Watch & Clockmakers' Guild
CADA Cotswold Antique Dealers' Association
CC Clockmakers' Company
CCCC Clarice Cliff Collectors' Club
CINOA Confédération Internationale des Négotiants en Oeuvres d'Art
CLPGS City of London Phonograph & Gramophone Society
CGCG Ceramics & Glass Conservation Group
CISS Channel Islands Specialists Society
CPADA Camden Passage Antique Dealers' Association
CPTA Camden Passage Traders' Association
CR Conservation Register
CSFAC Chartered Surveyors of Fine Art & Chattels
DADA Dorking Antique Dealers' Association
EADA Essex Antique Dealers' Association
ESoc Ephemera Society
FATG Fine Art Trade Guild
FNAVA Federation of National Auctioneers & Valuers
FSVA Fellow of the Society of Valuers & Auctioneers
GADR Guild of Antique Dealers & Restorers
GAI Guild of Architectural Ironmongers
GCS Golf Collectors' Society (GB, USA)
GOMC Guild of Master Craftsmen
HADA Hudson Antique Dealers' Association
IAA Institute of Antiques Auctioneers
IAB Irish Antiquarian Bookdealers
IADA Irish Antique Dealers' Association
IADAA International Association of Dealers in Ancient Art
IATA International Air Transport Association
IAVI Irish Auctioneers & Valuers Institute
IBNS International Bank Note Society
ICHAWI Institute for the Conservation of Historic & Artistic Works in Ireland
ICOM International Comittee for Conservation
IDDA Interior Decorators' & Designers' Association
IIC International Institute for Conservation of Historic & Artistic Work
ILAB International League of Antiquarian Booksellers
IMCOS International Map Collectors' Society
IMTA International Map Trade Association
IPAA International Porcelain Artists' Association
IPAV Institute of Professional Auctioneers & Valuers
IPC Institute of Paper Conservation
IPCRA Irish Professional Conservators' & Restorers' Association
ISVA Incorporated Society of Valuers & Auctioneers
IRRV Institute of Revenues, Ratings & Valuation
ITA Islington Trading Association
KCSADA Kensington Church Street Antique Dealers' Association
LAB London Antique Books

KEY TO MEMBER ORGANISATIONS

LAPADA	London & Provincial Antique Dealers' Association
LJAJDA	London & Japan Antique Jewellery Dealers' Association
LPC	League of Professional Craftsmen
MAPH	Member of the Association of Professional Horologists
MBHI	Member of British Horological Society
MBWCG	Member of British Watch & Clockmakers' Guild
NACF	National Art Collections Fund
NAEA	National Art Education Association
NAG	National Association of Goldsmiths
NAVA	National Association of Auctioneers & Valuers
NAWCC	National Association of Watch & Clock Collectors
NCCR	National Council for Conservation and Restoration
NIAVI	Northern Ireland Auctioneers & Valuers Institute
OCS	Oriental Ceramic Society
OMRS	Order Medals Research Society
PAADA	Petworth Art & Antique Dealers' Association
PADA	Portobello Antique Dealers' Association
PBFA	Provincial Book Fair Association
PBSA	Provincial Book Sellers' Association
PLA	Private Libraries Association
PNG	Professional Numismatists' Guild
PO	Pewter Organisation
PTA	Postcard Traders' Association
PTS	Philatellic Traders' Society
RADS	Registered Antique Dealers' Association
RICS	Royal Institute of Chartered Surveyors
RWHA	Royal Warrant Holders' Association
SAA	Scottish Association of Auctioneers
SAADA	Sherborne Art & Antique Dealers' Association
SDA	Stamp Dealers' Association
SDADA	Saintfield & District Antique Dealers' Association
SLAD	Society of London Art Dealers'
SIS	Scientific Instrument Society
SOBB	Society of Book Binders
SOFAA	Society of Fine Art Auctioneers
SPTA	Scottish Philatelic Traders' Association
SSA	Sussex Saleroom Association
SSCR	Scottish Society for Conservation & Restoration
TADA	Tetbury Antique Dealers' Association
TCS	Tennis Collectors' Society
TVADA	Thames Valley Antique Dealers' Association
UACC	United Autograph Collectors' Club
UKIC	United Kingdom Institute for Conservation
UKPCC	UK Perfume Collectors' Club
WCC	Worshipful Company of Clockmakers
WSADA	West Street Antique Dealers' Association
WKADA	West Kent Antique Dealers' Association

INDEX OF ADVERTISERS

Antiques Magazine 456
Amber Antiques 108
Architectural Heritage back cover
BACA 10, 554
The Brackley Antique Centre 278
Dollectable 356
Dukeries Antique Centre 282
Heanor Antiques Centre 272
Irish Antiques Online 443, 445
Ann Lingard 43
Lockson Services Ltd 5
Brian Loomes 324
Malvern Studios 311
Miller's Publications 504
Oxford Street Antiques Centre 273
Allan Smith 197
Alan & Kathy Stacey front inside cover
Station Mill Antiques Centre 262
Watsons Antiques back inside cover
Weather House Antiques 337

INDEX OF SPECIALISTS

ANTIQUITIES

Ancient and Gothic 171
Helios Gallery 95

ARCHITECTURAL

Aladdins Architectural Antiques 353
Angus Architectural Antiques 431
Antique Builders Suppliers 434
Architectural Antiques 233
Architectural Emporium 39
Architectural Heritage 243
Architectural Salvage 256
The Architectural Warehouse 118
Ballyalton House Architectural Antiques 437
Baron Antiques 361
Brighton Architectural Salvage 13
Brondesbury Architectural Reclamation 56
Camberwell Architectural Salvage & Antiques 58
Cast Offs 305
Cox's Architectural Salvage Yard Ltd 245
Crowther 62
Crowther of Syon Lodge Ltd 104
Cumbria Architectural Salvage 368
M R Dingle 150
Dorset Reclamation 167
Drummonds Architectural Antiques Ltd 132
EASY Edinburgh & Glasgow Architectural Salvage Yard 406
Easy Strip 260
Edenderry Architectural Salvage Ltd 453
The Emporium 316
Frome Reclamation 186
Goodwoods 443
Great Northern Architectural Antiques Co Ltd 363
Heritage Reclamations 229
Holyrood Architectural Salvage 406
Lakeland Architectural Antiques 366
LASSCO RBK 58
LASSCO St Michael's 46
Lindsay Court Architectural 344
McGovern's Corner 447
MDS Ltd 305
Robert Mills Architectural Antiques 182
Minchinhampton Architectural Salvage Co 240
Mongers Architectural Salvage 216
Nettlebed Antique Merchants 264
Pattison's Architectural Antiques 256
Plympton Reclamation and Architectural Salvage Ltd 163
Raven Reclaim & Architectural Salvage Ltd 305
Retrouvius Architectural Reclamation 57, 85
Ribble Reclamation 382
Small Wood Ltd 125
Southern Stoves & Fireplaces 170
Taymouth Architectural Antiques 42
Tynemouth Architectural Salvage 355
The Victorian Salvage and Joinery Co Ltd 448
Walcot Reclamation Ltd 180
Wells Reclamation Company 190
Willesden Green Architectural Salvage 57
Woodside Reclamation 352

BATHROOM FITTINGS

Alscot Bathroom Company 301
Catchpole and Rye 35
Thomas Crapper & Co 302

CAST-IRON RADIATORS

Cheshire Cast Company 360

CHURCH FURNISHINGS

Antique Church Furnishings 135
Architectural Antiques and Salvage 446
Chancellors Church Furnishings 135
McDonnell's Antique Furniture 451
Pew Corner Ltd 132

DOORS

LASSCO Warehouse 49
Original Door Specialist 58
Pipkins Antiques 379

FIREPLACES

Abacus Fireplaces 318
Antique Fireplaces 402
Any Old Iron 332
Architectural Rescue 58
Cardiff Reclamation 400
D & T Architectural Salvage 383
Decorative Heating 400
The Fireplace (Hungerford) Ltd 109
Fireplaces 'n' Things 109
Lindsay Architectural Antiques 305
T & J W Neilson Ltd 407
Nostalgia 375
Original Architectural Antiques 242
Past and Present Fireplaces 378
Pine-Apple Antiques 317
Rusty Grates 189
P J Smith (Fair Trades) 440
St Julien 321
The Fire & Stove Shop 399
Yesterdays Antiques 342

FLOORING

Abergavenny Reclamation 396
Holland & Welsh 400
LASSCO Flooring 57

STAINED GLASS

Architectural Artefacts 228
Gatehouse Workshops 284

STOVES

Ovne Antique Stoves 443

TELEPHONE BOXES

James Fuller and Son 201

ARMS & ARMOUR

Peter Finer 300
The Lanes Armoury 14
Michael D Long Ltd 285
M J M Antiques 110
St Pancras Antiques 139
West Street Antiques 128
Worldwide Arms Ltd 294

ARMOUR

Arbour Antiques Ltd 301
Peter Dale Ltd 62

ASIAN AND ISLAMIC

Robert Hales Antiques 89

JAPANESE SWORDS

Garth Vincent Antique Arms and Armour 341
Yazuka 385

ASIAN WORKS OF ART

Antiquewest Ltd at Patrick Sandberg Antiques 88
Gregg Baker Asian Art 88
Sebastiano Barbagallo Antiques 69, 93
David Bowden Chinese and Japanese Art 46
Brandt Oriental Antiques 79
Paul Champkins Oriental Art 79
Glade Antiques 237
Anita Gray 81
Grays Antique Market 81
Hanshan Tang Books 76
Gerard Hawthorn Ltd 82
Catherine Hunt 249
Imperial Antiques 375
Indigo 71, 178, 193
J A N Fine Art 90
Peter Kemp 90
Lini Designs 67
Jeremy Mason 64
Morris Namdar 84
Ormonde Gallery 96
Phoenix Oriental Art 50
Rossi & Rossi Ltd 65
Shiraz Antiques 85

CENTRAL ASIA

Artique 248

CERAMICS

Guest and Gray 81
Roger Keverne Ltd 82
Oriental Gallery 245
Daphne Rankin & Ian Conn Oriental Antiques 72
Marcus Ross Antiques 50

CHINESE ART

Eskenazi Ltd 80
S Marchant & Son 91
Priestley and Ferraro 77

CHINESE PORCELAIN
Geoffrey Waters Ltd 69

CHINESE SNUFF BOTTLES
Robert Hall 81

JAPANESE
Barry Davies Oriental Art 79

JAPANESE SATSUMA WARE
Mere Antiques 165

JAPANESE WOODCUT PRINTS
Japanese Gallery Ltd 49, 90

NORITAKE
Dragonlee Collectables 36
Yamamoto Antiques 87

BANKNOTES

Colin Narbeth and Son 101

BAROMETERS

Antique Barometers 203
Bar Street Antiques 326
Baskerville Antiques 142
Knole Barometers 188
Derek & Tina Rayment Antiques 360
Summersons 303
Alan Walker 111
Weather House Antiques 338

BLACK FOREST

Arenski Fine Art 93
Peter Petrou 96

BOOKS

Adam & Eve Books 73
Duncan M Allsop 305
Bath Old Books 177
Beaumont Travel Books 58
Bon-Accord Books 115
Book Art and Architecture Ltd 98
The Bookmark 13
Books & Maps 168
Boris Books 114
Bouquiniste 164
Bridport Old Books 170
Broadhursts of Southport Ltd 385
Iain Campbell 360
Canon Gate Bookshop 139
The Castle Book Shop 206
Castle Books 405
Coach House Bookshop 249
Cotham Hill Bookshop 182
Countryside Books 109
The Dartmoor Bookshop 152
G David 200
Deeside Books 112
Exeter Rare Books 156
Steven Ferdinando V
David Ferrow 216
Simon Finch 95
Fisher & Sperr 52
Fordham's 30
Paul Foster Books 76
Robert Frew Ltd 98
H M Gilbert 120
Gillmorehill Books 256
Simon Gough Books Ltd 216
Major Iain Grahame 222
Grant & Shaw Ltd 406
Peter J Hadley 218
Peter Hames 154
Adrian Harrington Antiquarian Bookseller 89
Frederick Harrison 162
Peter Herington Antiquarian Bookseller 67
Honiton Old Book Shop 159
Jiri Books 435
George Kelsall 372
Kings Quair 379
Robert Kirkman Ltd 233
E W Marchpane Ltd 101
New, Secondhand & Antiquarian Books 175
Nova Foresta Books 120
The Old Aberdeen Bookshop 350
Colin Page Antiquarian Books 15
Pedlar's Pack Books 167
Piccadilly Rare Books 24
Poor Richard's Books 224
Bertram Rota Ltd 102
P & B Rowan 433
Second Edition 408
Bernard J Shapero Rare Books 85
Clive Smith 208
Staniland Booksellers 347
Stothert Old Books 359
Stride & Son 139
Taikoo Books Ltd 331
Thomas Thorp 132
Till's Bookshop 408
Unsworths Booksellers Ltd 99, 265
R G Watkins 188
John & Shahin Wilbraham 19
Nigel Williams Rare Books 103

AFRICA
Heritage Books 123
Yesterdays Books 170

AFRICA, MIDDLE EAST
Oriental & African Books 289

ANTIQUES
Hay Cinema Bookshop 251
Ian K Pugh Books 312

ARCHAEOLOGY
The Old Bank Bookshop 277

ARCHITECTURE
Richard Axe Books 320
Camden Books 178
The Old Town Bookshop 407
Janette Ray Rare Books 330

ART
Thomas Heneage Art Books 63
Christopher Mayes 209
Nicholas Merchant 327
Savery Books 15
West Port Books 408

ARTHUR RACKHAM
Goldsworth Books and Prints 136

ARTS AND ANTIQUES
Howes Bookshop Ltd 19

ASIAN
Fine Books Oriental Ltd 98

BELLRINGING
Church Green Books 267

BINDINGS, FIRST EDITIONS
A & Y Cumming Ltd 21

PRODUCTION, DISTRIBUTION
Barry McKay Rare Books 364

BRIDGE
Beaver Booksearch 221

CARPETS & RUGS
Abington Books 224

CHESHIRE
Mereside Books 358

CHILDREN'S
Books Bought and Sold 129
The Bookshop Godmanchester 202
The Canterbury Book Shop 27
Minstergate Bookshop 330
The Old Children's Bookshelf 407
Rose's Books 252
Keith A Savage 228
John Williams 196

CINEMA
Keel Row Books 355
Michael Moon 369

CORNWALL
Bonython Bookshop 151
New Street Books 149

COUNTRYSIDE
Books Galore 185

CRICKET
Hambleton Books 328
J W McKenzie 130
Christopher Saunders 245
St Mary's Books & Prints 347

DECORATIVE ARTS
Potterton Books 326

DETECTIVE FICTION
Murder & Mayhem 252

EARLY PENGUIN
The Bookshop 185

EARLY PRINTED
Thomas Thorp 259
EARLY PENGUIN

INDEX OF SPECIALISTS

BOOKS

The Bookshop 182

EARLY PRINTED
Thomas Thorp 256

EAST ANGLIA
R G Archer Books 226

ENGLISH LITERATURE
Addyman Books 251
Jack Duncan 329
R A Gekoski Booksellers 98

FIELD SPORTS
John & Judith Head Barn Book Supply 195
Hereward Books 202
R E and G B Way 222

FILM AND TELEVISION
Yorkshire Relics 337

FIRST EDITIONS
Readers' Dream 214

GIRLS SCHOOL STORIES
The Haunted Bookshop 200

GLOUCESTERSHIRE AND WORCESTERSHIRE
Bookworms of Evesham 310

HAMPSHIRE
Book Academy 120

HEREFORD AND WORCESTER
Lechmere Antiquarian Books 311

HISTORY OF IDEAS
Tavistock Books 164
Clevedon Books 184

HORSE RACING
Byrkley Books Ltd 293

ICTHYOLOGY
Steven Simpson Natural History Books 225

ILLUSTRATED
Vanessa Parker Rare Books 452

ILLUSTRATED NATURAL HISTORY
Nicholas Goodyer 52

IRISH INTEREST
Antiquarian Booksellers 436
The Bantry Bookstore 442
The Bookshop 444
Cathach Books 446
Cathair Books 455
Davidson Books 436
Foyle Books 439
Royal Carberry Books 443
Stacks Bookshop 436
Stokes Books 448
Trinity Rare Books 451
The Winding Stair Bookshop 449

JUDAICA
Henry Pordes Books Ltd 101

LAKE DISTRICT
Maurice Dodd Books 368

LANGUAGES
Voltaire & Rousseau 325

LAW ENFORCEMENT
Undercover Books 347

LEATHER-BOUND
Sandwich Fine Books 37

LINCOLNSHIRE
P J Cassidy 344

LITERATURE
I D Edrich 45
The Winchester Bookshop 122

LOCAL HISTORY
Mereside Books 362

MARITIME
All Books 210
The Brazen Head Bookshop & Gallery 213
Fisher Nautical 144
Gaby Goldscheider 123
McLaren Books 130
Frank Smith Maritime Aviation Books 354

MEDITERANNEAN TRAVEL
Malcolm Hornsby 276

MILITARY
The Bookworm 405
Invicta Bookshop 111
Prospect Books 391
Schull Books 442
Ken Trotman Ltd 201

MOTORING
St Paul's Street Bookshop 347

MUSIC
Hancock & Monks 251
The Malvern Bookshop 311

NATURAL HISTORY
Chelsea Gallery and Il Libro 74
A & T Gibbard 17

NORFOLK
The Angel Bookshop 217

NORTHERN TOPOGRAPHY
R F G Hollett & Son 368

NUMISMATIC
Galata Print Ltd 399

ORNITHOLOGY
Isabelline Books 156

POETRY
Marchmont Bookshop 99

PRE-1700
P J Hilton Books 100

PRIVATE PRESS
Besley's Books 221

RAILWAY
The Chichester Bookshop 139

RELIGIOUS
Beckham Books 229
Kyrios Books 282
Murray and Kemmett 140

RUPERT BEAR BOOKS AND COLLECTABLES
More Books 359, 391

RUSSIAN
Anthony C Hall 105

SCIENCE
Austwick Hall Books 318
The Eagle Bookshop 233
Rogers Turner Books 60
Mark Westwood Books 252

SCI-FI AND CRIME
Carey's Bookshop 211

SCOTTISH INTEREST
Addendum Books 61
Ainslie Books 152
The Bookcellar 364
Book-ends 114
The Bookshop 390
Cooper Hay Rare Books 26
Grampian Books 222
Latto Books 351
Mair Wilkes Books 194
McNaughtan's Bookshop 407

SCULPTURE
Madalyn S Jones 331

SHERLOCK HOLMES
The Black Cat Bookshop 274

SPAIN, HISPANIC STUDIES
Paul Orssich 73

SUFFOLK
Blake's Books 230

TEXTILES
Avril Whittle, Bookseller 368

THEATRE
J C Books 220

TOLKEIN, C S LEWIS
Daeron's Books 238

TOPOGRAPHY
Kemp Booksellers 317
The Petersfield Bookshop 118

Stella Books 396
West Country Old Books 166

TRANSPORT
Simon Lewis Transport Books 243
Miss Ellany 127

TRAVEL
Atlas Books 46
The Garden House Bookshop 231
The Penny Farthing 450
Reg & Philip Remington 102
Peter Rhodes Books 120

VICTORIAN ILLUSTRATED
Armchair Books 405

WELSH INTEREST
Rhos Point Books 391
Julian Shelley Books 390
Ystwyth Books 390

WWII INTELLIGENCE
M & M Baldwin 309

YORKSHIRE
Fairburn Books 336
The Grove Bookshop 338
Grove Country Bookshop 319
Helmsley Antiquarian & Secondhand Books 322

BOXES

Cheyne House 23
Hampton Antiques 95
Gerald Mathias 68
Mostly Boxes 108
Alan and Kathy Stacey 191
Tremayne Applied Arts 151

LIMOGES BOXES
Michael's Boxes Ltd 68

MONEY BOXES
Collectors Old Toy Shop 336

TEA CADDIES
June and Tony Stone Fine Antique Boxes 97

TORTOISESHELL
Bazaar Boxes 234

CARPETS & RUGS

Atlantic Bay Gallery 73
Carpet Auctioneers Ltd 204
Uri Jacobi Oriental Carpet Gallery 357
James E McDougall 351
Desmond and Amanda North 30
The Rug Gallery 275
Samarkand Galleries 247

ORIENTAL
Isaac Carpets 90
Peter Linden Oriental Rugs and Carpets 445

Lindfield Galleries 141
Parvis 435

CARVINGS

IVORY
A and E Foster 237

CERAMICS

Ancient and Modern Collectables Centre 223
Aurea Carter 94
Church Street Antiques 131
Cohen & Cohen 89
Cohen & Cohen Portobello Road 94
Richard Dennis Gallery 89
Julian Eade 130
Forget-Me-Nots 402
Gabor Cossa Antiques 200
Jonathan Horne 90
Richard Scott Antiques 217
Thomond Antiques 366
B & T Thorn and Son 154
Tudor House Antiques 289

19TH-20THC
Delf Stream Gallery 37

ART DECO
Rick Hubbard Art Deco 119
Tango Art Deco & Antiques 303

CHILDREN'S PLATES
Rene Nicholls 193

CLARICE CLIFF
Banana Dance Ltd 46
Bona Art Deco Store 115
Castle Antiques 437
Nolton Antiques & Fine Art 394
Paddy Cliff's Clarice! 176
Riverside Antiques 302

COMMEMORATIVE
Farthings 165
Hope & Glory 90

GAUDY WELSH
Grandpa's Collectables 392

MEISSEN
Brian Haughton Antiques 82
London Antique Gallery 91

ROCKINGHAM
Holly Farm Antiques 334

ROYAL DOULTON
Millennium Collectables 282
Bart and Julie Lemmy 165

SOUTH DEVON TORQUAY WARE
The Spinning Wheel Antiques 385

STAFFORDSHIRE POTTERY
Frost Antiques & Pine 396

SUSIE COOPER
The Elephants Trunk 21

TUNBRIDGE WARE
Amherst Antiques 98

CINEMA

Steve's World Famous Movie Store 376

CLOCKS

Rodney Adams Antiques 393
Antique Clocks by Patrick Thomas 127
A & C Antique Clocks 181
The Barbers Clock 313
Jonathan Beech Antique Clocks 452
Bell Antiques 343
Big Ben Clocks and Antiques 69
Eric A Bird Jewellers 344
Ian Burton Antique Clocks 340
D Card 107
John Carlton-Smith 62
Chelsea Clocks and Antiques 66
Chobham Antique Clocks 126
Churchill Clocks 141
Bryan Clisby 116
The Clock Clinic Ltd 76
Clock Corner 362
The Clock House 125
The Clock Shop 120
The Clock Shop 298
The Clock Workshop 108
The Clockshop 136
The Clock-Work-Shop (Winchester) 121
Coach House Antiques 18
Combe Martin Clock Shop 155
Country Clocks 258
Derbyshire Clocks 272
Leigh Extence Antique Clocks 164
Fado Antiques 450
Fieldings Antiques & Clocks 377, 382
Jeffrey Formby Antiques 245
Robin Fowler Period Clocks 341
Gaby's Clocks and Things 38
Grandfather Clock Shop 246
Grantham Clocks 342
K Grosvenor 296
G K Hadfield 366
Gerald Hampton 171
Roy C Harris 294
Haworth Antiques 320
Tony Honan 442
Horological Workshops 131
Bernard G House Longcase Clocks 190
House of Clocks 232
It's About Time 212
Jester Antiques 249
Jillings 245
Kembery Antique Clocks 179
Roger Lascelles Clocks Ltd 71
Keith Lawson Antique Clocks 220
Robert Loomes Clock Restoration

346
Brian Loomes 324
J D Luffman 360
G E Marsh (Antique Clocks) Ltd 122
J Martinez Antiques 407
F J McAvenues & Son 442
Montpellier Clocks 241
Objets d'Art 359
The Old Clock Shop 41
Old Timers 277
The Old Village Clock Shop 123
Samuel Orr 141
Pendulum of Mayfair 84
Penman Clockcare 346
Phillips Antiques & French Polishing Service 389
Derek Roberts Antiques 39
Roderick Antiques 92
Second Time Around 343
Shrewsbury Clock Shop 292
Something Different 349
Stokes Clocks 443
Strike One Antique Clocks, Barometers & Music Boxes 52
Time and Motion 315
Timecraft Clocks 175
Timepiece Antique Clocks 448
W F Turk Fine Antique Clocks 77
Ty-Llwyd Antiques 401
Village Clocks 227
Woodward Antique Clocks Ltd 308

ANNIVERSARY, 400 DAY
David Ansell 103

AUSTRO-HUNGARIAN
Campbell and Archard 37

LANTERN CLOCKS
The Lewes Clock Shop 22

LONGCASE
Craig Barfoot Clocks 263
Browns Clocks 350
Castle Antique Clocks 401
Coppelia Antiques 361
The Essence of Time 297
Farmhouse Antiques 357
John Mann Fine Antique Clocks 364
Northern Clocks 376
P A Oxley Antique Clocks & Barometers 192
Allan Smith 196
W H Webber Antique Clocks 244
Chris Wilde Antiques 322

COINS & MEDALS

Alpha Coins & Medals 376
Ancient World 329
A H Baldwin and Son 99
Birmingham Coins 304
E J & C A Brooks 205
B J Dawson 370
Clive Dennett 218
Drizen Coins 209
Granta Coins, Collectables and Antiquities 200
Intercoin 354
Lockdale Coins Ltd 225
N S E Medal Department 285
Nottingham Coin Centre 285
R & J Coins 212
J Smith 330
Sterling Coins and Medals 170
World Coins 28

COINS
Coincraft 98
Format Coins 305
R W Jeffery 149
Jersey Coin Company 430
Robert Johnson Coin Co 99
Knightsbridge Coins 64
Michael Coins 91

MEDALS
Dixons Medals 315
Dutton & Smith Medal Collectors 284
Gainsborough House Antiques 163
Neate Militarian & Antiques 229
Romsey Medals 119
Toad Hall Medals 161
Yeovil Collectors Centre 191

OLD ENGLISH COINS
Studio Coins 122

ROMAN COINS
D M Regan 385

COLLECTABLES

ANTIQUE TINS
Michael Saffell Antiques 180

BEATRIX POTTER FIGURES
The Collector 184

CIGARETTE LIGHTERS
D'Eyncourt Antiques 126

HEAVY HORSE
Cloisters Antiques 201

HORSE BRASSES
www.horsebrass.co.uk 360

PENS
Classic Pen Engineering 74
The Pen & Pencil Gallery 368

PHONE CARDS
Phone Cards Centre 191

PHOTOGRAPHICA
Appledore Antiques Centre 25

POT LIDS
Rob Gee 165

SCI-FI
Suffolk Sci-fi Fantasy 225

TRADING CARDS
Cards Inc 259

COMMEMORATIVES
Antique and Collectors' Centre Diss 214
The Commemorative Man 172

CUTLERY
Portobello Antique Store 96
Taclow Coth 148

DECORATIVE ITEMS

Corrigan Antiques 450
The World of Antiques (UK) Ltd 69

DECORATIVE ARTS

A D Antiques 265
A D Antiques 420
A D Antiques 293
A S Antiques 374
Abstract/Noonstar 88
Art Deco Etc 13
Artemis Decorative Arts Ltd 88
Aspidistra Antiques 278
Peter Christian 377
Decorative Antiques 287
The Gooday Gallery 134
Mitofsky Antiques 447
New Century 91
Sylvia Powell Decorative Art 50
Puritan Values at the Dome 229
Ruskin Decorative Arts 247

ART DECO
Antiques & Interiors 218
Baron Art 216
Camel Art Deco 47
Ciancimino Ltd 62
Classical Deco 25
Decomania 59
Muir Hewitt 336
Metropolis Art Deco 186
Omega Decorative Arts 210
Tango Curios 350
Tymewarp 219

ARTS AND CRAFTS
Art Furniture 54
Clocktower Antiques Centre 120
Finnie Antiques 28
Hill House Antiques & Decorative Arts 67
Peter Hoare Antiques 40
Paul Reeves 91
Valmar Antiques 212

COTSWOLD ARTS AND CRAFTS
David Pickup 261

GLASGOW STYLE
The Studio 122

LIBERTY
Jag Applied and Decorative Arts 90

MIRRORED ART DECO FURNITURE
B and T Antiques Ltd 93

DISPLAY UNITS
Timbercraft 381

ELECTRICAL AND MECHANICAL
Early Technology 77

CAMERAS
Stuart Heggie 28

RADIOS
On The Air Ltd 392

TELEPHONES
Deja Vu Antiques 357
Traditional Telephones 166

EPHEMERA
The Autograph Collectors Gallery 284
Corinum Auctions 242

CIGARETTE CARDS
Bumbles 125
Marcel Cards 135
Murray Cards (International) Ltd 55, 101

POSTCARDS
Brighton Postcard Shop 13
Carlton Antiques 310
Francois Celada 16
Look 'N' Hear 212
Westport House Antique Shop 453

YORKSHIRE POSTCARDS
Mike Fineron Cigarette Cards & Postcards 330

FANS
L and D Collins 66

FURNITURE
A J Antiques 176
Acquisitions Antique & Handmade Furniture 353
Adams Rooms Antiques and Interiors 77
Aldershot Antiques 113
Alexander Antiques 435
Anthemion 365
Antiquarius 232
Antique Warehouse 58
Antiques and Fine Art 149
Antiques en France 278
Apollo Antiques Ltd 302
Archers 238
Avon Antiques 191
Ayuka Ltd 258
Bayliss Antiques 289
Clive Beardall 210
Berry Antiques 244
Bespoke Furniture 31
Christy Bird 446
H Blairman & Sons Ltd 78
G D Blay Antiques 127
M J Bowdery 132
Bowood Antiques 239
Brambridge Antiques 116
Breakspeare Antiques 249
Bristol Trade Antiques 181
Brown House Antiques 210
F G Bruschweiler Antiques Ltd 210
Burton Antiques 293
Butler's Furniture Galleries 158
Bygone Years 259
Bygones of Ireland Ltd 453
Ian Caldwell 135
Carrington House Antiques 391
Hugh Cash Antiques 451
Lennox Cato Antiques 30
Cheshunt Antiques 256
The Chest of Drawers 249
Chorley-Burdett Antiques 196
Collins Antiques 259
Comberton Antiques 201
J and M Coombes 127
Lisa Cordes Antiques 234
Marc Costantini Antiques 70
Cottage Antiques 204
Cottage Antiques 384
Country Antiques 431
Country House and Cottage Antiques 430
Country House Antiques 213
Cross Hayes Antiques 192
D K R Refurbishers 357
Dorking Desk Shop 125
English and Continental Antiques 223
English Rose Antiques 205
Eton Antiques 108
Falcon Antiques 18
Farrelly Antiques 258
Brian Fielden 55
Flower House Antiques 38
Forge Interiors 23
Forum Antiques 242
Franklin Antiques 109
Michael Gander 257
Georgian House Antiques 261
John Gilbert Antiques 325
Gladstone's Furniture 55
A Grice 381
Harmans Antiques 128
J Hartley Antiques Ltd 134
Kenneth Harvey Antiques 74
Hatherleigh Antiques 157
Hayter's Antique and Modern Furniture 123
Heath-Bullocks 131
Heritage Antiques 139
Christopher Hodsoll Ltd 63
Idvies Antiques 211
In Period Antiques 250
Simon and Frauke Jackson 178
Roger Lamb Antiques and Works of Art 247
Latchford Antiques 240
The Lemon Tree 361
Levenshulme Antiques Village 373
Lithgow & Partners 327
Alexander Lyall Antiques 226
MacHenry Antiques 435
Victor Mahy 194
Market House Antiques 213
Jeroen Markies Antiques Ltd 18
Maya Antiques 159
McBains Antiques 156
Richard Midwinter Antiques 297
Millcourt Antiques 444
Milton Antiques & Restoration 168
Patrick & Gillian Morley 303
John Nash Antiques and Interiors 253
F B Neill 207
Newark Antiques Warehouse Ltd 283
Old Barn Antiques 207
Old Barn Antiques 347
Old Corner House Antiques 43
The Old Malthouse 110
The Old Maltings Antique Centre 345
The Old Steam Bakery 150
O'Neil's Antiques Gosforth 352
O'Neil's Old Warehouse Antiques 351
Oola Boola Antiques London 61
Oxford Street Antiques Centre 275
Park Antiques 430
Park Antiques 340
Park Galleries Antiques 370
Gill Parkin Furniture 132
Partners Antiques 374
Christopher Peters Antiques 299
Phelps Ltd 105
Phoenix Green Antiques 116
Graham Pickett Antiques 346
Ludovic Potts Antiques 202
Priest's Antiques & Fine Arts 352
Quality Furniture Warehouse 55
Martin Quick Antiques 308
Radnor House Antiques 152
Randolph Antiques 224
The Refectory 128
Reindeer Antiques Ltd 280
Reindeer Antiques Ltd 92
Richmond Hill Antiques 134
The Salvage Shop 454
Mark Seabrook Antiques 281
Seaview Antiques 344
Second Time Around 359
Second Time Around 359
Selwoods Antiques 189
Shaston Antiques 174
At the Sign of the Chest of Drawers 52
At the Sign of the Chest of Drawers 51
Sitting Pretty 274
Sitting Pretty Antiques 230
Anthony Smith 106
Something Old, Something New 364
The Sovereign 237
Spurrier-Smith Antiques 269
Stable Antiques 141
Stalham Antique Gallery 220

INDEX OF SPECIALISTS

FURNITURE

Sutton Valence Antiques 38
Martin Taylor Antiques 308
Thakeham Furniture 144
Tomlinson Antiques 328
Treedale Antiques 287
Upper Court Manor Antiques 448
Warren Antiques 226
Waterfall Antiques 255
Mollie Webster 208
Anthony Welling 135
Westville House Antiques 188
Whitchurch Antique Centre 291
Wissinger Antiques 58
Witney Antiques 267
Year Dot Interiors 322
Yesteryears 166

17TH–18THC
Gwynedd Trading 391

17TH–19THC
Roger Grimes 452

18TH–19THC
Michael Andrews Antiques 130
Antiques and Restoration 224
Barnt Green Antiques 304
E W Cousins & Son 225
Nicholas Fowle Antiques 218
Norfolk House Galleries Ltd 128
Saracen Antiques Ltd 261
Stocks and Chairs 173
Vaughan Antiques 347
Wayside Antiques 272

18TH–19THC MAHOGANY
James Hardy Antiques Ltd 349

18TH–20THC
Phoenix Antiques 174

18THC
Nicholas Abbott 115
Barnet-Cattanach Antiques 255
Thomas Coulborn and Sons 307
Dunkeld Antiques 299
C. Fredericks and Son 89
John Heather 231
Michael Hughes 67
Scottish Antique and Arts Centre 180
Serendipity 253

18THC ENGLISH
John Keil Ltd 67
Brian Rolleston Antiques Ltd 92
Turpins Antiques 110

19THC
Adrian Alan Ltd 78
John Anthony 125
Birkdale Antiques 385
Lugley Street Antiques 123
Upper Court Manor Antiques 451
Wargrave Antiques 112

BARLEY TWIST
The Old Curiosity Shop 370

BEDROOM
David Cardoza Antiques 20
Forstal Farm Antique Workshops 33

BEDS
Antique Bed Company 114
The Antique Bed Shop 208
The Antique Brass Bedstead Co Ltd 207
Antiques and All Pine 196
The Bed Workshop 181
Bedsteads 177, 181
French House Antiques 73
J Girvan Antiques 305
Alexandra Gray 118
La Maison 44
Manor Farm Antiques 265
Morpheus Beds 249
Prestwich Antiques 374
Pughs Antiques 159
Seventh Heaven 391
Staveley Antiques 368
The Suffolk Antique Bed Centre 225
Victorian Imports 374
Works of Iron 339

BENTWOOD CHAIRS
Robert Whitfield 60

BILLIARD ROOM
Billiard Room Antiques 184

CHAIRS
Antique English Windsor Chairs 261
Chris Baylis Country Chairs 267
The Chair Set 267
Kantuta 77
The Odd Chair Company 381

CHESTS-OF-DRAWERS
Isabella Antiques 196

CHINESE
Nicholas Grindley 81
Orient Expressions Ltd 72, 179
Red Room 72
Snap Dragon 68
Two Dragons Oriental Antiques 394

CONTINENTAL
Birdie Fortescue Antiques 70
Mallett 8

COUNTRY
The Antiques Warehouse 227
Granary Antiques 191
Red Lion Antiques 143
Smith & Sons 170
Denzil Verey 239

DECORATIVE ITEMS
Decorative Antiques 70

DESKS
Dorking Desk Shop 127

DINING
Brook Farm Antiques 291
W J Casey Antiques 302
Coopers of Ilkley 338
The Country Furniture Shop 237
Dycheling Antiques 140
Freshfords 186
Andy Gibbs 254
Hill Farm Antiques 111
Pantiles Spa Antiques 40

ENGLISH
Callingham Antiques Ltd 142
Geary Antiques 340
Hare's Antiques Ltd 242
M Lees & Son 313
Peter Lipitch Ltd 68
Mallett 83
Mauleverer Antiques 318
Noel Mercer Antiques 226
Quinneys of Warwick 303
Patrick Sandberg Antiques 92
Stair & Company Ltd 86
Suffolk House Antiques 231
Simon Wingett Ltd 391

ENGLISH LACQUER
G T Ratcliff Ltd 209

FARMHOUSE TABLES
Simon Coleman Antiques 76

FRENCH
Deja Vu Antiques 209
French House Antiques 330
David Litt Antiques 232
Ripley Antiques 134

FRENCH AND ITALIAN
The French Room 142
Sayer Antiques 139

FRENCH BEDS
The French Warehouse 436

FRENCH COMMODES & ARMOIRES
The Decorator Source 249

FRENCH COUNTRY
Christopher's Antiques 130
Jan Hicks Antiques 112
Watson & Watson 269

FRENCH FARMHOUSE TABLES
Denzil Grant 223

FRENCH PAINTED FURNITURE
Pop Antiques 23

FRUITWOOD
Sieff 250

GEORGIAN
Aura Antiques 323
Dorchester Antiques 262

Fosse Way Antiques 246
J Green & Son 277
Hampshires of Dorking 128
C H Major 91
R N Myers & Son 319
Prichard Antiques 250

GEORGIAN MAHOGANY
Christopher Buck Antiques 36
Kingsley & Co 349

GEORGIAN–VICTORIAN
Kidwelly Antiques 388
Phoenix Trading Company - South Yorkshire 74
Wheatsheaf Antiques Centre 359

HAND-PAINTED
One Off 294

INDONESIAN
Steven Shell 195

IRISH GEORGIAN
Bobby Douglas 436

JAPANESE
Tansu 335

LIBRARY
Michael W Fitch Antiques 36

OAK
Beedham Antiques Ltd 109
Douglas Bryan Antiques 29
Stephen Cook Antiques 244
Country Antiques (Wales) 388
Day Antiques 249
Keith Hockin Antiques 247
Paul Hopwell Antiques 281
Huntington Antiques Ltd 247
J H S Antiques 269
Longmynd Antiques 288
C & J Mortimer & Son 207
Pateley Bridge Antiques 324
Priory Furnishing 335
Underwood Oak 113
Village Antique Centre 27

ORIENTAL
East Meets West Antiques 41

PAINTED
John Bird Antiques 142
Gilbert and Dale 186
Phoenix Antiques 41
Annette Puttnam Antiques 143

PAINTED PINE
Emscote Antiques 303

PAIRED ITEMS
Pairs Antiques 75

PINE
A B Period Pine 282
Annterior Antiques 162
Antique & Country Pine 360
Antique & Design 27
Antique Pine Stores 171
Attic Pine 438
M G Bassett 268
Mick Burt (Antique Pine) 340
Bygones Antiques 452
Capricorn Antiques 392
Clock Tower Antiques 14
Colystock Antiques 158
Cottage Farm Antiques 241
Country Pine Trading Co 294
Brian Davis Antiques 261
Delvin Farm Antiques 453
Ben Eggleston 367
Friargate Pine Co Ltd 271
Happers Antiques 236
Hardy Country 172
Harlequin Antiques 284
Heathfield Country Pine 216
Heritage Restorations 398
Bob Hoare Antiques 21
Holt Antique Centre 217
Ann Lingard Ropewalk Antiques 23
Millgate Antiques 328
Millgate Pine & Antiques 328
North Wilts Exporters 192
The Old Pine House 300
O'Marley's Ghost 448
One Step Back 222
Parkways Antiques 188
Partners in Pine 206
Pastorale Antiques 22
Pat's Antique and Reproduction Pine Furniture and Gift Shop 338
Penlan Pine 393
Phoenix Trading 207
Mr Pickett's 138
Pine and Country Furniture 224
Pine and Things 301
Pine for Pine Antiques 430
Pine Furniture Store 259
Pine Workshop 352
Pinestrip 204
Porcupine 372
Graham Price Antiques Ltd 22
Sambourne House Antiques 193
Seventeen Antiques 384
Thornbury Antiques 189
Times Past Antiques 109
Townhouse Antiques 373
Up Country Ltd 41
Westway Pine 322

REGENCY
Reeves Restoration at the Coach House Antiques 131

RUSSIAN
Antoine Chenevière Fine Arts Ltd 79

SOFT
Squirrel Antiques 114

UPHOLSTERED
Antics 332
Entente Cordiale 303

VERNACULAR
M & D Seligman 92

VICTORIAN
Ann's Antiques 452
Glenconnor Antiques 454
Miles Antiques 297
Nichols Antique Centre 333
The Old Grain Stores 215

VICTORIAN BALLOON BACK CHAIRS
Paul Ward Antiques 334

VICTORIAN–EDWARDIAN
Antique Workshop 208
Grantham Furniture Emporium 342
Riro D Mooney 201
The Old Bakery Antiques Ltd 259

WALNUT
Richard Courtney Ltd 66

WARDROBES
The Antiques Warehouse 177

WELSH
Adams Antiques 362
James Ash Antiques 388
T Evans Antiques 393
Michael Rowland Antiques 247

WING CHAIRS
Sebastian of Eton 108

GARDENING ANTIQUES

Antique Garden 356
Matthew Eden 192
Flaxton Antique Gardens 319
Jon Fox Antiques 245
Juro Farm and Garden Antiques 312
Padstow Antiques 148
Romantiques 150

STATUARY
Phoenix Trading Co 74

GLASS

Nigel Benson 20th Century Glass 88
Christine Bridge Antiques 75
Charis 165
The Coach House Antique Centre 28
Farmhouse Antiques 349
Templar Antiques 51
Brian Watson Antique Glass 217
Mark J West 77

DRINKING GLASSES
Jasmin Cameron 66
Jeanette Hayhurst 89
Somervale Antiques 187

BOTTLES
The Old Bottle Shop 59

COLOURED
Andrew Lineham Fine Glass 49

MONART
Perth Antiques 288

PERFUME BOTTLES
Lynda Brine Antiques 178

VICTORIAN COLOURED
Savery Antiques 15

GRAMOPHONES & RECORDS

Chris Baker Gramophones 37
Howard Hope Phonographs & Gramophones 129

HANDBAGS

Linda Bee 78

ICONS

Mark Gallery 87

JEWELLERY

Ancient and Modern 377
A K Campbell & Son 16
Corner House Antiques 244
Courtville Antiques 446
Sandra Cronan Ltd 79
Gem Antiques 34
Glydon and Guess 133
Sarah Groombridge 81
Hancocks and Co (Jewellers) Ltd 82
Harvey & Gore 63
Johnson Walker Ltd 82
John Joseph 82
Russell Lane Antiques 303
Lev Antiques Ltd 91
Linda's Antiques 443
The Little Gem 292
Massada Antiques 83
Christina Parker Antiques 223
Royal Mile Curios 408
Spectrum 85
Spectrum Fine Jewellery Ltd 12
Tempo Antiques 450
Timgems Jewellers 219
Tosi Gold Ltd 86
Sally Turner Antiques 239
Vinci Antiques 86
J R Webb Antiques 97
J W Weldon 449
Wimpole Antiques 87

DECORATIVE SILVER
Miwa Thorpe 69

ENGAGEMENT RINGS
Hallmark Jewellers 14

SCOTTISH
Bow-Well Antiques 405

SILVER
Leolinda 49
E P Mallory and Son Ltd 179
Stormont Antiques 433

VICTORIAN
Matthew Foster 80

JUKE BOXES

Juke Box World 346

KITCHENWARE

Sheila Hyson 165
Janie & Skip Smithson 343

T G GREEN
Gentry Antiques 80

LIGHTING

The Birdcage Antiques 369
Denton Antiques 89
Dernier and Hamlyn Ltd 67
Exeter Antique Lighting 156
Hector Finch Lighting 70
Gower House Antiques 402
La Belle Epoque 200
The Lamp Gallery 134
Magic Lanterns 258
Meadow Lamps Gallery 407
Number 38 165
Odeon Designs Ltd 296
O'Keeffe Antiques 398
Period Style Lighting 103
Post House Antiques 125
Saltney Restoration Services 359
Jeanne Temple Antiques 238

CHANDELIERS
Mrs Quick Chandeliers 91
Rainbow Antiques 72
Rainbow Too Interiors 72
Turnburrys Ltd 354

GLASS
Delomosne & Son Ltd 194

MAGAZINES

Tilleys Vintage Magazine Shop 334

AMERICAN COMICS
Wonderworld 170

BRITISH COMICS
The Border Bookshop 382

COMICS
Automattic Comics 192
Comic Book Postal Auctions Ltd 54
Comic Connections 259

MAPS & PRINTS

Cathedral Gallery 296
Magna Gallery 265
Melnick House Antiques 107
Neptune Gallery 447
Royal Mile Gallery 408
Town and Country Prints 228
David Windsor Gallery 392

1550–1850
The Witch Ball 16

20THC MONOGRAPH
Carol Manheim at Biblion 83

CHANNEL ISLANDS
Channel Islands Galleries Ltd 428

CUMBERLAND
Souvenir Antiques 365

MAPS
Altea Maps and Books 78
Gillmark Map Gallery 256
Hereford Map Centre 252
Simon Hunter Antique Maps 20
The Map House 68
Nicolson Maps 234
Pontcanna Old Books, Maps & Prints 401
Jonathan Potter Ltd 84
Tooley, Adams and Co 266

PRINTS
Antique Prints 445
Classic Prints 66
Dog Leap Antiques 353

SPORTING PRINTS
Pickwick Gallery 302

SUFFOLK
Claude Cox Books 225

MARITIME

The Jolly Roger 161
Langfords Marine Antiques 74
Peter Laurie Maritime Antiques 59
Marine Instruments 147
Nautical Antique Centre 176
Relcy Antiques 59
Woods Emporium 155

NAVAL ITEMS
Cobwebs 120

MEMORABILIA

BROOKLANDS BADGES
C A R S (Classic Automobilia and Regalia Specialists) 14

CHILDHOOD
The Museum of Childhood Memories 394

FOOTBALL
Brentside Programmes 203
D & D Programmes 79
Midland Football Programme Shop 305
John Priestley 285

FORMULA 1
Grand Prix Top Gear 258

MR PUNCH
Mr Punch's Antique Market 174

TRANSPORT
Paperchase 233

METALWARE

W A Pinn & Sons 212
Richard Sear 279

MILITARIA

Anything Old & Military Collectables 380
Bluebell Collectables 98
Blunderbuss Antiques 78
Bosleys Military Auctioneers 237
Casque and Gauntlet Militaria 130
Chelsea Military Antiques 66
Coldstream Military Antiques 237
Grenadiers 61
Ickleton Antiques 211
Jean's Military Memories 379
Just Military Ltd 333
Liverpool Militaria 384
Pastimes 183
Q & C Militaria 241
The Treasure Bunker Militaria Shop 132
Yesteryear Antiques 449

WEAPONS
Coltishall Antique Centre 214

WWII
Boscombe Militaria 168

MIRRORS

Chelsea Antique Mirrors 62
Molland Antique Mirrors 296
Richmond Antiques 370
Through The Looking Glass 92

19THC
Through The Looking Glass 72

FRENCH
Julian Antiques 141
The Old French Mirror Company 265

GESSO ORNAMENTED
Kilgarvan Antique Centre 454

GILDED
Ashton Gower Antiques 245

GILT
Boyle's Antiques 442

MUSIC

Lisa Cox Music 156
Travis & Emery Books on Music 102

INSTRUMENTS
C J C Antiques 388

MUSIC BOXES
Mayflower Antiques 96, 207
The Norfolk Polyphon Centre 213
Vanbrugh House Antiques 248
Graham Webb Musical Boxes 16

PIANOS
R R Limb Antiques 283
Music Room Antiques 138

PRINTED
Browsers Bookshop 147

STRING INSTRUMENTS
J and A Beare Ltd 78
Turner Violins 281

THE BEATLES
More Than Music Collectables 42

NEWSPAPERS

Antique Newspapers 428

19THC PRINTS
Craobh Rua Rare Book 435

OBJECTS OF VIRTUE

Magpie Antiques & Collectables 187

ONLINE ANTIQUES

Watsons Antiques 364

ORMOLU

Yellow Lantern Antiques 20

PAPERWEIGHTS

Sweetbriar Gallery Ltd 361
Wealth of Weights 18

SCOTTISH
Cabaret Antiques 405

PORCELAIN

Box of Porcelain 171
C and B Antiques 14
Davies Antiques 89
Folly Four Antiques & Collectables 118
Diana Huntley 49
Jade Antiques 205
Platt's of Lymington 117
Stable Antiques 328, 331

18TH–19THC
Mercury Antiques 96

18THC ENGLISH
Albert Amor 61
Roderick Jellicoe 90

18THC ENGLISH FIGURES
David & Sally March Antiques 176

ASIAN
Artemesia 113
Colin D Monk 91

BELLEEK
Cornmarket Curios 437

CHINA
Dunmore Antiques 434

CHINESE
Berwald Oriental Art 89
Heirloom & Howard Ltd 192
Santos 92
Jorge Welsh 92

DOULTON
Old Forge Collectables 437

ENGLISH
Stockspring Antiques 92

IRONSTONE
Valerie Howard 90

ROYAL CROWN DERBY
Friargate Antiques Company 271

SOUVENIR CHINA
The Crested China Co 316

WORCESTER
Bygones by the Cathedral 313
Simon Spero 92

POTTERY

Clamjamfrey 227
Nick & Janet's Antiques 234
Potteries Antique Centre 294
Potteries Specialist Auctions 294
Peter Scott 180
Special Auction Services 111
Julian Tatham-Losh 239

1780-1900 ENGLISH BLUE PRINTED
Gillian Neale Antiques 235

ART
Garners 205
John Lewis 340

BRITISH
Islwyn Watkins Antiques 398

BURLEIGH WARE
The Antiques Centre 115

DENBY
Mansfield Antique Centre 282

EARLY ENGLISH
John Reed Antiques 227

FRENCH SAIENCE
Homme de Quimper 346

MAJOLICA
Nicolaus Boston Antiques 89

MALING WARE
Antiques at H & S Collectables 353

MASON'S IRONSTONE
Paull's of Kenilworth 300

MOORCROFT
The Neville Pundole Gallery 28
Porchester Antiques 183
Rumours 51

STAFFORDSHIRE
Jacqueline Oosthuizen Antiques 68
Serendipity 30

SUNDERLAND LUSTREWARE
Ian Sharp Antiques 355

TORQUAY WARE
Corner Shop Antiques 146

WEMYSS
Fair Finds Antiques 282
Newburgh Antiques 399
Rogers de Rin 68

RAILWAYANA

Collectors Corner 329
Solent Railwayana 121
Solent Railwayana Auctions 121
Yesteryear Railwayana 35

REGIONAL ANTIQUES

ART ON ST IVES
The Book Gallery 150

FRENCH
Bristol Brocante 181
Anne Fowler 249

IRISH
Whyte's 449

SCIENTIFIC INSTRUMENTS

Victor Burness Antiques 57
Country Life Antiques 246
Ganymede Antiques 269
Grimes Militaria 182
David J Hansord and Son 345
Paul Howard 67
Mike Read Antique Sciences 151
Eric Tombs 128

BINOCULARS
Marine 288
Quicktest 259

GLOBES
Arthur Middleton Ltd 101

SLIDE RULES
Antique Scientific Instruments 357

TELESCOPES
Odin Antiques 15

WEATHER INSTRUMENTS
Richard Twort 190

SCRIPOPHILY

G K R Bonds Ltd 206

SCULPTURE

ANIMALIER
Victor Franses Gallery 63

BRONZE
Hickmet Fine Arts 140

EUROPEAN
Daniel Katz Ltd 64

SILVER

Advena Antiques & Fairs 343
Argenteus Ltd 99
Brian Beet 78
Daniel Bexfield Antiques 78
Barbara Cattle 329
Paul Daniel 100
Reginald Davis (Oxford) Ltd 264
D & B Dickinson 178
Bryan Douglas 100
R Feldman Ltd Antique Silver 100
O Frydman 80
Graus Antiques 81
Jonathan Green Antiques 195
Hedingham Antiques 211
Hock & Dough Antiques 279
Brand Inglis 144
Stephen Kalms Antiques 101
M P Levene Ltd 73
Leona Levine Silver Specialist 219
M Lexton 67
Sanda Lipton 82
C and T Mammon 101
Marks Antiques 83
Iain Marr 187
Otter Antiques 159
Payne and Son (Goldsmiths) Ltd 265
Percy's Ltd 101
Rare Art Ltd 102
Schredds of Portobello 97
Silstar Antiques Ltd 102
The Silver Fund Ltd 65
The Silver Shop 122
The Silver Shop 448
B Silverman 102
Jack Simons Antiques Ltd 102
Squires Antiques 369
S & J Stodel 102
Teme Valley Antiques 290
William Walter Antiques Ltd 102

18THC
ADC Heritage Ltd 61

BON BON DISHES
Tudor Antiques 227

CHESTER
Kayes 358

EXETER
D Lovell 165

FLATWARE
M & J Hamilton 100
Nat Leslie Ltd 101

GEORG JENSEN
Jeremy Sniders Antiques 180

GEORGIAN
Saintfield Antiques & Fine Books 438

IRISH
Weir and Sons 448

JEWELLERY
Chapel Place Antiques 40

PHOTO FRAMES
Tony Booth Antiques 94
Tony Booth 79

SCOTTISH, IRISH
Nicholas Shaw Antiques 138

SPORTING ANTIQUES

Books & Collectables Ltd 200
Evans and Partridge 121
Golfark International 352
Mullock & Madeley 293
Manfred Schotten Antiques 261
Warboys Antiques 204
Wot-a-Racket 29

ANGLING
Brindley John Ayers Antique Fishing Tackle 396
Neil Freeman Angling Auctions 97
David C Rogers Antiques & Interiors 279

BILLIARD TABLES
Academy Billiard Company 136
William Bentley Billiards 109

GOLF
Old St Andrews Gallery 203

SNOOKER TABLES
The Snooker Room 288

TEXTILES

Airlie Antiques (Textiles) 152

Antique Textiles and Lighting 177
The Aquarius 392
Brocante Antiques 391
Clifton Hill Textiles 182
Sheila Cook Textiles 94
Decades 377
Marilyn Garrow Fine Textile Art 223
The Green Room 224
Hart Antiques 394
Patsy Lewis 172
Betty Lovell 165
Past Caring 217
Catherine Shinn Decorative Textiles 241
Peta Smyth Antique Textiles 65
The Snug 153
Susannah 180
Textile-Art: The Textile Gallery 86

CLOTHING
Bizarre! 164
Bohemia 376
Echoes 382
Gladrags 406
Rufus the Cat 448
Saratoga Trunk Yesteryear Costume & Textiles 438
Jenny Vander 448
Vintage to Vogue 180
Wardrobe 16
Wartime Wardrobe 273

EUROPEAN
Classic Fabrics with Robin Haydock 66

LACE
Julia Craig 178
The Honiton Lace Shop 159

LINEN
The Linen Press 186

LINEN AND LACE
Antique Linens & Lace 177
Ceres Antiques 298

LINEN SHEETS
Penny Philip 179

SAMPLERS
Erna Hiscock 95

TAPESTRIES
Joanna Booth 66
C John Ltd 82

WELSH QUILTS
Jen Jones Antiques 389

TOOLS

Grandad's Attic 320
Woodville Antiques 32

WOODWORKING
Old Tools Feel Better! 166
David Stanley Auctions 277
The Tool Shop 228
Trinder's Fine Tools 223

TOYS

Abbey Models 168
Acme Toy Company 304
Antique Toys 158
Bearly Trading of London 60
Down To The Woods Ltd 173
Hobday Toys 104
Peter Le Vesconte Collectables 430
Pete McAskie Toys 83
Mimi Fifi 96
Now & Then 407
Off World 234
The Old Toyshop 119
Park House Antiques 247
Retrobuy 275
The Toy Shop 372
Wallis & Wallis 22

CHESS SETS
J & S Millard Antiques 179

DOLLS
Barbara Ann Newman 42
Bébés et Jouets 405
Dollectable 357
The Shrubbery 176

ROCKING HORSES
Rectory Rocking Horses 176
Stevenson Brothers 25

STAR WARS
Off World 211

STEIFF
Bears Galore 23
Dollies Bear-Gere Ltd 373
Dollyland 54
Teddy Bears of Witney 267

TEDDY BEARS
The Bear Room 234
Bears 'n' Bunnies 23
Bears on the Square 289
Bears on the Wold 246
Childhood Memories 130
Company of Bears 39
Sue Pearson Antique Dolls & Teddy Bears 15
Ursus 149

TREEN

Rebecca Calvert Antiques 345
Newsum Antiques 250

WATCHES

Atlam Sales and Service 93
Chamade Antiques 94
Samuel Elliot 446
Anthony Green Antiques 81
Harpers Jewellers Ltd 330
Pieces of Time 84
Mick & Fanny Wright 244

VINTAGE ROLEX
I Ehrnfeld 54

WRISTWATCHES
Brittons Jewellers 380
The Buying Centre 360
Sugar Antiques 51

WINE ANTIQUES

Bacchus Gallery 141

CORKSCREWS
Kaizen International Ltd 36
Christopher Sykes 235

WOOD CARVINGS

Celia Jennings 26

WORKS OF ART

C and L Burman 97

IMPERIAL RUSSIAN
Shapiro & Co. 85

INDEX OF PLACE NAMES

A

Abbeydorney, Co Kerry 448
Abbots Langley, Hertfordshire 253
Abbots Leigh, Somerset 176
Aberdare, Mid Glamorgan 392
Aberford, West Yorkshire 333
Abergavenny, Monmouthshire 393
Aberystwyth, Ceredigion 387
Abinger Hammer, Surrey 124
Accrington, Lancashire 374
Achill Sound, Co Mayo 450
Acle, Norfolk 213
Adare, Co Limerick 449
Addlestonemoor, Surrey 125
Aghadowey, Co Londonderry 436
Ahoghill, Co Antrim 429
Alcester, Warwickshire 297
Aldborough, Norfolk 213
Aldeburgh, Suffolk 221
Alderley Edge, Cheshire 354
Aldermaston, Berkshire 107
Aldershot, Hampshire 113
Alfreton, Derbyshire 266
Alfriston, East Sussex 12
Allerton Mauleverer, North Yorkshire 316
Allington, Lincolnshire 339
Alnwick, Northumberland 348
Alport, Derbyshire 266
Alresford, Hampshire 113
Alrewas, Staffordshire 291
Alsager, Cheshire 354
Alston, Cumbria 362
Alton, Hampshire 113
Altrincham, Greater Manchester 367
Amersham, Buckinghamshire 233
Ampthill, Bedfordshire 230
Andover, Hampshire 113
Andoversford, Gloucestershire 237
Antrim, Co Antrim 429
Appleby-in-Westmorland, Cumbria 362
Appledore, Kent 25
Ardingly, West Sussex 136
Armagh, Co Armagh 433
Arundel, West Sussex 137
Ascot, Berkshire 107
Ascott-under-Wychwood, Oxfordshire 257
Ash, Kent 25
Ashbourne, Derbyshire 266
Ashburton, Devon 152
Ashby-de-la-Zouch, Leicestershire 272
Ashford, Kent 25
Ashtead, Surrey 125
Askrigg, North Yorkshire 316
Astley Bridge, Greater Manchester 367
Atcham, Shropshire 285
Atherton, Greater Manchester 368
Athlone, Co Galway 447
Aughnacloy, Co Tyrone 437
Austwick, North Yorkshire 316
Axbridge, Somerset 176
Axminster, Devon 153
Aylesbury, Buckinghamshire 233
Aylesby, Lincolnshire 339
Aylsham, Norfolk 213

B

Baildon, West Yorkshire 333
Barnard Castle, Co Durham 347
Barnet, Hertfordshire 253
Barnham, West Sussex 138
Barnsley, Gloucestershire 237
Barnsley, South Yorkshire 329
Barnstaple, Devon 153
Barnt Green, West Midlands 302
Barrow-in-Furness, Cumbria 362
Barry, South Glamorgan 398
Barton upon Humber, Lincolnshire 339
Barton, Cambridgeshire 199
Barton, Lancashire, Lancashire 375
Basford, Staffordshire 291
Basingstoke, Hampshire 114
Bath, Somerset 176
Batley, West Yorkshire 333
Battle, East Sussex 12
Bakewell, Derbyshire 267
Balcombe, West Sussex 137
Balderton, Nottinghamshire 279
Baldock, Hertfordshire 253
Ballinamallard, Co Fermanagh 436
Ballinderry, Co Antrim 429
Ballinea, Co Cavan 440
Ballycastle, Co Antrim 429
Ballycolman, Co Tyrone 437
Ballydehob, Co Cork 440
Ballygawley, Co Tyrone 437
Ballymena, Co Antrim 429
Ballynahinch, Co Down 434
Balsham, Cambridgeshire 199
Bamford, Derbyshire 268
Banbury, Oxfordshire 257
Bandon, Co Cork 440
Bangor, Co Down, Co Down 434
Bangor, Gwynedd, Gwynedd 390
Bantry, Co Cork 440
Barking, Essex 204
Barlow, Derbyshire 268
Barmouth, Gwynedd 390
Barnard Castle, Co Durham 347
Barnet, Hertfordshire 253
Barnham, West Sussex 138
Barnsley, Gloucestershire 237
Barnsley, South Yorkshire 329
Battlesbridge, Essex 204
Bawdeswell, Norfolk 213
Bawtry, South Yorkshire 329
Baythorn End, Essex 205
Beaconsfield, Buckinghamshire 234
Beaminster, Dorset 167
Beaumaris, Isle of Anglesey 392
Beccles, Suffolk 221
Beckenham, Kent 25
Bedale, North Yorkshire 316
Bedford, Bedfordshire 231
Beer, Devon 154
Beeston, Cheshire 354
Belfast, Co Antrim 430
Belgrave, Cheshire 354
Belper, Derbyshire 268
Belton, Lincolnshire 339
Bembridge, Isle of Wight 122
Benenden, Kent 25
Benfleet, Essex 205
Bentley, South Yorkshire 329
Bere Regis, Dorset 167
Berkeley, Gloucestershire 237
Berkhamsted, Hertfordshire 253
Berwick-upon-Tweed, Northumberland 349
Betchworth, Surrey 125
Bethersden, Kent 25
Bethesda, Gwynedd 391
Beverley, East Riding of Yorkshire 313
Bewdley, Worcestershire 307
Bexhill-on-Sea, East Sussex 12
Bexley, Kent 25
Bibury, Gloucestershire 237
Bicester, Oxfordshire 258
Biddenden, Kent 25
Bideford, Devon 154
Bidford on Avon, Warwickshire 297
Biggleswade, Bedfordshire 231
Billingham, North Yorkshire 316
Billingshurst, West Sussex 138
Bilsington, Kent 26
Bingley, West Yorkshire 333
Birchington, Kent 26
Birdhill, Co Tipperary 452
Birdwell, South Yorkshire 329
Birkenhead, Merseyside 381
Birmingham, West Midlands 302
Birr, Co Offaly 451
Bishop Auckland, Co Durham 347
Bishops Castle, Shropshire 285
Bishopstone, East Sussex 13
Bisley, Gloucestershire 237
Bitton, Somerset 180
Bix, Oxfordshire 258
Blackburn, Lancashire 375
Blackrock, Co Dublin 442
Blandford Forum, Dorset 167
Bletchingley, Surrey 125
Blewbury, Oxfordshire 258
Bluewater, Kent 26
Blundellsands, Merseyside 381
Bodmin, Cornwall 146
Bolton Abbey, North Yorkshire 317
Bolton, Greater Manchester 368
Borehamwood, Hertfordshire 253
Boroughbridge, North Yorkshire 317
Borris, Co Carlow 440
Boscastle, Cornwall 146
Bosham, West Sussex 138
Boston, Lincolnshire 339
Bourne End, Buckinghamshire 234
Bournemouth, Dorset 168
Bourton-on-the-Water, Gloucestershire 237
Bowdon, Greater Manchester 368
Bowness-on-Windermere, Cumbria 362
Brackley, Northamptonshire 276
Bradford on Avon, Wiltshire 191
Bradford, West Yorkshire 333
Bradwell, Derbyshire 268
Bramham, West Yorkshire 333
Bramley, Surrey 125
Brampton, Cumbria 362
Brasted, Kent 26

Braunton, Devon 154
Bray, Co Wicklow 453
Brecon, Powys 396
Bredbury, Greater Manchester 368
Brentford, Middlesex 103
Brentwood, Essex 205
Bretherton, Lancashire 375
Brewood, Staffordshire 291
Bridgend, Mid Glamorgan 392
Bridgnorth, Shropshire 285
Bridgwater, Somerset 181
Bridlington, East Riding of Yorkshire 313
Bridport, Dorset 170
Brierley Hill, West Midlands 303
Brigg, Lincolnshire 340
Brighton, East Sussex 13
Brimpton, Berkshire 107
Brinklow, Warwickshire 297
Brinkworth, Wiltshire 192
Bristol, Somerset 181
Brixham, Devon 154
Broad Hinton, Wiltshire 192
Broadstairs, Kent 27
Broadway, Worcestershire 307
Brockenhurst, Hampshire 114
Brockham, Surrey 125
Bromborough, Merseyside 381
Bromham, Bedfordshire 231
Bromley Cross, Greater Manchester 369
Bromley, Kent 27
Bromsgrove, Worcestershire 307
Brooke, Norfolk 213
Broomfield, Essex 205
Brough, East Riding of Yorkshire 314
Bruton, Somerset 183
Buckingham, Buckinghamshire 234
Bucks Green, West Sussex 138
Budby, Nottinghamshire 279
Budleigh Salterton, Devon 154
Builth Wells, Powys 396
Bundoran, Co Donegal 442
Bungay, Suffolk 221
Burford, Oxfordshire 258
Burgess Hill, West Sussex 138
Burley In Wharfedale, West Yorkshire 334
Burlton, Shropshire 286
Burnham Market, Norfolk 213
Burnham-on-Sea, Somerset 183
Burnley, Lancashire 375
Burrough Green, Suffolk 222
Burscough, Lancashire 376
Burslem, Staffordshire 291
Burton Salmon, West Yorkshire 334
Burton-on-Trent, Staffordshire 291
Burwash, East Sussex 16
Burwell, Cambridgeshire 199
Bury St Edmunds, Suffolk 222
Bury, Greater Manchester 369
Bushey, Hertfordshire 253
Bushmills, Co Antrim 432
Buxton, Derbyshire 268

C

Caernarfon, Gwynedd 391
Caerphilly, Mid Glamorgan 392
Cahir, Co Tipperary 452
Cahirsiveen, Co Kerry 448
Caister-on-Sea, Norfolk 214
Camborne, Cornwall 146
Cambridge, Cambridgeshire 199
Camelford, Cornwall 146
Campsie Ash, Suffolk 222
Canonbie, Cumbria 362
Canterbury, Kent 27
Capel Iwan, Carmarthenshire 385
Cardiff, South Glamorgan 398
Cardigan, Ceredigion 388
Carlisle, Cumbria 362
Carmarthen, Carmarthenshire 385
Carndonagh, Co Donegal 442
Carrefour Selous, Jersey 427
Carrick on Shannon, Co Leitrim 449
Carrickfergus, Co Antrim 432
Carshalton, Surrey 125
Castle Cary, Somerset 184
Castle Donnington, Derbyshire 268
Castlecomer, Co Kilkenny 449
Castletol, Derbyshire 269
Caterham, Surrey 126
Cattledown, Devon 154
Cavendish, Suffolk 222
Caversham, Berkshire 107
Cawthorne, South Yorkshire 329
Chacewater, Cornwall 146
Chalfont St Giles, Buckinghamshire 234
Chalford, Gloucestershire 238
Chalgrove, Oxfordshire 259
Chandlers Ford, Hampshire 114
Chard, Somerset 184
Charleville, Co Cork 440
Charney Bassett, Oxfordshire 259
Charnock Richard, Lancashire 376
Chatham, Kent, Kent 28
Chatteris, Cambridgeshire 201
Chatton, Northumberland 349
Cheadle Hulme, Greater Manchester 369
Cheadle, Staffordshire 292
Cheam, Surrey 126
Chelmsford, Essex 205
Cheltenham, Gloucestershire 238
Chepstow, Monmouthshire 394
Cherhill, Wiltshire 192
Chertsey, Surrey 126
Chesham, Buckinghamshire 234
Cheshunt, Hertfordshire 254
Chester, Cheshire 354
Chesterfield, Derbyshire 269
Chichester, West Sussex 138
Chilcompton, Somerset 184
Chilton, Oxfordshire 259
Chippenham, Wiltshire 192
Chipping Camden, Gloucestershire 239
Chipping Norton, Oxfordshire 259
Chipping Ongar, Essex 205
Chipping Sodbury, Somerset 184
Chirk, Denbighshire 389
Chislehurst, Kent 28
Chittering, Cambridgeshire 201
Chobham, Surrey 126
Chorleywood, Hertfordshire 254
Christchurch, Dorset 171
Christian Malford, Wiltshire 192
Chulmleigh, Devon 155
Church Stretton, Shropshire 286
Churchill, Oxfordshire 260
Cilmery, Powys 396
Cirencester, Gloucestershire 240
Clacton-on-Sea, Essex 205
Clare, Suffolk 222
Clarecastle, Co Clare 440
Clarenbridge, Co Galway 448
Cleethorpes, Lincolnshire 340
Cleobury Mortimer, Worcestershire 307
Clevedon, Somerset 184
Cleveleys, Lancashire 376
Cley, Norfolk 214
Cliftonville, Kent 29
Clitheroe, Lancashire 376
Clonakilty, Co Cork 440
Clonmel, Co Tipperary 452
Clontarf, Co Dublin 443
Clydach, West Glamorgan 400
Coalville, Leicestershire 272
Cobham, Surrey 126
Cobridge, Staffordshire 292
Cockermouth, Cumbria 363
Coggeshall, Essex 205
Coleraine, Co Londonderry 437
Colesord, Gloucestershire 241
Colgate, West Sussex 139
Colne, Lancashire 376
Coltishall, Norfolk 214
Colwyn Bay, Conwy 388
Colyton, Devon 155
Comber, Co Down 434
Comberton, Cambridgeshire 201
Compton, Surrey 126
Congleton, Cheshire 357
Connah's Quay, Flintshire 390
Consett, Co Durham 347
Conwy, Conwy 388
Cookham, Berkshire 108
Cookstown, Co Tyrone 437
Corbridge, Northumberland 349
Cork, Co Cork 440
Corsham, Wiltshire 192
Cosford, Shropshire 286
Coventry, West Midlands 303
Cowbridge, South Glamorgan 399
Cowes, Isle of Wight 122
Coxley, Somerset 184
Cradley Heath, West Midlands 304
Cranborne, Dorset 171
Cranbrook, Kent 29
Craven Arms, Shropshire 286
Crawley, West Sussex 140
Crediton, Devon 155
Crewe, Cheshire 358
Crewkerne, Somerset 184
Criccieth, Gwynedd 391
Cromer, Norfolk 214
Cromford, Derbyshire 269
Cross Hands, Carmarthenshire 386
Cross Hills, West Yorkshire 334
Crowborough, East Sussex 16
Crowcombe, Somerset 185
Croydon, Surrey 127
Cuckfield, West Sussex 140
Cuddington, Cheshire 358

INDEX OF PLACE NAMES

D – G

Cullompton, Devon 155
Cutsdean, Gloucestershire 241

D

Dale Abbey, Derbyshire 269
Danbury, Essex 206
Darlington, Co DURHAM 348
Dartford, Kent 29
Dartmouth, Devon 156
Darwen, Lancashire 376
Davenham, Cheshire 358
Dawlish, Devon 156
Deal, Kent 29
Debenham, Suffolk 223
Deddington, Oxfordshire 260
Deganwy, Conwy 388
Denby Dale, West Yorkshire 334
Derby, Derbyshire 269
Dereham, Norfolk 214
Desborough, Northamptonshire 276
Devizes, Wiltshire 192
Dewsbury, West Yorkshire 334
Dingle, Co Kerry 448
Disley, Cheshire 358
Diss, Norfolk 214
Ditchling, West Sussex 140
Ditton Priors, Shropshire 287
Dolgellau, Gwynedd 391
Donaghadee, Co Down 434
Doncaster, South Yorkshire 330
Donegal, Co Donegal 442
Donnington, Berkshire 108
Dorchester , Oxfordshire 260
Dorchester, Dorset 171
Dorking, Surrey 127
Dovercourt, Essex 207
Downham Market, Norfolk 215
Driffield, East Riding of Yorkshire 314
Drinkstone, Suffolk 223
Drogheda, Co Louth 450
Droitwich Spa, Worcestershire 308
Dublin, Co Dublin 443
Duffield, Derbyshire 270
Dulverton, Somerset 185
Dun Laoghaire, Co Dublin 447
Dunchurch, Warwickshire 297
Dundalk, Co Louth 450
Dundonald, Co Down 434
Dunfanaghy, Co Donegal 442
Dunham Massey, Greater Manchester 369
Dunham on Trent, Nottinghamshire 279
Dunster, Somerset 186
Durham, Co Durham 348
Durrington, Wiltshire 193
Durrow, Co Laois 449
Duxford, Cambridgeshire 201

E

Easingwold, North Yorkshire 317
East Bolden, Tyne and Wear 350
East Hagbourne, Oxfordshire 261
East Leake, Leicestershire 272
East Molesey, Surrey 129
East Peckham, Kent 30
East Rudham, Norfolk 215
Eastbourne, East Sussex 16
Eastcote, Middlesex 103
Easton, Suffolk 223
Eastwood, Nottinghamshire 280
Eccles, Greater Manchester 369
Ecclesfield, South Yorkshire 330
Eccleshall, Staffordshire 292
Ecclestone, Lancashire 376
Edenbridge, Kent 30
Edenderry, Co Offaly 451
Edinburgh 403
Eggington, Bedfordshire 231
Elham, Kent 30
Ellesmere, Shropshire 287
Ely, Cambridgeshire 201
Emsworth, Hampshire 114
Enfield, Middlesex 103
Ennis, Co Clare 440
Enniskillen, Co Fermanagh 436
Epping, Essex 207
Epworth, Lincolnshire 340
Erbistock, Denbighshire 389
Erith, Kent 31
Esher, Surrey 129
Eton, Berkshire 108
Eversley, Hampshire 115
Evesham, Worcestershire 308
Ewell, Surrey 130
Ewenny, Mid Glamorgan 392
Ewloe, Flintshire 390
Exeter, Devon 156
Exning, Suffolk 223

F

Failsworth, Greater Manchester 369
Fairburn, West Yorkshire 334
Fairford, Gloucestershire 241
Fakenham, Norfolk 215
Falmouth, Cornwall 146
Faringdon, Oxfordshire 261
Farnborough, Kent 31
Farndon, Cheshire 358
Farnham, Surrey 130
Farningham, Kent 31
Farnsfield, Nottinghamshire 280
Faversham, Kent 31
Featherstone, West Yorkshire 334
Felixstowe, Suffolk 223
Fermoy, Co Cork 441
Fernhurst, Surrey 130
Finchingfield, Essex 207
Finedon, Northamptonshire 276
Finningham, Suffolk 224
Fir Tree, Co Durham 348
Fishguard, Pembrokeshire 395
Fladbury, Worcestershire 308
Flaxton, North Yorkshire 317
Fleet, Hampshire 115
Fleetwood, Lancashire 377
Flore, Northamptonshire 277
Folkestone, Kent 31
Ford, Northumberland 349
Fordham, Cambridgeshire 202
Fordingbridge, Hampshire 115
Forest Row, East Sussex 17
Four Crosses, Powys 396
Fowey, Cornwall 147
Framlingham, Suffolk 224
Freshford, Co Kilkenny 449
Freshwater, Isle of Wight 123
Frinton-on-sea, Essex 207
Frome, Somerset 186
Froncysyllte, Denbighshire 389

G

Gainsborough, Lincolnshire 340
Galway, Co Galway 448
Gargrave, North Yorkshire 317
Garstang, Lancashire 377
Gateshead, Tyne and Wear 350
Gillingham, Dorset 172
Glarryford, Co Antrim 432
Glasgow 409
Glastonbury, Somerset 186
Glengormley, Co Antrim 432
Glossop, Derbyshire 270
Gloucester, Gloucestershire 241
Godalming, Surrey 130
Godmanchester, Cambridgeshire 202
Godshill, Isle of Wight 123
Golden Cross, East Sussex 18
Gomershall, Surrey 131
Goole, East Riding of Yorkshire 314
Goring on Thames, Berkshire 109
Gormanstown, Co Meath 451
Gort, Co Galway 448
Gosforth, Tyne and Wear 350
Gosport, Hampshire 115
Gotham, Nottinghamshire 280
Goudhurst, Kent 32
Grampound, Cornwall 147
Grange-over-Sands, Cumbria 363
Grantham, Lincolnshire 340
Grasmere, Cumbria 364
Gravesend, Kent 32
Grays, Essex 207
Great Ayton, North Yorkshire 317
Great Baddow, Essex 207
Great Barrow, Cheshire 358
Great Bookham, Surrey 131
Great Chesterford, Essex 207
Great Glan, Leicestershire 272
Great Harwood, Lancashire 377
Great Houghton, South Yorkshire 330
Great Salkeld, Cumbria 364
Great Shelford, Cambridgeshire 202
Great Waltham, Essex 208
Great Yarmouth, Norfolk 216
Green Street Green, Kent 32
Greet, Gloucestershire 242
Greetland, West Yorkshire 334
Grey Abbey, Co Down 435
Greystoke, Cumbria 364
Greystones, Co Wicklow 453
Grimsby, Lincolnshire 341
Grimston, Leicestershire 272
Guestling, East Sussex 18
Guildford, Surrey 131
Guilsborough, Northamptonshire 277
Guisborough, North Yorkshire 317
Gurnos, West Glamorgan 400

H

cheston, Suffolk 224
ddenham, Cambridgeshire 202
dleigh, Suffolk 224
dlow Down, East Sussex 18
dlow, Kent 32
le, Greater Manchester 370
lebarns, Cheshire 358
lesowen, West Midlands 304
lesworth, Suffolk 224
lifax, West Yorkshire 334
lstead, Essex 208
m Common, Surrey 132
mpton Wick, Surrey 132
mpton, Middlesex 103
mstreet, Kent 32
nford, Staffordshire 292
pton, Lancashire 377
refield, Middlesex 103
rle Syke, Lancashire 377
low, Essex 208
pole, Northamptonshire 277
rrietsham, Kent 32
rriseahead, Staffordshire 293
rogate, North Yorkshire 318
rrow, Middlesex 104
rtley Wintney, Hampshire 115
tshill, Staffordshire 293
rwich, Essex 208
slemere, Surrey 132
slingden, Lancashire 377
stings, East Sussex 18
tch End, Middlesex 104
therleigh, Devon 157
tton, Cheshire 358
verfordwest, Pembrokeshire 395
warden, Flintshire 390
wes, North Yorkshire 320
worth, West Yorkshire 335
yes, Kent 32
yfield, Derbyshire 270
y-on-Wye, Herefordshire 249
ywards Heath, West Sussex 140
zel Grove, Greater Manchester 370
adcorn, Kent 32
adley, Hampshire 116
anor, Derbyshire 270
athfield, East Sussex 19
bden Bridge, West Yorkshire 335
e, Devon 158
msley, North Yorkshire 320
sby, Cheshire 359
ston, Cornwall 147
mel Hempstead, Hertfordshire 254
mingborough, North Yorkshire 320
mswell Cliff, Lincolnshire 341
nfield, West Sussex 140
nley-on-Thames, Oxfordshire 261
reford, Herefordshire 250
rne Bay, Kent 32
tford, Hertfordshire 254
skin Green, Lancashire 377
swall, Merseyside 381
xham, Northumberland 349
ywood, Greater Manchester 370
h Easter, Essex 208
h Halden, Kent 33
h Wycombe, Buckinghamshire 235
Highbridge, Hampshire 116
Hillsborough, Co Down 435
Hinckley, Leicestershire 272
Hindhead, Surrey 132
Hingham, Norfolk 216
Hitchin, Hertfordshire 255
Hoby, Leicestershire 272
Hockley, Nottinghamshire 280
Holbeach, Lincolnshire 342
Holland-on-Sea, Essex 208
Hollingworth, Greater Manchester 370
Holmfirth, West Yorkshire 336
Holsworthy, Devon 158
Holt, Norfolk 216
Holton le Clay, Lincolnshire 342
Holyhead, Isle of Anglesey 392
Holywood, Co Down 435
Honiton, Devon 158
Horam, East Sussex 19
Horbury, West Yorkshire 336
Horley, Surrey 133
Horncastle, Lincolnshire 342
Horndean, Hampshire 116
Hornsea, East Riding of Yorkshire 314
Horsham, West Sussex 140
Horwich, Greater Manchester 370
Houghton, West Sussex 140
Hove, East Sussex 19
Howden, East Riding of Yorkshire 315
Hoylake, Merseyside 381
Huddersfield, West Yorkshire 336
Hull, East Riding of Yorkshire 315
Hungerford, Berkshire 109
Huntingdon, Cambridgeshire 202
Huntington, Cheshire 359
Hurst Green, East Sussex 20
Hurst, Berkshire 110
Hurstpierpoint, West Sussex 140
Hythe, Kent 33

I

Ilchester, Somerset 186
Ilford, Essex 208
Ilfracombe, Devon 160
Ilkley, West Yorkshire 336
Ilmington, Warwickshire 298
Ilminster, Somerset 186
Impington, Cambridgeshire 202
Ingatestone, Essex 208
Ipswich, Suffolk 224
Ironbridge, Shropshire 287
Irthlingborough, Northamptonshire 277
Isleworth, Middlesex 104
Iver, Buckinghamshire 235
Ixworth, Suffolk 225

J

Jedburgh, Scottish Borders 421

K

Keighley, West Yorkshire 337
Kells, Co Antrim 432
Kelsale, Suffolk 225
Kelvedon, Essex 209
Kempsford, Gloucestershire 242
Kendal, Cumbria 364
Kenfig Hill, Mid Glamorgan 392
Kenilworth, Warwickshire 298
Keswick, Cumbria 365
Kettering, Northamptonshire 277
Kibworth, Leicestershire 272
Kidderminster, Worcestershire 308
Kidwelly, Carmarthenshire 386
Killamarsh, South Yorkshire 330
Killinghall, North Yorkshire 320
Killyleagh, Co Down 435
Kilrea, Co Londonderry 437
King's Langley, Hertfordshire 255
King's Lynn, Norfolk 217
Kingsbridge, Devon 160
Kingsclere, Berkshire 110
Kingston-upon-Thames, Surrey 133
Kingswinford, West Midlands 304
Kington, Herefordshire 251
Kinsale, Co Cork 441
Kinvara, Co Galway 448
Kirkby In Ashfield, Nottinghamshire 280
Kirkby Lonsdale, Lancashire 377
Kirkby Stephen, Cumbria 365
Kirton, Lincolnshire 342
Knaresborough, North Yorkshire 320
Knighton, Powys 396
Knutsford, Cheshire 359

L

Laleham, Middlesex 104
Lamberhurst, Kent 33
Lancaster, Lancashire 378
Langford, Nottinghamshire 280
Langport, Somerset 187
Larne, Co Antrim 432
Launceston, Cornwall 147
Lavenham, Suffolk 226
Lealholm, North Yorkshire 321
Leamington Spa, Warwickshire 298
Leap, Co Cork 441
Leatherhead, Surrey 133
Leavesden, Hertfordshire 255
Lechlade, Gloucestershire 242
Leckhampstead, Berkshire 111
Ledbury, Herefordshire 251
Leeds, West Yorkshire 337
Leek, Staffordshire 293
Leicester, Leicestershire 272
Leigh-on-sea, Essex 209
Leighton Buzzard, Bedfordshire 232
Leiston, Suffolk 226
Leominster, Herefordshire 251
Lepton, West Yorkshire 337
Lewes, East Sussex 20
Leyburn, North Yorkshire 321
Lichfield, Staffordshire 294
Limerick, Co Limerick 450
Lincoln, Lincolnshire 342
Lindfield, West Sussex 141
Lisburn, Co Antrim 433
Liskeard, Cornwall 147
Liss, Hampshire 116
Little Chalfont, Buckinghamshire 235
Little Downham, Cambridgeshire 202
Little Waltham, Essex 210

INDEX OF PLACE NAMES

M – O

Littleborough, Greater Manchester 370
Littlebourne, Kent 33
Littlehampton, West Sussex 141
Liverpool, Merseyside 382
Llanbadoc, Monmouthshire 394
Llandeilo, Carmarthenshire 386
Llandrindod Wells, Powys 396
Llandudno, Conwy 388
Llandysul, Ceredigion 388
Llanelli, Carmarthenshire 387
Llanerchymedd, Isle of Anglesey 392
Llanfair Caereinion, Powys 396
Llangollen, Denbighshire 389
Llanidloes, Powys 397
Llanrwst, Conwy 389
Llansantffraid, Powys 397
Llanvihangel Crucorney, Monmouthshire 394
Llanwrda, Carmarthenshire 387
London, East 44
London, North 46
London, South 57
London, West 78
Londonderry, Co Londonderry 437
Long Hanborough, Oxfordshire 262
Long Marston, Warwickshire 298
Long Marton, Cumbria 365
Long Melford, Suffolk 226
Long Sutton, Lincolnshire 343
Longnor, Shropshire 287
Longridge, Lancashire 378
Longtown, Cumbria 365
Looe, Cornwall 148
Loose, Kent 33
Lostwithiel, Cornwall 148
Loughall, Co Armagh 433
Loughborough, Leicestershire 274
Louth, Lincolnshire 343
Lower Stondon, Bedfordshire 232
Lowestoft, Suffolk 227
Lubenham, Leicestershire 274
Luddendenfoot, West Yorkshire 337
Ludlow, Shropshire 287
Luton, Bedfordshire 232
Lydeard St Lawrence, Somerset 187
Lyme Regis, Dorset 172
Lyminge, Kent 33
Lymington, Hampshire 116
Lymm, Cheshire 359
Lyndhurst, Hampshire 117
Lyneham, Wiltshire 193
Lynton, Devon 160
Lytham St Anne's, Lancashire 378

M

Macclesfield, Cheshire 359
Machynlleth, Powys 397
Maiden Newton, Dorset 172
Maidstone, Kent 33
Malahide, Co Dublin 447
Maldon, Essex 210
Mallow, Co Cork 441
Malmesbury, Wiltshire 193
Malton, North Yorkshire 321
Malvern, Worcestershire 308
Manchester, Greater Manchester 370
Maningford Bruce, Wiltshire 193
Manningtree, Essex 210
Mansfield, Nottinghamshire 280
Manton, Rutland 284
March, Cambridgeshire 202
Market Bosworth, Leicestershire 274
Market Deeping, Cambridgeshire 202
Market Drayton, Shropshire 288
Market Harborough, Leicestershire 274
Market Weighton, East Riding of Yorkshire 315
Marlborough, Wiltshire 193
Marlesford, Suffolk 227
Marlow, Buckinghamshire 235
Marple Bridge, Greater Manchester 371
Marsham, Norfolk 217
Martlesham, Suffolk 227
Martock, Somerset 187
Masham, North Yorkshire 321
Matlock, Derbyshire 271
Mattingley, Hampshire 117
Maymooth, Co Kildare 449
Melbury Osmond, Dorset 172
Melksham, Wiltshire 194
Melton Mowbray, Leicestershire 275
Melton, Suffolk 227
Menai Bridge, Isle of Anglesey 392
Menston, West Yorkshire 338
Mere, Wiltshire 194
Merstham, Surrey 133
Merthyr Tydfil, Mid Glamorgan 393
Mevagissey, Cornwall 148
Middle Aston, Oxfordshire 262
Middleham, North Yorkshire 321
Middleton In Teesdale, Co Durham 348
Middleton, Warwickshire 298
Midgham, Berkshire 111
Midhurst, West Sussex 141
Midsomer Norton, Somerset 187
Millendreath, Cornwall 148
Minchinhampton, Gloucestershire 242
Minehead, Somerset 187
Modbury, Devon 160
Moira, Co Armagh 434
Mold, Flintshire 390
Monkstown, Co Dublin 447
Monmouth, Monmouthshire 394
Morecambe, Lancashire 378
Moreton-in-Marsh, Gloucestershire 242
Morpeth, Northumberland 350
Mortimer, Berkshire 111
Mountain Ash, Mid Glamorgan 393
Moy, Co Tyrone 438
Moycullen, Co Galway 448
Much Wenlock, Shropshire 288
Mulbarton, Norfolk 217
Mumbles, West Glamorgan 400

N

Nantwich, Cheshire 360
Naphill, Buckinghamshire 235
Narberth, Pembrokeshire 395
Narborough, Leicestershire 275
Nayland, Suffolk 228
Neath, West Glamorgan 400
Needham Market, Suffolk 228
Nelson, Lancashire 378
Netherhampton, Wiltshire 194
Nettlebed, Oxfordshire 262
Nettleham, Lincolnshire 343
New Mills, Derbyshire 271
New Milton, Hampshire 117
New Romney, Kent 34
Newark, Nottinghamshire 281
Newbridge on Wye, Powys 397
Newbury, Berkshire 111
Newby Bridge, Cumbria 365
Newcastle Emlyn, Carmarthenshire 387
Newcastle-under-Lyme, Staffordshire 295
Newcastle-upon-Tyne, Tyne and Wear 351
Newent, Gloucestershire 243
Newhaven, East Sussex 22
Newmarket, Suffolk 228
Newnham on Severn, Gloucestershire 243
Newport Pagnell, Buckinghamshire 236
Newport, Co Tipperary 452
Newry, Co Down 435
Newton Abbot, Devon 161
Newtown, Powys 397
Newtownabbey, Co Antrim 433
Newtownards, Co Down 435
Norbury, Shropshire 289
North Petherton, Somerset 187
North Shields, Tyne and Wear 352
North Walsham, Norfolk 217
North Warnborough, Hampshire 117
North Wraxall, Wiltshire 194
Northallerton, North Yorkshire 321
Northampton, Northamptonshire 277
Northfleet, Kent 34
Northmoor, Oxfordshire 262
Northwood Hills, Middlesex 104
Norton, North Yorkshire 322
Norwich, Norfolk 218
Nottingham, Nottinghamshire 281
Nuneaton, Warwickshire 298
Nutley, East Sussex 22

O

Oakham, Rutland 284
Ockbrook, Derbyshire 271
Okehampton, Devon 161
Old Bedhampton, Hampshire 118
Oldbury, West Midlands 304
Oldcastle, Co Meath 451
Oldham, Greater Manchester 371
Olney, Buckinghamshire 236
Omagh, Co Tyrone 438
Orford, Suffolk 228
Ormskirk, Lancashire 379
Orpington, Kent 34
Osgathorpe, Leicestershire 275
Oswestry, Shropshire 289
Otford, Kent 34
Otley, West Yorkshire 338

Oundle, Cambridgeshire 202
Oxford, Oxfordshire 262
Oxted, Surrey 133

P

Padstow, Cornwall 149
Paignton, Devon 162
Painswick, Gloucestershire 243
Paisley, Renfrewshire 420
Par, Cornwall 149
Pateley Bridge, North Yorkshire 320
Patrington, East Riding of Yorkshire 314
Peasenhall, Suffolk 226
Peebles, Scottish Borders 421
Pembroke, Pembrokeshire 394
Pembroke Dock, Pembrokeshire 395
Penarth, South Glamorgan 398
Pencoed, Mid Glamorgan 392
Penistone, South Yorkshire 335
Penkridge, Staffordshire 295
Penmaenmawr, Conwy 388
Penrith, Cumbria 364
Penryn, Cornwall 149
Penygroes, Gwynedd 390
Penzance, Cornwall 149
Pershore, Worcestershire 309
Perth, Perth & Kinross 419
Peterborough, Cambridgeshire 200
Petersfield, Hampshire 115
Petworth, West Sussex 140
Pevensey, East Sussex 21
Pewsey, Wiltshire 192
Pickering, North Yorkshire 321
Pinner, Middlesex 104
Pitlochry, Perth & Kinross 420
Pittenweem, Fife 414
Plymouth, Devon 162
Plympton, Devon 164
Polegate, East Sussex 22
Polperro, Cornwall 150
Pontarddulais, West Glamorgan 399
Pontefract, West Yorkshire 332
Pontlyfni, Gwynedd 390
Pontrilas, Herefordshire 250
Pontyclun, Mid Glamorgan 392
Pontypool, Monmouthshire 394
Pontypridd, Mid Glamorgan 392
Poole, Dorset 172
Portaferry, Co Down 434
Portgordon, Moray 416
Porthcawl, Mid Glamorgan 392
Portrush, Co Antrim 432
Portslade, East Sussex 22
Portsmouth, Hampshire 116
Portsoy, Aberdeenshire 409
Portstewart, Co Londonderry 436
Potterspury, Northamptonshire 277
Potton, Bedfordshire 232
Poynton, Cheshire 359
Preston, Lancashire 378
Prestwich, Greater Manchester 371
Prestwick, South Ayrshire 422
Princes Risborough, Buckinghamshire 236
Pudsey, West Yorkshire 332
Pulborough, West Sussex 142
Purley, Surrey 132
Pwlldefaid, Gwynedd 390
Pwllheli, Gwynedd 390

Q

Queen Camel, Somerset V
Queniborough, Leicestershire 275

R

Radcliffe, Greater Manchester 372
Radhdrum, Co Wicklow 453
Radstock, Somerset 187
Rainham, Kent 35
Ramsbury, Wiltshire 195
Ramsey, Cambridgeshire 203
Ramsgate, Kent 35
Raughton Head, Cumbria 366
Raveningham, Norfolk 219
Ravensden, Bedfordshire 232
Rayleigh, Essex 210
Reading, Berkshire 111
Redbourne, Hertfordshire 255
Redditch, Worcestershire 310
Redhill, Surrey 133
Redruth, Cornwall 150
Reepham, Norfolk 219
Reigate, Surrey 133
Retford, Nottinghamshire 284
Rhayader, Powys 397
Rhos-on-Sea, Conwy 389
Rhyl, Denbighshire 390
Richmond, North Yorkshire 323
Rickmansworth, Hertfordshire 255
Riddings, Derbyshire 271
Ringwood, Hampshire 118
Ripley, Derbyshire 271
Ripon, North Yorkshire 323
Risby, Suffolk 228
Robin Hood's Bay, North Yorkshire 323
Rochdale, Greater Manchester 372
Rochester, Kent 35
Romford, Essex 211
Romiley, Greater Manchester 372
Romsey, Hampshire 119
Rossendale, Lancashire 380
Ross-on-Wye, Herefordshire 252
Rothbury, Northumberland 350
Rotherfield Greys, Oxfordshire 263
Rotherfield, East Sussex 23
Rotherham, South Yorkshire 330
Royston, Hertfordshire 255
Rugby, Warwickshire 299
Rugeley, Staffordshire 296
Ruislip, Middlesex 104
Runfold, Surrey 135
Rushden, Northamptonshire 278
Ruthin, Denbighshire 390
Ryde, Isle of Wight 123
Rye, East Sussex 23

S

Sabden, Lancashire 380
Saffron Walden, Essex 211
Saintfield, Co Down 436
Sale, Greater Manchester 372
Salisbury, Wiltshire 195
Saltaire, West Yorkshire 338
Saltash, Cornwall 150
Saltburn-by-the-sea, North Yorkshire 323
Sandbach, Cheshire 361
Sandgate, Kent 36
Sandiacre, Nottinghamshire 284
Sandown, Isle of Wight 124
Sandwich, Kent 37
Sandycove, Co Dublin 447
Sawbridgeworth, Hertfordshire 256
Saxmundham, Suffolk 228
Scarborough, North Yorkshire 323
Schull, Co Cork 442
Scratby, Norfolk 220
Scremerston, Northumberland 350
Scunthorpe, Lincolnshire 344
Seaford, East Sussex 24
Seagrave, Leicestershire 275
Seal, Kent 37
Seapatrick, Co Down 436
Seaton, Devon 163
Seaview, Isle of Wight 124
Sedbergh, Cumbria 366
Semley, Dorset 173
Sessay, North Yorkshire 324
Sevenoaks, Kent 37
Shaftesbury, Dorset 174
Shanklin, Isle of Wight 124
Shap, Cumbria 366
Shardlow, Derbyshire 271
Sheffield, South Yorkshire 330
Shefford, Bedfordshire 232
Shenton, Warwickshire 299
Shepton Mallet, Somerset 187
Sherborne, Dorset 174
Sherburn-in-Elmet, North Yorkshire 324
Shere, Surrey 135
Sheriffhales, Shropshire 289
Sheringham, Norfolk 220
Shifnal, Shropshire 289
Shipley, West Yorkshire 339
Shipston-on-Stour, Warwickshire 299
Shoreham by sea, West Sussex 144
Shrewsbury, Shropshire 289
Sible Hedingham, Essex 211
Sidcup, Kent 38
Sidmouth, Devon 163
Sittingbourne, Kent 38
Skelton, Cumbria 366
Sketty, West Glamorgan 400
Skibereen, Co Cork 442
Skipton, North Yorkshire 325
Slapton, Bedfordshire 232
Sligo, Co Sligo 451
Slingsby, North Yorkshire 325
Slough, Berkshire 112
Small Dole, West Sussex 144
Snitterfield, Warwickshire 299
Soham, Cambridgeshire 203
Solihull, West Midlands 305
Somerton, Somerset 188
Sonning-on-Thames, Berkshire 112
South Holmwood, Surrey 135
South Hykeham, Lincolnshire 344
South Molton, Devon 163
South Shields, Tyne and Wear 353

INDEX OF PLACE NAMES

T – W

South Walsham, Norfolk 220
Southampton, Hampshire 119
Southend-on-sea, Essex 212
Southport, Merseyside 383
Southsea, Hampshire 120
Southwell, Nottinghamshire 284
Southwold, Suffolk 228
Sowerby Bridge, West Yorkshire 339
Spalding, Lincolnshire 344
Sparkford, Somerset 188
Speldhurst, Kent 38
Spofforth, North Yorkshire 325
Sproughton, Suffolk 229
St Albans, Hertfordshire 256
St Austell, Cornwall 150
St Helier, Jersey 427
St Ives, Cambridgeshire 203
St Just, Cornwall 151
St Leonards-on-sea, East Sussex 24
St Mary, Jersey 428
St Neots, Cambridgeshire 203
St Ouen, Jersey 428
St Peter Port, Guernsey 426
St Saviour, Jersey 428
Stafford, Staffordshire 296
Staines, Middlesex 105
Stalham, Norfolk 220
Stalybridge, Greater Manchester 373
Stamford, Lincolnshire 344
Standish, Greater Manchester 373
Standlake, Oxfordshire 263
Standon, Hertfordshire 256
Stansted Mountfitchet, Essex 212
Stanton upon Hine Heath, Shropshire 290
Staveley, Cumbria 366
Stevenage, Hertfordshire 256
Steventon, Oxfordshire 263
Stewartstown, Co Tyrone 438
Stickney, Lincolnshire 345
Stillorgan, Co Dublin 447
Stock, Essex 212
Stockbridge, Hampshire 121
Stockbury, Kent 38
Stockport, Greater Manchester 373
Stockton Heath, Cheshire 361
Stockton-on-Tees, North Yorkshire 325
Stoke sub Hamdon, Somerset 188
Stoke-on-Trent, Staffordshire 296
Stokesley, North Yorkshire 325
Stone, Staffordshire 296
Stony Stratford, Buckinghamshire 236
Storrington, West Sussex 144
Stourbridge, West Midlands 305
Stowmarket, Suffolk 229
Stow-on-the-Wold, Gloucestershire 243
Stratford-upon-Avon, Warwickshire 299
Streat, West Sussex 144
Strensall, North Yorkshire 325
Stretford, Greater Manchester 374
Stretton, Cheshire 361
Stroud, Gloucestershire 246
Sudbury, Suffolk 229
Sunderland, Tyne and Wear 353
Surbiton, Surrey 135
Sutton Bridge, Lincolnshire 345
Sutton Coldfield, West Midlands 305
Sutton Valence, Kent 38
Sutton-in-Ashfield, Nottinghamshire 284
Swadlincote, Staffordshire 296
Swaffham, Norfolk 220
Swanage, Dorset 175
Swansea, West Glamorgan 400
Swinderby, Lincolnshire 345
Swindon, Wiltshire 196
Swinford, Leicestershire 275

T

Tadcaster, North Yorkshire 325
Tadworth, Surrey 135
Tamworth, Staffordshire 296
Tarporley, Cheshire 361
Tattershall, Lincolnshire 345
Taunton, Somerset 188
Tavistock, Devon 163
Teddington, Middlesex 105
Teignmouth, Devon 164
Templeton, Pembrokeshire 395
Tempo, Co Fermanagh 436
Tenbury Wells, Worcestershire 310
Tenby, Pembrokeshire 395
Tenterden, Kent 38
Tetbury, Gloucestershire 246
Tetsworth, Oxfordshire 263
Tewkesbury, Gloucestershire 248
Teynham, Kent 39
Thame, Oxfordshire 264
Thames Ditton, Surrey 135
Thetford, Norfolk 220
Thirsk, North Yorkshire 325
Thornbury, Gloucestershire 248
Thornton, East Riding of Yorkshire 316
Thornton-le-Dale, North Yorkshire 326
Thrapston, Northamptonshire 278
Thurcroft, South Yorkshire 332
Thursby, Cumbria 366
Ticehurst, East Sussex 24
Tiddington, Warwickshire 300
Timsbury, Somerset 189
Tintern, Monmouthshire 394
Titchfield, Hampshire 121
Tiverton, Devon 164
Tockwith, North Yorkshire 326
Todmorden, Lancashire 380
Tonbridge, Kent 39
Tonypandy, Mid Glamorgan 393
Topsham, Devon 164
Towcester, Northamptonshire 278
Tralee, Co Kerry 449
Trecastle, Powys 397
Tregare, Monmouthshire 394
Tregony, Cornwall 151
Treharris, Mid Glamorgan 393
Trevor, Denbighshire 390
Tring, Hertfordshire 256
Truro, Cornwall 151
Tunbridge Wells, Kent 39
Turners Hill, West Sussex 144
Tutbury, Staffordshire 296
Twickenham, Middlesex 105
Twyford, Berkshire 112
Tynemouth, Tyne and Wear 353
Tytherleigh, Devon 167

U

Ulverston, Cumbria 366
Upper Poppleton, North Yorkshire 326
Uppingham, Rutland 285
Upton-upon-Severn, Worcestershire 310
Uttoxeter, Staffordshire 297
Uxbridge, Middlesex

V

Vale, Guernsey 427
Ventnor, Isle of Wight 124

W

Waddesdon, Buckinghamshire 236
Wadebridge, Cornwall 152
Wadhurst, East Sussex 25
Wadworth, South Yorkshire 332
Wainfleet, Lincolnshire 345
Wakefield, West Yorkshire 339
Walesby, Lincolnshire 346
Wall under Heywood, Shropshire 291
Wallasey, Merseyside 384
Wallingford, Oxfordshire 264
Wallington, Surrey 135
Walmer, Kent 41
Walsall, West Midlands 305
Walton-on-Thames, Surrey 135
Warboys, Cambridgeshire 204
Wareham, Dorset 175
Warfield, Berkshire 112
Warlingham, Surrey 136
Warminster, Wiltshire 196
Warrington, Cheshire 361
Warsash, Hampshire 121
Warwick, Warwickshire 300
Waterford, Co Waterford 452
Watford, Hertfordshire 257
Watton, Norfolk 220
Wavendon, Buckinghamshire 236
Waverton, Cheshire 361
Wedmore, Somerset 189
Wednesbury, West Midlands 306
Weedon, Northamptonshire 278
Welling, Kent 41
Wellingborough, Northamptonshire 279
Wellington, Shropshire 291
Wells, Somerset 189
Wells-Next-the-Sea, Norfolk
Welshpool, Powys 397
Wem, Shropshire 291
Wendover, Buckinghamshire 236
Wentworth, South Yorkshire 332
West Bridgford, Nottinghamshire 284
West Byfleet, Surrey 136
West Haddon, Northamptonshire 279
West Kingsdown, Kent 41
West Ruislip, Middlesex 106

West Wickham, Kent 41
Westbury, Wiltshire 198
Westcliff-on-sea, Essex 212
Westerham, Kent 42
Weston Favell, Northamptonshire 279
Weston on The Green, Oxfordshire 264
Weston-super-Mare, Somerset 190
Westport, Co Mayo 450
Wexford, Co Wexford 452
Weybridge, Surrey 136
Weymouth, Dorset 175
Whaley Bridge, Derbyshire 272
Whalley, Lancashire 380
Wheathampstead, Hertfordshire 257
Wheatley, Oxfordshire 264
Whitbourne, Worcestershire 310
Whitby, North Yorkshire 326
Whitehaven, Cumbria 367
Whitley Bay, Tyne and Wear 353
Whitstable, Kent 43
Whittlesey, Cambridgeshire 204
Whixley, North Yorkshire 327
Whyteleafe, Surrey 136
Wickham, Hampshire 121
Wigan, Greater Manchester 374
Wilstone, Hertfordshire 257
Williton, Somerset 190
Wilmslow, Cheshire 361
Wilstead, Bedfordshire 232
Wilton, Wiltshire 198
Wimborne, Dorset 176
Wincanton, Somerset 190
Winchcombe, Gloucestershire 248
Winchester, Hampshire 121
Windermere, Cumbria 367
Windsor, Berkshire 112
Winslow, Buckinghamshire 237
Wisbech, Cambridgeshire 204
Withernsea, East Riding of Yorkshire 316
Witney, Oxfordshire 265
Wittersham, Kent 43
Wiveliscombe, Somerset 191
Woburn, Bedfordshire 232
Woking, Surrey 136
Wokingham, Berkshire 113
Wolverhampton, West Midlands 306
Woodbridge, Suffolk 230
Woodford Green, Essex 213
Woodford, Greater Manchester 374
Woodhall Spa, Lincolnshire 346
Woodhouse Eaves, Leicestershire 275
Woodseaves, Stafford 291
Woodstock, Oxfordshire 265
Wooler, Northumberland 350
Woolhampton, Berkshire 113
Woolpit, Suffolk 231
Wooton Bassett, Wiltshire 198
Wootton Wawen, Warwickshire 302
Worcester, Worcestershire 310
Workington, Cumbria 367
Worsley, Greater Manchester 374
Worthing, West Sussex 144
Wotton-under-Edge, Gloucestershire 249
Wraysbury, Middlesex 106
Wrentham, Suffolk 231
Wrexham, Denbighshire 390
Writtle, Essex 213
Wrotham, Kent 43
Wroxham, Norfolk 220
Wymeswold, Leicestershire 275
Wymondham, Norfolk 221

Y

Yarm, North Yorkshire 327
Yarmouth, Isle of Wight 124
Yarnton, Oxfordshire 265
Yeovil, Somerset 191
York, North Yorkshire 327
Yoxall, Staffordshire 297
Yoxford, Suffolk 231
Ystradgynlais, West Glamorgan 401

GENERAL INDEX

A

A & C Antique Clocks 181
A & H Antiques 399
A B Period Pine 282
A C Restorations 479
A D Antiques, Abernyte 420
A D Antiques, Tetsworth 265
A D Antiques, Woodseaves 293
A J Antiques, Bath 176
A P Sales, Spalding 346
A S Antiques 374
A645 Trading Post 336
Aaron Antiques 39
David Aaron 78
Abacus, Wednesbury 308
Abacus Books, Altrincham 369
Abacus Fireplaces, Thornton 318
Abacus Gallery, Stoke-on-Trent 298
Abbey Antique Restorers 477
Abbey Antiques, Ramsey 203
Abbey Antiques, Abbeydorney 450
Abbey Antiques, Cahir 454
Abbey Antiques, Whitby 328
Abbey Auctions, Leeds 339
Abbey Galleries, Bath 176
Abbey Models, Bournemouth 168
Abbeydale Antiques 332
A Abbott Antiques 224
Nicholas Abbott 115
Abbotts Auction Rooms 222
Aberdeen House Antiques 88
Aberford Country Furniture 335
Abergavenny Reclamation 396
Abingdon House Antique Centre 158
Abinger Bazaar 124
Abington Books 224
J Abrahart 467
Abram & Mitchell 384
Abstract/Noonstar 88
Academy Billiard Company 136
Acanthus, Garstang 379
Acanthus Antiques & Collectables, Nottingham 283
Acme Inc. 12
Acme Planet 44
Acme Toy Company 304
Acorn Antique Restoration Services 477
Acorn Antiques, Dulverton 185
Acorn Antiques, Sheffield 332
Acorn Antiques, Worthing 144
Acorns 434
Acquisitions Antique & Handmade Furniture 353
Acres Fine Art Auctioneers & Valuers 307
Adam & Eve Books 73
Adam Antiques 183
Adam Antiques & Restoration 490
James Adam 445
Adams Antiques, Nantwich 362
Adams Antiques of Chester 356
Rodney Adams Antiques, Pwllheli 393
Adams Arts & Antiques Ltd, Farningham 31
Adams Auctions 183
Adams Blackrock 444
Henry Adams Fine Art Auctioneers 138
Norman Adams Ltd 65
Adams Restorations 467
Adams Rooms Antiques and Interiors 77
ADC Heritage Ltd 61
Addington Antiques 111
Addington Studio Ceramic Repairs 460
Addyman Books 251
Philip Adler Antiques 248
Advena Antiques & Fairs 329, 343
Affordable Antiques, Ashby de la Zouch 274
Affordable Antiques, Hale 372
After Noah 46, 65
Agar Antiques 438
Agdar 243
Adrian F Ager, Ashburton Marbles 152
Graciela Ainsworth 497
T M Akers Antique Restoration 465
Aladdin's Antiques, Purley 133
Aladdins Architectural Antiques, Newcastle-upon-Tyne 353
Aladdin's Cave, Freshwater 123
Aladdins Cave, Swansea 402
Adrian Alan Ltd 78
Alan's Antiques 133
G Albanese 467
Albany Antiques 132
Alberts of Kensington 104
Albion House Antiques 144
Alcove Antiques 189
Aldergate Antiques 298
Aldershot Antiques 113
Alderson 176
David Aldous-Cook 135
F W Aldridge Ltd 492
Henry Aldridge & Son 192
Aldridges of Bath 176
Alexander Antiques, Portrush 435
Alexander Antiques, Small Dole 144
Alexandria Antiques, Brighton 13
Alfie's Antique Market 56
Alfreton Antique Centre 268
Alfriston Antiques 12
Alice's 93
Alicia Antiques 266
All Books 210
All Our Yesterdays 37
Roger Allan 497
Allbrooks 32
Michael Allcroft Antiques 273, 495
Anthony Allen Conservation, Restoration, Furniture and Artefacts 462, 483
Duncan M Allsop 305
Almonds House Clearances 376
Alpha Coins & Medals 376
Alphabets 206
Alpine Antiques 369
Alscot Bathroom Company 301
Alston Antiques 364
Altea Maps and Books 78
Altrincham Antiques 369
Amber Antiques, Caversham 107
Amber Antiques, Southampton 119
A A Ambergate Antiques 273
The American Comic Shop 28
The Amersham Auction Rooms 235
Cliff Amey & Son 501
Amherst Antiques 98
Amhuerst Auctions 35
Albert Amor 61
Ampthill Antiques Emporium 232
Anchor Antiques Ltd 99
Anchor Antiques (Wales) Ltd 400
Ancient and Gothic 171
Ancient and Modern, Blackburn 377
Ancient and Modern Collectables Centre, Felixstowe 223
Ancient and Oriental Ltd 274
Ancient World 329
Anderson & Garland 353
F E Anderson & Son 399
Anderson Antiques, Saltburn-by-the-Sea 325
Anderson Antiques (UK) Ltd, Hull 317
Anderson's Auction Rooms 432
Andover Saleroom (Pearsons) 113
Michael Andrews Antiques 130
Paul Andrews Antiques 74
Stephen Andrews Gallery 428
Andwells Antiques 115
Angel Antiques, Petworth 141
Angel Antiques, Redditch 312
The Angel Bookshop 217
Angela's Antiques 431
Anglo Pacific (Fine Art) Ltd 495
Anita's Antiques 162
Annatique 372
Annie's 12
Annie's Attic 299
Annie's Vintage Costume and Textiles 46
Anno Domini Antiques 61
Ann's Antiques, Limerick 452
Ann's Antiques, Stoke-on-Trent 298
Annterior Antiques 162
Ann-Tiques 347
David Ansell 103, 462
Anthea's Antiques 93
Anthemion 365
Anthony Antiques Ltd 445
John Anthony 125
Antica Antiques 32
Anticks, Basingstoke 114
Antics, Sheffield 332
Antics, Chichester 138
Antigone 133
Antiquarian 432
Antiquarian Booksellers 436
Antiquarius, Ampthill 232
Antiquarius Antique Centre, London SW03 66
Antiquary Antiques 336
Antiquated 141
Antique & Country Pine 360
Antique & Design 27
Antique and Collector's Centre, Scarborough 325
Antique and Collectors' Centre, Diss 214
The Antique & Interior Centre 248
Antique and Modern Restoration by Richard Parsons 480

Antique and Second Hand Traders 342
Antique Barometers 203
Antique Bed Company, Emsworth 114
The Antique Bed Shop, Halstead 208
The Antique Brass Bedstead Co Ltd, Great Baddow 207
Antique Builders Suppliers 434
The Antique Centre, Cowbridge 401
Antique Centre, East Molesey 129
The Antique Centre, Kidderminster 310
Antique Centre, Matlock 273
Antique Centre, Newcastle-upon-Tyne 353
Antique Centre, South Molton 163
The Antique Centre, Southampton 119
The Antique Centre, Tetbury 248
Antique Chairs and Museum 147
Antique China and Porcelain Restoration 460
Antique Church Furnishings 135
Antique Clocks by Patrick Thomas 127
Antique English Windsor Chairs 261
Antique Enterprises 119
Antique Exporters of Chester 363
Antique Fireplace Centre, Plymouth 162
Antique Fireplaces, Clydach 402
Antique Furniture Restoration, Edinburgh 490
Antique Furniture Restoration & Conservation, Darwen 488
Antique Furniture Warehouse 375
Antique Garden 356
Antique Glass 177
Antique Grove 16
Antique House 115
Antique Interiors, Bingley 335
Antique Interiors, Twickenham 105
Antique Interiors for Home & Garden, Lewes 20
Antique Leathers 493
Antique Linens & Lace 177
The Antique Loft 442
Antique Map and Bookshop 171
Antique Mart 133
The Antique Mirror Gallery 69
Antique Newspapers 428
Antique Pine Stores 171
Antique Prints 445
Antique Renovations, Lavenham 462
Antique Restoration, Rochester 465
Antique Restoration, Salisbury 474
Antique Restoration & Polishing, Chesham 480
Antique Restorations, Brasted 465
Antique Restorations, Brentford 467
Antique Restorations, London N17 494
Antique Restorers, Epsom 469
The Antique Rooms 210
Antique Scientific Instruments 357
Antique Services 491
The Antique Shop, Chester 357
The Antique Shop, St Leonards-on-Sea 24
The Antique Shop, Heswall 383
The Antique Store, Leek 295
The Antique Tea Shop 252
Antique Textiles and Lighting 177
Antique Toys 158
The Antique Trader at the Millinery Works, London N01 46
Antique Traders, Isleworth 104
Antique Warehouse, London SE8 58
Antique Workshop, High Easter 208
Antique Workshop Ltd, Boston 341
Antiques, Manningtree 210
Antiques & Anything, Tenbury Wells 312
Antiques & Bygones, Rochdale 374
Antiques & Clock Shop 282
Antiques & Curios, Derby 271
Antiques & Curios, Worcester 312
Antiques & Curios Centre, Cork 442
Antiques & Curios Shop, Peterborough 203
Antiques & Interiors 218
Antiques & Things 150
Antiques @ The George 260
Antiques Across the World 283
Antiques and All Pine 196
Antiques and Bygones, Chichester 138
Antiques and Collectables 157
Antiques and Country Living 186
Antiques and Country Pine 184
Antiques and Fine Art 149
Antiques and Gifts, Downham Market 215
Antiques and Restoration 224, 477
Antiques and Things 69
Antiques at 35 380
Antiques at H & S Collectables 353
Antiques at the Stile 438
Antiques at Wendover 238
The Antiques Centre, Hartley Wintney 115
Antiques Collectables & Furniture 257
Antiques Emporium, Burwell 199
The Antiques Emporium, Dorchester 171
The Antiques Emporium, Tetbury 248
Antiques en France 278
Antiques et Cetera, Hove 19
Antiques Etc, Brecon 398
Antiques Etc, Ryde 123
The Antiques Exchange, Bournemouth 168
The Antiques Exchange, London SE1 57
Antiques for All 167
Antiques Little Shop 255
Antiques Loft 271
The Antiques Market 195
Antiques of Bath 177
Antiques of Bloxham 260
Antiques of Penrith 367
Antiques of Sherborne 174
Antiques on High Ltd 264
The Antiques Shop, Tunbridge Wells 39
The Antiques Shop Bruton 183
Antiques Trade Warehouse, London SE1 57
Antiques Traders of Nantwich 362
Antiques Unlimited 309
The Antiques Warehouse, Bath 177
Antiques Warehouse, Buxton 270
The Antiques Warehouse, Farnham 130
The Antiques Warehouse, Marlesford 227
Antiques Warehouse, St Helier 429
The Antiques Warehouse, Worcester 312
Antiques Warehouse & Restoration, Uxbridge
The Antiques Warehouse Ltd, Bristol 181
Antiques Within 295
The Antiques Workshop 483
Antiquewest Ltd at Patrick Sandberg Antiques 88
Antiquiteas 114
Antiquities, Arundel 137
Antiquities, Wolverhampton 308
Antiquities of Hartshill 295
An-Toy-Ques 135
Anvil Antiques 295
Anvil Books 306
Any Amount of Books 99
Any Old Iron 332
Anything Old & Military Collectables 380
Apollo Antiques Ltd, Warwick 302
Apollo Galleries, Westerham 42
Appledore Antiques Centre 25
Appleton's Allsorts 208
Roger Appleyard Ltd 332
Jess Applin 199
Apter–Fredericks Ltd 66
Aquarius Antiques, Leeds 339
The Aquarius, Rhyl 392
Aquarius Books, Market Harborough 276
Aquarius Books Ltd, Bourton-on-the Water 239
Arbiter 386
Arbour Antiques Ltd 301
Arbras 93
Arcade Antiques, Bournemouth 168
Arcade Antiques, Falmouth 146
Arcade Arts Ltd 464
Arcadia, Oswestry 291
Arcadia Antiques, Bristol 181
Arcadia Antiques & Fine Art, Athlone 449
Arcadia Antiques Centre, Goole 316
Arcane Antiques Centre 258
Archaeological Conservator 464
Archaic Artifacts 32
R G Archer Books 226
Archers 238
Architectural Antiques, Bedford 233
Architectural Antiques and Salvage, Dublin 446
Architectural Artefacts, Southwold 228
Architectural Classics, Dublin 446
Architectural Emporium, Tunbridge Wells 39
Architectural Heritage, Cutsdean 243

GENERAL INDEX

A – B

Architectural Rescue, London SE5 58
Architectural Salvage, Hemel Hempstead 256
The Architectural Warehouse, Portsmouth 118
Architus Antiques & Collectables 379
Archive Books and Music 54
Archives Antique Centre 432
Archway Antiques, Grey Abbey 437
Archways, Tavistock 163
C Arden Bookseller 251
Ardingly Antiques 136
Arenski Fine Art 93
Argenteus Ltd 99
Argentum Antiques 205
Ariel Antiques 136
Armchair Books 405
John Armistead 494
The Armoury of St James 61
Armstrong Antiques 320
Armstrongs Auctions 298
Armstrong's Books & Collectables 305
John Arnold & Co 371
Phyllis Arnold Antiques 437
Arrow Auctions 312
Arrowsmith Antiques & Restoration 488
Art & Antiques, Cheltenham 240
Art and Antiques, Eton 108
Art Deco Etc 13
Art Furniture 54
Art Nouveau Originals C1900 46
Artemesia 113
Artemis Decorative Arts Ltd 88
Artique 248
Artisan Restoration 113
Artisans 461
The Arts and Crafts Furniture Co Ltd 76
Arts & Memorabilia 329
Arundel Antique Galleries 137
Arundel Antiques Centre 137
The Arundel Bookshop 137
As Time Goes By 382
Ascension Interiors 33
Ascot Antiques 377
Asenbaum Fine Arts Ltd 97
James Ash Antiques 388
Ashbourne Antiques Ltd 268
Ashcombe Coach House Antiques 20
Iain Ashcroft Furniture 489
Ashdale China Restoration 461
Ashdown Antiques, Crowborough 16
Ashdown Antiques Restoration, Uckfield 465
Ashe Antiques Warehouse 222
Ashley Pine 438
Ashton Gower Antiques 245
Ask Simon 357
Aspidistra, Kenilworth 300
Aspidistra Antiques, Finedon 278
Walter Aspinall Antiques 382
Assembly Antiques Centre 177
Astoria Art Deco 209
Astra House Antique Centre 343
Athelstan's Attic 193
Athena Antiques 120
G M Athey 488
Garry Atkins 88
Atlam Sales and Service 93
Atlantic Antiques 435
Atlantic Bay Gallery, London SW7 73
Atlas Books 46
The Attic, Chesham 236
The Attic, Newton Abbot 161
Attic Antiques, Saintfield 438
Attic Pine, Saintfield 438
Atticus Books, Grays 207
Atticus Bookshop, Lancaster 380
Atwell Martin 192
Auckinleck 405
The Auction House Bridport 170
Audley House Antiques 191
Audrey Bull Antiques 387
Aura Antiques 323
Austwick Hall Books 318
The Autograph Collectors Gallery 284
Autolycus 287
Automattic Comics 192
Autumn Leaves 345
Avaroot 376
Avon Antiques, Bradford on Avon 191
Avon House Antiques, Kingsbridge 160
Richard Axe Books 320
Aytac Antiques 78
Ayuka Ltd 258

B

B & B Antiques, Stickney 347
B & D Collectors' Toys 35
B and T Antiques Ltd 93
B B Collectables, Belfast 432
B H Woodfinishes 470
B S H Antique Restorers Ltd 467
B W Restorations 494
Bacchus Gallery 141
Back in Time 52
Back to Front 270
Back to the Wood 498
Baddow Antique Centre 207
Badgers Books 144
Bagatelle, Woodbridge 230
Bagatelle Antiques, Barton 199
Baggins Book Bazaar 35
Baggins too 35
Baggott Church Street Ltd 246
Duncan J Baggott 246
The Baildon Furniture Co 335
David Bailes of Knaresborough 486
E Bailey 130
Bailiff Forge Manufacturing 495
A Bainbridge & Co 106
Henry Baines 39
Anthony Baker 356
Chris Baker Gramophones 37
G Baker Antiques 344
Gregg Baker Asian Art 88
J & J Baker 226
Mark Baker 467
T Baker 282
A H Baldwin and Son 99
M & M Baldwin 309
David Ball Antiques 234
Ball & Claw Antiques 248
Ballantyne Booth Ltd 467
Ballinderry Antiques 431
Ballindullagh Barn 438
Ballyalton House Architectural Antiques 437
Balmuir House Antiques 248
Banana Dance Ltd 46, 75
Bangor Public Auctions 437
Simon Banks Antiques 279
Banners Collectors & Antiques Centre 333
The Bantry Bookstore 442
Bar Bookstore (The Antiquary Ltd) 326
Bar Street Antiques 326
Sebastiano Barbagallo Antiques 57, 69, 93
Barbara's Antiques and Bric-a-Brac 109
Barber Antiques 281
The Barbers Clock 313
Barbers Fine Art Auctioneers (West Sussex Estate Agents, Surveyors and Auctioneers) 136
Barbican Antique Centre 162
Barclay Antiques 264
Eddy Bardawil 88
Barden House Antiques 39
Craig Barfoot Clocks 263
P R Barham 94
Barham Antiques 94
Barkham Antiques Centre 113
Barleycorn Antiques 343
C & A J Barmby 458
Barmouth Court Antique Centre 333
Barn Antique Centre, Long Marston 300
The Barn Antiques, Barnstaple 153
Barn Antiques, Nantwich 362
The Barn at Bilsington, Bilsington 26
The Barn Collectors Market & Bookshop, Seaford 24
Barn Court Antiques, Templeton 397
Barnaby's Antiques, Wrotham 43
Barnaby's of Battle, Battle 12
Gloria Barnes of Clifton Antiques Centre 181
Jane Barnes Antiques and Interiors 158
Lorna Barnes Conservation 462, 492
R A Barnes Antiques 260
Barnet Bygones 255
Barnet–Cattanach Antiques 255
Roger Barnett 108
Barnett Antiques 139
D Barney 155
Barnstaple Auctions 153
Barnt Green Antiques 304
The Barometer Shop 463
Baron Antiques 361
Baron Art 216, 465
M Barrett Restoration 477
P Barrett 175
R F Barrett Rare Books 273
David Barrington 26
Edward Barrington-Doulby 349
Barrow Lodge Antiques 180
Richard Barry Southern Marketing Ltd 499
Barry's Antiques 216
Barter Books 350

Bartlett Street Antiques Centre 177
Carol Basing 459
Baskerville Antiques 142
M G Bassett 268, 483
David Bates 462
Eric Bates & Sons 218
Bath Antiquities Centre 177
Bath Old Books 177
Batley Auction House 335
Battersea Collectables 75
David Battle Antique Furniture Restoration and Conservation 474
Battlesbridge Antiques Centre 204
Keith Bawden 480
H C Baxter & Sons 76
Bay Books 355
Bay Tree Antiques 198
Chris Baylis Country Chairs 267
Bayliss Antiques 289
George Bayntun 177
Bazaar Boxes, Woburn 234
Bazar, London W10 93
BBM Jewellery, Coins & Antiques 310
BBR Auctions 331
Beacon Antiques 336
Beagle Books, Lymington 116
Beagle Gallery and Asian Antiques, London W11 94
The Bear Room 234
Bear Steps Antiques 291
Clive Beardall 210, 477
J and A Beare Ltd 78
Bearly Trading of London 60
Bearnes 156
Bears Galore 23
Bears 'n' Bunnies, Bromley 27
Bears 'n' Bunnies, Greenhithe 32
Bears on the Square 289
Bears on the Wold 246
P T Beasley 31
Beau Nash Antiques 39
Beaufield Mews Antiques 449
Beaumont Travel Books 58
Beaver Booksearch 221
John Beazor & Sons Ltd 200
Bébés et Jouets 405
James Beck Auctions 215
Beck Head Books & Gallery 380
Beckham Books 229
Beckwith and Son 256
Bed of Roses 240
The Bed Workshop 181
Bedale Antiques 318
Beddington Antiques and Clearance Centre at Lawmans 127
P E L Bedford 170
Margaret Bedi Antiques and Fine Art 318, 320, 329
Bedsteads 177, 181
Linda Bee 78
Beech House 333
Anthony James Beech 486
Jonathan Beech Antique Clocks 452
Beechams Furniture 477
Beechwood Antiques 396
Beedham Antiques Ltd 109
Beer Collectables 154
Bees Antiques 267
R Beesly 480
Beeston Reclamations 356
Beeswax Antiques 439
Brian Beet 78
Robert Belcher Antiques 310
Belford Antiques 405
Belgrave Antiques Centre 378
Bell Antiques, Grimsby 343
Bell Antiques, Romsey 119
Bell Antiques, Twyford 112
The Bell Gallery 432
Bell House Restoration 467
Bell Passage Antiques 251
Colin Bell, Ben Norris and Co 470
Bell, Book and Radnell 99
Belle Vue Restoration 483
C Bellinger Antiques 255
Belmont Jewellers 31
Below Stairs, Kendal 366
Below Stairs of Hungerford 109
Benezet Antiques 446
Bennett and Kerr Books 265
Alan Bennett 151
K Bennett 488
Bennetts Antiques & Collectables Ltd 318
Nigel Benson 20th Century Glass 88
William Bentley Billiards 109
Bentleys Fine Art Auctioneers 29
Benton Fine Art and Antiques 244
Berkeley Antiques 250
Berkeley Market 239
Berkhamsted Auction Rooms 255
Berkshire Antiques Centre 111
Berkshire Antiques Co Ltd 112
Bermondsey Antiques Market 57
Berry Antiques 244
Bertie's 77
Berwald Oriental Art 89
Besley's Books 221
Bespoke Furniture 31, 465
Beth–Nell Antiques 455
Better Days 394
Betty's Antiques 274
Beverley 56
Bewdley Antiques 309
Daniel Bexfield Antiques 78
Bexhill Antique Exporters 12
Biddle & Webb Ltd 304
Bidford Antique Centre 299
Big Ben Clocks and Antiques 69
Big Lamp Antiques 353
Biggs Antique Shop 450
Paula Biggs 181
Bigwood Antiques 26
Bigwood Auctioneers Ltd 302
Billiard Room Antiques 184
D and A Binder 56
Bingley Antiques 337
Peter Binnington 474
Birchington Antiques 26
Christy Bird 446
Eric A Bird Jewellers 344
John Bird Antiques 142
The Birdcage Antiques 369
Birdwell Lodge Craft & Antiques Centre 331
Birkdale Antiques 385
The Birmingham Antique Centre 304
Birmingham Coins 304
Bishopgate Antiques 329
Bishopston Books 181
Bizarre, London NW8 56
Bizarre!, Topsham 164
BK Art & Antiques 243
Black Cat Antiques 384
The Black Cat Bookshop 274
Black Dog Antiques 221
Black Horse Gallery 218
The Black Sheep 249
Adrian J Black 486
Laurance Black Ltd 405
Maxwell Black 465
The Blacksmiths Forge 281
Blackwater Pine Antiques 151
Steve Blackwell French Polishers 488
Blackwell's Rare Books 264
H Blairman & Sons Ltd 78
Blake's Books 230
Kitty Blakes Shop 220
Blanchard Ltd 61
G D Blay Antiques 127
Blenheim Antiques 243
Blestium Antique Centre 396
Blewbury Antiques 260
N Bloom and Son (1912) Ltd 78
Bloomfield Auctions 432
The Bloomsbury Bookshop 98
Blunderbuss Antiques 78
John Bly 61, 258
Bly Valley Antiques 221, 231
Blyburgate Antiques 221
Boadens Antiques 351
Clare Boam 344
Heather Boardman Antiques 140
Boar's Nest Trading 312
Bodmin Antiques Centre 146
Bogan House Antiques 167
Bohemia 376
Bold as Brass Polishers 494
Bolden Auction Galleries 352
Brian R Bolt Antiques 434
Bolton Antique Centre 370
Richard Bolton Furniture Restorer 480, 500
Bolton Pianos & Antique Export 377
Bona Art Deco Store 115
S Bond & Son 206
Bond Street Antiques, Cromer 214
The Bond Street Antiques Centre, London W1 78
The Bones Lane Antiques Centre 204
Bonhams & Brooks
Bedale 318
Bolton 370
Capel Iwan 387
Colchester 206
Fordingbridge 115
Hanford 294
Hemingborough 322
Henley-on-Thames 263
Hove 19
London SW7 73
London SW10 74
Monkstown 449
Nantwich 362
Newton Ferrers 161
Nottingham 284
Poole 173
Reepham 219
South Molton 163
Sparkford 188

GENERAL INDEX

B

Speldhurst 38
St Helier 429
St Peter Port 428
Strensall 327
Wallingford 266
Whitstable 43
Bonhams & Brooks North 375
Bonhams & Brooks Scotland 405
Bonhams & Brooks West Country 158
Bonstow and Crawshay Antiques 161
Bonython Bookshop 151
Book & Pieces 43
The Book & Stamp Shop 327
Book Academy 120
Book Aid Charitable Trust 60
Book and Comic Exchange 94
Book Art and Architecture Ltd 98
The Book Bug 257
Book Cellar 154
Book Centre 18
The Book Depot 458
The Book Exchange 255
The Book Gallery 150
The Book House 367
The Book Jungle 24
The Book Palace 60
The Book Passage 287
The Book Shop, Cambridge 200
The Book Shop, Hay-on-Wye 251
Bookbarn Ltd 186
Bookbox 246
Bookcase 364
Bookends, Emsworth 114
Bookends of Fowey 147
Bookfinders 432
Booklore 274
Bookman's Halt 24
The Bookmark, Brighton 13
Bookmark, Broad Hinton 192
The Bookmark, Rainham 35
Books 391
Books & Collectables Ltd 200
Books & Maps 168
Books Afloat 175
Books Bought and Sold 129
Books Etc. 214
Books Galore 185
Books in the Basement 133
Books, Maps & Prints 398
The Bookshop, Carndonagh 444
The Bookshop, Conwy 390
The Bookshop, Coventry 306
The Bookshop, Crewkerne 185
The Bookshop, Taunton 188
The Bookshop Blackheath Ltd 58
The Bookshop Godmanchester 202
Bookstack, Bridgnorth 287
Bookstack, Wolverhampton 308
Bookstop 31
Bookworld 291
The Bookworm, Edinburgh 405
Bookworm, Holland-on-Sea 208
Bookworms of Evesham 310
Bookworms of Shoreham 144
A E Booth and Son 130, 470
Joanna Booth 66
Mr Booth Antiques 261
Tony Booth, London W1 79
Tony Booth Antiques, London W11 94
Richard Booth's Bookshop Ltd 251
Malcolm Bord 99
The Border Bookshop 382
Borg's Antiques 357
Boris Books 114
Boscombe Militaria 168
Bosleys Military Auctioneers 237
Nicolaus Boston Antiques 89
Bosworth Antiques 276
John Botting 19
Boughey Antique Restoration 474
Boulevard Antiques 43
Boulton & Cooper Fine Art 323
C R Boumphrey 163
Bounty Antiques 164
Bourbon Hanby Antique Centre 66
J H Bourdon-Smith Ltd 62
Bourne End Antiques Centre 236
Bourne End Auction Rooms 236
Bourne Mill Antiques 130
Bourneville Books 252
Boutle and King 45
Bow Windows Bookshop 20
David Bowden Chinese and Japanese Art 46
M J Bowdery 132
Jason Bowen 474
Bowen & Co 187
Bowen, Son & Watson 289
Bowers' Auctioneers 437
Bowhouse Antiques 109
H & L Bowkett 322
Michael J Bowman ARICS 161
Bowood Antiques 239
Bowstead Antiques 357
Bow-Well Antiques 405
Box Bush Antiques 313
Box of Porcelain 171
K W Box 477
Boxroom Antiques 260
Symon E Boyd Clock Restorer 462
Patrick Boyd-Carpenter 79
Boydell Galleries 383
Boyle's Antiques 442
Boz Books 251
Bracketts Fine Arts 39
Brackley Antiques 278
The Brackley Antiques Cellar 278
J Bradburne-Price & Co 392
M and S Bradbury 474
Roger Bradbury Antiques 214
M Bradley 488
Robert Bradley Antiques 195
Bradley's Past and Present Shop 142
Emma Bradshaw Ceramic Restorations 460
Bradshaw Fine Wood Furniture Ltd 477
Bradwell Antiques Centre 270
Braemar Antiques 75
John Bragg Antiques 148
Bragge & Sons 23
Lesley Bragge Antiques 142
Brambridge Antiques 116
Brandt Oriental Antiques 79
Steve Vee Bransgrove Collectables 186
The Brazen Head Bookshop & Gallery 213
Breakspeare Antiques 249
Geoffrey Breeze 177
Ellen L Breheny 462
Brentside Programmes 203
Lorcan Brereton 446
Arthur Brett & Sons 218
Bric-a-Brac, Larne 434
Bric-a-Brac, Truro 151
Bridge Antiques 363
Christine Bridge Antiques 75
Bridge Collectables 224
Bridge End Antiques 364
Bridge House Antiques & Interiors 109
Bridgebarn Antiques 204
Bridgford Antiques 286
Bridgnorth Antiques Centre 287
Bridport Antique Centre 170
Bridport Old Books 170
Andy Briggs 480
Bright Helm Antiques & Interiors 13
Brightling Restoration 465
Brighton Architectural Salvage 13
Brighton Flea Market 13
Brighton Postcard Shop 13
Brighton Retro 13
Brightwells 253, 398
T & J Brindle Antiques 378
Brindle Fine Arts Ltd 382
Brindley John Ayers Antique Fishing Tackle 396
Lynda Brine Antiques 178
Bristol Auction Rooms 181
Bristol Brocante 181
Bristol Restoration Workshop 494
Bristol Trade Antiques 181
C T Bristow 470
Bristow and Garland 115
British Antique Replicas 138
Andrew Britten Antiques 193
Brittons Antiques 380
Brittons Jewellers 380
Tony Broadfoot Antiques 14
Broadhursts of Southport Ltd 385
Brocante Antiques, Chirk 391
Brocante Antiques & Interiors, Twyford 112
Brocante Antiques Centre, Marlborough 193
A F Brock & Co Ltd 372
Brogden Books 368
Bromlea and Jonkers 263
The Brompton Gallery 120
Brondesbury Architectural Reclamation 56
Michael Brook Antique Metal Restoration 494
Brook Farm Antiques 291
Brook Studio 460
T C S Brooke 220
E J & C A Brooks 205
Brooks Antiques 381
Broughton Books 405
David Brower 89
Browgate Antiques 335
Alasdair Brown 70
I and J L Brown Ltd 70, 252
P J Brown Antiques 379
S C Brown 483
Brown House Antiques 210
B Browning & Son 313

Brown's 74
Brown's Antiques & Collectables 350
Brown's Times Past Antiques 429
Browse Antiques 298
Browsers, Exmouth 157
Browsers, Llanrhaeadr-ym-Mochnant 399
Browsers Barn 25
Browsers Bookshop 147
Browzaround 381
Steven B Bruce Auctioneers Ltd 301
Sarah & Gary Brumfitt 474
Brun-Lea Antiques & Furnishings 377
S Brunswick 56
Brunswick Antiques 367
F G Bruschweiler Antiques Ltd 210
Douglas Bryan Antiques 29
Karen Bryan Antiques 226
N F Bryan-Peach Antiques 277
Bryden House Clocks & Antiques 246
Bryers Antiques 178
Christopher Buck Antiques 36
Buck House Antique Centre 236
Buckingham Antiques, Helmsley 322
Buckingham Antiques Centre Ltd, Buckingham 236
Wayne Buckner Antiques 118
Philip Buddell 151
Philip Buddell Antiques 151
Bullring Antiques 251
Bumbles 125
Peter Bunting 268
Burford Antiques Centre 260
C and L Burman 97
Victor Burness Antiques 57
The Burnham Model & Collectors Shop 184
Burns and Graham 121
David E Burrows Antiques 277
Burstow & Hewett 12
Mick Burt (Antique Pine) 340
Burton Antiques 293
Burwell Auctions 203
Bury & Hilton 295
Bush Antiques 211
Robert Bush Antiques 45
Bushwood Antiques 256
Butchers Antiques 147
Butchoff Interiors 94
Edward Butler 446
Jacob Butler – Period Joinery Specialist 458
R Butler 111
Roderick Butler 158
The Buying Centre 360
Byethorpe Furniture 483
Bygone Antiques, Swansea 402
Bygone Times, Ecclestone 378
Bygone Times International Plc, Ecclestone 379
Bygone Years, Watford 259
Bygones, Burford 260
Bygones Antiques, Limerick 452
Bygones by the Cathedral, Worcester 313
Bygones of Ireland Ltd, Westport 453
Bygones of Worcester 313
Bygones Reclamation (Canterbury) Ltd 27
Byrkley Books Ltd 293

C

C A R S (Classic Automobilia and Regalia Specialists) 14
C and B Antiques 255
C J C Antiques 388
Cabaret Antiques 405
The Cabinet Repair Shop 470
Andre de Cacqueray 62
Cadari Ltd 17
Cader Idris Bookshop 393
J E Cadman 474
Calder Valley Auctioneers 339
Ian Caldwell 135
Caledonia Antiques 182
Calico by Carol Anne 333
Callie's Curiosity Shop 396
Callingham Antiques Ltd 142
E Callister 501
Calton Gallery 405
Calverley Antiques 40
Calvers Collectables 104
Rebecca Calvert Antiques 345
Camberwell Architectural Salvage & Antiques 58
Cambridge Antiques 119
Cambridge House Antiques 304
Camden Art Gallery 56
Camden Books 178
Camden Passage Antiques Market 47
Camel Art Deco 47
Cameo Antiques 498
Jasmin Cameron 66
Cameron Preservation 496
Camillas Bookshop 16
Iain Campbell 360
Peter Campbell Antiques 194
Campbell and Archard 37
Peter Campion Restorations 480
Candle Lane Books 291
Cane and Rush Works 459
Cane Corner 459
The Cane Workshop 459
Caners & Upholders 459
M D Cannell 219
Elizabeth Cannon Antiques 206
Cannon Militaria 193
Cannonbury Antiques Southwold 228
Canon Gate Bookshop 139
Canonbury Antiques Ltd 94
Canter & Francis 346
The Canterbury Auction Galleries 27
The Canterbury Book Shop 27
Capel Mawr Collectors' Centre 393
Capes, Dunn & Co 372
Capital Bookshop 400
Patric Capon 47
Capricorn Antiques 392
D Card 107
Cardiff Antique Centre 400
Cardiff Reclamation 400
David Cardoza Antiques 20
Cards Inc 259
Cards 'N' Collectables 203
Mervyn Carey 25
Carey's Bookshop 211
Carl Ross Fireplaces 372
Carlisle Antique Centre 364
Carlsen's Antiques and Fine Arts 116
Carlton Antiques 310
Carlton Hollis Ltd 320
John Carlton-Smith 62
Carningli Centre 397
Carol's Antiques, Adare 451
Carol's Curiosity Shop, Seaton 163
Carol's Curiosity Shop, Sutton-in-Ashfield 286
J W Carpenter Antique Clock Restorer 462
Steve Carpenter 204
Carrington House Antiques 391
Carryduff Group Ltd 434
Cartels Auctioneers and Valuers 125
Aurea Carter 94
J S Carter 20
E Carty 498
Cary Antiques 184
Case & Dewing 214
Peter Casebow 470
W J Casey Antiques 302
Hugh Cash Antiques 451
Jack Casimir Ltd 94
Casque and Gauntlet Militaria 130
Cass Freshford Antiques 451
P J Cassells 364
P J Cassidy 344
Cassidy Antiques and Restorations 196
Cassidy's Gallery 59
Cast Offs 305
B Castle 470
Castle Antique Centre Ltd 42
Castle Antique Clocks 401
Castle Antiques, Arundel 137
Castle Antiques, Deganwy 390
Castle Antiques, Leigh-on-Sea 209
Castle Antiques, Lewes 21
Castle Antiques, Middleham 323
Castle Antiques, Newtownards 437
Castle Antiques, Nottingham 284
Castle Antiques, Orford 228
Castle Antiques, Thornbury 250
Castle Antiques, Warwick 302
Castle Antiques, Workington 369
Castle Antiques Ltd, Deddington 262
The Castle Book Shop, Colchester 206
Castle Books, Edinburgh 405
Castle Books, Poole 173
Castle Galleries 195
Castle Gibson 47
Castle Hill Books 253
Castle House 474
Castle Reclamation 187
Castle Restoration 490
Castlebridge Antiques 35
Castlegate Antique Centre 283
Cat in the Window Antiques 367
Catchpole and Rye 35
Cathach Books 446
Cathair Books 455
Cathay Oriental Antiques 284
Cathedral Antiques 35
Cathedral Gallery 296
Lennox Cato Antiques 30
Cato Crane & Co 384
Barbara Cattle 329
Causeway Books 434
D L Cavanagh Antiques 405

GENERAL INDEX

C

R G Cave & Sons Ltd 289
Rupert Cavendish Antiques 70
Cavendish Antiques & Collectors Centre 329
Cavendish Fine Art 112
Cavendish Rose Antiques 222
Cawthorne Antiques Centre 331
Caxton Prints 446
Cedar Antiques Centre Ltd 115, 116
Francois Celada 16
Cellar Antiques, Belfast 432
Cellar Antiques, Hawes 322
Central Auction Rooms 374
Century Tables 483
Ceramic Restoration, Abermule 462
Ceramic Restoration, Sherborne 460
Ceramic Restorations, Holt 460
Ceramics International 298
Cestrian Antiques 357
CG's Curiosity Shop 365
Chacewater Antiques 146
Chair Repair 459
The Chair Set 267
The Chair Shop 272
The Chairman of Bearsden 490
Chaldon Books and Records 126
Chalkwell Auctions Ltd 209
E Chalmers Hallam 118
Chamade Antiques 94
Ronald G Chambers – Fine Antiques 142
Paul Champkins Oriental Art 79
Chancellors Church Furnishings 135
Chancery Antiques Ltd 47
Chandlers Antiques 244
Nicholas Chandor Antiques 94
Chandos Books 182
Channel Islands Galleries Ltd 428
Chapel Antiques, Froncysyllte 391
Chapel Antiques, Glossop 272
Chapel Antiques, Nantwich 362
Chapel Antiques Centre, Barmouth 392
Chapel Antiques Centre, Sheffield 333
Chapel Emporium 345
Chapel Place Antiques 40
Chapel Street Arcades 149
Chapman Antiques 58
Peter Chapman Antiques and Restoration 47
Sylvia Chapman Antiques 295
Chapman, Moore & Mugford 174
Chappells & The Antiques Centre, Bakewell 269
Chapter & Verse Book Sellers 23
Chapter House Books 174
Chapters Book and Music Store 446
Chard Antiques Centre 184
Charing Cross Markets 100
Charis 165
Daniel Charles Antiques 269
Judith Charles Antiques & Collectables 291
Charlotte's Antiques 400
Benny Charlsworth's Snuff Box 379
Charlton House Antiques 47
Charnwood Antiques 480
Chateaubriand Antiques Centre 16
Chattels 171
Chaucer Bookshop 27
Checkley Interiors 295
Cheffins 200
Zygmunt Chelminski 458
Chelmsford Coin Centre 205
Chelsea Antique Mirrors 62
Chelsea Clocks and Antiques 66
Chelsea Gallery and Il Libro 74
Chelsea Military Antiques 66
Cheltenham Antique Market 240
Cheltenham Antiques Centre 240
Chemicals Ltd 499
Antoine Chenevière Fine Arts Ltd 79
Robert Cheney Antiques 279
Peter Cheney Auctioneers and Valuers 141
Cherry Antiques 256
Chertsey Antiques 126
Cherub Antiques, Carshalton 125
Cherub Antiques, Skipton 327
Cheshire Cast Company 360
Cheshunt Antiques 256
Chess Antique Restorations 480
Chess Antiques 236
The Chest of Drawers 249
Chester Antique Furniture Cave 357
Chesterfield Antiques 304
G & J Chesters 297
H Chesters & Sons 293
Chevertons of Edenbridge Ltd 30
Patrick Cheyne Auctions 369
Cheyne Galleries 105
Cheyne House 23
Chez Chalon 184
Chichester Antiques Centre 139
The Chichester Bookshop 139
Childhood Memories 130
The Children's Bookshop 251
Chiltern Strip & Polish 498
Chimney Pieces 354
China and Glass Restoration 460
The China Repairers 461
Chipping Norton Antique Centre 261
Chisholme Antiques 490
Chislehurst Antiques 28
Chiswick Auctions 87
Chiswick Park Antiques 87
Chit Chat Antiques 405
Chloe Antiques 144
Chobham Antique Clocks 126
Choice Antiques 196
Chorley–Burdett Antiques 168
Peter Christian 377
Robert Christie Antiques 434
Judith Christie 164
Christie's 62
Christie's South Kensington 73
Christina Grant 178
W J Christophers 28
Christopher's Antiques 130
Church End Antiques 52
Church Green Books 267
Church Hill Antique Centre 21
Church House Antiques 136
Church Lane Restorations 467
Church Street Antiques, Godalming 131
Church Street Antiques, Helmsley 322
Church Street Antiques, London NW8 56
Church Street Antiques, Wells-next-the-Sea
Church Street Antiques Centre, Stow-on-the-Wold 246
Church Street Antiques Ltd, Altrincham 369
Church Street Centre 230
Church Street Gallery 301
Church Stretton Books 288
Churchgate Auctions Ltd 274
Churchill Clocks 141
Lawrence Churchill London Ltd 134
Churchill Upholstery 501
Churchills Auction Room 361
Churt Curiosity Shop 130
Chylds Hall Fine Furniture Restoration 490
Ciancimino Ltd 62
Circa 1900 384
Circa Antiques 255
Circle Books 182
Cirencester Arcade 242
City Antiques Ltd 35
CJC Antiques 227
Clancy Chandeliers 455
Clare Antique Warehouse 222
Clare Hall Co 477
Claremont Antiques 40
Clarenbridge Antiques 450
Clarendon Books 275
Christopher Clarke Antiques 246
Robert Clark 264
Clarke Gammon Auctioneers and Valuers 131
Classic Bindings 62
Classic Fabrics with Robin Haydock 66
Classic Finishes 499
The Classic Library 74
Classic Pen Engineering 503
Classic Pictures 171
Classic Prints 66
Classical Deco 25
Classical Numismatic Group Inc. 79
Claymore Antiques 289
Michael Clayton French Polisher 488
Ralph Clee 470
Clee Tompkinson & Francis 389
Cleethorpes Collectables 342
Benedict Clegg 466
John M Clegg 289
Clegg & Son 316
J W Clements 364
Clevedon Books 184
Clewlow Antiques 328
Cliffe Antiques Centre 21
Kenneth F Clifford 486
Clifton Antique Centre 182
Clifton Hill Textiles 182
Clifton House Furniture 190
Cliftonville Antiques 29
Bryan Clisby 116
Clitheroe Collectables 378
The Clock Clinic Ltd 76
Clock Corner 362
The Clock House 125
The Clock Shop, North Shields 354
The Clock Shop, Southsea 120
The Clock Shop, Tutbury 298

Clock Tower Antiques, Brighton 14
Clock Tower Antiques, Tregony 151
The Clock Workshop, Caversham 108
Clockcraft 462
The Clockshop, Weybridge 136
Clocktower Antiques Centre, Southampton 120
The Clock-Work-Shop (Winchester), Winchester 121
Cloisters Antiques 201
Cloud Cuckoo Land, London N1 47
Cloud Cuckoo Land, Mevagissey 148
Cloughcor House Antiques 438
Clutter Antiques 287
Clydach Antiques 402
Clyde Antiques 317
Bobby Clyde Antiques 405
The Coach House, Lydeard St Lawrence 187
The Coach House Antique Centre, Canterbury 28
Coach House Antiques, Hastings 18
Coach House Books, Pershore 312
Coach House Bookshop, Tetbury 249
Coast Antiques 355
Cobham Galleries 126
Cobnar Books 33
Cobweb Books 328
Cobwebs, Coventry 306
Cobwebs, Galway 450
Cobwebs, Holt 216
Cobwebs, Larne 434
Cobwebs, London SE9 58
Cobwebs, Sheffield 333
Cobwebs, Southampton 120
Cobwebs Antiques and Collectables, Bembridge 122
Cobwebs Antiques & Collectables, Church Stretton 288
Cobwebs of Antiquities Ltd 374
Fergus Cochrane Leigh Warren 70
Cockermouth Antiques 365
Cockermouth Antiques & Craft Market 365
Tony Coda Antiques 341
Cofion Books & Postcards 397
Ray Coggins Antiques 198
Cohen & Cohen 89
Cohen & Cohen Portobello Road 94
Stephen Cohu Antiques 430
Coinage Hall Antique Centre 151
Coincraft 98
Coins and Bullion 100
Coldstream Military Antiques 237
Christopher Cole 474
Simon Coleman Antiques 76
T V Coles 203
Collage 147
Collectables, Darlington 350
Collectables, Honiton 158
Collectables, Rochester 36
Collector Centre, Edinburgh 406
The Collector, Belfast 432
The Collector, Clevedon 184
Collectors, Pontardulais 402
Collectors Books & CD Centre, Woodbridge 230
Collectors' Cabin 214
Collectors Carbooks 234
The Collectors Centre, Oldham 373
The Collectors Centre, St Peter Port 428
Collectors Centre, Walsall 307
Collectors Choice 160
Collectors' Corner, Barking 204
Collectors Corner, Carshalton 126
Collectors Corner, Chippenham 192
Collectors Corner, Cowbridge 401
Collectors Corner, Dewsbury 336
Collectors' Corner, Faversham 31
Collectors' Corner, Little Waltham 210
Collectors Corner, Ormskirk 381
Collectors Corner, St Ives 150
Collectors' Corner, Swansea 403
Collectors Corner, Truro 151
Collectors Corner, Watford 259
Collectors Corner, York 329
Collectors Gallery 291
Collectors Old Toy Shop 336
Collectors Place 291
The Collectors Shop, Harrow 104
The Collectors Shop, Northampton 279
The Collectors' Shop, Norwich 218
The Collector's Workshop, London N17 467
Collectors' World, Cromer 214
Collectors World, Nottingham 284
Collinge & Clark 98
Collinge Antiques 391
Peter Collingridge 47
Julie Collino 73
J Collins & Son 154
L and D Collins 66
Collins Antiques 259
Colliton Antique Centre 172
David Collyer Antique Restorations 474
Colonial Times 19
Colonial Times II 24
Coltishall Antique Centre 214
B J Coltman Antiques 353
Colton Antiques 206
Colwyn Books 390
Colystock Antiques 158
Colyton Antique Centre 155
Combe Martin Clock Shop 155
Comberton Antiques 201
Comic Book Postal Auctions Ltd 54
Comic Connections 259
The Commemorative Man 172
Company of Bears 39
Compton Mill Antique Emporium 295
Conlan Antiques 446
John & Noel Connell 19
Conquest House Antiques 28
Rosemary Conquest 47
Conservation Restoration Centre for Furniture and Wooden Artefacts 491
The Conservation Studio 459
Stephen Cook Antiques 244
Sheila Cook Textiles 94
W J Cook 467, 474
George Cooke 467
Sandy Cooke Antiques 226
Cookham Antiques 108
Cook's Cottage Antiques 319
Cookstown Antiques 439
J and M Coombes 127
Cooper and Tanner Chartered Surveyors 186
Alan Cooper Antique Restorations 470
John Cooper Antiques 430
Cooper Fine Arts 26
Cooper Hirst Auctions 205
Coopers of Ilkley 338
David J Cope 295
D A Copley 486
Copnal Books 360
N A Copp 480
Coppelia Antiques 361
Copperwheat Restoration 122, 470
Mark Coray Fine Antique Furniture Restoration 474
Corbitt's 353
Cordelia & Perdy's Antique Shop 296
Lisa Cordes Antiques 234
Corfield Ltd 117
Tim Corfield Professional Antiques Consultant 464
Corinum Auctions 242
Corn Exchange Antiques Centre 40
Corn Mill Antiques 327
Cornell Books Ltd 250
Corner Antiques 144
Corner Cottage Antiques 276
Corner Cupboard Antiques 375
Corner Farm Antiques 291
Corner House Antiques, Lechlade 244
Corner Shop Antiques, Bury St Edmunds 222
Corner Shop Antiques, Camelford 146
Cornerhouse Antiques, Leek 295
Cornfield Antiques & Collectables 16
Cornish Connection 272
Cornmarket Curios 437
Cornucopia 337
Coromandel 77
Corrib Antiques 450
Corry's Antiques 275
Corve Street Antiques 289
Corwell 470
N G and C Coryndon 474
Alison Cosserat 492
Marc Costantini Antiques 70
Cotham Antiques 182
Cotham Galleries 182
Cotham Hill Bookshop 182
The Cotswold Auction Co Ltd 240, 242, 243
Cotswold Pine 264
The Cottage 243
Cottage Antiques, Battlesbridge 204
Cottage Antiques, Cliftonville 29
Cottage Antiques, Glossop 272
Cottage Antiques, Halebarns 360
Cottage Antiques, Kells 434
Cottage Antiques, Leeds 339
Cottage Antiques, Liverpool 384
Cottage Antiques Ltd, Todmorden 382
Cottage Collectables, Holt 216
Cottage Collectibles, Eccleshall 294
The Cottage Collection 205

GENERAL INDEX

C – D

Cottage Farm Antiques 241
Cottage Style Antiques 36
Cottees of Wareham 175
Cottingly Antiques 335
Joan Cotton 286
Thomas Coulborn and Sons 307
Martin Coulborn Restorations 480
Count House Antiques 152
Country Antiques, Antrim 431
Country Antiques & Interiors, Cullompton 155
Country Antiques (Wales), Kidwelly 388
Country Chairmen and Dovetail Restoration 480
Country Clocks 258
Country Collections, Wheatley 266
Country Collector, Pickering 324
Country Cottage Antiques 273
Country Furniture, Fermoy 443
The Country Furniture Shop, High Wycombe 237
Country House and Cottage Antiques, St Mary 430
Country House Antiques, Brooke 213
Country House Furniture, Easingwold 319
Country Life Antiques, Bushey 255
Country Life Antiques, Stow-on-the-Wold 246
Country Markets Antiques & Collectables 261
Country Pine Trading Co 294
Country Rustics 126
The Country Seat 263
Countryside Books 109
County Auctions 148
Courthouse Antiques Centre 332
Richard Courtney Ltd 66
William Courtney & Son 383
Courtville Antiques 446
Courtyard Antiques, Brasted 26
Courtyard Antiques, Gravesend 32
Courtyard Antiques, Olney 238
Courtyard Antiques, Williton 190
Courtyard Books 186
Courtyard Collectables 151
Courtyard Restoration 491
E W Cousins & Son 225
Cowbridge Antiques Centre 401
John Cowderoy Antiques 16
The Coworth Gallery 107
Claude Cox Books 225
Lisa Cox Music 156
Cox's Architectural Salvage Yard Ltd 245
Peter Crabbe Antiques 200
Crackpots 34
Cradlewell Antiques 353
Craftsman Antiques 493
The Craftsman's Joint 468
Stuart Craig 95
Julia Craig 178
Brian and Caroline Craik Ltd 178
Cranbrook Antiques 29
Cranglegate Antiques 220
Craobh Rua Rare Book 435
Thomas Crapper & Co 302
Crawford Antiques 468
Robert H Crawley 468
Creek Antiques 59
Crescent Antiques, Disley 360
Crescent Antiques, Orpington 34
Crest Collectables 17
The Crested China Co 316
Crewkerne Antiques 185
Criccieth Gallery Antiques 393
M & A Cringle 213
J Crisp 493
Madeline Crispin Antiques 54
Criterion Auctioneers 47
Peter A Crofts 204
Sandra Cronan Ltd 79
The Crooked Window 186
Cross Hayes Antiques 192
Cross's Curios 304
Crowe's Antiquarian Books 218
Crown Auctions 325
Crown Furnishers 307
Crown Jewellers of Harrogate 320
Crows Auction Gallery 127
The Crows Nest 175
Crowther 62
Crowther of Syon Lodge Ltd 104
Croydon Coin Auctions 127
Crozier Antique Furniture Restoration 491
Cruck House Antiques 290
Mary Cruz Antiques 178
Crwys Antiques 400
Cryers Antiques 390
Cullompton Old Tannery Antiques 155
Culverden Antiques 40
Cumbria Architectural Salvage 368
Cumbria Auction Rooms 364
A & Y Cumming Ltd 21
Cundalls 323
Cura Antiques 95
Curborough Hall Farm Antiques Centre 297
Curio Corner, Tynemouth 355
Curio Corner, Whitby 328
CurioCity 212
Curios, Ventnor 124
Curiosity Corner, Guisborough 319
Curiosity Shop, Alfreton 268
Curiosity Shop, Kingsbridge 160
The Curiosity Shop, Pinner 104
The Curiosity Shop, South Shields 355
The Curiosity Shop on the Quay, Weymouth 175
Curiosity Too, Great Yarmouth 216
Curzon Pictures 165
The Cutlery Chest 379
Cwmgwili Mill Antiques 387
Cyjer Jewellery Ltd 79
Edmund Czajkowski & Son 486

D

D & C Antique Restorations 466
D & T Architectural Salvage 383
D H R Ltd 480
D K R Refurbishers 357
D M Antique Restoration 474
D M E Restorations Ltd 480
Da Capo Antiques 406
Clifford and Roger Dade 135
Daeron's Books 238
John Daffern Antiques 320
Dagfields Crafts & Antiques Centre 362
Dairy House Antiques 174
John Dale Antiques 95
Dale House 245
Peter Dale Ltd 62
Dalkeith Auctions Bournemouth 168
Danbury Antiques 206
The Dandelion Clock 17
Andrew Dando 178
Paul Daniel 100
Dann Antiques Ltd 194
The Dartmoor Bookshop 152
The Dartmouth Antique Company 156
M W Darwin & Son 318
Davenham Antiques Centre & Tea Room 360
K Davenport 501
Davenports Antiques 470
Davey & Davey 173
G David 200
Carlton Davidson Antiques 47
Davidson Books 436
Barry Davies Oriental Art 79
Bryan Davies & Associates 390
Edmund Davies & Son Antiques 383
Fred Davies & Co 390
Davies Antiques 89
Davies, White & Perry 290, 291
Andrew Davis Antiques 134
Brian Davis Antiques 261
G and D Davis Antique Restorers 468
Jesse Davis Antiques 66
Kenneth Davis (Works of Art) Ltd 62
M L Davis 475
Peter Davis Antiques 45
Reginald Davis (Oxford) Ltd 264
Christopher J L Dawes 338
Philip Dawes Antiques 257
B J Dawson 370
P Dawson Furniture Restorers 478
Day Antiques 249
Alan Day Antiques 406
Days Gone By 393
DDM Auction Rooms 342
M & J De Albuquerque 266
De Burca Rare Books 444
Adèle De Havilland 79
W De La Rue Antiques 428
Deacon Antiques 79
Deal Upholstery Services 500
Dealers 212
Deans Antiques 48
Dean's Antiques Emporium 53
Debden Antiques 211
Debenham Antiques 223
Deborah Paul 291
Decade Antiques & Textiles, Wallasey 386
Decades, Blackburn 377
Decodence 48
Decomania 59
Decorative Antiques, Bishops Castle 287
Decorative Antiques, Darlington 350
Decorative Antiques, Leek 295
Decorative Antiques, London SW6 70
Decorative Arts 14

Decorative Heating 400
The Decorator Source 249
Decorcraft Upholsterers 501
Decors 29
Decorum, Arundel 137
Decorum Antiques and Linens, Oakham 286
Deddington Antique Centre 262
Dee Cee Upholstery 500
Dee, Atkinson and Harrison 316
The Deermoss Gallery 293
Dee's Antique Pine 112
Deja Vu, Norwich 218
De-Ja-Vu, South Shields 355
Deja Vu Antiques, Chester 357
Deja Vu Antiques, Leigh-On-Sea 209
Deja-Vu Antiques & Collectables, Lostwithiel 148
Delaney Antiques 454
Delany Antiques 454
Delf Stream Gallery 37
Delmar Antiques 20
Delomosne & Son Ltd 194
Delphi Antiques 446
Delpierre Antiques 29
Delvin Farm Antiques 453
Sonia Demetriou 470
Den of Antiquity 164
Denham's 140
Clive Dennett 218
Denning Antiques 131
Richard Dennis Gallery 89
Guy Dennler 185
Denton Antiques 89
Deppner Antiques 290
Derbyshire Antiques Ltd 320
Derbyshire Clocks 272
Derbyshire Removals 495
Dernier and Hamlyn Ltd 67, 493
Derventio Books 271
Derwentside Antiques 270
Design Explosion 121
Designer Classics 103
Deva Antiques 116
Devizes Auction Centre 192
Devon Clocks 154
Devonshire Antiques 442
Ian Dewar 483
R G Dewdney 470
D'Eyncourt Antiques 126
Diamond Mills & Company 223
Arnold Dick Antiques 174
Dickens Curios 207
Alastair Dickenson Fine Silver Ltd 62
D & B Dickinson 178
J Dickinson 269
Dickinson Antiques 319
Robert Dickson and Lesley Rendall Antiques 67
Didier Aaron (London) Ltd 62
Didier Antiques 89
Didsbury Antiques 372
M R Dingle 150
Dip 'n' Strip, Clydebank 498
Dip 'n' Strip, Leeds 498
Dippers 234
Director Furniture Leathergilders 493
Discovery Antiques 281
Discretion Antiques Ltd 381
Diss Antiques & Interiors 215
Eric Distin Auctioneers & Chartered Surveyors 150, 162
DIVA (Digital Inventory and Visual Archive) 465
Dix Noonan Webb 79
Dixons Medals 315
Dix-Sept Antiques 230
Dobson's Antiques 255
Dockree's Fine Art Auctioneers & Valuers 371
Maurice Dodd Books 368
Simon Dodson 475
Gudrun Doel 165
Dog Leap Antiques 353
Louis J Doherty and Sons 453
Dollectable 357
Dollies Bear–Gere Ltd 373
Michael Dolling 478
Dollyland 54
Dolphin Antiques, Beer 154
Dolphin Quay Antique Centre, Emsworth 114
Dolphin Square Antiques, Dorking 127
Dome Antiques 52
Domino Restorations 461
The Door Stripping Company Ltd 498
Dorchester Antiques 262
The Dorchester Bookshop 172
Dorking Desk Shop 125, 127
Dorking House Antiques 127
Dorothy's Antiques 220
Dorridge Antiques 302
Dorridge Antiques & Collectables Centre 307
Dorset Coin Company 173
Dorset Reclamation 167
Bobby Douglas 436
Bryan Douglas 100
Christopher John Douglas 475
W H Douglas 400
Douglas & Kay 491
Doveridge House Antiques 308
Dovetail Interiors of Bedale 318
Dower House Antiques 366
Down To The Woods Ltd 173
Downham Market Antique Centre 215
Downland Furniture Restoration 471
Downlane Hall Antiques 40
A E Dowse & Son 333
The Dragon, South Molton 163
Dragon Antiques, Harrogate 320
Dragon Treasures, Petersfield 118
Dragonlee Collectables 36
Dragons Hoard 151
Andrew Drake Antiques 225
Draycott Books 241
Dreweatt Neate 108
Drewery and Wheeldon 342
C & K Dring 345
Drizen Coins 209
Dromore Road Auction Rooms 440
Drop Dial Antiques 371
Drummonds Architectural Antiques Ltd 132
Drums Malahide 449
Ann Drury Antiques 429
Du Cros Antiques 142
Dudley and Spencer 475
Michael Duffy Antiques 446
David Duggleby Fine Art 326
Hy Duke & Son 172, 176
Dukeries Antiques Centre 281
Jack Duncan 329
Duncan & Reid 406
Dunchurch Antiques Centre 299
Dunluce Antiques and Crafts 434
A Dunn and Son 494
Hamish Dunn Antiques 352
Dunn and Wright 471
Joe Dunne Auctioneers & Valuers 442
R D Dunning 486
K W Dunster Antiques 105
P M Dupuy 481
Durham House Antiques Centre 246
Durrants Auction Rooms 221
Dutton & Smith Medal Collectors 284
Frank Dux Antiques 178
Dycheling Antiques 140
Sue Dyer Antiques 292
Dyfed Antiques 397
Dyfi Valley Bookshop 399
Peter Dyke 42
Dynasty Antiques 172
Dyson & Son 223
Colin Dyte Exports Ltd 186

E

E K Antiques 279
E L R Auctions Ltd 333
E R Antiques Centre 375
Julian Eade 130
The Eagle Bookshop 233
W H Earles 466
Earlsdon Antiques 306
The Earlsfield Bookshop 77
East Meets West Antiques 41
East Street Antique Centre 185
Eastbourne Antiques Market 17
Eastcote Bookshop 103
Easter Antiques 115
Eastern Books of London 77
Eastgate Antiques 401
EASY Edinburgh & Glasgow Architectural Salvage Yard 406
Easy Strip 260
Eat My Handbag Bitch 44
J W Eaton 481
Eccles Road Antiques 75
Echo Antiques, Reepham 219
Echoes, Todmorden 382
Eclectic Antiques and Interiors, London SW3 67
Eclectica, London N1 48
Eclectique, Exeter 156
ECS 406
The Eddie Stobart Fan Club Shop 365
Eddie Stobart Promotions Ltd 365
A A Eddy and Son 475
Charles Ede Ltd 79
Matthew Eden 192
Eden House Antiques 349
Edenderry Architectural Salvage Ltd 453
G H Edkins and Son 349
David Edmonds Indian Furniture 87
I D Edrich 45

GENERAL INDEX

E – F

Charles Edwards 70
Christopher Edwards 110
K Edwards Antiques 22
Peter Edwards 80
Edwards and Elliott 107
Ben Eggleston 367
I Ehrnfeld 54
88 Antiques 93
R C Elderton 471
Eldreds Auctioneers and Valuers 162
Eldridge London 45
The Elephants Trunk 21
Elham Antiques 30
Elham Valley Book Shop 31
Elizabeth & Son 369
Elizabeth R Antiques 129
Elizabeth Street Antiques and Restoration Services 468
Ellenor Hospice Care Shop, Bexley 25
Ellenor Hospice Care Shop, Otford 34
Samuel Elliot 446
Elliott's 142
Donald Ellis Antiques 406
Joyce Ellis 496
R H Ellis and Son Auctioneers and Valuers 144
Ellis & Wedge Books 371
Richard Ellory 341
Ellory & Chaffer 342
Elm House Antiques 133
C G Elmer-Menage 481
Pamela Elsom Antiques 269
June Elsworth Beaconsfield Ltd 236
Elvisly Yours 80
Emlyn Antiques 395
Emma Antiques 37
Garry M Emms and Co Ltd 216
Empire Exchange 373
The Emporium, Atherton 370
The Emporium, Bridlington 316
Emporium, Dawlish 156
The Emporium, Pontardulais 402
Emporium Antiques, Sandgate 36
The Emporium Antiques and Collectors Centre, Southwold 229
The Emporium Antiques Centre, Bournemouth 168
The Emporium Antiques Centre, Lewes 21
The Emporium Antiques Centre Too, Lewes 21
The Emporium Antiques, Collectables & Crafts Centre, Welling 41
Emscote Antiques 303
Endeavour Books 328
Enfield Collectors Centre 103
Toby English Antique & Secondhand Books 266
English and Continental Antiques 223
English Antiques 303
English Country Antiques 155
English Garden Antiques 370
English Heritage 287
English Rose Antiques 205
Enhancements 14
Entente Cordiale 303
The Enterprise Collectors Market 17
Esher Antiques Centre 129
Eskdale Antiques 328
John Eskenazi Ltd 80
Eskenazi Ltd 80
Esox Antique Restoration 475
The Essence of Time 297
Essex Reupholstery Services 478
Etcetera, Rhayader 399
Etcetera Etc Antiques, Seaton 163
Eton Antiques 108
Eureka Antiques 193
Euro Antiques 217
European Accent 183
European Fine Arts & Antiques 381
Ann Evans 394
Luke Evans Antiques 466
T Evans Antiques 393
Evans and Partridge 121
Eversley Antiques 115
Ewbank Fine Art Auctioneers 136
The Exchange 167
Exeter Antique Lighting 156
Exeter Rare Books 156
Exeter's Antiques Centre on the Quay 156
Exning Antiques & Interiors 223
Expectations, Polperro 150
Expressions, Shrewsbury 292
Leigh Extence Antique Clocks 164
Extence Antiques 164

F

F and R Restorations 135, 471
Nicole Fabre French Antiques 70
Facets Glass Restoration 492
Fado Antiques 450
Fagin & Co, Todmorden 382
Fagins, March 202
Fagins Antiques, Hele 158
Failsworth Mill Antiques 371
Fair Deal Antiques 282
Fairburn Books 336
Fakenham Antiques Centre 215
Falcon Antiques 18
Trevor Falconer Antiques 435
Falstaff Antiques 36
Family Antiques 374
Famously Yours Ltd 26
Fandango 48
Faringdon Antiques Centre 263
Farleigh House Antiques 229
Farm Cottage Antiques 466
Farmhouse Antiques, Barnard Castle 349
Farmhouse Antiques, Chester 357
Farmhouse Antiques, Great Houghton 332
Farnborough Antiques 31
Farningham Pine 31
Farrelly Antiques 258
John Farrington Antiques 447
Farthing, Yarm 329
Farthings, Lynton 160, 165
Fauconberges 221
Faversham Antiques and Collectables 31
R Feldman Ltd Antique Silver 100
Feljoy Antiques 48
Fellows & Sons 304
J Felstead 237
Robin A Fenner and Co 164
James Fenning, Old and Rare Books 449
Fens Restoration and Sales 468
Fenwick & Fenwick Antiques 309
Steven Ferdinando V
Ferran's Antiques 436
The Ferret (Friday Street Antiques Centre) 263
Michael Ferris 492
David Ferrow 216
Ferry Antiques 112
Fiddlesticks 327
Field, Staff & Woods 36
Brian Fielden 55
Fieldings Antiques & Clocks 377, 382
The Fifteenth Century Bookshop 21
51 Antiques 93
Filibuster & Booth Ltd 333
Mark Finamore 492
Finan and Co 194
Hector Finch Lighting 70
Simon Finch 95
Simon Finch Rare Books 80
Finchingfield Antiques Centre 207
Finds 59
Fine Art Antiques 381
Fine Books Oriental Ltd 98
Fine Pine 167
Finedon Antiques Ltd 279
Peter Finer 300
Mike Fineron Cigarette Cards & Postcards 330
The Fingerplate Co 402
Finishing Touches 271
Finley's Finds 350
G W Finn and Son Auctioneers 28
The Fire & Stove Shop 399
The Fireplace (Hungerford) Ltd 109
Fireplaces 'n' Things 173
J First Antiques 80
Fisher & Sperr 52
Fisher Nautical 144
Fisherton Antiques Market 195
Michael W Fitch Antiques 36
Alan Fitchett Antiques 14
E Fitzpatrick 491
Fitzwilliam Antiques Centre 203
Flagstaff Antiques 122
Flagstones Pine and Country Furniture 277
Flanagans Ltd 447
Flaxton Antique Gardens 319
A Fleming (Southsea) Ltd 121
Fleury Antiques 447, 454
Flintlock Antiques 375
Flourish Farm Antiques 271
Flower House Antiques 38
Flying Duck Enterprises 59
Norman Flynn Restorations 460
Focus on the Past 182
Foley Furniture 310
Folly Four Antiques & Collectables 118
David Foord-Brown Antiques 140
G W Ford & Son Ltd 269
Fordham's 30
Fordington Antiques 172
Forest Books of Cheshire 373
Forest House Antiques 117
The Forge Antiques 439

'orge Interiors 23
'orge Studio Workshops 478
'orget-Me-Nots 402
'ormat Coins 305
effrey Formby Antiques 245
'ormer Glory 115
'orrest & Co Ltd 45
'orstal Farm Antique Workshops 33
.ucy Forsythe Antiques 439
3irdie Fortescue Antiques 70
'ortlands Antiques 442
'orum Antiques, Cirencester 242
'orum Antiques, Wexford 454
'osse Way Antiques 246
Graham Foster Antiques 141
A and E Foster 237
Matthew Foster 80
Michael Foster 67
Paul Foster Books 76
W A Foster 87
Fountain Antique Studios & Workshop, Coleraine 439
Fountain Antiques, Honiton 158
4b Antiques and Interiors 473
Four Winds Antiques 436
Fourways Antiques 284
Nicholas Fowle Antiques 218
A and J Fowle 77
Anne Fowler 249
Robin Fowler Period Clocks 341
Daniel Fox Upholstery 501
Jon Fox Antiques 245
Fox Cottage Antiques 246
Foxglove Antiques 396
Foyle Antiques 439
Foyle Books 439
Framing & Restoration Workshop 497
Peter Francis Antiques 438
Franklin Antiques 109
Alan Franklin Transport 495
N & I Franklin 62
J A L Franks and Co 62
Victor Franses Gallery 63
Rory Fraser 488
Frasers Autographs 100
G and R Fraser-Sinclair 471
A Frayling-Cork 495
C. Fredericks and Son 89
J Freeman 95
Neil Freeman Angling Auctions 97
Vincent Freeman 48
Freeman and Lloyd Antiques 36
Charles French 17
French Country Style 372
French House Antiques, London SW8 73
French House Antiques, York 330, 487
The French Room 142
The French Warehouse 436
Freshfords 186
Robert Frew Ltd 98
Friargate Antiques Company 271
Friargate Pine Co Ltd 271
Friend or Faux 221
Frogmore House Antiques 178
Frome Reclamation 186
Fron House Antiques Decorative Items 393
Frost Antiques & Pine 396
Frosts 56
O Frydman 80
Fritz Fryer 254
Fulham Antiques 70
Full of Beans 383
James Fuller and Son 201
Fullertons Booksearch 214
Furniture and Effects 37
The Furniture Cave 389
The Furniture Store 148
Furniture Vault 48
Furse Restoration 478
Fuschia Books 444
Jonathan Fyson Antiques 260

G

G B Antiques Centre 380
G K R Bonds Ltd 206
G M H Restoration 484
G W Conservation 459
Gabor Cossa Antiques 200
Gaby's Clocks and Things 38
Gainsborough House, Tewkesbury 250
Gainsborough House Antiques, Sidmouth 163
Galata Coins 398
Galata Print Ltd 399
Galleria Pinocchio 26
Gallerie 283
Gallerie Veronique 103
The Galleries Ltd, London SE1 57
The Gallery, Dunfanaghy 444
Gallery 23 Antiques 236
The Gallery Book Shop 270
Gallery Eleven 127
Gallery Kaleidoscope incorporating Scope Antiques 56
Gallery of Antique Costume & Textiles 56
Galliard Antiques 257
Gallimaufry 309
Galvins Antiques 442
Michael Gander 257
Gander and White Shipping Ltd 496
Ganymede Antiques 269
Garden Art 110
The Garden House Bookshop 231
John Gardiner 188
Richard Gardner Antiques 142
Gardiner & Gardiner 56
A D Gardner 471
Tony Gardner 471
Gargrave Gallery 319
Garland Antiques 75
John Garner Antiques 287
Garners 205
Garrard Antiques 289
Marilyn Garrow Fine Textile Art 223
Garth Antiques 320, 329
K M & J Garwood 19
Herbert G Gasson 23
Gatehouse Antiques 361
Gatehouse Workshops 284
Gateway Antiques, Burford 260
Gateway Arcade Antiques Market, London N1 48
Gathering Moss 52
Peter Gaunt 80
Thos Wm Gaze & Son 215
Gazebo 48
Geary Antiques 340
Gedyes Auctioneers & Estate Agents 365
Rob Gee 165
Ivo Geikie-Cobb 468
R A Gekoski Booksellers 98
Gem Antiques, Maidstone 34
Gem Antiques, Sevenoaks 37
Gemini Antiques & Gallery 310
Gems 139
Lionel Geneen Ltd 168
Rupert Gentle 195
Gentry Antiques, London W1 80
Gentry Antiques, Polperro 150
Geometrica 174
George Street Antiques Centre 19
Georgian Antiques, Cork 442
Georgian Antiques, Edinburgh 406
The Georgian Barn 396
Georgian House Antiques 261
The Georgian Rooms 316
The Georgian Village Antique Centre, London N1 48
Georgian Village Antiques, Sligo 453
Georgina's Antiques 14
Gerald Oliver Antiques 397
Michael German Antiques 89
A & T Gibbard 17
David Gibbins 230
Stanley Gibbons Auctions Ltd 100
Andy Gibbs 254
Paul Gibbs Antiques & Decorative Arts 390
Roderick Gibson 362
Nicholas Gifford-Mead 63
David Gilbert Antiques 36
John Gilbert Antiques 325
H M Gilbert 120
Martin Gilbert Antiques 294
Philip Gilbert 136
Gilbert and Dale 186
Gilboy's 475
The Gilded Lily 80
Gildings 276
G and F Gillingham Ltd 55
Gillmark Map Gallery 256
Gillycraft 27
Gilpin Antiques 238
Annabelle Giltsoff 196
Giltwood Gallery 240
The Ginnel Antiques Centre, Harrogate 320
Ginnell Gallery, Manchester 373
J Girvan Antiques 305
G J Gittins & Sons 394
T J Gittins 484
Glade Antiques 237
Martin Gladman Second-hand Books 52
Gladrags 406
Gladstone's Furniture 55
Glasheen's Bookshop 126
Glassdrummman 40

GENERAL INDEX

G – H

Glassenbury Antique Pine 466
The Glass-House 326
Glenbower Books 445
Glenconnor Antiques 454
Glencorse Antiques 132
Glendining's 80
The Globe Antiques & Art Centre 158
The Glory Hole, Oldbury 306
The Glory Hole, Sandiacre 286
Glory Hole Antiques, Leicester 275
Glossop Antique Centre 272
Gloucester Antique Centre 243
Gloucester House Antiques 243
Gloucester Road Bookshop 73
Gloucestershire Furniture Hospital 481
Glydon and Guess 133
Godalming Antiques 131
P Godden 478
Grenville Godfrey 459
Jemima Godfrey Antiques 228
Golden Cross Antiques 18
Golden Days 104
Golden Oldies 297
Gwendoline Golder Antiques 214
Golding, Young & Co 342
Goldmark Books 287
Gaby Goldscheider 123
Goldsmith & Perris 56
Goldsmiths Howard 202
Goldsworth Books and Prints 136
Golfark International 352
Roland Gomm 491
Good Day Antiques and Decor, Portsmouth 118
Good Hope Antiques 167
The Good Olde Days, Ockbrook 273
The Gooday Gallery, Richmond 134
Richard Goodbrey Antiques 224
Goodbye To All That 302
Goodison & Paraskeva 48
Guy Goodwin Restoration 484
John Goodwin & Sons 303
Nick Goodwin Exports 279
Pamela Goodwin 40
Goodwins 208
Goodwin's Antiques Ltd 406
Goodwood Furniture Restoration 471
Goodwood Pine Furniture 443
Goodwoods 443
Nicholas Goodyer 52
Gordon's Medals 80
Gormley Antique Gallery 440
Gorringes 40
Gorringes Auction Galleries 12
Gorringes Incorporating Julian Dawson 21
Alison Gosling Antiques 154
The Goss & Crested China Club 116
Simon Gough Books Ltd 216
Gillian Gould Antiques 55, 100, 265
Government House Quality Antique Lighting 240
Gow Antiques and Restoration 494
Gower House Antiques 402
Nicky Gowing 165
The Graham Gallery 81
Graham the Hat 347
Major Iain Grahame 222
Granary Antiques, Bradford on Avon 191
The Granary Antiques, Nuneaton 300
Granary Collectables 366
Grand Prix Top Gear 258
Grandad's Attic, Harrogate 320
Grandfather Clock Shop 246
Grandma's Attic, Walmer 41
Grandpa's Collectables, Ruthin 392
Granny's Attic, Ramsgate 35
Granny's Cupboard Antiques, Wisbech 204
Kym Grant Bookseller 190
Andrew Grant Fine Art Auctioneers 313
Denzil Grant 223
Grant & Shaw Ltd 406
Granta Coins, Collectables and Antiquities 200
Grantham Clocks 342
Grantham Furniture Emporium 342
Grantham Workshops Cabinet Makers 484
Granville Antiques 142
Graus Antiques 81
D J Gravell 489
Alexandra Gray 118
Anita Gray 81
Laila Gray Antiques 279
Gray Arts 461, 463
David A H Grayling 368
Grays Antique Market 81
Grays Antiques 313
Grayshott Pine 132
Great Expectations, Blackburn 377
Great Expectations, Horncastle 344
Great Expectations, Poole 173
Great Grooms Antique Centre, Billingshurst 138
Great Grooms of Hungerford 110
Great Malvern Antiques 310
Great Northern Architectural Antiques Co Ltd 363
The Great Oak Bookshop 399
Anthony Green Antiques 81
Ena Green 70
J Green & Son 277
Jonathan Green Antiques 195
Nicholas Green Antiques 306
Ron Green 280
Sally Green Designs 116
Green Dragon Antiques and Crafts Centre 190
Green Lane Antiques 381
The Green Room 224
The Green Shed 224
Greene's Antiques Galleries 452
Greens of Cheltenham Ltd 240
Greenslade Taylor Hunt 189
Greensleeves Books 261
Jonathan Greenwall Antiques 37
Colin Greenway Antiques 267
Greenwich Collectables 59
Judy Greenwood Antiques 70
George Gregory 178
Henry Gregory 95
Grenadiers 61
Gresham Books 185
Grey-Harris & Co 182
Greystoke Antiques 174
A Grice 381
Julie Griffin Antiques 14
Marcus Griffin Specialists in Silver Jewellery 439
Simon Griffin Antiques Ltd 81
Griffin Antiques 103
Griffith & Partners Ltd 98
G E Griffith 471
W John Griffiths Antiques 254
Roger Grimes 452
Grimes Militaria 182
Nicholas Grindley 81
Robert Gripper Restoration 481
Sarah Groombridge 81
K Grosvenor 296
Grosvenor Chambers Restoration 162
Grosvenor House Interiors 236
Grosvenor Prints 100
Grounds & Co 204
The Grove Antique Centre, Honiton 158
Grove Antiques, Darwen 378
Grove Antiques, Morpeth 352
The Grove Bookshop, Ilkley 338
Grove Country Bookshop 319
Guardroom Antiques 343
Claire Guest at Thomas Goode & Co. Ltd 81
Lynn Guest Antiques 286
Guest and Gray 81
Gullheath Ltd 484
Rex Gully Antiques 124
Alastair Gunn 491
John Gunning Antiques 452
Gurnos Sales 402
Gerard Guy Antiques 309
Gwydir Street Antiques 200
Gwynedd Trading 391
Gwynfair Antiques 394

H

H & H Classic Auctions Ltd 360
H L B Antiques 171
H P Book Finders 458
H R W Antiques Ltd 70
H S C Fine Arts & Antiques 324
Hackney House Antiques 270
Haddon Rocking Horses 500
G K Hadfield 366
Hadji Baba Ancient Art Ltd 81
Peter J Hadley 218
Hadlow Down Antiques 18
Haig and Hosford 478
David Hakeney Antiques 317
Halcyon Days 46, 81
Robert Hales Antiques 89
Halesworth Antiques Market 224
Halfway Trading 395
Halifax Antique Centre 336
Anthony C Hall 105
Fran Hall Glass Restoration 492
G J Hall, Antique Furniture Restoration 471
Robert Hall 81
Hall & Lloyd 288
Hallahan 298
Hallam Antique and Diamond Jewellery 284
Hallidays 189

ｌallidays (Fine Antiques) Ltd 263
ｌallmark Antiques 48
ｌallmark Jewellers 14
ｌarry Hall's Bookshop 432
ｌall's Curio Shop 452
ｌalls Fine Art (Chester) Ltd 357
ｌalls Fine Art Auctions 292
ｌambleton Books 328
eter Hames 154
/I & J Hamilton 100
:osemary Hamilton China Repairs 460
.oss Hamilton (Antiques) Ltd 63
ｌamilton Antique Restoration, Douglas 489
ｌamilton Antiques, Woodbridge 230
effery Hammond Antiques 253
ｌampshires of Dorking 128
ｌampstead Antique and Craft Emporium 55
ierald Hampton 171
ｌampton Antiques 95
ｌampton Court Antiques 129
he Hampton Court Emporium 129
ｌamptons International Auctioneers and Valuers 131
ｌanborough Antiques 264
ｌanbury Antiques 257
eter Hancock 139
ｌancock & Monks 251
ｌancocks and Co (Jewellers) Ltd 82
ｌandsworth Books 100
Hanlon Antiques 340
Hansen 494
ｌansen Chard Antiques 312
ｌanshan Tang Books 76
)avid J Hansord and Son 345
ｌappers Antiques 236
ames Hardy Antiques Ltd 349
ohn Hardy Antiques 275
ｌardy Country 172
ｌardy's Collectables 168
ｌarefield Antiques 103
ｌare's Antiques Ltd 242
irian Harkins 63
ｌarlequin Antiques, Edinburgh 406
ｌarlequin Antiques, Grantham 343
ｌarlequin Antiques, Nottingham 284
ｌarlequin Antiques, Porthcawl 395
ｌarlequin Antiques, Stretton 363
ｌarlequin Gallery 345
ｌarley Antiques 192
ｌarmans Antiques 128
ｌarmers of London Stamp Auctioneer Ltd 87
ｌarold's Place 88
/lartin and Dorothy Harper Antiques 270
ｌarpers Jewellers Ltd 330
ｌarpur Antiques 233
\drian Harrington Antiquarian Bookseller 89
irian Harris Furniture Restorations 478
ohn Harris Antiques and Restorations 142
Montague Harris & Co 398
ｌoy C Harris 294
ｌupert Harris Conservation 494
ｌarris Antiques Stansted 212
Anna Harrison Antiques 352
Frederick Harrison 162
Harrison Sales 332
Rosemary Hart 48
Hart & Rosenberg 95
Hart Antiques, Bridgend 394
Hart Antiques, Henley on Thames 481
Andrew Hartley Fine Arts 339
Caroline Hartley Books 271
J Hartley Antiques Ltd 134
Hartley & Co 384
Hartley Upholstery and Antique Restorations 501
Harvard Antiques 394
Harvatt Antiques 316
Kenneth Harvey Antiques 74
Patricia Harvey Antiques 56
W R Harvey & Co (Antiques) Ltd 267
Harvey & Gore 63
Harwich International Antique Centre 208
Harwood Antiques 340
Haslam Antiques 271
Bradley Hatch Jewellers 220
J E Hatcher & Son 501
Simon Hatchwell Antiques 74
H J Hatfield and Son 468
Hatherleigh Antiques 157
Hatter Antiques & Restoration 468
Haughey Antiques 367
Brian Haughton Antiques 82
The Haunted Bookshop 200
Havelocks Pine and Antiques 320
Havenplan Ltd 332
Havilland Antiques Ltd 429
Barry L Hawkins 215
Philip Hawkins Furniture 475
Ray Hawkins Antiques 400
Roger Hawkins Restoration 461
Hawkins Brothers Antiques 400
Hawkridge Books 271
Hawkswood Antiques 18
Hawley Antiques 315
Haworth Antiques 320
Gerard Hawthorn Ltd 82
Hay Antique Market 251
Hay Cinema Bookshop 251
Hay on Wye Booksellers 252
Roland Haycraft 481
Jeanette Hayhurst 89
The Hayloft Antiques 310
Hayman & Hayman 67
Roger Haynes Antique Finder 296
Hayter's Antique and Modern Furniture 123
Haywards Antiques & Avon House Antiques 160
W J Hazle 259
John & Judith Head Barn Book Supply 195
Headcorn Antiques 32
Headrow Antiques 339
Heanor Antiques Centre 272
Heape's 184
Heart of England Antiques 280
Hearth & Home 18
Mike Heath Antiques 123
Heath Upholstery 501
Heath-Bullocks 131
Heathcote Antiques 336
Heathcote Ball and Co Fine Art Auctioneers & Valuers 275
John Heather 231
Heather Antiques 48
Heathfield Country Pine 216
G B & P E Hebbord 252
Hedgecoe and Freeland 471
Hedingham Antiques 211
Hedleys Humpers 496
Hedley's of Hexham 351
William Heffer Antiques 458
Stuart Heggie 28
Heirloom & Howard Ltd 192
Heirloom Antiques, Tenterden 38
Heirloom Antiques, Chichester 139
Heirlooms, Worcester 313
Helena's Collectables 135
Helga's Antiques 443
Helios and Co, Weedon 280
Helios Gallery, London W11 95
Helmsley Antiquarian & Secondhand Books 322
The Helston Bookworm 147
Hemswell Antique Centres 343
The Hen Hoose 491
Hencotes Books and Prints 351
Thomas Heneage Art Books 63
Henfield Antiques and Collectables 140
Martin Henham 52
Henley Antique Centre 263
Hennessy 185
Henry's of Ash 25
Hens Teeth Antiques 468
Hera Antiques 400
Hera Restorations 490
Marcelline Herald Antiques 108
Heraldry Today 195
S Herberholz 484
Hereford Antique Centre 252
Hereford Map Centre 252
Hereward Books 202
Peter Herington Antiquarian Bookseller 67
Heritage Antiques, Chichester 139
Heritage Antiques, Loughall 435
Heritage Antiques, Wem 293
Heritage Architectural Restoration, Haddington 458
Heritage Books 123
Heritage Care 464
Heritage Reclamations, Sproughton 229
Heritage Restoration, Rainham 466
Heritage Restorations, Llanfair Caereinion 398, 497
Heritage Workshop 490
Herman & Wilkinson 447
Hermitage Antiques, Honiton 159
Hermitage Antiques Plc, London SW1 63
H W Heron & Son Ltd 299
Hertford Antiques 256
Herts & Essex Antiques Centre 258
Heskin Hall Antiques 379
Alan Hessel 481
Muir Hewitt 336
Hexham and Northern Mart 351
Hexham Antiques 351

GENERAL INDEX

H – I

Heywood Antiques 372
Stephen Hibberts Antiques 296
David Hick Antiques 429, 430
Hickley's Cards 114
Hickmet Fine Arts 140
Jan Hicks Antiques 112
Richard Higgins Conservation 463, 484
The Higgins Press 148
High Halden Antiques 33
High Peak Antiques 270
High Street Antiques 239
High Street Books 159
Highams Auctions 375
Highfield Antiques 120
Andrew Hilditch & Son Ltd 363
Hilditch Auction 193
D Hill 361
David Hill 367
Frank Hill & Son 317
Stephen Hill 481
Hill Farm Antiques 111
Hill House Antiques & Decorative Arts 67
P J Hilton Books 100
Nigel Hindley 71
Hingham Antiques 216
T C Hinton 466
Hirst Antiques 95
Erna Hiscock 95
Hitchcox's Antiques 261
The Hive 200
Bob Hoare Antiques 21
Peter Hoare Antiques 40
John Hobbs Ltd 63
Stuart Hobbs Antique Furniture Restoration 471
Hobbs Parker 25
Hobday Toys 104
Hobknobs Antiques and Gallery 229
Hock & Dough Antiques 279
Keith Hockin Antiques 247
Ian Hodgkins & Co Ltd 248
Christopher Hodsoll Ltd 63
Hogben Auctioneers & Valuers Ltd 31
HOK Fine Art 444
Henry Holden & Son 380
Holden Wood Antiques Centre 379
Raymond D Holdich 101
Hole in the Wall Antiques 375
Holland & Welsh 400, 465
E Hollander 463
R F G Hollett & Son 368
Chris Hollingshead 105
Holloways, Banbury 259
Holloway's Antiques, Bournemouth 169
Holly Farm Antiques 334
Andy Holmes 284
Brian and Lynn Holmes 82
D Holmes 90
Holmfirth Antiques 337
Holmwood Antiques 135
Michael Holroyd Restorations 489
Holt & Company, East Winch 215
Holt & Company, London SW6 71
Holt Antique Centre 217
Holt Antique Gallery 217
Holyrood Architectural Salvage 406
Homme de Quimper 346
Tony Honan 442
Honan's Antiques 450
Honey Pot Antiques Centre, Farnham 130
Honeypot Antiques, Godalming 131
The Honiton Lace Shop 159
Honiton Old Book Shop 159
Anthony Hook Antiques 42
Howard Hope Phonographs & Gramophones 129
Hope & Glory 90
Hope and Piaget 468
Hope Antiques 484
Hopkins Antique Restoration 489
J R Hopper & Co 318
Paul Hopwell Antiques 281
Horbury Antique Workshop 338
Horncastle Antique Centre 344
Jonathan Horne 90
Horners Auctioneers 213, 218
Edgar Horn's Fine Art Auctioneers 17
Malcolm Hornsby 276
Hornsby Furniture Restoration Ltd 468
R Hornsey & Sons 317
Hornsey Auctions Ltd 53
Hornsey's of Ripon 325
Horological Workshops 131, 463
Horsebridge Antique Centre 18
Horseshoe Antiques 261
The Horsham Antiques Centre 140
The Horsham Bookshop 140
Hotspur & Nimrod 269
Hotspur Ltd 63
Bernard G House Longcase Clocks 190
The House Clearance Shop 34
The House Hospital 77
The House of Antiques 14
House of Clocks 232
House Things Antiques 274
Housepoints 28
Patrick Howard Antiques 447
Paul Howard 67
Robin Howard Antiques 121
Valerie Howard 90
Howard Gallery 128
Howard's Reclamation 138
Howards of Broadway 309
Christopher Howe Antiques 63
W A Howe 173
Howes Bookshop Ltd 19
John Howkins Antiques Ltd 218
Jeff Howlett Restoration @ Great Grooms Antique Centres 471
Hoylake Antique Centre 383
John Hubbard Antiques Restoration & Conservation 484
Rick Hubbard Art Deco 119
Hubbard's Antiques 225
Huddersfield Picture Framing Co. 338
Russell Hudson Upholsterer 501
Hudsons of York 330
Hug & Plum 325
Geoffrey Hugall 235
David Hughes Antiques 190
P J Hughes Antiques 313
Michael Hughes 67
Val Hughes 491
John Hulme 481
Mac Humble Antiques 191
Owen Humble 353
Dudley Hume 14
Humphrey-Carrasco 63
Hungerford Arcade 110
Hungry Ghost 247
Catherine Hunt 249
Howard Hunt Antiques 471
Simon Hunter Antique Maps 20
Hunters of Hampton 103
Huntingdon Trading Post 202
Huntington Antiques 361
Huntington Antiques Ltd 247
Diana Huntley 49
Hunts Auctioneers 350
Hunts Pine 330
Hunts Pine Stripping Services 498
A M Hurrell 461
Anthony Hurst 230
Hurst Green Antiques 20
Hussar Military Miniatures 104
Gavin Hussey Antique Restoration 463
Hutchison Antiques and Interiors 205, 208
F Hutton (Bookbinder) 458
Hutton Antiques 292
Hyde Road Antiques 161
Hyperion Antique Centre 203
Hyperion Auction Centre 203
Sheila Hyson 165
Hythe Furnishings 501

I

Ibbett Mosely 38
Ichthus Antiques 397
Ickleton Antiques 211
Icknield Restorations 481
Ilminster Auctions 186
Imperial Antiques, Hull 317
Imperial Antiques, Stockport 375
Imperial Upholstery 502
In Period Antiques 250
Inchmartine Restorations 491
Inch's Books 324
Indigo, Bath 178
Indigo, London SW6 71
Indigo, Maningford Bruce 193
Jeff Ingall 478
D D & A Ingle 284
Inglenook Antiques 279
Ingleside Antiques 378
Brand Inglis 144
Gordon Inglis Antiques 406
Raymond P Inman 14
Inprint 248
Insitu 376
Intercoin 354
Intercol 52
Interiors and Antiques 144
International Furniture Exporters Ltd 496
The Inventory 218
Invicta Bookshop 111
Ipsden Woodcraft 481
Irish Art Group 439
Iron Wright 458
Ironchurch Antique Centre 370

Bruce Isaac 475
Isaac Carpets 90
Isabella Antiques 196
Isabelline Books 156
It's About Time 212
John Ives 105
Ivory Gate Antiques 284
Ivy Hall Antiques 453
Ivy House Antiques 213

J

J & A Antiques 394
J & M Collectables 38
J A N Fine Art 90
J C Books 220
J F F Militaria & Fire Brigade Collectables 118
J H S Antiques 269
J J Books and Antiques 164
J N Antiques 257
Jackdaw Antique Centres Ltd, Henley-on-Thames 263
Jackdaw Antique Centres Ltd, Marlow 237
Jackdawes, London SW6 71
Jack's 171
A E Jackson E, 237
Allan K L Jackson 407
John Jackson 44
Lee Jackson 101
Simon and Frauke Jackson 178
Jackson, Green & Preston 343
Jackson-Grant Antiques 39
Jacob & His Fiery Angel 148
Uri Jacobi Oriental Carpet Gallery 357
Jacobs and Hunt Fine Art Auctioneers 118
Jacobs Antique Centre 401
Jacquart Antiques 437
Jade Antiques 205
Jadis Antiques Ltd 179
Jaffray Antiques 194
Jag Applied and Decorative Arts 90
Anthony James & Son Ltd 67
Michael James Antiques & Curios 316
Japanese Gallery Ltd 49, 90
Jardinique 113
Jarndyce Antiquarian Booksellers 98
Jays Antiques and Collectables 187
Jeans Military Memories 379
R W Jeffery 149
Jefferys 148
Robin Jeffreys 165
Jeff's Antiques 395
Roderick Jellicoe 90
Jems Collectables 112
Adrian Jennings Antiques 309
Celia Jennings 26
Jeremiah's Fine Time Pieces and Antiques 430
Jeremy & Westerman 284
Jeremy Ltd 64
Jericho Books 264
Jericho Cottage 208
Jersey Coin Company 430
John Jesse 90
Jessops Antique Village 335
Jester Antiques 249
Francis Jevons 60
The Jewel Casket 447
S & H Jewell Ltd 101
Jezebel 14
Jillings 245
Jiri Books 435
Joan's Antiques 141
C John Ltd 82
John Nicholas Antiques 74
John's Corner Allsorts 142
Arthur Johnson & Sons 285
C A Johnson 344
Louis Johnson 352
Peter Johnson 149
Robert Johnson Coin Co 99
Johnson Walker Ltd 82
Johnsons 296
James Johnston 319
The Jolly Pedlars 137
The Jolly Roger 161
Jonathan Charles Antiques 296
Jonathan James 49
Alan Jones Antiques 161
B G Jones 490
Bob Jones Prytherch & Co Ltd 388
Christopher Jones Antiques 71
Howard Jones Antiques 90
Jen Jones Antiques 389
Kevin Jones Antiques 447
Leon Jones 289
Madalyn S Jones 331
R G Jones 466, 492
Jones & Llewelyn 388
James A Jordan 297
Jorgens Antiques 76
John Joseph 82
Margaret R Jubb 182
Jubilee Hall Antiques Centre 244
Juke Box World 346
Julian Antiques 141
Junk & Disorderly, Lamberhurst 33
Junk and Disorderly, Mulbarton 217
Junk and Disorderly, Waddesdon 238
The Junk Box 59
Junket Bargain Bygones 189
Junktion Antiques 342
Juno Antiques 278
Juro Farm and Garden Antiques 312
J R Jury & Son 481
Just a Second 77
Just Books 152
Just Chairs 501
Just Military Ltd 333

K

K C Antiques, Darwen 378
K C Antiques & K D Interiors at Samlesbury Hall, Preston 381
K D Antiques 358
K L M & Co 339
Kaimes Smithy Antiques 407
Kaizen International Ltd 36
Kaleidescope Porcelain and Pottery Restorers 461
Stephen Kalms Antiques 101
Kantuta 77, 500
Karim Restorations 493, 494
Katharine House Gallery 193
Daniel Katz Ltd 64
Kayes 358
Kear of Kennington Antiques 60
Kebo Antiques Market 169
Keeble Antiques 174
Keel Row Books 355
Mike Keeley 475
Keepence Antiques 401
R J Keighery 454
H W Keil (Cheltenham) Ltd 240
H W Keil Ltd 309
John Keil Ltd 67
Keith Gormley Antiques 303
Kellow Books 262
Kelly Antiques 440, 458
George Kelsall 372
Kembery Antique Clocks 179
Rodney S Kemble Fine Furniture 487
Peter Kemp 90
Kemp Booksellers 317
Kendal Studio Pottery Antiques 366
Kendons 209
Kennedy Wolfenden 432, 435
Ken's Paper Collectables 238
Kensington Church Street Antique Centre 90
Kent House Antiques 397
Gerald Kenyon Antiques 447
Norman Kerr 365
J Kershaw Fine Furniture Restoration 489
Keshishian 64
Kessler Ford Antiques 153
Keswick Bookshop 367
Keswick Collectables 367
Kev 'n' Di's Antiques 290
Roger Keverne Ltd 82
Key Antiques 262
Keymer Son & Co Ltd 26
Keys 213
Keystone Antiques 274
Kibworth Pine Co 274
Kidderminster Market Auctions 310
George Kidner 117
Kidwelly Antiques 388
Satch Kiely 453
Kilgarvan Antique Centre 454
Kilnsea Antiques 317
Richard Kimbell Ltd 276, 278
Kimber & Son 311
Ann King Antique Clothes 179
John King, London SW1 64
John King, Much Wenlock 290
Margaret King 221
Roger King Antiques 110
King Street Antiques, Knutsford 361
King Street Antiques, Southport 385
King Street Bookshop 216
King Street Curios 194
Kings Arms Antiques Centre 159
Kings Cottage Antiques 300
King's Court Galleries, Dorking 128
King's Court Galleries, London SW6 71
Kings Mill Antique Centre 379
Kings of Loughborough 484
Kingsbridge Collectors' Accessories in association with Salters Bookshelf 160
Kingsley & Co 349
Kingsleys Auctions Ltd 383

GENERAL INDEX

K – L

The Kingston Antiques Centre 133
Kingsway House Antiques 159
Robert Kirkman Ltd 233
Kirton Antiques 344
Kitchenalia 88
Kleanthous Antiques Ltd 95
Robert Kleiner and Co Ltd 464
Philip Knighton the Gramophone Man 492
Knights Gone By 390
Knight's Sporting Auctions 213
Knightsbridge Coins 64
Knole Barometers 188
Kopper Kettle Furniture 377
L & E Kreckovic 71
Krypton Komics 53
Kuwahara Ltd 496
Kyrios Books 282

L

La Belle Epoque 200
La Maison, Bourne End 236
La Maison, London E1 44
La Trouvaille 103
Laburnum Antiques 173
L'Accademia Antiques 71
The Lacquer Chest 91
Lacy Scott & Knight 222
Lake Antiques 124
Lakeland Architectural Antiques 366
Lakes Antiques & Collectables 367
Lakes Craft & Antiques Gallery 366
Laleham Antiques 104
Roger Lamb Antiques and Works of Art 247
Lamb Antique Fine Arts & Craft Originals 308
The Lamb Arcade 266
Raymond Lambert 230
Dorrian Lamberts 345
Lambert and Foster 38
Lambrays 152
Lamont Antiques Ltd 59
The Lamp Gallery 134
Penny Lampard 32
Lancastrian Antiques & Co 380
David M Lancefield Antiques 37
Landfall 117
Landgate Books 23
Russell Lane Antiques 303
W H Lane & Son, Fine Art Auctioneer and Valuers 149
Lane Antiques 121
The Lanes Armoury 14
Philip Laney 311
J & R Langford 392
Langford Antiques 121
Langfords Marine Antiques 74
Marion Langham 438
Lankester Antiques & Books 211
Lannowe Oriental Textiles 459, 499
Lansdown Antiques 179
Roger Lascelles Clocks Ltd 71
Judith Lassalle 49
LASSCO Flooring 57
LASSCO RBK 58
LASSCO St Michael's 46
LASSCO Warehouse 49
Latchford Antiques 240
Latto Books 351
Laurel Bank Antiques 330
Laurens Antiques 43
Peter Laurie Maritime Antiques 59
John Laurie 49
Lavande 12
D S Lavender Antiques Ltd 82
Law Fine Art Ltd 107
Alyson Lawrence 497
C and N Lawrence 496
F G Lawrence and Son 133
Lawrence Books 283
Lawrence Fine Art Auctioneers Ltd 185
Robert Lawrence-Jones 481
Lawrences Auctioneers Ltd 125
Lawrences Taunton Ltd 189
Peter Lawrenson 489
Alan Lawson & Son 407
E M Lawson and Co 263
F and T Lawson Antiques 134
Keith Lawson Antique Clocks 220
Lawton's Antiques 31
David Lay 149
S Layt 478
David Lazarus Antiques 116
M & J Lazenby Antique Restoration 475
Le Boudoir 179
Le Grenier 304
Peter Le Vesconte Collectables 430
Leather Conservation Centre 493, 500
P D Leatherland Antiques 111
Lechlade Arcade 244
Lechmere Antiquarian Books 311
Leeds Antique Centre 339
Leek Antiques Centre (Barclay House) 296
Leek Old Books 296
Bob Lees 373
M Lees & Son 313
Legends 279
E C Legg and Son 481
Legg of Dorchester 167, 172
Leiston Trading Post 226
Andrew Lelliott 481
Bart and Julie Lemmy 165
The Lemon Tree 361
L'Encoignure 74
Lennard Antiques 211
Lennox Auctions and Valuers 434, 502
Leolinda 49
Leominster Antique Centre 253
Leominster Antique Market 253
Le-Potier 205
Nat Leslie Ltd 101
Leslies Mount Road Auction Galleries 351
Letty's Antiques 275
Leuchers & Jefferson 82
Lev Antiques Ltd 91
M P Levene Ltd 73
Levenshulme Antiques Village 373
Leona Levine Silver Specialist 219
Lewes Antique Centre 21
Lewes Book Centre 22
The Lewes Clock Shop 22
Lewes Flea Market 22
John Lewis 340
M & D Lewis 64, 95, 96
Patsy Lewis 172
Simon Lewis Transport Books 243
Lewis & Lloyd 91
Lewis Antiques 270
David C E Lewry 472
M Lexton 67
Libra Antiques, Hurst Green 20
Libra Antiques, London W8 91
Libritz Stamps 256
Lights, Camera, Action 285
R R Limb Antiques 283
Lime Tree House Antiques 32
Limited Editions 375
Lincoln House Antiques 316
Lincoln Restorations 484
Lincolnshire Antiques and Fine Art 348
Linda's Antiques 443
Peter Linden Oriental Rugs and Carpets 445
Linden Antique Prints 134
Linden House Antiques, Leominster 253
Linden House Antiques, Stansted Mountfitchet 212
Lindfield Galleries 141
Lindsay Architectural Antiques 305
Lindsay Court Architectural 344
R Lindsell 466
Andrew Lineham Fine Glass 49
The Linen Press 186
Ann Lingard Ropewalk Antiques 23
Lini Designs 67
Lion Antiques 312
Lion Antiques Centre 299
Lion Fine Arts 252
Lion House Antiques Ltd 206
Lion Street Books 252
The Lion's Den 366
Michael Lipitch 67
Peter Lipitch Ltd 68
Sanda Lipton 82
Lisseters Antiques 260
Lister, Hugh and Favia 118
Lita Kaye Antiques 117
Lithgow & Partners 327
David Litt Antiques 232
Roger Little Antique Pottery 265
The Little Gem 292
Little Gems Rock Shop 214
Little Paws 290
Little River Oriental Antiques 68
The Little Shop 24
Little Theatre Antiques Centre 354
Liverpool Militaria 384
Llanelli Antiques 389
Llanishen Antiques 401
Llewellyn Clocks 463
David Lloyd 371
John Lloyd 472
Norman Lloyd & Co 400
Robin Lloyd Antiques 254
Lloyd Herbert & Jones 389
Lloyds International Auction Galleries Ltd 76
Monty Lo Antiques 82
Clive Loader Restorations 482
Lockdale Coins Ltd 225

Lockdales 225, 227
BBG Locke & England 300
Loddon Lily Antiques 112
Lodge and Thomas 152
Lomas Pigeon & Co Ltd 501
London Antique Gallery 91
London Cigarette Card Company Ltd 188
London House Antique Centre, Moreton-in-Marsh 245
London House Antiques, Westerham 42
London Road Antiques 407
Lonesome Pine Antiques 377
Michael D Long Ltd 285
Stephen Long 74
Timothy Long Restoration 466
Long Sutton Antique and Craft Centre 345
Michael Longmore and Trianon Antiques Ltd 83
Longmynd Antiques 288
R Longstaff & Co 346
Lonsdale Antiques 212
Look 'N' Hear 350
Looking Back 156
The Looking Glass 239
Brian Loomes 324
Robert Loomes Clock Restoration 346, 463
Loose Valley Antiques 33
C Lopez 472
Alan Lord Antiques 31
Lorraine's Antiques 431
Lots Road Galleries 74
Lotties 277
J D Loue 407
Loughborough Antiques Centre 276
Love Lane Antiques 362
Betty Lovell 165
D Lovell 165
Andrew Lowe Antiques 45
Lowestoft Auction Rooms 227
John Luce Antiques 154
Luckmans Antiques 306
Ludgershall Antiques Centre 114
Ludlow Antique Beds & Fireplaces 290
J D Luffman 360
Lugley Street Antiques 123
Charles Lumb & Sons Ltd 320
Luna 285
Lush Restoration 472
M Luther Antiques 71
Alexander Lyall Antiques 226
Lyme Regis Antique & Craft Centre 172
Lymington Antique Centre 117
Lymington Restoration 472
Lyndhurst Antique Centre 117

M

M & C Cards 243
M & C Stamps 243
M & J Antiques 348
M & M Restoration, London SW18 459, 499
M & M Restoration Work Ltd, Castletown 489
M B G Antiques 283
M G R Exports 183
M J M Antiques 110
M J R Upholstery 501
M K Restorations 482
Macdonalds Restoration 489
MacHenry Antiques 435
Mackenzie & Smith 484
Maddermarket Antiques 219
Made of Honour 358
Madison Gallery 143
Maen Dylan 393
Maggs Bros Ltd 83
Maggs Shipping Ltd 384
Magic Lanterns 258
Magical Restorations 468
Magna Gallery 265
Magnet Antiques 103
Magpie Antiques, Long Melford 226
Magpie Antiques, Malton 323
Magpie Antiques & Collectables, Hinckley 274
Magpie Antiques & Collectables, Porlock 187
The Magpie's Nest 316
Magpies 280
Maguire Antiques of Galway Ltd 450
Mahogany 429
Mah's Antiques 49, 91
Victor Mahy 194
Maisey Restoration 478
Peter Maitland 459
C H Major 91
Peter Makin 482
Makins & Bailey 24
Malahide Antique Shop 449
Malcolms No1 Auctioneers & Valuers 340
Malik Antiques 373
The Mall Antiques Arcade 49
Mallams 240, 265
Mallams incorporating Messengers 260
Mallett 8, 83
Mike Mallinson 380
E P Mallory and Son Ltd 179
The Malthouse 397
Malthouse Antiques, Bridgnorth 288
Malthouse Antiques, Dorking 128
Malthouse Antiques, Four Crosses 398
Malthouse Antiques Centre, Alcester 299
Malthouse Arcade 33
Malton Antique Market 323
The Malvern Bookshop 311
Malvern Link Antiques Centre 311
Malvern Studios 311, 484
C and T Mammon 101
Manchester Antique Company 375
Caira Mandaglio 96
Mandarin Gallery 34
Carol Manheim at Biblion 83
John Mann Fine Antique Clocks 364
Kathleen Mann Antiques 104
E and H Manners 91
Ken Mannion Fossils 341
Manor Antiques, Adare 451
Manor Antiques, Bournemouth 169
Manor Antiques, Wilstead 234
Manor Estate Auctions 389
Manor Farm Antiques 265
Mansell Antiques & Collectables 383
F C Manser & Son Ltd 292
Mansfield Antique Centre 282
Mansion House Antiques 489
Mantle Antiques 327
The Map House 68
Map World 83
Maple Antiques 135
Marcel Cards 256
Marcet Books 59
David & Sally March Antiques 176
S Marchant & Son 91
Marchmont Bookshop 99
E W Marchpane Ltd 101
Mariad Antiques 68
Marine, Craven Arms 288
Marine Instruments, Falmouth 147
Mario & Sabre 49
Mark Gallery 87
Market Antiques 394
Market Deeping Antiques & Craft Centre 202
Market Fayre 27
Market House Antiques 213
Market Place Antiques Restorations 475
Market Row Antiques & Collectables 211
Market Square Antiques 238
Jeroen Markies Antiques Ltd 18
Marks Antiques, London W1 83
Marks Antiques, Westerham 42
Marks Antiques, Jewellers/Pawnbrokers, Oldham 373
Mark's Mart 388
The Marlborough Parade Antique Centre 194
Marlborough Rare Books Ltd 83
Marlenes 182
Marlow Antiques Centre 237
Edward Marnier Antiques 187
G & DI Marrin & Son 32
Michael Marriott 71
Marryat Antiques Ltd 134
G E Marsh (Antique Clocks) Ltd 122
Frank R Marshall & Co 361
Marshall Buck and Casson 222
Peter Martin Ceramic Restoration 460
Peter J Martin 108
Robin Martin Antiques 96
Tony Martin 148
David Martin-Taylor Antiques 71
J Martinez Antiques 407
Martlesham Antiques 227
Martony Antiques and Collectables 235
Jeremy Mason 64
Masons Yard 23
Massada Antiques 83
Roy Massingham Antiques 26
Gerald Mathias 68
Mathy's Emporium 318
Matlock Antiques & Collectables 273
Andrew A Matthews Restoration 478

GENERAL INDEX

M

Christopher Matthews 321
Maud's Attic 225
Mauleverer Antiques 318
Sue Mautner Costume Jewellery 68
Matthew Maw 323
Thomas Mawer & Son Ltd 345
Maxey & Son 204
Maxwells of Wilmslow 376
Ann May 71
Greta May Antiques 39
May and Son 114
Maya Antiques 159
Nigel Mayall 484
Maybury Antique Restoration 472
Christopher Mayes 209
Mayfair Antiques, Dorking 128
Mayfair Antiques, Otley 340
Mayfair Gallery Ltd 83
Mayflower Antiques, Dovercourt 207
Mayflower Antiques, London W11 96
Mark Maynard 71
McAfee Auctions 432
Pete McAskie Toys 83
F J McAvenues & Son 442
McBains Antiques 156
Ann McCarthy 443
McCartneys, Builth Wells 398
McCartneys, Ludlow 290
McClenaghan 64
Joy McDonald Antiques 76
Stephen McDonnell 491
McDonnell's Antique Furniture 451
James E McDougall 351
McGovern's Corner 447
Vincent McGowan Antiques 444
P J McIlroy & Son 431
Alf McKay 475
Barry McKay Rare Books 364
J W McKenzie 130
McLarens Antiques & Interiors 358
Douglas McLeod Period Frames 465
McMahon's Antiques 444
John McMaster 37
MCN Antiques 96
McNally Antiques 127
McNaughtan's Bookshop 407
R J McPhee 478
MDS Ltd 305
Margaret Mead Antiques 193
Meadow Lamps Gallery 407
Meadowcroft Books 458
Mealy's Ltd 451
Medalcrest Ltd 110
Medway Auctions 36
Melbourne Antiques & Interiors 60, 61
Melbourne Hall Furniture 485
Melford Antiques Warehouse 226
Mellors & Kirk 285
Melluish & Davis 458
Melmount Auctions 439
Melnick House Antiques 107
Melody's Antique Galleries 358
Memories, Ashburton 153
Memories, Great Dunmow 207
Memories, Rochester 36
Memories, Tenterden 39
Memories Antiques 125
Memory Lane, Minehead 187
Memory Lane, Petts Wood 34
Memory Lane, Southampton 120
Memory Lane Antiques, Great Bookham 131
Memory Lane Antiques, Lower Stondon 234
Memory Lane Antiques, Ripley 273
Memory Lane Antiques, Stourbridge 307
Memory Lane Antiques and Collectables 38
Noel Mercer Antiques 226
Nicholas Merchant 327
The Merchant House 254
Merchant House Antiques, Honiton 159
Merchant House Antiques, Ipswich 225
Mercury Antiques 96
Mere Antiques 165
Mereside Books 362
Merlin Antiques 249
M Merritt 468
Merry's Auctions 280
Mersey Collectables 384
Metalwork Restoration Services 495
Metro Retro 49
Metropolis Art Deco 186
Mews Antique Emporium, Holt 217
The Mews Antique Market, London W1 83
Sarah Meysey-Thompson Antiques 230
Giuseppe Miceli 280
Judith Michael 351
Michael Coins 91
Michael's Boxes Ltd 68
Mid Devon Antiques 155
Middleham Antiques 323
Arthur Middleton Ltd 101
Bobbie Middleton 249
Middleton Hall Antiques 300
Nanette Midgley 326
Midland Football Programme Shop 305
Richard Midwinter Antiques 297
Milestone Antiques, Easingwold 319
Milestone Antiques, Lichfield 297
The Military History Bookshop 54
Mill Antiques, Colchester 206
Mill Antiques, Hull 317
Mill Antiques Etc, Bibury 239
Mill Court Antiques 438
The Mill Emporium 158
Mill Farm Antiques 360
Mill House Antiques 32
Mill Lane Antiques 213
J & S Millard Antiques 179
Millcourt Antiques 444
Millennium Collectables 282
James Miller 352
Thomas N Miller Auctioneers 354
Miller Services 277
Millers Antiques, Edinburgh 407
Millers Antiques Ltd, Ringwood 118
Millgate Antiques 328
Millgate Pine & Antiques 328
Mrs Mills' Antiques Etc., Ely 201
Robert Mills Architectural Antiques 182
Mills Antiques, Cork 443
Mary Milnthorpe & Daughters 326
Milton Antiques & Restoration 168
Frank Milward 111
Mimbridge Antiques and Collectables 126
Mimi Fifi 96
Minchinhampton Architectural Salvage Co 240
Ministry of Pine 189
Minster Antiques 330
Minster Books 176
Minstergate Bookshop 330
Mint Antiques 23
Mint Arcade 23
Miracle Finishing 482
Miracle Stripping 498
Miscellany Antiques, Malvern 311
Miss Ellany, Croydon 127
Mistermicawber.Co.Ltd 383
Mrs Mitchell 184
Paul Mitchell 485
Mitchell's Auction Company 365
Mitchells Lock Antiques 377
Mitofsky Antiques 447
MJM's 188
Modellers Loft 136
E C Molan 101
Mole Hall Antiques 221
Molland Antique Mirrors 296
Molloy's Furnishers Ltd 385
Monarch Antiques 24
George Monger 465
Mongers Architectural Salvage 216
Colin D Monk 91
Monogram Studios 462
Montague Antiques 179
Montpellier Clocks 241
Montpellier Mews Antique Market 321
Michael Moon 369
Riro D Mooney 201
Moor Antiques 153
Moor Hall Antiques 358
Eric T Moore 257
J Moore Restorations 482
Marcus Moore Antiques 292
Moore, Allen & Innocent 242
Patrick Moorhead Antiques 15
Roxane Moorhead Antiques 447
Mora & Upham Antiques 72
More Books, Chester 359
More Books, Llandudno 391
More Than Music Collectables 42
William Morey & Son 171
John Morgan and Sons 496
Robert Morgan Antiques 119
Morgan's Auctions 432
Michel André Morin 49, 50
David Morley Antiques 105
Patrick & Gillian Morley 303
Morphets of Harrogate 321
Morpheus Beds 249
A E Morris Books 393
Ian Morris, Chesterfield 271
J J Morris, Cardigan 390, 397
Peter Morris, Bromley 27
Morris Bricknell 254
Morris Marshall & Poole 399
Jan Morrison 182

Terence Morse & Son 96
C & J Mortimer & Son 207
Mortimers 156
David Morton 212
Moseley Emporium 305
C Moss 463
Ralph & Bruce Moss 255
Sydney L Moss Ltd 83
Trevor Moss Antiques 342
Moss End Antiques Centre 112
Mosstique 276
Mostly Boxes 108
Mother Hubbard Antiques 116
Mount Pleasant Antiques Centre 317
Mouse Mill Antique Centre 299
The Movie Shop 219
Moxhams Antiques 191
Moy Antique Pine 440
Moy Antiques 440
Moycullen Village Antiques 450
Moylurg Antiques 444
Moyrah Antiques 436
Mr Dip 498
Mr Gompy's Antiques & Curious 183
Mr Punch's Antique Market 174
A F Mrozinski 472
The Mulberry Bush Antique Shop 330
Mulberry House of Maldon 210
Mulbery Antiques 30
Mullen Bros Auctions 453
Mullock & Madeley 293
Mulroys Antiques 352
Munton & Russell 346
Murder & Mayhem 252
Murray and Kemmett 140
Murray Cards (International) Ltd 55, 101
The Museum of Childhood Memories 394
Musgrave Bickford Antiques 155
Music Room Antiques 138
Carol Musselwhite Antiques 198
R N Myers & Son 319
Myra's Antiques 290
Myriad, Salisbury 195
Myriad Antiques, London W11 96
Myrtle Antiques 187
Mytton Antiques 287

N

N S E Medal Department 285
Peter Nahum at the Leicester Galleries 64
Nakota Curios 19
Morris Namdar 84
Nanbooks 326
Nantwich Antiques 362
Napier House Antiques 229
Sylvia Napier Ltd 72
Colin Narbeth and Son 101
John Nash Antiques and Interiors 253
Nash & Company 53
Nassirzadeh Antiques 91
Naughton's Booksellers 449
Nautical Antique Centre 176
Rod Naylor 475
Timothy Naylor Associates 472
Naylors Auctions 346, 347
Neal Sons & Fletcher 230
Gillian Neale Antiques 235
Justin Neales Antiques & Interiors 299
Neales Auctioneers 271, 285
Neate Militarian & Antiques 229
Neath Antiques 402
Neath Market Curios 402
Needfull Things Ltd 324
A & A Needham 270
K Needham Restoration 485
Needham Market Antiques Centre 228
Needles Antique Centre 23
F B Neill 207
T & J W Neilson Ltd 407
V Nejus 398
Nelson Antiques 381
Neptune Gallery 447
D M Nesbit & Co 121
Nettlebed Antique Merchants 264
The Neville Pundole Gallery 28
The New Cavern Antiques & Collectors' Centre 371
New Century 91
The New Curiosity Shop 53
New England House Antiques 258
New Street Antique and Craft Centre 162
New Street Books 149
New, Secondhand & Antiquarian Books 175
Newark Antiques Centre 283
Newark Antiques Warehouse Ltd 283
Newbridge Antiques 399
Newbury Salvage Ltd 111
Newhampton Road Antiques 308
Newhaven Flea Market 22
Newington Antiques 38
Chris Newland Antiques 50
Mark Newland Enamel Restorer 465
Barbara Ann Newman 42
Newmans 185, 475
Newnham Court Antiques 34
Newsum Antiques 250
Newtons of Bury 371
Gordon Nichol Antiques 447
R J K Nicholas 280
Nicholas Antiques 129
Nicholas, Martin & Pole 113
Rene Nicholls 193
Nichols Antique Centre 333
John Nicholson Fine Art Auctioneers 130
Nick & Janet's Antiques 234
Nightingale Antiques, Little Chalfont 237
Nightingale Antiques and Craft Centre, West Wickham 41
Nimbus Antiques 274
Nimmo & Spooner 72
No 1 Castlegate Antiques 283
No. 9 Antiques 308
No. 12 68
No 24 of Frinton 207
No. 32 191
Nolton Antiques & Fine Art 394
The Nook Antiques 174
Nooks and Crannies 123
Noonan Antiques 452
John Noott Galleries 309
Peter Norden Antiques 249
Norfolk Galleries 478
Norfolk House Galleries Ltd 128
The Norfolk Polyphon Centre 213
Geoffrey Norman 257
Michael Norman Antiques Ltd 20
Peter Norman Antiques 199, 478
Norman D Landing Militaria 169
B J Norris 32
Norris of Blackheath 500
Desmond and Amanda North 30
North Devon Antiques Centre 153
North Shropshire Reclamation and Antique Salvage 288
North Street Antiques & Interiors 344
North Wales Antiques 390
North Wilts Exporters 192
Northallerton Auctions Ltd 323
Northcote Road Antiques Market 75
Northern Antiques Co 324
Northern Clocks 376
Northfleet Hill Antiques 34
Norwich Auction Rooms 219
Nostalgia, Clevedon 184
Nostalgia, Littleborough 372
Nostalgia, Porthcawl 395
Nostalgia, Stockport 375
Nostradamus 129
Nostradamus II 129
Not Just Antiques 169
Nothing Fancy 384
Notions Antiques 343
Nottingham Coin Centre 285
Notts Pine 187
Nova Foresta Books 120
Now & Then, Cardiff 401
Now & Then, Dunchurch 300
Now & Then, Edinburgh 407
Number 19 50
Number 38 165
Nutley Antiques 22
Simon Nutter and Thomas King-Smith 247

O

O Law I Law 393
G Oakes & Son 370
Oakfield Cabinet Makers 476
Oakland Antiques 432
Oaks and Partners 155
Oaktree Antiques 276
Oasis 15
Obelisk Antiques 196
Objets d'Art 359
R J O'Brien & Son Antiques Ltd 371
Octavia Antiques 143
The Odd Chair Company 381
Odds and Ends 227
Odeon Designs Ltd 296
Odiham Auction Sales 117
Odin Antiques 15
O'Donnell Antiques 266
Odyssey Fine Arts Ltd 64
Of Special Interest 53
Off The Wall Antique Mini Centre 256
Off World, Luton 234
Off World, Romford 211
Offa's Dyke Antique Centre 398

GENERAL INDEX

O – P

Ogee Restorations 487
Seamas O'Heocha Teoranta 497
O'Keeffe Antiques 359
O'Keeffe's Antiques and Interiors 451
Old & Gold 350
Old Amersham Auctions 235
The Old Apiary 12
The Old Bakery Antiques Ltd, Wheathampstead 259
The Old Bakery Antiques, Woolhampton 113
The Old Bakery Antiques, Wymondham 277
Old Barn Antiques, Compton 127
Old Barn Antiques, Epping 207
Old Barn Antiques, Sutton Bridge 347
Old Barn Antiques, Windsor 112
The Old Bottle Shop 59
The Old Brigade 280
Old Cawsey Antiques 341
The Old Chapel Antiques & Collectables Centre 299
The Old Chemist Shop Antique Centre 200
The Old Children's Bookshelf 407
The Old Cinema 87
The Old Clock Shop 41
Old Colonial 40
The Old Cop Shop 166
The Old Corn Mill Antique Centre 377
Old Corner House Antiques 43
The Old Cornstore Antiques Centre 137
The Old Curiosity Shop, Bredbury 370
The Old Curiosity Shop, King's Lynn 217
The Old Curiosity Shop, Sidmouth 163
The Old Curiosity Shop, St Sampsons 429
The Old Custom House 149
Old Exports Ltd 395
Old Forge Collectables 437
The Old Forge 466
The Old French Mirror Company 265
Old Friendship Antiques 338
The Old Grain Stores 215
The Old Granary Antique Centre 217
Old Hall Antiques 336
Old Hastings Bookshop 19
Old House Antiques Centre 138
The Old Ironmongers Antiques Centre 244
The Old Malthouse 110
The Old Maltings Antique Centre 345
Old Merchant's House Antiques Centre 254
The Old Mill, London SE6 58
Old Mill Antique Centre, Bridgnorth 288
Old Mill Antiques, Ballygawley 439
Old Mill Market Shop, Tetbury 250
The Old Mint House 22
Old Mother Hubbards 233
Old Oak Antiques Abercynon 395
The Old Orchard Antique Market 138
The Old Palace Antiques 148
The Old Picture Shop 15
The Old Pine House 300
The Old Post House, Axbridge 176
Old Post Office Antiques, Church Stretton 288
The Old Saddler's Antiques 389
The Old Salty 164
Old School, London N19 54
The Old School Antiques, Penryn 149
Old School House Antiques and Tea Room, Fir Tree 350
The Old Shop 449
The Old Sofa Warehouse 363
Old Soke Books 203
The Old Station 60
The Old Steam Bakery 150
The Old Tackle Box 29
Old Talbot Gallery 323
Old Timers 277
The Old Toll House 313
Old Tools Feel Better! 166
The Old Town Antiques Centre 17
The Old Town Bookshop 407
Old Town Hall Antiques, Falmouth 147
The Old Town Hall Antiques Centre, Midhurst 141
The Old Toyshop 119
The Old Trinket Box 105
The Old Vicarage Bookshop 341
The Old Village Clock Shop 123
The Old Warehouse Antiques 359
The Old Works Antiques 125
Old World Trading Co 72
The Olde Bakehouse Antiques 128
Olde Mill Antiques 377
Olden Days 147
Oldwoods Pine Furniture 497
Olinda House Antiques 23
Olivers 229
Olivers Bookshop 355
Diana O'Mahony Antiques & Jewellery 443
Oman Antique Galleries 448
O'Marley's Ghost 189
Omega Decorative Arts 210
On The Air Ltd 392
On the Hill Antiques 298
Once Upon a Time, St Austell 150
Once Upon a Time Antiques, Ahoghill 431
One Bell 226
One Off 294
One Step Back 222
O'Neil's Antiques Gosforth 352
O'Neil's Old Warehouse Antiques 351
Online 123
Onslow Auctions Ltd 72
Oola Boola Antiques London 61
Jacqueline Oosthuizen Antiques 68
O'Reillys 447
Orient Expressions Ltd 72, 179
Oriental & African Books 289
Oriental Gallery 245
Original Architectural Antiques 242
Original Door Specialist 58
Ormonde Antiques 455
Ormonde Gallery 96
Samuel Orr 141
Paul Orssich 73
M G Osborne 227
Osborne Antiques 497
The O'Shea Gallery 84
Osiris 385
Ossowski 64
O'Sullivan Antiques 448
Otford Antique and Collectors Centre 34
Othellos 209
O'Toole Antiques & Decorative Galleries 452
Otter Antiques, Honiton 159
Otter Antiques, Wallingford 266
Ottery Antique Restorers 476
Out of the Blue 185
Out of Time 50
Outhwaite & Litherland 384
Anthony Outred Antiques Ltd 64
Ovne Antique Stoves 443
Owlets 33
Oxfam Books 354
Oxford Furniture Warehouse 265
Oxford Longcase Clocks 463
Oxford Street Antiques Centre 275
Laurence Oxley 113

P

P A Oxley Antique Clocks & Barometers 192
P & P Antiques 285
P S I Collectables 147
The Packhouse Antiques Centre 135
Paddock Antiques 277
Paddy Cliff's Clarice! 176
Padstow Antiques 148
Colin Page Antiquarian Books 15
Kevin Page Oriental Art Ltd 50
Page Antiques 375
Pages Bookshop 436
Painswick Antiques 485
N St J Paint and Sons Ltd 429
Pairs Antiques 75
Palace Antiques 129
Pall Mall Antiques 209
Dermot & Jill Palmer Antiques 15
Palmers Green Antiques Centre 53
Pandora's Box, Castle Cary 184
Pandora's Box, Totnes 167
Pantiles Antiques 40
Pantiles Spa Antiques 40
Paperchase 233
Parade Antiques 162
Paragon Art 46
Paraphenalia, Sheffield 333
Paraphernalia, Stockton-On-Tees 327, 487
Paraphernalia Antiques, Birkenhead 383
Parasol Antiques 429
Michael Parfett 495
Paris Antiques, Ampthill 232
Paris Antiques, Leigh-On-Sea 209
Park Antiques, Menston 340
Park Antiques, St Helier 430
Park Galleries Antiques, Bolton 370
Park Hall 378
Park House Antiques 247

Park Lane Restoration 476
Park View Antiques 25, 466
Christina Parker Antiques 223
Vanessa Parker Rare Books 452
Gill Parkin Furniture 132
Parkins 126
G A Parkinson 490
K A Parkinson Books 385
Parkinson Auctioneers 25
Parkside Antiques 277
Parkways Antiques 188
Parlour Farm Antiques 242
Ian Parmiter 121
H & R L Parry Ltd 307
Partners Antiques 374
Partners in Pine 206
Timothy Partridge Antiques 17
Parvis 435
Passageway Antiques 137
Passers Buy 392
Past & Present, Belfast 433
Past & Present, Bromley 27
Past & Present, Edinburgh 407
Past & Present, Hingham 216
Past & Present Antiques and Collectables, King's Langley 257
Past & Presents, Knutsford 361
Past & Presents, Polperro 150
Past and Present, Risby 228
Past and Present Fireplaces, Clitheroe 378
Past and Present James Sturges Antiques, Totnes 167
Past Caring 217
Past 'n' Present, Christchurch 171
Past Present Toys, London N21 54
Past Sentence 38
Pastiche 490
Pastimes 183
Pastorale Antiques 22
Pateley Bridge Antiques 324
Paton Books 258
Pat's Antique and Reproduction Pine Furniture and Gift Shop 338
Richard Pattison 488
Pattison's Architectural Antiques 256
Alexander Paul Restorations 159, 476
Paull's of Kenilworth 300
Pavilion 379
K S Pawlowski 472
Clive Payne 262, 482
G Payne Antiques 301
Payne and Son (Goldsmiths) Ltd 265
PDQ Air Freight/Art Move 496
John Pearman 50
Pearman Antiques & Interiors 283
Martyn Pearson Glass 492
Sue Pearson Antique Dolls & Teddy Bears 15
Peasenhall Art & Antiques Gallery 228
Pedlar's Pack Books 167
Sarah Peek 460
Pegasus Antiques 285
Peggy's Pandora 203
Pembroke Antiques, Cambridge 201
Pembroke Antiques Centre, Pembroke 397
The Pen & Pencil Gallery 368
Pendelfin Studio Ltd 499
Pendle Antiques Centre Ltd 382
Pendulum of Mayfair 84
Peninsula Books 383
Penistone Pine & Antiques 332
Penlan Pine 393
Penman Clockcare 346
Pennard House Antiques 188
Pennies, Topsham 166
Pennies Antiques, Exeter 157
John Penny Antique Services, Southampton 499
Penny Farthing Antiques, Kinvara 450
Pennyfarthing Antiques, Boston 342
Pennyfarthing Antiques, Brough 316
Pennyfarthing Antiques, Salisbury 195
Pennyfarthing Antiques, Southampton 120
Penrith Farmers' & Kidd's Plc 368
Penybont Farm Antiques 403
Penzance Rare Books 149
R L Peploe 476
Eva-Louise Pepperall 472
Peppers Period Pieces 222
Percy's Ltd 101
Period Furniture Ltd, York 487
Period Furniture Showrooms, Beaconsfield 236
Period Piano Company 25
Period Pine 393
Period Style Lighting 103
Periplus Books 238
George Perkins 461
Perkins Stockwell and Co Ltd 485
J Perrin 476
Charles Perry Restorations Ltd 482
Perry & Phillips 288
Christopher Peters Antiques 299
Mark Peters Antiques 479
Paul M Peters 321
The Petersfield Bookshop 118
Simon Peterson 472
Peter Petrou 96
Petworth Antique Market 143
Petworth Collectables and Bookshop 143
Pew Corner Ltd 132
John M Peyto & Co Ltd 34
Phantique 157
Pharoahs Antiques 17
T L Phelps Fine Furniture Restoration 487
Phelps Ltd 105
Penny Philip 179
Elaine Phillips Antiques Ltd 321
Richard G Phillips Ltd 469
Ronald Phillips Ltd 84
S J Phillips Ltd 84
Trevor Philip & Son Ltd 64
Phillburys 466
Phillips Antiques & French Polishing Service 389
Phillips Auctioneers 225
Phillips Brothers 301
Phillips Fine Art Auctioneers 408
Phillips International Auctioneers and Valuers
Barnstaple 153
Bath 179
Cambridge 201
Canterbury 28
Cardiff 401
Carlisle 365
Carmarthen 388
Chester 359
Chichester 139
Exeter 157
Guildford 132
Leeds 339
London W1 84
London W2 87
Market Harborough 276
Newcastle-upon-Tyne 354
Norwich 219
Par 148
Retford 286
Ringwood 119
Sale 374
Sevenoaks 38
Sheffield 333
Sherborne 174
Solihull 307
Southport 385
Winchester 122
Phillips of Hitchin Antiques Ltd 257
Phipps & Pritchard 310
Phoenix Antiques, Fordham 202
Phoenix Antiques, Sherborne 174
Phoenix Antiques, Tunbridge Wells 41
Phoenix Conservation.com 490
Phoenix Design & Antiques 354
Phoenix Fireplaces 205
Phoenix Gallery 433
Phoenix Green Antiques 116
Phoenix Oriental Art 50
Phoenix Restoration 479
Phoenix Trading, Frinton-on-Sea 207
Phoenix Trading Co, London SW10 74
Phoenix Trading Company – South Yorkshire, Bentley 331
Phone Cards Centre 191
Piano Export 183
Piccadilly Antiques 179
Piccadilly Rare Books 24
Picfair Antiques 328
Pickering and Chatto 84
Pickering Antique Centre 324
Graham Pickett Antiques 346
Mr Pickett's 138, 472
Paul Pickford Antiques 272
David Pickup 261
Pickwick Antiques, Boscastle 146
Pickwick Gallery, Stratford-upon-Avon 302
Pickwicks Antiques, Stourbridge 307
Picton Collectables 397
Pieces of Time 84
Piers Furniture Repair Workshop 469
The Pig Sty 19
Pilgrim Antiques, Ampthill 233
Pilgrim Antiques, Honiton 159
Pilgrims Antique Centre, Dorking 128
Pilgrims Antiques Centre, Gainsborough 342
Pilgrim's Progress, Liverpool 384

GENERAL INDEX

P – R

Pilgrims Progress Antiques, Liverpool 489
Pillars Antiques 193
Pine & Country Antiques 301
Pine and Country Furniture 224
Pine & Period Furniture 147
Pine and Things 301
The Pine Barn 122
The Pine Cellars 122
Pine for Pine Antiques 430
Pine Furniture Store 259
Pine Love 235
The Pine Mine 497
The Pine Parlour 233
A Pine Romance 53
Pine Too 359
Pine Workshop 352
Pine-Apple Antiques 317
Pines Antique & Gift Centre 183
Pinestrip 204
Pinetum 28
Pinfold–Wilkinson Antiques 343
W A Pinn & Sons 212
Pipkins Antiques 379
Piers Pisani Antiques 175, 476
Nicholas S Pitcher Oriental Art 84
Marco Pitt 466
Places and Spaces 69
Planet Bazaar 54
Platt's of Lymington 117
Plestor Barn Antiques 116
Plough House Interiors 396
Plowden and Smith Ltd 464
Albert Plumb Furniture Co 472
Plumridge Antiques 124
Plymouth Auction Rooms 154
Plympton Antiques 159
Plympton Reclamation and Architectural Salvage Ltd 163
The Pocket Bookshop 161
A G Podmore & Son 487
Pokesdown Antique Centre 169
Poley Antiques 293
Nathan Polley Antique Restoration 482
Polly's Parlour 194
Polmorla Bookshop 152
Pontcanna Old Books, Maps & Prints 401
Ben Ponting Antiques 15
Pontypridd Sale Rooms & Auctions 395
Pool Auctions 150
Poor Richard's Books 224
Pop Antiques 235
Tony Popek Antiques 327
Porcelain Repairs 462
Porch House Antiques 250
Porchester Antiques 183
Porcupine 372
Henry Pordes Books Ltd 101
Portabellows 169
Portcullis Furniture 289
Portland Antiques 283
Portland Books 300
Portland House Antiques 345
Portobello Antique Store 96
Post House Antiques 125
Postcard Cabin 145
The Pot Board 388
D Potashnick 472
David & Carole Potter 285
Jonathan Potter Ltd 84
Potteries Antique Centre 294
Potteries Specialist Auctions 294
Potterton Books 326
The Pottery & Porcelain Restoration Co 461
Pottery Bank Antiques 352
The Pottery Buying Centre 293
Ludovic Potts Antiques 202
Ludovic Potts Restorations 479
T Potts 367
H W Poulter & Son 75
J Powell (Hove) Ltd 22
Sylvia Powell Decorative Arts 50
R J Poynter 482
Leo Pratt and Son 220
John Prestige Antiques 154
Preston Antique Centre Ltd 381
Prestwich Antiques 374
Prestwood Antiques 269
Pretty Bizarre 30
Pretty Things 429
Graham Price Antiques Ltd 22
Roderick Price & Co 388
Prichard Antiques 250
W D Priddy Antiques, Chichester Furniture Warehouse 139
Pride & Joy Antiques 183
John Priestley 285
Priestley and Ferraro 77
Priest's Antiques & Fine Arts 247
Priestpopple Books 352
Princess Antique Centre 292
Principia Fine Art, Hungerford 110
Principia Fine Art, London W11 96
Priors Reclamation 289
Priory Books 311
Priory Collectables 382
Priory Furnishing 335
Promenade Antiques, Cheltenham 241
Promenade Antiques & Books, Malvern 311
Prospect Books 391
Proudfoot Antiques 239
Pub Paraphernalia UK Ltd 60
Bernie Pugh at Oddfellows Corner 293
H J Pugh and Co 253
Ian K Pugh Books 312
Pughs Antiques 159
Pullman Gallery Ltd 64
The Pumping Station 401
Puritan Values at the Dome 229
Annette Puttnam Antiques 143
Pydar Antiques 152
John Pye & Sons Ltd 285

Q

Q & C Militaria 241
Quality Furniture Warehouse 55
Quality Restorations Limited 469
Bernard Quaritch Ltd 84
Quarter Deck Antiques 329
The Quay Centre 166
Quay Court Antiques 203
The Quay Gallery Antiques Emporium 157
Quayside Antiques, Rye 23
Quayside Antiques, Shrewsbury 292
The Queen's Shilling 495
Queens House Antiques 164
Quest 87
Martin Quick Antiques 308
Mrs Quick Chandeliers 91
Quicktest 259
Quiet Street Antiques 180
The Quiet Woman Antiques Centre 262
Quill Antiques, Bletchingley 125
Quill Antiques, Deal 30
Liz Quilter 235
Quinneys of Warwick 303
Quinto Bookshop 102

R

R & J Coins 212
R & L Furnishings 306
R G Antiques 281
R M Antiques 342
R M W Restorations 469
R S M Antique Restoration 489
Radio Days 58
Radnedge Architectural Antiques 389
Radnor House Antiques 152
Jim Railton 351
Rainbow Antiques 72
Rainbow Bridge 487
Rainbow Too Interiors 72
Harry Raine 349
Alan Ramsey Antiques 350
Randolph Antiques 224
Randtiques 112
Daphne Rankin & Ian Conn Oriental Antiques 72
George Rankin Coin Co Ltd 45
Piers Rankin 50
Rankine Taylor Antiques 242
Mark Ransom Ltd 65
Rapscallion Ltd 77
Rare Art Ltd 102
G T Ratcliff Ltd 209
M & A Ratcliffe 221
Rathmines Bookshop 448
Raven Reclaim & Architectural Salvage Ltd 305
Ravensdale Studios 461
Raw Deluxe 183
Paul Rawcliffe Upholstery Services 501
Rawlinsons 169
Jim Raw-Rees & Co 389
Janette Ray Rare Books 330
Ray & Scott Ltd 429
Derek & Tina Rayment Antiques 360
Alan Read 344
Mike Read Antique Sciences 151
Paul M Read Antique Furniture Restoration 466
Readers' Dream 214
Recollect, Leigh-on-Sea 209
Recollections, Bournemouth 169
Recollections, Poynton 362
Recollections, Richmond 325

Re-Collections, Hebden Bridge 337
Recollections Antiques Ltd 55
Record Detector 45
Rectory Rocking Horses 176
The Red House Antique Centre 330
Red House Glasscrafts 492
Red Lion Antiques 143
Red Room 72
Red Rose Cricket Books 369
Allen Reed 326
John Reed and Son Upholsterers 502
John Reed Antiques 227
T. Reed & Son 211
Reel Poster Gallery 87
Reeman, Dansie, Howe & Son 206
Paul Reeves 91
Reeves & Son 19
Reeves Restoration at the Coach House Antiques 131, 463
The Refectory 128
Reference Works 460
Reflections, Comber 436
Reflections, Lymm 361
Regal Antiques 42
D M Regan 385
Regency Antiques, Bognor Regis 460
Regency Antiques, Shanklin 124
Regency Furniture Restoration, Halesowen 485
Regency Restoration, London SW11 469
Regent Antiques 50
Reid & Reid 408
Reigate Galleries Ltd 133
Reindeer Antiques Ltd, London W8 92
Reindeer Antiques Ltd, Potterspury 280
Reindeer Restorations 485
Relcy Antiques 59
Relic Antiques, London N1 50
The Relic Antiques Trade Warehouse, London NW1 54
Relics, Ilfracombe 160
Relics, Wadebridge 152
Remains To Be Seen 292
Reg & Philip Remington 102
Remstone Contracts 469
Renaissance, Croydon 472
Renaissance, Sherborne 175
Renaissance Antiques 485
Renaissance China Restoration 462
Renaissance Ironwork 495
Rendells 153
Renishaw Antique & Pine Centre 334
Rennies 99
Repair Convert Furniture 479
Replay Period Clothing 241
The Restoration Co 472
Restoration Rooms 485
Restoration Supplies 499
Retro Products 310
Retrobuy 275
Retrospect 282
Retrouvius Architectural Reclamation 57, 85
Revival, Accrington 376
Revival, Colchester 206
Revival, Keighley 339
Revival, Timsbury 476
C H & D M Reynolds 324
Isobel Rhodes 231
Peter Rhodes Books 120
Rhombus 129
Rhos Point Books 391
Ribble Reclamation 382
David Richards & Sons 85
T N Richards 489, 490
Richard's Polishing 479
Richards Son & Murdoch 150
Gordon Richardson 464
Roderick Richardson 217
Richmond Antiques 370
Richmond Galleries 359
Richmond Hill Antiques 134
Riddetts of Bournemouth 169
Ridgeway Antiques 212
J and M Riley 139
R J H Rimmel 489
Rimmer Restoration 494
Rin-Tin-Tin 15
Ripley Antiques 134
Ripping Yarns 52
The Risby Barn Antique Centre 228
A & R Ritchie 430
Riverbank Gallery Ltd 143
Riverside Antiques, Newcastle Emlyn 389
Riverside Antiques, Stratford-upon-Avon 302
Riverside Antiques Centre, Sawbridgeworth 258
Sue Rivett Antiques 215
Roadside Antiques 366
Derek Roberts Antiques 39
Tyrone R Roberts 214
Roberts & Mudd Antiques 296
Robert's Antiques 430, 479
Roberts Emporium 401
Roberts Korner 305
Leon Robertson Antiques 149
John Robinson Antiques 376
Robinsons Timber Building Supplies Ltd 377
Rocco d'Ambrosio 501
Rochdale Book Company 374
Rocking Chair Antiques 363
Rocking Horse Antique Market 137
Roderick Antiques 92
John Roe Antiques 279
Roe and Moore 99
Rogers Antiques Gallery 96
Rogers de Rin 68
Rogers Turner Books 60
Rogers-Jones & Co 390
Rogier Antiques 65
Roland Gallery 180
Chris Rollason Home Counties Medal Services 495
Brian Rolleston Antiques Ltd 92
John Rolph 227
Romanov Restoration 492, 497
Romantiques, Redruth 150
Romantiques Antique Centre, Trevor 392
de Rome 335
Romiley Antiques & Jewellery 374
Romsey Auction Rooms 119
Romsey Medals 119
Ron's Emporium 30
Rookery Farm Antiques 50
The Rope Works 194
Rose and Crown Antiques 41
Rose Antiques 269
Rosebery Fine Art Ltd 61
Rosemary & Time 266
Roses Antiques 37
Rose's Books 252
Rosewood Restoration 476
John Ross & Company 433
Marcus Ross Antiques 50
Ross Antiques Market 254
Ross Old Books and Print Shop 254
Tim Ross-Bain 485
Rossi & Rossi Ltd 65
Ross-on-Wye Antique Gallery 254
Bertram Rota Ltd 102
Rother Reclamation 33
Rotherfold Antiqeus 167
Colin de Rouffignac 376
Roughshed 143
Round the Bend 313
Roundabout Antiques 140
Roundabout Shop 191
Roundstone Books 378
H Rowan 169
Mark Rowan 389
P & B Rowan 433
Michael Rowland Antiques 247
S H Rowland 205
Rowley Fine Art 202
Royal Carberry Books 443
Royal Mile Curios 408
Royal Mile Gallery 408
Royal Standard Antiques 123
E & C Royall 495
Ruddy Antiques 143
Rufus the Cat 448
The Rug Gallery 275
The Rugby Salerooms 301
Rugeley Antique Centre 298
Rule's Antiques 113
Simon & Penny Rumble Antiques 201
Rummages 272
Rumours 51
Ruskin Decorative Arts 247
Russell Books 189
Marlene Rutherford Antiques 271
Ryde Antiques 123
Rye Auction Galleries 24
Rye Old Books 24

S

S & J Antiques 307
S M Upholstery Ltd 501
S R Furnishings 306
S W Antiques 312
Sabine Antiques 212
F B Sadowski 476
Michael Saffell Antiques 180
Saffron Walden Antiques Centre 211
Saffron Walden Auctions 211
The Sage Door 169
John W Saggers 487
Sainsburys of Bournemouth Ltd 169
Saintfield Antiques & Fine Books 438
Dyala Salam Antiques 92
Salamanca 68
Salisbury Stripping Co 498

GENERAL INDEX

S

David N Salmon 469
N P and A Salt Antiques 334
F D Salter 223
Nicholas Salter Antiques 45
Saltney Restoration Services 359, 458
The Salvage Shop 454
Salvo 458
Samarkand Galleries 247
Sambourne House Antiques 193
Samiramis 85
Alistair Sampson Antiques Ltd 85
Anthony Sampson 185
Patrick Sandberg Antiques 92
Tony Sanders Gallery 149
Sandgate Passage 37
Sandwich Fine Books 37
Sandycove Fine Arts 449
Sandy's Antiques 169
Santiques 172
Santos 92
Sanz & Pottle 51
Saracen Antiques Ltd 261
Saracen Restoration 482
Sarah Rose Antiques 438
D H Sargeant 42
Sargeant Restorations 494
K J Sarginson Fine Furniture 487
Sasha 230
Christopher Saunders 245
Charles Saunders Antiques 68
H G Saunders Fine Antiques 143
Keith A Savage 228
Savery Antiques 15
Savery Books 15
G J Saville 337
Vigi Sawdon 492
Saxon Cross Antiques Emporium 363
David A Sayer Antique Furniture Restorer 473
Sayer Antiques 139
Scarborough Perry Fine Arts 20
Scarthingwell Antiques 327
Scarthingwell Auction Centre 327
Christine Schell 68
School Hill Antiques 22
Schoolhouse Antiques 241
T Schotte Antiques 229
Manfred Schotten Antiques 261
Schredds of Portobello 97
Michael Schryver Antiques 473
Schull Books 442
Sci-Fi World 119
James Scott 408
Peter Scott 180
Richard Scott Antiques 217
B Scott-Spencer 377
Sea View Antiques, Pontlyfni 393
Seabourne Mailpack Worldwide 496
Mark Seabrook Antiques, West Haddon 281
Seabrook Antiques, Long Melford 226
Seaford House Antiques 245
Arthur Seager Antiques 247
Seagers Restorations 473
Sealcraft 485
M G Seaman 301
Seaquel Antiques & Collectors Market 17
Richard Sear 279
Seaview Antiques, Horncastle 344
Sebastian of Eton 108
Second Chance Antique Centre 117
Second Edition 408
Second Time Around, Chester 359
Second Time Around, Hemswell Cliff 343
Second Time Around, Hornsea 317
Second Treasures 33
Secondhand & Rare Books 373
The Second-Hand Bookshop 133
Secondhand Department 27
Joel Segal Books 166
Select 373
Selected Antiques and Collectables 154
M & D Seligman 92
Selskar Abbey Antiques 454
Selwoods Antiques 189
Semley Auctioneers 173
Serendipity, Bicester 260
Serendipity, Deal 30
Serendipity, Haslemere 132
Serendipity, Huddersfield 338
Serendipity, Ledbury 253
Serpentine Antiques 369
Philip Serrell FSVA 313
Seventeen Antiques 384
Seventh Heaven 391
Severn Antiques 190
Esther Sexton Antiques 448
Sextons Auctioneers 452
Shabby Genteel 280
Shabby Tiger Antiques 248
The Shambles, Ashburton 153
Shambles Antiques, Kendal 366
Shanklin Auction Rooms 124
Bernard J Shapero Rare Books 85
Shapiro & Co. 85
Shardlow Antiques Warehouse 273
Andrew Sharp Antique Restoration Ltd 473
Ian Sharp Antiques 355
Shaston Antiques 174
Ann Shaw Antiques 437
Gerald Shaw 487
John Shaw Antiques Ltd 332
Nicholas Shaw Antiques 138
Stephen Shawcross & Son 371
Shawlan Antiques 495
Sheffield Antiques Emporium 334
Steven Shell 195
Julian Shelley Books 390
C B Sheppard & Son, Sutton-in-Ashfield 286
C Sheppard and Sons, Durrow 451
Sherborne World of Antiques 175
Sherbrook Antiques & Collectables 160
Shere Antiques Centre 135
Sherman Upholstery 501
D W Sherwood Ltd 280
Shieling Antiques 321
Shine's Antiques and Collectables 17
Shiners Snobs Knobs 354
Catherine Shinn Decorative Textiles 241
The Shipping Company 496
Shipwreck Centre 206
Shiraz Antiques 85
Shirley-Ann's Antiques & Decorative Furniture 20
Shiver Me Timbers 149
G S Shobrook and Co incorporating Fieldens 162
C Short 166
D J Short 479
Shortmead Antiques 233
Shrewsbury Antique Centre 292
Shrewsbury Antique Market 292
Shrewsbury Clock Shop 292
The Shrubbery 176
Sidmouth Antiques Centre 163
Sieff 250
Sigma Antiques 325
At the Sign of the Chest of Drawers 51, 52
Silstar Antiques Ltd 102
The Silver Fund Ltd 65
The Silver Shop, Dublin 448
The Silver Shop, Winchester 122
Silver Street Antiques 242
B Silverman 102
Silversaddle Antiques 440
Silvesters 26
Michael Sim 29
Simmons & Miles 485
J C Simmons & Son 325
Simmons & Sons 263
Simmons Gallery 99
Jack Simons Antiques Ltd 102
Simon's Books 188
Simply Oak 233
John Simpson 330
Steven Simpson Natural History Books 225
Simpsons 296
Sims Reed Ltd 65
Sitting Pretty, Great Glan 274
Sitting Pretty, Stoke-on-Trent 502
Sitting Pretty Antiques, Sudbury 230
Sivyer's 13
Keith Skeel Antiques 51
Skellgate Curios 325
Sketty Antiques 402
Barbara Skillen Porcelain and Pottery Restoration 461
Skipton Antiques & Collectors Centre 327
Skoob Books Ltd 99
Justin F Skrebowski Prints 97
Michael Slade 52, 469
Anderson Slater 326
Phillip Slater 485
Small Wood Ltd 125
Tony Smart Restorations 487
A H Smith & Son 501
Allan Smith 196
Anthony Smith, Uxbridge 106
Anthony Smith, Wolverhampton 485
Charles Smith & Son 326
Clive Smith 208
David Smith Antiques 286
Francis Smith Ltd 75
Frank Smith Maritime Aviation Books 354
Graham Smith Antiques 354
H A Smith & Son 469
J Smith, Wallingford 482
J Smith, York 330

John Smith of Alnwick Ltd 350
Keith Smith Books 253
Ken Smith Antiques Ltd 277
P J Smith (Fair Trades) 440
Peter Smith Antiques 355
R J Smith Restoration 479
Royden Smith 297
Sarah Smith Scent Bottles and Collectables 223
Smith & Smith Designs, Antique Pine and Country Furniture 316
Smith & Sons 170
Smithfield Antiques 398
Janie & Skip Smithson 343
Mark Smitten Cabinet Makers 485
John Smyth Antiques 366
Peta Smyth Antique Textiles 65
Smythe's 378
Snap Dragon, London SW3 68
Snapdragon, South Molton 163
Tim Snell Antiques 180
J A Snelson 485
The Snooker Room 288
Snooper's Paradise 15
Ruby Snowden Antiques 329
Snowdonia Antiques 490
The Snug 153
Soames Country Auctioneers 264
Sodbury Antiques 184
R Solaimany 85
Solaris Antiques 97
Solent Railwayana 121
Solent Railwayana Auctions 121
Nicholas Somers Chartered Arts and Antiques Surveyor 501
Somerton Antique Centre 188
Somervale Antiques 187
Something Different 349
Something Old, Something New 364
Somlo Antiques Ltd 65
Soosan 72
Sotheby's 85
Sotheby's (International Auctioneers) 502
Sotheby's South 138
Henry Sotheran Ltd 85
Source 180
South Coast Collectables 17
South Street Antiques, Axminster 153
South Street Trading Co, Riddings 273
Southam & Sons 280
Southbourne Antiques 170
Southdown House Antique Galleries 26
Southern Stoves & Fireplaces 170
Southgate Auction Rooms 53
Southgate Bookshop 53
Southport Furnishings 385
Sheila Southwell Studio 460
6a Antiques 23
Souvenir Antiques 365
The Sovereign 237
Spalding Antiques 346
Span Antiques 267
Graham Sparks Restoration 476
Special Auction Services 111
Specialised Postcard Auctions 242
Spectrum, London W1 85
Spectrum Fine Jewellery Ltd, Battle 12
J K Speed Antique Furniture Restoration 463, 487
A and J Speelman Ltd 85
Ken Spelman 330
Don Spencer Antiques 303
Martin Spencer-Thomas 157
Simon Spero 92
Spinning Wheel, Beaconsfield 236
The Spinning Wheel Antiques, Southport 385
Spires Restoration 487
Spongs Antique Centre 141
Sporting Antiques 41
Stephen Sprake Antiques 72
Springfield Antiques 13
Spurrier-Smith Antiques 269
Squires Antiques, Altrincham 369
Squires Antiques, Faversham 31
The Squirrel Antique & Collectors Centre, Basingstoke 114
Squirrels, Brockenhurst 114
St Clements Antiques 265
St David's Auctions 157
St Georges Antiques 346
St Helen's Restoration 490
St James Antiques 311
St James House Antiques & Restoration 319
St James's Gallery Ltd 429
St Julien 321
St Just Bygones 151
St Leonards Antiques and Craft Centre 161
St Martins Antique Centre 346
St Mary's Books & Prints 347
St Mary's Chapel Antiques 193
St Michael at Plea Antiques and Collectors Centre 219
St Nicholas Galleries Ltd 365
St Pancras Antiques 139
St Paul's Street Bookshop 347
St Petersburg Collection Ltd 86
St Thomas Antiques 476
Stable Antiques, Lindfield 141
Stable Antiques, Long Melford 226
Stable Antiques, Pickering 324
Stable Antiques, Sedbergh 368
Stable Antiques, Storrington 144
Stable Antiques, Thornton-Le-Dale 328
Stable Antiques, York 331
Stable Antiques at Houghton 140
Stable Doors, Hailsham 18
Stabledoors and Co, Beckenham 25
The Stables Antique Centre, Hatton 300
Stables Antiques Centre, Reading 111
John Stacey & Son 210
John Stacey & Son (Leigh Auction Rooms) 210
Alan and Kathy Stacey 191, 459
Stacks Bookshop 436
George Stacpoole 451
Staffordshire Pride 51
The Staffs Bookshop 297
Stage Door Prints 102
Stag's Head Antiques 372
Staines Antiques 105
Stair & Company Ltd 86
Stalham Antique Gallery 220
Kenneth Standrin 120
Stanfords 206
Staniland Booksellers 347
David Stanley Auctions 277
Stanstead Abbotts Leathers 493
Staple Grove Antiques Centre V
W M Stark 501
Starkadder 482
Station Mill Antiques Centre 262
Staveley Antiques 368
Robert D Steedman 354
Stefani Antiques 384
Stella Books 396
Steppes Hill Farm Antiques 38
Stepping Stones 323
Sterling Books 190
Sterling Coins and Medals 170
J W Stevens and Son 486
Stevenson Brothers 25, 500
Steve's World Famous Movie Store 376
David Steward Antiques 215
Stewart Antiques 143
Still Life 408
Still Useful 61
Stirling Antiques 124
Stocks and Chairs 173
Stocks and Chairs Antique Restoration 493
Stockspring Antiques 92
Jacob Stodel 86
S & J Stodel 102
William H Stokes 242
Stokes Books 448
Stokes Clocks 443
June and Tony Stone Fine Antique Boxes 97
Stonegate Antiques Centre 331
Dinah Stoodley 26
The Store 202
Stormont Antiques 433
Stothert Old Books 359
Stow Antiques 247
Julie Strachey 266
J Straker Chadwick & Sons 395
Strand Antiques, London W4 87
Strand Quay Antiques, Rye 24
Stratford Antiques and Interiors 302
T Straw Restoration 467
J Streamer 210
Streeton Antiques Ltd 281
Stretton Antiques Market 288
Jane Strickland & Daughters 160
Stride & Son 139
Strike One Antique Clocks, Barometers & Music Boxes 52
V Stringer 467
Strip It Ltd 498
Strippadoor Ltd 498
Stripped Pine Workshop 403, 499
The Stripper 499
The Stripping Store 499
M A Stroh Bookseller 53
Strouds of Southwell Antiques 286
Struwwelpeter 241
The Studio, Bromley 27
The Studio, Gomshall 131

Studio 101 109
Studio Bookshop 15
Studio Coins 122
Stuff, Bideford 154
Stuff & Nonsense, Chesham 237
Sturmans Antiques 322
Style 123
Succession 134
The Suffolk Antique Bed Centre 225
Suffolk Brass Ltd 499
Suffolk House Antiques 231
Suffolk Rare Books 230
Suffolk Sci-fi Fantasy 225
Sugar Antiques 51
Suite Dreams Upholstery 501
Summers Davis Antiques Ltd 266
Summersons 303
Sunburst Antiques & Art Furniture 18
F H Sunderland & Co 398
Sunderlands Sale Rooms 252
Sundial Antique Clock Service, Coulsdon 463
Sundial Antiques, Amersham 235
Sunningend Joiners and Cabinet Makers Ltd 482
Surrey Antiques 133
Surrey Restoration Ltd 473
R A Surridge 479
Susannah 180
Sussex Woodcraft 473
Suthburgh Antiques 227
Sutton Valence Antiques 34, 38
Spencer Swaffer 137
Marilyn Swain Auctions 343
Swan & Foxhole Antiques 29
Swan Antiques, Baythorn End 205
Swan Antiques, Chipping Camden 241
Swan Antiques, Saltaire 340
The Swan at Tetsworth 266
Swan Gallery 261
Swans Antiques and Interiors, Oakham 286
Swansea Antique Centre 403
Sweetbriar Gallery Ltd 361
Sweetings Antiques Belper 270
K W Swift 290
Swindon Auction Rooms 196
Swiss Cottage Furniture 339
E Swonnell Ltd 86
G E Sworder & Sons 212
Sydenham Antiques Centre 61
Christopher Sykes 235
William Sykes & Son 338
Symonds & Sampson 153
Sympathetic Restorations 486

T

T and S Blues Antiques 143
T J Upholstery 500
T L H & Company 371
T S Restorations 473
Taclow Coth 148
Tagore Ltd 86
Taikoo Books Ltd 331
Talbot Walk Antique Centre 134
The Talish Gallery 408
Talisman, Gillingham 172
Talisman 2, Bury St Edmunds 222
The Talking Machine 55
Talking Points Antiques 341, 492
Tamblyn Antiques 351
Tamlyn and Son 181
Robert P Tandy 463, 476
Tango Art Deco & Antiques 303
Tango Curios 350
Tankerton Antiques 43
Tansu 335
The Tao Antiques 303
Tapestry Antiques, Cheltenham 241
Tapestry Antiques, Hertford 256
Chris Tapsell at Christopher House 51
Tara Antiques 57
Tarka Antiques 161
Tarka Books 154
Tarporley Antique Centre 363
Lorraine Tarrant Antiques 119
Tarrant Street Antique Centre 137
Julian Tatham-Losh 239
Tattersalls 287
Taunton Antiques Market 189
Tavistock Books 164
Tavistock Furniture Store 164
Tayler & Fletcher 240
Louis Taylor Fine Art Auctioneers 294
M & R Taylor Antiques 290
Martin Taylor Antiques 308
Michael J Taylor Antiques 334
Pam Taylor Antiques 51
Peter Taylor and Son 257
Taylor Pearce Restoration Services Ltd 497
John Taylor's 345
Taylors, Ashburton 153
Taylors, Honiton 160
Taylors Collectables 152
Taylor-Smith Antiques 42
Tea and Antiques 224
Teddy Bears of Witney 267
Teme Valley Antiques 290
Templar Antiques 51
Jeanne Temple Antiques 238
Roy Temple Polishing 473
Temple Auctions Ltd 435
Temple Jones Restoration 467
Tempo Antiques 450
Tennants Auctioneers 321, 323
Tenterden Antique & Silver Vaults 39
Tenterden Antiques Centre 39
Terrace Antiques, Belfast 433
Terrace Antiques, London W5 88
Terry's Antiques and Collectables 190
Tess Antiques 452
Tewkesbury Antiques Centre 250
Textile Conservation, Banwell 464, 499
Textile Conservation Services, Worksop 464, 500
Textile-Art: The Textile Gallery 86
Teywood Ltd 479
Thakeham Furniture 144
Thanet Antiques Trading Centre 35
Thetford Antiques and Collectables 220
30th Century Comics 76
Thistlethwaite Antiques 326
Andrew Thomas 347
Ed Thomas Old Country Pine 497
Sean Thomas Antiques 444
The Thomas Chippendale School of Furniture 500
Thomond Antiques 366
John Thompson, Tunbridge Wells 41
John Thompson Antiques, Knaresborough 322
Jösef Thompson 325
M and A C Thompson 221
Thompson Auctioneers 322
Thomson, Roddick & Laurie Auctioneers 365
Thomson, Roddick & Medcalf 408
Thomson's Antiques 430
B & T Thorn and Son 154
Thornbridge Antiques 270
Thornbury Antiques 189
John Thornton 75
Thornton & Linley 323
Thorntons of Harrogate 321
Thornwood Auction 45
Thomas Thorp, Guildford 132
Thomas Thorp, Wheathampstead 259
John Thorpe Fine Furniture 476
Miwa Thorpe 69
Those Were The Days 201
Thread Bare Upholstery 473
Through the Looking Glass, Dun Laoghaire 449
Through The Looking Glass, London SW6 72
Through The Looking Glass, London W8 92
Kate Thurlow 98
Tilleys Vintage Magazine Shop 334
Tillmans Antiques 280
Till's Bookshop 408
Tillys Antiques 210
Timber Restorations 483
Timbercraft 381, 464
Timbers Antiques & Collectables 226
Time & Tide Antiques 437
Time and Motion 315
Time Restored 195, 463
Timecraft Clocks 175, 463
Timepiece Antique Clocks, Dublin 448
Timepiece Antiques, Teignmouth 164
Times Past, Waterford 454
Times Past Antiques, Eton 109
Timgems Jewellers 219
S and S Timms Antiques Ltd 234
Tin Tin Collectables 57
The Tinder Box 295
Tinkers Antiques 189
Tintern Antiques 396
The Titus Gallery 13
Toad Hall Antique Centre 19
Toad Hall Medals 161
Tobias & The Angel 76
Toby Jug Collectables 30
Tobys 157, 161, 166
M Tocci 496
Todd & Austin Antiques & Fine Art 122
Todd Antiques, Bangor 436
Todd's Antiques, Launceston 147
Todmorden Antique Centre 382
Tom Tom 102
Tombland Antiques Centre 219

Tombland Bookshop 219
Christopher Tombs 483
Eric Tombs 128
Tomlinson Antiques 328, 487
N S L Tomson 476
Tony's Antique Restoration 469
The Tool Shop 228
Tooley, Adams and Co 266
Rupert Toovey & Co 140
Top Drawer Antiques 269
Top Hat Antique Centre, Nottingham 286
Top Hat Antique Centre, Sheffield 334
Top of the Hill Antiques 293
Tosi Gold Ltd 86
The Totteridge Gallery 54
Tout Le Monde 437
Tower Antiques 171
The Tower Workshops 491
Town & Country Antiques 191
Town & Country Auctioneers 448
Town and Country Prints 228
Town Hall Antiques 235
Townhead Antiques 367
Townhouse Antiques 373
Townsford Mill Antiques Centre 208
James Townshend Antiques 180
The Toy Shop 372
Toynbee-Clarke Interiors Ltd 86
Clifford J Tracy 483
Traders Antiques and Country Pine Centre 113
Trading Post, Mountain Ash 395
The Trading Post Antique Centre, Tytherleigh 167
The Traditional Studio 461
Traditional Telephones 166
Transatlantic Antiques & Fine Art Ltd 233
Trash 'n' Treasure 356
Travers Antiques 55
Travis & Emery Books on Music 102
Charles W Traylen 132
Treasure Chest Antiques, Blackrock 445
Treasure Chest Antiques, Whitley Bay 355
The Treasure Chest Books, Felixstowe 224
Treasure Trove, Lymington 117
Treasure Trove Books, Leicester 276
The Treasury 22
Trecastle Antique Centre 399
Tredantiques 157
R J Tredwen 51
Treedale Antiques 287, 486
Treen Box Antiques 397
Treharris Antiques 395
Tremayne Applied Arts 151
Trembath Welch 208
Trengove Antiques 136
Trevan's Old Books 195
Trianon Antiques Ltd and Michael Longmore 86
Trident Antiques 227
Neil Trinder 488
Trinder's Fine Tools 223
Trinities 217
Trinity Curios 408
Trinity Rare Books 451
William Trist 491
Triton Gallery 241
Trojan Antiques 18
T R J Troke 473
Ken Trotman Ltd 201
Troubridge Antiques 241
Irene S Trudgett Collectables 122
Truman and Bates 483
The Truro Auction Centre 152
Tubbjoys Antiques 198
Martin Tucker Antique Restoration 473
Tudor Antiques, Llansantffraid 399
Tudor Antiques, Long Melford 227
Tudor Antiques and Fine Arts Ltd, Alresford 113
Tudor House, Stow-on-the-Wold 248
Tudor House Antiques, Christchurch 171
Tudor House Antiques, Cranbrook 29
Tudor House Antiques, Halesowen 306
Tudor House Antiques, Ironbridge 289
Tudor House Antiques and Collectables, Henley-on-Thames 263
Tudor Rose Antiques Centre, Newark 283
Tudor Rose Antique Centre, Petworth 143
Tunbridge Wells Antiques 41
W F Turk Fine Antique Clocks 77
Turks Head Antiques 109
Turnburrys Ltd 354
Alexis F J Turner Antiques 129
D Turner Antiques 341
David Turner 494, 495
Malcolm Turner 219
Sally Turner Antiques 239
Turner & Sons (1787) 385
Turner Violins 281
Turnpike Cottage Antiques & Tearoom 477
Turpins Antiques 110
Tutbury Mill Antique Centre 299
J C Tutt Antiques 143
20th Century Marks 42
Twice As Nice 450
The Twickenham Antiques Warehouse 105
Two Dragons Oriental Antiques 394
272 Antiques 301
275 Antiques 69
Richard Twort 190
Ty-Llwyd Antiques 401
Tymewarp 219
Tynemouth Architectural Salvage 355
Tything Antiques Centre 314

U

Andrew R Ullmann Ltd 46
Ultramarine 124
Un Français à Londres 65
Undercover Books 347
Clive Underwood Antiques 488
Underwood Hall Antiques 348
Underwood Oak 113
Unicorn Antiques, Edinburgh 408
Unicorn Antiques & Reproductions, Kingswinford 306
Robin Unsworth Antiques 238
Unsworths Booksellers Ltd 99, 265
Up Country Ltd 41
The Upholsterers Workshop 500
Upper Court Manor Antiques 448, 451
Upperbridge Antiques 338
Upstairs Antiques 403
Upstairs Downstairs 166
Ursus 149
Oliver Usher 453
Utility 394
Utopia Antiques Ltd 366
Utter Clutter 254

V

Vale Antiques, Easingwold 319
Vale Antiques, London W9 93
Valelink Ltd 15
Valley Auctions 33
Valmar Antiques 212
Valued History 201
Jan Van Beers Oriental Art 86
Vanbrugh House Antiques 248
Jenny Vander 448
Van-Lyn Antiques 435
Robert Vaughan Antiquarian Booksellers, Stratford-upon-Avon 302
Vaughan Antiques, Stamford 347
Vellantiques 134
The Venerable Bead 166
T Vennett-Smith Auctioneers and Valuers 282
Ventnor Antiques Centre 124
Ventnor Junction 124
Venus Trading 329
Denzil Verey 239
Angela Vernon Bates 469
G Vescovi 380
Vestry Antiques 29
Victor & Co 175
Victoria and Edward Antique Centre 128
Victoria Antiques, London E18 45
Victoria Antiques, Pembroke Dock 397
Victoria Antiques, Shipley 341
Victoria Antiques, Wadebridge 152
Victoria Antiques, Wallasey 386
The Victoria Centre 340
The Victoria Gallery and Bookshop 146
Victoria House 233
Victorian Chairman 170
Victorian Dreams 116
Victorian Imports 374
The Victorian Ironmonger 299
The Victorian Salvage and Joinery Co Ltd 448
The Victorian Shop 380
Victoriana Antiques and Kents Jewellers 157
Victoria's Antiques, Cork 443
Viewback Auctions 440

Villa Grisebach Art Auctions 55
Village Antique Centre, Brasted 27
Village Antiques, Antrim 431
Village Antiques, Cheam 126
Village Antiques, Cobham 126
Village Antiques, Finedon 279
Village Antiques, Prestwich 372374
Village Antiques, Weybridge 136
Village Antiques Aldermaston 107
Village Books 214
Village Clocks 227
Village Farm Antiques 371
The Village Market Antiques 281
Garth Vincent Antique Arms and Armour 341
Vincents of Clifton 183
Vinci Antiques 86
The Vinery Antiques 128
Elizabeth Viney 121
Vintage Antiques Centre 303
Vintage to Vogue 180
Virginia 97
Vision Thing 334
Visto 97
G Viventi 58
VOC Antiques 348
Vogue Antiques 373
Voitek Conservation of Works of Art 464, 498
Vokes Books Ltd 325
Volume One Books and Records 170
Vost's Fine Art Auctioneers & Valuers Ltd 228
S Vye 166

W

Rupert Wace Ancient Art Ltd 86
David Wainwright 55, 93, 97
The Wake Table 434
A E Wakeman and Sons Ltd 157
Walcot Reclamation Ltd 180
Waldegrave Antiques 105
Paul Waldmann Woodwork (Conservation Unit) 493
Patrick Waldron Antiques 243
Alan Walker 111
Brian Walker 477
John Walker Antiques 172
Richard Walker - Antique Restoration 486
Walker, Barnett & Hill 308
Walker Galleries 321
E F Wall Antiques 225
Wallis & Wallis 22
John Walsh & Co. 338
William Walter Antiques Ltd 102
P Walters Ltd 469
J D and R M Walters 36
Walters Antiques & Collectables 391
Walton & Hipkiss 307
Wanstead Antiques Centre 45
Warboys Antiques 204
Kerry Ward Antiques 77
Nigel Ward & Co. 254
Paul Ward Antiques 334
Ward and Chowen Auction Rooms 164
Ward Price Ltd 326
Wardrobe 16
Wards Collectables 340
Ward-Thomas Antiques 199
Wargrave Antiques 112
Waring's Antiques 253
Warley Antique Centre 307
Warminster Antique Centre 196
R Warner and Son 145
W W Warner Antiques 27
Warner Auctions Ltd 276
Helen Warren China Restoration 459
Jimmy Warren 33
Warren Antiques 226
Robert A Warry Auctioneer 168
Wartime Wardrobe 273
Warwick Antique Centre 303
Warwick Antique Restorations 464
Warwick Antiques 304
Warwick Auctions 306
The Warwick Leadlay Gallery 60
Warwick-Wright Restoration 461
Waterfall Antiques 255
Waterfront Antiques Market 147
Watergate Antiques 359
Simon Waterhouse Designs 486
Geoffrey Waters Ltd 69
Waterside Antiques 201
Islwyn Watkins Antiques 398
R G Watkins 188
Brian Watson Antique Glass 217
Gordon Watson Ltd 69
Graham Watson 491
Watson & Watson 269
Watsons Antiques 364
Watton Salerooms 220
Chris Watts Antiques 195
R E and G B Way 222
Way Back When 30
Wayfarer Books 147
Ways, Ryde 124
Ways Bookshop, Henley-On-Thames 264
Wayside Antiques, Duffield 272
Wayside Antiques, Tattershall 347
Wealth of Weights 18
Weather House Antiques 338
Weatherell's Antiques 321
Trude Weaver 97
Graham Webb Musical Boxes 16
W H Webber Antique Clocks 244
Mollie Webster 208
S J Webster-Speakman 229
Weedon Antiques 281
Weedon Bec Antiques 486
Mike Weedon 51
Weir and Sons 448
Peter K Weiss 102
P M Welch 483
J W Weldon 449
Well Cottage Antique Centre 238
Weller & Dufty Ltd 305
Weller King 503
Wellers Auctioneers 132
Anthony Welling 135
Wellington Gallery 57, 498
Wells Antique Centre 220
Wells Auction Rooms 190
Wells Reclamation Company 190
Jorge Welsh 92
Welsh Country Auctions 388
Welsh Salvage Co 396
Wendover Antiques 239
Wessex Antiques 175
Wesley J West & Son 234
Mark J West 77
West Country Auctions 158
West Country Old Books 166
West End Antiques 276
West Essex Antiques 208
West Essex Coin Investments 115
West Lancashire Antiques Export 378
West Middlesex Auction Rooms 103
West Midlands Collectors Centre 308
West of England Auctions 166
West Port Books 408
West Street Antiques, Dorking 128
West Street Antiques, Haslemere 132
West Vale Trading Post 336
West Wickham Bookshop 42
Westend Antiques & Jewellery 350
Westenholz Antiques Ltd 65
Westerham House Antiques 42
Westgate Auctions 43
Westland and Co 46
Westminster Group Antique Jewellery 86
Westmoor Furniture 477
D G Weston 473
Westport House Antique Shop 453
Westville House Antiques 188
Westway Pine 322, 488
Mark Westwood Books 252
Westwood House Antiques 250
Wharfdale Farmers Auction Mart Ltd 340
Tim Wharton 257
What Now Antiques 270
Whatever Comics 28, 34
The Whatnot, Londonderry 439
Whatnots, Lincoln 345
Whatnots Antiques of Tewkesbury, Tewkesbury 250
What-Not-Shop Antiques, Stowmarket 229
Noel Wheatcroft & Son 273
Nick Wheatley 194
Wheatsheaf Antiques Centre 359
Laurie Wheeler Restorations 459
Wheelers 464
N D Whibley Restorations 477
Whichcraft Jewellery 213
Whitchurch Antique Centre 291
Whitchurch Books Ltd 401
D P White 194
E & B White, Brighton 16
E White Antique Restoration, Derby 486
G White 376
M & M White Antiques and Reproduction Centre 133
The White Elephant 364
White House Antiques, Chalfont St Peter 236
White House Antiques & Stripped Pine, Waverton 363
Whitehead & Sons 392
Whiteladies Antiques & Collectables 183
Whitemoors Antique Centre 301
Whiteway & Waldron Ltd 73
David & Paula Whitfield 293

Robert Whitfield 60
Whitfield Restoration 479
B D Whitham 488
Whittaker & Biggs 359
Avril Whittle, Bookseller 368
Whittontique Curios & Collectables 334
Whyte's 449
Wick Antiques 117
Wickham Antiques 160
Wiend Books & Collectables 376
John & Shahin Wilbraham 19
Wild Rose Antiques 408
Chris Wilde Antiques 322
Wilfords 281
Wilkinson & Beighton 334
Colin Wilkinson and Co 434
T G Wilkinson Antiques Ltd 144
Wilkinsons 16
Willesden Green Architectural Salvage 57
William Antiques 259
A J Williams Shipping 496
Christopher Williams 173
G Williams, Betchworth 473
George Williams Antiques, Kells 453
John Williams, Swindon 196
John Williams Antique & Collectables, Warwick 304
Nigel Williams Rare Books 103
Paul Williams Antiques 395
Robert Williams 483
Williams & Watkins Auctioneers Ltd 255
Willroy Antiques Centre 201
Cyril C Wills 501
Wilmslow Antiques 363
O F Wilson Ltd 69
Peter Wilson 362
R S Wilson & Son 319
B B G Wilson Peacock 233
Wilson's Antiques 137, 145
Wilson's Auctions 435, 436
Agnes Wilton 51
Wimpole Antiques 87
Winchester Antiques 122
The Winchester Bookshop 122
Winchmore Antiques 54
P F Windibank 129
The Winding Stair Bookshop, Dublin 449
The Winding Stair, Galway 450
Windle & Co 335
Windmill Antiques 298
Windmill Bookshop 380
David Windsor Gallery 392
Windsor & Eton Antiques Centre 109
Windsor Antiques 499
Windsor House Antiques, Newcastle-Under-Lyme 297
Windsor House Antiques Centre, Moreton-In-Marsh 245
Simon Wingett Ltd 391
Wingett's 392
Winslow Antique Centre 239
Dominic Winter Book Auctions 196
Richard Winterton Auctioneers and Valuers 294
Wintertons Ltd 297
The Wireless Works 493
Mary Wise & Grosvenor Antiques 92
Wish Barn Antiques 24
Wissinger Antiques 58
The Wiston Project School 500
The Witch Ball 16
Withers of Leicester 274
Witney Antiques 267
Wizzards Furniture Transformers 486
Woburn Abbey Antiques Centre 235
Woburn Book Shop 99
D Wombell & Son 328
Wonderworld 170
Dale Wood & Co 335
Justin Wood Restoration 479
Michael Wood Fine Art 162
Richard Wood Antiques 408
Wood Be Good 127, 497
Wood 'n' Things, Bristol 477
Wood 'n' Things, Wolverhampton 308
Wood Pigeon 75
Wood Restorations 486
Woodage Antiques 51
Woodall & Emery Ltd 137
Woodbourne Antiques and Furniture Makers 469
Woodbridge Gallery 231
P Woodcock & Co 501
Woodcock House Antiques 202
Wooden Heart 298
Woodford Antiques & Collectables 162
Woodford Auctions 45
Geoffrey M Woodhead 160
Woodies Tools 170
Woodmans House 287
Wood's Antiques 160
Woods Emporium 155
Woods Wharf Antiques Market 132
Woodside Reclamation 352
Woodside Restoration Services 479
Woodstock Antiques, Leeds 339
Woodstock Antiques, St Leonards-on-Sea 24
The Woodstock Bookshop 267
Woodville Antiques 32
Joseph Woodward & Sons Ltd 443
Woodward Antique Clocks Ltd 308
The Woolahra Trading Co Ltd 92
Woolley and Wallis Salisbury Salerooms Ltd 196
Woolnough (AC) Ltd 493
Worcester Antiques Centre 314
Worcester Medal Service Ltd 309
The Works Antiques Centre 388
Works of Iron 339
World Coins 28
The World of Antiques (UK) Ltd 69
World War Books 41
Worlds Apart 336
World's End Bookshop 69
Worldwide Arms Ltd 294
The Worm Hole Antique Centre 264
J D Worrall 489
Worthing Auction Galleries Ltd 145
Wot-a-Racket 29
Wotruba and Son 473
Wotton Auction Rooms Ltd 251
Wrattan Antique & Craft Mews 29
Wren House Antiques 231
Wrentham Antiques 231
Gary Wright Antiques Ltd 245
Mick & Fanny Wright 244
Nigel Wright 488
Pamela Wright 16
Wright-Manley 356
www.horsebrass.co.uk 360
Stephen Wycherley 305
Wymondham Antique Centre 221
Wyrardisbury Antiques 106
Wyseby House Books 110

X

Ximenes Rare Books Inc 244

Y

Y S F Books Ltd 334
Yamamoto Antiques 87
Yarmouth Antiques and Books 124
Yarnton Antique Centre 267
Yazuka 385
Year Dot, Leeds 339
Year Dot Interiors, Harrogate 322
Yellow Lantern Antiques 20
Yeovil Collectors Centre 191
Yesterday and Today, Sutton-in-Ashfield 286
Yesterdays, Fleet 115
Yesterdays, Leamington Spa 300
Yesterdays, Lostwithiel 148
Yesterdays, Wareham 175
Yesterdays Antiques, Cleethorpes 342
Yesterdays Books, Bournemouth 170
Yesterdays Treasures, Cradley Heath 306
Yester-Year, Iver 237
Yesteryear Antiques, Dublin 449
Yesteryear Railwayana, Ramsgate 35
Yesteryears, Topsham 166
Yew Tree Antiques, Edenbridge 30
Yew Tree Antiques Warehouse, Wiveliscombe 191
York Antiques Centre 331
York Cottage Antiques 322
York Gallery Ltd 51, 73
York House (Antiques) 325
York Vale Antiques 331
Yorkshire Relics 337
Youll's Antiques, Chulmleigh 155
Youll's Antiques, Hungerford 110
John Young & Son Antiques 367
Michael Young 52
Peter Young Auctioneers 331, 500
R M Young Bookseller 163
Robert Young Antiques 75
Yoxall Antiques & Fine Arts 307
Ystwyth Books 390

Z

Richard Zabrocki & Son 488
Zeitgeist Antiques 93
Zoom 88

MILLER'S Antiques Shops, Fairs & Auctions 2002

ENTRY FORM

Please return a signed copy of this form to: Miller's Publications (Directory 2002), The Cellars, High Street, Tenterden, Kent TN30 6BN or fax to 01580 766100.

Name of Business: ....

Type of Entry *(Dealer/Auction House/Market or Centre/Associated Service)*: ....

Contact Name: ....

Street: ....

Town: .... County: .... Postcode: ....

Address for mailing *(if different from above)*: ....

....

Telephone: .... Fax: .... Mobile: ....

Email: .... Web address: ....

Trade only *(Yes/No)*: .... Parking nearby *(Yes/No)*: ....

Member of: .... Established: ....

Opening/Office hours: ....

Dealers only

Principal Stock: ....

If a Specialist Dealer, please give speciality *(one only)*: ....

Services offered *(Valuation/Restoration/Shipping/Book Search)*: ....

....

Exhibitor at which fairs? *(two only)*: ....

Quantity of stock held *(Small/Medium/Large)*: ....

Auction Houses only

Sale details: ....

Catalogues *(Yes/No)*: .... Frequency of main sale: ....

Markets/Centres only

Number of stalls/shops/dealers: ....

Associated Service only

Specialist area: ....

Services offered: ....

I agree that the above data may be included in the 2002 and future editions of Miller's Antiques Shops, Fairs & Auctions. I further acknowledge that it is my responsibility to keep this information up to date and agree to inform Octopus Publishing Group Ltd (OPG) of any changes to it.

Signature: ______________ Name: ______________ Date: ______________

Paragraph A: We Octopus Publishing Group Ltd (OPG) wish to share the information you have provided with Digital Octopus Ltd (DO) and our business partners for promotional and product development purposes, via a range of media including web sites and digital television. If you do not wish us to use your information in this way, then please tick here: ❑

If you no longer want to be included in the above publication or if you have any queries concerning the personal information held about you, please contact: Valerie Lewis, Miller's Publications, The Cellars, High Street, Tenterden, Kent TN30 6BN.